Fodor's

BUCKET LIST EUROPE

Welcome to Bucket List Europe

These are the experiences of a lifetime, the ones you'll recount to your children and friends long after you return from your European vacation. Marvel at natural wonders, explore big cities, stroll through picturesque villages. Ski in the Alps or climb the Eiffel Tower, take a cruise on the canals of Venice or the Rhine River. Visit the Sistine Chapel, shop in the luxury boutiques of Milan, climb to the top of the Acropolis, see the northern lights, or watch an English football match. As you plan your travels, please confirm that places are still open, and let us know when we need to make updates by writing to us at editors@fodors.com.

TOP REASONS TO GO

★ **Natural Wonders.** Mountain peaks, lakes, beaches, and forests offer stunning scenery.

★ **History.** Europe's story reaches back to the Greeks, Romans, Vikings, and Celts.

★ **World-class Museums.** Europe's museums hold myriad artistic and historic treasures.

★ **Cool Cities.** Explore the storied sights of Paris, Rome, Venice, Barcelona, and Prague.

★ **Exciting Activities.** Kayak in Norway, run with the bulls in Pamplona, hike the Cinque Terre.

Contents

MAPS

Chapter 1

EXPERIENCE BUCKET LIST EUROPE

WHAT'S WHERE

1 England, Scotland, and Wales. Travelers come to see such iconic attractions as Buckingham Palace, the whisky distilleries of the Scottish Highlands, and Snowdonia National Park.

2 Ireland and Northern Ireland. These powerhouse tourist destinations offer such highlights as the Cliffs of Moher, the Blarney Stone, and the Giant's Causeway.

3 France and the Low Countries. France is the most-visited country in Europe; just to the north are Belgium, the Netherlands, and Luxembourg (the so-called "Low Countries"). From the Eiffel Tower to the canals of Amsterdam, they offer some of Europe's most popular sights.

4 Spain and Portugal. The Iberian Peninsula offers wine, art, gorgeous scenery, and such iconic attractions as La Sagrada Família and the Alhambra.

5 Scandinavia and the Baltic Region. These eight northern European countries (Denmark, Estonia, Finland, Iceland, Latvia, Lithuania, Norway, and Sweden)

offer famous sights from Iceland's Blue Lagoon to Copenhagen's Tivoli amusement park.

6 Central Europe. The seven countries that make up Central Europe (Austria, the Czech Republic, Germany, Hungary, Poland, Slovakia, and Switzerland) have such iconic sights as the Brandenberg Gate, the Charles Bridge, and the Matterhorn.

7 Italy and Malta. Italy is known for famous sights like Rome's Trevi Fountain and Venice's Grand Canal; tiny Malta was once the headquarters of the mighty Knights Hospitaller.

8 The Balkans. The 10 countries in the Balkan Peninsula (Albania, Bosnia and Herzegovina, Bulgaria, Croatia, Kosovo, Montenegro, North Macedonia, Romania, Serbia, and Slovenia) make up the bulk of southern Europe.

9 Greece, Cyprus, and Istanbul. The two southernmost countries in Europe border the Aegean, offering such iconic sights as the Acropolis and Palace of Knossos, while Istanbul is also the only city to straddle two continents, making it a bucket list destination in its own right.

Iconic Landmarks

MONT-ST-MICHEL, FRANCE
The spire-top silhouette of this mighty offshore mound, dubbed the Marvel of the Occident, is one of the greatest sights in Europe. It's the third-most visited sight in France, after the Eiffel Tower and the Louvre. Plan to arrive at high tide, when the water races across the endless sands. *(Ch. 4)*

HOUSES OF PARLIAMENT, ENGLAND
Parliament's clock tower, the Elizabeth Tower, has become the symbol of London. Inside is Big Ben, the 13-ton bell (not the actual clock, as many mistakenly believe). But it's still a must-see attraction, especially after a massive 5-year renovation completed in 2022. *(Ch. 2)*

BRANDENBURGER TOR, GERMANY
Berlin's premier landmark, the Brandenburger Tor was left in a desolate no-man's-land when the wall was built. Since its dismantling, the sandstone gateway has become the scene of the city's Unification Day and New Year's Eve parties. It is the symbol of Berlin. *(Ch. 7)*

EIFFEL TOWER, FRANCE
The Eiffel Tower is to Paris what the Statue of Liberty is to New York: the ultimate civic emblem. But it wasn't supposed to be. Designed by Charles Eiffel for the 1899 Exposition Universelle, it was scheduled to be dismantled in 1909. Ironic, then, that it has become the one place in Paris everyone wants to visit at least once in life and the country's most popular tourist sight. *(Ch. 4)*

LEANING TOWER OF PISA, ITALY
Meant to be a campanile for Pisa's cathedral, the Torre Pendente began to lean shortly after its construction was begun in 1173, and the lean worsened until its completion in 1372. It may be the ultimate touristy attraction, but it's still a whole lot of fun to climb to the top and admire the view. Needless to say, reservations are essential. *(Ch. 8)*

CHARLES BRIDGE, CZECH REPUBLIC

The view from the foot of Prague's signature attraction on the Staré Město side, encompassing the towers and domes of Malá Strana and the soaring spires of Katedrála sv. Víta (St. Vitus Cathedral), is nothing short of breathtaking. Begun in 1357 by architect Peter Parler, it became one of the wonders of the world in the Middle Ages. *(Ch. 7)*

KINDERDIJK WINDMILLS, NETHERLANDS

At Kinderdijk, 55 km (34 miles) southwest of Amsterdam, you can see a collection of working 18th-century windmills, icons of the vast and flat Dutch landscape. On the UNESCO World Heritage list, the windmills, which are still maintained by resident families, are an impossibly romantic place to visit. *(Ch. 4)*

RIALTO BRIDGE, VENICE, ITALY

The first stone bridge over Venice's Grand Canal was completed in 1591 and designed by Antonio da Ponte. The view of the Grand Canal from its railing is one of the city's most famous. At the right time of day, you'll see all the busy boat traffic and the expanse of the city. *(Ch. 8)*

KAPELLBRÜCKE, SWITZERLAND

You may not know its name, but you've seen countless photos of this iconic, covered wooden footbridge over the River Reuss in Luzern, the oldest in Europe dating from the early 14th century. Heavily damaged by a fire in 1993, it was restored and reopened by 1994. Its shingle roof and grand stone water tower are to Luzern what the Matterhorn is to Zermatt. *(Ch. 7)*

COLOSSEUM, ITALY

The largest amphitheater of the Roman world was begun by Emperor Vespasian and inaugurated by his son Titus in AD 80. Although other Roman-era amphitheaters in Europe are better preserved, it is still the most spectacular extant edifice of that ancient empire, not to mention a symbol of Rome just as recognizable as St. Peter's Square. *(Ch. 8)*

Ancient Sights

NEOLITHIC ORKNEY, SCOTLAND
Among the many Neolithic treasures in Orkney are the Ring of Brodgar, a 3,000-year old circle of standing stones, and Skara Brae, the remarkable remains of a similarly ancient village uncovered on the grounds of delightful Skaill House. *(Ch. 2)*

THE ACROPOLIS, GREECE
A beacon of classical glory rising above Athens's architectural mishmash, this iconic citadel of upper Athens still evokes the spirit of the ancient heroes and gods who were once worshipped here. *(Ch. 10)*

POMPEII, ITALY
Once a city of some 15,000 people, this petrified memorial to the cataclysmic eruption of Mt. Vesuvius in AD 79, the excavated ruins of Pompeii offer a unique, occasionally spooky glimpse into life—and sudden death—in Roman times. *(Ch. 8)*

SOUNION, GREECE
The spectacular Temple of Poseidon in Sounion still summons strong emotions in this land of seafarers. The view from the summit is breathtaking. *(Ch. 10)*

LASCAUX CAVE, FRANCE
Discovered in 1940, this magnificently painted cave is like the Louvre of Paleolithic art, and millions have seen its spectacularly painted walls. Although the original cave can't be visited because of its fragility, a painstaking copy christened "Lascaux IV" opened to visitors in 2017. *(Ch. 4)*

VALLEY OF THE TEMPLES, ITALY
These ruins are proudly perched above the sea in a grove full of almond trees in Agrigento; not even in Athens will you find Greek temples this finely preserved. Akragas (the original Greek name) was celebrated by the Pindar as "the most beautiful city built by mortals." *(Ch. 8)*

STONEHENGE, ENGLAND
Almost five millennia after its construction, the power and mystery of this Neolithic stone circle on Salisbury Plain is still spellbinding and mysterious, having baffled archaeologists, not to mention the general public, for centuries. It is one of England's most-visited attractions. *(Ch. 2)*

The Acropolis, Athens, Greece

DELOS, GREECE
A short hop from Mykonos, the mythological birthplace of Apollo, despite having virtually no natural resources of its own, became the religious and political center of the Aegean as the headquarters of the Delian League in 454 BC. But after it was sacked in 88 BC (and again in 69 BC), it was abandoned. The excavations are among the most extensive in the Mediterranean. *(Ch. 10)*

ARÈNES DE NÎMES, FRANCE
Although it's not the biggest, it's certainly the best-preserved Roman amphitheater in the world. This arena is a miniature replica (approximately half the size) of the Colosseum in Rome, sitting in the city center of Nîmes, once a major city of Roman-era Gaul. The arena is still used for concerts and other events. *(Ch. 4)*

PALACE OF KNOSSOS, GREECE
The Minoan civilization flourished in Crete from around 2700 to 1450 BC, when it just disappeared, buried under layers of volcanic ash. Knossos was its center and is one of the most amazing archaeological sites in Greece. Its excavated only began in 1899 by British archaeologist Sir Arthur Evans. *(Ch. 10)*

Churches

TEMPLE EXPIATORI DE LA SAGRADA FAMÍLIA, BARCELONA, SPAIN
Barcelona's most emblematic architectural icon, Antoni Gaudí's Sagrada Família, is still incomplete 140 years after it was begun. This striking and surreal creation was conceived as nothing short of a Bible in stone. *(Ch. 5)*

WESTMINSTER ABBEY, LONDON, ENGLAND
Steeped in centuries of rich and occasionally bloody history, Westminster Abbey is one of England's most iconic buildings, most of which dates from the 1240s. It has hosted 38 coronations and 16 royal weddings, but it is equally known for its permanent residents, from kings to writers, who are buried here. *(Ch. 2)*

ST. PETER'S BASILICA, ROME, ITALY
The world's largest church, built over the tomb of St. Peter, is the most imposing and breathtaking architectural achievement of the Renaissance. No fewer than five of Italy's greatest artists—Bramante, Raphael, Peruzzi, Antonio da Sangallo the Younger, and Michelangelo—died while striving to erect this new St. Peter's. *(Ch. 8)*

SALISBURY CATHEDRAL, ENGLAND
Salisbury is dominated by the towering cathedral, a soaring hymn in stone. It is unique among cathedrals in that it was conceived and built as a whole in the amazingly short span of 38 years (1220–58). The spire, added in 1320, is the tallest in England and a miraculous feat of medieval engineering. *(Ch. 2)*

METEORA MONASTERIES, GREECE
Near Kalambaka, the legendary monasteries of Meteora—one of the wonders of the later Middle Ages—begin to appear along a circular road as it winds 6 km (4 miles) through an unearthly forest of gigantic rock pillars, atop six of which stand impregnable monasteries built in the turbulent 14th century. *(Ch. 10)*

COLOGNE CATHEDRAL, GERMANY
Germany's most-visited landmark embodies one of the purest expressions of the Gothic spirit in Europe. Begun in 1248, the magnificent cathedral in Cologne was not completed until 1880, and then only after the original plans were rediscovered. *(Ch. 7)*

ST. STEPHEN'S CATHEDRAL, VIENNA, AUSTRIA
Vienna's most famous landmark, its soaring 12th-century cathedral, is also Austria's most important Gothic building, and it holds a series of treasures, which you can see on a tour. Mozart's wedding and funeral were both held here. *(Ch. 7)*

DUOMO, FLORENCE, ITALY
It took almost 150 years to complete the Duomo, which was begun in 1295 but not finished until 1436. Its main feature, a work of engineering genius that has become the symbol of Florence, is the magnificent dome designed by Filippo Brunnelleschi. *(Ch. 8)*

Meteora Monasteries, Greece

BASILICA DI SAN MARCO, VENICE, ITALY
The Basilica di San Marco is not only the religious center of a great city, but also an expression of the political, intellectual, and economic aspiration and accomplishments of a place that, for centuries, was at the forefront of European culture. It is a monument not just to the glory of God, but also to the glory of Venice. *(Ch. 8)*

ALEXANDER NEVSKY CATHEDRAL, SOFIA, BULGARIA
You may recognize this neo-Byzantine structure with glittering interlocking domes from the pictures of it that appear on almost every piece of tourist literature about Bulgaria. It was built only at the beginning of the 20th century as a symbol of gratitude to Russia, which liberated Bulgaria from the Ottomon Empire. *(Ch. 9)*

NOTRE-DAME DE PARIS, FRANCE
Although much of the cathedral was destroyed by a fire in 2019, it is being reconstructed and is expected to reopen by the time of the Paris Olympics in 2024. *(Ch. 4)*

ST. JOHN'S CO-CATHEDRAL, MALTA
The plain exterior doesn't betray the spectacularly decorated Baroque interior of this church in Valletta. The floor is a patchwork of marble tombstones of the Knights of Malta (375 of them). *(Ch. 8)*

CHRIST CHURCH AND ST. PATRICK'S CATHEDRALS, DUBLIN
Dublin's two great churches are near each other in the center of the city. Christ Church is older, even though it looks more Victorian than Norman. Jonathan Swift was once the Dean of St. Patrick's, which was named after Ireland's patron saint. *(Ch. 3)*

ST. PAUL'S CATHEDRAL, ENGLAND
This is Sir Christopher Wren's breathtaking masterpiece, completed in 1710. As in Westminster Palace, prominent British subjects are buried here, including Wren himself, John Donne, the Duke of Wellington, and Admiral Lord Nelson. *(Ch. 2)*

Castles and Palaces

BRAN CASTLE, ROMANIA
Looming in the shadow of Mt. Bucegi, Castle Bran is a gloomy though beautifully preserved medieval-era fortress overlooking one of Romania's most important trade routes. It is often called "Dracula's Castle," but Vlad Ţepeş had little if any association with it. *(Ch. 9)*

TOPKAPI PALACE, ISTANBUL
This vast palace on Sarayburnu (Seraglio Point) was the residence of sultans and their harems in addition to being the seat of Ottoman rule from the 1460s until the mid-19th century, when Sultan Abdülmecid I moved his court to Dolmabahçe Palace. *(Ch. 10)*

THE ALHAMBRA, SOUTHERN SPAIN
Spain's most visited attraction is this sprawling palace-fortress that was the last bastion of the 800-year Moorish presence on the Iberian Peninsula. Its patios, courtyards, halls, baths, and gardens rank among the world's most magnificent building achievements. *(Ch. 5)*

WINDSOR CASTLE, ENGLAND
From William the Conqueror to Queen Victoria, the mystique of eight successive royal houses of the British monarchy permeates Windsor and its famous castle, where a fraction of the current King's vast wealth is displayed. It's the largest inhabited castle in the world. *(Ch. 2)*

NEUSCHWANSTEIN, GERMANY
Emerald lakes and the rugged peaks of the Alps surround what's become the world's most famous storybook castle. King Ludwig II commissioned the castle in 1868 (from a stage designer, no less) to pay tribute to the operas of Richard Wagner. Unfortunately, Ludwig died before it was completed. *(Ch. 7)*

CHÂTEAU DE VERSAILLES, FRANCE
Less a monument than a world unto itself, Versailles is the king of palaces. The end result of countless francs, 40 years, and 36,000 laborers, it was Louis XIV's monument to himself—the Sun King. It remains one of the most extravagant and well-known palaces in the world. *(Ch. 4)*

STIRLING CASTLE, SCOTLAND
Its magnificent strategic position on a steep-sided crag made Stirling Castle the grandest prize in the Scots Wars of Independence during the late 13th and early 14th centuries. Robert the Bruce's victory at Bannockburn won both

Royal Castle, Kraków, Poland

the castle and freedom from English subjugation for almost four centuries. *(Ch. 2)*

ROYAL CASTLE, KRAKÓW, POLAND

The Royal Castle that now stands on Wawel Hill dates from the early 16th century, when the Romanesque residence that stood on this site was destroyed by fire. King Sigismund the Old brought artists and craftsmen from Italy to create it. *(Ch. 7)*

REAL ALCÁZAR, SOUTHERN SPAIN

The official local residence of the king and queen was built by Pedro I (1350–69) on the site of Seville's former Moorish alcázar. Built more than 100 years after the Reconquest of Seville, this isn't a genuine Moorish palace but it's authentic enough—parts of the palace and gardens were re-created as a Dornish palace for the final seasons of *Game of Thrones*. *(Ch. 5)*

SCHLOSS SCHÖNBRUNN, VIENNA, AUSTRIA

Play royalty for a day in Vienna by visiting the summer residence of the Habsburgs with its elegant gardens, fountains, fake Roman ruins, a hilltop café, and Europe's oldest zoo. *(Ch. 7)*

ASHFORD CASTLE, IRELAND

Originally built in the 13th century and renovated in the late 19th century by the Guinness family, Ashford is now a luxurious hotel and one of the most magnificent places a visitor can stay in Ireland. *(Ch. 3)*

BRATISLAVA CASTLE

The wonderfully imposing Bratislavský hrad dates from AD 907, but it was largely rebuilt in the Renaissance style in the mid-16th century. It is especially known for its Baroque-era gardens.

Natural Wonders

THE MATTERHORN, SWITZERLAND
At 14,685 feet, the Matterhorn's elegant snaggletooth form rears up over the village of Zermatt. Its famous profile—which appears on candy wrappers, T-shirts, postcards, calendars—and even Disneyland—have made it the most famous mountain in the world. *(Ch. 7)*

SANTORINI SUNSET, GREECE
Even if you aren't a fan of sunset-watching, try to avoid the majesty of the setting sun from atop the thousand-foot-cliffs of the Aegean's most famous (and famously beautiful) island. The late-afternoon view, especially from Ia, at Santorini's northernmost point, is perhaps the most famous sunset viewing spot in the world. *(Ch. 10)*

PLITVICE LAKES, CROATIA
Plitvice Lakes National Park, a UNESCO World Heritage site, is one of Croatia's most visited destinations, with over 16 crystal-clear turquoise lakes connected by waterfalls and cascades. The whole area is encompassed in a 8,000-acre valley of lush green forests and steep hillsides that is also home to a wide variety of wildlife. *(Ch. 9)*

NAZARÉ GIANT WAVES, PORTUGAL
Nazaré, once a simple fishing village, is famed for the giant waves that form in winter thanks to an underground canyon just north of the town, which attracts the most daredevil of surfers. The best place to view the waves—and any surfers up to the challenge—is from the cliff-top fortress of Forte de São Miguel Arcanjo. *(Ch. 5)*

NORTHERN LIGHTS, FINLAND
Once you get away from the city lights, Finland offers great viewing of the aurora borealis. Many tour companies have expertise on how to witness this most memorable of natural phenomena, especially in the country's far northern reaches of Lapland. *(Ch. 6)*

CAUSEWAY COAST, NORTHERN IRELAND
Northern Ireland's most scenic seascape is a natural wonder that no visitor to the area should miss. The Giant's Causeway is a mass of almost 40,000 hexagonal pillars of volcanic basalt that was created (in mythology at least) by the Giant Finn MacCool. *(Ch. 3)*

GULFOSS WATERFALL, GOLDEN CIRCLE, ICELAND
A stop on the so-called Golden Circle tourist route, Iceland's most famous waterfall is a thundering, 105-foot-high double cascade that turns at right angles mid-drop into a dramatic chasm. Europe's largest, it's especially popular in winter, when the outer layers can freeze. *(Ch. 6)*

Loch Ness, Scotland

MT. ETNA, SICILY ITALY
The first time you see Mt. Etna, whether it's trailing clouds of smoke or emitting fiery streaks of lava, is certain to be unforgettable. The best-known symbol of Sicily and one of the world's major active volcanoes, Etna is the largest and highest volcano in Europe—the cone of the crater rises 11,014 feet above sea level. *(Ch. 8)*

LOCH NESS, SCOTLAND
Loch Ness has a greater volume of water than any other British lake, with a maximum depth of over 800 feet, not to mention a famously elusive monster in those depths. The loch and the romantic ruins of Urquhart Castle are among the most iconic sights in Scotland. *(Ch. 2)*

LAKE BLED, SLOVENIA
Surrounded by mountains and forests, picturesque Lake Bled is one of Europe's most beautiful. The island in the center (the only natural island in Slovenia) houses a popular pilgrimage church. *(Ch. 9)*

Museums

VATICAN MUSEUMS, ROME, ITALY
Other than the pope and his papal court, the occupants of the Vatican are some of the most famous artworks in the world. The collection includes the Stanze di Raffaello with their famous frescoes, Old Master paintings, sculptures, and the magnificent Sistine Chapel. *(Ch. 8)*

THE LOUVRE, PARIS, FRANCE
Simply put, the Louvre is the world's greatest art museum—and the largest, with 675,000 square feet of works from almost every civilization on earth. The three most iconic pieces here are, of course, the *Mona Lisa*, the *Venus de Milo*, and *Winged Victory*. *(Ch. 4)*

MUSEUM ISLAND, BERLIN, GERMANY
The architectural monuments and art treasures here hail from ancient Greece to Egypt to Rome to 18th-century Berlin. The highlights are the Neues Museum's Egyptian collection and the the Perganmonmuseum. *(Ch. 7)*

THE PRADO, MADRID, SPAIN
The Prado exhibits the art gathered by Spanish royalty since the time of Ferdinand and Isabella. The Prado's jewels are its works by the nation's three great masters—Goya, Velázquez, and El Greco—though the museum also holds many other masterpieces. *(Ch. 5)*

UFFIZZI GALLERY, FLORENCE, ITALY
The Medici installed their art collections at Europe's first modern museum, open to the public (at first only by request) since 1591. Among the highlights are the *Madonna and Child with Two Angels* by Fra Filippo Lippi; *Birth of Venus* by Sandro Botticelli; and the *Madonna of the Goldfinch* by Raphael. *(Ch. 8)*

RIJKSMUSEUM, AMSTERDAM, NETHERLANDS
The Rijksmuseum's most famous artwork, Rembrandt's monumental *The Night Watch*, has pride of place in its own gallery; other renowned works include Vermeer's *Woman Reading a Letter* and *The Milkmaid* and Frans Hals's *Portrait of a Couple*.If you want to see the Dutch masters, this is the world's best museum. *(Ch. 4)*

NATIONAL ARCHAEOLOGICAL MUSEUM, ATHENS, GREECE
Many of the greatest achievements in ancient Greek sculpture and painting are housed here in the most important museum in Greece. The collection contains highlights from every period of its ancient

Vasamuseet, Stockholm, Sweden

civilization, including the famous Mycenaean Antiquities and beautifully restored frescoes from Santorini. *(Ch. 10)*

GALLERIA DELL'ACCADEMIA, VENICE, ITALY

The greatest collection of Venetian paintings in the world hangs in these galleries founded by Napoléon in 1807 on the site of a religious complex he had suppressed. Highlights include the works of Jacopo Bellini and some of Tintoretto's finest works. *(Ch. 8)*

VASAMUSEET, TOCKHOLM, SWEDEN

The museum is built around the 17th-century warship Vasa, which sank 20 minutes into its maiden voyage but which was preserved in the mud at the bottom of the Baltic and now largely restored to her former glory. *(Ch. 6)*

BRITISH MUSEUM, LONDON, ENGLAND

The sheer scale and importance of the British Museum's many treasures is impossible to overstate or exaggerate; it truly is one of the world's great repositories of human civilization's works, including the Parthenon Sculptures (Elgin Marbles), the Rosetta Stone, and the Sutton Hoo Treasure. *(Ch. 2)*

Wine, Beer, and Spirits

GUINNESS STOREHOUSE, DUBLIN, IRELAND
Ireland's all-dominating brewery, which Arthur Guinness founded in 1759, is also one of Ireland's main tourist attractions. A high-tech museum tells the story of Guinness, Dublin's black blood. At the top, the newly extended Gravity Bar has the city's best views. *(Ch. 3)*

MADEIRA WINE, MADEIRA, PORTUGAL
The fortified wine from Maderia can be either dry or sweet, but it's all made on this Portuguese island in the Atlantic, where you can taste at numerous wineries, including Vinhos Barbeito, Henriques & Henriques, and the most famous, the Madeira Wine Company, which owns Blandy's Wine Lodge in Funchal. But just 15 minutes west of Funchal is Fajã dos Padres, a vineyard with a charming restaurant, where you can pair wine with your food. *(Ch. 5)*

MOSELLE WINE, LUXEMBOURG
Luxembourg's Moselle Valley is centered on the town of Remich, but as with its German counterpart, almost none of the wine is exported, so one of the only ways to enjoy it (and buy a bottle) is at the source. The largest of these wineries is the Caves de Wellenstein. *(Ch. 4)*

CHIANTI WINE, ITALY
Tuscany's most famous wine region is about halfway between Florence and Siena. With more than 5,000 wineries, there are plenty of options for tasting the classic wines of the region, but a visit to Castello di Brolio combines the region's finest castle with a wonderful wine-tasting experience. *(Ch. 8)*

MOSEL WINE, GERMANY
The German Mosel Valley is a beautiful region that has been producing delicious wines for over two centuries. Most of the wines produced here (the main varietal is Riesling, but also Pinot Blanc, Pinot Gris, and Elbling) are not exported and can only be enjoyed at one of the many wineries in the 75-mile span between Trier and Zell. The charming town of Bernkastel-Kues is a great place to start, with wineries and a wine museum in town and many other wineries in the surrounding hills. *(Ch. 7)*

CHÂTEAU MOUTON ROTHSCHILD, FRANCE
The Bordeaux region is France's largest wine-making region, and there are numerous options for wine-tasting at thousands of châteaux (all with an appointment, of course), but one of Bordeaux's most famous wineries, Château Mouton Rothschild, has long accepted visitors and has a welcoming visitor center, offering an excellent tasting experience for those lucky enough to get a reservation. *(Ch. 4)*

PILSNER URQUELL BREWERY, CZECH REPUBLIC
Beer is especially popular throughout Central Europe. In western Bohemia, the historic Pilsner Urquell Brewery, which began producing the first pilsner

Mosel Wine, Germany

beer in 1842, is a must-see for any beer lover. Guided tours (including a visit to the brewhouse and a tasting) are offered daily, and the brewery has its own restaurant, the largest in the Czech Republic. Nearby is a museum dedicated to the history of beer-brewing in the Czech Republic. *(Ch. 7)*

MALT WHISKY TRAIL, SCOTLAND

Nine iconic whisky sights in the Speyside region of the Scottish Highlands make up the Malt Whisky Trail, which includes some of the most famous names in Scotch whisky, including Glenlivet, Glenfiddich, and Strathisla, all located along the River Spey. But whisky production (and your chance to taste a wee dram) are not limited to this region. *(Ch. 2)*

PORT WINE TRAIL, PORTUGAL

Vila Nova de Gaia, just across the river from Porto, has been the headquarters of the port-wine trade since the late 17th century, and most of the famous port wine *bodegas* (wine storehouses) are here within a few minutes' walk of each other, including major names like Sandemann, Taylor, Graham, and Cálem. If you'd like to visit a vineyard (or even stay over), Fajã dos Padres is one of the oldest in the Douro Valley. *(Ch. 5)*

VISITING A WINERY IN SANTORINI, GREECE

Visitors to Santorini need something to do until they can watch its famous sunset. Well, the small island in the Agean produces more wine than any other in the Cyclades, and many of these wineries can be visited. While some offer drop-in tastings, you can also take a guided trip, led by certified sommeliers, with Santorini Wine Tours to visit (and taste) the island's excellent white wines. *(Ch. 10)*

THE CHAMPAGNE CELLARS OF REIMS, FRANCE

The Champagne region's largest city sits on a maze of 200 km of ancient cellars, recognized as a UNESCO World Heritage Site, that can be visited on guided walks. Many of the famed Champagne houses also offer tastings of their vintages, including such famous names as Taittinger, Mumm, Pommery, and Ruinart. *(Ch. 4)*

Towns and Villages

ROTHENBURG-OB-DER-TAUBER, GERMANY
The quintessential Medieval Bavarian town is filled with picturesque half-timber houses and is one of the most Instagram-worthy towns in Germany. Laid low by the havoc of the Thirty Years' War in the 17th century, modern tourism rediscovered the town and made it one of the most popular destinations in Germany. *(Ch. 7)*

THE COTSWOLDS, ENGLAND
With their stone cottages, Cotswold villages tend to be improbably picturesque. There are no unpretty villages in the Cotswolds, but Castle Combe in northwest Wiltshire may be one of the prettiest. *(Ch. 2)*

PERAST, MONTENGRO
This charming, tiny bayfront village is filled with stone villas, most with gardens filled with fig trees and oleander, that were built by local sea captains in the 17th and 18th centuries. *(Ch. 9)*

RAVELLO, ITALY
Overlooking the Bay of Salerno, Ravello shines on Italy's ravishing Amalfi Coast. Known for its refined beauty and gorgeous gardens, its highlight may be the cliff-perched Villa Cimbrone. *(Ch. 8)*

HAY-ON-WYE, WALES
With a crumbling old castle and low-slung buildings, this pretty village on the Welsh-English border has become world famous as a book-lover's paradise; every street is lined with secondhand bookstores. It's now the second-largest bookselling destination in the world. *(Ch. 2)*

ST-PAUL-DE-VENCE, FRANCE
The fortified medieval village in Provence had faded into near-oblivion before it was rediscovered by artists (including Signac, Modigliani, and Bonnard) in the 1920s, who frequented what is now one of France's most famous inns and restaurants, La Colombe d'Or. *(Ch. 4)*

BANSKÁ ŠTIAVNICA, SLOVAKIA
Since the 11th century, this picturesque little town (a UNESCO World Heritage Site and one of the most charming towns in Slovakia) has been devoted to mining. While the open-air mining museum is the biggest attraction, the fairy-tale castle is also a draw. *(Ch. 7)*

Perast, Montengro

BAEZA AND ÚBEDA, SPAIN
North of Granada, the historic town of Baeza, which is nestled between hills and olive groves, is one of the best-preserved old towns of Spain. Founded by the Romans, it was a Moorish capital and, later, was filled with a wealth of Renaissance palaces. Nearby the old town of Úbeda, a bit larger than Baeza, is one of the most outstanding enclaves of 16th-century architecture in Spain and a well-known center for artisanal ceramics. *(Ch. 5)*

NAOUSA, PAROS, GREECE
Lined with Venetian town houses, the charming taverna-filled waterfront of this Cycladic village discovered the power of tourism long ago and now draws more yachts than fishermen to its pretty harbor (now lined with tavernas, shops, and bars), but it's a chic and picturesque location in one of Greece's busiest tourist islands. *(Ch. 10)*

ST. WOLFGANG, AUSTRIA
This charming market town in Austria's Salzkammergut region (the country's lake district) is just southeast of Salzburg at the base of the Shafberg mountain. A popular summertime retreat of composers Samuel Barber and Gian Carlo Menotti, it overlooks the beautiful Wolfgangsee, a crystal-clear Alpine lake perfect for swimming and kayaking. The loveliest way to approach the village is by water, so visitors often leave their cars at Strobl and take one of the historic steamers. *(Ch. 7)*

Historic Sights

SZÉCHENYI FÜRDŐ, BUDAPEST, HUNGARY
The Széchenyi Thermal Bath is Budapest's largest thermal spa and one of Europe's largest, housed in a beautiful neo-Baroque building in the middle of Budapest's City Park with outdoor pools open all winter. Soaking and relaxing here is an essential experience. *(Ch. 7)*

LASCARIS WAR ROOMS, MALTA
In 1943, this underground tunnel complex beneath Valletta, a top-secret British war headquarters, may have decided the course of World War II, when the invasion of Sicily was planned here. It continued in service, being used by NATO until 1977. *(Ch. 8)*

YPRES, BELGIUM
This charming town was completely destroyed during World War I, but its major medieval buildings have been completely restored and now hosts moving memorials as well as the powerful In Flanders Fields Museum and the Memorial Museum Passchendaele 1917. *(Ch. 4)*

D-DAY BEACHES, NORTHERN FRANCE
Five beachheads (dubbed Utah, Omaha, Gold, Juno, and Sword) were established along the Normandy coast on June 6, 1944. Rugged Omaha Beach, near Bayeaux, is where you'll find the Monument du Débarquement and, not far away, the excellent Musée-Mémorial d'Omaha Beach and the nearby cemetery. Some 48 km (30 miles) east is Utah Beach, the other U.S. beachhead. *(Ch. 4)*

TOWER OF LONDON, LONDON, ENGLAND
Parts of this complex date back 11 centuries. The tower has been a prison (holding such famous prisoners as Anne Boleyn, Princess Elizabeth, Sir Walter Raleigh, Guy Fawkes, and even Rudolf Hess), an armory, and a mint, It now houses the Crown Jewels and the famous ravens and is one of London's iconic tourist sights. Looming nearby is the equally iconic, Victoria-era Tower Bridge. *(Ch. 2)*

DUBROVNIK OLD TOWN, CROATIA
Few sights in Croatia are as impressive or popular as this medieval wonder of a city. With its ancient walls and bell towers set high above the blue waters of the Adriatic, Dubrovnik commands a spectacular location. Walk the entire circuit of Dubrovnik's medieval city walls—which date back to the 13th century—for splendid views and a bit of that *Game of Thrones* feeling. *(Ch. 9)*

Dubrovnik Old Town, Croatia

ANNE FRANK HOUSE, AMSTERDAM, NETHERLANDS
This is the home of the most widely read Dutch author, and the setting of her famous book. Some might be too haunted by the story's tragic ending to relish a visit, but many can appreciate the Anne Frank Foundation's efforts to raise awareness about Europe's anti-Semitic past and discrimination everywhere. Visits are possible only with online timed tickets purchased in advance (it's one of Amsterdam's most popular sights). *(Ch. 4)*

BATH, ENGLAND
The original baths here date back to Roman times, but they became fashionable for English society in the 18th century; Bath is also known for its grand late-18th-century Palladian architecture and appearances in the works of Jane Austen, who set parts of both *Northanger Abbey* and *Persuasion* here. *(Ch. 2)*

WIELICZKA SALT MINE, POLAND
The vast, underground salt mines near Kraków are over 700 years old. Fans have included Polish kings, Nicolaus Copernicus, Johann Wolfgang von Goethe, Tsar Alexander I, and Emperor Franz Josef. The magnificent Chapel of the Blessed Kinga is a veritable cathedral hewn from salt. *(Ch. 7)*

MONET'S GARDEN, GIVERNY, NORTHERN FRANCE
Impressionist painter Claude Monet lived the second half of his life in the small village of Giverny, north of Paris, and his house (and also his more famous garden) still stands—along with its famous bridge and water lilies—as a reminder of what inspired some of his greatest work. *(Ch. 4)*

Activities

KAYAKING IN THE FJORDS, NORWAY
Norway's fjords are themselves bucket-list-worthy, among the most beautifully scenic waterways you could hope to explore, with raging waterfalls gushing down their steep cliff faces. The best way to experience the fjords is on water, especially up close on a kayak. *(Ch. 6)*

WATCHING A SHAKESPEARE PLAY, STRATFORD-UPON-AVON, ENGLAND
To see a play by Shakespeare in the town where he was born—and perhaps after you've visited his birthplace or other sights—is a magical experience. *(Ch. 2)*

WATCHING A FLAMENCO PERFORMANCE, SOUTHERN SPAIN
You'll find the Arab-influenced music and dance of flamenco almost everywhere in Andalusia, its spiritual home, but especially at La Casa del Flamenco in Seville, where performances are held in an atmospheric 15th-century house. *(Ch. 5)*

TRADITIONAL PUB TOUR, DUBLIN
The quintessential activity in Dublin is a visit to a local pub, ideally one with music. Dublin is still filled with traditional pubs such as the Brazen Head on Lower Bridge Street, where you can get a perfect pint of Guinness and hear traditional Irish music. You can also take an organized tour. *(Ch. 3)*

SHOPPING IN MILAN, ITALY
It should be no surprise that the center of the Italian fashion industry is also a great place to shop. The heart of Milan's shopping activity is the Quadrilatero della Moda district, north of the Duomo. But you don't want to miss the Galleria Vittorio Emanuele II, a spectacular covered arcade (with the original Prada store, among others). Corso Buenos Aires in northeastern Milan is one of the busiest in the city with more than 350 stores and outlets to choose from. *(Ch. 7)*

RIDING IN A GONDOLA, VENICE, ITALY
Despite its high price, taking a trip along the canals of Venice in a gondola with a singing driver is the quintessential Venice experience. Just try to avoid the middle of the day (there's no shade), and pick an engaging gondolier; the price itself is set, though it's slightly higher at night. *(Ch. 8)*

The Glacier Express, Switzerland

THE GLACIER EXPRESS, SWITZERLAND
Running between Zermatt and St. Moritz, the luxurious Glacier Express is a slow, daylong trip through some of Switzerland's most scenic areas, including the Rhine Gorge. All cars are panoramic, affording spectacular views, and you can add on a gourmet lunch. *(Ch. 7)*

EATING PIZZA IN NAPLES, ITALY
A highlight of any trip to Naples is the possibility of eating a *verace Pizza Napoletana* where it was invented in its modern form in the late 19th century. The most authentic pizzas are made from the freshest ingredients and baked in a wood-fired oven—simple and delicious. *(Ch. 8)*

WATCHING AN ENGLISH FOOTBALL MATCH, ENGLAND
Whether you take in a match from one of the members of England's Premier League or just a local club, watching a football (i.e., soccer) match can be the highlight of any trip for a true fan of the game. You can see great football not only in London but all over the country. *(Ch. 2)*

A NIGHT AT LA SCALA, MILAN, ITALY
Even if you aren't an opera aficionado, if you are able to score tickets, seeing an opera in Milan's La Scala, the home theater of Giuseppe Verdi, is an unforgettable experience. The attached museum is fascinating and will also give you a glimpse inside the celebrated theater. *(Ch. 8)*

Events

OKTOBERFEST, MUNICH, GERMANY
The original (and world's largest) fall beer festival is held annually beginning in late September in Munich's vast Oktoberfest grounds, where some 6 million people gather in tents to drink beer, eat copious amounts of food, sing, and celebrate Bavarian culture and folk traditions. *(Ch. 7)*

EDINBURGH FRINGE, SCOTLAND
Every August, the Fringe, the world's largest arts festival, is a decidedly down-to-earth companion to the high-arts Edinburgh Festival. *(Ch. 2)*

MONTREAUX JAZZ FESTIVAL, SWITZERLAND
This famous resort on the shores of Lac Léman is best known for its annual jazz festival over two weeks in July, which draws big-name artists. *(Ch. 7)*

MIDSUMMER, DALARNA, SWEDEN
For two weeks every summer, the most festive place in Sweden is the Dalarna region, the province around Lake Siljan, where Sweden's most beloved folk traditions are at their strongest. *(Ch. 6)*

SZIGET FESTIVAL, BUDAPEST, HUNGARY
The first Sziget Festival in 1993 was a small gathering, but it has since evolved into one of Europe's largest music festivals with over 1,000 shows across 60 stages, for seven days straight every August. It draws top names in music as well as DJs. *(Ch. 7)*

RUNNING OF THE BULLS, PAMPLONA, SPAIN
Since it was popularized by Ernest Hemingway's novel *The Sun Also Rises,*Pamplona's particular celebration of the festival of San Fermín each July has drawn the brave and foolhardy to run through the streets with the bulls that are released each morning. *(Ch. 5)*

WIMBLEDON, LONDON
Many tennis fans dream of making the pilgrimage to this famed tournament in London, the only tennis Grand Slam event played on traditional grass courts. Planning for this trip must start in mid-November, when the ticket lottery for the following summer's tournament is held. *(Ch. 2)*

Venice Carnevale, Italy

VENICE CARNEVALE, ITALY
Carnival celebrations are found all over Europe, but for the 12 days leading up to Ash Wednesday, none celebrates more than Venice, which sees throngs of masked revelers in the streets. Some come for the extravagantly priced masquerade balls, but many people some just to hang out and enjoy the street entertainment. *(Ch. 8)*

OBERAMMERGAU PASSION PLAY, GERMANY
Every decade since 1680, the small town of Oberammergau has presented a play based on the last days of Christ (performed solely by those who are born in or have lived in the village for over 20 years). The epic play stretches into the night (with a break for dinner), drawing a half-million spectators from May to October during performance years. *(Ch. 7)*

THE PALIO, SIENA, ITALY
Siena is often described as Italy's best-preserved medieval city, drawing visitors year-round to its magnificent Duomo, but this famed, twice-annual bareback horse race around the town's main piazza (on July 2 and August 16) has been held since 1633 (the second race was added in 1701), drawing even more visitors, including James Bond in *Quantum of Solace.* *(Ch. 8)*

Seasonal Travel

SKIING IN CHAMONIX-MONT-BLANC, FRANCE
The first winter Olympics was held in Chamonix in 1924. Since then, the resort on the slopes of Mont-Blanc has become one of the most popular ski resorts in Europe. It even has the world's highest cable car, at 12,000 feet, on Aiguille du Midi. *(Ch. 4)*

WHALE-WATCHING IN THE NORTH, ICELAND
Iceland's rich waters, especially around Húsavík, is widely considered the whale-watching capital of Europe, where whales are so accustomed to the daily tours that they will often come up extremely close to the boats and say "hi" during the season from April through October. *(Ch. 6)*

CHRISTMAS MARKET IN DRESDEN, GERMANY
During Advent, the four weeks leading up to Christmas, many German towns host festive Christmas markets, offering ornaments, food, and mulled wine. The oldest, which began in 1434, is in Dresden, which is known for its buttery stollen. *(Ch. 7)*

PETRA TOU ROMIOU, CYPRUS
Cyprus is known for its beautiful beaches, which draw thousands of tourists each year. Some of the best are along the country's western tip, where you'll also find the mythological birthplace of Aphrodite at Petra tou Romiou. Swimming around the rock is said to bring you eternal love. Nearby are more wonderful beaches around Paphos. *(Ch. 10)*

EL VALLE DEL JERTE, SPAIN
Spring in the Valle del Jerte in north Extremadura offers Spain's best display of cherry blossoms, backed by the snow-capped Gredos mountains. The valley is beautiful anytime in the spring or fall, but the cherry blossoms come out in mid-March, making this the prime time for regional tourism. *(Ch. 5)*

TULIP TIME, THE NETHERLANDS
Tulips are virtually synonymous with Holland, and tulip time, which typically runs from mid-March through mid-May sees huge crowds coming from all over the world to see the blooming bulb fields of South Holland, which are transformed into a vivid series of Mondrian paintings through the colors of millions of tulips and other flowers. *(Ch 4)*

SUMMER NIGHTLIFE IN MYKONOS, GREECE
Every summer, throngs of young (and sometimes not so young) partiers are drawn to tiny Mykonos,

Tulip Time, The Netherlands

known both for its raucous beach parties with top international DJs beginning in the late afternoon, as for its bars in the Little Venice area, which may not fill up until after 11. At both, the party goes on until the week hours. *(Ch. 10)*

THE LAVENDER ROUTE, PROVENCE, FRANCE
Lavender fields can be found all over Provence from June through August, when the purple flowers bloom and fill the air with their perfumed scent. The village of Sault holds its Fête de la Lavande on August 15. But the best place to see lavender blooms is the 12th-century Cistercian Abbaye Notre-Dame de Sénanque near Gordes. *(Ch. 4)*

SKIING IN KITZBÜHEL, AUSTRIA
Kitzbühel is indisputably one of Austria's most fashionable winter resorts, although the town boasts a busy summer season as well. In winter, many skiers are attracted by the famous Ski Safari—a carefully planned, clever combination of chairlifts, gondola lifts, draglifts, and runs that lets you ski for more than 145 km (91 miles) without having to walk a single foot. *(Ch. 7)*

HIKING IN THE CINQUE TERRE, ITALY
The five fishing villages that make up the "Cinque Terre" are connected by footpaths that draw throngs of tourists each summer to this gorgeous stretch of Ligurian Coast. But the best time to do the hike is in September or May, when the weather is milder and the crowds lighter. *(Ch. 8)*

Best Souvenirs to Take Home

"EVIL EYE" AMULET, GREECE AND TURKEY
Made of blue glass, this ubiquitous, eye-shaped amulet (*mati* in Greek, *nazar boncuğu* in Turkish) can be purchased in every souvenir shop in Greece and Turkey in the form of keychains and pendants. It protects you against the "evil eye" (the jealous or envious look of others).

GLOVES IN ITALY
Italy is known for its leather goods, but one of the best things to buy (at generally favorable prices) are leather gloves. Finely made, these will last for decades. One of the best places is Madova, a manufacturer in Florence just across the Ponte Vecchio from the Uffizzi Gallery.

MOZARTKUGEL, AUSTRIA
If you're sweet on Wolfgang Amadeus Mozart, you'll be nuts for these pistachio-, marzipan-, and nougat–filled chocolates, with a foil wrapper sporting the composer's likeness. Rival brands, each using a different portrait of Mozart, claim to be the original, but the blue-and-silver wrapped ones made by Fürst came first (appropriately).

WOODEN SPOONS, ROMANIA
The skill of carving intricately crafted wooden spoons is passed down through families in Romania. The handle is what gives the spoon its meaning. Most common is the solar symbol, which conveys protection. But you'll also find roosters (hope) and dragobetele (intertwined birds, which signify love).

TEA, TURKEY
In a country that has the most per-capita tea consumption in the world, it's not uncommon for you to get a glass of sweet apple tea after your meal. All manner of tea is available in the Spice Market in Istanbul, and you can also buy sets of tea glasses or a Turkish teapot to make it.

AMBER JEWELRY, POLAND AND LITHUANIA
Beautiful jewelry made from natural amber is common in countries that line the Baltic, where amber is often mined, and it's especially popular in Poland and Lithuania. Just be aware that there's a lot of fake amber out there made from resin, so buy from a reputable dealer.

WINE, GERMANY
You may first think of France and Italy for wine, but Germany produces excellent wine, especially from Riesling and Pinot Noir grapes. Why buy this as your souvenir? Most German wineries are small producers and don't export, so if you taste a good wine, you may not find it back home.

CHEESE, FRANCE
France produces some of the world's most famous (and best) cheese varieties, including Camembert, Brie, Roquefort, and Comté. But why buy cheese in France instead of your local Whole Foods? Most raw-milk cheeses cannot be imported commercially into the U.S., so French Camembert just tastes different (and better).

Cheese, France

However, individual travelers are allowed to carry in raw milk cheese.

SWEATERS, SCOTLAND
If you find yourself in western Scotland or in the Shetland Islands, you can find no better souvenir than an authentic Argyle or Fair Isle sweater that will remind you of your travels for years. Good-quality sweaters aren't cheap, but they are well-made and will last.

CHOCOLATE, SWITZERLAND
Known for its fine chocolate makers, Switzerland requires its chocolate to be made entirely in Switzerland using some locally sourced ingredients. The Swiss are particularly known for milk chocolate. Some of the best makers are Cailler in Broc, Teuscher in Zurich, Villars in Fribourg, Läderach in Bilten, and Lindt in Bern.

KUKSA, NORWAY AND FINLAND
If you are looking for an inexpensive but useful souvenir from your travels in Scandinavia, consider a *kuksa*, a carved wooden drinking cup (often with two finger holes on the handle). These are typically carved from birch wood by the Sami people, and the best are made from birch burls (but these are both rare and expensive).

OLIVE OIL, SPAIN
A useful souvenir of any trip to Spain is olive oil, which tends to have a fruitier flavor than Italian olive oil. Much Spanish olive oil originates in Jaén province (in Andalusia). Among the best companies are Castillo de Canena, Oro Bailén, Venta del Barón, and Oro del Desierto.

SEA SALT, CROATIA AND SLOVENIA
Europe's oldest salt pans are in the unassuming town of Ston, in Croatia's Pelješac Peninsula. But excellent salt is produced in Nin and also in Piran, in Slovenia. A small bag is a portable and useful souvenir.

GIN AND CHOCOLATE, ENGLAND
Gin has had a big resurgence in recent years, and a limited-batch artisanal gin is a great gift to bring home. Teetolaters may be more interested in British milk chocolate, which is richer and smoother (and not quite as sweet) as American chocolate.

What to Watch and Read

IF IT'S TUESDAY, THIS MUST BE BELGIUM

Directed by Mel Stuart, the comedy follows the misadventures of a group of American tourists doing a grand bus tour of Europe in the late 1960s. The cast includes Ian McShane and Suzanne Pleshette (and a cameo by a young Joan Collins).

MY LIFE IN RUINS

In the follow-up to her biggest hit *My Big Fat Greek Wedding,* Nia Vardalos plays a Greek-American tour guide leading a group of tourists through Greece while dealing with her own love life.

A ROOM WITH A VIEW BY E. M. FORSTER

Forster's comic novel of manners follows a young English woman, who eventually finds love through a trip to Italy with her spinster cousin. The equally well-received film starred Helena Bonham Carter, Daniel Day Lewis, and Maggie Smith.

SUMMERTIME

Katharine Hepburn stars as a middle-aged secretary visiting Venice, who falls in love with a married Italian man (Rossani Brazzi) in this film directed by David Lean (and based on the stage play *The Time of the Cuckoo* by Arthur Laurents).

TWO FOR THE ROAD

The film directed by Stanley Donen follows the complicated marriage of Audrey Hepburn and Albert Finney through several trips to France, constantly jumping back and forth in time.

THE LIGHT ON THE PIAZZA BY ELIZABETH SPENCER

An American woman travels in Italy with her developmentally disabled daughter, who falls in love with a handsome, younger Italian man. The novel was adapted into a film starring Olivia de Havilland and Yvette Mimieux as well as a popular stage musical.

DODSWORTH BY SINCLAIR LEWIS

A retired automobile executive tours Europe with his wife, and their marriage dissolves along with their travels, as they realize they have very different ideas of what they want in their golden years. It was adapted into a well-regarded film directed by William Wyler and starring Walter Huston.

ROMAN HOLIDAY

The classic starring Gregory Peck and Audrey Hepburn follows a European princess, who flees her duties to have a brief, fun day in Rome with an American journalist. Hepburn won a Best Actress Oscar for her role.

THE DA VINCI CODE BY DAN BROWN

The best-selling novel follows the adventures of an American professor, who has to follow clues to a veritable bucket list of major sights in Europe to solve an enduring mystery. The equally successful film adaptation starred Tom Hanks.

GAME OF THRONES

The HBO adaptation of George R.R. Martin's successful book series used bucket list sights in Europe to portray his fictional world of Westeros and Esteros. Large sections of the series were filmed in Northern Ireland, Seville, Dubrovnik, Malta, and Iceland.

TO CATCH A THIEF

The French Riviera is a co-star in this thriller from Alfred Hitchcock about a retired thief starring Cary Grant and Grace Kelly. The film was adapted from a less well-known novel by David Dodge.

THE TALENTED MR. RIPLEY BY PATRICIA HIGHSMITH

In this psychological thriller, amoral Tom Ripley falls accidentally into both good fortune and murder as he follows Dickie Greenleaf to Italy. The second successful film adaptation starring Matt Damon and Jude Law is just as well-known, but that was the second time the novel was filmed. The first, a predominately French-language adaptation titled *Purple Noon,* starred Alain Delon as Tom.

THE WAY

Martin Sheen finishes walking the Camino de Santiago in place of his son, who is killed in an accident along the pilgrimage route, in this film directed by Sheen's own son Emilio Estevez.

UNDER THE TUSCAN SUN BY FRANCES MAYES

Mayes's memoir details her experiences buying and renovating an abandoned Tuscan villa. The nonfiction memoir inspired a fictional film starring Diane Lane.

A YEAR IN PROVENCE BY PETER MAYLE

The British writer chronicles his attempt to relocate to Provence with his wife and their misadventures as they renovate a Provençal farmhouse in the late 1980s. The success of this first volume inspired Mayle to write three more books about his experiences in France.

NATIONAL LAMPOON'S EUROPEAN VACATION

The hapless Griswold family goes on a whirlwind tour of western Europe in this comedy starring Chevy Chase and Beverly D'Angelo.

THE SOUND OF MUSIC

No film has inspired travel to Salzburg more than this one. And since the film was made on-site, most of the set pieces can still be visited on a tour, as many people do every year.

AMÉLIE

Paris has rarely looked as attractive as in this whimsical French-language film about a young Parisian woman and the lives she touches.

NEITHER HERE NOR THERE: TRAVELS IN EUROPE BY BILL BRYSON

The American-born, but British-at-heart writer revisits the Europe of his youth, retracing a backpacking trip he took with a friend in the 1970s. Bryson is one of the best, with a beautiful command of writing and sense of place, not to mention great sense of humor.

FOR THE LOVE OF EUROPE: MY FAVORITE PLACES, PEOPLE, AND STORIES BY RICK STEVES

Few writers have done more to introduce Europe to Americans than Rick Steves, both through his tour company and also his best-selling travel guides. This is an easy read, but an important one, from a traveler who loves Europe and wants to share his love with others.

MY FAMILY AND OTHER ANIMALS BY GERALD DURRELL

British naturalist Gerald Durrell is better known to many for his trilogy about his family's travels and travails when they relocated to Corfu in the 1930s, the first of which was published in the mid-1950s. The books were adapted for the TV series *The Durrells in Corfu.*

Cultural Customs to Embrace

To truly *feel* like a local, you need to adopt their uniquely local ways of being. Each country has its own hard-to-translate cultural concepts or ways of being that contribute to the essence of the place and the people.

LA PASSEGGIATA, ITALY

What sounds like a delicious pasta is in fact an age-old after-dinner tradition. Every evening, Italians of all ages take a gentle stroll to connect with their community and to see and be seen. Leave the sportswear at home; this is a social, not a physical, workout.

HYGGE, DENMARK

First, learn how to pronounce it—"*hoogah.*" Defined as a "quality of coziness and comfortable conviviality that engenders a feeling of contentment or well-being," Danes practice *hygge* by actively creating daily space for peace and comfort through candles, soothing drinks, and cozy blankets.

FIKA, SWEDEN

Swedes consider it essential to make time for *fika* every day. It means making time to share a cup of coffee and something to eat (preferably cake) with loved ones. Rather than grabbing a coffee on the run, *fika* is an opportunity to stop and be present. And, yes, have cake.

THE CRAIC, IRELAND

It's not a drug, but you can get an endorphin high from embracing the general sense of fun and a love for life that is prized in Irish culture. *Craic* often goes with *ceoil* (music), so a traditional Irish session is a good place to start. For "mighty craic" add good stories and friends.

FRILUFTSLIV, NORWAY

Friluftsliv means "free air life" and spending time outdoors is an integral part of Norwegian life. The concept recognizes the importance of being connected to nature to improve your sense of well-being.

FLÂNER, FRANCE

The concept of *flâner* is so French that there is no English equivalent. It means to wander, both inward and outward, with no destination in mind. To practice, observe your surroundings with a philosophical spirit as you wander the charming streets of Paris.

LA SOBREMESA, SPAIN

Sobremesa literally means "over the table," and it means that you are expected to linger at/over the table after a meal is finished. For Spaniards, how you eat is as important as what you eat, and relaxed, leisurely after-dinner conversation and fun is prioritized. Note: you may need to partake in another Spanish custom the next day—*la siesta* (nap time).

LAGOM, SWEDEN

Lagom is all about balance in everything from how much cake you have at *fika* to how many hours you work. While traveling, it can mean balancing an overly ambitious agenda with time for breaks and spontaneous play.

GEZELLIGHEID, NETHERLANDS

Similar to the Scandinavian concept of *hygge*, the Dutch concept of *gezelligheid* is a revered practice of prioritizing cozy friendliness, usually in a snug pub with good beer. If anyone says " *Gezelligheid kent geen tijd* " (which means "being gezellig knows no time"), then you need to embrace the concept and buy another round instead of rushing off.

MERAKI, GREECE

The Greek concept of *meraki* means to put your heart and soul into what you do—to bring pride and care to your efforts. You can incorporate meraki into your daily life by bringing genuine passion to preparing a meal or to creating a photo album of your amazing Greek vacation.

Chapter 2

ENGLAND, SCOTLAND, AND WALES

WELCOME TO ENGLAND, SCOTLAND, AND WALES

TOP REASONS TO GO

★ **London's Icons:** From Big Ben to Buckingham Palace, London's landmarks are a must-see when visiting the U.K.

★ **Edinburgh:** With its Royal Mile, literary history, and renowned events and festivals, Edinburgh ticks most boxes.

★ **Snowdonia National Park:** Experience the Welsh countryside at its most gorgeous and dramatic in the home of Wales's highest mountain.

★ **Stonehenge:** Awe-inspiring and mystical, Stonehenge is one of the most famous prehistoric sites in England.

★ **Oxford and Cambridge:** England is home to these two prestigious universities, where you'll find centuries of history among ancient buildings and museums.

★ **Isle of Skye:** With the misty Cuillin Mountains and rocky shores, Skye has few rivals among Scotland's islands for sheer loveliness.

1 London and Vicinity. Not only Britain's financial and governmental center but also one of the world's great cities, London has mammoth museums, posh palaces, and iconic sights.

2 England. In England, historic, cultured, cosmopolitan towns and cities are liberally sprinkled between a richly diverse landscape that takes in pleasant green hills, dramatic moors, remote Broads, and glorious coastline.

3 Edinburgh. The captivating Scottish capital is a huge tourist draw, famous for its high-perched castle, Old Town and 18th-century New Town, and the most celebrated arts festival in the world.

4 Scotland. Between the Highlands and Lowlands, islands and lochs, Scotland is a land of immense wild beauty, with historic cities, mythical monsters, and no shortage of world-famous whisky distilleries to visit.

5 Wales. Clinging to the western edge of England, Wales is impossibly green and ruggedly beautiful, with soaring mountains, magnificent coastlines, and stunning castles.

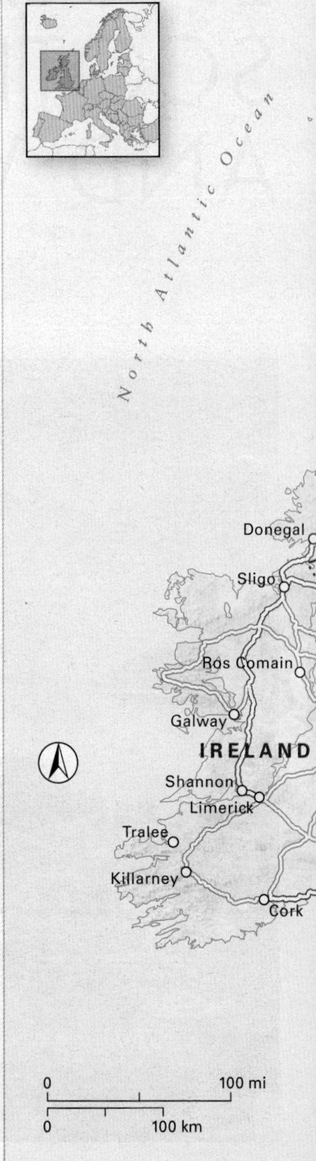

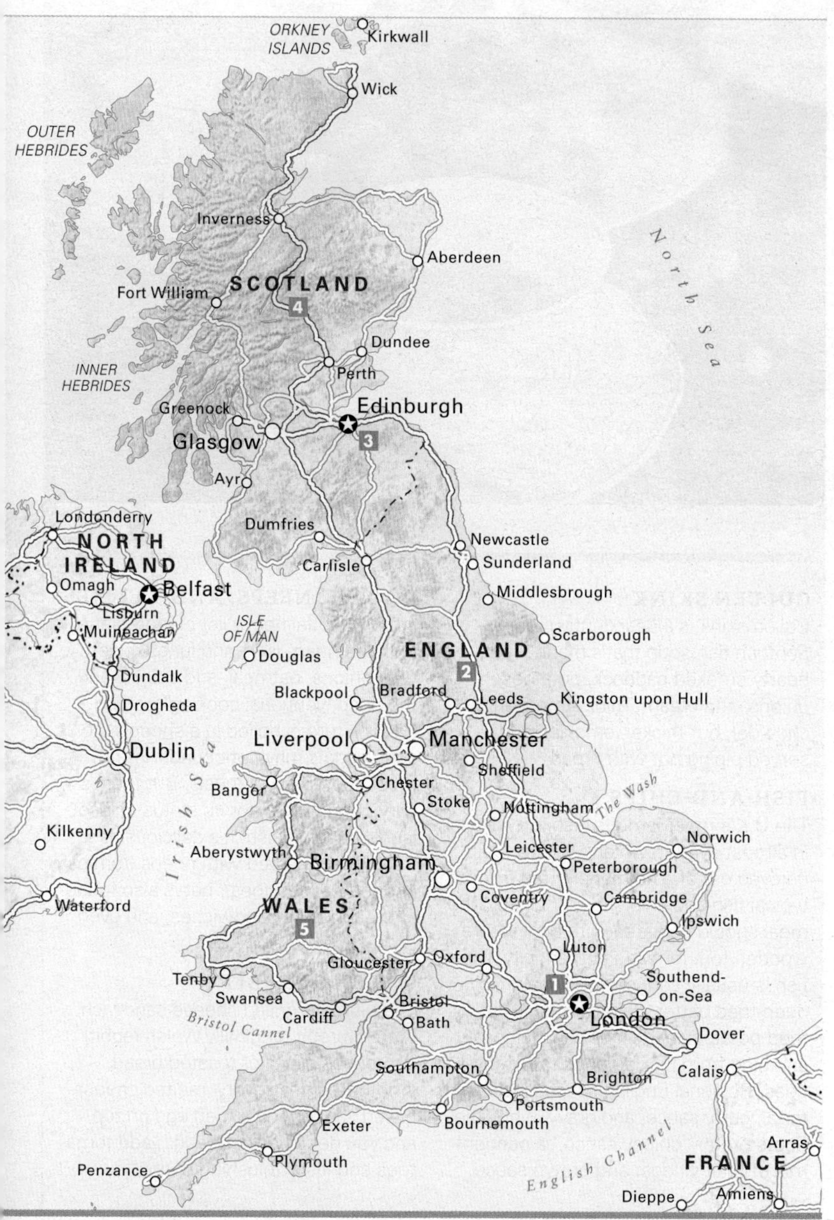
ORKNEY ISLANDS
Kirkwall
Wick
OUTER HEBRIDES
Inverness
Aberdeen
SCOTLAND
Fort William
4
North Sea
Dundee
Perth
INNER HEBRIDES
Greenock
Edinburgh
Glasgow
3
Ayr
Londonderry
Dumfries
NORTH IRELAND
Newcastle
Carlisle
Sunderland
Omagh
Belfast
Middlesbrough
Lisburn
ISLE OF MAN
Muineachan
Scarborough
Douglas
ENGLAND
Dundalk
2
Blackpool
Bradford
Leeds
Kingston upon Hull
Drogheda
Liverpool
Manchester
Dublin
Sheffield
Chester
Bangor
The Wash
Stoke
Nottingham
Irish Sea
Kilkenny
Norwich
Leicester
Aberystwyth
Birmingham
Peterborough
Waterford
Coventry
Cambridge
WALES
Ipswich
5
Luton
Gloucester
Oxford
Tenby
Southend-on-Sea
1
Swansea
Bristol
London
Cardiff
Bath
Bristol Cannel
Dover
Southampton
Calais
Brighton
Portsmouth
Exeter
Bournemouth
English Channel
Arras
Plymouth
Penzance
FRANCE
Dieppe
Amiens

WHAT TO EAT IN ENGLAND, SCOTLAND, AND WALES

Afternoon tea

CULLEN SKINK

Cullen skink is a decadently creamy Scottish fish soup that's made with hearty smoked haddock, potatoes, onions, and cream. Think American chowder, but thicker, smokier, and served piping hot with bread.

FISH-AND-CHIPS

The U.K.'s most famous dish is available in almost every town and village. Best enjoyed out of a hot paper wrap from a typical fish-and-chip shop, or chippy, the meal should be eaten with a miniature wooden fork for extra authenticity. The fish is usually cod, covered in a crispy deep-fried batter. Chips are thick-cut fried potatoes and sides can include anything from pickled eggs to mushy peas. Regional English sauces include tartar, curry sauce, and gravy, while the Scots prefer "chippy sauce," a pungent mix of malt vinegar and brown sauce.

HAGGIS, NEEPS, AND TATTIES

From the offal-heavy list of ingredients (minced heart, liver, and lungs mixed with onions, oatmeal, and spices) and the unconventional cooking method (the mixture is boiled in a sheep's stomach), haggis may not sound like the most appetizing of meals. But there's a very good reason for its status as Scotland's national dish: it's delicious. It's traditionally served with neeps (turnips) and tatties (potatoes), but is also found at breakfast, in sandwiches, and even on nachos.

WELSH RAREBIT

The ultimate grilled cheese sandwich, Welsh rarebit (originally Welsh rabbit) comprises slices of toasted bread smothered in a savory, melted cheese-based sauce. Add a fried egg on top and you get a "buck rarebit"; add tomatoes and it's a "blushing bunny."

CURRY

The 1970s saw a wave of South Asian immigrants arriving in the U.K. and setting up restaurants in big urban centers like London, Birmingham, and Manchester. These days, there's a mix of Indian, Bangladeshi, and Pakistani restaurants in almost every town and village, serving some of the finest curry anywhere outside of Asia.

CHEESE

The English stalwart Cheddar, Cheshire, Double Gloucester, and Stilton cheeses are complemented by traditional and experimental cheeses from small, local makers.

BANGERS AND MASH

Simple but effective, this pub grub staple comprises sausages served on a bed of mashed potatoes and topped with onion gravy. The "bangers" are usually Cumberlands—long, coiled, and particularly meaty pork sausages—but they can also be made from lamb or beef.

BARA BRITH

Literally translated as "speckled bread," this tasty, fruity Welsh loaf is made with flour, yeast, butter, eggs, dried fruits (usually raisins, currants, and sultanas) soaked overnight in tea, and mixed spices. When slathered with salted butter, it's the perfect tea time treat.

Bangers and mash

Fish-and-chips

ETON MESS

Named after the famous boarding school near Windsor, this traditional dessert consists of meringue, whipped cream, and strawberries (or other summer fruits). As the name suggests, it looks a little messy, but it tastes divine.

SMOKED FISH

From Arbroath smokies to Finnan haddie, smoked fish is a staple of Scottish dining tables. Smokies are haddock, salted and dried overnight, then smoked in a barrel over a hardwood fire, while Finnan haddies are cold-smoked haddock, cooked over green wood and peat. Visitors will also find menus featuring smoked herring (kippers), smoked trout, and, of course, smoked salmon.

AFTERNOON TEA

What is afternoon tea, exactly? Well, it means real loose-leaf tea—Earl Grey, English Breakfast, Ceylon, Darjeeling, or Assam—brewed in a fine bone china or porcelain pot, and served with fine bone cups and saucers, milk or lemon, and silver spoons, taken between noon and 6 pm. For the quintessential English ritual, enjoy a pot of tea alongside finger sandwiches, fruit scones, and cakes.

England, Scotland, and Wales Snapshot

Know Before You Go

CHECK TO SEE IF YOUR TRIP FALLS DURING A BANK HOLIDAY.

Several national "bank" holidays are celebrated throughout the year in the U.K.: May Day (first Monday in May), the last Monday in May, the last Monday in August, and Boxing Day (December 26). In Scotland, locals also get January 2 and usually St. Andrews Day (November 30) off, but not Easter Monday. Many stores and some attractions might be closed, and some restaurants and museums might be much busier than usual.

DO YOU SPEAK ENGLISH?

In England, an elevator is a lift; instead of waiting in line, you queue; the bathroom is known as the toilet, the loo, or the WC (for water-closet) so in public spaces you may see a W/C sign instead of a restroom sign; pants are trousers; underpants are pants or knickers; french fries are chips; potato chips are crisps; and soccer is football. Say "cheers" while clinking glasses or to say good-bye or thank you.

Planning Your Time

The land mass of England, Scotland, and Wales is relatively small, which makes covering ground by car a good choice. Bear in mind that in the countryside roads are windy, so journey times increase exponentially. By car, London to Edinburgh is eight hours and London to Cardiff is three. Otherwise planes and trains are convenient. Two weeks spent in England, Scotland, and Wales is enough to take in the main sites-although three is better.

Great Trips

3 days: Portmeirion to Snowdonia National Park to Aberystwyth.

4 days: Cambridge to Oxford to Cotswolds.

5 days: Edinburgh to Inverness to Isle of Skye.

Big Events

RHS Chelsea Flower Show. This five-day floral extravaganza in May is also a society event, held in London's upmarket Chelsea neighborhood.

Glastonbury Festival. Iconic and idiosyncratic, this not-quite-annual music event sprawls across Somerset farmland and features hundreds of big-name bands over three days in late June or early July.

Edinburgh's Festival. Taking over Scotland's capital every August, this cultural cornucopia is an amalgam of festivals running concurrently. Most prominent are the Edinburgh International Festival (www.eif.co.uk), featuring everything from opera to cutting-edge theater; the rowdier Edinburgh Fringe (www.edfringe.com), which highlights comedy and cabaret; and the Royal Edinburgh Military Tattoo (www.edintattoo.co.uk), a heady mix of music, dance, and military pageantry.

The Hay Festival. Every May and June, the world's leading writers, journalists, comedians, and philosophers descend on the small Welsh town of Hay for roughly ten days of talks, events, and workshops contributing to a dreamy literary experience in an even dreamier setting.

What To...

READ

Wuthering Heights, Emily Brontë. A passionate love story set in Yorkshire moors.

Clanlands, Sam Heughan and Graham McTavish. A wild and epic road trip around Scotland.

Collected Poems, Dylan Thomas. Emotive and lyrical as a writer, Dylan Thomas was also fiercely Welsh.

London: The Biography, Peter Ackroyd. The definitive history of the English capital.

WATCH

Notting Hill. An improbable romance with Notting Hill in a supporting role.

Braveheart. Stunning Scottish landscape and the epic tale of William Wallace.

Pride. The uplifting story of the LGBT activists supporting striking Welsh miners in 1984.

Withnail and I. Irreverent British humor at its best.

LISTEN TO

The Beatles, *Abbey Road*

Manic Street Preachers, *Everything Must Go*

The Proclaimers, *Sunshine on Leith*

Joy Division, *Unknown Pleasures*

BUY

Whisky from Scotland's distilleries

A traditional blanket from Wales

Tea (or a hamper) from Fortnum and Mason in London

An umbrella from James Smith & Sons in London

Contacts

AIR

Major Airports

London. Healthrow (LHR), Gatwick Airport (LGW), Stansted (STN)

Northern England. Manchester (MAN), Birmingham (BHX)

Scotland. Glasgow Airport (GLA), Edinburgh Airport (EDI), Aberdeen Airport (ABZ), Prestwick (PIK)

Wales. Cardiff (CWL), Bristol (BRS

BOAT

Caledonian MacBrayne (CalMac), Scotland. *www.calmac.co.uk*

DFDS Ferries. *www.dfds.com*

Northlink Ferries, Scotland. *www.northlinkferries.co.uk*

P&O Ferries. *www.poferries.com*

Western Ferries, Scotland. *www.western-ferries.co.uk*

BUS

National Express. *www.nationalexpress.com*

Mega Bus. *uk.megabus.com*

Arriva Bus. *www.arrivabus.co.uk*

SUBWAY

Transport for London (Tube). *tfl.gov.uk/modes/tube/*

TRAIN

National Rail. *www.nationalrail.co.uk*

Man in Seat 61. *www.seat61.com*

The Trainline. *www.thetrainline.com*

VISITOR INFORMATION

Visit England. *www.visitengland.com*

Visit Scotland. *www.visitscotland.com*

Visit Wales. *www.visitwales.com*

London

If London's only attractions were its famous landmarks, it would still be unmissable. From Big Ben to the British Museum to the Westminster Abbey, the city's famous attractions draw millions of visitors. But London is so much more. Though its long history is evident at every turn, it's also one of the world's most modern and vibrant cities.

London beckons with great museums, royal pageantry, and historically significant buildings. Unique Georgian terraces perch next to cutting-edge modern skyscrapers, and parks and squares provide unexpected oases of greenery amid the dense urban landscape. Modern central London still largely follows its winding medieval street pattern.

As well as visiting landmarks like St. Paul's Cathedral and the Tower of London, set aside time for random wandering; the city repays every moment spent exploring its backstreets and mews on foot. Go to lesser-known but thoroughly rewarding sites such as IWM London (the Imperial War Museum) and the historic Kensington Gardens, which were commissioned by King William III. Shop at Harrods, or visit one of London's many great markets, such as the Old Spitalfields Market or Portobello Road Market.

Today the city's art, style, fashion, and restaurant scenes make headlines around the world. London's chefs have become internationally influential, its fashion designers and art stars set global trends, its nightlife continues to produce exciting new acts, and its theater remains celebrated for superb classical and innovative productions, whether in the West End or in Shakespeare's Globe. Londoners are also obsessed with sports, so take in an English football match (that's soccer for Americans) if you have a chance.

Then there's that greatest living link with the past—the Royal Family. Don't let fear of looking like a tourist stop you from enjoying the pageantry of the Changing the Guard at Buckingham Palace, one of the greatest free shows in the world.

As the eminent 18th-century man of letters Samuel Johnson said, "When a man is tired of London, he is tired of life, for there is in London all that life can afford." Armed with energy and curiosity, you can discover its riches.

British Museum

Britain's Treasure Trove

The sheer scale and importance of the British Museum's many treasures is impossible to overstate or exaggerate; it truly is one of the world's great repositories of human civilization. Established in 1753 and initially based on the library and "cabinet of curiosities" of the Royal Physician Sir Hans Sloane, the collection grew exponentially over the following decades, partly due to bequests and acquisitions, but also as a result of plundering by the burgeoning British Empire. Now displayed in more than 60 galleries, the museum's contents include some of the greatest relics of humankind: the Parthenon Sculptures (Elgin Marbles), the Rosetta Stone, the Sutton Hoo Treasure, Egyptian mummies, a colossal statue of Ramesses II, fragments of the Seven Wonders of the Ancient World—almost everything, it seems, but the original Ten Commandments. The Americas are best represented by the North America Room (26), which holds one of the largest collections of native culture outside North America, while the Egyptian Sculpture Gallery (Room 4) gathers items from three millennia of pharaonic history. The museum's focal point is the Great Court, a brilliant modern design with a vast glass roof atop the museum's covered courtyard. Free tours cover the highlights in an economical 30 or 40 minutes.

Don't Miss

The Rosetta Stone, the key to deciphering Egyptian hieroglyphs, is the most famous rock in the world and a must-visit at the British Museum.

Getting Here and Around

Walk from Russell Square, Holborn, or Tottenham Court Road Tube stations.

✉ *Great Russell St., Bloomsbury* ☎ *020/7323–8000* 🌐 *www.britishmuseum.org* 🎫 *Free; donations encouraged*

Buckingham Palace

Royal Headquarters

Every summer London's most iconic royal residence, Buckingham Palace throws open its doors and admits visitors into 19 of its State Rooms, plus the sprawling palace gardens. Originally Buckingham House and the home of George III, the palace was begun in 1702 and remodelled by John Nash on the accession of George IV in 1820. Queen Victoria added the east front (by Edmund Blore, facing the Mall) to accommodate her prodigious state entertaining. Nash's gorgeous designs can still be admired at the core of the building. The north wing's private apartments always remain behind closed doors, but those State Rooms that are accessible are the grandest of the palace's 775 rooms, with fabulous gilt moldings and walls adorned with masterpieces by Rembrandt, Rubens, and other Old Masters.

Don't Miss

Arrive by 10:30 to grab a spot in the best viewing section for the ceremonial Changing the Guard—one of London's best free shows—that happens daily at 11 from May until the end of July (varies according to troop deployment requirements) and on alternate days for the rest of the year, weather permitting.

When to Go

The Changing of the Guard is year-round, but tours of the palace interior are only available from late July to early October, with selected dates in the winter and spring seasons.

Getting Here and Around

Nearest Tube stations: Victoria, St. James's Park, or Green Park.

✉ *Buckingham Palace Rd., St. James's* 🌐 *www.royalcollection.org.uk/visit* 🎫 *From £25 (timed tickets only)*

English Football Match

Sing "You'll Never Walk Alone" with Thousands of Fans

Football, aka soccer, may be the most popular sport in the world but it is arguably best experienced in England, where the modern rules of the game were established in 1863, and there are more clubs (40,000) than any other country. English clubs are cherished locally and celebrated globally, so attending a match is a near spiritual experience for fans as well as an authentic way to connect with locals. The English Premier League (August to May) is where you can see the top-20 teams in England. Think: Manchester United, Chelsea, Liverpool, and Arsenal. The FA Cup and Carabao Cup are other Bucket-List worthy experiences. For a less expensive and more local experience, look to the Football League and lower-tier teams. Visit a home club's website to get tickets.

Don't Miss

Iconic **Wembley Stadium** (✉ *Wembley, London* 🌐 *www.wembleystadium.com*) is home to the England national football team. **Old Trafford** (✉ *London Rd., Manchester* 🌐 *www.manutd.com*), the home of Manchester United, is one of the most famous stadiums in the world. **Tottenham Hotspur Stadium** (✉ *782 High Rd., London* 🌐 *www.tottenhamhotspur.com*) also offers behind-the-scenes tours.

Best Football Pub

In 1863, the English Football Association set down the rules of the sport at the Freemason's Arms in Covent Garden, London. The downstairs bar screens live matches. 🌐 *www.freemasonsarmscoventgarden.co.uk*

🌐 *www.thefa.com* 🌐 *www.premierleague.com* 🌐 *www.efl.com/carabao-cup*

Houses of Parliament

The Mother of Parliaments

Overlooking the Thames, the Houses of Parliament are, arguably, the city's most famous and photogenic sight, with the Clock Tower—renamed Elizabeth Tower in 2012 but everyone still calls it Big Ben—keeping watch on the corner and Westminster Abbey across Parliament Square. At the southwest end of the main Parliament building is the 336-foot-high Victoria Tower. The Palace of Westminster, as the complex is called, was first established on this site by Edward the Confessor in the 11th century. William II built a new palace in 1097, and this became the seat of English power. Fire destroyed most of the palace in 1834; the current complex dates largely from the mid-19th century. Tours include the chambers of both the House of Commons and the House of Lords, plus highlights such as the Royal Gallery, Central Lobby, and St. Stephen's Hall.

Don't Miss

Westminster Hall, with its remarkable hammer-beam roof, was the work of William the Conqueror's son William Rufus and is one of the largest remaining Norman halls.

When to Go

The Visitors' Galleries of the House of Commons are particularly popular during the Prime Minister's Questions at noon every Wednesday when Parliament is sitting (tickets are free, but noncitizens must line up and hope for no-shows). The public gallery of the House of Lords is an easier seat to score.

Getting Here and Around

Westminster Tube station is steps away.

✉ *St. Stephen's Entrance, St. Margaret St., Westminster* ☎ *020/7219–4114 for public tours* 🌐 *www.parliament.uk/visiting* 🎫 *Free; tours from £20*

National Gallery

World-Class Art

Standing proudly on the north side of Trafalgar Square is one of the world's supreme art museums, with more than 2,300 works on display. The collection includes masterpieces of British and Western European art by the likes of Van Eyck, Holbein, Velázquez, Turner, Monet, Seurat, van Gogh, and Picasso, to name but a few—and all for free. Watch out for outstanding temporary exhibitions, too, both free and ticketed. While you could allow a handful of paintings to fill your visit, there are enough to fill a full day. To one side of the main building—and currently holding the gallery's main entrance—is the large Sainsbury Wing, designed by American architects Robert Venturi and Denise Scott Brown. Here, you'll find one of the most visited parts of the gallery, the Renaissance collection, including important works by Michelangelo, Leonardo, Bellini, Titian, and Caravaggio. The gallery's collection of Dutch 17th-century paintings is one of the greatest in the world. Theme audio guides provide informative and entertaining insights into the art works on display, and two restaurants and an espresso bar supply welcome rest and refreshment.

Don't Miss

Masterpice hit-list: *The Virgin Of The Rocks* by Leonardo da Vinci; *The Arnolfini Portrait* by Jan Van Eyck; *A Young Woman Standing At A Virginal* by Johannes Vermeer; *Sunflowers* by Vincent van Gogh, and *Venus and Mars* by Sandro Botticelli.

Getting Here and Around

Charing Cross, Embankment, and Leicester Square are the nearest Tube stops.

✉ *Trafalgar Sq., Westminster* ☎ *020/7747–2885* 🌐 *www.nationalgallery.org.uk* 🎫 *Free; special exhibitions from £7; audio guide £5*

St. Paul's Cathedral

The Spiritual Heart of the Nation

This majestic structure where people and events are celebrated, mourned, and honored has for centuries held an important place in the heart, history, and skyline of London. St. Paul's Cathedral is Sir Christopher Wren's masterpiece, completed in 1710 after 35 years of building. It was actually Wren's third plan for the cathedral that was accepted, though the distinctive dome which crowns the center of the cathedral—an amazing feat of engineering, rising to 364 feet—was added later. Wren's maxim, "I build for eternity," proved no idle boast: in 1940, the dome and the rest of the cathedral were miraculously spared (mostly) by German bombs during World War II. As in Westminster Abbey, prominent people are buried inside the cathedral, including Wren himself, as well as the poet John Donne, the Duke of Wellington, and Admiral Lord Nelson. There are free, 90-minute, guided tours, bookable at the welcome desk.

Don't Miss

Gird your loins for the "great climb" (over 500 steps) to the dome's Golden Gallery, where you can walk outside for a spectacular panorama of London. En route, take a pause at the Whispering Gallery, where you can whisper something to the wall on one side, and a second later it transmits clearly to the other side, 112 feet away.

When to Go

Visit in the late afternoon for evensong, and let the choir's voices transport you to a world of absolute peace.

Getting Here and Around

Use the St. Paul's Tube station.

✉ *St. Paul's Churchyard, City of London* ☎ *020/7246–8350* 🌐 *www.stpauls.co.uk* 🎫 *£20*

Tower of London

Infamous Prison and Mighty Fortress

Nowhere else does London's history come to life so vividly as it does in this minicity of 20 towers that have housed a palace, barracks, the Royal Mint, archives, an armory, and even the Royal Menagerie. Conceived in 1078 by William the Conqueror, the Tower has been a place of imprisonment, torture, and execution for the realm's most notorious traitors and a few innocents as well. Notable inmates included Sir Thomas More, Anne Boleyn, Lady Jane Grey, Sir Walter Raleigh, and Guy Fawkes. You can learn more about these characters in the permanent exhibition in the Inner Ward, where a trio of towers—the Bloody Tower, Beauchamp Tower, and Queen's House—all have excellent views of the scaffold in Tower Green. Look out for the resident ravens, whose presence here is said to be essential to the survival of the kingdom. You should allow at least three hours for exploring, and take time to stroll along the battlements. Free tours by the Yeoman Warders, better known as the Beefeaters (who also mind the Tower's ravens), depart every half hour from the main entrance.

Don't Miss

Prebook tickets—months in advance, if possible—to the 700-year-old Ceremony of the Keys (the nightly locking of main gates).

Getting Here and Around

The tower is a short walk from Tower Hill tube station.

✉ *Tower Hill, City of London* 🌐 *www.hrp.org.uk* 🎫 *£28 (£25 online)*

Westminster Abbey

A Monument to the Nation's Past

Steeped in hundreds of years of rich and occasionally bloody history, Westminster Abbey is one of England's most iconic buildings, most of which dates from the 1240s. It has hosted 38 coronations—the first in 1066, when William the Conqueror was anointed here—and no fewer than 16 royal weddings, but it is equally well known for its permanent residents, from kings to writers, who are buried here, and many more who are memorialized. On entering, look up to your right to see the painted-glass rose window, the largest of its kind. The adjoining medieval Chapter House is adorned with 14th-century frescoes and has one of the finest surviving tiled floors in the country, dating from the 13th century. The King's Council met here between 1257 and 1547. The College Garden of medicinal herbs is a delightful diversion; it has been tended by monks for more than 900 years. Climb the Weston Tower for historical artifacts and remarkable views from the Queen's Diamond Jubilee Galleries.

Don't Miss

Highlights include the world's largest rose window, the Coronation Chair (dating from 1301), the Grave of the Unknown Warrior, and the Poet's Corner.

When to Go

Exact hours are complex and subject to change, so it's important to check before setting out. Beware: lines can be long during peak hours. Closed Sunday, except for worship.

Getting Here and Around

The closest Tube stops are Westminster and St. James's Park.

✉ *Broad Sanctuary, Westminster* ☎ *020/7222–5152* 🌐 *www.westminster-abbey.org* 🎟 *£22*

Wimbeldon

The Oldest and Most Prestigious Tennis Tournament in the World

For two weeks every summer, the planet becomes obsessed with the game of tennis as the world's top talent battles it out in crisp whites on the pristine grass courts of the All England Lawn Tennis and Croquet Club. Wimbledon's inaugural championship took place in 1877, with 22 men playing in the "Gentlemen's Singles." As the event grew in popularity, the Ladies' Singles and Men's Doubles events were introduced in 1884, and the Ladies' Doubles and Mixed Doubles events were added in 1913. The Wimbledon Championship is the only Grand Slam tournament played on traditional grass courts. It's also notable for its royal patronage and celebrity appearances, the absence of advertising around the courts, and the delightful spectator tradition of strawberries and cream and Pimm's. The Wimbledon Lawn Tennis Museum gets fans close to the trophies, grass, and history of the game year round.

Don't Miss

Wimbledon is a hot ticket. Register in advance for the public ballot (closes mid-November the year before), which enters fans in a lottery to win an opportunity to purchase tickets, priced around £50 to £200. Debenture tickets are the only legal resale tickets, starting at over £1,000 per person. You can also take your chances on the line outside with hundreds of other hopefuls.

Getting Here and Around

Take the tube to Southfields Station, which is a 15-minute walk away. By train, the nearest station is Wimbledon, a 20-minute walk away.

✉ *All England Lawn Tennis & Croquet Club. Church Rd., London* 🌐 *www.wimbledon.com* 🎫 *Event tickets from £50; museum tickets £25*

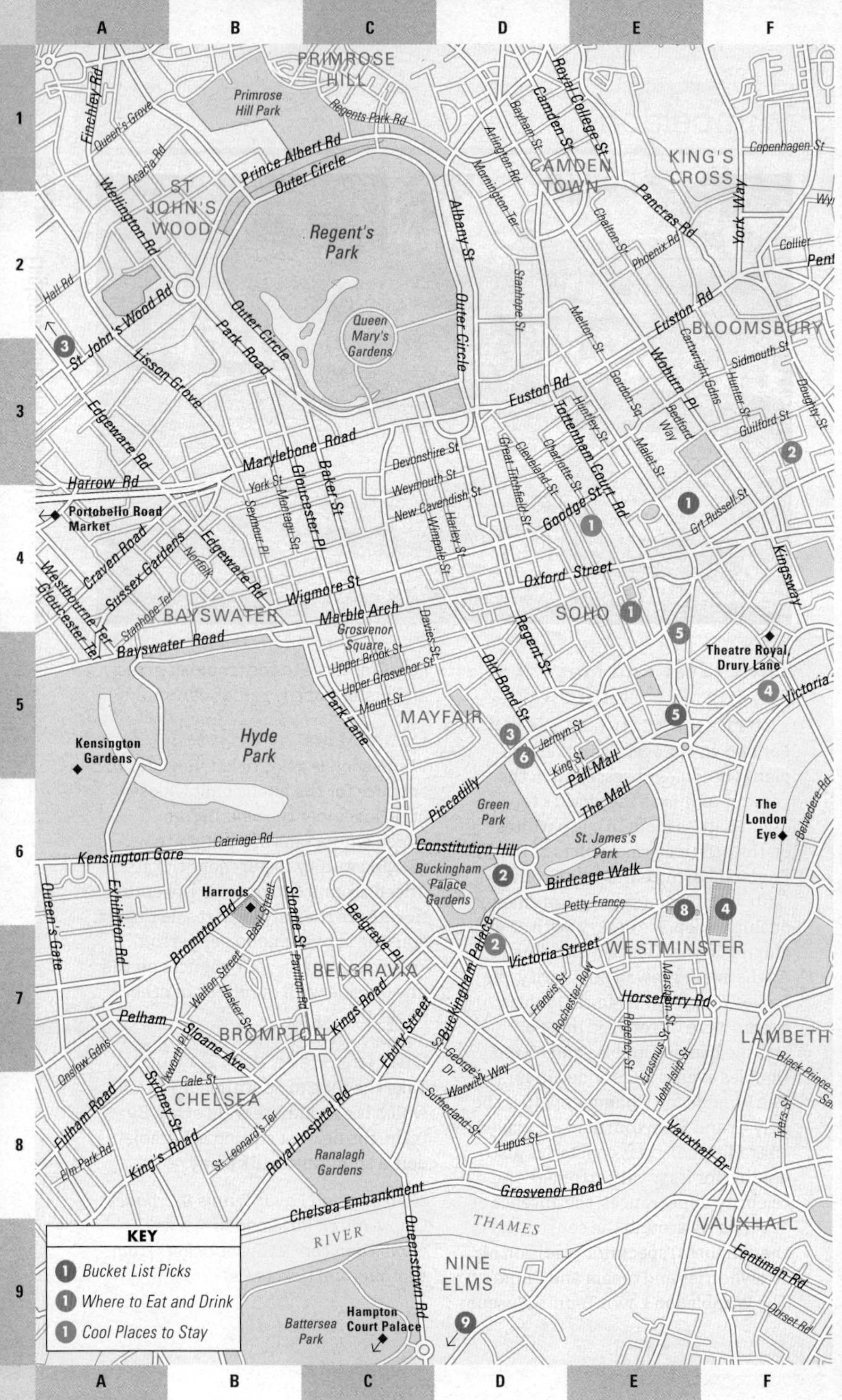
A B C D E F
1 2 3 4 5 6 7 8 9
PRIMROSE HILL
Primrose Hill Park
ST JOHN'S WOOD
Regent's Park
Queen Mary's Gardens
CAMDEN TOWN
KING'S CROSS
BLOOMSBURY
BAYSWATER
SOHO
MAYFAIR
Hyde Park
Kensington Gardens
Green Park
St. James's Park
Buckingham Palace Gardens
WESTMINSTER
BELGRAVIA
BROMPTON
CHELSEA
LAMBETH
Ranalagh Gardens
RIVER THAMES
VAUXHALL
NINE ELMS
Battersea Park
Portobello Road Market
Theatre Royal, Drury Lane
The London Eye
Harrods
Hampton Court Palace
KEY
Bucket List Picks
Where to Eat and Drink
Cool Places to Stay

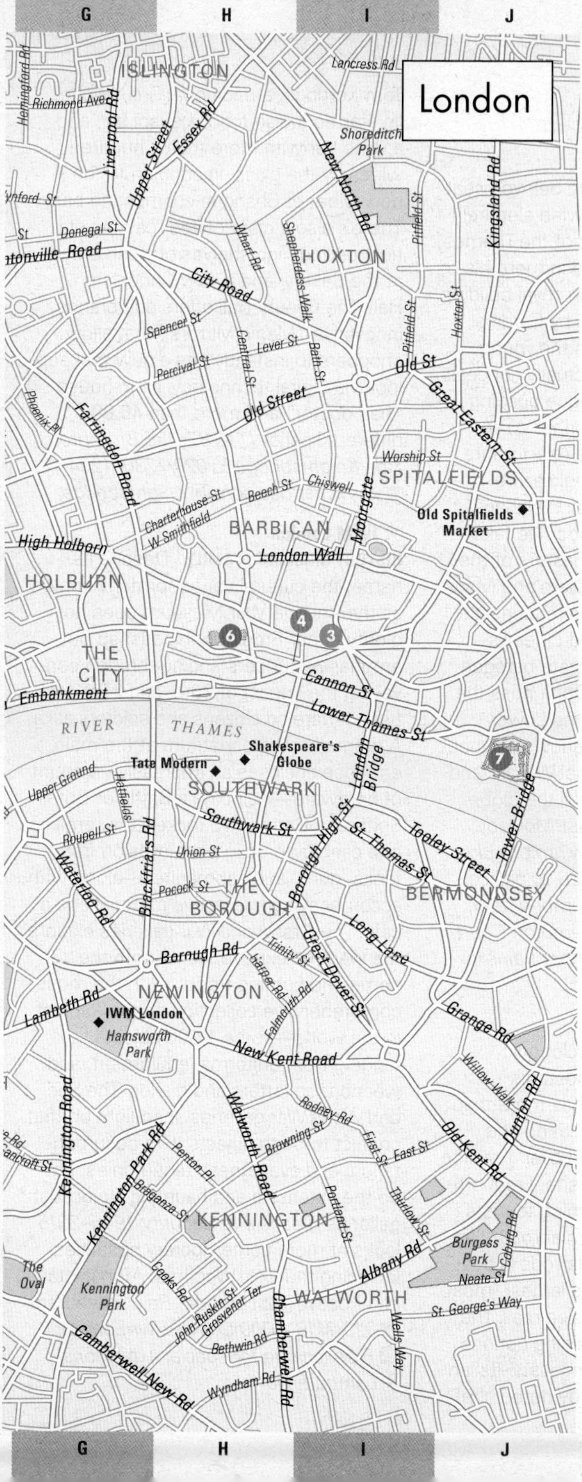

London

Bucket List Picks

1 British Museum E4
2 Buckingham Palace D6
3 English Football Match A3
4 Houses of Parliament F6
5 National Gallery E5
6 St. Paul's Cathedral H4
7 Tower of London J5
8 Westminster Abbey E6
9 Wimbledon D9

Where to Eat and Drink

1 The Dog and Duck E4
2 Noble Rot F3
3 The Ritz Restaurant D5
4 Sweetings I5
5 Two Brewers E4
6 The Wolseley D5

Cool Places to Stay

1 Charlotte Street Hotel E4
2 Hotel 41 .... D7
3 The Ned I4
4 The Savoy F5

When in London

★ Hampton Court Palace

CASTLE/PALACE | FAMILY | The beloved seat of Henry VIII's court, sprawled elegantly beside the languid waters of the Thames, Hampton Court is steeped in more history than virtually any other royal building in England. Begun in 1515 by Cardinal Wolsey to curry favor with the young Henry, the Tudor palace actually conceals a larger 17th-century baroque building partly designed by Christopher Wren. Wander through the State Apartments before taking in the strikingly azure ceiling of the Chapel Royal. Well-handled reconstructions of Tudor life take place all year. Latter-day masters of the palace, the joint rulers William and Mary (reigned 1689–1702), were responsible for the beautiful King's and Queen's Apartments and the elaborate baroque of the Georgian Rooms. Don't miss the famous hedge maze and the Lower Orangery Garden, which shows off thousands of exotic species that William and Mary gathered from around the globe. ✉ *Hampton Court Rd., East Molesey* ☎ *020/3166–6000* 🌐 *www.hrp.org.uk/hamptoncourtpalace* 🎫 *£26.10 palace, maze, and gardens* Ⓜ *Richmond, then Bus R68; National Rail: Hampton Court, 35 mins from Waterloo (most trains require change at Surbiton).*

Harrods

STORE/MALL | With an encyclopedic assortment of luxury brands, this Knightsbridge institution has more than 300 departments and 25 eating and drinking options, all spread over 1 million square feet on a 4½-acre site. Frequented more by window-shopping tourists and superrich visitors from abroad than by bling-averse natives, Harrods is best approached as the world's largest, most upscale, and most expensive mall. The dining hall offers on-site dining options ranging from a Pasta Evangelists' Italian offering to fish-and-chips by noted chef Tom Kerridge, a traditional Grill, Michelin-starred Indian food, a sushi bar, and a wine bar with more than a hundred wines by the glass, in addition to the new Moet et Chandon champagne bar. There's also a giant coffee-roasting station, ceiling-high shelves of fresh bread at the Bakery, and a new Chocolate Hall. The Beauty Hall offers cult brands, innovative "Magic Mirrors" that allow shoppers to instantly see a new makeup look via digital technology, an in-house "hair doctor," and more than 46,000 different lipsticks. ✉ *87–135 Brompton Rd., Knightsbridge* ☎ *020/7730–1234* 🌐 *www.harrods.com* Ⓜ *Knightsbridge.*

★ IWM London

HISTORY MUSEUM | FAMILY | Despite its name, the cultural venue formerly known as the Imperial War Museum does not glorify either Empire or bloodshed but emphasizes understanding through conveying the impact of 20th- and 21st-century warfare on citizens and soldiers alike. A dramatic six-story atrium at the main entrance encloses an impressive amount of hardware—including a Battle of Britain Spitfire, a German V2 rocket, the remains of a car blown up in post-invasion Iraq, tanks, guns, and submarines—along with accompanying interactive material and a café. The First World War galleries explore the wartime experience on both the home and fighting fronts, with the most comprehensive collection on the subject in the world—some 1,300 objects ranging from uniforms, equipment, and weapons to letters and diaries. The Second World War galleries shed light on that conflict through objects, film documentation, and eyewitness testimonies, as do the extensive and haunting Holocaust galleries. *Peace and Security 1945–2015* looks at more contemporary hostilities, including the Cold War, Iraq, Afghanistan, and Kosovo. ✉ *Lambeth Rd., South Bank* ☎ *020/7416–5000* 🌐 *www.iwm.org.uk* 🎫 *Free (charge for special exhibitions)* Ⓜ *Lambeth North.*

★ Kensington Gardens

GARDEN | FAMILY | Laid out in 1689 by William III, who commissioned Sir Christopher Wren to build Kensington Palace, the gardens are a formal counterpart to neighboring Hyde Park. Just to the north of the palace itself is the Dutch-style Sunken Garden. Nearby, the 1912 bronze statue of *Peter Pan* commemorates the boy in J. M. Barrie's story who lived on an island in the Serpentine and who never grew up. Kids will enjoy the magical Diana Memorial Playground, whose design was also inspired by Barrie's book. The Elfin Oak is a 900-year-old tree trunk that was carved with scores of tiny elves, fairies, and other fanciful creations in the 1920s. The Italian Gardens, an ornamental water garden commissioned by Prince Albert in 1860, is comprised of several ornamental ponds and fountains (there's also a nice café on-site), while the Round Pond attracts model-boat enthusiasts. ✉ *Kensington* ☎ *0330/061–2000* 🌐 *www.royalparks.org.uk* 🎫 *Free* Ⓜ *High St. Kensington, Lancaster Gate, Queensway, South Kensington.*

★ The London Eye

VIEWPOINT | FAMILY | To mark the start of the new millennium, architects David Marks and Julia Barfield devised an instant icon that allows Londoners and visitors alike to see the city from a completely new perspective. The giant Ferris wheel was the largest cantilevered observation wheel ever built at the time and remains one of the city's tallest structures. The 30-minute slow-motion ride inside one of the enclosed passenger capsules is so smooth you'd hardly know you were suspended over the Thames. **■ TIP→ Buy your ticket online to avoid the long lines and get a 15% discount.** ✉ *Jubilee Gardens, South Bank* ☎ *0871/781–3000* 🌐 *www.londoneye.com* 🎫 *From £30.50, cruise package from £46 (online only)* Ⓜ *Waterloo.*

London Walks

With walks available seven days a week, there's no need to book ahead with London's oldest established walking tours: just turn up at the meeting point at the allotted hour and pay £15 for a first-rate, guided two-hour tour. A multitude of themes includes Shakespeare's and Dickens's London, Beatles & Rock 'n Roll (which takes you to Abbey Road among other iconic sites), Harry Potter film locations, and the ever-popular Jack the Ripper tour which sets off at 7.30 pm every evening. ☎ *020/7624–3978* 🌐 *www.walks.com.*

★ Old Spitalfields Market

MARKET | Once the East End's wholesale fruit and vegetable market and now restored to its original architectural splendor, this fine example of a Victorian market hall is at the center of the area's gentrified revival. The original building is largely occupied by shops (mostly upscale, but some independents), with traders' stalls in the courtyard. A modern shopping precinct under a Norman Foster–designed glass canopy adjoins the old building and holds approximately 70 traders' stalls. Skip the stalls selling cheap imports and tacky T-shirts to find the good stuff, which includes vintage and new clothing, handmade rugs and jewelry, hand-carved toys, and more. Thursday is for antiques; Friday for a biweekly record fair; while weekends offer a little of everything. The Kitchens, 10 central dining venues showcasing small, independent chefs and restaurants, provide fresh takes on Mexican, Japanese, and other world cuisines. ✉ *16 Horner Sq., Brushfield St., Spitalfields* 🌐 *www.oldspitalfieldsmarket.com* Ⓜ *Liverpool St.; Overground: Shoreditch High St.*

★ Portobello Road Market

MARKET | Looking for a 19th-century snuff spoon? Perhaps a Georgian salt cellar? What about a 1960s-era minidress? Then head to Portobello Road's famous

Saturday market—and arrive at about 9 am to avoid the giant crowds. Stretching almost 2 miles from Notting Hill, the market is made up of four sections, each with a different emphasis: antiques, fresh produce, household goods, and a flea market. The antiques stalls are packed in between Chepstow Villas and Westbourne Grove, where you'll also find almost 100 antiques shops plus indoor markets, which are open on weekdays, when shopping is much less hectic. Where the road levels off, around Elgin Crescent, youth culture and a vibrant neighborhood life kicks in, with a variety of interesting small stores and food stalls. On Friday and Saturday, the section between Talbot Road and the Westway elevated highway becomes one of London's best flea markets. ✉ *Notting Hill* 🌐 *www.portobelloroad.co.uk* Ⓜ *Notting Hill Gate, Ladbroke Grove.*

★ Shakespeare's Globe

PERFORMANCE VENUE | FAMILY | This spectacular theater is a replica of Shakespeare's open-roof, wood-and-thatch Globe Playhouse (built in 1599 and burned down in 1613), where most of the Bard's greatest works premiered. American actor and director Sam Wanamaker worked ceaselessly for several decades to raise funds for the theater's reconstruction 200 yards from its original site, using authentic materials and techniques, a dream that was realized in 1997. "Groundlings"—patrons with £5 standing-only tickets—are not allowed to sit during the performance. Fortunately, you can reserve an actual seat on any one of the theater's three levels, but you will want to rent a cushion for £2 (or bring your own) to soften the backless wooden benches. Fifty-minute tours of the theater are offered hourly most days until 4 pm (unless there's a matinee performance or other major event). ✉ *21 New Globe Walk, Bankside* ☎ *020/7401–9919 general info* 🌐 *www.shakespearesglobe.com* 🎫 *Globe Theatre tour £25; Bankside tour £25; Wanamaker tour £13.50; Globe performances £5 (standing), from £25 (seated); Wanamaker performances £5 (standing), from £15 (seated)* ⏲ *No Globe performances mid-Oct.–mid-Apr.* Ⓜ *London Bridge; Mansion House, then cross Southwark Bridge.*

★ Tate Modern

ART MUSEUM | This spectacular renovation of a mid-20th-century power station is one of the most-visited museums of modern art in the world. Its great permanent collection, which starts in 1900 and ranges from modern masters like Matisse to the most cutting-edge contemporary artists, is arranged thematically (from "In the Studio" and "Artist and Society" to "Materials and Objects" and "Media Networks"). Its blockbuster temporary exhibitions have showcased the work of such disparate artists as Gaugin, Roy Lichtenstein, and Dorothea Tanning. The vast Turbine Hall is a dramatic entrance point used to showcase big audacious installations that tend to generate a lot of publicity. Past highlights include Olafur Eliasson's massive glowing sun and Carsten Holler's huge metal slides. ✉ *Bankside* ☎ *020/7887–8888* 🌐 *www.tate.org.uk/modern* 🎫 *Free (charge for special exhibitions)* Ⓜ *Southwark, Blackfriars, St. Paul's.*

★ Theatre Royal, Drury Lane

PERFORMANCE VENUE | FAMILY | This is London's most popular auditorium—most commonly known simply as Drury Lane—and almost its largest. Since World War II, its forte has been musicals (from *My Fair Lady* and *South Pacific* to *Miss Saigon* and *Shrek*), although David Garrick, who managed the theater from 1747 to 1776, made its name by reviving the works of the by-then-obscure William Shakespeare. Drury Lane enjoys all the romantic accessories of a London theater: a history of fires (it burned down three times), riots (in 1737, when a posse of footmen demanded free admission), attempted regicides (George II in 1716 and his grandson George III in 1800), and even sightings of the most famous phantom of the West End, the Man in Grey (seen in the Circle during matinees). Seventy-five-minute dramatized tours, led by actors, take place daily. ✉ *Catherine St., Covent Garden* ☎ *0844/412–4660* 🌐 *lwtheatres.co.uk/theatres/theatre-royal-drury-lane* 🎫 *Tickets from £26, tours £12* Ⓜ *Covent Garden, Holborn.*

Where to Eat and Drink

The Dog and Duck

PUBS | FAMILY | A beautiful example of a High Victorian pub, The Dog and Duck has a majestic interior overflowing with thousands of ornate glazed tiles, etched mirrors, chandeliers, and polished wood, although it's often so packed it can be hard to get a proper look. There's a fine selection of real ales at the bar and a restaurant serving superb pale ale–battered fish-and-chips with mushy peas. Originally built in 1734 and patronized by painters and poets like John Constable and Dante Gabriel Rossetti, the cozy upstairs dining room is named for writer and Dog and Duck regular George Orwell. ✉ *18 Bateman St., Soho* ☎ *020/7494–0697* 🌐 *www.nicholsonspubs.co.uk* Ⓜ *Oxford Circus, Tottenham Court Rd.*

★ Noble Rot

$$$ | BRITISH | There's an old Amsterdam coffeehouse vibe at this dark and creaky wine bar and restaurant on historic Lamb's Conduit Street in Bloomsbury. Run by two wine buffs and cult wine magazine publishers, you'll find deceptively simple ingredient-driven British dishes like roast Yorkshire pheasant with bread sauce and quince. **Known for:** paradise for oenophiles; unpretentious seasonal British and French wine-friendly fare; excellent value two- and three-course set lunch menu. $ *Average main: £28* ✉ *51 Lamb's Conduit St., Bloomsbury* ☎ *020/7242–8963* 🌐 *www.noblerot.co.uk* ⏲ *Closed Sun.* Ⓜ *Holborn.*

The Ritz Restaurant

$$$$ | BRITISH | London's most opulent dining salon here at The Ritz would impress even Marie Antoinette with its sumptuous Gilded Age rococo revival trompe-l'oeil frescoes, tasseled silk drapery, and towering marble columns. Sit at the late Margaret Thatcher's favorite seat overlooking Green Park (Table 1) and luxuriate in unreconstructed British haute cuisine, such as Bresse chicken with black Périgord truffles or beef Wellington carved table-side. **Known for:** luxurious dining made for the British elite; possibly London's best beef Wellington; legendary traditional Afternoon Tea in the Palm Court. $ *Average main: £64* ✉ *The Ritz, 150 Piccadilly, St. James's* ☎ *020/7493–8181* 🌐 *www.theritzlondon.com* 👔 *Jacket and tie* Ⓜ *Green Park.*

Sweetings

$$$ | SEAFOOD | Established in 1889 not far from St. Paul's Cathedral, little seems to have changed since the height of the British Empire at this quirky eatery. Although there are some things Sweetings doesn't do (dinner, reservations, coffee, or weekends), it does, mercifully, do great seafood. **Known for:** fresh Billingsgate fish served at raised linen-covered counters; tankards of "Black Velvet" Guinness and champagne; popular potted shrimp and Dover sole. $ *Average main: £30* ✉ *39 Queen Victoria St., City of London* ☎ *020/7248–3062* 🌐 *www.sweetingsrestaurant.co.uk* ⏲ *Closed weekends. No dinner* Ⓜ *Mansion House.*

★ Two Brewers

$$ | BRITISH | Locals congregate in a pair of low-ceiling rooms at this tiny 17th-century establishment by the gates of Windsor Great Park. Those under 18 aren't allowed inside the pub (although they can be served at a few outdoor tables), but adults will find a suitable collection of wine, espresso, and local beer, plus an excellent menu with dishes like roasted cod with butter sauce and samphire or steak frites with brandy and peppercorn.

Known for: classic, adults-only British pub; traditional lunchtime roast on Sunday; historic setting. *Average main: £16* *34 Park St., Windsor* *01753/855426* *www.twobrewerswindsor.co.uk.*

The Wolseley
$$$ | **AUSTRIAN** | **FAMILY** | A glitzy procession of famous faces, media moguls, and hedge-funders comes for the spectacle, swish service, and soaring elegance at this bustling Viennese-style grand café on Piccadilly. Located in a former Wolseley Motors luxury-car showroom, this brasserie begins its long decadent days with breakfast at 7 am (8 am on weekends) and serves Dual Monarchy delights until 11 pm (10 pm on Sunday). **Known for:** old-country central European delights; afternoon tea with a Viennese twist; classic grand café setting. *Average main: £28* *160 Piccadilly, St. James's* *020/7499–6996* *www.thewolseley.com* *Green Park.*

Cool Places to Stay

★ Charlotte Street Hotel
$$$ | **HOTEL** | Superstar London hotel designer Kit Kemp has taken the fabled Bloomsbury Group as her inspiration for this supremely stylish boutique hotel, which, if anything, feels more like a private members' club. **Pros:** elegant and luxurious; great attention to detail; excellent, lively location. **Cons:** the popular bar can be noisy; reservations essential for the restaurant; some rooms are small considering the price. *Rooms from: £400* *15–17 Charlotte St., Fitzrovia* *020/7806–2000, 888/559–5508 in U.S.* *www.firmdalehotels.com* *52 rooms* *No Meals* *Goodge St.*

★ Hotel 41
$$$$ | **HOTEL** | With faultless service, sumptuous designer furnishings, and a sense of fun to boot, this impeccable hotel breathes new life into the cliché "thinks of everything," yet the epithet is really quite apt. **Pros:** impeccable service; guests can charge restaurant and bar visits at next door Rubens hotel to their bill; Buckingham Palace is on your doorstep. **Cons:** unusual design is not for everyone; expensive; the private bar can feel stuffy. *Rooms from: £515* *41 Buckingham Palace Rd., Westminster* *020/7300–0041* *www.41hotel.com* *28 rooms* *No Meals* *Victoria.*

★ The Ned
$$ | **HOTEL** | Bursting with eye-catching art deco design and achingly hip interiors, The Ned is as close to the glamour of the 1920s Jazz Age as you'll find in contemporary London. **Pros:** amazing variety of bars and restaurants, all of high quality; rooftop pool with views of St. Paul's Cathedral; beautiful interiors in all rooms. **Cons:** location in The City means public spaces get very busy after work; neighborhood is deserted on weekends; also doubles as a private members club, so the vibe can get snooty. *Rooms from: £275* *27 Poultry, City of London* *020/3828–2000* *www.thened.com* *250 rooms* *No Meals* *Bank.*

★ The Savoy
$$$$ | **HOTEL** | **FAMILY** | One of London's most iconic hotels maintains its status at the top with winning attributes of impeccable service, stunning decor, and a desirable location on the Strand. **Pros:** one of the absolute top hotels in Europe; unbeatable pedigree and illustrious history; beautiful Thames-side location. **Cons:** everything comes with a price tag; street noise is surprisingly problematic, particularly on lower floors; some may find the opulence over the top. *Rooms from: £600* *The Strand, Covent Garden* *020/7836–4343, 888/265–0533 in U.S.* *www.thesavoylondon.com* *268 rooms* *Free Breakfast* *Charing Cross, Covent Garden.*

England

From medieval cathedrals to postmodern towers, from prehistoric stones to one-pub villages, England is a spectacular tribute to the strength—and flexibility—of tradition. However, while this is certainly the land of grand manors and royal castles steeped in history, it's also home to cutting-edge art, innovative cultural scenes, and trendy stores.

The capital city of London has all of these in abundance, not to mention a concentration of fashionable hotspots, sizzling nightlife, top-notch restaurants, and museums and galleries aplenty that reflect every area of its cultural and scientific life. But you'll find these draws in every other part of the nation too, strongly flavored by England's diverse regional characteristics and local quirks.

You don't have to venture far outside the capital to experience some of these, from the majesty of Windsor Castle to the theater scene in Stratford-upon-Avon (hometown to William Shakespeare) to the academic ambience of Oxford and Cambridge, but explore farther afield and you'll come to the ancient mysteries of Stonehenge, the evocative cathedral cities of Durham, Canterbury, and Salisbury, and such quintessential English treasures as the Georgian town of Bath, with its Roman roots and appearances in the works of Jane Austen.

Continue westward and you'll arrive at the sea-blown coasts of Devon and Cornwall, where Arthurian mythology is tangible in such spots as Tintagel Castle, while forays north will bring you through the gorgeous, sheep-pastured uplands of the Cotswolds to Stratford-upon-Avon for a feast of Shakespeare-related sights and experiences. You can encounter medieval history at first hand in such spots as Warwick and Kenilworth castles, and rekindle your nostalgia for the Beatles in the port of Liverpool.

In addition, northern England's attractions range from the silvery waters of the Lake District to the windswept moors and dales of Yorkshire—respectively Wordsworth and Brontë country. York and Durham exude pungent historical flavors, too, and you can walk in the footsteps of Roman soldiers along Hadrian's Wall.

Windsor Castle

The Largest Inhabited Castle in The World

This brooding, imposing castle is the only royal residence in continuous use by the British Royal Family since the Middle Ages. Highlights of a visit include the exquisite St. George's Chapel and the sumptuous State Apartments. St. George's Chapel, built in the Perpendicular style popular in the 15th and 16th centuries, boasts elegant stained-glass windows; a high, vaulted ceiling; and intricately carved choir stalls. Ten of the kings of England lie here, along with Queen Elizabeth II. Entered from the North Terrace, the State Apartments contain priceless furniture, carvings by Grinling Gibbons, and paintings by the likes of Canaletto, Rubens, Van Dyck, and Holbein. Changing of the Guard takes place at 11 am daily April to July and on alternate days August to March.

Don't Miss

After touring the castle, take a breather in the adjacent (and extensive) Windsor Great Park.

When to Go

St. George's Chapel is closed Sunday, and the State rooms (and sometimes the entire castle) are closed during official state occasions; consult the website or call ahead to check.

Getting Here and Around

Frequent buses (from the Colonnades opposite Victoria Coach Station) and trains (from Waterloo) connect Windsor to London. The drive from London takes around an hour on the M4.

✉ Castle Hill ☎ 0303/123–7304 🌐 www.rct.uk/visit/windsor-castle 🎫 £24; £13 when State Apartments are closed

The Royal Shakespeare Theatre

Experience Shakespeare in His Home Town

Just walking through the bustling, historic town of Stratford-upon-Avon, where Shakespeare was born and raised, provides a better understanding of the great playwright, but to see one of his plays at the stunning Royal Shakespeare Theatre is the icing on the cake. The Royal Shakespeare Company boasts three Stratford venues: the Royal Shakespeare Theatre, whose thrust stage is based on the original Globe Theater in London; the Swan Theatre, which stages plays by Shakespeare and his contemporaries; and The Other Place, the venue for contemporary works.

Don't Miss

Allow time to take The Royal Shakespeare Theatre's popular 60-minute Behind the Scenes tour, where you can visit backstage and the costume workshop, learn how a performance comes together, and ascend to the theater's tower for a panoramic view of Stratford. There's also a great rooftop restaurant.

When to Go

Avoid the crowds by visiting Stratford on weekends and during school vacations (to avoid frquent school groups). Or join them at Shakespeare's Birthday Celebrations, which usually take place on the weekend nearest to April 23.

Getting Here and Around

Stratford can be visited as a day-trip from London. Trains from London take two hours direct, more with transfers. Of Stratford's two stations, Stratford-upon-Avon is closest to the town center, an easy walk.

✉ *Waterside* *01789/403493* 🌐 *www.rsc.org.uk* 🎫 *General tickets from £16; prices start from £5 for rehearsals and previews. Seats book up fast, but day-of-performance and returned tickets are sometimes available*

Oxford University

See the Dreaming Spires

With arguably the most famous university in the world, Oxford has been a center of learning since 1167. Below the "dreaming spires" that Victorian writer Matthew Arnold so evocatively described, the old town curls around golden-stone buildings, ancient churches, good restaurants, and historic pubs. Oxford University isn't one easily identifiable campus, but a sprawling mixture of 38 colleges scattered around the city center, each with its own distinctive identity and focus. Most of the grounds and magnificent dining halls and chapels are open to visitors, though the opening times (displayed at the entrance gates) vary greatly. Allow a day or two to walk the winding streets, tour the ivy-covered colleges, and explore a brace of enthralling museums—the Ashmolean and Pitt Rivers.

Don't Miss

Allow time for an age-old Oxford tradition and hire a punt (flat-bottomed boat) to take in this historic city's placid and winding waterways. If you prefer more passive punting, hire a chauffered punt.

When to Go

Oxford receives visitors all year round but if you're hoping for a less crowded experience, visit between August and April. Peak season is from April to August, right after the exams finish.

Getting Here and Around

Megabus, Oxford Bus Company, and Stagecoach Oxford Tube offer bus service; the trip takes between one hour 40 minutes and two hours. A train takes about 90 minutes from London. Drivers from London should take the M40.

✉ *Oxfordshire* 🌐 *www.experienceoxfordshire.org*

Blenheim Palace

England's Versailles

This magnificent palace is Britain's only historic house to be named a World Heritage Site. Designed by Sir John Vanbrugh in the early 1700s in collaboration with Nicholas Hawksmoor, Blenheim was given by Queen Anne and the nation to General John Churchill, first duke of Marlborough, in gratitude for his military victories (including the Battle of Blenheim) against the French in 1704. The monumental exterior displays huge columns, enormous pediments, and obelisks, all exemplars of English Baroque. Inside, the lavish rooms are filled with family portraits, sumptuous furniture, elaborate carpets, fine Chinese porcelain, and immense pieces of silver. One of the most memorable rooms is the small, low-ceiling chamber where Winston Churchill was born in 1874; he's buried in nearby Bladon. Blenheim's grounds, the work of Capability Brown, are arguably the best example of the "cunningly natural" park in the country. The formal gardens, built in the 1920s, include water terraces and an Italian garden. You can join a free guided tour or simply walk through on your own; book a tour of the current duke's private apartments for a more intimate view of ducal life.

Don't Miss

Take the path that circles around the Great Lake and head toward the "Harry Potter Tree" for the best view (and photo) of a fantastic view of Vanbrugh's semi-submerged Grand Bridge and Blenheim Palace.

Getting Here and Around

The public bus service S3 runs (usually every half-hour) from Oxford, costs £3.30 one way. and drops you at the gates.

Off A4095, Woodstock *01993/810530*
www.blenheimpalace.com
Palace, park, and gardens £29; park and gardens £19

Bath

A Wellbeing Destination Since Roman Times

Bath is the only city in the U.K. that's a designated UNESCO World Heritage Site for the quality and harmony of its architecture. It was the Romans who put Bath on the map in the 1st century when they built a temple and a sophisticated baths complex here. Its popularity during the 17th and 18th centuries coincided with one of Britain's most creative architectural eras, when assembly rooms, theaters, and pleasure gardens were added to entertain the rich and titled. Bath is among the most alluring and harmonious small cities in Europe, its magnificent Georgian terraces a lasting reminder of a vanished world depicted by the likes of Jane Austen and Gainsborough. Bath reflects two great eras in human history: Be sure to honor both by seeing the remarkable Roman Baths as well as Georgian marvels like the Royal Crescent and the Assembly Rooms.

Don't Miss

For a complete healing-waters experience, take a dip at Thermae Bath Spa (🌐 *www.thermaebathspa.com*), which houses the only natural thermal hot springs in Britain you can bathe in. While the Romans bathed in the mineral-rich waters, the Georgians preferred to drink it. Take Afternoon Tea and sample the spa water at the elegant Pump Room Restaurant (🌐 *www.thepumproombath.co.uk*). Doctors once prescribed Bath Buns to offset the taste of the mineral waters: get yourself the most famous sweet brioche-style bun at Sally Lunn's (🌐 *www.sallylunns.co.uk*).

Getting Here and Around

Frequent trains and buses connect Bath with London. By car from London, take the M4, then the A46.

Bath Tourist Information Centre. ✉ *Bridgwater House, 2 Terrace Walk* ☎ *01225/614–420* 🌐 *www.visitbath.co.uk*

Salisbury Cathedral

A Medieval Masterpiece

The lofty silhouette of Salisbury Cathedral's majestic spire is visible long before you arrive. The building is unique among cathedrals in that it was conceived and built as a whole in the amazingly short span of 38 years (1220–58), and yet, it contains so many superlatives. The spire, added in 1320, is the tallest in England and a miraculous feat of medieval engineering.

In the north nave aisle, the medieval clock, dating from 1386, is the world's oldest working mechanical clock. The octagonal Chapter House contains the best preserved of the four surviving original copies of the Magna Carta (1215). You'll also find England's largest cathedral cloisters and cathedral close, the highest vault, and the original 13th-century oak stalls are the earliest complete set of choir stalls in England. Join a free one-hour tour of the cathedral, and the separate tour of the roof and spire for the spectacular views of the surrounding countryside.

Don't Miss

Covering over 80 acres, the highly atmospheric Cathedral Close offers vast lawns and gardens as well as 21 listed buildings reflecting architectural styles from the 13th to the 20th centuries. Allow time to visit the Salisbury Museum (home to one of the best collections relating to Stonehenge and local archaeology), the Rifles Museum, Arundells House, and Mompesson House.

Getting Here and Around

Salisbury is on main bus and train routes from London and Southampton, and is best explored on foot.

6 The Close, Salisbury, Wiltshire 01722/555120 www.salisburycathedral.org.uk Cathedral and Chapter House free, suggested donation £8; tower tour £14

Stonehenge

The World's Most Iconic and Enigmatic Archaeological Site

Mysterious and ancient, the circle of giant stones standing starkly against the wide sweep of Salisbury Plain for almost five millennia has spurred myth and legend and been the object of our collective awe, fascination, speculation, and emotion. Who built it? How? And why? It's probable that this was a religious site, and that worship here involved the earth's cycles around the sun. Construction began as early as 3,000 BC with the creation of a circular earthwork enclosure, followed by the construction of the stone circle itself, consisting of an inner circle of bluestones that was later surrounded by an outer circle of huge sarsen stones, many of them transported here from great distances. General visitors cannot enter the stone circle itself, but are free to roam the surrounding landscape with its Neolithic earthworks, some of which predate the stones.

Don't Miss

In the visitor center, a dramatic display using time-lapse photography puts you (virtually) in the center of the circle. If you want to physically go beyond the rope fence and walk among the stones, look for Inner Circle visits which take place outside public visiting hours (dawn or dusk). Demand for tickets far exceeds supply, and dates are often sold out months in advance, so plan ahead.

Getting Here and Around

Frequent Stonehenge Tour buses leave from Salisbury's train and bus stations or you can book a custom tour. Drivers can find the monument near the junction of the A303 with the A344.

✉ *Wiltshire, 8 miles north of Salisbury* ☎ *0370/333–1181* 🌐 *www.english-heritage.org.uk* 🎫 *£22 (walk-up); £19 (advance)*

King's College Chapel, Cambridge

A Gothic Masterpiece

Based on Sainte-Chapelle, the 13th-century royal chapel in Paris, this house of worship is perhaps the most glorious flowering of Perpendicular Gothic in Britain. Henry VI, the king after whom the college is named, oversaw the work. From the outside, the most prominent features are the massive flying buttresses and the fingerlike spires that line the length of the building. Inside, the most obvious impression is of great space and of light flooding in from its huge windows. The chapel's celebrated fan vaulting, the largest in the world, was completed in only three years by master mason John Wastell. The brilliantly colored bosses (carved panels at the intersections of the roof ribs) are particularly intense. An exhibition in the chantries, or side chapels, explains more about the chapel's construction. Behind the altar is *The Adoration of the Magi*, an enormous painting by Peter Paul Rubens.

Don't Miss

During regular terms, King's College Chapel has evensong services Monday through Saturday at 5:30 pm and Sunday at 10:30 am and 3:30 pm. Your best chance of seeing the full choir is Thursday to Sunday.

Getting Here and Around

Good bus and train services connect London and Cambridge. The long-distance bus terminal is very central, while local buses connect the train station with central Cambridge. Parking in the center is scarce and pricey. The city is best explored on foot, or you could join the throng by renting a bicycle.

King's College, Cambridge
01223/331212 *www.kings.cam.ac.uk*
£9, includes college and grounds

The Cotswolds

Quintessentially English Landscape

Prepare to fall in love with England. The beauty and charm of the Cotswolds—gently undulating limestone uplands stretching from Stratford-upon-Avon in the north to Bath in the south—have been immortalized in literature, paintings, and film. Suffused in vibrant greens and the honey yellows of Cotswold stone, the region's eloquently named and picture-postcard hamlets, time-defying churches, and sequestered ancient farmsteads embody the charm of rural England. The Cotswolds are deservedly popular with visitors, drawn to such imaginative garden displays as Hidcote Manor Garden, and such stately properties as Sudeley Castle, Stanway House, and Snowshill Manor—not to mention a profusion of art and antiques dealers, centered on the village of Stow-on-the-Wold.

Don't Miss

There are no unpretty villages in the Cotswolds, but Castle Combe in northwest Witlshire is often referred to as "England's prettiest town," and with good reason. There have been no new houses built here since about 1600, so you'll find plentiful character and history to go with that natural beauty and charm.

When to Go

It's best to avoid weekends, if possible. During the week, even in summer, you may hardly see a soul in the more remote spots. Hidcote Manor Garden is at its best in spring and fall, but this, along with many of the area's great houses, close in winter.

Getting Here and Around

Train and bus services within the Cotswolds are extremely limited. Driving is the ideal way of getting around.

🌐 *www.cotswolds.com*

A Tour of Jane Austen Country

Visit Your Favorite Fictional Worlds

Jane Austen country—verdant countryside interspersed with relatively unspoiled villages—still bears traces of the decorous early-19th-century life she described with wry wit in novels such as *Emma* and *Pride and Prejudice*. Serious Janeites will want to retrace her life in Bath, Chawton, Winchester, and Lyme Regis. Austen lived in Bath between 1801 and 1806, and it provided the setting for *Northanger Abbey* and *Persuasion*; the Jane Austen Centre explores her relationship to the city. The tiny village of Chawton, in the heart of Austen Country, is where you will find the tastefully understated house (now a museum), where Austen worked on three of her novels. In Winchester you can visit Austen's austere grave (she died at 8 College Street on July 18, 1817) within the cathedral and view an exhibit about her life. Lyme Regis is the 18th-century seaside resort on the Devon border where Austen spent two summers and set a turning point in *Persuasion*.

Don't Miss

At The Chawton House Library, you can see the dining room table where Austen joined her family for meals and also a manuscript written in her own hand.

Getting Here and Around

Chawton is about 83 miles southeast of Bath; Winchester is about 15 miles southwest of Chawton, and Lyme Regis is a further 110 miles southwest.

Jane Austen Centre. 🌐 *janeausten.co.uk*

Jane Austen's House Museum. 🌐 *www.jane-austens-house-museum.org.uk*

Lyme Regis Visitor Centre. 🌐 *www.visit-dorset.com*

Winchester Tourist Information Centre. 🌐 *www.visitwinchester.co.uk*

A Beatles Tour Around Liverpool

Walk in the Fab Four's Footsteps

Despite their international success, the Fab Four remained true sons of Liverpool, and the city remains a site of pilgrimage for fans more than half a century after the Beatles' early gigs here. Join one of the many organized tours available, or devise your own route. The three key shrines of Beatledom in Liverpool are John and Paul's childhood homes in south Liverpool and the legendary Cavern Club on Mathew Street downtown, where the Beatles were discovered by their future manager Brian Epstein in 1961. At two venues at the Albert Dock and Pier Head, The Beatles Story re-create stages in the Fab Four's lives—from early gigs in Germany and the Cavern Club to each member's solo career—with 3D computer animations, band artifacts, and more. All the mop-top knickknacks of your dreams are available for sale at these places and in the hugely popular official Beatles souvenir shop in Mathew St.

Don't Miss

Catch a live concert by a Beatles tribute band at Mathew Street's (re-created) Cavern Club, where the band played in its early days.

When to Go

At the annual International Beatleweek, usually held the last week in August, you can attend John and Yoko costume parties; listen to Beatles tribute bands; and check out record fairs, exhibitions, and conventions.

Getting Here and Around

Liverpool is well connected by bus, train, and road to the rest of the country. Liverpool John Lennon Airport lies about 5 miles southeast of the city.

🌐 *www.visitliverpool.com*

When in England

★ Canterbury Cathedral

CHURCH | The nucleus of worldwide Anglicanism, the Cathedral Church of Christ Canterbury (its formal name) is a living textbook of medieval architecture. The building was begun in 1070, demolished, begun anew in 1096, and then systematically expanded over the next three centuries. The cathedral was only a century old when Thomas Becket, the archbishop of Canterbury, was murdered here in 1170, possibly under orders of his friend Henry II. Becket was canonized, and Canterbury's position as the center of English Christianity was assured. The Norman staircase in the northwest corner of the Green Court dates from 1167 and is a unique example of the architecture of the times. Another highlight is the almost Disney-like stained glass window "Salvation" by artist Ervin Bossányi. ✉ *The Precincts, Canterbury* ☎ *01227/762862* 🌐 *www.canterbury-cathedral.org* 🎫 *£14; free for services; £5 tour; £2.50 audio guide.*

★ Durham Cathedral

CHURCH | A Norman masterpiece in the heart of the city, Durham Cathedral is a vision of strength and fortitude, a far cry from the airy lightness of later Gothic cathedrals. Construction began about 1090, and the main body was finished about 1150. The round arches of the nave and the deep zigzag patterns carved into them typify the heavy, gaunt style of Norman, or Romanesque, building. It was also the first European cathedral to be given a stone, rather than a wooden, roof. In good weather, you can climb the 325 steps up to the tower, which has spectacular views of Durham. The impressive Durham Cathedral Museum displays priceless Anglo-Saxon artifacts and offers access to previously hidden parts of the cathedral. Guided tours of the cathedral (one hour) are available Monday through Saturday. ✉ *Palace Green, Durham* ☎ *0191/386–4266* 🌐 *www.durhamcathedral.co.uk* 🎫 *Free (requested donation £3); museum £7.50; tower £5.50; guided tours £7.50* ⏲ *No tours Sun.*

★ Highclere Castle

CASTLE/PALACE | Set in 1,000 acres of parkland designed by Capability Brown, this is the historic home of the actual earls of Carnarvon—as opposed to the imaginary earls of Grantham that are portrayed living within it in the television drama *Downton Abbey*. Victorian Gothic rather than actual Gothic, this huge country house was designed by Sir Charles Barry, architect of the similar Houses of Parliament. Commissioned by the third earl in 1838 to transform a simpler Georgian mansion, Barry used golden Bath stone to create this fantasy castle bristling with turrets. Like its fictional counterpart, it served as a hospital during World War I. There's also an exhibit of Egyptian antiquities collected by the fifth earl, known for his pivotal role in the 1920s excavation of ancient Egyptian tombs, notably Tutankhamun's. The house is 25 miles north of Winchester and 5 miles south of Newbury. There's train service from London and Winchester to Newbury, and taxis can take you the 5 miles to Highclere. ✉ *Highclere Castle, Highclere Park, Newbury* ✥ *Off A34* ☎ *01635/253204* 🌐 *www.highclere-castle.co.uk* 🎫 *£27.50 castle, exhibition, and gardens; £20.50 castle and gardens* ⏲ *Closed weekends July–Sept. and Sept.–July except for select dates.*

★ Lake District National Park

NATIONAL PARK | **FAMILY** | In 1951, the Lake District National Park, filled with jagged mountains, waterfalls, wooded valleys, and stone-built villages, was created here from parts of the old counties of Cumberland, Westmorland, and Lancashire. No mountains in Britain give a greater impression of majesty; deeper and bluer lakes can be found, but none that fit so readily into the surrounding

England
Fort William
A9
Dundee
Perth
Greenock
Edinburgh
Glasgow
A1
SCOTLAND
Ayr
M74
North Sea
NORTH IRELAND
Dumfries
Newcastle
Carlisle
Sunderland
Durham Cathedral
Belfast
Middlesbrough
Lake District National Park
M6
A1
ISLE OF MAN
Scarborough
Douglas
ENGLAND
Dundalk
Irish Sea
York
Blackpool
Leeds
Drogheda
Bradford
Kingston upon Hull
Liverpool
Manchester
Dublin
A Beatles Tour Around Liverpool
Sheffield
Chester
IRELAND
The Wash
M6
Stoke
Nottingham
A1
Norwich
Leicester
Peterborough
Birmingham
Coventry
King's College Chapel, Cambridge
Warwick Castle
WALES
The Royal Shakespeare Theatre
Cambridge
Ipswich
M5
Luton
M40
Blenheim Palace
English Football Match
Oxford University
The Cotswolds
Southend-on-Sea
Swansea
M4
London
M4
Windsor Castle
Canterbury Cathedral
Cardiff
Bristol
Highclere Castle
Bath
M25
M20
Bristol Cannel
Stonehenge
A Tour of Jane Austen Country
Dover
Salisbury Cathedral
Calais
Southampton
Brighton
Portsmouth
Tintagel Castle
Bournemouth
Exeter
English Channel
Plymouth
Penzance
Dieppe
0
50 mi
Cherbourg
Le Havre
Rouen
0
50 km
Caen

scene. Outdoors enthusiasts flock to this region for boating or hiking, while literary types visit the homes of Beatrix Potter, William Wordsworth, Samuel Taylor Coleridge, and other famous writers. Covering an area of approximately 885 square miles and holding 16 major lakes and countless smaller stretches of water, its scenery is key to all the park's best activities: you can cross it by car in about an hour, but this is an area meant to be walked or boated or climbed. Seeing the homes and other sights associated with the writers who lived here and wrote about the area can also occupy part of a trip. ✉ *Lake District Visitor Centre, Ambleside Rd., Brockhole, Windermere* ☎ *015394/46601* 🌐 *www.brockhole.co.uk.*

★ Tintagel Castle

CASTLE/PALACE | Although all that remains of the ruined cliff-top Tintagel Castle, legendary birthplace of King Arthur, is the outline of its walls, moats, and towers, it requires only a little imagination to conjure up a picture of Sir Lancelot and Sir Galahad riding out in search of the Holy Grail. Archaeological evidence, however, suggests that the castle dates from much later—about 1150, when it was the stronghold of the earls of Cornwall. Long before that, Romans may have occupied the site. The earliest identified remains here are of Celtic (5th century AD) origin, and these may have some connection with the legendary Arthur. Legends aside, nothing can detract from the castle ruins, dramatically set off by the wild, windswept Cornish coast. Paths lead down to the pebble beach and a cavern known as Merlin's Cave. ✉ *Castle Rd., ½ mile west of the village, Tintagel* ☎ *01840/770328* 🌐 *www.english-heritage.org.uk* 🎫 *From £14.80* 🕐 *Closed Mon. and Tues. in late Feb.–Mar. and Nov., Mon.–Thurs. in Dec. (except week after Christmas), and weekdays Jan.–mid-Feb. (except one week in mid-Feb.).*

★ Warwick Castle

CASTLE/PALACE | **FAMILY** | The vast bulk of this medieval castle rests on a cliff overlooking the Avon River and is considered "the fairest monument of ancient and chivalrous splendor which yet remains uninjured by time," to use the words of Sir Walter Scott. Today, the company that runs the Madame Tussauds wax museums also owns the castle, and it has become more theme park than an authentic heritage site, but it is still a lot of fun. Warwick's two soaring towers, bristling with battlements, can be seen for miles: the 147-foot-high Caesar's Tower, built in 1356, and the 128-foot-high Guy's Tower, built in 1380. Warwick Castle's monumental walls enclose an impressive armory of medieval weapons. Below the castle, strutting peacocks patrol the 64 acres of grounds elegantly landscaped by Capability Brown in the 18th century. ✉ *Castle La. off Mill St., Warwick* ☎ *01926/406610* 🌐 *www.warwick-castle.com* 🎫 *Castle £37; £24 in advance.*

★ York

TOWN | Much of the historic cathedral city of York's medieval and 18th-century architecture has survived, making it a delight to explore and one of the most popular short-stay destinations in Britain. York was the military capital of Roman Britain, when it was known as Eboracum, and traces of Roman garrison buildings survive throughout the city. Vikings, who called the city Jorvik, used it as a base from which to subjugate the countryside. When the Normans arrived in the 11th century, they emulated the Vikings by using the city as a military base. They also established the foundations of York Minster, the largest Gothic cathedral in northern Europe. The timber-framed buildings on the medieval street known as the Shambles suggest what the city looked like in Tudor times. ✉ *Visit York, 1 Museum St., York* ✈ *3 hrs by train from London's King's Cross Station* 🌐 *www.visityork.org.*

Where to Eat and Drink

The Circus Restaurant

$$ | **MODERN EUROPEAN** | This sophisticated and popular restaurant on the corner of the Circus has an enticing seasonal menu that covers everything from morning coffee to late-night dinners. The husband-and-wife team prioritize locally sourced ingredients, and wines come from old-world small growers. **Known for:** local ingredients; family-run ethos; classic English cuisine. *Average main: £22* *34 Brock St., Bath* *01225/466020* *www.thecircusrestaurant.co.uk* *Closed Sun.*

★ Lambs of Sheep Street

$$ | **BRITISH** | Sit downstairs to appreciate the hardwood floors and oak beams of this local epicurean favorite; upstairs, the look is a bit more contemporary. The updates of tried-and-true dishes include herb-crusted rack of English lamb and panfried calf's liver with creamed potato, wilted spinach, pancetta, and crisp shallot. **Known for:** good-value set meals; one of the oldest buildings in Stratford; modern twists on British classics. *Average main: £20* *12 Sheep St., Stratford-upon-Avon* *01789/292554* *www.lambsrestaurant.co.uk* *No lunch Mon.*

★ Le Manoir aux Quat'Saisons

$$$$ | **FRENCH** | One of the original gastronomy-focused hotels, Le Manoir was opened in 1984 by chef Raymond Blanc, whose culinary talents have earned the hotel's restaurant two Michelin stars—now held for an incredible 38 years and running. Decide from among such innovative French creations as spiced cauliflower velouté with langoustines, beef fillet with braised Jacob's ladder, or Dover sole with brown butter and rosemary. **Known for:** one of the top restaurants in the country; flawless French-style fine dining; beautiful surroundings. *Average main: £229* *Church Rd., Great Milton* *01844/278881* *www.belmond.com/hotels/europe/uk/oxfordshire/belmond-le-manoir-aux-quat-saisons* *No lunch Mon.–Wed.*

★ Midsummer House

$$$$ | **FRENCH** | Beside the River Cam on the edge of Midsummer Common, this gray-brick 19th-century villa holds a two–Michelin star restaurant set in a comfortable conservatory. Fixed-price menus for lunch and dinner (with five to eight courses) present innovative dishes that place a focus on seasonal, often local, ingredients. **Known for:** great river views; beautiful historic setting; special-occasion dining. *Average main: £150* *Midsummer Common, Cambridge* *01223/369299* *www.midsummerhouse.co.uk* *Closed Sun.–Tues.*

Cool Places to Stay

★ Arden Hotel

$$$ | **HOTEL** | Bedrooms are spacious and discreet with splashes of green, violet, and dark crimson in this redbrick boutique hotel across the road from the Royal Shakespeare Theatre. **Pros:** convenient for theatergoers; crisp and modern style; gorgeous guest areas. **Cons:** gets booked up quickly; may be too noisy for some; can be popular with business travelers. *Rooms from: £230* *Waterside, Stratford-upon-Avon* *01789/298682* *www.theardenhotelstratford.com* *45 rooms* *Free Breakfast.*

★ Duke House

$$ | **B&B/INN** | This beautifully converted town house (home of the Duke of Gloucester when he was a student) is forever cropping up in British newspaper articles about the best B&Bs in the country. **Pros:** beautiful house; great location; suites are quite spacious. **Cons:** books up fast; two-night minimum on weekends; cheaper rooms are small. *Rooms from: £160* *1 Victoria St., Cambridge* *01223/314773* *www.dukehousecambridge.co.uk* *5 rooms* *Free Breakfast.*

Dukes Hotel

$$$ | HOTEL | At this small exclusive hotel in a discreet cul-de-sac, ample natural light brightens the classically elegant rooms. **Pros:** famous martini bar; peaceful setting in a central location; excellent restaurant. **Cons:** maybe a bit too quiet for some; price is still rather high for what's available; cheapest rooms book up well in advance. *Rooms from: £425 ✉ 35 St. James's Pl., St. James's ☎ 020/7941–4840, 800/381–4702 in U.S. 🌐 www.dukeshotel.com 87 rooms Free Breakfast Ⓜ Green Park.*

Old Parsonage

$$$ | HOTEL | A 17th-century gabled stone house in a small garden next to St. Giles Church, the Old Parsonage is a dignified retreat. **Pros:** beautiful vine-covered building; complimentary walking tours; free parking. **Cons:** pricey; some guest rooms are small; cool, contemporary look favored over period charm. *Rooms from: £300 ✉ 1 Banbury Rd., Oxford ☎ 01865/310210 🌐 www.oldparsonagehotel.co.uk 35 rooms Free Breakfast.*

Edinburgh

Edinburgh is "a city so beautiful it breaks the heart again and again," as Alexander McCall Smith once wrote. One of the world's stateliest cities and proudest capitals, it is—like Rome—built on seven hills, making it a striking backdrop for the ancient pageant of history. In a skyline of sheer drama, Edinburgh Castle looks out over the city, frowning down on Princes Street's glamour and glitz.

The city's Old Town, which bears a great symbolic weight as the "heart of Scotland's capital," is a boon for lovers of atmosphere and history. This is where you'll find the Royal Mile, which stretches from Edinburgh Castle down to the Palace of Holyroodhouse, and Grassmarket, one of the city's more picturesque areas filled with cute cafés, lively bars and restaurants, and streets brimming with history. In contrast, if you appreciate the unique architectural heritage of the city's Enlightenment, then the New Town's for you. You can take the word "new" with a pinch of salt; its foundation predates the United States *Declaration of Independence*.

As well as this rich past, Edinburgh's famous festivals, excellent museums and galleries, and the modernist Scottish Parliament, are all reminders that Edinburgh has its feet firmly in the 21st century.

Nearly everywhere in Edinburgh (the *burgh* is always pronounced *burra* in Scotland) are spectacular buildings, whose Doric, Ionic, and Corinthian pillars add touches of neoclassical grandeur to the largely Presbyterian backdrop. Large gardens are a strong feature of central Edinburgh, while Arthur's Seat, a craggy peak of bright green-and-yellow furze, rears up behind the spires of the Old Town. Even as Edinburgh moves through the 21st century, its tall guardian castle remains the focal point of the city and its venerable history.

Modern Edinburgh has become a cultural capital, staging the Edinburgh International Festival and the Festival Fringe in every possible venue each August. The stunning National Museum of Scotland complements the city's wealth of galleries and artsy hangouts. Add Edinburgh's growing reputation for food and nightlife and you have one of the world's most beguiling cities.

Royal Mile

Scotland's Most Famous Thoroughfare

History plays out before your eyes along the Royal Mile, a succession of storied streets. It begins below Edinburgh Castle on Castlehill, which is where alleged witches were burned at the stake in the 16th century. Just beyond Tolbooth Kirk—the 240-feet-high Gothic spire is the city's tallest—begins Lawnmarket, once the site of a produce market and today home to historic Gladstone's Land and the Writers' Museum. In the 1770s this area was frequented by the infamous Deacon Brodie, pillar of society by day and murderer by night—the likely inspiration for Dr. Jekyll and Mr. Hyde. Now begins the High Street, lined with impressive buildings. Beyond the dominating High Kirk of St. Giles (look for the heart mosaic set in cobbles outside) lies the Mercat Cross, an old mercantile center where royal proclamations were—and are still—read. Pass the Tron Kirk and you reach Canongate, known for its church graveyard and tolbooth. The Palace of Holyroodhouse marks the end of the Mile.

Don't Miss

Step inside the Royal Mile's High Kirk of St Giles to see the elaborate Chapel of the Order of the Thistle. Look out for the belligerent national motto "nemo me impune lacessit" ("No one provokes me with impunity") and the carved wooden angel playing bagpipes.

Getting Here and Around

The Royal Mile is best reached and explored by foot. Avoid the uphill walk from the New Town by taking a bus to George IV Bridge or North Bridge.

Grassmarket

Historic Marketplace and Hub of Activity

One of the most picturesque and popular areas of the city, Grassmarket's cobbled and winding streets are filled with cute cafés, lively bars and restaurants, and an exciting mix of mostly independent fashion and home stores. They're also brimming with history. Grassmarket dates to the 14th century, when it was an agricultural marketplace, but it is best known for its grisly history as the site of public executions in the 1600s and 1700s. Sections of the Old Town wall, Flodden Wall, can be viewed from the Vennel steps, along with some of the best views of Edinburgh Castle you'll find in the city.

Don't Miss

Cobbled Victoria Street is thought to be the inspiration for Diagon Alley from the Harry Potter series, while nearby Greyfriars Kirkyard is where you'll find the grave of John Gray. It is said that his dog (the famed Greyfriars Bobby) guarded the grave for 14 years and is now buried nearby.

Best Pubs

Grassmarket was once the site of the city's gallows, and two excellent Grassmarket pubs have names that reference the local hangings: The Last Drop and Maggie Dickson's. The latter references a woman who was hanged and proclaimed dead, but shortly before burial sprang back to life. She lived for another 40 years with the nickname Half-Hangit Maggie.

✉ *Grassmarket, Edinburgh* 🌐 *www.edinburgh.org*

Getting Here

Grassmarket is best reached by foot; it's a short, steep walk down from Edinburgh Castle and the Royal Mile, or a flatter walk from Princes Street Gardens and the New Town.

New Town

A Masterpiece of Urban Planning

It was not until the Scottish Enlightenment, a civilizing time of expansion in the 1700s, that the city's elite decided to break away from the Royal Mile's craggy slope and narrow closes to create a new neighborhood. This was to be the New Town, an area of elegant squares, classical facades, wide streets, and a harmonious geometric symmetry unusual in Britain. Princes Street, with its open vista facing the castle, is the southernmost of the New Town's thoroughfares, with Queen Street to the north and George Street as the axis, punctuated by St. Andrew and Charlotte squares. Today, the neoclassical buildings are home to a host of upmarket hotels, restaurants, and designer shops and all three national galleries. Take a stroll through beautiful Princes Street Gardens, home to the Scottish National Gallery, a functioning floral clock, and the Scott Monument, which looks like a snapped-off Gothic church spire.

Don't Miss

With its stunning vistas of the city, Calton Hill is a perfect setting for picnicking and watching festival fireworks. The hill is also home to a number of impressive monuments, including the Parthenon-like National Monument (also known as "Scotland's Disgrace," as it was never finished), the 100-foot-high Nelson Monument (topped with a "time ball" that's dropped at 1pm every day) and the City Observatory (which hosts regular contemporary art exhibitions).

Getting Here and Around

Princes Street is served by regular buses and trams from every corner of the city. It's a short (uphill) walk to the Royal Mile and the rest of the Old Town.

✉ *New Town, Edinburgh* 🌐 *edinburgh.org*

The Water of Leith

The Lifeblood of Edinburgh

The Water of Leith, Edinburgh's main river, rises in the Pentland Hills, skirts the edges of the city center, then heads out to Leith, where it flows into the Firth of Forth. For a scenic stroll, you can join the waterside walkway at the Scottish National Gallery of Modern Art, then follow it through pretty Dean Village—a charming assortment of old mill buildings, stone bridges, and lush greenery—to the arty neighborhood of Stockbridge. Continue to the Royal Botanic Garden, founded in 1670 as a physic garden and now home to 70 acres of rare and beautiful plants, before emerging at The Shore in Leith, just a short walk from the Royal Yacht *Britannia*. The whole route takes about 90 minutes at a leisurely pace—and with all the tree-lined paths, pretty stone bridges, colorful wild-flowers, and stunning birdlife (including herons, kingfishers, and buzzards) to see, you should definitely walk at a leisurely pace.

Don't Miss

During your walk, keep an eye out for Antony Gormley's evocative "6 Times" artwork, a series of life-size human sculptures dotted along the river.

Getting Here and Around

The Scottish National Gallery of Modern Art (the starting point for this walk) can be reached by free shuttle bus from the Scottish National Gallery on Princes Street. The Shore in Leith (the end point) is served by regular buses and trams from the city center.

Best Restaurants

Some of Scotland's most renowned chefs have made Leith their home. Treat yourself to a decadent tasting-menu meal at the likes of Restaurant Martin Wishart and The Little Chartroom.

🌐 *www.waterofleith.org.uk.*

Edinburgh Festival Fringe

The World's Greatest Celebration of Arts and Culture

With tens of thousands of performances held in hundreds of venues across Edinburgh over three weeks every August, the Edinburgh Festival Fringe is the largest arts festival in the world. Established in 1947 as an open and unvetted complement to the Edinburgh International Festival, it was formalized in 1958. Performers, both established and up-and-coming, take to mostly pop-up and nontraditional spaces repurposed for the month of August to showcase theater, music, comedy, puppetry, cabaret, and everything in between. Fire eaters, jugglers, string quartets, stand-up comedians, and magicians all throng into High Street and Princes Street for this uninhibited explosion of creativity. Many events are free; others cost less than £20. It's possible to arrange your own entertainment program from early morning to after midnight. The festival app will help you plan your calendar, but hotels are both expensive and booked up months in advance, so plan your trip as far in advance as possible and consider staying outside the city center.

Don't Miss

The city also hosts the Edinburgh International Festival (world-class classical music, theatre, and opera), the Edinburgh International Book Festival (attracting major international authors), the Edinburgh Art Festival (a free celebration of visual arts), and the Royal Edinburgh Military Tattoo (a bombastic display of military marching bands and motorcyclists).

Getting Here and Around

The Fringe mostly takes place in the Old Town.

✉ *Edinburgh Festival Fringe Society*
🌐 *www.edfringe.com*

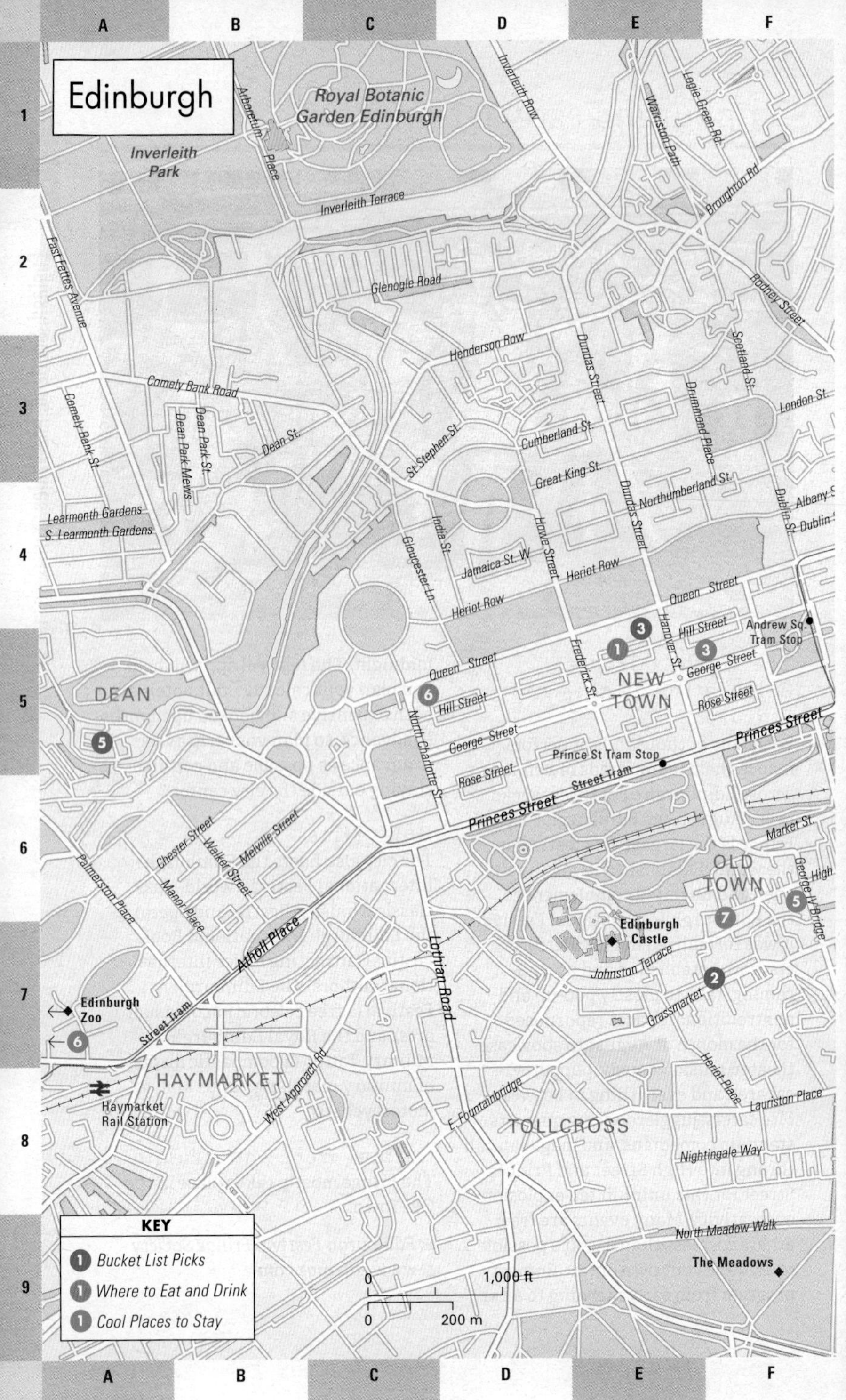
Edinburgh
A
B
C
D
E
F
1
2
3
4
5
6
7
8
9
Royal Botanic Garden Edinburgh
Inverleith Park
Arboretum Place
Inverleith Row
Warriston Path
Logie Green Rd.
Broughton Rd.
Inverleith Terrace
East Fettes Avenue
Glenogle Road
Rodney Street
Henderson Row
Scotland St.
Dundas Street
Drummond Place
Comely Bank Road
Comely Bank St.
Dean Park St.
Dean Park Mews
Dean St.
St Stephen St.
Cumberland St.
London St.
Great King St.
Northumberland St.
Dublin St.
Albany St.
S. Dublin St.
Learmonth Gardens
S. Learmonth Gardens
India St.
Howe Street
Gloucester Ln.
Jamaica St. W
Heriot Row
Queen Street
Hill Street
Andrew Sq. Tram Stop
Hanover St.
Frederick St.
George Street
NEW TOWN
Rose Street
DEAN
North Charlotte St.
Princes Street
Prince St Tram Stop
Street Tram
Chester Street
Walker Street
Melville Street
Market St.
OLD TOWN
Palmerston Place
Manor Place
George IV Bridge
High
Edinburgh Castle
Atholl Place
Lothian Road
Johnston Terrace
Edinburgh Zoo
Grassmarket
HAYMARKET
West Approach Rd
Heriot Place
Haymarket Rail Station
E. Fountainbridge
Lauriston Place
TOLLCROSS
Nightingale Way
KEY
Bucket List Picks
Where to Eat and Drink
Cool Places to Stay
North Meadow Walk
The Meadows
0
1,000 ft
0
200 m

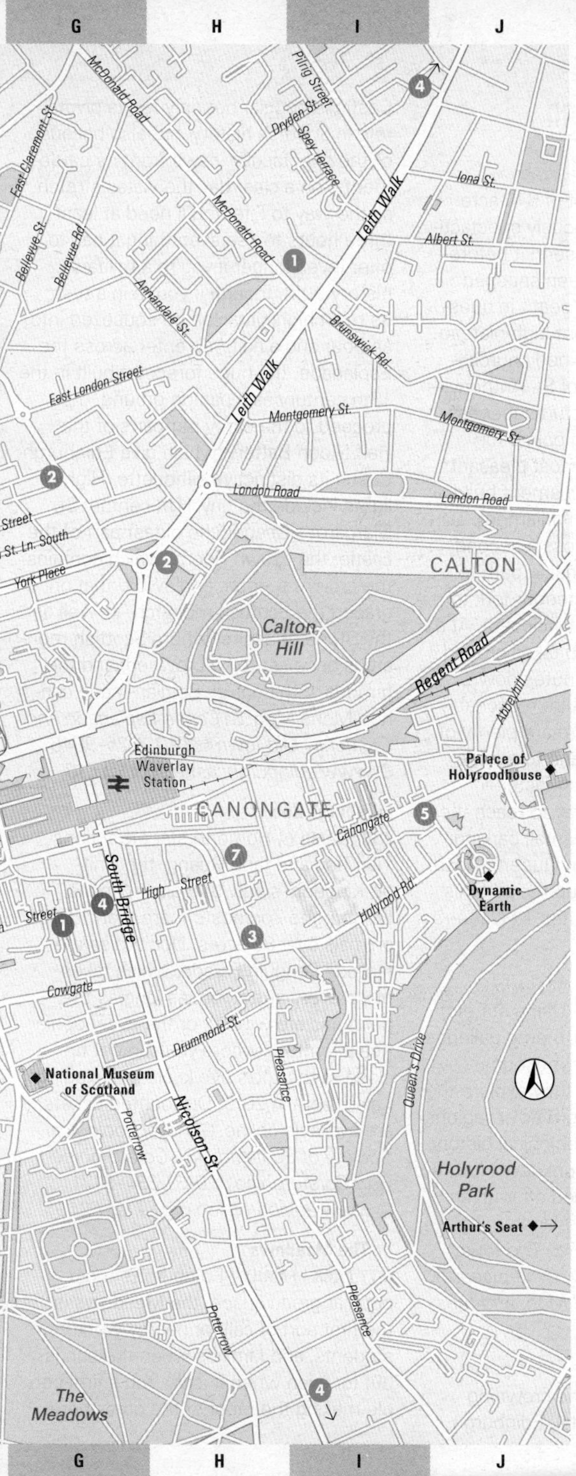

Bucket List Picks

1 Edinburgh Festival Fringe......... **G6**
2 Grassmarket......................... **F7**
3 New Town............................ **E5**
4 Royal Mile.......................... **G6**
5 The Water of Leith................. **A5**

Where to Eat and Drink

1 Dusit................................ **E5**
2 Fhior................................ **G3**
3 The Holyrood 9A..................... **H6**
4 The Little Chartroom................ **I1**
5 Oink................................. **I5**
6 Panda & Sons......................... **C5**
7 Wedgwood the Restaurant............. **H6**

Cool Places to Stay

1 Fingal............................... **I2**
2 The Glasshouse...................... **H4**
3 InterContinental Edinburgh The George............ **F5**
4 Prestonfield House.................. **I9**
5 Radisson Collection Royal Mile Edinburgh.......... **F6**
6 The Roseate Edinburgh............... **A7**
7 The Witchery by the Castle.......... **F6**

When in Edinburgh

Arthur's Seat

VIEWPOINT | The high point of 640-acre Holyrood Park is this famously spectacular viewpoint. You'll have seen it before—countless photos have been snapped from this very spot. The "seat" in question is actually the 822-foot-high plateau of a small mountain. A ruined church—the 15th-century Chapel of St. Anthony—adds to its impossible picturesqueness. There are various starting points for the walk, but one of the most pleasant begins at the Scottish Parliament building. Cross the road from Parliament, skirt around the parking lot, cross a second road, and join the gently rising path to the left (rather than the steeper fork to the right, which is currently closed). At a moderate pace, this climb takes around 45 minutes up and 30 minutes down, and is easy so long as you're reasonably fit. Even if you aren't, there are plenty of places to stop for a rest and to admire the views along the way. A faster—though less beautiful—way to reach the summit is to drive to the small parking area at Dunsapie Loch, on Queen's Road, then follow the footpath up the hill; this walk takes about 20 minutes. ✉ *Queen's Dr., Old Town.*

Dynamic Earth

HISTORY MUSEUM | **FAMILY** | Using state-of-the-art technology, the 11 theme galleries at this interactive science museum educate and entertain as they explore the wonders of the planet, from polar regions to tropical rain forests. Geological history, from the big bang to the unknown future, is also examined, all topped off with an eye-popping, 360-degree planetarium experience. ✉ *Holyrood Rd., Old Town* ☎ *0131/550–7800* 🌐 *www.dynamicearth.co.uk* 🎫 *£17.50* 🕒 *Closed Mon. and Tues. in Nov.–Feb.*

★ Edinburgh Castle

CASTLE/PALACE | **FAMILY** | The crowning glory of the Scottish capital, Edinburgh Castle is popular not only for its pivotal role in Scottish history, but also because of the spectacular views from its battlements: on a clear day the vistas stretch all the way to Fife. You'll need at least three hours to see everything it has to offer (even longer if you're a military history buff), though if you're in a rush, its main highlights can be squeezed into an hour and a half. You enter across the Esplanade, the huge forecourt built in the 18th century as a parade ground, then proceed to the curvy ramparts of the Half-Moon Battery, which give Edinburgh Castle its distinctive silhouette. Highlights include the tiny 11th-century St. Margaret's Chapel, the oldest part of the castle; the Crown Room, which contains the crown, scepter, and sword that once graced the Scottish monarch, as well as the Stone of Scone, where Scottish monarchs once sat to be crowned; and the famous 15th-century Belgian-made cannon Mons Meg. ✉ *Castle Esplanade and Castlehill, Old Town* ☎ *0131/225–9846* 🌐 *www.edinburghcastle.scot* 🎫 *£18.*

Edinburgh Zoo

ZOO | **FAMILY** | Home to star attractions Tian Tian and Yang Guang, the United Kingdom's only two giant pandas, Edinburgh's Zoo hosts more than 1,000 animals over 80 acres. Don't miss the famous Penguin Parade, which takes place every afternoon (as long as the penguins are willing), or the ever-popular Koala Territory, where you can get up close to the zoo's five koalas—including Kalari, born in 2019. Discounted tickets are available online. ✉ *Royal Zoological Society of Scotland, 134 Corstorphine Rd., Corstorphine* ☎ *0131/334–9171* 🌐 *www.edinburghzoo.org.uk* 🎫 *£21.95.*

★ The Meadows

CITY PARK | **FAMILY** | Edinburgh's most popular green space, the Meadows is the first port of call for nearby workers, students, and families when the sun is out (or even when it isn't). You'll find people making the most of the grass here:

picnicking, barbecuing, playing soccer, throwing frisbees, and flying kites. More formal sports facilities include tennis courts, a small golf putting course, and the biggest kids' play area in Edinburgh. Come during one of the city's many cultural festivals and there's likely to be a show on, too. ✉ *Melville Dr., South Side* ☎ *0131/529–5151* 🌐 *www.themeadowsofedinburgh.co.uk.*

★ National Museum of Scotland
HISTORY MUSEUM | FAMILY | This museum traces the country's fascinating story from the oldest fossils to the most recent popular culture, making it a must-see for first-time visitors to Scotland. Two of the most famous treasures are the Lewis Chessmen, a set of intricately carved 12th-century ivory chess pieces found on one of Scotland's Western Isles, and Dolly the sheep, the world's first cloned mammal and biggest ovine celebrity. A dramatic, cryptlike entrance gives way to the light-filled, birdcage wonders of the Victorian grand hall and the upper galleries. Other exhibition highlights include the hanging hippo and sea creatures of the Wildlife Panorama, beautiful Viking brooches, Pictish stones, and Queen Mary's *clarsach* (harp). Take the elevator to the lovely rooftop terrace for spectacular views of Edinburgh Castle and the city below. ✉ *Chambers St., Old Town* ☎ *0300/123–6789* 🌐 *www.nms.ac.uk.*

★ Palace of Holyroodhouse
CASTLE/PALACE | Onetime haunt of Mary, Queen of Scots, the Palace of Holyroodhouse has a long history of gruesome murders, destructive fires, and power-hungry personalities. Today, it's King Charles III's official residence in Scotland. A doughty, impressive palace standing at the foot of the Royal Mile, it's built around a graceful, lawned central court at the end of Canongate. And when royals are not in residence, you can take a tour. There's plenty to see here, so make sure you have at least two hours to tour the palace, gardens, and ruins of the 12th-century abbey; pick up the free audio guide for the full experience. The King James Tower is the oldest surviving section of the palace, containing Mary's rooms on the second floor and Lord Darnley's rooms below. The 150-foot-long Great Picture Gallery, on the north side, displays the portraits of 110 Scottish monarchs. ✉ *Canongate, Old Town* ☎ *0131/123–7306* 🌐 *www.rct.uk* 🎫 *£18* ⏲ *Closed Tues. and Wed. Oct.–June* ✍ *Advance booking required.*

Where to Eat and Drink

Dusit
$$ | THAI | Tucked down narrow Thistle Street, Dusit doesn't register on most travelers' radars, but it has been a local favorite since 2002. An authentic, contemporary Thai restaurant run by Bangkok-born Pom, the menu here delights with deliciously creamy curries, spicy stir-fries, and fragrant seafood specialties, all of which use a mix of fresh local produce and imported Thai vegetables. **Known for:** award-winning Thai food; local haunt; good value lunch menu. $ *Average main: £17* ✉ *49A Thistle St., New Town* ☎ *0131/220–6846* 🌐 *www.dusit.co.uk.*

Fhior
$$$$ | BRITISH | Owner and chef Scott Smith, who previously ran the award-winning Norn, serves seasonal, Scandinavian-inspired fare here with rare Scottish ingredients, from beremeal (an ancient form of barley) bread to sea buckthorn. Choose from seven to 10 courses for dinner (£65 to £90), with menus arriving sealed in envelopes; you're encouraged to trust the chef and leave them unopened until after dessert. **Known for:** modernist decor; old-school Scottish dishes with a Scandinavian flair; multi-course menu options chosen by the chef. $ *Average main: £35* ✉ *36 Broughton St., Edinburgh* ☎ *0131/477–5000* 🌐 *fhior.com* ⏲ *Closed Mon.–Wed.*

★ The Holyrood 9A

BARS | This warm, wood-paneled hipster hangout has a fine array of craft beers on tap, as well as an impressive whisky collection. It also serves some of Edinburgh's best gourmet burgers. ✉ *9A Holyrood Rd., Old Town* ☎ *0131/556–5044* 🌐 *www.theholyrood.co.uk.*

★ The Little Chartroom

$$$$ | BRITISH | For fine dining with a touch of theater, it's hard to beat this superb open-kitchen restaurant, where you can sit at the bar and watch the skilled chefs prepare and assemble each course. The à la carte menu is small—there's a choice of just three starters, three mains, and three desserts—but it's filled with innovative and exciting dishes, such as dressed crab with curry and smoked almonds or spatchcock partridge with haggis and celeriac. **Known for:** cozy kitchenside seating; small but varied menu; unique creations like sweetcorn custard. $ *Average main: £30* ✉ *14 Bonnington Rd., Leith* ☎ *0131/556–6600* 🌐 *www.thelittlechartroom.com* ⏲ *Closed Mon.–Wed. No lunch Thurs. and Fri.*

★ Oink

$ | BRITISH | For a quick, cheap bite while wandering the Royal Mile, you can't beat Oink—possibly the best hog roast (pulled pork) in Edinburgh. Located on Canongate (there are two other outlets, but this one is the best), it was founded by two farmers in 2008, and their high-quality, hand-reared pork has proved a huge hit ever since. **Known for:** unbelievable pulled pork; great-value lunch; no options for vegetarians. $ *Average main: £6* ✉ *82 Canongate, Old Town* ☎ *07584/637416* 🌐 *www.oinkhogroast.co.uk.*

★ Panda and Sons

BARS | The very definition of a hidden gem, this Prohibition-style speakeasy is cunningly tucked away behind a barbershop exterior. Venture inside and downstairs to discover a quirky bar serving some seriously refined cocktails. And yes, we're baffled by the fictional bar-owning panda, too. ✉ *79 Queen St., New Town* ☎ *0131/220–0443* 🌐 *www.pandaandsons.com.*

★ Wedgwood the Restaurant

$$$ | MODERN BRITISH | Rejecting the idea that fine dining should be a stuffy affair, owners Paul Wedgwood and Lisa Channon are in charge at this Royal Mile gem. Local produce and some unusual foraged fronds enliven the taste buds on menus that radically change with the seasons; expect deliciously quirky pairings like scallops in a cauliflower korma or roe deer with buttermilk. **Known for:** unfussy fine dining; delicious sticky toffee pudding; great value lunch deals. $ *Average main: £25* ✉ *267 Canongate, Old Town* ☎ *0131/558–8737* 🌐 *www.wedgwoodtherestaurant.co.uk.*

Cool Places to Stay

Fingal

$$$ | HOTEL | For something completely different, step aboard this floating boutique hotel, permanently moored near the Royal Yacht *Britannia* in Leith. **Pros:** out-of-the-ordinary luxury; close to Leith's best bars and restaurants; quiet and peaceful. **Cons:** no room service; dinner is underwhelming and overpriced; a little way out of the center. $ *Rooms from: £300* ✉ *Alexandra Dock, Leith* ☎ *0131/357–5000* 🌐 *www.fingal.co.uk* *23 rooms* 🍽 *Free Breakfast.*

★ The Glasshouse

$$$ | HOTEL | Glass walls extend from the 19th-century facade of a former church, foreshadowing the daring, modern interior of one of the city's original, and best, boutique hotels. **Pros:** truly stunning rooftop garden; very modern and stylish; near all the attractions. **Cons:** loud air-conditioning and toilet flushing; decor a little sterile for some; continental breakfast extra (hot breakfast even more). $ *Rooms from: £265* ✉ *2 Greenside Pl., New Town* ☎ *0131/525–8200* 🌐 *www.*

theglasshousehotel.co.uk 🛏 *77 rooms* 🍴 *No Meals.*

InterContinental Edinburgh The George
$$$ | **HOTEL** | Built in 1775 for Edinburgh's elite, this row of five Georgian town houses in the heart of the New Town now hosts a luxury hotel. **Pros:** excellent central location; stylish and comfortable bedrooms; in-room treat boxes with chips and candy. **Cons:** regular wedding parties in reception area; floors in older rooms are on a slight slope; breakfast is expensive. $ *Rooms from: £250* ✉ *19–21 George St., New Town* ☎ *0131/225–1251* 🌐 *edinburgh.intercontinental.com* 🛏 *240 rooms* 🍴 *No Meals.*

★ **Prestonfield House**
$$$$ | **HOTEL** | Baroque opulence reigns in this 1687 mansion, with rich velvet curtains, gold-framed portraits, and alabaster-sculpted busts adorning the grand and eccentric public rooms, and equally plush decorations in the guest rooms. **Pros:** baroque grandeur; great restaurant; extensive grounds. **Cons:** underwhelming showers in some rooms; brooding decor can look gloomy; bit pretentious for some. $ *Rooms from: £375* ✉ *Priestfield Rd., Prestonfield* ☎ *0131/225–7800* 🌐 *www.prestonfield.com* 🛏 *23 rooms* 🍴 *Free Breakfast.*

Radisson Collection Royal Mile Edinburgh
$$$ | **HOTEL** | The bright primary colors, striking stenciled wallpapers, and bold, eclectic furnishings inside this trendy design hotel contrast with the Gothic surroundings of the Royal Mile—and yet, somehow, it works. **Pros:** perfect location in the heart of the city; bold and fashionable decor; complimentary gin-and-tonic on arrival. **Cons:** decor a little Austin Powers in places; expensive during high season; street noise can leak into rooms. $ *Rooms from: £260* ✉ *1 George IV Bridge, Old Town* ☎ *0131/220–6666* 🌐 *www.radissonhotels.com* 🛏 *136 rooms* 🍴 *Free Breakfast.*

★ **The Roseate Edinburgh**
$$$ | **HOTEL** | Set within two Victorian town houses that sit across the road from one another, with each offering a selection of beautifully appointed rooms and suites, this hotel is one of Edinburgh's most luxurious boutique options. **Pros:** beautifully decorated; excellent food and service; quiet residential area. **Cons:** no elevator (and stairs to climb); a 20-minute walk to Princes Street; some traffic noise from outside. $ *Rooms from: £300* ✉ *4 W. Coates, Haymarket* ☎ *0131/337–6169* 🌐 *www.roseatehotels.com* 🛏 *35 rooms* 🍴 *Free Breakfast.*

The Witchery by the Castle
$$$$ | **HOTEL** | For a giant helping of Gothic romance, you can't beat the indulgent suites at this gorgeously appointed Castlehill hotel. **Pros:** unique and truly romantic retreat; plush antique furnishings; atmospheric dining. **Cons:** extravagant decor not for everybody; food is good but not top shelf; very expensive. $ *Rooms from: £695* ✉ *352 Castlehill, Old Town* ☎ *0131/225–5613* 🌐 *www.thewitchery.com* 🛏 *9 suites* 🍴 *Free Breakfast.*

Scotland

Most visitors to Scotland head straight to Edinburgh. That's understandable. Edinburgh is a stunning city with a rich history, century-old castles, a vibrant arts and festivals scene, and real charm and substance. But Scotland's magic extends beyond its captivating capital into the raw and poetic beauty of its ancient landscape where you will find not-to-be-missed experiences and dramatic scenery, on and off the beaten trail.

Scotland packs spectacular landscapes, as well as rich history and tradition, into a small country. From the Lowlands to the Highlands, its lush woodlands, windswept moors, and deep lochs will take your breath away. Impressive castles, whisky distilleries, golf courses and challenging long-distance walking trails through splendid scenery await. Formidable castles—some still grimly medieval, others rebuilt in Victorian times and redolent of aristocratic wealth and privilege—are among Scotland's historic glories, and haunting structures like the Calanais Standing Stones on the Isle of Lewis and Skara Brae on Orkney are testament to an even mistier and more ancient past. As the home of golf, Scotland claims some of the world's most challenging holes but has courses for all levels, many in splendid settings. Art lovers will find galleries and museums replete with works by renowned Scots and by some of the greatest of Europe's master painters and sculptors. Food lovers will find world-class fine-dining restaurants but also unpretentious brasseries and gastropubs where local chefs make the most of superb seafood, game such as grouse, pheasant and venison from Highland moors and glens, and distinctive locally grazed lamb and beef from the pastures of the Borders, Angus, Aberdeen and Orkney. Finally, no once-in-a-lifetime visit to Scotland is complete without a visit to one of the distinguished whisky distilleries—more than 130 of them—that are scattered from the Western and Northern Isles to the slopes of Speyside and the Lowlands.

Stirling Castle

A Royal Stronghold

Set high on volcanic rock, visible for many miles in every direction, the magnificent Stirling Castle is one of the largest and most important castles in Scotland and a source of great national pride. Its strategic location, guarding the lowest crossing point of the River Forth, made Stirling Castle the grandest prize in the Scots Wars of Independence during the late 13th and early 14th centuries. The Stewart monarchs made Stirling Castle their court and power base, hosting important celebrations like christenings and coronations here and creating fine Renaissance-style buildings within the walls. Today, you enter the castle through its outer defenses, which consist of a great curtained wall and batteries from 1708. Among the later works built for regiments stationed here, the Regimental Museum stands out; it's a 19th-century baronial revival on the site of an earlier building.

Don't Miss

Within the ramparts, the most conspicuous feature is the Palace, built by James V (1512–42) between 1538 and 1542. The decorative figures festooning the ornate outer walls show the influence of French masons. Also here are the Royal Apartments, which re-create the furnishings and tapestries found here during the reign of James V and his French queen, Mary of Guise.

Getting Here and Around

The M9 and M80 motorways connect Stirling with Edinburgh and Glasgow. Frequent buses from both cities take around 1 hour, as do trains. It's a steep uphill walk from the adjacent bus and train stations to the castle gateway.

✉ *Castlehill, Stirling* ☎ *01786/450000*
🌐 *www.stirlingcastle.gov.uk* 🎫 *£16*

Neolithic Orkney

Five Thousand Years of History

Orkney's stone circles, burial chambers, and ancient subterranean settlements testify to a deep human heritage and present a remarkable picture of life here around 5,000 years ago. An 1850 storm revealed the Neolithic village structures now known as Skara Brae—the most extensive Stone Age settlement in northern Europe. First occupied around 3000 BC, the underground homes contained stone beds, fireplaces, dressers, and cupboards. A reconstructed house can be seen in the visitor center. Beneath the grassy mound of Maeshowe is a vast chambered tomb dating to 2500 BC. Vikings who sheltered here in the 12th century AD carved runic inscriptions into its walls. Nearby, the Ring of Brodgar, dating to 2500–2000 BC, is an eerie circle of 36 Neolithic standing stones (originally 60) surrounded by a deep ditch. It's not hard to imagine strange rituals taking place here in the misty past.

Don't Miss

Skara Brae stands on the grounds of Skaill House, a splendid mansion built by the Bishop of Orkney in the 1600s.

Getting Here and Around

Skara Brae is 8 miles north of Stromness ferry port. Maeshowe is 6 miles northeast of Stromness and 1 mile from the Ring of Brodgar. Stagecoach Buses 7 and 8S link the Ring of Brodgar and Skara Brae with Kirkwall.

☏ *01856/841815* 🌐 *www.historicenvironment.scot* 🎫 *Maeshow £9; Skara Brae £7; Skara Brae and Skaill House £9* 🕒 *Skaill House closed Nov.–Mar.*

Inveraray Castle

Home of a Highland Dynasty

The seat of the Dukes of Argyll and chiefs of Clan Campbell since the 15th century, the castle that stands here today is testimony to their enduring wealth and power. Founded in 1746, this fusion of Baroque, Gothic, and Palladian architectural styles was completed in 1789. In 1877, after being damaged by fire, it was extended and embellished with the gray-green spires that surmount its corner towers, giving it something of the look of a French chateau. Inside are displays of luxurious furnishings and art, as well as a huge armory crammed with fearsome weaponry—a reminder that the Campbells did not accrue their riches by entirely peaceful methods. Tours of the castle follow the history of the powerful Campbell family and how they rose to be among the greatest potentates and landowners in the Highlands. The castle is surrounded by 16 acres of well-tended gardens and woodland, dominated by vivid rhododendrons and azaleas beneath towering cedars and sequoias.

Don't Miss

Inveraray Jail's realistic courtroom scenes, carefully re-created cells, and other paraphernalia provide a glimpse of life behind bars in Victorian times.

Getting Here and Around

Inveraray lies approximately 60 miles northwest of Glasgow, off the A83 highway.

✉ *Inveraray, Argyll* ☎ *01499/302203*
🌐 *www.inveraray-castle.com* 🎟 *£16*

Jacobite Steam Train

Scotland's Greatest Train Ride

This spectacularly scenic 84-mile round-trip between Fort William and Mallaig aboard a vintage train drawn by a historic steam locomotive is the most relaxing way to take in views of wild, birch-and bracken-covered slopes, mountains, lochs, beaches, and islands. En route, it crosses the 1,248-foot-long Glenfinnan Viaduct—a wonder when it was built in 1897, and which remains so today, especially for Harry Potter fans. The train gained worldwide fame as the "Hogwarts Express" that carried Harry Potter and his chums to their school for wizards in the movie versions of J.K. Rowling's books, and if you look out of your carriage window as the train crosses the picturesque viaduct you're likely to see a small throng of fans waiting to snap an unforgettable image.

Don't Miss

The 1815 Glenfinnan Monument tower overlooking Loch Shiel commemorates the place where Bonnie Prince Charlie raised his standard to begin his ill-fated bid for the throne in 1745. The full story is told in the nearby visitor center. 🌐 *www.nts.org.uk* 🎫 *£5*

When to Go

There are two trips a day between late April and late October. Weekend trips operate only in the height of summer.

Getting Here and Around

Long-distance Scottish Citylink (☎ *0871/266–3333* 🌐 *www.citylink.co.uk*) bus service connects Glasgow and Fort William. ScotRail (☎ *0344/811–0141* 🌐 *www.scotrail.co.uk*) has trains from London, as well as connections from Glasgow and Edinburgh.

✉ *Fort William Travel Centre, MacFarlane Way, Fort William* ☎ *0844/850–4685* 🌐 *www.westcoastrailways.co.uk*

Loch Ness

Here Be Monsters

Formidable Loch Ness is the biggest and best known of the chain of four long, narrow lochs that make up the Great Glen, a rift valley that carves across Scotland from the Moray Firth to the west coast. With a greater volume of water than any other British lake, the loch has a maximum depth of more than 800 feet, and according to local legend is home to a famous monster. Does something lurk in the gloomy depths? Maybe not—but "Monster Tourism" is said to be worth around £40 million to Scotland annually. At the lochside village of Drumnadrochit, the Loch Ness Centre and Exhibition walks you through fuzzy photographs, unexplained sonar readings, and eyewitness testimonies that true believers claim as evidence that "Nessie" exists. Monster or no monster, the loch, between pine and bracken-covered hillsides, is a spectacular slice of Highland scenery.

Don't Miss

The romantic lochside ruin, Urquhart Castle, was built in the 13th century and destroyed before the end of the 17th century to prevent its use by the Jacobites. A visitor center gives an idea of what medieval life was like here. ✣ *Off A82, 2 miles southeast of Drumnadrochit* 🌐 *www.historicenvironment.scot* 🎫 *£12*

Getting Here and Around

Buses between Inverness and Fort Augusts run along the loch on the A82, stopping at Drumnadrochit. Jacobite Cruises (🌐 *www.jacobite.co.uk*) runs cruises on Loch Ness.

✉ *Loch Ness Centre and Exhibition, Drumnadrochit* ☎ *01456/450573* 🌐 *www.lochness.com* 🎫 *£10*

West Highland Way

An Epic Walk

The long-distance West Highland Way stretches 96 miles from central Scotland to Fort William, through breathtaking scenery. Along its course the landscape changes as you walk from the shores of Loch Lomond into the hills beyond, past dramatic Glencoe, across Rannoch Moor—a vast expanse of bracken, heather, streams and lochs—and beyond it to the southern end of the Great Glen. The Way is divided into eight sections, none more than 15 miles in length, with accommodations at strategic points along the way. This is a trek that reasonably fit walkers can complete in 8-10 days, but there are challenging stretches, such as the steep stage between Rowardennan and Inverarnan at the head of Loch Lomond.

Don't Miss

Seen from the Way, Buachaille Etive Mor (the "Great Shepherd of Etive") is one of Scotland's most stunningly photogenic mountains, and often snowcapped even in early summer.

When to Go

The best months to walk the Way are May through September, but plan for rainy days. Snow lingers on higher ground as late as May; rainproof outerwear, warm inner layers, and tough, waterproof footwear are essential.

Getting Here and Around

The start of the route is marked with an obelisk on Douglas Street in the center of Milngavie, which has frequent Scotrail trains and Citylink bus services from Glasgow. Buses and trains between Glasgow and Fort William call at points along the route, including Inverarnan, Ardlui, Crianlarich, Tyndrum, Bridge of Orchy, and Ballachullish.

✉ *Milngavie* 🌐 *www.west-highland-way.co.uk*

Robert Burns Birthplace Museum

Meet Scotland's Bard

Robert Burns (1759–96) died young, but crammed a lot into his 37 years, penning poems and songs that are still much-loved today, including "A Man's a Man for A" and, of course, "Auld Lang Syne," sung every New Year's Eve in Scotland and worldwide. This museum brings to life the convivial farmboy-turned-poet, egalitarian, and philanderer with imaginative displays that present each of his poems in context, with commentaries sensitively written in a modern version of "Lallans," the Scots dialect in which he wrote. Headsets let you hear the poems sung or spoken. Interactive touch screens allow you to discuss politics, love, revolution, and Scottishness with a re-created Burns. In the grounds stand the medieval Brig (bridge) o' Doon, and the ruins of Auld Kirk Alloway, both famous for their roles in Burns's epic poem, "Tam o' Shanter," and the neoclassical Burns Monument, erected in 1832.

Don't Miss

Scotland's national poet lived in this thatched cottage, Burns Cottage, for his first seven years. It has a living room, a kitchen, and a stable, one behind the other. In the garden in summer grow the staple vegetables the poet's father might have cultivated. Videos re-create daily life in the 18th century.

Getting Here and Around

Alloway is 2½ miles south of Ayr, signposted from the A77, around 40 minutes from Glasgow by car. Regular trains from Glasgow to Ayr connect with local buses to Alloway, a 1–2 hour journey.

Murdoch's Lone, Alloway *01292/ 443700* *www.nts.org.uk* *£12, includes Robert Burns Birthplace Museum, Burns Cottage, and Burns Monument*

The Highland Games

Celebrating Scottish Traditions

From spring to late summer across a wide swath of northern Scotland, kilted competitors gather to toss, pull, fling, dance, and sing at various Highland events. No two "gatherings" are the same, but most incorporate agricultural shows, centuries-old sporting competitions, clan gatherings, and bagpiper playing. The Braemar Highland Gathering, held the first Saturday in September stands tall on ceremony and tradition, and the chance of seeing royalty up close means it attracts visitors from far and wide. Competitions and events include hammer throwing, caber tossing, tug-o-war, and bagpipe playing, and costume and historical displays. The British royal family has been connected to the event since the days of Queen Victoria and Prince Albert. Dufftown Games is the most competitive, with its race up the nearby Ben Rinnes, while the most picturesque is the Lochcarron Games, which are played and danced out under the massif of the Torridon Hills.

Don't Miss

The Cowal Highland Gathering is renowned for the quality of its Highland dancing, drawing in the best performers from around the globe as they compete in the Scottish and World Championships.

Getting Here and Around

Gathering locations are best reached by car. By train, you can reach Aberdeen directly from Edinburgh, Inverness, and Glasgow. Bus service is available to most towns. Reserve accommodations far in advance.

🌐 *www.visitscotland.com/see-do/events/highland-games*
🌐 *www.braemargathering.org*
🌐 *www.dufftownhighlandgames.com*
🌐 *www.lochcarrongames.org.uk*
🌐 *cowalgathering.com*

Golf at St. Andrews

Play Where Modern Golf Was Invented

With 550 golf courses for just 5.5 million residents, Scotland has the highest ratio of courses to people anywhere in the world, but the Holy Grail of courses is in St. Andrews where the game was invented and where fans come to follow in the footsteps of Hagen, Sarazen, Jones, and Hogan. Legend has it that the game was first played here with a piece of driftwood, a shore pebble, and a rabbit hole on the sandy, coastal turf. Residents were playing golf on the town links as far back as the 15th century, while the Royal & Ancient Golf Club of St. Andrews was founded in 1754. The town of St. Andrews prospers on golf, golf schools, and golf equipment (the manufacture of golf balls is a local industry), but it is also home to castle ruins, a botanical garden, and a grand university—the oldest in Scotland. Seven St. Andrews courses, all part of the St. Andrews Trust, are open to visitors, and more than 40 other courses in the region offer golf by the round or by the day.

Don't Miss

Considered the oldest golf course in the world, the Old Course was first played in the 15th century. Each year, more than 44,000 rounds are teed off. A handicap certificate is required to join the fun.

Getting Here and Around

St. Andrews is about 50 miles northeast of Edinburgh, and best experienced by car. The East Coast Main Line train stops at Leuchars, about 6 miles from St. Andrews.

St. Andrews Visitor Information.
✉ *70 Market St., St. Andrews*
☎ *01334/472021* 🌐 *www.standrews.com*

Malt Whisky Trail

The Ultimate Scotch Experience

Conjured from an innocuous mix of malted barley, water, and yeast, malt whisky is for many synonymous with Scotland. Lowlanders and Highlanders produced whisky for hundreds of years before it emerged as Scotland's national drink and major export. Today those centuries of expertise result in a sublimely subtle drink with many different layers of flavor. Each distillery produces a malt with—to the expert—instantly identifiable, predominant notes peculiarly its own. The Speyside region has the greatest concentration of distilleries, including nine iconic whisky sites connected by the signposted Malt Whisky Trail. Along the way, you'll find stunning scenery, working and historic distilleries, excellent bars, textiles mills, historic attractions, and lots of whisky.

Don't Miss

All the distilleries offer tours and tastings. Glenfiddich Distillery is home to the world's most-awarded single malt. The Strathisla Distillery was built in 1786 and now produces the main component of the Chivas Regal blend.

Getting Here and Around

The full trail can be driven in an hour and is best experienced with a car (and a designated driver). The key routes through malt whisky country are the A95 from Aviemore to Keith and the A96 from Inverness to Aberdeen. Sites on The Trail are clearly signposted.

The Malt Whisky Trail. ✉ *Speyside* 🌐 *maltwhiskytrail.com*

Glenfiddich Distillery. ✉ *Moray, Dufftown* 🌐 *www.glenfiddich.com*

Strathisla Distillery. ✉ *Moray, Keith* 🌐 *www.maltwhiskydistilleries.com/strathisla*

Abbottsford

Home of a Literary Legend

Georgian Scotland's greatest author, Sir Walter Scott, wrote his way out of bankruptcy to earn a knighthood, royal favor, international fame, and this splendid mock-baronial home by the River Tweed, replete with towers and turrets. Scott built the house from scratch on the site he bought in 1811 and lived here until his death in 1832. He filled it with books, antiques, works of art, arms and armor, and relics of the romantic past that he celebrated and brought to the world's attention in works like *Waverley*, *Ivanhoe*, and *Rob Roy*. Prizes of his collection include a jeweled crucifix owned by Mary, Queen of Scots; a lock of Bonnie Prince Charlie's hair, and a fearsome claymore once wielded by outlaw hero Rob Roy MacGregor. Scott surrounded his home with 120 acres of formal gardens and woodland and riverside trails that are a delight in summer.

Don't Miss

A free audio tour guides you around the salon, the circular study, and the library with its 9,000 leather-bound volumes.

When to Go

Abbotsford House is closed December to February; gardens are closed December to March. Visit April to May to see gardens at their most colorful or in September for fall foliage.

Getting Here and Around

Trains from Edinburgh Waverley to Tweedbank, 1 mile from Abbotsford, take 1 hour. Minibuses run from Tweedbank station and Melrose Abbey to Abbotsford Wednesday to Sunday. Check to see if service is operating before your visit.

✉ *B6360, Melrose* ☎ *01896/752043*
🌐 *www.scottsabbotsford.co.uk*
🎫 *House and gardens £14; gardens only £8*

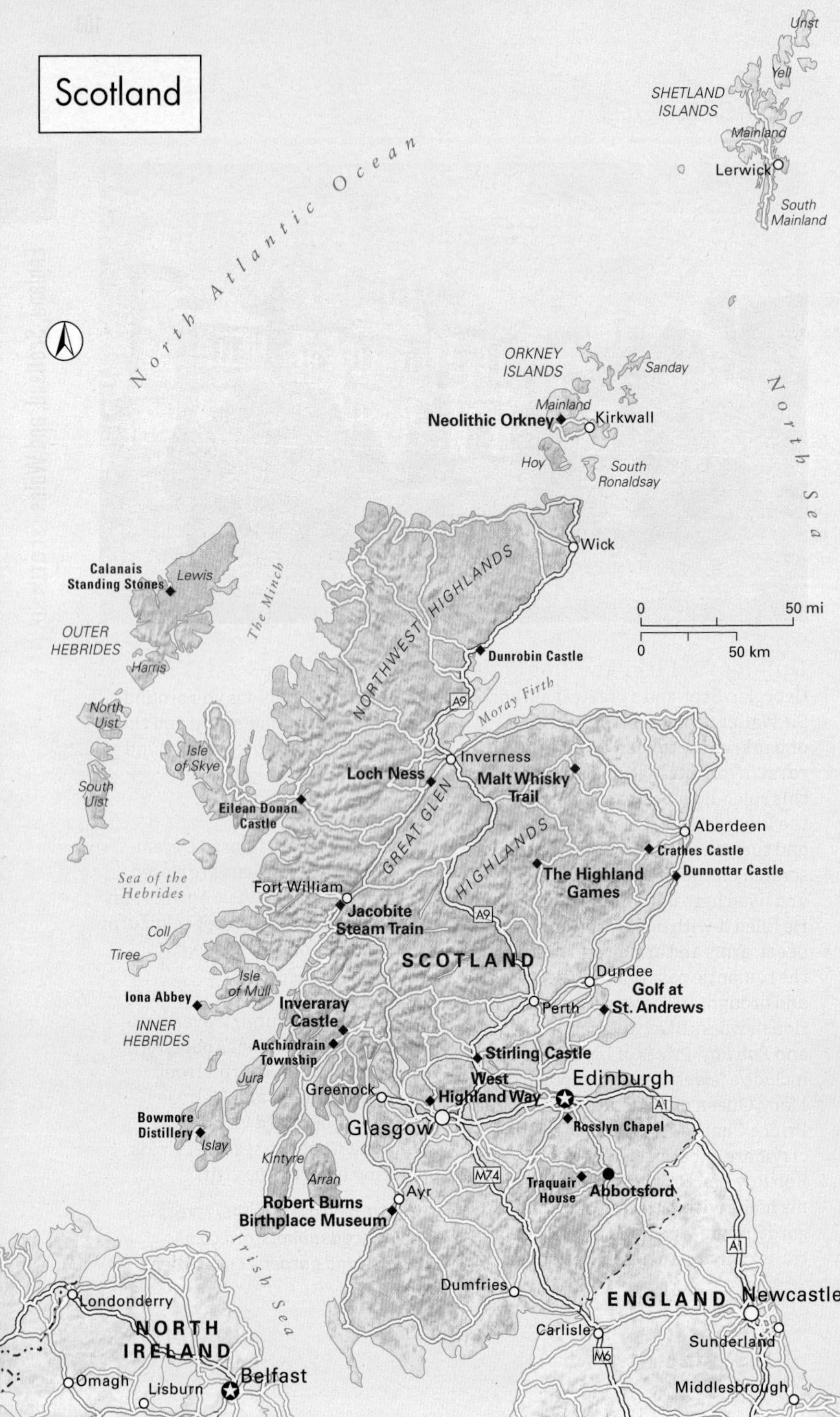
Scotland
North Atlantic Ocean
SHETLAND ISLANDS
Unst
Yell
Mainland
Lerwick
South Mainland
ORKNEY ISLANDS
Sanday
Mainland
Neolithic Orkney
Kirkwall
Hoy
South Ronaldsay
North Sea
Wick
0
50 mi
0
50 km
Calanais Standing Stones
Lewis
The Minch
OUTER HEBRIDES
Harris
North Uist
South Uist
NORTHWEST HIGHLANDS
Dunrobin Castle
A9
Moray Firth
Isle of Skye
Inverness
Loch Ness
Malt Whisky Trail
Eilean Donan Castle
GREAT GLEN
HIGHLANDS
Aberdeen
Crathes Castle
Dunnottar Castle
The Highland Games
Sea of the Hebrides
Fort William
Jacobite Steam Train
A9
Coll
Tiree
SCOTLAND
Isle of Mull
Iona Abbey
Inveraray Castle
Dundee
Golf at St. Andrews
Perth
INNER HEBRIDES
Auchindrain Township
Stirling Castle
Jura
West Highland Way
Edinburgh
Greenock
A1
Glasgow
Rosslyn Chapel
Bowmore Distillery
Islay
Kintyre
Arran
M74
Traquair House
Abbotsford
Ayr
Robert Burns Birthplace Museum
Irish Sea
A1
Londonderry
NORTH IRELAND
Dumfries
ENGLAND
Newcastle
Carlisle
Sunderland
M6
Omagh
Lisburn
Belfast
Middlesbrough

When in Scotland

★ Auchindrain Township

MUSEUM VILLAGE | FAMILY | Step a few centuries back in time at this open-air museum, a rare surviving example of an 18th-century communal-tenancy farm. About 250 years ago, there were several thousand working communities like Auchindrain, but this was the last of them, with its final tenant leaving in 1963. Today the bracken-thatch and iron-roof buildings, about 20 in all, give you a feel for early farming life in the Highland communities. Several houses are furnished and tell the story of their occupants. A tearoom is open morning to afternoon. ✉ *Auchindrain, Inveraray* ✣ *Off A83 about 6 miles south of Inveraray* ☎ *01499/500235* 🌐 *auchindrain.org.uk* 🎫 *£12 (£3 in winter)* ⏲ *Closed weekends Nov.–Mar.*

★ Bowmore Distillery

DISTILLERY | Bowmore is the grand old lady of Islay's distilleries, and a tour is a must for any visitor. In business since 1779, the distillery, like all Islay whisky makers, stands by the sea. Standard tours include a walk around the malting areas and the stills, and connoisseurs can opt for in-depth tours that include tutored tastings. ✉ *School St., Bowmore* ☎ *01496/810441* 🌐 *www.bowmore.com* 🎫 *From £18* ⏲ *Closed Sun. and Mon.*

★ Calanais Standing Stones (*Callanish Stones*)

RUINS | The west coast of Lewis is rich in prehistoric sites, and the most famous of these is the Calanais Standing Stones. Believed to have been positioned in several stages between 3000 BC and 1500 BC, this arrangement consists of an avenue of 19 monoliths extending northward from a circle of 13 stones, with other rows leading south, east, and west. Ruins of a cairn sit within the circle on the east side. Researchers believe they may have been used for astronomical observations, but you're free to cook up your own theories. The visitor center has an interesting exhibit on the stones, a very pleasant tearoom, and a gift shop. ✉ *Callanish* ☎ *01851/621422* 🌐 *www.historicenvironment.scot.*

★ Crathes Castle

CASTLE/PALACE | FAMILY | About 16 miles west of Aberdeen, Crathes Castle was once the home of the Burnett family and is one of the best-preserved castles in Britain. Keepers of the Forest of Drum for generations, the family acquired lands here by marriage and later built a castle, completed in 1596. The National Trust for Scotland cares for the castle, which is furnished with many original pieces and family portraits. The castle is open for guided tours only. Outside are grand yet lovingly tended gardens with calculated symmetry and flower-rich beds. There's an adventure park for kids, and the staff organizes activities that are fun and educational. ✉ *Off A93, Banchory* ☎ *01330/844525* 🌐 *www.nts.org.uk* 🎫 *£14.50* ⏲ *Closed weekdays Oct.–Feb. and Tues. and Wed. in May and Sept.*

★ Dunnottar Castle

CASTLE/PALACE | It's hard to beat the cinematic majesty of the magnificent cliff-top ruins of Dunnottar Castle, with its panoramic views of the North Sea. Building began in the 14th century, when Sir William Keith, Marischal of Scotland, decided to build a tower house to demonstrate his power. Subsequent generations added to the structure, and important visitors included Mary, Queen of Scots. The castle is most famous for holding out for eight months against Oliver Cromwell's army in 1651 and 1652, thereby saving the Scottish crown jewels, which had been stored here for safekeeping. Reach the castle via the A90; take the Stonehaven turnoff and follow the signs. Wear sensible shoes, and allow about two hours. ✉ *Off A92, Stonehaven* ☎ *01569/766320* 🌐 *www.dunnottarcastle.co.uk* 🎫 *£9.50.*

Dunrobin Castle

CASTLE/PALACE | FAMILY | Situated 12 miles north of Dornoch, flamboyant Dunrobin Castle is an ancient seat that became the home of the dukes of Sutherland, at which point it was transformed into the 19th-century white-turreted behemoth you see today. As well as its grand palatial facade and lavish interiors, the property also has falconry demonstrations and Versailles-inspired gardens. Head upstairs in the house for fine views over the garden and out to sea. The first duke, who was fascinated by trains, built his own railroad in the park and staffed it with his servants. Yet for all this frivolity, the duke has a controversial legacy: he was responsible for the Sutherland Clearances of 1810 to 1820, when people were forcibly removed from their farms to make room for sheep to graze. ✉ *Off A9, Golspie* ☎ *01408/633177* 🌐 *www.dunrobincastle.co.uk* 🎫 *£13.50* ⏲ *Closed Nov.–Mar.*

★ Eilean Donan Castle

CASTLE/PALACE | Guarding the confluence of lochs Long, Alsh, and Duich stands the most picturesque of all Scottish fortifications. Eilean Donan Castle, perched on an islet connected to the mainland by a stone-arched bridge, dates from the 14th century and has all the dramatic stone walls, timber ceilings, and winding stairs you could possibly desire. Empty and neglected for years after being bombarded by frigates of the Royal Navy during an abortive Spanish-Jacobite landing in 1719, this romantic Scottish icon was almost entirely rebuilt from a ruin in the early 20th century. The kitchen re-creates the busy scene before a grand banquet, and the upper floors show how the castle was transformed into a grand house. The picturesque cover of a thousand travel brochures, Eilean Donan has also appeared in a number of Hollywood movies and TV shows, from *The Wicker Man* to *Highlander*. There's a gift shop and a coffeehouse for the many visitors. The castle lies 8½ miles east of Kyle Lochalsh; you'll pass it if you're coming from the south. ✉ *Off A87, Dornie* ☎ *01599/555202* 🌐 *www.eileandonancastle.com* 🎫 *£10.*

★ Iona Abbey

RELIGIOUS BUILDING | Overseen by St. Columba, who traveled here from Ireland, Iona was the birthplace of Christianity in Scotland in the 6th century. It survived repeated Norse sackings before falling into disuse around the time of the Reformation. Restoration work began at the beginning of the 20th century. Today the restored buildings serve as a spiritual center under the jurisdiction of the Church of Scotland. Guided tours by the Iona Community, an ecumenical religious group, begin every half hour in summer and on demand in winter. ✉ *Iona* ☎ *01681/700512* 🌐 *www.historicenvironment.scot* 🎫 *£9.50.*

★ Rosslyn Chapel

RELIGIOUS BUILDING | This chapel has always beckoned curious visitors intrigued by the various legends surrounding its magnificent carvings, but today it pulses with tourists as never before. Much of this can be attributed to Dan Brown's best-selling 2003 mystery novel *The Da Vinci Code*, which featured the chapel heavily, claiming it has a secret sign that can lead you to the Holy Grail. Whether you're a fan of the book or not, this Episcopal chapel (services continue to be held here) remains an imperative stop on any traveler's itinerary. Originally conceived by Sir William Sinclair (circa 1404–80) and dedicated to St. Matthew in 1446, the chapel is outstanding for the quality and variety of the carving inside. Covering almost every square inch of stonework are human figures, animals, and plants. The meaning of these remains subject to many theories; some depict symbols from the medieval order of the Knights Templar and from Freemasonry. The chapel's design called for a cruciform structure, but only the choir and parts of the east transept walls were fully completed. Free talks about the building's history are held daily. ✉ *Chapel Loan, Roslin* ☎ *0131/440–2159* 🌐 *www.rosslynchapel.com* 🎫 *£9.50.*

★ **Traquair House**

HISTORIC HOME | Said to be the oldest continually occupied home in Scotland (since 1107), Traquair House has secret stairways and passages, a library with more than 3,000 books, and a bed said to be used by Mary, Queen of Scots in 1566. The top floor of the house is an interesting small museum. Outside is a reasonably scary maze, an adventure playground, and some lovely woodland walks as well as pigs, goats, and chickens. The 18th-century brew house still makes highly recommended ale, and there's a café on the grounds near the beautiful walled garden. You may even spend the night, if you wish. ✉ *Off B7062, Innerleithen* ✣ *From the A70 6 miles south of Peebles, take the B709 for 7 miles; the car entrance into the house is in the village* ☎ *01896/830323* 🌐 *www.traquair.co.uk* 🎫 *Grounds £6, house and grounds £12* ⏲ *Closed Nov.–Mar.*

Where to Eat and Drink

Brig o' Doon House

$$ | BRITISH | Originally built in 1827, this attractive hotel restaurant often has a piper by the door to greet hungry travelers ready for a Scottish setting and some Scottish fare. Tartan carpets, dark-wood paneling, and buck heads mounted on the walls set the mood, and the bar is a shrine to Robert Burns. **Known for:** riverside location; Scottish food and decor; great venison casserole. [$] *Average main: £15* ✉ *High Maybole Rd., Alloway* ☎ *01292/442466* 🌐 *www.brigodoonhouse.com.*

★ **Cail Bruich**

$$$$ | BRITISH | A Gaelic phrase that means "to eat well," the restaurant known as Cail Bruich certainly lives up to its name as evidenced by its many awards, including a coveted Michelin star (currently the only eatery in Glasgow with one). Run by two brothers, the ambitious and innovative menu makes use of local, high-quality Scottish ingredients, but it's really the delicate and clever cooking style that takes the menu to higher heights. **Known for:** Glasgow's only Michelin star; multicourse chef's table experience; elevated Scottish cuisine. [$] *Average main: £55* ✉ *725 Great Western Rd., West End* ☎ *0141/334–6265* 🌐 *www.cailbruich.co.uk* ⏲ *Closed Sun. and Mon. No lunch Tues.–Thurs.*

Lime Tree An Ealdhain

$$$ | MODERN BRITISH | One of Fort William's most upscale culinary spots, this restaurant is unfussy and modern inside, with low-hanging lamps, rich jewel-toned walls, and solid wood furniture. Expect filling dishes that, while not overly complex, are given an edge with embellishments such as fennel sauerkraut or marrowbone crumble. **Known for:** some of Fort William's most interesting food; inspired desserts; on-site art gallery. [$] *Average main: £21* ✉ *The Old Manse, Achintore Rd., Fort William* ☎ *01397/701806* 🌐 *www.limetreefortwilliam.co.uk* ⏲ *No lunch.*

★ **Loch Bay Restaurant**

$$$$ | SEAFOOD | Situated right on the waterfront, this distinctive black-and-white restaurant, where the island's top chefs come to unwind on their nights off, is a Skye foodie favorite. The seafood is freshly caught and simply prepared by renowned chef Michael Smith, with the aim of enhancing the natural flavors of the ingredients rather than overwhelming them with superfluous sauces. **Known for:** sublime yet simple seafood; beautiful bay views; impeccable service. [$] *Average main: £110* ✉ *1 Macleods Terr., Stein* ☎ *01470/592235* 🌐 *www.lochbay-restaurant.co.uk* ⏲ *Closed Sun.–Tues. and Jan.–Mar. No lunch.*

★ **Loch Fyne Oyster Bar**
$$ | **SEAFOOD** | The first of a chain of seafood restaurants that now stretches across the United Kingdom (though the rest are now owned by the Greene King brewery chain), this restaurant continues to please with its emphasis on ultrafresh, locally sourced seafood, simply prepared. Oysters, are, of course, a keynote, but the menu also features mussels, lobster, prawns, salmon, and much more from the sea, accompanied by perfect crunchy green vegetables such as peas, beans, and asparagus. **Known for:** plump oysters perfectly prepared; meltingly tender smoked salmon; seafood tapas. *Average main: £19 ✉ Clachan Farm, A83, Cairndow ☎ 01499/600482 ⊕ www.lochfyne.com.*

Oban Seafood Hut
$ | **SEAFOOD** | Serving arguably the best-value seafood in Oban, the late John Ogden's quayside fish shack is a local legend. Look for a green-painted shed on the pier, then join the line of cognoscenti waiting for simply sautéed scallops, grilled langoustine, and lobster, oysters, and mussels. **Known for:** king prawn sandwiches and scallops in garlic butter; cash or debit card only; limited seating. *Average main: £8 ✉ CalMac Pier, Oban ☎ 07881/418565 No credit cards Closed Nov.–Apr.*

Cool Places to Stay

★ **Cromlix House**
$$$ | **HOTEL** | A grand refurbished Victorian country house set amid beautiful grounds, Cromlix House is owned by Scottish tennis champion Andy Murray, and you might notice the sound of ball on racket from the tennis court. **Pros:** luxurious facilities; lovely grounds for walking; comfortable beds. **Cons:** not much for children; a little hard to find; an expensive indulgence. *Rooms from: £279 ✉ Off B8033, beyond the village of Kinbuck, Kinbuck ✣ Keep looking for the entrance, 4½ miles north of Dunblane ☎ 01786/822125 ⊕ www.cromlix.com 16 rooms Free Breakfast.*

★ **Eddrachilles Hotel**
$$ | **B&B/INN** | With one of the most spectacular vistas—out toward the picturesque islands of Badcall Bay—of any hotel in Scotland, Eddrachilles sits on a huge plot of private moorland just south of the Handa Island bird sanctuary. **Pros:** attractive garden; stunning shoreline nearby; close to bird sanctuary. **Cons:** needs a lick of paint; Wi-Fi limited to public areas; set menus only. *Rooms from: £145 ✉ Off A894, Scourie ☎ 01971/502080 ⊕ www.eddrachilles.com Closed Nov.–Mar. 10 rooms Free Breakfast.*

Foveran Hotel
$$ | **HOTEL** | About 34 acres of grounds surround this modern, ranch-style hotel overlooking Scapa Flow, about 3 miles southwest of Kirkwall. **Pros:** great views across Scapa Flow; super helpful management; food that's cooked to perfection. **Cons:** minimal staffing during the day; you must book the popular restaurant ahead of time; simple decor. *Rooms from: £130 ✉ Off A964, Kirkwall ☎ 01856/872389 ⊕ www.thefoveran.com 8 rooms Free Breakfast.*

★ **Gleneagles Hotel**
$$$$ | **HOTEL** | One of Britain's most famous hotels, Gleneagles is the very essence of modern grandeur, a vast palace that stands hidden in breathtaking countryside amid its world-famous golf courses. **Pros:** luxurious rooms; famous Andrew Fairlie restaurant; the three courses are a golfer's paradise. **Cons:** quite conservative decor; restaurants get very crowded; such luxury comes at a price. *Rooms from: £435 ✉ Off A823, Auchterarder ☎ 01764/662231 ⊕ www.gleneagles.com 258 rooms Free Breakfast.*

★ Isle of Eriska

$$$$ | **HOTEL** | **FAMILY** | On one of Scotland's few private islands, this sybaritic enclave conceals luxury facilities like a spa, pool, gym, golf course, and a Michelin-starred restaurant behind a severe baronial facade. **Pros:** exceptional food; gorgeous views; superb leisure facilities. **Cons:** usually booked out at least one year ahead in high season; dining out not an easy option; very popular with wedding parties. *Rooms from: £380 Off A828, Benderloch Island signposted from Benderloch village and connected to mainland by short bridge 01631/720371 www.eriska-hotel.co.uk 34 rooms Free Breakfast.*

★ Kinloch Lodge

$$$$ | **HOTEL** | An upscale hotel with an excellent restaurant, Kinloch Lodge peacefully overlooks the tidal Loch na Dal. The buildings date from the 17th century, although the best views are from the newer South House, which was built from the ground up with comfort and relaxation in mind. **Pros:** historic and characterful property; beautiful lochside setting; top-drawer dining. **Cons:** expensive stay; noisy bathroom fans; far from amenities. *Rooms from: £420 Off A851, Isleornsay 01471/833333 kinloch-lodge.co.uk 19 rooms Free Breakfast.*

The Torridon

$$$$ | **HOTEL** | The Victorian Gothic turrets of this former hunting lodge promise atmosphere and grandeur—and, with its log fires, handsome plasterwork ceilings, mounted stag heads, and antique mahogany furniture, The Torridon doesn't disappoint. **Pros:** wonderful countryside location; center for outdoor activities; two restaurants and a bar with more than 300 malts. **Cons:** very pricey; 6 miles out of town; activities must be booked in advance. *Rooms from: £595 Off A896, Shieldaig 01445/791242 www.thetorridon.com 18 rooms Free Breakfast.*

Traquair House

$$ | **B&B/INN** | Staying in one of the guest rooms in the 12th-century wing of Traquair House is to experience a slice of Scottish history. **Pros:** stunning grounds; spacious rooms; great breakfast. **Cons:** nearly 2 miles to restaurants and shops; rooms fill up quickly in summer; parking can be difficult in summer months. *Rooms from: £200 Off B7062, Innerleithen 01896/830323 www.traquair.co.uk 3 rooms Free Breakfast.*

Wales

Wales is a land of dramatic national parks; plunging, unspoiled coastlines; and awe-inspiring medieval castles. Its ancient history and deep-rooted Celtic culture make Wales similar in many ways to its more famous neighbors, Scotland and Ireland; and yet it doesn't attract the same hordes of visitors, which is a big part of the appeal.

Vast swaths of Wales were untouched by the industrial boom of the 19th century. Although pockets of the country were given over to industries such as coal mining and manufacturing (both of which have all but disappeared), most of Wales remained unspoiled. The country is largely rural, and there are more than 10 million sheep—but only 3 million people. Outside the urban areas, it has a Britain-as-it-used-to-be feel that can be hugely appealing.

The country has been politically autonomous since 1997, and Welsh culture is flourishing. Cardiff has the most successful creative economy in the U.K. outside of London, with a burgeoning television and film industry, as well as thriving art scenes in most towns and cities. Television shows such as *Doctor Who, Torchwood,* and *Sex Education* are all filmed in Wales. Welsh produce is constantly being celebrated and championed by a passionate new generation of chefs and artisan foodies. And of course, national rugby matches still bond the nation together. Simply put, Wales loves being Wales, and that enthusiasm is infectious to visitors.

Although Wales is a small country—on average, about 60 miles wide and 170 miles north to south—looking at it on a map is deceptive. It's quite a difficult place to get around, with a distinctly old-fashioned road network and poor public transport connections. To see it properly, you really need a car. The good news is that along the way you'll experience some beautiful drives. There are rewards to be found in the gentle folds of its valleys and in the shadow of its mountains.

Were some of the more remote attractions in Wales in, say, the west of Ireland, they'd be world famous and overrun with millions of visitors. Here, if you're lucky, you can almost have them to yourself.

Brecon

Gateway to Brecon Beacons

Moorlands, mountains, and valleys make up this rough and wild stretch of the Welsh midlands, as popular with hikers as with those who appreciate the scenic drive. The historic market town of Brecon nestles in the Usk Valley between the Brecon Beacons to the south and the Black Mountains to the east. It's packed with typical Welsh charm and known for its Georgian buildings, narrow passageways, and pleasant riverside walks. The town is particularly appealing on the second Saturday of each month for the local farmers' market, and during its annual jazz festival in August.

Don't Miss

About 5 miles southwest of Brecon you encounter the mountains and wild, windswept uplands of the 519-square-mile Brecon Beacons National Park, also an accredited International Dark Sky Reserve.

Getting Here and Around

Brecon is easily accessible from Cardiff by direct buses and can be enjoyed on foot. A car is useful for wider explorations of the Brecon Beacons (take the A470).

Best Restaurant

Felin Fach Griffin is renowned for its creative use of local products and the rustic-chic vibe. ✉ *A470, Felin Fach* ☎ *01874/620111* 🌐 *www.eatdrink-sleep.ltd.uk*

Best Activity

The Brecon Beacons contain some of the best mountain biking routes in Britain. Biped Cycles (✉ *10 Ship St.* 🌐 *www.bipedcycles.co.uk*) will rent you the right bike and equipment.

Brecon Beacons National Park. ✣ *Off A470* ☎ *01874/623366* 🌐 *www.brecon-beacons.org*

Tenby

The Perfect Seaside Town

Pastel-color Georgian houses cluster around a harbor in this seaside town, which became a fashionable resort in the 19th century and is still popular. Two golden sandy beaches stretch below the hotel-lined cliff top. Medieval Tenby's ancient town walls still stand, enclosing narrow streets and passageways full of shops, inns, and places to eat. From the harbor you can take a short boat trip to Caldey Island, with its active Cistercian community.

Don't Miss

Caldey Island, the beautiful little island off the coast at Tenby has whitewashed stone buildings that lend it a Mediterranean feel. The island is best known for its Cistercian order, whose black-and-white-robed monks make a famous perfume from the local plants. You can visit tiny St. Illtyd's Church to see the Caldey Stone, an early Christian artifact from circa AD 600, engraved in Latin and ancient Celtic. St. David's Church, on a hill above the village, is a simple Norman chapel noted for its art-deco stained glass. Boats to Caldey Island leave from Tenby's harbor every 20 minutes or so between Easter and October.

When to Go

Visit in summer when downtown Tenby closes to traffic and boat crossings to Caldey Island are running.

Getting Here and Around

Tenby is on the southwest Wales rail route from London's Paddington Station, with one change. The center of Tenby has parking restrictions. In summer, downtown is closed to traffic, so park in one of the lots and take the shuttle buses.

Tenby Tourist Information Centre.
✉ *Upper Park Rd.* ☎ *01437/775603*
🌐 *www.visitpembrokeshire.com*

Porthmadog

Beaches, Hikes, and a Sweet Train Ride

The little seaside town of Porthmadog, built as a harbor to export slate from nearby Blaenau Ffestiniog, stands at the gateway to the Llŷn Peninsula (pronounced like "lean," with your tongue touching your palate), with its virtually unspoiled coastline and undulating wildflower-covered hills. It's also near the town of Harlech, which contains one of the great castles of Wales, and the weird and wonderful Portmeirion, a tiny fantasy-Italianate village on a private peninsula surrounded by hills; it's said to be loosely modeled after Portofino in Italy.

Don't Miss

Founded in the early 19th century to carry slate, the Ffestiniog Railway starts at the quayside and climbs up 700 feet through a wooded vale, past a waterfall, and across the mountains. The northern terminus is in Blaenau Ffestiniog, where you can visit an old slate mine. The Ffestiniog Railway is perhaps the best of several small steam lines in this part of the country.

Getting Here and Around

Arrive by car via the A487 or in style aboard the Welsh Highland Railway. Porthmadog is a stop on the excellent Snowdon Sherpa bus service. The town itself is totally walkable and has good access to coastal trails.

Best Activity

Not only can you go on a tour of Llechwedd Slate Caverns, but you can take part in some breathtaking activities there, too. The highlight is Europe's largest zipwire zone, which includes the world's fastest and highest (and Europe's longest) zipline. ✉ *Blaenau-Ffestiniog* ☎ *01248/601444* 🌐 *www.zipworld.co.uk*

Porthmadog. ✣ *35 miles southeast of Lake Vyrnwy, 16 miles southeast of Caernarfon* 🌐 *www.porthmadog.com*

Eryri National Park

The Highest Mountain in Wales

Stretching from the Welsh midlands almost to its northern coast, Eryri (Snowdonia) National Park covers a vast swath of North Wales. The park consists of 823 square miles of rocky mountains, valleys clothed in oak woods, moorlands, lakes, and rivers, all guaranteeing natural beauty and, to a varying extent, solitude. Its most famous attraction, by far, is the towering peak of Mt. Snowdon ("Yr Wyddfa" in Welsh), the highest mountain in Wales. The view from the top is jaw-dropping: to the northwest you can see the Menai Strait and Anglesey; to the south, Harlech Castle and the Cadair Idris mountain range. There are six different walking paths to the top, but a far less punishing way is via the Snowdon Mountain Railway (🌐 *snowdonrailway.co.uk*) in nearby Llanberis.

Don't Miss

The rivers Llugwy and Conwy meet at the achingly beautiful Betws-y-Coed, a popular village surrounded by woodland and a great base to explore the park.

Best Restaurant

The Ty Gwyn, built in 1636, is one of the best places to eat in Snowdonia, offering traditional Welsh fare, beautifully prepared with local ingredients. 🌐 *www.tygwynhotel.co.uk*

Getting Here and Around

Betws-y-Coed is easy to reach on the Conwy Valley Railway that runs from Llandudno to Blaenau Ffestiniog. It is also a hub for the excellent Sherpa'r Wyddfa bus service that covers most of Eryri's beauty spots.

Eryri National Park Visitor Centre. ✉ *Royal Oak Stables, Station Rd., Betws-y-Coed* ☎ *01690/710426* 🌐 *www.snowdonia.gov.wales*

Hay-on-Wye

A Book Lover's Paradise

In 1961, the late Richard Booth established a small secondhand bookshop in the pretty little village of Hay-on-Wye. Other booksellers soon got in on the act, and now it's the largest secondhand bookselling center in the world, and alongside a crumbling old castle and low-slung buildings framed by lolloping green hills, every street is lined with bookstores. Priceless 14th-century manuscripts rub spines with "job lots" selling for a few pounds. For 10 days every May and June, Hay-on-Wye is taken over by its Literary Festival, a celebration of literature that attracts famous writers from all over the world.

Don't Miss

Richard Booth once tried to declare Hay an independent kingdom—with himself as king. Richard died in 2019 but his bookstore—Richard Booth Books—lives on and has a huge collection from all over the world, piled haphazardly, across two labyrinthine floors. There's also a tiny movie theater (around the corner on Brook Street) and a café.

When to Go

The annual Hay Festival takes place during May and June. A shorter winter weekend festival is held in November.

Getting Here and Around

A car is a must for getting to Hay—use the A438 and turn off at Clyro. Parking is tight in the town so use one of the public lots on the outskirts of town and stroll in.

Hay-on-Wye Tourist Information Bureau. ✉ *Chapel Cottage, Oxford Rd., Hay-on-wye* ☎ *01497/820144* 🌐 *www.hay-on-wye.co.uk/tourism*

Wales
Isle of Anglesey Coastal Path
ISLE OF ANGLESEY
Holyhead
Conwy Bay
Llandudno
Prestatyn
Dee
Liverpool
M53
Beaumaris
Conwy
Conwy Castle
Pensarn
A55
A5
Chester
Caernarfon
Snowdon Mountain Railway
Llanberis
Betws-y-Coed
A494
A483
A496
Irish Sea
Pant Glas
Blaenau Ffestiniog
Tyn-y-cefn
Llangollen
Chirk
Porthmadog
Portmeirion
Bala
Pwllheli
Eryri National Park
Oswestry
A470
Hells Mouth
BARDSEY ISLAND
Dolgellau
Barmouth
Mallwyd
A458
Welshpool
Machynlleth
Cemmaes Road
A487
Caersws
Newtown
Cardigan Bay
ENGLAND
Aberystwyth
A44
Llangurig
Llanrhystud
Rhayader
Hay-on-Wye
Aberaeron
Crossgates
Synod Inn
Builth Wells
Mynydd Preseli
Cardigan
Fishguard
Llandovery
Llyswen
Pembrokeshire Coast National Park
A40
Brecon
St. David's
St Davids Cathedral
Llandeilo
Brecon Beacons National Park
Carmarthen
Crickhowell
Abergavenny
St. Brides Bay
Haverfordwest
Milford Haven
Tintern Abbey
Merthyr Tydfil
A465
Llanelli
Tenby
Pembroke
Carmarthen Bay
M4
Pontypridd
Swansea
Gower Peninsula
Swansea Bay
Caerphilly Castle
Newport
CARDIFF
Barry
Bristol Cannel
M5
0
20 mi
0
20 km

When in Wales

★ Caerphilly Castle

CASTLE/PALACE | FAMILY | The largest and most impressive fortress in Wales, and one of the few still to be surrounded by its original moat, Caerphilly must have been awe-inspiring at the time of its construction in the 13th century. Built by an Anglo-Norman lord, the concentric fortification contained powerful inner and outer defenses. It was badly damaged during the English Civil War (check out the leaning tower), although extensive 20th-century renovations have restored much of its former glory. The original Great Hall is still intact, and near the edge of the inner courtyard there's a replica of a trebuchet—a giant catapult used to launch rocks and other projectiles at the enemy. Additionally, an interesting collection of modern interpretive sculptures has been placed around the castle, both inside and outside. A £5 million renovation led to the opening of a new visitor center, shop, and café in 2023. To celebrate the town's famous cheese, a free festival, the Big Cheese, is held here every year at the end of July. Caerphilly is 7 miles north of Cardiff. ✉ *Castle St., Caerphilly* ☎ *03000/252239* 🌐 *cadw.gov.wales* 🎫 *£10.10.*

★ Conwy Castle

CASTLE/PALACE | FAMILY | Of all Edward I's Welsh strongholds, it is perhaps Conwy Castle that best preserves a sheer sense of power and dominance. The eight large round towers and tall curtain wall, set on a rocky promontory, provide sweeping views of the area and the town walls, so be sure to take a walk around the battlements. Although the castle is roofless (and floorless in places), the signage does a pretty good job of helping you visualize how rooms such as the Great Hall must once have looked. Conwy Castle can be approached on foot by a dramatic suspension bridge completed in 1828; engineer Thomas Telford designed the bridge with turrets to blend in with the fortress's presence. ✉ *Rose Hill St., Conwy* ☎ *03000/252239* 🌐 *cadw.gov.wales* 🎫 *£11.10.*

★ Gower Peninsula

NATURE SIGHT | FAMILY | This peninsula, which stretches westward from Swansea, was the first part of Britain to be designated an Area of Outstanding Natural Beauty. Its shores are a succession of sheltered sandy bays and awesome headlands. The seaside resort of Mumbles, on the outskirts of Swansea, is the most famous town along the route. It's a pleasant place to wander on a sunny afternoon, with a Norman castle, an amusement pier, and a seaside promenade, as well as a variety of independent cafés and boutiques. Farther along the peninsula, the secluded Pwlldu Bay can only be reached on foot from nearby villages like Southgate. A few miles westward is the more accessible (and very popular) Three Cliffs Bay, with its sweeping views and wide, sandy beach. At the far western tip of the peninsula, Rhossili has perhaps the best beach of all. Its unusual, snaking causeway—known locally as the Worm's Head—is inaccessible at high tide. Gower is a popular destination with surfers and you'll find many other water sports offered here. ✉ *Swansea* 🌐 *www.visitswanseabay.com.*

Isle of Anglesey Coastal Path

HIKING & WALKING | FAMILY | Extending 130 miles around the island, this path leads past cliffs, sandy coves, and plenty of scenic variety. Pick up information at any of the regional tourist offices and choose a section; the west coast has the most dramatic scenery. 🌐 *www.visitanglesey.co.uk.*

★ Pembrokeshire Coast National Park

NATIONAL PARK | FAMILY | By far the smallest of the country's three national parks, Pembrokeshire Coast is no less strikingly beautiful than the other two. The park has several Blue Flag beaches and a host of spectacular cliff-top drives and walks, including some of the most popular stretches of the Wales Coast Path. The park has a smattering of historic sites, including the impossibly picturesque St. Davids Cathedral, built in a Viking-proof nook by the Irish Sea. The information center in St. Davids is a good place to start. ✉ *Oriel Y Parc Gallery and Visitor Centre, The Grove, St. Davids* ☎ *01437/720392* 🌐 *www.pembrokeshire-coast.wales* 🎫 *Free.*

★ Portmeirion

TOWN | FAMILY | One of the true highlights of North Wales is Portmeirion, a tiny fantasy-Italianate village on a private peninsula surrounded by hills; it's said to be loosely modeled after Portofino in Italy. Designed in the 1920s by architect Clough Williams-Ellis (1883–1978), the village has a hotel and restaurant among its multicolored buildings, and gift shops sell a distinctive local pottery. On the edge of town is a peaceful woodland trail punctuated here and there by such flourishes as a red iron bridge and a miniature pagoda. Williams-Ellis called it his "light-opera approach to architecture," and the result is magical, though distinctly un-Welsh. Portmeirion is about 2 miles east of Porthmadog. ✉ *Off A487, Portmeirion* ☎ *01766/770000* 🌐 *www.portmeirion.wales* 🎫 *£17.*

★ Snowdon Mountain Railway

TRAIN/TRAIN STATION | FAMILY | One of the most famous attractions in North Wales is the rack-and-pinion Snowdon Mountain Railway, with some of its track at a thrillingly steep grade. The 3,560-foot-high Snowdon—*Yr Wyddfa* in Welsh—is the highest peak south of Scotland and lies within the 823-square-mile national park. Weather permitting, trains go all the way to the summit; on a clear day you can see as far as the Wicklow Mountains in Ireland, about 90 miles away. You can take two types of train: a modern diesel-driven version, or a "heritage" version, complete with restored carriages and working steam engine. From mid-March to May, or in times of high winds, the journey is truncated so you don't get all the way up to the summit; if so, tickets are a few pounds cheaper.

TIP→ Tickets can sell out early on busy days, so try to book in advance. ✉ *A4086, Llanberis* ☎ *01286/870223* 🌐 *www.snowdonrailway.co.uk* 🎫 *Diesel service, £35 round-trip; heritage service, £45 round-trip* ⏱ *Closed Nov.–mid-Mar.*

★ St. Davids Cathedral

CHURCH | The idyllic valley location of this cathedral helped protect the church from Viking raiders by hiding it from the view of invaders who came by sea. Originally founded by St. David himself around AD 600, the current building dates from the 12th century, although it has been added to at various times since. You must climb down 39 steps (known locally as the Thirty-Nine Articles) to enter the grounds; then start at the Gatehouse, with its exhibition on the history of the building. In the cathedral itself, the 15th-century choir stalls still have their original floor tiles, while the Holy Trinity Chapel contains an intricate fan-vaulted ceiling and a casket said to contain the patron saint's bones. Don't miss the Treasury and its illuminated gospels, silver chalices, and 700-year-old golden bishop's crosier. At the rear of the grounds of St. Davids Cathedral are the ruins of the 13th-century Bishop's Palace, particularly beautiful at dusk. The cathedral has a good café serving lunch made with local produce. ✉ *The Close, St. Davids* ☎ *01437/720202* 🌐 *www.stdavidscathedral.org.uk* 🎫 *Free; £5 voluntary donation.*

Tintern Abbey

RELIGIOUS BUILDING | FAMILY | Literally a stone's throw from the English border, Tintern is one of the region's most romantic monastic ruins. Founded in 1131 by the Cistercians and dissolved by Henry VIII in 1536, it has inspired its fair share of poets and painters over the years—most famously J. M.

W. Turner, who painted the transept covered in moss and ivy, and William Wordsworth, who idolized the setting in his poem "Lines Composed a Few Miles Above Tintern Abbey." Come early or late to avoid the crowds. The abbey, 5 miles north of Chepstow and 19 miles southeast of Abergavenny, is on the banks of the River Wye. ✉ *A466, Tintern* ☎ *03000/252239* 🌐 *cadw.gov.wales* 🎫 *£8.30.*

Where to Eat and Drink

★ Beach House
$$$$ | MODERN BRITISH | On the beach at Oxwich, this stylish Michelin-starred eatery is considered one of the best in all of Wales. The beautifully presented dishes are made using excellent local ingredients, particularly seafood. **Known for:** beachside location; creative fish dishes; interesting wine list. $ *Average main: £80* ✉ *Oxwich Beach, Swansea* ☎ *01792/278–277* 🌐 *www.beachhouse-oxwich.co.uk* ⏲ *Closed Sun.–Tues.*

★ Park House
$$$ | MODERN FRENCH | In a building designed by William Burges (the same architect who helped design Cardiff Castle and Castell Coch), this upscale restaurant with a Welsh-French menu is one of the city's top eateries. The six-course dinner tasting menu is £59 plus £35 for matched wines, and there's also a simple bar menu featuring cheese and charcuterie. **Known for:** one of the best wine lists in the United Kingdom; charming building; local produce. $ *Average main: £28* ✉ *20 Park Pl., Cardiff* ☎ *029/2022–4343* 🌐 *www.parkhouserestaurant.co.uk* ⏲ *Closed Sun.–Tues.*

★ Plantagenet House
$$$ | BRITISH | Flickering candles, open fireplaces, exposed stone walls, and top-notch locally sourced food are hallmarks of this restaurant and bar, which dates back to the 10th century. The menu contains a selection of Welsh-reared steaks and other meat dishes, but outstanding seafood is the real specialty—try the shellfish platter for two. **Known for:** romantic setting; local produce; great seafood dishes. $ *Average main: £27* ✉ *Quay Hill, Tenby* ☎ *01834/842350* 🌐 *www.plantagenettenby.co.uk* ⏲ *Closed Mon. and Tues.*

The Plough and Harrow
$ | BRITISH | FAMILY | A short drive from Nash Point is this historic pub, on the edge of the tiny clifftop village of Monknash. The food is delicious and unfussy; the menu changes regularly, but features tasty pub classics like burgers and fish-and-chips. **Known for:** craft beer and cider; delicious pies; lively atmosphere. $ *Average main: £10* ✉ *Off Heol Las, Monknash* ☎ *01656/890209* 🌐 *www.ploughandharrowmonknash.co.uk.*

Tŷ Coch Inn
$ | BRITISH | In a seafront building in picture-postcard Porthdinllaen, this pub has what is undoubtedly one of the best locations in Wales. The lunches are honest and unpretentious: pies, sandwiches, or perhaps a plate of local mussels in garlic butter. **Known for:** stunning beach location; local craft beers; laid-back vibe. $ *Average main: £8* ✉ *Off B4417, Porthdinllaen* ☎ *01758/720498* 🌐 *www.tycoch.co.uk* ⏲ *No dinner.*

Tŷ Gwyn
$ | BRITISH | This coaching inn, built in 1636, is one of the best places to eat in Snowdonia. The food is traditional Welsh fare, beautifully prepared with local ingredients. **Known for:** charming, historic building in a beautiful setting; good choice of seafood dishes; nice options for vegetarians. $ *Average main: £14* ✉ *A5, Betws-y-Coed* ☎ *01690/710383* 🌐 *www.tygwynhotel.co.uk.*

★ The Walnut Tree
$$$$ | MODERN BRITISH | Regarded as one of the best chefs in the United Kingdom, Shaun Hill has been at the helm of this rustic-chic restaurant 3 miles northeast

of Abergavenny since 2008. The focus here is on local, seasonal produce with international influences; lunch is £40 for two courses. **Known for:** superb cooking; attractive dining room; peaceful location. *Average main: £34 Llanddewi Skirrid, Abergavenny Along the B4521 northeast of Abergavenny 01873/852797 www.thewalnuttree-inn.com Closed Sun.–Tues.*

★ Ynyshir Restaurant and Rooms
$$$$ | **MODERN BRITISH** | This two-Michelin-star restaurant, housed in a Georgian mansion set among parkland, is one of the best eateries in Wales thanks to its wonderful dishes featuring the best local, and international, meat and fish. There are just five tables next to the open kitchen and the only option offered by chef Gareth Ward is a tasting menu featuring a whopping 20 dishes—the whole experience takes 4 to 5 hours. **Known for:** tasting menu featuring creative meat dishes; award-winning wine list; stylish dining room. *Average main: £350 Eglwys Fach, Eglwys-fach 01654/781209 www.ynyshir.co.uk Closed Sun. and Mon. No lunch.*

Cool Places to Stay

★ Bodysgallen Hall
$$ | **HOTEL** | Tasteful antiques, polished wood, and comfortable chairs by cheery fires distinguish one of Wales's most luxurious country-house hotels. **Pros:** superb spa and pool; rare 17th-century knot garden; elegant dining and afternoon tea. **Cons:** too formal for some; hard to get to without a car; lots of steps and stairs. *Rooms from: £225 The Royal Welsh Way, Llandudno 01492/584466 www.bodysgallen.com 31 rooms Free Breakfast No children under the age of 6.*

Coach House
$ | **B&B/INN** | This former coach house in the center of Brecon has been converted into a luxurious place to stay, and the friendly hosts—a wealth of information about the local area—can arrange transport to and from the best walking paths in the Beacons. **Pros:** lovely staff; delicious breakfasts; private parking. **Cons:** on a main road; minimum two-night stay; not suitable for families. *Rooms from: £99 12 Orchard St., Brecon 01874/620043 www.coachhouse-brecon.com 6 rooms Free Breakfast No children under the age of 16.*

★ Hotel Portmeirion
$$$ | **HOTEL** | One of the most elegant and unusual places to stay in Wales, this waterfront mansion is located at the heart of Portmeirion. **Pros:** unique location; beautiful building; woodland walks. **Cons:** gets crowded with day-trippers; minimum stay on weekends; expensive food. *Rooms from: £304 Minffordd, Portmeirion 01766/770000 www.portmeirion.wales 55 rooms Free Breakfast.*

★ Lake Vyrnwy Hotel & Spa
$$ | **HOTEL** | **FAMILY** | Awesome views of mountain-ringed Lake Vyrnwy are just one asset of this country mansion on a 24,000-acre estate. **Pros:** perfect for outdoor pursuits; luxurious spa; excellent package deals. **Cons:** too remote for some; minimum stay on some summer weekends; decor could use updating. *Rooms from: £174 Off B4393, Llanwddyn 01691/870692 www.lakevyrnwy.com 52 rooms Free Breakfast.*

★ Llangoed Hall
$$ | **HOTEL** | This magnificent Jacobean mansion on the banks of the River Wye, about 7 miles west of Hay-on-Wye, has beautiful fabrics and furnishings, open fireplaces, a sweeping carved staircase, and a paneled library dating back to 1632. **Pros:** secluded setting by River Wye; wonderful art collection; regular special events and offers. **Cons:** often filled with wedding parties; minimum stay sometimes required; no attractions

within walking distance. *Rooms from: £220* *A470, Llyswen* *01874/754525* *www.llangoedhall.co.uk* *23 rooms* *Free Breakfast.*

★ Penally Abbey

$$ | **HOTEL** | Built on the site of a 6th-century abbey in 5 acres of lush forest overlooking Camarthen Bay, this dignified 18th-century house is awash with period details. **Pros:** informal luxury; great views; friendly hosts. **Cons:** cheaper rooms are in the Coach House; seven-day cancellation rule; no elevator. *Rooms from: £175* *Off A4139, Penally* *2 miles west of Tenby* *01834/843033* *www.penally-abbey.com* *12 rooms* *Free Breakfast.*

Squirrel's Nest Treehouse Retreat

$$$$ | **HOUSE** | **FAMILY** | These well-equipped wooden treehouses on a working sheep farm six miles from the nearest town offer a wonderful luxury retreat. **Pros:** peaceful location; comfortable glamping; good walking trails. **Cons:** patchy 4G coverage; two-night minimum stay; not easily accessible for all. *Rooms from: £400* *Nantygelli, Llanbister Rd., Llandrindod Wells* *01597/840506* *www.squirrels-nest.co.uk* *3 treehouses* *No Meals.*

Three Cliffs Bay Holiday Park

$ | **HOUSE** | **FAMILY** | Not only is this five-star campsite in an Area of Outstanding Natural Beauty (aka the Gower Peninsula), it overlooks what has been voted one of Britain's best beaches. **Pros:** stunning location; on-site shop selling local produce; good bathroom facilities. **Cons:** minimum stay on weekends and school holidays; payments are non-refundable; patchy Wi-Fi. *Rooms from: £29* *North Hills Farm, Penmaen, Swansea* *01792/371218* *www.threecliffsbay.com* *Closed Nov.–Mar.* *20 yurts, 23 caravan pitches, 90 tent pitches* *No Meals.*

Chapter 3

IRELAND AND NORTHERN IRELAND

WELCOME TO IRELAND AND NORTHERN IRELAND

TOP REASONS TO GO

★ **The Wild Atlantic Way:** This epic driving, biking, or hiking journey along Ireland's stunning west coast includes mystical Connemara and the rugged Dingle Peninsula.

★ **Rock of Cashel:** With a history going back over 1000 years, this medieval settlement became the seat of the Munster kings in the 5th century.

★ **The Ancient East:** A string of awesome sites along the eastern side of the country spans the neolithic wonders of Newgrange, to 6th-century monastic Glendalough, and on to Kilkenny Castle.

★ **The Craic in a Dublin Pub:** Besides being home to the best pint of Guinness on the planet, a quality public house in the capital will be full of music, chat, and wild, let-your-hair-down fun.

★ **Drive the Giant's Causeway Coast:** Along Northern Ireland's Atlantic shore, this pristine stretch of coast holds many of Northern Ireland's don't-miss attractions, including the world-famous natural wonder that is the Giant's Causeway.

1 **Dublin.** A transformed city since the days of O'Casey and Joyce, Ireland's capital may have replaced its legendary tenements with modern high-rises, but its essential spirit remains intact.

2 **Ireland.** Half an hour from Dublin you'll find yourself in the stunning, wild Irish landscape, from the midland lakes, to the mountain's and islands of the west, and the sea-battered shores of Kerry and West Cork. On the way take in the history-soaked, culture-loving cities of Galway, Cork, and Kilkenny.

3 **Northern Ireland.** From the beauty of Antrim's coastline to the vibrant cultural renaissance of Belfast and Derry, Northern Ireland is full of promise and possibility. Cross the Giant's Causeway and trail after the island's ancient Celtic mysteries in the shimmery Glens of Antrim.

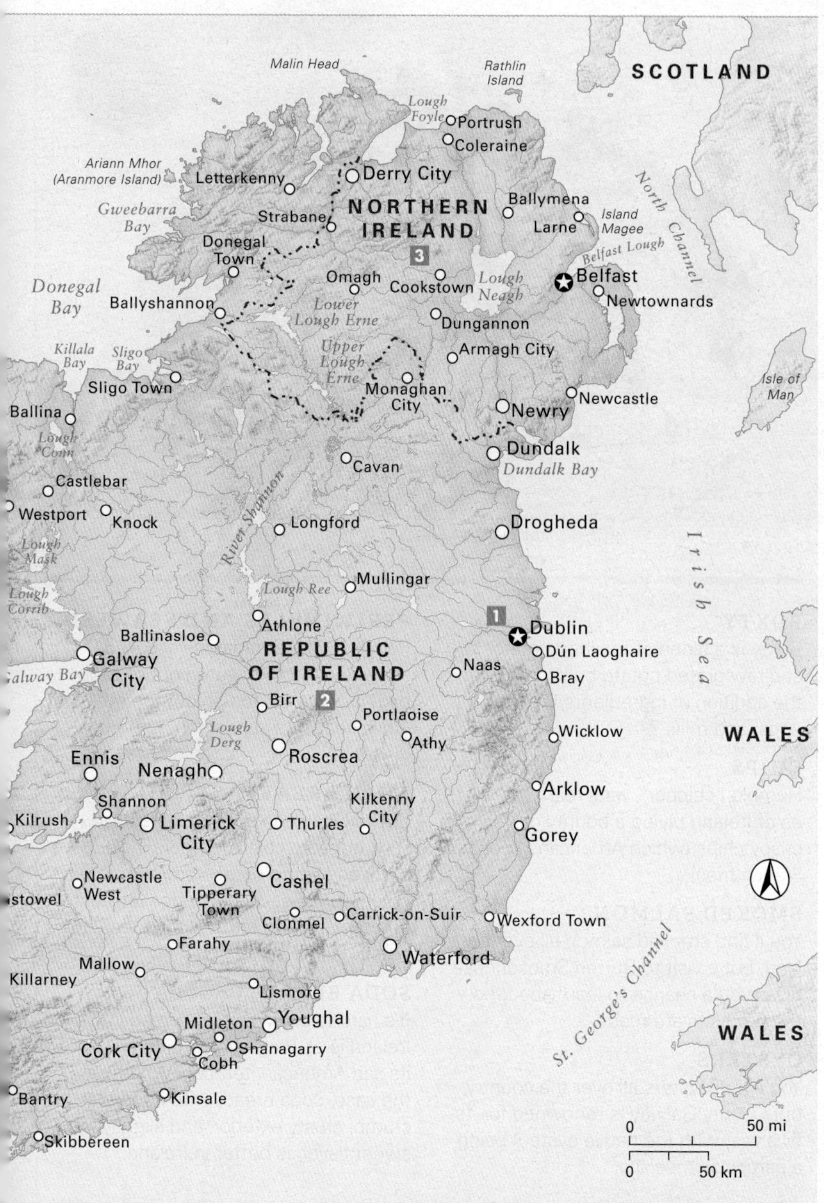

Malin Head
Rathlin Island
SCOTLAND
Lough Foyle
Portrush
Coleraine
Ariann Mhor (Aranmore Island)
Letterkenny
Derry City
Gweebarra Bay
NORTHERN IRELAND
Ballymena
Strabane
Larne
Island Magee
North Channel
Donegal Town
3
Belfast Lough
Omagh
Cookstown
Lough Neagh
Belfast
Donegal Bay
Ballyshannon
Lower Lough Erne
Newtownards
Dungannon
Killala Bay
Sligo Bay
Upper Lough Erne
Armagh City
Sligo Town
Monaghan City
Isle of Man
Newcastle
Ballina
Newry
Lough Conn
Dundalk
Dundalk Bay
Cavan
Castlebar
Westport
Knock
River Shannon
Longford
Drogheda
Lough Mask
Irish Sea
Mullingar
Lough Ree
Lough Corrib
1
Athlone
Dublin
Ballinasloe
REPUBLIC OF IRELAND
Dún Laoghaire
Galway City
Naas
Galway Bay
Bray
Birr
2
Portlaoise
Lough Derg
Athy
Wicklow
WALES
Roscrea
Ennis
Nenagh
Arklow
Shannon
Kilkenny City
Kilrush
Limerick City
Thurles
Gorey
Newcastle West
Cashel
Tipperary Town
stowel
Clonmel
Carrick-on-Suir
Wexford Town
Farahy
St. George's Channel
Waterford
Mallow
Killarney
Lismore
Youghal
Midleton
WALES
Cork City
Shanagarry
Cobh
Bantry
Kinsale
Skibbereen
0
50 mi
0
50 km

WHAT TO EAT AND DRINK IN IRELAND AND NORTHERN IRELAND

Soda bread

BOXTY
Boxty is a blend of mashed potatoes and raw grated potato bulked up with the addition of ingredients like flour, eggs, and milk.

CHIPS
Humble "chipper" vans roam the villages of Ireland plying a bounty of fresh, crispy chips (which Americans know as French fries).

SMOKED SALMON
You'll find smoked salmon all over Ireland, but a visit to Burren Smokehouse gives you a chance to learn about how the products are made.

OYSTERS
You'll find oysters all over the country, but County Galway is renowned for its bivalves, with the native oysters being a particular specialty.

PERIWINKLES AND SEAWEED
Periwinkles are traditionally boiled in seawater and then eaten out of paper bags using a pin to fish out the meat, while seaweed appears in numerous dishes.

IRISH BREAKFAST
Specific items in a full breakfast may vary, but core cast members include black and white pudding, browned mushrooms, sausages, eggs, at least one tomato, and either soda bread or a potato farl.

SODA BREAD
It's hard to say why soda bread in Ireland is so dramatically different from its sad American iteration. Whatever the case, soda bread, with its tender crumb, crusty exterior, and slightly sweet flavor, is better in Ireland.

TEA AND SCONES

You'll find that teatime can come with different food options, governed in part by the time of day you're taking your tea.

POITÍN

In Tunisia, it's called boukha. In Italy, grappa. In the United States, moonshine. In Ireland, this beast is called poitín and—once illegal—it's making a comeback.

WHISKEY

Jamesons and Bushmills are fine examples of Irish whiskey, but Ireland has number of newer craft distillers. Look for Dingle, the Connacht Whiskey Company, Knappogue Castle, and Pearse.

CIDER

While you can find cider in a variety of styles, and with varying levels of sweetness and fermented funk, it's said that the apples of County Armagh are of particularly high quality.

CRAFT BEER

Craft beer is finding fans across the globe and Ireland is no exception. Ireland's craft-beer scene is small, but growing interest helps provide a counterpoint to the behemoth that is Guinness.

Oysters

Whiskey

GUINNESS

Guinness is ubiquitous, omnipresent, and an easy choice for those disinclined to roll the dice on the undulating flavor wheel that modern craft beer represents.

COLCANNON

Colcannon is a traditional dish of mashed potatoes mixed with kale or cabbage. It's simple, hearty, and a good match for Ireland's frequently blustery weather.

CHEESE

Whether it's funky, washed-rind cheeses from Gubbeen and Durrus or the squat, veined cakes of Cashel Blue, there's a variety of high-quality cheeses for you to look for and enjoy.

Ireland and Northern Ireland Snapshot

Know Before You Go

ONE ISLAND, TWO COUNTRIES.
Since 1921, the Republic of Ireland and Northern Ireland have been separate countries, sharing the same history and (in most ways) the same culture, but with their own currencies and differences in language. Since 2005, you haven't been stopped at the now inconspicuously labeled border (you may not even notice it). Maintaining this ease of travel was one of the most contentious parts of Brexit, but fortunately, little has changed for the visitor to Ireland and Northern Ireland.

IT JUST RAINS, AND IT WILL PASS.
It's not exactly news that it rains in Ireland—hence the lush green valleys and meadows—but it may be a surprise that the weather can be so changeable. Ireland's weather is generally temperate, but storms can roll in without warning, and foggy, chilly conditions are common year-round. The morning weather forecast may leave you none the wiser. In fact, you may laugh to see every weather possibility proposed for your day, from hail, a "chance of showers," and treacherous roads due to frost, to "sunny spells" and sun showers. You can get four seasons in one day, sometimes in one hour. All you need to know is that you should not let the weather interfere with your plans, because it will pass. Pack accordingly with layers, a waterproof jacket regardless of the season, and good waterproof shoes or boots. And if you find yourself in need of new layers, you have a good excuse to shop for tweed caps and cable-knit sweaters.

Planning Your Time

Distances are short and major roads are good, so two weeks is time to really see the whole of Ireland at your own pace. You can do Dublin, the West, and even venture into the undiscovered Midlands. A trip to Northern Ireland should also be in the cards. The sunny Southeast is a good stop before heading back to Dublin. If your time is shorter focus on Dublin and the West.

Great Trips

3 days: Dip your toe into the culture of Dublin and take half-day trips out to Wicklow and Newgrange.

3 days: After a day of history and food in Belfast, drive the Giant's Causeway Coast from Carrickfergus Castle all the way to Derry.

7 days: Combine a few days in Dublin with a trip along the spectacular Wild Atlantic Way, staying in Galway and Kerry.

Big Events

Puck Fair. Puck Fair in Kerry is the oldest festival in Ireland, dating back to pagan times, where a goat is made king for three days of drinking, dancing, and general abandon. Held on the second weekend in August, it's truly one of Ireland's most unusual festivals.

Blooomsday. Even though it is now reckoned that more Americans and Japanese attend the events surrounding Bloomsday (🌐 *jamesjoyce.ie*) than Irish people, it hasn't taken away a jot from an event that continues to grow regardless. Bloomsday is June 16.

Six Nations Rugby Tournament. Every spring rugby fever grips the country as the Six Nations Tournament begins. The beloved Irish team takes on the might of Wales, France, Scotland, Italy, and its old enemy

England in a series of bone-crunching encounters.

What To...

READ

We Don't Know Ourselves: A Personal History of Modern Ireland, Fintan O'Toole. Journalist recounts the spectacular changes that have occurred in Ireland over the past six decades.

Dubliners, James Joyce. Classic, much-loved stories of early 20th-century Dublin life.

Normal People, Sally Rooney. A novel about class, art, life, and love in contemporary Ireland.

Country Girls, Edna O'Brien. Once-banned, a trilogy set in 1960s Ireland about two young Irish women who move to Dublin.

WATCH

Brooklyn. The story of one young woman's emigration from and heartbreaking return to rural Ireland.

The Banshees of Inisherin. A tragicomedy set on a remote island off the west coast of Ireland.

Derry Girls. An ensemble sitcom about a group of adolescent schoolgirls and their lives near the end of the Troubles.

The Commitments. A Dublin soul band tries to make it in the early 1990s.

LISTEN TO

Planxty, *Planxty*

U2, *The Joshua Tree*

Cranberries, *Everybody Else is Doing It, So Why Can't We?*

Fontaines DC, *Skinty Fia*

The Pogues, *Rum, Sodomy & the Lash*

Van Morrison, *Astral Weeks*

Sinead O'Connor, *I Do Not Want What I Haven't Got*

BUY

Irish Pottery. Choose designs from Ardmore Pottery in Waterford or Shannagarry Potters in Cork.

Sweaters. Electronic sheep's quirky, unisex sweaters and scarves are everything Grandma's aren't.

Whiskey. Boutique, small-batch distilleries have sprung up all over Ireland, with Glendalough Distillery a standout.

Irish salmon. Frank Hederman and the Burren Smokehouse have both won awards.

Contacts

AIR

Major Airports: **Dublin** (DUB), **Shannon** (SNN). **Cork** (ORK), **Belfast International Airport** (BFS), **George Best Belfast City Airport** (BHD)

BOAT

Irish Ferries. 🌐 *www.irishferries.com*

Stena Line. 🌐 *www.stenaline.ie*

P & O. 🌐 *www.poferries.com*

BUS

Aircoach. 🌐 *www.aircoach.ie*

Bus Éireann. 🌐 *www.buseireann.ie*

Citylink. 🌐 *www.citylink.ie*

Dublin Coach. 🌐 *www.dudblincoach.ie*

Translink Goldline. 🌐 *www.translink.co.uk*

Ulsterbus. 🌐 *www.translink.co.uk*

TRAIN

Irish Rail. 🌐 *www.irishrail.ie*

Northern Ireland Railways. 🌐 *www.translink.co.uk*

VISITOR INFORMATION

Discover Ireland. 🌐 *www.discoverireland.ie*

Discover Northern Ireland. 🌐 *www.discovernorthernireland.com*

Dublin

For so long a provincial town on the periphery of Europe, the last few decades have seen Dublin blossom into a bustling, modern city of quality restaurants and elegant hotels, along with soaring house prices and traffic gridlock. But behind the shining glass and steel, the old Dublin still flourishes in the Victorian parks, Georgian squares, and history-soaked streets. Whether you're out to enjoy the old or new Dublin, you'll find it a colossally entertaining city, all the more astonishing considering its intimate size.

It is ironic and telling that James Joyce chose Dublin as the setting for his famous *Ulysses, Dubliners,* and *A Portrait of the Artist as a Young Man* because it was a "center of paralysis" where nothing much ever changed. Which only proves that even the greats get it wrong sometimes. Indeed, if Joyce were to return to his once-genteel hometown today what would he make of Temple Bar—the city's erstwhile down-at-the-heels neighborhood, now crammed with cafés and trendy hotels and suffused with a nonstop international-party atmosphere? Today, Ireland's capital is packed with elegant shops and hotels, theaters, galleries, coffeehouses, and a stunning variety of new, creative little restaurants can be found on almost every street in Dublin, transforming the provincial city that suffocated Joyce into a place almost as cosmopolitan as the Paris to which he fled. Yet, the fundamentals—the Georgian elegance of Merrion Square, the Norman drama of Christ Church Cathedral, the foamy pint at an atmospheric pub—are still on hand to gratify. And most of all, there are the locals themselves: the nod and grin when you catch their eye on the street, the eagerness to hear half your life story before they tell you all of theirs, and their paradoxically dark but warm sense of humor.

Guinness Storehouse

Temple to the Gods of the Perfect Pint

Going to Dublin without paying tribute to Guinness is like going to New Orleans and ignoring jazz. Ireland's all-dominating brewery—founded by Arthur Guinness in 1759—spans a 60-acre spread west of Christ Church Cathedral. The actual brewery is closed to the public, but the Guinness Storehouse is one of Ireland's most popular attractions, designed to woo—some might say brainwash—you with the wonders of the "dark stuff." In a 1904 cast-iron-and-brick warehouse, the museum display covers six floors built around a huge, central glass atrium, which is shaped like a giant pint glass. Beneath the glass floor of the lobby you can see Arthur Guinness's original lease on the site, for a whopping 9,000 years. The exhibition elucidates the brewing process and its history and offers a chance to pull your own perfect pint. The star attraction is undoubtedly the top-floor Gravity bar, with 360-degree floor-to-ceiling glass walls that offer a nonpareil view out over the city at sunset while you sip your "free" pint.

Don't Miss

Across the street from Guinness, take the fun and interesting tour of the working Roe + Co. whiskey distillery, set in the the former Guinness Power Station.

Getting Here and Around

The Storehouse is only a 15-minute walk from the city center, with nearby bus and LUAS stops on Thomas and James's Streets.

✉ *St. James' Gate, Dublin West* ☎ *01/408–4800* 🌐 *www.guinness-storehouse.com* 🎫 *From €31*

Trinity College and the Book of Kells

Ireland's Own Oxford

Founded in 1592 by Queen Elizabeth I to "civilize" (Her Majesty's word) Dublin, Trinity's memorably atmospheric campus has housed Jonathan Swift, Oscar Wilde, Bram Stoker, Samuel Beckett and Sally Rooney. College grounds cover 40 acres, and most buildings date from the 18th and early 19th centuries. The looming campanile, or bell tower, is the symbolic heart of the college; erected in 1853, it dominates the center of the square.

The highlight of any visit to Trinity has to be the sumptuous Old Library, Ireland's largest collection of books and manuscripts, and home to Book of Kells, generally considered to be one of the great masterpieces of early Christian art. Such is the incredible workmanship of this illuminated version of the Gospels that one folio alone is as exciting as the entirety of many other painted manuscripts. But don't overlook the other treasures, including the spectacular Long Room; the carved Royal Arms of Queen Elizabeth I; and the Book of Armagh, a 9th-century copy of the New Testament that also contains St. Patrick's Confession.

Don't Miss

The majestic Long Room, with its famous row of marble busts of great writers and thinkers, including Roubiliac's iconic sculpture of Trinity's own Jonathan Swift.

Getting Here and Around

Trinity is located at the very center of Dublin, on the Southside, a minute's walk from Grafton street, and beside bus, LUAS and DART hubs.

✉ *Front Sq., Southside* ☎ *01/896–2320* 🌐 *tcd.ie/visitors/book-of-kells* 🎫 *From €18, includes Book of Kells*

Chapter One and the Abbey Theatre

Dublin's Finest Restaurant and Most Storied Theater

Named for its location, downstairs in the vaulted, stone-wall basement of the now-closed Dublin Writers Museum, Chapter One is a two-star Michelin restaurant with a devoted clientele and an innovative and precise menu featuring carefully sourced Irish ingredients. Joyce himself would have purred and poetized over the roast pigeon, brussels sprouts, pear, and offal tart all with sauce perigourdine. Plan a pretheater meal then take a five-minute stroll to the Abbey for curtain up.

Opened in 1904 by W. B. Yeats and friends, the Abbey Theatre quickly became one of the world's most fabled playhouses, and the beating heart of Irish drama. Early successes included the works of J. M. Synge and Sean O'Casey, and plays by recent heavyweights Brian Friel, Tom Murphy, Hugh Leonard, and John B. Keane. Unfortunately, the original structure burned down in 1951. A starkly modernist auditorium was built in its place—but what it may lack in aesthetics it makes up for in space, acoustics, and simmering Irish creativity.

Don't Miss

Spring for the famed Tasting Menu at Chapter One; each of the six staggeringly creative courses are paired with superior wines.

Getting Here and Around

Chapter One and the Abbey and are both just off O'Connell Street on Dublin's Northside, where numerous buses and the LUAS stop. **Abbey Theatre.** ✉ *Lower Abbey St., Dublin North* ☎ *01/878–7222* 🌐 *abbeytheatre.ie* **Chapter One by Mickael Viljanen.** ✉ *18–19 Parnell Sq., Dublin North* ☎ *01/873–2266* 🌐 *chapteronerestaurant.com*

Traditional Music Pub Crawl

A Moving Concert

Led by two professional musicians who perform tunes and songs and tell the story of Irish music, this award-winning listening tour offers authentic immersion taking you to two storied traditional Irish music pubs in Dublin, where the *craic (wild, carefree fun)*is guaranteed. At each stop you'll settle in for a "session" of musicians playing traditional songs, jigs, and reels, then your guides will discuss the history of the Irish music and its influence on contemporary music all over the world. Fiddle, whistle, accordion, *bodhran* (a Celtic, handheld drum), and uilleann pipes (think bagpipes, but sweeter and played sitting down) are some of the traditional instruments you'll hear during the tour. Toe-tapping is included; drinks are not.

Don't Miss

The Musical Pub Crawl Dinner Show includes a three-course meal with dishes like Beef & Guinness Pie and Irish Oak-Smoked Salmon served up with live music, history, and traditional Irish dancing performances.

Getting Here and Around

Tours are seven nights a week from May to September and reduced to weekends in March, April, and October. The dinner show is at 5:30 and lasts three hours; the regular music tour is at 7:30 and takes 2½ hours. Bars visited in the tour include The Ha'Penny Bridge Inn and Flanagan's Bar & Restaurant. For the dinner show, the meal is served at Flanagan's. Meet upstairs at the Ha'penny Bridge Inn pub in Temple Bar. ✉ *20 Lower Stephens St., Southside* ☎ *01/478–0191* 🌐 *www.musicalpubcrawl.com* 🎫 *From €19*

Christ Church and St. Patrick's

Dublin's Twin Cathedrals

Only the throw of a Viking handaxe separates Dublin's two great churches, both steeped in history dating to Dublin's foundation. From Christ Church's exterior, you'd never guess that the first Christianized Danish king built a wooden church at this site in 1038; because of the extensive 19th-century renovation the cathedral looks more Victorian than Anglo-Norman, including a Bridge of Sighs–like structure that connects the cathedral to the old Synod Hall, which now holds the Viking multimedia exhibition, Dublinia. The vast, sturdy crypt, with is Dublin's oldest surviving structure, houses the excellent exhibition *Treasures of Christ Church.*

St. Patrick's was built in honor of Ireland's patron saint, who—according to legend—baptized many converts at a well on this site. Make sure you see the gloriously heraldic Choir of St. Patrick's, hung with colorful medieval banners, and find the tomb of Jonathan Swift, the most famous of St. Patrick's many illustrious deans. If you're a music lover, you're in for a treat; matins (9:40 am) and evensong (5:45 pm) are still sung on many days.

Don't Miss

Christ Church's Tom and Jerry—the mummified bodies of a cat and rat who were trapped in an organ pipe in the 1860s, are caught in a cartoon chase for all eternity.

Getting Here and Around

Both cathedrals are on the west side of the city, about 15 minutes from the center, and on numerous bus routes.

Christ Church Cathedral. ✉ *Christ Church Pl. and Wine-tavern St., Dublin West* ☎ *01/677–8099* 🌐 *christchurchcathedral.ie* 🎫 *€10*

St. Patrick's Cathedral. ✉ *Patrick St., Dublin West* ☎ *01/453–9472* 🌐 *stpatrickscathedral.ie* 🎫 *€8*

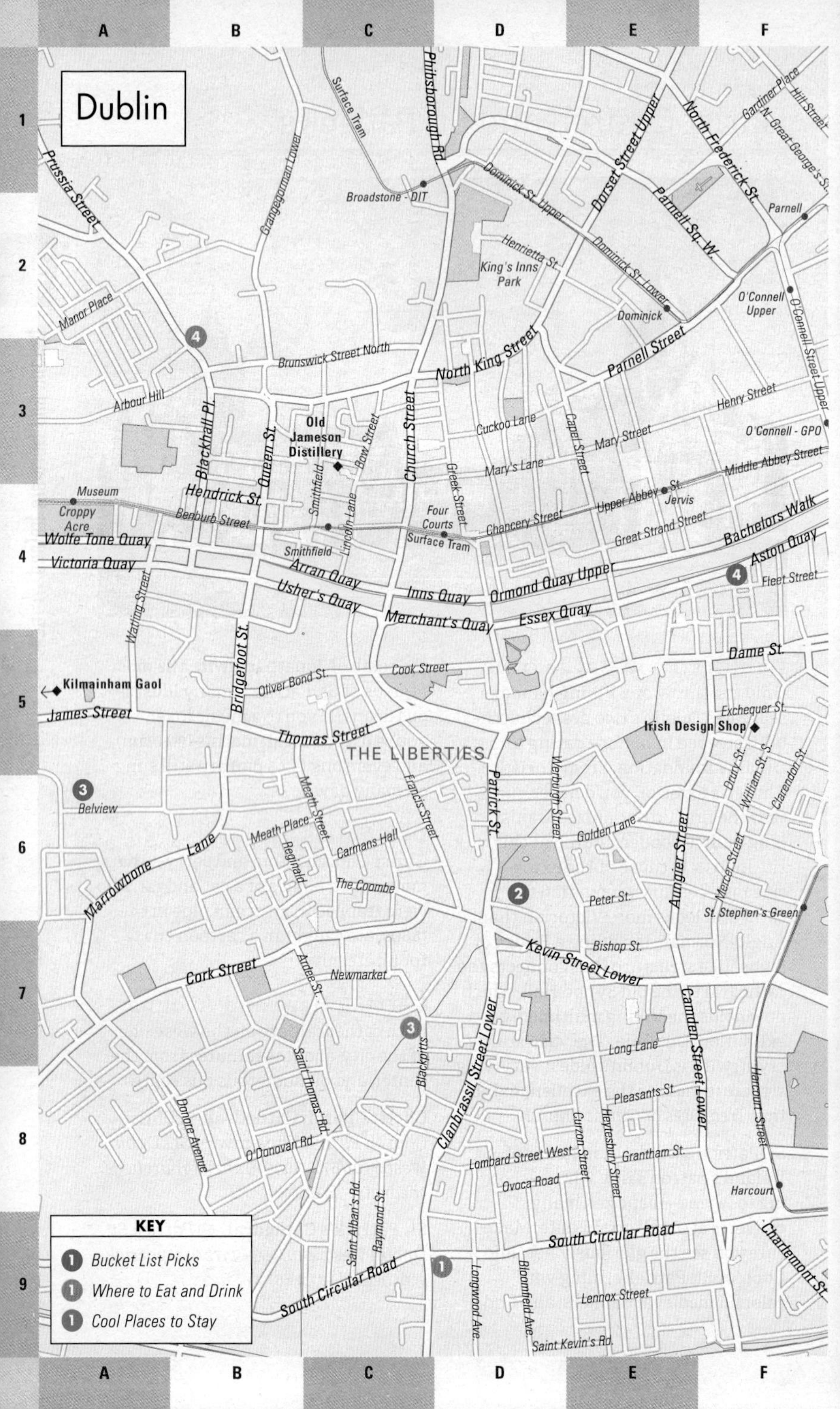

Dublin
A
B
C
D
E
F
1
2
3
4
5
6
7
8
9
Prussia Street
Surface Tram
Phibsborough Rd.
Dorset Street Upper
North Frederick St.
Gardiner Place
Hill Street
N. Great George's St.
Grangegorman Lower
Dominick St. Upper
Parnell Sq. W.
Broadstone - DIT
Parnell
Henrietta St.
Dominick St. Lower
King's Inns Park
O'Connell Upper
Manor Place
Dominick
O'Connell Street Upper
Brunswick Street North
North King Street
Parnell Street
Arbour Hill
Henry Street
Blackhall Pl.
Queen St.
Old Jameson Distillery
Bow Street
Church Street
Cuckoo Lane
Capel Street
O'Connell - GPO
Mary Street
Greek Street
Mary's Lane
Middle Abbey Street
Museum
Hendrick St.
Smithfield
Upper Abbey St.
Jervis
Croppy Acre
Benburb Street
Lincoln Lane
Four Courts
Chancery Street
Great Strand Street
Bachelors Walk
Wolfe Tone Quay
Surface Tram
Smithfield
Victoria Quay
Arran Quay
Aston Quay
Ormond Quay Upper
Fleet Street
Usher's Quay
Inns Quay
Watling Street
Merchant's Quay
Essex Quay
Bridgefoot St.
Dame St.
Cook Street
Kilmainham Gaol
Oliver Bond St.
James Street
Exchequer St.
Irish Design Shop
Thomas Street
THE LIBERTIES
Patrick St.
Werburgh Street
Drury St.
William St. S.
Clarendon St.
Belview
Meath Street
Francis Street
Meath Place
Golden Lane
Aungier Street
Mercer Street
Marrowbone Lane
Reginald
Carmans Hall
The Coombe
Peter St.
St. Stephen's Green
Bishop St.
Kevin Street Lower
Cork Street
Ardee St.
Newmarket
Camden Street Lower
Clanbrassil Street Lower
Long Lane
Blackpitts
Saint Thomas' Rd.
Harcourt Street
Donore Avenue
Pleasants St.
Curzon Street
Heytesbury Street
O'Donovan Rd.
Lombard Street West
Grantham St.
Ovoca Road
Harcourt
Saint Alban's Rd.
Raymond St.
South Circular Road
Charlemont St.
South Circular Road
Longwood Ave.
Bloomfield Ave.
Lennox Street
Saint Kevin's Rd.
KEY
Bucket List Picks
Where to Eat and Drink
Cool Places to Stay

Bucket List Picks

1 Chapter One and the Abbey Theatre **G3**

2 Christ Church and St Patrick's......................... **D6**

3 Guinness Storehouse **A6**

4 Traditional Music Pub Crawl **F4**

5 Trinity College and the Book of Kells **G5**

Where to Eat and Drink

1 Bastible **D9**

2 Forest Avenue.................................. **H9**

3 Hen's Teeth **C7**

4 L. Mulligan Grocer......................... **B2**

5 Restaurant Patrick Guilbaud **H7**

Cool Places to Stay

1 The Gibson Hotel **J3**

2 The Merrion Hotel........................ **H6**

3 Number 31....................................... **H8**

4 The Shelbourne Hotel................... **G6**

When in Dublin

★ The Forty Foot

SWIMMING | With so much live music to hear, pubs to visit, and great food to eat, there's a good chance that the bulk of your visit to Ireland may be focused on how you end the day, but you'd be missing out on one of Dublin's secret and storied traditions if you didn't allow time to start the day with a dip in the Irish Sea. The Forty Foot, a historic bathing pool on a promontory on the southern tip of Dublin Bay, has been welcoming brave locals for an invigorating morning swim for over 250 years (well, women were not welcome here until the 1970s.) It is a quick DART trip from Dublin city center, a 2-minute walk from the James Joyce Tower (the sea here is described by Buck Mulligan in *Ulysses* as "the snotgreen sea,") and a 20-minute cliffside walk to Dalkey Castle and village for lunch after. Rest assured, the waves at Forty Foot are not forty feet high, nor is the water forty feet deep. Rather, it is said to be named for the British Army's 40th Regiment of Foot. The test is to see if you can last longer than 40 seconds in the Baltic temperatures! ✉ *The Battery, Sandycove Point.*

Irish Design Shop

HOUSEWARES | Two young jewelers got together to open this exciting shop dedicated to the best in Irish design and designers. They sell the work of some of Ireland's best makers with everything from bird feeders, Aran hats and other woolens, and Irish cookbooks to pottery, prints, their own jewelry line, and assorted other treasures. ✉ *41 Drury St., Southside* ☎ *01/679–8871* 🌐 *irishdesignshop.com.*

★ Kilmainham Gaol

JAIL/PRISON | Leaders of many failed Irish rebellions spent their last days in this grim, forbidding structure, and it holds a special place in the myth and memory of the country. The 1916 commanders Pádraig Pearse and James Connolly were held here before being executed in the prison yard. Other famous inmates included the revolutionary Robert Emmet and Charles Stewart Parnell, a leading politician. You can visit the prison only as part of a very moving and exciting guided tour, which leaves every hour on the hour. The cells are a chilling sight, and the guided tour and a 30-minute audiovisual presentation relate a graphic account of Ireland's political history over the past 200 years—from an Irish Nationalist viewpoint. A newer exhibition explores the history of the prison and its restoration. A small tearoom is on the premises. **■ TIP→ It is almost essential to book ahead for the guided tour, especially during high season. You really don't want to chance a three-hour wait.** ✉ *Inchicore Rd., Dublin West* ☎ *01/453–5984* 🌐 *kilmainhamgaolmuseum.ie* 🎫 *€8.*

★ National Gallery of Ireland

ART MUSEUM | Caravaggio's *The Taking of Christ* (1602), Van Gogh's *Rooftops of Paris* (1886), Vermeer's *Lady Writing a Letter with Her Maid* (circa 1670) ... you get the picture, or rather, you'll *find* the picture here. Established in 1864, and designed by Francis Fowke (who also designed London's Victoria & Albert Museum), the National Gallery of Ireland is one of Europe's finest smaller art museums, with "smaller" being a relative term: the collection holds more than 2,500 paintings and some 10,000 other works. But unlike Europe's largest art museums, the National Gallery can be thoroughly covered in a morning or afternoon without inducing exhaustion.

A highlight of the museum is the major collection of paintings by Irish artists from the 17th through 20th centuries, including works by Roderic O'Conor (1860–1940), Sir William Orpen (1878–1931), and William Leech (1881–1968). The Yeats Museum section contains works by members of the Yeats family, including Jack B. Yeats (1871–1957), the brother of writer W.B. Yeats, and by far the best-known Irish painter of the 20th century.

The collection also claims exceptional paintings from the 17th-century French, Dutch, Italian, and Spanish schools, and works by French Impressionists Monet, Sisley, and Renoir. If you are in Dublin in January, catch the sumptuous annual Turner exhibition, with paintings only displayed in the winter light that best enhances their wonders. The amply stocked gift shop is a good place to pick up books on Irish artists. Free guided tours are available on Saturday at 12:30 and on Sunday at 12:30 and 1:30. ✉ *Merrion Sq. W, Georgian Dublin* ☎ *01/661–5133* 🌐 *nationalgallery.ie* 🎫 *Free; special exhibits €15.*

★ National Museum of Archaeology

HISTORY MUSEUM | Just south of Leinster House is Ireland's National Museum of Archaeology, one of four branches of the National Museum of Ireland, and home to a fabled collection of Irish artifacts dating from 7000 BC to the present. Organized around a grand rotunda, the museum is elaborately decorated, with mosaic floors, marble columns, balustrades, and fancy ironwork. It has the largest collection of Celtic antiquities in the world, including gold jewelry, carved stones, bronze tools, and weapons.

The Treasury collection, including some of the museum's most renowned pieces, is open on a permanent basis. Among the priceless relics on display are the 8th-century Ardagh Chalice, a two-handled silver cup with gold filigree ornamentation; the bronze-coated iron St. Patrick's Bell, the oldest surviving example (5th–8th century) of Irish metalwork; the 8th-century Tara Brooch, an intricately decorated piece made of white bronze, amber, and glass; and the 12th-century bejeweled oak Cross of Cong, covered with silver and bronze panels.

The exhibition Ór- *Ireland's Gold* gathers together the most impressive pieces of surprisingly delicate and intricate prehistoric goldwork—including sun disks and the late Bronze Age gold collar known as the Gleninsheen Gorget—that range in dates from 2200 to 500 BC. Upstairs, Viking Ireland is a permanent exhibit on the Norsemen, featuring a full-size Viking skeleton, swords, leatherworks recovered in Dublin and surrounding areas, and a replica of a small Viking boat. A newer attraction is an exhibition entitled *Kinship and Sacrifice,* centering on a number of Iron Age "bog bodies" found along with other objects in Ireland's peat bogs.

The 18th-century Collins Barracks, near Phoenix Park, houses the National Museum of Decorative Arts and History, a collection of glass, silver, furniture, and other decorative arts, as well as a military history section. ✉ *Kildare St. Annex, 7–9 Merrion Row, Georgian Dublin* ☎ *01/677–7444* 🌐 *museum.ie* 🎫 *Free* ⏲ *Closed Mon.*

Old Jameson Distillery

DISTILLERY | Founded in 1791, this distillery produced one of Ireland's most famous whiskeys for nearly 200 years, until 1966, when local distilleries merged to form Irish Distillers and moved to a purpose-built, ultramodern distillery in Middleton, County Cork. A major recent renovation has turned this original distillery into a state-of-the-art museum and whiskey experience to rival Guinness's storehouse. In fact, Jameson claims to be the most visited distillery in the world. Tours focus on either exploring the history of the old place, blending your own whiskey, or honing your whiskey-cocktail-making skills. Tours include a complimentary tasting; four attendees are invited to taste different brands of Irish whiskey and compare them against bourbon and Scotch. If you have a large group and everyone wants to do this, phone in advance to arrange it. You can even bottle your own whiskey, with a personalized label. ✉ *Bow St., Dublin West* ☎ *01/807–2348* 🌐 *jamesonwhiskey.com* 🎫 *From €25.*

★ St. Stephen's Green

CITY PARK | FAMILY | Dubliners call it simply Stephen's Green, and green it is (year-round)—a verdant, 27-acre Southside square that was used for the public punishment of criminals until 1664. After a long period of decline, it became a private park in 1814—the first time in its history that it was closed to the public. Its fortunes changed again in 1880, when Sir Arthur Guinness paid for it to be laid out anew. Flower gardens, formal lawns, a Victorian bandstand, and an ornamental lake with lots of waterfowl are all within the park's borders, connected by paths guaranteeing that strolling here or just passing through will offer up unexpected delights (such as palm trees). Among the park's many statues are a memorial to W.B. Yeats and another to Joyce by Henry Moore. A large outdoor market springs up around the park at Christmastime. ✉ *Southside* 🎫 *Free.*

Where to Eat and Drink

★ Bastible

$$$$ | BISTRO | Even with its location in a relatively unfashionable corner of the city, this high-end bistro has the natives traveling miles to get a treasured table. The five-course set menu manages to be daring and traditional at the same time, with game and fish transformed in particularly ingenious ways. **Known for:** trendy crowd; booking up; ample wines by the glass, pairings offered. [$] *Average main: €85* ✉ *111 S. Circular Rd., Dublin West* ☎ *01/473–7409* 🌐 *bastible.com* ⏲ *Closed Sun.–Tues. No lunch.*

★ Forest Avenue

$$$$ | CONTEMPORARY | Named after the street in Queens where chef-owner Sandy Wyer grew up, Forest Avenue is a star on the Dublin food stage. The menu is a five-course taster, and while choice is limited, quality and value are off the charts. **Known for:** warm, friendly vibe; daring tasting menu; pairing wine with food. [$] *Average main: €78* ✉ *8 Sussex Terr., Georgian Dublin* ☎ *01/667–8337* 🌐 *forestavenuerestaurant.ie* ⏲ *Closed Sun.–Tues.*

★ Hen's Teeth

$$ | TAPAS | This effortlessly cool, award-winning eatery slots neatly into the gallery/shop that makes up the rest of the Hen's Teeth empire. Located in the working-class Blackpitts area of the Liberties, the atmosphere is diner casual, while the food is a tapas-inspired trip into small-plate adventure. **Known for:** Sunday roast dinners; DJs on weekends; fun cocktails. [$] *Average main: €21* ✉ *Blackpits, Merchant Quay, The Liberties* ☎ *01/561–3036* 🌐 *hensteethstore.com* ⏲ *Closed Mon. and Tues.*

★ L. Mulligan Grocer

$$ | IRISH | This gem of an old Dublin boozer—which was once also the local grocer—has been turned into a gastropub and world-beer emporium, without losing too much of its real Dublin feel. It's the perfect spot for a quick pint of ale and a plate of black pudding (with pear relish and red chard) if you don't feel like a full sit-down meal. **Known for:** huge beer selection; popularity with hipsters; welcoming, friendly staff. [$] *Average main: €21* ✉ *18 Stoneybatter, Dublin North* ☎ *01/670–9889* 🌐 *lmulligangrocer.com* ⏲ *No lunch weekdays.*

★ Restaurant Patrick Guilbaud

$$$$ | FRENCH | Also known as "Dublin's finest restaurant," this Michelin-starred place on the ground floor of the Merrion Hotel boasts a menu described as French, but chef Guillaume Lebrun's genius lies in his occasional daring use of traditional Irish ingredients—so often taken for granted—to create the unexpected. The ambience is just as delicious, if you're into lofty, minimalist dining rooms and Irish modern art (the Roderic O'Conors and Louis le Brocquys are all from the owner's private collection). **Known for:** award-winning chef; Annagassan blue lobster; Irish modern art collection. $ *Average main: €64* ✉ *Merrion Hotel, 21 Upper Merrion St., Georgian Dublin* ☎ *01/676–4192* 🌐 *restaurantpatrickguilbaud.ie* ⏲ *Closed Sun. and Mon.*

Cool Places to Stay

★ The Gibson Hotel

$$$ | HOTEL | The terrace bar at the tastefully modern Gibson Hotel has to be the dream spot to view the impressive skyline and shimmering waterways of Dublin's trendy docklands area. **Pros:** fitness center with sauna; restaurant serves fantastic breakfasts; LUAS right outside for easy transit to Dublin center. **Cons:** slightly off the beaten track; can get busy and loud on concert nights; extra fee for parking. $ *Rooms from: €289* ✉ *Point Village, Dublin North* ☎ *01/681–5000* 🌐 *thegibsonhotel.ie* *252 rooms* *No Meals.*

★ The Merrion Hotel

$$$$ | HOTEL | Stately and spiffy, and splendidly situated directly across from the Government Buildings between St. Stephen's Green and Merrion Square, this luxurious hotel actually comprises four exactingly restored Georgian town houses. **Pros:** Michelin-starred restaurant; impressive art collection; city-center location. **Cons:** you'll pay extra for a room in the original house; some rooms are overdecorated; some may find the atmosphere a bit formal. $ *Rooms from: €440* ✉ *Upper Merrion St., Georgian Dublin* ☎ *01/603–0600* 🌐 *merrionhotel.com* *142 rooms* *No Meals.*

★ Number 31

$$$ | B&B/INN | Whether your lodging style is sublime Georgian elegance or cool modern, this one-in-a-million guesthouse, a short walk from St. Stephen's Green, serves up both—as well as the best made-to-order breakfast in town. **Pros:** the king and queen of guesthouse hosts; serene decor and art; fantastic breakfasts. **Cons:** a few rooms can be a little noisy; no elevator; minimum two-night stay on summer weekends. $ *Rooms from: €250* ✉ *31 Leeson Close, Georgian Dublin* ☎ *01/676–5011* 🌐 *number31.ie* *21 rooms* *Free Breakfast.*

★ The Shelbourne

$$$$ | HOTEL | Paris has the Ritz, New York has the St. Regis, and Dublin has the Shelbourne—resplendent in its broad, ornamented, pink-and-white mid-Victorian facade right off Grafton Street. **Pros:** rooms in front overlook Stephen's Green; history at every turn; spa and wellness center. **Cons:** some noise in front rooms; feels a little stuffy at times; pricey. $ *Rooms from: €460* ✉ *27 St. Stephen's Green, Southside* ☎ *01/663–4500, 800/543–4300 in U.S.* 🌐 *theshelbourne.com* *265 rooms* *No Meals.*

Ireland

As your plane breaks through the mists on your flight into Ireland, you'll see the land for which the Emerald Isle was named: a lovely patchwork of rolling green fields speckled with farmhouses, cows, and sheep.

Shimmering lakes, meandering rivers, narrow roads, and stone walls add to the impression that rolled out before you is a luxurious welcome carpet, one knit of the legendary "forty shades of green."

This age-old view of misty Ireland may be just what you imagined. But don't expect to still find Eire the land of leprechauns, shillelaghs, shamrocks, and mist. Those can only be found in souvenir shop windows or embroidered on Irish linen handkerchiefs and tablecloths; and the mists—in reality a soft, apologetic rain—can envelop the entire country, in a matter of minutes.

Today's Ireland is a complex place where the mystic lyricism of the great poet W. B. Yeats, the hard Rabelaisian passions of James Joyce, and the spare, aloof dissections of Samuel Beckett grew not only from a rich and ancient culture but also from 20th-century upheavals, few of which have been as dramatic as the transformation that has changed Ireland since the 1990s.

Ireland's economy—christened the "Celtic Tiger"—was one of the fastest-growing in the industrialized world until 2008, when it crashed with a mighty thud. No longer a simple provincial capital, Dublin is a thriving tech capital filled with large financial institutions. While there are still echoes of its Georgian history, it's every bit the modern European city these days.

Outside Dublin, life is more relaxed. Indeed, the farther you travel from the capital, the more you'll be inclined to linger. And once you take a deep breath of some of the best air in the Western world and look around, you'll find some dazzling sights: the fabled Rock of Cashel, the fun and gourmet-friendly city of Cork, the lively Galway City, Kilkenny's Medieval Mile, and the spectacularly scenic Ring of Kerry. In one of the villages on this peninsula in Ireland's extreme southwest, you'll be able to venture down a back road, find an old pub, and meet the locals. Undoubtedly, you'll be on first-name terms in no time.

The Burren and Cliffs of Moher

Ireland's Wild West

Visitors never cease to be shocked at how suddenly the ubiquitous green Irish landscape gives way to the rugged, gray wilderness of The Burren in west County Clare. The name is an Anglicization of the Irish word *bhoireann* (a rocky place), and as far as the eye can see are vast slabs of fissured limestone, known as karst, with deep cracks harboring plant life that's as alien as the setting. Burial sites like the iconic Poulnabrone Dolmen or Roughan Hill's extensive network of homes, walls, and wedge tombs dating back more than 5,000 years identify a lifestyle that changed very slowly in the millennia that followed. No visit to the Burren is complete without taking in the magnificent Cliffs of Moher, rising vertically out of the sea in a giant mass of sandstone and shale that stretches over an 8-km (5-mile) swath of County Clare's coastline, reaching a height of 710 feet at their apex. On a clear day you can see the Aran Islands and the mountains of Connemara to the north, as well as the lighthouse on Loop Head and the mountains of Kerry to the south.

Don't Miss

The Burren Food Trail: artisanal chocolatiers, cheese makers, confectioners, farmers, and beekeepers are harnessing the Burren's unique landscape, putting the area at the helm of Ireland's emerging food scene.

Getting Here and Around

From the south take the R476 road from Ennis. Coming from Galway and the north take the N67. Buses go to nearby Lahinch and Ballyvaughan.

A Stay in Ashford Castle

Live the Fairy Tale

Enjoy the royal treatment and get your fill of history, luxury, adventure, and charm with a stay in an Irish castle-hotel. Glorious Ashford Castle, which dates from the 13th century and was rebuilt in 1870 for the Guinness family, has long been wowing presidents and celebrities. Now housing a five star, uberluxurious hotel, its regal setting is the epitome of a romantic Irish castle, with flamboyant turrets and 350 acres hugging Lake Corrib. For something truly romantic, consider the Hideaway Cottage, a former boathouse on the shore of the lough with its own gated gardens and pier. Sample high-Victorian style with afternoon tea in the splendidly ornate Connaught Room or predinner drinks at The Prince of Wales Bar (named for the one who visited in the 1890s).

Don't Miss

With clay-pigeon shooting, horse riding, angling, tree-climbing, ziplining, a 9-hole golf course, and spa and indoor pool, you can be as active or inactive as your royal self pleases. At the very least, don't miss the chance to take a morning walk with a noble Irish wolfhound or with a hawk on your arm at the on-site School of Falconry.

Getting Here and Around

Ashford Castle is 23 km (14 miles) northeast of Maam Cross on the N59, a scenic drive skirting the shores of Lough Corrib.

Ashford Castle. ✉ *Ashford Castle Dr., Cong* ☎ *094/954–6003* 🌐 *www.ashford-castle.com*

Biking Through Killarney National Park

Freewheeling Through Paradise

Feeling the wind on your face and the scent of damp woods and heather moors in the air as you pedal through woods of oak, holly, and yew (populated by red deer) and down to the sapphire lakes of Killarney has to be one of Ireland's most stimulating experiences. The three Lakes of Killarney and the mountains, woods, and 25,000 acres that surround them make up this beautiful national park in the kingdom of Kerry. While a jaunting car (pony and cart) is the traditional way to tour the park, renting a bike allows more freedom and connection with the landscape. Highlights of the different cycling routes you can take include Ross Castle, Muckross Abbey, Brickeen Bridge, the Meeting of the Waters, Old Weir Bridge, and Torc Waterfall. The heart of the park is the pristine Muckross House and Gardens, an ivy-clad Victorian manor next door to the Visitor Centre.

Don't Miss

For stunning views of the three lakes and surrounding mountains, don't miss Ladies' View.

When to Go

The red fruits of the Mediterranean strawberry tree are at their peak in October and November, which is also about the time when the bracken turns rust color. In late April and early May, the purple flowers of the rhododendron come out.

Getting Here and Around

Killarney is well served by Expressway buses and has a rail link to Dublin and Cork.

Killarney National Park. ✉ *Muckross Rd., Killarney* 🌐 *killarneynationalpark.ie* 🎫 *Free*

O'Sullivan Cycles. ✉ *Beech Rd., Killarney* 🌐 *www.killarneyrentabike.com* 🎫 *From €20/day*

Newgrange

Older Than Stonehenge and the Great Pyramids of Giza

One of the most spectacular prehistoric sites in the world, Newgrange's Neolithic tomb inexplicably remains something of a hidden gem when compared with less-ancient Stonehenge. The wondrous site is shrouded in myth and mystery, including how the people who built Newgrange transported the huge stones to the spot. The mound above the tomb measures more than 330 feet across and reaches a height of 36 feet. White quartz was used for the retaining wall, and egg-shape gray stones were studded at intervals. The passage grave may have been the world's earliest solar observatory. It was so carefully constructed that, for five days on and around the winter solstice, the rays of the rising sun shine for about 20 minutes down the main interior passageway to illuminate the burial chamber. The geometric designs on some stones at the center of the burial chamber continue to baffle experts. Tours of the site depart from the Brú na Bóinne Visitor Centre. Be sure to reserve tickets in advance to visit Newgrange; same day tickets are rarely available.

Don't Miss

Prehistoric Knowth has 150 beautifully decorated stones surrounding its central burial mound. Much of the Knowth site is still under excavation so you might see archaeologists at work.

Getting Here and Around

From Dublin it's about a 50-minute drive to Newgrange: take the M1 motorway north to the Donore exit. The Bus Éireann route from Dublin to Drogheda stops at Newgrange.

Brú na Bóinne Visitor Centre. ✉ *Slane, Co. Meath* ☎ *041/988–0300* 🌐 *heritageireland.ie/visit/places-to-visit/bru-na-boinne-visitor-centre-newgrange-and-knowth*

Skellig Michael

Unforgettable Remote Island Monastery

Rising 700 feet from the Atlantic Ocean almost 12 km (7½ miles) west of the lveragh Peninsula in County Kerry is the most spectacularly situated of all Early Medieval island monastic sites. The UNESCO World Heritage site of Skellig Michael, or Great Skellig, holds the amazing remains of a 7th- to 12th-century village of monastic beehive dwellings that were home to early Christian monks. In spite of a thousand years of battering by Atlantic storms, the church, oratory, and living cells are surprisingly well preserved. The site is reached by climbing more than 600 increasingly precipitous steps, offering vertigo-inducing views. Despite the island's pivotal appearance in *The Force Awakens* and *The Last Jedi*, access to this fragile site is still limited to 180 visitors a day, so book in advance (booking opens in early spring) and hope for good weather.

Don't Miss

During the journey to Michael you'll pass Little Skellig, the breeding ground of more than 22,000 pairs of gannets. Puffin Island, to the north, has a large population of shearwaters and storm petrel.

When to Go

Due to choppy seas at the best of times, June, July, and early August are the best months to take the boat trip. Access is limited so be sure to book several months ahead.

Getting Here and Around

As scheduled boat departures may change with the weather, it is best to rent a car so that you can adapt as needed. Plan to stay in Portmagee the night before your sailing.

Skelligs Rock Cruises. ✉ *Portmagee.* ☎ *087/236-2344* 🌐 *www.skelligsrock.com* ⏲ *No sailings Oct.–mid-May*

Glendalough

A Sacred Place By the Lakes

Nestled in a lush, quiet valley deep in the rugged Wicklow Mountains, among two lakes and acres of windswept heather, Gleann dá Loch ("glen of two lakes") is one of Ireland's premier monastic sites. The hermit monks of early Christian Ireland were drawn to the Edenic quality of some of the valleys in this area, and this evocative settlement remains to this day a sight to calm a troubled soul. The oldest building, presumed to date from St. Kevin's time, is the Teampaill na Skellig (Church of the Oratory), on the south shore of the Upper Lake. At the southeast corner of the Upper Lake is the 11th-century Reefert Church, with the ruins of a nave and a chancel. The ruins by the edge of the Lower Lake are Glendalough's most important. The gateway, beside the Glendalough Hotel, is the only surviving entrance to an ancient monastic site anywhere in Ireland. An extensive graveyard lies within, with hundreds of elaborately decorated crosses.

Don't Miss

The perfectly preserved six-story Round Tower, built in the 11th or 12th century, stands 100 feet high, with an entrance 25 feet above ground level.

Getting Here and Around

If you're driving, the N11 is the fastest route but the R115 is the most scenic. St. Kevin's Bus has daily service between Dublin and Glendalough, with a stop in Bray.

Glendalough Visitor Center. *Off R757* ☎ *040/445–325* 🌐 *heritageireland.ie* 🎫 *Ruins free, visitor center €5*

Gaelic Games

Hurling and Gaelic Football

Ireland's national sports, Hurling and Gaelic Football, feature prominently in Ireland's past and present, and are integral to Irish culture, community, and life. The sports are played, supported, and celebrated widely: every county has teams; every small town has a club, and every young hurler or footballer dreams of representing their county in the All Ireland Championships. Hurling, the fastest field sport in the world, has been played in Ireland for over 3,000 years. Tales of the sport are recorded in Irish legend and mythology, most notably in the epic tales of Ulster hero Cú Chulainn, who became a warrior through the practice of hurling. The game is still the stuff of legend today and still very much a "warrior's game," given the speed, skill, and ferocity required in the battle for a win. Gaelic Football has not been around as long (earliest references date to the 1600s) but is beloved by the Irish with the same manic intensity that it is played.

Don't Miss

While hurling and Gaelic football play is at its highest level at the inter-county games, some of the greatest rivalries are at parish or club level. Even the best county players will play for their parish club and the passion and team rivalry witnessed at this level is an incredible experience. Kilkenny, Cork, and Tipperary are considered "the big three" of hurling with the most championship wins between them, while Kerry, Dublin, and Galway have the most wins in football. Check the GAA's website for match listings around your travel.

Gaelic Athletic Association. 🌐 *www.gaa.ie*

Kilkenny's Medieval Mile

A Walk Through a Medieval, Vibrant City

Dubbed "Ireland's Medieval Capital" by its tourist board, and also called "the Oasis of Ireland" for its many pubs and watering holes, Kilkenny is an impressively preserved city best explored on a medieval discovery trail that takes you from a magnificent castle to an iconic cathedral, with much to see along the way. The highlight is the Gothic masterpiece, Kilkenny Castle. Built in 1172, for more than 500 years it served as the seat of the earls of Ormonde. Be sure to stroll the grounds, and the Celtic cross–shape rose garden, after a spot of tea in the old Victorian kitchen.

Rothe House, one of Ireland's finest examples of a Tudor-era merchant's dwelling, is now home to a collection of Bronze Age artifacts, ogham stones (carved with an early Celtic alphabet), and period costumes.

In spite of Cromwell's defacements, 13th-century St. Canice's is still one of the finest cathedrals in Ireland. Many of the memorials and tombstone effigies represent distinguished descendants of the Normans, some depicted in full suits of armor. The biggest attraction on the grounds is the 102-foot-high Round Tower, which was built in 847 by King O'Carroll of Ossory.

Don't Miss

Kyteler's Inn, where Dame Alice, an alleged witch and "brothel keeper," was accused in 1324 of poisoning her four husbands.

Getting Here and Around

From Dublin, take the N7/M7 to the M9 and exit at junction 8 to Kilkenny. Buses and trains run daily from Dublin.

Kilkenny Tourist Office. 🌐 *visitkilkenny.ie*

The Wild Atlantic Way

Ireland's Spectacular Coastal Route

Ireland's Wild Atlantic Way is one of the longest defined coastal routes in the world, winding its way for 1,600 miles (2,600 km) along the Irish west coast from the Inishowen Peninsula in the north down to the picturesque town of Kinsale in the south. There are over 150 official "Discovery Points" on the route, with a further 15 highlighted as "Signature Discovery Points of special merit." Highlights along the way include the stunning cliffs on the Slieve League coast; the sinuous roads skirting the Connemara coast, where you will see shimmering lakes mirroring mountains, miles of bogland, islands surrounded by a supernatural fog, and higgledy-piggledy stone walls; the Dingle Peninsula, where you will find the the longest beach on the Wild Atlantic Way as well as Conor Pass, Ireland's highest mountain pass; and the dramatic cliffs, magical fishing villages, and emigrant history of West Cork's Mizen Head Peninsula.

Don't Miss

One of Ireland's top attractions, the Cliffs of Moher, can be found in the magical landscape of the Burren and West Clare section of the route. Allow time to walk the striking coastal trail to the cliffs.

Getting Here and Around

To experience the full coast or segments at your leisure, allowing for spontaneous stops and sightseeing along the way, you will want to rent a car. Guided bus tours package the highlights of the route with accommodation and dining, while guided and self-guided biking and hiking tours are also available.

🌐 *www.thewildatlanticway.com*

Kissing the Blarney Stone

Steal the Gift of the Gab

Kissing a famed ancient stone in this mid-15th-century stronghold is said to endow the kisser with the fabled "gift of the gab," and cheesy as it seems, it is still an exhilarating right-of-passage for any visitor to the Emerald Isle.

In the center of Blarney, the ruined keep is all that's left of the castle that was the 15th-century seat of the great McCarthy Clan. To kiss the stone, you must climb 127-steps, lie down on the battlements, hold on to a guardrail, and lean your head way back. It's a surprising, blood-rushing thrill. And apparently, you will come away with a tongue so sweet "you could tell someone to go to hell in such a way that they will look forward to the journey." You can take pleasant walks around the castle grounds. Rock Close contains oddly shaped limestone rocks landscaped in the 18th century and a grove of ancient yew trees that is said to have been a site of Druid worship.

Don't Miss

A trip to the nearby, world-famous Blarney Woollen Mills, one of the largest and most celebrated shops for Irish craft and design.

Getting Here and Around

Blarney is about a 20-minute drive west of Cork City Center, midway between the N22 Killarney road and the N20 to Limerick. Local buses depart from Cork Bus Station and drop you at the Blarney Green.

Blarney Castle. ✉ *Blarney, Co. Cork* ☎ *021/438–5252* 🌐 *www.blarneycastle.ie* 🎫 *€18*

When in Ireland

The Aran Islands

No one knows for certain when the Aran Islands—Inis Mór (Inishmore), Inis Meáin (Inishmaan), and Inis Oírr (Inisheer)—were first inhabited, but judging from the number of Bronze Age and Iron Age forts found here (especially on Inis Mór), 3000 BC is a safe guess. Each island has a hotel, and there's no shortage of guesthouses, campsites, hostels, and B&Bs. All three offer breathtaking scenery, a patchwork of fields in every shade of green trimmed with stone walls, and windswept walks. Dún Aengus Hillfort is the main draw to Inis Mór, the largest and most populated. Stretching more than 16 km (10 miles) long and about 2 km (1 mile) wide at most points, with an area of 7,640 acres, it's too large to fully explore on foot on a day trip, so hire a bicycle near the pier to navigate its lanes. Inis Meáin has a population of about 300 and its empty beaches and gorgeous scenery can be explored on foot or bicycle with relative ease. Inis Oírr, the smallest island, can be explored on foot in an afternoon ✉ *Aran Islands* 🌐 *www.galwaytourism.ie.*

Ardmore

TOWN | Historic spiritual sites, white beaches, dramatic cliff walks, local fishermen—little Ardmore is a picture postcard Irish town that packs a whole lot of wonder into a small peninsula at the base of a tall cliff. With a few notable exceptions the cute but very real village, with a highly lauded restaurant, is often overlooked by most overseas tourists. Ardmore and other nearby beaches offer access to surfing, snorkeling, kayaking, and anything else that involves fun and the sea. Don't miss the weathered but stunningly abstract biblical scenes carved on the west gable of the 12th-century Cathedral of St. Declan, along with the most pristine Round Tower in Ireland next door. ✉ *Ardmore* 🌐 *www.dungarvantourism.com/ardmore.*

★ Connemara National Park

NATIONAL PARK | The Irish people are well aware of what a jewel they have in the largely unspoiled wilderness, grazed by sheep and herds of wild ponies, that is the 5,000-acre Connemara National Park, the result of a successful lobby for landscape preservation. Like the American West, Connemara is an area of spectacular, almost myth-making geography—of glacial lakes; gorgeous, silent mountains; lonely roads; and hushed, uninhabited boglands. Letterfrack is the gateway village to the park and it makes a good base for exploring the park and nearby attractions, including Kylemore Abbey. Its visitor center covers the area's history and ecology, particularly the origins and growth of peat. You can also get advice and details on the many excellent walks and beaches in the area. One trail includes part of the famous Twelve Bens mountain range, which is best suited for experienced hill walkers. An easier hike is the Lower Diamond Hill Walk, at about 3 km (less than 2 miles). ✉ *Park and Visitor Centre, on N59 near Letterfrack, Letterfrack* ☎ *095/41054* 🌐 *www.connemaranationalpark.ie* 🎫 *Free* 🕒 *Visitor center closed Nov.–mid-Mar.*

★ Croagh Patrick

MOUNTAIN | Look out as you travel north for the great bulk of 2,500-foot-high Croagh Patrick; its size and conical shape make it one of the West's most distinctive landmarks. On clear days a small white oratory is visible at its summit (it stands on a ½-acre plateau), as is the wide path that ascends to it. The latter is the Pilgrim's Path. Each year about 25,000 people, many of them barefoot, follow the path to pray to St. Patrick in the oratory on its peak. St. Patrick, who converted Ireland to Christianity, spent the 40 days and nights of Lent here in 441. The traditional date for the pilgrimage is the last Sunday in July. The climb involves a gentle uphill slope, but you need to be fit and agile to complete the last half hour, over scree (small loose

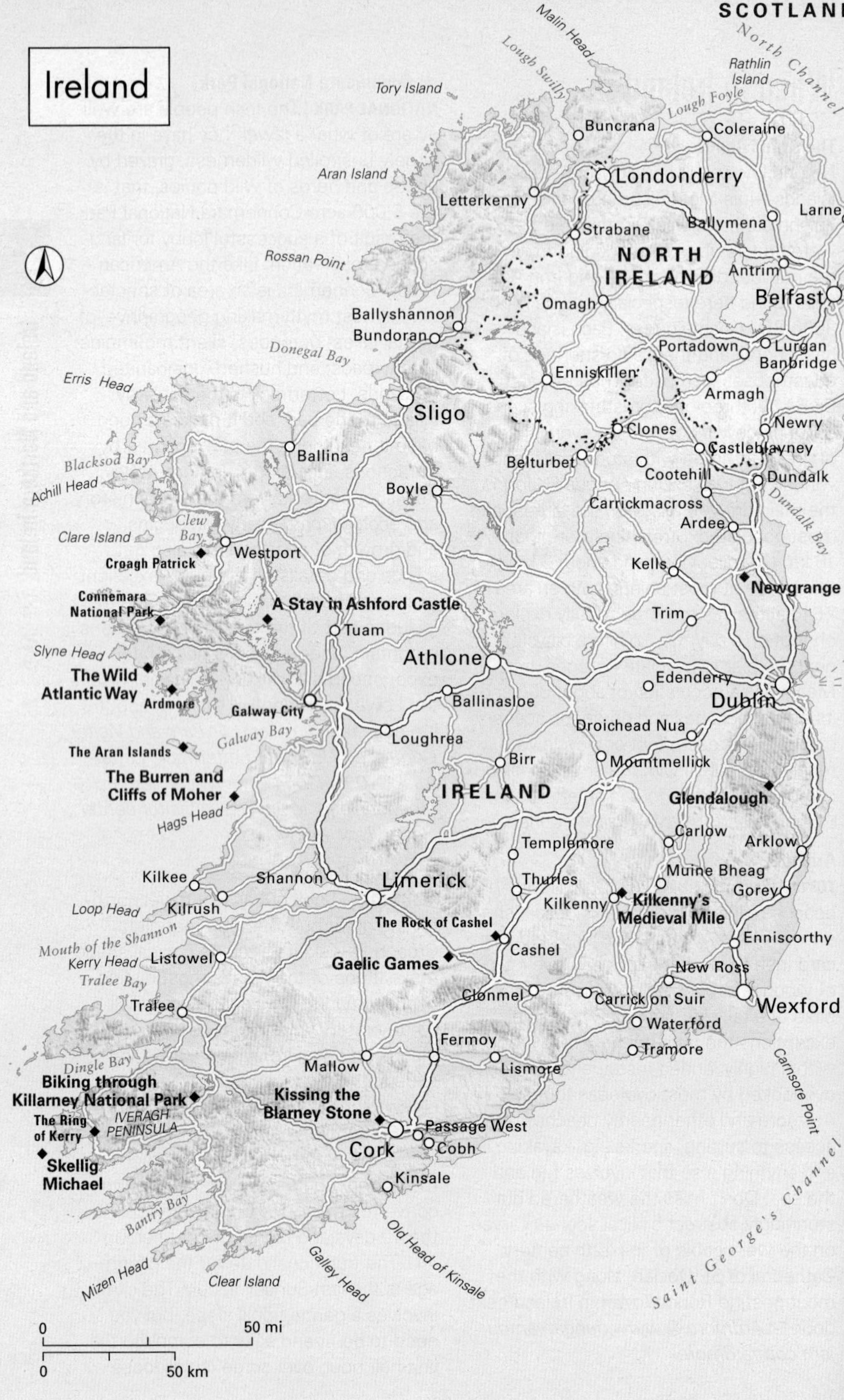

Ireland
SCOTLAND
North Channel
Malin Head
Lough Swilly
Rathlin Island
Tory Island
Lough Foyle
Buncrana
Coleraine
Aran Island
Londonderry
Letterkenny
Larne
Ballymena
Strabane
Rossan Point
NORTH IRELAND
Antrim
Belfast
Omagh
Ballyshannon
Bundoran
Portadown
Lurgan
Banbridge
Donegal Bay
Erris Head
Enniskillen
Armagh
Sligo
Newry
Clones
Castleblayney
Blacksod Bay
Ballina
Belturbet
Cootehill
Dundalk
Achill Head
Boyle
Carrickmacross
Dundalk Bay
Clew Bay
Ardee
Clare Island
Westport
Croagh Patrick
Kells
Newgrange
Connemara National Park
A Stay in Ashford Castle
Trim
Tuam
Slyne Head
Athlone
The Wild Atlantic Way
Edenderry
Ardmore
Dublin
Galway City
Ballinasloe
Galway Bay
Droichead Nua
Loughrea
The Aran Islands
Mountmellick
Birr
The Burren and Cliffs of Moher
IRELAND
Glendalough
Hags Head
Carlow
Templemore
Arklow
Muine Bheag
Kilkee
Shannon
Limerick
Thurles
Gorey
Kilkenny
Kilkenny's Medieval Mile
Loop Head
Kilrush
The Rock of Cashel
Enniscorthy
Mouth of the Shannon
Cashel
Kerry Head
Listowel
Gaelic Games
New Ross
Tralee Bay
Clonmel
Carrick on Suir
Wexford
Tralee
Waterford
Fermoy
Tramore
Carnsore Point
Mallow
Lismore
Dingle Bay
Biking through Killarney National Park
Kissing the Blarney Stone
The Ring of Kerry
IVERAGH PENINSULA
Passage West
Cork
Cobh
Skellig Michael
Kinsale
Bantry Bay
Saint George's Channel
Old Head of Kinsale
Galley Head
Mizen Head
Clear Island
0
50 mi
0
50 km

rocks with no trail). The hike can be made in about three hours (round-trip) on any fine day and is well worth the effort for the magnificent views. ✉ *Westport*.

Galway City

TOWN | The harbor city of Galway is the unofficial capital of western Ireland and a stronghold of traditional Irish ways, from its rapturous music scene to its artisanal seafood restaurants. Its streets, with their famed boho bars and cafés, are a magnet for visitors. Despite its size, it has retained the essence of a much smaller town, particularly in its compact and very walkable nucleus, which is most alive later in the evening when street lights come on and the sound of uilleann pipes, harps, and bodhráns filters through the air. Highlights include the food scene, The Druid Lane Theatre, The Claddagh and Katie's Cottage and Arts Centre, Tigh Neachtain and the Róisín Dubh pubs, and the seaside suburb of Salthill. In late July, you can catch the twin highlights of the social calendar: the wondrous Galway Arts Festival followed by the raucous Galway Races. ✉ *Galway City* 🌐 *www.discoverireland.ie/ places-to-go/galway*.

★ The Ring of Kerry

SCENIC DRIVE | Along the perimeter of the Iveragh Peninsula, the dramatic coastal road from Kenmare to Killorglin known as the Ring of Kerry is probably Ireland's single most popular tourist route. Stunning mountain and coastal views are around almost every turn. The only drawback: on a sunny day, it seems like half the nation's visitors are traveling along this two-lane road, driving, packed into buses, riding bikes, or hiking. The route is narrow and curvy, and the local sheep think nothing of using it for a nap; take it slowly. Tour buses tend to start in Killarney and ply the Ring counter-clockwise, so consider jumping ahead and starting in Killorglin or following the route clockwise, starting in Kenmare (although this means you risk meeting tour buses head-on on narrow roads). Either way, bear in mind that most of the buses leave Killarney between 9 and 10 am. The trip covers 179 km (111 miles) on N70 (and briefly R562 and N71) if you start and finish in Killarney. The journey will be 40 km (25 miles) shorter if you only venture between Kenmare and Killorglin. Because rain blocks views across the water to the Beara Peninsula in the east and the Dingle Peninsula in the west, hope for sunshine. It makes all the difference.

★ The Rock of Cashel

HISTORIC SIGHT | Seat of the Kings of Munster and the hallowed spot where St. Patrick first plucked a shamrock to explain the mystery of the Trinity, the Rock of Cashel is Ireland's greatest group of ecclesiastical ruins. Standing in the middle of a sloped, treeless valley, the Rock's titanic grandeur and majesty creates what one ancient scribe called "a fingerpost to Heaven." Today, the great limestone mass still rises 300 feet to command a panorama over all it surveys—fittingly, the name derives from the Irish *caiseal,* meaning "stone fort," and this gives a good idea of its strategic importance.

For centuries, Cashel was known as the "city of the kings"—from the 5th century, the lords of Munster ruled over much of southern Ireland from here. In 1101, however, they handed Cashel over to the Christian fathers, and the rock soon became the center of the reform movement that reshaped the Irish Church. Along the way, the church fathers embarked on a centuries-long building campaign that resulted in the magnificent group of chapels, Round Towers, and walls you see at Cashel today.

Built in the 15th century—though topped with a modern reconstruction of a beautifully corbelled medieval ceiling—the **Hall of the Vicar's Choral** was once the domain of the cathedral choristers. Located in the hall's undercroft, the museum includes the original St. Patrick's Cross.

The real showpiece of Cashel is **Cormac's Chapel,** completed in 1134 by Cormac McCarthy, King of Desmond and Bishop of Cashel. It is the finest example of Hiberno-Romanesque architecture. Preserved within the chapel is a splendid but broken sarcophagus, once believed to be Cormac's final resting place. At the opposite end of the chapel is the nave, where you can look for wonderful medieval paintings now showing through old plasterwork.

With thick walls that attest to its origin as a fortress, the now roofless **St. Patrick's Cathedral** is the largest building on the site. In the choir, look for the noted tomb of Myler McGrath. Note the tombs in the north transept, whose carvings—of the apostles, other saints, and the beasts of the Apocalypse—are remarkably detailed. The octagonal staircase turret that ascends the cathedral's central tower leads to a series of defensive passages built into the thick walls—from the top of the tower, you'll have wonderful views. At the center of the cathedral is the area known as **The Crossing,** a magnificently detailed arch where the four sections of the building come together.

Directly beyond the Rock's main entrance is the 7-foot-tall **High Cross,** carved from one large block and resting upon what is said to have been the original coronation stone of the Munster kings. The cross was erected in St. Patrick's honor to commemorate his famous visit to Cashel in AD 450. This cross is a faithfully rendered replica—the original now rests in the Rock's museum. As the oldest building on the Rock, the **Round Tower** rises 92 feet to command a panoramic view of the entire Vale of Tipperary. A constant lookout was posted here to warn of any advancing armies. ✉ *Rock of Cashel, Cashel* ☏ *062/61437* 🌐 *heritageireland.ie/places-to-visit/rock-of-cashel* 🎫 *€8.*

Where to Eat and Drink

★ Aimsir

$$$$ | **IRISH** | This new sensation of Irish cuisine was awarded not one but two Michelin stars only months after it opened. It didn't come as a surprise to those in the know, with the husband-and-wife team of Jordan and Majken Bech Bailey both having worked in some of Europe's most feted eateries. **Known for:** unique nonalcoholic pairing menu (as well as wine, beer, and cider pairings); impeccable service; bucket-list dining experience with 18 small courses. $ *Average main: €€220* ✉ *Cliff at Lyons, Lyons Rd., Celbridge* ☏ *01/630–3500* 🌐 *aimsir.ie* ⏲ *Closed Sun.–Tues. No lunch.*

★ Campagne

$$$$ | **FRENCH** | When Garrett Byrne, the former head chef of Dublin's celebrated Chapter One, returns home and opens a restaurant, people take notice, and the awards (including a Michelin star)—and diners from all of Ireland—start flooding in. The menu is a work of art, with common French themes toyed with and expanded. **Known for:** modern French cuisine; destination dining; relaxed contemporary setting. $ *Average main: €38* ✉ *5 The Arches, Gashouse La., Kilkenny* ☏ *056/777–2858* 🌐 *campagne.ie* ⏲ *Closed Mon. and Tues. No dinner Sun. No lunch Wed.–Sat.*

★ The Moorings-Bridge Bar

$ | **IRISH** | The dramatic location of this simple bar on the windswept waterfront of the tiny fishing village of Portmagee draws year round visitors to this corner of the Iveragh Peninsula. A simple menu with the emphasis on local seafood, fish-and-chips, and lamb is served in the low-beamed bar's rustic pine interior. **Known for:** local seafood chowder; unpretentious hospitality; popularity with locals. $ *Average main: €15* ✉ *Main St., Portmagee* ☏ *066/947–7108* 🌐 *moorings.ie.*

★ **Wild Honey Inn**

$$ | **MODERN IRISH** | Owner-chef Aidan McGrath and Kate Sweeney's modest Victorian premises on the outskirts of Lisdoonvarna have become something of a culinary landmark by becoming Ireland's first pub to be awarded a Michelin star. A brief, well-thought-out menu showcases the best of local produce, which includes hake, lamb, rib-eye steak, and pork. **Known for:** perfectly presented and executed dishes; friendly and attentive staff; inn is a good base for Burren. *Average main: €24* *Kincora Rd., Lisdoonvarna* *065/707–4300* *wildhoneyinn.com* *Closed Nov.–Feb.*

Cool Places to Stay

★ **Adare Manor Hotel**

$$$$ | **HOTEL** | This spectacular, recently overhauled, Victorian mansion, once the abode of the Quin family (earls of Dunraven) is an ostentatious Gothic wonderland, thanks to 840 well-manicured acres outside and the 26-foot-high, 100-foot-long Minstrels' Gallery with its decorated ceiling and stained-glass windows inside. **Pros:** fully updated Gothic mansion; one of Ireland's best golf courses; excellent amenities including a cinema, spa, and pool. **Cons:** off the beaten track as a touring base; fitness facilities and pool are modest in size; expensive. *Rooms from: €850* *Limerick Rd., Adare* *061/396–566* *www.adaremanor.ie* *108 rooms* *Free Breakfast.*

★ **Aran Camping and Glamping**

$$ | **APARTMENT** | Aran's glamping units, or *clocháns,* are igloo-shape (inspired by monks' medieval beehive huts) and fully heated, with en suite and cooking facilities. **Pros:** unique units; atmospheric setting on beach; heated, with cooking facilities. **Cons:** no Wi-Fi; groups discouraged; no TV. *Rooms from: €150* *Inis Mor, Frenchman's Beach, Aran Islands* *086/189–5823* *irelandglamping.ie* *9 units* *No Meals.*

★ **Cliff House**

$$$$ | **HOTEL** | Tucked into the cliffs overlooking the fishing village of Ardmore, ageless nature confronts modernist design at Cliff House—and this luxury hotel and spa remains one of the most innovative additions to Irish accommodations in the last few decades. **Pros:** the sea is everywhere; great spa and pool; up the road from the wonderful Ardmore Pottery shop. **Cons:** pricey for the region; sometimes has two-day minimum in summer; younger staff still learning the trade. *Rooms from: €450* *Cliff Rd., Ardmore* *thecliffhousehotel.com* *39 rooms* *No Meals.*

★ **The K Club**

$$$$ | **RESORT** | Manicured gardens and the renowned Arnold Palmer–designed K Club golf course surround this mansard-roof country mansion. **Pros:** restaurant has one of Ireland's finest wine cellars; luxurious spa; championship golf course. **Cons:** attracts golf crowd; rooms vary in quality; can get very busy in summer. *Rooms from: €450* *Off Baberstown Rd., Straffan* *01/601–7200* *kclub.ie* *69 rooms, 23 apartments* *Free Breakfast.*

★ **Sheen Falls Lodge Kerry Hotel**

$$$$ | **HOTEL** | The magnificence of this bright-yellow, slate-roofed former hunting lodge is matched only by its setting on 300 secluded acres of lawns, gardens, and forest between Kenmare Bay and the falls of the River Sheen. **Pros:** impeccable service from attentive staff; gourmet picnics available from the lodge; Skellig Island trips (boat or helicopter) by arrangement. **Cons:** Less than 2 km (1 mile) from the village; small swimming pool; spa gets busy, book in advance. *Rooms from: €615* *Off N71, Kenmare* *064/664–1600* *sheenfallslodge.ie* *Closed Jan. 3–Feb. 4* *66 rooms* *Free Breakfast.*

Northern Ireland

Northern Ireland has changed beyond recognition since the beginning of the 21st century. Regeneration of its two major cities, Belfast and Derry, has led to a creative and cultural renaissance and a surge of interest from all over the world. New luxury hotels, trendy bars, and chic restaurants have created a huge number of opportunities for travelers.

Northern Ireland is less than one-fifth the size of its southern neighbor, the Republic of Ireland. But within its boundaries are some of the unspoiled scenery you could ever hope to see: the Mountains of Mourne and the panoramic summit of Slieve Donard and the Glens of Antrim; the extraordinary Giant's Causeway; a 320 km (200 mile) coastline of long sandy beaches and hidden coves; and rivers and leaf-sheltered lakes, including the U.K.'s largest freshwater lake, Lough Neagh, that provide fabled fishing grounds. Ancient castles and Palladian-perfect 18th-century stately homes are as numerous here as almost anywhere else in Europe, standing amid leafy country estates or dominating rugged headlands.

Don't tell the Scots, but it's also a golfing powerhouse, with a staggering total of 95 courses from which to choose. Its young bands and its writers and poets have been internationally acclaimed, and its biggest city is home to Titanic Belfast, one of Europe's leading visitor attractions. South of the inspiring skyline of Derry lie the border counties, where quaint towns dot the scenic landscapes around the Lakes of Fermanagh. Complementing Northern Ireland's built and natural heritage is a vibrant cultural patrimony, epitomized not least by the foot-tapping fiddle music that trickles from multiple city-center bars and at events such as Ballycastle's annual Ould Lammas Fair.

These days, the border with the Republic of Ireland is of little consequence if you're just here to see the country. There are no checkpoints, no one is stopped and questioned, and no passports are checked. Having said that, Brexit did bring a new trade border in the Irish Sea. To the relief of many, however, it didn't lead to a "hard border" of customs, trade, or security being reintroduced.

Causeway Coast

Castles, Distilleries, and a Giant's Path

Stretching 80 miles from Belfast to Derry, the Causeway Coast is studded with Northern Ireland's most spectacular locations, from the natural beauty of the Nine Glens of Antrim to the storied castles of Carrickfergus and Dunluce and the giddy Carrick-a-Rede rope bridge. For whiskey connoisseurs, the historic Bushmills Distillery offers tours and tastings, while Game of Thrones fans can discover a wealth of filming locations including the Dark Hedges (known in the series as the Kingsroad). Thrill seekers love the dramatic Gobbins Cliff Path, cut into the towering rock of the Islandmagee peninsula.

Don't Miss

Northern Ireland's only UNESCO World Heritage site, the Giant's Causeway is a mass of almost 40,000 mostly hexagonal pillars of volcanic basalt, clustered like a giant honeycomb and extending hundreds of yards into the sea. Legend has it that the causeway was built by an Irish giant to battle with a Scottish giant.

When to Go

The Causeway Coast is at its best in summer, with long hours of daylight and vivid sunsets—but that's also when its attractions are most crowded. Arguably, the Giant's Causeway itself is most memorable when being pounded by mighty winter-gray combers.

Getting Here and Around

The A2 highway from Belfast skirts the Causeway Coast. The Translink Causeway Rambler coach service operates June through mid-September and hits all the main visitor attractions.

Giant's Causeway Visitor Experience. ✉ *44 Causeway Rd., Bushmills* ☎ *028/2073–1855* 🌐 *nationaltrust.org.uk/giants-causeway*

Belfast's Murals

A Graphic History

Bold, untutored, and colorful, Belfast's murals—originating in the sectarian divisions of The Troubles—still draw the eye and visitors more than 25 years after the Good Friday Peace Agreement of 1998 drew a veil over that violent era in Northern Ireland's history. Today, they increasingly reflect a wider, less sectarian view of global themes such as human rights, climate change, and other hot topics. Loyalist murals at points like Freedom Corner in east Belfast often portray balaclava-wearing paramilitaries. In Nationalist neighborhoods, some murals no longer glorify gunmen but are inspired by international events. The International Wall is a tapestry of themes as diverse as Basque independence and the Cuban Revolution. Elsewhere, some murals are inspired by Celtic mythology. In Belfast's Cathedral Quarter, you'll find a huge concentration of new and imaginative murals by international artists, such as "The Duel of Belfast, Dance by Candlelight."

Don't Miss

Enhance your understanding of the Troubles with a visit to Crumlin Road Gaol. Built in 1846, this once-grim prison in North Belfast held some of the North's most notorious paramilitary killers during the worst years of The Troubles, between 1969 and 1996, when the prison closed. An engrossing 75-minute tour takes in the punishment and condemned cells and the spine-chilling execution chamber.

Getting Here and Around

The best way to see the political murals is on a Black Taxi tour, which will take you to all the main political sights and murals with added context.

The Official Black Taxi Tours. ☎ *028/9064–2264* 🌐 *www.belfasttours.com* 🎫 *£40 up to 2 passengers*

The Titanic Experience

A Monument to Belfast's Maritime Heritage

The keystone of Belfast's rejuvenated docklands, now appropriately known as the Titanic Quarter, and gateway to the Maritime Mile, this world-class visitor attraction headlines an engrossing multimedia exhibition along with showcasing nine linked interpretative galleries that outline the RMS *Titanic*'s dramatic story as well as the wider theme of Belfast's long seafaring and industrial heritage. The stunning bow-shape facade of the six-story building reflects the lines of the great ship, the shard-like appearance created from 3,000 differently shaped panels, each folded from into asymmetrical geometries from silver anodized aluminum sheets. Within, a self-guided audio tour leads you through experiences including a "dark ride," re-creations of the ship's cabins. An underwater exploration movie theater designed by the Titanic explorer Robert Ballard, who discovered the wreck of the great ship 12,500 feet beneath the surface of the Atlantic in 1985, shows films of the wreck taken by the cameras of Ballard's submersible vessel *Alvin*.

Don't Miss

Six giant stained-glass windows commissioned by Tourism Ireland and depicting key scenes from the renowned Game of Thrones series, filmed in Northern Ireland, comprise the Glass of Thrones Walking Trail. You'll find all six along the nearby Maritime Mile.

Getting Here and Around

Titanic Experience is 1½ miles (a 30-minute walk) from central Belfast. Translink Metro Bus 26 runs from the Belfast Welcome Centre on Donegall Square, opposite City Hall.

Titanic Belfast. ✉ *Olympic Way, 6 Queen's Rd., Titanic Quarter* ☎ *028/9076–6386* 🌐 *www.titanicbelfast.com* 🎫 *£25*

Derry City Walls

A Ring of Ramparts

With the imprint of a sometimes turbulent past around every corner, lively Derry oozes character. Also known as Londonderry, it's proud of its 400-year-old walls and architectural heritage. The city's history is told in expressive visual terms by mural walls and stained glass, the rejuvenated Guildhall, and the spectacular Peace Bridge that swoops across the River Foyle. It's one of an elite coterie of cities that have preserved intact their historic ramparts (built between 1614 and 1618), which now comprise Northern Ireland's largest state monument. To get a feel for the city's history, stroll around the parapet walkway, atop a 1-mile circuit of massive ramparts, where 17th-century cannons still stand. Beneath the walls, on Orchard Street, look out for the Derry Girls mural, celebrating the characters of the hit TV series. There are more highly politicized murals, commemorating events from the Troubles era, on Rossville Street, in the heart of the Catholic Bogside neighborhood.

Don't Miss

Outside the walls, on Whitaker Street, the rejuvenated Victorian Guildhall houses a visitor center where interactive exhibits tell the story of the Plantation (British colonization) of Ulster, the construction of the walled city, and how these events shaped present-day Derry.

Getting Here and Around

Frequent Translink Goldline express buses connect Belfast and Derry, taking one hour and 40 minutes. Northern Ireland Railways trains from Belfast take around two hours.

Visit Derry Tourist Information Centre. ✉ *1–3 Waterloo Pl., West Bank* ☎ *028/7126–7284* 🌐 *www.visitderry.com*

Ulster American Folk Park

From Old Ulster to the New World

The excellent museum village evokes Northern Ireland's historic links with North America, recreating a Tyrone village of two centuries ago, a log-built American settlement of the same period, and the docks that emigrants to America would have used. The centerpiece is an old whitewashed cottage, the ancestral home of Thomas Mellon (1813–1908), the Ulster-born banker and philanthropist. Another thatched cottage is a reconstruction of the boyhood home of Archbishop John Hughes, founder of New York's St. Patrick's Cathedral. There are full-scale replicas of Irish peasant cottages, a schoolroom, and other buildings, and reenactors in period costume stay in character as local folk to tell you about their way of life. From a reconstructed small-town high street lined with old-time storefronts including William Murray's drapery store and W.G. O'Doherty's candy store, you pass through the spartan passenger quarters of a wooden emigrant ship *Brig Union* to emerge in a New World of sturdy wooden cabins, barns, and farmhouses set among paddocks and pine woods.

Don't Miss

The Mellon Centre for Migration Studies is a must for history buffs or those seeking to trace their Ulster roots, with a collection of historic books, maps, periodicals, and an emigration database, including passenger lists spanning the decades 1800–60.

Getting Here and Around

The park is 6 miles north of Omagh on the A5 highway. By bus, take the 273 Metrobus service to Omagh, then the 97 Ulsterbus.

2 Mellon Rd., Castletown, Omagh *028/8224–3292* *www.ulsteramericanfolkpark.org* *£10* *Closed Mon.*

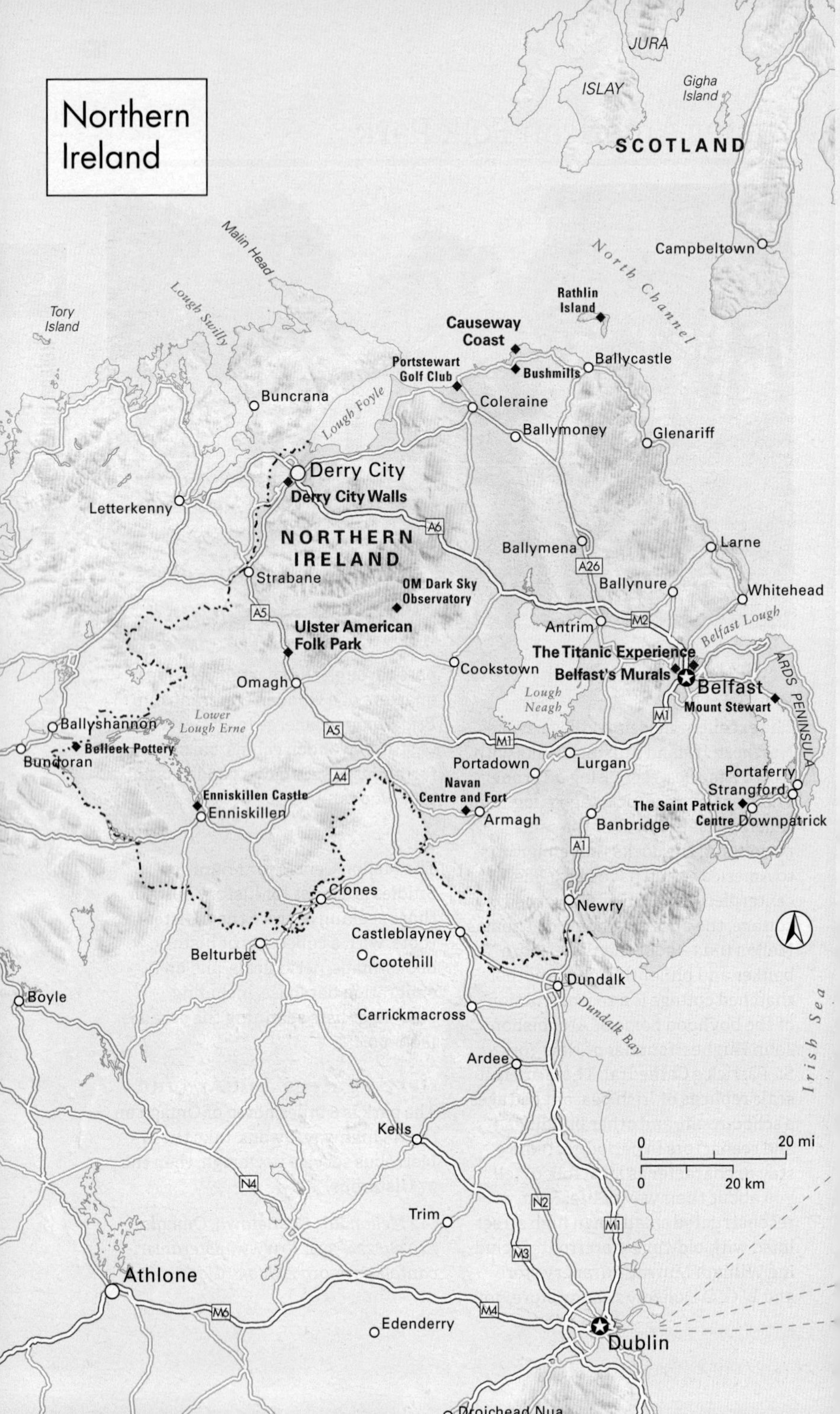

Northern Ireland
JURA
ISLAY
Gigha Island
SCOTLAND
Campbeltown
North Channel
Malin Head
Lough Swilly
Tory Island
Rathlin Island
Causeway Coast
Portstewart Golf Club
Bushmills
Ballycastle
Buncrana
Lough Foyle
Coleraine
Ballymoney
Glenariff
Derry City
Derry City Walls
Letterkenny
A6
NORTHERN IRELAND
Ballymena
Larne
A26
Strabane
OM Dark Sky Observatory
Ballynure
Whitehead
A5
Ulster American Folk Park
Antrim
M2
Belfast Lough
The Titanic Experience
Belfast's Murals
Belfast
Cookstown
Omagh
Lough Neagh
Mount Stewart
ARDS PENINSULA
M1
Lower Lough Erne
Ballyshannon
Belleek Pottery
Bundoran
A5
M1
Portadown
Lurgan
A4
Navan Centre and Fort
Portaferry
Strangford
Enniskillen Castle
Enniskillen
Armagh
The Saint Patrick Centre
Downpatrick
Banbridge
A1
Clones
Newry
Castleblayney
Belturbet
Cootehill
Dundalk
Boyle
Dundalk Bay
Carrickmacross
Irish Sea
Ardee
Kells
0
20 mi
0
20 km
N4
N2
Trim
M1
M3
Athlone
M6
M4
Edenderry
Dublin
Droichead Nua

When in Northern Ireland

★ Belleek Pottery

FACTORY | On the riverbank stands the visitor center of Belleek Pottery Ltd., producers of Parian china; a fine, egg-shell-thin, ivory porcelain shaped into dishes, figurines, vases, and baskets. There's a factory, showroom, exhibition, museum, and café. You can watch a 20-minute audiovisual presentation or join a 30-minute tour of the factory, where you can get up close and talk to craftspeople—there's hardly any noise coming from machinery in the workshops. Everything here is made by hand just as workers did back in 1857. The showroom is filled with beautiful but pricey gifts. ✉ *3 Main St., Belleek* ☎ *028/6865–8501* 🌐 *www.belleek.ie* 🎫 *£6 for tour.*

★ Bushmills

DISTILLERY | Reputedly the oldest licensed distillery in the world, Bushmills was first granted a charter by King James I in 1608, though historical records refer to a distillery here as early as 1276. Bushmills produces the most famous of Irish whiskeys—its namesake—and a rarer black-label version, Black Bush, widely regarded as the best of the best. On the guided tour, discover the secrets of the special water from St. Columb's Rill, the story behind malted Irish barley, and learn about triple distillation in copper stills and aging (which happens for long years in oak casks). ✉ *2 Distillery Rd., off A2, Bushmills* ☎ *028/2073–3218* 🌐 *www.bushmills.eu* 🎫 *Tours from £15; children under 8 not permitted on tour.*

Enniskillen Castle

CASTLE/PALACE | Strategically sited overlooking the River Erne, Enniskillen's 600-year-old waterfront castle is one of the best-preserved monuments in the north, and has undergone a multimillion-pound redevelopment, which has seen the tourist office merging with the castle complex, creating a new gateway to the region. Built in the early 15th century by the Gaelic Maguires to command the waterway, the castle was of tremendous importance in guarding one of the few passes into Ulster and the crossing point between Upper and Lower Lough Erne. After a yearlong program of work costing £3.3 million, four new galleries spread over two floors are now in place in the restored barrack coach house. A new building, in the shape of the original armory, links the visitor center with the coach house, allowing tourists a glimpse of the original castle wall. The center, styling itself as a "history hub," combines tourism, genealogy, archive, and heritage services alongside a café and shop. ✉ *Castlebarracks, Wellington Rd., Enniskillen* ☎ *028/6632–5000* 🌐 *www.enniskillencastle.co.uk* 🎫 *£5.*

★ Mount Stewart

HISTORIC HOME | Now in the care of the National Trust, and completely renovated in 2015, this stately Neoclassical home near Belfast was formerly the country estate of the marquesses of Londonderry. Mount Stewart was constructed in two stages where an earlier house had stood: George Dance designed the west facade (1804–05), and William Vitruvius Morrison designed the Neoclassical main part of the building (1845–49), complete with an awe-inspiring Grecian portico facade. The 7th Marchioness, Edith, managed to wave her wand over the interior—after a fashion: Chinese vases, Louis-Philippe tables, and Spanish oak chairs do their worst to clutter up the rooms here. Still, the house does have some noted 18th-century interiors, including the central hall and the grand staircase hung with one of George Stubbs's most famous portraits, that of the celebrated racehorse Hambletonian—this is perhaps the greatest in situ setting for a painting in Ireland. There are no fewer than 18 named garden walks to choose between. ✉ *Portaferry Rd., Newtownards* ✣ *Ulsterbus 10 on Belfast to Portaferry route stops near front entrance*

☎ *028/4278–8387* 🌐 *www.nationaltrust.org.uk/mount-stewart* 💷 *£11.*

Navan Centre and Fort

HISTORIC SIGHT | FAMILY | Just outside Armagh is Ulster's Camelot—the region's ancient capital. Excavations date activity to 700 BC. Legend has it that thousands of years ago this was the site of the palace of Queen Macha; subsequent tales call it the barracks of the legendary Ulster warrior Cuchulainn and his Red Branch Knights. Remains dating from 94 BC are particularly intriguing: a great conical structure, 120 feet in diameter, was formed from five concentric circles made of 275 wooden posts, with a 276th, about 12 yards high, situated in the center. In 2020 the center underwent a modern-day rebranding making it a more immersive Iron Age Celtic experience for visitors. On arrival you are welcomed into the clan with a cleansing ceremony and purification involving smoke and fire. Traditional herb bread and mead is offered as stories of Ulster's heroes and warriors are recounted; those who feel the need may connect with the land and energy through some calming Celtic Mindfulness, all served up with music and mythology. ✉ *81 Killyleagh Rd., 3 km (2 miles) west of Armagh on A28, Armagh* ☎ *028/3752–9644* 🌐 *www.visitarmagh.com/places-to-explore/navan-centre-fort* 💷 *Apr.–Sept. £13; Oct.–Mar. £7* ⏲ *Closed Mon.*

OM Dark Sky Observatory

OBSERVATORY | Deep in the wild Sperrin Mountains of Tyrone, a lack of light pollution allows for astonishing views of the night sky and creates an ideal location for seeing crystal-clear star constellations. Northern Ireland's first dark-sky observatory opened in Davagh Forest in the foothills of the mountains in spring 2020. The new center houses a retractable roof, observatory, and telescope showcasing the dark-sky site, combining technology from holographic installations to virtual reality headsets and interpretation panels so you can explore the solar system. On a cloud-free night, you may be lucky enough to see the Milky Way, the Perseid meteor shower (if here in August), or deep-sky objects such as the Pleiades, the Orion Nebula, and depending on conditions, the northern lights.

■ TIP→ Without your own transport, a taxi from Cookstown is the only way to reach the site and costs around £20. ✉ *Davagh Forest, Omagh* ✣ *Located 24 km (15 miles) northwest of Cookstown signposted off the main A505 Cookstown to Omagh Rd.* ☎ *028/8876–0681* 🌐 *www.omdarksky.com* 💷 *£5.*

Portstewart Golf Club

GOLF | More than 120 years old, Portstewart may scare you with its opening hole, known as "Tubber Patrick," generally regarded as the toughest starter in Ireland. Picture a 425-yard par-4 that descends from an elevated tee to a small green tucked between the dunes. The Strand Course is affectionately called "The Sleeping Giant," and the manicured greens are known for uniformity and speed. Eight of the holes have been redesigned to toughen the course and two have been lengthened. From its rolling fairways and undulating dunes the views stretch across the Atlantic Ocean to north Donegal. ✉ *117 Strand Rd., Portstewart* ☎ *028/7083–2015* 🌐 *www.portstewartgc.co.uk* 💷 *The Strand: Apr. £165; May–Oct. daily £215; Nov.–Mar. £70; Old Course: summer weekdays £15, winter £10, weekends £15 all year; Riverside: weekdays £25, weekends £30* 🏌 *The Strand: 18 holes, 7118 yards, par 72; Old Course: 18 holes, 4730 yards, par 64; Riverside: 18 holes, 5725 yards, par 68.*

Rathlin Island

ISLAND | There's a sense of dreamy loneliness about this spot, rising 8 km (5 miles) offshore beyond the tide rip of Sloch na Marra (Valley of the Sea). One hundred people still live on Northern Ireland's only offshore island, amid the twin delights of history and wildlife. In 1306, the Scottish king Robert the Bruce took shelter in a cave (under the east lighthouse) and, according to the popular legend, was inspired to continue his armed struggle against the English by watching a spider patiently spinning its web. It was on Rathlin in 1898 that Guglielmo Marconi set up the world's first cross-water radio link, from the island's lighthouse to Ballycastle. Hiking and bird-watching—look out for the Atlantic nomads: choughs, puffins, guillemots, and razorbills nesting on the cliffs and sea stacks in the summer—as well as visiting the Rathlin West Light Seabird Centre and Lighthouse are the island's main activities. A high-speed passenger-only catamaran, the M.V. *Rathlin Express,* cuts the 10-km (6-mile) journey time crossing over the Sea of Moyle to 25 minutes; from July to September it runs six round-trips daily (£12; reservations 24 hours ahead essential). ✉ *Rathlin Island, 9½ km (6 miles) from Ballycastle, Ballycastle* ☎ *028/2076–9299* 🌐 *www.rathlinballycastleferry.com* 🎫 *Lighthouse £5; Boathouse Visitor Centre free.*

The Saint Patrick Centre

HISTORY MUSEUM | FAMILY | The interactive exhibits here bring the ancient myths and stories of early Christian Ireland to life. You can explore how St. Patrick's legacy developed in early Christian times, examine the art and metalwork that were produced during this golden age, and listen to modern debates about Ireland's patron saint. Interpretative boards outline local sites connected with the saint. Self-guided tours of sites linked with St. Patrick last about 70 minutes and take you across a bridge over the River of Words. ✉ *St. Patrick's Sq., 53A Lower Market St., Downpatrick* ☎ *028/4461–9000* 🌐 *www.saintpatrickcentre.com* 🎫 *£6* 🕒 *Closed Sun., Nov.–Feb.*

Where to Eat and Drink

Badger's

$ | IRISH | The famous *Derry Girls* mural adorns one outside wall of this old-school tavern. Inside, wood-paneled walls are covered with photos of local sporting legends. **Known for:** traditional Irish pub decorations; Sunday roast dinners; Guinness pints. 💲 *Average main: £13* ✉ *18 Orchard St., Central District* ☎ *028/7136–3306.*

Bert's Jazz Bar

LIVE MUSIC | Belfast's only dedicated jazz bar offers live music seven nights a week and excellent cocktails in surroundings calculated to evoke New York at the height of the golden age of jazz. ✉ *The Merchant Hotel, 16 Skipper St., Cathedral Quarter* ☎ *028/9026–2713* 🌐 *www.themerchanthotel.com/berts-jazz-bar.*

★ Crown Liquor Saloon

OTHER ATTRACTION | Belfast is blessed with some exceptional pubs, but the Crown is one of the city's glories. Owned by the National Trust (the U.K.'s official conservation organization), it's an ostentatious box of delights and immaculately preserved. Opposite the Europa Hotel, it began life in 1826 as the Railway Tavern and is still lighted by gas; in 1885 the owner asked Italian craftsmen working on churches in Ireland to moonlight on rebuilding it, and its place in Irish architectural pub history was assured. Richly carved woodwork around cozy snugs (cubicles—known to regulars as "confessional boxes"), leather seats, color tile work, and an abundance of mirrors make up the decor. But the pièce de résistance is the embossed ceiling with its swirling arabesques and rosettes of burnished primrose, amber, and gold, as dazzling now as the day it was installed. If you wish to eat, choose the upstairs dining room, which has a much wider and better selection of food. ✉ *46 Great Victoria St., Golden Mile* ☎ *028/9024–3187* 🌐 *www.nicholsons-pubs.co.uk.*

★ Fish City

$ | **SEAFOOD** | A cut above the average fish-and-chips restaurant, award-winning Fish City serves sustainably sourced seafood including Carlingford oysters, cod, scampi, and other treats. For nonpescatarians there are vegan and vegetarian options, too. **Known for:** Fish City Kiev; fisherman's curry; gourmet burgers. [$] *Average main: £19* ✉ *33 Ann St., Central District* ☎ *028/9023–1000* 🌐 *www.fish-city.com.*

★ Harry's Shack

$ | **IRISH** | With its raw wooden tables, wood-burning stove, sand on the floor, and outdoor terrace, this beachside restaurant in Portstewart, about 20 minutes from Dunluce, is *the* destination restaurant par excellence of the north coast. Brunches might consist of pancakes with maple syrup, smoked salmon and scrambled eggs, or pasta. **Known for:** fresh, tasty lobster; local pale ale; on-the-beach dining with outdoor bar. [$] *Average main: £15* ✉ *118 Strand Rd., Portstewart* ☎ *028/7083–1783* ⌚ *Closed for dinner Sun.–Wed.*

Observatory

COCKTAIL LOUNGES | Spectacular sunsets and nighttime views over the city are the key selling points of the Grand Central Hotel's posh penthouse lounge. It's the highest bar in Ireland, with an imaginative cocktail list and a swank clientele. Reserve a table ahead of time and dress to impress. ✉ *Grand Central Hotel, 9–15 Bedford St., Central District* ☎ *028/9023–1066* 🌐 *www.grandcentralhotelbelfast.com/observatory.*

★ Pyke 'N' Pommes

$ | **IRISH** | Starting life as a street food truck, PNP is now a full-service restaurant (with a liquor license) but is still serving up its authentic street-food dishes such as Legenderry, Veganderry, and jalapeño burgers. Long bare bulbs hang over rough-hewn tables made with thick wooden scaffold planks and 1960s reclaimed school chairs. **Known for:** classic street-style burgers; squid tacos; charcoal-grilled whole fish. [$] *Average main: £7* ✉ *57 Strand Rd., West Bank* ☎ *028/7167–2691* 🌐 *www.pyken-pommes.ie* ⌚ *Closed Mon. and Tues.*

Ramore Restaurants

$ | **ECLECTIC** | **FAMILY** | Creative, moderately priced fare, alongside panoramic views in an elegant setting, attract locals and tourists to this popular restaurant and wine bar complex with multiple venues. The light-filled Mermaid Kitchen and Bar, serving seafood, conjures up a beachside feel evocative of coastal Maine, except you're looking out on Portrush's West Strand (although admittedly Belfast is only 100 km [60 miles] south); the more informal Harbour Bistro serves wood-fired steaks and burgers; Neptune and Prawn, on the other side of the harbor, serves Asian-inspired fare; and the Tourist Restaurant has a Mexican theme with burritos, nachos, and tacos and specializes in pizzas and burgers. **Known for:** multiple venues; wood-fired burgers and grilled fish; sea and sunset views. [$] *Average main: £13* ✉ *Landsdown Harbour, Portrush* ☎ *07506/990345* 🌐 *www.ramorerestaurant.com.*

★ Seahorse

$$$$ | **ECLECTIC** | The Grand Central Hotel's first-floor brasserie is a bright, stylish space and a favorite rendezvous for well-heeled locals, especially on weekends. Entrées lean toward modern Irish treatments of local surf-and-turf dishes, but there are tasty vegetarian options, too. **Known for:** rack of Mourne lamb; roast monkfish; tender sirloin steaks. [$] *Average main: £34* ✉ *Grand Central Hotel, 9–15 Bedford St., Central District* ☎ *028/9023–1066* 🌐 *www.grandcentral-hotelbelfast.com/seahorse.*

Cool Places to Stay

Ballygally Castle

$$$ | **HOTEL** | Connoisseurs of sea views love this little mock-baronial castle, originally built by a Scottish lord in 1625. **Pros:** deluxe rooms have coastal views; afternoon tea packages; free parking. **Cons:** popular with wedding parties; somewhat bland, if comfortable, furnishings; service can be hit or miss. *Rooms from: £130 274 Coast Rd., Ballygally 028/2858–1066 www.hastingshotels.com 54 rooms Free Breakfast.*

★ **Bishop's Gate Hotel**

$$$ | **HOTEL** | Restored from a historic city-center building that was once a gentleman's club, Bishop's Gate Hotel has kept its Edwardian craftsmanship and original architectural details but the plush rooms with velvet furnishings are all fit for the 21st century; just for fun, the guest rooms have retained their antique telephones with rotary dials—and yes, they do work. **Pros:** elegant restoration; central location; valet parking available. **Cons:** surrounding streets can be noisy at night; short on amenities; popular with wedding parties. *Rooms from: £129 24 Bishop St., Central District 028/7114–0300 www.bishopsgatehotelderry.com 31 rooms Free Breakfast.*

The Bushmills Inn

$$$$ | **B&B/INN** | This comfortable old coach inn dating from the 1600s welcomes with peat fires and cozy rooms; the master distiller's suite even comes with fluffy slippers and bathrobes. **Pros:** close to distillery and the Giant's Causeway; easy to find in central location; secure off-street parking. **Cons:** if you're tall, look out for the low timber beams; very expensive for what you get; overrated menu. *Rooms from: £230 9 Dunluce Rd., Bushmills 028/2073–3000 www.bushmillsinn.com 41 rooms Free Breakfast.*

Causeway Hotel

$$$ | **HOTEL** | Owned by the U.K.'s National Trust and flaunting a stunning location overlooking the Atlantic Ocean, this 1840s hotel is less than a half mile from the celebrated Giant's Causeway. Older rooms have been fully refurbished and freshened with a calming shade of duck-egg blue. **Pros:** free parking; old-world charm with modern comforts; as close as it gets to the Giant's Causeway. **Cons:** too many family parties; service can be a tad churlish; isolated with nowhere to eat or drink nearby. *Rooms from: £140 40 Causeway Rd., Bushmills 028/2073–1210 www.thecausewayhotel.com 28 rooms Free Breakfast.*

Grand Central Hotel

$$$$ | **HOTEL** | Beyond a doubt the coolest place to stay, dine, and hang out in Belfast, this swish 23-floor venue is part of the Hastings portfolio and boasts the highest bar in Ireland. **Pros:** top location; valet parking; panoramic views from top-floor bar. **Cons:** no on-site parking; no pool; frustrating waits for elevators. *Rooms from: £220 Bedford St., Central District City center, 5-min walk from City Hall 028/9023–1066 www.grandcentralhotelbelfast.com 300 rooms Free Breakfast.*

★ **The Londonderry Arms Hotel**

$$$ | **HOTEL** | What awaits at this lovely traditional inn are ivy-clad walls, gorgeous antiques, regional paintings, prints and maps, rare whiskeys, and lots of fresh flowers—all time-burnished accents well befitting an estate once inhabited by Sir Winston Churchill. **Pros:** fine historic vibe; good in-house dining and drinking options; spacious rooms. **Cons:** no good local alternative spots to eat and drink; old-fashioned hotels (and creaky floorboards) aren't to everyone's taste; service sometimes moves at a slow pace. *Rooms from: £120 20 Harbor Rd., Carnlough 028/2888–5255 www.londonderryarmshotel.com 35 rooms Free Breakfast.*

★ **The Merchant Hotel**
$$$$ | **HOTEL** | A mix of glorious Victorian grandeur and Art Deco–inspired modernity, this hotel—regarded by some as Ireland's most spectacular—was built as the headquarters of Ulster Bank in the mid-19th century and still leads the way in style and sophistication. **Pros:** superhelpful staff; fabulous gym and spa; discounted off-street parking available just steps away. **Cons:** elevator occasionally unreliable; Wi-Fi access intermittent in some rooms; labyrinthine corridors. *Rooms from: £289* ✉ *16 Skipper St., Cathedral Quarter* ☎ *028/9023–4888* 🌐 *www.themerchanthotel.com* *67 rooms* 🍴 *Free Breakfast.*

Chapter 4

FRANCE AND THE LOW COUNTRIES

WELCOME TO FRANCE AND THE LOW COUNTRIES

TOP REASONS TO GO

★ **Marvelous Food:** From stroopwafels in Amsterdam to haute cuisine in France to chocolate and mussels in Belgium, you'll find plenty of great things to eat.

★ **Awesome Art:** From the grand, sprawling Louvre to the Rijksmuseum to the Magritte Museum.

★ **Wineries and Breweries:** White to red, you can sip your way across the countryside in France, while Belgium and the Netherlands are more attuned to beer.

★ **Battlefield Tours:** From Napoléon's final stand at Waterloo to the Ardennes Forest to the D-Day Beaches of Normandy, the fate of Europe and the world was decided here.

★ **Architecture:** From Amsterdam's canal houses, to medieval Bruges and Ghent, to the elegant fairy-tale castles and chateaus of France and Luxembourg.

1 Paris and the Île de France. A quayside vista that takes in the Seine, Notre-Dame, the Eiffel Tower, and mansard roofs all in one generous sweep is enough to convince you that Paris is indeed the most beautiful city on Earth.

2 Provence and the French Riviera. In this magical part of France you'll discover scenic perched villages and charming farmer's markets, historic towns and long, luxurious beaches fronting the glittering Mediterranean—all under an azure sky.

3 Northern France. From the Normandy D-Day beaches and charming Honfleur, to the many charms of Lille, bubbly Champagne, and the delicious specialties and wines of Alsace-Lorraine, this is a region to take your time and savor as you go.

4 Southern France and Corsica. The Pyrenees' vertiginous forests, the Dordogne's prehistoric caves, Bordeaux's world-class vineyards, and the countless historic villages and cities along the way—the south harbors untold treasure. Not to mention sundrenched Corsica's wild landscapes and gorgeous beaches.

5 Belgium. Like two worlds in one, this is a land of delightful contrasts. Between Dutch-speaking Flanders and French-speaking Wallonia, you'll find romantic landscapes and villages, superb food and drink, and lively Brussels all within relatively short distances.

6 Luxembourg. One of the wealthiest nations in the world, tiny Luxembourg distills all the best of its three neighboring countries in a cosmopolitan mix of natural beauty, eye-popping chateaus, charming villages, and a sophisticated city.

7 The Netherlands. Amsterdam may have old-fashioned charm to spare, but this lively contemporary city is also a cultural hub par excellence, complete with vibrant dining, shopping, and nightlife scenes. Art lovers do not miss The Hague, and this compact country offers many coastal pleasures.

North Sea
Isle of Man
IRELAND
Dublin
Middlesbrou
Scarborough
Leeds
Kingston up
Liverpool
Manchester
Stoke
Nottingham
Birmingham
UNITED KINGDOM
Cambridge
Oxford
London
Cardiff
Bath
Dover
Exeter
Portsmouth
Plymouth
Penzance
English Channel
Flensburg
Kiel
Hamburg
Leeuwarden
Groningen
Bremen
NETHERLANDS
Hannover
Amsterdam
The Hague
Utrecht
Rotterdam
GERMANY
Brugge
Antwerpen
Brussels
Calais
Lille
BELGIUM
Cologne
Bonn
Frankfurt
Cherbourg
Dieppe
Amiens
LUXEMBOURG
Luxembourg
Le Havre
Rouen
Nürnberg
Caen
Reims
Metz
Paris
Brest
Nancy
Stuttgart
Rennes
Troyes
Strasbourg
Ulm
Le Mans
Orleans
Freiburg
Lorient
Auxerre
Mulhouse
Nantes
Tours
Dijon
Zürich
Vaduz
Bourges
Nevers
Bern
SWITZERLAND
FRANCE
Geneva
La Rochelle
Vichy
Lugano
Limoges
Lyon
ALPS
Milan
Bay of Biscay
Brive
Bordeaux
Grenoble
Turin
ITALY
Agen
Genoa
Avignon
Nimes
Monte-Carlo
San Sebasti
Toulouse
MONACO
Nice
Bilbao
Montpellier
PYRENEES
Beziers
Marseille
Toulon
Pamplona
ANDORRA
Bastia
Andorra
CORSICA
SPAIN
Mediterranean Sea
Zaragoza
Ajaccio
Barcelona
Tarragona
0
100 mi
0
100 km
Sassari
SARDINIA
1
2
3
4
5
6
7

WHAT TO EAT IN FRANCE AND THE LOW COUNTRIES

Galettes

FRENCH PASTRIES

For many, the only way to start a morning in France is with a buttery, flaky croissant. Other typical breakfast viennoiseries include the pain au chocolat, the custardy pain aux raisins, brioche with sugar or chocolate chips, and the chouquette, a small unfilled puff with sugar crystals.

CREPES AND GALETTES

The crepe and its heartier sibling, the galette, can be found in creperies all over the country. The darker galette is made with tender buckwheat, and is best paired with savory fillings. The golden *sucré crêpe* is made with a lighter batter, and best with sweeter fillings.

CANCALE OYSTERS

After the Roman invasion some 2,000 years ago, France and its 2,000 miles of coastline became the first European country to practice *l'ostréiculture* (oyster farming) on a large scale. In particular, Cancale's oyster beds produce some of the finest varieties.

CHEESE

There are more than 1,200 varieties of cheese in France, 45 of which have a Protected Designation of Origin (AOP) certification. Don't miss tangy chèvre goat cheese from the Loire Valley; opulently creamy Camembert from Normandy; earthy (and not for the faint of heart) époisses from Burgundy; and gooey Brie from the Île de France. Dutch cheeses include creamy, yellow Gouda and semi-hard Edam.

NOUVELLE CUISINE

Hands down the most influential culinary innovation of the later 20th century, nouvelle cuisine was pioneered by Lyon native son the late chef Paul Bocuse. A lighter, healthier fare, this new cuisine favors simpler recipes, the freshest possible ingredients, and quick cooking times to highlight the natural flavors of vegetables and meat. For a taste, head to his eponymous restaurant in Lyon, which is widely considered one of the greatest restaurants in the world.

PROVENÇAL ROSÉ WINE

Provence is the world's largest rosé producer, using Grenache, Cinsault, Mourvedre, and Syrah grapes, which help create that distinguished pale orange-tinted pink color. While in Provence, you'll find plenty of expensive and affordable options to sample.

BURGUNDY AND BORDEAUX RED WINES

Bordeaux produces four times as much *vin* as Burgundy and its wines are typically a blend of a variety of grapes, including Cabernet Sauvignon, Merlot, Malbec, Cabernet Franc, and Petit Verdot. Meanwhile, Burgundy wine, known for its distinctive sloping bottle, uses the single varietal terroir, like Pinot Noir and Chardonnay, and has a more acidic or mineral taste than the polished Bordeaux.

MOULES

Mussels (*moules* in French; *moulessen* in Dutch) are a Belgian staple. They are usually steamed in white wine and served with *frites*—the two are almost inseparable.

French Pastries

Moules

FRITES

So-called "French fries" actually originated in Belgium. The secret to Belgian fries (*frites* in French; *friet* in Dutch) is the potato. The *bintje* variety is most commonly used here, cut thickly and double-fried in beef tallow for a golden, crunchy outer texture.

WAFFLES

The scent of Belgian waffles invades everywhere you find tourists. Sprinkle on simple icing sugar for a classic taste, or top with any manner of heart-stopping ingredients (usually chocolate sauce and whipped cream). For an alternative, try the humble *stroopwaffel*—a delicious Dutch biscuit made with two waffle wafers sandwiching a caramel filling.

BELGIAN AND DUTCH BEER

The Trappist monks of Notre-Dame de Scourmont are some of the more prolific abbey brewers, producing the blue-, red-, and white-labeled Chimay beers that are now ubiquitous across Europe. Some of the most popular beers in the world are made in the Netherlands, including Heineken and Amstel, but also more celebrated beers like La Trappe Trappist and Grolsch.

France and the Low Countries Snapshot

Know Before You Go

BELGIUM IS NOT ALL CHOCOLATES AND BEER.

All the clichés you've heard are true: Belgium is one of the best places in the world to sip a great ale and to nibble on exquisitely tempered chocolate. But there are plenty of other local treats waiting to be discovered. Don't miss out on trying the creamy stew *waterzooi,* originally from Ghent, or the Liège specialty *boulets* (succulent meatballs, now found across Wallonia), to name but two.

BE BIKE-SAVVY IN AMSTERDAM.

As you watch the thousands of bikes gliding down Amsterdam's 400 km (249 miles) of bike paths, you may be tempted to join them. Trying to pedal with the locals can be a nerve-wracking experience, to say the least, as the Dutch like to bike fast and aggressively. Unless you're an experienced biker, consider riding in one of the parks to start or joining a bike tour to help you navigate around the native bikers. And though you may stick out, wearing a helmet helps to increase your sense of safety. Make sure you use hand signals and having a bell is a good idea. As a pedestrian, be sure to watch for bikes, too. You can easily get hit while crossing the street if not vigilant.

IN FRANCE RENTING A CAR CAN BE A GREAT IDEA.

Driving is the best option if you want to explore all those picturesque villages, but a few pointers go a long way. First, forget the SUV and rent a small car that's easy to maneuver and parallel park along tiny cobblestone streets—and be sure to specify automatic transmission when renting, unless you're fully comfortable with a manual car. France's tolls on the autoroutes can add up quickly: Paris to Nice is around €80 one-way. If you have the time, stick to the National (RN) and District (RD) roads. Generally, driving here isn't much different than driving in the States (yes, they drive on the same side of the road as us). But there's no turning right on a red light, a triangle with an X means to yield to the right at the next junction (that's the opposite in the United States), and when entering a roundabout, priority is to the left.

Planning Your Time

PARIS AND THE ÎLE DE FRANCE

You could easily spend a month in Paris and not see everything. But in a week or even a long weekend, you can start to get a good feel for all this spectacular city has to offer. Don't forget the many riches just outside Paris, from Chartres Cathedral (an easy hour-long train ride) to Monet's Giverny and the Château de Fontainebleau, there's much to see within an hour from the city.

PROVENCE AND THE FRENCH RIVIERA

There are many ways to see Provence: focus on its major cities—Marseille, Aix, Avignon—or take some time to see its spectacular countryside, savoring the Mediterranean lifestyle as you go. You can travel between the major cities by train or bus, but to explore the countryside's many charming villages a car is essential. Distances in Provence are short, so you can take in a lot in a week.

SOUTHERN FRANCE AND CORSICA

There's a lot to see here, and you can cover a lot of ground by train, but not all routes are direct. If you can rent a car you'll appreciate the flexibility. Consider starting with a city and branching out into the countryside. If you're a wine connoisseur, the scenic wine routes are a good bet—by car or by bicycle. Corsica's wild beauty is best seen by car, and if you don't drive just stay put on the beach!

BELGIUM

Many visitors fly into Brussels, but train connections on the high-speed TGV from Amsterdam, Paris, and other cities are fast, convenient, and inexpensive. Consider Brussels as a first stop, then branch out to Bruges and other towns and regions depending on your time. Brussels is a land of many contrasts: in Dutch-speaking Flanders you'll find romantic villages and in French-speaking Wallonia a picturesque countryside. Consider following a beer route to take you to places you might otherwise overlook.

THE NETHERLANDS

As a world-class cultural center brimming with sights, Amsterdam is the central attraction. But there's plenty to see outside the city, too. Train and bus networks within the country and beyond are excellent, and because The Netherlands is quite small, you can see a lot in a short time. Art lovers should not miss The Hague, but historic Rotterdam and Utrecht have their own pleasures. Seaside fishermen's villages and long, sprawling beaches offer a nice reprieve from city life, too.

LUXEMBOURG

Tiny, landlocked Luxembourg has outsized charms: from cosmopolitan Luxembourg City to a captivating countryside dotted with scenic villages. What's more, in a bid to mitigate automobile traffic, all public transport in the country is free. You can drive the country end to end in no time. But you can just as easily hop on a wine tour bus in the Moselle or join a hiking or bike-riding tour along its scenic gorges.

Great Trips

4 days in Belgium: 2 days in Brussels, with side-trips to Bruges and Ghent (or Antwerp).

5 days in the Netherlands: 2 days in Amsterdam, with day trips to Rotterdam, the windmills in Kinderdijk, and The Hague.

5 days in France: Paris (with Versailles), Honfleur, Bayeux, and Mont-St-Michel.

Big Events

Gentse Feesten, Belgium. A 10-day celebration of indulgence in mid-July, this was originally intended to curb summer drinking by workers in Ghent. However, it seems to have had the opposite effect, and includes music making, entertainment, and assorted happenings in the streets of the city, and a world-class dance music festival that lasts until the wee hours. 🌐 *gentsefeesten.stad.gent*

Open Garden Days, Amsterdam. On the third weekend in June you can visit more than 25 canal house gardens not usually accessible to the public. 🌐 *www.opentuinend-agen.nl*

Fête des Lumières, France. Every year in early December, Lyon puts on the incredible Festival of Lights, during which more than 70 light installations transform the city's streetscapes into thrilling works of art. 🌐 *www.fetedeslumieres.lyon.fr*

What To...

READ

A Food Lover's Guide To France, Patricia Wells. For lovers of food and wine.

France Today, John Ardagh. The best primer on modern France.

Flawless: Inside the Largest Diamond Heist in History, Scott Andrew Selby and Greg Campbell. A true crime thriller, set in Antwerp.

Good Beer Guide Belgium, Tim Webb. The definitive guide.

Anne Frank: The Diary of a Young Girl, Anne Frank. An essential classic.

The UnDutchables, Colin White and Laurie Boucke. A funny and honest look at Dutch culture.

WATCH

The Intouchables. A touching tale of an unlikely friendship.

Jean de Florette. A view of rural Provençal life.

Meet the Fokkens. Documentary on elderly twin Dutch prostitutes.

Turkish Delight. Paul Verhoeven's tale of a bohemian Amsterdam sculptor.

La Promesse. The tale of immigrants on the edge of Belgian society.

Man Bites Dog. A darkly funny Brussels-set mockumentary.

LISTEN TO

Serge Gainsbourg, *La Javanaise*

Jacques Dutronc, *Il est cinq heures, Paris s'éveille*

MC Solaar, *Qui Sème le Vent Récolte le Tempo*

Erik Satie, *Trois Gymnopédies*

BUY

Chocolate in Belgium, the Netherlands, and Luxembourg

Wine in France and Luxembourg

Licorice and Jenever in the Netherlands

Cheese in the Netherlands and France

Contacts

AIR

Major Airports:

Paris. Orly (ORY), Charles de Gaulle (CDG), Beauvais (BVA)

France. Lyon (LYS), Marseille (MRS), Nice (NCE), Bordeaux (BOD), Toulouse (TLS)

Belgium. Brussels Airport (BRU), Brussels South Charleroi (CRL), Antwerp International Airport (ANR)

Netherlands. Amsterdam Schipol (AMS), Rotterdam The Hague (RTM)

Luxembourg. Luxembourg (LUX), 352/24–65–24–65 www.lux-airport.lu

BOAT

Brittany Ferries. ✉ *France* 🌐 *www.brittany-ferries.com* **DFDS Seaways.** ✉ *France/Netherlands* 🌐 *www.dfdsseaways.co.uk* **P&O European Ferries.** ✉ *France/Netherlands* 🌐 *www.poferries.com* **Stena Line.** ✉ *Netherlands* 🌐 *www.stenaline.nl*

BUS

Connexxion Bus Company. ✉ *Netherlands* 🌐 *www.connexxion.nl/en* **De Lijn.** ✉ *Belgium* 🌐 *www.delijn.be* **Flixbus.** ✉ *France* 🌐 *www.flixbus.fr* **Mobiliteit.lu.** ✉ *Luxembourg* 🌐 *www.mobiliteit.lu/en* **STIB/MIVB.** ✉ *Belgium* 🌐 *www.stib.be* **TEC.** ✉ *Belgium* 🌐 *www.letec.be*

TRAIN

NS–Nederlandse Spoorwegen/Dutch Railways. ✉ *Netherlands* 🌐 *www.ns.nl* **SNCB/NMBS.** ✉ *Belgium* 🌐 *www.belgiantrain.be* **SNCF.** ✉ *France* 🌐 *www.sncf.com* **Société Nationale des Chemins de Fer Luxembourgeois (CFL).** ✉ *Luxembourg* 🌐 *www.cfl.lu* **TGV.** ✉ *France* 🌐 *en.oui.ncf/en/tgv* **Thalys.** ✉ *Belgium/France/Netherlands* 🌐 *www.thalys.com*

VISITOR INFORMATION

France Tourism. 🌐 *www.france.fr* **Amsterdam Visitor Centre.** 🌐 *www.iamsterdam.com* **Visit Brussels.** 🌐 *visit.brussels* **Visit Flanders.** 🌐 *www.visitflanders.com* **Visit Luxembourg.** 🌐 *www.visitluxembourg.com/en* **Visit Wallonia.** 🌐 *www.wallonia-belgiumtourism.co.uk* **VVV—Netherlands Board of Tourism.** 🌐 *www.vvv.nl*

Paris

If there's a problem with a trip to Paris, it's the embarrassment of riches you're confronted with. No matter which aspect of Paris you choose—touristy, historic, fashion-conscious, pretentious-bourgeois, thrifty, or the legendary bohemian, arty Paris of undying attraction—one thing is certain: you will carve out your own Paris, one that is vivid, exciting, ultimately unforgettable.

As world capitals go, Paris is surprisingly compact. The city is divided in two by the River Seine, with two islands (Île de la Cité and Île St-Louis) in the middle. Each bank of the Seine has its own personality; the Rive Droite (Right Bank), with its spacious boulevards and formal buildings, generally has a more genteel, dignified feel than the carefree and chic Rive Gauche (Left Bank), to the south. The east–west axis from Châtelet to the Arc de Triomphe, via rue de Rivoli and the Champs-Élysées, is the Right Bank's principal thoroughfare for sightseeing and shopping.

Each quartier, or neighborhood, has its own personality, which is best discovered by foot. Ultimately, your route will be marked by your preferences, your curiosity, and your energy level. You can wander for hours without getting bored—though not, perhaps, without getting lost.

But the riches of Paris do not stop at its borders. For centuries the city's influence fanned out over the farmland and forests of the Île-de-France, the region circling Paris, in the form of country chateaus and their manicured gardens. If there had not been the world-class cultural hub nearby, would Monet have retreated to his Japanese gardens at Giverny? Louis XIV, tired of treacherous aristocrats and rebellious Parisians, decamped to a swampy hunting ground, where his father had kept a modest lodge, and the rest is history—in the 17th century, the new power base was going to be Versailles. Built over 40 years, the sprawling, gilt-laden chateau was the new power base from which the Sun King's rays could radiate unfettered, keeping his friends close and potential enemies closer.

The Louvre

The World's Most Famous (and Visited) Museum

Simply put, the Louvre is the world's greatest art museum—and the largest, with 780,000 square feet of works from almost every civilization on earth. The three most popular pieces here are, of course, the *Mona Lisa*,the *Venus de Milo*, and *Winged Victory*. Beyond these must-sees, your best bet is to focus on whatever interests you the most, from 5th-century sculpture to 17th-century paintings to the newest addition, the 30,000-square-foot Arts of Islam wing, one of the world's largest collections of Islamic art. Pick up an excellent color-coded map at the information desk. To save time, buy your ticket online, and avoid the crowds at the Pyramide by entering through the Carrousel du Louvre. The shortest lines tend to be in the morning and on Wednesday and Friday night, when the museum is open late.

Don't Miss

The Louvre has one of the world's best Egyptian collections, while the Islamic wing contains 30,000 square feet of treasures, and the Galerie d'Apollon houses the French crown jewels.

Getting Here

The best way to get to the Louvre is on foot or by metro. Enter the Louvre's central Place du Carousel from the Rue de Rivoli, the Quai François Mitterand on the Seine side, or through the Tuileries Gardens. By metro, get off at the Palais-Royal–Musée de Louvre metro stop to arrive underground at the Carousel du Louvre entrance. The Louvre–Rivoli metro stop puts you outside the building's eastern edge.

✉ *Palais du Louvre, Rue de Rivoli* ☎ *01–40–20– 53–17* 🌐 *www.louvre.fr* 🎫 *€15 or €17 online (includes 48-hr entry to Musée Eugène Delacroix)* 🕐 *Closed Tues. Fri. open til 9:45 pm*

Eiffel Tower

The Most Iconic Landmark of Paris

The Eiffel Tower is to Paris what the Statue of Liberty is to New York and what Big Ben is to London: the ultimate civic emblem. French engineer Gustave Eiffel spent two years working to erect this monument for the World Exhibition of 1889. Because its colossal bulk exudes a feeling of mighty permanence, you may have trouble believing that it nearly became 7,000 tons of scrap metal (the 1,063-foot *tour* contains 12,000 pieces of metal and 2,500,000 rivets) when its concession expired in 1909. You can stride up the stairs as far as the second floor, but if you want to go to the top you'll have to hop on an elevator. (Be sure to take a close look at the fantastic ironwork.) You can skirt the crushing lines by reserving your ticket online, booking a tour, or reserving a table at one of the two restaurants.

Don't Miss

The Eiffel Tower is most breathtaking at night, when 20,000 glittering lights perform a sparkling display five minutes every hour on the hour until 1 am.

Restaurants

Madame Brasserie (open for breakfast, lunch, and dinner) or the gastronomic Jules Verne are pricey, but the views—needless to say—are spectacular.

Getting Here

The closest metro stops are Trocadéro, Bir-Hakeim, École Militaire, or the RER stop Champ de Mars–Tour Eiffel.

✉ *Quai Branly, 7e, Eiffel Tower* 🌐 *www.toureiffel.paris* ⏲ *Stairs close at 6 pm in off-season (Oct.–June). Closed last 2 wks in Jan. for annual maintenance* 🎫 *By elevator from €18; by stairs from €11*

The Marais

The City's Epicenter of Cool

In the Marais (which literally means "swamp") you'll notice the vestiges of times past everywhere, and it's the juxtaposition of ancient and modern, culture and commercialism that creates the neighborhood's enormous appeal. King Henry II and Queen Catherine de Medici held court at the Place des Vosges, still Paris's most elegant square. In modern times, the area hosted the city's first gay bar. Its streets are still an epicenter of culture and artistic life, with dozens of art galleries and some of the city's most fascinating museums. Not to mention the shopping, with everything from hipster boutiques and bargain vintage shops to the reigning names in haute-couture. You'll also find chic cafés and coffee shops, fantastic food stalls, fancy restaurants, stylish wine bars, and romantic boutique hotels.

Don't Miss

If it has to do with Parisian history, you'll find it at the Musée Carnavalet (✉ *16 rue des Francs-Bourgeois* 🌐 *www.carnavalet.paris.fr* 🚇 *St-Paul*). Spruced up after a four-year renovation. And it's all free. The museum's sculpted garden at 16 rue des Francs-Bourgeois is open from April to the end of October.

Eat Here

Breizh Café. Eating a crepe in Paris might seem clichéd, until you venture into this modern offshoot of a Breton creperie that uses the finest local ingredients. $ *Average main: €12* ✉ *109 rue Vieille du Temple* ☎ *01–42–72–13–77* 🌐 *www.breizhcafe.com* ⏲ *Closed Aug.* 🚇 *St-Sébastien–Froissart*

Getting Here

The closest metros are Saint-Paul and Hotel de Ville, both on metro line no. 1. It's a quick walk from the Bastille stop or from Chemin Vert, too.

Avenue des Champs-Élysées

The Most Famous Avenue in Paris

Marcel Proust lovingly described the genteel elegance of the storied Champs-Élysées (pronounced "chahnz-eleezay," with an "n" sound instead of "m," and no "p") during its Belle Époque heyday, when its cobblestones resounded with the clatter of horses and carriages. Today, despite unrelenting traffic and the intrusion of chain stores and fast-food franchises, the avenue still sparkles. There's always something happening here: stores are open late (and many are open on Sunday, a rarity in Paris); nightclubs remain top destinations (especially for jet-setters); and cafés offer prime people-watching, though you'll pay for the privilege—after all, this is Europe's most expensive piece of real estate. By 2024, Paris plans to transform the avenue, drastically reducing automobile traffic in favor of expanded pedestrian walkways and hundreds of new trees.

Don't Miss

Inspired by Rome's Arch of Titus, the colossal **Arc de Triomphe**, 164-foot triumphal arch, was ordered by Napoléon to celebrate his military successes. The Arc de Triomphe is notable for magnificent sculptures by François Rude. Climb the stairs to the top of the arch to see the star effect of the 12 radiating avenues and the vista down the Champs-Élysées toward Place de la Concorde and the distant Musée du Louvre. ✉ *Pl. Charles-de-Gaulle, Champs Élysées* 🌐 *www.paris-arc-de-triomphe.fr* 🎫 *€13*

Getting Here

You can arrive at the Étoile metro stop on any number of metros, or the faster RER. Be sure to follow the exit marked "Champs-Élysées" or you risk circling the entire ring road. You can also start at Place de la Concord (metro Concorde, line nos. 1, 8, 12) and walk up from there. The George V metro stop drops you off roughly in the middle.

St-Germain-des-Prés

The Classic Paris Neighborhood

If you had to choose the most classically Parisian neighborhood, this would be it. St-Germain-des-Prés has it all: genteel blocks lined with upscale art galleries, storied cafés, designer boutiques, atmospheric restaurants, and a fine selection of museums. Cast your eyes upward after dark and you may spy a frescoed ceiling in a tony apartment. The epicenter of Paris's Bohemian Left Bank, this is where writers, artists, and designers wrote, argued, and created in the famous cafés of the Boulevard Saint-Germain—Cafés Flore, Deux Magots, Lipp—and the artists' studios around the famous Montmartre cemetery (where some of them repose).

Don't Miss

Musée d'Orsay. This gorgeously renovated Belle Époque train station displays a world-famous collection of Impressionist and Postimpressionist paintings on three floors, including Monet's series on the cathedral at Rouen and samples of his water lilies. ✉ *1 rue de la Légion d'Honneur, St-Germain-des-Prés* 🌐 *www.musee-orsay.fr* 🎫 *€14* 🕓 *Closed Mon.*

Getting Here

The St-Germain neighborhood is in the 6e arrondissement and a bit of the 7e. To get to the heart of this area, take the Line 4 metro to St-Germain-des-Prés. For shopping, use this station or St-Sulpice. From either of those stops, it's a short walk to the Jardin du Luxembourg, or take the RER B line to the Luxembourg station. For the Musée d'Orsay, take the Line 12 metro to Solferino or the RER C line to the Musée d'Orsay.

Sainte-Chapelle

A Glittering Gothic Jewel

Built by the obsessively pious Louis IX (1226–70), St-Chapelle is a Gothic jewel, constructed over seven years at phenomenal expense, is home to the oldest stained-glass windows in Paris. It was originally built to house the Crown of Thorns, which was later moved to Notre Dame (and survived the fire there). The chapel is essentially an enormous magic lantern illuminating 1,130 figures from the Bible. Come on a sunny day to appreciate the full effect of the light filtering through all of that glorious stained glass, though sunset is the optimal time to see the rose window.

Don't Miss

The Seine's famous islands, Île de la Cité and Île St-Louis, are linked to the banks of the Seine by a series of bridges, offering postcard-worthy views all around. Although mighty Notre-Dame was severely damaged by a fire, it is still standing; farther east, the atmospheric Île St-Louis is dotted with charming hotels, cozy restaurants, small specialty shops, and Paris's most famous *glacier* (ice-cream maker), Bertillon. Among the rare survivors is the Conciergerie, the cavernous former prison where Marie-Antoinette and other victims of the French Revolution spent their final days.

Getting Here

Île de la Cité and Île St-Louis are in the 1er and 4e arrondissements (Boulevard du Palais is the dividing line between the 1er and 4e arrondissements on Île de la Cité). If you're too far away to get here on foot, take the metro to St-Michel station or Cité.

✉ *4 bd. du Palais, Île de la Cité* 🌐 *www.sainte-chapelle.fr* 🎫 *€12; €19 with the Conciergerie*

Cathédrale Notre-Dame de Paris

The Heart of France

Looming above Place du Parvis, this Gothic sanctuary is the symbolic heart of Paris and, for many, of France itself, now more than ever. A heart-breaking 2019 fire almost destroyed the entire cathedral. The roof was devastated, and the 300-foot spire collapsed, but after the fire was extinguished, the structure was deemed sound, and most of the priceless relics inside survived, including the famed rose windows and the "Crown of Thorns" said to have been worn by Jesus Christ. France vowed to rebuild the cathedral before the 2024 Paris Olympics, and the project seems to be on schedule.

Don't Miss

The Pont Neuf, which crosses the Seine at the tip of the Isle de la Cité, is not only one of the most famous bridges in Paris but also the city's oldest—and looks out onto Place Dauphine, the grand public square at the end of the island, as well as the Square du Vert Galant, the public garden on the island's tip.

Best Place to Eat

Berthillon. While it's a treat to get a boule on the go, at Bertillon's salon de thé you can order any combination of their more than 80 all-natural flavors—made simply with cream, sugar and fruit, nuts, chocolate, and other delights according to the season—and topped with a billowing crown of crème Chantilly. ✉ *31 rue St-Louis-en-l'Île, Île Saint-Louis* 🌐 *www.berthillon.fr* 🕓 *Closed Mon. and Tues.* 🚇 *Pont-Marie*

Getting Here

The closest metro stop is Cité, from which it is a short stroll to the cathedral.

✉ *6 parvis Notre-Dame–Pl. Jean-Paul II, Île de la Cité* ☎ *01–42–34–56–10* 🌐 *www.notredamedeparis.fr*

Versailles

An Opulent Jewel in the French Crown

A two-century spree of indulgence by the consecutive reigns of three French kings produced two of the world's most historic landmarks: gloriously, the Palace of Versailles and, momentously, the French Revolution. The history and glory of both are encapsulated in the historic city of Versailles, where the world's most famous palace is less a monument than a world unto itself. Versailles is indisputably the king of palaces. The end result of countless francs, 40 years, and 36,000 laborers, it was Louis XIV's monument to himself—the Sun King. Construction of the sprawling palace and gardens, which Louis personally and meticulously oversaw, started in 1661 and took 40 years to complete.

Don't Miss

Versailles's most famous getaway, the **Hameau de la Reine**, was added under the reign of Louis XVI at the request of his relentlessly scrutinized wife, Marie-Antoinette. Seeking to create a simpler "country" life away from the court's endless intrigues, between 1783 and 1787, the queen had her own rustic hamlet built in the image of a charming Normandy village, complete with a mill and dairy, roving livestock, and delightfully natural gardens.

Getting Here

Versailles has three train stations, but its Rive Gauche gare—on the RER-C line from Paris, with trains departing from Austerlitz, St-Michel, Invalides, and Champ-de-Mars—provides the easiest access and puts you within a five-minute walk of the chateau (45 minutes, €3.65).

Pl. d'Armes,Versailles www.chateauversailles.fr Closed Mon. €18, all-attractions pass, €20, Hameau de la Reine, €12, park free (weekend fountain show €10, Apr.–Oct.) €12; €17 with joint ticket to Conciergerie

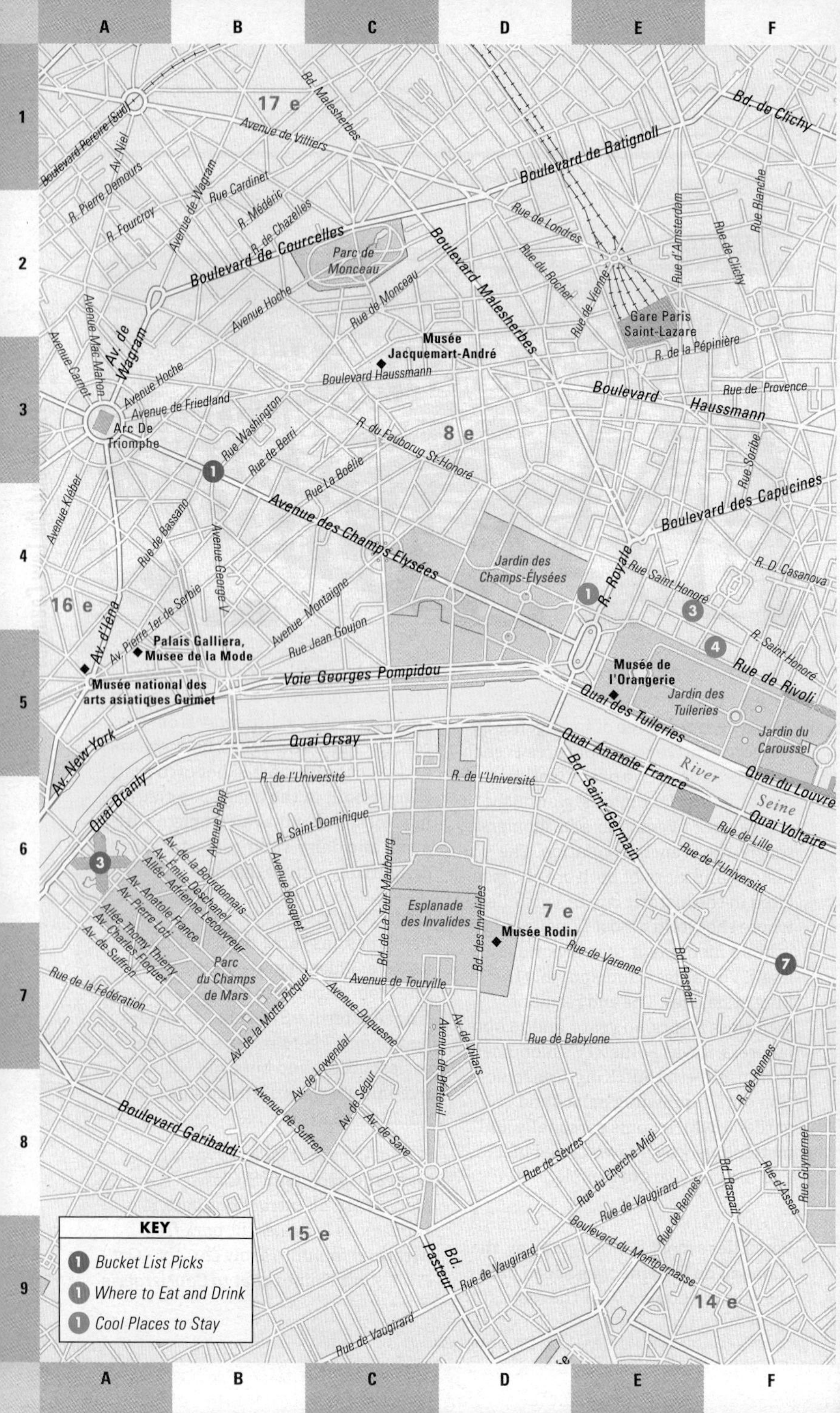

A
B
C
D
E
F
1
2
3
4
5
6
7
8
9
17 e
8 e
16 e
7 e
15 e
14 e
Bd. de Clichy
Boulevard de Batignoll
Boulevard Pereire (Sud)
Av. Niel
R. Pierre Demours
Avenue de Villiers
Bd. Malesherbes
Rue Cardinet
R. Médéric
R. Fourcroy
Avenue de Wagram
R. de Chazelles
Boulevard de Courcelles
Parc de Monceau
Rue de Londres
Rue du Rocher
Rue de Vienne
Rue d'Amsterdam
Rue de Clichy
Rue Blanche
Boulevard Malesherbes
Gare Paris Saint-Lazare
R. de la Pépinière
Avenue Mac Mahon
Avenue Carnot
Av. de Wagram
Avenue Hoche
Rue de Monceau
Musée Jacquemart-André
Boulevard Haussmann
Boulevard Haussmann
Rue de Provence
Avenue de Friedland
Arc De Triomphe
Rue Washington
Rue de Berri
R. du Faubourg St-Honoré
Rue Scribe
Rue La Boëtie
Avenue des Champs Elysées
Boulevard des Capucines
Avenue Kléber
Rue de Bassano
Avenue George V
Jardin des Champs-Élysées
R. Royale
Rue Saint Honoré
R. D. Casanova
Av. Pierre 1er de Serbie
Avenue Montaigne
Rue Jean Goujon
R. Saint Honoré
Av. d'Iéna
Palais Galliera, Musee de la Mode
Musée national des arts asiatiques Guimet
Voie Georges Pompidou
Musée de l'Orangerie
Rue de Rivoli
Quai des Tuileries
Jardin des Tuileries
Jardin du Carousel
Av. New York
Quai Orsay
Quai Anatole France
River Seine
Quai du Louvre
Quai Voltaire
Quai Branly
R. de l'Université
R. de l'Université
Bd. Saint-Germain
Rue de Lille
Rue de l'Université
R. Saint Dominique
Avenue Rapp
Av. de la Bourdonnais
Av. Émile Deschanel
Allée Adrienne Lecouvreur
Av. Anatole France
Av. Pierre Loti
Allée Thomy Thierry
Av. Charles Floquet
Av. de Suffren
Avenue Bosquet
Bd. de La Tour Maubourg
Esplanade des Invalides
Bd. des Invalides
Musée Rodin
Rue de Varenne
Bd. Raspail
Rue de la Fédération
Parc du Champs de Mars
Av. de la Motte Picquet
Avenue de Tourville
Avenue Duquesne
Av. de Villars
Avenue de Breteuil
Rue de Babylone
Av. de Lowendal
Avenue de Suffren
Av. de Ségur
Av. de Saxe
R. de Rennes
Boulevard Garibaldi
Rue de Sèvres
Rue du Cherche Midi
Rue de Vaugirard
Rue de Rennes
Bd. Raspail
Rue d'Assas
Rue Guynemer
Boulevard du Montparnasse
Bd. Pasteur
Rue de Vaugirard
Rue de Vaugirard
KEY
Bucket List Picks
Where to Eat and Drink
Cool Places to Stay

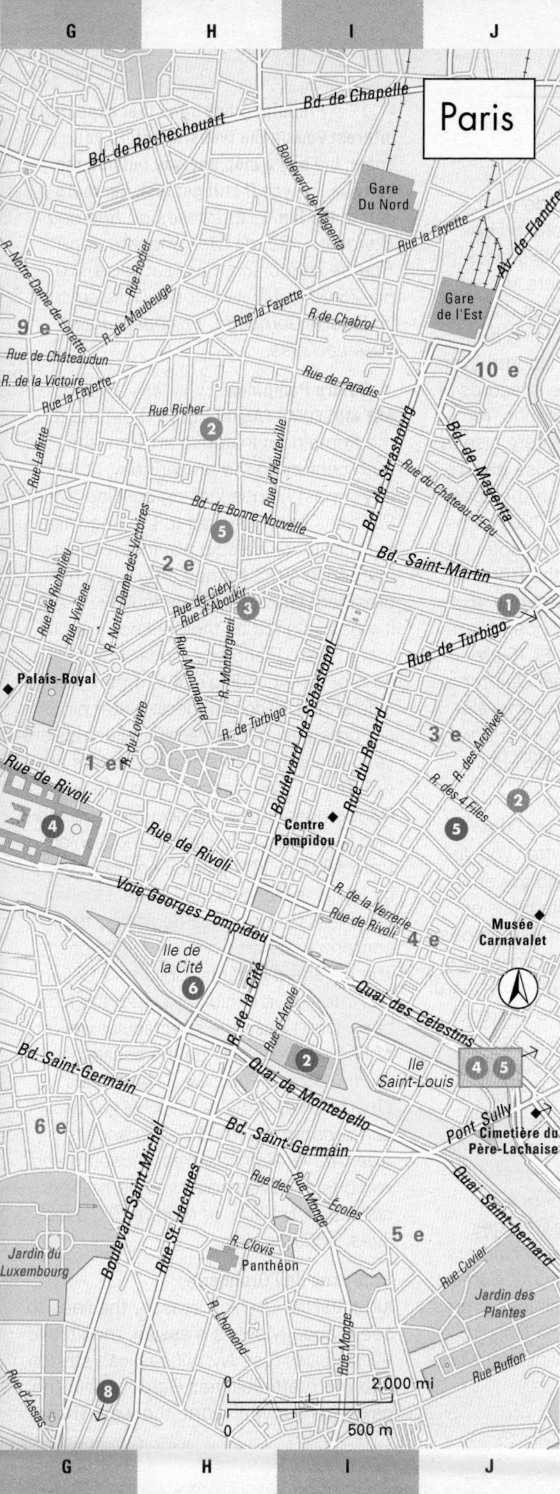

Bucket List Picks

1. Avenue des Champs-Élysées B3
2. Cathédrale Notre-Dame de Paris.............. I7
3. Eiffel Tower......................... A6
4. The Louvre.......................... G5
5. The Marais J6
6. Sainte Chapelle H7
7. St-Germain-des-Prés F7
8. Versailles G9

Where to Eat and Drink

1. Astier.................................. J4
2. Breizh Café J5
3. Frenchie H4
4. Le Bistrot Paul Bert................ J7
5. Septime J7

Cool Places to Stay

1. Hôtel de Crillon..................... E4
2. Hôtel de Nell H3
3. Hôtel du Continent................. E4
4. Hôtel Le Meurice F5
5. The Hoxton Paris H4

When in Paris

★ Musée Carnavalet

HISTORY MUSEUM | If it has to do with Parisian history, it's here. Spruced up after a four-year renovation, this fascinating hodgepodge of artifacts and art ranges from prehistoric canoes used by the Parisii tribes to the cork-lined bedroom where Marcel Proust labored over his evocative novels. Thanks to scores of paintings, drawings, photographs, furniture, and scale models, nowhere else in Paris can you get such a precise picture of the city's evolution through the ages. The museum fills more than 100 rooms in two adjacent mansions, the Hôtel Le Peletier de St-Fargeau and the Hôtel Carnavalet. The sculpted garden at 16 rue des Francs-Bourgeois is open from April to the end of October. ✉ *16 rue des Francs-Bourgeois, 4e, Marais Quarter* ☎ *01–44–59–58–58* 🌐 *www.carnavalet.paris.fr* 🎫 *Free; around €7 for temporary exhibitions* ⏲ *Closed Mon.* Ⓜ *St-Paul.*

★ Cimetière du Père-Lachaise

CEMETERY | Bring a red rose for "the Little Sparrow" Edith Piaf when you visit the cobblestone avenues and towering trees that make this 118-acre oasis of green perhaps the world's most famous cemetery. Two of the biggest draws are Jim Morrison's grave (with its own guard) and the life-size bronze figure of French journalist Victor Noir, whose alleged fertility-enhancing power accounts for the patches rubbed smooth by hopeful hands. Other significant grave sites include those of writers Colette, Marcel Proust, Gertrude Stein, and Oscar Wilde; actress Sarah Bernhardt; opera singer Maria Callas; composers Georges Bizet and Frédéric Chopin; and painters including Georges-Pierre Seurat, Camille Pissaro, Jean-Auguste-Dominique Ingres, Jacques-Louis David, Eugène Delacroix, Amedeo Clemente Modigliani, and Max Ernst.

■ TIP→ Pinpoint grave sites that especially interest you on the website before you come, but buy a map anyway outside the entrances—you'll still get lost, but that's part of the fun. ✉ *Entrances on Rue des Rondeaux, Bd. de Ménilmontant, and Rue de la Réunion, Père Lachaise* ☎ *01–55–25–82–10* 🌐 *www.pere-lachaise.com* 🎫 *Free* Ⓜ *Gambetta, Philippe-Auguste, Père-Lachaise.*

★ Centre Pompidou

ART MUSEUM | FAMILY | Love it or hate it, the Pompidou, featuring art from the 20th century to the present day, is the city's most unique-looking building. Most Parisians have warmed to the Lego-like exterior that caused a scandal when it opened in 1977. Named after French president Georges Pompidou (1911–74), it was designed by then-unknown architects Renzo Piano and Richard Rogers, who put the building's guts on the outside and color-coded them: water pipes are green, air ducts are blue, electrics are yellow, and elevators and escalators are red. The Musée National d'Art Moderne (Modern Art Museum) occupies the top two levels. Level 5 displays modern art from 1905 to 1960, including major works by Matisse, Modigliani, Marcel Duchamp, and Picasso. Level 4 is dedicated to contemporary art from the 1960s on. The Galerie d'Enfants (Children's Gallery) has interactive exhibits to keep the kids busy. Don't miss the spectacular views of Paris on your way up the escalator. ✉ *Pl. Georges-Pompidou, 4e, Marais Quarter* ☎ *01–44–78–12–33* 🌐 *www.centrepompidou.fr* 🎫 *Center access free, Atelier Brancusi free, museum and exhibits €17 (free access to permanent collection 1st Sun. of month)* ⏲ *Closed Tues.* Ⓜ *Rambuteau.*

★ Musée de l'Orangerie

ART MUSEUM | In high season, the lines to see Claude Monet's massive, meditative *Water Lilies* (*Les Nymphéas*) can stretch into the pretty Tuileries Gardens, but the paintings are well worth the wait. These works, displayed in two curved galleries designed in 1914 by the master himself, are the highlight of the Orangerie's small but excellent collection, which also features early-20th-century paintings by other Impressionist masters like Renoir, Cézanne, and Matisse. Temporary exhibitions are typically quirky and well-curated. Originally built in 1852 to shelter orange trees, the long rectangular building, a twin of the Jeu de Paume across the garden, includes a portion of the city's 16th-century wall. Timed entrances, easily bookable online, are strongly recommended. ✉ *Jardin des Tuileries at Pl. de la Concorde, Louvre* ☎ *01–44–77–80–07* 🌐 *www.musee-orangerie.fr* 🎫 *€12.50* 🕐 *Closed Tues.* Ⓜ *Concorde.*

★ Musée Jacquemart-André

ART MUSEUM | Perhaps the city's best small museum, the opulent Musée Jacquemart-André is home to a huge collection of art and furnishings lovingly assembled in the late 19th century by banking heir Edouard André and his artist wife, Nélie Jacquemart. Their collection includes Renaissance works, as well as works from French painters Fragonard, Jacques-Louis David, and François Boucher, plus Dutch masters Van Dyke and Rembrandt. The Belle Époque mansion itself is a major attraction, with highlights including an elegant ballroom and a winter garden that was the wonder of its day. Don't forget to pick up the free audioguide in English, and do inquire about the current temporary exhibition, which is usually top-notch. Plan on a Sunday visit and enjoy the popular brunch (€29.50) in the café from 11 am to 2:30 pm. Reservations are not accepted, so come early or late to avoid waiting in line. ✉ *158 bd. Haussmann, 8e, Grands Boulevards* ☎ *01–45–62–11–59* 🌐 *www.musee-jacquemart-andre.com* 🎫 *€12* Ⓜ *St-Philippe du Roule, Miromesnil.*

★ Musée Rodin

ART MUSEUM | **FAMILY** | Auguste Rodin (1840–1917) briefly made his home and studio in the Hôtel Biron, a magnificent 18th-century mansion that now houses a museum dedicated to his work. The front garden is dominated by *The Gates of Hell* (circa 1880), which Rodin, who was inspired by the monumental bronze doors of the Italian Renaissance churches, spent more than 30 years sculpting in stories from Dante's *Divine Comedy.* Inside the museum, look for *The Bronze Age,* inspired by the sculptures of Michelangelo. There's also a room of works by Camille Claudel (1864–1943), Rodin's student and longtime mistress. An English audioguide (€6) is available for the permanent collection and for temporary exhibitions. L'Augustine serves meals and snacks in the shade of the garden's linden trees. **TIP→ Skip the line by buying a ticket online.** ✉ *77 rue de Varenne, 7e, Eiffel Tower* ☎ *01–44–18–61–10* 🌐 *www.musee-rodin.fr* 🎫 *€13 (free 1st Sun. of month)* 🕐 *Closed Mon.* Ⓜ *Varenne.*

★ Palais-Royal

OTHER ATTRACTION | This truly Parisian garden is enclosed within the former home of Cardinal Richelieu (1585–1642). The 400-year-old arcades now house boutiques and one of the city's oldest restaurants, the haute-cuisine Le Grand Véfour, where brass plaques recall former regulars like Napoléon and Victor Hugo. Built in 1629, the *palais* became royal when Richelieu bequeathed it to Louis XIII. Other famous residents include Jean Cocteau and Colette, who wrote of her pleasurable "country" view of the *province à Paris.* It was also here, two days before the Bastille was stormed in 1789, that Camille Desmoulins gave an impassioned speech sowing the seeds of Revolution. Today, the garden often hosts giant temporary art installations sponsored by another tenant, the Ministry of Culture. The courtyard off Place Colette is outfitted with an eye-catching collection of squat black-and-white columns created in 1986 by artist Daniel Buren. ✉ *Pl. du Palais-Royal, Louvre* Ⓜ *Palais-Royal–Louvre.*

Where to Eat and Drink

Astier

$$$ | BISTRO | FAMILY | There are three good reasons to go to Astier: the generous cheese platter plunked on your table atop a help-yourself wicker tray, the exceptional wine cellar with bottles dating back to the 1970s, and the French bistro fare (even if portions seem to have diminished over the years). Dishes like marinated herring with warm potato salad, sausage with lentils, and baba au rhum are classics on the frequently changing set menu, which includes a selection of no less than 20 cheeses. **Known for:** same-day reservations possible; traditional atmosphere; excellent choice for authentic French cooking. $ *Average main: €29* ✉ *44 rue Jean-Pierre Timbaud, 11e, République* ☎ *01–43–57–16–35* 🌐 *www.restaurant-astier.com* Ⓜ *Parmentier.*

★ Breizh Café

$ | FRENCH | FAMILY | Eating a crêpe in Paris might seem clichéd, until you venture into this modern offshoot of a Breton crêperie. The plain, pale-wood decor is refreshing, but what really makes the difference are the ingredients—farmers' eggs, unpasteurized Gruyère, shiitake mushrooms, Valrhona chocolate, homemade caramel, and extraordinary butter from a Breton dairy farmer. **Known for:** some of the best crêpes in Paris; adventurous ingredients; Cancale oysters on the half shell. $ *Average main: €12* ✉ *109 rue Vieille du Temple, 3e, Marais Quarter* ☎ *01–42–72–13–77* 🌐 *www.breizhcafe.com* ⏲ *Closed Aug.* Ⓜ *St-Sébastien–Froissart.*

★ Frenchie

$$$$ | BISTRO | Set in a brick-and-stone-walled building on a pedestrian street near Rue Montorgueil, Frenchie has quickly become one of the most hard-to-book bistros in town, with tables booked months in advance, despite two seatings each evening. This success is due to the good-value, €140 five-course dinner menu (prix fixe only); boldly flavored dishes such as calamari gazpacho with squash blossoms or melt-in-the-mouth braised lamb with roasted eggplant and spinach are excellent options. **Known for:** casual laid-back atmosphere that belies the ultrasophisticated dishes; extensive and original wine list; graciously accommodating to vegetarians. $ *Average main: €40* ✉ *5 rue du Nil, 2e, Grands Boulevards* ☎ *01–40–39–96–19* 🌐 *www.frenchie-restaurant.com* ⏲ *Closed weekends, 2 wks in Aug., and 10 days at Christmas. No lunch* Ⓜ *Sentier.*

★ Le Bistrot Paul Bert

$$$ | BISTRO | The Paul Bert delivers everything you could want from a traditional Paris bistro (faded 1930s decor, thick steak with real frites, and good value), so it's no wonder its two dining rooms fill every night with a cosmopolitan crowd. The impressively stocked wine cellar helps, as does the heaping cheese cart, the laid-back yet efficient staff, and hearty dishes such as monkfish with white beans and duck with pears. **Known for:** excellent, and abundant, cheese trolley; delicious dessert soufflés; sidewalk seating in summer. $ *Average main: €25* ✉ *18 rue Paul Bert, 11e, Charonne* ☎ *01–43–72–24–01* 🌐 *www.bistrotpaulbert.fr* ⏲ *Closed Sun. and Mon.* Ⓜ *Rue des Boulets.*

★ Septime

$$$ | BISTRO | With amazing food and a convivial, unpretentious atmosphere, Septime has become one of the hottest tables in town. Seasonal ingredients, inventive pairings, and excellent natural wines bring in diners ready for exciting and sophisticated dishes like creamy gnochetti in an orange-rind-flecked Gouda sauce sprinkled with coriander flowers. **Known for:** exceptional Parisian bistro; one Michelin star; reservations needed far in advance. $ *Average main: €32* ✉ *80 rue de Charonne, 11e, Charonne* ☎ *01–43–67–38–29* 🌐 *www.*

septime-charonne.fr Ⓒ *Closed weekends* Ⓜ *Ledru Rollin, Charonne.*

Cool Places to Stay

★ Hôtel de Crillon

$$$$ | **HOTEL** | One of the city's most historic properties reopened in 2017 after a four-year renovation and is now more sumptuous and majestic than ever. **Pros:** "Grands Appartements" designed by Karl Lagerfeld; well-equipped gym with personal trainers available on request; beautiful bar with a mile-long Champagne list. **Cons:** small pool with tough-to-find changing rooms; extra beds not available in smaller rooms; very expensive. Ⓢ *Rooms from: €1800* ✉ *10 pl. de la Concorde, Louvre* ☎ *01–44–71–15–00* 🌐 *www.rosewoodhotels.com* *124 rooms* 🍽 *No Meals* Ⓜ *Concorde.*

★ Hôtel de Nell

$$$ | **HOTEL** | Tucked in a picturesque corner of a chic, up-and-coming neighborhood ripe for exploration, this serenely beautiful hotel offers contemporary luxury with clean lines and uncluttered spaces designed by French starchitect Jean-Michelle Wilmotte. **Pros:** good dining and bar on premises; interesting neighborhood to explore; beautiful rooms. **Cons:** area deserted at night; far from the major Paris attractions; lacks a spa. Ⓢ *Rooms from: €351* ✉ *9 rue du Conservatoire, Grands Boulevards* ☎ *01–44–83–83–60* 🌐 *www.hoteldenell.com* *33 rooms* 🍽 *No Meals* Ⓜ *Bonne Nouvelle.*

★ Hôtel du Continent

$ | **HOTEL** | You'd be hard-pressed to find a budget hotel this stylish anywhere in Paris, let alone in an upscale neighborhood close to many of the city's top attractions. **Pros:** very friendly staff; all modern amenities; prime Parisian location just steps from Rue St-Honoré, arguably the city's best shopping street. **Cons:** no lobby; tiny bathrooms; bold decor not for everyone. Ⓢ *Rooms from: €159* ✉ *30 rue du Mont-Thabor, Louvre* ☎ *01–42–60–75–32* 🌐 *www.hotelcontinent.com* *25 rooms* 🍽 *No Meals* Ⓜ *Concorde, Tuileries.*

★ Hôtel Le Meurice

$$$$ | **HOTEL** | **FAMILY** | Since 1835, Paris's first palace hotel has welcomed royalty and celebrities from the Duchess of Windsor to Salvador Dalí and continues to enchant with service, style, and views. **Pros:** stunning art and architecture; views over the Tuileries gardens; Michelin-starred dining. **Cons:** some amenities lacking like in-room coffee machine; front-desk service at times inattentive; very expensive. Ⓢ *Rooms from: €1845* ✉ *228 rue de Rivoli, Louvre* ☎ *01–44–58–10–09* 🌐 *www.dorchestercollection.com* *208 rooms* 🍽 *No Meals* Ⓜ *Tuileries, Concorde.*

The Hoxton Paris

$$ | **HOTEL** | In 2017, the urban-chic trendsetting Hoxton brand transformed an 18th-century mansion in Paris's up-and-coming Sentier district into this hip hostelry with a chic restaurant, three cocktail bars—including the charming Jacques Bar tucked away on the second floor—and a welcoming community vibe. **Pros:** cool neighborhood with lots to explore; historic mansion setting; memorable bar scene. **Cons:** off-the-radar neighborhood not for everyone; restaurant is just average; the most affordable rooms have very few frills. Ⓢ *Rooms from: €345* ✉ *30–32 rue du Sentier, Grands Boulevards* ☎ *01–85–65–75–00* 🌐 *www.thehoxton.com* *172 rooms* 🍽 *Free Breakfast* Ⓜ *Grands Boulevards, Bonne Nouvelle.*

Northern France

Northern France, with its medieval towns, rugged coastline, historic sights, and world famous vineyards, is rich in both culture and beauty; the diversity across its regions contributes to its appeal.

To the west, the Loire Valley is a fairy-tale realm par excellence, studded with storybook villages and the famous *châteaux de la Loire*. It's also a great wine-producing region, with 60 appelations producing some of the best-known white wines in France.

Normandy sprawls across France's northwestern corner where, due to its geographic position, the region is blessed with a stunning natural beauty that once inspired Maupassant and Monet. The latter's garden in Giverny is still a major draw for tourists, but Mont-St-Michel is among the most-visited sights in France.

In Brittany, wherever you wander you'll hear the primal pulse of Celtic music that tells you that you are in the land of the Bretons. Burgundy, in the heart of northern France, is wine country.

Producing a rarefied concentration of what many consider the world's greatest wines and harboring a sigh-worthy collection of magnificent Romanesque abbeys, Burgundy hardly needs to be beautiful—but it is. Its green-hedgerow countryside, medieval villages, and stellar vineyards deserve to be rolled on the palate and savored.

Few drinks in the world pull on the imagination quite like Champagne, yet surprisingly few tourists visit the pretty vineyards of Reims in the Champagne region. The region's reputation as a bit of a backwater, halfway between Paris and Luxembourg, shifted with the arrival of the TGV line serving eastern France and Germany, and the UNESCO World Heritage status awarded to the vineyards, cellars, and sales houses in 2015. But the region is also rich in Gothic architecture, and no fewer than 10 Gothic cathedrals dot the region.

On the eastern border only the Rhine separates Germany from Alsace-Lorraine, a region that often looks—and even sounds—German. But at its heart, just to prove how deceptive appearances can be, it is passionately French. That Strasbourg, which is famous for its German-style Christmas markets, was the birthplace of the national anthem ("La Marseillaise") illustrates how Alsace and Lorraine are among the most intensely French of all France's provinces.

Monet's Garden, Giverny

The Most Famous Garden in France

The small village of Giverny (pronounced "jee-vair-knee"), just beyond the Epte River, which marks the boundary of the Île-de-France, has become a place of pilgrimage for art lovers. It was here that Claude Monet lived for 43 years, until his death at the age of 86 in 1926. Although his house is now prized by connoisseurs of 19th-century interior decoration, it's his garden, with its Japanese-inspired water-lily pond and bridge, that remains the high point for many—a 5-acre, three-dimensional Impressionist painting you can stroll around at leisure. The garden—planted with nearly 100,000 annuals and even more perennials—is a place of wonder. No matter that about 500,000 visitors troop through each year; they seem to fade in the presence of beautiful roses, carnations, lady's slipper, tulips, irises, hollyhocks, poppies, daisies, nasturtiums, larkspur, azaleas, and more.

Don't Miss

Although the gardens are most beautiful in spring, Monet's famous water lilies—the ones he painted to much acclaim—bloom in the latter part of July and the first weeks of August.

Getting Here

Frequent main-line trains connect Paris's Gare St-Lazare with Vernon (50 minutes); you can then cover the remaining 10 km (6 miles) to Giverny by taxi, bus, or bike (the last of these can be rented at the café opposite Vernon station). April through October, shuttle buses meet trains daily and whisk passengers to Giverny (20 minutes) for €10.

⊠ 84 rue Claude Monet, Giverny ☎ 02–32–51–28–21 🌐 www.fondation-monet.com 🎫 €11 ⏲ Closed Nov.–late Mar.

Lille

The Quintessential Flemish City

Lille blends history with thriving contemporary culture. Born from the ancient marshes that gave its name, Lille is the 10th-largest city in France and sports a distinct Flemish flavor, thanks to its close proximity to Belgium. Devastated during the two World Wars, Lille suffered further setbacks from the decline of regional coal, mining, and textile industries. But there's been a revival thanks to the opening of the Channel Tunnel and the arrival of the Eurostar train linking Lille with Paris (1 hour), London (1½ hours), and Brussels (35 minutes). Extensive urban renovation has added parks, shopping areas, art museums, restaurants, and a concert hall.

Don't Miss

Vieille Bourse. Lille's finest efforts in architecture can be witnessed at the Old Stock Exchange in the heart of the old city. Built in the mid-17th century, the building rose in grand fashion, adopting a Flemish Renaissance design laden with elaborate reliefs, cherubs, and garlands. Today, the central courtyard, wrapped by 24 houses and connecting arcades, is home to secondhand bookshops, florists, and chess competitions.

Best Restaurant

Crêperie Beaurepaire. No trip to France is complete without eating at least one crepe, and any visit to Lille should include a meal at this Old Town creperie. ✉ *1 rue de St-Etienne, Lille* ☎ *03–20–54–60–54* ⏲ *Closed Sun.*

Getting Here

Take the Eurostar from Paris, Brussels, or London. Explore the Old Town on foot and take the metro for longer journeys.

Office de Tourisme de Lille. 🌐 *www.lilletourism.com*

Mont Saint-Michel

A Tidal Island Cradling an Architectural Jewel

Mont-St-Michel is the third-most-visited sight in France, after the Eiffel Tower and the Louvre. This beached mass of granite, rising some 400 feet, was begun in AD 709 and is crowned with the "Marvel," or great monastery, which was built during the 13th century. Wrought by nature and centuries of tireless human toil, the sea-surrounded mass of granite adorned with the soul-lifting silhouette of the Abbaye du Mont-St-Michel may well be your most lasting image of Normandy.

Don't Miss

Abbaye du Mont-St-Michel. The history-shrouded abbey on the mountain's peak remains the crowning glory of medieval France. It's worth lingering to see the Mont spectacularly illuminated at night, or spend the night if you want to see the abbey before the tourist hordes arrive. ✉ *Le Mont-Saint-Michel* 🌐 *www.mont-saint-michel.monuments-nationaux.fr* 🎫 *From €9*

Best Restaurant

Le Pré Sale. While not on the Mont itself, Le Pré Sale makes up for this with a tasty menu of Normandy favorites. 🌐 *www.restaurantlepresale-montsaintmichel.com*

Getting Here

From Paris, take the TGV from Gare Montparnasse to Rennes and connect by bus. From Caen, take either an early-morning or an afternoon train to Pontorson, and then hop a cab or bus for the 15-minute drive to the foot of the abbey.

Mont-St-Michel Tourist Office.
✉ *Corps de Garde, Bd. de l'Avancée, Le Mont-Saint-Michel* ☎ *02–33–60–14–30* 🌐 *www.ot-mont-saintmichel.com*

Champagne Cellars of Reims

The City Built on Champagne

Behind a facade of austerity, the Champagne region's largest city remains one of France's richest tourist sites, thanks especially to the fact that it sparkles with some of the biggest names in Champagne production. The maze of cellars constitutes a leading attraction here. Several of these producers organize visits with guided tours of their cavernous, hewn-chalk underground warehouses, including Taittinger. Although many of Reims's historic buildings were flattened in World War I and replaced by drab, modern architecture, those that do remain are of royal magnitude.

Don't Miss

Cathédrale Notre-Dame de Reims. Restored for its 800th birthday in 2011, this magnificent Gothic cathedral long provided the setting for the coronations of French kings. The glory of Reims's cathedral is its facade: it's so skillfully proportioned that initially you have little idea of its monumental size.

Best Restaurant

Cafe du Palais. The walls at this 1930s restaurant are crammed with gilt-edged mirrors, golden cherubs, and old paintings, while crystal chandeliers hang from the ceiling, which itself is topped by a magnificent Art Deco glass roof signed by Jacques Simon. *www.cafedupalais.fr*

Getting Here

You can make it to Reims in 50 minutes on the TGV express from Gare de l'Est, Paris. Plenty of Champagne houses are within walking distance of the city.

Taittinger. *9 pl. St-Nicaise, Reims* *03–26–85–45–35* *www.taittinger.com* *From €25* *Closed Mon.*

Belle-Île-en-Mer

A Magical, Beautiful Island off the Breton Coast

Covering 84 square km (32 square miles), Belle-Île is the largest of Brittany's islands; and, as its name implies, it is beautiful. Being less commercialized than its mainland counterpart, Quiberon (a spa town on the eastern side of the Quiberon Peninsula), Belle-Île maintains a natural appeal. Monet created several famous paintings on the island, and the pristine terrain may tempt you to set up an easel yourself.

Don't Miss

Citadel Vauban. Your first stop on Belle-Île will most likely be Le Palais, the island's largest community. As you enter the port, it's impossible to miss the star-shape Citadelle Vauban, named for the famous military engineer who, in the early 1700s, oversaw a redesign of the original fort here (which dated back to the 11th century). Stroll the grounds, savor the views, and then bone up on local lore at the on-site Musée de la Citadelle Vauban.

Getting Here

Ferries, which run hourly in July and August, connect Belle-Île's Le Palais with Quiberon's Gare Maritime. Because of the cost, it's best to make the crossing as a foot passenger. Bad weather can affect ferry crossings in winter.

Do This

The ideal way to get around to the island's 90 spectacular beaches is by bike. The best place to rent two-wheelers (and cars—this is also the island's Avis outlet) is at Roue Libre in Le Palais (🌐 *www.velobelleile.fr*).

Belle-Île-en-Mer Tourist Office. ✉ *Le Palais, Quai Bonnelle* ☎ *02–97–31–81–93* 🌐 *www.belle-ile.com*

Cathédrale Notre-Dame de Rouen

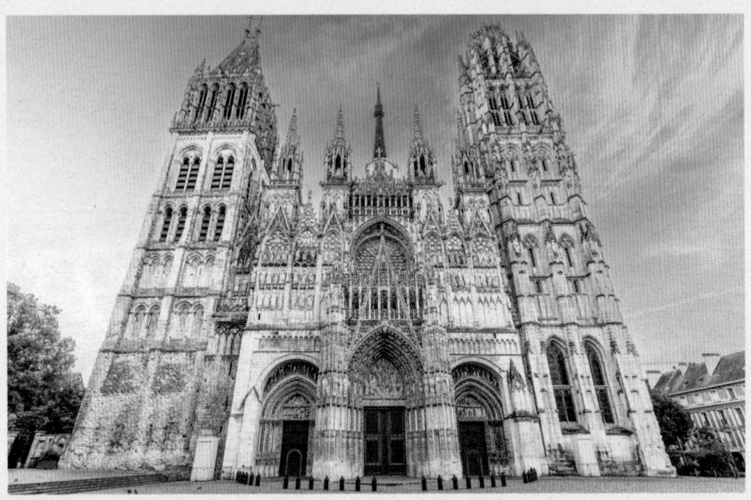

The Lively Norman Capital

"O Rouen, art thou then to be my final abode!" was the agonized cry of Joan of Arc as the English dragged her out to be burned alive in the market square on May 30, 1431. The city was hit hard during World War II, but a wealth of medieval half-timber houses still line the tiny cobblestone streets of Vieux Rouen. Of course, the glorious cathedral itself is nothing to scoff at: Claude Monet immortalized it in a memorable series of paintings. Even in the so-called City of 100 Spires, the one crowning its main cathedral stands out. Erected in 1876, it's the highest in France—a cast-iron tour de force rising 490 feet above the crossing. Interior highlights include the 13th-century choir, with its pointed arcades; vibrant stained glass depicting the crucified Christ; and massive stone columns topped by some intriguing carved faces.

Don't Miss

The exact location of Joan of Arc's pyre is marked by a concrete-and-metal cross in front of the modern Église Jeanne-d'Arc—and that eye-catching, flame-evoking church is just one of the many landmarks that makes this sizable port city so fascinating.

When to Go

The city is beautifully illuminated during winter, and Christmas markets arrive at the end of November.

Getting Here

Rouen-bound trains leave Paris's Gare St-Lazare every half hour or so.

Cathédrale Notre-Dame. ✉ *Pl. de la Cathédrale* ☎ *02–35–71–85–85* 🌐 *www.cathedrale-rouen.net* 🎫 *Tours €2*

Église Ste-Jeanne-d'Arc. ✉ *Pl. du Vieux-Marché, Le Vieux-Marché* ☎ *02–32–08–13–90*

Modernist Architecture in Le Havre

A Love Letter to Modernist Architecture

Considering it was bombarded 146 times during World War II, you might think there'd be little left to see in Le Havre—France's second-largest port (after Marseille). Think again. The rebuilt city, with its uncompromising recourse to reinforced concrete and open spaces, looks like no other city in the country, thanks in part to its share of some of France's most spectacular 20th-century edifices. The rational planning and audacious architecture of Auguste Perret (1874–1954) have earned the city UNESCO World Heritage status. His unforgettable Église St-Joseph—half rocket ship, half church—is alone worth the trip.

Don't Miss

Auguste Perret Model Apartment. This fascinating relic of post–World War II Le Havre is a testament to the city's postwar destruction—and to the determination of architects and city planners to create new homes for displaced residents. Sign up for a guided tour at the city's well-appointed Maison du Patrimoine; while the tour is in French, even nonspeakers will find plenty to admire in the collection of midcentury furniture and utility-minded ceramics and artwork. The apartment makes an interesting counterpoint to Perret's nearby masterpiece, the Église St-Joseph.

Getting Here

Direct trains from Paris's Gare St-Lazare arrive here 13 times a day (2 hours 10 minutes). If you're coming from the United Kingdom, Brittany Ferries provides sea links between Portsmouth and Le Havre.

Le Havre Tourist Office. ✉ *186 bd. Clemenceau* ☎ *02–32–74–04–04* 🌐 *www.lehavre-etretat-tourisme.com*

Bayeux Tapestry

A Mesmerizing Story of Conquest

Essentially a 225-foot-long embroidered scroll stitched in 1067, the Bayeux Tapestry, known in French as the Tapisserie de la Reine Mathilde (Queen Matilda's Tapestry), depicts the epic story of William of Normandy's conquest of England, narrating Will's trials and victory over his cousin Harold, culminating in the Battle of Hastings on October 14, 1066. The extremely detailed, often homey scenes provide an unequaled record of the clothes, weapons, ships, and lifestyles of the day. It's showcased in the Musée de la Tapisserie (Tapestry Museum).

Don't Miss

Bayeux itself was never bombed by either side; hence, its Norman Gothic cathedral and beautiful Old Town emerged intact. Although the highlight here for most visitors is the world's most celebrated piece of needlework, for a different take on the past, plan to come for the boisterous **Fêtes Médiévales**, a market-cum-carnival held in the streets around the cathedral on the first weekend of July. A more conventional market is held every Saturday morning in the Place St-Patrice.

Getting Here

Buses run from Caen to Bayeux regularly (50 minutes) and trains from Paris also arrive frequently (2 hours 20 minutes).

✉ *Centre Guillaume-le-Conquérant, 13 bis rue de Nesmond, Bayeux* ☎ *02–31–51–25–50* 🌐 *www.bayeuxmuseum.com* 🎫 *€10* ⏱ *Closed Jan.*

D-Day Beaches

A Remembrance of the Longest Day

History set its sights along the coast of Normandy at 6:30 am on June 6, 1944, as the 135,000 men and 20,000 vehicles of the Allied forces made land in their first incursion in France in World War II. The entire operation on this "Longest Day" was called Operation Overlord—the code name for the invasion of Normandy. Five beachheads (dubbed Utah, Omaha, Gold, Juno, and Sword) were established along the coast to either side of Arromanches.

Don't Miss

Omaha Beach. You won't be disappointed by the rugged terrain and windswept sand of Omaha Beach, 16 km (10 miles) northwest of Bayeux. Here you can find the Monument du Débarquement (Monument to the Normandy Landings) and the Musée-Mémorial d'Omaha Beach, a large shedlike structure packed with tanks, dioramas, and archival photographs that stand silent witness to "Bloody Omaha." In Colleville-sur-Mer, overlooking Omaha Beach, is the hilltop American Cemetery and Memorial, designed by landscape architect Markley Stevenson. ✉ *Les Moulins, Av. de la Libération, Saint-Laurent-sur-Mer* 🌐 *www.musee-memorial-omaha.com* 🎫 *€8* ⏲ *Closed late Nov.–early Feb.*

Utah Beach

Head east on D67 from Ste-Mère to Utah Beach, which, being sheltered from the Atlantic winds by the Cotentin Peninsula and surveyed by lowly sand dunes rather than rocky cliffs, proved easier to attack than Omaha. Allied troops stormed the beach at dawn, and just a few hours later had managed to conquer the German defenses, heading inland to join up with the airborne troops. ✉ *Utah Beach, Ste-Marie-du-Mont*

Strasbourg's Old Town

The Unofficial Capital of Europe

Although it's in the heart of Alsace and draws appealingly on Alsatian *gemütlichkeit* (coziness), Strasbourg is a cosmopolitan French cultural center and the symbolic, if unofficial, capital of Europe. Against an irresistible backdrop of old half-timber houses, waterways, and the colossal single spire of its red-sandstone cathedral, Strasbourg embodies Franco-German reconciliation and the wider idea of a united Europe. You'll discover an incongruously sophisticated mix of museums, charming neighborhoods like La Petite France, elite schools, international think tanks, and the European Parliament.

Don't Miss

With gingerbread, half-timber houses that seem to lean precariously over the canals of the Ill, plus old-fashioned shops and inviting little restaurants, Petite France ("Little France") is the most magical neighborhood in Strasbourg.

Best Restaurant

Chez Yvonne. Artists, tourists, lovers, and heads of state sit elbow-to-elbow in this classic weinstube, founded in 1873. All come to savor steaming platters of local specialties.

Do This

Strasbourg is a big town, but its center is easily explored on foot, or, more romantically, by boat. The company **Batorama** organizes 70-minute boat tours along the Ill. 🌐 *www.batorama.com* 🎫 *€14*

Getting Here

Strasbourg is served by excellent train links from numerous French cities. Once here, walk where possible and hop the tram for longer journeys.

Strasbourg Tourist Office. ✉ *17 pl. de la Cathédrale, Strasbourg* 🌐 *www.visitstrasbourg.fr*

When in Northern France

Beaune

TOWN | Beaune is sometimes considered the wine capital of Burgundy because it is at the heart of the region's vineyards, with the Côte de Nuits to the north and the Côte de Beaune to the south. It's also a popular spot for festivals, with top draws including the International Festival of Baroque Opera in July, Jazz O'Verre in September, and the wine-themed Les Trois Glorieuses in November. That combination makes Beaune one of Burgundy's most visited communities. Despite the hordes, however, it remains a very attractive provincial town, teeming with art above ground and wine barrels down below. With its steep, gabled roof colorfully tiled in intricate patterns, the famed Hospices de Beaune is this city's top attraction—and one of Burgundy's most iconic sights. It was founded in 1443 as a hospital to provide free care for the poor after the Hundred Years' War. ✉ *Beaune* 🌐 *www.beaune-tourisme.fr.*

★ Château de Chambord

CASTLE/PALACE | **FAMILY** | As you travel the gigantic, tree-shaded roadways that converge on Chambord, you first spot the château's incredible towers—19th-century novelist Henry James said they were "more like the spires of a city than the salient points of a single building"—rising above the forest. When the entire palace breaks into view, it is an unforgettable sight.

With a 420-foot-long facade, 440 rooms, 365 chimneys, and a wall that extends 32 km (20 miles) to enclose a 13,000-acre forest, the Château de Chambord is one of the greatest buildings in France. Under François I, building began in 1519, a job that took 12 years and required 1,800 workers. His original grandiose idea was to divert the Loire to form a moat, but someone (perhaps his adviser, Leonardo da Vinci, who some feel may have provided the inspiration behind the entire complex) persuaded him to make do with the River Cosson. François I used the château only for short stays; yet 12,000 horses were required to transport his luggage, servants, and entourage when he came. Later kings also used Chambord as an occasional retreat, and Louis XIV, the Sun King, had Molière perform here. In the 18th century Louis XV gave the château to the Maréchal de Saxe as a reward for his victory over the English and Dutch at Fontenoy (southern Belgium) in 1745. When not indulging in wine, women, and song, the marshal planted himself on the roof to oversee the exercises of his personal regiment of 1,000 cavalry. Now, after long neglect—all the original furnishings vanished during the French Revolution—Chambord belongs to the state.

There's plenty to see inside. You can wander freely through the vast rooms, filled with exhibits (including a hunting museum)—not all concerned with Chambord, but interesting nonetheless—and lots of Ancien Régime furnishings. The enormous double-helix staircase (probably envisioned by Leonardo, who had a thing about spirals) looks like a single staircase, but an entire regiment could march up one spiral while a second came down the other, and never the twain would meet. The real high point here in more ways than one is the spectacular chimneyscape—the roof terrace whose forest of Italianate towers, turrets, cupolas, gables, and chimneys has been compared to everything from the minarets of Constantinople to a bizarre chessboard. During the year there's a packed calendar of activities on tap, from 90-minute tours of the park in a 4x4 vehicle (€18) to guided carriage tours (€11). A soaring three-story-tall hall has been fitted out to offer lunches and dinners. ✉ *Chambord* ☎ *02–54–50–40–00* 🌐 *www.chambord.org/en* 🎫 *€14.50.*

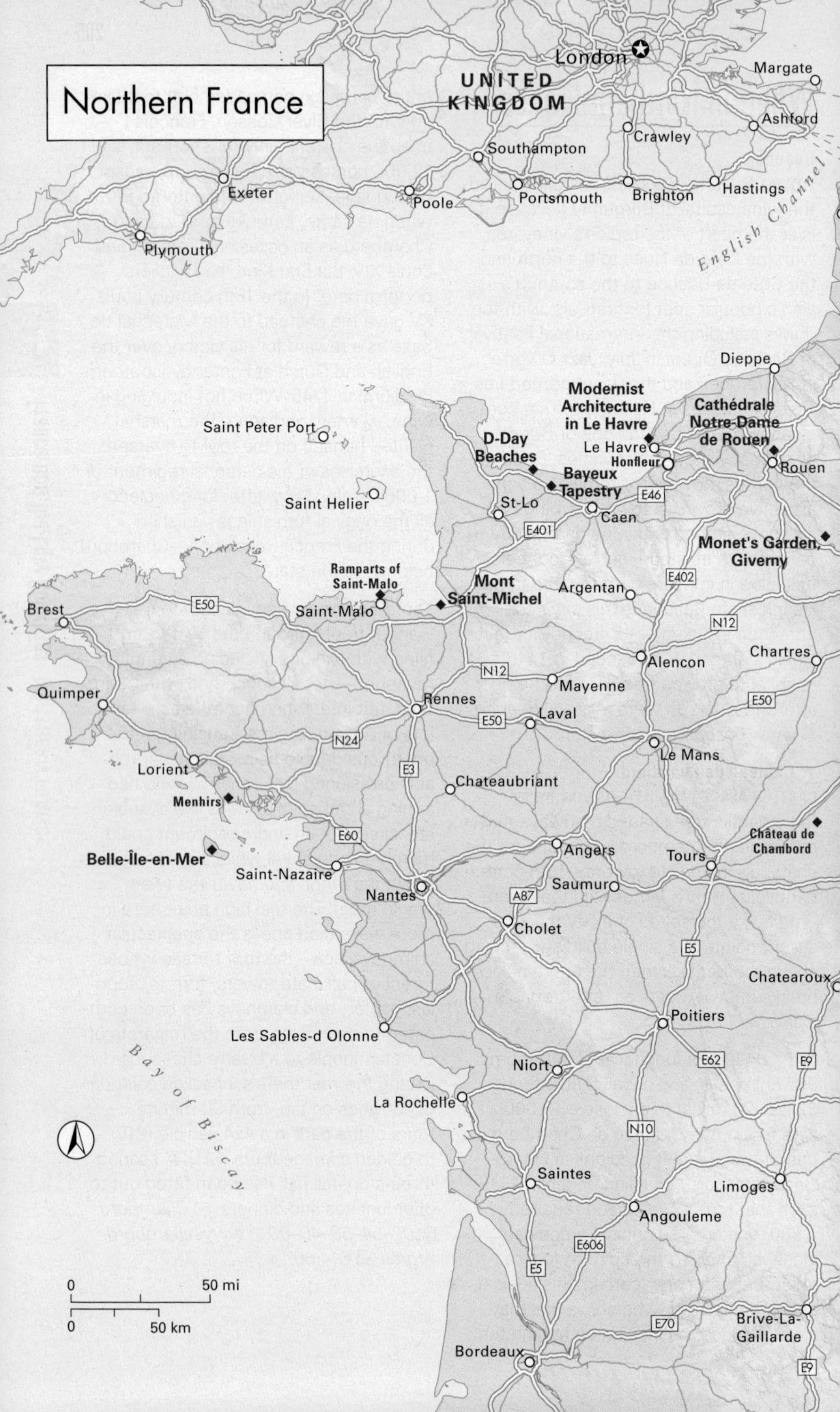

Northern France
UNITED KINGDOM
London
Margate
Ashford
Crawley
Southampton
Exeter
Poole
Portsmouth
Brighton
Hastings
Plymouth
English Channel
Dieppe
Modernist Architecture in Le Havre
Cathédrale Notre-Dame de Rouen
Saint Peter Port
D-Day Beaches
Le Havre
Honfleur
Rouen
Bayeux Tapestry
Saint Helier
St-Lo
E46
Caen
E401
Monet's Garden, Giverny
Ramparts of Saint-Malo
Mont Saint-Michel
Argentan
E402
Brest
E50
Saint-Malo
N12
Chartres
Alencon
N12
Mayenne
Quimper
Rennes
E50
Laval
E50
N24
Le Mans
Lorient
E3
Chateaubriant
Menhirs
E60
Château de Chambord
Angers
Belle-Île-en-Mer
Saint-Nazaire
Tours
Nantes
Saumur
A87
Cholet
E5
Chatearoux
Poitiers
Les Sables-d Olonne
Bay of Biscay
E62
E9
Niort
La Rochelle
N10
Saintes
Limoges
Angouleme
E606
E5
0
50 mi
0
50 km
E70
Brive-La-Gaillarde
Bordeaux
E9

Breda
Moers
Dortmund
Duisburg
Eindhoven
Düsseldorf
Oostende
Brugge
Antwerp
Dunkerque
E40
Gent
BELGIUM
Cologne
Siegen
Calais
Maastricht
Brussels
Bonn
LiÃ¨ge
Boulogne-Sur-Mer
E15
Lille
GERMANY
Namur
Lens
Charleroi
Koblenz
E402
N25
Cambrai
Wiesbaden
Abbeville
E41
Mainz
Amiens
LUXEMBOURG
Saint-Quentin
Trier
E17
Luxembourg
E46
Kaiserslautern
Soissons
Champagne Cellars of Reims
Reims
A16
E19
N2
E50
Metz
N14
E50
Chalons-Sur-Marne
E5
Paris
E25
N12
Versailles
N4
N4
Nancy
Strasbourg
E50
Saint Dizier
E17
Strasbourg's Old Town
E54
E23
E15
Troyes
E25
E5
Colmar
Freiburg
E17
Mulhouse
Orléans
Auxerre
A77
Vesoul
Basel
E15
Dijon
Besançon
Vierzon
FRANCE
Bern
Bourges
Beaune
N83
SWITZERLAND
E11
Lausanne
Moulins
A39
E62
Paray-Le-Monial
Geneva
E62
N7
E15
E25
E70
E712
Clermont-Ferrand
Lyon
Chambery
ITALY
E70
Saint-Étienne
E15
E70
N88
Saint Vallier
Torino
Grenoble
Valence
E11
E712

Colmar

TOWN | An atmospheric maze of narrow streets lined with candy-color, half-timber Renaissance houses hanging over cobblestone lanes in a disarmingly ramshackle way—Colmar out-charms even Strasbourg. Each shop-lined backstreet winds its way to the 15th-century customs house, the Ancienne Douane, and the square and canals that surround it. During the first half of August, Colmar celebrates with its annual **Foire Régionale des Vins d'Alsace,** an Alsatian wine fair in the Parc des Expositions. Events include folk music, theater performances, and, above all, the tasting and selling of wine. ✉ *Colmar* ✣ *2½ hrs by train from Paris Gare de l'Est* 🌐 *www.tourisme-colmar.com.*

Honfleur

TOWN | The most picturesque of the Côte Fleurie's seaside towns is a time-burnished place with a surplus of half-timber houses and cobbled streets that are lined with a solid selection of stylish boutiques. Much of its Renaissance architecture remains intact—especially around the 17th-century Vieux Bassin harbor, where the water is fronted on one side by two-story stone houses with low, sloping roofs and on the other by tall slate-topped houses with wooden facades. Maritime expeditions (including some of the first voyages to Canada) departed from here; later, Impressionists were inspired to capture it on canvas. ✉ *Honfleur* 🌐 *www.honfleur-tourism.co.uk.*

Menhirs

RUINS | Dating to around 4500 BC, Carnac's menhirs remain as mysterious in origin as their English contemporaries at Stonehenge, although religious beliefs and astronomy were doubtless an influence. The 2,395 monuments that make up the three *alignements*—Kermario, Kerlescan, and Ménec—form the largest megalithic site in the world, and are positioned with astounding astronomical accuracy in semicircles and parallel lines over about a kilometer (half a mile). The site, just north of the town, is fenced off for protection, and you can examine the menhirs up close only from October through March; in summer you must join a €11 guided tour (some are in English). This visitor center explains the menhirs' history and significance, plus it offers an excellent selection of interesting books in all languages as well as regional gifts. ✉ *D196, Carnac* ☎ *02–97–52–29–81 for Maison des Mégalithes* 🌐 *www.menhirs-carnac.fr.*

Ramparts

MILITARY SIGHT | St-Malo's imposing stone ramparts have withstood the pounding of the Atlantic since the 12th century. They were considerably enlarged and modified in the 18th century, and now extend from the château for almost 2 km (1 mile) around the Vieille Ville—known as *intra-muros* (within walls). The views from them are stupendous, especially at high tide. Look for the statues of celebrated explorer Jacques Cartier and swashbuckling corsair Robert Surcouf; the latter, a hero of many daring 18th-century raids on the British navy, eternally wags an angry finger over the waves at England. ✉ *St-Malo.*

Where to Eat and Drink

★ Au Crocodile

$$$$ | **FRENCH** | At one of the temples of Alsatian-French haute cuisine, you get a real taste of old Alsace with a nouvelle spin. Founded in the early 1800s, its grand salon is still aglow with skylights, and a spectacular 19th-century painting showing the Strasbourgeoisie at a country fair continues to set the tasteful tone. **Known for:** extensive wine list; reasonably priced lunch menus Thursday and Friday; top-notch cuisine and masterful sauces. $ *Average main: €60* ✉ *10 rue de l'Outre,*

Strasbourg ☎ *03–88–32–13–02* 🌐 *www.au-crocodile.com* ⏲ *Closed Sun. and Mon. No lunch Tues.and Wed.* 👔 *Jacket and tie required.*

★ Breizh Café

$ | FRENCH | FAMILY | Not all crêpes are created equal, and you'll taste the difference at Bertrand Larcher's original Cancale flagship (his Paris outpost is the city's go-to crêperie). Traditional crispy buckwheat galettes are given a modern gourmet twist with the best locally sourced ingredients—organic eggs and vegetables, artisanal cheeses, local oysters and seafood, free-range meats, smoked or seaweed butter from the St-Malo–based dairy superstar Jean-Yves Bordier—and the tender white-flour dessert crêpes are to die for. **Known for:** a cut above the usual crêpe; laid-back setting good for families; nice cider list. 💲 *Average main: €14* ✉ *7 quai Thomas, Cancale* ☎ *02–99–89–61–76* 🌐 *www.breizhcafe.com.*

★ La Couronne

$$$$ | MODERN FRENCH | Behind a half-timber facade filled with geraniums, the "oldest inn in France," dating from 1345, is crammed with stained leaded glass, sculpted wood beams, marble Norman chimneys, leather-upholstered chairs, and damask curtains. Of its many famous guests over the centuries, perhaps the most celebrated here is Julia Child, who ate her first meal in France—"the most exciting meal of my life"—here. **Known for:** cozy, wood-lined Salon des Rôtisseurs, an antiquarian's delight; cool history; excellent value, prix-fixe dinner menu. 💲 *Average main: €50* ✉ *31 pl. du Vieux-Marché, Le Vieux-Marché* ☎ *02–35–71–40–90* 🌐 *www.lacouronne-rouen.co.uk.*

La Maison d'à Côté

$$$$ | MODERN FRENCH | Just a five-minute drive from Chambord in a tiny village, two-Michelin-star La Maison d'à Côté serves French haute cuisine in an intimate yet contemporary dining room. Chef Christophe Hay insists on local whenever possible, and his frequently changing menus, which vary with the seasons, include line-caught fish from the Loire, local Wagyu beef, and caviar de Sologne. **Known for:** gorgeous presentation; superb natural wine list; gorgeous village setting. 💲 *Average main: €36* ✉ *25 rte. de Chambord, Montlivault* ☎ *02–54–20–62–30* 🌐 *www.lamaisondacote.fr* ⏲ *Closed Tues., and Wed. Sept.–Apr.*

★ Le Parc

$$$$ | FRENCH | Legendary chef Gérard Boyer made Le Parc the most famous haute gastronomic restaurant in Reims, and now Philippe Mille has regained the heights of Boyer's era with his talent for modern, but generous, cuisine. Prepared with precision, the product-inspired dishes ooze enthusiasm, including scallops with white-truffle sauce and foie gras poached in borscht. **Known for:** famous haute dining pedigree; extensive wine listing with plenty of Champagne options; high sophistication which means reservations and jacket and tie are essential. 💲 *Average main: €90* ✉ *Château Les Crayères, 64 bd. Henry-Vasnier, Reims* ☎ *03–26–24–90–00* 🌐 *www.lescrayeres.com* ⏲ *Closed Mon. and Tues.*

★ Les Chants d'Avril

$ | BISTRO | It may not be the fanciest restaurant in Nantes or the most central, but Les Chants d'Avril is where the locals go for affordable "bistronomic" fare. Murals, dark-wood paneling, and leather banquettes lend a warm, traditional look; the attention to market-driven ingredients and interesting wines, however, puts it on par with the best modern *bistrôts à vin.* **Known for:** amazingly priced modern bistro cuisine; fresh seasonal ingredients; lively atmosphere. 💲 *Average main: €16* ✉ *2 rue Laënnec, Nantes* ☎ *02–40–89–34–76* 🌐 *www.leschantsdavril.fr* ⏲ *Closed weekends.*

★ SaQuaNa
$$$$ | **MODERN FRENCH** | Chef Alexandre Bourdas earned his second Michelin here after putting Honfleur on the gastronomic map with his first over a decade ago. From the ravishing dining room to the impeccable presentation, his restaurant is a study in getting it right down to the smallest detail, with surprising combinations like sea bream with nori and marinated sanshō or cabbage tempura with a truffle crust. **Known for:** elements of Bourdas's native Midi-Pyrénées cuisine; sweet masterpieces from pâtissier par excellence Justine Rethore; great wine list. *Average main: €98* *22 pl. Hamelin, Honfleur* *02–31–89–40–80* *saquana-alexandre-bourdas.com* *Closed Mon.–Tues.*

Cool Places to Stay

★ Château Richeux
$$$ | **HOTEL** | Retired chef Olivier Roellinger and his wife, Jane, still preside over their family's luxurious hotel empire, which includes the beautiful, castellated, 1920s waterfront Château Richeux. **Pros:** famous cuisine; grounds designed specifically for those seeking quiet; beautiful sea views. **Cons:** isolated for those seeking crowds; breakfast is expensive; must have a car. *Rooms from: €240* *Le Point du Jour, Saint-Méloir-des-Ondes* *02–99–89–64–76* *www.maisons-de-bricourt.com* *Closed mid-Jan.–Feb.* *13 rooms* *No Meals.*

★ Hotel Barrière Le Normandy Deauville
$$$$ | **HOTEL** | This hotel—its facade a riot of pastel-green timbering, checkerboard walls, and Anglo-Norman balconies—has been a town landmark since it opened in 1912, and crowds still pack the place. **Pros:** grand interiors; luxurious amenities; Deauville's place to be seen. **Cons:** some elements of kitschy bombast; service can be patronizing; pretty pricey. *Rooms from: €375* *38 rue Jean-Mermoz, Deauville* *02–31–98–66–22* *www.hotelsbarriere.com* *271 rooms* *Free Breakfast.*

Hôtel Cour du Corbeau
$$ | **HOTEL** | Opened as an inn in 1580 and restored to its former half-timber glory, the "courtyard of the crow" retains its Middle Ages facade, but its interiors are another story: luxe design, crystal chandeliers, period furniture, and colorful fabrics are the essence of modern style, sumptuousness, and comfort. **Pros:** dazzling and luxurious; great location a short walk from the cathedral; old-world charm. **Cons:** has a tea salon but no restaurant; pricey breakfast; the rooms around the courtyard can get noisy. *Rooms from: €210* *6–8 rue des Couples, Strasbourg* *03–90–00–26–26* *www.cour-corbeau.com* *57 rooms* *No Meals.*

★ Hôtel Le Cep
$$$$ | **HOTEL** | This stylish ensemble of buildings spanning the 14th to 16th centuries oozes history from every arcade of its Renaissance courtyard, and, even better, all guest rooms—named for different Burgundy wines—have been luxuriously modernized and decorated with individual panache; some have wood beams, others canopied or four-poster beds. **Pros:** luxurious rooms; wonderful spa; friendly staff. **Cons:** breakfast is extra; the basic rooms are small and best avoided if you have a lot of luggage; pricey. *Rooms from: €366* *27 rue Jean François Maufoux, Beaune* *03–80–22–35–48* *www.hotel-cep-beaune.com* *65 rooms* *No Meals.*

Le Manoir des Impressionnistes
$$$ | **HOTEL** | Set atop a small wooded hill 200 yards from the sea, this gorgeous half-timber, dormer-roof manor has a pretty green-and-white facade in the Anglo-Norman style, plus accommodations that promise sweeping views. **Pros:** exquisitely decorated and furnished; great views; stylish bathrooms. **Cons:** away from town center; no elevator; breakfast not included. *Rooms from: €190* *23 rte. de Trouville, Honfleur* *02–31–81–63–00* *www.manoirdes-impressionnistes.com* *11 rooms* *No Meals.*

★ **Les Sources de Cheverny**
$$$ | **HOTEL** | It's a winning formula: find a stately manor on a wooded estate in the middle of wine country, add a luxe restaurant and spa, and focus on sustainability and wellness, and this spot has nailed it. **Pros:** lovely quiet setting; privacy when you want it, conviviality when you don't; sustainability is taken as seriously as luxury. **Cons:** the newer buildings are strangely charmless; only one unisex steam room and no sauna in the spa; must have a car to get there. *Rooms from: €300* *Chemin du Breuil, Cheverny* *02–54–44–20–20* *www.sources-cheverny.com* *49 rooms* *No Meals.*

★ **Saint-Pierre**
$$ | **HOTEL** | At the very epicenter of historic Saumur, this little 15th- to 17th-century house is hidden beneath the medieval walls of the church of St-Pierre—look for its entrance on one of the pedestrian passages that circle the nave. **Pros:** central location; sophisticated decor; lovely courtyard and bar. **Cons:** no restaurant; some rooms face busy road; some rooms on the small side. *Rooms from: €125* *Rue Haute-St-Pierre, Saumur* *02–41–50–33–00* *www.saintpierre-saumur.com* *15 rooms* *No Meals.*

Ty Mad
$ | **HOTEL** | This landmark hotel—frequented by artists and writers such as Picasso and Breton native Max Jacob in the 1920s—has been completely refitted with cool, light, modern furnishings that blend perfectly with its cove and beach setting. **Pros:** delightful seaside setting; stylish modern interior; fabulous prices. **Cons:** rooms are small and modestly equipped; breakfast not included in all bookings; small parking area. *Rooms from: €122* *Plage St-Jean, Douarnenez* *02–98–74–00–53* *www.hoteltymad.com* *Closed mid-Nov.–mid-Mar.* *15 rooms* *No Meals.*

Provence and the French Riviera

As you approach Provence there's a magical moment when you finally leave the north behind: cypresses and red-tile roofs appear; you hear the screech of cicadas and breathe the scent of wild thyme and lavender. What many visitors remember best about Provence is the light.

The vibrant sun here bathes vineyards, olive groves, fields full of lavender, and tall stands of sunflowers with an intensity that captivated Cézanne and Van Gogh. Bordering the Mediterranean and flanked by the Alps and the Rhône River, Provence attracts hordes of visitors. Fortunately, many of them are siphoned off to the resorts along the Riviera, which is part of Provence but whose jet-set image doesn't fit in with the tranquil charm of the rest of the region.

It's no wonder this enchanted idyll of sun-kissed Mediterranean-inflected cuisine, wines, and landscape, and Provençal-style cooking attracts droves of Parisians in all seasons along with a slew of European and American expats, some have probably been inspired by the popular series of memoirs by Peter Mayle, who lived in Provence and wrote about his life there for some 25 years. This bon-chic-bon-genre city crowd languishes stylishly at Provence's country inns and restaurants but also rents villas in the countryside.

And as you move east toward the French Riviera the effect is even more pronounced as the euros pile up and the bling factor intensifies. Here one can slip easily into the life of the idle rich, which can supply visitors with everything their hearts desire (and their wallet can stand). Home to sophisticated resorts beloved by billionaires, remote hill villages colonized by artists, Mediterranean beaches, and magnificent views, the Côte d'Azur (to use the French name) stretches from Marseille to Menton. Thrust out like two gigantic arms, divided by the Valley of the Var at Nice, the peaks of the Alpes-Maritimes throw their massive protection, east and west, the length of the favored coast all the way from St-Tropez to the Italian frontier.

Marseille

France's Greatest Seaport

The city used to be given wide berth by travelers in search of a Provençal idyll. A huge mistake. Marseille, even from its earliest history, has maintained its contradictions with a kind of fierce and independent pride. Yes, there are rough neighborhoods and some modern eyesores, but there is also tremendous beauty and culture. Cubist jumbles of white stone rise up over a picture-book seaport, bathed in light of blinding clarity, crowned by larger-than-life neo-Byzantine churches, and framed by massive fortifications; neighborhoods teem with diversity; souklike African markets smell deliciously of spices and coffees; and the labyrinthine Old Town radiates pastel shades of saffron, marigold, and robin's-egg blue.

Don't Miss

Notre-Dame-de-la-Garde. Towering above the city and visible for miles around, this overscaled neo-Byzantine monument was erected in 1853 by Napoleon III. Referred to fondly by the Marseillais as "La Bonne Mère," the cathedral sits at the city's highest point, as a beacon to sailors and fishermen for safety at sea. ✉ *Rue Fort du Sanctuaire, off Bd. André Aune, Garde Hill* 🌐 *www.notredamedelagarde.com*

Getting Here and Around

The main train station is Gare St-Charles on the TGV line, with frequent trains from Paris, the main coast route (Nice–Italy), and Arles. The gare routière is on Place Victor Hugo. Marseille has a very good local bus, tram, and métro system, and the César ferry boat (immortalized in Pagnol's 1931 film *Marius*) crosses the Vieux Port every few minutes and is free of charge.

Marseille Office du Tourisme. 🌐 *www.marseille-tourisme.com*

Arles

The Quintessential Gateway to Provence

If there were only one city to visit in Provence, lovely little Arles might be it. The city's wealth of vestiges, from antiquity, medieval times up through the Renaissance, provide a contrast with the contemporary Fondation Luma. Sitting on the banks of the Rhône River, the city's Vieille Ville is where time seems to have stood still since 1888—the year Vincent van Gogh immortalized Arles in his paintings. Arles is far too charming—and lived in—to become museum-like, yet it has a wealth of classical antiquities, including a well-preserved Roman arena; quarried-stone edifices and shuttered town houses shading graceful Old Town streets and squares; and one of Provence's most vibrant and extensive Saturday morning markets.

Don't Miss

The Camargue. The vast, marshy landscapes of the Camargue will swamp you with their strange beauty, white horses, pink flamingoes, and black bulls. For 1,500 square km (580 square miles), the vast alluvial delta of the Rhône River stretches to the horizon, an austere marshland unrelievedly flat. If people find the Camargue interesting, birds find it irresistible. Its protected marshes lure some 400 species, including more than 160 in migration—little egrets, gray herons, spoonbills, bitterns, cormorants, redshanks, grebes, and its famous flamingos. ✉ *Camargue Tourist Office, 5 av. Van Gogh, Saintes-Maries-de-la-Mer* 🌐 *www.saintes-maries.com*

Getting Here

You can take the TGV to Avignon from Paris and jump on the local connection to Arles. You can also reach Arles directly by train from Marseille or by bus from Avignon or Nîmes.

Office de Tourisme Arles. 🌐 *www.arlestourisme.com*

Palais des Papes, Avignon

A Medieval Alternative to the Vatican

Wrapped in a crenellated wall punctuated by towers and Gothic slit windows, Avignon's historic center stands distinct from modern extensions, crowned by the Palais des Papes, a 14th-century fortress-castle that's nothing short of spectacular. The colossal palace creates a disconcertingly fortress-like impression, underlined by the austerity of its interior. Most of the original furnishings were returned to Rome with the papacy; others were lost during the French Revolution. However, the main rooms are decorated with some excellent 14th-century frescoes by Simone Martini and Matteo Giovanetti; the Grand Tinel, or Salle des Festins (Feast Hall), has a majestic vaulted roof and a series of 18th-century Gobelin tapestries.

Don't Miss

For the French, Avignon is almost synonymous with the **Festival D'Avignon**, a theater festival held every July; thousands pack the city's hotels to bursting for the official festival and Le Festival OFF, the fringe festival with an incredible 1,300 performances each day. If your French isn't up to a radical take on Molière, look for English-language productions or try the circus and mime—there are plenty of shows for children, and street performers abound.

Getting Here

The high-speed TGV Méditerranée line connects Paris and Avignon (2 hours 40 minutes). The Gare Avignon TGV is a few miles southwest of the city (a train shuttle bus connects with the train station in town every 15 minutes from early morning to late at night).

✉ *Pl. du Palais, Avignon* 🌐 *www.palais-des-papes.com* 🎫 *€12; audio tour €2*

Le Sentier du Littoral, Cap d'Antibes

One of the World's Most Spectacular Footpaths

Bordering Cap-d'Antibes's zillion-dollar hotels and over-the-top estates, one of France's best walking paths stretches about 5 km (3 miles) along the outermost tip of the peninsula, bringing it "full circle" around the gardens at Eilenroc over to l'Anse de l'Argent Faux. Start at Plage de la Garoupe (where Cole Porter and Gerald Murphy used to hang out), with a paved walkway and dazzling views over the Baie de la Garoupe and the faraway Alps. Round the far end of the cap, however, and the paved promenade soon gives way to a boulder-studded pathway that picks its way along 50-foot cliffs, dizzying switchbacks, and thundering breakers.The walk takes about two hours to complete but is unforgettable.

Don't Miss

With its broad stone ramparts scalloping in and out over the waves and backed by blunt medieval towers, it's easy to understand why Antibes (pronounced "Awn-teeb") inspired Picasso to paint on a panoramic scale. From the Promenade Amiral-de-Grasse to the souklike maze of Vieil Antibes, Monet fell in love with the town, and his most famous paintings show the fortified Vieil Antibes against the sea.

Getting Here

The train station in Antibes is within walking distance of Vieil Antibes and only a block or so from the beach. From the station, take Bus No. 2 to Fontaine. To return, follow the Pl. de la Garoupe until Bd. de la Garoupe, where you'll make a left to reconnect with the bus.

🌐 *www.antibesjuanlespins.com* ✣ *Note that the path can be dangerous during bad weather (gates will typically be closed, so don't go around them). You can arrange a guided walk at the Antibes Tourist Office.*

Nice

High Culture and Provençal Grace

France's fifth-largest city strikes an engaging balance. Port-town exotica, lazy Mediterranean cafés, urban excitement, and fun-in-the-sun have made it a favorite destination for French and international travelers as well as a coveted place for well-heeled Europeans to establish a second home. You could easily spend your entire vacation here, attuned to Nice's quirks, its rhythms, its very multicultural population, and its Mediterranean tides. Now it's being transformed into the "the Green City of the Mediterranean." For proof, witness the 30-acre Promenade de Paillon Park in the middle of town or the east-west T2 tramline that uses a power supply of rechargeable Ecopack supercapacitors—so no ugly overhead wires can be seen.

Don't Miss

Musée Matisse. In the 1960s, the city of Nice bought this lovely, light-bathed, 17th-century villa and restored it to house a large collection of Henri Matisse's works. The Fauvist artist settled along Nice's waterfront in 1917 and remained here until his death in 1954. The collection includes several pieces the artist donated to the city and represents the evolution of his art, from still lifes to exuberant dancing paper dolls. ✉ *164 av. des Arènes-de-Cimiez, Cimiez* 🌐 *www.musee-matisse-nice.org* 🎫 *€15, includes entry to all municipal museums for 48 hrs* ⏲ *Closed Tues.*

Getting Here

Nice has seasonal direct flights from the U.S. as well as high-speed train service from Paris in as little as 6 hours.

Office du Tourisme Nice Côte d'Azur. 🌐 *www.explorenicecotedazur.com*

Arènes de Nîmes

Roman-Era Treasures

Nîmes is a feisty town in transition. Yet its rumpled and rebellious ways trace directly back to its Roman incarnation, when its population swelled with soldiers, arrogant and newly victorious after their conquest of Egypt in 31 BC. A 24,000-seat coliseum, a thriving forum with a magnificent temple patterned after Rome's Temple of Apollo, and a public water network fed by the Pont du Gard (which is actually in Provence) attest to its classical prosperity. Nîmes has opted against becoming a staid, atmospheric Provençal market town and has invested in progressive modern architecture.

Don't Miss

The **Arènes,** the best-preserved Roman amphitheater in the world, is a miniature of the Colosseum in Rome (note the small carvings of Romulus and Remus, the mythological founders of Rome, on the exterior and the intricate bulls' heads etched into the stone over the entrance on the north side). Nearby, the Maison Carrée stands lovely and forlorn in the middle of a busy downtown square, an exquisitely preserved temple striking a timeless balance between symmetry and whimsy, purity of line and richness of decoration. Modeled on the Temple of Apollo in Rome, adorned with magnificent marble columns and elegant pediment, the Maison Carrée remains one of the most noble surviving structures of ancient Roman civilization anywhere. ✉ *Pl. de la Maison Carrée, Nîmes* 🌐 *www.arenes-nimes.com* 🎫 *From €6.*

Getting Here and Around

Although all the sites in Nîmes are walkable, the useful Tango bus runs a good loop from the station and passes by many of the principal sites along the way for €1.30.

Office du Tourisme de Nîmes.
🌐 *www.nimes-tourisme.com*

St-Paul-de-Vence

A Gorgeous Hilltop Village

Medieval St-Paul-de-Vence can be seen from afar, standing out against the skyline. Having faded into near oblivion by the early 20th century, it was rediscovered in the 1920s, when a few penniless artists began paying for their drinks at the local auberge with paintings. Those artists turned out to be Signac, Modigliani, and Bonnard, who met at the Auberge de la Colombe d'Or, now a sumptuous inn and restaurant, where the walls are still covered with their ink sketches and daubs. It's a magical place, where artists are still drawn to its light, its pure air, and its wraparound views.

Don't Miss

Fondation Maeght. Many people come to St-Paul-de-Vence just to visit France's most important private art foundation, founded in 1964 by art dealer Aimé Maeght. High above the medieval town, it's an extraordinary marriage of the arc-and-plane architecture of Josep Sert; the looming sculptures of Miró, Moore, and Giacometti; the mural mosaics of Chagall; and the humbling hilltop setting, complete with pines, vines, and flowing planes of water. ✉ *623 ch. des Gardettes, St-Paul-de-Vence* 🌐 *www.fondation-maeght.com* 🎫 *€16*

Contact the tourist office for a private guided visit in English (€7 plus discounted admission rate of €11).

Getting Here

It's only 15 minutes from the coast by car; take the Cagnes-sur-Mer highway to Exit 47 or 48 (depending on the direction you're coming from) and look for signs on the RD 436 to La Collle sur Loup/Vence. St-Paul-de-Vence is between the two. There's no train station; take Bus No. 400 from Nice (25 minutes) or Cannes (2 hours).

Office du Tourisme. 🌐 *www.saint-pauldevence.com*

The Lavender Route, Provence

The Soul of Haute-Provence

Van Gogh may have made the sunflower into the icon of Provence, but it is another flower—one that is unprepossessing, fragrant, and tiny—that draws thousands of travelers every year to Provence. They come to journey the famous "Route de la Lavande" (the Lavender Route), a wide blue-purple swath that connects over 2,000 producers across the south of France.

Don't Miss

Cistercian Abbaye Notre-Dame de Sénanque. The greatest spot for lavender worship in the world is the 12th-century abbey, near Gordes, which in July and August seems to float above a sea of lavender, a setting immortalized in a thousand travel posters. ✉ *D177, 4 km (2½ miles) north of Gordes* ☎ *04–90–72–05–72* 🌐 *www.senanque.fr* 🎫 *€8*

When to Go

To see lavender in bloom, you have to go in season, which (if you're lucky) runs from June to early August. Like Holland's May tulips, the lavender of Haute-Provence is in its true glory only once a year: the last two weeks of July, when the harvesting begins—but fields bloom throughout the summer months for the most part. The village of Sault hosts the not-to-be-missed **Fête de la Lavande,** a day-long festival entirely dedicated to lavender, the best in the region, and usually held around August 15. 🌐 *www.ventoux-provence.fr*

Getting Here

Gordes is 39 km (24 miles) east of Avignon. There's no bus or train service, so you'll need a car. Although you could take a taxi as far as Gordes (approx. €75), the only practical way to explore this region is by rental car.

When in Provence and the French Riviera

Aix-en-Provence

TOWN | Longtime rival of edgier, more exotic Marseille, the lovely town of Aix-en-Provence (pronounced "ex") is gracious, cultivated, and made all the more cosmopolitan by the presence of some 40,000 university students. Although it is true that Aix owns up to a few modern-day eyesores, the overall impression is one of beautifully preserved stone monuments, quietly sophisticated nightlife, leafy plane trees, and gently splashing fountains. With its thriving market, vibrant café life, spectacularly chic shops, and superlative music festival, it's one Provence town that really should not be missed. Be sure to see the **Caumont Centre d'Art** (⊠ *3 rue Joseph Cabassol, Aixen-Provence* 🌐 *www.caumont-centredart.com*), one of the city's top cultural attractions, with elegant gardens and a great restaurant. ⊠ *Aix-en-Provence* 🌐 *www.aixenprovencetourism.com.*

Cannes International Film Festival

FILM FESTIVALS | The Riviera's cultural calendar is splashy and star-studded, and never more so than during May's Cannes International Film Festival. Screenings aren't open to the public, so unless you have a pass, your stargazing will be on the streets or in restaurants (though if you hang around the back street exits of the big hotels around 7 pm, you may bump into a few celebs on their way to the red carpet). Cinéma de la Plage shows Cannes classics and out-of-competition films free at Macé beach at 9:30 pm. In addition, Cannes Cinéphiles (🌐🌐 *www.cannes-cinema.com*) gives 4,000 film buffs a chance to view Official Selections; you can apply online starting in February. ⊠ *Cannes* 🌐 *www.festival-cannes.com.*

Grasse

TOWN | If you are interested in perfume, then there's no better place in the world to visit. Its unusual art museum, famed perfume museum, and picturesque backstreets also hold the laboratories where the great blends of Chanel, Dior, and Guerlain are produced. You can't visit those private laboratories, but Grasse does have three functioning perfume factories that create simple blends and demonstrate production techniques for free. The skills linked to cultivating flowers and blending fragrances in Grasse are so prestigious that they've been added to the UNESCO list of protected treasures. ⊠ *Grasse* 🌐 *www.tourisme.paysdegrasse.fr.*

Les Baux-de-Provence

TOWN | When you first search the craggy hilltops of Les Baux-de-Provence (that's "boh"), you may not quite be able to distinguish between bedrock and building, so naturally does the ragged skyline of towers and crenellation blend into the sawtooth jags of stone. It was from this intimidating vantage point that the lords of Baux ruled throughout the 11th and 12th centuries over one of the largest fiefdoms in the south, commanding some 80 towns and villages. But by the 15th century the lords of Baux had fallen from power, their stronghold destroyed. As dramatic in its perched isolation as Mont-St-Michel and St-Paul-de-Vence, this tiny chateau-village ranks as one of the most visited tourist sites in France, yet has somehow escaped the usual tourist-trap tawdriness. Lovely 16th-century stone houses, with even their window frames still intact, shelter elegant shops, cafés, and galleries that line the car-free main street, overwhelmed by day with the smell of lavender-scented souvenirs. ⊠ *Les Baux-de-Provence* ✥ *Take the A7 until you reach Exit 25, then the D99 between Tarascon and Cavaillon. Les Baux is 10 km (6 miles) south of St-Rémy via the D5 and the D27* 🌐 *www.lesbauxdeprovence.com.*

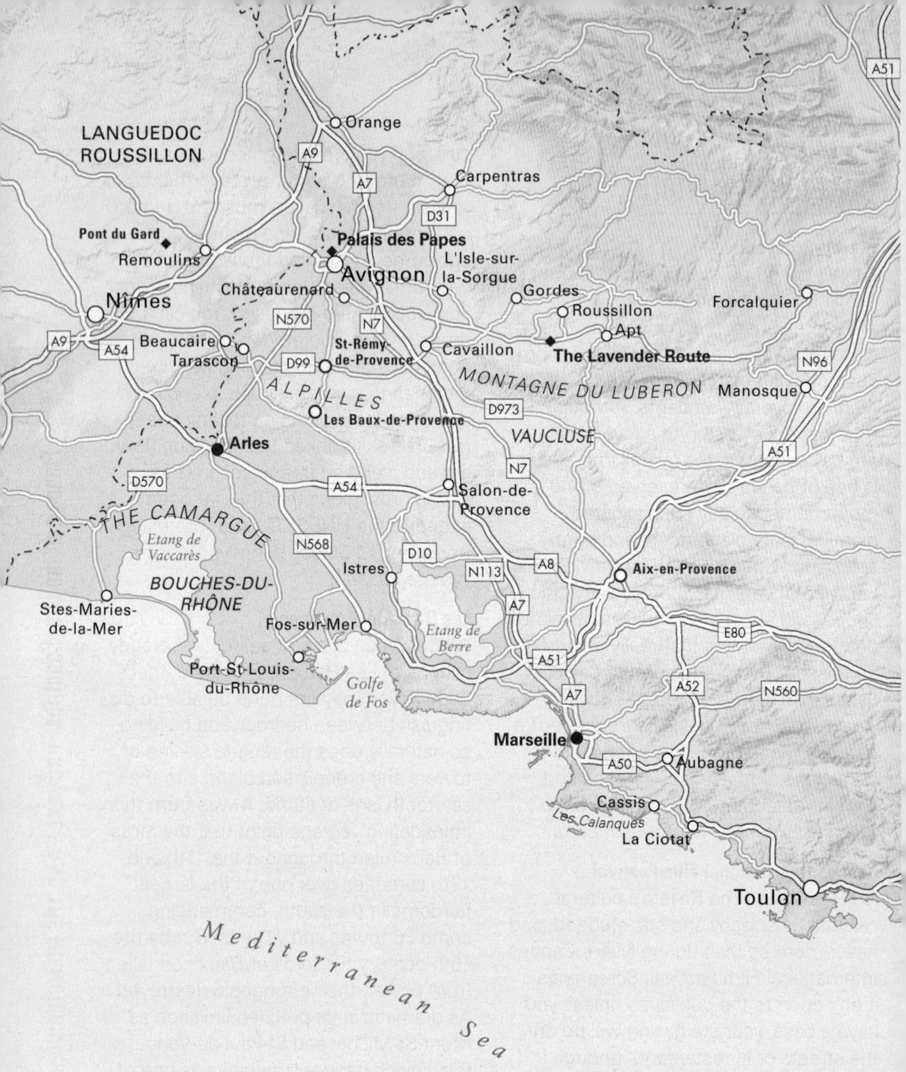

Provence and the French Riviera

Sisteron
Digne
N85
Entrevaux
N202
Moostiers-Ste-Marie
Castellane
Riez
L'Escarène
ITALY
D952
N202
N85
A8
Villefranche-sur-Mer
Monte-Carlo
Menton
Vence
Casino de Monte Carlo
D955
St-Paul-de-Vence
Nice
N7
Eze
MONACO
St-Jean-Cap-Ferrat
Grasse
Cagnes-sur-Mer
Arènes de Nîmes
Aups
Fayence
N7
Baie des Anges
EASTERN CÔTE d'AZUR
PROVENCE-ALPES-CÔTE D'AZUR
D562
Antibes
Cannes
Le Sentier du Littoral, Cap d'Antibes
Draguignan
D4
A8
Mandelieu-La Napoule
N7
Brignoles
Fréjus
St Raphael
Cannes International Film Festival
A8
Musée d'Art Classique de Mougins
Golfe de Fréjus
Cap du Dramont
D558
D25
N98
D43
MASSIF DES MAURES
Ste-Maxime
A57
Golfe Juan
Port-Grimaud
St-Tropez
WESTERN CÔTE d'AZUR
Gassin
Ramatuelle
N98
D559
Cap Camarat
Mediterranean Sea
Hyères
Cap Lardier
La Tour-Fondue
Ile de Port-Cros
Ile du Levant
0
10 mi
0
10 km

★ Musée d'Art Classique de Mougins

ART MUSEUM | This hidden gem "highlights the dialogue between the old and the new" with Roman, Greek, and Egyptian art rubbing shoulders with pieces by Picasso, Matisse, Cézanne, Warhol, and Dalí. Expect to come across a sarcophagus alongside a Cocteau or a Hirst sculpture next to an ancient bust. Spread over four floors, the museum also houses antique jewelry and the world's largest private armory collection. *32 rue Commandeur, Mougins 04–93–75–18–22 www.mouginsmusee.com €14.*

★ Pont du Gard

RUINS | The ancient Roman aqueduct is shockingly noble in its symmetry. The rhythmic repetition of arches resonates with strength, a testimony to an engineering concept that was relatively new in the 1st century AD, when the structure was built under Emperor Claudius. Today, unsullied by tourists, the surrounding nature is just as resonant, with the river flowing through its rocky gorge unperturbed by the work of master engineering that straddles it. In fact, one of the preferred ways of viewing the bridge is via canoe or kayak, easily rentable upstream. You can approach the aqueduct from either side of the Gardon River. If you choose the south side (Rive Droite), the walk to the *pont* (bridge) is shorter and the views arguably better. *400 rte. du Pont du Gard, Vers-Pont-du-Gard 04–66–37–50–99 www.pont-dugard.fr Guided tour €15, includes Espaces Culturels.*

St-Rémy-de-Provence

TOWN | Something felicitous has happened in this market town in the heart of the Alpilles—a steady infusion of style, of art, of imagination—all brought by people with a respect for local traditions and a love of Provençal ways. Here, more than anywhere, you can meditate quietly on antiquity, browse aromatic markets with basket in hand, peer down the very row of plane trees you remember from a Van Gogh, and also enjoy urbane galleries, cosmopolitan shops, and specialty food boutiques. It might be considered the Hamptons of Provence. *St-Rémy-de-Provence www.alpillesenprovence.com.*

St-Tropez

TOWN | With a pretty port, inviting cafés, and a photogenic old town in sugar-almond hues, St-Tropez might not stand out at first glance. There are sandy beaches and old-fashioned squares with plane trees and pétanque players, but these are a dime a dozen throughout Provence. So what made St-Tropez an internationally known locale? Two words: Brigitte Bardot. When this *pulpeuse* (voluptuous) actress showed up in St-Tropez on the arm of Roger Vadim in 1956 to film *And God Created Woman,*the heads of the world snapped around. The glitterati have followed ever since, and the city has remained one of the top destinations on the French Riviera. Be aware that the city can only be reached by car, bus, or boat. *St-Tropez www.sainttropeztourisme.com.*

Where to Eat and Drink

★ Chez Tata Simone

$$ | **FRENCH** | **FAMILY** | Set in an 18th-century Provençal mas once owned by the *grand mère* of one of the owners, this countrified restaurant is a short drive outside the city but well worth the small effort. Sit inside at wooden tables or out under towering plane trees to enjoy delicious dishes made with locally sourced ingredients that mix classic recipes (yes, from Tata Simone) with a modern touch. **Known for:** country atmosphere; welcoming service; hearty home-cooked dishes. *Average main: €18 Chemin du Mas de Jacquet 04–90–99–65–12 chez-tata-simone.business.site Closed Mon. and Tues. No lunch Wed. to Sat. No dinner Sun.*

Dior Café des Lices

$$$ | **FRENCH** | What could be more fashionable than tucking into exquisite cuisine—prepared by Michelin-starred guest chefs such as Yannick Alleno and Arnaud Donckele—in an enchanting sheltered garden designed by Peter Wirtz at the House of Dior? Meals are reasonably priced for St-Tropez, and the dessert selection is large (consider trying the much-lauded, tiny, round D'Choux pastries, which come in a variety of flavors). **Known for:** huge dessert menu, including famed caramel D'Choux; comparatively reasonable prices; secret garden vibe. *Average main: €32* *13 rue François Sibilli, St-Tropez* *04–98–12–67–65* *www.dior.com* *Closed mid-Oct.–March.*

★ **La Chassagnette**

$$$$ | **FRENCH** | Reputedly the original registered "organic" restaurant in Provence, this sophisticated yet comfortable spot, 12 km (7½ miles) south of Arles at the entrance of the Camargue, is fetchingly designed and has a dining area that extends outdoors, where large family-style picnic tables await under a wooden-slate canopy overlooking the extensive gardens. Using ingredients that are grown right on the property, innovative master chef Armand Arnal serves only prix-fixe menus that are a refreshing, though not inexpensive, mix of modern and classic French country cuisine. **Known for:** bucolic setting; outdoor dining; local, seasonal products. *Average main: €38* *Rte. du Sambuc, D36, Arles* *04–90–97–26–96* *www.chassagnette.fr* *Closed Tues. Wed. and Dec. to mid-Mar. No dinner Thur., Sun. and Mon.*

★ **Les Baux Jus**

$$ | **VEGETARIAN** | Who would have thought to find this caliber of 100% organic, raw, gluten-free, and vegan restaurant in the heart of Provence? Like foodie heaven to those with restricted diets, Les Baux Jus offers a tantalizing range of cold-pressed juices, salads, pastries, and smoothies—the food is so good that even carnivores will appreciate its innovation and freshness. **Known for:** vegan and gluten-free dishes; 100% organic ingredients; friendly atmosphere. *Average main: €20* *Rue de la Calade, Les Baux-de-Provence* *Closed Tues.*

Cool Places to Stay

★ **Baumanière Les Baux-de-Provence**

$$$$ | **HOTEL** | Spread over five historic buildings just outside the village of Les Baux, guest rooms at this fabled hotel—sheltered by rocky cliffs and set amid formal landscaped terraces and gardens—are the last word in Provençal chic: breezy, private, and beautifully furnished. **Pros:** two of the great restaurants of Provence; full-service spa; three pools. **Cons:** a bit of a snobby atmosphere; service hit-or-miss; expensive. *Rooms from: €380* *Val d'Enfer, Les Baux-de-Provence* *04–90–54–33–07* *www.baumaniere.com/en* *Closed Mon. and Tues. early Jan.–early Mar. Restaurant closed Jan., Feb., and Mon. year-round* *54 rooms* *No Meals.*

★ **Château des Alpilles**

$$$$ | **HOTEL** | Reached via a lane of majestic plane trees and set on 8 acres of luxuriant parkland, this gracious five-star manor (it's not exactly a château) dates back to medieval times, and it's one of St-Rémy's dreamiest spots—and that's saying a lot in this château-saturated territory. **Pros:** service that anticipates your every need; top-notch—and reasonably priced—dining on the premises; spectacular grounds in the country only a 5-minute drive from St-Rémy. **Cons:** expensive; not a lot to do after dark; if you prefer contemporary design it isn't for you. *Rooms from: €389* *Rte. de Rougadou, St-Rémy-de-Provence* *04–90–92–03–33* *www.chateaudesalpilles.com* *Closed Jan.–mid-Mar.* *21 rooms* *No Meals.*

★ Hôtel L'Arlatan

$$$ | **HOTEL** | Once home to the counts of Arlatan, this ideally located 15th-century stone house, close to the Fondation Vincent Van Gogh, stands on the site of a 4th-century basilica, and a glass floor reveals the excavated vestiges under the lobby. **Pros:** whimsical decor with a cool history; lively atmosphere in the bar and restaurant; exceptional value. **Cons:** heated pool is small; rooms range dramatically in price; mad color schemes may prove distracting to some. *Rooms from: €240* *26 rue du Sauvage, Arles* *04–90–93–56–66* *www.arlatan.com* *45 rooms* *No Meals.*

La Bastide Saint-Antoine

$$$$ | **HOTEL** | This ocher mansion, once the home of an industrialist who hosted the Kennedys and the Rolling Stones, is now the Relais & Chateaux domain of celebrated chef Jacques Chibois, who welcomes you with old stone walls, shaded walkways, an enormous pool, and guest rooms that glossily mix Louis XVI, Provençal, and high-tech delights. **Pros:** choice of Provençal or modern room decor; coffee machine and organic tea in each room; 1,000 wine references and over 25,000 bottles. **Cons:** restaurant is very expensive; books up far in advance; deposit of 50% of the total stay is charged at time of booking. *Rooms from: €336* *48 av. Henri-Dunant, Grasse* *04–93–70–94–94* *www.jacques-chibois.com* *Closed 3 wks in Nov.* *16 rooms* *No Meals.*

★ Les Lodges Sainte-Victoire

$$$$ | **HOTEL** | Although it's just outside Aix and amid 10 acres of woods, olive groves, and vineyards, with Cézanne-immortalized Mont Ste-Victoire as a backdrop, this hotel eschews the rustic-country-inn aesthetic in favor of a sophisticated, deluxe-contemporary style. **Pros:** has one of the city's best restaurants; four swanky private villas; beautiful grounds and views of Mont Ste-Victoire from the infinity pool. **Cons:** outside the city center; some first-floor rooms lack views; decor a little dark on cloudy days. *Rooms from: €400* *2250 rte. Cézanne, Le Tholonet* *04–42–24–80–40* *www.leslodgessaintevictoire.com* *35 rooms* *No Meals.*

Lou Cagnard

$$$ | **HOTEL** | Ground-floor rooms at this pretty little villa with a pool opens onto the flower-filled, manicured garden, where breakfast (€18) is served in the shade of a fig tree. **Pros:** walking distance to everything; free parking; accessible for those mobility issues. **Cons:** 3- and 5-night minimum stays June–Sept.; strict cancellation policy; breakfast not included. *Rooms from: €340* *18 av. Paul-Roussel, St-Tropez* *04–94–97–04–24* *www.hotel-lou-cagnard.com* *Closed Jan.–Mar.* *27 rooms* *No Meals.*

★ Mas de Peint

$$$$ | **HOTEL** | Sitting on roughly 1,250 acres of Camargue ranch land, this exquisite 17th-century farmhouse may just offer the ultimate mas experience. **Pros:** isolated setting makes for a

romantic getaway; on-site pool and lots of activities offered; no detail is missed in service or style. **Cons:** not all rooms have showers; a bit rustic, including lots of mosquitoes; not much to do once sun goes down, which some appreciate. *Rooms from: €350* *D36, Le Sambuc* *04–90–97–20–62* *www.masdepeint.com* *Closed mid-Nov.–Mar.* *15 rooms* *No Meals.*

★ **Villa Gallici**

$$$$ | HOTEL | Rooms here are bathed in the lavenders, blues, ochers, and oranges of Aix and feature elegant antiques and gorgeous Souleiado and Rubelli fabrics—a design scheme that truly evokes the swank 19th-century Provence colonized by Parisian barons and dukes. **Pros:** rich fabrics and dashing interiors; beautiful garden spot; 15-minute walk to town and shops. **Cons:** meals are pricey; no elevator; antique style not for everyone. *Rooms from: €520* *Av. de la Violette, Aix-en-Provence* *04–42–23–29–23* *www.villagallici.com* *Closed Jan.* *22 rooms* *No Meals.*

Southern France and Corsica

Paris's great rival, Lyon, is often called the doorway to the south, where Mediterranean influences begin to creep in. Like predestined lovers, the Rhône joins the Saône at the heart of Lyon, to form a fluvial force rolling south to the Mediterranean. The Rhône Valley's bounty includes hundreds of steep vineyards and small-town winemakers tempting you with their vintages.

West of Provence, Toulouse, a major French urban center, offers a bustling market and delightful old town, not to mention the fairy-tale ramparts of perched Carcassonne and beautiful, historic Albi. Farther west toward the coast (and the Spanish border), is Basque country, another distinctive culture. The most popular gateway to the region is Biarritz, the "king" of France's Atlantic coast resorts, whose refinements once drew the crowned heads of Europe, and its beaches now attract the international surf set for their roaring Atlantic tides. East, toward the towering peaks of the central Pyrenees are lovely towns and even lovelier natural scenery.

Northeast of the Basque country, the Dordogne, in France's Périgord region, is famed for its prehistoric art, truffle-rich cuisine, and storybook villages. This living postcard is threaded by the picturesque Dordogne River, which weaves westward past prehistoric sites like Lascaux, where millions have witnessed prehistory writ large on its spectacularly painted cave walls.

West of the Dordogne toward the Atlantic coast lies Bordeaux, one of the France's great cities and even greater wine regions. As the capital of the historic province of Aquitaine, Bordeaux is both the commercial and cultural center of southwest France.

But a coastal drive in Corsica may well convince you that this most southerly of French destinations is indeed an enchanted island of fairy tales, with its rugged, mountainous terrain sheltering oak forests and vineyards, all giving way to a ring of endless sandy beaches and the glittering blue Mediterranean beyond.

Lascaux Cave Paintings

The Louvre of Paleolithic Art

In 1940, four schoolchildren looking for their lost dog discovered hundreds of wall paintings in this cave just south of Montignac; the paintings of horses, cows, black bulls, and unicorns were determined to be thousands of years old, making the cave famous and attracting throngs of visitors to the site. Over time, the original Lascaux cave paintings began to deteriorate due to exhaled carbon dioxide. To make the mysterious paintings accessible to the general public, the French authorities spent years perfecting a facsimile. In 2017, the most complete replica to date, opened within a sophisticated new complex—the International Center for Cave Art—that incorporates the latest technologies, including virtual reality, 3-D cinema, and digital tablets, for a totally immersive experience.

Don't Miss

The region is centered on Sarlat and its impeccably restored medieval buildings, but the area is honeycombed with dozens of *grottes* (caves) filled with Paleolithic drawings, etchings, and carvings. Lascaux is just south of Sarlat. To do justice to Sarlat, meander through its Cité Médiévale in the late afternoon or early evening, aided by the tourist office's walking map.

Getting Here

Trains make the trip from Paris to Sarlat in six hours, with a change in Souillac. The best way to reach Lascaux is by car, but you can also take the 07 bus serving Sarlat-la-Caděna-Montignac-Lascaux-Périgueux (🌐 *transports.nouvelle-aquitaine.fr*) to Montignac and then a taxi.

✉ *Rte. de la Grotte de Lascaux* ☎ *05–53–05–65–60* 🌐 *www.lascaux.fr* 🎫 *€20 Closed Jan. (timed ticket req.)*

Biarritz

The King of the Atlantic Coast Resorts

Biarritz, the gateway to France's Basque region, may no longer draw actual kings, but there's no shortage of deluxe hotel rooms or bow-tied gamblers ambling over to the casino. The city first rose to prominence when rich and royal Carlist exiles from Spain set up shop here in 1838. Unable to visit San Sebastién—just across the border on the Basque Coast—they sought a summer watering spot as close as possible to their old stomping ground. Among the exiles was Eugénie de Montijo, destined to become empress of France, whose villa is now the Hôtel du Palais, on Biarritz's main seaside promenade. If you want to rediscover yesteryear Biarritz, start by exploring the narrow streets around the cozy 16th-century church of St-Martin.

Don't Miss

Back in 1660, Louis XIV chose the tiny fishing village of St-Jean-de-Luz as the place to marry the Infanta Maria Teresa of Spain. Along the coast between Biarritz and the Spanish border, it remains memorable for its colorful harbor, old streets, curious church, and elegant beach. Its iconic port shares a harbor with its sister town Ciboure, on the other side of the Nivelle River. The historic multihued houses around the docks are evocative of its former glory.

Getting Here

TGV Inoui trains connect Paris and Biarritz six times daily (4 hours 16 minutes). The train station is southeast of the city core, so catch Bus No. 2 to reach the centrally located Hôtel de Ville. It's a quick train or bus ride to St-Jean-de-Luz.

Destination Biarritz. 🌐 *tourisme.biarritz.fr*

Carcassonne

France's Best-Preserved Medieval Village

Poised atop a hill overlooking lush green countryside and the Aude River, Carcassonne's fortified upper town, known as La Cité, looks lifted from the pages of a storybook—literally, perhaps, as its circle of towers and battlements is said to be the setting for Charles Perrault's classic tale *Puss in Boots*. With its turrets and castellated walls, it appeals to children and those with a penchant for the Middle Ages.

Don't Miss

Carcassonne usually goes medieval in mid-August with Les Médiévales, a festival of troubadour song, rich costumes, and jousting performances. And don't forget the spectacular Bastille Day (July 14) fireworks over La Cité.

Where to Stay

Hôtel de la Cité. Enjoying the finest location within the walls of the old city, this ivy-covered former Episcopal palace provides a high level of creature comfort, which the ascetic Cathars would most definitely have deprived themselves of. $ *Rooms from: €205* ✉ *Pl. August-Pierre Pont, La Cité* ☎ *04–68–71–98–71* 🌐 *www.cite-hotels.com*

Getting Here

There are 15 trains daily from Toulouse; from the station you can take a cab, hop a navette shuttle, or make the 30-minute walk up to La Cité. Bus service is available from Toulouse as well. If you're driving, park across the road from the drawbridge.

Destination Carcassone. 🌐 *www.tourisme-carcassonne.fr*

The Food of Lyon

The Birthplace of Modern French Cuisine

No other city in France teases the taste buds like Lyon, birthplace of traditional French cuisine. Home to both the workingman's *bouchons* and many celebrity chefs, the capital of the Rhône-Alpes region has become the engine room for France's modern cooking canon. Lyon's development owes much to its riverside location halfway between Paris and the Mediterranean, and within striking distance of Switzerland, Italy, and the Alps. The Lyonnais are proud that their city has been important for more than 2,000 years and has 12 restaurants with one or more Michelin stars.

Don't Miss

The charming Vieux Lyon has narrow cobblestone streets, 15th- and 16th-century mansions, loads of small museums, and a divine cathedral. Officially cataloged as national monuments, the courtyards and passageways are open to the public during the morning. Look for the quaint *traboules*, passageways under and through townhouses dating to the Renaissance (in Vieux Lyon) and the 19th century (in La Croix Rousse). Originally designed as shortcuts for silk weavers delivering their wares, they were used by the French Resistance during World War II to elude German street patrols. A map is available at the tourist office and in most hotel lobbies.

Getting Here

Lyon is easily reachable by rail from Paris and other places in France. Perrache is closer to the older parts of the city. There's also a metro system, and funiculars reach the higher parts of the old city.

Lyon Tourisme. 🌐 *en.lyon-france.com*

Château Mouton Rothschild

One of France's Greatest Wineries

Bordeaux as a whole, rather than any particular points within it, is what you'll want to visit in order to understand why it has always been so special. If you are a wine drinker, you must visit one of the famous châteaux. Most of the great vineyards in this area are strictly private, although owners are usually receptive to inquiries from bona fide wine connoisseurs. One, however, has long boasted a welcoming visitor center: Mouton Rothschild, whose eponymous wine was brought to perfection in the 1930s by that flamboyant figure Baron Philippe de Rothschild. Wine fans flock here for visits that might include a trip to the cellars, the *chai* (wine warehouse), and the museum, including a display of wine labels. There is, of course, a wine tasting at the end. All visits are by appointment only; be sure to reserve at least two weeks in advance.

Don't Miss

La Cité du Vin. Rising up on the Bordeaux cityscape like a silvery, wine decanter, the exterior of this contemporary building is inspired by the way wine swirls when it is poured into a glass. Inside, you'll find an interactive museum highlighting every aspect of the world of wine and wine making. ✉ *1 Esplanade de Pontac, Bordeaux* 🌐 *www.laciteduvin.com* 🎫 *€20*

Getting Here and Around

Bordeaux has an airport but is a bit more than two hours by train from Paris. Local trains take you to Pauillac, from where you can take a taxi to the chateau, but it's much easier if you have a car.

✉ *Le Pouyalet, Pauillac* ✈ *56 miles north of Bordeaux* ☎ *05–56–73–21–29* 🌐 *www.chateau-mouton-rothschild.com* 🕒 *Closed weekends* 🎫 *From €50*

Maison Bonaparte, Corsica

The Birthplace of an Emperor

"The best way to know Corsica," according to Napoléon, "is to be born there." Not everyone has had his luck, so chances are you'll be arriving on the overnight ferry from Marseille or flying in from Paris or Rome to discover "the Isle of Beauty." This vertical, chalky, granite Mediterranean island remains France's very own Wild West: a powerful natural setting and, literally, a breath of fresh air. Ajaccio, its largest city, is located on the west coast. Founded in 1492, most of this ville impériale's tourist trade revolves around its most famous son, Napoléon Bonaparte. The luminous seaside city is surrounded by snowcapped mountains and pretty beaches and offers numerous sites, eateries, side streets, and a popular harbor.

Don't Miss

One of four national historic museums dedicated to Napoléon, the multilevel house where the emperor was born on August 15, 1769, contains memorabilia and paintings of the extended Bonaparte family. History aficionados can tour the rooms where Charles and Letitzia Bonaparte raised their eight children. Visit the trapdoor room and find the opening next to the door through which Napoléon allegedly escaped in 1799.

Getting Here

You can fly to Ajaccio, then take a shuttle or taxi into town. Ferries from Nice, Toulon, and Marseilles are also frequent, taking about six hours.

Maison Bonaparte. ✉ *Rue St-Charles* 🌐 *www.musees-nationaux-malmaison.fr* 🎫 €7 🕓 *Closed Mon.*

Office de Tourisme d'Ajaccio. ✉ *www.ajaccio-tourisme.com*

Skiing in Chamonix-Mont-Blanc

France's Venerable Ski Resort

Chamonix-Mont-Blanc is the oldest and biggest of the French winter-sports resort towns and was the site of the first Winter Olympics, held in 1924. Although the ski areas are spread out, it's more approachable and affordable than Courchevel, its more upscale cousin. Some runs are extremely memorable, such as the 20-km (12-mile) one through the Vallée Blanche or the off-trail area of Les Grands Montets. And the situation is getting better: many lifts have been added, improving access to the slopes as well as shortening lift lines. In summer it's a great place for hiking, climbing, and enjoying dazzling views. If you're heading to Italy via the Mont Blanc Tunnel, Chamonix will be your gateway.

Don't Miss

Aiguille du Midi, a 12,619-foot granite peak, is topped with a needle-like observation tower, terrace, and restaurants. The world's highest cable car soars 12,000 feet up, almost to the top (an elevator completes the journey to the summit), providing positively staggering views of 15,700-foot Mont Blanc, Europe's loftiest peak. ✉ *100 pl. de l'aiguille du Midi, Chamonix-Mont-Blanc* 🌐 *www.montblancnaturalresort.com* 🎫 *Cable car €67 round-trip*

Getting Here

TGV trains from Lyon-Saint-Exupéry airport take 1 hour 55 minutes. There's also TGV service from Paris's Gare de Lyon (3 hours 42 minutes). The required train ride from St-Gervais-Les-Bains to Chamonix is in itself an incredible trip, up the steepest railway in Europe. You'll feel your body doing strange things to adjust to the pressure change.

Chamonix Tourist Office. ✉ *85 pl. du Triangle de l'Amitié, Chamonix-Mont-Blanc* ☎ *04–50–53–00–24* 🌐 *www.chamonix.com*

Southern France and Corsica
Le Mans
Orléans
Auxerre
Tours
Nantes
Saumur
Cholet
Vierzon
Bourges
Chatearoux
Poitiers
Les Sables-d Olonne
Niort
La Rochelle
Moulins
Montlucon
Gueret
Bellac
Gannat
Saintes
Limoges
Angouleme
Clermont-Ferrand
FRANCE
Château Mouton Rothschild
Perigueux
Tulle
Brive-La-Gaillarde
Lascaux Cave Paintings
Bordeaux
Bergerac
Saint-Flour
Aurillac
Bay of Biscay
Langon
Cahors
Rodez
Agen
Roquefort
Caussade
Montauban
Albi
Mont-de-Marsan
Aire-sur-L'adour
Auch
Toulouse
Castres
Mazamet
Lodeve
Montpellier
Biarritz
Pau
Tarbes
Beziers
Sete
Carcassonne
Narbonne
Pamplona
ANDORRA
Andorra la Vella
Perpignan
SPAIN
Zaragoza
Lleida
Barcelona
E5
A77
E15
E9
E62
A83
E11
N7
E70
E606
E72
N88
E80
E7
N240
A2
E90

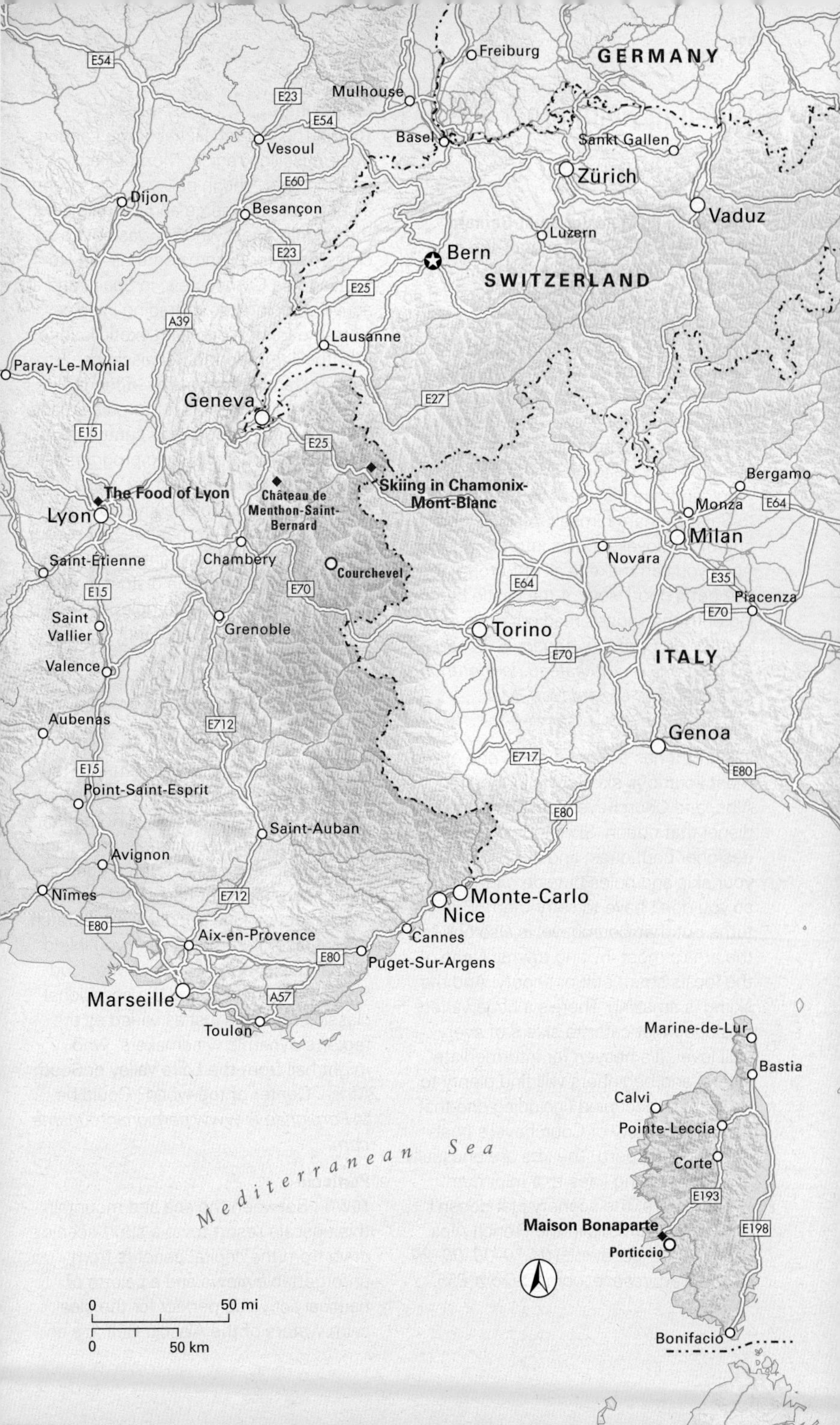

GERMANY
Freiburg
Mulhouse
Basel
Sankt Gallen
Zürich
Vaduz
Vesoul
Dijon
Besançon
Luzern
Bern
SWITZERLAND
Lausanne
Paray-Le-Monial
Geneva
The Food of Lyon
Château de Menthon-Saint-Bernard
Skiing in Chamonix-Mont-Blanc
Lyon
Bergamo
Monza
Milan
Saint-Étienne
Chambery
Courchevel
Novara
Saint Vallier
Grenoble
Torino
Piacenza
Valence
ITALY
Aubenas
Genoa
Point-Saint-Esprit
Saint-Auban
Avignon
Nîmes
Monte-Carlo
Nice
Aix-en-Provence
Cannes
Puget-Sur-Argens
Marseille
Toulon
Marine-de-Lur
Bastia
Calvi
Pointe-Leccia
Corte
Maison Bonaparte
Porticcio
Bonifacio
Mediterranean Sea
E54
E23
E60
E25
A39
E27
E15
E70
E64
E35
E712
E717
E80
A57
E193
E198
0
50 mi
0
50 km

When in Southern France and Corsica

★ Château de Menthon-Saint-Bernard

CASTLE/PALACE | The exterior of the magnificent Château de Menthon-Saint-Bernard is the stuff of fairy tales (so much so that Walt Disney modeled his version of Sleeping Beauty's castle on it); the interior is even better. The castle's medieval rooms—many adorned with tapestries, Romanesque frescoes, Netherlandish sideboards, and heraldic motifs—have been lovingly restored by the owner, who can trace his ancestry directly back to Saint-Bernard himself. All in all, this is one of the loveliest dips into the Middle Ages you can make in all of Europe. You can get a good view of the castle by turning onto the Thones road out of Veyrier. ✉ *Allée du Château, Annecy* ☎ *04–50–60–12–05* 🌐 *www.chateau-de-menthon.com* 🎫 *€11* 🕒 *Closed Nov.–Mar.*

Courchevel

RESORT | It has a reputation as one of the most luxurious ski resorts in the French Alps, and Courchevel doesn't do much to dispel that notion. Ski shops glitter like designer boutiques, and ski valets place your skis and poles outside on the snow so you don't have to carry them. But it turns out that Courchevel is also one of the area's most inviting towns. None of the locals seem stiff or snooty. And the skiing is amazing. There's a huge variety of slopes that cater to skiers of every skill level. It's heaven for intermediate skiers, and beginners will find plenty to keep them occupied (including one that has a great view of Courchevel's postage-stamp airport). The lifts are unusually speedy, keeping lines to a minimum. What's more, the scenery just doesn't get better than this in the French Alps. ✉ *D91A, Courchevel* ☎ *04-79-08-00-29* 🌐 *www.courchevel.com* 🎫 *From €55.*

Montpellier

TOWN | The vibrant capital of the Languedoc-Roussillon region, Montpellier (pronounced "monh-pell-yay") has been a center of commerce and learning since the Middle Ages, when it was both a crossroads for pilgrims on their way to Santiago de Compostela, in Spain, and an active shipping center trading in spices from the East. Along with exotic luxuries, Montpellier imported Renaissance learning, and its university—founded in the 13th century—has nurtured a steady influx of ideas through the centuries. An imaginative urban planning program has streamlined the 17th-century Vieille Ville, and monumental perspectives dwarf passersby on the Promenade du Peyrou. An even more utopian venture in urban planning is the Antigone district, a vast, harmonious, 100-acre complex designed in 1984 by Barcelona architect Ricardo Bofill. ✉ *Montpellier* 🌐 *www.montpellier-france.com.*

Perpignan

TOWN | Salvador Dalí once called Perpignan's train station "the center of the world." That may not be true, but the city certainly is the capital hub of Roussillon. Perpignan tends to echo its surrounding agricultural landscape, rough around the edges and full of yet-unrealized potential that attracts a kind of bold spirit. Scratch the surface of Perpignan and you'll find Roma music, deep Catalan pride, loud Spanish influences, and the occasional classic crepe. It's just as varied as the region's dynamic winemakers, who might hail from the Loire Valley or South Africa. Center of the world? Could be. ✉ *Perpignan* 🌐 *www.perpignantourisme.com.*

Porticcio

TOWN | Between the sea and mountain, this upscale resort town a short scenic drive from the capital benefits from unforgettable views and a palette of nautical activities perfect for the clear, calm waters of the Ajaccio Gulf. It's an oasis, dotted with a number of luxury resorts, notable for its beaches, verdant countryside, and ancient Tower of Capitello. Discover the stunning landscape with boat excursions offered by Découvertes Naturelle (*www.promenades-en-mer.org*). *Porticcio* *www.ornanotaravo-tourisme.corsica*.

Where to Eat and Drink

★ Auberge du Père Bise
$$$$ | FRENCH | For anyone who's never dined in one of France's grand old restaurants, this two-star stunner would be a fine start. Set in a century-old chalet-inn in the tiny storybook village of Talloires, on the incomparably beautiful Lac d'Annecy, from start to finish you'll be pampered in the old style. **Known for:** stunning lakeside setting; distinguished menu of French classics; legendary restaurant. *Average main: €84* *303 rte. du Port, Annecy* *04–50–60–72–01* *www.perebise.com* *Closed Tues., Wed., and mid-Dec.–mid-Feb.*

★ Garriane
$$$$ | INTERNATIONAL | Foodies appreciate Garriane's direct approach to eating and drinking well. Here a plain-Jane decor and a dim neighborhood spectacularly contrast with immaculate plates presented by the Aussie-bred chef (who incidentally shook up Perpignan's sleepy food scene with a strictly seasonal menu emphasizing local produce boldly prepared for an exotic outcome). **Known for:** nine-course degustation menu that's the best meal in Perpignan; affordable lunch menu; booking ahead a must. *Average main: €37* *18 Carrer Frédéric Valette, Perpignan* *04–68–67–07–44* *Closed Sun.–Tues. No lunch Wed. and Sat.*

La Cave des Creux
$$$ | FRENCH | An amazing view of Mont Blanc is yours at the Cave des Creux, opened by a couple of ski instructors on top of what was once a shelter for shepherds and their flocks (you can still see some of the old cheese cellar and its equipment on the lower level). It's hard to resist the stone-trimmed dining room, where huge iron beams, industrial lighting, and a sleek fireplace give the place a modern feel. **Known for:** fabulous decor and setting, including a wraparound deck; menu of forward-thinking French classics; organic wine list. *Average main: €32* *Courchevel 1850, Courchevel* *04–79–06–76–14* *www.cavedescreux-courchevel.com* *Closed May–Nov.*

Le Cabanon Bleu
$$$ | SEAFOOD | About a mile outside Ajaccio, this restaurant provides wonderful views across Ajaccio Bay from its attractive terrace at the edge of the sea. Given its location, it's no surprise that Le Cabanon Bleu specializes in fresh fish and seafood dishes such as grilled langoustine and tuna, but duck and beef are also on the menu. **Known for:** John Dory tartare; fresh seafood platters; excellent lobster. *Average main: €26* *65 cours Lucien Bonaparte, Ajaccio* *04–95–51–02–15* *www.cabanon-bleu.com*.

Le Chat Perché
$$$ | FRENCH | This eatery is a popular choice, especially when sunny weather encourages taking a seat on the terrace, overlooking the square below. The cuisine varies with the seasons, the markets, and the humor of the chef, but everything is homemade and reasonably priced. **Known for:** warm bistro ambience; carefully curated regional wine list; traditional dishes served with flair. *Average main: €26* *Pl. de la Chapelle Neuve, 10 rue college Duvergier, Montpellier* *04–67–60–88–59* *www.le-chat-perche-restaurant.fr* *Closed Sun. No lunch.*

Cool Places to Stay

★ **Baudon de Mauny**

$$ | B&B/INN | The finest rooms in Montpellier (and quite possibly the whole region) can be found at this chic guesthouse on one of the historic district's nicest streets. **Pros:** gorgeous architectural design; extra-spacious rooms; flawless service. **Cons:** no on-site parking; several flights of stairs; expensive for the area. *Rooms from: €220* *1 rue de la Carbonnerie, Montpellier* *04–67–02–21–77* *www.baudondemauny.com* *9 rooms* *No Meals.*

★ **Casa 9**

$$ | HOTEL | Among the orchards and vineyards in the countryside surrounding Perpignan sits Casa 9, a 15th-century *mas* (farm) with a barn that's been converted into lavish lodgings. **Pros:** all rooms look onto a patio or garden; property shaded by lush palms and 100-year old trees; stylish interiors. **Cons:** no on-site restaurant; a car is essential; breakfast not included. *Rooms from: €129* *Mas Petit, Rte. de Corbère, Perpignan* *07–78–80–54–35* *www.casa9hotel.fr* *Closed early Jan.* *9 rooms* *No Meals.*

★ **Le Maquis**

$$$$ | HOTEL | FAMILY | One of the island's finest *hôtels de charme,* this graceful, ivy-covered Genoese-style retreat rambles down through terraced gardens to a private beach overlooking the Golfe d'Ajaccio. **Pros:** exceptional restaurant with terrace; its own beach with naturally protected cove; a massage and treatment room. **Cons:** near airport, so there is some airplane noise; no gym; nonheated outdoor pool (but heated one inside). *Rooms from: €580* *Bd. Marie-Jeanne Bozzi, Porticcio* *19 km (12 miles) south of Ajacio* *04–95–25–05–55* *www.lemaquis.com* *Closed Jan.–Feb. 14* *25 rooms* *No Meals.*

★ **Le Strato**

$$$$ | HOTEL | Despite its undeniable sophistication, Le Strato manages to convey a delicious coziness that extends from the contemporary dining room to the beautifully appointed guest rooms and pristine-white marble baths. **Pros:** superb views; fun programs for kids; cozy elegance. **Cons:** room lighting can be tricky but allows for subtlety; live bar entertainment sometimes amateurish; off-the-charts expensive. *Rooms from: €3430* *Rue de Bellecôte, Courchevel* *04–79–41–51–60* *www.hotelstrato.com* *Closed Apr.–mid-Dec.* *26 rooms* *Free Breakfast.*

★ **Splendid Hotel**

$$ | HOTEL | Just steps from crystalline Lac d'Annecy, overlooking a lovely canal running through Annecy's Old Town, this nicely renovated hotel has all the comfort and charm you could want plus the best location possible. **Pros:** hotel-subsidized parking nearby; some rooms have balconies; nice contemporary decor. **Cons:** some noise due to hardwood floors; not all rooms have showers; service varies. *Rooms from: €168* *4 quai Eustache Chappuis, Annecy* *04–50–45–20–00* *www.hotel-annecy-lac.fr* *47 rooms* *No Meals.*

Belgium

Belgium has attractions far out of proportion to its diminutive size. From medieval cities and abbeys where Trappist monks still run their own breweries to its wide stretches of countryside and famous World War I and II battlegrounds, it's a little country that packs a big punch.

Capital Brussels is vibrant, cosmopolitan, and far more than Europe's administrative hub. The city was home to Victor Horta, Jacques Brel, René Magritte, Georges Remi (better known as Hergé, creator of Tintin), and many other famous people you thought were actually French and brims with museums celebrating their achievements. But for all its world-class dining, architecture, and art, the city keeps a low profile; that means you'll have plenty of breathing room to relish its Art Nouveau townhouses, graffiti trails, grand square, and the siren call of its *friteries* and chocolate shops.

With around a million inhabitants, Brussels has the boulevards and palaces one would expect from a European capital. Its closest rival in terms of size is the port of Antwerp, although the two differ greatly in character. While the capital draws visitors for its sights, its sister city remains more of a shopping destination, filled with high-end boutiques and enough diamond stores to bankrupt the most prudent of billionaires. Brussels has the culture, but Antwerp is where the cool kids go.

For pure history, head instead to Bruges, a medieval city on a more manageable scale. Its cobbled streets, Gothic wonders, and fine eateries are no secret though. Ypres, in southern Flanders, is a destination shaped by more recent history, namely World War I, which virtually destroyed the town, which now hosts several moving museums and monuments to the Great War's destruction. To escape the tourist beat, lively Mons and stately Tournai (the only part of Belgium ever to be conquered by the British) offer a fine alternative and are only a short hop from the Ardennes of southern Wallonia, a beautiful area of ancient villages riddled with caves and wrapped by looping rivers and pristine forests. Dinant is one of the most charismatic of those towns.

Brussels

Stroll the City of Art Nouveau

Brussels is a capital of paradoxes. For all its reputation as a city of architectural blunders (fueled by rampant postwar redevelopment), it was also the playground of early-20th-century "starchitect" Victor Horta, whose light touch can still be seen in the airy town houses of the Schaerbeek, Ixelles, and Saint-Gilles districts. In the latter, his former home has been turned into an intriguing museum. Elsewhere, Art Nouveau walking tours offer a slower take on the capital and unravel some other gems, such as the Paul Cauchie house near Parc du Cinquantenaire (itself an architectural wonder), whose dazzling *sgraffito* facade glitters in the midday sun. Everywhere you look, from the gilded excess of the Grand Place to the austere Neoclassical mansions of Upper Town, this is a city that rewards *flâneurs*.

Don't Miss

Upper Town is the cultural heartbeat of the capital, filled with excellent museums ranging from the royal art collections to the Coudenberg, still lie beneath the street. You can visit the current royal home in the summer months, but spare time, too, for the Musical Instrument Museum, quietly the most engaging escape in the city.

Getting Here and Around

The capital is well-connected by buses, trams, and metro lines, and has trains to most major Belgian cities as well as Amsterdam, Paris, Luxembourg City, and others. It is also served by a pair of international airports (Zaventem and Charleroi) with direct flights from the U.S.

Brussels Tourist Information. ✉ *Grand Place, Lower Town* ☎ *02/513–8940* 🌐 *visit.brussels/en*

Musée Horta. ✉ *Rue Américaine 25, Saint-Gilles* 🌐 *hortamuseum.be*

Antwerp

Party in Belgium's Capital of Style

Like many port cities, Antwerp retains an outsized influence in some unexpected realms. Its diamond district is world-famous, and some 80% of the planet's rough diamonds are still traded here. It is also a leader in fashion. Since the 1980s, Antwerp-trained fashion designers have been renowned for their experimental styles, as seen in the many boutiques that lie off the Meir and in the MoMu design museum. This is naturally where Belgium's bright young things come to shop and to spend. Areas such as the Wilde Zee, a five-street-wide shopping mecca of boutiques and pop-ups, fill during the day; by night the likes of the two-Michelin-starred The Jane restaurant (in a former military hospital) transform Antwerp's dining scene. This is a city of excess, so arrive ready to indulge.

Don't Miss

Antwerp's art scene was once the envy of Europe, and masterpieces by Peter Paul Rubens (whose house lies off the Meir), Pieter Bruegel, and other Flemish greats are seen in the Museum Mayer Van den Bergh and the Snijders & Rockoxhuis. But, for all its culture, perhaps the best day out is De Ruien, 8 km (5 miles) of underground sewers, canals, and tunnels that were covered up in the 1800s.

Getting Here and Around

Antwerp is threaded by a "premetro" tram network that dives underground and links most areas. Regular trains arrive at the city's Centraal Station from Brussels, Bruges, and Ghent.

MoMu. ✉ *Nationalestraat 28* 🌐 *momu.be*

Visit Antwerpen. ✉ *Steenplein 1, Oude Stad* 🌐 *www.visitantwerpen.be*

Dinant

Follow Your "Meuse" Down to Dinant

The most charismatic part of Belgium's Ardennes region lies south of the old Roman town of Namur, gateway to the region. Here you'll find Dinant, simultaneously hanging off and tucked under spectacular cliffs on the Meuse river. It has a surprisingly industrial past, and once rode the crest of the 12th- and 15th-century copper booms; now it caters to the many visitors who flock here to discover the city's historic ruins. Climb the 408 steps carved into the rockface that lead up to its citadel; visit the nearby Châteaux de Freyr, an impressive Renaissance home filled with 17th-century woodwork; then kayak the looping river waters beneath the old town. There is plenty of charm to be found and a culinary scene to rival any of Belgium's big cities.

Don't Miss

The Ardennes stretches across most of southern Wallonia, from the beer-brewing abbeys of Chimay and Rochefort in the west to the German-speaking High Fens (Hautes Fagnes) of the east, where a large expanse of peat bogs, heath, and marshland switches up the landscape. Along the way, make stops at the scenic La-Roche-en-Ardennes and historic Bastogne, famed for its World War II siege by the Germans, a time when the Battle of the Bulge tore this land apart.

Getting Here and Around

Buses connect up many of the small towns and regular trains connect Dinant to Namur, but to reach the many castles and houses that dot the region, you'll need your own set of wheels.

Visit Ardennes. 🌐 *www.visitardenne.com*

Bruges

Discover the Flemish Primitives

The well-preserved cobbles, churches, and canals of Bruges recall when this was one of the wealthiest medieval cities in Europe. By the time Flanders became a Burgundian state in the 15th century, it was already a playground for wealthy patrons and artists, spawning the local Flemish Primitive style of painting. It became a revolution in realism, portraiture, and perspective, capturing the era in astonishing detail. The work of prominent artists from this time, such as Hans Memling and Jan van Eyck, can be seen in Bruges' excellent Groeningemuseum, which offers a crash course in Flemish art. You'll also find artistic treasures across the city, from Michelangelo's *Madonna and Child* at the Church of Our Lady to the impressive collection of Memling paintings at the Sint-Janshospitaal Museum.

Don't Miss

Boat the canals, visit the excellent Gruuthusemuseum, take a tour of the iconic Halve Maan Brewery, and buy chocolate. If you're not tired after that, rent a bike and pedal the lesser-seen fringes of town where you'll find fewer crowds.

When to Go

On Ascension Day, a vial, thought to contain a few drops of the blood of Christ, is carried through the streets from the Gothic basilica.

Getting Here and Around

Direct trains connect Bruges to Ghent and Brussels on the same line. Cars are only a burden in this pedestrianized town.

Bruges Tourist Information. 🌐 *www.visitbruges*

Groeningemuseum. ✉ *Dijver 12* 🌐 *museabrugge.be*

Ypres

Remembering the Battles of World War I

Eastern Belgium was the setting for some of the most brutal fighting of the 20th century as Europe clashed in the fields of Flanders during World War I (1914–18). It was here that Ypres (Ieper), a quiet convent town, was drawn into the crossfire after neutral Belgium was forced into the Great War. The area became the site of four major battles, culminating in 1918, when the Allies finally broke the German lines. Around Ypres, guided tours relive the horrors of its battlefield sites, while museums in the surrounding towns break them down in finer detail. In the city, In Flanders Fields museum and the Menenpoort memorial (an area once dubbed "Hellfire Corner" by Allied soldiers) both offer an unvarnished glimpse of this era. At the latter is inscribed the names of 55,000 soldiers, many of whom were never found, such was the carnage.

Don't Miss

Not far from Ypres lies the Memorial Museum Passchenge 1917 in Zonnebeke, which re-creates the tragic Third Battle of Ypres and is home to the largest collection of World War I memorabilia in Flanders.

Getting Here and Around

Hourly trains run directly from Ghent to Ypres in 1 hour and 10 minutes; those from Brussels and Bruges must change at Kortrijk. There is little public transport around the battlefield sites. To visit them properly, you will require your own vehicle or a guided tour.

In Flanders Fields Museum. ✉ *Grote Markt 34, Ypres* 🌐 *www.inflandersfields.be* 🎫 €10 🕒 *Closed Mon. mid-Nov.–Mar.*

Tourist Office Ieper. 🌐 *www.toerismeieper.be*

Carnaval de Binche

Join the Carnival

Western Wallonia is filled with strange and colorful folkloric festivals. The Doudou of Mons, the *Geants* (giants) parade of Ath, the silent procession of Lessines all conjure another era. But none are so unusual (and drunken) as that of tiny Binche, a celebration said to date from a week of festivities held for the visit of Charles V in 1549. It requires six months of planning, with events beginning on the Sunday before Ash Wednesday. At its center are the Gilles, local Binchois costumed somewhat eerily in identical waxed masks painted with green spectacles and large mustaches. They march the town in a two-step shuffle accompanied by all sorts of medieval figures as visitors spill out of the bars on the town square to egg them on.

Don't Miss

If you can't make it for the festival, it's worth popping into Binche's Musée du Carnaval et du Masque, a museum that delves into the histories of folkloric festivals in the Wallonia region. It also has VR headsets that drop you into the action of carnivals gone by.

Where to Eat

Brasserie la Binchoise. A go-to restaurant in Binche for a good meal and a beer. This old-school brasserie-cum-brewpub, at the foot of the city ramparts, has been brewing here since the 1800s. *brasserielabinchoise.be*

Getting Here

Binche is on the same railway line that runs through Tournai, Mons, and Charleroi, all of which have connections to Brussels.

Binche Tourism. 🌐 *www.binche.be*

Musée du Carnaval et du Masque. ✉ *Rue Saint-Moustier 10* 🌐 *museedu-masque.be*

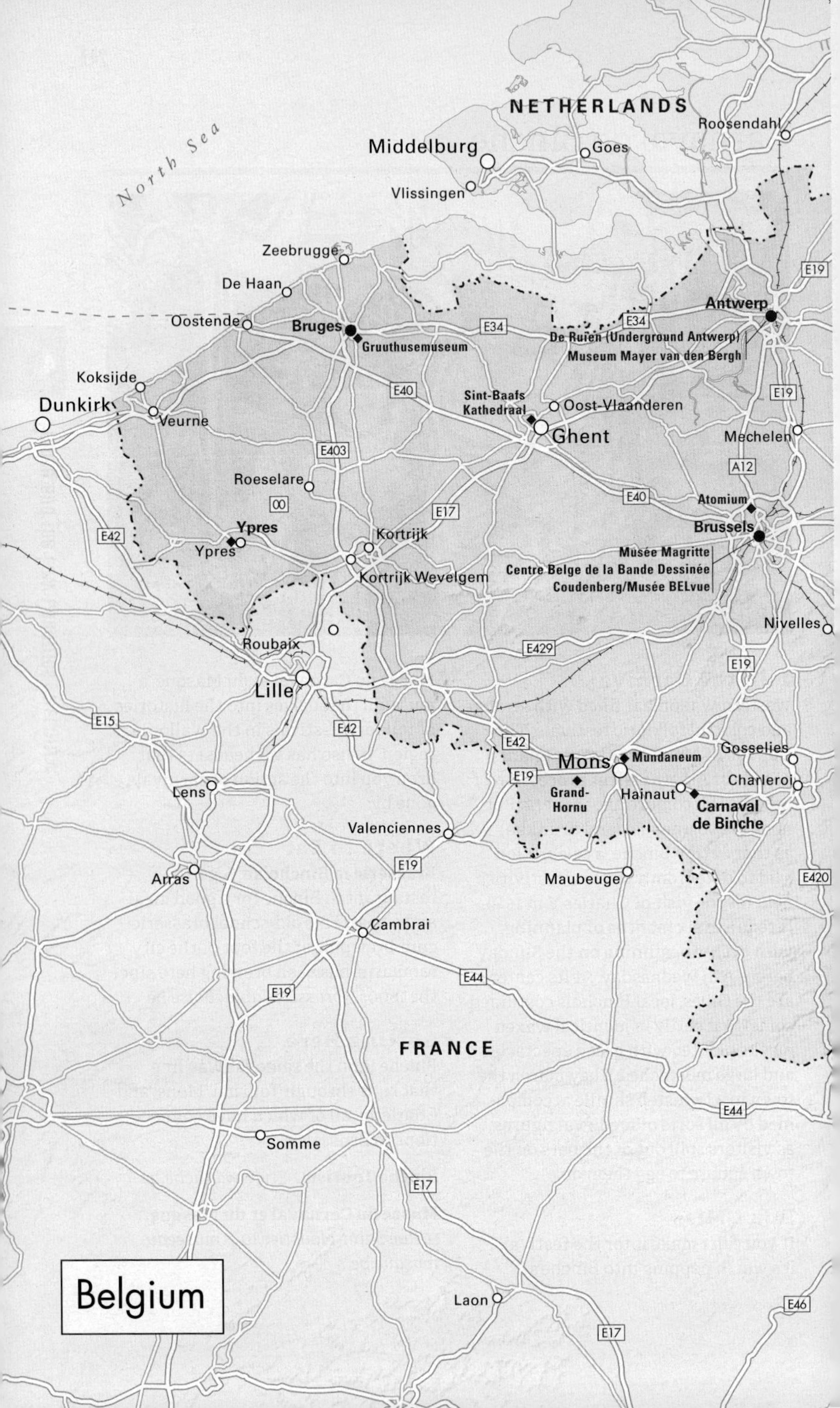
North Sea
NETHERLANDS
Middelburg
Goes
Roosendahl
Vlissingen
Zeebrugge
De Haan
Oostende
Bruges
Gruuthusemuseum
E34
De Ruïen (Underground Antwerp)
Museum Mayer van den Bergh
Antwerp
E19
Koksijde
Dunkirk
Veurne
E40
Sint-Baafs Kathedraal
Oost-Vlaanderen
Ghent
Mechelen
A12
E403
Roeselare
00
E17
Atomium
Brussels
Musée Magritte
Centre Belge de la Bande Dessinée
Coudenberg/Musée BELvue
E42
Ypres
Kortrijk
Kortrijk Wevelgem
Nivelles
Roubaix
E429
Lille
E15
Gosselies
Mons
Mundaneum
Charleroi
Grand-Hornu
Hainaut
Carnaval de Binche
Lens
Valenciennes
Arras
Maubeuge
E420
Cambrai
E44
FRANCE
Somme
Belgium
Laon
E46

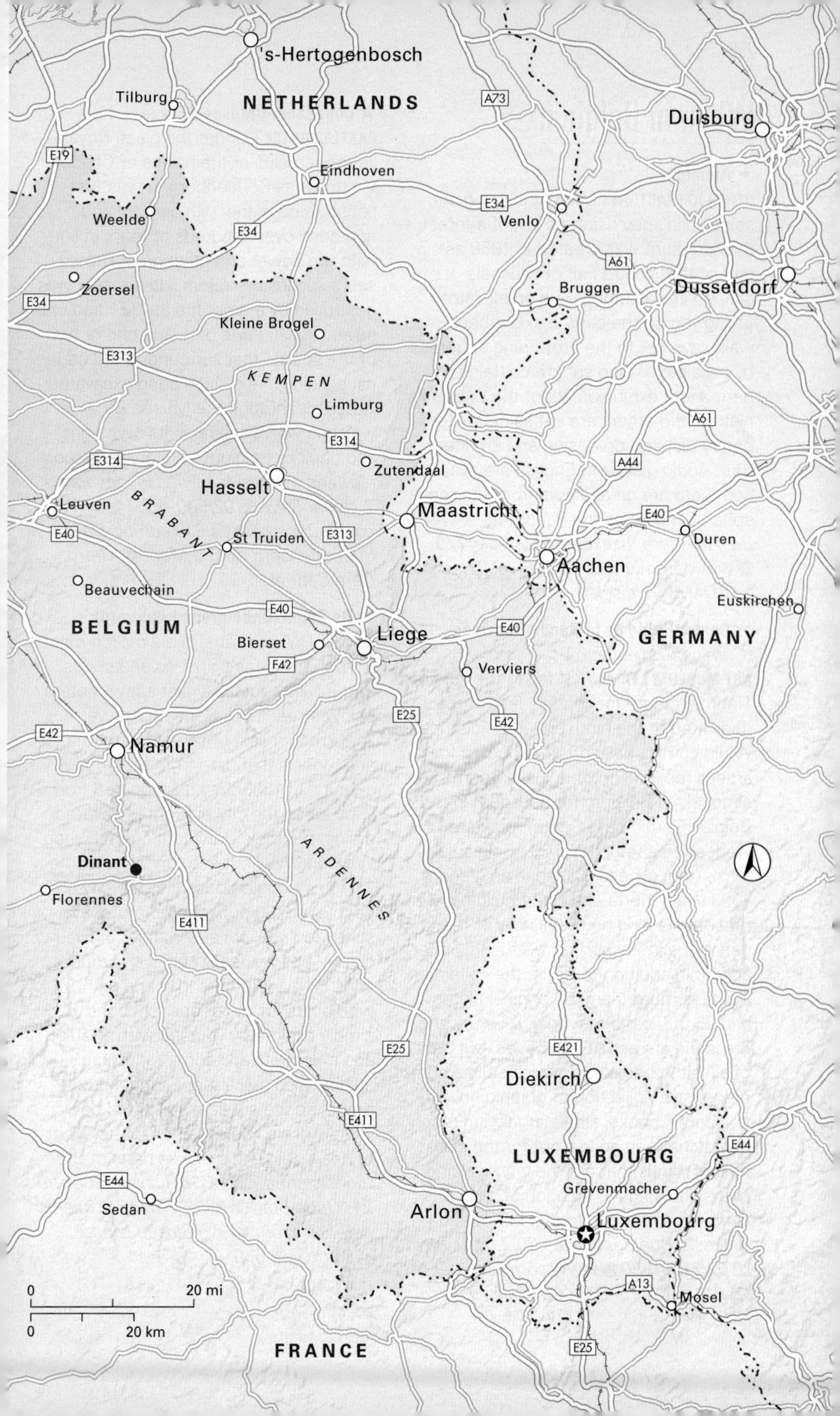

's-Hertogenbosch
NETHERLANDS
Tilburg
A73
Duisburg
E19
Eindhoven
E34
Weelde
Venlo
E34
A61
Zoersel
Bruggen
Dusseldorf
E34
Kleine Brogel
E313
KEMPEN
Limburg
A61
E314
A44
E314
Zutendaal
Hasselt
BRABANT
Leuven
Maastricht
E40
E40
Duren
St Truiden
E313
Aachen
Beauvechain
Euskirchen
E40
BELGIUM
E40
Liege
GERMANY
Bierset
E42
Verviers
E25
E42
E42
Namur
ARDENNES
Dinant
Florennes
E411
E421
E25
Diekirch
E411
E44
LUXEMBOURG
E44
Grevenmacher
Sedan
Arlon
Luxembourg
A13
Mosel
0
20 mi
0
20 km
FRANCE
E25

When in Belgium

★ Atomium

OTHER ATTRACTION | FAMILY | Like a giant, shiny child's toy rising up out of a forest, the Atomium was created in 1958 as part of the World's Fair of Brussels. It's shaped like an atom, with an elevator taking you up the central axis where walkways link to the protruding spheres by escalators. One sphere contains a permanent exhibition about the building's history; the others are set aside for temporary displays on design and architecture. Audio guides in English are available and there are great views from the top sphere, known as the Panorama. ✉ *Av. de l'Atomium, Laeken* ☎ *02/475–4775* 🌐 *www.atomium.be* 🎫 *€16; includes visit to ADAM* Ⓜ *Heisel.*

★ Centre Belge de la Bande Dessinée (*Comics Art Museum*)

ART MUSEUM | FAMILY | It fell to the land of Tintin to create the world's first museum dedicated to the ninth art—comic strips. While comics have often struggled for artistic recognition, they have been taken seriously in Belgium for decades. In the Belgian Comic Strip Center, they are wedded to another strongly Belgian art form: Art Nouveau. Based in an elegant 1903 Victor Horta–designed building, the museum is long on the history of the genre, if a little short on kid-friendly interaction. In addition to Tintin, the collection includes more than 400 original plates and 25,000 cartoon works. A library and brasserie are added incentives, but best of all is the bookshop, which sells a comprehensive collection of graphic novels and comic books, albeit largely in French or Dutch. Keep an eye out for the **comic-strip murals** that dot the city; walking maps showing the location of each one can be found at the tourist information office. ✉ *Rue des Sables 20, Lower Town* ☎ *02/219–1980* 🌐 *www.comicscenter.net* 🎫 *€10* Ⓜ *Metro: Gare Centrale.*

★ Coudenberg/Musée BELvue

CASTLE/PALACE | Under the place Royale lie the remains of the palace of Charles V. Known as Coudenberg, it was first constructed in the 11th century and upgraded over hundreds of years in line with the power and prestige of Brussels's successive rulers. However, it was destroyed by a great fire in 1731 and was never rebuilt. Parts of it, and one or two of the streets that surrounded the original building, have since been excavated. Access is through the Musée BELvue, which is worth seeing in its own right and unpicks Belgium's history of democracy and its royal family. ✉ *Pl. des Palais 7, Upper Town* ☎ *02/500–4554* 🌐 *www.coudenberg.com* 🎫 *€18 combo ticket* 🕓 *Coudenberg closed Mon.* Ⓜ *Metro: Gare Central.*

★ De Ruien (Underground Antwerp)

TUNNEL | What seems like a million miles from the Rubens paintings and shops of the Meir is actually just a few meters below street level. Beneath Antwerp lie 8 km (5 miles) of sewers, streams, and tunnels that date from the 16th century. In 1885 they disappeared from view when the city brought in covered drains, but their story continued. During WWI and WWII, these tunnels became a way to smuggle goods into the city and people out. Suit up (special protective suits are supplied) and wander old vaults, canals, bridges, and medieval fortifications on guided tours (day and night), with boats for the deeper sections; or simply explore by yourself with a tablet and map. Rats and some rather big spiders also make these tunnels their home, so the squeamish should beware. Tours will also be called off in the event of heavy rain—this makes parts of the tunnels unnavigable. ✉ *Ruihuis, Suikerrui 21, Oude Stad* ☎ *03/344–0755* 🌐 *ruien.be/en* 🎫 *From €19* 🕓 *Closed Mon.* Ⓜ *Tram 3, 4, 5, 9.*

★ **Grand-Hornu**

ART MUSEUM | Around 12 km (7½ miles) west of Mons, the Borinage yields one of its grandest visions. Many of the industrialists of the late-18th and 19th centuries built accommodation for their workers. These were typically squalid, pragmatic affairs, but the Grand-Hornu was different. It was the dream child of the French industrialist Henri de Gorge (1774–1832), who created a vast neoclassical hub for his workers in 1810. Its 450 homes were spacious, had hot water, and the facilities were plentiful. Workers had access to a school, clinic, dance hall, and library. In 1829, some 2,500 people lived here, but by 1954, the local mines had closed and the site was abandoned. It has since been restored and is now home to an acclaimed contemporary art museum, yet it's worth visiting just to see the grounds, encircled by redbrick arches like some industrial colosseum. This remains a curious anachronism, out of step with what was mostly a dehumanizing era for workers, and was designated a UNESCO World Heritage site in 2012. ✉ *Rue Sainte-Louise 82, Boussu* ✥ *10 km (6 miles) east of Mons* ☏ *065/613–881* 🌐 *www.cid-grand-hornu.be* 🎫 *€10* 🕒 *Closed Mon.* Ⓜ *Bus: 7, 9.*

★ **Gruuthusemuseum**

HISTORY MUSEUM | Arguably the city's finest museum lies within a house built in the 15th century for the Gruuthuses, a powerful family who made their money on the exclusive right to sell "gruut," an herbal mixture used for flavoring beer. Louis, the patriarch behind its rise, was a businessman, diplomat, patron, and a lover of culture. Of course, its history didn't end there, and it has stood throughout the ups and downs of one of the great medieval cities. The museum tells the story of Bruges through its most powerful family and their legacy of art and relics, but also through the museum's own collection of crafts—lace, amber, porcelain, jewels—that formed the backbone of the city's trade. ✉ *Dijver 17C, Bruges* ☏ *050/448–743* 🌐 *www.museabrugge.be* 🎫 *From €14* 🕒 *Closed Mon.* Ⓜ *Bus: 1, 11.*

★ **Mundaneum**

HISTORY MUSEUM | This UNESCO-recognized endeavor tells a little-known story. At the dawn of the 20th century, a pair of human-rights lawyers, Paul Otlet and Henri La Fontaine (Belgium's only Nobel Peace Prize winner), had the idea for a paper database of all knowledge. They called it the Mundaneum. By 1972 it held 12 million bibliographic records (index cards). The building is now a fascinating museum. ✉ *Rue de Nimy 76, Mons* ☏ *065/315–343* 🌐 *www.mundaneum.org* 🎫 *€7* 🕒 *Closed Mon. and Tues.*

★ **Musée Magritte**

ART MUSEUM | After years of sharing display space in the neighboring museum complex on rue de la Régence, Surrealist genius René Magritte (1898–1967) finally got his own, much-deserved space. The collection starts on level three, tracing Magritte's life and work chronologically. The artist's mother committed suicide when he was 13; certainly, her profession as a milliner is difficult to separate from his later obsession with hats. The museum expands key moments through letters, sculptures, films, and, of course, some 200 paintings, including the haunting *The Domain of Arnheim.* ✉ *Entrance at pl. Royale 1; buy tickets at rue de la Régence 3, Upper Town* ☏ *02/508–3211* 🌐 *www.musee-magritte-museum.be* 🎫 *€10, combo ticket €15 (includes entry to Oldmasters and Fin-de-Siècle museums)* 🕒 *Closed Mon.* Ⓜ *Metro: Gare Centrale.*

★ **Museum Mayer Van den Bergh**

ART MUSEUM | Pieter Bruegel the Elder's arguably greatest and most enigmatic painting, *Dulle Griet*, is the showpiece of the 4,000 works that passionate art connoisseur Mayer Van den Bergh amassed in the 19th century. It has been restored to its full, hellish glory and is the prize of a collection that also includes Bruegel's witty, miniature illustrations in the *Twelve Proverbs,* based on popular Flemish sayings, and such treasures as a life-sized polychrome statue from about 1300 of St. John resting his head on Christ's chest. There's an English-language pamphlet included with admission that reviews part of the collection. ✉ *Lange Gasthuisstraat 19, Meir* ☎ *03/338–8188* 🌐 *www.mayervandenbergh.be* 🎫 *€10* ⏲ *Closed Mon.* Ⓜ *Tram: 4, 7.*

★ **Sint-Baafs Kathedraal** (*St. Bavo's Cathedral*)

CHURCH | Construction on the cathedral of St. Bavo (or Sint-Baaf) began in the 12th century but it wasn't finished for hundreds of years. Inside is breathtaking, and since 2021 its crown jewel, the Ghent Altarpiece, one of the most beautiful and influential paintings of the Middle Ages, has been resting in a newly built visitor center. ✉ *Sint-Baafsplein, Ghent* ☎ *09/397–1500* 🌐 *www.sintbaafskathedraal.be* 🎫 *Cathedral free; Altarpiece visit €13; AR tours €16* ⏲ *Closed during mass* Ⓜ *Tram: 1.*

Where to Eat and Drink

★ **Comme Chez Soi**

$$$$ | FRENCH | With superb cuisine, excellent wines, and attentive service, this two-star Michelin restaurant remains a regal choice, with an interior (and prices) to match. Lionel Rigolet, who took over the reins as chef from his father-in-law Pierre Wynants in 2006, is a ceaselessly inventive character with one foot in tradition, dishing up elegant racks of veal dashed with sweetbreads or cockerel breasts crowned with crayfish. **Known for:** very busy—book before you step on the plane, let alone through the door; sumptuous cooking from a genuine star of the Belgian dining scene; an excellent, and often surprising, wine list. Ⓢ *Average main: €53* ✉ *Pl. Rouppe 23, Lower Town* ☎ *02/512–2921* 🌐 *www.commechezsoi.be* ⏲ *Closed Sun.–Tues.* 👔 *Jacket and tie* Ⓜ *Metro: Anneessens.*

★ **The Jane**

$$$$ | EUROPEAN | Having held two Michelin stars since 2017, this shooting star on the Belgian gastronomy scene is located in the chapel of a former military hospital, albeit an open kitchen has replaced the altar and stained glass takes its inspiration from the tattoo parlor. The wine list is vast and the average dining experience usually runs past three hours thanks to its 10-course (€215) tasting menu, which is heavily slanted toward fish and seafood. **Known for:** lengthy tasting menus with international inspiration; a fantastic wine list with well-thought-out pairing options; fabulous setting in a former chapel. Ⓢ *Average main: €50* ✉ *Paradeplein 1, South of the Center* ☎ *03/808–4465* 🌐 *www.thejaneantwerp.com* ⏲ *Closed Mon.–Wed.* Ⓜ *Tram: 4.*

★ **Maison Antoine**

$ | BELGIAN | FAMILY | The Maison Antoine frites stand sells the best fries in the capital, say some people, accompanied by a dizzying range of condiments; try either local fave "Bicky" or the indulgent vol-au-vent sauce. **Known for:** excellent fries; condiment heaven; picky management (be sure to clean up after yourself). Ⓢ *Average main: €4* ✉ *Pl. Jourdan 1, Schuman* ☎ *02/230–5456* 🌐 *www.maisonantoine.be* Ⓜ *Metro: Maelbeek.*

★ **Publiek**

$$$ | BISTRO | Dishes at this Michelin-starred bistro from established Ghent chef Olly Ceulenaere are intricately prepared with a depth of flavor that belies their often simple ingredients. A small, ever-changing set menu invariably delivers. **Known for:** exquisitely prepared bistro food; boundless culinary creativity; great value considering the quality of the cooking. Ⓢ *Average main: €25* ✉ *Ham 39, Ghent* ☎ *09/330–0486* 🌐 *www.publiekgent.be* ⏲ *Closed Sun. and Mon.* Ⓜ *Bus: 3, 8, 39.*

Rebelge

$$$$ | **BELGIAN** | The fine-dining restaurant by acclaimed local chef Jean-Phi is as eclectic as his frites-sandwich joint Mitraillette. The menu is defiantly local, with a wide choice of regional beers often accompanying either a sharing-plate (around €15) or main-sized version of the same dishes. **Known for:** an inspired selection of beers and wines; inventive local cooking by a bonified "Top Chef"; it's a bit far out, so you'll have at least a 15-minute walk from the center. *Average main: €31* *Av. Reine Astrid 31, Mons* *0493/999–666* *re-belge.be* *Closed Sun.–Tues.*

Cool Places to Stay

★ De Witte Lelie

$$$$ | **HOTEL** | Three step-gabled 17th-century houses have been combined to create Antwerp's most exclusive hotel. **Pros:** large rooms; friendly, attentive service; complimentary minibars. **Cons:** some rooms have no elevator access; breakfast not included in room rate; its rates make it something of an indulgence. *Rooms from: €266* *Keizerstraat 16–18, Meir* *03/226–1966* *www.dewittelelie.be* *10 rooms* *No Meals* *Tram: 10, 11.*

★ 1898 The Post

$$$ | **HOTEL** | This stately boutique hotel, on the quayside of the Graslei, set hearts aflutter when it opened in 2018. **Pros:** the city-center location means you're never far from the action; the Cobbler is one of the better cocktail bars in the city; it's a fascinating piece of local history. **Cons:** there's no pool, gym, spa, or restaurant; the noise from the bars in the center does drift up; it's a bit of a labyrinth inside. *Rooms from: €179* *Graslei 16, Ghent* *09/277–0960* *1898the-post.com* *38 rooms* *Free Breakfast* *Tram: 1.*

★ Hotel de Orangerie

$$$ | **HOTEL** | Hotel de Orangerie, one of a swarm of boutique hotels that have colonized central Bruges, is family owned—and perhaps the most enchanting of its kind. **Pros:** perfect location with picturesque views; wonderful old building; heavenly afternoon teas. **Cons:** canal-view rooms come at a hefty price; parking costs are steep, even by Bruges's standards; the entry-level "comfort" rooms are a little tight. *Rooms from: €178* *Kartuizerinnestraat 10, Bruges* *050/341–649* *www.hotelorangerie.be* *20 rooms* *No Meals* *Bus: 1, 11.*

★ Juliana Hotel Brussels

$$$$ | **HOTEL** | The newest big boutique stay in the center sits on place des Martyrs, which holds a monument to the 445 patriots who died in the brief but successful 1830 war of independence. **Pros:** noon checkouts are always a plus; everything oozes class, from the service to the design; check out the afternoon tea (2–5) in the bar for a dash of civilized fun. **Cons:** hard to pick fault, but all that luxury does get a bit much; it's just darn expensive; parking is pricey. *Rooms from: €279* *Pl. des Martyrs 1–4, Lower Town* *02/214–0800* *www.juliana-brussels.com* *43 rooms* *Free Breakfast* *Metro: De Brouckère.*

Luxembourg

Tiny Luxembourg, nestled between Germany, France, and Belgium, has been a pawn of larger powers for much of its 1,000 years. Yet, from its history of siege and invasion, you would think it was filled with gold. In fact, it was the very defenses against these centuries of attacks that made it so desirable. An impregnable gem that all of Europe wanted—until they no longer did.

Today, Luxembourg is the little country that could: a world financial powerhouse filled with more Michelin-starred restaurants per capita than any nation outside Japan, and surrounded by winelands, medieval villages, hilltop castles, World War II sites, and huge swathes of the Ardennes. All this is packed into a country smaller in size than the state of Rhode Island. But it didn't come easy.

The region was first inhabited more than 3,000 years ago by pre-Celtic tribes, though its modern history didn't start until AD 963, when Charlemagne's descendant Siegfried, Count of the Ardennes, chose a meander on the Alzette River to fortify the capital of his domain. Over the following centuries, everyone wanted a piece of Luxembourg: France, the Habsburgs, the Burgundians, the Netherlands, Prussia, Germany. There were few centuries when it didn't change hands.

By 1815, the country had become a Grand Duchy, albeit one beholden to the Netherlands. Its lands were trimmed in return for more autonomy, finally achieving full independence in 1867. Ironically, it would then spend the latter parts of the following century becoming one of the founders of the European Union (E.U.).

Today, it's the world's only remaining Grand Duchy, albeit with a constitutional monarch and a democratically elected parliament. It's one of the smallest countries in Europe, with a population of under 650,000, not to mention the smallest member of NATO. Wearied by its experiences in World War II, Luxembourg's rulers sought to make sure it never happened again. In turn, its financial center grew and, along with its newfound political clout, it now has the third-highest per capita income in the world.

Luxembourg City

Explore a Historical Wonder

The UNESCO-listed old town of Luxembourg City is of necessity small, bound by the same rock walls that once made it impregnable. As a result, the capital perches spectacularly atop cliffs at the crux of the Pétrusse and Alzette rivers, its stone belly riddled with defensive tunnels, known as the casements, that were dug in the 17th century. And while the capital's once-famous fortifications were torn down in the late 1800s in return for the Grand Duchy's independence, you can still soak up relics of its earliest days, from the glorious Cathédrale Notre-Dame to the Flemish Renaissance palace that flings open its doors in summer. Spare some time also to visit Fort Thungen, on the Kirchberg Plateau, a rare surviving defense that now serves as a museum on the history of the old citadel.

Don't Miss

The newly opened Pétrusse Casements were only made accessible to the public in mid-2022. Built by Spain in the 17th century, they were bricked up as the city's fortifications were dismantled in 1867.

Getting Here

Luxembourg International Airport lies just 7 km (4½ miles) from the capital. You can also take a train from Belgium, France, or Germany; once there, the Grand Duchy has a free public transport network.

Where to Stay

La Pipistrelle is a wonderful B&B in The Grund area that incorporates the old city walls into the building's construction. It's like living history. 🌐 *pipistrelle.lu*

Luxembourg City Tourism. 🌐 *luxembourg-city.com*

Pétrusse Casements. ✉ *Pl. de la Constitution, Luxembourg City*

Clervaux

The Family of Man

Found deep in Luxembourg's Ardennes, the small town of Clervaux is surrounded by deep-cleft hills and nestled in a loop of the Clerve river. It is an unassuming place and a popular base for hikers, yet at its heart lies a 12th-century castle that is home to the greatest artistic sight in the Grand Duchy. In 1951, Luxembourg-born photographer Edward J. Steichen (1879–1973) invited entries for a collection of images, now known as *The Family of Man*, that would record humanity in all its flawed wonder and mystery. He whittled them down from 2 million to around 500 and toured the collection around the world. Since 1994, it has been exhibited in Clervaux and remains one of Europe's great cultural sights.

Don't Miss

Clervaux's Benedictine Abbey of Sts. Maurice and Maur was built in 1910 in neo-Gothic style and sits perched high above the town. Its monks are famed for their Gregorian plainchant, which has even been released on albums. Guided visits (call 92/0072 to book) afford a rare chance to hear it live.

When to Go

The shoulder seasons of spring and autumn are a great time to explore the hills and forests of the Ardennes, before the summer months bring tourists in their droves.

Getting Here and Around

Trains run direct from Luxembourg City to Clervaux, taking one hour. There is no need for a car unless you're going to tour the area.

Château de Clervaux. ✉ *Montée du Château 6, Clervaux* 🌐 *clervaux.lu*

World War II Sites

Learn About the Battle of the Bulge

Occupied Luxembourg was scarred by its experiences during World War II (1939–45) as the Ardennes was turned into the bloodiest of battlefields. It witnessed one of the last big dice throws by Germany, for whom the writing was on the wall after the United States entered the war. The Ardennes Counteroffensive (or Battle of the Bulge) was designed to swiftly split the Allied armies along the Western Front so Germany could sue for peace on its own terms; instead, it devolved into one of the century's most brutal battles. You'll find sites across the Grand Duchy both marking and examining this era, from American and German military cemeteries on the fringes of the capital to statues of General George S. Patton (who liberated the Grand Duchy in 1944). Museums and memorials spread across the far north in particular, with those in Diekirch, Wiltz, and Clervaux among the most poignant.

Don't Miss

For the best overview, leave the Ardennes and head south to Esch-sur-Alzette, where the recently refurbished **Musée National de la Résistance** delves into Luxembourg's occupation during World War II, documenting local resistance groups and life in the camps. ✉ *Pl. de la Résistance, Esch-sur-Alzette* ☎ 54/8472 *mnr.lu* ⏲ *Closed Mon.*

Getting Here and Around

Trains run direct from Luxembourg City to Diekirch, Clervaux and Esch-sur-Alzette. The No. 223 bus connects to Hamm, where you'll find the American Military Cemetery, while the No. 411 leads to its German equivalent in Sandweiler.

Moselle Wineries

Taste the Wines of the Moselle Valley

The Moselle Valley has been producing wine for over 2,000 years, but the lack of exports outside Luxembourg meant that its growers have stayed a secret, keeping prices low. The gateway to the region's vineyards is the riverside town of Remich, from where a number of wine cruises depart. About two-thirds of Luxembourg's wine production is controlled by Les Domaines de Vinsmoselle, a collection of cooperatives dating back to the 1920s. There are also some 50 independent vintners, with many cellars (caves) open for tastings and as departure points for tours, including Caves St. Martin. Look out for their signs as you drive or cycle the Route du Vin wine tour through the valley.

Don't Miss

The Musée du Vin in Ehnen lays out the story of the region. For tastings, head to the cellars of the huge Caves de Wellenstein in Bech-Kleinmacher or hop on one of Navitours' wine cruises from Remich.

Getting Here and Around

By car, Remich is a half-hour drive from Luxembourg City along the E29. From there the Route du Vin (or N10) runs alongside the Moselle between Schengen and Grevenmacher.

What to Try

Look out for local specialties such as *crémant*, a sparkling white wine often drunk as an aperitif. If you're lucky, you'll also find ice wine (*aiswain*), harvested in winter at temperatures of -7°C, and *stréiwain* (straw wine), made from mature grapes laid out to dry on straw mats.

Centre Visit Remich. ✉ *Rte. du Vin 11, Remich* ☎ *75/8275* 🌐 *entente-moselle.lu*

Hiking in Mullerthal

Go Hiking in "Little Switzerland"

The eastern fringe of Luxembourg is a hilly terrain of dense fir and beech forests, high limestone bluffs, and twisting brooks. It is known to locals as *Petit Suisse* (Little Switzerland), and it's no surprise that it has become a popular spot for hikers, spelunkers, and climbers. The town of Berdorf in particular has built up a name for itself as a vibrant center for walkers and is surrounded by trails rising up from the plateau and passing through gorges, grottoes, rocks, and fissures. Try the 13.5-km (8-mile) Gorge du Loup or, for a bigger challenge, take on the Mullerthal Trail 112 km (69.5 miles).

Don't Miss

The region's oldest and largest town is Echternach, known for its basilica, which was named after 7th-century monk St Willibrord. Just next door, the abbey has been converted into a museum that is filled with exquisite medieval illuminations.

When to Go

Arrive in time for Whit Sunday (late May/June) and you can see one of Europe's more unusual UNESCO-inscribed religious processions, when local pilgrims "hop" through Echternach to pay their respects at the tomb of its founder, St Willibrord.

Getting Here and Around

While there is a decent bus service (No. 110 runs from Luxembourg City to Echternach), a car is the easiest way to get around. Take the E29 northeast of the capital to Echternach; from there, Route 364 connects to Berdorf.

Berdorf Tourist Information. ✉ *Beim Martbusch 3, Berdorf* 🌐 *visitberdorf.lu*

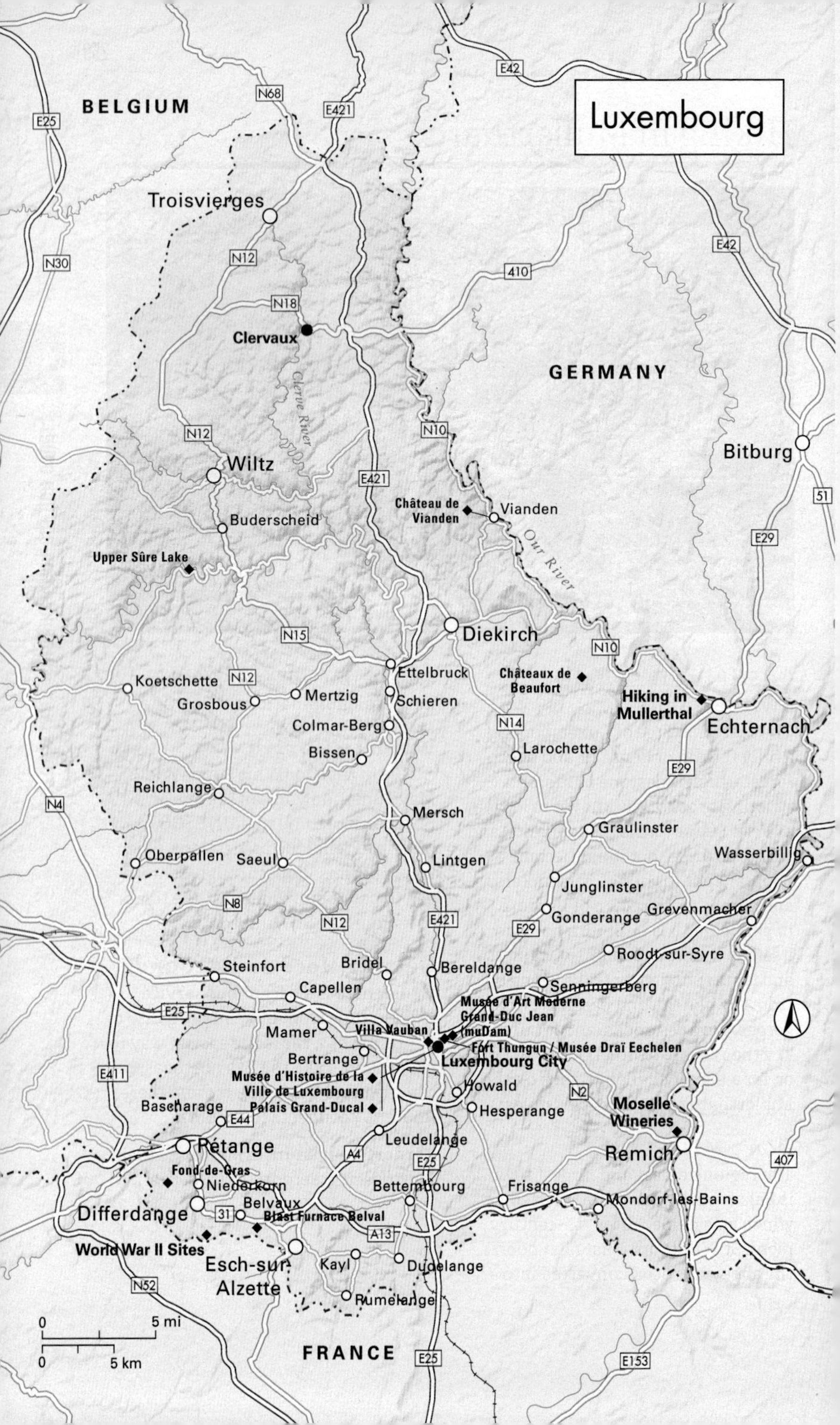

Luxembourg
BELGIUM
GERMANY
FRANCE
E42
N68
E421
E25
Troisvierges
N12
N30
N18
Clervaux
Clerve River
410
E42
N12
Wiltz
N10
E421
Bitburg
Château de
Vianden
Vianden
51
Buderscheid
Our River
E29
Upper Sûre Lake
Diekirch
N15
N10
N12
Ettelbruck
Châteaux de
Beaufort
Koetschette
Hiking in
Mullerthal
Schieren
Grosbous
Mertzig
Echternach
Colmar-Berg
N14
Larochette
Bissen
E29
Reichlange
N4
Mersch
Graulinster
Oberpallen
Saeul
Lintgen
Wasserbillig
Junglinster
N8
Grevenmacher
N12
E421
Gonderange
E29
Roodt-sur-Syre
Steinfort
Bridel
Bereldange
Capellen
Senningerberg
Musée d'Art Moderne
Grand-Duc Jean
(muDam)
E25
Mamer
Villa Vauban
Fort Thungun / Musée Draï Eechelen
Bertrange
Luxembourg City
E411
Musée d'Histoire de la
Ville de Luxembourg
Howald
N2
Bascharage
Palais Grand-Ducal
Hesperange
Moselle
Wineries
E44
Pétange
Leudelange
Remich
A4
E25
407
Fond-de-Gras
Niederkorn
Bettembourg
Frisange
Mondorf-les-Bains
Differdange
31
Belvaux
Blast Furnace Belval
A13
World War II Sites
Esch-sur-
Alzette
Kayl
Dudelange
N52
Rumelange
0
5 mi
0
5 km
E25
E153

When in Luxembourg

Blast Furnace Belval

FACTORY | In the early 1900s, the town's Belval neighborhood was home to the biggest ironworks site in Luxembourg. The last furnace was decommissioned in 1997 and the complex now houses a university and the country's biggest music venue, **Rockhal**. The renovated Furnace A is now open to the public. ✉ *Av. du Rock'n'Roll, opposite the Rockhal, Esch-sur-Alzette* ☎ *26/8401* 🌐 *www.minetttour.lu* 🎫 *€5; guided tours €10* ⏲ *Closed Mon. and Tues.* Ⓜ *Bus: 3, 332.*

★ **Châteaux de Beaufort** (*Castles of Beaufort*)

CASTLE/PALACE | Around 15 km (9 miles) west of Echternach, at the top of the Ernz Noire valley, a short detour leads to Beaufort. Near the village stand two splendid castles, side by side: a magnificently imposing medieval shell only partially restored after World War II bombing left it in ruins, and a Renaissance-style chateau dating from the 17th century. ✉ *Rue du Château, Beaufort* ☎ *83/6601* 🌐 *www.visitbeaufort.lu* 🎫 *€5; €10 with a guided tour* ⏲ *Renaissance castle: closed to tours Mon.–Wed. (Apr.–Oct.); Nov.–Mar. by appt. only; the medieval castle is closed Nov.–Mar.* Ⓜ *Bus: 502.*

★ **Château de Vianden** (*Vianden Castle*)

CASTLE/PALACE | Driving around the last bend into Vianden, you're greeted by a full-length view of Vianden Castle rearing up on the hill, replete with conical spires, crenellation, step gables, and massive bulwarks. The castle was built on Roman foundations at the turn of the first millennium, though its most spectacular portions date from the 11th, 12th, and 15th centuries. Its near-pristine appearance is the result of massive restoration in the 20th century. ✉ *Mnt. du Château, Vianden* ☎ *83/41081 Castle* 🌐 *www.castle-vianden.lu* 🎫 *€10.*

★ **Fond-de-Gras**

MINE | FAMILY | This small valley lies around 10 km (6 miles) northwest of Esch-sur-Alzette, and was once the heart of the country's mining industry, connected via a pair of railway lines: one to ship equipment and ore in and out of nearby Pétange; another to transport the workers to the mining village of Lasauvage or into France. It was still operating by the 1960s. In summer, visitors can ride trains into the old mining tunnels, pedal a "draisine" (€10) along the tracks, see rail and mining museums, and tour the old villages where the miners once lived. July also sees the arrival of blues and steampunk festivals. ✉ *Fond-de-Gras 2* ✣ *South of Pétange* ☎ *26/582–069* 🌐 *minettpark.lu* 🎫 *Museum: free; mining train: €7; train 1900: €14* ⏲ *Closed Oct.–Apr.* Ⓜ *Bus: 2 and 6 (change at Differdange).*

Fort Thungun / Musée Draï Eechelen

HISTORY MUSEUM | In 1732, the Austrian rulers of the city strengthened the Grunewald Front, expanding the original fortifications to the northeast. They built Fort Thungen, which was enlarged and reinforced a century later. Today, its casements, tunnels, and mines host the excellent Musée Draï Eechelen that details the building's history and eventual demolition along with the rest of the city's defenses in the 1867 Treaty of London. ✉ *Park Dräi Eechelen 5, Luxembourg City* ☎ *26/4335* 🌐 *m3e.public.lu* 🎫 *Free; €7 for temporary exhibitions* ⏲ *Museum closed Mon.* Ⓜ *Tram: T1.*

Musée d'Art Moderne Grand-Duc Jean (*muDam*)

ART MUSEUM | FAMILY | This gem of a gallery, on the western edge of the Kirchberg plateau, is as much an architectural landmark as it is a museum. The designs of architect I.M. Pei make this stunning edifice as eye-catching as the works of modern art on show within. The building is a mix of limestone and glass—the latter formed into pyramids that both mimic the church spires of the old city across the Alzette valley and echo Pei's similar work for the Louvre in Paris. The museum's interior is light and airy and the perfect foil for the changing exhibitions by internationally renowned contemporary artists. There are no permanent displays, so repeat visits are always rewarding. Entrance is free between 6 and 9 pm on Wednesday. ✉ *Park Dräi Eechelen 3, Luxembourg City* ☎ *45/37851* 🌐 *mudam.lu* ⏲ *Closed Tues.*

Musée d'Histoire de la Ville de Luxembourg (*Luxembourg City Historical Museum*)
HISTORY MUSEUM | Partially underground, this clever museum traces the development of the city over 1,000 years, working its way up through the centuries as you ascend floors. Its lowest levels show the town's preserved ancient stonework. From a glass-wall elevator, you can also enjoy a wonderful view of the ravine from the upper floors. There's free entry every Thursday from 6 to 8. ✉ *Rue du St-Esprit 14, Luxembourg City* ☎ *47/964–500* 🌐 *www.citymuseum.lu* 🎫 *€5* ⏲ *Closed Mon.* Ⓜ *Bus: 2, 4.*

Palais Grand-Ducal
CASTLE/PALACE | **FAMILY** | The city's finest building dates from the 16th century. Its elaborate facade shows a Flemish Renaissance influence, with ornate balconies and a symmetrical exterior, and it was formerly the home to the Grand Ducal royal family. It is now mainly used for business and entertaining, though in July and August it opens its doors to visitors, offering the chance to explore its extensive art collection, which was dispersed during World War II before being returned, and the Hall of Kings where foreign envoys are officially received. ✉ *Rue du Marché-aux- Herbes 17* ☎ *22/2809* ⏲ *Closed Sept.–June.* (Grand-Ducal Palace)

★ **Upper Sûre Lake**
NATIONAL PARK | **FAMILY** | The reservoir was dammed in 1961 to create a long-term source of drinking water for Luxembourg. Chunks of it are still off-limits because of this, but there's plenty to explore. In summer, solar-powered boats (May–October) take you on two-hour tours of the water. Mercifully, no motorboats are allowed here, but on warm days the lake fills with windsurfers, paddlers, and wild swimmers. You can rent canoes, kayaks, and SUPs from the youth hostel in Lultzhausen in July and August, and for walkers, there are some 90 km (56 miles) of trails to explore (maps are at the visitor center). But if you'd rather relax, several beaches line the shores at **Insenborn**, **Lultzhausen**, and across the water at **Liefrange**, with a more secluded stretch found just past the Burfelt viewing platform. This is where locals come to escape for the day. ✉ *Upper Sûre Lake, Esch-sur-Sûre* 🎫 *Free.*

Villa Vauban
ART GALLERY | Also billed as the Musée d'Art de la Ville de Luxembourg (City of Luxembourg Art Museum), this lovely white mansion house is surrounded by perfectly tended gardens and feels like a haven of peace in the heart of the bustling city. Having undergone several face-lifts and changes of use since it was first built by the wealthy owner of a glove factory in 1873, major renovation work has given the building a new life as a permanent home for Luxembourg City's collection of Old Masters. Works by Canaletto and Van Dyck, to name but two, are juxtaposed with new pieces on matching themes by contemporary artists. Entry is free between 6 and 9 pm on Friday. ✉ *Av. Emile Reuter 18, Luxembourg City* ☎ *47/964–900* 🌐 *www.villavauban.lu* 🎫 *€5* ⏲ *Closed Tues.* Ⓜ *Tram: T1.*

Where to Eat and Drink

Am Tiirmschen

$$$ | BRASSERIE | Those after good Luxembourgish food inevitably boil their choice down to Am Tiirmschen or Um Dierfgen (on Côte d'Eich). Neither restaurant will let you down, but this old hand gets the nod because of its setting. **Known for:** good, swift service; Luxembourgish classics you need to try at least once; a romantic setting in a building wonderfully hidden off a side street. *Average main: €24 Rue de l'Eau 32, Luxembourg City 26/270–733 www.amtiirmschen.lu Closed Sun. and Mon. Bus: 2, 4.*

★ Clairefontaine

$$$$ | FRENCH | Having always been the go-to for government ministers and visiting dignitaries, long-standing owner-chef Arnaud Magnier has attempted to shake things up a bit. Out went the old red leather, in came a bolder new look. **Known for:** a spot on one of the city's most attractive squares; the terrace is delightful in summer; simply some of the best cooking in Luxembourg. *Average main: €105 Pl. de Clairefontaine 9, Luxembourg City 46/2211 www.restaurantclairefontaine.lu Closed weekends Jacket and tie Bus: 4, 10.*

Mesa Verde

$$$ | VEGETARIAN | This was the first meat-free restaurant in Luxembourg back in 1990. Today, its vegetarian, vegan, and seafood menu typically piles on myriad flavors (some more successfully than others) as tofu, seitan, spring rolls, veggies, samosas, rice, vol-au-vents, and creamy Thai curry sauces spill across the plate. **Known for:** a nice tree-shaded terrace opens up across the street in summer; the occasional band livens up the evening; veggie comfort food to bring a smile to your face. *Average main: €24 Rue du St. Esprit 11, Luxembourg City 46/4126 Closed Sun. and Mon. Bus: 2, 4.*

★ Restaurant du Château

$$$$ | FRENCH | The culinary gem of the city. The setting, nestled within the courtyard of the castle, is a peach, and its terrace makes a grand alfresco escape on a summer's evening. **Known for:** a beautiful castle garden setting; elaborate gastronomy in a town sorely lacking high-end alternatives; excellent wine menu. *Average main: €56 Montée du Château 4, Clervaux 26/904–857 www.rdcc.lu Closed Mon. and Tues.*

Cool Places to Stay

★ Escher Bamhaiser

$$ | APARTMENT | This trio of duplex tree houses (for four or six people) lies on the edge of the deer park, high in the Gaalgebierg area is simply one of the best stays in Luxembourg. **Pros:** great views from the private terraces; the café serves nice food if you can't be bothered to find a restaurant nearby; there's no other sleep quite like it in Luxembourg. **Cons:** breakfast is an extra €15; it's a bit of a walk into town; the sound of the animals can be quite noisy. *Rooms from: €120 Gaalgebierg 64, Esch-sur-Alzette 27/542–233 bamhaiser.esch.lu 3 tree houses No Meals.*

★ Hôtel de L'Ecluse

$$ | HOTEL | This family-run hotel holds more than a few surprises, including a huge green space to its rear complete with outdoor pool (closed in winter), putting green, and views over the neighboring vineyard. **Pros:** it's really good value; free covered parking area; a peaceful quiet stay. **Cons:** the front is on a rather busy road; you're not near any of the better-equipped towns or villages; you really need a car to get here. *Rooms from: €105 Waistrooss 29, 4 km (2½ miles) north of Remich, Wormeldange 23/619–191 www.hotel-ecluse.lu 35 rooms Free Breakfast Bus: 160, 450.*

★ **La Pipistrelle B&B**

$$$ | **B&B/INN** | This historic B&B of just four rooms lies on the fringes of the Grund, next to Cafe des Artistes and only a steep, five-minute walk up to the city (or just take the handy elevator). **Pros:** it's living history; you've got a wealth of drinking and dining close by; great setting on the edge of the Grund. **Cons:** no parking; there's no elevator or disabled access to rooms and the staircase is narrow; it's a B&B, so there are few facilities. *Rooms from: €215* ✉ *Montée du Grund 26, Luxembourg City* ☎ *621/300–351* 🌐 *www.pipistrelle.lu* *4 rooms* *Free Breakfast* Ⓜ *Bus: 23.*

★ **Le Place d'Armes**

$$$$ | **HOTEL** | Simply the nicest-looking rooms in the city. **Pros:** you're in the shopping heart of the city; guests have access to a digital magazine subscription; the rooms really are something special. **Cons:** the square outside can be noisy for overlooking rooms; no pool or wellness facilities; none of it comes cheap. *Rooms from: €280* ✉ *Pl. d'Armes 18, Luxembourg City* ☎ *27/4737* 🌐 *www.hotel-leplacedarmes.com* *28 rooms* *Free Breakfast* Ⓜ *Tram: T1.*

The Netherlands

The Netherlands is every cliché you imagine and more. While the wooden clogs may be largely confined to the souvenir shops these days, this really is a land of windmills, tulips, canals, and bicycles, albeit with the backdrop of a fast-paced 21st-century nation. At its heart is one of Europe's most important capitals, a famously open and tolerant place where almost anything goes.

The Netherlands only assumed its current form in 1830, when Belgium broke away as an independent state, but the country has existed in one form or another for around a thousand years. A proud seafaring nation that built its wealth on international trade, it has also waged a war on the sea itself that is still ongoing. With much of the land lying below sea level, it owes its continued existence to a complex series of dikes, barriers, and polders reclaimed from the waters.

While Amsterdam has all the waterways, gabled town houses, and rusty pushbikes you could possibly shake a stick at, it is only one aspect of The Netherlands. To get the full picture you'll need to head out to the other towns, or to the countryside that is just as flat as you've been told. The country's best-known city may be the national capital, but Rotterdam is where you'll find the modern architecture and melting-pot cultures; Delft is a wonderful, dollhouse-like city; while the brightly colored patchwork of flowers of the Bulb Fields—if you time your visit to coincide with the spring blooms—is an experience you won't soon forget.

The Netherlands is at its best when the temperatures climb, and cafés and restaurants spill across sidewalks to invite leisurely alfresco meals. Spring is the driest time of year, and because it's also when the tulip fields bloom, this is the most popular time to visit.

Amsterdam Canal Cruise

A Boat Trip Along an Iconic Waterway

No visit to Amsterdam would be complete without taking a boat trip. Joining a canal-boat cruise is the quickest, easiest, and most delightful way to get your bearings in the Dutch capital. The most picturesque area is the canal "belt" of the Golden Age that was built around the medieval city center, and consists of four main encircling canals. The Singelgracht was constructed in the 15th century, but two phases of 17th-century construction yielded the Herengracht (Gentlemen's Canal, built in 1612), and some 50 years later the Keizersgracht (Emperor's Canal) and Prinsengracht (Prince's Canal). Together they became the premier addresses of historic Amsterdam, where wealthy bankers and famous merchants ordered homes built in the latest fashionable styles, ranging from Baroque to Neoclassical. The area's significance was recognized in 2010 with the awarding of UNESCO World Heritage status.

Don't Miss

Brouwersgracht (Brewers' Canal) is regularly voted Amsterdam's most beautiful street, lined with residences and former warehouses for the brewers, fish processors, and tanneries who operated here in the 17th century. Although most of the buildings are now luxury apartments, an old-world charm still reigns.

Getting Here

Standard boat trips last one to two hours. To join a standard daytime cruise, simply walk up to any of the various boating companies docked throughout the city center.

Amsterdam Tourism. 🌐 *www.iamsterdam.com*

Blue Boat. ✉ *Stadhouderskade 30, Eastern Canal Ring* 🌐 *www.blueboat.nl/en*

Anne Frank House

The Tragic Tale of a Teenage Innocent

In the pages of her diary, the young Anne Frank recorded two increasingly fraught years living in secret, in a warren of rooms at the back of what is now known as Anne Frankhuis (Anne Frank House), a 1635 canal house, hidden from the Nazis. Anne was born in Germany in 1929; when she was four, her family moved to the Netherlands to escape growing anti-Jewish sentiment. After the war reached the Netherlands in 1940, Anne's father Otto took his wife and daughters into hiding in July 1942. They were later joined by the Van Pels family, and a dentist named Fritz Pfeffer. Together, the five adults and three children sought refuge in the attic of the rear annex, or *achterhuis*, of Otto's pectin business in the center of Amsterdam. The entrance was hidden behind a hinged bookcase, and five of Otto's trusted employees provided food and supplies. In August 1944, the Franks were betrayed, and the Gestapo invaded this hideaway. Everyone was transported to camps, and Anne died in Bergen-Belsen a few months before the liberation. Otto Frank was the only survivor.

Don't Miss

In Anne's bedroom, newspaper clippings and movie-star pictures that she pasted on the walls are still on view, now preserved behind glass.

Getting Here

To reach the house, take Tram No. 13, 14, or 17 to Westermarkt, or walk 15 minutes from Centraal Station.

✉ *Westermarkt 20, Amsterdam* ☎ *020/556–7105* 🌐 *www.annefrank.org* 🎫 *€14 Make reservations as far in advance as possible; tickets always sell out, especially in summer*

Rijksmuseum Amsterdam

Dutch Masters

The quantity of quality of the art on display in Amsterdam's museums is jaw-dropping. The Rijksmuseum Amsterdam (State Museum) houses the world's largest concentration of Dutch masterworks, as well as paintings, sculpture, and objects from East and West that provide global context for the history of the Netherlands. But the nearby Stedelijk Museum houses a treasury of modern and contemporary art by such giants of modernism as Chagall, Cézanne, Picasso, Monet, and Mondrian, as well as pieces by American Pop artists, Abstract Expressionists, and works from the De Stijl school. And the Van Gogh Museum venerates the short but productive career of the tortured 19th-century artist, offering 200 of his paintings and 500 drawings on permanent display, from *The Potato Eaters* to his later and more technicolor still lifes—including the famous series of Sunflowers.

Don't Miss

If time is limited, head directly for the Rijksmuseum's Gallery of Honor to admire Rembrandt's *The Night Watch*. *The Night Watch* is really the *Day Watch*, but it received its name in the 18th century when the varnish had darkened.

Getting Here

Tram Nos. 2, 5, and 12 all stop at Museumplein. All three museums require timed tickets, and those for the Rijksmuseum and Van Gogh Museum almost always sell out, so they should be booked as far ahead as possible.

Rijksmuseum Amsterdam. ✉ *Museumstraat 1, Amsterdam* 🌐 *www.rijksmuseum.nl* 🎫 *€20*

Stedelijk Museum. ✉ *Museumplein 10, Amsterdam* 🌐 *www.stedelijk.nl* 🎫 *€19*

Van Gogh Museum. ✉ *Museumplein 6, Amsterdam* 🌐 *www.vangoghmuseum.nl* 🎫 *€19*

Tulip Time at the Keukenhof

Oceans of Color

In springtime the bulb fields of South Holland are transformed into a vivid series of Mondrian paintings through the colors of millions of tulips and other flowers. The Bollenstreek (Bulb Fields district) extends from Leiden to Haarlem, with the greatest concentration of blooms around the town of Lisse and the famed Keukenhof Gardens. This 79-acre park and greenhouse complex is one of the largest open-air flower exhibitions in the world, and draws huge crowds during the eight weeks it's open. Its hothouses and lakeside flower beds are home to 7 million tulip bulbs.

Don't Miss

Head for the Keukenhof's windmill for a vista over the surrounding patchwork of fields, or view the crowds from a distance with an hour-long boat tour (book this near the windmill, €9).

When to Go

The Keukenhof Gardens are open late March to mid-May, and carefully timed planting ensures they remain at their best throughout. An early or late spring can shift the time frame in the surrounding bulb fields by as much as two weeks.

Getting Here

By car from Amsterdam, take the A4 in the direction of Den Haag, then Exit 4. Continue on the N207 to Lisse and follow signs for the Keukenhof. By train, head for Haarlem and take Bus No. 50, or to Schiphol Airport and take Bus No. 361.

✉ Stationsweg 166a, Lisse ☎ 0252/465–555 🌐 keukenhof.nl 🎫 €19 (tickets are cheaper if booked online in advance)

Vermeer's Delft

Amsterdam in Miniature—Without the Crowds

With canal-lined streets and medieval houses, Delft is like a scaled-down version of Amsterdam, with smaller canals, narrower bridges, and fewer people. It's easy to understand how Johannes Vermeer (1632–75) found inspiration here. Few spots in the Netherlands are as intimate and attractive as this charming little town. With time-burnished canals and cobblestone streets, Delft possesses a calm that recalls the quieter pace of the 17th-century Golden Age, back when Vermeer was counted among its citizens. There are plenty of quiet residential corners where the modern world is easy to escape—you could easily imagine the artist strolling the streets looking for his next subject.

Don't Miss

The Vermeer Centrum takes visitors on a multimedia journey through the life and work of the great artist. Touch screens, projections, and other interactive features are interspersed with giant reproductions of the master's work. ⊕ *www.vermeerdelft.nl*

Getting Here

Direct trains leave Amsterdam Centraal Station for Delft every half hour throughout the day—the journey is a little less than one hour. Central Delft is compact and easily covered on foot.

Best Restaurants

With terrace tables on a small square overlooking a narrow canal, De Wijnhaven is a great place to soak up Delft's medieval atmosphere while enjoying Dutch and international classics. ⊕ ✉ *www.wijnhaven.nl*

Delft Tourist Information (VVV).
✉ *Kerkstraat 3* ☎ *015/205–4052*
⊕ *www.delft.com*

Escher in Het Paleis Museum

M. C. Escher's Impossible Worlds

In the 18th century, Lange Voorhout Palace in The Hague was the residence of Caroline of Nassau, daughter of Prince Willem IV. More recently, it was transformed into the Escher in Het Paleis Museum, devoted to Dutch graphic artist M. C. Escher (1892–1972). His prints and engravings of unforgettable imagery—roofs becoming floors, water flowing uphill, fish transforming into birds—became world famous in the 1960s and '70s. Replete with ever-repeating Baroque pillars, Palladian portals, and parallel horizons, Escher's visual trickery presaged the "virtual reality" worlds of today. Fittingly, the museum features an Escher Experience where you don a helmet and take a digital trip through his unique world. Don't forget to look up as you walk around—dangling glitteringly from the ceiling is a series of custom-designed chandeliers by Dutch sculptor Hans van Bentem that are inspired by Escher's work. These delightfully playful creations include umbrellas, sea horses, birds, and even a giant skull and crossbones.

Don't Miss

The nearby Mauritshuis is a relatively conventional art gallery, but its collection is almost unrivaled in Europe, featuring as it does 14 Rembrandts and 3 masterpieces by Vermeer—including his *View of Delft* and the haunting *Girl with a Pearl Earring.* 🌐 *www.mauritshuis.nl*

Getting Here

Two trains every hour connect Amsterdam with Den Haag Centraal station, taking 50 minutes. Both museums are a five-minute walk from the station. ✉ *Lange Voorhout 74, Den Haag* ☎ *070/427–7730* 🌐 *www.escherinhetpaleis.nl* 🎫 *€10* 🕒 *Closed Mon.*

Deltapark Neeltje Jans

The Story of the Dutch Against the Sea

Surpassing even the Afsluitdijk (Closure Dike) that in the 1930s turned the shallow Zuiderzee inland sea into the freshwater IJsselmeer lake, the Delta Works were a response to a catastrophic storm surge in 1953 that inundated large swaths of the Netherlands, much of which lies below sea level. As mammoth an undertaking as it was, it shortened the Dutch coastline and thus actually reduced the amount of work that would have been needed to strengthen existing dykes. On an island near what remains, Deltapark Neeltje Jans—the world's largest flood barrier—tells the story of this most important achievement of Dutch hydraulic engineering. There are also exhibits documenting the 2,000-year history of the nation's struggle with the sea, as well as a shark-filled aquarium and other attractions aimed at younger visitors.

Don't Miss

The centerpiece of the Deltapark, the Delta Experience tells the story of what happened on the night of January 31, 1953, when breached dikes led to the biggest postwar natural disaster in the Netherlands. A 4D panoramic animation lets you experience the unstoppable destructive powers of the sea.

Do This

Take a walk on the nearby dunes and get a close-up view of the more natural side of Dutch sea defenses.

Getting Here

Deltapark Neeltje Jans is 150 km (94 miles) southwest from Amsterdam. The drive takes around 1 hour 45 minutes, or one hour from Rotterdam.

Faelweg 5, Vrouwenpolder
0111/655–655 www.neeltjejans.nl
€20 Closed weekdays Nov.–Mar.

Utrecht's Oudegracht

The Netherlands' Only Dual-level Canal

With a history longer than Amsterdam's, picturesque Utrecht is the site where the Dutch Republic was established in 1579, with the signing of the Union of Utrecht. The city's central, sunken canal is unique in the Netherlands, for its towpath has upper and lower levels, with shops and galleries opening onto street level, and restaurants and cafés on the walkway just above the water. It's especially charming in summer, when café and restaurant tables cover both levels.

Don't Miss

Steps from Oudegracht, the Domtoren is the country's tallest church tower, albeit the remainder of the 14th-century house of worship was destroyed by a storm in the 17th century. The tower is 367 feet high, and if you are up to tackling the 465 steps, the panoramic view from the top is unsurpassed. 🌐 *www.domtoren.nl*

Best Restaurant

Bakery Broodje Mario is a city institution, which has been serving a variety of rolls and pizza slices from its shop window on Oudegracht for over 45 years. Follow the lead of most locals by ordering the signature "broodje Mario": a must-try warm bun, stuffed with cheese, salami, chorizo, shredded veg, and chili. 🌐 *broodjemario.nl*

Getting Here

Utrecht Centraal Station is the hub of the national rail network, and trains connect it with every city. The journey time from Amsterdam is 30 minutes. Central Utrecht is easy to cover on foot, with many streets reserved for pedestrians only.

Toerisme Utrecht. ✉ *Domplein 9* ☎ *030/236–0004* 🌐 *www.visit-utrecht.com*

Kinderdijk Windmills

The View Made for Chocolate Boxes

The windmills of Kinderdijk are some of the most photographed sights in Holland. The sight of its 19 windmills under sail is magnificently and romantically impressive. Not surprisingly, this landmark sight (on the UNESCO World Heritage list) is one of the most visited places in the Netherlands. These are water-pumping mills whose job was to drain water from the Alblasserwaard polder enclosed by the Noord and Lek rivers—a function now performed by the 1950 pumping station with its humongous water screws, which you pass on the way to the site. The name Kinderdijk (which means "children's dike") comes from a legend involving a baby in a cradle who washed up here after the great floods of 1421, with a cat sitting on its tummy to keep them both from tumbling out. Rarer than ever, these windmills date all the way back to 1740.

Don't Miss

The windmills are open in rotation, so there is always one interior to visit. A walk through a working windmill gives fascinating insight into how the millers and their families lived.

Getting Here

By car, Kinderdijk is 20 km (12 miles) from Rotterdam. Follow directions to Rotterdam, then take the A15 to Exit 22. Waterbus (*www.waterbus.nl*) runs a fast ferry service from the Erasmusbrug in Rotterdam to the city of Dordrecht, via Kinderdijk. Ferries run hourly in each direction from May to October, and the trip takes half an hour.

Molenkade, Alblasserdam *078/691–2830* *www.kinderdijk.nl* *€16*

Hoge Veluwe National Park

Nature and Art in Perfect Harmony

When German heiress Hélène Müller married Dutch industrialist Anton Kröller at the turn of the 20th century, they formed a unique partnership. She collected art; he bought up land and created a foundation to maintain it as a national park, building a museum at its center to house his wife's purchases. Today you can wander the forests, heath, dunes, and moors that together form the Netherlands' largest national park, covering 13,300 acres. Then you can visit the Kröller-Müller Museum at its heart, containing one of the world's best collections of Van Goghs, as well as works by Seurat, Picasso, and Mondrian.

Don't Miss

The gardens and woods around the museum form the largest open-air gallery in Europe, with a collection of 20th-century sculptures that include works by Auguste Rodin, Barbara Hepworth, and Alberto Giacometti.

Getting Here

By car, take the A1, A12, or A50, following signs for "Park Hoge Veluwe." There are three entrances: at Otterlo (Houtkamperweg 9), Hoenderloo (Houtkamperweg 13), and Schaarsbergen (Koningsweg 17).

Do This

Park admission includes the use of one of 1,800 white bicycles. You'll find them at the park entrances, at the visitor center, Parkrestaurant De Hoge Veluwe, and at the Kröller-Müller Museum. Return them to any bike rack when you are finished.

Kröller-Müller Museum. ✉ *Houtkampweg 6, Otterlo* ☎ *0318/591–241* 🌐 *krollermuller.nl* 🎟 *€12* 🕓 *Closed Mon.*

Visitor Center. ✉ *Houtkampweg 9b, Otterlo* ☎ *055/833–0833* 🌐 *www.hogeveluwe.nl* 🎟 *€13*

The Netherlands

When in the Netherlands

★ A'DAM Lookout

VIEWPOINT | Originally constructed in 1971 as the headquarters of Royal Dutch Shell, the A'DAM Tower has now been repurposed as a hotel, and several bars and restaurants. For most day visitors, however, the best way to experience it is to ride the glass-ceilinged elevator—you'll be entertained by a sound and light show as you ascend—to A'DAM Lookout, a rooftop observation deck with a superb panoramic view of the IJ River, Centraal Station, and across the old city beyond. The visit includes a multimedia exhibition about Amsterdam history and culture. Daredevils can also sign up for "Over the Edge," which is Europe's highest swing and does exactly what it says: it will swing you out beyond the edge of the tower and leave your feet dangling 330 feet above the street below. ✉ *Overhoeksplein 5, Amsterdam-Noord* ☎ *020/242–0100* 🌐 *www.adamlookout.com* 🎟 *€14.50 (€2 discount for booking online), additional €5 for swing.*

★ Binnenhof and the Ridderzaal (*Inner Court and the Knights' Hall*)

GOVERNMENT BUILDING | The governmental heart of the Netherlands, the Binnenhof (or Inner Court) complex is in the very center of town yet tranquilly set apart, thanks to the charming Hofvijver (court lake). The setting creates a poetic contrast to the endlessly dull debates that go on within its walls—the basis of everyday Dutch politics. Pomp and decorum are in full fig every third Tuesday of September, when Queen Beatrix arrives at the 13th-century Ridderzaal, or Knights' Hall, in a golden coach to open the new session of Parliament. For many centuries the Binnenhof was the court for the Counts of Holland; it is now a complex of buildings from several eras. You can wander freely around the open outer courtyard, but entrance to the Knights' Hall (a highlight) and other interior rooms is by guided tour only. Buy tickets for guided visits at the visitor center at Hofweg 1, across the road from the west entrance to the Binnenhof. ✉ *Binnenhof 8a, The Hague* ☎ *070/757–0200* 🌐 *prodemos.nl* 🎟 *€9.50 Ridderzaal plus Dutch House of Representatives* ⏲ *Closed Sun. Some areas may be closed when government meetings are taking place.*

Depot Boijmans Van Beuningen

NOTABLE BUILDING | Opening in 2021, and resembling a giant mirror-clad bowl designed to reflect the Rotterdam skyline, this storage facility for artworks owned by the Museum Boijmans Van Beuningen is both a stunning reaffirmation of the city's reputation for architectural innovation and yet another symbol of its cultural importance. The adjacent museum is undergoing major renovation that will not be completed until 2026, but in the meantime visitors who cannot wait for it to reopen can tour the depot, with a guide and a guard, and check out the entire 151,000-strong collection—containing works by Monet, Rembrandt, Mondriaan, Warhol, and many others—on pull-out racks. For an alternative view of the city, check out the rooftop garden, which is home to 75 trees. ✉ *Melkkoppad 15, Rotterdam* ☎ *010/441–9400* 🌐 *www.boijmans.nl* 🎟 *€20* ⏲ *Closed Sun.*

★ Frans Hals Museum

Named after the celebrated man himself, this not-to-be-missed museum holds a collection of some 250 amazingly virile and lively group portraits by the Golden Age painter, depicting the merrymaking civic guards and congregating regents for which he became world famous, as well as a series of doll houses by Sara Rothè and works by his son, Nicholaes Hals. The building itself is one of the town's smarter *hofjes:* an entire block of almshouses grouped around an attractive courtyard. In the 17th century, this was an *oudemannenhuis,* or home for elderly men, so it is only fitting that their cottages now form a sequence of galleries for the paintings of Hals and other 17th-century masters of the Haarlem School, along with period furniture, antique silver, and ceramics. From mid-March to mid-May, during bulb season, the museum is made even more resplendent, with a liberal splash of tulip bouquets and other floral art displays adding extra color to the galleries and hallways. ✉ *Groot Heiligland 62, Haarlem* ☎ *023/511-5775* 🌐 *www.franshalsmuseum.com* 🎫 *€16 (including De Hallen)* ⏲ *Closed Mon.*

Heineken Experience

Founded by Gerard Heineken in 1864, the Heineken label has become one of the most famous in the world. The beer is no longer brewed here, but the former brewery has been transformed into the "Heineken Experience," an interactive visitor center that offers tours of the facilities. Everything from vast copper vats to multimedia exhibits are on view, and if you've ever wanted to know what it feels like to be brewed and bottled, the 4D virtual-reality ride "Brew Your Ride" will clue you in. At the end of the tour you get to taste the goods. (No beer is served to visitors under the age of 18.) **TIP→ Buy your ticket in advance; you'll save €3, and they often sell out.** ✉ *Stadhouderskade 78, De Pijp* ☎ *020/523–9222* 🌐 *www.heinekenexperience.com* 🎫 *€21 (€18 online).*

★ Hermitage Amsterdam

OTHER MUSEUM | Taking advantage of 300 years of historical links between Amsterdam and St. Petersburg, the directors of the State Hermitage Museum in St. Petersburg and of the Nieuwe Kerk museum in Amsterdam chose this spot on the Amstel for a new outpost. In 2009, the final refurbishment stage of the former home for the elderly Amstelhof was completed, with high white interiors and smaller side rooms connected by long unadorned corridors. The amount of exhibition space is actually much smaller than you might imagine from the outside (or from the entry price), but the quality of the shows is generally excellent. ✉ *Amstel 51, Plantage* ☎ *020/530–8755* 🌐 *www.hermitage.nl* 🎫 *€19.50.*

★ Kasteel de Haar

The spectacular Kasteel de Haar is not only the largest castle in the Netherlands, but also the most sumptuously furnished. The castle was founded back in 1165, but several renovations and many millions later, the family expanded the house under the eye of P.J.H. Cuypers, designer of Amsterdam's Centraal Station and Rijksmuseum, in 1892. Inside the castle are acres of tapestries, medieval iron chandeliers, and the requisite ancestral portraits snootily studying you as you wander through chivalric halls so opulent and vast they could be opera sets. You can view its grand interiors only via one of the guided tours (no kids under age 5), which leave on the hour and are led only in Dutch. No matter, the objects of beauty on display can be understood in any language. For public transport, take Bus No. 127 leaving hourly from Vleuten Station, direction Breukelen/Kockengen, until the Brink stop in Haarzuilens, a 15-minute walk from the castle. ✉ *Kasteellaan 1, near Haarzuilens, Haarzuilen* ☎ *030/677–8515* 🌐 *www.kasteeldehaar.nl* 🎫 *€18, €7 grounds only; €6 parking.*

★ Markthal

MARKET | Rotterdam's indoor market is a giant archlike structure that houses 228 apartments in its "shell," and provides a roof for more than 100 permanent food stalls. But the real star is the breathtaking interior—in particular the vast mural of colorful insects, fruit, flowers, and vegetables that fills the curving walls and ceiling. Named *Hoorn des Overvloeds* (Horn of Plenty), it's the work of Dutch artist Arno Coenen. Originally created in 4,000 separate pieces before being transferred to its current home, it covers an area of 120,000 square feet and has reasonable claim to being the world's largest painting. ✉ *Dominee Jan Scharpstraat 298, Rotterdam* ☎ *030/234–6464* 🌐 *www.markthal.nl* 🎫 *Free.*

Where to Eat and Drink

★ De Kas

$$$$ | MEDITERRANEAN | Situated in a 1926-built former municipal greenhouse is a lovely, modern, and light-filled restaurant (you're surrounded by glass) serving Mediterranean-influenced food. Wim de Beer and Jos Timmer took over the menu in 2018, changing the focus to include more freshly grown vegetables, often from the restaurant's own greenhouses and garden, though the restaurant is not strictly vegetarian because both meat and fish are served. **Known for:** fresh ingredients "picked in the morning, served in the afternoon"; daily changing vegetable-forward menus; a beautiful and airy glass building and delightful garden terrace. *$ Average main: €59.50 ✉ Kamerlingh Onneslaan 3, Amsterdam-Oost ☎ 020/462–4562 🌐 www.restaurant-dekas.com ⏲ No dinner Sun.*

ML

$$$$ | DUTCH | This long-standing city favorite, housed in the hotel of the same name, is a showpiece for the talents of chef Mark Gratema. The spacious, airy dining room is a seamless blend of modern and traditional, with wood-paneled walls, crisp linens, and chic furniture—the perfect backdrop for sampling an endlessly changing menu of cutting-edge and creative dishes that are as big a treat for the eye as they are for the palate. **Known for:** award-winning high-end cuisine; stylish decor; playful flavor combinations. *$ Average main: €35 ✉ Klokhuisplein 9, Haarlem ☎ 023/512–3910 🌐 www.mlinhaarlem.nl ⏲ Closed Sun. and Mon. No lunch.*

★ Parkheuvel

$$$$ | CONTEMPORARY | In a tastefully modern, semicircular building, with bay windows overlooking the Maas, this posh restaurant run by chef-owner Erik van Loo is one of the Netherlands' finest eateries—with service as effortlessly attentive as you would expect. Luxuries such as truffles are added to the freshest ingredients, with the day's menu dictated by the availability of the best produce at that morning's markets. **Known for:** high-end refined dining; award-winning cuisine; reservations essential. *$ Average main: €48 ✉ Heuvellaan 21, Centrum ☎ 010/436–0766 🌐 www.parkheuvel.nl ⏲ Closed Mon. and Tues.; no dinner Sun.; no lunch Sat.*

★ Restaurant As

$$$$ | MEDITERRANEAN | A Chez Panisse–trained chef whips up frequently changing menus with local ingredients and a Mediterranean flair at this lively restaurant in a former chapel; all dishes are cooked on an open fire in an outdoor wood oven. The three-course dinner menus are a great value and make it worth venturing to Amsterdam's far southern reaches (Tram No. 5 stops a block away)—there is always a choice of meat or fish, and you can add an "in-between" course for a little bit more. (You can also order à la carte at lunch.) Most of the seating is at long communal tables, which makes for a convivial atmosphere. **Known for:** "pure cooking" with local, seasonal ingredients; well-priced prix-fixe menus; beautiful park-facing terrace. *$ Average main: €38.50 ✉ Prinses Irenestraat 19, Oud-Zuid ☎ 020/644–0100 🌐 www.restaurantas.nl ⏲ Closed Mon.-Tues.*

★ Restaurant Sinne

$$$$ | MEDITERRANEAN | This candlelit French-Mediterranean restaurant with exposed brick walls and whimsical cartoon paintings is a true local favorite. Choose a set menu by picking from several appetizers, mains, and desserts—the minimum order is three courses and ranges all the way up to eight. **Known for:** accessibly priced Michelin-starred cuisine; signature dish: celeriac with black truffle and celeriac foam, egg yolk, and Hollandaise sauce; elegant, romantic setting. *$ Average main: €42 ✉ Ceintuurbaan 342, De Pijp ☎ 020/682–7290 🌐 www.restaurantsinne.nl ⏲ Closed Mon. and Tues. No lunch Wed.–Fri.*

Cool Places to Stay

★ Ambassade

$$$$ | **HOTEL** | **FAMILY** | Friday's book market on nearby Spui Square lends a literary ambience to these 10 connected, stylishly decorated 17th- and 18th-century houses, where charming guest rooms are decked out in rich fabrics and colors, with striking details (wood-beam ceilings, elegant chandeliers), and modern 20th-century paintings. **Pros:** intimate, homely atmosphere; some guest rooms overlook the picturesque Herengracht canal; hub for literati. **Cons:** breakfast is not included; hotel has an elevator, but some rooms can only be reached via narrow stairs; no in-house spa, though there is an affiliation with a spa down the street. *Rooms from: €270 Herengracht 341, Western Canal Ring 020/555–0222 www.ambassade-hotel.nl 56 rooms No Meals.*

★ Conservatorium Hotel

$$$$ | **HOTEL** | Located across the street from the Stedelijk Museum—the surrounding area chockablock with scenic parks, super-deluxe shops, restaurants and concert halls, and tram lines giving quick access into the city center—the Conservatorium is a convenient retreat for travelers looking for a stay with style. **Pros:** luxurious spa; great location only yards away from the big three museums; one of the best design hotels in town. **Cons:** breakfast service can be slow; duplex rooms (bed upstairs, shower downstairs) not to every guest's liking; very expensive rates. *Rooms from: €485 Van Baerlestraat 27, Museum District 20/570–0000 www.conservatoriumhotel.com 129 rooms No Meals.*

★ Hotel Arena

$ | **HOTEL** | Located inside Oosterpark, this former 19th-century orphanage is an open, accessible space, which seamlessly merges the landmark's historic character with contemporary glass, greenery, and gentle earthy hues to suit its surroundings. **Pros:** Amsterdam's first true "city park hotel" combines a stylish interior and peaceful views; a brilliant boutique-style option that offers value for money; stunning surroundings near enough to everything, but without those crushing crowds. **Cons:** no connecting rooms or triple/quad rooms, but most can fit an extra bed; if you're looking for a very central location, this isn't it; there's no gym, but there is a tennis court and the park's ideal for a morning run. *Rooms from: €112 's-Gravesandestraat 55, Amsterdam-Oost 020/850–2400 www.hotelarena.nl 139 rooms No Meals.*

★ Hotel Des Indes

$$$ | **HOTEL** | What was once a 19th-century mansion is one of the world's premier hotels, with a harmonious blend of fluted marble columns, brocaded walls, and gilding, as well as ample bedrooms with all the best facilities. **Pros:** sumptuous; elegant; centrally located. **Cons:** some rooms small for the price; on-site parking expensive; too old-fashioned for some. *Rooms from: €195 Lange Voorhout 54-56, The Hague 070/361–2345 www.hoteldesindesthehague.com 92 rooms No Meals.*

Hotel New York

$$ | **HOTEL** | An atmospheric standout on Rotterdam's business-oriented hotel scene occupies the former twin-towered, waterside headquarters of the Holland-America Line, offering individually decorated rooms with high ceilings that contrast with the modernist, vaguely nautical decor, and excellent views. **Pros:** great riverside location; historic building; nice room decor. **Cons:** away from main sights; cheapest rooms have no views; restaurant food just okay. *Rooms from: €160 Koninginnenhoofd 1, Kop van Zuid 010/439–0500 www.hotelnewyork.nl 72 rooms No Meals.*

Chapter 5

SPAIN AND PORTUGAL

WELCOME TO SPAIN AND PORTUGAL

TOP REASONS TO GO

★ **Gorgeous Cathedrals:** Towering temples have presided over Spanish cities for centuries and are some of the greatest marvels in Spain.

★ **Beaches:** You can't go wrong on the mainland or the Canary and Balearic Islands.

★ **Amazing Architecture:** From Roman engineering feats to modern delights, Spain has stunning monuments from every century.

★ **Lisbon:** The vibrant capital encompasses cobblestone streets, funicular railways, and world-class museums, combining old-time charm with top-notch dining and buzzing nightlife.

★ **Cruising the Douro River:** A cruise is a relaxing way to explore the eye-opening landscapes of the Douro River Valley, with its steeply terraced vineyards.

★ **Hiking the Rota Vicentina:** Stretching from Alentejo to the Algarve, the 250-mile Rota Vicentina is one of the most beautiful coastal trails in Europe.

1 **Madrid.** The Spanish capital since 1561 is a vibrant and increasingly international metropolis.

2 **Barcelona.** From the medieval Barri Gòtic to the modernist Eixample, Barcelona demands your full attention.

3 **Southern Spain.** Southern Spain is a veritable feast of sights, sounds, tastes, and warm sunshine.

4 **Northern Spain.** From the plains of Castile to the Pyrenees and the Mediterranean in the east, Northern Spain delivers on all accounts.

5 **Canary Islands.** These eight islands are a historic way station between the old- and new worlds.

6 **Portugal.** Packed with vibrant culture, history, and natural beauty, Portugal contains striking landscapes ripe for exploration.

7 **Madeira and the Azores.** The colorful volcanic islands are among Portugal's most enchanting regions.

Bordeaux
Bay of Biscay
FRANCE
Gijón
Santander
E70
viedo
San Sebastián
Bilbao
Toulouse
León
Vitoria-Gasteiz
Pamplona
PYRENEES
ANDORRA
Andorra la Vella
Logroño
Burgos
4
A6
Valladolid
Zaragoza
Lleida
Mataró
E90
2
Barcelona
Salamanca
A50
A6
E5
E90
Tarragona
E803
E15
A23
Madrid
1
SPAIN
COSTA DEL AZAHAR
Castellón de la Plana
E90
E5
E901
BALEARIC ISLANDS
Palma
MALLORCA
Valencia
IBIZA
Formentera
Albacete
E15
A31
N322
E5
A30
Elche
Alicante
Córdoba
Jaén
Murcia
3
Cartagena
Mediterranean Sea
Granada
E15
Málaga
Almería
Algiers
arbella
COSTA DEL SOL
E15
GIBRALTAR
Gibraltar
Chlef
N11
Mostaganem
N4
Oran
Relizane
N2
ALGERIA
MOROCCO
Oujda
Tlemcen
Saida

WHAT TO EAT AND DRINK IN SPAIN AND PORTUGAL

Paella

TAPAS

Itinerant grazing from tavern to tavern is popular throughout Spain and gives you the chance to try all types of tapas, from traditional favorites such as *boquerones en vinagre* (cured anchovies), *albóndigas* (meatballs) and *ensaladilla rusa* (potato salad), to local specialties, including *pintxos* in the Basque Country and *espinacas con garbanzos* (spinach with chickpeas) in Seville.

PORTUGUESE WINE

Portugal is most famous for Port wine, from the Douro Valley. Often served with dessert, port comes in several varieties, ranging from the citrusy white to more caramel and nutty aromas of the tawny and ruby. Chilled Vinho Verde is a favorite with the Portuguese in the summer. Produced in the region between Minho and Douro, this popular wine (sometimes slightly effervescent) is available all over the country.

PASTÉIS DE NATA

Portugal has plenty of tasty pastries, but if you can only pick one, make it the *pastel de nata*—a custard tart that is best purchased in a specialized store. Egg yolk, milk, and sugar are the main ingredients in the creamy filling, which is held together by a flaky pastry cup.

BACALHAU À BRÁS

Portugal's national dish is codfish, better known as *bacalhau*, and one of the many creative cod-based recipes to try is *bacalhau à brás*, scrambled eggs with shredded cod, onion, and thin potato sticks topped with black olives.

SPANISH WINE

Almost every region of Spain produces fine wines. Galicia is famous for its citrusy, slate-y white Albariño; central Spain produces bold, oaky reds including Ribera del Duero's famed Tempranillo by Pingus and Protos; in Catalonia, sparkling cava is made using the same method as Champagne, and the Penedès region produces fine whites and reds; Rioja is the prime wine region, most famous for its reds; and in Andalusia, the seven types of sherry reign supreme, particularly around Jerez de la Frontera.

SWEET BITES

The Spaniards' sweet tooth becomes apparent in the vast array of cakes and pastries on display in *pastelería* windows or sold at convents across the country. Desserts tend to be low-key; among the most popular are *crema catalana*, a Catalan version of the French crème brûlée, and *pestiños*, cylinders or twists of fried dough in anise-honey syrup. Almonds feature in many sweets, including *mazapán* (marzipan) and *turrón* nougat, in its soft or hard version, typically eaten during the festive season.

FISH AND SEAFOOD

Spain's Mediterranean and Atlantic coastlines are a treasure trove of fresh fish and seafood. In Galicia, *pulpo a la gallega* stars boiled octopus with olive oil and smoky paprika; cod (*bacalao*) takes center stage in the Basque Country in various guises; and in Andalucia,

Pastéis de nata

Pulpo a la Gallega

frituras (fried fish) with crisp whitebait and squid rings feature on restaurant menus throughout the region.

RICE

Rice grows in parts of Catalonia and Valencia. The most famous rice dish is, of course, *paella valenciana*, one of Spain's most significant gastronomic contributions. The "real thing" is made with short-grain rice, chicken, rabbit, *garrofó* (a local white bean), tomatoes, green beans, and saffron. However, you'll also come across *paella marinera* with seafood and fish, and *paella negra*, made with squid ink.

STEWS

Guisos, the ultimate comfort foods, are made according to recipes handed down through the generations. They usually include pulses, vegetables, potatoes, and meat or fish. In Madrid, try *cocido madrileño*, made with chickpeas; in central Spain, *pisto manchego* with fried egg on top; in Asturias, *fabada*, showcasing creamy white beans and smoky sausage; in Catalonia, *suquet de peix*, with fish and *sèpia amb pésols* with cuttlefish and tomatoes; and in Andalusia, *rabo de toro* (oxtail), stewed with vegetables.

Spain and Portugal Snapshot

Know Before You Go

GET YOUR TIMING RIGHT.

High summer is not the best time to enjoy Spain or Portugal, particularly the baking hot interior. If you want good weather but smaller crowds, time your visit for the shoulder seasons of June or September.

A SLOWER WAY OF LIFE.

Both Spain and Portugal are late countries, with dinner in Portugal coming around 8 or 9 (it's even later in Spain... more like 10). Sundays are especially quiet except in tourist areas. But siestas are a thing of the past.

BOOK AHEAD.

You'll need to plan ahead for big-ticket sights like the Alhambra, the Sagrada Família, Park Güell, and the Picasso Museum (book tickets before you arrive if you want to be assured entry). There is zero flexibility with this at most attractions, so be sure to arrive at your appointed time.

SPANISH ISN'T THE SAME AS PORTUGUESE.

In large cities and major resorts towns in Portugal, many people speak English and will immediately switch languages if you seem to be struggling. But off the beaten path they might not speak any English. Any attempt you make to speak Portuguese in Portugal will be well received; a smattering of Spanish less so.

THERE'S A COOL WIND BLOWING.

Portugal is not, strictly speaking, a Mediterranean country, but an Atlantic one. The ocean has a strong influence on the climate, and temperatures often plummet and the wind picks up even on summer nights, so pack a jacket or shawl in July or August.

Planning Your Time

You could easily spend a week in either Madrid or Barcelona and still have plenty more to see. Devote a minimum of three or four days in each of these major cities and save a day for a day trip. Spain is a large country, and there's an especially large amount to see in Southern Spain; Northern Spain is equally fascinating but somewhat less visited. You'll need at least a week in Portugal to see Lisbon, Porto, and Sintra, but if you have more time, there's a lot to explore. The Canary Islands, Azores, and Madeira are separate trips that require at least a week each.

Great Trips

5 days: Madrid plus Seville or Granada

7 days: Barcelona, Bilbao, and San Sebastian

7 days: Madrid, Toledo, Córdoba, Granada

5 days: Lisbon to Porto

6 days: The Alentejo and the Ribatejo

Big Events

Carnaval (Carnival). The final festival before Lent, Carnaval is held throughout Spain and Portugal, with processions of masked participants, singing competitions, parades, and displays of flowers.

Peixe em Lisboa. Lisbon's biggest gastronomic event (in April) features top Portuguese and foreign chefs, who set up food stalls and do cooking demonstrations and talks. 🌐 *www.peixemlisboa.com*

Fiesta de Otoño (Autumn Festival). In September, this festival in Jerez de la Frontera in Andalusia celebrates the grape harvest and includes a procession, the blessing of the harvest, and traditional-style grape treading.

What To...

READ

For Whom the Bell Tolls, Ernest Hemingway

Monsignor Quixote, Graham Greene

The New Spaniards, John Hooper

Baltasar and Blimunda, José Saramago

The High Mountains of Portugal, Yann Martel

WATCH

¡Ay Carmela! director Carlos Saura

Women on the Verge of a Nervous Breakdown, director Pedro Almodóvar

Family United, director Daniel Sánchez Arévalo

Lisbon Story, director Wim Wenders

Porto, director Gabe Klinger

BUY

Damascene (metalwork inlaid with gold or silver), pottery, embroidery, and marzipan in Toledo.

Embroidered linen tablecloths and place mats, made using the traditional *calado* method in the Canary Islands.

Shoes and leather clothing, porcelain and handblown glass, and artificial pearls on Mallorca.

Hand-painted *azulejos* (tiles) in Portugal.

Traditional handcrafted embroidery items, such as pillow cases and tablecloths in Madeira.

Contacts

AIR

Major Airports: Adolfo Suárez Madrid–Barajas Airport (MAD); Barcelona International Airport (BCN); Málaga Airport (AGP); Bilbao (BIO); Mallorca (PMI), Ibiza (IBZ); Lisbon Humberto Delgado Airport (LIS), Porto Francisco Sá Carneiro Airport (OPO); Madeira Airport (FNC); Ponta Delgada Airport João Paulo II (PDL)

BOAT

Brittany Ferries. 🌐 *www.brittany-ferries.com*

FRS. 🌐 *www.frs.es*

Trasmediterránea. 🌐 *www.trasmediterranea.es*

BUS

SPAIN

ALSA. ☎ *902/242–2242* 🌐 *www.alsa.es*

Flixbus. 🌐 *www.flixbus.es*

PORTUGAL

Eva Transportes. ☎ *707/223–344* 🌐 *www.eva-bus.com*

Rede Expressos. ☎ *707/223–344 or 217/524–524* 🌐 *www.rede-expressos.pt*

Rodo Norte. ☎ *259/340–710* 🌐 *www.rodonorte.pt*

TRAIN

SPAIN

RENFE. 🌐 *www.renfe.es.*

PORTUGAL

Comboios de Portugal. 🌐 *www.cp.pt*

VISITOR INFORMATION

SPAIN

🌐 *www.spain.info/en*

🌐 *www.parador.es*

🌐 *www.spainisculture.com*

PORTUGAL

🌐 *www.visitportugal.com*

🌐 *www.winesofportugal.info*

Madrid

Madrid, the Spanish capital since 1561, is Europe's third-largest city and a vibrant, international metropolis with an infectious appetite for art, music, and epicurean pleasures. In the span of a single block, you might find a century-old taverna, a Senegalese textile supplier, a Sichuan hot pot restaurant, and a glitzy boutique hotel.

In other words, the Madrid of Ernest Hemingway—of bullfights and siestas and sherry wine and frilly fans—has largely faded into the past. Expect instead a cosmopolitan, open-minded city with enough youth-driven verve to keep you on your toes but enough history and old-world charm to remind you that you're on vacation.

There are many modern barrios such as Salamanca, Chamberí, and Chamartín, but the historic center—between the Royal Palace and Parque del Buen Retiro—is the main attraction for international visitors. Here you'll find a conglomeration of Belle Époque buildings with intricate facades, terra-cotta-roofed residences, redbrick Mudejar Revival churches, and grand public squares.

Then there's the art—the legacy of one of the most important global empires ever assembled. King Carlos I (1500–58), who later became Emperor Carlos V (or Charles V), set out to collect the best specimens from all European schools of art, many of which found their way to Spain's palaces and, later, to the Prado Museum, not to mention the contemporary Reina Sofía and the wide-ranging Thyssen-Bornemisza.

Madrileños love being outdoors as much as possible. Restaurant patios (*terrazas*), flea markets, and parks and plazas are always teeming when the sun's out. Year-round, the city's buzzy tapas scene draws crowds of locals and tourists alike, with a number of standbys on Cava Baja in La Latina, eye-popping *nueva cocina* numbers along Chamberí's Calle Ponzano, and in the barrios' old-school markets, many of which have been transformed into experimental (and affordable) tapas emporiums.

If time allows, a day trip to the monumental Renaissance-style palace complex of El Escorial offers a deep dive into the life of Spanish royalty.

Madrid's Markets

Shop for the City's Best

Traditional Spanish ingredients, freshly prepared tapas, antiques, and souvenirs: Madrid's wonderfully varied markets offer a bit of everything. The most popular is Mercado de San Miguel, with its bustling mix of upscale tapas spots and grab-and-go counters set beneath a gorgeous fin-de-siècle glass dome. Enjoy a glass of wine and classic snacks like croquetas and jamón, or try a futuristic-flavored ice cream from Rocambolesc. For a more authentic experience, head to Malasaña's Mercado de Los Mostenses, where you'll spot locals buying meat and produce; at lunchtime, it teems with families and workers scoping out affordable food. If you're ready to rummage, the legendary open-air El Rastro flea market takes place every Sunday on the streets and squares of La Latina. Its 3,000-plus stalls brim with unique finds and tchotchkes—from vintage furniture to old vinyl to second-hand clothing.

Don't Miss

Plaza General Vara del Rey has some of El Rastro's best antiques, and the streets beyond—Calles Mira el Río Alta and Mira el Río Baja—boast all sorts of miscellany.

When to Go

Come early to Mercado de San Miguel and El Rastro. Note that Mercado de Los Mostenses is closed on Sunday.

El Rastro. ✉ *Barrio de las Letras* 🚇 *Metro: La Latina, Puerta de Toledo*

Mercado de Los Mostenses. ✉ *Pl. de Los Mostenses, Malasaña* ☎ *91/542–5838* 🚇 *Metro: Plaza de España, Noviciado*

Mercado de San Miguel. ✉ *Pl. de San Miguel, Sol* ☎ *91/542–4936* 🌐 *www.mercadodesanmiguel.es* 🚇 *Metro: Ópera*

Plaza Mayor

Madrid's Grandest Square

A symbol of imperial Spain's might and grandeur, this vast public square is one of the largest in Europe, measuring 360 feet by 300 feet. It was completed in 1619 under Felipe III, whose equestrian statue stands in the center. Steeped in four centuries of history, the plaza has seen it all: *autos-da-fé* (public burnings of heretics), the canonization of saints, executions, royal marriages, masked balls, and bullfights (until 1847). It also once housed a city market, and many of the surrounding streets retain the names of associated trades and foods, including Calle de Lechuga (Lettuce Street), Calle de Fresa (Strawberry Street), and Calle de Botoneros (Button Makers' Street). Closed to motorized traffic and framed by arcades and cafés, it's a pleasant place for sidewalk-sitting and coffee- or cava-sipping as buskers put on impromptu shows. Sunday morning brings a stamp and coin market.

Don't Miss

The plaza's oldest building, dating from 1590, Casa de la Panadería (Bakery House) stands out with its bright Baroque-style murals and gray spires; you can visit the tourist information office on the ground floor.

When to Go

While the plaza is bustling year-round, at Christmastime it takes on a particularly festive air. From late November to the end of December, more than 100 stalls sell all manner of holiday items, including wreathes, ornaments, toys, and Nativity scenes. 🌐 *www.mercadonavidadplazamayor.com*

Plaza Mayor. 🚆 *Metro: Sol, Opera*

Watch a Real Madrid Soccer Match

Madrid's True Passion

Fútbol (or soccer) is Spain's number one sport, and Madrid has four teams: Real Madrid, Atlético Madrid, Rayo Vallecano, and Getafe, though Real Madrid is by far the most famed. Its success goes far beyond Spanish borders; FIFA considers Real Madrid the most successful soccer team in the 20th century and one of the most successful sports franchises ever, having won five FIFA World Cup tournaments. The team's home base is in the Chamartín neighborhood at Santiago Bernabéu Stadium, which holds 85,400 (and also offers daytime tours of its facilities). A €590 million gut renovation of the stadium is on track to be completed in 2023. You can book tickets online about a week in advance, or if the match isn't sold out, tickets are sold in the stadium box office.

Don't Miss

To enjoy a spirited match without the long lines and inflated price tag of Real Madrid, step up to Rayo Vallecano's box office. The team's second-tier status doesn't make the games any less thrilling (think college ball vs. NBA), especially when you catch them on their home turf in Vallecas, which seats 14,708. You can feel good about your ticket purchase, too, since Rayo is known for its community activism. When the pandemic hit, the team's charitable foundation sewed and distributed 12,000 masks for under-supplied hospitals.

Rayo Vallecano: Campo de Fútbol de Vallecas. ✉ *Calle del Payaso Fofó 0, Puente de Vallecas* ☎ *91/478–4329* 🌐 *www.rayovallecano.es* 🚇 *Portazgo*

Real Madrid: Santiago Bernabéu Stadium. ✉ *Paseo de la Castellana 140, Chamartín* ☎ *91/398–4300* 🌐 *www.realmadrid.es* 🚇 *Santiago Bernabéu*

Palacio Real

Madrid's Own Version of Versailles

The largest palace in Western Europe, the Royal Palace awes visitors with its sheer size and monumental presence. It was commissioned in 1738 by the first of Spain's Bourbon rulers, Felipe V. Outside, you can see the classical French architecture on the graceful Patio de Armas; inside, more than 3,000 rooms (a fraction of which are open to the public) compete with one another for over-the-top opulence. A two-hour guided tour points out highlights including the Salón de Gasparini, King Carlos III's private apartments; the Salón del Trono, a grand throne room; and the banquet hall, set with gleaming china. Also within are the Painting Gallery, with works by Spanish, Flemish, and Italian artists; the Royal Armory, with tailored suits of armor; the Royal Library, with a first edition of *Don Quixote*; and Stradivarius's Royal Quartet, the world's largest collection of five-stringed instruments by the famed violin maker.

Don't Miss

Every Wednesday and Saturday, the Changing of the Guard takes place (11–2 and 10–noon in summer) at the Puerta del Príncipe, across Plaza de Oriente, with a more lavish ceremony (with up to 100 guards and horses) the first Wednesday of most months at noon.

Best Room

The 8,600-square-foot Royal Kitchen has remained largely unchanged since the late 18th century. Its framed handwritten menus, antediluvian wood-burning ovens, copper cauldrons, wooden iceboxes, and nearly 3,000 antique kitchen utensils make it a must-stop for foodies.

✉ *Calle Bailén, Palacio* ☎ *91/454–8800* 🌐 *www.patrimonionacional.es* 🚆 *Metro: Opera* 🎫 *From €12*

Museo del Prado

A Treasury of Spanish Masterpieces

The Prado was first commissioned in 1785 as a natural science museum, but by the time the building was completed in 1819, its purpose had changed to exhibiting the art gathered by Spanish royalty since the time of Ferdinand and Isabella. The museum's jewels are its works by the nation's three great masters Goya, Velázquez, and El Greco—though it also holds masterpieces by Flemish, Dutch, German, French, and Italian artists, collected when their lands were part of the Spanish Empire. Highlights include Goya's 14 nightmarish "black paintings," executed by the artist to decorate the walls of his home; two of El Greco's greatest works, *The Resurrection*and *The Adoration of the Shepherds*; and Hieronymus Bosch's eerie triptych *The Garden of Earthly Delights*. With 2,000-plus paintings and sculptures on display, a visit here can easily be an all-day affair.

Don't Miss

The Prado's most famous canvas, Velázquez's *Las Meninas (The Maids of Honor)*, is a masterpiece of spatial perspective. In this complex visual game, *you* are the king and queen of Spain, reflected in a distant mirror as the court painter (Velázquez) pauses in front of his easel to observe your features.

Top Tip

More than 3 million visitors stream through the Prado's doors each year. Book a timed ticket online to skip the lines and try for 10 am, when the museum opens, to avoid the worst of the crowds.

✉ *Retiro* ☎ *91/330–2800* 🌐 *www.museo-delprado.es* 🚇 *Metro: Banco de España, Estación del Arte* 🎫 *€15*

Museo Thyssen-Bornemisza

One of the Greatest Private Art Collections

The far-reaching collection of the Thyssen's almost 1,000 paintings traces the history of Western art with examples from every important movement, from 13th-century Italian Gothic through 20th-century American pop art. The works were gathered from the 1920s to the 1980s by wealthy industrialist Baron Hans Heinrich Thyssen-Bornemisza and his father, Heinrich Sr. The museum occupies the spacious late-18th-century Villahermosa Palace, just across from the Prado. The baron donated the entire collection to Spain in 1993, and a subsequent renovation added the baroness's personal collection. Spanish heavyweights like Goya, Picasso, and Dalí are represented, as are Dutch masters Rembrandt and Van Gogh, plus a wide array of important Impressionist, Postimpressionist, and German Expressionist paintings. The temporary exhibits, which have featured fashion icons like Coco Chanel and retrospectives of top artists such as Lucien Freud, are fascinating.

Don't Miss

Perusing the massive collection can take hours, but be sure to zero in on major works including El Greco's *The Annunciation*, Picasso's *Harlequin with a Mirror*, Edward Hopper's *Hotel Room*; Roy Lichtenstein's *Woman in Bath;* and Hans Holbein the Younger's iconic *Portrait of Henry VIII.*

Best Break

In spring and summer, the rooftop café is an appealing place to unwind with a coffee or cocktail and offers lovely views of the courtyard garden below. It stays open until 11:30 pm on Friday and Saturday.

✉ *Paseo del Prado 8, Barrio de las Letras* ☎ *91/791–1370* 🌐 *www.museo-thyssen.org* 🚇 *Metro: Banco de España* 🎫 *€13*

Parque del Buen Retiro

Stroll Through the City's Favorite Green Space

Once the private playground of royalty—and a UNESCO World Heritage site since 2021— Madrid's crowning park is a vast expanse of green (some 300 acres) encompassing formal gardens, fountains, lakes, exhibition halls, children's play areas, and outdoor cafés. The park, especially lively on weekends, also hosts a book fair in May and occasional concerts in summer. From the entrance at the Puerta de Alcalá, head straight toward the center to find the Estanque Grande (big pond), presided over by a grandiose equestrian statue of King Alfonso XII. The 19th-century Palacio de Cristal (Glass Palace) was built to house exotic plants but today hosts temporary exhibitions. The Rosaleda (Rose Garden) is bursting with color and heady with floral scents for most of the summer.

Don't Miss

Near the southern edge of the park, look for the *Fuente del Ángel Caído* (*Fallen Angel Fountain*); the statue here is the only one in the world depicting the Prince of Darkness before his fall from grace.

Best Break

El Retiro is now a nightlife destination, thanks to **Florida Park**, the see-and-be-seen leisure complex with multiple venues: El Pabellón, a white-tablecloth restaurant; La Galería, an informal tapas bar; La Terraza, a chic rooftop terrace; Los Kioskos, an indoor-outdoor bar with live flamenco; and La Sala, a tony nightclub that stays open until 6 am on weekends. 🌐 *www.floridapark.es*

✉ *Puerta de Alcalá* 🚆 *Metro: Retiro.*

Museo Nacional Centro de Arte Reina Sofía

Home to Picasso's Most Iconic Painting

A towering sculpture by Roy Lichtenstein greets you at the door to Spain's preeminent modern art museum, housed in an 18th-century hospital building with a snazzy postmodern extension by Jean Nouvel (added in 2005). It features more than 1,000 works on four floors—the tip of the iceberg from a collection of over 23,000 works. Painting is the focus here, but photography and cinema are also represented. The museum contextualizes the works of the great modern masters—Picasso, Miró, and Dalí—and of other famed artists, such as Juan Gris, Yves Klein, Julio Gonzalez, Eduardo Chillida, and Antoni Tàpies, into broad historical narratives to explain the evolution of modern art. This means, for instance, that the Dalís are not all displayed together in a single area, but scattered around the 38 rooms. The museum also mounts insightful temporary exhibitions, mainly focusing on contemporary artists.

Don't Miss

The museum's showpiece is Picasso's *Guernica*: the huge black-and-white canvas depicts the horror of the Nazi Condor Legion's ruthless bombing of innocent civilians in the Basque town of Gernika in 1937 during the Spanish Civil War.

Where to Eat

Housed in a striking, modern space in the Jean Nouvel–designed addition, **NuBel** offers upscale international dishes presented with an artistic flair. It's open for breakfast, lunch, and dinner, and the set weekend brunch features live DJs. 🌐 *www.nubel.es*

✉ *Calle de Santa Isabel 52, Lavapiés* ☎ *91/467–5062* 🌐 *www.museoreinasofia.es* 🚇 *Metro: Estación del Arte* 🎫 *€12*

El Escorial

A Monument to the Spanish Golden Age

A UNESCO World Heritage Site and one of Spain's most visited landmarks, the imposing Monastery and Real Sitio de San Lorenzo de El Escorial (or just El Escorial) was commissioned by Felipe II after the death of his father in the 1500s and remains the most complete and impressive monument of the later Renaissance in Spain. The monastery was built as an eternal memorial for his relatives and the crypt here is the resting place of the majority of Spain's kings, from Charles V to Alfonso XIII. A fantasy land of gilded halls, gleaming marble floors, hand-painted frescoes, rich tapestries, and ceramic tiles, the gargantuan royal residence also houses an important collection of paintings by Renaissance and baroque artists donated by the crown. Outside, it's surrounded by beautifully manicured French gardens.

Getting Here

An hour from Madrid, San Lorenzo del Escorial makes for a leisurely day trip. A dozen or so trains leave daily from the Madrid Sol train station, or you can take the C3 regional line from Atocha, Chamartín, Nuevos Ministerios, or Recoletos. The entrance to El Escorial is about a 15-minute walk from the station.

Best Room

El Escorial's magnificent, 177-foot-long library is adorned with vibrant frescoes and houses a rare collection of more than 4,700 manuscripts, many of them illuminated, and 40,000 printed books.

✉ *Av Juan de Borbón y Battemberg, s/n, San Lorenzo de El Escorial* ☎ *91/890–5903* 🌐 *www.sanlorenzoturismo.es* 🎫 *€12*

Madrid
A
B
C
D
E
F
1
2
3
4
5
6
7
8
9
C. de José Abascal
C. de José Abascal
C. de Joaquín María López
C. de Donoso Cortés
C. de Donoso Cortés
C. de Fernández de los Ríos
C. de Fernando el Católico
Calle de Eloy Gonzalo
C. de Isaac Peral
C. de Hilarión Eslava
C. de Galileo
C. de Vallehermoso
C. de Magallanes
C. de Bravo Murillo
C. de Santa Engracia
C. de Juan de Austria
Parque del Oeste
Calle de la Princesa
C. de Gaztambide
C. de Andrés Mellado
C. de Guzmán el Bueno
C. de Blasco de Garay
C. de Rodríguez San Pedro
C. de Fuencarral
C. del Cardenal Cisneros
C. de Trafalgar
Paseo del Pintor Rosales
C. de Romero Robledo
C. de Benito Gutiérrez
C. de Altamirano
C. del Marqués de Urquijo
C. de Alberto Aguilera
C. de Luchana
C. de Sagasta
Western Park
C. de Tutor
C. de Martín de los Heros
C. de Ferraz
Palacio de Liria
C. del Conde Duque
C. de Montserrat
C. de Monteleón
C. de San Andrés
C. de Fuencarral
C. de Churruca
C. de Larra
C. de Quintana
C. del Rey Francisco
C. de Evaristo San Miguel
C. de la Princesa
C. de Noviciado
C. de Amaniel
C. del Acuerdo
C. de San Bernardo
MALASAÑA
C. de la Palma
C. de Barceló
Calle de la Rosaleda
Paseo del Rey
C. de Luisa Fernanda
C. de San Vicente Ferrer
C. de San Bernardino
C. de la Madera
Corredera Alta de San Pablo
Plaza de España
C. del Pez
C. de San Bernardo
Gran Vía
Paseo de la Florida
Cuesta de San Vicente
Calle de Silva
CHUECA
C. de Valverde
C. de Hortaleza
Gran Vía
Calle de Bailén
Monasterio de las Descalzas Reales
C. del Carmen
C. Preciados
Calle de la Montera
C. de la Aduana
Paseo de la Virgen del Puerto
Teatro Real
C. de Alcalá
Puerta del Sol
Calle Mayor
Calle Mayor
Calle de la Cruz
C. del Sacramento
Calle de Atocha
Pl. de Jacinto Benavente
Calle de Segovia
C. de Manzanares
BARRIO DE LA LATINA
Plaza de Tirso de Molina
Ronda de Segovia
Calle de Bailén
Calle de la Cabeza
Calle del Calvario
Carrera de San Francisco
C. de Jesús y María
Calle de Linneo
Calle de Juan Duque
Calle de Toledo
Calle Ribera de Curtidores
Calle de los Embajadores
Calle del Mesón de Paredes
Calle del Amparo
C. de Zurita
Paseo Imperial
Ronda de Segovia
Ronda de Toledo
Calle del Casino
C. de Valencia
KEY
Bucket List Picks
Where to Eat and Drink
Cool Places to Stay

Bucket List Picks

1 El Escorial A5
2 Madrid's Markets D7
3 Museo del Prado H7
4 Museo Nacional Centro de Arte Reina Sofía G9
5 Museo Thyssen-Bornemisza G7
6 Palacio Real C6
7 Parque del Buen Retiro I7
8 Plaza Mayor E7
9 Watch a Real Madrid Soccer Match H1

Where to Eat and Drink

1 Casa Botín E7
2 Casa Salvador G5
3 La Dolores G7
4 La Venencia F7
5 Melo's F8
6 Robuchon I4
7 Salmon Guru F7

Cool Places to Stay

1 Barceló Torre de Madrid D5
2 CoolRooms Palacio de Atocha F8
3 Gran Meliá Palacio de Los Duques D6
4 Iberostar Las Letras Gran Vía F6
5 Mandarin Oriental Ritz, Madrid H7
6 Rosewood Villa Magna I3

When in Madrid

CaixaForum

ART MUSEUM | Swiss architects Jacques Herzog and Pierre de Meuron (who designed London's Tate Modern) converted an early-20th-century power station into a stunning arts complex that arguably turns Madrid's "Golden Triangle" of art museums into a quadrilateral. Belonging to one of the country's wealthiest foundations (La Caixa bank), the structure seems to float above the sloped public plaza, with a tall vertical garden designed by French botanist Patrick Blanc on its northern side contrasting with a geometric rust-color roof. Inside, the soaring exhibition halls display ancient as well as contemporary art including pieces from La Caixa's proprietary collection. ✉ *Paseo del Prado 36, Barrio de las Letras* ☎ *91/330–7300* 🌐 *www.caixaforum.es* 🎫 *€6* Ⓜ *Estación del Arte.*

★ Monasterio de las Descalzas Reales

(*Monastery of the Royal Discalced/Barefoot Nuns*)

RELIGIOUS BUILDING | After a 20-month closure for renovations, this important 16th-century monastery reopened to the public in late 2021 with 200 new works from its art collection on display. The plain brick-and-stone facade belies an opulent interior strewn with paintings by Francisco de Zurbarán, Titian, and Pieter Brueghel the Elder—all part of the dowry of new monastery inductees—as well as a hall of sumptuous tapestries crafted from drawings by Peter Paul Rubens. Fifty works from the collection were meticulously restored as part of the recent renovations. The convent was founded in 1559 by Juana of Austria, one of Felipe II's sisters, who ruled Spain while he was in England and the Netherlands. It houses 33 different chapels—the age of Christ when he died and the maximum number of nuns allowed to live at the monastery—with more than 120 immaculately preserved crucifixes among them. About a dozen nuns still live here and grow vegetables in the garden. **TIP→ You must take a tour in order to visit the convent, and tickets must be bought online ahead of time (they sell out fast); those who don't speak Spanish can access an English guide through the app.** ✉ *Pl. de las Descalzas Reales 3, Palacio* ☎ *91/454–8800* 🌐 *www.patrimonionacional.es/en/real-sitio/monasterio-de-las-descalzas-reales* 🎫 *€6* ⏲ *Closed Mon.* ✍ *Reservations and pre-purchased tickets required* Ⓜ *Sol.*

★ Museo Sorolla

ART MUSEUM | See the world through the once-in-a-generation eye of Spain's most famous impressionist painter, Joaquín Sorolla (1863–1923), who lived and worked most of his life at this home and garden that he designed and decorated. Every corner is filled with exquisite artwork—including plenty of original Sorollas—and impeccably selected furnishings, which pop against brightly colored walls that evoke the Mediterranean coast, where the painter was born. The museum can be seen as part of the Abono Cinco Palacios, a €12 pass that grants access to five mansion-museums. ✉ *Paseo del General Martínez Campos 37, Chamberí* ☎ *91/310–1584* 🌐 *museosorolla.mcu.es* 🎫 *€3 (free Sat. after 2 and Sun.)* ⏲ *Closed Mon.* Ⓜ *Rubén Darío, Gregorio Marañón.*

Palacio de Liria (*Liria Palace*)

HISTORIC HOME | In 2019, this working palace belonging to the House of Alba, one of Spain's most powerful noble families, formally opened to the public. Its sumptuous halls and creaky passages are hung with works selected from what many consider to be Spain's finest private art collection—you'll spot Titians, Rubens, Velázquezes, and other instantly recognizable paintings. In the library, Columbus's diaries from his voyage to the New World are on display as well as the first Spanish-language Bible and other priceless official documents. The

Neoclassical palace was built in the 18th century but was bombed during the Spanish Civil War (only the facade survived), its works thankfully safeguarded during the conflict. The Duchess of Alba oversaw the reconstruction of the palace to its precise original specifications. **TIP→ Visits are by tour only, but if online tickets are sold out, try your luck as a walk-in.** ✉ *Calle de la Princesa 20, Malasaña* ☎ *91/230–2200* 🌐 *www.palaciodeliria.com* 🎫 *€15 (includes tour)* Ⓜ *Ventura Rodríguez.*

★ Parque del Oeste

CITY PARK | FAMILY | This is many Madrileños' favorite park for its pristine yet unmobbed paths and well-pruned lawns and flower beds. From dawn to dusk, expect to see dogs cavorting off leash, couples sprawled out beneath the trees, and groups of friends playing frisbee and fútbol. From Paseo del Pintor Rosales, meander downhill toward Avenida de Valladolid, crossing the train tracks, and you'll hit Madrid Río; walk southwest and you'll find Templo de Debod and, beyond, the newly pedestrianized Plaza de España. This park also contains the city's only cable car (see "Teleférico") and, 100 yards beneath it, a rose garden (Rosaleda; free entry) containing some 20,000 specimens of more than 650 rose varieties that reach their peak in May. In the quieter northern section of the park (along Avenida Séneca), you'll happen upon Civil War–era bunkers interspersed among plane-tree-lined promenades, a sobering reminder that Parque del Oeste was the western front of Madrid's resistance against Franco's armies. ✉ *Paseo del Pintor Rosales, Moncloa* Ⓜ *Argüelles, Moncloa, Ventura Rodríguez, Pl. de España.*

★ Puerta del Sol

PLAZA/SQUARE | Crowded with locals, tourists, hawkers, and street performers, the Puerta del Sol is the nerve center of Madrid. It was renovated in 2023, and not all Madrileños are wild about its new, more austere look. A brass plaque in the sidewalk on the south side of the plaza marks Kilometer Zero, the point from which all distances in Spain are measured. Across the square are two important statues: *El oso y el madroño* (a bear climbing a strawberry tree, Madrid's official symbol), and an equestrian statue of King and Mayor Carlos III. Watch your belongings when passing through as the area is often packed with pedestrians. ✉ *Sol* Ⓜ *Sol.*

Teatro Real

OPERA | This resplendent neoclassical theater is the city's premier venue for opera and dance performances. Built in 1850, it fell into disuse from 1925 to 1966 because of political upheaval. A major restoration project endowed it with golden balconies, plush seats, and state-of-the-art stage equipment. Opera buffs rave about the choir, said to be one of the best in the world. The theater sometimes hosts flamenco on Friday evenings in the smaller auditorium. ✉ *Pl. de Isabel II s/n, Palacio* ☎ *91/516–0600* 🌐 *www.teatroreal.es* Ⓜ *Ópera.*

Where to Eat and Drink

Casa Botín

$$$ | SPANISH | Botín, established in 1725, is the world's oldest restaurant (according to *Guinness World Records)*, and was a favorite of Ernest Hemingway—the final scene of *The Sun Also Rises* is set in this very place. The *cochinillo asado* (roast suckling pig), stuffed with aromatics, doused with wine, and crisped in the original wood-burning oven, is a must. **Known for:** world's oldest restaurant; roast lamb and suckling pig; roving music ensembles. Ⓢ *Average main: €27* ✉ *Calle Cuchilleros 17, La Latina* ☎ *91/366–4217* 🌐 *www.botin.es* Ⓜ *Tirso de Molina.*

★ Casa Salvador

$$ | SPANISH | Whether you approve of bullfighting or not, the culinary excellence of Casa Salvador—a checkered-tablecloth, taurine-themed restaurant that opened in 1941—isn't up for debate. Sit down to generous servings of featherlight fried hake, hearty oxtail stew, and other stodgy (in the best way) Spanish classics, all served by hale old-school waiters clad in white jackets. **Known for:** time-warpy decor; walls packed with bullfighting paraphernalia; cloud-light fried hake and stewed oxtail. *Average main: €23 ✉ Calle de Barbieri 12, Chueca ☎ 91/521–4524 🌐 www.casasalvadormadrid.com ⏲ Closed Sun. No dinner Mon. Ⓜ Chueca.*

La Dolores

$ | TAPAS | A lively corner bar (established in 1908) with a colorful trencadís-tiled facade, this is a solid spot for a cold beer and a nosh after visiting the nearby museums. Try the *matrimonio* ("marriage") tapa, which weds one pickled and one cured anchovy on a slice of crusty baguette. **Known for:** affordable no-nonsense tapas; refreshing cañas; mixed crowd of foreigners and locals. *Average main: €12 ✉ Pl. de Jesús 4, Barrio de las Letras ☎ 91/429–2243 Ⓜ Antón Martín.*

La Venencia

WINE BARS | This dusty sherry-only bar hasn't changed a lick since the Spanish Civil War, from its no-tipping policy to its salty waiters to its chalked bar tabs. The establishment is named for the tool used to extract sherry through the bunghole of a barrel. *✉ Calle de Echegaray 7, Barrio de las Letras ☎ 91/429–7313 🌐 www.lavenencia.com Ⓜ Sol.*

★ Melo's

$ | SPANISH | This beloved old Galician bar changed hands in 2021—it's now run by three twentysomething Madrid natives who couldn't bear to see their favorite neighborhood hangout disappear—but the menu of eight infallible dishes has miraculously stayed the same (save for the addition of battered cod, a secret family recipe of one of the new business partners). Come for the jamón-flecked croquetas, blistered Padrón peppers, and griddled football-size *zapatilla* sandwiches; stay for the dressed-down conviviality and the *cuncos* (ceramic bowls) overflowing with slatey Albariño. **Known for:** old-school Galician bar food; oversize ham croquetas; battered cod grandfathered in from Casa Revuelta. *Average main: €11 ✉ Calle del Ave María 44, Lavapiés ☎ 91/527–5054 Ⓜ Lavapiés.*

Robuchon

$$$$ | BISTRO | Opened in fall 2022, this restaurant complex offers different experiences on three separate floors of the same historic building. The casual ground-floor bistro L'Ambassade pays homage to the former Embassy tea room that stood here since 1931, with a selection of teas, tarts, and tapas. **Known for:** swanky underground cocktails; haute cuisine tasting menus; pastries, scones, and casual fare on the main floor. *Average main: €155 ✉ Paseo de la Castellana, 12, Salamanca ☎ 91/453–8728 🌐 www.jrobuchonespana.es Ⓜ Colon.*

Salmon Guru

COCKTAIL LOUNGES | Regularly featured on best-of lists, Salmon Guru is Madrid's—and perhaps Spain's—most innovative coctelería. Come here to impress and to geek out over eye-popping concoctions like the Chipotle Chillón, made with mezcal, absinthe, and chipotle syrup. The nueva cocina tapas are almost as impressive as the drinks. *✉ Calle de Echegaray 21, Barrio de las Letras ☎ 91/000–6185 🌐 www.salmonguru.es Ⓜ Antón Martín.*

Cool Places to Stay

Barceló Torre de Madrid

$$$ | HOTEL | A jewel box of glowing lights, harlequin furniture, and gilded mirrors, the soaring Barceló Torre de Madrid opened in 2017 and remains one of the trendiest hotels in town. **Pros:** cutting-edge design by local artists; sleek pool and spa area; excellent Somos restaurant. **Cons:** feels understaffed;

limited pool hours; confusing elevators. *$ Rooms from: €240 ✉ Pl. de España 18, Moncloa ☎ 91/524–2339 🌐 www.barcelo.com ⇆ 256 rooms 🍽 No Meals Ⓜ Pl. de España.*

CoolRooms Palacio de Atocha
$$$$ | **HOTEL** | Arguably the splashiest hotel in this part of town, CoolRooms is situated at the northern edge of Lavapiés, five minutes on foot from both Sol and Antón Martín market. **Pros:** exceptionally spacious rooms even at the entry level; fresh flowers and plants galore; neon signs and clubby, young atmosphere. **Cons:** no gym; overeager and occasionally harried staff; unheated shallow pool. *$ Rooms from: €317 ✉ Calle de Atocha 34, Lavapiés ☎ 91/088–7780 🌐 www.coolrooms.com ⇆ 35 rooms 🍽 No Meals Ⓜ Antón Martín, Sol.*

Gran Meliá Palacio de Los Duques
$$$$ | **HOTEL** | In this luxurious urban oasis with an expansive courtyard tucked behind Gran Vía, reproductions of famous Diego Velázquez paintings feature in every room. **Pros:** Dos Cielos, one of the city's best hotel restaurants; underfloor heating and deep-soak tubs; rooftop bar and splash pool. **Cons:** rooms are less attractive than public areas; rooftop often off-limits because of private events; no great views from rooms. *$ Rooms from: €437 ✉ Cuesta Santo Domingo 5, Palacio ☎ 91/276–4747 🌐 www.melia.com ⇆ 180 rooms 🍽 No Meals Ⓜ Santo Domingo.*

Iberostar Las Letras Gran Vía
$$$ | **HOTEL** | A modern, clubby hotel on the stately avenue of Gran Vía, Iberostar Las Letras is a welcoming oasis from the area's constant hubbub of tourists and shoppers. **Pros:** state-of-the-art gym; many rooms have balconies; happening rooftop bar. **Cons:** lackluster service and food in Gran Clavel; no spa; awkward bathroom design. *$ Rooms from: €235 ✉ Gran Vía 11, Sol ☎ 91/523–7980 🌐 www.iberostar.com ⇆ 110 rooms 🍽 No Meals Ⓜ Banco de España.*

★ **Mandarin Oriental Ritz, Madrid**
$$$$ | **HOTEL** | A €99-million renovation by Mandarin Oriental completed in 2021 breathed new life to this grande dame overlooking the Prado, replacing mustard-colored drapes, dim sconces, and faded carpets with bright whites, gold accents, and stunning contemporary art. **Pros:** celebrity chef restaurant Deessa; new fitness center and chandelier-lighted pool; the epitome of modern luxury. **Cons:** many museum-grade antiques were auctioned off in the revamp; inconsistent El Jardín restaurant; priced too high for the vast majority of travelers. *$ Rooms from: €1,195 ✉ Pl. de la Lealtad 5, Retiro ☎ 91/701–6767 🌐 www.mandarinoriental.com ⇆ 153 rooms 🍽 No Meals Ⓜ Banco de España.*

★ **Rosewood Villa Magna**
$$$$ | **HOTEL** | Barrio Salamanca's most distinctive hotel, which reopened in late 2021 under the Rosewood umbrella after a yearlong eight-figure renovation, is now one of the swankiest properties in Spain. **Pros:** inviting spa and public areas with fireplaces and cushy sofas; Madrid's best hotel breakfast and high tea; impeccable service. **Cons:** Amós restaurant still getting its footing; big-city surroundings lack charm; unrenovated bathrooms feel old-fashioned. *$ Rooms from: €982 ✉ Paseo de la Castellana 22, Salamanca ☎ 91/587–1234 🌐 www.rosewoodhotels.com/en/villa-magna ⇆ 154 rooms 🍽 No Meals Ⓜ Rubén Darío, Colón.*

Barcelona

Barcelona is Spain's most visited city, and it's no wonder: it's a 2,000-year-old master of the art of perpetual novelty. More Mediterranean than Spanish, historically closer and more akin to Marseille or Milan than to Madrid, Barcelona has always been ambitious, decidedly modern (even in the 2nd century), and quick to accept the latest innovations.

Barcelona's Consell de Cent (Council of 100), constituted in 1274, was Europe's first parliament and one of the cradles of Western democracy. The center of an important seafaring commercial empire with colonies spread around the Mediterranean as far away as Athens, when Madrid was still a Moorish outpost on the arid Castilian steppe—it was Barcelona that absorbed new ideas and styles first. It borrowed navigation techniques from the Moors. It embraced the ideals of the French Revolution. It nurtured artists like Pablo Picasso and Joan Miró, who blossomed in the city's air of freedom and individualism. Barcelona, in short, has always been ahead of the curve.

The infinite variety and throb of street life, the nooks and crannies of the medieval Barri Gòtic, the ceramic tile and stained glass of flamboyant Moderniste facades in the Eixample, and everywhere art, music, and food (ah, the food!)—one way or another, Catalonia's beguiling capital will find a way to get your full attention. Topping the list of attractions are the dazzling architectural creations of Antoni Gaudí—there are seven important Gaudí buildings in the city alone, including his tour de force, La Sagrada Familia. Locals and visitors alike flock to La Rambla, the city's iconic pedestrian thoroughfare, home to the world-famous market, La Boquería, an intoxicating foodie destination. For art aficionados, Barcelona's world-class museums showcase everything from Romanesque church frescoes to major works by Picasso. Miles of sandy coastline offer an urban beach escape for sun-worshippers; the lush, green spaces atop Montjuïc await exploration by nature-lovers. But it's by night that Barcelona truly comes alive, when you can linger over regional wines and cuisine at buzzing tapas bars. One thing is for sure, you will never run out of things to do in the Catalan capital.

La Sagrada Família

Barcelona's Architectural Icon

Antoni Gaudí's striking, surreal masterpiece was conceived as nothing short of a Bible in stone, an arresting representation of the history of Christianity. Looming over the city like a manmade massif of grottoes and peaks, La Sagrada Família strains skyward in piles of stalagmites. The towers include those dedicated to the four evangelists—Matthew, Mark, Luke, and John—and the highest of all, dedicated to Christ the Savior. Inside, the basilica's main nave and the apse create an immense, immaculate space culminating in the highest point: the main altar's hyperboloid skylight 250 feet above the floor. The vaulting is perforated with 288 skylights admitting abundant light. The sharp-edged, treelike leaning columns shape the interior spaces and will support the six towers being built above them. Vaults are decorated with green and gold Venetian mosaics that diffuse the light as if they were leaves in a forest. Still under construction 140 years after it was begun, La Sagrada Família, once completed, will soar to a height of 564 feet, making it Barcelona's tallest building.

Don't Miss

The Nativity Facade, featuring the organic or so-called melting wax look that became Gaudí's signature, is the only part of the Sagrada Familia built during his lifetime.

Best Views

You can take an elevator skyward to the top of the bell towers for spectacular views across the city.

✉ *Pl. de la Sagrada Família, Carrer Mallorca 401, Eixample Dreta* ☎ *93/207–3031, 93/208–0414 visitor info* 🌐 *sagradafamilia.org* 🚇 *Metro: Sagrada Família* 🎫 *From €26 (booking online in advance is essential)*

La Boqueria

An Essential Foodie Pilgrimage

The largest and most spectacular of Barcelona's food markets, La Boqueria, also known as the Mercat de Sant Josep, is an explosion of life and color. As you turn in from La Rambla, you're greeted by bar-restaurants serving tapas at counters and stall after stall selling fruit, herbs, veggies, nuts, candied preserves, cheese, ham, fish, and poultry. Under a Moderniste hangar of wrought-iron girders and stained glass, the market occupies a neoclassical square built in 1840, with a sidewalk mosaic by Joan Miró added in 1970. Highlights include the sunny greengrocer's market outside, along with Pinotxo (Pinocchio), just inside to the right, which serves one of the most authentic Catalan breakfasts in Barcelona. Look for the *fruits del bosc* (fruits of the forest) stand at the back of La Boqueria, with its display of wild mushrooms, herbs, nuts, and berries.

When to Go

To avoid the worst of the crowds, visit when it opens at 8 am or after 5 pm. The market is closed on Sunday.

Best Restaurant

Local gourmands squeeze in to the tiny, unassuming-looking **Direkte Boqueria**, on the edge of the famous Boquería market, where Catalan chef Arnau Muñío flexes his culinary chops in full view of the diners at his chef's-table-style counter. There are two tasting menus, one long, one short, both of which showcase Muñío's unique approach to Catalan-Asian fusion food. *www.direkte.cat*

La Rambla 91 *93/413–2345* *www.boqueria.barcelona* *Metro Liceu*

Barri Gòtic

Barcelona's Beautifully Preserved Medieval Core

No city in Europe has an ancient quarter to rival Barcelona's Barri Gòtic in terms of both historic atmosphere and the sheer density of monumental buildings. It's a stroller's delight, teeming with narrow cobblestone streets, charming squares, and medieval buildings; the area around the Catedral de la Seu is built over Roman ruins you can still visit. Historic churches abound, including the Catedral de Barcelona, a marvelous Gothic structure with soaring columns and arches, and behind, a palm tree–shaded 14th-century cloister populated by 13 white geese. You can also discover one of Europe's oldest synagogues and secret Jewish baths in the ancient Jewish quarter, El Call. Other highlights include Plaça Reial, a large square surrounded by stately arcades and lined with bustling cafes; in the center is the Fountain of the Three Graces flanked by decorative lampposts designed by Gaudí in 1879.

When to Go

Visit before 1:30 or after 4:30 or you'll miss a lot of street life; some churches are closed mid-afternoon as well. Plaça Reial is most colorful on Sunday morning, when collectors gather to trade stamps and coins.

Best Restaurant

Linger over a coffee or glass of wine at the legendary **Els Quatre Gats**, an Art Nouveau masterpiece and former meeting place for Barcelona's bohemians. Catalan artists mingled here, Antoni Gaudí was a regular, and a young Picasso mounted his first exhibition on its walls. 🌐 *4gats.com*

Palau de la Música Catalana

A Feast for the Eyes and Ears

One of the world's most extraordinary music halls—a riot of color and form both inside and out—was designed in 1908 by Lluís Domènech i Montaner. Floral mosaics and ornate sculptures decorate the facade; inside, the decor is just as arresting. Wagner's Valkyries burst from the right side of the stage over a heavy-browed bust of Beethoven; Catalonia's popular music is represented by the graceful maidens of Lluís Millet's song *Flors de Maig* (*Flowers of May*) on the left. Overhead, an inverted stained-glass cupola seems to channel the divine gift of music straight from heaven. Painted rosettes and giant peacock feathers adorn the walls and columns, and, across the entire back wall of the stage, is a relief of muselike Art Nouveau musicians in costume.

Top Tip

If you can't fit a performance into your itinerary, you owe it to yourself to take a tour of this amazing building. The standard guided tour in English takes place at 10 am and 3 pm, and you can add a 20-minute live piano or organ recital on select dates, or take a self-guided audio tour, downloaded to your personal device.

Best Break

Pop by for a coffee or glass of wine at **Café Palau**, set in a beautiful Art Nouveau space on the ground floor of the music hall.

4–6, Born-Ribera *93/295–7200, 90/247–5485 box office* *www.palaumusica.cat* *Metro: Urquinaona* *Tours from €16*

Casa Batlló

Gaudí's Modernista Masterpiece

Gaudí's marvelously eccentric Casa Batlló is actually a makeover: it was originally built in 1877 by one of Gaudí's teachers, Emili Sala Cortés, and acquired by the Batlló family in 1900. Batlló wanted to tear down the undistinguished building and start over, but Gaudí persuaded him to remodel the facade and the interior, and the result is astonishing. The facade—with its rainbow of colored glass and *trencadís* (polychromatic tile fragments) and the toothy masks of the wrought-iron balconies projecting outward toward the street—is an irresistible photo op. The scaly roof line represents the Dragon of Evil impaled on St. George's cross, and the skulls and bones on the balconies are the dragon's victims, allusions to medieval Catalonia's code of chivalry and religious piety. Inside, the translucent windows on the landings of the central staircase light up the maritime motif and the details; Gaudí opted for natural shapes and rejected straight lines, as seen in the swirling ceilings and sinuous architectural details.

Don't Miss

Head down to the remodeled cellar to see the Gaudí Cube, a new immersive video and sound installation inspired by the architect, featuring LED projections on all sides, including the floor and the ceiling.

When to Go

From April to November, Casa Batlló hosts magical open-air evening concerts on the roof; tickets include a free glass of cava.

Passeig de Gràcia 43, Eixample Dreta *93/216–0306* *www.casabatllo.es* *From €35* *Metro: Passeig de Gràcia*

Casa Milà (La Pedrera)

Coolest Rooftop Sculpture Garden

Usually referred to as *La Pedrera* (*The Stone Quarry*), with a curving stone facade that undulates around the corner of the block, this building, unveiled in 1910, is one of Gaudí's most celebrated yet initially reviled designs. Seemingly defying the laws of gravity, the exterior has no straight lines, and is adorned with winding balconies covered with wrought-iron foliage sculpted by Josep Maria Jujol. Gaudí's rooftop chimney park, alternately interpreted as veiled Saharan women or helmeted warriors, is as spectacular as anything in Barcelona, especially in late afternoon when the sunlight slants over the city into the Mediterranean. Inside, the handsome Àtic de la Balena (Whale Attic) has excellent critical displays of Gaudí's works from all over Spain. The Pis dels veïns (Tenants' Apartment) is an interesting look into the life of a family who lived in La Pedrera in the early 20th century.

Don't Miss

On the roof, Gaudí built a parabolic arch that perfectly frames the towers of his masterpiece, La Sagrada Familia; it's the ultimate Barcelona photo op.

When to Go

While the rooftop is fabulous by day, it's even better come evening: "The Night Experience" features spectacular illuminated projections on the swirling chimneys, accompanied by a rousing soundtrack. In June and July, the Àtic de la Balena and the roof terrace are open for drinks and live jazz concerts.

✉ *Passeig de Gràcia 92, Eixample Dreta* ☎ *93/214–2576* 🌐 *www.lapedrera.com/en* 🚆 *Metro: Diagonal* 🎫 *From €25 (plus €3 fee if not booked in advance online)*

Park Güell

An Open-air Art Nouveau Extravaganza

Gaudí's delightfully eccentric constructions make this hilly park one of the city's top attractions. Named for and commissioned by the architect's main patron, Count Eusebi Güell, it was originally intended as a gated residential community. Though the real estate venture failed, Gaudí successfully engineered many of the public areas. Among them are the gingerbread gatehouses, the central plaza with its fabulous serpentine polychrome bench and jaw-dropping city and sea views, and (below it) the Room of a Hundred Columns—a covered market supported by tilted Doric-style columns and mosaic medallions. Other highlights include the double set of stairs and the iconic lizard guarding the fountain between them.

Don't Miss

Up the steps of Park Güell and to the right is the whimsical house where Gaudí lived with his niece from 1906 until 1925. Now a small museum, exhibits include Gaudí-designed furniture and decorations. *sagrada-familia.org*

When to Go

Avoid the worst of the summer heat by booking a timed entry ticket for the morning (the park opens at 8 am).

Getting Here

From the Lesseps metro station, take Bus No. 24 or V19 to the park entrance. Or from the Bus Turístic stop on Travessera de Dalt, make the steep 10-minute climb up Carrer de Lallard or Avinguda del Santuari de Sant Josep de la Muntanya.

Carretera del Carmel, 23, Gràcia
93/409–1830 *parkguell.barcelona*
From €10

Montjuïc

Top Sights, Great Views

Though a bit removed from the hustle and bustle of Barcelona street life, scenic, hilly Montjuïc has a number of high-profile attractions to lure visitors. The Museu Nacional d'Art de Catalunya, housed in the magnificent Palau Nacional, contains what is considered the world's best collection of medieval Romanesque frescoes—removed from dilapidated churches in the Pyrenees and restored with their original contours. At Fundació Joan Miró, colorful abstract masterpieces by the native Barcelona artist are on display in an all-white hilltop museum; the roof terrace, dotted with his playful sculptures, boasts panoramic city views. Sports fans can peek inside the open-air Olympic Stadium, built for the International Exhibition of 1929, renovated for the 1992 Olympic Games, and now hosting concerts as well as FC Barcelona soccer games through 2024.

Best View

Scattered across Montjuïc are several *miradores* (viewpoints), including Mirador Jardins de Miramar, with its garden terraces overlooking the port and the sea.

Getting Here

You can take the cross-harbor Telefèric de Montjuïc from Barceloneta; Bus No. 150 from Plaça d'Espanya, which stops at major sites; or the funicular from the Paral·lel metro stop.

Estadi Olímpic. ✉ *Lluís Companys, Passeig Olímpic, 15–17, Montjuïc* 🌐 *estadiolimpic.barcelona/en*

Fundació Joan Miró. ✉ *Parc de Montjuïc* 🌐 *www.fmirobcn.org* 🕒 *Closed Mon.* 🎫 *€14*

Museu Nacional d'Art de Catalunya. ✉ *Parc de Montjuïc* 🌐 *www.museunacional.cat* 🕒 *Closed Mon.* 🎫 *Entry from €2, permanent collection from €12*

When in Barcelona

★ Casa Vicens

HISTORIC HOME | Antoni Gaudí's first important commission as a young architect began in 1883 and finished in 1885. For this house Gaudí still used his traditional architect's tools, particularly the T square. The historical eclecticism (that is, borrowing freely from past architectural styles around the world) of the early Art Nouveau movement is evident in the Orientalist themes and Mudejar (Moorish-inspired) motifs lavished throughout the design. Casa Vicens stands out for its polychromatic façade, made with green and white checkered tiles, in combination with tiles with floral patterns. ✉ *Carrer de les Carolines 20–26, Gràcia* ☎ *93/271–1064* 🌐 *www.casavicens.org* 🎫 *€16* Ⓜ *Fontana, Lesseps.*

★ Ciutadella Park (*Parc de la Ciutadella*)

CITY PARK | **FAMILY** | Once a fortress designed to consolidate Madrid's military occupation of Barcelona, the Ciutadella is now the city's main downtown park. The clearing dates from shortly after the War of the Spanish Succession in the early 18th century, when Felipe V demolished some 1,000 houses in what was then the Barri de la Ribera to build a fortress and barracks for his soldiers and a *glacis* (open space) between rebellious Barcelona and his artillery positions. The fortress walls were pulled down in 1868 and replaced by gardens laid out by Josep Fontseré. In 1888 the park was the site of the Universal Exposition that put Barcelona on the map as a truly European city. ✉ *Passeig de Picasso 21, La Ciutadella* Ⓜ *L4 Barceloneta, Ciutadella–Vila Olímpica, L1 Arc de Triomf.*

La Rambla

STREET | The poet-playwright Federico García Lorca called this the only street in the world he wished would never end—and in a sense, it doesn't. A river of humanity flows down past the mimes, acrobats, jugglers, musicians, puppeteers, portrait artists, break dancers, rappers, and rockers competing for the crowd's attention. Couples sit at café tables no bigger than tea trays while nimble-footed waiters dodge traffic, bringing food and drink from kitchens. With the din of taxis and motorbikes in the traffic lanes on either side of the promenade, the revelers and rubberneckers, and the Babel of languages, the scene is as animated at 3 am as it is at 3 pm. A stroll here is essential to your Barcelona experience, but keep a close eye on your valuables, as this part of the city is sadly teeming with pickpockets. ✉ *La Rambla, Barcelona.*

★ Museu d'Història de Barcelona (MUHBA) (*Museum of the History of Barcelona*)

HISTORY MUSEUM | This fascinating museum just off Plaça del Rei traces Barcelona's evolution from its first Iberian settlement through its Roman and Visigothic ages and beyond. You can tour underground remains of the original Roman settlement via metal walkways. Some 43,000 square feet of archaeological artifacts, from the walls of houses, to mosaics and fluted columns, olive presses, and street systems, can be found in large part beneath the plaça. See how the Visigoths and their descendants built the early medieval walls on top of these ruins, recycling chunks of Roman stone and concrete, bits of columns, and even headstones. Guided tours are available in English at 10:30 am daily, but have to be reserved in advance. ✉ *Palau Padellàs, Pl. del Rei s/n, Barri Gòtic* ☎ *93/256–2100* 🌐 *www.barcelona.cat/museuhistoria/en* 🎫 *From €7; free with Barcelona Card, Sat. and the first Sun. of month* 🕓 *Closed Mon.* Ⓜ *Jaume I.*

★ Museu Picasso (*Picasso Museum*)

ART MUSEUM | The Picasso Museum is housed in five adjoining palaces on Carrer Montcada, a street known for Barcelona's most elegant medieval mansions. Picasso spent his key formative years in Barcelona (1895–1904), and although

Barcelona
A
B
C
D
E
F
1
2
3
4
5
6
7
8
9
Casa Vicens
Real Monestir de Santa Maria de Pedralbes
Carrer de Còrsega
Carrer de Rosselló
Carrer de Provença
DRETA DE L'EIXAMPLE
C. de Mallorca
C. de València
Avinguda de Roma
Carrer d'Aragó Gali
EIXAMPLE
Carrer del consell de Cent
Carrer de la Diputació
Universitat de Barcelona
Gran Via de les Corts Catalanes
Universitat
Plaça de la Universitat
Carrer de Sepúlveda
SANT ANTONI
Carrer de Floridablance
Carrer de Tamarit
Carrer de Manso
Sant Antoni
Carrer Parlament
C. de Viladomat
Carrer de viladomat
C. del Comte d'Urgell
C. del Comte Borrell
Carrer del Comte d'Urgell
C. de Casanova
C. de Muntaner
C. d'Aribau
C. d'Enric
Carrer de Balmes
Commuter Rail
Rambla de Catalunya
Passeig de Gràcia
Diagonal
C. de Pau Claris
Carrer de Llúna
C. Bonavista
Carrer de Còrsega
Avinguda Diagonal
C. del Rosselló
Verdaguer
Carrer de Mallorca
Carrer de València
Carrer de d'Aragó
Passeig de Gràcia
Carrer de Roger
Carrer del Bruc
Carrer de Enric
Carrer de Ballèn
C. de la Diputació
Gran Via de les Corts Catalanes
Carrer de Casp
Catalunya
Ronda Universitat
Carrer de Pelai
Plaça de Catalunya
Catalunya
Urquinaona
Carrer d'Ausiás Ma
Ronda de Sant Pere
Carrer Fontanella
La Rambla
Ronda de Sant Antoni
C. Valldenzella
Carrer dels Tallers
MACBA Museu d'Art Contemporani
C. Elisabets
C. de Sant Vicenç
C. Joaquim Costa
C. dels Àngels
C. Pintor Fortuny
EL RAVAL
C. del Carme
C. de la Cera
C. de la Riereta
C. d'en Rolg
C. de Hospita
C. de Sant Pacià
Rambla del Raval
C. Robador
Liceu
C. de Santa Anna
C. Comtat
C. Montsió
C. d'Ortigosa de Trafalgar
C. Portaferrissa
La Rambla
BARRI GÒTIC
Av. Catedral
Av. F.Cambó
C. del Bisbe
Catedral de la Seu
C. de Montcada
C. Fonglilar
C. Carders
Carrer del Comerç
Museu d'Història de Barcelona (MUHBA)
C. Llibreteria
C. Jaume I
C. de la Princesa
Jaume I
Museu Picasso
C. de Ferran
C. de la Lleona
Avinguda del Paral·lel
Ronda de Sant Pau
BARRI XINÈS
C. de Sant Pau
C. de Marquès de Barbera
C. Nou de la Rambla
C. de les Tàpies
Paral·lel
Carrer de Blai
C. del Roser
C. d'en Fontrodona
C. Nou de la Rambla
C. de Lafont
C. de Blesa
Carrer de Vila i Vilà
Av. de les Drassanes
C. des Escudellers
C. d'Avinyó
C. d'Ataolf
Santa Maria del Mar
C. Mosques
LA RIBERA
C. d'en Gignás
Via Laietana
Av. Marquès de l'Argenterá
Estació de França
POBLE SEC
Pg. de Montjuïc
C. de Palaudàries
C. Puig Xoriguer
C. Carrera
C. Portal de Santa
Museu Marítim & Drassanes Reials
Drassanes
C. de Josep Anseim Clavé
C. de la Mercè
Passeig de Colom
Barceloneta
B10
Torre Miramar
Passèig de Josp Carner
Plaça de les Drassanes
Plaça Portal de la Pau
Dàrsena Nacional
Museu d'Història de Catalunya
Carrer Balboa
Ronda del Litoral
Terminal Maritime Transmediterránea
MOLL DE BARCELONA
Terminal Maritime Drassanes
PORT VELL
Pg. d'itaca
MOLL D'ESPANYA
Dàrsena del Comerç
LA BARCELONETA
Aquàrium
Torre de Jaume I
Terminal Maritime Internacional Maremagnum
Carrer Sant Carles
C. Almirall Cervera
Pg. de Joan de Borbó
Terminal Maritime Internacional Sud
Terminal Maritime Internacional Nord
Terminal Maritime Internacional Italie and Algérie
Dàrsena Sant Bertrán
Grand Marina
Cable Car
MOLL BALEARS
C. Escar
Platja de Sant Sebastià

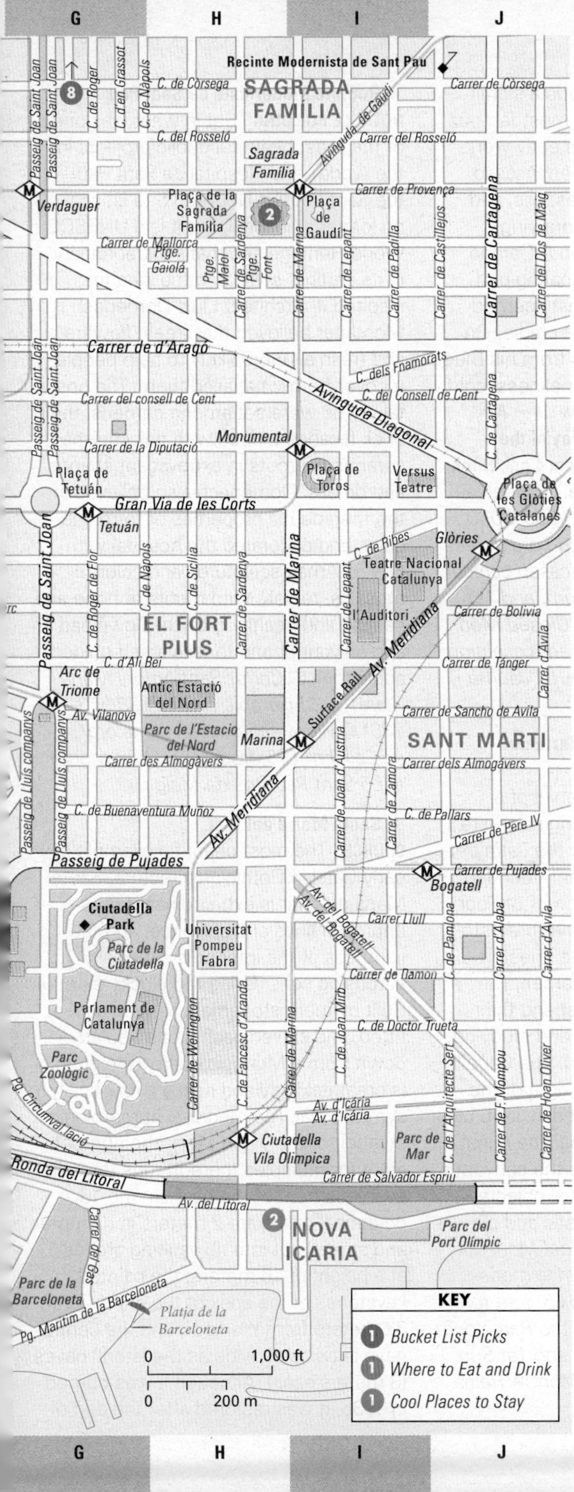

Bucket List Picks

1 Barri Gòtic D6
2 Basilica de la Sagrada Família H2
3 Casa Batlló D3
4 Casa Milà (La Pedrera) E1
5 La Boqueria C5
6 Montjuïc A8
7 Palau de la Música Catalana E5
8 Park Güell G1

Where to Eat and Drink

1 Cal Pep F7
2 La Cova Fumada F9
3 La Pepita E1
4 Lasarte D2
5 Paradiso F7
6 Suculent C6

Cool Places to Stay

1 The Barcelona EDITION E6
2 Hotel Arts Barcelona H8
3 Hotel El Palace Barcelona E4
4 Majestic Hotel & Spa E2
5 Seventy Barcelona E1

this collection doesn't include a significant number of the artist's most famous paintings, it is strong on his early work, showcasing the link between Picasso and Barcelona. The sketches, oils, and schoolboy caricatures and drawings from Picasso's early years in A Coruña are perhaps the most fascinating part, showing the facility the artist seemed to possess almost from the cradle. On the second floor are works from his Blue Period in Paris, a time of loneliness, cold, and hunger for the artist. **TIP→ Admission is free the first Sunday of the month and every Thursday from 4 pm. Book online to avoid the long lines.** ✉ *Montcada 15–19, Born-Ribera* ☎ *93/256–3000, 93/256–3022 guided tour and group reservations* 🌐 *www.museupicasso.bcn.cat* 🎟 *€12; free Thurs. from 4 pm, and 1st Sun. of month. Tours €6* ⏲ *Closed Mon.* ☞ *Guided tours of permanent collection (in English) are Sun. at 11* Ⓜ *L4 Jaume I, L1 Arc de Triomf.*

★ Real Monestir de Santa Maria de Pedralbes

RELIGIOUS BUILDING | This marvel of a monastery, named for its original white stones (*pedres albes, from the Latin petras albas*), is really a convent, founded in 1326 for the Franciscan order of Poor Clares by Reina Elisenda. The three-story Gothic cloister, one of the finest in Europe, surrounds a lush garden. The day cells, where the nuns spend their mornings praying, sewing, and studying, circle the arcaded courtyard. The Capella de Sant Miquel, just to the right of the entrance, has murals painted in 1346 by Catalan master Ferrer Bassa. The nuns' upstairs dormitory contains the convent's treasures: paintings, liturgical objects, and seven centuries of artistic and cultural patrimony. ✉ *Baixada del Monestir 9, Pedralbes* ☎ *93/256–3434* 🌐 *monestirpedralbes.bcn.cat/en* 🎟 *€5; free for visitors under 16, and with the Barcelona Card; free Sun. after 3 pm, and 1st Sun. of every month* ⏲ *Closed Mon.* Ⓜ *Reina Elisenda (FGC).*

★ Recinte Modernista de Sant Pau

NOTABLE BUILDING | Set in what was one of the most beautiful public projects in the world—the Hospital de Sant Pau—the Sant Pau Art Nouveau Site is, sadly, no longer a hospital, but it is a UNESCO World Heritage site that's extraordinary in its setting, style, and the idea that inspired it. Architect Lluis Domènech i Montaner believed that trees, flowers, and fresh air were likely to help people recover from what ailed them. The hospital wards were set among gardens, their brick facades topped with polychrome ceramic tile roofs in extravagant shapes and details. Domènech also believed in the therapeutic properties of form and color, and decorated the hospital with Eusebi Arnau sculptures and colorful mosaics, replete with motifs of hope and healing and healthy growth. Download an app on your phone to take a self-guided audio tour. ✉ *Carrer Sant Antoni Maria Claret 167, Eixample Dreta* ☎ *93/553–7801* 🌐 *www.santpaubarcelona.org/en* 🎟 *From €15; free 1st Sun. of month* Ⓜ *L5 Sant Pau/Dos de Maig.*

★ Santa Maria del Mar

CHURCH | The most beautiful example of early Catalan Gothic architecture, Santa Maria del Mar is extraordinary for its unbroken lines and elegance, and the lightness of the interior is especially surprising considering the blocky exterior. Built by mere stonemasons who chose, fitted, and carved each stone hauled down from a Montjuïc quarry, the church is breathtakingly and nearly hypnotically symmetrical. The medieval numerological symbol for the Virgin Mary, the number eight (or multiples thereof) runs through every element of the basilica: the 16 octagonal pillars are 2 meters in diameter and spread out into rib vaulting arches at a height of 16 meters; the painted keystones at the apex of the arches are 32 meters from the floor; and the central nave is twice as wide as the lateral naves (8 meters each). Although it was burned in 1936, it was restored after the end of the Spanish Civil War by Bauhaus-trained architects. ✉ *Pl. de Santa Maria 1, Born-Ribera* ☎ *93/310–2390* 🌐 *www.santamariadelmarbarcelona.org* 🎫 *From €5* Ⓜ *L4 Jaume I.*

Where to Eat and Drink

★ Cal Pep

$$ | TAPAS | It's has been in a permanent feeding frenzy for more than 30 years, intensified by hordes of tourists, but this loud, hectic bar manages to keep delivering the very highest quality tapas, year in year out. Be prepared to wait up to an hour for a place at the counter; reservations for the tables in the tiny back room and on the outdoor terrace are accepted, but the counter is where the action is. **Known for:** excellent fish fry; delicious tortilla de patatas; lively counter scene. $ *Average main: €20* ✉ *Pl. de les Olles 8, Born-Ribera* ☎ *93/310–7961* 🌐 *www.calpep.com* ⏲ *Closed Sun. and 3 wks in Aug. No lunch Mon.* Ⓜ *Jaume I, Barceloneta.*

★ La Cova Fumada

$ | TAPAS | There's no glitz, no glamour, and not even a sign outside, but the battered wooden doors of this old, family-owned tavern hide a tapas bar to be treasured. Loyal customers and hordes of tourists queue for the market-fresh seafood, served from the furiously busy kitchen. **Known for:** blink and you'll miss it; "bomba" (fried potato croquette); lunch only. $ *Average main: €12* ✉ *Baluard 56, Barceloneta* ☎ *93/221–4061* ⏲ *Closed Sun.* Ⓜ *Barceloneta.*

★ La Pepita

$$ | TAPAS | Don't be distracted by the graffitied walls and highly Instagrammable dishes: the innovative tapas at La Pepita lives up to the hipster hype. The room is dominated by long marble-topped bar—there are only a handful of tables in the narrow space—so it's best for couples or small groups. **Known for:** popcorn-topped ice cream; shrimp croquetas; Spanish fried eggs and potatoes with foie gras. $ *Average main: €20* ✉ *Còrsega 343, Gràcia* ☎ *93/238–4893* 🌐 *www.lapepitabcn.com* Ⓜ *Diagonal.*

★ Lasarte

$$$$ | BASQUE | While Martin Berasategui, one of San Sebastián's corps of master chefs, no longer runs the day-to-day operations of this Barcelona kitchen (it's in the capable hands of chef Paolo Casagrande) the restaurant continues to be a culinary triumph. Expect an eclectic selection of Basque, Mediterranean, and off-the-map creations, a hefty bill, and fierce perfectionism apparent in every dish. **Known for:** inventive cuisine at one of the best restaurants in Barcelona; magnificent tasting menu; heavenly grilled pigeon. $ *Average main: €70* ✉ *Mallorca 259, Eixample* ☎ *93/445–3242* 🌐 *www.restaurantlasarte.com* ⏲ *Closed Sun., Mon., Tues., 2 wks in Jan., 1 wk at Easter, and 3 wks in Aug./Sept.* Ⓜ *Diagonal, Passeig de Gràcia, Provença (FGC).*

Paradiso

COCKTAIL LOUNGES | Hidden behind the fridge door in an unassuming-looking pastrami bar, this speakeasy is one of the city's worst-kept secrets. Cocktail maestro Giacomo Giannotti's creations are works of art, bursting with fire, smoke, and dry ice. And they taste absolutely delicious. Prepare to stand in line for up to an hour to get in. ✉ *Rera Palau 4, Born-Ribera* ☎ 🌐 *paradiso.cat/en* Ⓜ *Barceloneta L4.*

★ Suculent

$$ | CATALAN | This is a strong contender for the crown of Barcelona's best bistro, where chef Toni Romero turns out Catalan tapas and dishes that have roots in rustic classics but reach high modern standards of execution. The name is a twist on the Catalan *sucar lent* (to dip slowly), and excellent bread is duly provided to soak up the sauces, which you won't want to let go to waste. **Known for:** set menus but à la carte available at the bar; must-try steak tartare on marrow bone; big, bold flavors. $ *Average main: €18* ✉ *Rambla del Raval 45, El Raval* ☎ *93/443–6579* 🌐 *www.suculent.com* ⏲ *Closed Sat. and Sun.* Ⓜ *Liceu.*

Cool Places to Stay

★ **The Barcelona EDITION**
$$$$ | **HOTEL** | The Edition hotels are known for their sleek, minimalist design and top-notch food and drink options and the Barcelona outpost adds a breezy 10th-floor terrace with sweeping views. **Pros:** excellent service; dreamy views from the rooftop; great food and drink options. **Cons:** pricey; only upgraded rooms have balconies; tiny swimming pool. $ *Rooms from: €380* ✉ *Av. de Francesc Cambó 14, Born-Ribera* ☎ *93/626–3330* 🌐 *www.editionhotels.com/es/barcelona* *100 rooms* 🍽 *No Meals* Ⓜ *Jaume I L4.*

★ **Hotel Arts Barcelona**
$$$$ | **HOTEL** | This luxurious Ritz-Carlton-owned, 44-story hotel is just steps from the beach and all the nightlife of Port Olímpic. **Pros:** superb restaurant on-site; fantastic views from rooms, especially on higher floors; seafront pool area with loungers. **Cons:** far from the city center; very pricey; reception area can get quite busy. $ *Rooms from: €420* ✉ *Carrer de la Marina 19–21, Port Olímpic* ☎ *93/221–1000* 🌐 *www.hotelartsbarcelona.com* *483 rooms* 🍽 *No Meals* Ⓜ *L4 Ciutadella–Vila Olímpica.*

★ **Hotel El Palace Barcelona**
$$$$ | **HOTEL** | Founded in 1919 by Caesar Ritz, the original Ritz (the grande dame of Barcelona hotels) was renamed in 2005 but kept its lavish, timeless style intact blending its grand style with contemporary experiences, from the liveried doorman in top hat and lobby's massive crystal chandelier to seasonal immersive pop-up experiences on the seventh floor rooftop garden. **Pros:** historic grand-dame luxury; legendary cocktail bar; Mayan-style sauna in the award-winning spa. **Cons:** may feel slightly intimidating; painfully pricey; formal atmosphere. $ *Rooms from: €339* ✉ *Gran Vía de les Corts Catalanes 668, Eixample Dreta* ☎ *93/510–1130* 🌐 *www.hotelpalacebarcelona.com* *120 rooms* 🍽 *No Meals* Ⓜ *L2/L3/L4 Passeig de Gràcia.*

★ **Majestic Hotel & Spa**
$$$$ | **HOTEL** | With an unbeatable location on Barcelona's most stylish boulevard—steps from Gaudí's La Pedrera and near the area's swankiest shops—and a stunning rooftop terrace with killer views of the city's landmarks, this hotel is a near-perfect place to stay. **Pros:** very good restaurant and spa; beloved city landmark with interesting history; superb, personalized service. **Cons:** some standard rooms a bit small for the price; pricey but excellent buffet breakfast; street outside often bustling. $ *Rooms from: €323* ✉ *Passeig de Gràcia 68-70, Eixample Dreta* ☎ *93/488–1717* 🌐 *majestichotelgroup.com/en/barcelona/hotel-majestic* *275 rooms* 🍽 *No Meals* Ⓜ *L2/L3/L4 Passeig de Gràcia, Provença (FGC).*

★ **Seventy Barcelona**
$$ | **HOTEL** | On the southern border of Gràcia, a short stroll to the Passeig de Gràcia, this boutique hotel is in an ideal spot for travelers who like to be close to the action, without being in the thick of it. **Pros:** good location; thoughtful staff; good quality for the price. **Cons:** few rooms with patios or balconies; outdoor pool is small; busy street outside. $ *Rooms from: €160* ✉ *Còrsega 344–352, Barcelona* ☎ *93/012–1270* 🌐 *www.seventybarcelona.com* *145 rooms* 🍽 *No Meals* Ⓜ *Diagonal.*

Southern Spain

Bordering Portugal in the west, stretching along the Atlantic in the southwest and then sweeping along the Mediterranean to the south and east before encircling the Balearic Islands in the northeast, Southern Spain is a veritable feast of sights, sounds, and tastes.

From historic cities to quaint white villages, from foot-stomping flamenco to Michelin-star dining, and all in warm sunshine most of the year, this southern half of Spain will whet your appetite for more. Bordering Portugal lies Extremadura, a wild isolated region and the heartland of most of the explorers and conquerors of the so-called New World. The landscape rolls green and lush on the wooded *dehesa* plains, and rugged and lofty in the great sierras. Outdoor activities come into their own, while medieval Cáceres has one of the best-preserved old quarters in Europe.

Occupying the entire southern swath of Spain, Andalusia is the country's second-largest region and the most populated. Perhaps the traveler's vision of quintessential Spain, this is a land of evocative flamenco, delicate orange blossom, Moorish kingdoms, and a warm welcome. Its greatest cities, Córdoba, Granada, Málaga, and Seville, all house historical and cultural treasures. In tandem, its landscapes range from rolling hills to snow-capped mountains via Europe's only desert, vast sandy beaches and endless olive groves. Andalusia is also home to some of Spain's prettiest villages.

Some 50 to 190 miles off the eastern coast of Spain, the cluster of the Balearic Islands (four are inhabited) offers the quintessential Mediterranean: turquoise sea, white sand, rolling olive groves, and ocher towns and villages.

Mallorca, easily the largest, sits in the center and is home to high mountains, the elegant capital city of Palma de Mallorca, and medieval towns. To the west lies Ibiza, one of Europe's top vacation destinations, offering secluded coves and luxury lodging in the north and sandy beaches and party venues in the south. Next-door Formentera is small and quiet but boasts some of the finest sands in the Mediterranean. Menorca, the northernmost isle, is mostly flat and windswept. Prehistoric monuments dot all corners of the central plain while two fine towns, Ciutadella and Mahón, stand guard on either side.

Real Alcázar, Seville

Quintessential Southern Spain

Seville's whitewashed houses, bright with bougainvillea, ocher-color palaces, and Baroque facades, have long enchanted locals and travelers. It's a city for the senses—the fragrance of orange blossom suffuses the air in spring, the sound of flamenco echoes through the alleyways, and views of the great Guadalquivir River accompany you at every turn. Seville offers a bewitching mosaic of flamenco, matadors, horses, refreshing patios, and religious fervor. Add to this, rich Baroque and Renaissance monuments, colonial palaces, and delicious cuisine, and the city brings vibrant color to any vacation.

At the top of your must-see list sit the Real Alcázar (fortress)—a Mudejar delight whisking you straight to the land of Scheherazade—and the Cathedral (the largest in Spain), which is topped with the Giralda minaret tower. Continue your architectural feast with one of the city's splendid palaces, excellent museums, and fine churches, while taking in Seville's nod to modernity in the Gaudí-style Metropol Parasol, and the elegant contemporary bridges.

Don't Miss

The romantic neighborhood of Santa Cruz, with its whitewashed houses, colorful geraniums cascading down the facades, winding alleyways, and intimate squares—all lit by old-style lamps at night.

Getting Here

Seville's airport has domestic and some European flights; train connections include the high-speed AVE service from Madrid, with a journey time of less than 2½ hours.

Real Alcázar. ✉ *Pl. del Triunfo, Santa Cruz* ☎ *954/502324* 🌐 *www.alcazarsevilla.org* 🎫 *€14; Cuarto Real €5*

Seville Tourism. 🌐 *www.visitasevilla.es*

The Alhambra, Granada

An Exquisite Moorish Palace

The Alhambra is Spain's top attraction (around 3 million people visit every year). Something of an architectural gem, it's composed of royal residential quarters, court chambers, baths, and gardens, surrounded by defense towers and massive walls. The courtyards, patios, and halls offer an ethereal maze of Moorish arches, columns, and domes containing intricate stucco carvings and patterned ceramic tiling.

The heart of the Alhambra, the Palacios Nazaríes contain delicate apartments, and fountains, and are divided into three sections: the *mexuar*, where business, government, and palace administration were headquartered; the *serrallo*, staterooms where the sultans held court; and the harem. Above them all is Generalife, the ancient summer palace of the Nasrid kings with stunning city views.

Don't Miss

The view of the Alhambra and the snowy peaks of the Sierra Nevada from the opposite side of the Darro ravine in the Albayzín Moorish quarter. Make your way up to the Mirador de San Nicolás at the most magical times of day, dawn and dusk.

Getting Here

There are regular trains from Seville, and a twice-daily fast service from Málaga, taking 70 minutes. From the train station, the L4 bus takes you to the Gran Vía to the C30 service to the Alhambra. Cabs are also available outside the station.

✉ Cuesta de Gomérez, Alhambra ☎ 858/889002 tickets, 958/027971 information 🌐 tickets.alhambra-patronato.es/en 🎫 From €8, Museo de la Alhambra and Palacio de Carlos V free ✍ Advance reservations essential ⏲ Closed Mon. **TIP→ You must carry your passport for entry.**

Mosque-Cathedral of Córdoba

850 Columns of Spanish Islamic Architecture

Córdoba's famous Mezquita remains are one of the country's grandest and yet most intimate examples of its Moorish heritage. Built between the 8th and 10th centuries, the mosque's plain, crenellated exterior walls do little to prepare you for the sublime beauty of the interior. Here, 850 columns rise before you in a forest of jasper, marble, granite, and onyx. Crowning them, red-and-white-stripe arches curve up to the ceiling of delicately carved cedar.

The beautiful 10th-century *mihrab* (prayer niche) is the mezquita's brightest jewel, and sits behind the *maksoureh*, whose mosaics and plasterwork make it a masterpiece of Islamic art. After the Reconquest, the Christians left the mezquita largely undisturbed apart from their most visible addition, the heavy, incongruous baroque structure, sanctioned for Christian worship in the 1520s.

Don't Miss

Calleja de las Flores, a few yards off the northeastern corner of the Mezquita, is a tiny street packed with the city's prettiest patios. They bloom at their most marvelous in May but are a delight at any time of year with their flowers, ceramics, foliage, and iron grilles.

Getting Here

The city's modern train station is the hub for a comprehensive network of regional trains, with regular high-speed train service to Granada, Seville, Málaga, Madrid, and Barcelona.

✉ Calle de Torrijos, Judería ☎ 957/470512 🌐 mezquita-catedraldecordoba.es 🎫 Mezquita €11, free Mon.–Sat. 8.30–9.30 am, Torre del Alminar €3

Picasso in Málaga

In the Footsteps of a Great Artist

Pablo Picasso was born in Málaga in 1881. Although he lived there for just the first decade of his life, the city houses an important legacy of his life and work. Start your discovery trail at Casa Natal de Picasso (Picasso's Birthplace), furnished in the style of the era and home to a permanent exhibition of the artist's early sketches and sculptures, as well as family memorabilia.

Continue to Iglesia de Santiago church on Calle Granada to see the record of Picasso's baptism, before reaching the Museo Picasso. The museum's small collection showcases the works Picasso kept for himself or gave to his family, displayed in chronological order according to the periods that marked his 73-year development as an artist. The museum also displays some Roman and Moorish remains in the basement.

Don't Miss

A stroll around Pasaje Chinitas, off Plaza de la Constitución and named for the notorious Chinitas cabaret. Pop into the dark, vaulted bodegas selling local wines made from Málaga muscat grapes, silversmiths, and religious artifact stores that have changed little since Picasso was a boy in the late 1890s.

Getting Here

Málaga Airport has a wide range of domestic and international flights. Regular high-speed AVE trains connect with Madrid (2½ hours), Seville (under two hours), and Granada (one hour and ten minutes).

Museo Casa Natal de Picasso. ✉ *Pl. de la Merced 15, Málaga* 🌐 *www.fundacionpicasso.malaga.eu* 🎫 *From €3*

Museo Picasso Málaga. ✉ *Calle San Agustín, Málaga* 🌐 *www.museopicassomalaga.org* 🎫 *From €9 (free last 2 hrs on Sun.)*

Flamenco

The Soundtrack to Andalusia

Expect to come across the awe-inspiring song, music, and dance of flamenco almost everywhere in Andalusia, its spiritual home. The music is largely Arabic and has echoes of Greek dirges and Jewish chants, while Hindu sways, Roman mimes, and other movements inform the dance. There are more than 50 different styles (or *palos*) of flamenco, four of which are the stylistic pillars others branch off from: *toná, soleá, fandango,* and *seguidilla.* In its simplest form, a flamenco performance consists of people seated around a singer and clapping, known as a *tablao*, with perhaps a six-stringed guitar, a *cajón* (wooden box) and a dancer, enhancing the experience.

You'll come across spontaneous flamenco in the Santa Cruz and Triana districts in Seville, in Jerez de la Frontera, or in the Sacromonte area in Granada. Professionals regularly perform at *tablaos* in the main cities. Jerez de la Frontera (February–March) and Granada (December) hold festivals, while bi-annual flamenco festivals take place in Málaga (odd-numbered years) and Seville (even-numbered years). The Festival Nacional de Cante Flamenco held in September in Ogijares, near Granada, is a treat for fans of flamenco song.

Don't Miss

A professional performance of flamenco in the heart of Seville's Santa Cruz district at La Casa del Flamenco. The atmospheric patio in the 15th-century house has excellent acoustics, so there's no need for microphones or amplifiers.

La Casa del Flamenco. ✉ *Calle Ximénez de Enciso 28, Barrio de Santa Cruz, Seville* ☎ *954/029999* 🌐 *www.lacasadelflamencosevilla.com* 🎫 *From €10*

Ibiza Beaches

Simply Stunning Sands

When it comes to oceanfront property, the Balearic Islands have everything from long sweeps of beach on sheltered bays to tiny crescents of sand in coves, some so isolated you can reach them only by boat. Skip the main developed beaches and head to their simpler and smaller counterparts in or adjoining the islands' admirable number of nature reserves and the best destinations for sun and sand. The best are on Ibiza.

Head straight for *Ses Salines*, a relatively narrow, but fine golden stretch of sand along the curve of Ibiza's southernmost bay. Or, on the east coast, try *Cala Mastella*, a tiny cove tucked away in pine woods where a kiosk on the wharf serves the fresh catch of the day, and *Cala Llenya*, a family-friendly beach in a protected bay with shallow water. *Benirrás* is a small cove backed by pine-clad hills on the northern coast of Ibiza. It's known for its sunsets and laid-back vibe and for the Sunday sunset ritualistic drum circles, one of the island's most popular events.

Don't Miss

If the Ibiza scene is too much for you, there are others. In Mallorca, Es Trenc is one of the few long beaches spared development. The pristine stretch of soft, white sand is backed by crystal-clear blue water, and the 10-km (6-mile) walk along the beach from Colònia Sant Jordi to the Cap Salines lighthouse is one of Mallorca's treasures. And in Menorca, make for Cala Macarella and Cala Macarelleta, a pair of beautiful, secluded coves edged with pines, accessed by walking through the woods from the more developed beach at Santa Galdana.

Ibiza. 🌐 *tourism.eivissa.es*

Mallorca. 🌐 *www.infomallorca.net*

Menorca. 🌐 *www.menorca.es*

Baeza and Úbeda

Renaissance Architectural Gems

The historic towns of Baeza and Úbeda are two stunning surprises in the heart of Jaén's olive groves, set in the shadow of the wild Sierra de Cazorla mountain range. Both rank among the most outstanding enclaves of 16th-century architecture in Spain and boast a wealth of Renaissance palaces, churches, and stately mansions.

In Baeza, feast your eyes on the Gothic facade of the town hall, the fine 14th-century rose window in the Cathedral, also home to a baroque silver monstrance, and the remains of the original mosque in the Gothic Cloisters. Climb the clock tower to view the best views. Highlights in Úbeda include the Hospital de Santiago, whose plain facade leads to an arcaded patio and a grand staircase; the Sinagoga de Agua, known as the Water Synagogue for the wells and natural spring under the mikvah; and the Sacra Capilla de El Salvador, considered one of the masterpieces of Spanish Renaissance religious art.

Don't Miss

Úbeda's famous ceramics are known for their classic, green-glazed items. See the potters at their wheels and kilns, and buy their wares in the barrio alfarero, centered on Calle Valencia.

When to Go

Spring and fall are ideal for sightseeing and pleasant temperatures.

Getting Here

Frequent buses connect Úbeda and Baeza with Jaén (around one hour), which is 91 km (57 miles) north of Granada and 113 km (70 miles) east of Córdoba, but a private car is the best option given the area's remoteness.

Semer Turismo & Cultura. 🌐 *visitasguiadasubedaybaeza.com*

Cáceres

Europe's Best-Preserved Medieval Old Quarter

One of Spain's oldest cities, Cáceres is known for its UNESCO-protected old town, complete with 22 Moorish towers from the 8th to 13th centuries, and a pristine medieval and Renaissance quarter. This Ciudad Monumental—so convincingly ancient that Game of Thrones used it as a filming location—has several must-sees. They include the 12th-century Moorish Casa de las Veletas, the city museum home to a superbly preserved Moorish cistern with horseshoe arches supported by stone pillars; the Palacio de los Golfines de Abajo, one of the city's great noble homes with a sumptuous plateresque facade; and the 16th-century Gothic Cathedral.

Don't Miss

The Museo Helga de Alvear houses a great collection of contemporary art, including paintings by Josef Albers and John Baldessari, and sculptures by Ai Weiwei and Dan Graham.

When to Go

Spring and fall make ideal seasons for bearable temperatures. Avoid July and August, when the region is blisteringly hot, and also the winter if you don't like it cold.

Best Restaurant

Atrio Restaurante Hotel. Jaw-droppingly elegant, the hotel's ground-floor restaurant specializes in refined contemporary cooking, while the interiors come with bespoke furniture and original works by Warhol. 🌐 *www.restauranteatrio.com*

Getting Here

Trains from Madrid take about 2½ hours; the historic quarter is a 15-minute walk from the station.

Cáceres Tourism. 🌐 *turismo.caceres.es*

El Valle del Jerte

Cherry Blossoms and Snow-Capped Peaks

Get a front-row seat to one of Spain's most breathtaking natural displays in spring when the Jerte Valley in northern Extremadura offers a riot of cherry blossoms, backed by the snow-capped Gredos mountains. Catch your first glimpse of this spectacular sight from the Puerto de Tornavacas—literally, the point "where the cows turn back." Part of the N110 road northeast of Plasencia, the pass has an elevation of 4,183 feet, affording a breathtaking view of the valley formed by the fast-flowing Jerte River. The lower slopes are covered with a dense mantle of ash, chestnut, and cherry trees, all pink and white in early spring. Their richness contrasts with the granite cliffs of the Sierra de Gredos, blanketed in Garnacha grapevines. Be sure to visit Cabezuela del Valle, one of the valley's best-preserved villages, full of half-timber stone houses.

Don't Miss

A visit to the Monasterio de Yuste, southeast of the valley and one of the most impressive monasteries in all of Spain. Carlos V (1500–58), the founder of Spain's vast 16th-century empire, spent his last two years in this remote but starkly beautiful spot.

When to Go

Mid-March onward heralds the start of the blossom—monitor the bloom date estimates on the tourist board's website. The valley is also beautiful at any time during spring and fall. Avoid the boiling hot summer months.

Getting Here

You will need a car to get here and explore the valley. For a scenic route, follow N110 southwest from Ávila to Plasencia.

🌐 *www.turismovalledeljerte.com*

When in Southern Spain

★ Baelo Claudia

RUINS | On the Atlantic coast, 24 km (15 miles) north of Tarifa, stand the impressive Roman ruins of Baelo Claudia, once a thriving production center of garum, a salty, pungent fish paste appreciated in Rome. The visitor center includes a museum. Concerts are regularly held at the restored amphitheater during the summer months. ✉ *Tarifa* ⊕ *Take N340 toward Cádiz 16 km (10 miles), then turn left for Bolonia on CA8202* ☎ *956/106797* 🎫 *€2* ⏲ *Closed Mon.*

★ Bodegas Tradición

WINERY | Tucked away on the north side of the old quarter and founded in 1998, this is one of the city's youngest bodegas, but it has the oldest sherry. The five types sit in the casks for at least 20 years—most for longer. Visits (book in advance by phone or email) include a tour of the winery, a lesson in how to pair each sherry type, and a tour of the unique Spanish art collection that includes works by El Greco, Zurburán, Goya, and Velázquez. ✉ *Pl. de los Cordobeses 3, Jerez de la Frontera* ☎ *956/168628* 🌐 *www.bodegastradicion.es* 🎫 *€50.*

★ Caminito del Rey

TRAIL | Clinging to the cliff side in the valley, the "King's Walk" is a suspended catwalk built for a visit by King Alfonso XIII at the beginning of the 19th century. It reopened in March 2015 after many years and a €9 million restoration and is now one of the province's main tourist attractions—as well as one of the world's dizziest. No more than 400 visitors are admitted daily for the walk, which includes nearly 3 km (2 miles) on the boardwalk itself and nearly 5 km (3 miles) on the access paths. It takes four to five hours to complete, and it's a one-way walk, so you need to make your own way back to the start point at the visitor center at the Ardales end (shuttle buses take you back). A certain level of fitness is required and the walk is not permitted for the under 8s or recommended for anyone who suffers from vertigo. **■TIP→ This is one of the Costa del Sol's busiest attractions; book well ahead.** ✉ *Valle del Guadalhorce* 🌐 *caminitodelrey.info* 🎫 *From €10* ⏲ *Closed Mon.*

Festival de los Patios, Córdoba

CULTURAL FESTIVALS | This celebration, awarded UNESCO World Heritage status in 2012, is held during the second week of May, a fun time to be in Córdoba, when owners throw open their flower-decked patios to visitors (and to judges, who nominate the best), and the city celebrates with food, drink, and flamenco. ✉ *Córdoba* 🌐 *turismodecordoba.org.*

Parque Natural Marítimo y Terrestre Cabo de Gata–Níjar

NATURE PRESERVE | Birds are the main attraction at this nature reserve just south of San José; it's home to several species native to Africa, including the *camachuelo trompetero* (large-beaked bullfinch), which is not found anywhere else outside Africa. Check out the Punto de Información visitor center in Rodalquilar, which has an exhibit and information on the region and organizes guided walks and tours of the area. ✉ *Calle Fundición, San José* ⊕ *Rodalquilar* ☎ *671/594419* ⏲ *Open weekends only Nov.—April.*

Palma de Mallorca

TOWN | Capital of the Balearics, Palma is one of the great unsung cities of the Mediterranean—a showcase of medieval and modern architecture, a venue for art and music, a mecca for sailors, and a killer place to shop for shoes. Palma's cathedral is an architectural wonder that took almost 400 years to build. Begun in 1230, the wide expanse of the nave is supported by 14 70-foot-tall columns that fan out at the top like palm trees. A ceramic mural by the late Catalan artist and Mallorca resident Joan Miró, facing the cathedral across the pool that runs the length of Parc de la Mar. And don't

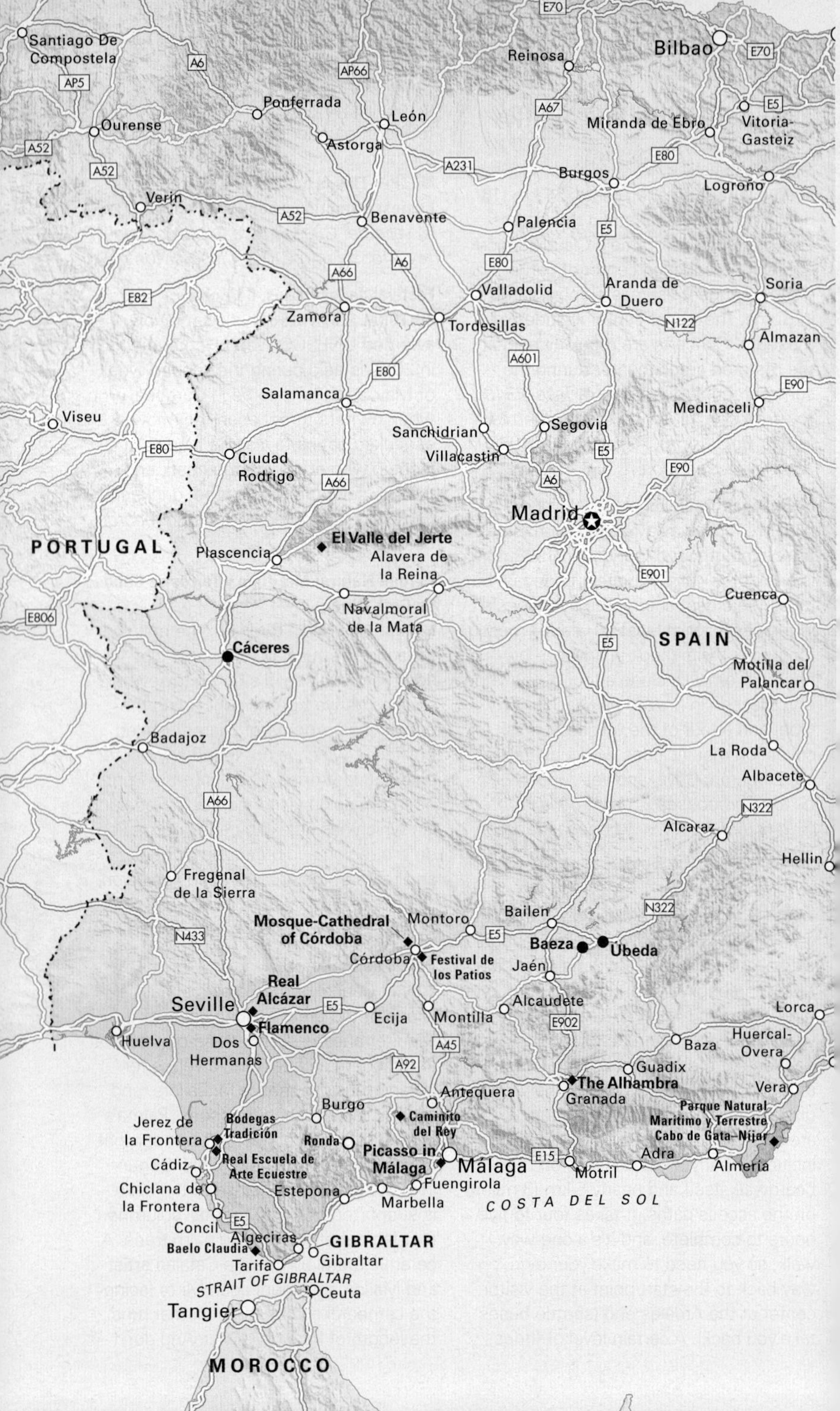
Santiago De Compostela
Ourense
Ponferrada
León
Astorga
Reinosa
Bilbao
Miranda de Ebro
Vitoria-Gasteiz
Burgos
Logrono
Verín
Benavente
Palencia
Valladolid
Aranda de Duero
Soria
Zamora
Tordesillas
Almazan
Salamanca
Medinaceli
Viseu
Sanchidrian
Segovia
Villacastin
Ciudad Rodrigo
Madrid
PORTUGAL
Plascencia
El Valle del Jerte
Alavera de la Reina
Navalmoral de la Mata
Cuenca
Cáceres
SPAIN
Motilla del Palancar
Badajoz
La Roda
Albacete
Alcaraz
Hellin
Fregenal de la Sierra
Mosque-Cathedral of Córdoba
Montoro
Bailen
Baeza
Úbeda
Córdoba
Festival de los Patios
Jaén
Real Alcázar
Seville
Flamenco
Ecija
Montilla
Alcaudete
Lorca
Huelva
Dos Hermanas
Baza
Huercal-Overa
Guadix
The Alhambra
Granada
Vera
Antequera
Burgo
Caminito del Rey
Parque Natural Maritimo y Terrestre Cabo de Gata-Nijar
Jerez de la Frontera
Bodegas Tradición
Ronda
Picasso in Málaga
Málaga
Real Escuela de Arte Ecuestre
Cádiz
Motril
Adra
Almería
Chiclana de la Frontera
Estepona
Fuengirola
Marbella
COSTA DEL SOL
Concil
Algeciras
GIBRALTAR
Baelo Claudia
Tarifa
Gibraltar
STRAIT OF GIBRALTAR
Ceuta
Tangier
MOROCCO
E70
A6
AP66
AP5
A67
E5
A52
E80
A231
A6
A66
E82
E80
N122
A601
E90
E5
E80
A66
A6
E90
E901
E806
E5
A66
N322
N433
E5
N322
E5
E902
A45
A92
E15
E5

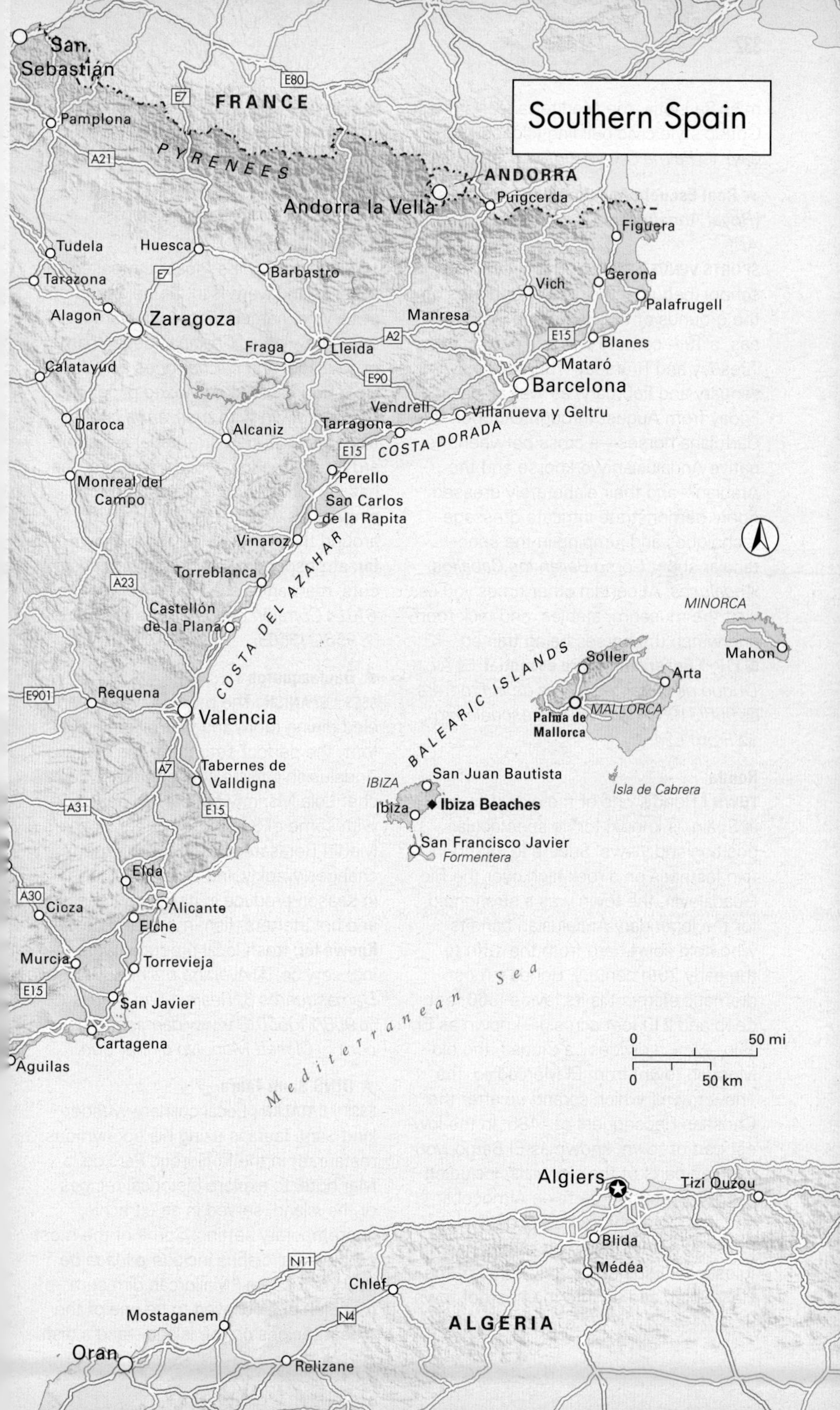

Southern Spain
FRANCE
PYRENEES
ANDORRA
Andorra la Vella
San Sebastián
Pamplona
Puigcerda
Figuera
Tudela
Huesca
Barbastro
Tarazona
Gerona
Vich
Palafrugell
Alagon
Zaragoza
Manresa
Blanes
Fraga
Lleida
Mataró
Calatayud
Barcelona
Vendrell
Villanueva y Geltru
Daroca
Alcaniz
Tarragona
COSTA DORADA
Perello
Monreal del Campo
San Carlos de la Rapita
Vinaroz
Torreblanca
COSTA DEL AZAHAR
Castellón de la Plana
MINORCA
Mahon
BALEARIC ISLANDS
Soller
Arta
Requena
Valencia
Palma de Mallorca
MALLORCA
Tabernes de Valldigna
IBIZA
San Juan Bautista
Ibiza
Ibiza Beaches
Isla de Cabrera
San Francisco Javier
Formentera
Elda
Cicza
Alicante
Elche
Murcia
Torrevieja
San Javier
Cartagena
Aguilas
Mediterranean Sea
0
50 mi
50 km
Algiers
Tizi Ouzou
Blida
Médéa
Chlef
Mostaganem
ALGERIA
Oran
Relizane
E80
E7
A21
A2
E15
E90
A23
E901
A7
A31
A30
N11
N4

miss Sa Llotja, the Mediterranean's finest Gothic-style civic building (closed Monday). ✉ *Palma* 🌐 *www.infomallorca.net.*

★ **Real Escuela Andaluza del Arte Ecuestre** (*Royal Andalusian School of Equestrian Art*)

SPORTS VENUE | **FAMILY** | This prestigious school (begun in the 1970s) operates on the grounds of the Recreo de las Cadenas, a 19th-century palace. At noon every Tuesday and Thursday (Thursday only in January and February) as well as each Friday from August through October, the Cartujana horses—a cross between the native Andalusian workhorse and the Arabian—and their elaborately dressed riders demonstrate intricate dressage techniques and jumping in the spectacular show *Cómo Bailan los Caballos Andaluces*. At certain other times you can visit the museum, stables, and tack room and watch the horses being trained. **TIP→ Reservations are essential.** ✉ *Av. Duque de Abrantes, Jerez de la Frontera* ☎ *956/319635* 🌐 *www.realescuela.org* 🎫 *From €24.*

Ronda

TOWN | Ronda, one of the oldest towns in Spain, is known for its spectacular position and views. Secure in its mountain fastness on a rock high over the Río Guadalevín, the town was a stronghold for the legendary Andalusian bandits who held court here from the 18th to the early 20th century. Ronda's most dramatic element is its ravine (360 feet deep and 210 feet across)—known as El Tajo—which divides La Ciudad, the old Moorish town, from El Mercadillo, the "new town," which sprang up after the Christian Reconquest of 1485. In the lowest part of town, known as El Barrio, you can see parts of the old walls, including the 13th-century Puerta de Almocobar and the 16th-century Puerta de Carlos V. From here, the main road climbs past the Iglesia del Espíritu Santo (Church of the Holy Spirit) and up into the heart of town. ✉ *Ronda* ✣ *147 km (91 miles) southeast of Seville* 🌐 *www. turismoderonda.es.*

Where to Eat and Drink

★ **Casa Manteca**

$ | **SPANISH** | Cádiz's most quintessentially Andalusian tavern is in the neighborhood of La Viña, named for the vineyard that once grew here. *Chacina* (Iberian ham or sausage) and *chicharrones de Cádiz* (cold pork) served on waxed paper and washed down with *manzanilla* (sherry from Sanlúcar de Barrameda) are standard fare at the low wooden counter that has served bullfighters and flamenco singers, as well as dignitaries from around the world, since 1953. **Known for:** atmospheric interior; delicious cold cuts; manzanilla sherry. $ *Average main: €10* ✉ *Corralón de los Carros 66, Cádiz* ☎ *956/213603.*

★ **Damasqueros**

$$$$ | **SPANISH** | The modern, wood-paneled dining room and warm lighting form the perfect setting for the creative Andalusian cuisine cooked here by local chef Lola Marín, who learned her trade with some of Spain's top chefs, such as Martín Berasategui. The tasting menu changes weekly and always includes in-season produce in its six courses (cold and hot starters, fish, meat, and dessert). **Known for:** fresh local produce; wine pairing; service. $ *Average main: €55* ✉ *Calle Damasqueros 3, Realejo-San Matías* ☎ *958/210550* 🌐 *www.damasqueros.com* 🕒 *Closed Mon. No dinner Sun.*

★ **DINS Santi Taura**

$$$$ | **CATALAN** | Local culinary wunderkind Santi Taura is using his eponymous restaurant in the El Llorenç Parc de la Mar hotel to explore historical recipes of the island, served in an ultrachic, contemporary setting. Some of the most emblematic dishes include *panada de peix de roca*—a "Mallorcan dim sum" of rock fish pie, believed to be one of the oldest recipes on the island—and a dish of rabbit with lobster, which combines the sea and the mountains. **Known for:** awarded one Michelin star in 2023; bar seating lets you see the chef at work; no menu; only an 11-step tasting "journey". *Average main: €95 Pl. de Llorenç Villalonga 4, Centro 656/738214 www.dinssantitaura.com Mon. closed. Lunch only served Fri. and Sat. Dinner served Tues.-Sat.*

★ El Choco

$$$$ | SPANISH | The city's most exciting restaurant, which has renewed its Michelin star annually since 2012, El Choco has renowned chef Kisko Garcia at the helm whipping up innovative dishes based on his 10 Commandments to preserve good cooking. One of them is that taste always comes first, and that plays out well during a meal at this minimalist restaurant with charcoal-colored walls, glossy parquet floors, and dishes offering new sensations and amazing presentations. **Known for:** creative Andalusian cooking; good value Michelin-star tasting menu; innovative presentation. *Average main: €110 Compositor Serrano Lucena 14, Centro 957/264863 www.restaurantechoco.com Closed Mon.–Wed. and Aug. No dinner Sun.*

★ Es Molí de Foc

$$$$ | SPANISH | Originally a flour mill, this is the oldest building in the village of Sant Climent, and both the atmosphere and the food are exceptional. Taste seasonal dishes, which can include prawn carpaccio with cured Mahón cheese and guacamole, black paella with monkfish and squid, and *carrilleras de ternera* (beef cheeks) with potato. **Known for:** summer terrace; brewery on-site; one entire menu dedicated to rice dishes. *Average main: €24 Carrer Sant Llorenç 65, Sant Climent ⊕ 4 km (2½ miles) southwest of town 971/153222 www.esmolidefoc.es Closed Mon.*

★ La Carboná

$$$ | SPANISH | In a former bodega, this eatery has a rustic atmosphere with arches, wooden beams, and a fireplace for winter nights, and in summer you can often enjoy live music and sometimes flamenco dancing while you dine. The chef has worked at several top restaurants, and his menu includes traditional grilled meats as well as innovative twists on classic dishes, such as Iberian ham croquettes with curry and Amontillado mayo or *rodaballo con velouté de palo cortado* (skate with sherry velouté). **Known for:** multiple-course sherry-tasting menu; bodega setting; innovative dishes. *Average main: €25 Calle San Francisco de Paula 2, Jerez de la Frontera 956/347475 No dinner Mon. Closed Tues. and July.*

★ Sollo

$$$$ | SPANISH | Perched high in the hills above Fuengirola, this is one of the best fish restaurants on the Costa del Sol. Michelin-starred chef Diego Gallegos champions sustainable and healthy cuisine, and his on-site aquaponics facility raises most of the fish and vegetables used here. **Known for:** sustainable and innovative cuisine; Latin American touches in dishes; coastal views. *Average main: €150 Higuerón Hotel, Avda. del Higuerón 48, Reserva del Higuerón, Fuengirola 951/385622 www.sollo.es Closed Sun. and Mon. No lunch.*

Cool Places to Stay

★ Can Gall

$$$$ | B&B/INN | Santi Marí Ferrer remade his family's *finca* (farmhouse), with its massive stone walls and native savina wood beams, into one of the island's friendliest and most comfortable country inns. **Pros:** family-friendly; oasis of quiet; poolside pergola for events and yoga sessions. **Cons:** 15-minute drive to beaches; some private terraces a bit small; often booked out for weddings. *Rooms from: €230 Ctra. Sant Joan, Km 17.2, San Lorenzo de Balafia 971/337031,*

670/876054 🌐 www.cangall.com 🛏 11 rooms 🍽 Free Breakfast.

★ Casa Palacio Maria Luisa

$$$$ | **HOTEL** | Once home to Jerez's gentlemen's club (known as the Casino) and a symbol of the city's sherry heyday, this restored 19th-century mansion is the most comfortable luxury hotel and the only five-star grand-luxe hotel in town. **Pros:** beautifully designed, über-comfortable rooms; excellent service; lovely outside terrace. **Cons:** might be too grandiose for some; expensive breakfast; small pool. *$ Rooms from: €340 ✉ Calle Tornería 22, Jerez de la Frontera ☎ 956/926263 🌐 casapalaciomarialuisa.com 🛏 21 rooms 🍽 No Meals.*

Gran Hotel Miramar

$$$$ | **HOTEL** | Málaga's giant "wedding-cake" palace was opened by King Alfonso XIII in 1926 as one of the city's first hotels and fully restored to its former glory in 2017; if you can't splurge on a room, at least treat yourself to a coffee or cocktail here. **Pros:** most luxurious accommodations in town; personal butler service; stunning interior patio. **Cons:** faces a busy road; short walk from city center; pricey. *$ Rooms from: €350 ✉ Paseo de Reding 22, Málaga ☎ 952/603000 🌐 www.granhotelmiramarmalaga.com 🛏 190 rooms 🍽 No Meals.*

★ Hospes Palacio del Bailío

$$$$ | **HOTEL** | One of the city's top lodging options, this tastefully renovated 17th-century mansion is built over the ruins of a Roman house (visible beneath glass floors) in the historic center of town. **Pros:** dazzling interiors; impeccable comforts; pleasant patio gardens. **Cons:** not easy to access by car; pricey; not all rooms have views. *$ Rooms from: €250 ✉ Calle Ramírez de las Casas Deza 10–12, Plaza de la Corredera ☎ 957/498993 🌐 www.hospes.com/palacio-bailio 🛏 53 rooms 🍽 No Meals.*

★ Hotel Alfonso XIII

$$$$ | **HOTEL** | Inaugurated by King Alfonso XIII in 1929 when he visited the World's Fair, this grand hotel next to the university is a splendid, historic, Mudejar-style palace, built around a central patio and surrounded by ornate brick arches. **Pros:** both stately and hip; impeccable service; historic surroundings. **Cons:** a tourist colony; expensive; too sophisticated for some. *$ Rooms from: €550 ✉ Calle San Fernando 2, El Arenal ☎ 954/917000 🌐 marriott.com 🛏 148 rooms 🍽 No Meals.*

★ Mirabó de Valldemossa

$$$$ | **B&B/INN** | At the far end of a winding dirt road in the hills overlooking the Real Cartuja, across the valley of Valldemossa, this luxurious little agroturismo is a romantic hideaway that's hard to reach and even harder to tear yourself away from. **Pros:** friendly personal service; peace and quiet; incredible views. **Cons:** no restaurants nearby; three-night minimum stay in summer; those low stone doorways can be a headache. *$ Rooms from: €275 ✉ Ctra. Valldemossa, Km 15.950, Valldemossa ☎ 661/285215 🌐 mirabo.es/en ⏲ Closed Dec. and Jan. 🛏 9 rooms 🍽 Free Breakfast.*

★ Parador de Granada

$$$$ | **HOTEL** | This is Spain's most expensive and most popular parador, right within the walls of the Alhambra. **Pros:** good location for the Alhambra; lovely interiors; garden restaurant. **Cons:** no views in some rooms; removed from city life; very expensive. *$ Rooms from: €450 ✉ Calle Real de la Alhambra, Alhambra ☎ 958/221440 🌐 www.paradorsofspain.com 🛏 40 rooms 🍽 No Meals.*

Northern Spain

Encircling the Atlantic Ocean to the north and west, sweeping down to the plains of Castile in the south and stretching to the Pyrenees and the Mediterranean in the east, Northern Spain delivers on all accounts. Whether it's scenic, cultural, architectural, or culinary, this vast region will set your senses alive.

The two Castiles—Castile-La Mancha and Castile and León—straddle the center with windswept steppe, planted with olive trees, grain and grapevines, punctuated with tiny medieval villages, noble cities, and a treasure trove of palaces, castles, and cathedrals. Gems in the Castile crown include Ávila, Burgos, Salamanca, Toledo, Cuenca, and Almagro.

The high mountainous north with a rugged coastline is home to Galicia, Asturias, and Cantabria, three regions of emerald landscapes, swirling sea mists, and Celtic folklore. Highlights include the cathedral city of Santiago de Compostela, the finish line for Europe's most famous pilgrim trail; glorious beaches; and the Picos de Europa soaring mountain range, one of Spain's best-kept secrets.

The far eastern corner borders France and is a land of rolling hills, colorful fishing villages, cutting-edge art and architecture and Spain's best food. In the Basque Country, the Museo Guggenheim Bilbao provides a striking modern contrast to its aristocratic neighbor, San Sebastían, the home of pintxos tapas. To the south, Navarra and its bull-running capital, Pamplona, rolls towards the Pyrenees, while La Rioja is a patchwork of highlands, plains, and vineyards, watered by the mighty Ebro River.

The Pyrenees form the gateway between the Iberian Peninsula and the rest of Europe, and this soaring range (several peaks top 11,000 feet) houses three dozen gorgeous valleys. Outdoor activities, including skiing, reign supreme, but architectural delights such as Alquézar also await you.

Tucked between the Pyrenees and the Mediterranean, Catalonia alone is one of the top reasons to visit Spain. Its list of musts runs long and includes the delights of Girona, Dalí country, ancient monasteries, one of the world's top restaurants, and the Costa Brava with its pine-studded coves.

Toledo

Medieval Treasure Trove

The spiritual capital of Castile, Toledo sits atop a rocky mount surrounded on three sides by the Río Tajo. Once home to the Romans, Moors, and then Christians, the city has a rich history of religious, intellectual, and economic prowess. The winding streets and steep hills can be tough to navigate, especially when you're searching for a specific sight, so take a full day (or three) to absorb the town's medieval trappings—and relish in getting lost from time to time. Its wealth of treasures includes the Cathedral, one of the most impressive structures in all of Spain and home to a stunning Mozarabic chapel and several paintings by El Greco; the city's two main synagogues, Sinagoga de Santa María La Blanca (founded in 1203 and a wonder of Mudejar architecture) and the Sinagoga del Tránsito (whose plain exterior belies sumptuous interior walls); plus numerous convents and churches, and the imposing Alcázar Fortress.

Don't Miss

The Iglesia de Santo Tomé was built to house El Greco's most masterful painting, *The Burial of Count Orgaz*. Time your visit as soon as the building opens to avoid the crowds.

Getting Here

The best way to get to Toledo from Madrid is the high-speed AVE train, which leaves from Madrid some nine times daily from Atocha station and gets you there in 30 minutes. From the ornate Neo-Mudejar train station, take a taxi or bus (L61 or L62), or walk the 1½ km (1 mile) to the city center.

Toledo Tourist Office. ✉ *Pl. de Zocodover 8, Toledo* ☎ *92/526–7666, 68/785–4965, 92/523–9121* 🌐 *www.turismo.toledo.es*

Camino de Santiago

Ninth-Century Pilgrimage Trails

With seven main routes and crossing meadows, mountains, and villages across Spain, this pilgrimage attracts around 350,000 travelers each year on their way to the sacred city of St. James. A spiritual—not necessarily religious—quest is generally their motivation; some complete the hike alone, while many more do it with friends or family. The most popular route is the *Camino francés* (French Way) that runs 791 km (480 miles) east–west from the French border to Santiago de Compostela. Pilgrims generally walk around 19 miles per day for a month, although some divide their route into smaller chunks and take longer to complete it. You can also cycle or ride a horse.

Don't Miss

You triumphantly enter through the Pilgrim's Door and hug the statue of St. James before collecting your Compostela certificate from the pilgrim's office, only awarded to those who have walked at least 62 miles (100 km) or cycled twice the distance and have the stamped passport to show for it.

Best Restaurant

Casa Marcelo. The restaurant fuses traditional Galician with international flavors, whipping up creatively plated dishes in an open-plan kitchen for the jovial dining area—always full and always loud—seating guests at long communal tables. ✉ *Rúa das Hortas 1, Santiago de Compostela* 🌐 *www.casamarcelo.co.*

When to Go

June–September is the busiest time, while April, May, and late September are more tranquil. The winter months have soggy, unpredictable weather.

🌐 *www.caminodesantiago.gal* 🌐 *www.caminodesantiago.me* 🌐 *www.camino-adventures.com*

Islas Cíes

Pristine Nature Reserve

The Cíes Islands, 35 km (21 miles) west of Vigo, are among Spain's best-kept secrets, forming one of the last unspoiled refuges on the Spanish coast. The three islands are designated a nature conservation and wildlife sight and are home to seven beautiful beaches. The white sands are surrounded by turquoise waters brimming with marine life; there's also great birding and several well-marked trails across the islands. The only way to get around is on your own two feet, and it takes about an hour to traverse the main island. To cross to the islands, you must obtain authorization from the Xunta de Galicia online portal.

Don't Miss

An overnight stay on the island at the designated camping area, giving you the chance to experience the sunset over the ocean and a night under the stars. Book your spot well in advance.

When to Go

Full service runs only during the summer (roughly late May to mid-September).

Best Restaurant

Serafín Restaurant on Illa do Faro, one of the three on the islands, are specialists in fish and seafood, caught daily in the Vigo estuary, and served on the pleasant shady terrace. ⊕ *679/349065*

Getting Here

Starting weekends in May and then daily June–late September, Naviera Mar de Ons runs about eight boats from Vigo's harbor. The journey (45 minutes each way) must be booked in advance.

Xunta de Galicia. ⊕ *autorizacionillas-atlanticas.xunta.gal*

Islas Cies Camping. ⊕ *www.camping-islascies.com*

Naviera Mar de Ons. ⊕ *www.marde-ons.com*

Salvador Dalí Trail

A Surrealist Triangle

With a painterly technique that rivaled that of Jan van Eyck, a flair for publicity so aggressive it would have put P.T. Barnum to shame, and a penchant for the shocking, artist Salvador Dalí entered art history as one of the foremost proponents of surrealism. He was born in Figueres, where he created a museum-monument to himself during the last 20 years of his life (he died in 1989). The Teatre-Museu Dalí has a glass geodesic dome, studded with iconic egg shapes and pays homage to his fertile imagination and artistic creativity. Casa Salvador Dalí in Portlligat was the artist's summerhouse and is packed with bits of the surrealist's colorful daily life. Reservations at all are essential.

Don't Miss

Castell Gala Dalí in Púbol, a medieval castle, is home to lush gardens decorated with hybrid elephants and Wagner masks. Gala is buried in the castle crypt.

Getting Here and Around

Figueres is one of the stops on the regular train service from Barcelona to the French border and there are also frequent local buses, especially from nearby Cadaqués. Portlligat is a 15-minute walk from the town of Cadaqués, Púbol is a 4 km (2½ mile) walk or taxi ride from the Flaçà train station or bus stop.

Casa Salvador Dalí. ✉ *Portlligat s/n, Cadaqués* 🌐 *www.salvador-dali.org* 🎫 *From €15* 🕒 *Closed Mon. Nov.–Mar.*

Castell Gala Dalí Púbol-la Pera. ✉ *Púbol-la Pera, Púbol* 🌐 *www.salvador-dali.org* 🎫 *From €9* 🕒 *Actual hrs may vary monthly*

Teatre-Museu Dalí. ✉ *Gala-Salvador Dalí 5, Figueres* 🌐 *www.salvador-dali.org* 🎫 *From €17* 🕒 *Closed Mon. (except July and Aug.)*

Salamanca

Spain's Oldest University

Salamanca's radiant sandstone buildings, mathematically proportioned Plaza Mayor, and meandering river make it one of the most majestic and beloved cities in Spain as well as a veritable showpiece of the Spanish Renaissance. If you approach from Madrid or Ávila, your first glimpse of Salamanca will be the city rising from the wide and winding Tormes River. In the foreground is a 15-arch Roman bridge; soaring above it are the old and new cathedrals. Piercing the skyline to their right is the Renaissance monastery and church of San Esteban. Behind these lies a medieval warren of palaces, convents, and university buildings that culminates in the Plaza Mayor.

Don't Miss

The symbol of Salamanca, an eroded "lucky" frog on the elaborate facade of the Escuelas Mayores at the University. Legend has it that students who spot it first time will pass all their exams.

Best Food Shopping

Visit the Mercado Central, Salamanca's most historic market with more than 50 stalls, where you can stock up on local gourmet specialties and round out your shopping spree with a glass of wine at any of the traditional tapas counters. ✉ *Pl. del Mercado, Salamanca.*

Getting Here and Around

From Madrid, approximately 13 trains depart for Salamanca daily, several of which are high-speed and take just over 1½ hours. Avanza buses leave from the Estación Sur de Autobuses. Once in Salamanca, local buses run routes throughout the city, including to and from the train and bus stations.

Salamanca City Tourist Office.
✉ *Pl. Mayor 32, Salamanca*
☎ *92/321–8342* 🌐 *www.salamanca.es*

Parc Nacional d'Aiguestortes i Estany de Sant Maurici

Arresting Mountain Scenery

The terrain of this national park (whose name translates to 'twisted waters' in Catalan) is formed by jagged peaks, steep rock walls, and deep glacial depressions filled with crystalline water, all of which lie in the shadow of the twin peaks of Els Encantats. The park's 200-some streams, lakes, and lagoons intersperse with fir and birch forests and empty into the Noguera River watercourses. The land range sweeps from wildflower-blanketed meadows below 5,000 feet to rocky crests at nearly double that height. Look out for Pyrenean chamois, golden eagles and capercaillies.

Don't Miss

The one-day scenic walking trail across the park, from east to west, starting at the village of Espet and finishing in Boi. If you're fit and experienced, the ascent of the highest peak, the 11,168-foot Aneto above Benasque, makes a tough but rewarding day-long hike in the summer.

When to Go

If you're a hiker, stick to the summer (June–September, especially July), when the weather is better and there's less chance of a serious snowfall—not to mention blizzards or lightning storms at high altitudes.

Getting Here and Around

The C13 covers 34 km (21 miles) from Sort to Espot. One of the main entrances to the park is 4 km (2 miles) west of Espot, where you can park (no private cars are allowed inside the park). Be sure to arrive early—preferably before 9 am—as parking lots fill up quickly in high season.

✉ *Espot* ☏ *973/696189* 🌐 *parcsnaturals.gencat.cat* 🎫 *Free*

El Celler de Can Roca

A Life-Changing Culinary Experience

Widely considered among the world's best restaurants (and according to some *the* best restaurant), this Girona fine-dining spot helmed by the Roca brothers—Joan, Josep, and Jordi—has unsurprisingly maintained its three Michelin stars since 2009. Expect wildly inventive dishes and daring presentations on your plates during the tasting menu (a choice of two is offered) as well as perfectly paired wine in your glass. True to its status, reservations are required many months or even a year in advance. Yes, people plan a trip to Spain just to have dinner here.

Don't Miss

A predinner stroll around the old quarter of Girona. Highlights include El Call, the 13th-century Jewish Quarter with its crisscross network of medieval stone streets; and the Cathedral, dating back to the 11th century and famous for housing the widest nave in the world.

Best Helado

Not your average ice-cream parlor, Rocambolesc is the brainchild of master confectioner Jordi Roca. Expect exquisite helados, fanciful toppings, and popsicles in the shape of Girona's famous climbing bear. ✉ *Carrer Santa Clara 50, Girona* 🌐 *www.rocambolesc.com*

Getting Here

More than 20 trains run daily from Barcelona to Girona, the regional taking take one to two hours and the high-speed AVE train service under 40 minutes. The train station is about a 30-minute walk from El Celler de Can Roca; alternatively, pick up a taxi outside the station on arrival.

[$] *Average main: €200* ✉ *Can Sunyer 48, Girona* ☎ *972/222157* 🌐 *cellercanroca.com* 🕓 *Closed Sun. and Mon. and most of Aug. No lunch Tues.*

Almagro Theater

Authentic 17th-Century Atmosphere

Appearing almost as it did in 1628 when it was built, this theater has wooden balconies on four sides and a stage at one end of its open patio. During the golden age of Spanish theater—the time of playwrights Pedro Calderón de la Barca, Cervantes, and Lope de Vega—touring actors came from all over Europe to Almagro. Give the tourist-oriented spectacles a miss unless you're thoroughly bilingual or a Spanish theater buff, but if you're in town in July, do catch a performance at the international classical theater festival. Next-door is the ancient Plaza Mayor, where 85 Roman columns form two colonnades supporting green-frame 16th-century buildings. Near the plaza are granite mansions emblazoned with the heraldic shields of their former owners.

Don't Miss

Take an evening stroll in the Plaza Mayor and sample the local tapas. Highlights include pickled baby eggplant (*berenjena de Almagro*) and rustic Manchegan wines.

Best Hotel

Parador de Almagro is five minutes from the Plaza Mayor in a finely restored 16th-century Franciscan convent with cells, cloisters, and pretty indoor courtyards. There's free parking and an outdoor pool. 🌐 *www.parador.es*

Getting Here

Almagro has once-daily train from Madrid (2½-hours), but it's probably best to rent a car. The drive south from the capital takes you across the plains of La Mancha, the land of Don Quixote.

Almagro Theatre. 🌐 *www.corraldecomedias.com* **Almagro Tourism.** 🌐 *www.ciudad-almagro.com*

Segovia Aqueduct

A Working Roman Aqueduct

Segovia's aqueduct is one of the greatest surviving examples of Roman engineering and the city's main sight. Stretching from the walls of the old town to the lower slopes of the Sierra de Guadarrama, it's about 2,952 feet long and rises in two tiers to a height of 115 feet. The raised section of stonework in the center originally carried an inscription, of which only the holes for the bronze letters remain. Neither mortar nor clamps hold the massive granite blocks together, but miraculously, the aqueduct has stood since the end of the 1st century AD and still carries water.

Don't Miss

A visit to the nearby Alcázar castle, whose silhouette is widely believed to be the inspiration for the Walt Disney logo. Highlights inside include intricate woodwork on the ceiling and knights in shining armor.

Best Restaurant

Mesón de José María. Near the Plaza Mayor, this old-timey traditional tavern-restaurant serves, according to foodies, the most delectable *cochinillo* (suckling pig) in town, but there are plenty of lighter, fresher dishes to choose from as well. Expect a boisterous mix of locals and tourists. $ *Average main: €28* ✉ *Calle Cronista Lecea 11, Segovia off Pl. Mayor* ☎ *92/146–1111, 92/146–6017* 🌐 *www.restaurantejose-maria.com*

Getting Here and Around

High-speed AVE trains from Madrid's Chamartín station—the fastest option—take 30 minutes and drop you at Guiomar station, about 7 km (4 miles) outside Segovia's center. City Bus 11 is timed to coincide with arriving trains and will take you to the foot of the aqueduct after about a 15-minute ride.

Running of the Bulls, Pamplona

A Mad (and Dangerous) Dash

Of course, Pamplona (*Iruña* or *Iruñea* in Euskera) is best known for its running of the bulls, made famous by Ernest Hemingway in his 1926 novel, *The Sun Also Rises.* Every morning of the festival, a rocket is shot off at 8 sharp, and the bulls kept overnight in the corrals at the edge of town are run through a series of closed-off streets leading to the bullring, an 850-meter (½-mile) dash. Running among them are Spaniards and foreigners feeling audacious (or perhaps foolhardy) enough to risk getting gored. The degree of peril for the runners is difficult to gauge. Serious injuries are reported daily during the festival; deaths are rare but do occur. Some say the human cost is beside the point: after the bulls' desperate gallop through town, every one of them is killed slowly to cheers in the bullring, a reality that draws ire from many antibullfighting Spaniards and animal rights groups—and, in many cases, from uninitiated Americans who aren't as prepared as they think for the gory spectacle. Running is free, but tickets to *corridas* (bullfights) are pricey and can be difficult to finagle.

When to Go

The occasion is the festival of San Fermín, July 6–14, when Pamplona's population triples (along with its hotel rates). Given the fate of the unfortunate bulls, the festival comes under more scrutiny with each passing year, even if most attendees are not there to run but rather to party.

Getting Here

Pamplona is 79 km (47 miles) south of San Sebastián. If you aren't flying into the small airport, it's probably easier to take a bus or train from San Sebastián, a trip of less than two hours.

🌐 *www.pamplona.es/en/turismo*

Bay of Biscay
Vivero
Ribadeo
A Coruña
Betanzo
E70
Santa Maria del Naranco and San Miguel de Lillo
Gijón
Ribadesella
Llanes
Santander
Oviedo
Camino de Santiago
E70
Museum Guggenheim Bilbao
Bilbao
Santiago De Compostela
Reinosa
E1
A6
AP66
AP5
Islas Cíes
Ponferrada
A67
León
Miranda de Ebro
Vigo
Ourense
Las Médulas
Astorga
A52
E80
A231
A52
Burgos
Verín
E1
A52
Benavente
Palencia
E5
A6
E80
Braga
A66
Valladolid
Aranda de Duero
E82
Zamora
Tordesillas
N122
Porto
A601
E80
Salamanca
Segovia Aqueduct
A-velha
Viseu
Sanchidrian
Segovia
E80
E80
Ciudad Rodrigo
Villacastin
E5
E90
A6
A66
Coimbra
Madrid
PORTUGAL
Leiria
Plascencia
Alavera de la Reina
E901
Navalmoral de la Mata
Toledo
E806
E5
Caceres
Badajoz
A66
Almagro Theater
Alcaraz
Fregenal de la Sierra
N322
Bailen
Montoro
N433
Córdoba
E5
Úbeda
Jaén
Seville
E5
Ecija
Montilla
E902
Huelva
Dos Hermanas
A92
Guadix
Granada

Northern Spain
FRANCE
SPAIN
ANDORRA
PYRENEES
Bordeaux
Langon
Albi
Aire-sur-L'adour
Auch
Toulouse
San Sebastián
Flysch
Day of the Joaldunak
Beziers
Narbonne
Pamplona
Running of the Bulls
Vitoria-Gasteiz
Logroño
Parc Nacional d'Aiguestortes i Estany de Sant Maurici
Perpignan
Andorra la Vella
Puigcerda
Vall de Núria Rack Railway (Cremallera)
Figuera
Salvador Dalí Trail
El Celler de Can Roca
Pasarelas de Alquézar
Huesca
Tudela
Tarazona
Barbastro
Soria
Alagon
Zaragoza
Vich
Gerona
Palafrugell
Manresa
Almazan
Fraga
Lleida
Blanes
Calatayud
Mataró
Barcelona
Medinaceli
Daroca
Vendrell
Villanueva y Geltru
Alcaniz
Tarragona
COSTA DORADA
Perello
Monreal del Campo
San Carlos de la Rapita
Vinaroz
Casas Colgadas
Cuenca
Torreblanca
Castellón de la Plana
COSTA DEL AZAHAR
BALEARIC ISLANDS
Motilla del Palancar
Requena
Valencia
Palma
MALLORCA
La Roda
Albacete
Tabernes de Valldigna
Isla de Cabrera
IBIZA
Formentera
Hellin
Elda
Alicante
Cieza
Elche
Murcia
Torrevieja
Mediterranean Sea
San Javier
Lorca
Cartagena
Huercal-Overa
Aguilas
Vera
E70
E5
A21
E7
E80
A2
E15
E90
A23
E901
A7
N322
A31
A30
0
50 mi
0
50 km

When in Northern Spain

★ **Casas Colgadas** (*Hanging Houses*)
NOTABLE BUILDING | As if Cuenca's famous Casas Colgadas, suspended impossibly over the cliffs below, were not eye-popping enough, they also house one of Spain's finest museums, the Museo de Arte Abstracto Español (Museum of Spanish Abstract Art)—not to be confused with the adjacent Museo Municipal de Arte Moderno. Projecting over the town's eastern precipice, these houses originally formed a 15th-century palace, which later served as a town hall before falling into disrepair in the 19th century. In 1927 the cantilevered balconies were rebuilt, and in 1966 the painter Fernando Zóbel created the world's first museum devoted exclusively to abstract art. The works he gathered—by such renowned names as Carlos Saura, Eduardo Chillida, Lucio Muñoz, and Antoni Tàpies—are primarily by exiled Spanish artists who grew up under Franco's regime. The museum has free smartphone audio guides that can be downloaded from the website. ✉ *Calle de los Canónigos, Cuenca* ☎ *96/921–2983* 🌐 *www.march.es/arte/cuenca* 🎫 *Free* ⏲ *Closed Mon.*

Day of the Joaldunak
ARTS FESTIVALS | If you're in the Baztan Valley in the Pyrenees, try to be in the village of Ituren in late September for its carnival, the Day of the Joaldunak, which has been recognized as one of the oldest celebrations in Europe. Here you can see striking costumes hung with clanging cowbells as participants parade from farm to farm and house to house paying homage to their ancestors; some anthropologists argue that the rituals go back to pagan times. Check the exact dates of the event with the tourist office as each year's schedule depends on the phases of the moon. ✉ *Ituren* 🌐 *www.valledebaztan.com.*

★ **Flysch**
NATURE SIGHT | **FAMILY** | The Flysch is the crown jewel of the Basque Coast Geopark, a 13-km (8-mile) stretch of coastline distinguished by spectacular cliffs and rock formations. Taking its name from the German for "slippery"—a reference to the slipping of tectonic plates that thrust the horizontal rock layers into vertical panels—the Flysch contains innumerable layers of sedimentary rock displaying some 20 million years of geological history. One such layer is black and devoid of fossils; it was identified by scientists as marking the Cretaceous–Paleogene extinction event, which caused the extinction of the dinosaurs. ✉ *Playa de Itzurun, Zumaia* 🎫 *Free.*

★ **Las Médulas**
RUINS | **FAMILY** | One of northern Spain's most impressive archaeological sites, this mountainous area of former Roman gold mines—located 24 km (15 miles) south of town—is a UNESCO World Heritage Site. The landscape is the result of an ancient mining technique in which myriad water tunnels were burrowed into a mountain, causing it to collapse. Miners would then sift through the rubble for gold. What's left at Las Médulas are half-collapsed mountains of golden clay with exposed tunnels peeking through lush green forest. Take in the best panorama from the Orellán viewpoint. There are hiking paths, a small archaeology exhibit, and a visitor center; the latter organizes 3-km (2-mile) walking tours—check schedules online, and call or email ahead to book (✉ medulas@ccbierzo.com). **■ TIP→ A parking lot was added in 2021; the price is €3 per vehicle.** ✉ *Carucedo* ☎ *98/742–0708* 🌐 *www.patrimoniocastillayleon.com/en/las-medulas* 🎫 *Free, archaeology center €2, Orellán tunnel €3, guided walking tour €5.*

★ **Museo Guggenheim Bilbao**
ART MUSEUM | A beacon of modernity built in the ruins of Bilbao's scruffy shipyards and steelworks, the Guggenheim

dramatically reanimated this one-time industrial city when it opened in 1997. At once suggestive of a silver-scaled fish and a mechanical heart, Frank Gehry's sculpture in titanium, limestone, and glass is the perfect habitat for the 250-some Contemporary and Postmodern artworks it contains. Artists synonymous with the 20th century (Kandinsky, Picasso, Miró, Pollock, Calder, et al.), particularly European artists of the 1950s and '60s (Eduardo Chillida, Antoni Tàpies, Jose Maria Iglesias, Francesco Clemente, Anselm Kiefer, et al.) are joined by contemporary figures (Bruce Nauman, Juan Muñoz, Julian Schnabel, Miquel Barceló, Jean-Michel Basquiat, et al.). **TIP→ Buy tickets in advance online to save a few euros.** ✉ *Abandoibarra Etorbidea 2, El Ensanche* ☎ *94/435–9080* 🌐 *www.guggenheim-bilbao.eus* 🎫 *€18* 🕒 *Closed Mon. Sept.–June* Ⓜ *Moyúa.*

★ Pasarelas de Alquézar

TRAIL | FAMILY | Take a breathtaking riverside hike (1½ hours) on the Ruta de las Pasarelas loop, which hugs near-sheer cliffs that plunge into rushing turquoise waters. There's a waterfall, a cave, and plenty of placards with information on the surrounding nature and historical buildings. Be sure to bring plenty of water and to arrive early, since parking (follow the signs) is limited. Certain stretches are on metal pathways with steep drops, so those with limited mobility or a fear of heights should skip this one. The trail starts at Plaza de Rafael Ayerbe beside the ayuntamiento (town hall). No bikes or pets are allowed. ✉ *Pl. Rafael Ayerbe, Alquézar* ☎ *682/932809* 🌐 *www.pasarelasdealquezar.com* 🎫 *€4.*

★ Santa María del Naranco and San Miguel de Lillo

CHURCH | These two churches—the first with superb views and its plainer sister 300 yards uphill—are the jewels of an early architectural style called Asturian pre-Romanesque, a more primitive, hulking, defensive line that preceded Romanesque architecture by nearly three centuries. Commissioned as part of a summer palace by King Ramiro I when Oviedo was the capital of Christian Spain, these masterpieces have survived for more than 1,000 years. Tickets for both sites are available in the church of Santa María del Naranco. ✉ *Monte Naranco, Oviedo* ✣ *2 km (1 mile) north of Oviedo* ☎ *638/260163* 🌐 *www.santamariadel-naranco.es* 🎫 *€4, includes guided tour (free Mon., without guide).*

★ Vall de Núria Rack Railway (Cremallera)

TRAIN/TRAIN STATION | FAMILY | The 45-minute train ride from the town of Ribes de Freser up to Núria provides one of Catalonia's most eclectic excursions—in few other places in Spain does a train make such a precipitous ascent. The cogwheel train, nicknamed *La Cremallera* ("The Zipper" in English), was completed in 1931 to connect Ribes with the Santuari de la Mare de Déu de Núria (Mother of God of Núria) and with hiking trails and ski runs. ✉ *Estación de Ribes-Enllaç, Ribes de Freser* ☎ *972/732020* 🌐 *www.valldenuria.cat/en/summer/rack-railway/presentation* 🎫 *€30 round-trip* 🕒 *Closed weekdays in Nov.*

Where to Eat and Drink

★ Antonio Bar

$$ | TAPAS | Tuna carpaccio with pickled Basque peppers, battered hake cheeks, tripe and pork jowl stew—these are some of the classics you'll find on the menu at Antonio, a neighborhood standby that serves unpretentious pintxos at fair prices. Ask about specials, which vary depending on what's in season. **Known for:** no-nonsense pintxo bar; packed with locals; regional beers and wines. 💲 *Average main: €21* ✉ *Calle Bergara 3, Centro* 🌐 *www.antoniobar.com* 🕒 *Closed Sun.*

★ Arzak

$$$$ | BASQUE | One of the world's great culinary meccas, award-winning Arzak embodies the prestige, novelty, and science-driven creativity of the Basque culinary zeitgeist. The restaurant and its high-tech food lab—both helmed by founder Juan Mari Arzak's daughter Elena these days—are situated in the family's 19th-century home on the outskirts of San Sebastián. **Known for:** scintillating yet unpretentious culinary experience; old-school hospitality; fresh flavors and striking plating. *Average main: €230 Av. Alcalde Jose Elosegui 273, Alto de Miracruz 94/327–8465, 94/328–5593 www.arzak.es Closed Mon., June 15–July 2, and 3 wks in early Nov.*

★ Azurmendi

$$$$ | BASQUE | The immersive gastro-experience at the envelope-pushing eco-restaurant by renowned Basque chef Eneko Atxa starts with nibbles in the indoor garden, continues on to the kitchen with a quick tour, and culminates in the dining room with a conceptual tasting menu featuring dishes like "dew water" and "essence of the forest." **Known for:** three-Michelin-star dining; Bilbao's most innovative and sustainable restaurant; a 10-minute drive from town. *Average main: €300 Legina Auzoa, Bilbao 94/455–8866 www.azurmendi.restaurant Closed Sun. and Mon. No dinner Tues.–Thu.*

★ Can Ventura

$$$ | CATALAN | In a flower-festooned 17th-century stone house is one of La Cerdanya's finest restaurants, which serves elevated Catalan fare with French touches. Beef a la llosa and duck with orange and spices are house specialties, and the wide selection of *entretenimientos* (hors d'oeuvres or tapas) is the perfect way to begin. **Known for:** beef seared on hot slate; cozy mountain lodge setting; additional bar area for drinks and tapas. *Average main: €25 Pl. Major 1, Llívia 972/896178 www.canventura.com Closed Mon. and Thurs. No dinner Sun.*

★ La Hoja 21

$$$ | SPANISH | Just off the Plaza Mayor, this upscale restaurant has a glass facade, high ceilings, butter-yellow walls, and minimalist art—a welcome relief from the dime-a-dozen Castilian mesones. Savor traditional fare with a twist, such as ibérico pork ravioli and langoustine-stuffed trotters at dinner, or spring for the €20 lunch prix fixe, an absolute steal, served Tuesday through Friday mid-day. **Known for:** nuanced yet unpretentious modern fare; phenomenally affordable menú del día; romantic, low-key atmosphere. *Average main: €22 Calle San Pablo 21, Salamanca 92/326–4028 www.lahoja21.com Closed Mon. No dinner Sun.*

★ Martín Berasategui

$$$$ | CONTEMPORARY | Basque chef Martín Berasategui has more Michelin stars than any other chef in Spain, and at his flagship in the dewy village of Lasarte-Oria, it's easy to see why. Dishes are Basque at heart but prepared with exacting, French-inflected technique that comes through in dishes like artfully composed salads, elegant caviar preparations, and eel-and-foie-gras mille-feuilles—a Berasategui signature. **Known for:** once-in-a-lifetime dining experience; idyllic, white-tablecloth outdoor terrace; artful mix of classic and avant-garde. *Average main: €88 Calle Loidi 4, Lasarte ⊕ 8 km (5 miles) south of San Sebastián 94/336–6471, 94/336–1599 www.martinberasategui.com Closed Mon., Tues., and mid-Dec.–mid-Jan. No dinner Sun.*

★ Mercado de la Ribera

MARKET | This renovated triple-decker ocean liner, with its prow facing down the estuary toward the open sea, houses one of the best markets of its kind in Europe—and one of the biggest, with some 400 retail stands that run the gamut from fish markets to pintxo bars to wine shops. This is a good place to stock upon culinary souvenirs while indulging in a pintxo or three. ✉ *Calle de la Ribera 22, Casco Viejo* ☎ *94/602–3791* 🌐 *mercadodelaribera.biz* 🕓 *Closed Sat. from 3 pm and Sun.* Ⓜ *Casco Viejo.*

★ **Restaurante Iván Cerdeño**

$$$$ | SPANISH | Chef Iván Cerdeño's namesake restaurant is a beacon of Castilian alta gastronomía—think architectural dishes composed of foams, spherified sauces, and edible flowers served in a minimal white-tablecloth dining room. The ever-rotating tasting menus (5, 7, or 10 courses) almost always feature local game such as partridge or roe deer. **Known for:** two-Michelin-star dining; culinary hot spot; secluded location across the Tagus. $ *Average main: €85* ✉ *Cigarral del Ángel, Ctra. de la Puebla, Toledo* ☎ *92/522–3674* 🌐 *www.ivancerdeno.com* 🕓 *Closed Mon. and Tues., Dinner only served Fri. and Sat.*

★ **Restaurant Pont Vell**

$$$$ | CATALAN | Book in advance for a table on the romantic riverfront terrace and you'll be rewarded with exceptional views of Besalu's medieval bridge. The prix-fixe menu changes monthly and offers a wide array of traditional Catalan dishes of superb quality, with seasonal ingredients sourced from the nearby Banyols market. **Known for:** seasonal menu; terrace with views; warm, friendly service. $ *Average main: €45* ✉ *Pont Vell 24, Besalú* ☎ *972/591027* 🌐 *www.restaurantpontvell.com* 🕓 *Closed Mon. and Tues. Dinner Fri. and Sat. only.*

Cool Places to Stay

Caravan Cinema

$$$ | B&B/INN | This cozy, cinema-themed pension with in-room Nespresso machines and huge TV is a good value. **Pros:** independently owned; convenient to main sights; cheerful staff. **Cons:** some rooms overlook a gritty little courtyard; inadequate soundproofing; contact proprietor to schedule check-in time. $ *Rooms from: €205* ✉ *Calle Correo 11, Casco Viejo* ☎ *68/886–0907* 🌐 *www.caravan-cinema.com* 🛏 *11 rooms* 🍴 *No Meals* Ⓜ *Arriaga.*

★ **Casa Irene**

$$$ | B&B/INN | Casa Irene exudes old-fashioned coziness with wood-beamed ceilings and plush armchairs, plus modern amenities. **Pros:** individualized attention; understated yet tasteful decor; free shuttle to the slopes. **Cons:** street-facing rooms can be noisy on summer nights; dated decor; often booked up. $ *Rooms from: €180* ✉ *Carrer Major 22, Arties* ☎ *973/644364* 🌐 *www.hotelcasairene.com* 🕓 *Closed May, June, Oct., and Nov.* 🛏 *22 rooms* 🍴 *Free Breakfast.*

★ **Hotel Diana**

$$ | HOTEL | Built in 1906 by architect Antoni de Falguera i Sivilla, a disciple of Antoni Gaudí, this Moderniste gem sits on the square in the heart of the Vila Vella, steps from the beach. **Pros:** attentive service; ideal location, with sea views; Moderniste touches. **Cons:** minimal amenities; room rates unpredictable; some rooms are small. $ *Rooms from: €101* ✉ *Pl. de Espanya 6, Tossa de Mar* ☎ *972/341886* 🌐 *www.hotelesdante.com* 🕓 *Closed Nov.–late Mar.* 🛏 *21 rooms* 🍴 *No Meals.*

★ **Hotel María Cristina**

$$$$ | HOTEL | Belle Époque grace and opulence are embodied here, in San Sebastián's most legendary hotel looming over the Urumea. **Pros:** elaborate white-tablecloth breakfasts; old-world elegance with new-world amenities; grand historic building. **Cons:** staff can be a bit stiff; views aren't as dramatic as from other top hotels; wildly expensive. $ *Rooms from: €837* ✉ *Paseo República Argentina 4, Centro* ☎ *94/343–7600* 🌐 *www.hotel-mariacristina.com* 🛏 *136 rooms* 🍴 *No Meals.*

★ **Hotel Marqués de Riscal, A Luxury Collection Hotel, Elciego**
$$$$ | **HOTEL** | Frank Gehry's post-Guggenheim hotel looks like an extraterrestrial colony in the middle of one of La Rioja's oldest vineyards. **Pros:** dazzling architecture; dependable big-brand (Marriott) luxury; superb dining. **Cons:** phenomenally expensive; interiors pale in comparison to the exterior; service isn't always five-star. *Rooms from: €594* ✉ *Calle Torrea 1, Elciego* ✣ *6 km (4 miles) southwest of Laguardia* ☎ *94/518–0880* 🌐 *www.hotel-marquesderiscal.com* *43 rooms* *Free Breakfast.*

★ **Hotel Spa Relais & Châteaux A Quinta da Auga**
$$$$ | **HOTEL** | Tastefully converted from a 14th-century printing factory, this restored stone building is set among manicured gardens and beside the burbling Río Sar. Rooms drip with French crystal chandeliers and opulent antique furniture—handpicked by the owner—a level of attention to detail that's mirrored by the above-and-beyond service. **Pros:** destination restaurant; attentive service; tranquil spa with pool. **Cons:** 10-minute drive from town; Wi-Fi spotty in some rooms; small beds. *Rooms from: €215* ✉ *Paseo da Amaia 23B, Santiago de Compostela* ☎ *981/534636* 🌐 *www.aquintadaauga.com* *51 rooms* *Free Breakfast.*

★ **Landa**
$$$$ | **HOTEL** | **FAMILY** | If you've ever dreamed of holing up in a luxurious castle, consider booking a room at Landa, a converted 14th-century palace some 5 km (3 miles) from the city center surrounded by lush gardens. **Pros:** stunning indoor-outdoor swimming pool; surprisingly affordable for level of luxury; beautiful lobby. **Cons:** roads to and from town are busy; car required; inconsistent food quality and unprofessional restaurant staff. *Rooms from: €233* ✉ *Ctra. de Madrid–Irún, Km 235, Burgos* ☎ *94/725–7777* 🌐 *www.landa.as* *37 rooms* *No Meals.*

★ **Parador de Sigüenza**
$$$ | **HOTEL** | **FAMILY** | This fairy-tale 12th-century castle has hosted royalty for centuries, from Ferdinand and Isabella right up to Spain's present king, Felipe VI. **Pros:** excellent food; sense of history and place; plenty of parking. **Cons:** much of castle is a neo-medieval replica; bland, modern furniture that doesn't jibe with the space; occasionally surly service. *Rooms from: €140* ✉ *Pl. del Castillo, Sigüenza* ☎ *94/939–0100* 🌐 *www.parador.es* *81 rooms* *No Meals.*

Canary Islands

A historic way station between the old and new worlds, the eight Canary Islands sit 800 miles off southwest Spain and just 70 miles from southern Morocco. Between them, the octet provides a mosaic of landscapes from black-sand beaches, lofty volcanoes, and lush banana plantations to pretty villages, colonial cities, and some of Europe's most vibrant festivals.

Their make-up is just as varied. Geographically, the Canary Islands are African—the windswept plains of the easternmost islands of Fuerteventura and Lanzarote almost mirror the Sahara Desert. Climatically, the islands enjoy pleasant weather all year, with little variation in temperature. Not for nothing are they known as the Land of the Eternal Spring. Culturally, they're European—the art and architecture have clear roots in Spanish tastes and trends.

Our bucket list highlights musts on five islands: Tenerife, Gran Canaria, Lanzarote, Fuerteventura, and La Palma. The smaller islands of El Hierro, La Gomera, and La Graciosa are no less attractive, but slightly less accessible. Nonetheless, make time for them if you can.

Tenerife is the largest of the islands and also home to Spain's highest mountain, El Teide. The dry and built-up south of the island has the busiest tourist resorts, while the wetter north is blanketed in banana plantations and vineyards. La Palma, northwest of Tenerife, is known as the Isla Bonita for its breathtaking scenery in almost pristine surroundings.

Gran Canaria, an almost circular island, has three distinct identities: its capital, Las Palmas, is a thriving business center; the white-sand beaches of the south are tourist magnets; and the spectacular rural landscapes inland have a forgotten-in-time allure.

Farther east are Lanzarote and Fuerteventura, the driest islands where it rarely rains and both popular year-round tourist destinations. Lanzarote is a UNESCO biosphere reserve, and its volcanic landscapes and beaches give it a surreal vibe. Flat and windy Fuerteventura is home to a small population, little development, and probably the best beaches.

Parque Natural de Timanfaya

Volcanic Landscapes and Lagoons

Popularly known as the "Fire Mountains," this national park of barren volcanic landscapes takes up much of southern Lanzarote. The terrain is a violent jumble of exploded craters, cinder cones, lava formations, and heat fissures. The only access to the central volcanic area is on a 14-km (9-mile) bus circuit.

A taped English commentary explains how a local priest took notes during the 1730 eruption that buried two villages. He had plenty of time—the eruption lasted six years, making it the longest-known eruption in volcanic history. By the time it was over, more than 75% of Lanzarote was covered in lava. Throughout the park, look out for a little devil with a pitchfork, designed by César Manrique, the Lanzarote-born architect.

Outside the park near Yaiza is El Charco Verde, a bizarre green lagoon, which looks like something out of a sci-fi thriller. It gets its radioactive hue from its sulfuric content and Ruppia maritima seagrass. A viewpoint at the turnoff to El Golfo is the nearest you can get to the lake and an excellent spot for photos, especially at sunset.

Don't Miss

A meal at El Diablo restaurant in the heart of the park where everything on the menu is cooked over a volcanic crater using the natural heat created by volcanos underneath is unforgettable. 🌐 *cactlanzarote.com/en/menus/el-diablo-restaurant/*

Getting Here and Around

Once on Lanzarote, you'll need a car to reach the park; bus service is irregular.

✉ *Centro de Visitantes Mancha Blancha, Ctra. de Yaiza a Tinajo, Km 11.5, Tinajo* ☎ *928/118042* 🎫 *€10*

Parque Nacional del Teide

Spain's Highest Peak

The dormant volcano El Teide, Spain's highest peak (at 12,198 feet), looms on the horizon wherever you are in Tenerife, and its (often snow-capped) peak is visible from the neighboring islands of Gran Canaria and La Palma on clear days. Its slopes are blanketed with pines in the north and barren lava fields in the south. You need a special permit to reach the highest point, but most hikers and tourists will be content with hitching a ride up most of the way on the cable car.

Within the park, you can find blue-tinged hills (the result of a process called hydrothermal alteration); spiky, knobby rock protrusions; and lava in varied colors and textures. The bizarre, photogenic rock formations known as Los Roques de García are especially memorable.

Don't Miss

A hike along one of the park's 30 well-marked trails. A particular highlight is the two-hour walk around Los Roques de García, bizarre rock formations that showcase the park's volcanic roots.

When to Go

Visit in late May and early June to catch the display of crimson, horn-shaped tajinaste flowers in bloom, a dramatic sight. Permits are available at ⊕ *www.reservasparquesnacionales.es* (allow two months to process).

Getting Here and Around

Four roads lead to El Teide, each getting you to the park in about an hour, but the most beautiful approach is from Orotava. Roads into the park are occasionally closed due to icy conditions in winter.

Cable Car. ✉ *La Orotava* ⊕ *www.volcanoteide.com* 🎫 *From €37*

Parque Nacional del Teide. ✉ *La Orotava* ⊕ *www.reservasparquesnacionales.es* ✍ *Climbing reservation required at least 2 months in advance*

César Manrique House Museum

The Essence of Lanzarote

Lanzarote is synonymous with César Manrique (1919–92), the acclaimed artist and architect who helped shape modern-day Canarian culture and share it on the world stage. He designed many of the island's tourist attractions and convinced authorities to require that all new buildings be painted white with green or brown trim (white with blue on the coast), to suggest coolness and fertility. He also helped local activists fight overdevelopment.

Overlooking the sleepy town of Haría, his final home is preserved as if in amber. The artist lived in this architecturally stunning estate, which he built for himself, until his untimely death by auto accident. Plant-filled courtyards lead into living areas brimming with sculptures, paintings, and iconic furniture; the bathroom, with a floor-to-ceiling window into a leafy garden, is a highlight, as is the outdoor pool and art studio, kept precisely how it was left on the day he died.

Don't Miss

The Fundación César Manrique, Manrique's high-design bachelor pad in Tahíche, contains his studio with original paintings, cave dwellings, and crystalline pools; the Jardín de Cactus, also in Costa Teguise, is home to 10,000 specimens, all planted by Manrique.

Getting Around

Lanzarote Intercity buses connect the Costa Teguise and Arrecife.

César Manrique House Museum. ✉ *Calle Elvira Sanchez 30, Haria* 🌐 *www.fcmanrique.org* 🎟 *€10*

Fundación César Manrique. ✉ *Calle Jorge Luis Borges 16, Tahíche* 🌐 *www.fcmanrique.org* 🎟 *€8*

Jardín de Cactus. ✉ *Ctra. General del Norte, Guatiza* 🌐 *www.cactlanzarote.com* 🎟 *€7*

Canary Islands Beaches

Volcanic Beaches at Their Best

Each island offers its own visual contrasts of beaches. Pure white sands are lapped by pristine turquoise sea in Fuerteventura; the Atlantic laps at crest after crest of sand dunes on Gran Canaria; white surf caresses black volcanic sands in Tenerife; and the fire mountains of Timanfaya form the backdrop to many beaches in Lanzarote.

Absolute highlights include: Corralejo, Playa de Sotavento, and Jandia Peninsula in Fuerteventura, famed as some of Spain's best beaches and perfect spots for wind and kite surfing; Playa de los Guios in Tenerife is a small, placid cove with natural black sand and dwarfed by Los Gigantes, the towering cliffs nearby; Maspalomas in Gran Canaria has golden sand that stretches for 1¾ miles along the island's southern tip and is backed by dunes, palm groves, and a saltwater lagoon; and Playa de Famara in Lanzarote, the island's most breathtaking beach, sits in a natural cove and its 4 miles of sand are flanked by spectacularly high cliffs. The riptide here makes for excellent surfing and windsurfing.

Don't Miss

A walk along Playa de Corralejo in Fuerteventura where 2 miles (3½ km) of white sands are fringed by high dunes on one side and the ocean and Isla de Lobos on the other. The views are simply magnificent.

When to Go

Winds with an average speed of 12 mph blow from the northeast more or less all summer, so avoid beaches such as Famara on Lanzarote and Corralejo on Fuerteventura unless, of course, you're riding the waves!

Caldera de Taburiente National Park

A Natural Visual Feast

What strikes you first about Caldera de Taburiente National Park in La Palma is its sheer verticality, jutting over 3,000 feet above sea level, which feels dramatic considering that the ocean is only a couple of miles away as the crow flies. Trails here take you through dense Canarian pine forests, meadows of wildflowers, dramatic gorges, and burbling streams. All around you are even higher, jagged cliff tops whose peaks are often hidden above the cloud line.

Don't Miss

The jaw-dropping indigo tajinaste flowers, known as "towers of jewels" and reaching up to 9 feet in height, can be seen in late spring and early summer across the meadows along with deep blue bugloss and dark red Canary Island spurge.

Best Activity

Picturesque hiking on the two main routes: one uphill and one downhill. The latter is far and away more enjoyable, but you'll have to hire a taxi (approximately €55; try to split the fee with other hikers) at the Barranco de las Angustias (aka Parking de la Villa) to drop you at the trailhead at Mirador Los Brecitos. You then walk the scenic route from Los Brecitos back down to the taxi stand, four- to seven hours depending on how pokey you are. The hike is steep with lots of uneven surfaces and not suited to all travelers. Bring plenty of water and snacks.

Getting Here and Around

Buses between Santa Cruz de la Palma and Los Llanos de Aridane stop at the visitor center parking lot.

Caldera de Taburiente National Park. ☎ 922/922280 🌐 *www.reservasparquesnacionales.es*

Isla Bonita Tours. 🌐 *www.islabonitatours.com*

When in the Canary Islands

★ Casa del Vino

WINERY | Wine and food lovers shouldn't miss this wine museum and tasting room, opened by the Canary Islands' government to promote local vintners. The surprisingly well-appointed museum, which describes local grapes, viticultural methods, and history, has English-language placards; reasonably priced tastings in various formats are held in the abutting bar area, and you can buy your favorite bottle in the shop. The complex also has a tapas bar and a restaurant with creative Canarian fare and a curious little honey museum with exhibits and tastings. Casa del Vino lies about halfway between Puerto de la Cruz and Tenerife North Airport, at the El Sauzal exit on the main highway. ✉ *Calle San Simon 49, at Autopista General del Norte, Km 21, Sauzal* ☎ *922/572535* 🌐 *www.casadelvinotenerife.com* 🎫 *Free* ⏲ *Closed Mon.*

★ Casa Museo Colón (*Columbus Museum*)

HISTORY MUSEUM | **FAMILY** | In a palace where Christopher Columbus may have stayed when he stopped to repair the *Pinta*'s rudder, nautical instruments, copies of early navigational maps, and models of Columbus's three ships are on display in addition to interactive exhibits. The palace, which retains many original features, has two rooms holding pre-Columbian artifacts and one floor dedicated to paintings from the 16th to the 19th century. There's a glaring absence of criticism of Columbus's complicated legacy. ✉ *Calle Colón 1, Vegueta* ☎ *928/312373* 🌐 *www.casadecolon.com* 🎫 *€4 (free Sun.).*

Piscinas Naturales El Caletón

HOT SPRING | **FAMILY** | Lava flows formed these seaside natural pools, to which stairs, paths, and railings have been added for easy access. There's a pleasant café selling drinks and snacks and a conventional swimming pool that comes in handy when the surf is rough. Far from luxurious or exclusive, the pools are owned by the town and popular with born-and-bred *Ti nerfeños* of all ages. ✉ *Av. Tome Cano 5, Garachico* 🎫 *Free.*

Roque de Los Muchachos Observatory

OBSERVATORY | **FAMILY** | Little do many science buffs know that La Palma boasts the second-best astronomy observatory in the Northern Hemisphere, outdone only by Mauna Kea in Hawaii. Situated within the Caldera de Taburiente National Park, it has three extremely powerful telescopes and sits above the clouds at an altitude of 7,861 feet (2,396 meters). Though the site is operated by an astrophysics institute, small-group visits, lasting 70–90 minutes and always held at dawn, are subcontracted to a company called Ad Astra. The tour with a certified guide includes entry into one of the telescopes. ✉ *Parque Nacional Caldera de Taburiente* ☎ *696/186633* 🌐 *www.adastralapalma.com/tours-en/observatory-tour* 🎫 *From €20* ✍ *Reservations essential.*

★ Tenerife Espacio de las Artes (*TEA*)

ART MUSEUM | This museum is the leader in contemporary art on the islands due to its sleek low-rise design and avant-garde exhibitions. Designed by the Swiss architects Herzog & de Meuron, it's next to the Museo de la Naturaleza. Expect 20th- and 21st-century art with a political or sociological bent. TEA's crown jewel is the hall dedicated to *Tinerfeño* surrealist artist Óscar Domínguez. ✉ *Av. San Sebastián 8, Santa Cruz de Tenerife* ☎ *922/849057* 🌐 *www.teatenerife.es* 🎫 *Free* ⏲ *Closed Mon.*

Where to Eat and Drink

★ Bodegas Monje

$$ | **SPANISH** | A five-minute drive from the Casa del Vino, in the township of El Sauzal, you'll find this award-winning winery and restaurant perched on a bluff overlooking the ocean. After a lunch of crackly pulled (local heritage-breed *cochino*

Canary Islands

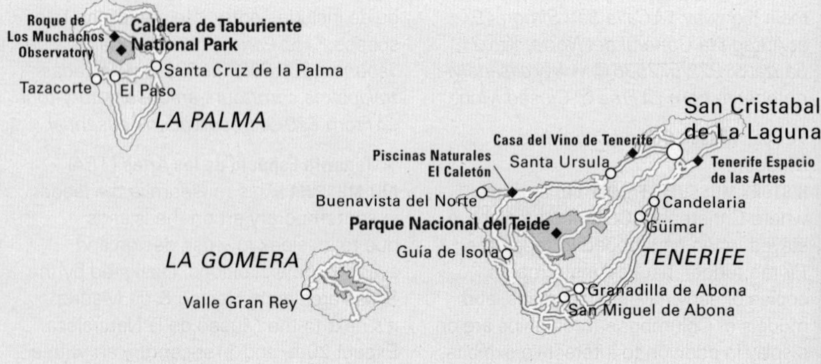

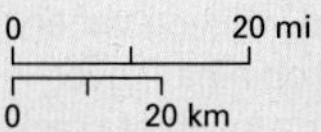

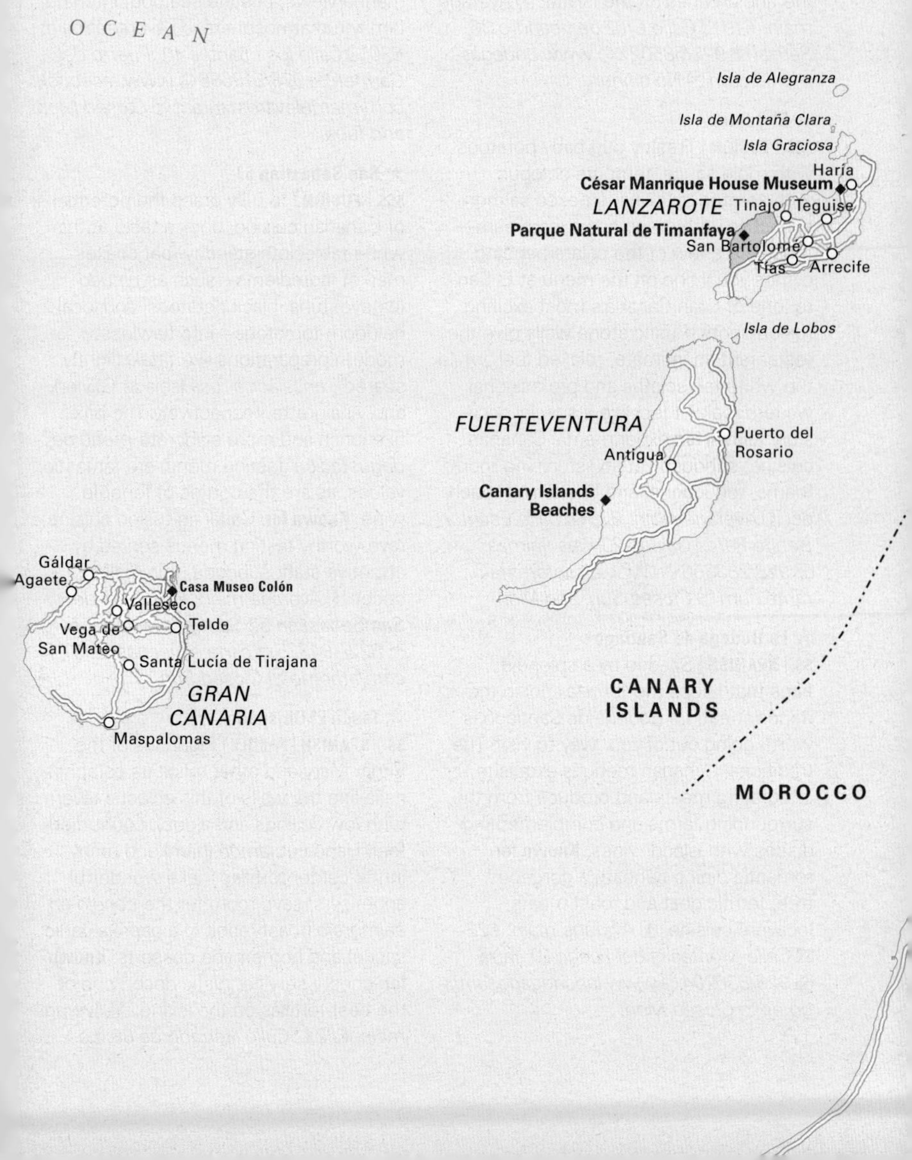

OCEAN

Isla de Alegranza

Isla de Montaña Clara

Isla Graciosa

Haría

César Manrique House Museum

LANZAROTE

Tinajo

Teguise

Parque Natural de Timanfaya

San Bartolomé

Tías

Arrecife

Isla de Lobos

FUERTEVENTURA

Puerto del Rosario

Antigua

Canary Islands Beaches

Gáldar

Agaete

Casa Museo Colón

Valleseco

Vega de San Mateo

Telde

Santa Lucía de Tirajana

GRAN CANARIA

Maspalomas

CANARY ISLANDS

MOROCCO

negro) pork and roasted potatoes, waddle over to the bodega for a tour and tasting, and if you're looking for a gluggable souvenir, snap up a bottle of the tintilla, a smoky, complex red aged in French oak barrels that's nearly impossible to find in shops. **Known for:** heritage-breed pulled pork; mojo-making demonstrations (call ahead to book); production of some of the finest wines on the island. *Average main: €19 Calle Cruz de Leandro 36, Sauzal 922/585027 www.bodegas-monje.com No dinner.*

★ El Santo

$$$ | FUSION | Freshly dug baby potatoes with mole sauce, tempura octopus with aerated spirulina, smoked salmon aguachile with green apple ice cream—these are a few of the palate-bending dishes you'll find on the menu at El Santo, one of Gran Canaria's most exciting fusion spots. Rustic stone walls give the restaurant an intimate, relaxed feel, while the white tablecloths and professional waiters make it feel like a special occasion. **Known for:** experimental Canarian cuisine; subdued yet stylish dining room; foams, reductions, and fine-dining touches. *Average main: €29 Calle Escritor Benito Pérez Galdós 23, Las Palmas 928/283366 www.elsantorestaurante.com Closed Sun. and Mon.*

★ La Bodega de Santiago

$$ | SPANISH | Shaded by a splendid ficus that keeps the *terraza* cool in the midday heat, La Bodega de Santiago is worth going out of your way to visit. The traditional Canarian menu is exquisite, integrating meats and produce from the surrounding farms and complementing dishes with island wines. **Known for:** romantic dining beneath a gorgeous tree; terrific goat and roast meats; locavore cuisine. *Average main: €22 Calle Montañas del Fuego 27, Yaiza 928/836204 www.labodegadesantiago.es Closed Mon.*

★ Mardeleva

$$ | SEAFOOD | On a hill overlooking the port, this small family-run restaurant is all about the catch of the day (try the barracuda if available), served either fried or grilled and always accompanied by papas arrugadas. *Arroz caldoso con bogavante* (soupy rice with lobster) is another highlight. **Known for:** pleasant marina views; pristine seafood; intimate, family-run atmosphere. *Average main: €20 Calle los Infantes 10, Puerto del Carmen 928/510686 www.facebook.com/mardelevarestaurant Closed Mon. and Tues.*

★ San Sebastián 57

$$$ | FUSION | To fully grasp the potential of Canarian cuisine, book a table at this white-tablecloth standby that coaxes market ingredients—such as *patudo* (bigeye) tuna, black potatoes, and local heirloom tomatoes—into flawless, modern preparations like *tataki* (lightly seared), *ensaladilla rusa* (salade Olivier), and vinaigrette, respectively. The prix-fixe lunch and more elaborate *menú de degustación* (tasting menu) are fantastic values, as are the bottles of Tenerife wine. **Known for:** Canarian fusion cuisine; rave-worthy tasting menus served by attentive staff; subdued, minimalist decor. *Average main: €26 Av. de San Sebastián 57, Santa Cruz de Tenerife 822/104325 carta.sansebastian57.com/athome Closed Sun.*

★ Tasca El Obispado

$$ | SPANISH | FAMILY | Figurines of the Virgin Mary and other religious paraphernalia line the walls of this eclectic tavern with low ceilings and a cozy, countrified feel. Hand-cut *jamón* (ham) and runny-in-the-center tortillas make wonderful appetizers; save room for the *conejo en salmorejo* (roast rabbit in a paprika-garlic sauce) and homemade desserts. **Known for:** cheery service; rustic decor; one of the best tortillas on the island. *Average main: €22 Calle Herradores 88, La*

Laguna ☎ 922/251450 🌐 www.facebook.com/tascaobispado.

Cool Places to Stay

★ Bahía del Duque

$$$$ | RESORT | FAMILY | Built to resemble a 19th-century Canarian village—complete with a bell tower, Italianate villas, and leafy courtyards—this sprawling luxury resort takes in eight restaurants, five swimming pools, a 24-hour gym, and two tennis courts. **Pros:** warm, helpful staff; good breakfast buffet with made-to-order eggs; bountiful poolside real estate. **Cons:** most pools aren't climatized; leaks in public areas when it rains; overpriced spa. *$ Rooms from: €314 ✉ Av. de Bruselas, Adeje ☎ 922/746932 🌐 www.thetaishotels.com ⇆ 351 rooms 🍴 No Meals.*

★ Bohemia Suites & Spa

$$$ | RESORT | When Swiss architect Pia Smith was tasked with refurbishing the Hotel Apolo, the first hotel on the Playa del Inglés, she reached for the sledgehammer. **Pros:** standout spa and brand-new wellness facilities; most avant-garde cocktail bar in the Canaries; characterful modern decor. **Cons:** garden-view rooms face noisy construction site; poolside waiter service is slow; certain areas undergoing renovation or repair. *$ Rooms from: €240 ✉ Av. Estados Unidos 28, Maspalomas ☎ 928/563400 🌐 www.bohemia-grancanaria.com ⇆ 67 rooms 🍴 Free Breakfast.*

★ Hacienda Cuatro Ventanas

$$$ | HOUSE | Until recently, if you wanted luxury on Tenerife, you had to settle for one of the big-brand resorts in the south—no longer; Cuatro Ventanas, hidden among rolling banana plantations that tumble into the sea, is the kind of place a celebrity might rent to disappear to for a few weeks. **Pros:** highly Instagrammable infinity pool; a world away from the tourist hubbub; high-design interiors. **Cons:** minimum three-night stay; no full-time staff or daily cleaning service; slow Wi-Fi. *$ Rooms from: €200 ✉ Calle Playa del Socorro 1–2, Puerto de la Cruz ☎ 660/866678 🌐 www.haciendacuatroventanas.com ⇆ 4 rooms 🍴 No Meals.*

★ Iberostar Heritage Grand Mencey

$$ | HOTEL | The ancient Guanches' name for their kings was *mencey,* and you'll feel like one at this grand, white stucco-and-marble hotel north of the city center. **Pros:** quiet, leafy neighborhood; well-oiled-machine staff; fairy-tale garden. **Cons:** far from the action; high fees for parking and spa access; no kid-centric areas or programming. *$ Rooms from: €169 ✉ Calle Dr. José Naveiras 38, Santa Crùz de Tenerife ☎ 922/609900 🌐 www.iberostar.com ⇆ 286 rooms 🍴 No Meals.*

★ La Laguna Gran Hotel

$$ | HOTEL | This chic four-star housed in an 18th-century palace opened in 2017. **Pros:** rooftop pool, gym, and bar; varied breakfasts with local items; Michelin-starred restaurant. **Cons:** poor soundproofing; strong-smelling cleaning products; inconsistent service. *$ Rooms from: €110 ✉ Calle Nava y Grimón 18, La Laguna ☎ 922/108080 🌐 www.lalagunagranhotel.com ⇆ 123 rooms 🍴 No Meals.*

★ Veintiuno

$ | HOTEL | This boutique adults-only hotel is a social-media darling, thanks to its drool-worthy rooftop pool overlooking the cathedral. **Pros:** serene and stylish decor; rooftop splash pool; local art and quirky library. **Cons:** noisy ground-floor room; cramped breakfast area; no tea- and coffee-making facilities in entry-level rooms. *$ Rooms from: €120 ✉ Calle Espíritu Santo 21, Las Palmas ☎ 683/369723 🌐 www.hotelveintiuno.com ⇆ 11 rooms 🍴 No Meals.*

Portugal

Don't be fooled by Portugal's size: the landscapes of this small country unfold in astonishing diversity. Squeezed in between Spain and the North Atlantic, its striking topography varies from its mountainous, green interior, to its wild and sweeping coastline, battered by monster waves here, and stretched out over tranquil bays of golden sand there.

Its elemental blessings are far from its only draws. Whether you're admiring azulejo-studded palaces in Lisbon, sipping world-famous port in a Douro Valley bodega, or tucking into hearty *bacalhau-à-brás* in a countryside tasquinha, the Mediterranean culture that runs so deep here, influenced by centuries of migration, never fails to enchant visitors—many of whom continue to return, year after year.

Traces of a Celtic, Roman, and Islamic past are evident on the land, in its people, and their tongue. The long Atlantic coastline means that most of Portugal's tumultuous history has centered on the sea. From the charting of the Azores archipelago in 1427 to their arrival in Japan in 1540, Portuguese explorers unlocked sea routes to southern Africa, India, eastern Asia, and the Americas.

The great era of exploration, known as the *Descobrimentos,* reached its height during the 15th century under the influence of Prince Henry the Navigator. But the next several centuries saw dynastic instability, extravagant spending by monarchs, natural disasters, and foreign invasion.

Order came in the 20th century in the form of a right-wing dictatorship by António de Oliveira Salazar that began in 1933 and lasted more than 40 years, until a near-bloodless coup established democracy in 1974. Portugal remained mostly neutral during World War II, finally allowing the U.S. to use an airbase in the Azores only in 1944.

Today Portugal is politically stable, and its people enjoy the prosperity brought by integration into the European Union (EU). The highway system, in particular, has been overhauled with the help of EU money, making traveling around the region far easier than it once was.

The Alfama, Lisbon

Lisbon's Oldest Neighborhood

Before there was Lisbon, there was Alfama: the neighborhood that miraculously survived the devastating earthquake of 1755, which flattened much of the city. As such, its historic architecture is still largely intact—or rather, it decays in a delightfully rustic way. In spring and summer, the heady aroma of grilled fish, meat, and vegetables wafts through Alfama's buzzing warren of narrow streets and alleyways, along with the sultry sound of fado music—allow them to draw you to the neighborhood's heart, clustered around the 12th-century Sé Cathedral, where pop-up barbecues and bars, packed with locals and tourists alike, are guaranteed to spark a festive mood.

Don't Miss

Although Castelo de São Jorge was constructed by the Moors, the site was previously fortified by Romans and Visigoths. Notice a statue of Dom Afonso Henriques as you pass through the main entrance—his forces in 1147 besieged the castle and drove the Moors from Lisbon. A residence of the kings of Portugal until the 16th century, the palace now contains a museum and a stately restaurant, Casa do Leão, offering dining with spectacular sunset views.

Getting Here

Tram 28 or 12 serves the boundaries of Alfama. The neighborhood is best seen on foot, but beware, as in the rest of the city, the streets are steep and hilly. Getting a little lost is guaranteed, but simply walk downhill to get back to the city center.

Castelo de São Jorge. ✉ *Rua de Santa Cruz do Castelo, Alfama* 🌐 *www.castelodesaojorge.pt* 🎫 *€10*

Museu Nacional do Azulejo, Lisbon

Portugal's Famous Tiles

Of all Portugal's artistic images, it's the *azulejo* that's perhaps the best known. This centuries-old marriage of glazed ornamental tiles and Portuguese architecture is a match made in heaven, and elaborate designs depicting a variety of religious or pastoral scenes can be seen decorating the facades and interiors of buildings, fountains, or more recently, metro stations, throughout the country. It's thought that the Moors introduced the tiles to Iberia, and although many are blue, the term "azulejo" may not come from *azul*, the Portuguese word for that color, but rather from the Arabic *az-zulayj* (little stones).

Don't Miss

In Lisbon's Museu do Azulejo you can trace the development of tiles in Portugal from their beginnings to the present day. Housed in the 16th century Madre de Deus convent and cloister, the museum displays a range of both individual glazed tiles and elaborate pictorial panels. The 118-foot-long *Panorama of Lisbon* (1730) is a detailed study of the city and its waterfront, and is reputedly the country's longest azulejo mosaic. The richly furnished convent church contains some sights of its own: of note are the gilt baroque decoration and lively azulejo works depicting the life of St. Anthony.

Getting Here

The Museu do Azulejo is situated on the waterfront, easily reachable from the center of town on foot. The nearest train station is Santa Apolónia.

✉ *Rua da Madre de Deus 4* ☎ *218/100–340* 🌐 *www.museudoazulejo.gov.pt* 🎫 *€5* 🕒 *Closed Mon.* 🚆 *Blue line to Santa Apolónia*

Palácio Nacional da Pena, Sintra

Sintra's Fairy-Tale Castle

This fairy-tale castle, completed in 1885 by German architect Baron Wilhelm Ludwig von Eschwege, is undoubtedly Sintra's biggest draw. Formerly the residence of King Ferdinand II and Queen Maria II, it's set in the lofty Serra de Sintra, and is a glorious conglomeration of turrets and domes awash in pastels, whose interior is decorated with a flamboyant collection of Victorian and Edwardian furniture, ornaments, and paintings. The grounds are a sprawling maze of plants from every corner of the globe, hidden temples, greenhouses, and ethereal grottoes. The dreamlike Valley of the Lakes, the highlight of the grounds, is where swans glide eerily dark waters, shaded by towering trees.

Don't Miss

There are exceptional views of the Serra de Sintra and the North Atlantic from The Queen's Terrace. To the south, spot the Cruz Alta (High Cross), set on the Serra de Sintra's highest point, 528 meters above sea level, and on the left, an enormous statue of a knight (thought to be Baron Eschwege).

Getting Here

Sintra is easy and fast to reach by train from Lisbon. From there it's an arduous uphill walk, or, catch Bus 434. It's not recommended to drive in the center of Sintra: the roads are busy, winding, and narrow, and parking is extremely limited. The palace can get very busy: arrive as it opens to avoid the crowds. The park, however, remains quiet throughout the day.

Estrada da Pena. ☎ *219/237–300*
🌐 *www.parquesdesintra.pt*
🎫 *€14 palace and park, €8 park only*

Food in the Alentejo

Portugal's Gastronomic Heart

Alentejano cuisine is considered Portugal's best, with centuries-old farming practices that were organic long before it was trendy. As it's dubbed the country's granary, bread here is a major part of meals. It's the basis of a popular dish known as *açorda*, a thick, stick-to-your-ribs porridge to which various ingredients such as fish, meat, and eggs are added. *Cação*, also called baby shark or dogfish, is a white-meat fish mostly served in soup or porridge. Serpa cheese is one of Portugal's most renowned, which is tangy, but mellow when properly ripened. Alentejo wines—especially those from Borba, Reguengos de Monsaraz, and Vidigueira—are regular prize-winners at national tasting contests. Elvas is known for its tasty sugar plums. They were exported to England and the Americas, where they became a popular Christmas sweet.

Don't Miss

Alentejo's most prized product is *porco preto*—the pork of free-range black pigs that graze on acorns under Alentejo's famous cork trees. It's often served in the classic dish, *carne de porco à alentejana*.

When to Go

April to June is a wonderful time to visit, when fields are full of wildflowers. July and August are brutally hot, but by mid-September things cool off considerably.

Getting Here and Around

Évora (the regional capital) and Beja are connected to Lisbon by buses and trains daily, which take under two hours. Getting around the region is best by bus or car.

Alentejo Tourism. 🌐 *www.visitalentejo.pt*

Rotas dos Vinhos do Alentejo. 🌐 *www.vinhosdoalentejo.pt*

The Giant Waves of Nazaré

The World's Biggest Waves

Nazaré is the surf capital of Portugal, famed for its monster winter waves that form thanks to an underground canyon north of the town, which attracts the most daredevil of surfers. The best place to view the waves—and any surfers up to the challenge—is from the ancient cliff-top fortress of Forte de São Miguel Arcanjo. Nazaré offers plenty of appeal for less-adventurous visitors, too. The beachfront boulevard is lined with restaurants and bars, and in summer the broad, sandy beach is suitable for swimming. The *sete saias Nazarenas* or "seven skirts Nazarean women," can be seen all around the town, dressed in colorful mismatching attire and, of course, wearing seven skirts, said to represent biblical and magical concepts including the seven virtues, the seven colors of the rainbow, or the seven waves of the sea.

Don't Miss

It's on Praia do Norte that German surfer Sebastian Steudtner hit a world record in 2020 for surfing an 86-foot wave. See his surfboard, as well as others donated by big wave surfers including that of previous record-holder Garrett McNamara, at the Nazaré Surfer Wall, located in Farol de Nazaré, within the Forte de São Miguel Arcanjo fortress.

When to Go

The giant wave season begins in November and ends in February, and that's when surfers come here. In summer, the beaches draw another variety of tourists seeking out the sun and sand.

Getting Here

Nazaré can be reached by bus or train from Lisbon, but buses are faster, taking under two hours.

Peneda-Gerês National Park

Portugal's Only National Park

The 172,900-acre Peneda-Gerês National Park, situated on the border with Spain, was created in 1970 to preserve the region's rare species, which includes golden eagles, Iberian wolves, wild cats, and many other rare flora and fauna. It remains Portugal's only national park and protected area, and has a multitude of marked trails. Even a short trip allows for gentle grass mountains, medieval villages, and thermal baths to unfurl before you, with plenty of opportunities for swimming and hiking. The park's headquarters is in Braga, but you can get a map of the more than 30 marked trails at any local tourism office in the surrounding towns.

Don't Miss

The park also has a rich historic and cultural heritage. There are Roman roads, castles, granaries, mills, and dams to explore, as well as a megalithic necropolis. Many ancient traditions are still practiced at one of its medieval villages.

Best Activities

A wide range of single and multiday tours can be booked with National Park Tours, which include pick-up from Porto or Braga.

Getting Here

The national park has three main sections and is most easily explored by car. The southern, most easily accessible part is a two-hour drive from Braga. The central region is accessible from Ponte da Barca, or from Arcos de Valdevez. The northern region, encompassing the Serra da Peneda, is best approached from Melgaço.

National Park Tours. 🌐 *www.nationalparktours.pt*

Peneda-Gerês National Park. ✉ *Sede do Parque Nacional, Av. António Macedo, Braga* ☎ *253/203–480* 🌐 *www.natural.pt*

The Port Wine Trail, Porto

The Nectar of the Douro Valley

Portugal's finest producers of port wine operate in and around the Douro Valley, near the city of Porto (which is how it got its name). It's often served with dessert, and varieties range from the citrusy white to more caramel, as well as those with nutty aromas, like the "tawny" and "ruby." Can't choose? Explore every flavor in the city of Vila Nova de Gaia, headquarters of the port wine trade since the late-17th century. You can spend the whole day visiting and sampling the wines, but Porto Cálem, one of the biggest names, may also be the best.

Don't Miss

A vineyard visit is a must. Quinta Do Vallado, established in 1716, is one of the oldest quintas in the Douro Valley. It once belonged to Antónia Adelaide Ferreira, a woman known for her leadership in port wine cultivation. Tours, tastings, and workshops take place year-round. Like many other quintas throughout the region, it also has rooms for guests.

Best Restaurant

Taylor's Barão Fladgate. Some bodegas also have restaurants with sophisticated menus; this one has a garden and terrace with magnificent views of Porto. ✉ *Rua do Choupelo 250* 🌐 *www.tresseculos.pt*

Getting Here and Around

Vila Nova de Gaia is short bus journey from Porto. Bodegas are signposted and within a few minutes' walk of each other. Quinta Do Vallado, 122 km (76 miles) east of Vila Nova de Gaia, is best reached by car.

Porto Cálem. ✉ *Av. Diogo Leite, 344, Vila Nova de Gaia* 🌐 *tour.calem.pt* 🎫 *€13 tour and tasting* 🚊 *Jardim do Morro*

Quinta Do Vallado. ✉ *Vilarinho dos Freires* ☎ *254/323–147* 🌐 *www.quintado-vallado.com*

Coimbra

A Historic University Town

Coimbra, Portugal's one-time capital, is a city that oozes history. Its renowned university is one of the oldest in Europe, dating from the 16th century. The latter is where the majority of the city's highlights reside, from the jaw-dropping 18th-century library, Biblioteca Joanina, and the azulejo-bedecked Capela de São Miguel; to the sprawling botanic gardens, and physics lab, the Cabinet of Curiosities. Beyond the university, medieval marvels dot every cobbled street corner, and students can be seen marching to and from class in their traditional black capes. Providing the soundtrack for it all is Coimbra's sorrowful brand of fado, whose somber tones you can hear reverberating from one of many fado houses.

Don't Miss

For a little more history, head to Conímbriga, whose extraordinary mosaics, fountains, and baths make it Portugal's best-preserved Roman site. The most intact villa here is the 3rd-century House of the Fountains, covered with mosaics depicting Perseus offering the head of Medusa to a monster from the deep.

Getting Here and Around

Coimbra is easy to reach from Porto or Lisbon, with regular trains and buses, each taking around two hours. The hilltop university is a steep uphill walk, but it's served by the number 34 bus. Getting to Conímbriga is by bus, which takes 45 minutes.

Conímbriga. ✉ *Rua das Ruinas 7, Condeixa-a-Velha* 🌐 *www.conimbriga.gov.pt* 🕙 *Closed Sat.* 🎟 *€5*

Universidade de Coimbra. ✉ *Largo da Porta Férrea* 🌐 *visit.uc.pt/turismo* 🎟 *€13 (includes all university ticketed sights; limited number of library visitors allowed daily)*

When in Portugal

Aveiro

TOWN | The canals and lagoons in and around the old port of Aveiro are steeped in tradition, closely tied both to the sea and to the Ria de Aveiro—the vast, shallow lagoon that fans out to the north and west of town, from where salt is extracted and kelp harvested for use as fertilizer. Swan-neck *moliceiros* (kelp boats) glide along canals that run through the center, leading to the town to be called "little Venice". The best place for viewing is along the Canal Central and Canal de São Roque, crossed by several attractive bridges. On the banks, to the west of these canals, are checkerboard fields of gleaming, white salt pans. In much of the older part of town, sidewalks and squares are paved with *calçada* (traditional Portuguese hand-laid pavement) in intricate nautical patterns. The town's most attractive buildings showcase the art nouveau style that has made Aveiro celebrated by architecture fans around the world. The old fishermen's quarter, just off the main canal, has been turned into a delightful little area of small bars and restaurants ✉ *Aveiro* 🌐 *visitportugal.com.*

Paiva Walkways

TRAIL | This zigzag wooden walkway along the Paiva River offering scenic views of the river and the Arouca Geopark is widely celebrated. From start to finish, the 8-km-long (5-mile-long) trail hike takes about 2½ hours and allows visitors to experience the surrounding landscape—waterfalls, granite cliffs, endangered species, five geosites—without disrupting it. There's river beach access from the walkway, in case you want to take a dip, and there's a suspension bridge that provides amazing views. You can access the walkway from either Espiunca or Areinho. **■ TIP→ While there are cafés located at both ends of the trail, make sure you pack enough water and snacks and wear comfortable walking shoes as this is a strenuous hike, requiring you to climb a lot of stairs.** ✉ *Arouca Geopark, Arouca, Ovar* ☎ *256 940 258* 🌐 *www.passadicos-dopaiva.pt.*

★ **Parreirinha de Alfama**

LIVE MUSIC | This little club has been owned by fado legend Argentina Santos since the 1960s, and although she no longer sings, she sits by the door most nights greeting newcomers and listening to other highly rated singers. Chef Jaqueline Silva ensures the food, which includes rich seafood stews and other traditional dishes, is as appealing as the music. ✉ *Beco do Espírito Santo 1, Alfama* ☎ *218 868 209* 🌐 *www.parreirinhadealfama.com* Ⓜ *Blue Line to Santa Apolónia.*

Praia do Camilo

BEACH | They say the best things come in small packages, and that's certainly the case here. A short way beyond Praia de Dona Ana, little Praia do Camilo is a hugely popular cove. Just beyond it is the Ponta da Piedade, a much-photographed group of rock arches and grottoes. Praia do Camilo is accessed via a long, wooden walkway through picturesque cliffs. At the top of the cliff restaurant O Camilo offers stunning views over the beach, and serves great oysters. **Amenities:** none. **Best for:** snorkeling. ✉ *South of Praia Dona Ana, Lagos.*

★ **Sir Henry Cotton Championship Golf Course**

GOLF | On what was once a flat, uninteresting rice paddy, Sir Henry Cotton created his most famous course. It is considered his masterpiece because of the beautiful setting he created by planting more than 100,000 trees. Cotton held court here for years, welcoming the great and good from the golf world to the lavish resort. The course has had a face-lift and remains a stern test of your skills—the par-3 13th hole has been ranked among the best in the world. Although the course gets busy, golfers on different holes seldom come into contact due

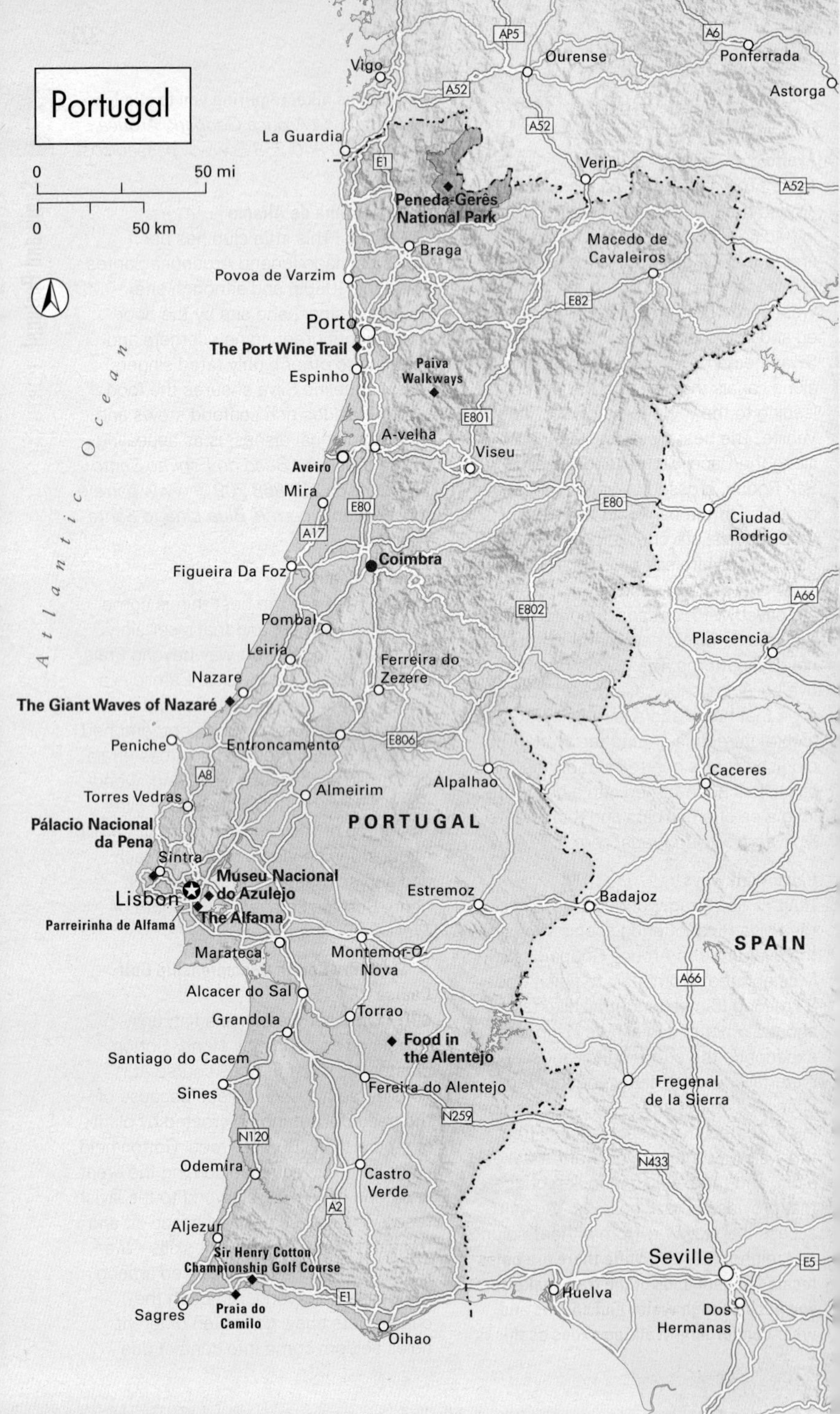

Portugal
0
50 mi
0
50 km
Atlantic Ocean
AP5
A6
Vigo
Ourense
Ponferrada
Astorga
A52
La Guardia
E1
Verin
A52
Peneda-Gerês National Park
Macedo de Cavaleiros
Braga
Povoa de Varzim
E82
Porto
The Port Wine Trail
Paiva Walkways
Espinho
E801
A-velha
Viseu
Aveiro
Mira
E80
A17
Ciudad Rodrigo
Coimbra
Figueira Da Foz
A66
E802
Pombal
Plascencia
Leiria
Ferreira do Zezere
Nazare
The Giant Waves of Nazaré
Peniche
Entroncamento
E806
Caceres
A8
Alpalhao
Torres Vedras
Almeirim
PORTUGAL
Pálacio Nacional da Pena
Sintra
Museu Nacional do Azulejo
Lisbon
Estremoz
Badajoz
Parreirinha de Alfama
The Alfama
SPAIN
Marateca
Montemor-O-Nova
A66
Alcacer do Sal
Torrao
Grandola
Food in the Alentejo
Santiago do Cacem
Fregenal de la Sierra
Sines
Fereira do Alentejo
N259
N120
N433
Odemira
Castro Verde
A2
Aljezur
Sir Henry Cotton Championship Golf Course
Seville
E5
Huelva
E1
Sagres
Praia do Camilo
Dos Hermanas
Oihao

to the mature trees and wide fairways. Penina Hotel & Golf Resort guests are entitled to special green fee rates. On the championship course, a handicap of 28 is required for men and 36 for women to play. *Penina Hotel & Golf Resort, N125, Alvor 282 420 200 penina.com €150 18 holes, 6860 yds, par 73.*

Where to Eat and Drink

★ Belcanto

$$$$ | PORTUGUESE | With two Michelin stars, Belcanto is another jewel in the crown of celebrity chef José Avillez and is one of Lisbon's most celebrated restaurants. Widely credited with putting Avillez (and Portuguese cuisine) on the culinary world stage, the restaurant uses the latest gastronomic techniques to update traditional dishes. **Known for:** tasting menus and chef's table experience; huge list of the finest regional wines; witty presentations. *$ Average main: €55 Rua Serpa Pinto 10A, Chiado 213 420 607 belcanto.pt Closed Sun. and Mon. M Blue or Green Line to Baixa-Chiado.*

★ Fialho

$$$ | PORTUGUESE | The charming elderly owner, Amor Fialho, is the third generation of Fialhos to operate this popular restaurant. He has handed off daily operations to his children, Helena and Rui, but he's still present most evenings in the kitchen, and has been known to give foreign visitors a tour, pointing out photos of the former Spanish king's visit. **Known for:** wide selection of Alentejo wines; homemade sweets for dessert; game dishes like partridge and lamb. *$ Average main: €25 Travessa das Mascarenhas 14, Évora 266 703 079 restaurantefialho.pt Closed Mon.*

★ Majestic Café

$$$ | CAFÉ | Full of art nouveau grandeur—think leaded-glass doorways, elaborately carved woodwork, and ornate chandeliers—the Majestic Café has been the preferred hangout of Portugal's intellectual and social elite since the 1920s. After years of neglect, it was restored to its former glory and is once again an elegant place for coffee, cakes, and evening piano music. **Known for:** Belle Epoque grandeur; famous afternoon tea with sandwiches and scones; indulgent breakfasts with a flute of sparkling wine. *$ Average main: €25 Rua de Santa Catarina 112, Baixa 222 003 887 www.cafemajestic.com Closed Sun. M Bolhão.*

★ Memmo Alfama Terrace

$$ | PORTUGUESE | The terrace at the chic Memmo Alfama Hotel has some of the neighborhood's best views, with tables and chairs arranged around a small infinity pool overlooking the city and the river. The menu centers around tapas-style small plates—the selection of Portuguese cheeses and meats, served with a basket of fresh-baked bread, is a good place to start. **Known for:** popular weekend brunch; fantastic sunset views; creative house cocktails. *$ Average main: €18 Memmo Alfama Hotel, Travessa das Merceeiras 27, Alfama 964 150 453 www.memmohotels.com/alfama/the-terrace M Blue Line to Terreiro do Paço.*

★ Noélia e Jerónimo

$$$$ | PORTUGUESE | From the outside, owner Noélia's restaurant (which she shares with her partner, Jerónimo) looks like just another unassuming local place, but inside the flavors sing and the senses are delighted, particularly with the tomato rice with seafood or, to be even more indulgent, the rice with champagne and local oysters. Make reservations, or be prepared to wait. **Known for:** beautifully presented dishes; draws foodies from all over; open-air dining room. *$ Average main: €35 Rua da Fortaleza, Edifício Cabanas-Mar, Loja 6, Tavira 281 370 649 Closed Wed.*

★ Tasquinha do Oliveira

$$ | PORTUGUESE | The charming husband-and-wife duo of Manuel and Carolina Oliveira own and operate this tiny upscale dining room with huge taste. There are only 14 seats in the entire restaurant, creating the atmosphere of a family dining room. **Known for:** delicious codfish fritters and other favorites; excellent selections of Alentejo wines; warm service. *$ Average main: €18 ✉ Rua Cándido dos Reis 45-A, Évora ☎ 266 744 841 ⊗ Closed Sun. and early Aug.*

Cool Places to Stay

★ Hotel Infante Sagres

$$$ | HOTEL | Intricately carved wood, beautiful rugs and tapestries, heavenly stained-glass windows, and a vintage elevator make Porto's first luxury hotel still a standout today. **Pros:** fashion-themed Vogue Cafe has art deco fabulousness; great views from upper floors, sundeck, and pool; full of historic charm. **Cons:** some rooms get street noise; in a very busy area; small pool. *$ Rooms from: €242 ✉ Praça D. Filipa de Lencastre 62, Baixa ☎ 223 398 500 ⊕ www.infantesagres.com ⇨ 85 rooms ǀ◎ǀ Free Breakfast Ⓜ Aliados.*

★ Lawrence's Hotel

$$$ | B&B/INN | The oldest lodging on the Iberian peninsula, this 18th-century grande dame has hosted such illustrious guests as Lord Byron and, more recently, Queen Beatrix of the Netherlands (as well as one former U.S. president who is rumored to be a regular guest). **Pros:** terrace restaurant has spectacular views; light meals served in the cozy bar; lovely gardens. **Cons:** no gym or swimming pool; some rooms are small; decor can feel twee. *$ Rooms from: €210 ✉ Rua Consiglieri Pedroso 38–40, Sintra ☎ 219 105 500 ⊕ lawrenceshotel.com ⇨ 16 rooms ǀ◎ǀ Free Breakfast.*

★ Pestana Palace Lisboa

$$$$ | HOTEL | FAMILY | Madonna based herself at this restored 19th-century palace while house hunting in Lisbon, and it's not hard to see why the Queen of Pop fell in love with the place: the former home of the Marquis of Valle Flôr and its gardens are classified as national monuments, and the elegant property harbors a collection of fine art. **Pros:** dine in the elegant Valle Flôr restaurant; beautiful outdoor and indoor swimming pools; spa offers an exclusive range of treatments. **Cons:** some distance from the major attractions; outdoor pool area busy in summer; all this luxury doesn't come cheap. *$ Rooms from: €275 ✉ Rua Jau 54, Ajuda ☎ 213 615 600 ⊕ www.pestanacollection.com/en/hotel/pestana-palace ⇨ 193 rooms ǀ◎ǀ Free Breakfast.*

★ Pousada da Rainha Santa Isabel

$$ | HOTEL | If there's one pousada in all of Portugal that you splurge on, this should be it; dubbed the "museum of all pousadas," this hotel is housed in the medieval Castelo de Estremoz. **Pros:** an architectural gem; a favorite for history buffs; great breakfast selection. **Cons:** few activities for children; decor might not be to everyone's taste; pricey restaurant. *$ Rooms from: €175 ✉ Largo D. Dinis 1, Estremoz ☎ 268 332 075 ⊕ pousadas.pt ⇨ 33 rooms ǀ◎ǀ Free Breakfast.*

★ Quinta das Lágrimas

$$ | HOTEL | FAMILY | The gardens of this elegant castle are part of Portuguese history: it was here where Pedro, son of King Afonso IV, and Inês de Castro, lady in waiting to the royal court, met secretly and fell deeply in love. **Pros:** fairy-tale setting in the truest sense; scrumptuous breakfast buffet; restaurant, pools, golf course, and Turkish bath and sauna on-site. **Cons:** a bit far from city center attractions; some rooms a bit small and boxy; visitors to gardens walk directly past some rooms. *$ Rooms from: €198 ✉ Rua António Augusto Gonçalves, Coimbra ☎ 239 802 380 ⊕ quintadaslagrimas.pt ⇨ 57 rooms ǀ◎ǀ Free Breakfast.*

Madeira and the Azores

The islands of Madeira and the Azores are among Portugal's most enchanting regions. The islands (as well as the even more remote Cape Verde Islands) became Portuguese possessions in 1480 with the signing of the Treaty of Alcáçovas-Toledo, which also gave Spain ownership of the Canary Islands.

Madeira, made up of a series of dramatic volcanic peaks rising from the sea, lies around 600 km (373 miles) off the west coast of Morocco, ensuring an alluring, balmy year-round temperature. The natural beauty of this island is like no other, from the cliffs that plummet seaward to mountain summits cloaked in silent fog. You'll find everything from black-sand beaches to thundering waterfalls, manicured gardens to wild, rugged volcanos. It's a place for hiking, but also for relaxing on the beach; a place for gorging yourself on seafood, and then working it off with a swim in the ocean. Wine connoisseurs have always savored Madeira's eponymous export, but a sip of this heady elixir provides only a taste of the island's many delights. Other draws include the carpets of flowers, the waterfalls that cascade down green canyons, and the great hiking along the island's famous network of *levadas*, former irrigation channels turned walking trails.

The enchanting Azores archipelago consists of nine volcanic islands spread over about 600 km (370 miles) in the Atlantic Ocean, roughly 2,454 km (1,525 miles) from North America and 1,600 km (994 miles) from the Portuguese mainland. The Azores offer green, rolling hills straight out of Ireland blended with the dramatic volcanic landscapes and hot springs of Iceland and the black sand beaches and lush greenery of Hawaii—all in one. Nature lovers come to witness the stunning beauty of the isles, with their volcanoes, natural swimming holes, and—in spring—millions of wild, blooming hydrangeas. More adventurous travelers take advantage of the hiking, world-class fishing, and excellent whale-watching available. Still others come for a brief glimpse into a simpler life that is rarely seen today in mainland Europe.

Parque Terra Nostra, Azores

Lush Gardens and Volcanic Hot Springs

These sprawling gardens within the Furnas Valley in the Azorean island of São Miguel sit atop a gigantic volcanic crater, much like Yellowstone National Park in the United States. The park dates back to 1775, when Boston merchant Thomas Hickling built a summer house called Yankee Hall, planted trees brought in from North America, and constructed the thermal water pool, still a highlight of the park today. The gardens were enlarged in the mid-19th century, adding Australian King and Canary Islands palm trees and other imported species, all still thriving today. The garden is particularly well known for its collections of camellias, cycadales, and ferns, as well as its thermal pool, which is an orange-brown color due to its high iron content.

Don't Miss

The nearby Poça da Dona Beija Hot Springs features rustic hot springs surrounded by greenery. There are four stone pools with water at 39°C, some with waterfall features, and one cooler pool with 28°C water.

Best Restaurant

Terra Nostra Garden Restaurant. It seems like everyone at this old-school restaurant is here to partake of the signature dish: *cozido nas Caldeiras das Furnas*, stew cooked underground in the hot springs. ✉ *Terra Nostra Garden Hotel, Rua Padre Jose Jacinto Botelho 5, Furnas* 🌐 *www.terranostra-gardenhotel.com*

Parque Terra Nostra. ✉ *Rua Padre Jose Jacinto Botelho, Furnas* 🌐 *www.parqueterranostra.com* 🎫 *€8*

Poça da Dona Beija Hot Springs. ✉ *Lomba das Barracas* 🌐 *www.pocadonabeija.com*

Lagoa dos Sete Cidades, Azores

The Most Photographed Sight in the Azores

The caldeira das Sete Cidades, an enormous volcanic crater on the Azorean island of São Miguel that collapsed during a prehistoric eruption, is truly an unmissable sight. The major attractions within the crater are the stunning Lagoa das Sete Cidades (Sete Cidades Lakes). The Blue and Green Lakes (Lagoa Azul and Lagoa Verde) can be seen from a variety of viewpoints. If at all possible, visit on a clear day, when one lake appears to be robin's egg blue and the other jade green. The best way to see the lakes is from one of the vantage points high above, especially Vista do Rei. The viewpoint at Boca do Inferno offers what many visitors consider an even better view, overlooking not only the lakes, but also the entire volcano-shape landscape.

Don't Miss

Drive farther down the west coast to stop at Ponta da Ferraria, which differs from the other natural hot springs on São Miguel because it's actually in the ocean. Surrounded by basalt cliffs, the cold ocean water mixes with the hot thermal water to create a unique bathing experience—just keep an eye on the tides, as at high tide, the waters can feel chilly, while at low tide they can be steamy. But time it right, and you'll never want to leave.

Lagoa dos Sete Cidades. ✉ *Sete Cidades* ✣ *27 km (17 miles) northwest of Ponta Delaga, about a 40-minute drive* 🌐 *visitazores.com*

Ponta da Ferraria. ✉ *Rua Padre Fernando Vieira Gomes 11, Sete Cidades* 🎫 *Free*

Carreiros do Monte, Madeira

Exhilarating Urban Sledding

The village of Monte is home to one of Madeira's oldest and most eccentric attractions: a snowless sled ride down the mountain. The toboggan sleds were first created to carry supplies from Monte to Funchal. Nowadays the rides are just for fun, and no visitor to Madeira should miss out on this white-knuckle adventure. Dressed in white and wearing goatskin boots with soles made of rubber tires, drivers line up on the street below the Igreja de Nossa Senhora do Monte. Resembling big wicker baskets, the sleds have wooden runners that are greased with pig fat so they'll go even faster. Two drivers run alongside the sled, controlling it with ropes as it races downhill on a 10-minute trip halfway to Funchal. At the end of the ride, there are several souvenir shops where you can pick up a photograph of yourself taken by a sneaky photographer.

Don't Miss

Close to the sled ride, the colorful Monte Palace Tropical Garden is known around the world, and for good reason. Tiled panels recall the adventures of Portuguese explorers, pagodas and gateways lend touches of Asia, and cannons pour their salvos of water from a stone galleon in a lake.

Getting Here

Take the cable car from Funchal, Bus 20, 21, or 48, or a short taxi ride up to Monte.

Carreiros do Monte. ✉ *Caminho do Monte 4, Monte* 🌐 *www.carreirosdo-monte.com* 🎟 *€30*

Monte Palace Tropical Garden. ✉ *Caminho do Monte 174, Monte* 🌐 *montepalacemadeira.com* 🎟 *€13*

Piscinas Naturais do Porto Moniz, Madeira

Otherworldly Sea Pools

Madeira's northernmost village of Porto Moniz is one of the island's best day trips. Though not a beach per se, the unique natural sea pools are one of the most popular sights in Madeira, with children and adults splashing in the waters around the volcanic rocks or soaking up some sun on the concrete "beach." There are pools of varying sizes, some shallow and calm (perfect for kids) and some deeper and rougher for more adventurous types (one even has a diving board). You can rent deck chairs and umbrellas and dine at the snack bar during the summer months. The water here is significantly colder than elsewhere on the island.

Don't Miss

About 12 km (7 miles) south of Porto Moniz is the Achadas da Cruz cable car—an engineering marvel that transports visitors down the almost vertical drop to the windswept farming area of Fajã da Quebrada Nova. Before the cable car was built, the only way to get there was by boat. The tiny carriages operate only when needed, so press the button to confirm you're ready to go. At the bottom, you'll find a truly beautiful part of Madeira, with wind-contoured fields, black-stone beaches, deafening waves, and a tangle of grape vines used for local winemaking.

Getting Here

Porto Moniz is 50 km (31 miles) northwest of Funchal, about a 55-minute drive.

Piscinas Naturais do Porto Moniz. ✉ *Rua do Lugar, Porto Moniz* 🌐 *www.portomoniz.pt* 🎫 *€3*

Teleférico das Achadas da Cruz. ✉ *Caminho do Teleférico, Achadas da Cruz* 🌐 *www.portomoniz.pt* 🎫 *€3*

Sampling Madeira Wine, Madeira

The Island's Famed Libation

Madeira has long been known for its namesake fortified wine. Producers throughout the island create their own Madeira; the most well-known is the Blandy family, who has been making Madeira wine for more than 200 years. At Blandy's Wine Lodge in Funchal, visitors can hear how the wine is made, visit the cellars, and listen to tales about Madeira wine from knowledgeable guides. There's plenty of time for a generous tasting at the end of the visit. Another lovely place to try Madeira wine with a meal—and to spend the night—is Quinta do Furão, in Madeira's north. In the autumn, you can help out with the harvest.

Don't Miss

Fajã dos Padres (✉ *Rua Padres António Dinis Henrique 1, Quinta Grande* 🌐 *fajadospadres.com*), about a 15-minute drive west of Funchal, is a self-proclaimed "island within Madeira island" between Câmara de Lobos and Ribeira Brava, only accessible by a steep, though short, cable car ride. Spend a few hours touring the fascinating organic farm and vineyards and enjoying lunch at the charming restaurant, which serves authentic and inexpensive local food and their homemade Madeira wine.

Getting Here

Blandy's Wine Lodge is an easy walk to the center of Funchal. Quinta do Furão is a 45-km (28-mile) drive north of Funchal.

Blandy's Wine Lodge. ✉ *Av. Arriaga 28, Funchal* ☎ *291/228–978* 🌐 *www.blandyswinelodge.com* 🎫 *Guided tours with tastings from €11*

Quinta do Furão. ✉ *Estrada da Quinta do Furão nº 6, Santana* ☎ *291/ 570–100* 🌐 *www.quintadofurao.com*

When in Madeira and the Azores

★ Algar do Carvão

CAVE | FAMILY | Climb deep inside an extinct volcano at this 1,804-foot volcanic cave located toward the middle of Terceira. You'll be guided 148 feet down a set of stairs to the floor of the cavern before descending another 115 feet to a crystal clear lake fed by rainwater (which completely disappears during dry summers). Though the stairs are on the steep side, they have handrails and are not challenging to descend or ascend—just be sure to dress warmly, as the cave becomes colder and wetter the farther down you go. Along the way you'll see unique stalactites and stalagmites. Opening times vary depending on the season, but are generally limited to a few hours in the afternoons, so check before you go. ✉ *Estrada Algar Do Carvao* ✥ *11 km (7 miles) from Angra do Heroísmo* ☎ *295 212 992* 🌐 *www.montanheiros.com* 🎫 *€8; €12 with Grutal do Natal* ⏲ *Closed Mon., Thurs., and Sun. Oct.–Mar.*

★ Cabo Girão

VIEWPOINT | FAMILY | At 1,900 feet, Cabo Girão is on one of the highest sea cliffs in the world, and the observation platform—with a clear glass floor so you can gaze straight down—gives you a bird's-eye view down to the coast. From here you can see the ribbons of terraces carved out of steep slopes where farmers daringly cultivate grapes and garden vegetables. During high season, the walkway can get crowded with bus tours, so get there early if you want to beat the crowds. ✉ *Estrada do Cabo Girão* 🎫 *Free.*

★ Caldeira

VOLCANO | Located toward the center of the island (and therefore best accessed by car), this stunning ancient volcanic crater with a diameter of 2 km (more than 1 mile) and a depth of 1,312 feet started forming at least 400,000 years ago, with the last volcanic event taking place 1,000 years ago. There's a scenic viewpoint to snap a few pictures, or opt for the fairly easy hike around the 7-km (4-mile) circular trail that winds around the rim's perimeter; there are some narrow sections, so bring your hiking shoes. The perimeter walk takes two to three hours to complete and offers lovely views of the lush laurel forest and, if you're lucky and the day is clear, to Mt. Pico in the distance. ✥ *15 km (9¼ miles) northwest of Horta* 🎫 *Free.*

★ Eira do Serrado

VIEWPOINT | FAMILY | About 16 km (10 miles) northwest of Funchal, this *miradouro* (viewpoint) overlooks the Grande Curral, once thought to be the crater of a long-extinct volcano in the center of the island. Local legend says the surrounding peaks are the fortress of a princess who wanted to live in the clouds so badly that her father—the volcano god—caused an earthquake that pushed the rocky cliffs high into the sky. Today the views are breathtaking in all directions; you can appreciate them even more if you stay the night or dine at the panoramic Eira do Serrado Hotel & Spa. If you are driving here from Funchal, head north toward Curral das Freiras and turn at the sign for Eira do Serrado. The roads do get a little narrow and nerve-wracking at times, but they're worth embracing for the view. ✉ *Off Route 107, Curral das Freiras* ☎ *291 710 060 hotel* 🌐 *www.eiradoserrado.com* 🎫 *Free.*

★ Montanha do Pico (*Mt. Pico*)

MOUNTAIN | Visible from many locations around Pico—unless it's shrouded in fog and clouds, as is often the case—and even more visible from across the water in Faial, 7,713-foot Mt. Pico is the highest mountain in Portugal. Past eruptions have occurred on its flanks rather than from the summit, the most recent back in 1720. If you want to hike up Mt. Pico, you can start at the Casa da Montanha

Madeira and the Azores Islands

CORVO

Santa Cruz

FLORES

ATLANTIC

SAO JORGE

Velas

Caldeira

FAIAL

Horta

Montanha do Pico

Sao Mateus

PICO

AZORES ISLANDS

OCEAN
Santa Cruz
GRACIOSA
Algar do Carvão
Lajes
TERCEIRA
Sao Sebastiao
Topo
SAO MIGUEL
Mosteiros
Lagoa dos Sete Cidades
Ponta Delgada
Parque Terra Nostra
Fumas
Bar Caloura

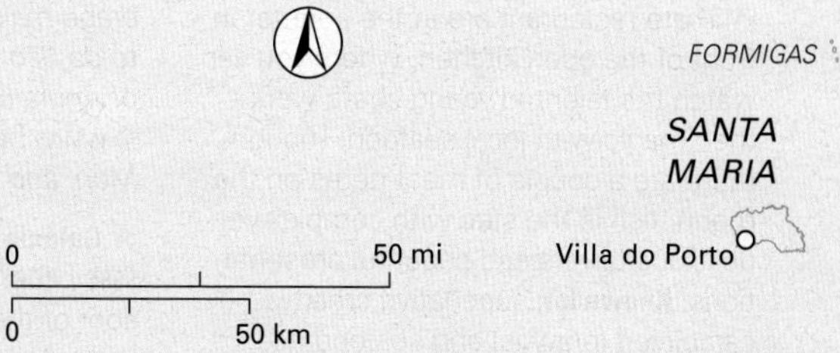
FORMIGAS
SANTA MARIA
Villa do Porto
0
50 mi
0
50 km

(Mountain House) at 4,035 feet. Though it's not a difficult climb, it can still be quite challenging as the path is steep with uneven rocks; depending on your experience level, consider hiring a guide to accompany you. Come early or book online to be guaranteed a hiking spot, as hikers are limited to 120 per day. Bring photo ID to register. ✉ *Casa da Montanha, Caminho Florestal 9, Candelária* ☎ *967 303 519* 🌐 *montanhapico.azores.gov.pt* 🎫 *€15 for hiking permit.*

★ **Teleférico da Madeira** (*Madeira Cable Car*)

TRANSPORTATION | FAMILY | The sleek, Austrian-engineered cable car service travels from Funchal's waterfront up to Monte at 1,804 feet above sea level. The trip takes 15 minutes each way, and there are great views to enjoy as you float silently up and over the city's white-washed houses. The orange roofs form a patchwork from above, complemented by swooping birds of prey, scampering mountain goats, and new blooms on the trees. A great option is to ride the cable car up, then take one of the renowned snowless "basket toboggans" part of the way back down. ✉ *Av. do Mar e das Comunidades Madeirenses,, Funchal* ☎ *291 780 280* 🌐 *madeiracablecar.com* 🎫 *€18 round-trip, €12.50 one-way.*

Where to Eat and Drink

★ **Ákua**

$$$ | SEAFOOD | The best seats in this intimate restaurant are at the counter in front of the open kitchen, where you can watch the talented young chefs work their magic with local seafood. Though there are a couple of meat items on the menu, fish is the star, with complex yet delicious flavors and beautiful presentations. **Known for:** superlative creamy carabinieri (prawns) and seafood rice, and codfish tacos; delicious house-made sourdough bread; attentive and knowledgeable service. [$] *Average main: €23* ✉ *Rua dos Murças 6, Funchal* ☎ *938 034 758* 🌐 *akuafunchal.pt.*

★ **Bar Caloura**

$ | SEAFOOD | FAMILY | It's more than worth a trip 20 km (12 miles) east of Ponta Delgada to dine at this popular open-air seafood restaurant with lovely water views; since the place doesn't take reservations, bring your swimsuit for a dip in the adjacent pool while you wait. The friendly staff will grill up your choice of the fresh local fish on display—perhaps tuna, stingray, or barracuda—but you can't go wrong with baked mussels in a buttery garlic sauce or just-caught limpet, plus (a rarity for the islands) a well-stocked salad bar. **Known for:** the freshest fish around; lively atmosphere; homemade desserts. [$] *Average main: €15* ✉ *Rua da Caloura 20, Água de Pau* ☎ *296 913 283* 🌐 *www.facebook.com/barcaloura.*

★ **Beira Mar São Mateus**

$ | SEAFOOD | Be sure to make reservations for this always-bustling fish and seafood spot—rightfully thought by many to be the best on the island—with pretty views overlooking the marina in the tiny fishing village of São Mateus. You can't go wrong with any of the freshly caught fish (the restaurant has its own fishing boat), along with limpets, slipper lobsters, and barnacles, which you coax from their shells with tiny forks. **Known for:** save room for the gingerbread-like "cake of the Indies"; snappy service keeps things moving along; indoor and outdoor seating with water views. [$] *Average main: €13* ✉ *Canada Porto 46, Porto de São Mateus* ✥ *5 km (3 miles) west of Angra do Heroísmo* ☎ *295 642 392* 🌐 *www.beiramarazores.com* ⏲ *Closed Mon. and 3 wks in Nov.*

★ **Galáxia Skyfood**

$$$$ | PORTUGUESE | Seated on the 16th floor of the Savoy Palace, in a cozy room with painted ceilings, you'll feel like you're dining under the stars—and the food will truly transport you to another world. Chef Carlos Gonçalves serves up innovative five- to seven-course tasting menus (à la carte is also available) using local ingredients but with a twist—think traditional *cozido panelo* (vegetables and sausage) transformed into tasty tacos and creamy rice with nori seaweed and lemon puree. **Known for:** wonderful Portuguese wine pairings; inventive tasting menus; creative desserts using local fruits, such as pineapples and bananas. *Average main: €34* *Savoy Palace, Av. do Infante 23, Funchal* *969 882 020* *www.savoysignature.com* *Closed Mon. No lunch.*

★ Õtaka

$$$$ | ASIAN FUSION | The sophisticated Nikkei-style tasting menus, which mix South American and Japanese style with Azorean ingredients, combined with knowledgeable servers and a welcoming atmosphere (think minimalist wood tables and an open kitchen) add up to one of the finest dining experiences in Ponta Delgada at this always-packed restaurant. Chef José Pereira, who worked for many years in Geneva before heading home to the Azores, uses as many local ingredients as possible in his artfully presented dishes such as crispy nigiri with tuna tartare and Azorean whitefish sashimi with miso and yuzu; his wife Anne Teixeira prepares the decadent tropical desserts. **Known for:** unique takes on Japanese cuisine; exquisite food presentations; Azorean wine pairings. *Average main: €45* *Rua Hintze Ribeiro 5* *919 312 080* *www.facebook.com/restauranteotaka* *Closed Sun. and Mon. No lunch.*

★ The Wanderer

$$$$ | ECLECTIC | For the most unique dining experience in Madeira, head to the ground floor of a nondescript shopping mall, where you'll enter into another world—one only experienced by six lucky diners at a time, who sit communally at one long table. Self-taught Swiss-born chef-owner Selim Latrous, who spent many years in Southeast Asia, incorporates Thai and Indian flavors into his five-course tasting menus; friendly sommelier Christian pairs every dish with unique drinks (either alcoholic or non) while Selim shares the story behind each dish, making for an entertaining and culinarily satisfying evening you won't soon forget. **Known for:** ingredients foraged from throughout Madeira; beautifully presented surprise menus; delightful beverage pairings, including poncha and stout beer. *Average main: €125* *Centro Commercial Olimpo 11, Av. do Infante, Funchal* *915 682 872* *thewanderermadeira.com* *Closed Sun. and Mon. No lunch.*

Cool Places to Stay

★ Aqua Natura Bay

$$ | HOTEL | FAMILY | In the quieter eastern part of town, with a spectacular view of the cliffs, this bright and modern hotel provides a welcome respite from the often tourist-clogged sea pools area, yet is still only a short walk away from the action. **Pros:** room rate includes entrance to sea pools; contemporary furnishings and decor; all rooms have balconies. **Cons:** gym a bit basic; some rooms on the small side; restaurant can feel crowded. *Rooms from: €152* *Rua do Forte de São João Baptista 7* *291 850 150* *www.aquanaturahotels.com* *45 rooms* *Free Breakfast.*

★ Pocinho Bay

$$$ | B&B/INN | FAMILY | Owners Jose and Louisa, former sociologists from Lisbon, have transformed their summer vacation property into a truly unique place to stay, with a collection of six elegant volcanic rock cottages and two sophisticated two-bedroom villas, all decorated with artifacts collected during their extensive travels around the world. **Pros:** beautiful grounds just outside your door; natural rock pool sits nearby; personalized service. **Cons:** somewhat isolated location; no restaurant or bar; no fitness center or spa. $ *Rooms from: €215* ✉ *Pocinho* ✣ *6 km (4 miles) southwest of Madalena* ☎ *292 629 135* 🌐 *www.pocinhobay.com* ⏱ *Closed Dec.–Feb.* 🛏 *6 rooms, 2 villas* 🍽 *Free Breakfast.*

★ **Pousada Forte Angra do Heroísmo**

$ | HOTEL | FAMILY | From the outside, you'd never know that a modern hotel sits inside the walls of a 16th-century fort perched on a hilltop overlooking the sea on the edge of Angra (but only about a 10-minute walk into town); beyond the historical significance, the cool, contemporary guest rooms, outdoor pools and bar, and sea views make the Pousada a great place to spend the night. **Pros:** highly atmospheric place to stay; spacious rooms and bathrooms; quiet location. **Cons:** very small TVs in rooms; no gym; steep walk up and down the hill to town center. $ *Rooms from: €120* ✉ *Rua do Castelinho* ☎ *295 403 560* 🌐 *www.pousadas.pt* 🛏 *29 rooms* 🍽 *Free Breakfast.*

★ **Reid's Palace, A Belmond Hotel, Madeira**

$$$$ | HOTEL | On a rocky point surrounded by 10 acres of gardens, Reid's—which first opened its doors in 1891—is synonymous with luxurious lodgings in Madeira. **Pros:** hotel seems tranquil even when it's busy; solicitous staff caters to your every whim; restaurants have amazing views of the sea. **Cons:** classic decor not to everyone's taste; somewhat confusing layout; extremely pricey. $ *Rooms from: €790* ✉ *Estrada Monumental 139, Funchal* ☎ *291 717 171* 🌐 *www.belmond.com* 🛏 *158 rooms* 🍽 *Free Breakfast.*

★ **Senhora da Rosa**

$$ | HOTEL | FAMILY | On the lovely grounds of an 18th-century farm, this boutique hotel just east of Ponta Delgada offers thoroughly modern comforts including an outdoor pool, spa with sauna and Turkish bath, and pilates reformer room. **Pros:** fun kids' club programs; peaceful location away from urban noise; thoughtful design details. **Cons:** not enough umbrellas near the pool; not walkable to town; Wi-Fi doesn't always work. $ *Rooms from: €171* ✉ *Rua Senhora da Rosa 3* ✣ *4 km (2.5 miles) east of Ponta Delgada* ☎ *296 100 900* 🌐 *www.senhoradarosa.com* 🛏 *35 rooms* 🍽 *Free Breakfast.*

★ **White Exclusive Suites & Villas**

$$$$ | HOTEL | You'll get a taste of modern Azorean volcanic style when stepping inside the sleek black-and-white rooms and chic public spaces in this exclusive 10-room boutique hotel created out of a cluster of 18th-century manor houses perched above the ocean. **Pros:** a 15-minute drive east of Ponta Delgada; unique design for the islands; staff willing to go the extra mile. **Cons:** no gym; can hear outside noise in some rooms; not very child-friendly. $ *Rooms from: €504* ✉ *Rua Rocha Quebrada 10* ✣ *8 km (5 miles) east of Ponta Delgada* ☎ *296 249 153* 🌐 *www.whiteazores.com* 🛏 *10 rooms* 🍽 *Free Breakfast.*

Chapter 6

SCANDINAVIA AND THE BALTIC REGION

WELCOME TO SCANDINAVIA AND THE BALTIC REGION

TOP REASONS TO GO

★ **Great Food (Sweden):** Industry investment, the finest raw ingredients, and a thirst for the exotic have made new Swedish cuisine climb to Europe's heights.

★ **Modern Design (Denmark):** Denmark's capital is *the* place to experience one of the nation's top exports.

★ **Lapland (Finland):** The north of Finland is a world unlike any other and an ideal spot to see the twinkling Northern Lights.

★ **The Fjords (Norway):** The Norwegian fjords are known for their beauty, including the Oslofjord, which runs south from Oslo to the sea, and Geirangerfjord, the most famous.

★ **Geothermal Spas (Iceland):** Bubbling pools dot the Iceland countryside from the famed Blue Lagoon to Húsavík's beloved GeoSea baths.

★ **Art Nouveau (Rīga):** One-third of Latvia's capital is composed of delightful Art Nouveau–style architecture, including stunning Albert Street.

1 Baltic States. Estonia, Latvia and Lithuania are best known for once being Soviet-occupied lands, but their capital cities are charming and full of history.

2 Denmark. The Kingdom of Denmark is an archipelago of some 450 islands, the arc of one peninsula, and the far off lands of the Faroe Islands and Greenland.

3 Finland. Finland's vast tracts of forest add to the feeling of remoteness in this northern land. The capital, Helsinki, shows the influence of both Swedish and Russian dominance.

4 Iceland. The Land of Fire and Ice holds some of the most stunning and rugged landscape on the planet. Reykjavík is the world's most northerly capital.

5 Norway. Long and narrow, Norway is about 30% wilderness. Oslo, the capital, is a friendly, manageable city.

6 Sweden. Bordered by Norway on the west and Finland to the east, Sweden has lush forests covering half the country and a landscape dotted with 100,000 lakes. The capital, Stockholm, is built on 14 small islands.

20°W
0°
20°E
Longyearbyen
SVALBARD
(Norway)
Arctic Ocean
Barents Sea
70°N
JAN
MAYEN
(Norway)
Hammerfest
Vadsl
Murmansk
Alta
Tromsø
Norwegian Sea
Svolvar
Kiruna
Kemijarvi
Bodi
Kemi
Mo i Rana
Lulen
Oulu
RUSSIA
FINLAND
3
SWEDEN
6
Namsos
Umei
Kokkola
Joensuu
Prnskaldsvik
Vaasa
Trondheim
Astersund
Molde
Sundsvall
St.
Petersburg
Tampere
Lahti
NORWAY
5
Turku
Helsinki
Lillehammer
Tallinn
Bergen
Uppsala
Oslo
ESTONIA
Pskov
Haugesund
Stockholm
Skien
Stavanger
Riga
UNITED
KINGDOM
LATVIA
1
Kristiansand
Gdteborg
North Sea
Prime Meridian
LITHUANIA
Vilnius
Prhus
Copenhagen
DENMARK
2
Kaliningrad
Minsk
BELARUS
Gdansk
GERMANY
POLAND

WHAT TO EAT IN SCANDINAVIA AND THE BALTIC REGION

Reindeer

SKOLEBOLLER

"School buns," which feature a custard filling and grated coconut, are so called as they were once a common lunch for schoolchildren.

LOBSTER

In Iceland it is technically called a langoustine, but it's very similar in appearance and flavor to its southerly cousin. There is an annual lobster festival in Höfn.

SKYR

Ever since the first explorers arrived in Iceland 1,000 years ago, yogurt-like skyr has been a staple of the local diet, often with bilberries or lingonberries mixed in.

REINDEER

Many of Scandinavia's indigenous Sámi people still herd reindeer, and you simply can't visit without trying reindeer meat. It's traditionally served with mashed potatoes and cranberry or lingonberry sauce, or in a hot dog.

MEATBALLS

Meatballs are a popular dish throughout the nordic region. In Sweden, *köttbullar* are usually a mix of beef and pork. Finland's *lihapullat* can sometimes incorporate reindeer meat. Danish *frikadeller* are often boiled, minced pork. Norwegian *Kjøttkaker* are thicker and less round than their Swedish counterparts.

ÆBLESKIVER

A holiday classic, these perfectly round baked balls made out of vanilla-flavored pancake dough are a perennial favorite among Danish kids and grown-ups, dipped in jam and powdered sugar.

HERRING
Herring is about as Scandinavian as it gets. You'll find it smoked and fried across the Nordic region, but you have to try fermented herring, *surströmming*, in Sweden and pickled herring in Denmark.

SMØRREBRØD
Open-faced sandwiches, *smørrebrød*, are a must in Denmark. Rye bread is piled high with Danish delicacies such as pickled herring, cold cuts, meatballs, fried fish, and cheese. Typically washed down with beer and aquavit.

FISH SOUP
You'll find a version of creamy fish soup made with hunks of cod and lots of vegetables across the Nordic region.

FRIED VENDACE
One of the most popular snacks in Finland is vendace, a small fish covered in rye flour and fried until it's golden, crispy, and fatty, served with a squeeze of lemon and garlicky mayonnaise.

KNÄCKEBRÖD
Forget bread, it's all about crackers for breakfast or lunch in Sweden. The hard, crackly bread, crispbread, is often topped with butter, cheese, and cold cuts and makes for an excellent picnic lunch.

Lobster

Skoleboller

KOLDSKÅL MED KAMMERJUNKERE
The taste of Danish summers and many a childhood, this type of buttermilk is mixed with eggs, sugar, vanilla, and often lemon and topped with crushed pieces of crispy cookies and, if you're feeling extra Danish, chopped strawberries.

HOT DOGS
Denmark can't claim to have invented the hot dog, but the country has developed a creative take on it. *Pølsevogne* (hot dog carts) are strategically positioned in Danish cities, dishing up grilled sausages in buns, topped with mustard, ketchup, and sometimes remoulade.

STEGT FLÆSK MED PERSILLESOVS
One of the most beloved classics in Danish cuisine, this dish consists of crispy fried pork, boiled potatoes, and creamy parsley sauce.

LEIPÄJUUSTO
Known as Finnish squeaky cheese or bread cheese, this fresh cheese made from cow's milk is traditionally eaten as a dessert topped with cloudberry jam or as a snack on rye crackers or rye bread.

Scandinavia and the Baltic Region Snapshot

Know Before You Go

DRINK TAP WATER.

Some of the world's purest water is found in this pocket of the world. Drink up.

THE NORTHERN LIGHTS ARE NOT GUARANTEED.

The aurora borealis dazzles when the skies are clear and there's lots of solar activity. It happens between autumn and early spring, especially up north in areas with minimal light pollution. It's always a lucky strike—you may just get a couple of green streaks or a full dance of red and purple.

LET IT ALL HANG OUT IN THE SAUNA.

No need to be prudish. Saunas and thermal baths are a big part of the culture, and it's a communal activity—meaning mom, dad, and grandma all sweat it out in the buff together. Be aware that saunas are mostly mixed-sex. You can wrap a towel around you and no one will bother you if you do choose to wear a swimsuit.

Planning Your Time

Scandinavia and the Baltics are absolutely made for road trips, so don't be afraid to grab a car and venture out on your own. Roads are well-maintained and many areas have designated tourist routes, covering the best sites and wonders. A week is a good amount of time to spend in Iceland, Sweden, or Finland, but two weeks is certainly ideal for a country as varied as Norway or a region as vast as the Baltics.

Great Trips

5 days. The Ring Road, Iceland. Reykjavík to Vík to Höfn to Seyðisfjörður to Akureyri to Reykjavík.

3 days. The Faroe Islands. Vágar to Mykines to Streymoy.

4 days. Bergen to Voss to Leon to Molde to Ålesund.

Big Events

Midsummer. A happy time for social gatherings, flowered hair, and maypole dancing in all of Scandinavia.

Reykjavík Pride. An 11-day city-wide celebration and parade in August. 🌐 *www.hinsegindagar.is*

Christmas in Tivoli Gardens. More than a million visitors flock to this pretty Christmas market in Copenhagen. 🌐 *www.tivoli.dk*

What To...

READ

On Time And Water, Andri Snær Magnason

A Doll's House, Henrik Ibsen

*Tales from Moominvalley,*Tove Jansson

My Struggle. Karl Ove Knausgård

WATCH

Rams, Grímur Hákonarson (Icelandic movie filmed in Iceland)

The Kingdom, Lars Von Trier (Danish TV show filmed in Denmark)

Trollhunter, André Øvredal (Norwegian movie filmed in Norway)

The Girl With The Dragon Tattoo, Niels Arden Oplev (Swedish-Danish movie filmed in Sweden)

LISTEN TO

ABBA, *Arrival* (Sweden)

Arvo Pärt, *Tabul a Rosa* (Estonia)

Sigur Rós, *Ágætis byrjun* (Iceland)

Wardruna, *Runaljod - Ragnarok* (Norway)

BUY

Wool sweaters (called *lopapeysa*) in Iceland

Salty licorice in Finland

Wickerwork baskets in the Baltic countries

Design objects in Copenhagen

Contacts

AIR

MAJOR AIRPORTS

Sweden. Stockholm Arlanda Airport (ARN)

Denmark. Copenhagen Airport, Kastrup (CPH)

Norway. Oslo Gardermoen Airport (OSL), Bergen Flesland Airport (BGO)

Finland. Helsinki-Vantaa Airport (HEL)

Iceland. Reykjavík–Keflavík Airport (KEF)

Baltic States. Riga International Airport (RIX), Vilnius International Airport (VNO), Linnart Meri Tallinn Airport (TLL)

BOAT

Destination Gotland. ☒ *Sweden* 🌐 *www.destinationgotland.se*

DFDS Seaways. ☒ *Denmark* 🌐 *www.dfdsseaways.dk*

Eckerö Line. ☒ *Finland www.eckeroline.fi*

Fjord 1. ☒ *Norway* ☎ *57–75–70–00* 🌐 *www.fjord1.no*

ForSea. ☒ *Sweden* 🌐 *www.forsea.se*

Hurtigruten. ☒ *Norway* 🌐 *www.hurtigruten.com*

Molslinjen. ☒ *Denmark* 🌐 *www.molslinjen.dk*

Norled. ☒ *Norway* ☎ *51–86–87–00, press 9 for English* 🌐 *www.norled.no*

Polferries. ☒ *Sweden* 🌐 *www.polferries.se*

Ruteinformasjonen (Route information). ☒ *Norway* 🌐 *www.ruteinfo.no*

Scandlines. ☒ *Denmark/Germany* 🌐 *www.scandlines.com*

Smyril Line. ☒ *Iceland* ☎ *470–2803* 🌐 *www.smyrilline.is*

Stena Line. ☒ *Sweden* 🌐 *www.stenaline.se*

Tallink-Silja Line. ☒ *Estonia/Finland/Sweden* 🌐 *www.tallink.com*

Viking Line. ☒ *Sweden* 🌐 *www.vikingline.se*

TRAIN

Arriva. ☒ *Denmark* 🌐 *www.arriva.dk*

DSB. ☒ *Denmark* 🌐 *www.dsb.dk*

Elron. ☒ *Estonia* 🌐 *elron.ee*

Finnish State Railways. ☒ *Finland* 🌐 *www.vr.fi*

Lithuanian Railways. ☒ *Lithuania* 🌐 *www.litrail.lt/en/*

NSB. ☒ *Norway* 🌐 *www.nsb.no*

Pasažieru Vilciens. ☒ *Latvia* 🌐 *www.pv.lv/en/*

SJ. ☒ *Sweden* 🌐 *www.sj.se*

VISITOR INFORMATION

Denmark. 🌐 *visitdenmark.com* 🌐 *visitfaroeislands.com*

Estonia. 🌐 *visitestonia.com*

Finland. 🌐 *visitfinland.com* 🌐 *discoveringfinland.com*

Iceland. 🌐 *visiticeland.com* 🌐 *inspiredbyiceland.com*

Latvia. 🌐 *latvia.travel*

Lithuania. 🌐 *lithuania.travel*

Norway. 🌐 *visitnorway.com*

Sweden. 🌐 *visitsweden.com*

Baltic States

The Baltic states are commonly referred to as one region. Sharing a similar complex history, it is true that these three countries do have several common denominators. They were the first to declare independence from the USSR, in 1990–91, after being occupied for large parts of the 20th century. All three of their capitals are UNESCO World Heritage Sites, and each country also offers a wide range of other cultural attractions, such as nature, wellness, and top-class gastronomy.

Estonia is the northernmost country, located just a short ferry trip from Finland and Sweden. With its picturesque and well-preserved Old Town, Tallinn, the capital, dates from the 13th century. From there on, extend your stay to the university city of Tartu or the coastal wellness resort of Pärnu.

Latvia is a small and compact country with one-third of the population living in its capital, Riga, also the largest city in the Baltics. Rīga has a wonderful variety of Art Nouveau architecture and characteristic wooden houses, in addition to its lively central market. Only a short ride away from Rīga in either direction lies the two lovely cities of Jurmala, by the coast, and Sigulda, which is surrounded by the beautiful Gauja National Park.

Lithuania is the largest and southernmost Baltic country, as well as the first to declare its independence, in 1990. The capital Vilnius is located inland, a few hours' drive from the coast, and features a charming medieval and Gothic city center, as well as the bohemian, creative, and somewhat rebellious area of Uzupis. Other highlights include Kaunas, previously the temporary capital, as well as the neighboring coastal towns of Palanga and Klaipėda, wherein lies the Curonian Spit, another of the country's World Heritage Sites.

Rīga Old Town

An Architectural Pearl

From stunning architecture and a lively central market to a UNESCO designation, the Baltic capital city of Rīga truly has it all. Rīga's medieval Old Town and its surrounding city center was designated a UNESCO World Heritage site in 1997, recognized for having the finest collection of Art Nouveau buildings in Europe. The fabric of this medieval core remains remarkably intact, with Gothic spires sheltering church naves and winding cobbled streets revealing sturdy gables. Albert Street houses some of Rīga's most stunning Art Deco buildings—as well as their famed Art Nouveau Museum. Elizabetes Street's period architecture is a testament to the wealth generated here by shipping and trade in the early 20th century. Today, Rīga is a creative and welcoming city.

Don't Miss

Originally opened in 1930, Riga's Central Market is located in five historic Zeppelin hangars just outside the Old Town. It offers a wide range of meats, spices, beer, spirits, and handicraft products, as well as a food court. There are also stalls outside, with high-quality produce from smaller companies and farmers. Enjoy sampling and buying authentic Latvian (and also some international) delicacies.

Getting Here and Around

Rīga's airport is a 20-minute ride from the city center, which is extremely walkable; Rīga also has a well-developed public transport system.

Rīga Tourism Information Center. ✉ *Rātslaukums 6, Centra rajons, Riga* ☎ *67/037–900* 🌐 *liveriga.com*

Hot-Air Balloon Ride in Vilnius

Float Above a UNESCO World Heritage Centre

If you were wondering how popular a pastime hot-air ballooning is in Lithuania, the fact that Lithuania has the highest number of hot air balloons per capita should give you an idea. Vilnius is the only European capital to allow hot air balloon rides within the town limits, and the fiery, shining dots in the sky have become emblematic of the historic capital. While the sight of balloons floating over the melange of Baroque, Gothic, Renaissance, and medieval-style architecture is a wonder to behold, the view of Vilnius' Old Town and its lush surroundings from above is even better. When you come back down to earth, you'll want to take time to walk the winding cobblestone streets, learn about this city's history of oppression and resilience, stop for traditional Šakotis cake, and explore a vibrant food and arts scene.

Don't Miss

While a flight above the Vilnius' Old City—a UNESCO world heritage site—is an unparalleled experience, don't miss the view of the island castle of Trakai. Surrounded by clouds and charming red towers, it's a sight straight out of a fairy tale.

When to Go

Flight season is between April and November.

Best Tour

Hot Air Lines is one of the most popular operators. Flights usually last around one hour. 🌐 *www.orobalionai.lt*

Getting Here and Around

Several international operators offer good connections in Europe. Vilnius Airport is small and close to the city center, which can be reached by bus, train, or taxi.

Visit Vilnius. 🌐 *www.govilnius.lt/visit-vilnius*

The Hill of Crosses

100,000-Plus Crosses, One Potent Symbol

One of the most unique places in the Baltics is the Hill of Crosses, a pilgrimage site where more than 100,000 crosses decorate a small hillside. Piled on top of each other in all shapes and sizes, the collage has become a nationwide symbol of Lithuania's faith and resilience. The collection began after Lithuania's failed 1831 revolution against the Russians. Many locals, unable to retrieve the bodies of their fallen family members, put crosses on the hill to commemorate these loved ones. As attempts to revolt continued through the 1800s, more crosses were added, eventually becoming a field of silent dissent against their unwanted rulers. Even during the Soviet occupation in the 20th century—when Soviet guards patrolled the hill, physically preventing Lithuanians from entering—locals continued to plant down crosses in secret, a dangerous rebellion against their occupiers. Today, in modern-day independent Lithuania, the collection continues to grow. Pope John Paul II planted a cross on his 1993 visit to the site, and you can add one in memory of a loved one or in homage to the strength and bravery of the Lithuanian people.

Don't Miss

Nearby Šiauliai is Lithuania's fourth largest city and home to Gubernija brewery, Lithuania's oldest brewery, dating to 1665. It's worth stopping for a tour and tasting.

Getting Here and Around

The hill is located 12 km (7½ miles) north of Šiauliai, a 2½ hour drive from Vilnius or 1½ hours from Rīga.

✉ *81439 Jurgaičiai, Lithuania* ☎ *41/370–860* 🌐 *www.kryziukalnas.lt*

Lahemaa National Park

Situated on the northern coast of the country, Lahemaa National Park is the largest nature reserve in Estonia, spanning 725 sq km (275 square miles) and offering stunning coastline dotted with quaint fishing villages and grand manor estates (look for Palmse, Vihula, and Sagadi manors), beautiful woodland walks, bogs, beaches, grasslands, flora and fauna, as well as Estonia's highest waterfall, Jägala juga. Estonians believe this area to be filled with spirits, while others just find it otherworldly in its beauty; decide for yourself. Allow time to explore the peaceful and charming villages of Käsmu and Altja. Resting on Käsmu Bay, the village of Käsmu is picture-postcard cute with white picket fences, rustic houses, and quintessential rural Estononian charm. Altja has traditional cottages, an Estonian wooden swing, and an age-old tavern. There are 20 hiking trails to lead you through this diverse landscape.

Don't Miss

The 3.8-mile Viru Bog trail, perched on a narrow boardwalk, brings you through some iconically Estonian forests and peat bogs. Make sure to stay on the well-marked paths—bogs are a delicate ecosystem. The Oandu Forest Nature Trail is another must, especially for forest lovers.

When to Go

Take advantage of the up to 18 hours of sunlight per day in the summer.

Getting Here

Lahemaa is a one-hour drive from Tallinn. The visitor center is next to Palmse Manor, opposite the Palmse bus stop.

✉ *Palmse, Haljala Municipality, Lääne-Viru County* 🌐 *kaitsealad.ee/en/protected-areas/lahemaa-national-park* 🎫 *Free*

Old Town Tallinn

A Medieval-but-Modern Baltic Capital

Tallinn's picturesque and well-preserved Old Town dates back to the 13th century and is listed by UNESCO as a World Heritage site.The city center is divided into the Upper and Lower Town, its meandering cobbled streets taking you to a wealth of historic sights, including churches and fortifications alongside beautiful residential and commercial buildings and restaurants serving both traditional and modern Estonian and Nordic cuisine. Other areas to explore are Kalamaja, with its characteristic wooden houses and the vast Kadriorg Park where you will find a palace and several museums. While much of Tallinn's immediate appeal is its history, but you will also find a vibrant and vital new Tallinn with an emerging tech industry, contemporary street art, Telliskivi Cultural City, and Depoo Market where you can find street food, soviet memorabilia, bars, cafés, and more.

Dont Miss

The early-20th-century Russian Orthodox Alexander Nevsky Cathedral was originally a symbol of the centuries of Russification endured by Estonia. If possible, arrive at the cathedral sometime in the early afternoon when the golden mosaics that decorate the church will shimmer like diamonds. St. Mary's, another church down the street, exemplifies Estonian Christianity, so a stop after the Nevsky Cathedral will provide an interesting contrast.

Getting Here and Around

Tallinn is a short ferry trip from Helsinki, an overnight sailing from Stockholm, and an easy flight from anywhere in Europe.

Visit Tallinn. ☎ *645/7722*
🌐 *www.visittallinn.ee*

A Võrumaa Smoke Sauna Experience

A Sweaty UNESCO Cultural Heritage Experience

Sauna culture has deep roots in the Baltics. In fact, the area is one of the originators of the practice. For the Võrumaa region in southern Estonia, the smoke sauna is the most revered iteration and so intrinsically tied to their identity that in 2014, it was named a UNESCO Intangible Cultural Heritage of Humanity practice. A smoke sauna is typical to a normal sauna, sans the chimney, meaning that the smoke meanders about you rather than instantly floating out of the wooden building (don't worry, the door of a smoke sauna is kept open to maintain the flow of oxygen). The practice is more than just a physical cleansing; for Estonians, it's a distinctly spiritual experience, one that should be savored and treated with the upmost respect. Mooska Farm, run by the Veeroja family, has been one of the most careful guardians of the practice, and for those looking to experience an authentic Estonian smoke sauna, there's no better place to visit.

Don't Miss

Follow everything your guides say to have the true sauna experience, and yes, that includes jumping into the pond and trying some sauna-smoked meat at the end.

Getting Here and Around

Mooska Farm is a three hour drive southeast from Tallinn or northeast from Riga.

Best Activities

The Võrumaa region is any outdoor-lovers paradise, full of great snowshoeing, skiing, and walking trails.

Mooska Farm. ✉ *Haanja parish, Võru county, Estonia* ☎ *503/2341* 🌐 *mooska.eu* 🎫 *From €300*

When in the Baltic States

Curonian Spit

NATIONAL PARK | Extending from Klaipėda to the Sambian Peninsula in Russia, this UNESCO World Heritage Site is a series of forested barrier islands across the mouth of the Curonian Lagoon. Running for 98 kilometers (61 miles), the very narrow—4 km (2½ miles) at its widest point and only 400 meters (1,312 feet) at its thinnest—spit contains Europe's highest moving sand dunes. The nearby town of Nida is a cozy gem that offers a great viewpoint, the Hill of Urbas. A visit to seaside resort area Juodkrantė and its Witches Hill sculpture garden is also recommended. ✉ *Curonian Spit National Park, Nida* ☎ *469–51224* 🌐 *www.nerija.lrv.lt/* 🎫 *€30 ($32) June 6–Aug. 8, €5 ($6) during off-season.*

★ Museum of Occupation and Freedom Fights (*Okupacijų ir laisvės kovų muziejus*)

In the New Town, housed in a late 19th-century building on the emblematic Gedimino Avenue, this museum's home was first the Vilnius headquarters of the German Gestapo and later the Soviet KGB, who also utilized it for interrogations and as a prison. It was converted to this commemorative museum, which has proven to be a powerful reminder of all those killed during the many long occupations of Lithuania, and its facade is covered by plaques with names, in remembrance of those who were executed here or deported to Siberia during the Soviet regime. ✉ *Auku g. 2A, Vilnius* ☎ *85/249–8156* 🌐 *www.genocid.lt* 🎫 *€4* ⏲ *Closed Mon. and Tues.*

★ Raekoja Plats

GOVERNMENT BUILDING | Tallinn's picturesque Town Hall Square has a long history of trade, social meetings, and at least one execution, which was the result of a dispute over a bad omelet. You can tour the only surviving Gothic **town hall** in northern Europe, where Old Thomas, its weathervane, has been atop the **tower** since 1530. Across the square sits the **Raeapteek,** the town hall pharmacy, which dates from 1422 and is one of the oldest continuously running pharmacies in Europe. From the round stone marked with a compass rose in the middle of the square, it should be possible to see the tops of all five spires of the Old Town. The square is lined with beautiful and elaborate merchant houses alongside lively cafés and restaurants. Throughout the year, it hosts several festivals, markets, and events, not the least Tallinn's wonderful Christmas market, including its famed Christmas tree. ✉ *Raekoja plats, Tallinn* ☎ *645/7905 town hall, 558/75701 pharmacy* 🌐 *www.raekoda.tallinn.ee* 🎫 *Town Hall €5; tower €4 (cash only)* ⏲ *Town Hall closed Sun. Town Hall open by reservation only Oct.–June. Tower closed mid-Sept.–mid-May.*

Ragakapa Nature Park (*Ragakāpas dabas parks*)

Spanning more than 370 acres along the sea, this nature reserve was established in 1962 to protect the local sand dunes. It consists of lush and untouched pine forest, with a high level of biodiversity and some trees dating back several hundred years. There are two nature trails and an open-air museum to discover, but there's also plenty of space for leisurely strolls without a set goal. ✉ *Tiklu iela 1A, Jurmala* ☎ *67/730–078* 🎫 *Free.*

★ Rīga Art Nouveau Centre (*muzejs "Rīgas Jūgendstila centrs"*)

In a former residential building surrounded by other beautiful Jugendstil structures, Rīga's Art Nouveau Center showcases a historic apartment with authentic period furniture, tableware, artworks, kitchen utensils, clothing, and other precious objects. Just outside the museum apartment is a wonderful spiral staircase that is considered one of the most magnificent Art Nouveau masterpieces in Europe. Once you see it, you will know why. ✉ *Alberta iela 12, Riga*

Baltic States
0
50 mi
0
50 km
FINLAND
Turku
Vantaa
Espoo
Helsinki
Kotka
Vyborg
Gulf of Finland
Raekoja Plats
Tallinn Christmas Market
Telliskivi Creative City
Old Town Tallinn
Lahemaa National Park
Kunda
Kingisepp
Johvi
Keila
Vormsi
Hiiumaa
Paide
Mustvee
Lake Peipus
Lihula
Muhu
Poltsamaa
ESTONIA
Saaremaa
Kuressaare
Parnu
Tartu
Lake Pihkva
Võrtsjärv
Kihnu
Haademeeste
Baltic Sea
Sorve
Gulf of Riga
Ainaži
Voru
Pskov
Kolka
A Võrumaa Smoke Sauna Experience
Salacgriva
Ovisi
Valmiera
Tuja
Ape
RUSSIA
Mersrags
Skulte
Rīga Old Town
Turaida Museum Reserve
Ragakāpa Nature Park
Riga Art Nouveau Center
Pavilosta
Jurmala
Rīga
Ergli
Madona
Saldus
LATVIA
Lubans
Liepaja
Gostini
Jekabpils
Klampji
Mazeikiai
Birzai
Palanga
The Hill of Crosses
Plunge
Šiauliai
Rokiskis
Daugavpils
Klaipeda
Seduva
Panevėžys
Priekule
Curonian Spit
LITHUANIA
Utena
Ukmerge
Hot Air Balloon Ride in Vilnius
Kaunas
Kaliningrad
RUSSIA
(Kaliningrad Oblast)
Vilnius
Museum of Occupation and Freedom Fights
Mariampole
Vilnius Cathedral
Kalvarija
BELARUS
Suwalki
Merkine
Lida
Minsk
Olsztyn
Elk
Grodno
POLAND
Lomza
Ostroleka
Bialystok

☎ *67/181–465* 🌐 *www.jugendstils.riga.lv* 🎫 *€9* ⏲ *Closed Mon.*

★ Tallinn Christmas Market

MARKET | Less-known and trafficked than other Christmas markets in Europe, Tallinn's Christmas market has a hidden gem appeal and authentic feel, all the more authentic because its impressive Christmas tree has been set up in Tallinn Town Hall Square since 1441, making it the first Christmas tree ever to be put on display in Europe. Held for the month of December in Town Hall Square, you'll find wooden chalets filled with treasures, crafts, and foodstalls where local merchants offer Estonian Christmas cuisine and drinks. Be sure to try the hot, rum-based Vana Tallinn liqueur. ✉ *Raekoja plats, Tallinn* 🌐 *www.visitestonia.com* 🎫 *Free* ⏲ *Closed early Jan. to late Nov.*

★ Telliskivi Creative City (*Telliskivi Loomelinnak*)

BUSINESS DISTRICT | Telliskivi Creative City is a complex of shops, eateries, workshops, pop-up stores, event venues, and other creative spaces. It is located in a reclaimed factory, just a short walk outside the historical city center, next to a large indoor market hall and the beautiful residential quarters of Kalamaja, known for their characteristic wooden architecture. Here you will find artisinal bread and ice cream, select Estonian and Nordic design items, and a range of great restaurants and cafés. ✉ *Telliskivi tn. 60A, Tallinn* 🌐 *telliskivi.cc.*

Turaida Museum Reserve (*Turaidas muzejrezervāts*)

MUSEUM VILLAGE | Turaida Museum Reserve is one of the most popular museums in Latvia and one of the country's top attractions. Covering over more than 98 acres, it is divided into several parts and includes the remnants of an impressive medieval-era castle and a modern sculpture park dedicated to Latvian folk songs, which are a crucial part of the national heritage. Another important feature of the park is the place where the so-called Rose of Turaida is buried. As the story goes, a baby was found in the arms of her dead mother after a siege on Turaida Castle; she grew up to be a beautiful young woman and was betrothed to the gardener of Sigulda Castle; however, she was killed by a Polish soldier, choosing to die rather than betray her true love. Buried on the Turaida Castle grounds under a linden tree, her grave is a popular spot for newlyweds to leave flowers in the hope that their love will prove just as strong. ✉ *Turaidas iela 10, Sigulda* ☎ *67/972–376* 🌐 *www.turaida-muzejs.lv* 🎫 *€6 May–Oct., €4 Nov.–Apr.*

★ Vilnius Cathedral (*Vilnius katedra*)

Vilnius's beautiful cathedral is the most important place for worship for Lithuania's Catholic community and has been a national symbol for centuries. The building itself was completed in the 18th century, but some original portions of the church date from the 13th and 15th centuries. In 1922, the church was named a basilica by Pope Pius XI. It is centrally located on Cathedral Square, next to the bell tower, which was originally a watch tower, and the recently reconstructed Palace of the Grand Dukes of Lithuania. In its catacombs, several key figures of Lithuanian history are buried, including Saint Casimir, Alexander Jagiellon, and the heart of the Polish king Władysław IV Vasa. ✉ *Katedros a. 1, Vilnius* ☎ *85/261–0731* 🌐 *www.katedra.lt.*

Where to Eat and Drink

Monai

$$ | **INTERNATIONAL** | One of the best restaurants in Lithuania and the Nordic region, Monai serves fresh, modern dishes made with local seasonal ingredients. The dining room is chic and stylish with a relaxed atmosphere, friendly service, and an open kitchen, where skilled chefs are hard at work. **Known for:** considered one of the country's top restaurants; homey feeling with open kitchen; alternating and exciting desserts. $ *Average main: €16* ✉ *Liepu g. 4, Klaipeda* ☎ *86/266–3662* 🌐 *www.restoranasmonai.lt* 🕓 *Closed Mon. No dinner Sun.*

★ Muusu Restorans

$$$ | **EUROPEAN** | The innovative European and traditional Latvian dishes are packed with flavor and texture and include zander (pike-perch) and wild game. The relaxed, welcoming restaurant is located at the heart of Rīga's historical center. **Known for:** a modern menu including traditional Latvian elements; great location at the heart of Old Town; beautiful plating on sleek, artisinal pottery. $ *Average main: €22* ✉ *Skarnu iela 6, Riga* ☎ *25/772–552* 🌐 *www.muusu.lv* 🕓 *Closed Sun. No lunch Mon. or Sat.*

★ NOA

$$$ | **INTERNATIONAL** | NOA Restaurant is one of the better restaurants in Estonia and the Nordic countries. The menu focuses on brasserie-style dishes with international influences that are largely based on local produce. **Known for:** the Chef's Hall, for a more exclusive experience; consistently ranked as one of Estonia's top restaurants; the location, with beautiful views of the sea and Tallinn's skyline. $ *Average main: €22* ✉ *Ranna tee 3, Tallinn* ☎ *508/0589* 🌐 *www.noaresto.ee.*

★ Olde Hansa

$$ | **EASTERN EUROPEAN** | In a 15th-century building in the Old Town, this welcoming and lively restaurant re-creates medieval times and cooking, with waiters in period costume, candlelit tables, and historic Eastern European recipes for such dishes as game pot and wild boar. The honey beer is claimed to be out of this world, and the old-fashioned food is always fresh and tasty. **Known for:** genuine medieval atmosphere; hearty dishes of game and meat; flavored craft beer. $ *Average main: €20* ✉ *Vana turg 1, Vanalinn* ☎ *627/9020* 🌐 *www.oldehansa.ee.*

★ Sweet Root

$$$$ | **INTERNATIONAL** | One of Lithuania's best fine-dining restaurants serves an unparalleled tasting menu based exclusively on local and seasonal ingredients. Many of the dishes feature new takes on traditional Lithuanian recipes and/or surprising elements of texture, flavor, and design, and you're likely to get your protein served in several different ways (e.g., quail with lingonberries, quail with beets and plums, quail with cabbage and black currant leaves). **Known for:** strictly local and seasonal produce; inventive flavors and textures; elaborate tasting menus with wine pairings, all at about a third the price of Noma. $ *Average main: €75* ✉ *Uzupio g. 22, Vilnius* ☎ *86/856–0767* 🌐 *www.sweetroot.lt* 🕓 *Closed Mon., Tues., and Sun. No lunch.*

★ Vegan Restoran V

$$ | **VEGETARIAN** | Vegan Restoran V indeed serves a modern and innovative, international à la carte menu including only vegan dishes, filled with flavor and nutrients. The restaurant is located at the heart of Tallinn's historical center, in a small and cozy venue with ancient stone vaults and a small terrace during summer. **Known for:** beetroot ravioli with cashew cheese for starter; showcasing the best of vegan food; being busy (reservations are highly recommended). $ *Average main: €11* ✉ *Rataskaevu 12, Tallinn* ☎ *626/9087* 🌐 *veganrestoran.ee* 🕓 *Closed Mon.*

★ Vila Komoda Restaurant

$$$ | **INTERNATIONAL** | The restaurant of family-run boutique hotel Vila Komoda serves seasonal dishes in Nordic style, based on local ingredients that sometimes are picked by the restaurant's own staff. It is owned and managed by an internationally acclaimed Lithuanian chef known for his inventiveness and attention to detail. **Known for:** run by internationally acclaimed chef; inventive menu; focus on local ingredients and traditions. $ *Average main: €21* ✉ *Meiles*

al. 5, Palanga ☎ 8460/20490 🌐 www.vilakomoda.lt.

★ **Vincents**

$$$ | **INTERNATIONAL** | This renowned restaurant and foodie favorite serves a menu of international delicacies made with carefully selected ingredients, both local and imported. Included in its celebrity-rich clientele have been, among others, Elton John, José Carreras, German Chancellor Angela Merkel, and George Bush. **Known for:** modern, international haute cuisine; extensive wine list, reflecting both the Old and the New World; celebrity clientele. *$ Average main: €25 ✉ Elizabetes iela 19, Riga ☎ 67/332–830 🌐 www.restorans.lv ⏲ Closed Sun. and Mon. No lunch.*

Cool Places to Stay

★ **AC Hotel Rīga**

$ | **HOTEL** | This stylish and well-designed hotel with friendly service has a great location in Rīga's beautiful Art Nouveau district, just outside the historical city center. **Pros:** central location near the Art Nouveau quarter; beautiful views from some rooms and the fitness studio; spacious lounge and bar. **Cons:** large and somewhat impersonal; not possible to prebook parking; location slightly outside the historical center. *$ Rooms from: €90 ✉ Dzirnavu iela 33, Riga ☎ 67/331–717 🌐 www.marriott.com 239 rooms Free Breakfast.*

Grand Palace Hotel

$$$ | **HOTEL** | Sophisticated amenities, 19th-century furnishings, and an enviable location in the heart of Rīga make this award-winning hotel a grand place in which to relax in luxury. **Pros:** old-world elegance; excellent service; central location. **Cons:** upper price level; rooms are small; smoking allowed in the bar. *$ Rooms from: €175 ✉ Pils iela 12, Riga ☎ 67/044–000 🌐 www.grandpalaceriga.com 56 rooms Free Breakfast.*

Hotel Schlössle

$$$$ | **HOTEL** | Located at the heart of Old Town, this luxurious and beautiful Tallinn hotel has authentic interior details and attentive, welcoming service. **Pros:** excellent location; lots of charm; on-site restaurant. **Cons:** rooms accessible by stairs only; expensive; relatively small rooms. *$ Rooms from: €220 ✉ Püha-vaimu tn. 13–15, Tallinn ☎ 699/7700 🌐 www.schlossle-hotels.com 23 rooms Free Breakfast.*

Kurshi Hotel & Spa

$ | **HOTEL** | A small and chic boutique hotel near the beach was designed by Latvian architect Juris Lasis, with modern interiors and some industrial touches. **Pros:** chic design; restaurant on-site, serving modern Latvian cuisine; spa with treatments and small relaxation area. **Cons:** use of relaxation area not included for all rooms; limited spa facilities for a spa hotel; location is a little bit away from the city center. *$ Rooms from: €90 ✉ Cernu iela 22, Jurmala ☎ 67/878–900 🌐 www.kurshihotel.lv 34 rooms Free Breakfast.*

★ **Pacai**

$$$$ | **HOTEL** | A beautiful, gently restored Baroque palace from the 17th century has been turned into a hotel that's named after its noble founders. **Pros:** unique building and atmosphere; exclusive on-site spa; attentive and professional service. **Cons:** a historic building that may be difficult to navigate; may be difficult to access by car due to location in the Old Town; high room rates. *$ Rooms from: €240 ✉ Didzioji g. 7, Vilnius ☎ 85/277–0000 🌐 hotelpacai.com 104 rooms Free Breakfast.*

Shakespeare Boutique Hotel

$$ | **HOTEL** | Foregoing Nordic minimalism, this elegant boutique hotel in a historic building is decorated in a rich English style, with individually and lovingly designed rooms themed around famous writers. **Pros:** central location; beautiful interiors; elegant on-site restaurant. **Cons:**

limited space for outdoor seating; some aspects of the historic building are inconvenient; fairly high price point. $ *Rooms from: €140* ✉ *Bernardinu g. 8, Vilnius* ☎ *85/266–5885* 🌐 *www.shakespeare.lt* *31 rooms* 🍽 *Free Breakfast.*

★ **Villa Ammende Luxury Art Nouveau Hotel**
$$$ | **HOTEL** | This small but high-end boutique hotel is in a beautiful Art Nouveau villa from the early 20th century, originally established as the wedding location for a merchant's daughter. **Pros:** beautiful and unique atmosphere; location near beach and city center; fine-dining restaurant on-site. **Cons:** upper price level; no spa available; location not directly on the beach or right in the city center. $ *Rooms from: €159* ✉ *Mere pst.7, Pärnu* ☎ *447/3888* 🌐 *ammende.ee* *19 rooms* 🍽 *Free Breakfast.*

Denmark

Denmark is a liberal, modern state with a strong focus on equality and the environment. Here, tradition mixes with new ideas, age-old buildings stand next to cutting-edge restaurants serving New Nordic cuisine, and many residents ride their bicycles to work.

The history of the country stretches back 250,000 years, when Jutland was inhabited by nomadic hunters, but it wasn't until AD 500 that a tribe from Sweden, called the Danes, migrated south and christened the land Denmark. The Viking expansion that followed was based on the country's strategic position in the north. Intrepid navies navigated to Europe and Canada, invading and often pillaging, until, under King Knud (Canute) the Great (995–1035), they captured England by 1018.

After the British conquest, Viking supremacy declined as feudal Europe learned to defend itself. Under the leadership of Valdemar IV, Sweden, Norway, Iceland, Greenland, and the Faroe Islands became a part of Denmark, though Sweden broke away again by the mid-15th century and battled Denmark for much of the next several hundred years, whereas Norway remained under Danish rule until 1814 and Iceland until 1943. Greenland and the Faroe Islands are still self-governing Danish provinces.

Denmark prospered in the 16th century, but King Christian IV's fantasy spires and castles—which can be explored today—and the Thirty Years' War led to state bankruptcy. By the 18th century, absolute monarchy had given way to representative democracy, and culture flourished. But when Denmark refused to surrender its navy to the English during the Napoleonic Wars, Lord Nelson bombed Copenhagen to bits. Denmark lost Norway to Sweden, and Denmark's glory days were over.

Though Denmark was unaligned during World War II, the Nazis invaded in 1940. The small but strong resistance movement that was active throughout the war is greatly celebrated. Since then Denmark has become a highly developed social-welfare system, financed by hefty taxes that are the subject of grumbles and jokes. But the Danes are proud of their state-funded medical and educational systems and high standard of living. It's part of the reason the Danes have been crowned as the world's happiest people several times, and why Copenhagen has repeatedly been named one of the world's most liveable cities.

Copenhagen's Palaces

Rosenborg, Amalienborg, and Christiansborg

Denmark is home to one of the world's oldest monarchies, and the city of Copenhagen is home to three of the Danish royal family's exquisite homes, all packed with royal treasures and heirlooms that provide a window into the past and present of the royal family. King Christian IV built Rosenborg Castle in the 17th century as a summer residence but loved it so much that he lived here until his death. The castle features 400 years of royal treasures, coronation thrones, royal portraits, and the Crown Jewels and Royal Regalia. Stately Amalienborg Palace has been the official royal residence since 1784 and it is still the queen's winter residence. Christiansborg Palace is where the Queen officially receives guests and from where the parliament—and the prime minister—rule the country. Several parts of the palace can be visited, including the Royal Kitchen, Royal Stables, and the tower.

Don't Miss

The Royal Danish Guard leaves its barracks at Rosenborg Castle at approximately 11:30 am and marches through the city to Amalienborg Palace for the changing of the guard at noon.

Getting Here and Around

All three castles are within easy walking distance of each other.

Amalienborg Slot. 🌐 *www.kongernessamling.dk/en/amalienborg* 🎫 *Museum DKr 95*

Christiansborg Slot. 🌐 *kongeligeslotte.dk* 🎫 *Tower free, Royal Reception Chamber DKr 95*

Rosenborg Slot. 🌐 *www.kongernessamling.dk/rosenborg* 🎫 *DKr 115*

Louisiana Museum of Modern Art

Art, Architecture, and Nature

The must-see Louisiana is one of Denmark's top attractions, admired for its exceptional modern art collection and its memorable setting and experience. Even if you're not an art lover, it's well worth the 30-minute trip from Copenhagen to experience its striking combination of art, architecture, and nature. Set in a sprawling sculpture garden with panoramic views of the Øresund sound, a 19th-century villa is surrounded by three modernist pavilions and connected by glass-walled passages to seamlessly blend indoors and outdoors. If you are an art lover, Louisiana's collection of modern art is one of Scandinavia's largest, with more than 4,000 artworks. Allow ample time to explore the sculpture park and the two-story museum store where you will find an excellent selection of Scandinavian and Danish design.

Don't Miss

"Gleaming Lights of the Souls" by Yayoi Kusama is one of the Louisiana's most popular exhibits. The walls and ceilings are covered with mirrors; the floor is a reflecting pool; and you stand in the middle of the water on a platform.

When to Go

In late August the museum is home to Louisiana Literature, a literature festival with visits from some of the literary world's most famous authors.

Getting Here and Around

Trains run to Humlebæk from Copenhagen every 20 minutes, and it's a 30-minute trip. The trains, called Øresundstoget, originate in the Swedish city of Malmö and run in the other direction from Helsingør.

✉ *Strandvej 13* ☎ *49/19–07–19* 🌐 *www.louisiana.dk* 🎫 *DKr 145*

Odense

Home to All Things Hans Christian Andersen

Once upon a time there was a city named Odense, the capital of Funen and Denmark's third-largest city, that felt like a storybook world—perhaps because fairy-tale fans the world over have kept the magic alive for over 200 years as they retrace the footsteps of its most famous son, author Hans Christian Andersen. There are character sculptures throughout the city and several attractions dedicated to the author, including the new Hans Christian Andersen House, designed by Japanese architect Kengo Kuma, which brings Andersen's literary universe to life through interactive exhibits and gardens. After immersing yourself in the worlds imagined by the author, be sure to visit the more intimate H. C. Andersen's Childhood Home, a tiny, sparsely decorated house where the young boy lived with his parents in the early 1800s.

Don't Miss

The historical half-timbered houses and the fairy-tale charm are one face of this city; allow time for its more contemporary aspects, such as the Brandts Museum and the buzzing gastronomic scene.

When to Go

One of the city's most popular festivals is a tribute to Hans Christian Andersen with a week of cabaret, concerts, parades, and artistic experiences in late August. 🌐 *www.hcafestivals.com*

Getting Here

Direct trains from Copenhagen's main station depart for the 75-minute trip to Odense every half hour. You also can take the train to Odense directly from Copenhagen airport. By car, you'll want to take E20 heading west.

VisitOdense. ☎ *63/75–75–20* 🌐 *www.visitodense.com*

Egeskov Slot (Egeskov Castle)

A Romantic Renaissance Castle

There are castles, and then there are castles. Located in southern Funen, Egeskov Castle dates back 460 years and is considered the best-preserved moat castle in Europe. Built by sheriff Frands Brockenhuus and completed in 1554, Egeskov is still inhabited but open to the public. Classified as a Renaissance-style water castle (a castle whose site is largely defended by water), the castle features an impressive moat and setting, delicate spires, detailed masonry with whimsical creatures in its thick walls, extensive grounds and gardens, and grand halls. After losing yourself in the Hunting Room, the Yellow Room, and the loft, check out the vintage car and motorcycle collections as well as the world's largest dollhouse, the treetop walk, and mazes.

Don't Miss

The first gardens were laid out around 1713 and were inspired by the castle gardens at Fredensborg, Frederiksborg, and Versailles. Today, the castle park includes various mazes, a scented garden, an English garden, a fuchsia garden, a white garden, rose garden, water garden, and a peaceful Garden of Life.

When to Go

The castle is home to the annual Heartland Festival, which brings together Denmark's creative elite for several days every June.

Getting Here and Around

There are several direct trains every hour from Odense to Svendborg (40 minutes). The town is best explored by bike or car; it's possible to rent both at multiple locations.

Svendborg Tourist Information. ✉ *Havnepladsen 2, Svendborg* 🌐 *www.visitsvendborg.dk*

Ærø

Island Idyll

A jewel of an island located in the heart of the South Funen Archipelago, Ærø is the stuff of Danish fairy tales with bustling harbors, friendly locals, and charming villages as well as utterly enchanting coastline, scenic hiking and bicycling trails, and beautiful beaches complete with colorful beach houses. Quaint small towns dot the coast, but it's in Ærøskøbing, Denmark's most carefully preserved medieval village, dating from the 13th century, that you'll feel you stepped right into the fairy tale. The half-timbered houses and narrow cobblestone streets look exactly as they did a century ago. Pause to smell the day's fresh bread in a bakery, to shop handmade crafts, to hear the church bells, and to wonder at the intricate hand-carved doors and cast-iron lamps. Ærø is also a popular base for island-hopping to Tåsinge, Als, Drejø, Skarø, and more... if you can leave, that is.

Don't Miss

At Ærø Brewery, take a guided tour, have a beer tasting, and eat lunch in their garden. It's one of the larger micro-breweries in Denmark.

Best Restaurant

Den Gamle Købmandsgaard is a combined farmers' market, café, and bar and the main meeting point on the town's central square. Stop by for local products or for a meal in the atmospheric café. ✉ *Torvet 5, Ærøskøbing.* ☎ *64/81–14–57* 🌐 *www.dgkshop.com*

Getting Here

You need to board a boat to get to Ærø, whether you're bringing a car or not. The most frequent route is between Svendborg and Ærøskøbing (which takes 75 minutes), but there are also ferry connections to Søby and Fynshavn.

Ærø Tourism Office. 🌐 *www.visitaeroe.com*

Møns Klint

Denmark's Most Dramatic Landscape

Seventy-million-year-old chalk cliffs crumble to the jade green waters of the Baltic Sea on the stunning coast of the island of Møn. This is some of Denmark's most dramatic scenery and one of its most visited natural attractions. Circled by a beech forest, the milky-white bluffs of Møns Klint plunge 400 feet to a small, craggy beach with sparkling waters, accessible by more than 500 steps. Here you can join in the hunt for ancient fossils of cephalopods, sea urchins, and algae in the lime-rich soil, which you can then have identified at Geo-Center Møns Klint, a spectacular natural history museum with aquariums, interactive exhibits, and a Mosasaurus skeleton. In addition to the spectacular cliffs and waters, hikers and bicyclists will enjoy the coastal network of trails, bird-watchers can observe local and migrating specimens, and Dark-Sky lovers will appreciate the magnificent Danish starry skies.

Don't Miss

This area is known for its variety of rare orchid species. Stop at the Geo Center to pick up a booklet about the 18 varieties to be spotted and their whereabouts.

Getting Here

You can reach Møn by car across bridges linking it to Zealand and the nearby island of Falster. It's about a 90-minute drive from Copenhagen. There's no direct train link to Møn: you must take a train to Falster and then switch to a bus.

House of Møn. ✉ *Sttoregade 2, Stege* ☎ *52/24–63–88* 🌐 *www.sydkystdanmark.dk*

Aarhus Ø

Denmark's Coolest City

Copenhagen has long been known as one of the art and design capitals of the world, but its little sister Aarhus, Denmark's "second city," is the Solange to Denmark's Beyonce—interesting, cool, and coming for the title. Specifically, Aarhus Ø, a recently developed neighborhood located on an artificial island and home to unique architecture and a modern maritime vibe. New and fascinating structures keep rising in this quarter. Highlights include Dokk1, a stunning library and cultural space with floor-to-ceiling windows and a minimal tubular bell (the world's largest) suspended from the ceiling, which is rung via a button in the local hospital whenever an Aarhus baby is born; the triangular Harbor Bath complex, which was designed by the office of the Danish starchitect Bjarke Ingels, and a unique residential building that looks like floating icebergs, appropriately named "the Iceberg."

Don't Miss

Make time to visit ARoS Aarhus Kunstmuseum with its much-Instagrammed rooftop rainbow walkway; Kulbroen—a former coal bridge that has received the High Line treatment with art and events, and the Latin Quarter's cute cafés and cobblestoned streets.

Best Activity

Do as the Danes and swim in the open sea swimming course at Aarhus Havbane. You'll need a wetsuit and a healthy tolerance for cold water. *havbanen.dk*

Getting Here

The train from Copenhagen takes less than three hours. FlixBus offers cheap, direct bus service as well.

VisitAarhus. *Store Torv* *87/31–50–10* *www.visitaarhus.com*

The Faroe Islands

Extraordinary Landscapes

The 18 volcanic, rocky, and rugged islands that make up the Faroe Islands, a self-governing archipelago located between Iceland, Scotland, and Norway, are home to dramatic mountains, steep coastal cliffs, and green heathlands where wild-roaming sheep graze. The islands have been attracting nature lovers for decades, but in recent years Tórshavn's restaurants, hotels, and shops have begun attracting urban travelers to its winding medieval streets. Tórshavn is a great base, but you're here for the sheep—and in summer, puffin—photos. The landscape is postcard perfect at every turn so you don't have to work too hard to find awe-inspiring beauty, but the Insta-famous hitlist includes the candy-striped Kallur Lighthouse on Kalsoy in Trøllanes, the optical illusion at Lake Sørvágsvatn on Vagar, and the Mullafossur Waterfall in Gasadalur.

Don't Miss

Guðrun & Guðrun, run by two local women, who use the Faroes' isolation and natural beauty as inspiration for their designs of sweaters, hats, and other woollen souvenirs.

Best Activity

If visiting in summer, hire a tour guide to take you on a scenic hike of Mykines and its infamous puffin colony. 🌐 *visitmykines.com*

Getting Here and Around

There are daily year-round flights to Tórshavn from Copenhagen and Billund. Smyrnil Line offers a year-round 40-hour ferry between Denmark and the Faroe Islands. Public transport is excellent but you'll want to rent a car to explore at your own pace. You can also arrange day-trip tours from Tórshavn. Plan ahead as availability for all of these is limited.

Visit Faroe Islands. ✉ *Niels Finsens gøta, Tórshavn* 🌐 *visitfaroeislands.com*

Skagen

Denmark's Northern Light

For more than a century, Skagen, a picturesque area where the North Sea meets the Baltic Sea, has been known for its natural light and beauty, not least because of the group of painters—The Skagen Painters—who tried to re-create its special quality of light and idyllic seascapes in their paintings. This 600-year-old market town on Jutland's windswept northern tip has long pebbly beaches, dune-covered heathland and huge, open skies, which shower the beach town in an almost mythical light. Sunsets are tremendous events, drawing crowds to the beaches, while nights are spent dining, drinking, and dancing at romantic beach hotels, scenic bistros, and small bars.

Don't Miss

The Skagens Museum is a wonderful homage to the talented 19th-century Danish artist and poet Holger Drachmann and his friends who founded the Skagen School of painting. Their work depicted everyday life in Skagen from the turn of the 20th century until the 1920s. You'll recognize the painted light and landscapes as you walk on the beach or in the dunes.

Best Hotel

Brøndum was the main haunt of the Skagen Painters, and its bistro is still popular with Denmark's artistic elite. www.broendums-hotel.dk

Getting Here

Despite its relative distance from Denmark's main cities, Skagen is easy to get to. You will have to change trains in Aalborg: from here it's a scenic two-hour train ride north. To drive; from Aalborg, take E45 north to Frederikshavn, then continue north on Route 40 to Skagen.

Skagen Turistbureau. ✉ *Vestre Strandvej* ☎ *10 98/44–13–77* 🌐 *www.skagen-tourist.dk*

When in Denmark

Bike Tours Denmark
BICYCLE TOURS | Denmark is a cyclist's utopia, with thousands of miles of bike lanes, bicycles outnumbering cars in the capital city, mostly flat terrain, and incredibly scenic tour options. This Europe-wide operator offers guided and self-guided biking tour options for Denmark's most beautiful rides, like a 7-night tour of Northern Zealand and Copenhagen that includes charming villages, wild forests, beautiful coastlines, beaches, castles, and the top sights of Copenhagen. A Southern Fyn option includes Odense, the idyllic island of Ærø, Svendborg, and Nyborg. ☎ *833/216–0635* ✉ *info@biketours.com* 🌐 *www.biketours.com/denmark* 🎫 *From € 952 self-guided.*

Carlsberg Bryggeri (*Carlsberg Brewery*)
BREWERY | A large, ornate chimney makes this mid-19th-century brewery visible from a distance. J. C. Jacobsen, one of Denmark's most important historical figures, named the brewery after his son Carl; *berg,* or mountain, signifies the brewery's location on Valby Hill. The four giant granite elephants that guard the main entrance were inspired by Bernini's famous obelisk in Rome. In the visitor center, interactive displays, also in English, take you step by step through the brewing process. At the end of your visit, you can sample some of the company's beers for an additional fee. The Carlsberg Museum, also on the grounds, tells the story of the Jacobsen family, their beer empire, and Carlsberg's extensive philanthropy, which still greatly benefits Danish culture. Large-scale beer production has now moved outside of the city, and the old brewery complex is being developed for residential and cultural use. The visitor center has been closed for years due to major renovation work, but it was scheduled to reopen in mid-2023. ✉ *Gamle Carlsberg Vej 11, Vesterbro* ☎ *33/27–12–82* 🌐 *www.visitcarlsberg.com.*

★ **Hammershus and Hammerknuden**
MOUNTAIN | FAMILY | Hammerknuden, the northernmost tip of Bornholm, is home to the island's most dramatic cliffs and some stunning coastal walks and also to northern Europe's biggest fortress ruin, Hammershus. The medieval fortress is perched atop a windy cliff with views of the Baltic Sea, and it's the perfect crowning of a walk around the coast. Close to the ruin you'll find Opalsøen, a jade-green lake in a former granite quarry. It's popular for swimming, and the brave try the 8-meter (26-foot) cliffside jump. Scale the steep hill behind the lake to access a heath-clad area where sheep graze between lighthouses. The top of the island offers stunning views of Hammershus and a beautiful walk around the tip of Bornholm and back into charming Sandvig. ✉ *Langebjergvej 26* ☎ *56/48–11–40* 🎫 *Free.*

★ **Kronborg Slot** (*Kronborg Castle*)
CASTLE/PALACE | Kronborg Castle dominates the city of Helsingør. Built in the late 1500s, it's the inspiration for Elsinore castle in Shakespeare's *Hamlet* (1601). Shakespeare probably never saw the castle in person, but he managed to capture its spirit—it's a gloomy, chilly place, where it's clear that an ordinary person today lives much better than kings once did. The castle was built as a Renaissance tollbooth: from its cannon-studded bastions, forces collected a tariff from all ships crossing the sliver of water between Denmark and Sweden. Well worth seeing are the 200-foot-long dining hall and the dungeons, where there is a brooding statue of Holger Danske (Ogier the Dane). According to legend, the sleeping Viking chief will awaken to defend Denmark when it's in danger. (The largest Danish resistance group during World War II called itself Holger Danske.) ✉ *Kronborg 2C, Helsingør* ✣ *At the point, on the harbor front* ☎ *49/21–30–78* 🌐 *kongeligeslotte.dk* 🎫 *DKr 125* ⏲ *Closed Mon. Oct.–Mar.*

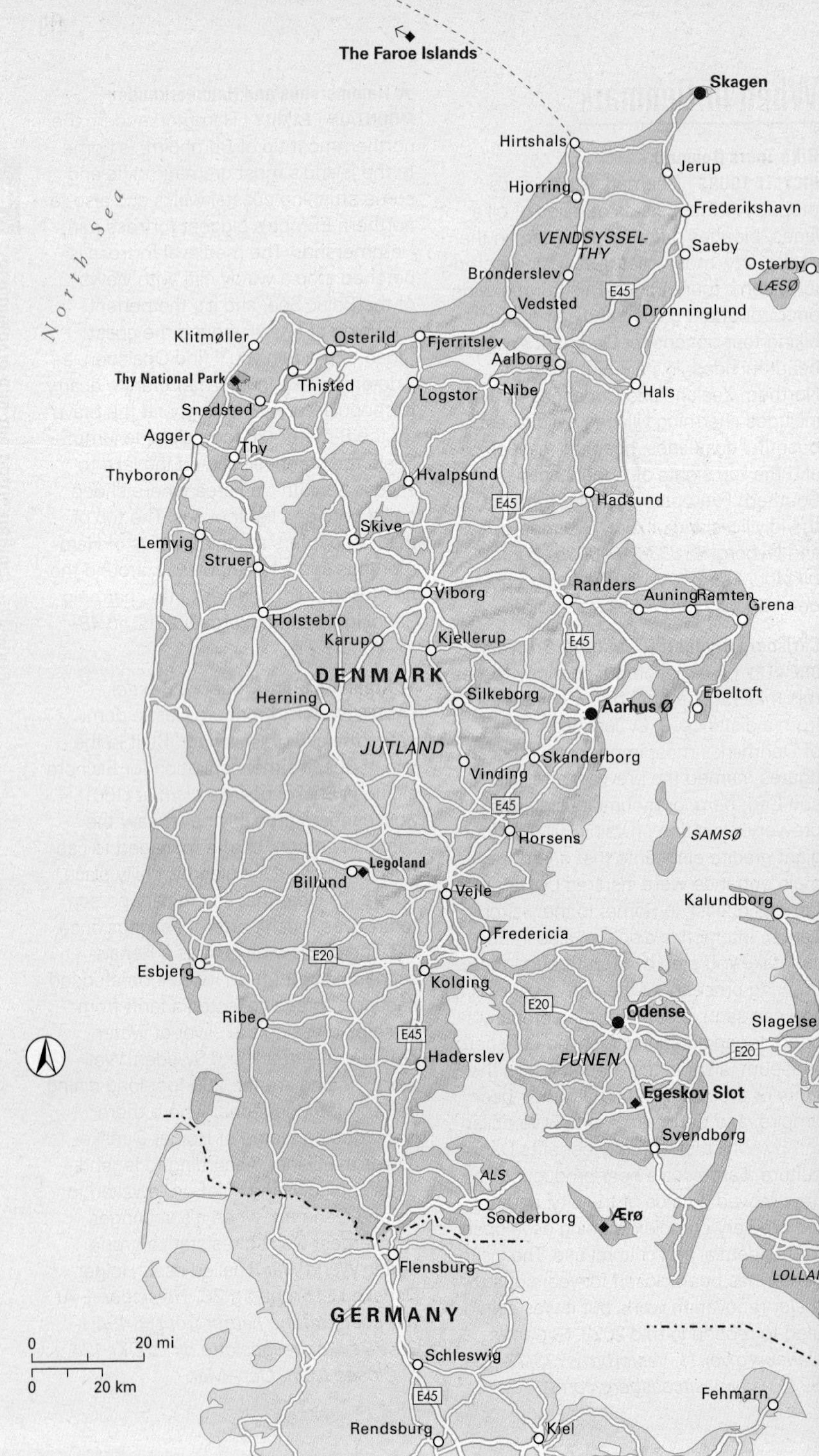

The Faroe Islands
Skagen
Hirtshals
Jerup
Hjorring
Frederikshavn
VENDSYSSEL-
THY
Saeby
North Sea
Osterby
LÆSØ
Bronderslev
E45
Vedsted
Dronninglund
Klitmøller
Osterild
Fjerritslev
Aalborg
Thy National Park
Thisted
Logstor
Nibe
Hals
Snedsted
Agger
Thy
Thyboron
Hvalpsund
Hadsund
E45
Skive
Lemvig
Struer
Randers
Auning
Ramten
Grena
Viborg
Holstebro
Karup
Kjellerup
E45
DENMARK
Herning
Silkeborg
Aarhus Ø
Ebeltoft
JUTLAND
Skanderborg
Vinding
E45
Horsens
SAMSØ
Legoland
Billund
Vejle
Kalundborg
Fredericia
E20
Esbjerg
Kolding
E20
Odense
Ribe
Slagelse
E45
Haderslev
E20
FUNEN
Egeskov Slot
Svendborg
ALS
Sonderborg
Ærø
Flensburg
LOLLAN
GERMANY
0
20 mi
0
20 km
Schleswig
E45
Fehmarn
Rendsburg
Kiel

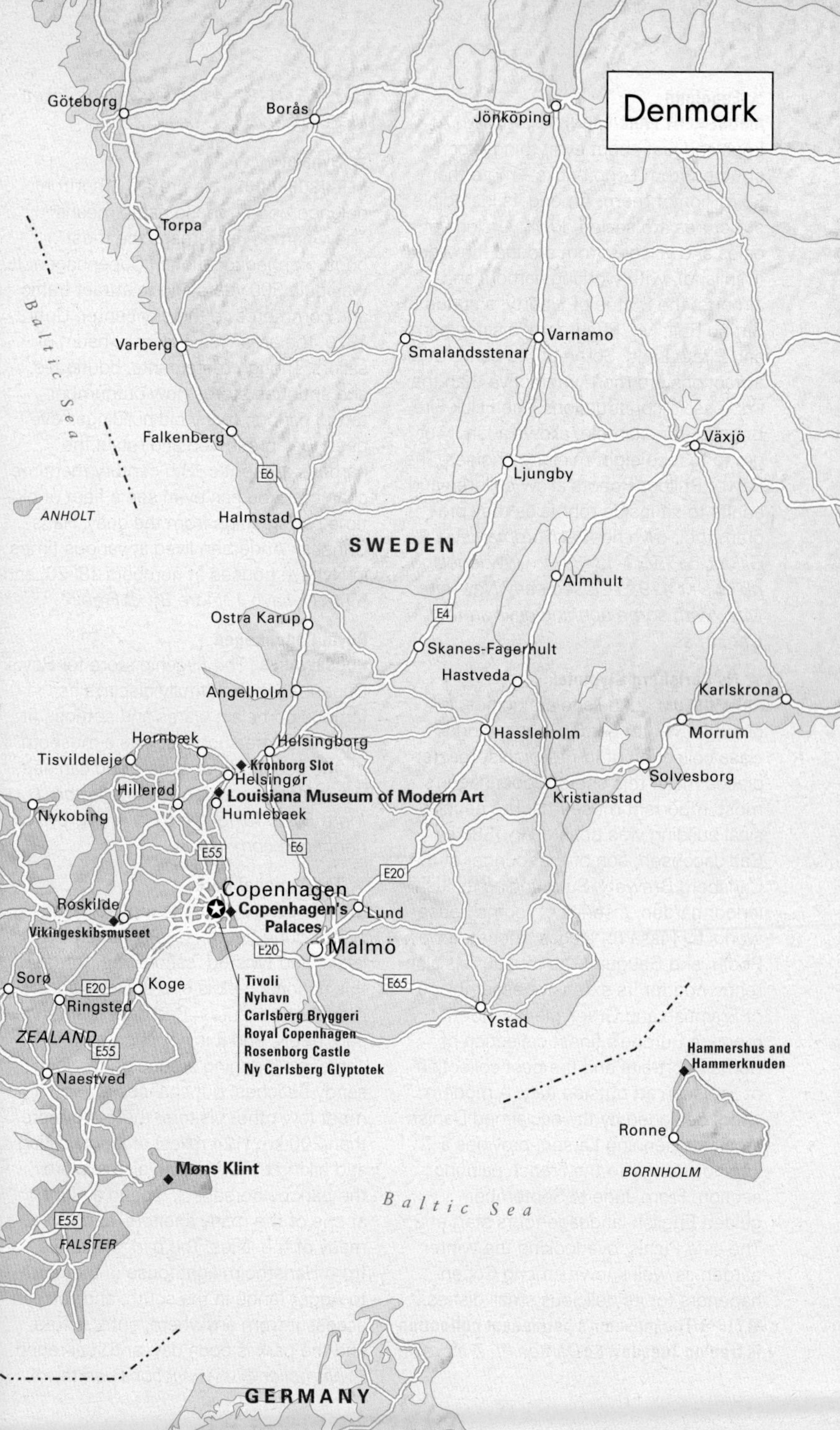

Denmark
Göteborg
Borås
Jönköping
Torpa
Baltic Sea
Varberg
Smalandsstenar
Varnamo
Falkenberg
Växjö
E6
Ljungby
ANHOLT
Halmstad
SWEDEN
Almhult
Ostra Karup
E4
Skanes-Fagerhult
Hastveda
Angelholm
Karlskrona
Hornbæk
Helsingborg
Hassleholm
Morrum
Tisvildeleje
Kronborg Slot
Helsingør
Solvesborg
Hillerød
Louisiana Museum of Modern Art
Kristianstad
Nykobing
Humlebaek
E55
E6
E20
Copenhagen
Roskilde
Copenhagen's Palaces
Lund
Vikingeskibsmuseet
E20
Malmö
Sorø
Koge
E65
E20
Tivoli
Nyhavn
Ringsted
Carlsberg Bryggeri
Ystad
ZEALAND
Royal Copenhagen
E55
Rosenborg Castle
Hammershus and Hammerknuden
Ny Carlsberg Glyptotek
Naestved
Ronne
BORNHOLM
Møns Klint
Baltic Sea
E55
FALSTER
GERMANY

★ Legoland

AMUSEMENT PARK/CARNIVAL | FAMILY | At Legoland just about everything is constructed from Lego bricks—more than 58 million of them. Among its incredible structures are scaled-down versions of cities and villages from around the world (Miniland), with working harbors and airports; the Statue of Liberty; a statue of Sitting Bull; Mt. Rushmore; a safari park; and Pirate Land. Some of the park's other attractions are more interactive than the impressive constructions. The Falck Fire Brigade, for example, allows a family or group to race eight mini fire engines. The Power Builder Robots allow children and adults to sit inside robots as they program their own ride. ✉ *Nordmarksvej 9, Billund* ☎ *75/33–13–33* 🌐 *www.legoland.dk* 🎫 *DKr 429* ⏲ *Closed early Nov.–late Mar., with some opening days around Christmas.*

★ Ny Carlsberg Glyptotek

ART MUSEUM | Exquisite antiquities, a beautiful winter garden, and a world-class collection of Impressionist masterpieces make this one of Copenhagen's most important museums. The neoclassical building was donated in 1888 by Carl Jacobsen, son of the founder of the Carlsberg Brewery. Surrounding its lush indoor garden, a series of rooms house works by Pissarro, Degas, Monet, Sisley, Rodin, and Gauguin. The museum is also renowned for its extensive assemblage of Egyptian and Greek pieces, not to mention Europe's finest collection of Roman portraits and the best collection of Etruscan art outside Italy. A modern wing, designed by the acclaimed Danish architect Henning Larsen, provides a luminous entry to the French painting section. From June to September, guided English-language tours start at 2. The café Picnic, overlooking the winter garden, is well known among Copenhageners for its delicious small dishes. **■ TIP→ The museum's permanent collection is free on Tuesday.** ✉ *Dantes Pl. 7, Indre By* ☎ *33/41–81–41* 🌐 *www.glyptoteket.dk* 🎫 *DKr 125* ⏲ *Closed Mon.*

★ Nyhavn

NEIGHBORHOOD | This pretty harborfront neighborhood, whose name means "new harbor," is perhaps the most photographed location in Copenhagen. It was built 300 years ago to attract traffic and commerce to the city center. Until 1970, the area was a favorite haunt of sailors. Though restaurants, boutiques, and antiques stores now outnumber tattoo parlors, many old buildings have been well preserved and retain the harbor's authentic 18th-century maritime character. You can even see a fleet of old-time sailing ships from the quay. Hans Christian Andersen lived at various times in Nyhavn houses at numbers 18, 20, and 67. ✉ *Nyhavn 1, Indre By* 🎫 *Free.*

Royal Copenhagen

HOUSEWARES | The flagship store for Royal Copenhagen beautifully displays its famous porcelain wares and settings fit for royals. The shop also has a museum on the second floor, where you can see the painters in action. ✉ *Amagertorv 6, Indre By* ☎ *33/13–71–81* 🌐 *www.royalcopenhagen.com.*

★ Thy National Park

NATIONAL PARK | With its rugged, windswept dune heath, several hundred lakes, and twisted, sand-swept forest, this national park is one of Denmark's proudest treasures. Red deer roam the park freely, and it is not uncommon to see seals lounging around on the long, sandy beaches, but chances are you'll meet few other visitors; there are more than 200 km (124 miles) of lonely biking and hiking trails. You can also explore the park by horseback, spend a night at one of the many shelters, and fish at many of the lakes. The park stretches from Hanstholm lighthouse in the north to Agger Tange in the south, and you can access it from anywhere; entry is free, and the park is open day- and year-round. ✉ *Klitmøller* 🌐 *www.nationalparkthy.dk.*

★ **Tivoli**

AMUSEMENT PARK/CARNIVAL | FAMILY | Tivoli is not only Copenhagen's best-known attraction, but also the city's most charming one. The amusement park, the second-oldest in the world, is located conveniently next to the city's main train station and attracts more than 4 million people from mid-April to mid-September. It is a pleasure garden as well as an amusement park. Among its attractions are a pantomime theater, an open-air stage, several dozen restaurants (some of them very elegant and with Michelin stars), and frequent concerts—from classical to rock to jazz. The Tivoli Guard, a youth version of the Queen's Royal Guard, performs every day. Try to see Tivoli at least once by night, when 100,000 colored lanterns illuminate the Chinese pagoda and the main fountain. Some evenings there are also fireworks displays. ✉ *Vesterbrogade 3, Indre By* ☎ *33/15–10–01* 🌐 *www.tivoli.dk* 🎫 *DKr 145–155, entrance and unlimited ride pass DKr 379* 🕒 *Closed late Sept.–mid-Oct., early to mid-Nov., most of Jan., and late Feb.–May.*

Vikingeskibsmuseet (*Viking Ship Museum*)

HISTORY MUSEUM | Less than 1 km (½ mile) north of the cathedral, on the fjord, is the modern Viking Ship Museum, containing five Viking ships sunk in the fjord 1,000 years ago. Submerged to block the passage of enemy ships, they were discovered in 1957. The painstaking recovery involved building a watertight dam and then draining the water from that section of the fjord. The splinters of wreckage were then preserved and reassembled. A deep-sea trader, warship, ferry, merchant ship, and fierce 92½-foot man-of-war attest to the Vikings' sophisticated and artful boat-making skills. The museum café serves excellent Nordic Viking-inspired meals. ✉ *Vindeboder 12, Roskilde* ☎ *46/30–02–00* 🌐 *www.vikingeskibsmuseet.dk* 🎫 *DKr 160.*

Where to Eat and Drink

★ **Christianshavn Bådudlejning**

$ | EUROPEAN | One of Copenhagen's most charming cafés isn't just located by the water but directly on it. This combined café, restaurant, and bar is floating on Christianshavn Kanal, giving it one of the best locations in the city. **Known for:** unique location on the water; creative, contemporary cuisine; creative crowd and good people-watching. $ *Average main: DKr85* ✉ *Overgaden Neden Vandet 29, Christianshavn* ☎ *32/96–53–53* 🌐 *baadudlejningen.dk* 🕒 *Usually closed Oct., Nov., Feb., and Mar.*

★ **Domestic**

$$$$ | SCANDINAVIAN | The brick walls, wooden floors, and high-beamed ceilings wow visitors at this gourmet restaurant, but only until the snacks start to arrive; then it's all about the food. The menu—four or eight courses—changes depending on the season, but it's always based on high-quality local ingredients and imaginative culinary thinking. **Known for:** creative menus and snacks; excellent wine and juice pairings; seasonal, local produce. $ *Average main: DKr800* ✉ *Mejlgade 35B, Århus* ☎ *61/43–70–10* 🌐 *restaurantdomestic.dk* 🕒 *Closed Sun.–Tues. No lunch.*

Frederikshøj

$$$$ | SCANDINAVIAN | One of Denmark's most celebrated and uncompromising chefs, Wassim Hallal, concocts brilliant dishes at this Michelin-starred restaurant with floor-to-ceiling windows offering views of a beautiful garden and the sea. The menus are a tour de force of local ingredients and sky-high gastronomic ambitions. **Known for:** elaborate, elegant dishes; first-class local produce; contemporary design and service. $ *Average main: DKr2500* ✉ *Oddervej 19, Århus* ☎ *86/14–22–80* 🌐 *frederikshoj.com* 🕒 *Closed Sun.–Tues.*

★ Geranium

$$$$ | SCANDINAVIAN | This modern northern European kitchen is giving acclaimed Noma a run for its money. Chefs Rasmus Kofoed and Søren Ledet put a modern touch on classic Scandinavian cooking by using molecular gastronomy and sourcing vegetarian products from biodynamic farmers; it made headlines when the restaurant removed all meat from the menu in 2021. **Known for:** location atop the soccer stadium parking garage; great media acclaim; vegetable-centric masterpieces. *$ Average main: DKr3800 ✉ Parken, Per Henrik Lings Allé 4, 8th fl., Nørrebro ☎ 69/96–00–20 🌐 www.geranium.dk ⏲ Closed Sun.–Tues. No lunch Wed. and Thurs.*

★ Hart Bageri

$ | BAKERY | Delicious fresh-baked bread, made by a former Tartine chef is always a consolation, regardless of the cause of your sadness, but especially if you are lamenting the fact that you never got to eat at now-closed, world-famous Noma. In this case, bread *really* is the next best thing as Hart Bageri was opened with the support of Noma's René Redzepi and it supplied the acclaimed restaurant with sourdough bread. **Known for:** tartine chef; supplier of bread to Noma; Danish pastries. *$ Average main: DKr1 ✉ Gammel Kongevej 109, Frederiksberg ☎ 31/11–18–50 🌐 hartbageri.com.*

★ Hviids Vinstue

BARS | Around since the 1720s, Hviids Vinstue attracts all kinds, young and old, singles and couples, for a glass of wine or cognac in its atmospheric basement with dark, wooden furniture, stained-glass windows, and leather couches. *✉ Kongens Nytorv 19, Indre By ☎ 33/15–10–64 🌐 www.hviidsvinstue.dk.*

★ Kadeau

$$$$ | SCANDINAVIAN | Located in the sand dunes on the idyllic southern stretch of the island, this New Nordic disciple serves Michelin-starred dishes with a strong focus on local produce. It looks like a traditional Danish summer house, but the food is anything but traditional; the lofty ambitions and equally high culinary capabilities of the young chefs have made it one of Denmark's most daring, darling restaurants. **Known for:** beautiful location on sandy beach; ambitious, creative dishes; excellent wine list. *$ Average main: DKr2150 ✉ Baunevej 18, Aakirkeby ☎ 56/97–82–50 🌐 www.kadeau.dk ⏲ Closed Oct.–Apr.*

Maison

$$ | FRENCH | Offering a menu of French classics including snails from Burgundy, foie gras, steak au poivre, sole meunière, and crème brûlée, Maison is decked out with a zinc bar, marble countertops, and French bistro chairs. Frankly, it's a dream of a brasserie, one of the best in Copenhagen. **Known for:** knowledgeable sommeliers and extensive wine list; stylish clientele; high-quality ingredients. *$ Average main: DKr235 ✉ Dronningens Tværgade 43 ☎ 33/18–15–16 🌐 www.restaurantmaison.dk ⏲ Closed Sun. No lunch.*

Restaurant Alouette

$$$$ | MODERN EUROPEAN | The Danish-American couple behind this restaurant met when Camilla Hansen walked into Nick Curtin's restaurant in New York to go on a blind date with another man, and the rest is history. The restaurant, which serves French-inspired menus in a former band room in Islands Brygge, quickly got its first Michelin star. **Known for:** transforming high-quality ingredients into playful dishes; elegant setting; seasonal approach. *$ Average main: DKr1195 ✉ Sturlasgade 14, Christianshavn ☎ 31/67–66–06 🌐 www.restaurant-alouette.dk ⏲ Closed Sun.–Wed. No lunch.*

TorvehallerneKBH

MARKET | FAMILY | Ever since opening in 2011, this covered marketplace with vendors selling culinary specialties has been busy. Vendors range from natural wine bars to stalls selling Vietnamese sandwiches, Danish licorice, raw food, and specialty coffee. There are many stalls selling delicacies to go and fresh vegetables, fish, meat, and poultry as well. ✉ *Frederiksborggade 21, Indre By* ☎ *70/10–60–70* 🌐 *torvehallernekbh.dk* 🎫 *Free.*

Cool Places to Stay

★ Coco Hotel

$$$ | **HOTEL** | This stylish newcomer on Copenhagen's hotel scene charms with its atmospheric courtyard, light-filled rooms, and mix of Scandinavian and French design. **Pros:** atmospheric garden and living room; light-filled rooms overlooking the courtyard; colorful, playful design throughout. **Cons:** some rooms are on the small side; located on a busy stretch of Vesterbrogade; the café is popular with locals, so there might be a wait for tables. $ *Rooms from: DKr1350* ✉ *Vesterbrogade 41, Vesterbro* ☎ *33/21–21–66* 🌐 *www.coco-hotel.com* 🛏 *83 rooms* 🍴 *Free Breakfast.*

★ Brøndums Hotel

$$ | **HOTEL** | Located among the most interesting attractions in Skagen and steeped in local history, this beach hotel is one of the most charming places to stay not only in Skagen but in all of Denmark. **Pros:** atmospheric rooms and beautiful main building; first-class Danish-French bistro restaurant; historical atmosphere. **Cons:** books up in the summer; not located directly on the beach; not all rooms are in the main building. $ *Rooms from: DKr895* ✉ *Anchersvej 3, Skagen* ☎ *98/44–15–55* 🌐 *www.broendums-hotel.dk* 🛏 *47 rooms* 🍴 *Free Breakfast.*

★ Helenekilde Badehotel

$$$$ | **HOTEL** | Perched atop the steep cliffs leading down to a pretty beach and offering grand views of the sea, this beachside beauty, in business since 1904, is one of the best hotels in Denmark. **Pros:** many rooms have sea views and some have terraces; beautiful decor; excellent restaurant and bar. **Cons:** books out months in advance in peak season; sometimes closed because of weddings or conferences; luxury comes with a price. $ *Rooms from: DKr3045* ✉ *Strandvejen 25, Tisvildeleje* ☎ *48/70–70–01* 🌐 *helenekilde.com* ⏲ *Closed January* 🛏 *27 rooms* 🍴 *Free Breakfast.*

★ Hotel d'Angleterre

$$$$ | **HOTEL** | With gorgeous rooms and impeccable service, this elegant luxury hotel has been a favorite of royalty for centuries and, more recently, of rock stars. **Pros:** sparkling, albeit classic, rooms; central location; the grande dame on Copenhagen's hotel scene. **Cons:** pricey; restaurant and spa can be busy; breakfast service can be spotty. $ *Rooms from: DKr4950* ✉ *Kongens Nytorv 34, Indre By* ☎ *33/12–00–95* 🌐 *www.dangleterre.dk* 🛏 *92 rooms* 🍴 *No Meals.*

Hotel Føroyar

$$$ | **HOTEL** | High in the hills above Tórshavn, and high in guests' estimation, this is considered to be one of the best accommodations in town, combining boutique design sensibilities with the natural life of the island. **Pros:** fabulous views; interesting architecture; nature setting. **Cons:** a 20-to-30-minute walk to town, uphill on the way back; some rooms are a little dated; no elevator. $ *Rooms from: DKr1600* ✉ *Oyggjarvegur 45, Tórshavn* ☎ *298/317–500* 🌐 *www.hotelforoyar.com* 🛏 *106 rooms* 🍴 *Free Breakfast.*

Manon Les Suites

$$$$ | **HOTEL** | It's easy to forget you're in Copenhagen when you walk into this adults-only hotel and see the indoor pool, surrounded by jungle-like plants and plush daybeds—you may think you're in Bali. **Pros:** stylish interior and common areas; popular with Copenhagen creatives; great location. **Cons:** pool area can be noisy; popular with non-guests; windows don't open in some rooms.

[$] *Rooms from: DKr2695* ✉ *Gyldenløvesgade 19, Indre By* ☎ *45/70–00–15* 🌐 *guldsmedenhotels.com/manon-les-suites* 🛏 *87 suites* 🍽 *Free Breakfast.*

★ Nordlandet

$$$ | HOTEL | Perched atop the cliff that separates Allinge from Sandvig, this contemporary hotel boasts grand views of the Baltic Sea, one of Bornholm's best restaurants, and bright, airy rooms and apartments dressed in a mix of classic and contemporary designer furniture. **Pros:** great sea views; excellent restaurant and hotel bar; location at the meeting point between Allinge and Sandvig. **Cons:** not all rooms are in the main building; café and bar can be busy with non-guests; pricey. [$] *Rooms from: DKr1790* ✉ *Strandvejen 68, Allinge* ☎ *56/48–03–44* 🌐 *hotelnordlandet.com* ⏲ *Closed Jan.–Mar.; Mon.–Wed. in Apr.; and Sun.–Tues. in Oct.–Dec.* 🛏 *27 rooms* 🍽 *Free Breakfast* ☞ *2-night min on some rooms.*

★ Villa Copenhagen

$$$$ | HOTEL | A forgotten landmark, the former Danish post office has been turned into a justifiably hyped luxury hotel with stylish rooms by the Scandinavian hotel emperor Petter Stordalen. **Pros:** stylish Scandinavian design throughout; plush cocktail bar and a hip brasserie; sustainable focus throughout the hotel. **Cons:** some rooms have views of Tivoli, but not all; luxury comes with a price; located on a busy, noisy intersection. [$] *Rooms from: DKr2331* ✉ *Tietgensgade 35-39, Indre By* ☎ *78/73–00–00* 🌐 *www.villacopenhagen.com* 🛏 *390 rooms* 🍽 *No Meals.*

★ Villa Provence

$$$$ | HOTEL | As promised by the name, this boutique hotel is a little slice of Provence in the heart of Aarhus. **Pros:** atmospheric courtyard and lounge areas; excellent breakfast with handpicked cheeses, fresh fruit, and homemade bread; friendly owners. **Cons:** some rooms are newer than others; breakfast room is cute but small; some rooms are decorated with more love than others. [$] *Rooms from: DKr1895* ✉ *Fredens Torv 12, Århus* ☎ *86/18–24–00* 🌐 *villaprovence.dk* 🛏 *39 rooms* 🍽 *Free Breakfast.*

Finland

The contrasts of nature and seasonal extremes dictate unforgettable experiences in this Nordic land, where winter brings perpetual darkness, and summer, perpetual light. Crystal-clear streams and rivers feed vast lakes and run through endless forests, home to varied wildlife, illuminated by midnight sun in summer and enchanted by dancing Northern Lights at other times, while reindeer roam free above the Arctic Circle.

The architecture of Alvar Aalto and the Saarinens—Eliel and son Eero—visible in many U.S. cities, confirms the Finnish affinity with nature, evoking echoes of Finland's vast forests. The music of Jean Sibelius, Finland's most famous son, swings from a somber midwinter nocturne to the tremolo of sunlight slanting through pine and birch. If you are drawn to majestic open spaces, linked by efficient infrastructure, and all the outdoor options they provide, and appreciate courteous, honest locals, Finland is for you.

In tune with those seasonal extremes, you might also notice an annual cycle of character in Finland's inhabitants which is more pronounced than elsewhere, whereby the gloom of midwinter is reflected in introspection, and the continuous summer light is expressed in more extroverted behavior. The average Finn has become harder to define, as a more urbanized, well-traveled, and often multilingual generation comes to the fore, gradually eroding the surly, reticent stereotype. In fact, Finland has been designated as World's Happiest Nation for five consecutive years (as of 2022) in the UN's World Happiness Report, although their definition of happiness is more complex than mere material wealth. Finns still like their silent spaces, especially in the sauna, regarded by many as cleansing to the soul as well as to the body.

Löyly Sauna, Helsinki

Sauna Where It Was Invented

While saunas are considered a luxury for most of the rest of the world, in Finland, the sauna is an integral part of daily Finnish life and culture—a place to cleanse the body and mind. One of the coolest, or maybe hottest, saunas to visit in Finland is located on a stretch of Helsinki waterfront. Löyly (the name in Finnish for the steam released when water is tossed on the sauna stove) is a modern sauna, restaurant, and bar complex in a striking and angular wooden structure, with stunning views and direct access to the refreshing Baltic Sea between sessions. There are three different saunas available: a traditional Finnish smoke sauna, and two other wood-heated options. In winter, there is an "avanto," a hole in the ice for an invigorating winter dip. While many Finnish saunas are nude, you'll need a bathing suit here (rentals are available).

Don't Miss

When reserving your sauna experience, be sure to make a reservation to dine at the on-site restaurant. The à la carte dinner menu includes Finnish dishes such as pike perch and reindeer, while the lunch selection includes moose meatballs and salmon soup. Dine on the sun-soaked terrace after sessions in summer or by an open fire in winter.

Getting Here and Around

Take the 6 train from Helsinki's Central Railway Station to the last stop in the Hernesaari district, from which Löyly is a short walk.

✉ *Hernesaarenranta 4, Helsinki*
☎ *09/6128–6550* 🌐 *www.loylyhelsinki.fi*
🎫 *From €21*

The Northern Lights in Lapland

Experience Magical Lights Dancing Across the Sky

The aurora borealis or Northern Lights is a mesmerizing natural phenomenon occurring in a roughly oval belt around the Arctic zone as a reaction in the earth's magnetic fields to solar activity, and Finnish Lapland is one of the best places—with the highest probability—for aurora viewing in the world. While there are no absolute guarantees of the skies dancing in light, your chances increase the farther north you go. In Saariselkä, aurora displays are visible up to 200 times per year. Many hotels here have glass igloos or roofs for viewing and there are also plentiful photographers and experts leading tours and workshops to help you capture the magic.

Don't Miss

Lapland Safaris offers Aurora Viewing tours that include thermal gear, traditional reindeer burgers by an open fire, an igloo visit, and aurora viewing. 🌐 *www.laplandsafaris.com*

When to Go

If possible, plan your visit from September to November or February to March; December and January are more crowded and often snowier.

Best Hotel

Muotka Wilderness Hotel offers elevated luxury in one of Europe's most remote and wild landscapes, with lodging options that include riverside log cabins and en suite glass-roofed pods. 🌐 *wildernesshotels.fi*

Getting Here and Around

Finnair flies to Rovaniemi, Ivalo, and Kittilä from Helsinki, or there are trains from Helsinki to Rovaniemi.

Visit Finland. 🌐 *www.visitfinland.com/en/places-to-go/lapland*

Finnish Meteorological Institute Aurora alerts. 🌐 *www.aurorasnow.fmi.fi*

The Midnight Sun in Sodankylä

Adventures When the Sun Doesn't Set

Venture north of the Arctic Circle in Summer and you will find the land of the Midnight Sun, where the curtains never drop on day and the stars and moon are supplanted by endless sunlight. Almost all of Lapland lies above the Arctic Circle, which means that night doesn't fall for several months every summer. 24 hours of sunlight means late-night adventures and a breaking of traditional rules and nap times. Most Finns take to the countryside to revel in the light, understandable after dark Arctic winters. The glorious extension of daylight lends itself to hiking or fat-biking across secluded upland trails, canoeing on lakes and river rapids, or all-night postsauna lake swimming.

Don't Miss

The annual Midnight Sun Film Festival at Soldankylä makes the most of its daylight hours with 24-hour film screenings.

When to Go

The period of true nightless night is when the sun never falls below the horizon and lengthens as you travel farther north. At Rovaniemi on the Arctic Circle it lasts from early June to early July. At Utsjoki on Finland's northern tip, it lasts from mid-May to late July.

Best Activity

According to the data provided by WHO, the world's cleanest air is measured at Pallas, Lapland.

Getting Here

Rovaniemi is connected with Helsinki and the south by road, rail, and air links. There are regular bus services between Rovaniemi and Sodankylä.

Visit Finland. 🌐 *www.visitfinland.com/en/places-to-go/lapland*

Santa Claus Village

The Home of Santa Claus

It's always Christmas in Rovaniemi, the one true home of the one and only true Santa. Santa Claus—known as *joulupukki* in Finnish, which literally means "Christmas goat"—is a legend, a source of magic for children, an ambassador of good will for Finland, and a big business in northern Finland. The main attraction, located directly on the Arctic Circle, is Santa Claus Village, open year-round for kids of all ages to meet Santa and his elves. There are restaurants and souvenir shops, gift workshops, and you can even meet Santa's reindeer. At Santa's Main Post Office, you can send Christmas postcards stamped with the special Arctic Circle postmark or even order a letter from the big man himself. You can also pick up an Arctic Circle Crossing Certificate at the information office. In winter, with the thick snow and frost on the trees, this is an enchanting place to visit, obviously especially for younger family members.

Don't Miss

SantaPark is an imaginative, subterranean, Christmas theme park built into the side of a hill just a few miles outside Rovaniemi. You'll find a magic train, an ice gallery, a lively elf show, a Christmas post office, and naturally another chance to meet the man of the moment, Santa Claus. However, it's a seasonal attraction, open for the Christmas season only. 🌐 *www.santaparkarcticworld.com*

Getting Here

Rovaniemi is connected with Helsinki and the south by road, rail, and air links. To visit Santa Claus Village, take local Bus 8 or Santa's Express Bus from Rovaniemi; see website for timetables.

✉ *Tähtikuja 1, Rovaniemi* ☎ *016/356–2096* 🌐 *www.santaclausvillage.info*

Savonlinna

A Lakeside Retreat

Finland's lakes are one of its best known attractions, numbering about 188,000 of every shape and size, and you don't need to travel far in the Lakelands region to appreciate their beauty, whether in winter or summer. Savonlinna, hugged by gigantic Lake Saimaa, is the best-placed town in the Lakelands and a convenient base from which to begin exploring the region. It's also a stunning town in itself, known for its water-bound views, cultural life, and for having the finest castle in all of Finland dominating its own craggy island. Built in 1475 to protect Finland's eastern border, Olavinlinna retains its medieval character and is one of Scandinavia's best-preserved historic monuments.

Don't Miss

The monthlong Savonlinna Opera Festival in July is one of Finland's—and Europe's—greatest. Most events are staged at the 14th-century Olavinlinna Castle, splendidly positioned just offshore.

Best Activity

SaimaaHoliday Oravi offers seal-watching safaris to see the rare Saimaa ringed seal in the Saimaa region from May to September. There are almost 400 of the animals in the lake, representing a conservation success story for a species that had dropped to a dangerously low population. 🌐 *www.oravivillage.com/en/Activities/Summer/Safaris-and-Seal-watching* 🎫 *From €75*

Getting Here

It's a six-hour ride/drive from Helsinki to Savonlinna traveling Route 5 to Route 14 in Juva, then another 60 km (37 miles) from Juva. The train trip from Helsinki to Savonlinna takes 4½ hours.

Savonlinna Tourist Information. 🌐 *www.visitsavonlinna.fi*

When in Finland

★ Amos Rex

ART MUSEUM | Opened in 2018 beneath the newly renovated 1930s Lasipalatsi (Glass Palace), this impressive contemporary art museum with 24,000 square feet of subterranean exhibition space is the expanded new home of the Amos Anderson Art Museum, the 590-seat handsome Bio Rex cinema (restored to its 1930s glory), a café, and a restaurant. The roof of the sizeable exhibition hall is a series of giant domes with angled roof lights that frame surrounding views and light the galleries. From outside, the roof's gently rolling forms are part of a popular public square that beckons to children and skateboarders and serves as a very modern counterpoint to the 1930s functionalist surroundings. Originally dedicated to Finnish and Swedish art of the 19th and 20th centuries, the museum is now also focused on international contemporary art. ✉ *Mannerheimintie 22–24, Keskusta* ☎ *09/6844–4633* 🌐 *amosrex.fi* 🎫 *€20* 🕒 *Closed Tues.*

★ Hanko

TOWN | In the coastal town of Hanko (Hangö) on Finland's southernmost tip, you'll find long stretches of beach—about 30 km (19 miles) of it—some sandy and some with sea-smoothed boulders. Sailing abounds here, thanks to Finland's largest guest harbor. A sampling of the grandest and most fanciful wooden villas in Finland dot the coast, their porches edged with gingerbread iron detail and woodwork and crazy towers sprouting from their roofs. Favorite pastimes here are beachside strolls; bike rides along well-kept paths; and, best of all, long walks along the main avenue past those great wooden houses with their wraparound porches. Clean sands and shallow waters make it a popular tourist hotspot, especially during the Hanko Regatta yacht race held every July. ✉ *Hanko* ✣ *146 km (91 miles), or 2½ hours by train, from Turku.*

★ Icebreaker Sampo Cruise

CRUISES | Sea Lapland, in the southwest region of Finnish Lapland, is one of the few extraordinary places in the world where the sea completely freezes over in the winter. The Icebreaker Sampo Cruise offers an unforgettable sea, snow, and ice adventure from the Baltic port of Kemi, with a half-day cruise crunching through the ice on the frozen Gulf of Bothnia. Morning and afternoon cruises take passengers several miles out to sea, stopping to let you walk down a gangway to stroll on this temporary, dazzling, frozen plain, with the option of donning a waterproof survival suit in which to float around in open pools next to the ship. The tour also includes free entrance to the SnowCastle area where you will find ice sculptures, snow slides, and a winter park. ✉ *Lumilinnankatu 15A* ☎ *016/258–878* 🌐 *https://experience365.fi/icebreakersampo.*

★ Marimekko

MIXED CLOTHING | Since the 1950s Marimekko has been selling bright, unusual clothes for men, women, and children in quality fabrics, and it is perhaps the most durable, recognizable, and iconic of all Finnish design brands, popular globally. Though the products are expensive, they're worth a look even if you don't plan to buy. There are several locations in central Helsinki and others throughout Finland, in addition to this flagship concept store. ✉ *Kämp Galleria, Pohjoisesplanadi 33, Keskusta* ☎ *09/572–5632* 🌐 *www.marimekko.com.*

Moominworld

THEME PARK | FAMILY | The Moominworld theme park brings to life all the famous characters of the beloved children's stories written by Finnish author Tove Jansson. The stories emphasize family, respect for the environment, and new adventures. Obviously, it's a very popular family destination—though somewhat

Finland
NORWAY
Tromsø
Utsjoki
Kaamanen
Sami Museum and the Northern Lapland Nature Center Siida
Reindeer Farm Petri Mattus
E6
E75
Enontekio
Muonio
Sirkka
The Northern Lights in Lapland
Kandalaksha
E10
Sodankylä
The Midnight Sun in Sodankylä
Saarenpuhdas
E105
Kemijärvi
E63
Santa Claus Village
Pello
Kayla
E45
E10
Rovaniemi
Kuusamo
Tallvik
E75
Raiskio
Tore
Peranka
Kemi
Icebreaker Sampo Cruise
Olhava
Pudasjarvi
Arvidsjaur
Luleå
Suomussalmi
RUSSIA
Wild Taiga Wildlife Tours
Oulu
SWEDEN
Gulf of Bothnia
E4
Raahe
E75
Kuhmo
Skelleftea
Kajaani
Sotkamo
E8
Kalajoki
FINLAND
Himanka
Nurmes
Kokkola
Iisalmi
Lieksa
Pyhasalmi
Umeå
Pannainen
E63
Holmsund
Lestijarvi
Joensuu
Kuopio
Vaasa
Airaksela
Örnsköldsvik
Laihia
Seinajoki
Varkaus
E4
E8
Jyväskylä
Savonlinna
Leivonmaki
Sundsvall
Kristinestad
Mikkeli
Parkano
Kankaanpaa
E63
E75
E12
Lappeenranta
Pori
Tampere
Lahti
Kouvola
Rauma
Hämeenlinna
Hamina
0
50 mi
0
50 km
E18
E8
Hyvinkaa
Lovisa
St. Petersburg
Porvoo
Moominworld
Turku Cathedral
Helsinki
Turku
Amos Rex
Marimekko
Oodi Central Library
Suomenlinna
Löyly Sauna, Helsinki
RUSSIA
Storby
Svensbole
Ekenas
Hanko
Tallinn
ESTONIA

overpriced as such—but it's a draw for tourists of all ages. Sadly, it's open only in summer. ✉ *Kaivokatu 5, Naantali* ☎ *02/511–1111* 🌐 *www.moominworld.fi* 🎫 *€35, 2-day ticket €43* ⏲ *Closed mid-Aug–mid-June.*

★ Oodi Central Library

LIBRARY | FAMILY | Opened at the beginning of 2019 and conceived as a gift to its citizens marking the centenary of Finland's independence in 1917, sleek, ultramodern Oodi, made of steel, glass, and wood, is much more than a conventional book-lending library, although it serves that function too. A huge, convivial living room for the people, Oodi houses two cafés, a kids' area, 3-D printers, sewing machines, computer workstations, a music studio, and a movie theater, as well as a fair collection of books and magazines. The view from the balcony on the top floor (closed in the slippery winter months) extends across a broad plaza—the "People's Square"—bordered by the Music Center and the Kiasma Museum of Contemporary Art, with Finlandia Hall also nearby. It is a manifestation of Nordic service planning at its finest, most imaginative and most elegant. ✉ *Töölönlahdenkatu 4, Keskusta* ☎ *09/3108–5000* 🌐 *www.oodihelsinki.fi* 🎫 *Free.*

Reindeer Farm Petri Mattus

FARM/RANCH | Visits to this working reindeer farm, located near Menesjärvi Lake toward the Lemmenjoki National Park, are hosted by the reindeer herder and owner Petri Mattus. He'll take you by sled, lined with reindeer pelts and towed by snowmobile, to show you the reindeer and let you hand-feed them, and if you're there at the right time, you can watch a spectacular roundup or witness calves being born and earmarked in spring. Coffee, tea, and light lunch can be included in the program price. This is one of the most authentic reindeer farms in Finnish Lapland, offering a genuine insight into the traditional Sámi lifestyle. ✉ *Kittiläntie 3070B, Inari* ☎ *0400/193–950* 🌐 *www.reindeerfarmpetrimattus.com* 🎫 *From €120 per person (depending on group size)* ⏲ *By reservation only.*

★ Sámi Museum and the Northern Lapland Nature Center Siida

OTHER MUSEUM | The museum of the culture of the Sámi people is close to the westernmost corner of Inarijärvi Lake in the village of Inari and houses an absorbing exhibition describing every aspect of Sámi history and life (Siida is a traditional reindeer herding site and community). It also gives fascinating explanations of the natural environment and harsh arctic climate in which these people, predominantly reindeer herders, have traditionally forged a seminomadic livelihood. There's an open-air museum behind the main building, comprising traditional Lapp dwellings and farm buildings. A souvenir shop sells Sámi handicrafts, and café-restaurant Sarrit serves good lunches. Siida has been expanding, and some exhibits were still in the process of being transferred to a new annex in fall 2022 as renovations proceeded, but the museum has remained open throughout the expansion work. ✉ *Inarintie 46, Inari* ☎ *0400/898–212* 🌐 *www.siida.fi* 🎫 *€15* ⏲ *Closed Sun. in Oct.–May.*

★ Suomenlinna (*Fortress of Finland*)

HISTORIC SIGHT | It feels like another world, but the sea views and rugged shorelines of this sea fortress, Helsinki's top historical destination, are a 15-minute harbor ferry hop from the Market Square in the center of town. It's a perennially popular collection of fortifications, museums, parks, and gardens and has been designated a UNESCO World Heritage Site. In 1748, Finland's Swedish rulers started to build the impregnable fortress, long referred to as the Gibraltar of the North, across a series of interlinked islands. Although Suomenlinna has never been taken by assault, it came under Russian governance with the rest of Finland in 1808 and came under fire from British and French ships in 1855 during the Crimean War. Today Suomenlinna makes a lovely excursion from Helsinki at any time of the year but particularly in early summer when the island is carpeted by wildflowers and engulfed in a mauve-and-purple mist of lilacs. There are several cafés and restaurants on the islands. ✉ *Suomenlinna C40, Suomenlinna* ✣ *In the entrance to Helsinki's South Harbour* ☎ *0295/338–410 tourist info* 🌐 *www.suomenlinna.fi/en* 🎫 *Fortress free, museum €7, other fees vary.*

Turku Cathedral

CHURCH | The "mother church" of the Finnish Lutheran faith and Finland's national shrine, this medieval cathedral was first consecrated in 1300 (before the Reformation) and its 101-meter-tall stone tower is one of the city's main landmarks in its most historic quarter next to a broad cobbled square and close to the river. It contains a small museum of historic items as well as the tomb of Bishop Hemming, one of the cathedral's first benefactors. ✉ *Tuomiokirkonkatu 1, Turku* ☎ *040/341–7100* 🌐 *www.turuntuomiokirkko.fi* 🎫 *Free.*

★ Wild Taiga Wildlife Tours

SPECIAL-INTEREST TOURS | Operating mainly in Finland's unspoiled eastern Kainuu region, mostly in Suomussalmi and Kuhmo, Wild Taiga offers wildlife viewing and photography tours that get you thrillingly close to majestic wild brown bears, wolves, wolverines, and birds of prey from special hides designed for photography. Hiking, skiing, snowshoeing, auora-photography, and cultural activities can also be added. Wildlife-watching tours are offered in spring, summer, and autumn; bears are hibernating through the winter. 🌐 *wildtaiga.fi/en* 🎫 *Overnight bear-watching tour from €159.*

Where to Eat and Drink

★ Juttutupa

LIVE MUSIC | Steeped in history, this bar was first opened in 1906 by the Helsinki Workers' Association. If that gives a staid impression, don't be deterred: Juttutupa hosts great jazz, blues, and other music nights (admission is free) and has a convivial, authentically Helsinki atmosphere, making it one of the city's best live music venues. At the bar's "revolutionary table," Vladimir Lenin met with fellow conspirators and plotted Russia's revolution, just one element of a fascinating and eventful history. The bar is inside the Graniittilinna restaurant, behind the Scandic Paasi hotel, a magnificent National Romantic–style stone fortress overlooking an inlet from the sea. The menu includes good pizzas and salads, and there is an outdoor terrace that catches the evening sun. ✉ *Graniittilinna, Säästöpankinranta 6, Kallio* ☎ *020/742–4240* 🌐 *www.juttutupa.fi.*

Kaskis

$$$$ | FINNISH | Local, in-season, and fresh ingredients, including foraged herbs and salad ingredients from nearby forests, are featured on set menus at this sustainably principled gourmet restaurant, voted Finnish Restaurant of the Year in 2018. A popular venue for special events or celebrations, Kaskis reopened after renovations in 2020 and lists rainbow trout, whitefish, venison, and forest berries on its menu, with matching wine packages. **Known for:** sustainably sourced ingredients; intimate and friendly ambience; award-winning prestige. [$] *Average main: €119* ✉ *Kaskenkatu 6A, Turku* ☎ *044/723–0200* 🌐 *www.kaskis.fi* ⏲ *Closed Sun.–Tues. No lunch.*

Moro Sky Bar

COCKTAIL LOUNGES | Perched on top of Tampere's tallest building, the Solo Sokos Hotel Torni, this lively cocktail bar offers the best view in town to go with your drinks. The line for the elevator from the hotel lobby can extend a bit, especially on weekend evenings, but most punters seem to think it's worth the wait. ✉ *Solo Sokos Hotel Torni, Ratapihankatu 43, Tampere* ☎ *020/123–4634* 🌐 *www.raflaamo.fi.*

★ Nili

$$$ | **FINNISH** | Probably the coziest and best place in town to sample authentic, top-quality Lapp dishes, Nili offers a prix-fixe "Rovaniemi Menu" that includes bear-meat consommé, caramelized pork, arctic pike perch, and a final course of homemade "squeaky" cheese, which is a hard cheese that is baked in the oven to soften it and usually served with cloudberry jam. The à la carte menu includes sautéed reindeer—poronkäristys—with mashed potatoes and lingonberry sauce, a local classic. **Known for:** sautéed reindeer; authentic Lapp dishes; rustic wood-and-hide decor. [$] *Average main: €30* ✉ *Valtakatu 20, Rovaniemi* ☎ *0400/369–669* 🌐 *www.nili.fi* 🕓 *Closed Sun. No lunch.*

★ Ora Restaurant

$$$$ | **MODERN EUROPEAN** | Hidden away in the Eira district on Helsinki's most elegant art nouveau residential street, tiny Ora is the antithesis of pretentious gourmet dining, although its creativity and sense of fun has earned it a Michelin star. All ingredients—apart from salt—are produced or foraged locally, and the menu is exquisitely crafted, with foraged herbs and fresh seasonal vegetables complementing fish and meat creations. **Known for:** open kitchen; exciting and innovative menu; Michelin star. [$] *Average main: €89* ✉ *Huvilakatu 28A, Eira* ☎ *0400/959–440* 🌐 *www.orarestaurant.fi* 🕓 *Closed Sun.–Tues. No lunch.*

★ Smör

$$$$ | **SCANDINAVIAN** | An elegant riverside restaurant, Smör (Swedish for "butter") prides itself on being an ambassador of local food and a master of Nordic cuisine, and has earned a reputation for its discerning wine cellar filled with small vineyard labels. A selection of cold or hot small plates comprise the à la carte menu (four items minimum recommended), but the highlight is an all-Nordic-ingredient prix-fixe menu that includes duck, herring, and venison. **Known for:** new menu every eight weeks; all-Nordic ingredients; carefully curated wine cellar. [$] *Average main: €89* ✉ *Läntinen Rantakatu 3, Turku* ☎ *02/536–9444* 🌐 *www.smor.fi* 🕓 *Closed July and Sun.–Tues. No lunch.*

Cool Places to Stay

★ Arctic Light Hotel

$$$$ | **HOTEL** | The kind of genuine boutique hotel that Finland needs more of, the Arctic Light is a wonderful luxury haven in downtown Rovaniemi, the perfect retreat after a cold winter day of snowmobile or reindeer safaris, but it's just as comfortable at other times of the year. **Pros:** central location; excellent breakfast; cozy boutique character. **Cons:** an unnecessary profusion of pillows; confusing lighting controls; dark fittings. [$] *Rooms from: €350* ✉ *Valtakatu 18, Rovaniemi* ☎ *020/96200* 🌐 *www.arcticlighthotel.fi* *52 rooms* 🍽 *Free Breakfast.*

★ Hotel Kämp

$$$$ | **HOTEL** | Situated opposite the Esplanade, this luxurious, late-19th-century cultural landmark has long been the meeting point for Finland's most prominent politicians, artists, and celebrities in accordance with its unofficial status as Finland's ritziest hotel. **Pros:** lavish rooms; five-star service; fantastic spa. **Cons:** high rates; slightly over-formal ambience; high rates, again. [$] *Rooms from: €300* ✉ *Pohjoisesplanadi 29, Keskusta* ☎ *09/5619–2701* 🌐 *www.hotelkamp.com* *179 rooms* 🍽 *Free Breakfast.*

★ Hotel Punkaharju

$$$ | **HOTEL** | Situated on the idyllic Punkaharju esker ridge a 30-minute drive southeast of Savonlinna, surrounded by quintessential Finnish lake-and-forest

scenery, this is one of the most beautifully located hotels in Finland, if not *the* most beautifully located. **Pros:** scenic location; modern with historic character; excellent restaurant. **Cons:** some rooms are a little small; weak Wi-Fi; distant from other dining options and amenities. *Rooms from: €250 Punkaharjun Harjutie 596, Punkaharju 015/511–311 www.hotellipunkaharju.fi Closed late Dec.–mid-Feb.; closed Mon. and Tues. mid-Feb.–late Apr. and late Sept.–mid-Dec. 20 rooms, 12 cabins Free Breakfast.*

★ Hotel St. George

$$$$ | HOTEL | Competing with the Hotel Kämp at the pinnacle of Finnish luxury, the St. George opened in 2018 in converted apartment buildings on one corner of the Vanha Kirkkopuisto (Old Church Park). **Pros:** stylish and luxurious; park and city rooftop views on the upper floors; excellent breakfast. **Cons:** pricey; confusing reception entrance; art not to everyone's taste. *Rooms from: €350 Yrjönkatu 13, Keskusta 09/4246–0011 www.stgeorgehelsinki.com 153 rooms No Meals.*

★ Kakslauttanen Arctic Resort

$$$$ | RESORT | FAMILY | What started as a roadside restaurant grew into a cozy scattering of wood cabins and eventually a sprawling resort with a variety of lodgings from traditional log cabins to glass igloos, snow igloos, and apartment-sized chalets with hemispherical glass extensions for aurora viewing, all of them at premium prices. **Pros:** variety of unique lodging styles; beautiful location surrounded by forest; amenities include reindeer farm and smoke saunas. **Cons:** resort feel, especially in the West Village; distance to walk from cabins to restaurant in West Village; very pricey. *Rooms from: €450 Kiilopääntie 9, Saariselkä 016/667–100 www.kakslauttanen.fi 145 rooms Free Breakfast.*

★ Naantali Spa Hotel and Spa Residence

$$$ | RESORT | This modern spa complex offers spiritual and physical replenishment in a tranquil seaside setting and is often voted Finland's best hotel in travel awards. **Pros:** 100 listed spa treatments; variety of restaurants and bars; spa, gym, and sauna included in most rates. **Cons:** lacks the intimacy of smaller retreats; menu of treatments can be confusing; slightly at odds with small-town local atmosphere. *Rooms from: €210 Matkailijantie 2, Naantali 02/445–5100 www.naantalispa.fi 169 rooms Free Breakfast.*

Iceland

Iceland is like no other place on earth. Its landscapes are so otherworldly that they represent fictional worlds in many fantasy epics. The air smells different here—clean and crisp—and it's so clear that on a sunny day you can see for miles. Welcome to Iceland, a land of dazzling white glaciers, rugged black sand beaches, bubbling hot springs, perilous lava fields, and awe-inspiring waterfalls.

This North Atlantic island exemplifies the ferocious powers of nature, ranging from the still-warm lava from the 2020–21 Fagradalsfjall eruption to the chilling splendor of the Vatnajökull Glacier. More than 80% of the island's 103,000 square km (40,000 square miles) is uninhabited. Ice caps cover 11% of the country, more than 50% is barren, 6% consists of lakes and rivers, and less than 2% of the land is cultivated. There's hardly a tree to be seen in most of the country, making the few birches, wildflowers, and delicate vegetation all the more lovely in contrast.

Surrounded by the sea, the Icelanders have become great fishermen, and fish remains, along with tourism, the cornerstone of the economy. Because of importation needs and high value-added taxes on most goods and services, prices tend toward the steep side. Hotels and restaurants are pricey, but with a little digging you can usually find reasonably inexpensive alternatives.

So far north—the country touches the Arctic Circle—Iceland has the usual Scandinavian long hours of darkness in winter. Maybe this is why Icelanders are such good chess players (Iceland played host to the memorable 1972 Fischer–Spassky match). Such long nights may also explain why, per capita, more books are written, printed, purchased, and read in Iceland than anywhere else worldwide. Of course, there's more to do in the winter than just read, for one would be remiss to not go hunt those famed twinkling Northern Lights.

The Blue Lagoon

A Wellspring of Wonder

The most famous bathing spot in the world and Iceland's most iconic attraction, the breathtaking Blue Lagoon is a steaming, milky-blue geothermal pool and spa, set in a rocky, lava-filled landscape.This world-renowned therapeutic pool is famous for its mineral-rich seawater and soft white silica mud, both of which have healing effects on the skin. The visit experience is designed as a relaxing spa day where you submerge yourself in the bath-warm water and simply unwind in the ethereal landscape. To add to the relaxation, you can pick up a mud mask from the in-water mask bar, reserve an in-water massage, and hang out in the grotto-like steam room carved into the volcanic rock. A reception area includes concessions and boutique shops where you can buy health products made from the lagoon's mineral-rich ingredients. Make a day of it with a postsoak lunch at Lava restaurant, where you will find contemporary Icelandic cuisine and those incredible views.

Don't Miss

A stay at the lagoon's luxury Retreat Hotel includes unlimited access to the healing waters, spa, and landscape.

When to Go

The thermal waters stay warm year-round, so really there's no bad time to visit. In winter, the experience is enhanced with snow falling and the Northern Lights dancing above you.

Getting Here

The lagoon is only 20 minutes from Keflavík Airport and 50 minutes from Reykjavík by car. Buses run from the BSÍ bus terminal in Reykjavík to the Blue Lagoon frequently. Booking in advance is essential.

✉ *Bláa lónið, Norðurljósavegur 9, Grindavík* ☎ *354/420–8800* 🌐 *www.bluelagoon.com* 🎫 *From ISK 11,990*

The Golden Circle

Iceland's Holy Trinity

One of the most scenic routes in all of Europe, the Golden Circle loops for 186 miles, taking in some of the most spectacular sites in the country. The first big stop on the route is where the original settlers of Iceland had their Alþingi, one of the oldest parliamentary institutions in the world. It is both culturally and naturally unique. Next stop is the Geysir hot spring area with the Strokkuur geyser that erupts every few minutes more than 100 feet into the sky. The third and last stop is the most famous waterfall in all of Iceland: Gullfoss, or "Golden Waterfall." White glacial water pours down from the highlands and into a deep canyon at a volume, speed, and power that seems incomprehensible.

Don't Miss

For a quick bite, most gas stations or service centers offer the traditional Icelandic *pylsur*—hot dog. For the true experience, ask for "eina með öllu" which will give you the hot dog along with all the toppings, including raw onions, cooked onions, and two unique sauces. While gas station hot dogs might not be popular in other countries, in Iceland they are a delicacy enjoyed by all.

When to Go

Summer brings long days and luscious landscapes. In winter, it's all even more breathtaking against the snow, and there's nothing like a frosty stroll around the winding paths of Þingvellir.

Getting Here and Around

Driving is the most popular way to see this region. The Golden Circle route should take you seven or eight hours by car, if you make stops at the various sights.

Reykjanes Visitor Center. ✉ *Duusgata 2–8, Reykjanesbær, Southern Peninsula* 🌐 *reykjanesgeopark.is* 🎫 *Free*

Whale-Watching in Húsavík

Gentle Giants, Up-Close-and-Personal

Many whale, dolphin, and porpoise species call Iceland's rich waters home—in fact, Iceland is considered the whale-watching capital of Europe—and a multitude of whale-watching tours embark from the larger coastal towns. But when it comes to seeing humpbacks and more as close as possible, Húsavík is the undisputed capital (it was also the site where NASA astronauts trained before going to the moon in the 1960s). In this small northern town, whales are so accustomed to the daily tours that they will often come up extremely close to the boats and say "hi." Keep your eyes peeled and if you're lucky, you might see a rare breaching.

Don't Miss

The two standout tour companies in Húsavík are Gentle Giants and North Sailing. Gentle Giants offers both classic tours on traditional wooden boats as well as shorter tours on RIB speedboats for those looking for a little more adrenaline. North Sailing, meanwhile, has an impressive fleet of old fishing boats and schooners, two of which have been modified with an electric engine to offer an eco-friendly carbon-neutral whale-watching experience.

When to Go

April through October is the best time to visit, but tours are offered year-round.

Getting Here

From Akureyri, take Highway 1 east before turning left onto Highway 85 north to Húsavík. The drive is about one hour. Driving is really your only option.

Gentle Giants. ☎ 464–1500 🌐 *www.gentlegiants.is*

North Sailing. ☎ 464–7272 🌐 *www.northsailing.is*

Fagradalsfjall Volcano

A Still-Steaming Volcano

The Fagradalsfjall volcano eruption site is a must-visit in Iceland. Where else can you stand but feet away from newly made continental crust? A wasteland of spiky jagged lava, this tuya volcano, which last erupted in August 2022, is still steaming, with fields of fresh basalt covered in blankets of mist. There are a few different paths to explore within the volcano's vicinity, varying in difficulty from easy to advanced, but there are also numerous tour operators that offer trips to the volcano via guided hikes, helicopter, or airplane. That said, don't be afraid to just go yourself and have a long picnic there. ⚠ **If your visit coincides with an active period of the volcano, check in advance to make sure the current hiking conditions are safe.**

Don't Miss

Path A will get you the closest to the cooled magma. While there are a few strenuous portions, it's doable for anyone that's moderately in shape. Expect to spend around four to five hours actually walking. Hiking boots are strongly recommended.

Best Restaurants

A steaming cup of lobster soup from the nearby Bryggjan café in Grindavík—about a 10 minute drive away—is just what's needed after a day of trekking. ✉ *Miðgarður 2, 240 Grindavík* ☎ *354/426–7100* 🌐 *www.bryggjan.com*

Getting Here

The site itself is just an hour's drive from Reykjavík—take Highway 41 toward Keflavík and turn onto Highway 43 toward Grindavík, then follow Highway 427 until you see a plethora of well-parked parking lots.

✣ *Hwy. 427 from Grindavík* 🎫 *Parking ISK 1000*

The Westfjords Way

Drive the Real Iceland

The land of fire and ice offers several incredibly scenic drives and while most head to the iconic (but heavily touristed) Golden Circle, the Westfjords Way in Iceland's North West offers almost 600 miles of breathtaking scenery minus the tour buses and traffic. This dramatic driving loop navigates the edges of the Westfjords peninsula, including towns like Ísafjörður, Flateyri, Þingeyri, Patreksfjörður, Hólmavík, and Drangsnes. Break up the driving with overnights in Ísafjörður and Patreksfjörður, both great bases for exploring, and consider immersing yourself in the landscape, nature, and the way of life by building breaks for tours and activities into your itinerary. From Ísafjörður, book ATV, bus, and horseback-riding tours of the area, while in Patreksfjörður, you'll want to allow time to walk the red sand of Rauðasandur Beach and to soak in Birkimelur Swimming Pool's geothermal water.

Don't Miss

Showstoppers along the Westfjords Way include the Látrabjarg Sea Cliffs; the Dynjandi waterfalls; the Sorceror's Cottage; the pass between Hrafnseyri and Þingeyri; the road around Klofningur; Hvítanes Seal colony, and the Neshringur loop, and basically every time you look out your window.

When to Go

While the new Dýrafjarðargöng tunnel makes it possible to travel to this region year-round, June to August is the best time to drive the loop.

Getting Here

Take a ferry to the Southern Westfjords from the Snæfellsnes Peninsula or drive from Reykjavik (70 miles). Plan at least three days (preferably four) to drive around the Westfjords region and visit its main attractions.

Visit Westfjords. ☎ *354/450–8060*
🌐 *www.westfjords.is*

Mývatn Nature Baths

Soak Like an Icelander

While many opt for the iconic Blue Lagoon, the Mývatn Nature Baths offer a much more scenic, much less crowded and much more authentic Icelandic geothermal experience. Containing a unique blend of minerals, silicates and microorganisms, the waters of Mývatn are much paler than its southern counterpart and it's a warm and wonderful place to relax. Plus, if it gets too hot you can order an in-bath glass of cold beer. While it's rare to find Icelanders at the Blue Lagoon, at Mývatn, you'll find locals who have visited weekly for their whole lives and swear by its healing powers. Believe them!

Best Activities

The surrounding area is filled with some of Iceland's top attractions. For example, Dimmuborgir, Goðafoss, Hverir and Krafla Volcano are all within driving distance. Sigurgeir's Bird Museum is a quirky stop, too.

Don't Miss

Plan your visit around sunset—the views over the lake are especially enchanting then.

Best Restaurant

There's farm to table and then there's cowshed to coffee cup. Vogafjós Cowshed Café, just 10 minutes from the baths is known for its homemade local food, views of cows grazing, and its superfresh whole milk and cream to go with your coffee and delicious fresh-baked cakes. ✉ *Vogar, 660 Myvatn* 🌐 *www.vogafjosfarmresort.is*

Getting Here and Around

From Akureyri, take Highway 1 west until the well-marked turnoff on the right. The drive is just over one hour.

✉ *Jarðbaðshólar, Mývatn* ☎ *354/464–4411* 🌐 *www.myvatnnaturebaths.is*
🎫 *ISK 5900*

Vatnajökull National Park

Hike Europe's Largest Glacier and Visit an Ice Cave

Home to Europe's largest glacier and 3,00 square miles of ice, Vatnajökull National Park is said to put the "ice" in Iceland, and with seven volcano systems under all that ice, it could also explain the "land of fire and ice" nickname. Within this massive park, you'll find spectacular displays of nearly every geological feature and landscape Iceland has to offer: horseshoe-shape cliffs, thundering waterfalls, endless glacier tongues, active volcanoes, otherworldly lava fields, and more. The Skaftafell region of the park receives more than 500,000 visitors each year, who come to hike its numerous scenic trails, marvel at dripping glacial tongues, or simply just witness its magnificence. The Vatnajökull glacier has numerous glacial outlets that are popular for hikes, but Skaftafellsjökull is an easy one to visit, with the trail to the edge of the glacier paved half the way there. Explore moulins and crevasses, see sapphire blue ice caves, and soak in the glorious scenery.

Don't Miss

Iceland's tap water is some of the cleanest in the world; try some straight from the glacier.

Best Tour

IceGuide specializes in glacier-theme tours with thrilling visits to glacier ice caves or kayaking excursions between creaking icebergs on a glacier lagoon, plus glacier walks and hikes, too. 🌐 *www.iceguide.is/tours*

Getting Here

The glacier is located just off Highway 1, about a 4½-hour drive east from Reykjavík.

Skaftafell Visitor Center. ✣ *Just off Hwy. 1 in Vatnajökull National Park* ☎ *354/470–8300* 🌐 *www.vjp.is*

Fimmvörðuháls

The Most Epic Mountain Trail

Journeying between the ice caps of both Eyjafjallajökull and Mýrdalsjökull, the Fimmvörðuháls trail offers the best of Iceland in one day. The nine-hour hike goes through a plethora of iconically Icelandic landscapes, from moss-covered lava fields to desolate Highland deserts to lush valleys, black sand dunes, and snowfields and glaciers. It just might be the most spectacular hike you'll ever do.

Don't Miss

Every segment of Fimmvörðuháls is stunning, but make sure to leave time to appreciate the magnificent splendor of Hvannárgil Canyon, which begins in the last third of the trail on the descent down into Þórsmörk.

When to Go

The hike is only open during the summer months.

Best Accommodation

Volcano Huts offers comfortable—albeit austere—lodging for the night in Þórsmörk. The best part? Their hearty dinner buffet will knock your socks off after the grueling hike. 🌐 *www.volcanotrails.com*

Best Tour

Útivist Travel Association expert guide service is famous for its summer solstice hikes of this trail. 🌐 *www.utivist.is*

Getting Here

If you are in decent shape and prepared for changeable weather and some significant elevation gain in spots, you can do this 15½-mile hike in 8 to 10 hours. The trail begins at Skógafoss. Reykjavík Excursions offers buses to the trailhead as well as back from Þórsmörk.

Visit South Iceland. 🌐 *www.south.is/en/place/fimmvorduhals*

Seljalandsfoss

Walk Behind a Glacial Waterfall

Iceland is known for its magnificent waterfalls, each with their unique beauty and appeal, from the zigzagging Klifbrekkufoss to the most powerful Dettifoss, the mythological "Waterfall of the Gods," Godafoss, and the Golden Circle's famous Gullfoss. The majestic Seljalandsfoss glacial waterfall, situated right off the Ring Road, is one of the country's most picturesque waterfalls and boasts the rare feature of a trail that allows you to walk behind it. Your reward for getting wet is a great view as well as being able to see, hear, and feel the mighty pounding waters sourced from the Seljalandsá river and the Eyjafjallajökull Glacier.

Don't Miss

Just a short five-minute hike from Seljalandsfoss is the hidden waterfall Gljúfrabúifoss. This 40-meter high beauty, tucked snugly into a mossy cave, has a particularly big rock you can stand on for a truly epic photo.

When to Go

Seljalandsfoss is open year-round and easiest to visit in summer. If you visit in winter, be sure to bring spikes for your shoes. Regardless of season, bring waterproof gear or a change of clothes.

Getting Here

Take Highway 1 south from Reykjavík until the well-marked right hand turn into Seljalandsfoss. It's about a one hour and 45 minute drive. It's very popular and never closes, so try to visit early or late (taking advantage of the Midnight Sun) to avoid crowds in summer.

✉ *Efiórsmerkurvegur, Hvolsvöllur* 🌐 *www.south.is/en/destinations/sights-along-the-ring-road* 🎫 *Free*

Hornstrandir Nature Reserve

Remote Wilderness in Northwest Iceland

Known as the Edge of the World, Hornstrandir Nature Reserve is a remote wilderness, only accessible in Summer and by boat, which makes it one of the wildest and best preserved parts of Iceland. It also makes it a hiker's and nature-lover's dream. On the northern edge of the Westfjords, this 220-mile reserve was established as a protected region in the 1970s and has been uninhabited since the 1950s, save for the flora and fauna that thrive here undisturbed by hunting, grazing, and tour buses. You're likely to spot whales and seals while crossing on the ferry, and thousands of seabirds—Arctic terns, puffins, kittiwakes, black guillemots, and more—at the dramatic cliffs surrounding the bay of Hornvík. You will also likely see the area's most popular local, the adorable Arctic Fox, as you explore. You can hike all day without seeing anyone, so make sure you come prepared.

Don't Miss

Borea Adventures offers single- or multiday kayak trips around the Hornstrandir Peninsula, combined with some hiking excursions during the days. Their four-day glacier fjords kayaking trip combines kayaking adventures with wildlife sightseeing.

Best Activity

The Adalvik to Hesteyri trail (from where the ferry drops you off and picks you up) is a convenient and scenic hike that you can easily complete in five to six hours.

Getting Here

Most tours, especially day tours, depart from Ísafjörður, but you can take a boat from Norðurfjörður.

Westfjords Regional Information Center. ✉ *Neðstikaupstaður 400, Ísafjörður* 🌐 *www.westfjords.is*

Iceland
Greenland Sea
Hornstrandir Nature Reserve
HORNSTRANDIR
Smidhjuvik
Furufjordhur
Minnibakki
Unadhsdalur
Ísafjörður
Arctic Fox Center
Hamar
Arnes
Pingetri
61
The Westfjords Way
Arngerdhareyi
Selardalur
Bildudalur
Kaldranes
Drangsnes
Nordhurbotn
60
Hvallatur
Brekkuvellir
Fjardharhorn
Stadharholskirkja
Breidafjordur
Hvammur
Bordheyri
Stykkisholmur
Budhardalur
57
Sandur
Olafsvik
SNÆFELLSNES PENINSULA
54
Hellnar
Snæfellsjökull National Park
Faxafloi
Akrar
Haugar
Snorralaug
Borgarnes
Lundur
1
Akranes
Reykjavík Art Museum
Reykjavik
Alafoss
Thingvellir
Keflavik
41
Hafnir
The Blue Lagoon
Fagradalsfjall Volcano
Grindavik
427
Stokkseyri
Eldhestar
Selfoss
Skalholt
Pingvellir National Park
Geysir
Gullfoss Falls
The Golden Circle
Porisvatn
Hveravellir
Langjökull Glacier
Hvitárvatn
Keta
Fell
Skagafjordur
Hofsos
Hvammur
Skagastrond
1238 The Battle of Iceland
Saudharkrokur
Tjorn
Blondous
75
Thingeyrar
Hvammstangi
Silfrastadhir
Landmannalaugar
Hvolsvollur
Storidalur
Seljalandsfoss
Fimmvörðuháls
Ribsafari Boat Tours
Vestmannaeyjar
Heimaey
Skeidflotur
Reynisfjara
North Atlantic Ocean
0
20 mi
0
20 km

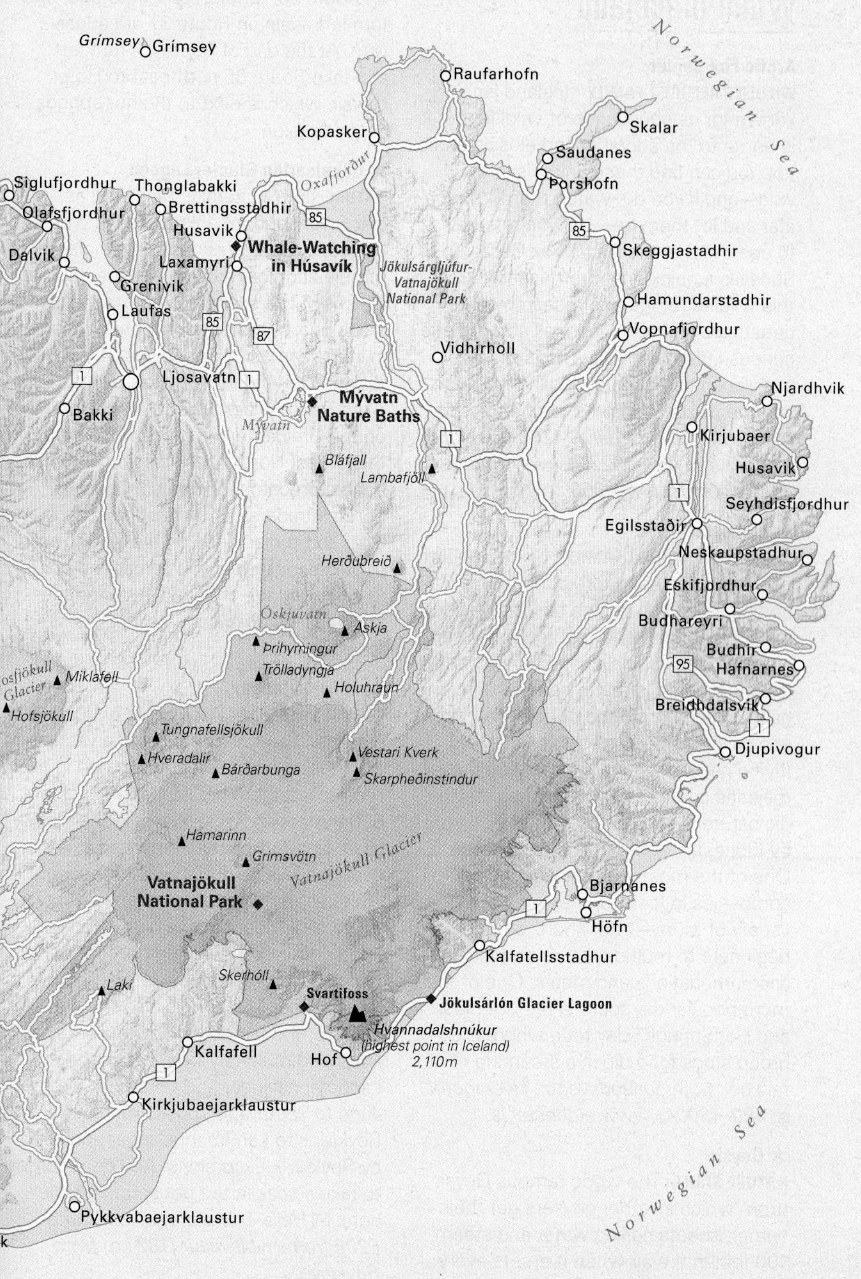
Grímsey
Grímsey
Raufarhofn
Norwegian Sea
Skalar
Kopasker
Saudanes
Oxafjordur
Þorshofn
Siglufjordhur
Thonglabakki
Olafsfjordhur
Brettingsstadhir
85
Husavik
85
Whale-Watching in Húsavík
Skeggjastadhir
Dalvik
Laxamyri
Jökulsárgljúfur-Vatnajökull National Park
Grenivik
Hamundarstadhir
Laufas
85
87
Vopnafjordhur
Vidhirholl
1
Ljosavatn
1
Njardhvik
Bakki
Mývatn Nature Baths
Mývatn
Kirjubaer
1
Bláfjall
Lambafjöll
Husavik
1
Seyhdisfjordhur
Egilsstaðir
Neskaupstadhur
Herðubreið
Eskifjordhur
Óskjuvatn
Askja
Budhareyri
Þrihyrningur
Budhir
95
Hafnarnes
Trölladyngja
Hofsjökull Glacier
Miklafell
Holuhraun
Hofsjökull
Breidhdalsvik
1
Tungnafellsjökull
Djupivogur
Vestari Kverk
Hveradalir
Bárðarbunga
Skarpheðinstindur
Hamarinn
Grimsvötn
Vatnajökull Glacier
Bjarnanes
Vatnajökull National Park
1
Höfn
Kalfatellsstadhur
Skerhóll
Laki
Svartifoss
Jökulsárlón Glacier Lagoon
Hvannadalshnúkur (highest point in Iceland) 2,110m
Kalfafell
Hof
1
Kirkjubaejarklaustur
Norwegian Sea
Þykkvabaejarklaustur

When in Iceland

Arctic Fox Center

WILDLIFE REFUGE | FAMILY | Iceland isn't known for its abundance of wildlife, but it is home to the adorable and elusive arctic fox. You can find these animals in the wild—and if you do, watch them from afar and let them be—but you're sure to see them at the Arctic Fox Center in Súðavík, a quick drive from Ísafjörður. At this wildlife refuge and research center, guests are invited to learn all about these curious little mammals. The arctic fox population has been dwindling for years, and the center also puts forth efforts to maintain it. ✉ *Eyrardalur, 420 Súðavík, Ísafjörður* ☎ *456–4922* 🌐 *www.arcticfox-centre.com* 💳 *ISK 1,500.*

★ Eldhestar

HORSEBACK RIDING | FAMILY | Since the 10th century, it has been forbidden to import horses to Iceland, which has resulted in a unique horse breed that Icelanders take pride in. One special characteristic of the Icelandic horse is that it has five different gaits: in addition to the normal walk, trot, and gallop, there is also *tölt* and *skeið* (flying pace). If you fancy meeting these majestic creatures and exploring Icelandic nature in a new way, you should stop by Eldhestar, right outside of Hveragerði. One of the most well-established riding companies in Iceland, they offer a wide variety of tours—from short tours for beginners to multiday tours that include accommodations and meals. One of their more popular day tours is the "Horses and Hot Springs" day tour, where the group stops for a dip in a steaming natural pool. ✉ *Suðurlandsvegur, Hveragerði* ☎ *480–4800* 🌐 *www.eldhestar.is.*

★ Geysir

NATURE SIGHT | The world-famous Geysir (from which all other geysers get their name), shoots boiling water and steam 100 feet in the air when it erupts every few months. From Þingvellir, the first stop in the Golden Circle, continue east on Route 36, turn left on Route 365, and turn left again on Route 37 at Laugarvatn. At the end of Route 37, turn left and take Route 35 northeast to Hótel Geysir, which is next to the hot springs. ✉ *Haukadalur.*

★ Jökulsárlón Glacier Lagoon

NATURE SIGHT | Literally translated as "Glacier River Lagoon", Jökulsárlón is where you can see large chunks of the glacier tumble and float around in a spectacular ice show. The scenery is so magnificent, it has been used as a location for scenes in some James Bond movies (*A View to a Kill* and *Die Another Day*), as well as *Lara Croft Tomb Raider.* West of the lagoon, on the Breiðamerkur sands, you'll find the largest North Atlantic colony of skua, sizable predatory seabirds that dive-bomb intruders during nesting season. Boat and zodiac rides on the lagoon are hugely popular, but you can spend hours just walking the area and admiring the spectacle. ✉ *Jökulsárlón, Höfn* 🌐 *www.icelagoon.com.*

Landmannalaugar

NATURE PRESERVE | Accessible only during summer, Landmannalaugar is a vast area of stunning natural beauty located in the remote southern highlands. It sits about 600 meters above sea level in the Fjallabak Nature Reserve, between a glacial river and lava field that was formed in the 15th century. With its dazzling multicolored rhyolite mountains, a blue lake inside a red crater, and bubbling geothermal areas, it becomes a popular hang-out in the summer. The spot is also the starting point for the famed Laugavegur hike, an advanced multi-day trek that connects Landmannalaugar and Þórsmörk. From June to September, buses run daily from Reykjavík to Landmannalaugar and back by Reykjavík Excursions. And don't forget to take a soak in the hot springs while here. ✉ *Hella* ✣ *Hrauneyjar via Route F208 from Hvolsvöllur (182 km from Reykjavík).*

★ **Reykjavík Art Museum**

ART MUSEUM | FAMILY | Also known as Hafnarhús, this former warehouse of the Port of Reykjavík now houses the city's main art museum. The six galleries occupy two floors, and there's a courtyard and "multipurpose" space. The museum's permanent collection includes a large number of works donated by the contemporary Icelandic artist Erró. There are also regular temporary exhibitions. Admission is free with the Reykjavík City Card. ✉ *Tryggvagata 17, Miðbær* ☎ *411–6400* 🌐 *www.listasafnreykjavikur.is* 🎫 *ISK 1,950.*

★ **Reynisfjara**

BEACH | Take route 215 for 5 km (3 miles) to reach the popular black sand beach, Reynisfjara, located on the western side of Reynisfjall. The surrounding cliffs are the home to thousands of puffins in the summer, as well as arctic terns and fulmars. The dramatic splattering of the explosive waves on the obsidian black beach is a thrill to watch, but for safety reasons visitors must stay far from the edge of the water. The waves off Reynisfjara can rise quickly, sweeping people up in seconds, which has resulted in many accidents and even deaths. Offshore are the towering basalt sea stacks, Reynisdrangar. Their silhouette is seen from both Vík and Reynisfara. ✉ *Route 215, Vík.*

★ **Ribsafari Boat Tours**

ADVENTURE TOURS | If you're up for a bumpy ride, Ribsafari tours offer a fun way to spot puffins and marvel at and explore the hidden sea caves under the islands as well as learn about the history and nature of the islands. They offer one- and two-hour boat trips that are sure to get your adrenaline going. ✉ *Tangagata 7* ☎ *661–1810* 🌐 *www.ribsafari.is* 🎫 *From ISK 14,900 for one hour.*

Snorralaug

HOT SPRING | What may well be the oldest hot spring in Iceland was first mentioned in the writings of medieval Icelandic historian and poet Snorri Sturluson, who used to bathe here. The water is often far too hot for a dip, so visit the nearby Snorrastofa instead to learn about Sturluson himself. ✉ *Snorrastofa.*

★ **Svartifoss**

WATERFALL | Prepare to have your breath taken away twice by Svartifoss (literally, 'Black Falls'): once by the trail, which is rather steep, and again by the waterfall itself, a wonder of natural architecture. The falls feature a single torrent of water plunging over a wall of symmetrical basalt columns that look like a pipe organ. The mile-long, rubber-lined trail starts from the campsite at Skaftafell. Do not be tempted to drive up the access road—this is for staff only and strictly prohibited. ✉ *Svartifoss, Höfn.*

★ **1238 The Battle of Iceland**

HISTORY MUSEUM | This Sauðárkrókur attraction, enhanced by VR technology, presents an immersive exhibition based on the legendary and bloody chapter of Iceland's history known as the Age of the Sturlungs (1220–1264), which marked the end of Iceland's independence. At the on-site restaurant Grána Bistro, you can fill up on good local food. ✉ *1238 The Battle of Iceland, Aðalgata 21* ☎ *588–1238* 🌐 *www.1238.is* 🎫 *ISK 3,450.*

Where to Eat and Drink

★ **Áshús**

$$$ | ICELANDIC | Glaumbær's cozy tea room is an unforgettable stop, particularly after a meander around the historical grounds. Either get their soup, cakes, and coffee buffet or just order something á la carte. **Known for:** every traditional Icelandic pastry there is; top-tier pancakes; looks like grandma's house, tastes like grandma's secret family recipes. 💲 *Average main: ISK3,100* ✉ *Glaumbær, Varmahlíð* ☎ *453–6173* 🌐 *www.glaumbaer.is/is/en/ashus-tea-room-cafe* 🕘 *Closed late Sept.–early May.*

★ Bæjarins Beztu Pylsur

$ | FAST FOOD | FAMILY | In a parking lot facing the harbor, this tiny yet famous fast-food hut is known for serving the original Icelandic hot dog—and a single person serves about a thousand of them a day from the window. Ask for *eina með öllu* (pronounced "*ayn*-ah med *utl*-lou"), or "one with everything," which gets you mustard, tomato sauce, rémoulade (mayonnaise with finely chopped pickles), and chopped raw and fried onions. **Known for:** quick service; a wide variety of locally loved condiments; incredibly helpful hot dog holders on the nearby tables. *Average main: ISK400 ✉ Tryggvagata and Pósthússtræti, Austurströnd 3, Miðbær ☎ 511–1566 www.bbp.is.*

Bruggsmiðjan Kaldi Brewery

BREWERY | Learning about how beer is made does not take away the pleasure of drinking it, and at Kaldi, Iceland's first microbrewery, you can do both. You even get to keep your glass as a souvenir. Make sure to call and schedule an appointment in advance. The brewery is located in the town of Árskógssandi, just south of Dalvik. *✉ Öldugata 22, Árskógssandi ☎ 466–2505 www.bruggsmidjan.is ISK 2,500.*

★ Dill Restaurant

$$$$ | SEAFOOD | There's only one option at Dill: a tasting menu with a modern spin on traditional Icelandic dishes. In 2017, Dill was the first restaurant in Iceland to be awarded a Michelin star, with chef Gunnar Karl Gíslason at the helm. **Known for:** spectacular tasting menu; careful attention to detail with presentation; downright delicious takes on Icelandic dishes. *Average main: ISK15,900 ✉ Laugavegur 59, Miðbær ☎ 552–1522 www.dillrestaurant.is Closed Sun. and Mon. year-round, Sat. every other week, and Tues. every other week. No lunch.*

★ Lava Restaurant

$$$$ | ICELANDIC | Eating world-class food at a restaurant built into a lava cliff with views of the milky Blue Lagoon is a once-in-a-lifetime opportunity you will never forget. The set menu offers a gourmet meal for pescatarians, vegetarians, and carnivores at a reasonable price (by Icelandic standards). **Known for:** combines fine dining with the wild spirit of Icelandic nature; the perfect dine-in-your-robe post-spa meal; stunning lava rock wall. *Average main: ISK6,000 ✉ Blue Lagoon, Norðurljosavegur 9, Grindavík ☎ 420–8800 www.bluelagoon.is.*

★ Norð Austur Sushi&Bar

$$$ | JAPANESE FUSION | Winning high-pedigree accolades for its food that creatively fuses fresh local fish with Japanese techniques and flavors, Norð Austur is worth booking ahead for. It is open in the summer only and is in high demand for its beautifully presented morsels, creative cocktails, and cozy atmosphere. **Known for:** omakase for the table; sake and Japanese whiskey; maki rolls. *Average main: ISK3,400 ✉ Norðurgata 2 ☎ 787–4000 www.nordaustur.is Closed Mon. and Tues.*

★ Simbahöllin

$$ | CAFÉ | Built in 1915, this former general store is now a restaurant loved by locals and visitors alike. Go for Belgian waffles in the morning or afternoon, and visit again at night for the local catch of the day and lamb tagine. **Known for:** superb Belgian waffles; soup of the day; local institution. *Average main: ISK1,600 ✉ Fjarðargata 5, Þingeyri ☎ 899–6659 www.simbahollin.is.*

★ Skál!

$ | SCANDINAVIAN | Located in the Hlemmur Mathöll food hall, Skál! offers elegant Icelandic platings in a casual setting. The best part is that prices are much more reasonable than you'd see in most restaurants around the city, but you really aren't giving up any quality when it comes to the food. **Known for:** exellent arctic char; reasonable portions; fun food hall location. *Average main: ISK2,350*

✉ *Laugavegur 107, Hlíðar* ☎ *519–6515* 🌐 *www.skalrvk.com.*

★ Slippurinn

$$$$ | ICELANDIC | For those looking to try authentic Icelandic food, look no further than this beloved family-run eatery. Specializing in fresh fish, their ethos is all about sustainability and slow food. **Known for:** bright and welcoming interior; seven-course set menu that covers the best of Icelandic cuisine; pan-fried fish that you'll later dream about. $ *Average main: ISK5,000* ✉ *Strandvegur 76* ☎ *481–1515* 🌐 *www.slippurinn.com* ⏲ *Closed Sun.–Tues. and late Sept.-May.*

★ Tjöruhúsið

$$$ | SEAFOOD | FAMILY | You never know exactly what the menu will be at the family-owned Tjöruhúsið, and for good reason: it all depends on what the local fishermen catch. You have your pick of two dinner seatings, at 7 pm and 9 pm (so don't be late), and three menu options—soup only, fish only, or fish and soup. **Known for:** super fresh catch of the day; delicious soups; strict dinner seatings and small menu. $ *Average main: ISK3,200* ✉ *Nedsti kaupstadur, Ísafjörður* ☎ *456–4419* ⏲ *Closed Mon.*

★ Yuzu Burger

$$ | BURGER | FAMILY | From the classic cornerstore Sjoppu burger to the BBQ and bacon burger, the menu is far from one-sided at this lunchtime favorite. Plus, there are plenty of vegan options. **Known for:** quick service; Instagram-worthy interiors; unique burger combos. $ *Average main: ISK2,690* ✉ *Hverfisgata 44, Reykjavík* ☎ *588–8818* 🌐 *www.yuzu.is.*

Cool Places to Stay

Bubble Hotel Iceland

$$$ | HOTEL | For a once in a lifetime experience, sleep under the Midnight Sun or the northern lights in a luxurious bubble, with unforgettable nighttime vistas. **Pros:** peaceful and quiet; comfortable and warm beds; insane views if the weather is good. **Cons:** experience is largely dependent on weather; shared bathrooms and showers; bubbles are somewhat close together. $ *Rooms from: ISK34,900* ✉ *Ölvisholt, Selfoss* ☎ *773–4444* 🌐 *www.buubble.com* ⏲ *Closed Sept.–May* 🛏 *5 bubbles* 🍴 *No Meals.*

★ Englendingavík

$ | B&B/INN | FAMILY | The loudest noise you'll hear at this beautiful 1890 house is birdsong, and although luxury amenities are not the focus, there's no substitute for the coziness of staying at this family's home. **Pros:** good on-site restaurant; family-run with a very welcoming environment; prime location near Borgarnes. **Cons:** communal living is stressed over privacy; breakfast not included; no luxury amenities. $ *Rooms from: ISK19,373* ✉ *Skúlagata 17, Borgarnes* ☎ *896–8926* 🌐 *www.englendingavik.is* 🛏 *5 rooms* 🍴 *No Meals.*

★ Hotel Búdir

$$$$ | HOTEL | After you see the iconic Búðakirkja church, you'll dream of nights of peaceful slumber under the stars surrounded by fields, and the Hotel Búdir is the closest you'll come to that. **Pros:** fantastic restaurant; prime location in Snæfellsjökull National Park; perhaps the quietest hotel you'll ever stay in. **Cons:** expensive; breakfast not included with room rate; not much to do in the area if you're not into the outdoors. $ *Rooms from: ISK47,430* ✉ *356 Snæfellsbær* ☎ *435–6700* 🌐 *www.hotelbudir.is* 🛏 *28 rooms* 🍴 *No Meals.*

★ Hotel Húsafell

$$$$ | HOTEL | There are few hotel options here, but Hotel Hísafell has everything you need for a solid home base while exploring the region. **Pros:** beautiful design; great location for outdoor activities; access to geothermal pools and float gear. **Cons:** rooms can get quite hot; lackluster buffet breakfast; basic amenities given room rate. $ *Rooms from:*

ISK45,900 ✉ *Stórarjóður* ☎ *435–1551* 🌐 *www.hotelhusafell.com* 🛏 *48 rooms* 🍴 *Free Breakfast.*

★ ION Adventure Hotel

$$$$ | **HOTEL** | Clean, green, and emerging from the landscape, the ION Hotel is a striking sight in the primordial surrounds of Nesjavellir, a geothermal area close to Þingvellir National Park. **Pros:** well serviced by tour operators providing a range of outdoor activities; striking design in an unusual landscape; luxury spa with an oudoor hot tub and bar. **Cons:** culturally speaking, it's completely off-piste (no nearby shops, bars, or restaurants); proven difficult for some cars to reach in winter; right next to a geothermal power plant. $ *Rooms from: ISK63,000* ✉ *Nesjavöllum við Þingvallarvatn, Selfoss* ☎ *578–3720* 🌐 *www.ioniceland.is* 🛏 *46 rooms* 🍴 *No Meals.*

★ Radagerdi Guesthouse

$$ | **B&B/INN** | This is the very picture of a Nordic guesthouse on the coast—the design is minimalist and on point, breakfast is included, and there's a terrace area for taking in the scenery. **Pros:** free breakfast; beautiful terrace area; modern design. **Cons:** shared bathrooms in some rooms; small rooms; loud plumbing. $ *Rooms from: ISK24,600* ✉ *Aðalstræti, Patreksfjörður* ☎ *456–1560* 🌐 *www.radagerdi.net* 🛏 *11 rooms* 🍴 *Free Breakfast.*

★ The Reykjavik EDITION

$$$$ | **HOTEL** | From the moment you step into this hotel, you'll know you're somewhere special: the staff is friendly and alert, the on-site spa is worth a visit, and the rooms showcase the best of Scandinavian design taste. **Pros:** next-level service; incredible on-site restaurant; stunning interiors. **Cons:** some rooms feel a bit small; quite expensive; a bit of a walk to the downtown neighborhood. $ *Rooms from: ISK102,527* ✉ *Austurbakki 2, Reykjavík* ☎ *582–0000* 🌐 *www.marriott.com* 🛏 *253 rooms* 🍴 *Free Breakfast.*

★ Skálakot Manor Hotel

$$$$ | **B&B/INN** | Right by the root of a mountain lies this horse farm that has been in the same family for seven generations and their meticulously built, incredibly cozy yet luxurious manor. **Pros:** guided horseback rides to Seljalandsfoss from the hotel; luxurious guestrooms with cozy bathrobes and lovely selection of soaps; candlelit farm-to-table dinners in the dining room. **Cons:** standard breakfast; sauna and hot tub access costs extra; expensive. $ *Rooms from: ISK60,000* ✉ *Skálakoti, Hvolsvöllur* ☎ *487–8953* 🌐 *www.skalakot.is* 🛏 *14 rooms* 🍴 *Free Breakfast.*

★ Torfhús Retreat

$$$$ | **HOTEL** | Despite being in a simple turf house, the Torfhús Retreat is one of the most luxurious hotels in all of Iceland. **Pros:** so peaceful, you'll feel far away from the modern world; prix-fixe dinner that'll wow you; houses are true architectural marvels. **Cons:** not as many amenities as you'd expect for the price; extremely expensive; far away from restaurants, stores, and shops. $ *Rooms from: ISK100,000* ✉ *Dalsholt, Selfoss* ☎ *788–8868* 🌐 *www.torfhus.is* 🛏 *25 suites* 🍴 *Free Breakfast.*

Norway

One of the world's most beautiful countries, Norway has long been a popular cruise destination, especially along its rugged west coast, famed for its stunning fjords. Formed during the last ice age's meltdown when the inland valleys carved by huge glaciers filled with seawater, fjords are undoubtedly Norway's top attractions—they shape the country's unique landscape and never fail to take your breath away.

Although the fjords are Norway's most dramatic scenic features, there is much else to see, from vast expanses of rugged tundra in the north to huge evergreen forests along the Swedish border, from fertile coastal plains in the southwest to the snow-covered peaks and glaciers of the center. In almost any kind of weather, blasting or balmy, large numbers of Norwegians are outdoors, fishing, biking, skiing, hiking, or sailing. On the urban front, Oslo, Bergen, and Stavanger are all vibrant cities with rich culture, including many festivals and world-class artists (homegrown and imported) performing regularly to discerning audiences.

One of the least densely populated countries in Europe, Norway is also one of the richest (thanks to the discovery of oil and gas in the North Sea in the late 1960s), and this wealth has changed both the economy and self-confidence of the Norwegian people, transforming cities like Stavanger into global players. Norway regularly tops surveys as the country with the highest quality of life in the world, owing a great deal to the well-developed welfare system.

When discussing the size of their country, Norwegians like to say that if Oslo remained fixed and the northern part of the country were swung south, it would reach all the way to Rome. Perched at the very top of the globe, this northern land stretches 2,750 km (1,705 miles) from north to south with vast expanses of unspoiled terrain—a fantastic playground for nature lovers, wildlife enthusiasts, and sporty types.

Kayak the Fjords

Stunning World Heritage Landscapes

Formed during the last ice age's meltdown when the inland valleys carved by huge glaciers filled with seawater, Norway's fjords are undoubtedly its top attractions—they shape the country's unique landscape and never fail to take your breath away. From the shimmering waterways, lush green farmlands edge up rounded mountainsides where craggy steep peaks seem to touch the blue skies. There are more than a thousand fjords in Norway, all along the coast, but the most iconic fjords are located in the western part of the country. In spectacular inlets like Nærøyfjord and the Geirangerfjord—both UNESCO World Heritage Sites—walls of water shoot up the mountainsides, jagged snowcapped peaks blot out the sky, and water tumbles down the mountains in an endless variety of colors. The best way to appreciate the scenery of the fjords is by boat, and while cruise ships are a popular option, there's something about getting up-close-and-personal with the sparkling water that makes kayaking the fjords a true once-in-a-lifetime experience.

Don't Miss

You can rent your own kayak, but a guided tour is recommended. Geiranger Fjordservice AS is an established tour company with a number of kayak tours, including one that ventures into the spectacular Seven Sisters Falls. 🌐 *www.geirangerfjord.no*

Getting Here

The closest airport is Ålesund International Airport, though one can also get to the area by train from Oslo, which takes around 5 and a half hours. By car, take the Trollstigen highway.

Norsk Fjordsenter. ✉ *Gjørvahaugen 35, Geiranger* ☎ *70–26–38–10* 🌐 *www.fjordsenter.com*

Jotunheimen Nasjonalpark

Home of the Giants

With the largest concentration of peaks higher than 2,000 meters (6,561 feet) in northern Europe, it is easy to see why Jotunheimen Nasjonalpark is one of most popular areas in Norway for hiking and mountain climbing. Jotunheimen is Norwegian for "Home of the Giants" and this park includes the country's two highest mountains, Galdhøpiggen and Glittertind, as well as several lakes, the largest being Gjende. There is an extensive network of tracks and trails, and you will find hikes and treks suitable for all levels of experience. Plan to spend a couple of days away from civilization in this stunning, quintessentially Norwegian wilderness.

Don't Miss

About 60,000 people walk the Besseggen Ridge every year, making this Norway's most popular day hike. In Jotunheimen Nasjonalpark, the mountain ridge is between Gjende and Bessvatnet, two clear alpine lakes, and the trail offers beautiful views of the landscape.The best time to visit is when the Gjendebåten boat is running from mid-June to mid-October. Park at Reinsvangen where the shuttle bus takes you to Gjendeosen and the Gjendebåten boat.

Getting Here

It's recommended to arrive to the national park by car. From Oslo, take the E18 to Fagernes. Then take the RV 51, which includes the famed Valdresflya scenic route. There are also daily express buses to Jotunheiman from Oslo, Bergen, and Trondheim, as well as local buses to the most popular trailheads during the summer.

Jotunheimen Nasjonalpark. ☎ *61–24–14–44* 🌐 *www.nasjonalparkriket.no*

The Flåm Railway

The Most Scenic Train Ride in Scandinavia

Although this trip covers only 20 km (12 miles), the one-way journey takes nearly an hour to travel through 20 tunnels and 2,850 feet up a steep mountain gorge. The masterpiece of Norwegian engineering took 20 years to complete, and today it's one of Norway's top attractions, drawing more than 1 million travelers each year. The train runs year-round, with 8 to 10 round-trips from mid-April through mid-October and 4 round-trips the rest of the year. Most tourists take the train round-trip, returning on the same train after arriving in Myrdal. However, after the day-trippers have departed, Flåm is a wonderful place to extend your tour and spend the night. Located at the end of the Sognefjord, Norway's longest fjord, this beautiful village is an ideal base for exploring the area.

Don't Miss

For the best experience, grab a seat on the left side of the train if heading from Myrdal, or right side if heading from Flåm. This'll provide you the best views of Norway's jagged volcanic peaks, vast mossy valleys, and sparkling waterfalls.

Best Restaurant

Microbrewery Ægir Bryggeri og Pub—just a three-minute walk from the line—offers some of the region's best beer and local meats. ✉ *A-feltvegen 23 Flåm* ☎ *57–63–20–50* 🌐 *flamsbrygga.no/aegir-bryggeripub*

Getting Here

From Voss take the E16 heading northeast—it takes about an hour to get to Flåm and the railway station. Buses also link Flåm with Voss and Bergen.

Flåm Train Station. ✉ *A-Feltvegen, Flåm* ☎ *57–63–14–00* 🌐 *www.visitflam.no/flamsbana* 🎫 *NOK 650*

Vigeland Sculpture Park

The Largest Sculpture Park by a Single Artist in the World

Sprawling across 80 acres, and featuring more than 200 sculptures in bronze, granite, and cast iron by acclaimed Norwegian sculptor Gustav Vigeland, this sculpture park is beloved by locals and one of Norway's top attractions, with over a million visitors a year. Vigeland's realistic works represent the cycle of human life and all its emotions. Highlights include the famed *The Angry Boy*, a bronze of an enraged cherubic child stamping his foot, which has drawn legions of visitors and has been filmed, parodied, painted red, and even stolen; the 56-foot-high granite *Monolith*, a column of 121 upward-striving nudes in an apotheotic, eternal struggle toward heaven; *The Fountain* surrounded by 20 statues from representing childhood to death and one of the most iconic images of the park, and *Man Attacked By Babies*, which represents a man struggling with the responsibility of parenthood.

Don't Miss

The Vigelandsmuseet was the Norwegian sculptor's studio and residence, housing models of almost all his works, as well as drawings, woodcuts, and the original molds and plans for Vigeland Park. The building is considered one of the finest examples of neo-classical architecture in Norway.

Getting Here

The Line 3 subway or Line 12 tram is the easiest way to get to the park. It's a 2-mile walk from the city center, so you could also walk or bike to the park. Allow two to three hours to explore the park.

✉ *Frognerparken, Frogner* ☎ *23–49–37–00 for museum* 🌐 *www.vigeland.museum.no* 🎫 *Free*

The Northern Lights in Tromsø

The City with Consistently High Aurora Activity

The Northern Lights, also known as Aurora Borealis, is high on every traveler's wishlist for Scandinavia, and there's no better place to see them in Norway (and some would say, all of Scandinavia) than Tromsø. Known as the Paris of the North for both its culture and proximity to the North Pole, Tromsø offers ice-capped mountain ridges and jagged architecture that echoes the peaks, as well as the world's most northerly university, brewery, and planetarium—all under magical skies that dance in green light from September to April. Endless entertainments, guided tours, and viewing spots maximize the experience.

Don't Miss

Head to Fjellheisen Mountain to catch the lights from the highest point in the city. Accessible via a spectacular cable car ride, the viewing area offers panoramic views and a cozy café. Tromsø's Botanical Garden has no set hours, so you can walk its terraces under a glowing sky while the Science Center of Northern Norway explains the science behind the northern lights.

Best Tour

Chasing Lights is a Tromsø-based tour company that offers diverse packages to help you witness the Northern Lights. ✉ *Storgata 64, Tromsø* ☎ *455–17–551* 🌐 *chasinglights.com*

Getting Here

There are both domestic and international flights to Tromsø but no train service. Once there, you should rent a car to see all the sights

Visit Tromsø. ☎ *77–61–00–00* 🌐 *www.visittromso.no*

Bergen

The Heart of the Fjords

It may be known as Norway's Second City but with seven rounded lush mountains, pastel wood houses, the historic and picturesque wharf of Bryggen, winding cobblestone streets, and Hanseatic relics, you will fall in love with Bergen's charms at first sight. Surrounded by forested hills and glittering fjords, the area is a natural draw for visitors interested in skiing, biking, walking, fishing, and boating. On any sunny day you'll see locals taking the Mount Fløyen Funicular to the top of Mount Fløyen for a quick hike or just to soak in the views. Bergen gets its share of rainy days, too, which means there are plentiful indoor amusements, including Bergenhus Fortress, KODE 1 museum, the Bergen Fish Market, and the museum and home of Norway's most famous composer, Edvard Grieg. Situated between the two biggest fjords in Norway, Bergen is also an ideal starting point for fjord excursions.

Don't Miss

A row of mostly reconstructed 14th-century wooden buildings that face the harbor makes the UNESCO World Heritage Site and historic Hanseatic harborside, Bryggen, one of the most charming (and photographed) walkways in Europe.

Best Restaurant

Enhjørningen is housed in one of Bryggen's old wooden buildings, but the menu is contemporary Norwegian and it changes according to the day's catch. www.enhjorningen.no

To Kokker, set in a 300-year-old building on the wharf, serves up traditional Norwegian dishes cooked to perfection. www.tokokker.no

Getting Here and Around

Flesland Airport is a 30-minute bus ride from Bergen, with a convenient shuttle to the downtown area.

Visit Bergen. ☎ *55–55–20–00* 🌐 *www.visitbergen.com*

The Atlantic Ocean Road

A Gravity-Defying Scenic Drive

The *Atlanterhavsvegen* or the Atlantic Ocean Road—a 5-mile stretch of Norwegian Road 64 connecting the mainland with Avery Island—is one of the world's most scenic drives and considered Norway's Engineering Feat of the Century. Connecting the island of Averøy with Eide via a series of small islands and islets spanned by a total of eight bridges, including Storseisundbrua, the longest (850 feet) and highest (75 feet). The beauty of the Atlantic Ocean Road comes not only from its location, perched above the roaring Norwegian Sea, but also the death-defying roller-coaster of the highway's engineering. Bridges twist and turn through salty air connecting the little islets and skerries, making a drive that is as adrenaline-packed as it is beautiful. Though it's meant to be driven by car, opting for a bike provides an even more spectacular experience—just watch out for bad weather.

Don't Miss

You'll need to concentrate on the road as you drive, so the Atlantic Ocean Road requires stops, lots of stops. Take advantage of all viewing points along the way to breathe in the fresh sea air and marvel at the road teetering on the edge of the ocean. The Eldhusøya rest area has a scenic coastal walk and a café, too.

Getting Here

The drive is 8.3-kilometers (5.2 miles) long and officially begins at Utheim on Averøy and ends after the Vevang-straumen Bridge. The drive—with time at all the stops—will take between two to three hours.

Nasjonale turistveger. ☎ 22–07–30–00 🌐 *www.nasjonaleturistveger.no/en/routes/atlanterhavsvegen*

Svalbard

A Genuine Arctic Fairy Tale

At this Arctic archipelago, midway between the North Pole and mainland Norway, you can spot a polar bear or walrus, go dog sledding, hike a glacier, see the Northern Lights, and experience extreme midnight sun or polar night. In short, have all your Arctic adventure dreams come true. A visit here is a once-in-a-lifetime experience, whether you're hiking in the starkly beautiful mountains, exploring the wilderness on a snowmobile or expedition sailboat, or watching wildlife from afar. Svalbard's main settlement, the world's northernmost urban community, Longyearbyen, offers a good selection of hotels, restaurants, cafes, and bars. **TIP→ Polar bears are a real danger here; you'll need an armed guide with you when you leave town.**

When to Go

Visit in winter for the best chances of seeing the northern lights, between March and May if you'd like to try winter sports, and during the summer if you want great hiking, kayaking, and mountain biking.

Best Accommodation

The Isfjord Radio Adventure Hotel is not accessible by road, only via snowmobile, dog sled, or boat safari. This remote outpost is the perfect basecamp to see walruses, arctic foxes, and more in relative comfort. The sauna is the icing. 🌐 *www.basecampexplorer.com*

Best Tour

Basecamp Explorer offers dogsledding tours with 100 Alaskan huskies eager to take you on half-day, full-day, and multiple day tours into the wilderness. 🌐 *www.basecampexplorer.com/svalbard*

Getting Here and Around

You can fly to Svalbard from mainland Norway.

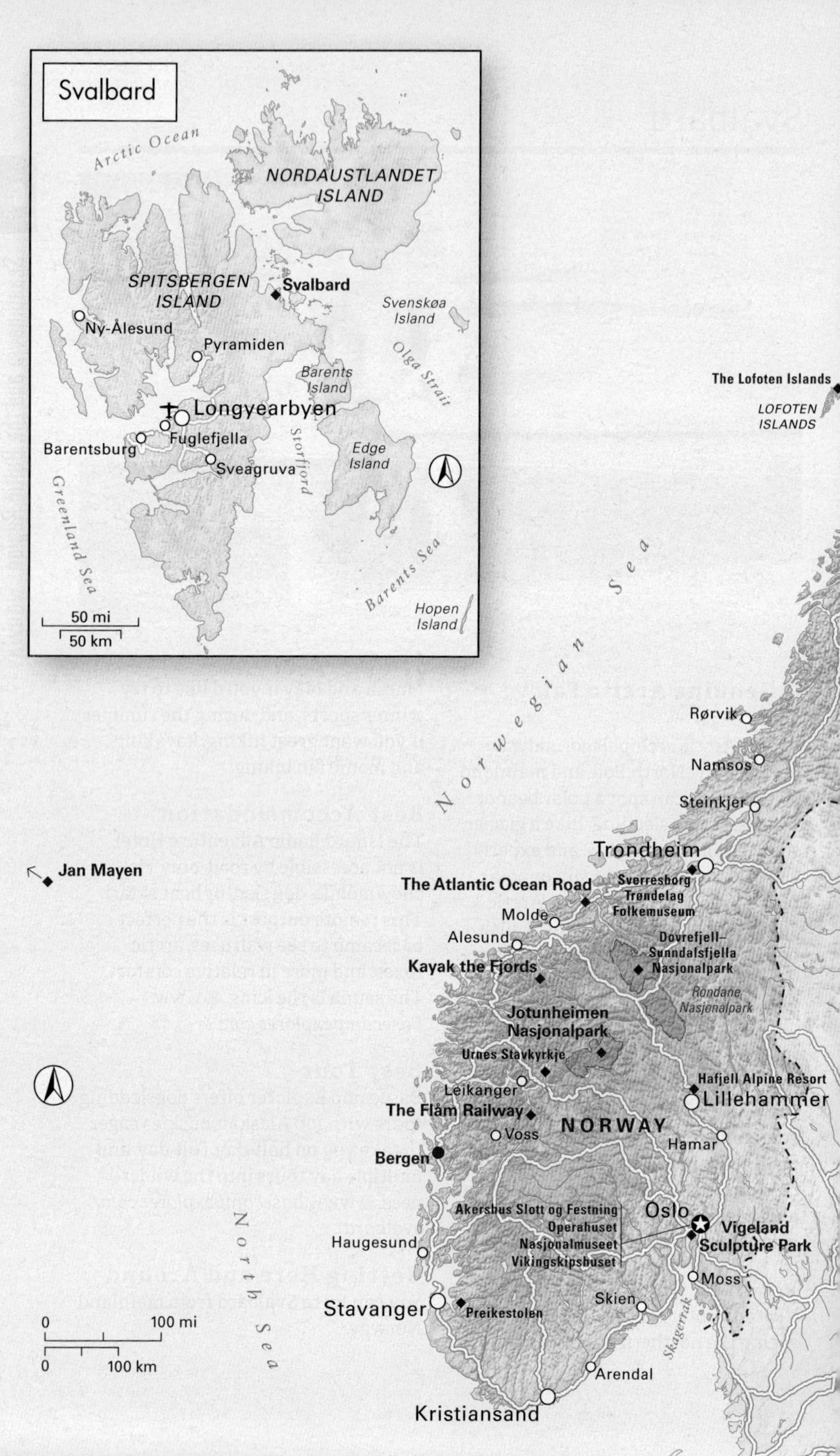

Svalbard
Arctic Ocean
NORDAUSTLANDET ISLAND
SPITSBERGEN ISLAND
Svalbard
Svenskøa Island
Ny-Ålesund
Pyramiden
Olga Strait
Barents Island
Longyearbyen
Fuglefjella
Barentsburg
Sveagruva
Storfjord
Edge Island
Greenland Sea
Barents Sea
Hopen Island
50 mi
50 km
The Lofoten Islands
LOFOTEN ISLANDS
Norwegian Sea
Rørvik
Namsos
Steinkjer
Trondheim
Jan Mayen
The Atlantic Ocean Road
Sverresborg Trøndelag Folkemuseum
Molde
Alesund
Dovrefjell–Sunndalsfjella Nasjonalpark
Kayak the Fjords
Rondane Nasjonalpark
Jotunheimen Nasjonalpark
Urnes Stavkyrkje
Hafjell Alpine Resort
Leikanger
Lillehammer
The Flåm Railway
Voss
NORWAY
Hamar
Bergen
Akershus Slott og Festning
Operahuset
Nasjonalmuseet
Vikingskipshuset
Oslo
Vigeland Sculpture Park
Haugesund
North Sea
Moss
Skien
Stavanger
Preikestolen
Skagerrak
0
100 mi
0
100 km
Arendal
Kristiansand

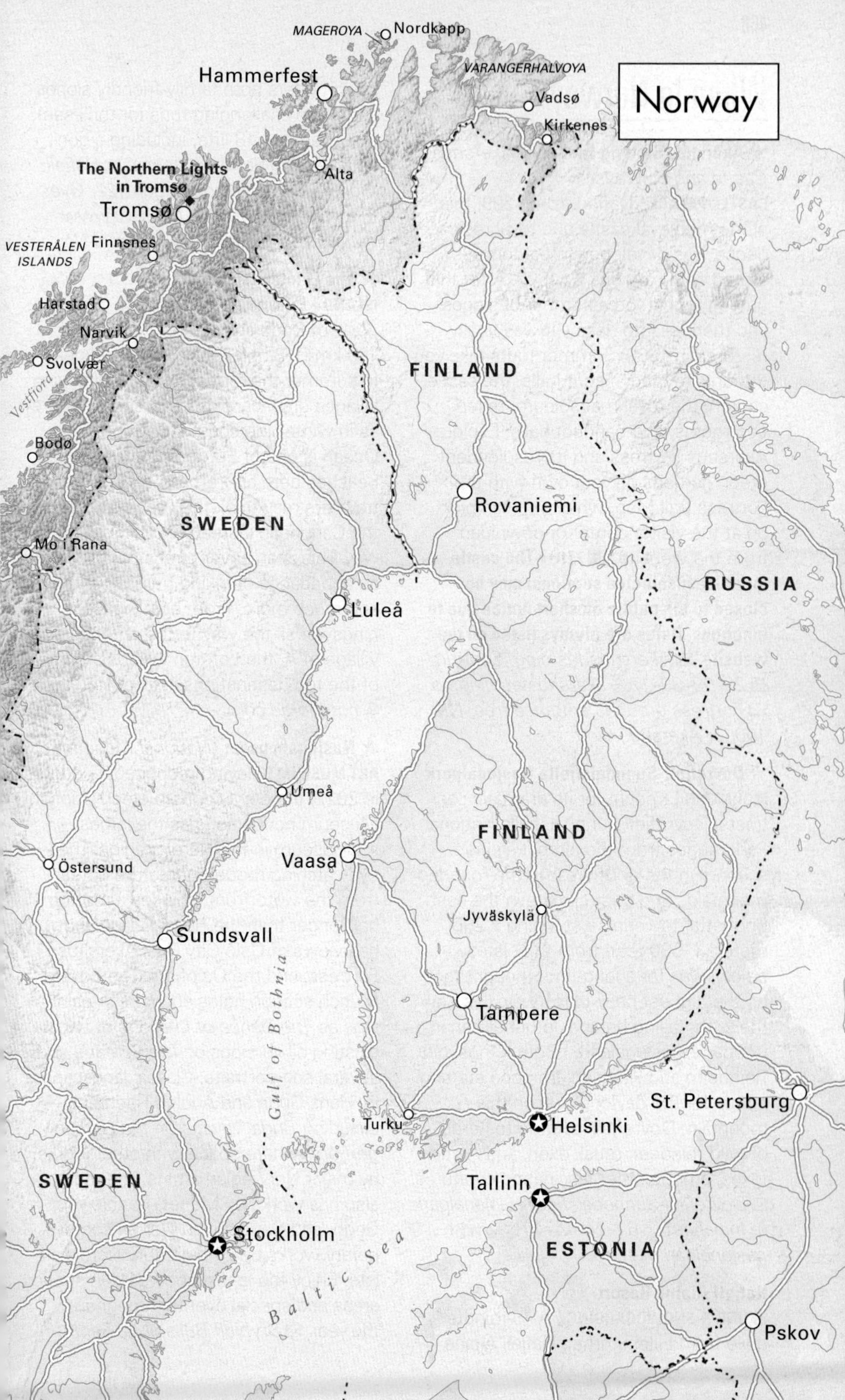

Norway
MAGEROYA
Nordkapp
VARANGERHALVOYA
Hammerfest
Vadsø
Kirkenes
The Northern Lights in Tromsø
Alta
Tromsø
VESTERÅLEN ISLANDS
Finnsnes
Harstad
Narvik
Svolvær
Vestfjord
FINLAND
Bodø
Rovaniemi
SWEDEN
Mo i Rana
RUSSIA
Luleå
Umeå
FINLAND
Vaasa
Östersund
Jyväskylä
Sundsvall
Gulf of Bothnia
Tampere
St. Petersburg
Turku
Helsinki
SWEDEN
Tallinn
Stockholm
ESTONIA
Baltic Sea
Pskov

When in Norway

★ **Akershus Slott og Festning** (*Akershus Castle and Fortress*)

CASTLE/PALACE | Dating from 1299, this stone medieval castle and royal residence was developed into a fortress armed with cannons by 1592. After that time, it withstood a number of sieges and then fell into decay. It was finally restored in 1899. Summer tours take you through its magnificent halls, the castle church, the royal mausoleum, reception rooms, and banquet halls. Explore Akershus Fortress and its resplendent green gardens on your own with the Fortress Trail Map, which you can pick up at the visitor center or download from the website. **TIP→ The castle (or at least selected sections) may be closed to the public on short notice due to functions. Dates are always listed on the website.** ✉ *Akershus festning, Sentrum* ☎ *23–09–39–17* 🌐 *akershusfestning.no* 🎫 *Fortress grounds entrance free, NKr 100 for Akershus Slott.*

★ **Dovrefjell-Sunndalsfjella Nasjonalpark**

MOUNTAIN | Known for its dramatic contrasts, Dovrefjell-Sunndalsfjella National Park ranges from the almost alpine scenery in the northwest to the rounded mountains and drier climate in the east. Snøhetta, towering a stunning 2,286 meters (7,500 feet) from the plateau below, was for a long time thought to be the highest peak in Norway. (It's now the 24th, falling behind Jotunheimen in Rondane Nasjonalpark.) Both Kongsvold/Reinheim and Hjerkinn are good starting points for the daylong trek up this mountain. Dovrefjell is home to herds of wild reindeer, musk oxen, and Arctic foxes, among other fascinating creatures. ✉ *Dovrefjell-Sunnedalsfjella Nasjonalpark* ✣ *Innlandet* ☎ *61–24–14–44* 🌐 *www.nasjonalparkriket.no.*

Hafjell Alpine Resort

SKIING & SNOWBOARDING | A 15-minute drive from Lillehammer, Hafjell Alpine Resort offers both family-friendly slopes and more challenging runs for thrill-seekers. There are 18 lifts, including a gondola, leading up to 33 slopes. ✉ *Hafjell Alpine Resort, Hundervegen 122, Øyer* ✣ *Innlandet* ☎ *40–40–15–00* 🌐 *www.hafjell.no* ⏱ *Closed mid-Apr.–mid-Nov.*

★ **The Lofoten Islands**

ISLAND | Extending out into the ocean north of Bodø are the Lofoten Islands, a 190-km (118-mile) chain of jagged peaks. In summer the farms, fjords, and fishing villages draw caravans of visitors, whereas in winter the coast facing the Arctic Ocean is one of Europe's stormiest. The beaches here are remarkably clear, and travelers may think they have landed in the Caribbean instead of Northern Norway. This is an adventurer's paradise with an abundance of hiking trails, boat trips, and much more. From bustling Henningsvær all the way to the photogenic village of Å, the Lofoten Islands are one of the top destinations in all of Norway. 🌐 *nordnorge.com.*

★ **Nasjonalmuseet** (*National Museum*)

ART MUSEUM | Having reopened its doors in 2022, the newly constructed National Museum now stands as the largest art museum in the Nordic region. The eye-catching modern structure not far from the waterfront includes a rooftop hall longer than the Royal Palace and has views of Oslo City Hall, Akershus Fortress, and the Oslofjord. The Edvard Munch section holds such major paintings as *The Dance of Life,* one of two existing oil versions of *The Scream,* and several self-portraits. Classic landscapes by Hans Gude and Adolph Tidemand—including *Bridal Voyage on the Hardangerfjord*—share space with other works by major Norwegian artists. The museum also has works by Monet, Renoir, Van Gogh, and Gauguin, as well as contemporary works by 20th-century Nordic artists. Enjoy the landscaped garden seating areas and special events throughout the year. ✉ *Brynjulf Bulls pl. 3, Sentrum*

☎ *21–98–20–00* 🌐 *www.nasjonalmuseet.no* Ⓜ *Nationaltheatret.*

★ **Operahuset** (*Opera House*)
PERFORMANCE VENUE | One of the crown jewels of Scandinavian architecture, the Oslo Opera House is a stunning addition to the city's waterfront. When it first opened its doors, the gala ceremony attracted Denmark's royal family, the leaders of several countries, and a host of celebrities. Designed by the renowned Norwegian architect firm Snøhetta, the white marble and glass building slopes downward toward the water's edge, giving visitors spectacular views of the fjord, the surrounding mountains, and the city skyline. And it doesn't just look good: the acoustics inside the 1,364-seat auditorium are excellent, as are those in the two smaller performance spaces. The space is the permanent home of the Norwegian National Opera and Ballet and also hosts a full calendar of music, theater, and dance. The Oslo Biennale will be staging performances on the rooftop through 2023. The bistro restaurant, though typically Norwegian in priceyness, is gorgeous and offers seafood and wines you don't want to miss on this memorable visit. ✉ *Kirsten Flagstads pl. 1, Sentrum* ☎ *21–42–21–21* 🌐 *www.operaen.no* 🎫 *Free; guided tours NKr 120* Ⓜ *Jernbanetorget.*

★ **Preikestolen** (*Pulpit Rock*)
VIEWPOINT | A huge cube with a vertical drop of 2,000 feet, Pulpit Rock is not a good destination if you suffer from vertigo—it has a heart-stopping view. The clifflike rock sits on the banks of the finger-shape Lysefjord. You can join a boat tour from Stavanger to see the rock from below, or you can hike for about two hours to the top on a marked trail. The track goes from Preikestolhytta, where there is a big parking lot.

★ **Sverresborg Trøndelag Folkemuseum** (*Sverresborg Trondelag Folk Museum*)
OTHER MUSEUM | **FAMILY** | Near the ruins of King Sverre's medieval castle is this open-air historical museum that depicts everyday life in Trøndelag during the 18th and 19th centuries. The stave church here, built in the 1170s, is the northernmost preserved church of its type in Norway. In the Old Town, you can visit a 1900s dentist's office and an old-fashioned grocery store that sells sweets. In the summer there are farm animals on-site, and a range of activities for children. There's a copy of the main house at Walt Disney World's Epcot in the Norway pavilion. ✉ *Sverresborg allé 13, Trondheim* ☎ *73–89–01–00* 🌐 *www.sverresborg.no* 🎫 *NKr 115* 🕒 *Closed Mon. Sept.–May.*

Urnes Stavkyrkje (*Urnes Stave Church*)
CHURCH | In the village of Ornes, this beautiful stave church is one of the oldest in the area. It's believed to have been completed in 1132 (although some say 1140). Take the ferry to get here. ✉ *Fv 331, Solvorn* ✣ *Vestland* 🌐 *www.stavechurch.com.*

★ **Vikingskipshuset** (*Viking Ship Museum*)
HISTORY MUSEUM | **FAMILY** | The Viking legacy in all its glory lives on at this classic Oslo museum. Chances are you'll come away fascinated by the *Gokstad, Oseberg,* and *Tune,* three blackened wooden Viking ships that date from AD 800. Discovered in Viking tombs around the Oslo fjords between 1860 and 1904, the boats are the best-preserved Viking ships ever found; they have been on display since the museum's 1957 opening. In Viking times, it was customary to bury the dead with food, drink, useful and decorative objects, and even their horses and dogs. Many of the well-preserved tapestries, household utensils, dragon-style wood carvings, and sledges were found aboard ships. The museum's rounded white walls give the feeling of a burial mound. Avoid summertime crowds by visiting at lunchtime. ✉ *Huk Aveny 35, Bygdøy* ☎ *22–13–52–80* 🌐 *www.khm.uio.no* 🎫 *NKr 100.*

Where to Eat and Drink

★ Ægir Bryggeri og Pub

$$$ | **NORWEGIAN** | It started out as a straightforward microbrewery, but Ægir has been transformed into a complete culinary experience. Conveniently located near the cruise port in Flåm, its local dishes pair beautifully with the award-winning beer. **Known for:** interesting architecture; some of the region's best beer; local meats. *Average main: NKr300 ✉ A-feltvegen 23 ✢ Vestland ☎ 57–63–20–50 🌐 flamsbrygga.no.*

★ Bakeriet på Å

$ | **NORWEGIAN** | **FAMILY** | If you drive to the end of the Lofoten Islands, you absolutely must stop at this traditional Norwegian bakery famous for its cinnamon buns. The bakers use traditional methods, so the pastries are always at their freshest. **Known for:** locals say these are the region's best cinnamon buns; traditional flatbreads and other delights; freshly baked breads. *Average main: NKr60 ✉ Å ☎ 76–09–14–88.*

Bare

$$$$ | **NORWEGIAN** | The elegant but spare mirrored dining room at this local favorite puts all the emphasis where it should be: on the creative dishes coming out of the kitchen. And you'll get to sample quite a few of them, depending on whether you opt for the "half menu" consisting of 7 courses or go all the way with an 11-course extravaganza. **Known for:** fine dining at its best in Bergen; wine pairings couldn't be better; attentive service. *Average main: NKr1250 ✉ Bergen Børs Hotel, Torgallmenningen 2, Vågsbunnen ☎ 400–02–455 🌐 www.barerestaurant.no ⏲ Closed Sun. and Mon. No lunch.*

★ Brasserie France

$$$ | **FRENCH** | As its name suggests, this wine bar is straight out of Paris: the long white aprons on the waiters, the Art Nouveau flourishes in the dining room, the old French posters on the walls, and the closely packed tables all add to the illusion. The sumptuous menu includes the classics: steak tartare, entrecôte, and duck confit. **Known for:** an indulgent "bouillabaisse à la maison"; an impressive vegetarian set menu; perfect location near Parliament. *Average main: NKr300 ✉ Øvre Slottsgt. 16, Sentrum ☎ 23–10–01–65 🌐 www.brasseriefrance.no ⏲ Closed July and Sun. No lunch weekdays Ⓜ Stortinget.*

Crowbar and Bryggeri

PUBS | Spread across two floors, Oslo's largest microbrewery offers tasty beers and hearty pub fare like whole suckling pig. The menu changes weekly, and there's always a friendly bearded face to talk you through all the options. *✉ Torggata 32, Sentrum ☎ 21–38–67–57 🌐 crowbryggeri.com Ⓜ Jernbanetorget.*

★ Flåmstova

$$$ | **NORWEGIAN** | Looking for all the world like a traditional chalet, thanks to the massive beams and honey-color wood floors, you'll feel the Scandinavian *hygge* (coziness) as soon as you walk inside. The restaurant focuses on fresh local ingredients while encouraging creativity among its chefs. **Known for:** dishes prepared with local beer; new takes on traditional dishes; locally sourced ingredients. *Average main: NKr285 ✉ Flåmsbrygga Hotel, A-Feltvegen 25 ✢ Vestland ☎ 57–63–20–50 🌐 flamsbrygga.no ⏲ Closed Oct.–mid-June ☞ Available for groups on request in low season.*

★ Magic Ice Bar

BARS | Everything on the premises is made of ice, down to the barstools, the tables, and even the glasses. Ice sculptures of some of Norway's most intrepid explorers make you feel like you're getting a history lesson along with your beer. If you're a little chilly, the staff will loan you a parka. *✉ Kaigata 4, Tromsø ☎ 413–01–050 🌐 www.magicice.no/listings/tromso-norway/.*

★ **Restaurant Smak**
$$$$ | **NORWEGIAN** | You'll be impressed by the attention to detail shown by the chefs at this elegant dining room, with well-composed dishes that blend exciting and unexpected flavors. The menu changes with the season and takes advantage of the freshest ingredients available, with meats and cheeses from nearby farms. **Known for:** great set menu; impressive wine selection; local cheeses. *$ Average main: NKr795 ✉ Skippergata 16B, Tromsø ☎ 941–76–110 ⊕ www.restaurant-smak.no ⏲ Closed Sun. and Mon.*

★ **Restaurant Under**
$$$$ | **NORWEGIAN** | Europe's first underwater restaurant, Under sits well below sea level, with a massive wall of glass that gives you a look into the icy waters of the North Sea. It's an architectural and engineering marvel, looking like a modern building tipping gently into the ocean and connected to onshore rocks by a bridge. **Known for:** panoramic views; fresh seafood; Norwegian classics. *$ Average main: NKr2450 ✉ Bålyveien 48, Mandal ✥ Agder ⊕ under.no ⏲ Closed Sun.–Tues. in low season.*

★ **Theatercafeen**
$$$ | **NORWEGIAN** | An Oslo institution, Theatercafeen has been a meeting place for artists and intellectuals for more than a century. Today it still attracts Oslo's beau monde, and as it's right across the street from the National Theater, it's a good bet for celebrity spotting. **Known for:** traditional dishes like spicy moules frites; desserts like wild strawberry sorbet; sublime fish cakes. *$ Average main: NKr300 ✉ Continental Hotel, Stortingsgt. 24–26, Sentrum ☎ 22–82–40–50 ⊕ www.theatercafeen.no ⏲ Closed July M Nationaltheatret.*

Cool Places to Stay

★ **Amerikalinjen Hotel**
$$$$ | **HOTEL** | The handsome headquarters of the Norwegian America Line opened its doors in 1919, and 100 years later it was transformed into this boutique hotel appealing to the design-conscious explorer. **Pros:** sophisticated design throughout; wonderful gym and sauna; room-service cocktails. **Cons:** extremely steep rates; can be a bit of a scene; no space for extra beds. *$ Rooms from: NKr2092 ✉ Jernbanetorget 2, Oslo ☎ 21–40–59–00 ⊕ www.amerikalinjen.com 122 rooms No Meals M Jernbanetorget.*

★ **Fleischer's Hotel**
$$$$ | **HOTEL** | By the train station in the center of the city, this hotel dating from 1864 has plenty of details that call to mind a bygone era—bay windows, wooden balconies, and steeply pitched mansard roofs; even the newer wings have a pleasingly traditional look. **Pros:** indoor pool and sauna; central location; period charm. **Cons:** some noise from the train station; expensive rates; some amenities open only in summer. *$ Rooms from: NKr2100 ✉ Evangerveien 13, Voss ☎ 56–52–05–00 ⊕ fleischers.no 110 rooms Free Breakfast.*

Fretheim Hotel
$$$$ | **HOTEL** | One of western Norway's most beautiful hotels, the Fretheim has a classic, timeless look thanks to its whitewashed facade topped with a tower. **Pros:** superb location; excellent food; long history. **Cons:** not all the rooms have fjord views; expensive rates; simple decor in some rooms. *$ Rooms from: NKr3100 ✉ Nedre Fretheimsvegen ✥ Vestland ☎ 57–63–63–00 ⊕ fretheimhotel.no/en 122 rooms Free Breakfast.*

★ **Grand Hotel**
$$$$ | **HOTEL** | Looking like it would be at home on any street in Paris, this grand dame with a mansard roof and Beaux Arts entrance is the choice of visiting

heads of state, rock musicians, and Nobel Peace Prize winners. **Pros:** period touches have been preserved throughout; step-out balconies overlooking the town square; beautiful pool and spa facilities. **Cons:** gets busy during any of the city's festivals; spa and pool are short walk away from hotel; occasionally overrun by conference attendees. *Rooms from: NKr2000 ✉ Karl Johans gt. 31, Sentrum ☎ 23–21–20–00 🌐 www.grand.no 283 rooms 🍽 No Meals Ⓜ Stortinget.*

★ Guldsmeden Hotel

$$$ | **HOTEL** | The inviting reception area with soft leather couches, a crackling fireplace, and charm to spare let you know you're in the ultimate Oslo escape. **Pros:** close to the neighborhood's top attractions; on-site hammam big enough for two; rooms are selfie-ready. **Cons:** 20-minute walk to Oslo Central Station; no fitness center; no room service. *Rooms from: NKr1300 ✉ Parkveien 78, Frogner ☎ 23–27–40–00 🌐 guldsmeden-hotels.com 50 rooms 🍽 No Meals.*

★ Hindsæter Mountain Hotel

$$$ | **HOTEL** | **FAMILY** | This historic hotel has stunning views of the Sjodalen Valley and Jotunheimen National Park. **Pros:** wellness room with whirlpool and saunas; family rooms available; ski- and snowshoe rentals. **Cons:** no à la carte dinner options; rooms on the small size; books up fast. *Rooms from: NKr1650 ✉ Sjodalsveien 1549, Tessanden ✣ Innlandet ☎ 61–23–89–16 🌐 www.hindseter.no 26 rooms 🍽 Free Breakfast.*

★ Sorrisniva Igloo Hotel

$$$$ | **HOTEL** | This hotel is magical, melting away each spring and reappearing when winter settles in over the region. **Pros:** free sauna; free parking; free shuttle service. **Cons:** sauna available only in the morning; no luggage allowed in rooms; shared bathroom and changing area. *Rooms from: NKr4320 ✉ Sorrisniva 20, Alta ☎ 78–43–33–78 🌐 sorrisniva.no/igloo-hotel ⏲ Closed late spring–mid-Dec. 30 rooms 🍽 Free Breakfast.*

★ The Thief

$$$$ | **HOTEL** | Oslo's most tongue-in-cheek boutique hotel is located on Tjuvholmen, meaning Thief Islet, hence the unusual name. **Pros:** free admission to museum next door; a sumptuous breakfast spread; excellent location by the water. **Cons:** expensive rates; small swimming pool; isolated location. *Rooms from: NKr3000 ✉ Landgangen 1, Tjuvholmen ☎ 24–00–40–00 🌐 thethief.com 118 rooms 🍽 Free Breakfast.*

Sweden

Sweden requires the visitor to travel far, in both distance and attitude. Approximately the size of California, Sweden stretches up to the Arctic fringes, where glacier-topped mountains and thousands of acres of forests are broken only by wild rivers, pristine lakes, and desolate moorland. In the more populous south, roads meander through softly undulating countryside, skirting lakes, and passing small villages with sharp-pointed church spires.

Once the dominant power of the region, Sweden has traditionally looked inward for its own Nordic solutions. During the Cold War, its citizens were in effect subjected to a giant social experiment aimed at creating a perfectly just society with an all-embracing welfare state that adopted the best aspects of socialism and capitalism.

Sweden is today one of the world's dominant players in the information-based economy, especially mobile technology, and new technology is widely used throughout the country. On the social front, an influx of immigrants is reshaping the once-homogeneous society. Sweden continues to face political and social difficulties in the areas of immigration and integration.

Sweden is an arresting mixture of ancient and modern, its countryside dotted with runestones and timbered farmhouses, recalling its Viking past and more recent agrarian culture. Its cities, however, are modern, their shop windows filled with the latest in consumer goods and fashions.

Swedes are reluctant urbanites: their hearts and souls are in the forests and the archipelagos, to which they faithfully retreat, whenever possible, to enjoy the quiet. The country, frankly, is stunning, with natural assets in spades. Moose, reindeer, and lynx roam the forests, coexisting with the whine of chainsaws and the rumble of logging machines.

Stadshuset Stockholm

Walk in Nobel Footsteps

Famous for its grand ceremonial halls and as the venue of the annual Nobel Prize banquet, the dark red bricks and tall spire featuring three golden crowns (Sweden's national emblem) of Stockholm's City Hall make it one of the city's most impressive and recognizable landmarks. Designed by architect Ragnar Östberg and completed in 1923, this working center of city government is functional but ornate and can only be explored on a tour. Highlights include the immense Blå Hallen (Blue Hall—a hall that is not actually blue), the venue for the annual Nobel Prize dinner; and the ornate Council Chamber designed to resemble the open roof of a Viking longhouse. In summer months, visit the top of the 348-foot tower to enjoy a breathtaking panorama of the city and Riddarfjärden. Admission to the tower is separate from the guided tour, and requires walking stairs.

Don't Miss

Upstairs from Blå Hallen, the Gyllene Salen (Golden Hall) glitters with stunning golden mosaics depicting people and scenes from Swedish history rendered in the Byzantine style. Note the "Queen of Lake Mälaren" on the northern wall, which depicts a woman holding Stockholm in her lap.

Getting Here

Stadshuset sits by the water on the southeastern tip of Kungsholmen, a few hundred yards southwest of the central station. Closest t-bana stations: Rådhuset or T-Centralen.

✉ *Hantverkarg. 1, Stockholm* ☎ *08/50829058* 🌐 *www.cityhall.stockholm* 🎫 *Tour: SKr 130, tower SKr 90*

Vasamuseet

A Preserved 16th-Century Flagship

The mighty warship *Vasa* sank just minutes into her maiden voyage in August 1628, scuppered by a gust of wind and a fault in her design. The crowds who had come out to celebrate her glory instead witnessed her demise. Consigned to a watery grave, the *Vasa* was discovered in the late 1950s before being raised from the seabed in 1961. Its hull had been preserved by the Baltic mud, free of the shipworms (really clams) that can eat through timbers. Now largely restored to her former glory (however short-lived that may have been), the man-of-war resides in a handsome museum. The sheer size of this cannon-laden hulk inspires awe and fear in equal measure. The political history of the world might have been different had she made it out of the harbor. Engaging exhibitions illustrate the ship's history, the aftermath of the tragedy, and the raising of the *Vasa* some three centuries later.

Don't Miss

Outside the museum, a waterfront path skirts past a number of other museums and farther onto the island of Djurgården, the charming forests and green spaces of which once only the king was allowed to enjoy. These days, though, Djurgården is a popular spot for summer picnics, inspiring museum visits, and lazy strolls by the water and through leafy glades.

Getting Here

Tram line 7 from Sergels Torg stops a short walk from the museum.

✉ *Galärvarvsv. 14, Stockholm* ☎ *08/51954880* 🌐 *www.vasamuseet.se* 🎫 *From SKr 170*

Götaplatsen

The Cultural Heart of Göteborg

Built in 1923 in celebration of the city's 300th anniversary, and located at the end of Göteborg's main boulevard Avenyn, this square is home to the city's oldest cultural institutions and one of the city's best photo opportunities. In the center is the Swedish American sculptor Carl Milles's breathtaking fountain statue of Poseidon holding a codfish. Behind the statue stands the Göteborg Konstmuseum (Gothenburg Museum of Art), flanked by the city's main concert hall and municipal theater, important buildings in which the city celebrates its contributions to Swedish cultural life. The Konstmuseum is the best known with its majestic steps leading up to the building and its monumental pillars. The view from the steps—with Poseidon in the foreground and Avenyn stretching out in the background—is one of the city's most iconic.

Don't Miss

Göteborg's Konstmuseum extensive and impressive collection of leading Scandinavian painters and sculptors including works by Swedes such as Carl Milles, Johan Tobias Sergel, impressionist Anders Zorn, Victorian idealist Carl Larsson, and Prince Eugen. The museum's collection of 19th- and 20th-century French art is the best in Sweden, and there's also a small collection of old masters. The ground floor Hasselblad Center hosts exhibits devoted to showcasing progress in the art of photography.

Getting Here

Göteborg begs to be explored on foot but buses and trams stop nearby.

Gothenburg Visitor Centre. ✉ *Kungsportsplatsen. 2* ☎ *031/3684200* 🌐 *www.goteborg.com*

Bohuslän

Picture-Perfect West Coast

There's a bit of rivalry between Sweden's coasts, and many who favor the Bohuslän region north of Göteborg are quick to call it not just the west coast but the *best* coast. It's a place of brilliant colors, vibrant flavors, and simple pleasures: strolling through a pretty fishing village, dining on fresh seafood at a dockside restaurant, enjoying a picnic on a sun- warmed cliff, and cooling off with a dip in the ocean. The ideal way to explore the area is by meandering slowly north from Göteborg, taking full advantage of the gorgeous scenery and charming towns along the way. Marstrand, once the preferred summer retreat of King Oscar II, is regarded a summer paradise with excellent hiking, pretty white houses, and great swimming spots. Fiskebäckskil is a peaceful village with a picturesque harbor and many beautiful houses that once belonged to local sea captains. Lysekil, with its sea safaris and nature reserve, has been one of Sweden's most popular summer resorts since the 19th century.

Don't Miss

A popular motif for postcards from Bohuslän, Smögen is one of Sweden's prettiest villages with its colorful fishing huts along Smögenbryggan—painted in vivid shades of red, yellow, blue, and green—and cobbled lanes and streets lined with shops and restaurants selling Räkmacka (open shrimp sandwiches).

Getting Here

The best way to explore Bohuslän is by car. The E6 highway runs the length of the coast from Göteborg to Strömstad.

West Sweden Tourist Board. 🌐 *www.westsweden.com*

Kulturen i Lund

Historic Buildings and Beautiful Gardens

The second-oldest open-air museum in the country, Kulturen consists of a beautiful collection of farmhouses, town houses, a church, and other buildings that offer a glimpse at how people have lived in southern Sweden over the centuries. Some have always stood on this spot, while others have been moved here from locations across Skåne. Step inside and see what daily life was like for people from different time periods and social classes, from the medieval up to the 1930s. The museum also houses a variety of exhibitions—both permanent and seasonal—exploring Lund's history, folk art, design, and textiles, as well as toys, books, and a broad range of other topics.

Don't Miss

Thomanderska Huset (the Thomanders' House) was the home of theology professor and member of parliament Johan Henrik Thomander and his family between 1833 and 1850. The half-timbered house, which was moved to Kulturen in 1925, has been furnished with items that once belonged to the Thomanders and shows how the family would have lived in the early 19th century. Outside, an inviting ornamental garden has been planted with flowers that would have been familiar to the Thomanders.

Getting Here

Kulturen is located in the center of Lund, just a couple of blocks from Lunds Domkyrkan and a few minutes' walk from the train station. Lund is 19 km (12 miles) northeast of Malmö.

✉ *Tegnérsplatsen 6, Lund* ☎ *046/350400*
🌐 *www.kulturen.com* 🎫 *SKr 90*
🕒 *Closed Mon. mid-Sept.–Apr.*

Fårö

Get Away From It All

It takes just over five minutes south by ferry from Gotland to reach the tiny, secluded island of Fårö, a popular summer retreat for Scandinavians. If you really want to hide away from the world, Fårö is it—the island has just 500 year-round residents. Legendary Swedish filmmaker Ingmar Bergman once called this island home, and every June, film fanatics head there to celebrate Bergman Week, a festival of film, music, and talks organized by the Bergman Center. In September, the island celebrates Fårönatta—a night when its shops, restaurants, and attractions stay open all night and the church holds a midnight mass. Bear in mind that basic services, including police, medical services, and banks, are virtually nonexistent on Fårö itself, but they are all available back across the water on Gotland.

Don't Miss

Head to the Digerhuvud area, on the island's northwest coast, to find hundreds of impressive natural "sea stacks," weathered rock formations known as raukar that can be up to 8 meters (26 feet) tall. Carl Linneaus, the Swedish botanist, called them "stone giants," and it's easy to see why; they often take on human profiles, fueling local myths and legends.

Getting Here

A six-minute ferry is all it takes to reach Fårö from the island of Gotland. Flights arrive at Visby airport on Gotland regularly from Stockholm, while ferries to Gotland leave from Nynäshamn (south of Stockholm) and Oskarshamn (north of Kalmar).

Destination Gotland. ✉ *Korg. 2, Visby* ☎ *0771/223300* 🌐 *www.destinationgotland.se*

Midsummer in Dalarna

The Most Swedish of Holidays

There is nowhere better to celebrate the festival of Midsummer, when Swedes don folk costumes and dance to fiddle and accordion music around maypoles covered in wildflower garlands, than in Dalarna, the most traditional of Sweden's 25 provinces. Around Lake Siljan, celebrations kick off with Siljansrodden, with teams of rowers competing in "church boats," traditional longboats that once transported people across the lake to Sunday church services. Races are held in communities around the lake for a two-week period. Midsummer Day in Rättvik sees the festive arrival of church boats, bearing people in traditional costumes to attend services in the town's whitewashed 13th-century church. In Leksand, Sweden's tallest maypole is decorated and raised, with thousands of people joining in the festivities.

Tällberg is considered by many to be Midsummer at its most traditional. Start the day by picking flowers in the surrounding meadows, before helping to decorate the maypole, which is raised in the evening, ready for the dancing to begin.

Don't Miss

Join the fun. Don't worry, you'll soon get the hang of dancing around the maypole like little frogs ("små grodorna") or a crow ("Prästens lilla kråka").

When to Go

Midsummer is celebrated on the Friday in June closest to the Summer Solstice.

Getting Here

The Dalarna region is around three hours by car northwest of Stockholm and six hours northeast of Gothenburg. You can also take a train.

Visit Dalarna. 🌐 *www.visitdalarna.se*

Jokkmokk Market

A Festival of Sámi Art, Culture, and Crafts

Located just a few kilometers into the Arctic Circle, Jokkmokk is an important cultural center for the indigenous Sámi people, whose territory spreads over the far north of Norway, Sweden, Finland, and Russia. Since 1605, this town of just under 3,000 people has been the site of the annual Jokkmokk Market, a winter gathering taking place over several days in early February when the Sámi people parade their culture with pride. The festivities draw more than 35,000 visitors, including Sámi from across northern Scandinavia, as well as other travelers. In addition to market stalls selling traditional foods and handicrafts, there is a full program of cultural events, concerts, and lectures, as well as skiing, Northern Lights viewing, dogsled riding, and reindeer racing. The rest of the year, Jokkmokk is a quiet town that makes a good jumping-off point for exploring the Laponia World Heritage Area, about an hour and 45 minutes farther north.

Don't Miss

At first glance, Ájtte, Swedish Mountain, and Sámi Museum, look simple, but exhibit areas open off the central core like petals on a flower. Impressive displays explore the culture and history of the Sámi people, their crafts, traditional clothing, reindeer herding, religion, education, the Arctic landscape, and wildlife, along with the impact of outsiders.

When to Go

To experience Sámi culture, visit during early February. But book accommodations up to a year ahead.

Getting Here

Jokkmokk is 200 km (124 miles) south of Kiruna (the nearest airport).

Swedish Lapland. 🌐 *www.swedishlapland.com/jokkmokk*

Sweden
Norwegian Sea
Vestfjord
Tromsø
Jukkasjärvi
Kiruna
Sarek Nat'l Park
Muddus Nat'l Park
Jokkmokk Market
Rovaniemi
Luleå
Skellefteå
Umeå
Örnsköldsvik
Gulf of Bothnia
Trondheim
Östersund
Vaasa
FINLAND
Härnösand
Sundsvall
SWEDEN
NORWAY
Midsummer in Dalarna
Bollnäs
Lillehammer
Nusnäs
Naturum Dalarna
Sundborn
Gävle
Dalarna
Borlänge
Tampere
Turku
Helsinki
Oslo
Uppsala
Uppsala Domkyrka
Sigtuna
Västerås
Vaxholm
Stadshuset Stockholm
Vasamuseet
Stockholm
Karlstad
Örebro
Mariefred
Fotografiska
Kungliga Slottet
Tallinn
ESTONIA
Skagerrak
Mariestad
Nyköping
Norrköping
Bohuslän
Vannersborg
Kristiansand
Linköping
Fårö
Öland
Visby
Götaplatsen
Trädgårdsföreningen i Göteborg
Borås
Jönköping
Riga
LATVIA
Kosta Boda Glasbruk
Växjö
Kalmar
Baltic Sea
Halmstad
DENMARK
Helsingborg
Karlskrona
Kristianstad
LITHUANIA
Lund
Copenhagen
Kulturen i Lund
Malmöhus
Malmö
Ystad
RUSSIA
Kaliningrad
E6
E45
E75
E12
E8
E4
E18
E22
0
100 mi
100 km

When in Sweden

★ Fotografiska

ART MUSEUM | Opened in 2010, this contemporary photography museum housed in a 1906 redbrick Art Nouveau building along the Södermalm waterfront spotlights edgy fine art photography. Past exhibitions have included celebrity photographer Annie Leibovitz and director Anton Corbijn. ✉ *Stadsgårdshamnen 22, Södermalm* ☎ *08/50900500* 🌐 *www.fotografiska.com* 🎫 *From SKr 175* ✍ *Online booking recommended; additional fee for drop-in tickets.*

Kosta Boda Glasbruk

FACTORY | The Kingdom of Crystal's oldest works, dating from 1742, was named for the two former generals who founded it, Anders Koskull and Georg Bogislaus Stael von Holstein. Faced with a dearth of local talent, they initially imported glassblowers from Bohemia. The Kosta works pioneered the production of crystal (to qualify for that label, glass must contain at least 24% lead oxide). The Kosta complex includes a glass hut where you can watch glassblowers at work, a glass art gallery, outlet stores, and a glass studio where you can try your own hand at glassblowing (booking required). Since 1990 Kosta Boda also owns the renowned Orrefors glass brand, which has its own outlet shop here. To get to the village of Kosta from Kalmar, drive 59 km (36 miles) west on Route 25, then 15 km (9 miles) north on Route 28. ✉ *Stora Vägen 96, Kosta* ☎ *0478/34529* 🌐 *www.kostaboda.se/kosta-art-gallery* 🎫 *Guided tours SKr 70 (reservations required).*

★ Kungliga Slottet (*Royal Palace*)

CASTLE/PALACE | Designed by Nicodemus Tessin the Younger, the Royal Palace was completed in the 1770s to replace the Tre Kronor palace, which burned down in 1697. Each of the four facades has a distinct style. Watch the changing of the guard in the curved terrace entrance, and view the palace's fine furnishings and Gobelin tapestries on a tour of Representationsvåningarna (the State Apartments). Remnants of the earlier palace, as well as artifacts recovered after the fire, can be seen at the Tre Kronor Museum on the ground floor of the north side. To survey the crown jewels, head to Skattkammaren (the Treasury). Livrustkammaren (the Royal Armory)—Sweden's oldest museum, dating back nearly 400 years—has an outstanding collection and a separate admission fee. **TIP→ Entrances to the Treasury and Armory are on the Slottsbacken side of the palace.** ✉ *Slottsbacken 1, Gamla Stan* ☎ *08/4026100* 🌐 *www.kungligaslotten.se* 🎫 *SKr 170; SKr 150 for Livrustkammaren.*

Malmöhus

HISTORY MUSEUM | The city's castle, Malmöhus, completed in the 1540s, was for many years used as a prison (James Hepburn, 4th Earl of Boswell and third husband of Mary, Queen of Scots, was one of its notable inmates). Exhibits trace the dramatic history of the castle and the city of Malmö over the past 500 years. Malmöhus is also home to the Malmö Art Museum and an aquarium, which together with the adjacent Technology and Maritime Museum are part of a complex called Malmö Museer. A single admission ticket gets you into all the museums. ✉ *Malmöhusv., Malmö* ☎ *040/344400* 🌐 *www.malmo.se* 🎫 *SKr 40 for all museums.*

Naturum Dalarna

NATURE SIGHT | Perched on a hill overlooking Siljansnäs, Naturum Dalarna offers enchanting forest walks and a new observation tower—opened in 2021—that offers jaw-dropping views over the forested hills around Lake Siljan from three different viewing levels at 24 meters (79 feet), 27 meters (89 feet), and 32 meters (105 feet). (All but the highest viewing level can be accessed by elevator.) The visitor center offers exhibitions exploring the local Dalarna nature, wildlife, and geology, while outside, different wildlife trails wind through the forest. ✉ *Buffils Anna Väg 36, Siljansnäs* ☎ *010/2250329* 🌐 *www.naturumdalarna.se* 🎫 *Free* ⏲ *Closed Mon.–Thurs. in Apr. Closed Mon. and Tues. in Sept.*

★ Nusnäs

TOWN | The lakeside village of Nusnäs is where the famous painted wooden Dala horses are made. These were originally carved by the peasants of Dalarna as toys for their children, but their popularity rapidly spread in the 20th century. In 1939 they achieved international popularity after being shown at the New York World's Fair, and since then they have become a Swedish symbol. Founded in the 1920s by brothers from a poor family, the companies Grannas A. Olsson Hemslöjd (🌐 *www.grannas.com*) and Nils Olsson Dalahästar (🌐 *www.nilsolsson.se*) still make Dala horses today. At their factories, you can see the horses being made and purchase finished horses in many different sizes and colors, including the classic bright red. You can even have them personalized with your name or other text while you wait. ✉ *Nusnäs.*

Sundborn

HISTORIC HOME | In this small village you can visit Carl Larsson-gården, the lakeside home of the internationally famous Swedish artist (1853–1919), especially known for his watercolor paintings of his family's busy domestic life. The house itself was creatively painted and decorated by Larsson's wife, Karin, who also trained as an artist. Admission is by guided tour only, and tickets are timed; advance booking is recommended, especially in summer. If you do need to wait, you can stroll around the garden or lake, visit the café, or browse the shop, which sells items based on designs in the house and other work by the Larssons. In summer, tour tickets also include entry to the Kvarnen Gallery, which has special exhibits related to Carl Larsson and his work. ✉ *Carl Larsson-gården, Carl Larssons Väg 12, Sundborn* ✣ *14 km (8½ miles) northeast of Falun* ☎ *023/60053* 🌐 *www.carllarsson.se* 🎫 *SKr 240* ⏲ *Guided tours only. Check website for English tour times.*

★ Trädgårdsföreningen i Göteborg (*Garden Society of Gothenburg*)

GARDEN | These beautiful open green spaces, manicured gardens, and tree-lined paths are the perfect place to escape for some peace and rest. Rose fanciers can head for the magnificent rose garden, where there are 2,500 roses of 1,200 varieties. Also worth a visit is the Palm House, whose late-19th-century design echoes that of London's Crystal Palace. ✉ *Slussg. 1, Centrum* ☎ *031/3650000* 🌐 *www.tradgardsforeningen.se* 🎫 *Free.*

★ Uppsala Domkyrka (*Uppsala Cathedral*)

CHURCH | The 390-foot twin towers of Uppsala Cathedral—whose height equals the length of the nave—dominate the city skyline. Work on the cathedral began in the early 13th century; it was consecrated in 1435 and restored between 1885 and 1893. Still the seat of Sweden's archbishop, the cathedral is also the site of the tomb of Gustav Vasa, the king who established Sweden's independence in the 16th century. Inside is a silver casket containing the relics of St. Erik, who was assassinated in 1160, and it is also the burial place of other notable figures, including Carl von Linné. ✉ *Domkyrkoplan, Uppsala* ☎ *018/4303630* 🌐 *www.uppsalacathedral.com* 🎫 *Free.*

Where to Eat and Drink

★ AIRA

$$$$ | **SWEDISH** | AIRA's dark and moody exterior, tucked away on the island of Djurgården, belies its light, airy interior, scattered with white-clothed tables and seats and banquettes of chocolate-brown velvet. The cuisine from one of Sweden's best known chefs, Tommy Myllymäki, skews toward local ingredients infused with international flavors, offering the best of land and sea, all prepared in an open kitchen alongside the high-ceilinged dining space. **Known for:** handcrafted nonalcoholic-drinks pairing menu; Nordic dishes with an international twist; prix-fixe menu. *Average main: SKr995* *Biskopsv. 9, Djurgården* *08/48004900* *www.aira.se* *Closed Sun.–Tues.*

Årstiderna i Kockska Huset

$$$ | SCANDINAVIAN | This cozy, atmospheric restaurant occupies a series of interconnected cellar vaults in one of Malmö's best-preserved 16th-century buildings. Traditional Swedish dishes, often centered on beef, game, and seafood, are given a contemporary twist. **Known for:** traditional Swedish dishes; historic setting; excellent wine list. *Average main: SKr370* *Frans Suellsg. 3, Malmö* *040/230910* *arstiderna.pieplowsrestauranger.se* *Closed Sun. No lunch Sat.*

★ Lilla Bjers

$$$$ | SWEDISH | Situated 7 km (4½ miles) south of Visby in the midst of farmland, Lilla Bjers prides itself on creating seasonal menus largely from its own-grown produce, complimented with locally sourced organic ingredients. Meals are served in light, airy repurposed greenhouses in the shade of the olive trees interspersed between the wooden tables, and heated in the winter months by a wood-burning stove. **Known for:** restaurant's own nonalcoholic drinks; organic wines from Europe; farm-to-table experience. *Average main: SKr830* *Lilla Bjers 410, Gotland* *Just off Rte. 410 south out of Visby* *0498/652440* *www.lillabjers.se/restaurant* *Closed Mon.–Wed. No lunch Thurs. No dinner Sun.*

SK Mat & Människor

$$$ | SCANDINAVIAN | The connection between people and food is at the heart of this stylish yet intimate restaurant where you can watch your meals being prepared in the completely open kitchen—in fact, chefs often bring dishes to the tables themselves. The focus is on seasonal Scandinavian cuisine expertly prepared and complemented by an extensive wine list. **Known for:** creative cuisine; relaxed fine dining; list of more exclusive wines by the glass. *Average main: SKr287* *Johannebergsg. 24, Vasastan* *031/812580* *www.skmat.se* *Closed Sun. No lunch.*

Wedholms Fisk

$$$$ | SEAFOOD | On the Nybroviken waterfront in central Stockholm, Wedholms Fisk serves almost exclusively seafood that is simply but beautifully prepared. The menu is divided by fish type, with a number of options for each type of fish. **Known for:** outstanding seafood; extensive wine list; elegant setting. *Average main: SKr619* *Arsenalsg. 1, Norrmalm* *08/6117874* *www.wedholmsfisk.se* *Closed Sun. No lunch Sat.*

Cool Places to Stay

Berns Hotel

$$$ | HOTEL | Berns Hotel has been a hotspot since the late 19th century; rooms here have hardwood floors, off-white walls, feather-stuffed quilts, and throw pillows and curtains in muted tones, all complemented with modern artwork. **Pros:** stylish rooms; stunning restaurant; great location. **Cons:** some rooms are on the smaller side; the bar can be loud on weekends or during events; corridors could use updating. *Rooms from: SKr2500* *Näckströmsg. 8, Norrmalm* *08/56632200* *www.berns.se* *81 rooms* *Free Breakfast.*

Diplomat

$$$$ | HOTEL | Within easy walking distance of Djurgården, this elegant hotel is less flashy than most in its price range, but it's chic with subtle, tasteful designs and has an efficient staff. **Pros:** wonderful location; mix of old-world charm and modern comfort; fantastic views. **Cons:** antique elevator is small and a bit slow;

some rooms are small; rooms can get hot in summer. $ *Rooms from: SKr3900* ✉ *Strandv. 7C, Östermalm* ☎ *08/4596800* 🌐 *www.diplomathotel.com* 🛏 *130 rooms* 🍴 *Free Breakfast.*

★ **Ett Hem**

$$$$ | HOTEL | Feel free to grab a drink or snack from the fridge—at Ett Hem (meaning "A Home"), guests are encouraged to act like they're at home in these restored Arts and Crafts town houses with only 22 rooms. **Pros:** excellent food; private-home feel; beautiful rooms and common areas. **Cons:** 20-minute walk to city center; books up fast; atypical setup may not be for some. $ *Rooms from: SKr4995* ✉ *Sköldungag. 2, Östermalm* ☎ *08/200590* 🌐 *www.etthem.se* 🛏 *22 rooms* 🍴 *Free Breakfast.*

★ **Grand Hôtel**

$$$$ | HOTEL | At first glance the Grand seems like any other world-class international hotel, and in many ways it is: its location is one of the best in the city, on the quayside just across the water from the Royal Palace, and service is slick and professional. **Pros:** unadulterated luxury; location can't be beat; excellent amenities. **Cons:** gym is shared with non-guests and can be crowded; faded in parts; breakfast (not included) on the expensive side. $ *Rooms from: SKr4700* ✉ *Södra Blasieholmshamnen 8, Norrmalm* ☎ *08/6793500* 🌐 *www.grandhotel.se* 🛏 *279 rooms* 🍴 *No Meals.*

★ **Hotell Oskar**

$$ | B&B/INN | At this charming boutique-style inn made up of two 19th-century town houses, the rooms are spacious, modern, and bright, with white walls, colorful art, and polished oak floors. **Pros:** central location; well-designed, cozy rooms; excellent breakfast. **Cons:** no restaurant; limited amenities; self-service check-in. $ *Rooms from: SKr1695* ✉ *Bytareg. 3, Lund* ☎ *046/188085* 🌐 *www.hotelloskar.se* 🛏 *8 rooms* 🍴 *Free Breakfast.*

★ **Icehotel**

$$$ | HOTEL | It's no wonder that Jukkasjärvi's famed Icehotel was first conceived and constructed as an art installation in 1989—this fantastical structure is a sensory extravaganza. **Pros:** cool accommodations, both literally and figuratively; beautiful riverside setting; gorgeous ice art everywhere. **Cons:** ice rooms are expensive; some guests find it hard to sleep in the cold, despite warm sleeping bags; bathroom use at night requires some unwrapping. $ *Rooms from: SKr2385* ✉ *Marknadsv. 63, Jukkasjärvi* ☎ *0980/66800* 🌐 *www.icehotel.com* 🛏 *50 ice rooms (can vary from yr to yr), 44 warm rooms, 28 chalet apartments* 🍴 *Free Breakfast.*

Chapter 7

CENTRAL EUROPE

7

WELCOME TO CENTRAL EUROPE

TOP REASONS TO GO

★ **Stunning Cities:** Discover everywhere from fairy-tale Prague to fast-changing Berlin, lakeside Zürich to thermal bath–filled Budapest.

★ **Churches:** Take your pick among stand-outs in splendid styles from Renaissance to Rococo to Baroque.

★ **Outdoor Activities:** In winter, skiers take to the slopes of Switzerland and Austria. In summer, swimmers hit the shores of northern Poland or of Hungary's Lake Balaton.

★ **Wine Tasting:** Whether it's German Riesling, Austrian Grüner Veltliner, or Hungarian Tokaji, wine has quenched the thirst of visitors to Central Europe for centuries.

★ **Music:** This region means classical music. From grand opera houses to Baroque churches, the music of Mozart, Chopin, Dvořák, Liszt, and Beethoven fills the air.

★ **Sport:** Germany is a mecca for soccer, but winter sports rule here. Visit the toboggan runs of Switzerland or the ice hockey rinks of Slovakia.

1 **Austria.** Come for great landscapes and even greater culture, from skiing in the Tyrolean Alps to nights at the Vienna opera.

2 **Germany.** From Berlin's cutting-edge art to Hamburg's historic harbor to Munich's famous Oktoberfest, Germany offers diverse experiences.

3 **Switzerland.** Zürich mixes old-world charm with a youthful vibe. But it is in Switzerland's lakes, valleys, and peaks where you'll find its soul.

4 **Czech Republic.** Prague offers Gothic splendors, while the castle-dotted countryside showcases dazzling relics of Europe's past.

5 **Hungary.** Once ruled by the Turks and Habsburgs, modern Hungary has a confident cultural capital, spectacular lakes, and flourishing vineyards.

6 **Poland.** Whether you're into sleeping in an old palace or camping by the lake, folk crafts, or fine dining, Poland has it all.

7 **Slovakia.** From the cobbled streets of Bratislava to the hiking trails of the High Tatras, Slovakia is made to explore on foot.

SWEDEN
Aarhus
DENMARK
Copenhagen
Malmö
Baltic Sea
Liepaga
LATVIA
LITHUANIA
RUSSIA
(Kaliningrad Oblast)
Kaliningrad
Vilnius
Gdańsk
BELARUS
POLAND
6
Berlin
Warsaw
Brest
Łódź
Dresden
Prague
Kraków
Lvov
CZECH REPUBLIC
4
Nürnberg
SLOVAKIA
7
UKRAINE
Munich
Vienna
Bratislava
AUSTRIA
1
Budapest
HUNGARY
5
Cluj-Napoca
ROMANIA
SLOVENIA
Ljubljana
Zagreb
Venice
CROATIA
Belgrade
BOSNIA AND
HERZEGOVINA
SERBIA

WHAT TO EAT IN CENTRAL EUROPE

Sachertorte

FONDUE

Whether a mix of Gruyère and Vacherin (known as moitié-moitié) or a less pungent mix of hard cheeses, fondue is a Swiss staple. Too rich for you? Try raclette, a heated half wheel of full-bodied cheese, melted onto potatoes or bread.

GOULASH

Meaning "herdsman," goulash is one of Hungary's national dishes. The classic recipe is created using beef, potatoes, vegetables, pinched egg noodles, paprika, and various other Hungarian spices. The Czech Republic and Slovakia have their own variations on "guláš."

KÄSESPÄTZLE

This Austrian take on macaroni and cheese, also popular in parts of Germany, Switzerland, and Liechtenstein, has strips of egg pasta called Spätzle layered with onions and grated cheese, then panfried to a golden brown and topped with fried onions.

PICKLED CHEESE

A staple of Czech pubs,*nakládaný hermelín* is a Camembert-like cheese that's marinated in oil and spices. Is it a little like Prague's Astronomical Clock: overhyped? Perhaps. But you're going to remember it. Best enjoyed spread on dark Czech bread.

PIEROGI

In Poland, pierogi is the fast food of choice. These boiled dumplings come in two main versions:*pierogi ruskie* (the Russian pierogi), with potatoes, cottage cheese, onion, salt, and pepper, and the*pierogi z kapustą i grzybami*, with cabbage and mushrooms.

SACHERTORTE

The famous chocolate cake with a layer of apricot jam and dark chocolate icing is synonymous with Vienna. Developed in the 19th century, the Hotel Sacher lays claim to the "original" recipe, which is allegedly kept under lock and key.

BIRCHERMÜESL

Created by raw food pioneer Dr. Bircher-Benner at the turn of the 20th century, Birchermüesli is a Swiss breakfast dish made with soaked, rolled oats, grated apples, nuts, and cream. It comes in several varieties but often contains fresh berries.

LÁNGOS

This is a traditional Hungarian fried bread, sold everywhere by street carts and vendors. The usual toppings for this deep-fried delight are a dollop of sour cream and shredded cheese, but other options include bacon, sausage, red onion, garlic, and paprika.

WHITE WINE

From Germany's Mosel Valley and the Czech Republic's Moravian wine region to the hilly terraces overlooking Vienna and the shores of Lake Balaton, white wine is big business in Central Europe. Look out for varieties including Riseling, Grüner Veltliner, and Pinot Blanc.

Goulash

Fondue

BEER AND PLUM BRANDY

All Central European countries have their favorite pilsner (pale lager), but the original can be found at the Pilsner Urquell brewery, 40 miles south of Prague. Need something stronger? Try a*slivovitz* (plum brandy), popular in the Czech Republic, Slovakia, Poland, and Hungary.

BRATWURST

In a country that loves sausages, the bratwurst is, by far, the German favorite. Perhaps the most beloved of all Bratwürste (sausages) is the small, thin sausage from the city of Nuremberg. Thuringian bratwurst is larger and is made from lean pork shoulder flavored with garlic and marjoram.

RÖSTI

Basically glorified hash browns, these are grated, fried potatoes covered in toppings like bacon. They've become known as Switzerland's national dish.

Central Europe Snapshot

Know Before You Go

CURRENCY MATTERS.

Not every country in Central Europe is part of the Euro zone, so don't assume you won't need to change currencies. While the euro is used in Austria, Germany, and Slovakia, you'll need francs for Switzerland, crowns for the Czech Republic, forints for Hungary, and złoty for Poland. Many hotels and bars in the major regional capitals will take euros anyway, but prepare for a poor exchange rate.

HOW DO YOU SAY...?

There are several different languages spoken throughout this region, with four in Switzerland alone. You can get by in English, but learning a few key phrases will always be appreciated.

DITCH THE WHEELS.

All the big cities of Central Europe are conveniently connected by public transport, including by cross-border trains and buses. Even smaller towns and villages are usually accessible by local buses, so there's no need to have your own car. There are also quick and cheap flight connections across the region, though obviously on-the-ground transport is a greener option.

Planning Your Time

While Central Europe is a relatively compact area, it's close to 1,000 miles from one extreme (southwestern Switzerland) to the other (northeastern Poland). Plan around four weeks for a "big city" itinerary that starts in Zürich, visits Munich, Salzburg, Vienna, Bratislava, Budapest, Kraków, and Prague, and ends in Berlin. Only a week to spare? Limit yourself to two or three cities.

Great Trips

4 days. Zürich to St Gallen to Bregenz to Munich.

5 days. Prague to Kraków.

5 days. Budapest to Bratislava to Vienna.

Big Events

Febiofest. Film lovers will want to catch Febiofest, the largest film festival in Central Europe, held in April or May in Prague.

Montreux Jazz Festival . This legendary lakeside event—the world's second-largest annual jazz festival—offers three weeks of exemplary jazz throughout July.

Budapest Wine Festival. Taste the best of Hungarian and international wines every September at this popular Buda Castle festival.

What To...

READ

Sherlock Holmes: The Final Problem, Arthur Conan Doyle. A classic set at Switzerland's Reichenbach Falls.

The Trial, Franz Kafka. A dystopian novel by Prague's famous author, who wrote in German.

Géza Gárdonyi. A journey into medieval Hungary.

The Third Man, Graham Greene. The novel (and film) is set in Vienna just after World War II.

WATCH

Amadeus. The tale of Austrian composer Wolfgang Mozart told by Czech director Miloš Forman.

The Witness. Péter Bacsó's satire about the communist regime in Hungary is a cult classic.

Schindler's List. Set in Kraków, Steven Spielberg's harrowing historical drama won seven Oscars.

*The Swissmakers.*This comedy by Rolf Lyssy is Switzerland's most successful movie.

LISTEN TO

Wolfgang Amadeus Mozart, *Eine Kleine Nachtmusik*

Kraftwerk, *The Model*

Frédéric Chopin, *The Polonaise*

Karel Gott, *Lady Karneval*

BUY

Nobody does lager better than the Czechs and the Germans.

Take your pick of crystal from Swarovski (Austria), Moser (Czech), or Ajka (Hungary).

Popular in Slovakia, bryndza sheep-milk cheese is deliciously pungent.

Fürst Mozartkugel marzipan and nougat–filled chocolates are an Austrian essential.

Contacts

AIR

MAJOR AIRPORTS

Austria. Vienna (VIE)

Germany. Frankfurt (FRA), Munich (MUC), Berlin Brandenburg (BER)

Switzerland. Zürich (ZRH), Geneva (GVA)

Czech Republic. Prague (PRG)

Hungary. Budapest (BUD)

Poland. Warsaw (WAW), Krakow (KRK)

Slovakia. Bratislava (BTS)

BUS

Flixbus. 🌐 *www.flixbus.com*

Austria. Blaguss Reisen 🌐 *www.blaguss.at*

Germany. Eurolines 🌐 *www.eurolines.de*

Switzerland. PostBus 🌐 *www.postauto.ch*

Czech Republic. Regiojet 🌐 *www.regiojet.cz*

Hungary. Volán 🌐 *www.volanbusz.hu*

TRAIN

Austria. ÖBB (Österreichische Bundesbahnen) 🌐 *www.oebb.at*

Germany. Deutsche Bahn 🌐 *www.deutschebahn.com*

Switzerland. Swiss Federal Railways 🌐 *www.sbb.ch*

Czech Republic. Czech Railways 🌐 *www.cd.cz*

Slovakia. Slovak Rail 🌐 *www.zssk.sk*

Hungary. MAV 🌐 *www.mavcsoport.hu*

Poland. PKP 🌐 *www.pkp.pl*

VISITOR INFORMATION

Austria. 🌐 www.austria.info

Germany. 🌐 www.germany.travel

Switzerland. 🌐 www.myswitzerland.com

Czech Republic. 🌐 www.visitczechrepublic.com

Slovakia. 🌐 www.slovakia.travel

Hungary. 🌐 www.visithungary.com

Poland. 🌐 www.poland.travel

Austria

Austria is where children laugh at marionette shows in the parks, couples linger for hours over pastries at gilt-ceiling cafés, and Lipizzaner stallions dance to Mozart minuets. It's a country that embraces the elegance of a time gone by. But look beyond the postcard clichés of dancing white horses and the Vienna Boys' Choir, and you'll find a conservative-mannered yet modern country, where there's an exciting juxtaposition of old and new.

While Vienna has sumptuous palaces—plus UN organizations housed in a wholly modern complex—it's also a modern city with high-rise office buildings beyond the historic core. The Salzburg area is where *The Sound of Music* took place, but is also home to avant-garde art in its Museum de Moderne.

Start with Vienna's historical and artistic heritage, home to the legacies of Beethoven, Freud, and Klimt. This city is a mélange of Apfelstrudel and psychoanalysis, Schubert and schnitzel. Its grand Kunsthistorisches Museum holds one of the greatest art collections anywhere, while the Staatsoper is one of the continent's finest opera houses, and Schönbrunn Palace flaunts the glories of Imperial Austria.

Move on to Salzburg, Mozart's birthplace and home to one of the world's ritziest summer music festivals as well as sights from *The Sound of Music*. And nestled in the alps is Innsbruck, where the baroque architecture in the Altstadt (or Old City) remains much as it was 400 years ago. The protective vaulted arcades along main thoroughfares, the tiny passage-ways giving way to noble squares, and the ornate restored houses all contribute to an unforgettable picture.Don't miss a spot of skiing or hiking in the Aus-trian alps, or embrace the staggering mountainscapes with a drive on the Grossglockner High Alpine Road. Then indulge in wine tasting on the banks of the majestic Danube river or take a dip in one of the pristine, tranquil lakes of the Austrian countryside.

Schloss Schönbrunn

Marvel at Vienna's Hapsburg Palace

This huge Hapsburg summer residence was originally designed by Johann Bernhard Fischer von Erlach in 1696 but altered considerably for Maria Theresa. The impressive approach to the palace and its gardens through the front gate yields the vast main courtyard, which unfolds to a supreme achievement of baroque planning. Formal *Allées* (promenades) shoot off diagonally, one on the right toward the zoo, one on the left toward a rock-mounted obelisk and a fine false Roman ruin. But these are merely a frame for the composition in the center: the sculpted marble fountain; the carefully planted screen of trees behind; the sudden, almost vertical rise of the grass-covered hill beyond, with the Gloriette a fitting crown. Within the palace, the state salons are quite up to the splendor of the exterior and the gardens, but note the contrast between these chambers and far more modest rooms where the rulers lived most of their time.

Don't Miss

The Hall of Mirrors, where the six-year-old Mozart performed for Empress Maria Theresa in 1762, and the Grand Gallery, where the Congress of Vienna (1815) danced at night after carving up Napoléon's collapsed empire during the day.

Getting Here

Take the U4 subway and get off at Schönbrunn.

✉ *Schönbrunner-Schloss-Strasse, Vienna* ☎ *01-811-13-239* 🌐 *www.schoenbrunn.at* 🎫 *From €22*

Eating a Traditional Wiener Schnitzel

Indulge in a Staple Bigger than a Dinner Plate

The crispy, unfussy breaded, fried cutlet—traditionally made with veal, though you'll also find it made with pork, and occasionally turkey or chicken—is as iconic to Vienna (and Austria) as the baguette is to France. This national dish even incorporates the name of the country's capital, Vienna (*Wiener*). Legend says it was brought to Austria around 1857 by Austrian Field Marshal Radetzky. Allegedly, he enjoyed a similar dish *cotoletta a la Milanese* in Italy so much that he brought the recipe back with him. But this origin story may or may not be true: the first known mention of Wiener Schnitzel in Austrian cuisine actually dates back to 1831.

It's not just a dish for tourists. Locals like to eat it at restaurants, but it's a popular dish people make at home, too. In principle, it's a simple dish that requires specific steps. The meat is pounded so it's evenly thin, coated in flour, then egg, then bread crumbs. Then it's fried to a golden brown: the secret to a good schnitzel is that the breading becomes airy and fluffy, not heavy. And it's also famously enormous, often spilling over the plate. Wiener schnitzel is traditionally served with a wedge of lemon and a side of cold potato salad. Try it at Pfarrwirt, one of the oldest taverns in Vienna.

Don't Miss

Go superlocal and order it with a side of lingonberry sauce—it's a tart berry similar to cranberry.

Eat Here

Pfarrwirt. ✉ *Pfarrpl. 5* ☎ *01 3707373* 🌐 *www.pfarrwirt.com* 🚊 *Tram D to Grinzinger Strasse*

Coffee in a Viennese Coffee House

Press Pause as the Viennese Do

The coffeehouse culture is as much a part of the Austrian—and Viennese—soul as Mozart is. The city boasts more than 1,600 coffeehouses (*Wiener Kaffeehäuser* in German). And while these cafés have been known for centuries as "Vienna's parlors," they face stiff competition today from both Starbucks and more modern, hipster coffee shops. Still, nothing will ever diminish the sentimental feelings Austrians have for these coffeehouses. Newspapers were run from them; revolutions started within them; and many an hour whiled away. The traditional coffeehouse experience is appealingly old-school: think sumptuous, red-velvet-padded chairs and coffee served on small silver platters. Then there's the waiters, dressed in Sunday-best outfits; the pastries, cakes, strudels, and rich tortes; the newspapers, magazines, and journals; and a sense that here time stands still. There's no need to worry about overstaying your welcome, even over a single small cup of coffee. Experience the ambience at Cafe Sperl, featured in Hollywood films *A Dangerous Method* and *Before Sunrise.*

Don't Miss

Take a look at the coffee menu. In Austria, coffee is never merely coffee. It comes in countless forms and under many names. Ask a waiter for *ein Kaffee* and you'll get a vacant stare. Study the 20-plus options, and look out for some of the most decadent, including the coffee-and-whipped-cream concoctions, universally cherished as *Kaffee mit Schlag* (or in summer, it's cold coffee with ice cream *and*whipped cream).

Stop Here

Cafe Sperl. ✉ *Gumpendorferstrass 11*
☎ *01–586–4158* 🌐 *www.cafesperl.com*
🚆 *U1, U2, U4 to Karlsplatz*

Lipizzaner Horses

The Miraculous Viennese Stallions

On the grounds of the Imperial Palace is the world-famous Spanish Riding School, a favorite for centuries, and no wonder: who can resist the sight of the white Lipizzaner horses going through their masterful paces? For the last 300 years they have been perfecting their haute école riding demonstrations to the sound of Baroque music in a ballroom that seems to be a crystal-chandeliered stable. The interior of the riding school, the 1735 work of Fischer von Erlach the Younger, makes it Europe's most elegant sports arena. What's even more miraculous is that the horses are born dark and only turn white (actually light gray) as they get older.

Don't Miss

Even if you are in Vienna at a time when the horses aren't performing (or if you don't have time for or can't get tickets to a performance), you can take a guided tour of the Spanische Reitschule, their home in the Hofburg every Tuesday through Sunday.

When to Go

Performances are held most weekends throughout the year except in July and the first half of August. Sunday is the most common performance day. Morning training sessions are also held throughout the year on many weekdays except in July and early August. There are multiple tours offered on most days from Tuesday through Sunday.

Spanische Reitschule. ✉ *Michaelerplatz 1, 1st District* ☎ *01/533–9031* 🌐 *www.srs.at* 🎫 *From €30; morning exercises from €16; guided tour €21* ⏲ *Closed late July and early Aug. No tours Mon.* 🚇 *U3/Herrengasse*

Grossglockner High Alpine Road

Austria's Most Scenic Drive

One of the best-known roads in the Alps, the *Grossglockner Hochalpenstrasse* (Grossglockner High Alpine Road) rises to more than 2438 meters (8,000 feet) and contains 36 hairpin bends, with mountain panoramas the whole way. It leads you deep into the Hohe Tauern National Park where you'll be rewarded with absolutely breathtaking views of the 3,798-m (12,460-foot) Grossglockner peak and surrounding Alps, of the vast glaciers in the valley below, and, on a clear day, even into Italy. This is the best way to see Austria's highest peaks from the comfort of your car.

Don't Miss

The best scenic vantage point is at the Edelweissspitze. It's an unbelievable view out over East Tyrol, Carinthia, and Salzburg, including a whopping 19 glaciers and 37 peaks scraping the sky above 3,000 meters (9,600 feet).

When to Go

It's easier to drive (and the scenery is more beautiful) in the summer or early fall, but the road is typically closed from early November to early May.

Getting Here

The road is a gated section of some 46 km (29 miles) from Bruck to Heiligenblut. From Zell am See, head south toward Bruck an der Grossglocknerstrasse, and continue on the B107. After the toll station in Ferleitern, the highway begins its many hairpin turns and continues to Heiligenblut.

☎ (0662) 873673, road information www.grossglockner.at 🎫 1-day pass: €40 regular or hybrid vehicle; €32 (100% electric or hydrogen): 3-wk pass: €73 (all vehicle types) ⏲ Last entry 45 mins before closing

Salzburg

Mozart's Hometown

Art lovers call Salzburg the "Golden City of High Baroque"; historians refer to it as the Florence of the North or the German Rome; music lovers know it as the birthplace of one of the world's most beloved composers, Wolfgang Amadeus Mozart (1756–91). The house he was born in, the *Mozart-geburtshaus*, is a homage to Salzburg's prodigal son and offers fascinating insights into his life and works, with carefully curated relics of Mozart's youth, listening rooms, and models of famous productions of his operas. And the best example of Baroque is the old town's *Dom zu Salzburg*, a cathedral set within the beautiful Domplatz with the Virgin's Column in its center. This is considered to be the first early-Italian Baroque building north of the Alps. Its facade is of marble, its towers reach 250 feet into the air, and it holds 10,000 people.

Don't Miss

The renaissance-inspired pleasure Schloss Hellbrunn has famous trick fountains, a lush green lawn, and the gazebo that witnessed so much wooing in *The Sound of Music.* Be sure to ascend to Fortress Hohensalzburg on the peak and find the soul-stirring combination of gorgeous architecture in a stunning natural location.

Getting Here

Salzburg Airport is Austria's second-largest international airport. The city is 2½ hours (198 miles) from Vienna or 2 hours (93 miles) from Munich by train. Once in Salzburg, you can get around by bus; a single bus ticket costs €2.10.

Salzburg Tourism. 🌐 *www.salzburg.info*

Innsbruck

Get a Glimpse of the Jagged Alps

The capital of Tyrol owes much of its charm and fame to its location next to the steep, sheer sides of the Alps that rise from the edge of the city like a shimmering blue-sky-and-snow-white wall—an impressive backdrop for the mellowed green domes and red roofs of the lively Baroque town tucked below.

Don't Miss

The *Goldenes Dachl* (Golden Roof) has become the symbol of Innsbruck and made famous the late-Gothic mansion whose balcony it covers. The roof is capped with 2,657 gilded copper tiles, and its regilding is said to have taken nearly 31 pounds of gold. The house was built in 1420 for Frederick IV as the residence of the Tirolean sovereign. Legend persists that he added the golden look to counter rumors that he was penniless, but the balcony was, in fact, added by Emperor Maximilian I in the late 15th century as a "royal box" for watching various performances in the square below. He had the roof gilded to symbolize the wealth and power of Tirol, which had recently undergone massive financial reform. The building is now a museum displaying memorabilia and paintings from the life of the emperor.

Getting Here

Innsbruck is 166 km (103 miles) southwest of Salzburg, 476 km (295 miles) southwest of Vienna. A train takes 2½ hours to Vienna and 2 hours to Munich. Local public transit is by bus and streetcar (single tickets €2.80).

Goldenes Dachl Museum. ✉ *MaximilianHerzog-Friedrich-Strasse 15, Innsbruck* 🎫 *€60* 🕓 *Closed Mon. Oct.–Apr.*

Innsbruck Tourism.
🌐 *www.innsbruck.info*

Dürnstein

Wine Tasting with Views of the Danube

The Wachau is a stunning stretch of the river-hugging Danube Valley best known for the cultivation of vines since prehistoric times. And if a beauty contest were held among the towns along the Danube, chances are the small town of Dürnstein, would be the winner. The main street, Hauptstrasse, is lined with picturesque medieval and baroque structures and romantic, cobbled streets. Wine walks are well-marked, and you can sample wine at the many wine bars in town or directly on the grounds of the wineries, among the vines or in a wine cellar.

Don't Miss

Be sure to hike up to the ruins of Durnstein Castle, 20 minutes from the center of town. Legend says that upon his return from the crusades, English King Richard the Lionheart tore up the Austrian flag and refused to share his spoils of war with Austrian Duke Leopold V., so the duke held him prisoner in the castle for a year.

When to Go

Avoid winter and weekdays, when many of the wineries are closed for tasting. The best time of year is October and November, when the grapes from the surrounding hills are harvested by volunteers from villages throughout the valley—and members of the local wine cooperative garnish their front doors with straw wreaths to show they can offer tastes of the new wine.

Getting Here

Durnstein is 85 km (53 miles) northwest of Vienna, approximately 1½ hours by train.

Durnstein Tourism.
🌐 *www.duernstein.at*

St. Wolfgang

A Charming Village on a Majestic Lake

Situated on the steep banks of the Wolfgangersee (Wolfgang Lake), St. Wolfgang is a picturesque town in Austria's lake district with panoramic views of the mountains surrounding it. The crystal clear, pristine lake is ideal for swimming, kayaking, and general relaxing. The village boasts a small cluster of chalet-like houses ideal for a tranquil stroll, and the forested lakeshore is lined with gently creaking wooden boathouses. In town, check out the altarpiece in the 15th-century Wallfahrtskirche, one of the finest examples of late-Gothic woodcarving to be found anywhere. On a bright day, sunlight off the lake dances on the ceiling in brilliant reflections through the stained-glass windows.

Don't Miss

Take a trip on a steamer boat that plies the waters of the lake. The earliest paddleboat on the lake is still in service, a genuine 1873 steamer called the The view of the town against the dramatic mountain backdrop is one you'll see again and again on posters and postcards.

Getting Here

St. Wolfgang is 19 km (12 miles) southeast of St. Gilgen, 50 km (31 miles) southeast of Salzburg. The town is busy and traffic heavy, so if you drive, park in Strobl and take the steamer in; otherwise, consider a bus.

Wolgangsee Ferry. *www.5schaetze.at/en/wolfgangseeschifffahrt.html* *Closed mid-Oct.–Apr.* *€13*

Wolfgangsee Tourist Office. *wolfgangsee.salzkammergut.at*

Skiing in Kitzbühel

Austria's Most Fashionable Ski Resort

Kitzbühel is indisputably one of Austria's most fashionable winter resorts, although the town boasts a busy summer season as well. In winter, many skiers are attracted by the famous Ski Safari—a carefully planned, clever combination of chair-lifts, gondola lifts, draglifts, and runs that lets you ski for more than 145 km (91 miles) without having to walk a single foot. There are both challenging and easy slopes; the ski network here is vast and spectacular, with 60 lovely mountain huts scattered over the slopes offering excellent food and drink to break the ski day. There are 192 km (119 miles) of slopes—106 of them blue, 66 red and 20 black—all served by 57 ski lifts throughout winter and spring (often until early May). In the summer, visitors are offered free guest cards that provide free or discounted activities.

Where to Stay

Rasmushof. It's hard to imagine a better choice for a Kitzbühel stay than this superluxurious but relaxed former farmstead, with unrivaled year-round proximity to outdoor activities. **Pros:** fabulous location; breathtaking views; ski-in ski-out in winter. **Cons:** pretty pricey for the area; away from the town center; service in bar can be curt. $ *Rooms from: €255* ✉ *Hermann Reisch Weg 15* ☎ *05356/652520* 🌐 *www.rasmushof.at* 🍽 *Free breakfast*

When to Go

The main ski season lasts from mid-December to mid-March, but there's sometimes skiing into early May. The resort is home to the Hahnenkamm World Cup Downhill, one of the most daunting events on the ski-racing calendar in January.

Kitzbühel Tourismus.
🌐 *www.kitzbuehel.com*

When in Austria

★ Albertina Museum
One of the largest of the Habsburg residences, the Albertina rests on one of the last remaining fortresses of Vienna's Old City. Its must-see collection of nearly 65,000 drawings and almost a million prints is one of the most prized graphic collections in the world. All the Old Masters are showcased here: Leonardo da Vinci, Michelangelo, Raphael, Rembrandt. The Batliner Collection includes excellent examples of French and German Impressionism and Russian avant-garde. The mansion's early-19th-century salons—all gilt boiserie and mirrors—provide a jewel-box setting. ✉ *Augustinerstrasse 1, 1st District* ☎ *01/534–830* 🌐 *www.albertina.at* 🎫 *€16.90; €23 Albertina and Albertina Modern* Ⓜ *U3/Herrengasse.*

★ Dachstein Ice Caves
CAVE | This is one of the most impressive sights of the eastern Alps—vast ice caverns, many of which are hundreds of years old and aglitter with ice stalactites and stalagmites, illuminated by an eerie light. The most famous sights are the Rieseneishöhle (Giant Ice Cave) and the Mammuthöhle (Mammoth Cave), but there are other caves and assorted frozen waterfalls in the area. **■ TIP→ Be sure to wear warm, weatherproof clothing and good shoes. Start before 2 pm to see both caves.** ✉ *34 Winkl, Hallstatt* ✣ *From Hallstatt, take the scenic road around the bottom of the lake to Obertraun; then follow the signs to the cable car (Dachsteinseilbahn). From the cable-car landing, a 15-minute hike up takes you to the entrance (follow signs "Dachsteineishöhle")* ☎ *05/0140* 🌐 *www.dachstein-salzkammergut.com/en/* 🎫 *Giant Ice and Mammoth Cave €37.50 each; combined ticket €44.00; cable car €33 round-trip; Ice Sounds concert €75* ⏲ *Closed Nov.–Apr.*

★ Kunsthistorisches Museum (*Museum of Fine Art*)
The collection of Old Master paintings here reveals the royal taste and style of many members of the mighty House of Hapsburg, which ruled a vast empire in the 16th and 17th centuries. The museum is most famous for the largest collection of paintings under one roof by, among others, the Dutch master Pieter Brueghel the Elder—many art historians say that seeing his sublime *Hunters in the Snow* is worth a trip to Vienna. The Italian wing features Titian, Giorgione, Raphael, and Caravaggio. One level down is the remarkable Kunstkammer, displaying priceless objects created for the Hapsburg emperors. ✉ *Maria-Theresien-Platz, 1st District* ☎ *01/525–240* 🌐 *www.khm.at* 🎫 *€16* ⏲ *Closed Mon. in Sept.–May* Ⓜ *U2/MuseumsQuartier; U2 or U3/Volkstheater.*

★ Mozarthaus
This is Mozart's only still-existing abode in Vienna, where he lived for 2½ years and write dozens of piano concertos, as well as *The Marriage of Figaro* and the six quartets dedicated to Joseph Haydn. You'll also have access to an excellent audio guide. For two weeks in April 1787, Mozart taught a pupil here who would become famous in his own right, the 16-year-old Beethoven. **■ TIP→ You can purchase a combined ticket for Mozarthaus Vienna and Haus der Musik for €18.** ✉ *Domgasse 5, 1st District* ☎ *01/512–1791* 🌐 *www.mozarthausvienna.at* 🎫 *€11* Ⓜ *U1 or U3/Stephansplatz.*

★ Stephansdom (*St. Stephen's Cathedral*)
Vienna's soaring centerpiece, this beloved 12th-century cathedral enshrines the heart of the city. Originally the structure was to have had matching 445-foot-high spires, but funds ran out, and the lack of symmetry makes the cathedral instantly identifiable from its profile. It's a stylistic jumble ranging from 13th-century Romanesque to 15th-century Gothic. One particularly masterly work: the stone

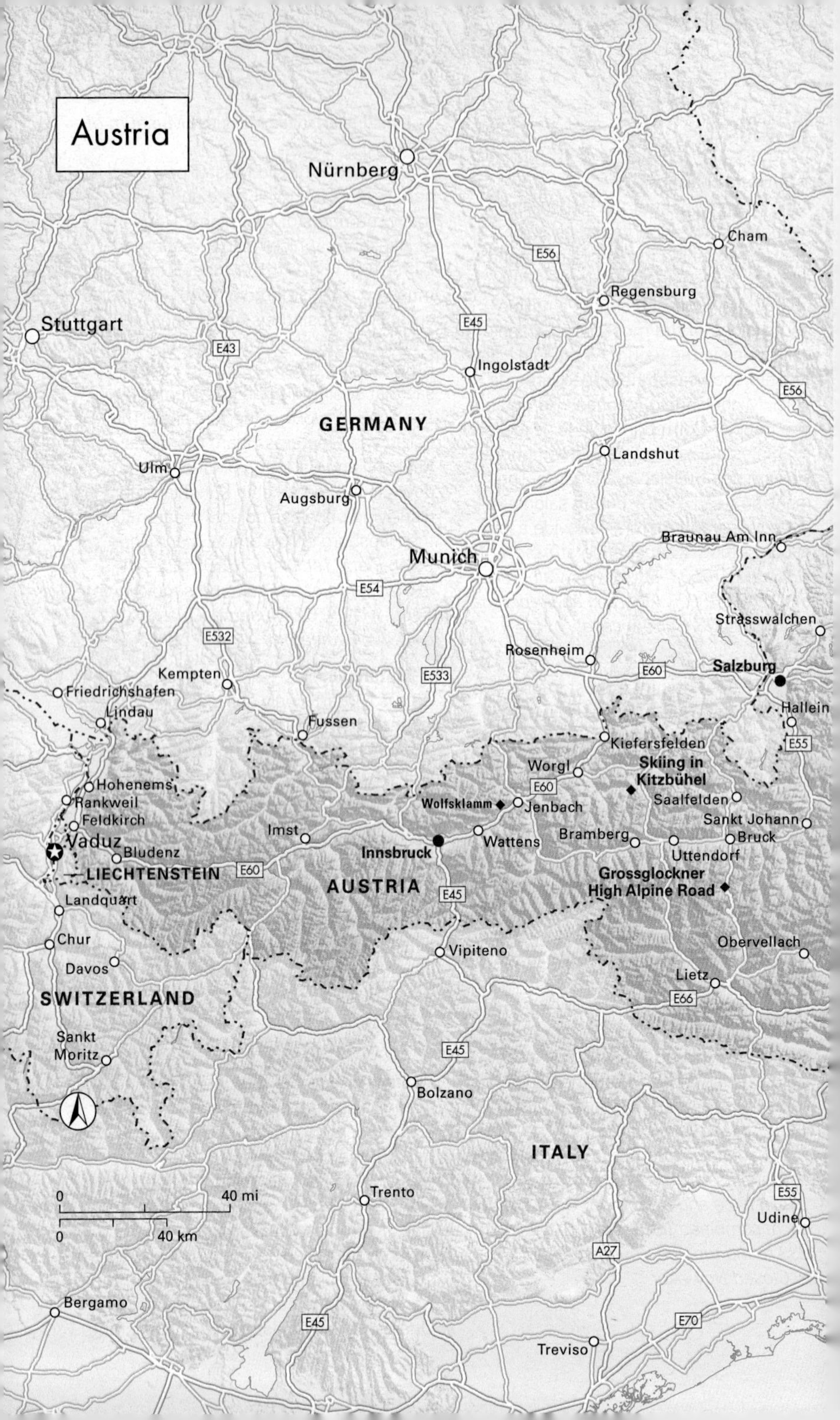
Austria
Nürnberg
Cham
E56
Regensburg
Stuttgart
E45
E43
Ingolstadt
E56
GERMANY
Landshut
Ulm
Augsburg
Braunau Am Inn
Munich
E54
Strasswalchen
E532
Rosenheim
Salzburg
E60
E533
Kempten
Friedrichshafen
Lindau
Hallein
Fussen
Kiefersfelden
E55
Skiing in Kitzbühel
Worgl
Hohenems
E60
Rankweil
Wolfsklamm
Jenbach
Saalfelden
Feldkirch
Sankt Johann
Imst
Bramberg
Bruck
Vaduz
Wattens
Innsbruck
Bludenz
Uttendorf
LIECHTENSTEIN
E60
AUSTRIA
Grossglockner High Alpine Road
E45
Landquart
Chur
Vipiteno
Obervellach
Davos
Lietz
SWITZERLAND
E66
Sankt Moritz
E45
Bolzano
ITALY
0
40 mi
0
40 km
Trento
E55
Udine
A27
Bergamo
E45
E70
Treviso

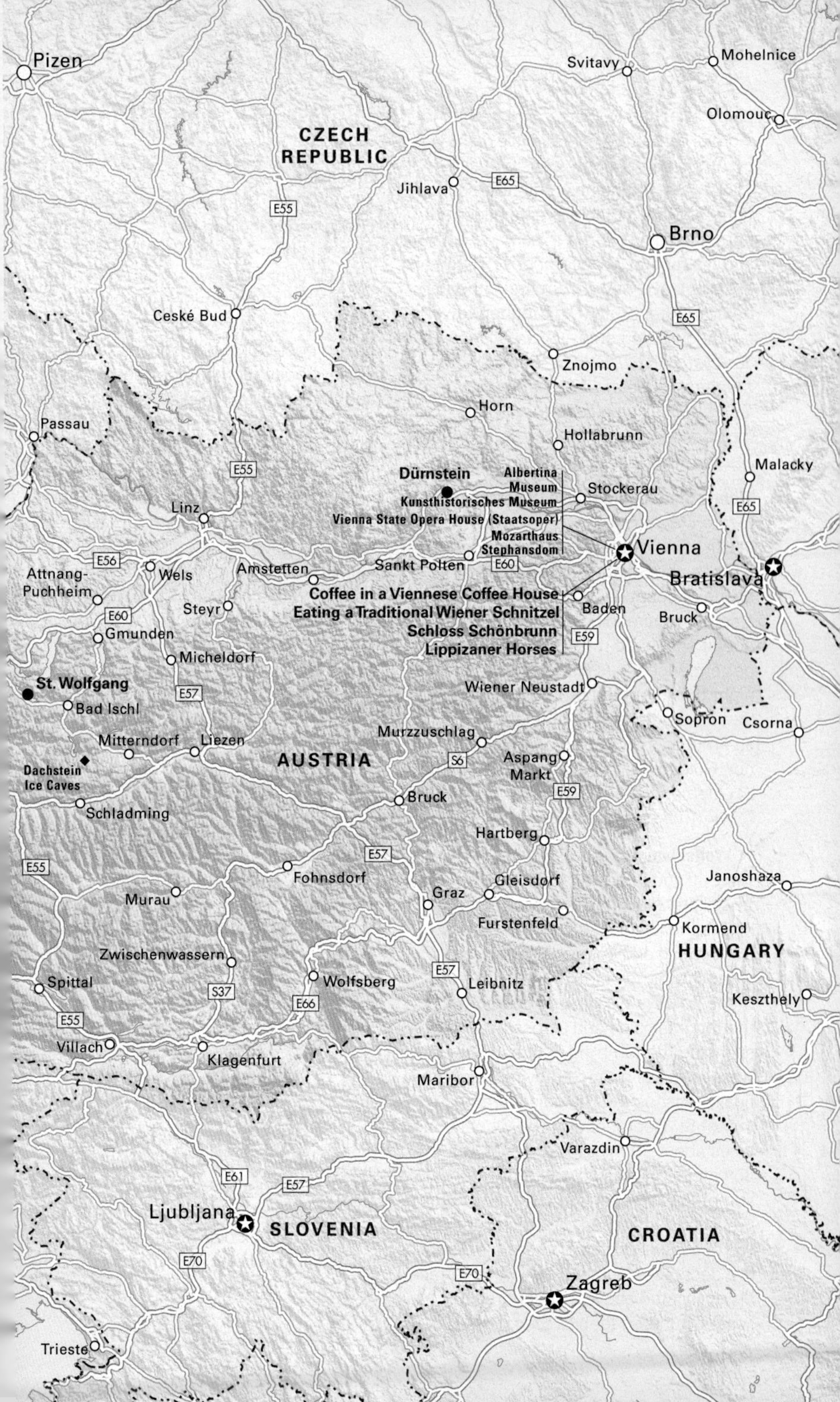
Pizen
Svitavy
Mohelnice
Olomouc
CZECH REPUBLIC
Jihlava
E65
E55
Brno
Ceské Bud
E65
Znojmo
Horn
Passau
Hollabrunn
Malacky
E55
Dürnstein
Albertina Museum
Kunsthistorisches Museum
Vienna State Opera House (Staatsoper)
Mozarthaus
Stephansdom
Stockerau
Linz
E65
Vienna
Bratislava
E56
Wels
Amstetten
Sankt Polten
E60
Attnang-Puchheim
Coffee in a Viennese Coffee House
Eating a Traditional Wiener Schnitzel
Schloss Schönbrunn
Lippizaner Horses
Baden
Steyr
E60
Bruck
Gmunden
E59
Micheldorf
St. Wolfgang
E57
Wiener Neustadt
Bad Ischl
Sopron
Csorna
Murzzuschlag
Mitterndorf
Liezen
AUSTRIA
S6
Aspang Markt
Dachstein Ice Caves
E59
Schladming
Bruck
Hartberg
E57
E55
Fohnsdorf
Janoshaza
Gleisdorf
Murau
Graz
Furstenfeld
Kormend
HUNGARY
Zwischenwassern
E57
Spittal
Wolfsberg
Leibnitz
S37
E66
Keszthely
E55
Villach
Klagenfurt
Maribor
Varazdin
E61
E57
Ljubljana
SLOVENIA
CROATIA
E70
E70
Zagreb
Trieste

pulpit attached to the second freestanding pier left of the central nave, carved by Anton Pilgram between 1510 and 1550; most intriguing are its five sculpted figures. Many notable events occurred here, including Mozart's marriage in 1782 and his funeral in December 1791. Enjoy the bird's-eye views from the cathedral's beloved Alter Steffl (Old Stephen Tower), reached via 343 steps. ✉ *Stephansplatz, 1st District* ☎ *01/515–52–3054* 🌐 *www.stephanskirche.at* 🎫 *Cathedral only free. // €6 all-inclusive guided tour tickets include the catacombs, North Tower, and South Tower.* Ⓜ *U1 or U3/Stephansplatz.*

Vienna State Opera House (Staatsoper)
(*State Opera House*)
OPERA | One of the world's great opera houses, the Staatsoper has been the scene of countless musical triumphs and a center of unending controversy over how it should be run and by whom. A performance takes place virtually every night from September to June, drawing on the vast repertoire of the house, with an emphasis on Mozart, Verdi, and Wagner. Guided tours are given year-round. ✉ *Opernring 2, 1st District* ☎ *01/514–440* 🌐 *www.wiener-staatsoper.at.*

★ Wolfsklamm
TRAIL | If you're driving from Hall in Tirol to Zell am Ziller, this impressive gorge hike is the perfect stop along the way. Exhilarating and spectacular (but very safe), the climb starts in the village of Stans, follows walkways hewn from the mountainside and across bridges spanning the tumbling river and beside waterfalls—all protected by railings—and finally reaches the Benedictine monastery of St. Georgenberg. The whole thing takes about 90 minutes and features 354 steps. At the top, the monastery's sumptuously decorated Baroque church, precariously perched on a rocky peak, is worth a few minutes of your time. There is a decent restaurant, too, with a terrace dizzily located above a sheer drop of several hundred feet. ✉ *Stans.*

Where to Eat and Drink

Drechsler
$ | **AUSTRIAN** | This lively cafe-restaurant, conveniently located next to the Naschmarkt, is best known for its breakfast (served until 4 pm every day) and for its classic coffee house feel with contemporary decor (one wall is decorated with ripped posters.) Lunch options like baked sweet potato, homemade sage gnocchi, and Styrian baked chicken (a classic dish from Styria, a region in Austria known for its wine and food) hold their own to brunch favorites like avocado toast with poached eggs and salmon and blueberry pancakes. It's a popular stop for a late-afternoon cocktail or late-night coffee. **Known for:** excellent breakfasts; open late; popular with a cool crowd. 💲 *Average main: €12* ✉ *Linke Wienzeile 22, 6th District/Mariahilf* ☎ *01/581-2044* 🌐 *www.drechsler-wien.at.*

Figlmüller
$$ | **AUSTRIAN** | This Wiener schnitzel institution might be touristy, but it's known for breaded veal and pork cutlets so large they overflow the plate and still attracts locals, too. The cutlet is hammered—you can hear the mallets pounding from a block away—so that the schnitzel winds up wafer-thin. **Known for:** huge schnitzel; delicious potato salad; second location at Bäckerstrasse 6. 💲 *Average main: €19* ✉ *Wollzeile 5, 1st District* ☎ *01/512–6177* 🌐 *www.figlmueller.at* Ⓜ *U1 or U3/Stephansplatz.*

★ Herberstein
$$$$ | **EUROPEAN** | Tucked away inside the historic Kremsmünsterhaus, this elegant restaurant rocks a mod-retro look with cozy tables, muted lighting, and attractive stonework. The cuisine is Austrian with a touch of Asia, as evidenced by the selection of wok dishes and an excellent sushi bar. **Known for:** delicious corn cream soup; courtyard seating; sushi making classes available. 💲 *Average main: €25* ✉ *Altstadt 10, Linz* ☎ *0732/786161*

🌐 *www.herberstein-linz.at* ⏲ *Closed Sun. No lunch.*

★ **Ikarus**

$$$$ | MODERN EUROPEAN | This extraordinary Michelin-starred restaurant, set with the ultramodern Hangar-7 and overlooking its gleaming vehicle collection, features a different renowned guest chef every month from all over the world who serve a mind-boggling array of cuisines—the only guarantees are that the ingredients will be fresh and set, high-quality menus (usually at least six courses). Visiting chefs are announced several months in advance, so you can plan your trip to Salzburg accordingly; though getting a table can prove tricky so book as early as you can. **Known for:** unique setting and concept; extensive wine list and expert pairing; incredibly expensive. $ *Average main: €250* ✉ *Hangar-7, Wilhelm-Spazier-Strasse 7A, Salzburg* ☎ *0662/21970* 🌐 *www.hangar-7.com* ⏲ *No lunch Mon.–Thu.*

★ **Wirtshaus Schoneck**

$$$$ | AUSTRIAN | With fine views of the city, an atmospheric bar, and veranda and garden for summer dining, this is one of Innsbruck's most exquisite restaurants. Housed in a former imperial hunting lodge across the River Inn from the city center, it's been earning fine-dining accolades since 1899, thanks to a menu that features Austrian staples with a sophisticated twist. **Known for:** excellent-value business lunches; impressive and historic setting; an ever-changing menu with Austrian classics. $ *Average main: €26* ✉ *Weiherburggasse 6, Innsbruck* ☎ *0512/272728* 🌐 *www.wirtshaus-schoeneck.com* ⏲ *Closed Sun.–Tues.*

Cool Places to Stay

★ **Hotel Sacher Wien**

$$$$ | HOTEL | FAMILY | One of Europe's legends, originally founded by Franz Sacher, chef to Prince Metternich—for whom the famous chocolate cake was invented—this hotel dates from 1876 but has delightfully retained its old-world atmosphere-mit-Schlag while also providing luxurious, modern-day comfort. **Pros:** retains its hisotrical ambience; decadent breakfast; family-run and service-oriented –ratio of staff to guests is more than two to one. **Cons:** you'll need reservations for the bar and dining as it is popular; located on a busy street; popular dining options mean public areas are not always restful. $ *Rooms from: €560* ✉ *Philharmonikerstrasse 4, 1st District* ☎ *01/514–560* 🌐 *www.sacher.com* *149 rooms* 🍽 *No Meals.*

Hotel Wolf

$$ | B&B/INN | The embodiment of Austrian gemütlichkeit, just off Mozartplatz, the small, family-owned, in-the-center-of-everything Hotel Wolf offers spotlessly clean and cozy rooms in a rustic building from the year 1429. **Pros:** plenty of atmosphere; in a historic house; lovely breakfast. **Cons:** parking is a problem; no air-conditioning or fans; staff can sometimes be unhelpful. $ *Rooms from: €150* ✉ *Kaigasse 7, Salzburg* ☎ *0662/843–453–0* 🌐 *www.hotelwolf.at* *16 rooms* 🍽 *Free Breakfast.*

Nala Individuell Hotel

$$ | HOTEL | Quirky, colorful, and unapologetically contemporary, Nala is a breath of fresh air in a city dominated by heritage hotels. **Pros:** quirky and colorful rooms; inviting terrace with mountain views; breakfast buffet includes strudel. **Cons:** check out is at 10:30 am; a short walk from the center; too primary colored for some. $ *Rooms from: €189* ✉ *Müllerstrasse 15, Innsbruck* ☎ *0512/584444* 🌐 *www.nala-hotel.at* *57 rooms* 🍽 *Free Breakfast.*

Berlin

Since the fall of the Iron Curtain, no city in Europe has seen more development and change than Berlin, the German capital. The two Berlins that had been physically separated for almost 30 years have become one, and the reunited city has become a cutting-edge destination for architecture, culture, entertainment, nightlife, and shopping.

After successfully uniting its own East and West, Berlin now plays a pivotal role in the European Union. But even as the capital thinks and moves forward, history is always tugging at its sleeve. Between the wealth of neoclassical and 21st-century buildings there are constant reminders, both subtle and stark, of the events of the 20th century.

Young by European standards, Berlin began prospering in the 1300s, thanks to its location at the intersection of important trade routes. Later, Frederick the Great (1712–86) made Berlin and nearby Potsdam his glorious centers of the enlightened yet autocratic Prussian monarchy. In 1871, Prussia, ruled by the "Iron Chancellor" Count Otto von Bismarck, unified the many independent German states into the German Empire and made Berlin the capital. World War I ended the German monarchy. But it also brought an end to Prussian autocracy, resulting in Berlin's golden years during the 1920s. The city became a center for the cultural avant-garde. The golden era came to an end with the Depression and the rise of Hitler, who also made Berlin his capital.

By World War II's end, 70% of the city lay in ruins. Berlin was partitioned and finally divided by the Berlin Wall, with Soviet-controlled East Berlin as the capital of its new communist puppet state, the German Democratic Republic (GDR), and West Berlin an outpost of Western democracy completely surrounded by the communist GDR (although the German capital was moved to Bonn). Today, Berlin is once again the heart and soul of Germany, and though you can still feel its history everywhere, one of the world's hippest cities looks toward its future as an international capital with a zeal rarely found elsewhere.

Museum Island

World-Class Museums in the Heart of Berlin

On the site of one of Berlin's two original settlements, this unique complex of five state museums is a UNESCO World Heritage site and a must-visit in Berlin. The museums are the **Alte Nationalgalerie**, the **Altes Museum** (Old Museum), the **Bode-Museum**, the **Pergamonmuseum**, and the **Neues Museum** (New Museum). If you get tired of antiques and paintings, drop by any of the museums' cafés. The David Chipperfield–designed James-Simon-Galerie state-of-the-art visitor center serves as a central space to buy tickets, and also includes a gift shop, café, and temporary exhibition space, as well as direct access to the Pergamonmuseum and Neues Museum.

Don't Miss

The Neues Museum is home to the Egyptian Museum, including the famous bust of Nefertiti (who, after some 70 years, has returned to her first museum location in Berlin). It also features the Papyrus Collection and the Museum of Prehistory and Early History. The Pergamonmuseum's name is derived from its principal display, the Pergamon Altar, a monumental Greek temple discovered in what is now Turkey and dating from 180 BC. it is still very much worth a visit. Equally impressive are the gateway to the Roman town of Miletus, the Ishtar Gate, and the Babylonian processional way. Though the altar is inaccessible until at least 2025, the museum is still very much worthwhile.

Bodestr. 1–3, Mitte *smb.museum* *€29 combined ticket for all Museum Island museums* *U-bahn to Museumsinsel or S-bahn to Hackescher Markt*

Brandenburger Tor

The Symbol of Berlin

Once the pride of Prussian Berlin, the Brandenburger Tor was left in a desolate no-man's-land when the wall was built. Since the wall's dismantling, the sandstone gateway has become the scene of the city's Unification Day and New Year's Eve parties. This is the sole remaining gate of 14 built by Carl Langhans in 1788–91, designed as a triumphal arch for King Frederick Wilhelm II. Troops paraded through the gate after successful campaigns—the last time in 1945, when victorious Red Army troops took Berlin. The upper part of the gate, together with its chariot and Goddess of Victory, was destroyed in the war. In 1957 the original molds were discovered in West Berlin, and a new quadriga was cast in copper and presented as a gift to the people of East Berlin.

Don't Miss

Not far from the Brandenburg Gate, Tiergarten, a bucolic 630-acre park with lakes, meadows, wide paths, and two beer gardens, is the "green heart" of Berlin. In the 17th century, it served as the hunting grounds of the Great Elector (its name translates as "animal garden"). Now it's the Berliners' backyard for sunbathing and summer strolls. Tiergarten is the third-largest urban green space in Germany. Garden architect Peter Joseph Lenné landscaped the park's 6½ acres of lakes and ponds in the mid-1800s. The park's most popular attraction is the Berlin Zoo.

✉ *Pariser Pl., Mitte* 🚆 *U-bahn or S-bahn to Brandenburger Tor*

East Side Gallery

Berlin Wall Turns Artists' Playground

This 1-km (½-mile) stretch of concrete went from guarded border to open-air gallery within three months. East Berliners breached the wall on November 9, 1989, and between February and June of 1990, 118 artists from around the globe created unique works of art on its longest remaining section. One of the best-known works, by Russian artist Dmitri Vrubel, depicts Brezhnev and Honecker (the former East German leader) kissing, with the caption "My God. Help me survive this deadly love." The stretch along the Spree Canal runs between the Warschauer Strasse S- and U-bahn station and Ostbahnhof. The red brick Oberbaumbrücke (an 1896 bridge) at Warschauer Strasse makes that end more scenic.

Don't Miss

The East Side Gallery is located off of the cobblestone streets of Friedrichshain, bustling with bars, cafés, and shops that have an alternative feel. There's plenty to see here, including Karl-Marx-Allee, a long, monumental boulevard lined by grand Stalinist apartment buildings (conceived of as "palaces for the people" that would show the superiority of the Communist system over the capitalist one); the area's funky parks; Urban Spree, a sprawling arts and event space largely focused on urban graffiti, photography, and street art; and lively Simon-Dach-Strasse, home to shops and eateries. It's cool, it's hip, it's historical. If you're into street art, this is a good place to wander.

✉ *Mühlenstr., Friedrichshain* 🚆 *U-bahn or S-bahn to Warschauer Strasse or S-bahn to Ostbahnhof*

Remembering Berlin's History

The Weight of the Past

You can't visit Berlin without being reminded of the 20th-century atrocities committed there. The **Topography of Terror** (Topographie des Terrors) is partially an open-air exhibit and partially a stunning indoor exhibition center, where you can view photos and documents explaining the secret state police and intelligence organizations that planned Nazi crimes against humanity. The **Memorial to the Murdered Jews of Europe** (Denkmal für die Ermordeten Juden Europas) is an expansive memorial dedicated to the 6 million Jews who were killed in the Holocaust, which consists of a grid of more than 2,700 concrete stelae. The **Jewish Museum** (Jüdisches Museum Berlin) uses a mix of historical objects, art exhibitions, and interactive exhibits to tell the history of Germany's Jews from the Middle Ages through today. An attraction in itself is the highly conceptual building, designed by Daniel Libeskind.

Don't Miss

At the Topography of Terror, the outdoor cellar remains of the Nazis' Reich Security Main Office (composed of the SS, SD, and Gestapo) uses photos, newspaper articles, and other documents to examine National Socialist policy in Berlin between 1933 and 1945.

Jewish Museum. ✉ *Lindenstr. 9–14, Kreuzberg* 🌐 *jmberlin.de* 🎫 *Free (but you must book a timed ticket online)* 🚆 *U-bahn to Hallesches Tor*

Memorial to the Murdered Jews of Europe. ✉ *Cora-Berliner-Str. 1, Mitte* 🎫 *www.stiftung-denkmal.de* 🎫 *Free* 🚆 *S-bahn to Unter den Linden*

Topography of Terror. ✉ *Niederkirchnerstr. 8, Kreuzberg* 🌐 *www.topographie.de* 🎫 *Free* 🚆 *U-bahn to Kochstrasse or U-bahn or S-bahn to Potsdamer Platz*

Reichstag

A Symbol of Democracy Restored

The Bundestag, Germany's federal parliament, returned to its traditional seat in the spring of 1999 for the first time since 1933. British architect Sir Norman Foster lightened up the gray monolith with a glass dome: you can circle up a gently rising ramp while taking in the rooftops of Berlin and the parliamentary chamber below. Completed in 1894, the Reichstag housed the imperial German parliament and later served a similar function during the ill-fated Weimar Republic. On the night of February 27, 1933, the Reichstag was burned down in an act of arson, a pivotal event in Third Reich history. It was rebuilt but again badly damaged in 1945.

Don't Miss

A riverwalk with great views of the government buildings begins behind the Reichstag.

You Should Know

All visitors must register their names and birth dates in advance for a visit to the dome, either with or without a 90-minute guided tour, which you can do online; space permitting, you can also book a dome visit at least two hours in advance at the visitors' service on the south side of Schiedemannstrasse, near the Reichstag.

✉ *Pl. der Republik 1, Tiergarten* ☎ *030/2273–2152* 🌐 *bundestag.de* 🎫 *Free with prior registration online* 🚆 *Unter den Linden (S-bahn), Bundestag (U-bahn)*

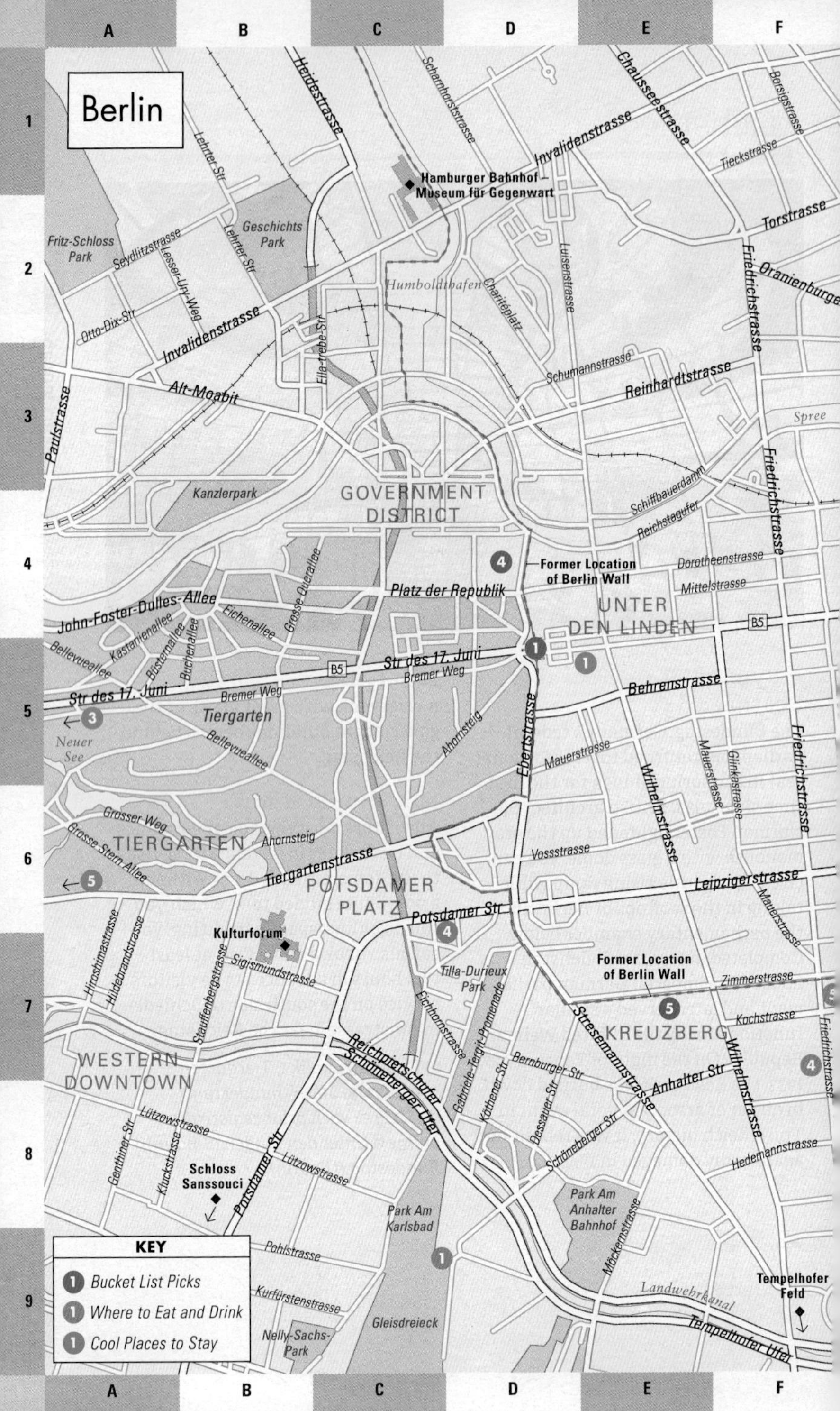
Berlin
A
B
C
D
E
F
1
2
3
4
5
6
7
8
9
Hamburger Bahnhof – Museum für Gegenwart
Heidestrasse
Scharnhorststrasse
Chausseestrasse
Invalidenstrasse
Borsigstrasse
Tieckstrasse
Torstrasse
Lehrter Str
Geschichts Park
Fritz-Schloss Park
Seydlitzstrasse
Lesser-Ury-Weg
Humboldthafen
Charitéplatz
Luisenstrasse
Friedrichstrasse
Oranienburger
Otto-Dix-Str
Ella-Trebe-Str
Schumannstrasse
Reinhardtstrasse
Alt-Moabit
Paulstrasse
Spree
Kanzlerpark
GOVERNMENT DISTRICT
Schiffbauerdamm
Reichstagufer
Former Location of Berlin Wall
Dorotheenstrasse
Mittelstrasse
Platz der Republik
UNTER DEN LINDEN
B5
John-Foster-Dulles-Allee
Eichenallee
Grosse Querallee
Kastanienallee
Bellevueallee
Büsternallee
Buchenallee
Str des 17. Juni
Bremer Weg
Behrenstrasse
Tiergarten
Neuer See
Ahornsteig
Ebertstrasse
Mauerstrasse
Wilhelmstrasse
Glinkastrasse
Grosser Weg
Grosse Stern Allee
TIERGARTEN
Vossstrasse
Tiergartenstrasse
POTSDAMER PLATZ
Leipzigerstrasse
Potsdamer Str
Kulturforum
Hiroshimastrasse
Hildebrandstrasse
Stauffenbergstrasse
Sigismundstrasse
Tilla-Durieux Park
Zimmerstrasse
Kochstrasse
Eichhornstrasse
Gabriele-Tergit-Promenade
Stresemannstrasse
KREUZBERG
Reichpietschufer
Schöneberger Ufer
Bernburger Str
Köthener Str
Anhalter Str
WESTERN DOWNTOWN
Lützowstrasse
Dessauer Str
Schöneberger Str
Hedemannstrasse
Genthiner Str
Kluckstrasse
Schloss Sanssouci
Park Am Karlsbad
Park Am Anhalter Bahnhof
Möckernstrasse
Pohlstrasse
Kurfürstenstrasse
Landwehrkanal
Tempelhofer Feld
Tempelhofer Ufer
Gleisdreieck
Nelly-Sachs-Park
KEY
Bucket List Picks
Where to Eat and Drink
Cool Places to Stay

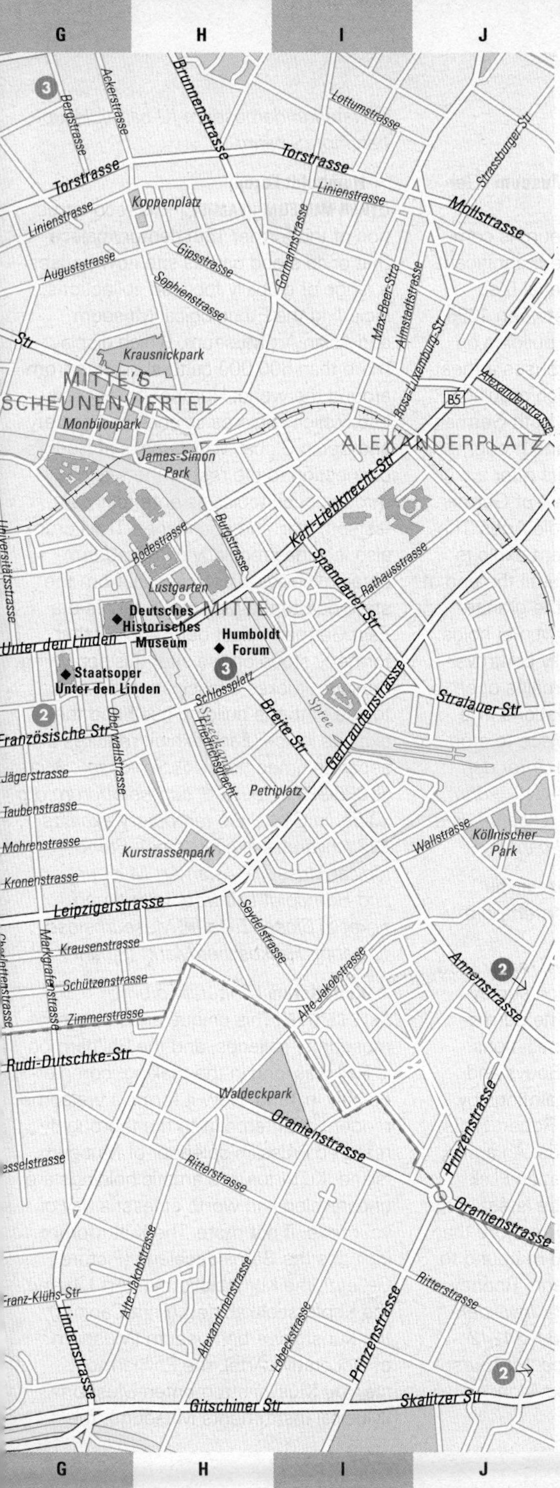

Bucket List Picks ▼

1 Brandenburger Tor D5
2 East Side Gallery..................... J6
3 Museum Island H4
4 Reichstag.................................. D4
5 Remembering Berlin's History...... E7

Where to Eat and Drink ▼

1 BRLO Brwhouse C9
2 Horváth J9
3 Katz Orange G1
4 Nobelhart und Schmutzig.......... F7
5 Restaurant Tim Raue F7

Cool Places to Stay ▼

1 Hotel Adlon Kempinski Berlin E5
2 Hotel de Rome G5
3 KPM Berlin
Hotel & Residences A5
4 The Mandala Hotel C6
5 SO/ Berlin Das Stue A6

When in Berlin

★ **Deutsches Historisches Museum** (*German History Museum*)

HISTORY MUSEUM | The museum is composed of two buildings. The magnificent pink, baroque Prussian arsenal (Zeughaus) was constructed between 1695 and 1730 and is the oldest building on Unter den Linden. It also houses a theater, the Zeughaus Kino, which regularly presents a variety of films, both German and international, historic and modern. The new permanent exhibits offer a modern and fascinating view of German history since the early Middle Ages. The Zeughaus and the permanent exhibits are closed for renovations until the end of 2025. Behind the arsenal, the granite-and-glass Pei building by I. M. Pei holds often stunning and politically controversial changing exhibits; it remains open during the Zeughaus renovations. The museum's café is a great place to stop and restore your energy. ✉ *Unter den Linden 2, Mitte* ☎ *030/203–040* 🌐 *dhm.de* 🎫 *€8* Ⓜ *Museumsinsel (U-bahn), Friedrichstrasse (S-bahn and U-bahn).*

★ **Hamburger Bahnhof—Museum für Gegenwart** (*Museum of Contemporary Art*)

ART MUSEUM | This light-filled, remodeled train station is home to a rich survey of post-1960 Western art. The permanent collection includes installations by German artists Joseph Beuys and Anselm Kiefer, as well as paintings by Andy Warhol, Cy Twombly, Robert Rauschenberg, and Robert Morris. An annex presents the Friedrich Christian Flick Collection, a collection of the latest in the world's contemporary art. The more than 1,500 works rotate, but you're bound to see some by Bruce Naumann, Rodney Graham, and Pipilotti Rist. ✉ *Invalidenstr. 50–51, Mitte* ☎ *030/2664–24242* 🌐 *smb.museum* 🎫 *€14 (free 1st Thurs. of month 4–8 pm)* ⏲ *Closed Mon.* Ⓜ *Naturkundemuseum (U-bahn), Hauptbahnhof (S-bahn).*

★ **Humboldt Forum**

OTHER MUSEUM | FAMILY | This reconstruction of the former 15th-century palace that once stood on this site now houses a range of globally focused collections, including the Ethnological Museum and Asian Art Museum, which display more than 500,000 cultural objects from around the world; Humboldt University Lab, which explores science and society; and Berlin Global, which looks at Berlin's connection to the rest of the world through such topics as entertainment, fashion, war, and boundaries. The Forum also includes regularly changing temporary displays. Controversial from the start, due to the razing of the '70s-era East German Palast der Republik that formerly stood on the site, this sprawling museum makes a fascinating day out to see both the building itself and the exhibits inside. Each exhibit requires a separate timed ticket. ✉ *Schlosspl., Mitte* ☎ *030/9921–18989* 🌐 *humboldtforum.org* 🎫 *Berlin Global €7; temporary exhibits €12 (children's exhibits free); Ethnological Museum, Asian Art Museum, and Humboldt Lab free, with timed ticket* ⏲ *Closed Tues.* Ⓜ *Museumsinsel (U-bahn), Hackescher Markt (S-bahn).*

★ **Kulturforum** (*Cultural Forum*)

ARTS CENTER | This unique ensemble of museums, galleries, and the Philharmonic Hall was long in the making, completed only in 1998. Now it forms a welcome modern counterpoint to the thoroughly restored Prussian splendor of Museum Island. Kulturforum's artistic holdings are unparalleled and worth at least a day of your time, if not more. The Kulturforum includes the Gemäldegalerie (Picture Gallery), the Kunstbibliothek (Art Library), the Kupferstichkabinett (Print Cabinet), the Kunstgewerbemuseum (Museum of Decorative Arts), the Philharmonie, the Musikinstrumenten-Museum (Musical Instruments Museum), the

Staatsbibliothek (National Library), and the Neue Nationalgalerie (New National Gallery). ✉ *Potsdamer Platz* 🌐 *smb.museum/en/museums-institutions/kulturforum/home.html* 🎫 *Prices vary for each museum* ⏲ *Closed Mon.* Ⓜ *Potsdamer Platz (U-bahn and S-bahn).*

★ **Schloss Sanssouci**

CASTLE/PALACE | FAMILY | Prussia's most famous king, Friedrich II—Frederick the Great—spent more time at his summer residence than in the capital. Executed according to Frederick's impeccable French-influenced taste, the palace, which lies on the northeastern edge of Sanssouci Park, was built between 1745 and 1747. It is extravagantly rococo, with scarcely a patch of wall left unadorned. Visits to the palace are only allowed at fixed times scheduled when tickets are purchased and sell out early. The extravagant terraced gardens are filled with climbing grapevines, trellises, and fountains to reach the Italianate Friedenskirche, which houses a 13th-century Byzantine mosaic taken from an island near Venice. ✉ *Park Sanssouci, Potsdam* ☎ *0331/969–4200* 🌐 *spsg.de* 🎫 *Schloss Sanssouci €14; Friedenskirche free* ⏲ *Schloss Sanssouci closed Mon. Friedenskirche closed weekdays Nov.–mid-Mar.*

★ **Staatsoper Unter den Linden** (*State Opera*)

NOTABLE BUILDING | Frederick the Great was a music lover and he made the Staatsoper Unter den Linden, on the east side of Bebelplatz, his first priority. The lavish opera house was completed in 1743 by the same architect who built Sanssouci in Potsdam, Georg Wenzeslaus von Knobelsdorff. The house reopened in late 2017 after a major seven-year renovation. There are guided 90-minute tours of the opera house's interior on weekends (book online), but they are offered in German only. ✉ *Unter den Linden 7, Mitte* ☎ *030/2035–4555* 🌐 *staatsoper-berlin.de* 🎫 *Tours €15* Ⓜ *Museumsinsel (U-bahn), Unter den Linden (U-bahn).*

★ **Tempelhofer Feld** (*Tempelhofer Park*)

CITY PARK | Of all Berlin's many transformations, this one—from airport to park—might be the quickest. The iconic airport (it was the site of the 1948–49 Berlin airlift) had its last flight in 2008. Only two years later, it opened as a park, complete with untouched runways. It's now one of the city's most beloved and impressive outdoor spots, where bikers, skaters, kite flyers, urban gardeners, picnickers, and grillers all gather. Although the Nazi-era airport buildings are not open for wandering, you can explore them on a two-hour tour (book online). ✉ *Bordered by Columbiadamm and Tempelhoferdamm, Neukölln* ☎ *030/7009–06710* 🌐 *thf-berlin.de* 🎫 *Park free; airport building guided tour €16.50* ⏲ *No tours Tues. and Wed.* Ⓜ *Tempelhof (S-bahn and U-bahn).*

Where to Eat and Drink

★ **BRLO Brwhouse**

$$ | ECLECTIC | FAMILY | A cross between a craft brewery, a hip outdoor beer garden (spring through fall only), and a casual indoor restaurant inside reused shipping containers, BRLO is a quintessential Berlin spot to spend an afternoon drinking and eating. If the weather's nice, grab a striped lounge chair outside and choose from a range of modern bar snacks at the beer garden, open every day except in winter; otherwise, head indoors for a choice of vegetable-focused mains along with meats cooked in their own smoker. **Known for:** cool, fun outdoor and indoor setting; tasty barbecue and vegetables; beers brewed on-site. $ *Average main: €19* ✉ *Schöneberger Str. 16, Kreuzberg* ☎ *030/5557–7606* 🌐 *en.brlo.de* ⏲ *Restaurant closed Sun. and Mon. No lunch Tues.–Fri. Beer garden closed Mon.* Ⓜ *Gleisdreieck (U-bahn).*

★ **Horváth**

$$$$ | **AUSTRIAN** | In a cozy wood-paneled room with a colorful mural of Berlin scenes along the wall and a sleek open kitchen, Austrian chef Sebastian Frank puts a creative spin on dishes from his native country. Vegetables (along with touches of meat and fish) become the stars of the show with innovative cooking techniques and a judicious use of herbs, many grown on his roof terrace, in a choice of five- or eight-course menus; each dish pairs perfectly with unique wines primarily from Eastern Europe. **Known for:** mushroom liver "foie gras" with apple balsam reduction; celeriac baked in salt dough and matured for 12 months; wonderful wine selection from the former Austro-Hungarian empire. *Average main: €170 Paul-Lincke-Ufer 44A, Kreuzberg 030/6128–9992 restaurant-horvath.de Closed Mon. No lunch Kottbusser Tor (U-bahn).*

★ **Katz Orange**

$$ | **CONTEMPORARY** | This lovely restaurant, hidden in a courtyard off a quiet residential street, is both elegant enough for a special occasion and homey enough to be a favorite local haunt. Local ingredients are used whenever possible on the inventive menu, and the restaurant is best known for its slow-cooked meats for two: choose pork or lamb, along with fresh vegetable-focused side dishes. **Known for:** beautiful setting with courtyard seating; 12-hour slow-roasted Duroc pork; interesting craft cocktails. *Average main: €20 Bergstr. 22, Mitte 030/9832–08430 katzorange.com No lunch Nordbahnhof (S-bahn).*

★ **Nobelhart und Schmutzig**

$$$$ | **GERMAN** | The locavore obsession is taken seriously at this trendy spot that uses only the most local ingredients in the simple but sublime preparations that come from the open kitchen and are served at a long, shared counter. One 10-course menu is served each evening (dietary restrictions can usually be accommodated) and everything—from the bread and butter through several vegetable, meat, and fish courses—is gorgeously presented and delicious. **Known for:** one nightly 10-course tasting menu (slightly cheaper on Tues. and Wed.); all-natural wines, best experienced when paired with each dish; friendly servers who share the stories behind every plate. *Average main: €130 Friedrichstr. 218, Mitte 030/2594–0610 nobelhartundschmutzig.com Closed Sun. and Mon. Kochstrasse (U-bahn).*

★ **Restaurant Tim Raue**

$$$$ | **ASIAN FUSION** | The conservative decor belies the artistry on offer at this Michelin-starred restaurant from Germany's most famous celebrity chef. Upscale Asian-influenced cuisine, combining Japanese, Thai, and Chinese flavors and techniques, can be sampled in either classic or seasonal seven-course tasting menus for dinner or four- to eight-course tasting menus for lunch; pair your food with splendid wines from one of the most comprehensive lists in Berlin. **Known for:** Peking duck "TR" (duck three ways); langoustine with wasabi Cantonese-style; more than 800 wine choices. *Average main: €240 Rudi-Dutschke-Str. 26, Kreuzberg 030/2593–7930 tim-raue.com Closed Sun. and Mon. No lunch Tues.–Thurs. Kochstrasse (U-bahn).*

Cool Places to Stay

★ **Hotel Adlon Kempinski Berlin**

$$$$ | **HOTEL** | The Adlon's prime setting adjacent to the Brandenburg Gate, wonderful spa, and highly regarded restaurants (including Michelin-starred Lorenz Adlon) make this one of the top addresses to stay in Berlin. **Pros:** top-notch luxury hotel; surprisingly large rooms; excellent in-house restaurants. **Cons:** sometimes-stiff service with an attitude; rooms off Linden are noisy with the windows open; interiors a bit dated.

$ *Rooms from: €348* ✉ *Unter den Linden 77, Mitte* ☎ *030/22610* 🌐 *kempinski.com* ⇄ *382 rooms* 🍴 *No Meals* Ⓜ *Brandenburger Tor (U-bahn and S-bahn).*

★ **Hotel de Rome**

$$$$ | HOTEL | In a 19th-century former bank, the luxurious Hotel de Rome offers well-designed rooms with fantastic views of Berlin landmarks around Unter den Linden, a unique spa and pool area in the old bank vault, and extremely helpful service. **Pros:** great location near top tourist attractions; large rooms and bathrooms; roof terrace with amazing views. **Cons:** some rooms need minor fixes; expensive compared to other Berlin hotels; service at breakfast can be slow when it's busy. $ *Rooms from: €320* ✉ *Behrenstr. 37, Mitte* ☎ *030/460–6090* 🌐 *roccofortehotels.com* ⇄ *146 rooms* 🍴 *No Meals* Ⓜ *Französische Strasse (U-bahn), Unter den Linden (U-bahn).*

★ **KPM Berlin Hotel & Residences**

$$ | HOTEL | The renowned porcelain manufacturer KPM uses its own products in this stylish hotel close to Tiergarten and the Berlin Zoo. Sleek black, white, and grey rooms with wood floors have an urban vibe and a comfy feel, with lounging chairs and large-size desks; some include floor-to-ceiling windows and balconies. **Pros:** spacious guest rooms; comfortable beds; lovely views from top-floor terrace. **Cons:** technology in rooms (light switches, TV) overly confusing to some; breakfast could be better; sauna on the small side. $ *Rooms from: €166* ✉ *Englische Str. 6, Tiergarten* ☎ *030/374–0990* 🌐 *kpmhotel.de* ⇄ *117 rooms* 🍴 *No Meals* Ⓜ *Tiergarten (S-bahn).*

★ **SO/ Berlin Das Stue**

$$$$ | HOTEL | FAMILY | History meets contemporary style on the edge of the leafy Tiergarten, in a building that once housed the Royal Danish Embassy and still retains governmental grandeur—from the classical facade to the dramatic entry staircase—now mixed with warming touches from designer Patricia Uriquola and modern tapas at The Casual restaurant. **Pros:** quiet location on Tiergarten park and next to the zoo (with direct access); kind and helpful staff; lovely spa, including pool and sauna. **Cons:** can be on the pricey side; a bit far from main Berlin sights and restaurants; not all rooms have views. $ *Rooms from: €259* ✉ *Drakestr. 1, Tiergarten* ☎ *030/311–7220* 🌐 *so-berlin-das-stue.com* ⇄ *78 rooms* 🍴 *No Meals* Ⓜ *Tiergarten (S-bahn).*

★ **The Mandala Hotel**

$$$$ | HOTEL | This privately owned luxury hotel exudes a cool, serene, Zen-like ambience, with understated floral arrangements and calming, neutral tones throughout, along with some of the largest rooms in the city, a spa and gym with amazing views, and the elegant Michelin-starred restaurant Facil. **Pros:** free laundry facilities on several floors; relaxing spa area with multiple saunas; fabulous modern restaurant in a stunning setting. **Cons:** in a busy, noisy (though central) Potsdamer Platz location; breakfast on the pricey side; tiny lobby. $ *Rooms from: €230* ✉ *Potsdammer Str. 3, Tiergarten* ☎ *030/5909–50000* 🌐 *the-mandala.de* ⇄ *159 rooms* 🍴 *No Meals* Ⓜ *Potsdamer Platz (U-bahn and S-bahn).*

Germany

Germany is a land full of contrast and surprises, with an ever-changing landscape. A journey from the sand dunes of the Baltic Sea coast in the north, to the soaring mountain peaks in the south, will take you past half-timber towns, and across pastoral landscapes with castles, churches, and hillside vineyards. It is filled with a strong sense of cultural heritage, where men still don traditional *Lederhosen* and women *Dirndln*, at least in southern regions like Bavaria.

There is beer to be consumed by the stein under the shade of old chestnut trees, and chilled Riesling wines to be sipped on riverside terraces. No matter what part of Germany you visit, there are thick layers of history: from Roman relics to medieval castles and from Baroque palaces to Communist-era apartment blocks. Almost every city boasts a handsomely restored Altstadt (Old Town) at its center.

But, for all the tradition, Germany is very much a modern country. High-speed autobahns and clean, comfortable trains link its cities. It's also a global leader in avant-garde fashion, culture, and art, which is reflected in its many museums and galleries.

Perhaps above all else, Germans take their leisure seriously. The great outdoors has always been an important escape, with great beaches in the north, Alpine skiing in the south, and world-class hiking almost anywhere. Big-city party neighborhoods like Hamburg's infamously seedy Reeperbahn shake things up.

Each season has its own festivities: Fasching (Carnival) heralds the end of winter, beer gardens open up with the first warm rays of sunshine, fall is celebrated with Munich's Oktoberfest, and Advent brings colorful Christmas markets.

Oktoberfest in Munich

Europe's Biggest Party

Oktoberfests are now found everywhere, but the original in Munich has never been equaled. Conceived as a royal wedding celebration in 1810, today some 6 million participants over 16–18 days congregate for a glorious celebration of beer, Bavarian culture, beer, folk traditions, and still more beer. More than 7 million liters (2 million gallons) are put away, along with 650,000 sausages, 530,000 roast chickens, and 110 oxen. You could be forgiven for reducing everything to a string of clichés—drunken revelers, deafening brass bands, and red-faced men in leather shorts singing uproariously—but Oktoberfest is also a great day out for families, or a fun night for couples.

Don't Miss

The ceremonial arrival of the brewers and beer tent landlords starts at 10:50 am on the first day. Setting off from Josephspitalstrasse a mile east of the Theresienwiese, they arrive at the Oktoberfest grounds on horse-drawn carriages festooned with flowers. This is followed at noon by the tapping of the first barrel, performed by the mayor of Munich with a cry of "O'zapft is!" ("It's tapped!") in the Schottenhamel tent.

When to Go

Oktoberfest takes place the third weekend in September through the first weekend in October.

Getting Here

The Theresienwiese U-bahn (subway) stop is right outside the Oktoberfest grounds. Goetheplatz or Poccistrasse are the next-closest stations. The Hauptbahnhof is just a 10- to 15-minute walk away.

✉ *Theresienwiese, Munich* 🌐 *www.oktoberfest.de* ✍ *You can reserve seats up to 6 months in advance; otherwise, arrive very early for a walk-in spot*

BMW Welt

Bavaria's Prime Car Maker

BMW is one of the big four German automakers (Mercedes-Benz, Volkswagen, and Porsche are the other three), and its headquarters has the most to offer. Opened in 2007, the cutting-edge design of BMW Welt, with its sweeping, futuristic facade, is one structure helping to overcome the conservative image Munich has had in the realm of architecture since 1945. Even if you have just a passing interest in cars and engines, this showroom is a must—it has averaged 2 million visitors a year since its opening. In addition to tours of the building, there are readings, concerts, and exhibitions. Tours are in high demand, so it's best to book ahead via phone or email. You can also visit the BMW Plant to see how a BMW car is made. It can be toured on weekdays (minimum age to participate is six, with an adult, reservations at least two weeks in advance required).

BMW Museum

The circular tower of the auto-maker's museum in the Olympiapark is one of the defining icons of Munich's modern cityscape. It contains not only a dazzling collection of BMWs old and new but also items and exhibitions relating to the company's social history and its technical developments.

Best Restaurants

BMW Welt has four dining options, ranging from a snackbar to a restaurant with two Michelin stars; there's also a restaurant in the BMW Museum.

BMW Museum. ✉ *Am Olympiapark 2, Milbertshofen* 🌐 *bmw-welt.com* 🎫 *€10* 🕓 *Closed Mon.* 🚆 *Olympiazentrum*

BMW Welt. ✉ *Am Olympiapark 1, Milbertshofen* 🌐 *bmw-welt.com Tours from €8* 🕓 *BMW Plant closed weekends* 🚆 *Olympiazentrum*

A Hamburg Boat Tour

Germany's Most Historic Seaport

Hamburg has an unbreakable bond with water. It is Germany's largest port, while the twin lakes of the Binnenalster (Inner Alster) and Aussenalster (Outer Alster) provide fabulous vistas. Every Hamburger dreams of living within sight of the lakes, but only the wealthiest can afford it. Those who can't still have plenty of opportunities to enjoy the waterfront, however, and the Outer Alster is ringed by tree-lined public pathways. There are few better ways to get to know the city than by taking a trip on its waterways. Various tour operators offer a wide variety of options.

Don't Miss

A great alternative to joining a cruise is to board one of the scheduled HADAG harbor ferries, which have been operating around Hamburg's docks since 1888 and offer an inexpensive way to get out on the water.

Best Water Activities

Another lovely way to see Hamburg is to rent paddleboats, canoes, or rowboats on the Outer Alster in summer between 10 am and 9 pm, starting at €20 an hour.

Getting Here and Around

Hamburg Hauptbahnhof has train connections from across Germany; it's approximately 3½ hours from Frankfurt, 5¾ hours from Munich. The boat landing at Jungfernstieg, below the Alsterpavillon, is the starting point for lake and canal cruises.

Alster Touristik. *www.alstertouristik* *Alster Lake cruises from €17*

HADAG Harbor Ferries. *www.hadag.de* *Harbor cruises from €19*

Maritime Circle Line. *www.maritime-circle-line.de* *From €20*

Dresden's Christmas Market

Germany's Oldest Yuletide Festival

Few places do Christmas as well as Germany, and the country's Christmas markets (Weihnachtsmärtke) sparkle with white fairy lights and are rich with the smells of gingerbread and mulled wine. More than 2,000 spring up outside town halls and in village squares across the country each year, their stalls brimming with ornate tree decorations and candy. Kids munch on candy apples and ride old-fashioned carousels while their parents shop for trinkets and toast the season with steaming mugs of Glühwein. The oldest market of all, in Dresden—it dates back to 1434—is also among the most popular, drawing 2 million visitors. With 250 stands occupying large swaths of the city center, the Striezelmarkt is named after the city's famous Stollen, a buttery Christmas fruitcake made with marzipan.

Don't Miss

Dresden was destroyed during World War II, but most of its Altstadt has been restored, including the Frauenkirche (Church of Our Lady), a masterpiece of Baroque architecture. Originally completed in 1743, with a huge dome set on a smaller square base, it was designed to look as if it was a single stone.

When to Go

The Christmas market runs during the four weeks leading up to Christmas Eve, usually beginning in late November.

Getting Here

Dresden is two hours by train from Berlin.

Dresden Tourism. 🌐 *www.dresden.de*

Frauenkirche. ✉ *Georg-Treu-Platz 3, Dresden* 🌐 *www.frauenkirche-dresden.org* 🎫 *Free; cupola and tower €8; audio guides in English €3*

Wine Tasting in the Mosel

Riesling Country

Germany's Mittelmosel (Middle Mosel) is a beautiful valley, where vineyards tumble down steep slate slopes to riverside villages full of half-timbered, Baroque, and Belle Époque architecture. Famed for its mild climate and 2,000-year-old wine-making tradition, it produces some of the world's best Rieslings. Its many wineries and tasting rooms are concentrated along a meandering 75-mile stretch of lush valley, picturesque towns, and rural estates between Trier and Zell, allowing for multiple sips in a short amount of time. While other varietals are produced here, the staple of most estates is Riesling. The wineries are predominantly small, family-owned operations, and there tends to be an emphasis on the production of high-quality, low-quantity wines. Their tasting rooms, when not part of the winery itself, are frequently extensions of family homes, affording visitors intimate contact with the winemakers.

Don't Miss

In Bernkastel-Kues, the Mosel Wine Cultural Center has a small wine museum, and a vaulted cellar, where you can sample more than 100 wines from the region. Just 10 km (6 miles) upstream from Bernkastel is the Paulinshof winery, whose Auslese impressed Thomas Jefferson in 1788.

Getting Here and Around

By car, Bernkastel-Kues is about 45 minutes northeast of Trier and 90 minutes southwest of Koblenz. You can also bike in the summer.

Mosel Wine Cultural Center. ✉ *Cusanusstr. 2, Bernkastel-Kues* 🎫 *Museum €5, Vinothek free, wine tasting €18*

Paulinshof: ✉ *Paulinsstr. 14, Kesten, 10½ km (6½ miles) from Berkastel-Kues* 🌐 *www.paulinshof.de* ⏲ *Closed Sun.*

Neuschwanstein Castle

A Gravity-Defying Masterpiece

Emerald lakes and rugged Alpine peaks surround Neuschwanstein, the world's most famous storybook castle. In 1868, Bavaria's King Ludwig II commissioned a stage designer to create this over-the-top architectural gem atop Swan's Rock, and overlooking the Alpsee lake. The five-story castle was conceived to pay tribute to the operas of Richard Wagner. While the exterior was constructed in Romanesque style, the interior contains murals alluding to sagas and legends, such as "Swan's Corner," a living room dedicated to the Swan Knight Lohengrin.

Don't Miss

Far older than Neuschwanstein, Schloss Hohenschwangau was built in the 12th century, although it was updated in the 19th, and it actually feels like a noble home.

Best View

There are some spectacular walks around Neuschwanstein, but the delicate Marienbrücke (Mary's Bridge) is spun like a medieval maiden's hair across a deep, narrow gorge, offering great views of the castle.

Getting Here

Hohenschwangau is a 2-hour drive from Munich (about 2½ hours by train, via Fussen). Schloss Neuschwanstein itself is a strenuous climb, but you can also make the trip by horse-drawn carriage or bus.

Schloss Hohenschwangau.
www.hohenschwangau.de €24

Schloss Neuschwanstein.
www.neuschwanstein.de €18

Ticket Center Hohenschwangau.
www.ticket-center-hohenschwangau.de *Reservations essential*

A Rhine River Cruise

Germany's Watery Superhighway

The romance of the Rhine is most apparent in a 40-mile stretch known as the Mittlerhein, designated a UNESCO World Heritage site for its concentration of magnificent castles, medieval towns, and vineyards of the Rhine Gorge. It begins in Bingen and passes St. Goarshausen before ending in Koblenz, at the confluence of the Rhine and Mosel rivers. While the fastest way to get around is by car or train, the river has been navigated by ship for thousands of years, and this option remains the most scenic, not to mention the safest for visitors looking to drink wine while soaking up a little history.

Don't Miss

One of the Rhineland's most famous and beloved attractions is the steep (430-foot-high) slate cliff named after the beautiful blonde nymph Loreley, from the story written in 1801 by author Clemens Brentano. Brentano drew inspiration from the sirens of Greek mythology, and his poem describes her sitting on the ledge, singing songs so lovely that sailors were lured to their demise in the treacherous rapids. The rapids really are treacherous; the Rhine is at its narrowest here and the current the swiftest.

When to Go

The main tourist season typically runs from Easter to October.

Getting Here

Koblenz is one hour from Cologne by train or car, or 90 minutes from Frankfurt.

Koblenz Tourist-Information. *www.koblenz-tourism.com*

Köln-Düsseldorfer Deutsche Rhein-schiffahrt. *www.k-d.com*

Rheinschifffahrt Hölzenbein. *www.hoelzenbein.de*

Zugspitze

Germany's Tallest Mountain

The awe-inspiring view from 10,000 feet at the summit of the Zugspitze takes in 400 peaks in four countries. You can't see Germany's highest mountain from nearby Garmisch-Partenkirchen, so it's worth braving the glass-bottom cable car, which ascends 6,381 feet over a distance of 10,451 feet in around 10 minutes. Combined with the panoramic vistas from the three restaurants' sunny terraces at the summit, it makes a visit to the Zugspitze unforgettable. There are even some 20 km (12 miles) of slopes for skiing and snowboarding near the summit on its perfectly groomed natural snow.

Don't Miss

Outdoor activities abound in this region. In spring and summer, cowbells tinkle and wild flowers blanket meadows beside trails that course up and down the mountainsides; these are popular with both mountain bikers and hikers. In winter, snow engulfs the region, turning trails into paths for cross-country skiers and the mountainsides into pistes for snowboarders and downhill skiers to carve their way down.

When to Go

Snow is promised by most resorts from December through March, although there's skiing on the glacier slopes at the top of the Zugspitze at least through May. Spring and autumn are ideal times for leisurely hikes.

Getting Here

Garmisch-Partenkirchen, the regional hub, is 90 minutes south of Munich by train or car. The Zugspitze cable car starts in Grainau, 10 km (6 miles) outside town on the road to Austria.

Zugspitze Cable Car. ✉ *Olympiastr. 31, Garmisch-Partenkirchen* 🌐 *zugspitze.de* 🎫 *€52 round-trip (€63 in summer)*

Oberammergau Passion Play

A Once-in-a-Decade Spectacular

Spectacularly situated in an Alpine valley, Oberammergau is best known for its Passion Play, first presented in 1634 as an offering of thanks after the Black Death stopped just short of the village. In faithful accordance with a solemn vow, it has been performed every 10 years since 1680; it will next be performed in 2030. Its 16 acts, which take 5½ hours (there's a break for dinner), depict the final days of Christ, from the Last Supper through the Crucifixion and Resurrection. It's presented daily on a partly open-air stage against a mountain backdrop from late May to late September. The entire village is swept up in the production, with some 1,500 residents directly involved in its preparation and presentation (only Oberammergau residents can take part). When the play isn't being performed, you can take a guided tour of the theater and the nearby Oberammergau Museum.

Don't Miss

A few miles away, Kloster Ettal is a remarkable monastery founded in 1330 by Emperor Ludwig the Bavarian. It's the largest Benedictine monastery in Germany. It has its own brewery, distillery, and hotel. Its domed basilica can be toured on Monday and Thursday.

Getting Here and Around

Oberammergau is 90 km (56 miles) south of Munich, reachable by regional train from Murnau. It's also connected to Garmisch and Füssen by bus.

Kloster Ettal. ✉ *Kaiser-Ludwig-Pl. 1, Ettal* 🌐 *kloster-ettal.de* 🎫 *Basilica tour €5; brewery tour €12, distillery tour €9* ⏲ *No tours Nov. and Jan.–June*

Oberammergau Passion Play Theater. ✉ *Passionswiese, Theaterstr. 16, Oberammergau* 🌐 *passionstheater.de* 🎫 *€4; €5 including Oberammergau Museum* ⏲ *Closed Mon.*

Cologne Cathedral

Germany's Largest Church

Cologne's Cathedral is a feast of lacy spires, flying buttresses, and ornate stained-glass windows, embodying one of the purest expressions of the Gothic spirit in Europe. Meant to be a tangible expression of God's kingdom on Earth, it was conceived with such immense dimensions that construction, begun in 1248, was not completed until 1880, after the original plan was rediscovered. At 515 feet high, the two west towers were briefly the tallest structures in the world, before they were surpassed by the Washington Monument. Conceived to house relics of the Magi, the three kings who paid homage to the infant Jesus, it was designed on a scale to accommodate vast numbers of pilgrims.

Don't Miss

If you're up to it, climb to the top of the bell tower to get the complete vertical experience.

Best Restaurant

Früh am Dom. Within sight of the Dom, this is a good place to try home-style German dishes while sampling the city's beloved Kölsch beer. Your waiter will replace your empty glass with a full one whether you order it or not—cover your glass with a coaster if you don't want more. It's often crowded, but the mood's fantastic. $ *Average main: €14* ✉ *Am Hof 12–18, Altstadt* ☎ *0221/261–3215* 🌐 *www.frueham-dom.de* 💳 *No credit cards*

Getting Here

Cologne's main station (Hauptbahnhof) is connected with all major cities in Germany. The cathedral is just a few steps away and unmissable as you exit the station.

✉ *Domplatz, Altstadt* ☎ *0221/9258–4730* 🌐 *www.koelner-dom.de, www.domforum.de (guided tours)* 🎫 *Treasury €5; guided tours from €10*

Rothenburg-ob-der-Tauber

Perfectly Preserved Medieval Charm

Rothenburg-ob-der-Tauber is the kind of medieval town that even Walt Disney might have thought too picturesque to be true, with half-timber architecture galore and a wealth of fountains and flowers against a backdrop of towers and turrets. As late as the 17th century, it was a thriving market town. Then it was laid low economically by the havoc of the Thirty Years' War, and with its economic base devastated, the town remained a backwater until it was rediscovered by modern tourism.

Don't Miss

Rothenburg's city walls are dotted with 42 red-roofed watchtowers. Only about half can still be accessed on foot, but it provides an excellent way of circumnavigating the town from above. Let your imagination take you back 600 years as you explore covered sentries' walkways punctuated by cannons and turrets. There are superb views of the tangle of pointed and tiled red roofs.

Best Restaurant

In a building dating back to AD 900—claimed to be the oldest in town—Restaurant-Zur Höll ("To Hell") has an extensive selection of regional dishes, as well as Franconian wine. 🌐 www.hoell.rothenburg.de

Getting Here

If you arrive by car, there are large metered parking lots just outside the town wall. The local train takes about 2½ hours from Augsburg; 3 hours from Nuremberg or Stuttgart. Once you arrive, everything in the walled town can easily be reached on foot.

Rothenburg Tourist Information. ✉ *Rathaus, Am Marktpl. 2, Rothenburg ob der Tauber* ☎ *09861/404–800* 🌐 *www.tourismus.ruthenburg.de*

Romantic Heidelberg

Germany in a Nutshell

If any city encapsulates the spirit and history of Germany, it is Heidelberg. Scores of poets and composers—virtually the entire 19th-century German Romantic movement—have sung its praises: Goethe and Mark Twain both fell in love with the city; and composer Robert Schumann was a student at the university. Heidelberg was the political center of the Lower Palatinate, and French King Louis XIV sacked the city twice, in 1689 and 1693. But from its ashes arose a lovely Baroque town built on Gothic foundations, with narrow, twisting streets and alleyways, dominated by a dramatic hilltop castle, and an intact Altstadt (Old Town) full of lively restaurants and pubs. Walk under the twin towers of Heidelberg's Alte Brücke (Old Bridge), and look back for a picture-postcard view of the city that exudes the spirit of romantic Germany.

Don't Miss

Schloss Heidelberg is arguably Germany's most beautiful castle. The oldest parts date from the 15th century, though most was built during the Renaissance in the Baroque styles of the 16th and 17th centuries.

Best Restaurant

Zum Roten Ochsen. Many of the rough-hewn oak tables here have initials carved into them, a legacy of the thousands who have visited this famous old tavern. $ *Average main: €15* ✉ *Hauptstr. 217, Heidelberg* ☎ *06221/20977* 🌐 *www.roterochsen.de* 🕓 *Closed Sun. and Mon., and mid-Dec.–mid-Jan. No lunch Nov.–Mar.*

Getting Here

Heidelberg is 60 minutes from Frankfurt by rail. To reach the castle, take the Königstuhl Bergbahn (funicular).

Schloss Heidelberg. ✉ *Schlosshof, Heidelberg* 🌐 *www.schloss-heidelberg.de* 🎫 *€9*

When in Germany

Bamberg

TOWN | Sitting majestically on seven hills above the Regnitz River, the entire Alstadt area of this beautiful, historic town is a UNESCO World Heritage Site. Few towns in Germany survived the war with so little damage. Although it exploded onto the European political scene as the capital of the Holy Roman Empire under Emperor Heinrich II, its winding cobblestone streets contain one of the best-preserved collections of early-medieval half-timber structures in Europe, dominated by a cathedral consecrated in 1237. ✉ *Bamberg* ✣ *65 km (40 miles) west of Bayreuth, 80 km (50 miles) north of Nuremberg* 🌐 *bamberg.info.*

Görlitz

TOWN | Tucked away in the country's easternmost corner (bordering Poland), Görlitz's quiet, narrow cobblestone alleys and exquisite architecture make it one of Germany's most beautifully preserved cities. It emerged from World War II relatively unscathed, and as a result has more than 4,000 historic houses in various styles. Although the city has impressive museums, theater, and music, it's the casual dignity of these buildings, in their jumble of styles, that makes Görlitz so attractive. Notably absent are the typical socialist eyesores and the glass-and-steel modernism found in many eastern German towns. It's overlooked by far too many tourists. ✉ *Görlitz* ✣ *48 km (30 miles) east of Bautzen, 60 km (38 miles) northeast of Dresden* 🌐 *www. goerlitz. de.*

Hofbräuhaus

RESTAURANT | Duke Wilhelm V founded Munich's Hofbräuhaus (court brewery) in 1589; it's been at its present location since 1607, where the golden beer is consumed from a one-liter mug called a *Mass*. If the cavernous ground-floor hall or beer garden is too noisy, there's a quieter restaurant upstairs. Visitors to the city far outnumber locals, who regard HBH as a tourist trap. The brass band that performs here most days adds modern pop and American folk music to the traditional German numbers. ✉ *Platzl 9, Altstadt* ☎ *089/2901–36100* 🌐 *hofbraeuhaus.de/en* Ⓜ *Marienplatz, Isartor.*

Königssee

BODY OF WATER | One less strenuous way into the Berchtesgaden National Park is via electric boat. Only the skipper of these excursion boats is allowed to shatter the silence on the Königssee (King's Lake)—his trumpet fanfare demonstrates a remarkable echo as notes reverberate between the almost vertical cliffs that plunge into the dark green water. Smaller than the Königssee but equally beautiful, the Obersee can be reached by a 15-minute walk from the second stop (Salet) on the boat tour. The lake's backdrop of jagged mountains and precipitous cliffs is broken by a waterfall, the Rothbachfall, which plunges more than 1,000 feet to the valley floor. Boat service on the Königssee runs year-round, except when the lake freezes. ✉ *Boat service, Seestr. 29, Schönau* ☎ *08652/96360* 🌐 *seenschifffahrt.de* 🎫 *€20 round-trip from Schonau to St. Bartholomä and Salet.*

Pilgrimage Church of Wies (*Wieskirche*)

CHURCH | This church, also known simply as Wieskirche (church in the meadow), is a glorious example of German rococo architecture, in an Alpine meadow just off the Romantic Road. Its yellow-and-white walls and steep red roof are set off by the dark backdrop of the Trauchgauer Mountains. Visit it on a bright day if you can, when light streaming through its high windows displays the full glory of the glittering gold and white interior. Concerts are presented in the church from the end of June through the beginning of August. ✉ *Wies 12, Steingaden* ✣ *To get here from village of Steingaden (22 km [14 miles] north of Füssen on B-17),*

Germany
0
50 mi
0
50 km
North Sea
Baltic Sea
DENMARK
SWEDEN
Helsingborg
Copenhagen
Roskilde
Malmö
Esbjerg
Odense
Svendborg
Flensburg
E45
Kiel
Stralsund
Rostock
Lübeck
E251
Bremerhaven
Emden
A Hamburg Boat Tour
Hamburg
E55
Groningen
Szczecin
E26
NETHERLANDS
Oldenburg
Bremen
Schnoorviertel
E28
E37
E45
Hannover
Berlin
Osnabrück
Braunschwei
Potsdam
A31
E30
E30
E30
Münster
Bielefeld
Magdeburg
E55
E51
E45
Duisburg
Dortmund
E331
Göttingen
Cottbus
Wuppertal
A38
Düsseldorf
Leipzig
Kassel
Cologne
Cologne Cathedral
GERMANY
Dresden's Christmas Market
Görlitz
Dresden
Bonn
E41
E40
Liège
Erfurt
Jena
Gera
E31
E35
Gießen
Chemnitz
E45
Koblenz
Königsee
A Rhine River Cruise
A71
Coburg
Hof
E55
LUXEMBOURG
Frankfurt
Wiesbaden
A73
Prague
Wine Tasting in the Mosel
Würzburg
Bamberg
Luxembourg
E51
Mannheim
E50
Pizen
Heidelberg
Saarbrücke
Nürnberg
CZECH REPUBLIC
Metz
Romantic Heidelberg
Rothenburg-ob-der-Tauber
Karlsruhe
Regensburg
Ceské Bud
Nancy
Stuttgart
E43
E56
FRANCE
E52
Ingolstadt
BMW Welt
E41
Oktoberfest in Munich
E25
Passau
E45
E35
Schwarzwaldbahn
Ulm
Hofbräuhaus
Linz
Schloss Nymphenburg
Munich
Mulhouse
Freiburg
Neuschwanstein Castle
Pilgrimage Church of Wies
Rosenheim
Basel
E52
Salzburg
Oberammergau Passion Play
Zürich
LIECHTENSTEIN
Zugspitze
AUSTRIA
Biel
E60
Bern
Luzern
Vaduz
Innsbruck
Lausanne
SWITZERLAND
ITALY
Klagenfurt

turn east and follow signs to Wieskirche ☎ *8862/932–930* 🌐 *www.wieskirche.de* 🎫 *Free (donations accepted)* 🕓 *Closed to tourists Sun. until 1 pm and during hrs of worship.*

★ **Schloss Nymphenburg**

CASTLE/PALACE | FAMILY | This glorious Baroque and Rococo palace, the largest in Germany, grew in size and scope over more than 200 years. Begun in 1662 by the Italian architect Agostino Barelli, it was completed by his successor, Enrico Zuccalli. It represents a tremendous high point of Italian cultural influence, in what is undoubtedly Germany's most Italian city. Grandiose frescoes are by masters such as François Cuvilliés the Elder and Johann Baptist Zimmermann. The palace park is laid out in formal French style, with low hedges and gravel walks extending into woodland. It's also worth visiting the former royal stables, now the Marstallmuseum, which houses a fleet of carriages, coaches, and sleighs. In its upper rooms are examples of the world-renowned Nymphenburg porcelain. ✉ *Schloss Nymphenburg, Nymphenburg* ☎ *089/179–080* 🌐 *www.schloss-nymphenburg.de* 🎫 *From €5* 🕓 *Amalienburg, Badenburg, Pagodenburg, and Magdalenenklause closed mid-Oct.–Apr.* Ⓜ *Schloss Nymphenburg (Tram or Bus).*

★ **Schnoorviertel**

HISTORIC DISTRICT | Stroll through the narrow streets of this idyllic district, a jumble of houses, taverns, and shops. This is Bremen's oldest district, dating back to the 15th and 16th centuries. The neighborhood is fashionable among artists and craftspeople, who have restored the tiny cottages to serve as galleries and workshops. Other buildings have been converted into popular antiques shops, cafés, and pubs. The area's definitely a great source for souvenirs, with incredibly specialized stores selling porcelain dolls, teddy bears, African jewelry, and smoking pipes, among many other things. There's even a year-round Christmas store. ✉ *Bremen.*

★ **Schwarzwaldbahn** (*Black Forest Railway*)

TRAIN/TRAIN STATION | FAMILY | The Hornberg–Triberg–St. Georgen segment of the Schwarzwaldbahn is one of Germany's most scenic train rides. The 149-km (93-mile) Schwarzwaldbahn, built from 1866 to 1873, runs from Offenburg to Lake Constance via Triberg. It has no fewer than 39 tunnels, and at one point climbs almost 2,000 feet in just 11 km (6½ miles). It's part of the German Railway, and you can make inquiries at any station. ✉ *Triberg* ☎ *030/2970* 🌐 *www.bahn.de.*

Where to Eat and Drink

★ **L.A. Jordan im Ketschauer Hof**

$$$$ | FUSION | An 18th-century complex is the home to the Bassermann-Jordan wine estate and an elegant restaurant, which has one Michelin star. Choose a six-, seven- or eight-course menu from the selection of Mediterranean-influenced Asian dishes, or order à la carte; and select a wine from more than 500 bottles from all over the world, including every vintage of Bassermann-Jordan wine since 1870. **Known for:** sleek, mod ern decor in historic buildings; creative modern cooking; excellent service. 💲 *Average main: €35* ✉ *Ketschauerhofstr. 1, Deidesheim* ☎ *06326/70000* 🌐 *ketschauer-hof.com* 🕓 *Closed Sun. and Mon. No lunch.*

★ **Landhaus Scherrer**

$$$$ | GERMAN | A proud owner of a Michelin star since it opened its doors in 1978, Landhaus Scherrer continues to be one of the city's best-known and most celebrated restaurants. The focus is on the use of organic, sustainable ingredients to produce classic and modern German cuisine with international touches, and unsurprisingly, the accompanying wine list is exceptional. **Known for:** Vierländer duck; parklike setting; on-site bistro for similar fare at lower prices. *$ Average main: €40 ✉ Elbchaussee 130, Ottensen ☎ 040/8830–70030 🌐 www.landhausscherrer.de ⏲ Closed Sun. M Hohenzollernring (Bus Nos. M15 and 36).*

★ Tantris Maison Culinaire

$$$$ | EUROPEAN | Recently reimagined as a trio of restaurants under one roof, Tantris, which has been around since 1971, has smartly broadened its range of modern French culinary offerings. There's the classic Restaurant Tantris, with its pricey prix-fixe lunch and dinner menus of haute cuisine (around 300 euro per person); Tantris DNA, featuring an upscale à la carte lunch and dinner menu; and Tantris Bar, serving cocktails and a short menu of French favorites like beef tartare. **Known for:** gourmet tasting menus; distinctive interior design; flawless service. *$ Average main: €90 ✉ Johann-Fichte-Str. 7, Schwabing ☎ 089/361–9590 🌐 tantris.de/en ⏲ Restaurant Tantris closed Sun.–Tues.; Tantris DNA closed Wed. and Thurs. M Münchener Freiheit, Dietlindenstrasse.*

★ Waldhotel Sonnora Restaurant

$$$$ | FRENCH | At this elegant country hotel in the forested Eifel Hills, guests are offered one of Germany's absolute finest dining experiences in a room plush with gold and white wood furnishings and red carpet. Choose a spectacular five-, seven-, or eight-course menu or dine à la carte: the chef is renowned for transforming truffles, foie gras, and Persian caviar into masterful dishes, and challans duck in an orange-tarragon sauce is his specialty. **Known for:** elegant surroundings; excellent wine list; numerous accolades. *$ Average main: €90 ✉ Waldhotel Sonnora, 1 Auf dem Eichelfeld, Dreis ☎ 06578/406 🌐 www.hotel-sonnora.de ⏲ Closed Mon.–Wed. and 2 wks in summer and winter.*

★ Zur Forelle

$$ | GERMAN | For more than 350 years Forelle (Trout) has stood over the small, clear River Blau, which flows through a large trout basin right under the restaurant. In addition to the variations of trout, including smoked and tartare, there are pasta dishes and excellent venison in season. **Known for:** variations on local trout; pasta dishes; game dishes in season. *$ Average main: €20 ✉ Fischerg. 25, Ulm ☎ 0731/63924 🌐 www.ulmer-forelle.de ⏲ Closed Sun.*

Cool Places to Stay

★ Bareiss

$$$$ | RESORT | FAMILY | A much-loved luxury hotel founded by Hermine Bareiss in 1951, this is one of the top hotels in Europe and one of the very best in Germany. **Pros:** beautiful, secluded location; excellent pools and sauna; fine choice of restaurants. **Cons:** very expensive; rooms feel old-fashioned to some; minimum stays in high season. *$ Rooms from: €640 ✉ Hermine-Bareiss-Weg 1, Mitteltal ☎ 07442/470 🌐 www.bareiss.com 🛏 100 rooms 🍽 Free Breakfast ☞ Rates include breakfast and dinner.*

★ Brenners Park-Hotel & Spa

$$$$ | HOTEL | This stately and exclusive hotel on the Lichtentaler Allee is one of Germany's most celebrated and storied retreats—a favorite of royalty, from Queen Victoria to Czar Alexander II, and their contemporaries— that today features individually decorated rooms and suites with both modern and antique furnishings, good-sized balconies, and grand marble bathrooms. **Pros:** elegant rooms; extremely central location; world-class spa and pool. **Cons:** fellow guests can be aloof; quite expensive; noise in some rooms when hotel hosts private events. *$ Rooms from: €555 ✉ Schillerstr. 4/6, Baden-Baden ☎ 07221/9000 🌐 www.oetkercollection.com 🛏 100 rooms 🍽 No Meals.*

★ **Fairmont Hotel Vier Jahreszeiten**

$$$$ | HOTEL | Some claim that this beautiful 19th-century town house on the edge of the Binnenalster is the best hotel in Germany. **Pros:** luxury hotel with great view of Alster lakes; close to shopping on Jungfernstieg; large, charming rooms. **Cons:** high prices even in off-season; not much in way of nightlife outside of the hotel; some consider bathrooms too small. *Rooms from: €339* *Neuer Jungfernstieg 9–14, Neustadt* *040/34940* *www.fairmont.com* *156 rooms* *No Meals* *Jungfernstieg (U-bahn and S-bahn).*

★ **Grand Hotel Russischer Hof**

$$ | HOTEL | This historic, classical hotel, once the haunt of European nobility and intellectual society, continues to be a luxurious gem in the heart of Weimar—it's one of Germany's finest hotels. **Pros:** quiet location in the city center; service is impeccable; good restaurant Anastasia ($$) serves fine Austrian-Thuringian fusion cuisine. **Cons:** rooms are on the small side; rooms have thin walls; some rooms overlook an unsightly back courtyard. *Rooms from: €155* *Goethepl. 2, Weimar* *03643/7740* *www.russischerhof.com* *125 rooms* *No Meals.*

★ **Radisson Blu Schwarzer Bock Hotel**

$$ | HOTEL | The Schwarzer Bock first opened as a bathhouse in 1486 and is now a sophisticated hotel that maintains stunning architectural features such as marble columns and an exceptionally charming wood-paneled room adjacent to the classically decorated bar. **Pros:** fully air-conditioned; excellent location; wonderful old furnishings. **Cons:** extra cost for cots; parking is expensive and 100 meters away; rooms on the first floor facing the street can be noisy at night. *Rooms from: €134* *Kranzpl. 12, Wiesbaden* *0611/1550* *www.radissonblu.com* *142 rooms* *No Meals.*

★ **Steigenberger Hotel Frankfurter Hof**

$$$$ | HOTEL | Since 1876, this neo-Gothic gem has been the first choice of visiting heads of state, business moguls, and others who keep coming back because of its impeccable service, luxurious rooms, endless-seeming amenities, and central location. **Pros:** old-fashioned elegance; central location close to Altstadt and museums; marble baths with whirlpool tubs. **Cons:** expensive rates; on a busy street; limited parking. *Rooms from: €249* *Am Kaiserpl., City Center* *069/21502* *www.frankfurter-hof.steigenberger.de* *303 rooms* *No Meals* *Willy-Brandt-Platz (U-bahn).*

Switzerland

The paradox of Switzerland pitches rustic homeyness against high-tech urban efficiency. While digital screens tick off beef futures in Zürich, the crude harmony of cowbells echoes in the velvet mountain pastures of the Berner Oberland. While fur-clad socialites raise jeweled fingers to bid at auctions in Geneva, the women of Appenzell, in Central Switzerland, did not get the right to vote until 1991.

Switzerland is a haven of private banking, serious shopping, major music festivals, fabulous art collections, palace hotels, state-of-the-art spas, some of the finest gastronomy in the world, and a burgeoning contemporary scene of filmmakers, architects, artists, and designers making international names for themselves.

The country's Roman ruins, decorated medieval facades, castles, churches, and ornately carved wooden chalets point to its rich history, as do folk traditions like "banishing winter," where bell ringing, whip cracking, fire, and fearsome costumes are meant to frighten off the old spirits and usher in the spring.

This home of William Tell, heartland of the Reformation, birthplace of the Red Cross, and one of the world's oldest democracies also boasts extraordinary scenery.

There are times when the reality of Switzerland puts postcard idealization to shame, surpassing advertising-image peaks and skies. Its rugged Alpine regions concentrate some of the best features of rural Switzerland: awesome mountain panoramas, massive glaciers, crystalline lakes, dramatic gorges and waterfalls, chic ski resorts, dense pine forests, and charming gingerbread chalets.

Agriculture, once the country's prime industry, is still important, evidenced by the frequent sight of cattle dotting the hillsides—for purposes beyond photo-ops.

The Matterhorn

Climb Every Mountain

Try to take your eyes off this glorious enigma, be it from a luxury hotel room, from the ski slopes, or the sky-high Gornergrat Bahn. Set in the shadow of the Matterhorn is tourist-beloved Zermatt, a car-free town where you can amble through the bustling village streets before heading to even higher elevations. There's fun to be had by all—whether you're here to swoosh down first-class slopes in a snowy winter wonderland or hike up the flower-covered valley in the warm summer months. It sometimes suffers from mass tourism, but despite the throngs of tourists, you're never far from a solitary moment along the roaring glacial river or a pine fragrant mountain path.

Don't Miss

Take the Gornergrat Bahn to witness majestic views of the Matterhorn, Monte Rosa, Gorner Glacier, and an expanse of other peaks. Atop there is the chance to pose with St. Bernard dogs—it's touristy, yes, but memorable. Those who dare can ski or hike back down.

Best Activities

Particularly special is the 9-km (6-mile) hiking route from Blauherd to Sunnegga, passing lakes like Stelli, Grindji, and Grün along the way.

Zermatt's skiable terrain lives up to its reputation: the 54 lifts and mountain railways boast 360 km (224 miles) of marked pistes. Thanks to the glacier, there is skiing year-round.

Getting Here

Zermatt is 28 km (18 miles) south of Visp, plus a spectacular 10-km (6-mile) train ride from Täsch.

Gornergrat Bahn. ✉ *Bahnhofpl. 1, Zermatt* ☎ *084/8642442* 🌐 *www.gornergrat.ch* 🎫 *SF88 round-trip, SF44 one-way*

Luzern

The Heart of Switzerland

Luzern has rightly earned the must-see spot on every Switzerland tour. No wonder: you can take a paddleboat steamer on the Vierwaldstättersee (Lake Luzern) past some of the most beautiful lakeside vistas to the Rütli Meadow—the "birthplace of Switzerland"—and the fabled Wilhelm Tell chapel. Luzern itself has an Old Town so clean, it could be mistaken for a museum exhibit. With the mist rising off the water and the mountains looming above in the morning sun, it's easy to understand why people are mesmerized by the inspiring terrain around this pretty city. Where else can you sit and gaze at mountains, a river, and a lake plus architectural treasures like a late-medieval wooden bridge and a Baroque church—all from the same perfect table for two under the chestnut trees on the lakeside? One of the joys of traveling in this region is touring Lake Luzern and its fjord-like inlets on one of its time-stained 20th-century paddle steamers. These are a slow but extremely scenic and therefore worthwhile mode of transportation; you'll find locals on day trips traveling along with you.

Don't Miss

Visit the Kapellbrücke (Chapel Bridge), the oldest wooden bridge in Europe, which snakes diagonally across the Reuss. When it was constructed in the early 14th century, the bridge served as a rampart in case of attacks from the lake. Its shingle roof and grand stone water tower are to Luzern what the Matterhorn is to Zermatt.

Getting Here

Luzern is 52 km (32 miles) southwest of Zurich, and easily reached by car or train.

Lake Lucerne Navigation Company. ✉ *Werftestr. 5, Luzern* ☎ *041/3676767* 🌐 *www.lakelucerne.ch*

Luzern Tourism. 🌐 *www.luzern*

Locarno and Ascona

Ticino's Star-Studded Duo

Superbly placed on the sheltered curve of the northernmost tip of Lago Maggiore and surrounded on all sides by mountains, Locarno is Switzerland's sunniest town. Subtropical flora flourishes here, with date palms, fig trees, bougainvillea, and rhododendron burgeoning on the waterfront. Don't forget your sunglasses—you don't show your face here without a stylish set of shades, especially during August, when the town makes worldwide news with its film festival and showcases the latest cinema on an outdoor screen in the Piazza Grande. Just across the peninsula lies its tiny twin, Ascona, whose lakeside promenades have been so beloved by painters. The town was little more than a fishing village until the end of the 19th century, when it was adopted by vegetarians, socialists, mystics, nudists, and other progressive sorts.

Don't Miss

Breathtaking alpine scenery and vivid colors are wed on the protected Brissago Islands, set like jewels in the lake and reached only by ferry. Wander their botanical gardens that teem with more than a thousand species of subtropical plants.

Getting Here

From Milan Malpensa it's a two-hour train or bus (102 km (63 miles) to Locarno. Ferries to the Isola Grande depart regularly from Ascona and Locarno.

Isola Grande. 🌐 *www.isolebrissago.ch/en*

Sportello Informativo di Locarno. 🌐 *www.ascona-locarno.com*

Fondue in Fribourg

Stir the Melting Pot

Fondue famously originated in the Neuchâtel region of Switzerland, but it is now *derigueur* in every Alpine setting. However, it's the charming city of Fribourg that has a fanatical stronghold on the molten meal. The recipe is surprisingly simple—cheese melted together with white wine, garlic, and a dash of kirsch (brandy distilled from cherries). Aficionados debate the perfect blend of cheeses—try the two-cheese fondue *neuchâteloise* that honors Switzerland's fabulous Gruyère and Emmental cheeses, or opt for the less pungent four-cheese mountain fondue (sometimes known as hard cheese fondue). But whatever you do, don't miss tasting the classic *moitié-moitié* (half-and-half) combination of Canton Fribourg's two greatest cheeses— Gruyère and Vacherin Fribourgeois. The Vacherin can be melted alone for an even creamier fondue, and potatoes can be dipped instead of bread.

Don't Miss

Right out of a fairy tale, Gruyères village is crowned with one of the most picture-perfect castles in Switzerland. Its only street climbs steeply past souvenir shops, the H. R. Giger Museum, and a selection of local restaurants featuring pots of rich, bubbly fondue.

Best Fondue Restaurant

Café du Midi. This classic spot has been serving fondue since 1877. [$] *Average main: SF28* ✉ *25 rue de Romont, Fribourg* ☎ *026/3223133* 🌐 *www.lemidi.ch*

Getting Here

Fribourg is 34 km (21 miles) southwest of Bern and 74 km (46 miles) northeast of Lausanne. Gruyerès is an hour from Fribourg by train and bus.

Fribourg Tourisme.
🌐 *www.fribourgtourism.ch*

Gruyère Tourisme.
🌐 *www.la-gruyere.ch*

Appenzell

A Hidden Culinary Gem for Foodies

Isolated by a ridge of green hills, Appenzell is one of Switzerland's least explored regions. The Appenzellers are known for their quirky senses of humor, old-fashioned costumes (including hoop earrings for most men), and good natured Anstand, which loosely translates as "decorum" or "decency." But more than anything, Appenzell is cheese and beer country, and you would be remiss to leave without a taste of either. To get your bearings in Appenzell, head to the Landsgemeindeplatz, the town square where the famous open-air elections (men-only until 1991) take place the last Sunday in April. The streets are lined with brightly painted homes and bakeries full of Birnebrot (pear bread) and souvenir Biber (almond-and-honey cakes).

Don't Miss

Appenzell has a long tradition of fine embroidery, easily seen during the Alpfahrten Festival, when cows are herded up or down the mountains. Women's hair is coiffed in tulle, and their dresses have intricate embroidery and lace, often with an edelweiss motif; men wear embroidered red vests and suspenders decorated with edelweiss or cow figures.

Best Activity

Explore the lush green hills and jagged peak of Mt. Säntis following the Whiskytrek, where hikers can visit some of the 25 mountain inns that brew their own excellent whiskey.

Getting Here

Appenzell is about 97 km (60 miles) east of Zurich. Take a train to St. Gallen, and then it's just 48 more minutes to Appenzell.

Appenzell Tourism.
www.appenzell.ch

Lauterbrunnen

Waterfalls, Waterfalls, and More Waterfalls

The Lauterbrunnen Valley is often ranked as one of the most beautiful places in Switzerland. A Swiss Shangri-La, it encloses a nearly perfect set piece of earth, sky, and water. The mountains here seem to part like the Red Sea as two awesome, bluff-lined rock faces line the vast valley, where grassy meadows often lie in shadow as 1,508-foot rocky shoulders rise on either side. What really sets this mountainous masterpiece apart are the 72 waterfalls (Lauterbrunnen means "only springs") that line the length of the 3-km-long (2 mile-long) valley. Some plummet from sky-high crags, others cascade out of cliff-face crevasses, and many are hidden within the rocks themselves; the largest, the Staubbach Falls, were immortalized by Johann Wolfgang von Goethe, William Wordsworth, and Lord Byron, who described them as "the tail of a white horse blowing in the breeze."

Don't Miss

A series of 10 glacier waterfalls hidden deep inside rock walls make up the Trümmelbachfälle (Trümmelbach Falls), a spectacular sight that you can access by a tunnel lift. Approach the departure point via a pretty creek-side walkway and brace yourself for some steep stair climbing. Bring a jacket—the wet mist can feel awfully cold in summer attire.

Getting Here

The Bernese Oberland Railway runs trains from Interlaken Ost station to Lauterbrunnen, a distance of about 10 km (6 miles) south of Interlaken; tthe trip takes 20 minutes.

✉ *Lauterbrunnen* ☎ *033/8553232* 🌐 *www.truemmel-bachfaelle.ch* 🎟 *SF11* 🕒 *Closed early Nov.–early Apr.*

Montreux Jazz Festival

Switzerland's Biggest Music Event

Montreaux is where Igor Stravinsky composed Petrouchka and where Vladimir Nabokov resided in splendor. Montreux and its suburbs have attracted artists and literati for 200 years: Byron, Shelley, Tolstoy, and Flaubert were all drawn to its lush shoreline. The resort is best known for its annual jazz festival, which now includes rock, R&B, Latin, and hip-hop. Each July, Montreux's usually composed promenade explodes in a street festival of food tents, vendor kiosks, and open band shells, which complement standing-room-only concert hall venues. The most popular events sell out within hours. Montreux might be called the Cannes of Lac Léman—though it might raise an eyebrow at the slur. Spilling down steep hillsides into a sunny south-facing bay, its waterfront thick with magnolias, cypresses, and palm trees, the historic resort earns its reputation for glitz and glamour.

Don't Miss

One of Switzerland's must-sees is the Château de Chillon, the awe-inspiringly picturesque 12th-century castle that rears out of the water at nearby Veytaux. Its 19th-century Romantic-era restoration is so evocative and so convincing that even the jaded castle hound may become carried away.

Getting Here

Nestled at the eastern edge of Lac Léman, Montreux is on the main train line, just 21 km (13 miles) from Lausanne.

Château de Chillon. ✉ *21 av. de Chillon, Veytaux* 🌐 *www.chillon.ch* 🎫 *SF14*

Montreaux Jazz Festival.
🌐 *www.montreuxjazzfestival.com*

The Glacier Express

The Prettiest Swiss Rail Journey

The queen of all scenic routes, the Glacier Express (christened the world's slowest express train), begins and ends in two of Switzerland's most frequented and fashionable resorts: St. Moritz and Zermatt. Glaciated valleys, steep gorges, high meadows, and ancient townships are all viewed through panoramic cars while the train passes over 291 bridges and through 91 tunnels.The Swiss have a world-class transportation network, and the country makes the most of its Alpine rail engineering, which cuts through the icy granite landscape above 6,560 feet. It's easy to explore Switzerland by rail (as well as boat, bus, and city tram), and riding the Glacier Express is no exception. The trip takes seven and a half hours and is punctuated by a three-course meal—starter, dinner, and dessert—that is prepared from scratch onboard and delivered right to your seat. Foodies may choose to upgrade to the Excellence Class, which includes a five-course extravaganza served at the special window seat you'll voyage in.

Don't Miss

A major highlight is the trip through the Rhine Gorge, Switzerland's very own Grand Canyon.

Getting Here

You can begin at either St. Moritz in eastern Switzerland's Grabünden region (Switzerland's ritziest resort), or Zermatt, in the southern Valais region in the shadow of the Matterhorn.

Glacier Express. *www.glacier-express.ch* *SF152 (plus SF49 for seat reservation in summer; SF39 in winter)* *7 hrs, 30 min*

When in Switzerland

★ **Fraumünster** (*Church of Our Lady*)
CHURCH | Of the church spires that are Zürich's signature, the Fraumünster's is the most delicate, a graceful sweep to a narrow point. It was added to the Gothic structure in 1732; the remains of Louis the German's original 9th-century abbey are below. Its Romanesque choir is a perfect spot for meditation beneath the ocher, sapphire, and ruby glow of the 1970 stained-glass windows by the Russian-born Marc Chagall, who loved Zürich. The Graubünden sculptor Alberto Giacometti's cousin, Augusto Giacometti, executed the fine painted window, made in 1930, in the north transept. ✉ *Stadthausquai, Kreis 1* 🌐 *www.fraumuenster.ch* 🎫 *SF5.*

Maison Cailler
FACTORY | **FAMILY** | On the way from Fribourg to Gruyères, chocoholics should consider stopping at this tantalizing chocolate factory in the otherwise unassuming town of Broc. A name in Swiss chocolate since 1819, Cailler offers a 90-minute tour complete with chocolate tasting. ✉ *7 rue Jules Bellet, Broc* ☎ *026/9215960* 🌐 *www.cailler.ch* 🎫 *SF15.*

★ **Mt. Pilatus**
MOUNTAIN | **FAMILY** | To reach the mountain by cable car, get a bus from the train station in Luzern to the suburb of Kriens, where you catch a tiny, four-seat cable car that flies silently up to Fräkmüntegg (4,600 feet). From there, change to the sleek, multilevel 55-passenger cable car that sails through open air up the rock cliff to the summit station (5,560 feet). A 10-minute walk takes you to **Esel**, one of the central peaks that make up Pilatus. From a platform here, views unfold over the Alps and the sprawling, angular Lake Luzern. Once you reach the top, glorious views are everywhere. The flat main trail on the top leads in and out of the mountain, and comes replete with striking cavern windows that offer drop-dead-gorgeous vistas. ☎ *041/3291111* 🌐 *www.pilatus.ch.*

Murten
TOWN | The ancient town of Murten, known in French as Morat, is a popular resort on the Murtensee/Lac de Morat (Lake Murten). The bilingual town has a boat-lined waterfront, windsurfing rentals, a lakeside public pool complex, grassy picnic areas, and a promenade as well as a superbly preserved medieval center. From the town's 13th-century gates, take a stroll through the fountain-studded cobblestone streets. Climb up the worn wooden steps to the town ramparts for a view of the lake over a charming montage of red roofs and stone chimneys. Although a small town, Murten looms large in the history of Switzerland. Its most memorable moment came on June 22, 1476, when the Swiss Confederates—already a fearsomely efficient military machine—attacked with surprising ferocity and won a significant victory over the Burgundians, who were threatening Fribourg. The Swiss lost 410 men, the Burgundians 12,000. ✉ *Murten* ✥ *17 km (11 miles) north of Fribourg* 🌐 *www.fribourgregion.ch/en/regionmurtensee/.*

Reichenbachfälle (*Reichenbach Falls*)
WATERFALL | **FAMILY** | Meiringen's one showstopper is the Reichenbachfälle, where Sir Arthur Conan Doyle's fictional detective Sherlock Holmes and his archenemy, Professor Moriarty, plunged into the "cauldron of swirling water and seething foam in that bottomless abyss above Meiringen." This was the climax of the "last" Holmes story, "The Final Problem" (the uproar over the detective's untimely end was such that the author was forced to resurrect his hero for further fictional adventures). The falls, 2,730 feet up a mountain a little way outside of town, can be visited via a funicular. Buy your funicular ticket online or from the driver (cash only). ✉ *Hausenstr. 34,*

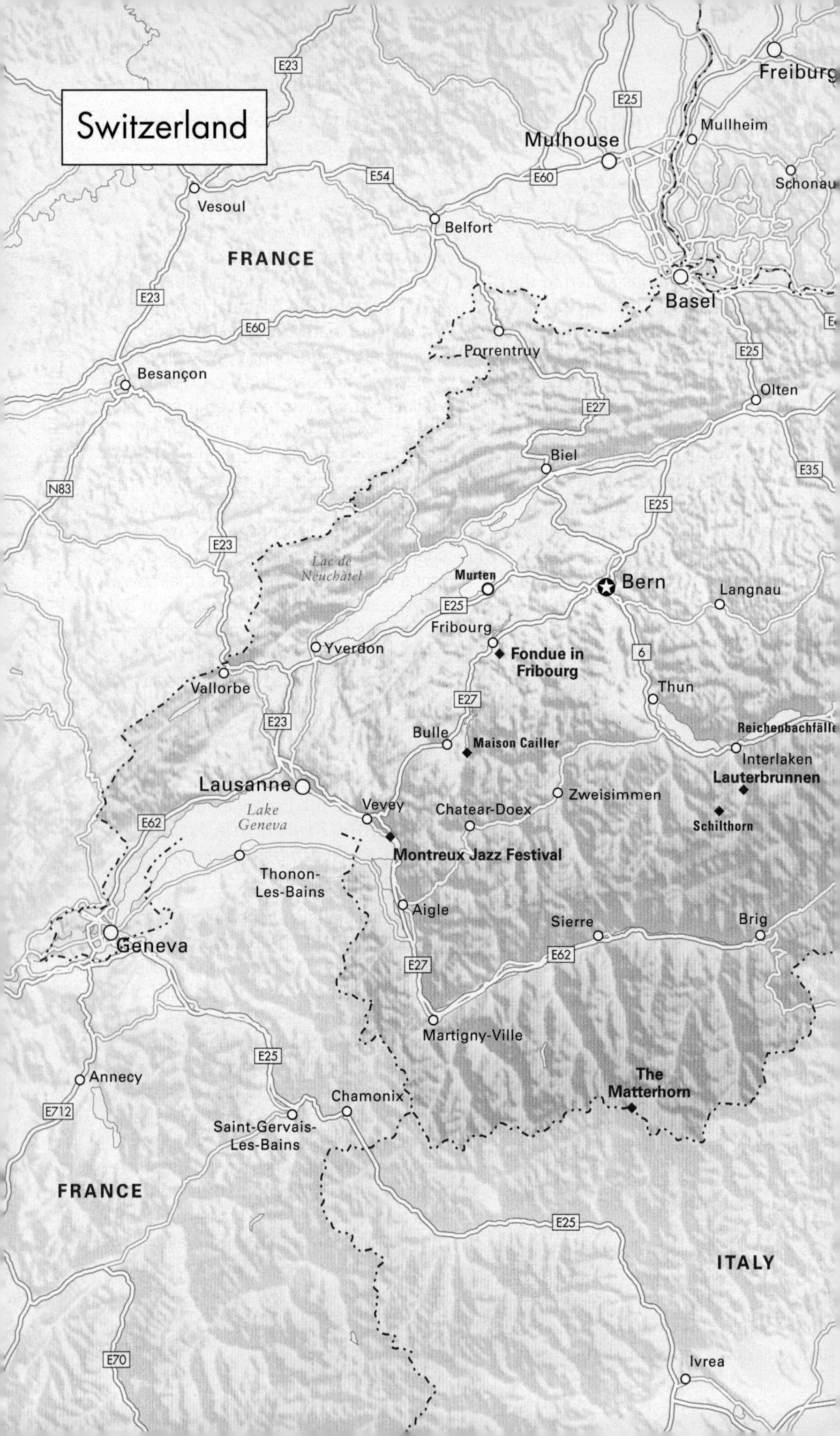

Switzerland
FRANCE
E23
Vesoul
E54
Belfort
Mulhouse
E60
E25
Mullheim
Freiburg
Schonau
Basel
Porrentruy
E60
E23
Besançon
E25
Olten
E27
Biel
E35
N83
E25
E23
Lac de Neuchâtel
Murten
Bern
Langnau
E25
Fribourg
Fondue in Fribourg
6
Yverdon
Vallorbe
Thun
E27
E23
Bulle
Maison Cailler
Reichenbachfälle
Interlaken
Lauterbrunnen
Lausanne
Lake Geneva
Vevey
Chatear-Doex
Zweisimmen
Schilthorn
E62
Montreux Jazz Festival
Thonon-Les-Bains
Aigle
Sierre
Brig
Geneva
E62
E27
Martigny-Ville
E25
Annecy
The Matterhorn
Chamonix
E712
Saint-Gervais-Les-Bains
FRANCE
E25
ITALY
E70
Ivrea

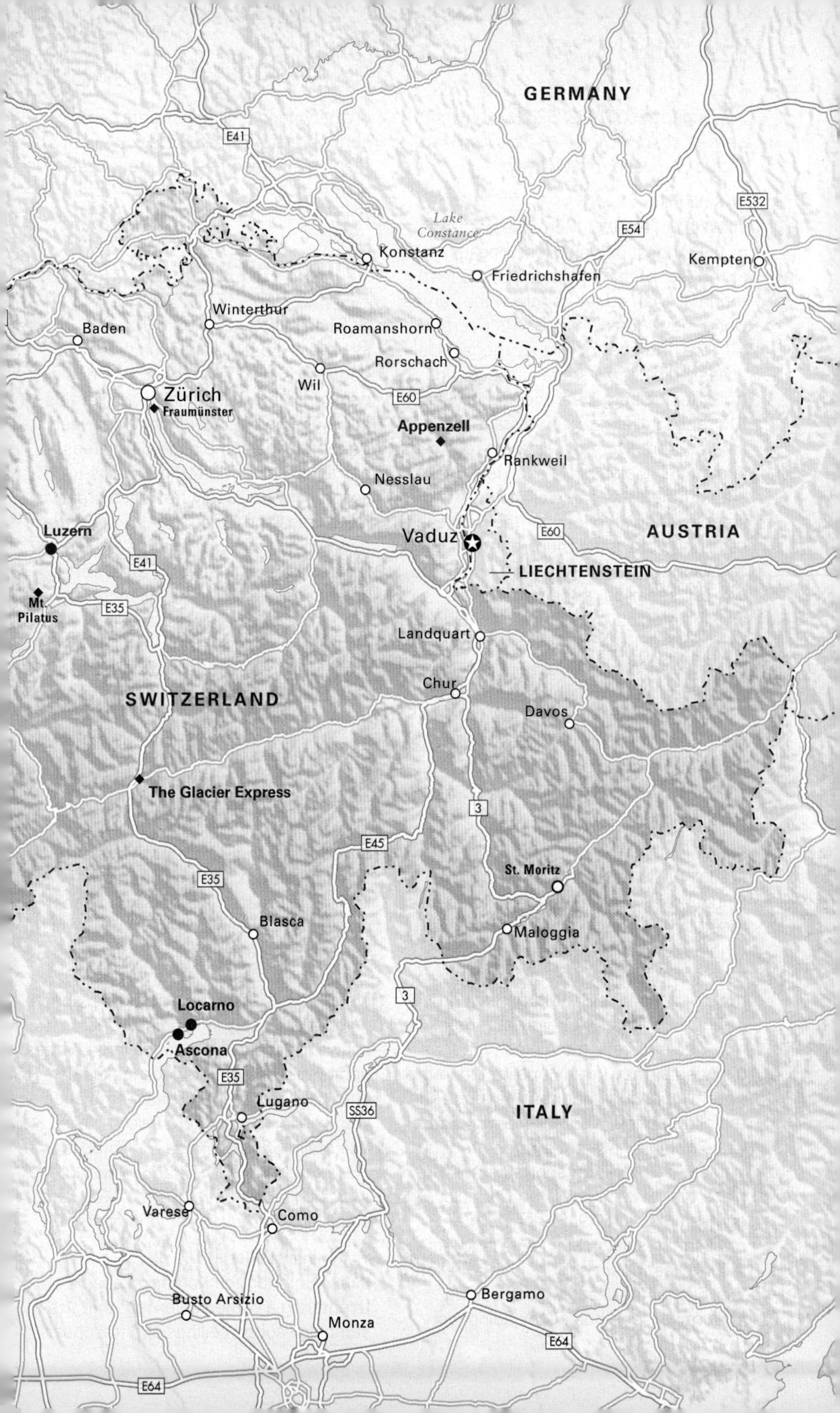
GERMANY
E41
E532
Lake Constance
E54
Konstanz
Kempten
Friedrichshafen
Winterthur
Baden
Roamanshorn
Rorschach
Wil
Zürich
Fraumünster
E60
Appenzell
Rankweil
Nesslau
Luzern
Vaduz
E60
AUSTRIA
E41
LIECHTENSTEIN
Mt. Pilatus
E35
Landquart
Chur
SWITZERLAND
Davos
The Glacier Express
3
E45
E35
St. Moritz
Blasca
Maloggia
3
Locarno
Ascona
E35
Lugano
SS36
ITALY
Varese
Como
Busto Arsizio
Bergamo
Monza
E64
E64

Meiringen ☎ *033/9822626* 🌐 *www.grimselwelt.ch* 🎫 *SF12; SF18 including Aare Gorge* ⏲ *Closed mid-Oct.–Apr.*

★ Schilthorn

VIEWPOINT | FAMILY | Mürren boasts some of the longest downhill runs because it is at the foot of the Schilthorn (9,748 feet) mountain, famed for its role in the James Bond movie *On Her Majesty's Secret Service*. The peak of this icy megalith is accessed by a four-stage cable car ride from Stechelberg (near the spectacular Mürrenbach Falls) or a two-stage cable car ride from Mürren, past bare-rock cliffs and stunning slopes. At each level you step off the cable car, walk across the station, and wait briefly for the next cable car. At the top is the much-photographed revolving restaurant Piz Gloria, where you can see clips of the film. There's also an interactive, multimedia exhibition that is a must-see for James Bond fans called *Bond World*. Attractions include a flight simulator inside a helicopter and a 35-seat theater showing 007's Alpine adventures. ✉ *Mürren* ☎ *033/8260007* 🌐 *schilthorn.ch* 🎫 *Cable car SF108 round-trip from Stechelberg, SF86 round-trip from Mürren.*

St. Moritz

RESORT | Who put the ritz in St. Moritz? Undoubtedly, St. Moritz's reputation was made by the people who go there and who have been going there, generation after generation, since 1864, when hotelier Johannes Badrutt dared a group of English tourists—already summer regulars—to brave the Alpine winter as his guests. They loved it, delighted in the novelty of snowy mountain beauty, and the glitterati followed. Even a hundred years of hype have not exaggerated its attraction as a winter sports center. The place that twice hosted the Olympic games (1928 and 1948)—and trademarked the shining sun as its logo—is still well set up for sports, with excellent facilities for ice-skating, bobsledding, ski jumping, and horseback riding. Very ordinary people fill the streets come summer—the same hikers you might meet in any resort—and hotel prices plummet. ✉ *St. Moritz* 🌐 *www.stmoritz.com.*

Where to Eat and Drink

★ Findlerhof

$$ | SWISS | Ideal for long lunches between sessions on the slopes or a panoramic break on an all-day hike, this place perched in tiny Findeln, between the Sunnegga and Blauherd ski areas, has astonishing Matterhorn views to accompany decidedly fresh and creative food. Franz and Heidi Schwery tend their own Alpine garden to provide lettuce for their salads and berries for vinaigrettes and hot desserts. **Known for:** astonishing Matterhorn views; cozy atmosphere; local Swiss specialties. Ⓢ *Average main: SF30* ✉ *Findeln, Findeln* ☎ *027/9672588* 🌐 *www.findlerhof.ch* ⏲ *Closed May–mid-June and mid-Oct.–Nov.*

Galleria Arté al Lago

$$$ | SEAFOOD | Extraordinary art in all forms is the trademark of this Michelin-starred location at the atmospheric Villa Castagnola, where paintings and sculptures from a variety of artists line the walls and halls and exhibitions change twice yearly. Chef Frank Oerthle has a way with seafood: specialties change seasonally but can include steamed oysters with caramelized spring onion and wasabi-infused scallops. **Known for:** capable of seating large parties upon request; sunlit terrace looks out onto Lake Lugano; art gallery ambience you won't find anywhere else. Ⓢ *Average main: SF58* ✉ *Piazza Emilio Bossi 7, Lungolago* ☎ *091/9732555* 🌐 *www.villacastagnola.com* ⏲ *Closed Mon. and Tues.* 👔 *Men must wear long pants.*

★ Kornhauskeller

BARS | Entering the Kornhauskeller is akin to entering a cathedral, except that the stunning vaulted ceilings and frescoes are underground and the lounge-bar in the gallery stocks an incredible array of whiskeys, rums, and bourbons. The building has focused on food throughout its long life, first as a wine cellar–granary, then as a beer hall. In addition to its vast lounge of leather sofas and chairs, the Kornhauskeller houses a classy restaurant. ✉ *Kornhauspl. 18, Altstadt* ☎ *031/3277272* 🌐 *www.kornhauskeller.ch.*

★ Old Swiss House
$$$ | **SWISS** | This popular establishment has been feeding travelers since 1931 in what was originally built as a farmhouse in 1858, now containing a beautifully contrived collection of 17th-century antiques, leaded glass, and an old-world style—everything pleasantly burnished by more than 90 years of service. The standing menu includes specialties from around the country: cubed fillet of beef in a green-pepper mustard sauce, pike perch with ratatouille, and chocolate mousse. **Known for:** more than 30,000 bottles of wine in stock; plush and elegant atmosphere; kitchen that's open all day. $ *Average main: SF56* ✉ *Löwenpl. 4, Luzern* ☎ *041/4106171* 🌐 *www.oldswiss-house.ch* ⏲ *Closed Sun. and Mon. in Jan. and Feb.; closed Mon., Mar.–Dec.*

★ Restaurant de l'Hôtel de Ville
$$$$ | **FRENCH** | Since the tragic loss of world-renowned chef Benoit Violier, his determined widow, Brigitte, has continued to oversee the three-Michelin-star restaurant, propelling it to even higher accolades. Chef Franck Giovannini is winning hearts—and stomachs—with his fresh twist on haute cuisine. **Known for:** finely orchestrated prix-fixe menus; consistently ranked one of the best restaurants in the world; exceptional service with a smile that is rare for such establishments. $ *Average main: SF95* ✉ *1 rue d'Yverdon, Crissier* ✣ *7 km (4 miles) west of Lausanne* ☎ *021/6340505* 🌐 *www.restaurantcrissier.com* ⏲ *Closed Sun. and Mon.*

Talvò by Dalsass
$$$$ | **MEDITERRANEAN** | With a focus on the highest-quality ingredients and a simplistic, Mediterranean cooking style that allows each individual taste to shine, dining here is a true culinary experience, though be prepared to spend almost as much on a meal as on a hotel room. Though the menu changes seasonally, it always includes a tempting mix of fish, game, meat, and poultry dishes, with a blend of local and international ingredients. **Known for:** refined Mediterranean cuisine; historic 17th-century farmhouse setting; olive oil chocolate mousse. $ *Average main: SF78* ✉ *Via Gunels 15, Champfèr* ✣ *3 km (2 miles) southwest of St. Moritz, about 330 feet from postbus stop* ☎ *081/8334455* 🌐 *www.talvo.ch* ⏲ *Closed mid-Apr.–late June and mid-Oct.–early Dec. Closed Mon. and Tues. in summer. No lunch Mon. and Tues. in winter.*

Cool Places to Stay

★ The Alpina Gstaad
$$$$ | **RESORT** | In a vast park above the village, this exquisite hotel manages to be posh and homey at the same time. **Pros:** every room has a balcony with a beautiful view; excellent food in three restaurants, including Japanese; large spa with indoor and outdoor pools. **Cons:** uphill walk from town; awfully high prices for drinks and spa treatments; you'll have to check out eventually. $ *Rooms from: SF800* ✉ *Alpinastr. 23, Gstaad* ☎ *033/8889888* 🌐 *www.thealpinagstaad.ch* ⏲ *Closed mid-Mar.–early June and Oct.–early Dec.* *56 rooms* *Free Breakfast.*

★ Der Teufelhof Basel
$ | **HOTEL** | The Teufelhof is actually two hotels in one: the Art Hotel has nine rooms that are works of art in their own right and were stunningly reconceived by well-known artists such as Switzerland's Dieter Meyer, while the simple rooms of the adjoining Gallery Hotel function as

a canvas for a single artist to show off recent work or for an exhibit on a particular theme (such as historic photographs of Basel). **Pros:** great location—only three tram stops away from the main station; excellent service; good choice of food and drink options. **Cons:** no air-conditioning; no elevator in the Art Hotel; some noise in rooms facing the tram. *Rooms from: SF198 Leonhardsgraben 49, Altstadt 061/2611010 www.teufelhof.com 33 rooms No Meals.*

★ Grand Hotel Kronenhof

$$$ | HOTEL | A grand Versailles set amid mountain peaks, the Kronenhof is the pinnacle for rest, relaxation, and pampering, with gorgeous designs inside and out, a keen attention to detail, and a sprawling lawn perfect for admiring the views of Roseg Valley. **Pros:** beautiful grounds and location; excellent dining options; top-of-the-line children's facility. **Cons:** expensive for this area; hotel check-out could be more streamlined; more modern rooms lack character of the traditional ones. *Rooms from: SF485 Via Maistra 1, Pontresina 081/8303030 www.kronenhof.com Closed early Apr.–mid-June and mid-Oct.–early Dec. 112 rooms Free Breakfast.*

★ Hôtel Palafitte

$$$$ | HOTEL | Unique in Europe, this one-level hotel is partly built on piles on Lac de Neuchâtel, giving it unbeatable clear-day views that include the distant Alps. **Pros:** some rooms have ladders so you can descend directly into the lake for a swim; golf-cart-style vehicle shuttles guests to rooms; unique structure with loads of character. **Cons:** despite air-conditioning, strong sun may heat your room up; some glitches in maintenance; breakfast is expensive. *Rooms from: SF560 2 rte. des Gouttes d'Or, Monruz 032/7230202 www.palafitte.ch 40 suites No Meals.*

★ Hotel Royal Savoy Lausanne

$$$ | HOTEL | After a six-year, top-to-bottom renovation, the historic Royal Savoy has been unveiled as the latest—and perhaps the finest—five-star hotel in all of Suisse Romande. **Pros:** excellent value for a five-star property; rooftop lounge provides a panoramic view over the lake; large spa area for a pampered soak in various marbled pools. **Cons:** gray interiors are not for those who dislike a neutral palette; moneyed guests (and some staff) give off a haughty vibe; outdoor pool is quite small. *Rooms from: SF370 40 av. d'Ouchy, Ouchy 021/6148888 royalsavoylausanne.com 186 rooms No Meals.*

★ Victoria-Jungfrau Grand Hotel & Spa

$$$$ | RESORT | FAMILY | Restoration has taken this 1865 grande dame firmly into the 21st century, with glitzy touches such as the burled-wood entryway, a vast belle époque lobby that spirals off into innumerable bars and tea salons, and a sprawling spa with an elegant 1940s-style indoor pool, outdoor saltwater pool with lovely views, and substantial gym. **Pros:** central Interlaken location with view of Jungfrau; wonderful spa; elegant common areas. **Cons:** hotel layout can be confusing to navigate; some call this place overpriced; not all rooms have balconies. *Rooms from: SF655 Höheweg 41, Interlaken 033/8282828 www.victoria-jungfrau.ch 216 rooms Free Breakfast.*

Czech Republic

The experience of visiting the Czech Republic involves stepping back in time. The country's capital Prague is one of Europe's best-preserved (and justifiably popular) cities, with a romantic riverside location enhanced by graceful bridges and a magnificent skyline punctuated with medieval church spires. Its time-honored Old Town follows a plan laid out 1,000 years ago, with ancient squares and winding cobblestone streets. Everywhere you turn, there's history to see.

But, as the saying goes, the world is a book, and those who don't travel read only one page. The same applies to visitors who come to the Czech Republic but visit only Prague. Don't get us wrong: it's a great page to read. But if you want the whole story—and to really get to grips with Czech history—you need to get out of the capital and embrace the adventures beyond.

Venture outside of Prague's borders and you'll discover a whole world of wonderful attractions. There are the myriad castles that dot the landscape around the capital, from the fairy-tale chateau of Karlštejn to the historical hunting lodge of Konopiště. There are the charming towns of Bohemia, from the graceful colonnades and dilapidated villas of spa resort Karlovy Vary to the impossibly pretty castle and gardens of red-roofed Český Krumlov. And there is the beer, including the famous Pilsner Urquell, the world's first pale lager—as well as the lesser known (but equally excellent) wines of Moravia.

In between the big-name sights, you'll find plenty of Gothic towers, Renaissance facades and Baroque interiors, as well as glorious mountain ranges and forest-covered countryside, to keep you entertained for weeks on end.

Old Town Square, Prague

One of Europe's Prettiest Squares

The hype about Staroměstské náměstí (Old Town Square) is completely justified. Picture a perimeter of colorful Baroque houses contrasting with the sweeping old-Gothic style of the Týn Church in the background. As the heart of the Old Town, the majestic square grew to its present proportions when Prague's original marketplace moved away from the river in the 12th century. Its shape and appearance have changed little since that time. During the day the square pulses with activity: in summer the square's south end is dominated by sprawling (pricey!) outdoor restaurants; during the Easter and Christmas seasons it fills with wooden booths of holiday vendors. At night, the brightly lit twin towers of the Týn Church rise gloriously over the glowing Baroque facades. The square's history has also seen violence, from defenestrations (throwing people from windows) in the 15th century to 27 Bohemian noblemen killed by Austrian Habsburgs in 1621; 27 white crosses embedded in the square's paving stones commemorate the spot.

Don't Miss

Hundreds of visitors gravitate outside Staroměstská radnice (Old Town Hall) throughout the day to see the hour struck by the mechanical figures of the Astronomical Clock. Don't be disappointed by the lack of drama, but focus on its astonishing age: it was first installed on the tower in 1410.

Getting Here

If you are in Prague, there's almost no way to miss Old Town Square, which is at the very heart of the old city. It's a five-minute walk from the nearest metro station (Staroměstská; Line A) and not much farther from the Charles Bridge. The square is pedestrianized, as are most streets around, so wear comfortable shoes.

Charles Bridge, Prague

A Medieval Masterpiece

This is Prague's signature monument, and rightly so. The view from the foot of Karlův most (Charles Bridge) on the Old Town side, encompassing the towers and domes of Malá Strana (Lesser Town) and the soaring spires of St. Vitus Cathedral, is nothing short of breathtaking. This heavenly vista subtly changes in perspective as you walk across the bridge, attended by a host of baroque saints that decorate the bridge's peaceful Gothic stones. At night its drama is spellbinding: St. Vitus Cathedral lit in a ghostly green, Prague Castle in monumental yellow, and the Church of St. Nicholas in a voluptuous pink, all viewed through the menacing silhouettes of the bowed statues and the Gothic towers. Night is the best time to visit the bridge, which is choked with visitors, vendors, and beggars by day. The later the hour, the thinner the crowds—though the bridge is never truly empty, even at daybreak.

Don't Miss

Eighth on the right is the statue of St. John of Nepomuk, who according to legend was wrapped in chains and thrown to his death from this bridge. Touching the statue is supposed to bring good luck or, according to some versions of the story, a return visit to Prague.

Getting Here

On the Old Town side, the nearest metro station is Staroměstská (Line A). On the Lesser Town side, it's best to take a tram to Malostranské náměstí.

✉ *Between Karlova (Staré Město) and Mostecká (Malá Strana)*

St. Vitus Cathedral

The Spiritual Heart of Prague

Despite its monolithic presence, Prague Castle is not a single structure but a whole of complex of them—and the most significant is Katedrála sv. Víta (St. Vitus Cathedral). With its graceful, soaring towers, this Gothic house of worship is among Europe's most beautiful, with a long history beginning in the 10th century and continuing to its completion in 1929. Inside, the six stained-glass windows to your left and right and the large rose window behind are modern masterpieces; see if you can spot the contributions of art nouveau master Alfons Mucha. Other highlights include the Svatováclavská kaple (Chapel of St. Wenceslas); the Kralovské oratorium (Royal Oratory), a perfect example of late Gothic architecture; the ornate silver sarcophagus of St. John of Nepomuk; and the eight chapels around the back of the cathedral. Don't miss the mosaic on the south side of the cathedral's exterior, constructed from a million glass and stone tesserae in the 1370s.

Don't Miss

Prague Castle is also home to Bazilika sv. Jiří (St. George's Basilica), virtually unchanged since the 12th century; Starý královský palác (Old Royal Palace), with the largest secular Gothic interior space in Central Europe; and Zlatá ulička (Golden Lane), a jumbled collection of brightly colored houses crouched under the fortification wall, where Franz Kafka lived briefly with his sister.

✉ Hrad III nádvoří 2 ☎ 224–372–434 🌐 www.katedralasvatehovita 🎫 Included in 2-day castle ticket (from 250 Kč) 🚆 Line A: Malostranská plus Tram 22 to Pražský Hrad

Karlštejn Castle

A Picture-Perfect Castle

If it's a picture-book European castle you're after, look no further. Perched atop a wooded hillside, Hrad Karlštejn (Karlštejn Castle) comes complete with battlements, turrets, and towers. Once Charles IV's summer palace, Karlštejn was originally built to hold and guard the crown jewels (which were moved to Prague Castle in 1619). There is a fairly strenuous hike up to the castle—lined with souvenir stands and overpriced snack bars—but it's worth the journey. Once you've reached the top, take time to walk the ramparts and drink in the panorama of the village and countryside below, before embarking on a tour to see the castle's greatest treasure, the Chapel of the Holy Cross. Because of its proximity to Prague, Karlštejn is the most-visited site outside of the Czech capital, so be prepared for crowds.

Don't Miss

There are two other castles nearby: Konopiště, the country retreat of Archduke Franz Ferdinand; and Křivoklát, a beautiful fortification with an atmospheric courtyard.

Getting Here

Karlštejn is a quick, simple, and scenic train journey from Prague's Hlavní nádraží; when you arrive, follow the crowds to the castle. Check the schedule for trains heading to Beroun.

Hrad Karlštejn. ✉ *Karlštejn 18* 🌐 *www.hrad-karlstejn.cz* 🎫 *Tours from 190 Kč* ⏲ *Closed Mon. Tower closed Oct.–Apr., chapel closed Nov.–Apr.*

Křivoklát. ✉ *Křivoklát 47* 🌐 *www.hrad-krivoklat.cz* 🎫 *Tours from 240 Kč* ⏲ *Closed Mon. Closed weekdays Nov.–Mar.*

Zámek Konopiště. 🌐 *www.zamek-konopiste.cz* 🎫 *Tours from 240 Kč* ⏲ *Closed Mon. and Dec.–Mar.*

Pilsner Urquell Brewery

A Mecca for Beer Lovers

Plzeň—or Pilsen in German—is the industrial heart of Western Bohemia and the region's biggest city. It's also a must-see for intellectual beer aficionados, with anyone who loves the stuff flocking to pay homage to the Plzeňský prazdroj (Pilsner Urquell) brewery. The first pilsner beer was created here in 1842 using the excellent Plzeň water, a special malt fermented on the premises, and hops grown in the region around Žatec (which remains in great demand today.) Guided tours of the brewery, complete with a visit to the brewhouse and beer tastings, are offered daily. Just a short walk away is Pivotéka v Pivovarském muzeu (Brewery Museum), with all kinds of fascinating paraphernalia that trace the region's brewing history, including the horse-drawn carts used to haul the kegs.

Don't Miss

Plzeň's Náměstí Republiky (Republic Square) is one of Bohemia's largest. It's dominated by the looming Gothic Church of St. Bartholomew, but look out for other architectural jewels around, like the Renaissance Town Hall, built by Italian architects and adorned with*sgraffiti*.

Best Restaurant

U Mansfelda. A gleaming copper hood floats above the taps in this pub with an inviting patio. $ *Average main: Kč260* ✉ *Dřevěná 9* ☎ *377–333–844* 🌐 *umansfelda.cz*

Getting Here

There are frequent trains between Prague and Plzeň (about 1 hour 15 minutes, 260 Kč each way). The brewery is a 15-minute walk from the train station.

✉ *U Prazdroje 7, Plzeň* 🌐 *www.prazdrojvisit.cz* 🎫 *Pilsner Brewery: 300 Kč; Gambrinus Brewery: 200 Kč*

Karlovy Vary

Playground of the Rich and Famous

Karlovy Vary—often known by its German name, Karlsbad—is the most famous of the Bohemian spa towns. It's named for the omnipresent Emperor Charles IV, who allegedly happened upon the springs in 1358 while on a hunting expedition. As the story goes, the emperor's hound fell into a boiling spring and was scalded. Charles had the water tested and, familiar with spas in Italy, ordered the village of Vary to be transformed into a haven for baths. The spa reached its golden age in the 19th century, when aristocrats from all over Europe came for treatments. The long list of those who "took the cure" includes Peter the Great, Goethe, and Chopin. Even Karl Marx, when he wasn't decrying wealth and privilege, spent time at the wealthy resort; he wrote some of*Das Kapital*here. The Karlovy Vary International Film Festival, which began in 1946 and is held during every July, attracts movie stars and film fans from all over the world.

Getting Here

Frequent bus service between Prague and Karlovy Vary makes the journey only about two hours each way; tickets cost 160 Kč to 200 Kč. The train takes longer (more than three hours) and costs about 250 Kč. Once in town, you can easily get around on foot.

Stay Here

Grandhotel Pupp. The granddaddy of them all, this is one of Central Europe's most famous resorts, going back some 220 years. It's been featured in movies from *Last Holiday* to *Casino Royale.* $ *Rooms from: Kč6500* ✉ *Mírové nám. 2, Karlovy Vary* ☎ *353–109–631* 🌐 *www.pupp.cz* 🍽 *Free Breakfast*

Český Krumlov

The Jewel of Southern Bohemia

It's rare that a place not only lives up to its hype but exceeds it. Český Krumlov, the official residence of the Rožmberk (Rosenberg) family for centuries, is *the* must-see destination in Southern Bohemia, with a storybook landscape so perfect it resembles a movie set. It gets very busy with visitors, but if you stay overnight you can experience the city after the tour buses have departed, and in the evening when quiet descends, the town is twice as spellbinding. Český Krumlov's lovely looks can be put down to a castle and a river. Hrad Český Krumlov (Český Krumlov Castle) is one of the most gorgeous in the country, perched on a hill and watching over its quaint village with the Vltava River doing its picturesque winding best. The castle area offers plenty of sightseeing, and the extensive gardens are worth an hour or two. Down in the town, the medieval streets are beyond charming.

Don't Miss

Gorgeous sgraffiti facades decorate the **Hotel Růže**, a former Jesuit school. The abundant Renaissance flourishes are a result of city once being on the Bavarian-Italian trade route. Be sure to visit the parking area (really!); the view is perfect.

Stay Here

Hotel Růže. Converted from a Jesuit school, this excellent, centrally located hotel with spacious rooms is a two-minute walk from the main square. *Rooms from: Kč4157* ✉ *Horní 154* ☎ *380–772–100* 🌐 *www.hotelruze.cz* *Free Breakfast*

Getting Here

Direct buses to Český Krumlov leave Prague several times a day. The trip lasts a hair under three hours, and costs in the region of 200 Kč.

Sedlec Ossuary

A Bone-Chilling Sight

Forget all the beautiful baroque architecture in Kutná Hora. This is the reason many outside the Czech Republic have heard of (and make the trip to) the small town an hour outside of Prague. The skeletal remains of around 40,000 people have been lovingly arranged in the Kaple Všech svatých (All Saints Chapel), more commonly called the Bone Church. Look out for the chandelier, which is made with every bone in the human body, as well as the Schwarzenberg coat of arms, which includes a raven (assembled from various small bones) pecking the eye of a Turkish warrior.

Don't Miss

Definitely venture into Kutná Hora itself, if only to see the dramatically beautiful Chrám sv. Barbory. Getting to this Gothic church is nearly as pleasurable as a visit; it's about a 10-minute walk from the main square along a road lined with baroque statues, from which you can gaze at the surrounding countryside. The walk is particularly lovely in the fall, when the leaves change.

Best Restaurant

Dačický. A medieval tavern feel and big plates of Czech food make Dačický a warm, authentic experience. $ *Average main: Kč240* ✉ *Rakova 8* ☎ *603 434–367* 🌐 *www.dacicky.com*

Getting Here

A train to the main station from Prague takes about an hour. The Bone Church is a 10-minute walk from the train station, and the town of Kutná Hora is about 30 minutes by foot; there's a riverside path that takes slightly longer but is a lovely stroll in good weather.

✉ *Zámecká* 🌐 *www.sedlec.info* 🎫 *160 Kč (incl. Church of the Assumption); 300 Kč (also incl. St. Barbara's Cathedral)* ⏲ *Closed Mon. Nov.–Jan.*

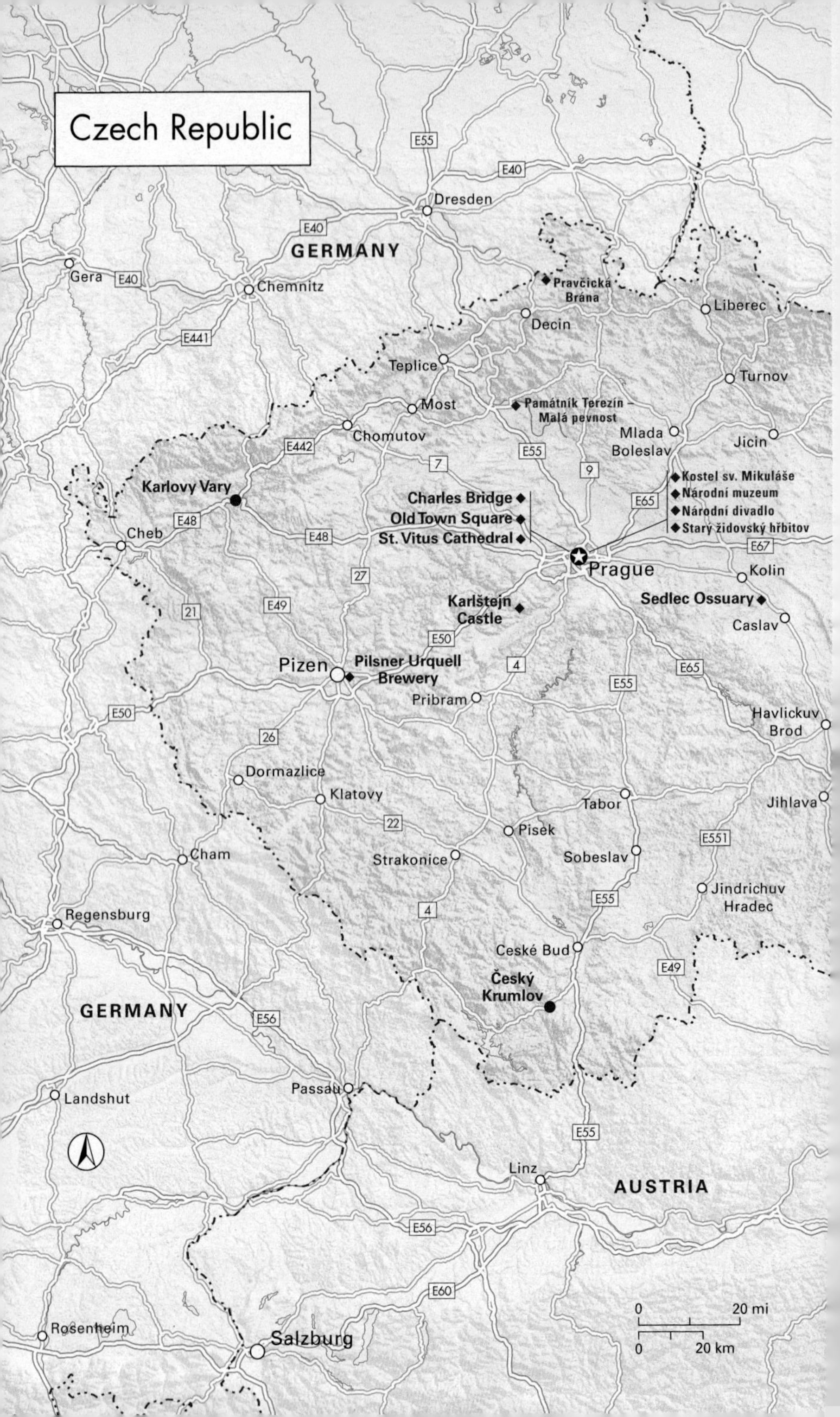
Czech Republic
GERMANY
Dresden
E55
E40
Gera
Chemnitz
E441
Pravčická Brána
Liberec
Decin
Teplice
Turnov
Most
Památník Terezín – Malá pevnost
Chomutov
Mlada Boleslav
Jicin
E442
E55
7
9
Karlovy Vary
Charles Bridge
Old Town Square
St. Vitus Cathedral
Kostel sv. Mikuláše
Národní muzeum
Národní divadlo
Starý židovský hřbitov
E65
E48
Cheb
E67
Prague
Kolin
27
Karlštejn Castle
Sedlec Ossuary
21
E49
Caslav
E50
Pizen
Pilsner Urquell Brewery
4
E65
E55
Pribram
Havlickuv Brod
26
Dormazlice
Klatovy
Tabor
Jihlava
22
Pisek
E551
Cham
Strakonice
Sobeslav
Jindrichuv Hradec
Regensburg
4
E55
Ceské Bud
E49
Český Krumlov
GERMANY
E56
Landshut
Passau
E55
Linz
AUSTRIA
E56
E60
0
20 mi
0
20 km
Rosenheim
Salzburg

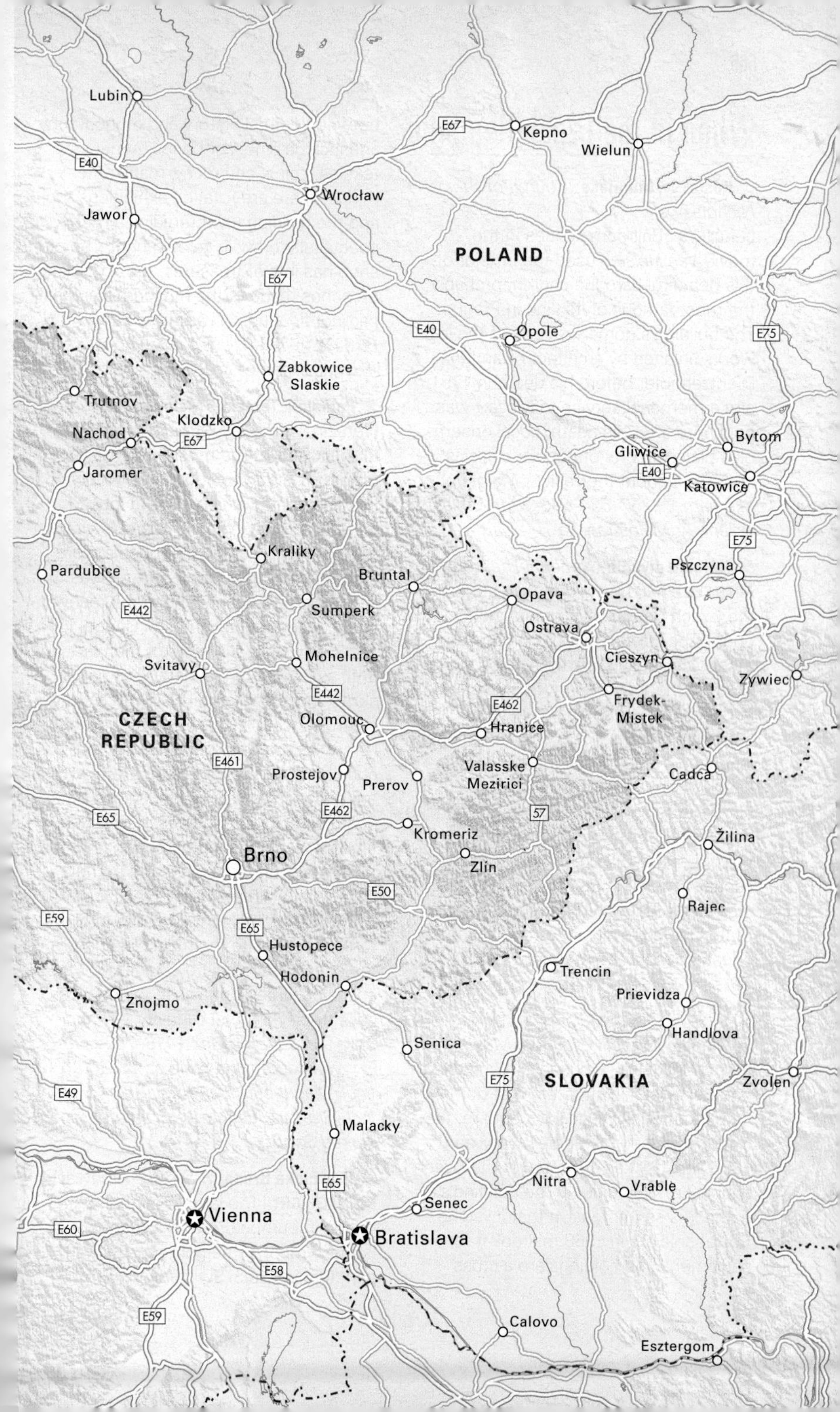

Lubin
Kepno
Wielun
E67
E40
Wrocław
Jawor
POLAND
E67
E40
Opole
E75
Zabkowice
Slaskie
Trutnov
Klodzko
Nachod
E67
Bytom
Gliwice
E40
Katowice
Jaromer
E75
Kraliky
Pszczyna
Pardubice
Bruntal
Opava
Sumperk
E442
Ostrava
Mohelnice
Cieszyn
Svitavy
Zywiec
E442
Frydek-
Mistek
E462
CZECH
REPUBLIC
Olomouc
Hranice
E461
Valasske
Mezirici
Cadca
Prostejov
Prerov
E462
57
E65
Kromeriz
Žilina
Brno
Zlin
E50
Rajec
E59
E65
Hustopece
Trencin
Hodonin
Znojmo
Prievidza
Handlova
Senica
E75
SLOVAKIA
Zvolen
E49
Malacky
E65
Nitra
Vrable
Senec
Vienna
Bratislava
E60
E58
E59
Calovo
Esztergom

When in the Czech Republic

★ **Kostel sv. Mikuláše** (*Church of St. Nicholas*)
CONCERTS | Ballroom scenes in the movie *Van Helsing* used the interior of this beautiful baroque church, probably the most famous of its kind in Prague. The building's dome was one of the last works finished by architect Kilian Ignaz Dientzenhofer before his death in 1751, and a memorial service to Mozart was held here after his death. Local ensembles play concerts of popular classics here throughout the year. ✉ *Malostranské nám.* ☎ *257–534–215* 🌐 *stnicholas.cz* Ⓜ *Line A: Malostranská.*

★ **Národní divadlo** (*National Theater*)
ARTS CENTERS | This is the main stage in the Czech Republic for drama, dance, and opera. The interior, with its ornate and etched ceilings, is worth the visit alone. Most of the theater performances are in Czech, but some operas have English supertitles, and ballet is an international language—right? Book the opera online ahead of time for fantastic discounts; you'll get to see top-quality performances in sumptuous surroundings at a snip of the price you could pay in other European capitals. The New Stage, next door, as well as the Estates Theater and Prague State Opera are all part of the National Theater system. ✉ *Národní 2* ☎ *224–901–448* 🌐 *narodni-divadlo.cz* Ⓜ *Line B: Národní třída.*

★ **Národní muzeum** (*National Museum*)
HISTORY MUSEUM | Housed in a grandiose neo-Renaissance structure that dominates the top of Wenceslas Square, the National Museum was built between 1885 and 1890 as a symbol of the Czech national revival. Indeed, the building's exterior is so impressive that invading Soviet soldiers in 1968 mistook it for parliament. The holdings are a cross between natural history and ethnography and include dinosaur bones, minerals, textiles, coins, and many, many other things. There are rotating exhibitions too, and the building itself remains a pretty spectacular draw in its own right. The gift shop has lots of treasures, too, including brooches made of the museum's original parquet flooring. ✉ *Václavské nám. 68* ☎ *224–497–111* 🌐 *nm.cz* 🎫 *250 Kč* Ⓜ *Lines A and C: Muzeum.*

★ **Památník Terezín – Malá pevnost** (*Terezín Memorial – Small Fortress*)
HISTORIC SIGHT | The most powerful aspect of Terezín is that you don't need much imagination to visualize how it looked under Nazi rule. When it was a Jewish ghetto, more than 59,000 people were crammed into this camp. Terezín was actually an exception among the many Nazi concentration camps in Central Europe. In the early years of the war—until as late as 1944—detainees had a semblance of a normal life, with limited self-rule, schools, a theater, and even a library. As the Nazi war effort soured, the conditions for the people in Terezín worsened. Transports to Auschwitz and other death camps were increased to several times a week. Above the entrance to the main courtyard stands the horribly false motto "Arbeit macht Frei" (Work Brings Freedom). At the far end of the fortress, opposite the main entrance, is the special wing built by the Nazis when space became tight. These windowless cells display a brutal captivity. ✉ *Principova alej 304, Terezín* ☎ *416–782–225* 🌐 *www.pamatnik-terezin.cz* 🎫 *210 Kč (incl. Magdeburg Barracks); 260 Kč (also incl. Ghetto Museum)* ⏲ *Crematorium closed Sat.*

★ **Pravčická Brána** (*Pravčická Archway*)
NATURE SIGHT | The largest natural rock bridge in Europe, Pravčická Archway is the symbol of the gorgeous national park that is Czech Switzerland, which

sits on the border with Germany. To reach the archway, you can either start walking from Hřensko (follow the red hiking route) or take a local bus to a stop called Tři Prameny. From here, it's a lovely and atmospheric walk up through the forest to reach the rock formation, which comes complete with a museum and restaurant called Falcon's Nest—supplies are brought in via pulley. There's also a pub where you can order fine beer in the shadow of the bridge itself. For an entrance fee, you can scramble around nearby rock formations, which have a similarly alien appeal, for a better vantage point. ✉ *Hrensko* 🌐 *www.pbrana.cz* 🎫 *95 Kč* ⏲ *Closed weekdays Nov.–Mar.*

★ **Starý židovský hřbitov** (*Old Jewish Cemetery*)
CEMETERY | An unforgettable sight, this cemetery is where all Jews living in Prague from the 15th century to 1787 were laid to rest. The lack of any space in the tiny ghetto forced graves to be piled on top of one another. Tilted at crazy angles, the 12,000 visible tombstones are but a fraction of thousands more buried below. Walk the path amid the gravestones; the relief symbols you see represent the names and professions of the deceased. The oldest marked grave belongs to the poet Avigdor Kara, who died in 1439; the original tombstone can be seen in the Maisel Synagogue. The best-known marker belongs to Jehuda ben Bezalel, the famed Rabbi Loew (died 1609), a chief rabbi of Prague and a profound scholar, credited with creating the mythical golem. ✉ *Široká 3* ✣ *Entrance through Pinkas Synagogue* ☎ *222–749–211* 🌐 *jewishmuseum.cz* 🎫 *Jewish Museum combination ticket 350 Kč (excl. Old-New Synagogue) or 500 Kč (incl. Old-New Synagogue)* ⏲ *Closed Sat. and Jewish holidays* Ⓜ *Line A: Staroměstská.*

Where to Eat and Drink

★ **Café Savoy**
$$ | CZECH | One of the best of Prague's traditional turn-of-the-century-style grand cafés, the Savoy is popular day and night for its brunches, coffees, Czech classics, and pastries. In particular, try the *větrník*, a Czech classic made of choux pastry with cream and caramel. **Known for:** lavish interior; warm and efficient staff; long lines. $ *Average main: Kč150* ✉ *Vítězná 5* ☎ *731–136–144* 🌐 *cafesavoy.ambi.cz* Ⓜ *Tram 1, 9, 20, 22, 23, 25, 97, 98, or 99 to Újezd.*

★ **La Degustation Bohême Bourgeoise**
$$$$ | ECLECTIC | One of Prague's two Michelin star holders is this elegant tasting room, where diners are taken on a superlative culinary adventure via a Czech-inspired tasting menu over an extended evening. The menu roves around Czech and European cuisine playfully and stylishly, including classic local specialties with a twist, like pork belly, cabbage, and mustard or a dessert of cream, blueberry, and basil. **Known for:** probably Prague's best food and service; playful and inventive takes on classic dishes; wine-paired tasting menu. $ *Average main: Kč2450* ✉ *Haštalská 18* ☎ *222–311–234* 🌐 *ladegustation.cz* Ⓜ *Line A: Staroměstská.*

Rango
$$ | MEDITERRANEAN | Part of a hotel of the same name, the interior of Rango is a mash-up of medieval, baroque, and modern style—think Gothic arched ceilings and '60s modern light fixtures. Similarly, the cuisine ranges from Italy to Greece; in addition to panini, they serve excellent pasta dishes, pizzas, and grilled meat. **Known for:** historical space; friendly and quick service; superior pizza and pasta. $ *Average main: Kč270* ✉ *Pražská 10, Plzen* ☎ *377–329–969* 🌐 *www.rango.cz.*

★ **Terasa U Zlaté studně**
$$$$ | **INTERNATIONAL** | On top of the boutique Golden Well Hotel, lunch or dinner, either inside or on the terrace of this Michelin-rated restaurant overlooking the city's rooftops, is a delicious experience that more than lives up to the views and prices. The menu runs the gamut from the full degustation (3,400 Kč) to more reasonably priced à **Known for:** exceptional cooking of an inventive international menu; among the best views in Prague; feeling of exclusivity. *Average main: Kč1000 ✉ Golden Well Hotel, U Zlaté studně 4 ☎ 257–533–322 🌐 terasauzlatestudne.cz Ⓜ Line A: Malostranská.*

Cool Places to Stay

★ **Alchymist Grand Hotel and Spa**
$$$ | **HOTEL** | A baroque fever dream of Prague masterminded by an Italian developer, the Alchymist doesn't go the understated route. **Pros:** astonishing renovation of a 16th-century building; afternoon wine tastings; central yet tucked away. **Cons:** steep uphill walk from the tram; loud a/c; some rooms and suites in need of a refresh. *Rooms from: Kč5500 ✉ Tržiště 19 ☎ 257–286–011 🌐 alchymisthotel.com 46 rooms Free Breakfast Ⓜ Line A: Malostranská plus Tram 12, 20, or 22 to Malostranské náměstí.*

★ **Augustine, a Luxury Collection Hotel, Prague**
$$$$ | **HOTEL** | There's plenty of competition in Prague's high-end hotel market, but the Augustine—now part of Marriott's Luxury Collection—continues to come out on top. **Pros:** impeccable service and tranquil feel; clever design, with hidden garden spaces; impressive spa and restaurant. **Cons:** breakfast not always included; sometimes noisy wood floors; no swimming pool. *Rooms from: Kč10000 ✉ Letenská 12 ☎ 266–112–234 🌐 marriott.com 101 rooms No Meals Ⓜ Line A: Malostranská.*

Falkensteiner Spa Resort Marienbad
$$$$ | **HOTEL** | Formerly the Grand Spa Marienbad, this Austrian-owned hotel is made up of three interconnected buildings and boasts the most rooms and the biggest wellness center in Mariánské Lázně. **Pros:** huge spa; excellent spa services; sleek rooms. **Cons:** officious staff; expensive; overly Teutonic vibe. *Rooms from: Kč7100 ✉ Ruska 123, Mariánské Lázne ☎ 354–929–399 🌐 www.falkensteiner.com/en/spa-resort-marianske-lazne 164 rooms Free Breakfast.*

★ **Tři Lilie**
$$$ | **HOTEL** | "Three Lilies" is thoroughly elegant, from its brasserie to its guest rooms, some of which have balconies with French doors. **Pros:** glorious a/c; rooms with balconies; extremely efficient service. **Cons:** no restaurant in the hotel (just breakfast); if you don't want spa services, much of its appeal is lost; guests report issues with Wi-Fi. *Rooms from: Kč2500 ✉ Národní 3, Františkovy Lázne ☎ 354–208–900 🌐 www.trililie.cz 31 rooms Free Breakfast.*

Hungary

Budapest, an old-world city with a throbbing urban pulse, is a must-stop on any trip to Central Europe. Szentendre and Eger have their own charms, including majestic hilltop castles and cobblestone streets winding among lovely Baroque buildings. All this, and the generosity of the Magyar soul, sustains visitors to this land of vital spirit and beauty.

Hungary sits at the crossroads of Central Europe, having retained its own identity by absorbing countless invasions and foreign occupations. Its industrious, resilient people have a history of brave but unfortunate uprisings: against the Ottomans in the 17th century, the Habsburgs in 1848, and the Soviet Union in 1956. With the withdrawal of the last Soviet soldiers from Hungarian soil in 1991, Hungary embarked on a decade of sweeping changes.

Adjusting to a free-market economy has not been easy sailing, but Hungary has regained self-determination and a chance to rebuild an economy devastated by years of Communist misrule. Hungary joined NATO in 1999, and the country joined the European Union (EU) in May 2004, though it has not yet adopted the euro as its official currency. It has been a rollercoaster of good times and bad ever since. Two rivers cross the country: the famous Duna (Danube) flows from the west through Budapest on its way to the southern frontier, and the smaller Tisza flows from the northeast across the Nagyalföld (Great Plain). What Hungary lacks in size, it makes up for in beauty and charm. Hungarians are known for their hospitality.

Although the unusual and difficult language is anything but a quick study, English is fast becoming the second language of Hungary, even superseding German. But what all Hungarians share is a deep love of music, and the calendar is studded with it.

Széchenyi Fürdő

Budapest's Best Thermal Bath

Széchenyi Fürdő, the largest medicinal bathing complex in Europe, is housed in a beautiful neo-Baroque building in the middle of City Park. There are several thermal pools indoors as well as two outdoor pools, which remain open even in winter when dense steam hangs thick over the hot water's surface—you can barely make out the figures of elderly men, submerged shoulder deep, crowded around waterproof chessboards. To use the baths, you pay a standard price (unless you get a doctor's prescription, in which case entry is free), plus a small surcharge if you prefer having a private changing cabin instead of a locker. Facilities include medical and underwater massage treatments, carbonated bath treatments, and mud wraps. A great way to sweat away last night's *pálinka* (fruit brandy).

Don't Miss

It might seem somewhat counter-intuitive, but the famous Szechenyi Baths have developed a reputation for being a major party place, which is no small feat in a party-mad city like Budapest. Spa parties (okay, spa-rties) take place most Saturdays throughout the year and are truly dizzying experiences. Tickets cost €59 (Ft25,000), and parties usually begin at 9:30 pm and last until 2 am. To take photos, a permit is required, but why are you taking your phone into a thermal bath anyway?

✉ *Állatkerti körút 9–11, Budapest* ☎ *13–633–210 www.szechenyibath.hu* 🎫 *Weekdays 7100ft (with locker usage), weekends 8200ft (with locker usage)*

Sziget Festival

One of Europe's Biggest and Best Festivals

Mighty oaks from little acorns grow. That is the saying, right? The Sziget Festival is the perfect example, having come a long way from its humble beginnings in 1993. That small gathering has grown to a festival attracting around half a million visitors annually; what was once a handful of stages has become 60 stages showcasing more than 1,000 performances over a week-long run in August, when Obudai Island in Budapest becomes the center of the European festival scene. And Sziget is not limited to music. There's a circus, theater, amusement park, and museum quarter, and the festival encompasses all genres and art forms, including a focus on sustainability and education.

Don't Miss

This is a music festival at heart, so be sure to single out performances that you don't want to miss. Some of the biggest names in music have made the Sziget stage their own over the years, so check out the line-up as early as possible and get circling those names.

Getting Here

During the festival, free bike storage and repair facilities are offered on the festival grounds, and a ferry shuttles between the festival and Jászai Mari Square, and there are also bus and car options.

✉ *Óbudai-sziget, Május 9. park* 🌐 *szigetfestival.com* 🎫 *Festival pass from €240*

Lake Balaton

Central Europe's Largest Lake

Surrounded by mysterious mountains and wonderful wineries, it is no surprise that Central Europe's largest lake was once a magnet for wealthy Hungarians in search of respite. Those days are over, and Lake Balaton is now a beloved destination for locals and visitors of all means. Stretching almost 80 km (50 miles) and ringed by some marvelous resorts, Balaton is a year-round lake that is perfect for bathing (it is one of the most shallow large bodies of water in Europe) and swimming in summer, or ice-fishing and skating in winter (if the weather is sufficiently cold, of course). The gorgeous Szigliget Fortress stands proud on the lake's northern shore, and the vast Benedictine Abbey in nearby Tihany is an absolute must. Balaton is also home to some gorgeous lake caves, a subterranean network of mysteries that have developed alongside the growing number of visitors; these are the first electrified caves in Hungary.

Don't Miss

Lake Balaton is busy but serene throughout the year. But for four days in the middle of summer, when Balaton Sound festival takes over the southern bank of the lake, around 100,000 electronic music devotees make the pilgrimage to see some of the biggest names in the genre, with Massive Attack, Kraftwerk, Moby, and The Prodigy among past headliners.

Getting Here

Several trains leave Budapest daily. For the north bank, head to Balatonfüred, while Siofok is the hub on the south.

Anna Grand. The hotel is Balatonfüred's grandest accommodation option. $ *Rooms from: 67,000 HUF* ✉ *Gyógy Tér 1, Balatonfüred* ☎ *87/581–200* 🌐 *www.annagrandhotel.hu*

Visegrád Citadel

A Castle with Stunning Views over the Danube Bend

Crowning the top of a 1,148-foot hill, the dramatic Fellegvár was built in the 13th century and served as the seat of Hungarian kings in the early 14th century. A *panoptikum* (akin to slide projection) show portraying the era of the kings is included with admission. The breathtaking views of the Danube Bend below are ample reward for the strenuous 40-minute hike up. Then again, you can always drive up the hill. The Citadel is packed with interesting tidbits and tangible history, but there is something about those views that really takes the biscuit. Make sure the camera is fully charged.

Don't Miss

Be sure to check out the Holy Crown of the Hungarian Kingdom while here, although be aware that it isn't the original. That was swiped by a chambermaid back in 1440 and smuggled out of the citadel in a red velvet pillow. If anything, that story makes the replica even more fascinating. There is also an exceptional historical exhibition telling the storied tale of this marvelous citadel.

Getting Here

Visegrád is easily accessible from Budapest, with several trains leaving daily and stopping at Nagymaros-Visegrád (the citadel is just across the river from the station). The journey takes approximately 45 minutes. The drive to Visegrád is a simple 50-minute one along Route 11.

✉ *Várhegy, Visegrád 2025* ☎ *26–398–101* 🌐 *www.visitvisegrad.hu* 🎫 *2700ft, parking 300ft* 🕒 *Closed weekdays Jan. and Feb.*

Eger

An Oenophile's Dream in Northern Hungary

Surrounded by vineyards and more than 175 of Hungary's historic monuments—a figure surpassed only by Budapest and Sopron—the picture-book Baroque city of Eger is ripe for exploration. The city, which lies in a fertile valley between the Mátra Mountains and their eastern neighbor, the Bükk range, has borne witness to much history, heartbreak, and glory. One of Hungary's great legends tells of the women of Eger pouring hot pitch onto the heads of the Ottomans as they attempted to scale the castle walls (the event is depicted in a famous painting now in the National Gallery in Budapest). Today, restored Baroque and Rococo buildings line Eger's cobblestone streets, making for excellent strolling and sightseeing. Wherever you wander, make a point of peeking into open courtyards, where you may find otherwise hidden architectural gems.

Don't Miss

Eger wine is renowned beyond Hungary. The best-known variety is Egri Bikavér (Bull's Blood of Eger), a full-bodied red wine. Other outstanding vintages are the Medoc Noir, a dark red dessert wine; Leányka, a delightful dry white; and the sweeter white Muskotály. The place to sample them is the Szépasszony-völgy (Valley of the Beautiful Women), a vineyard area on the southwestern edge of Eger's city limits. More than 200 small wine cellars (some literal holes-in-the-wall) stand open and inviting in warm weather, and a few are open in winter, too.

Getting Here

Eger is a 90-minute drive north of Budapest. The bus and train are also an option, with multiple departures daily from Keleti station in Budapest.

Eger Tourism. 🌐 *visiteger.com*

Hortobágy National Park

Hungary's Great Plain

The largest protected area in the country, Hortobágy National Park is the pride of the nation. Located just a short drive from Debrecen, the park is a magnificent steppe packed with grazing animals, sweeping grasslands, swamps, lakes, floodplain forests, migrating birds, and everything else one would expect from a vast national park in the heart of the Great Plain. The range of experiences available is seemingly endless, from embracing shepherd life to animal-watching and more, including a magical star walk in the evening. A steppe safari is a must, where visitors can see buffalo, pelicans, vultures, wolves, wild horses, and so much more. Hortobágy National Park is a significant stop on the migration route for countless species of birds, so bust out the binoculars when here.

Don't Miss

The most iconic symbol of Hortobágy National Park is the Nine-arched bridge, a self-explanatory structure packed with history and heritage. The bridge was completed in 1833 (a rickety wooden structure stood here before then) and spans a whopping 167 meters, and legend has it the bricks used were bound by mortar made with sand wine. The excellent Hortobágy Inn and fascinating Herdsmen Museum are located by the bridge, so be sure to check out both of those once you've filled up the photo library.

Getting Here

Debrecen is a three-hour train trip from Budapest. Hortobágy National Park is a simple 40-minute drive west of Debrecen, and there are also direct buses from the city to Hortobágy.

✉ *Sumen u. 2, Debrecen* 4024 ☎ 52–529–920 🌐 *www.hnp.hu* 🎫 *2000ft*

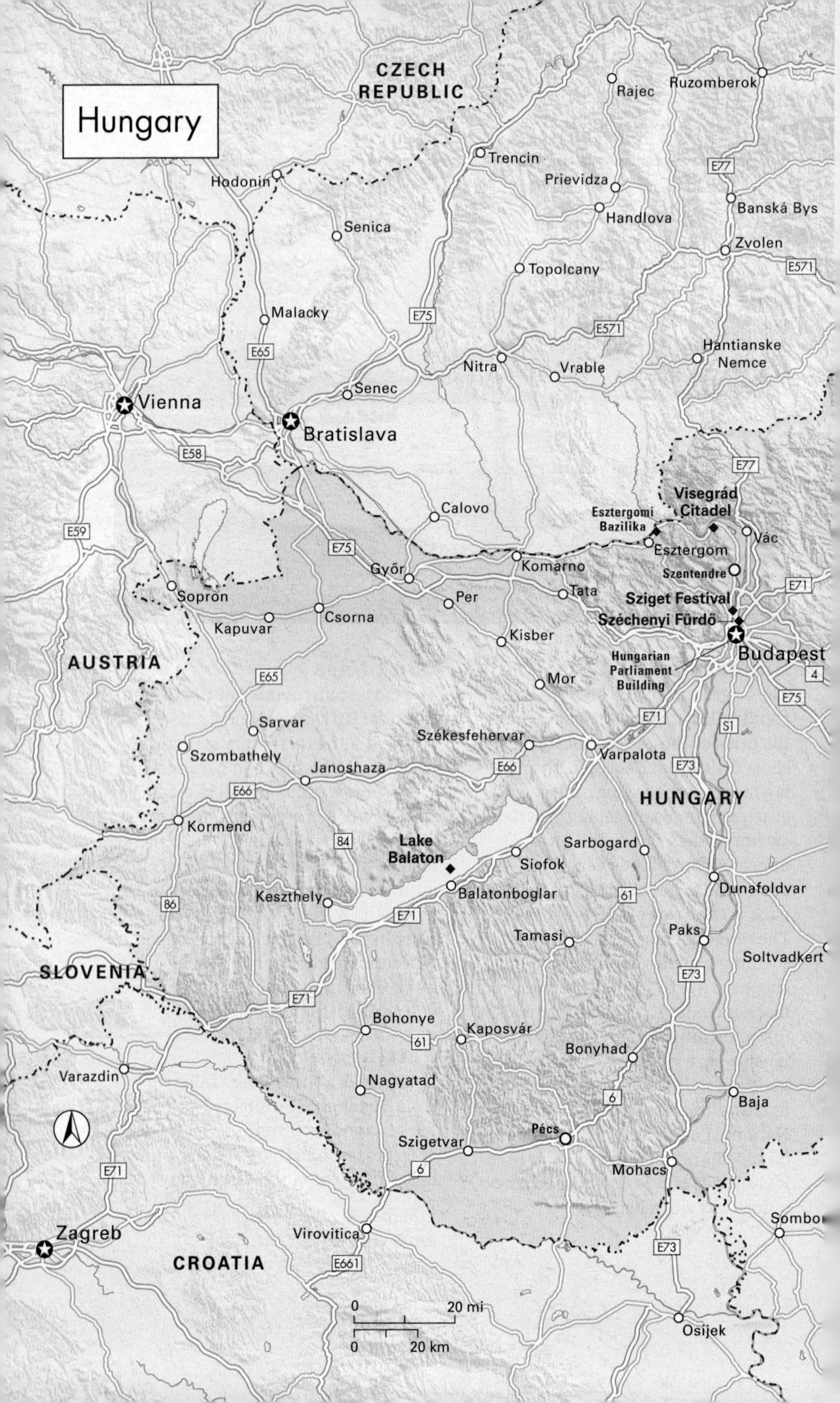
Hungary
CZECH REPUBLIC
AUSTRIA
SLOVENIA
CROATIA
HUNGARY
Rajec
Ruzomberok
Trencin
Hodonin
Prievidza
Handlova
Banská Bys
Zvolen
Senica
Topolcany
Malacky
Nitra
Vrable
Hantianske Nemce
Senec
Vienna
Bratislava
Calovo
Visegrád Citadel
Esztergomi Bazilika
Esztergom
Vác
Szentendre
Győr
Komarno
Tata
Sziget Festival
Széchenyi Fürdő
Budapest
Hungarian Parliament Building
Sopron
Kapuvar
Csorna
Per
Kisber
Mor
Sarvar
Székesfehervar
Varpalota
Szombathely
Janoshaza
Kormend
Lake Balaton
Sarbogard
Siofok
Balatonboglar
Keszthely
Dunafoldvar
Tamasi
Paks
Soltvadkert
Bohonye
Kaposvár
Bonyhad
Varazdin
Nagyatad
Baja
Pécs
Szigetvar
Mohacs
Zagreb
Virovitica
Sombor
Osijek
E77
E571
E75
E65
E58
E59
E71
E66
E73
S1
4
84
86
61
6
E661
0
20 mi
20 km

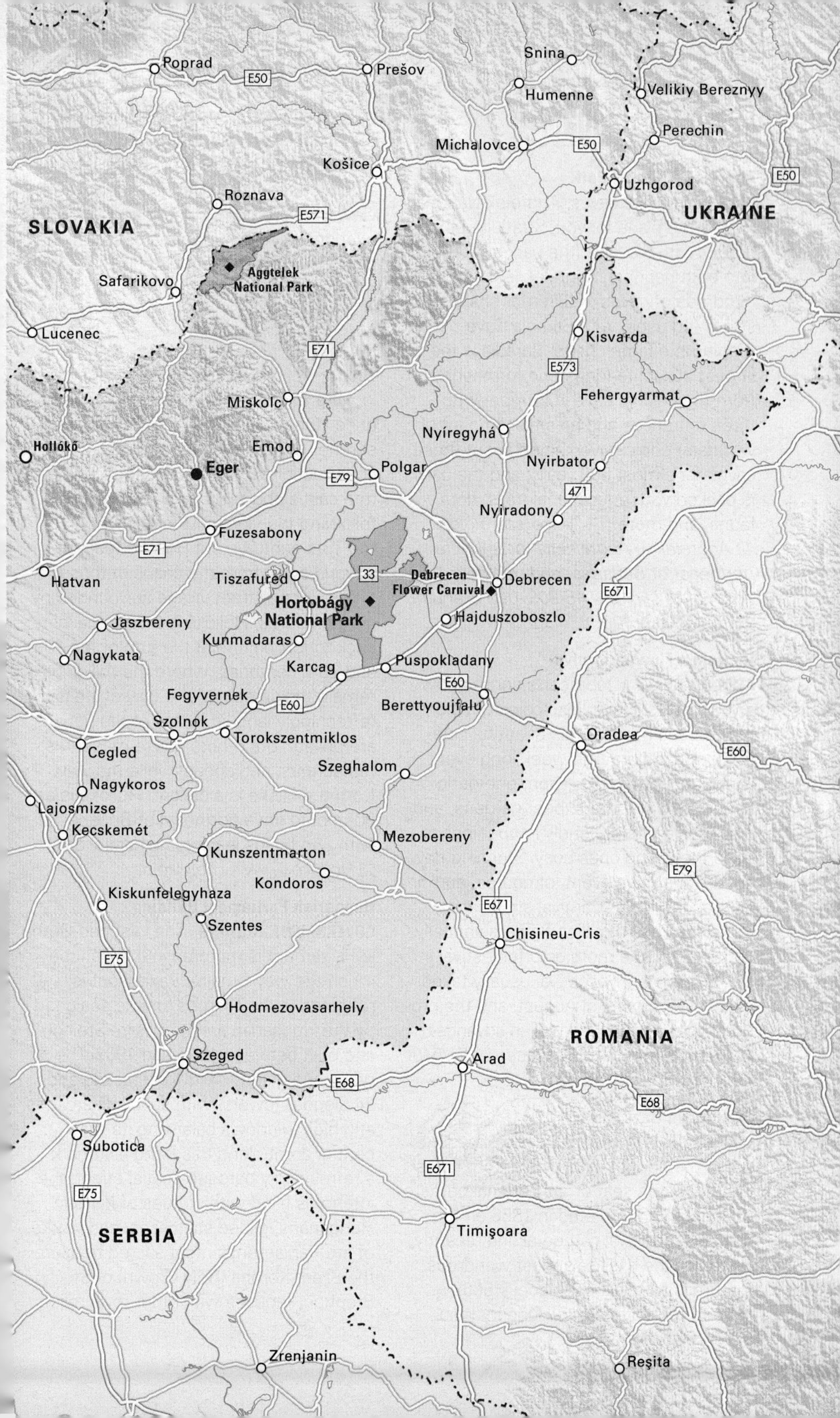

Poprad
Prešov
E50
Snina
Humenne
Velikiy Bereznyy
Perechin
Michalovce
E50
Košice
E50
Uzhgorod
UKRAINE
Roznava
E571
SLOVAKIA
Aggtelek
National Park
Safarikovo
Lucenec
E71
Kisvarda
E573
Fehergyarmat
Miskolc
Nyíregyhá
Hollókő
Emod
Nyirbator
Eger
E79
Polgar
471
Nyiradony
Fuzesabony
E71
Hatvan
Tiszafured
33
Debrecen
Flower Carnival
Debrecen
E671
Hortobágy
National Park
Hajduszoboszlo
Jaszbereny
Kunmadaras
Nagykata
Karcag
Puspokladany
E60
Fegyvernek
E60
Berettyoujfalu
Szolnok
Torokszentmiklos
Oradea
E60
Cegled
Szeghalom
Nagykoros
Lajosmizse
Kecskemét
Mezobereny
Kunszentmarton
Kondoros
E79
Kiskunfelegyhaza
E671
Szentes
Chisineu-Cris
E75
Hodmezovasarhely
ROMANIA
Szeged
Arad
E68
E68
Subotica
E671
E75
Timişoara
SERBIA
Zrenjanin
Reşita

When in Hungary

Aggtelek National Park

CAVE | If you like caves, Aggtelek National Park is the place for you. Straddling the border with Slovakia (the park stretches into both nations), Aggtelek is home to hundreds of caves of different shapes, sizes, and uses, with Baradla Cave topping the fame charts. Baradla is the largest stalactite (dripstone formations from the ceiling) cave in Europe, with three entrances and no small amount of wonder. People have known about these caves for almost 500 years, and the park is packed with educational trails, flora, fauna, and more. ✉ *Tengerszem oldal 1., Aggtelek* ✈ *Aggtelek is three hours northeast of Budapest and one hour north of Miskolc.* ☎ *48/503–003* 🌐 *anp.hu* 🎫 *Tours from 4000ft.*

Debrecen Flower Carnival

ARTS FESTIVALS | Debrecen's annual Flower Carnival is a joyful explosion of color, but there is more to this beautiful celebration than flora. The week-long event is packed with events, from energetic concerts to craft fairs, beer gardens, and a schedule of kid-friendly happenings to keep the young ones busy. Stunning flowers are the main event, of course, and Debrecen Flower Carnival showcases more than half a million flowers annually. You won't find a more colorful festival in all of Hungary. The festival usually takes place over a week in August, and the program gets announced well in advance. ✉ *Hunyadi utca 1–3, Debrecen* ☎ *52/518-400* 🌐 *visitdebrecen.com.*

Esztergomi Bazilika

CHURCH | This immense basilica, the largest in the country and visible from miles around, is the seat of the cardinal primate of Hungary. Completed in 1856 on the site of a medieval cathedral and recently restored, the basilica's most wondrous feature is the Bakócz Chapel (1506). Named for a primate of Hungary who only narrowly missed becoming pope, the chapel—on your left as you enter—is the most beautiful work of Renaissance architecture in all of Hungary. For a great view of Esztergom, climb the long, winding staircase up to the observation platform in the cathedral's cupola. ✉ *Szent István tér 1, Esztergom* ☎ *33/402–354* 🌐 *www.bazilika-esztergom.hu* 🎫 *1,200ft.*

Hollókő

TOWN | Hollókő is a must for anyone looking to step back in time and experience Hungarian folk culture at its most serene. Okay, the circumstances of its construction weren't exactly peaceful (the castle above the village was built following the violent Mongol invasion of the 13th century), but Hollókő today is a world away from the chaos of those times. A one-street village surrounded by gorgeous hills, Hollókő is a time machine back to folk culture at the turn of the 19th and 20th centuries, where the buildings remain the same and the way of life is refreshingly languid. Many of the houses are private, but others house museums, restaurants, and shops, while the view from the castle is a delight. Hollókő is a 90-minute drive northeast of Budapest, with two buses leaving the capital daily. ✉ *Hollóko* 🌐 *www.holloko.hu.*

Hungarian Parliament Building

GOVERNMENT BUILDING | The vast neo-Gothic Parliament is mirrored in the Danube much the way Britain's Parliament is reflected in the Thames. It was designed by the Hungarian architect Imre Steindl and built between 1885 and 1902. The grace and dignity of its long facade and 24 slender towers, with spacious arcades and high windows balancing its vast central dome, lend this living landmark a refreshingly baroque spatial effect; the interior is filled with statues of historic Hungarians, gilded staircases, and works of art. Parliament's most sacred treasure, the Szent Korona (Holy Crown) of St. Stephen, reposes with other royal relics under the cupola. The only way you can visit the newly renovated Parliament and see the crown is on one of the daily tours, which depart from a visitor center next door. The building is closed to the public when the legislature is in session. ✉ *Kossuth Lajos tér 1-3* ☎ *1/441-4000* ✉ *tourist.office@parlament.hu* 🎫 *3000ft.*

Pécs

TOWN | First-time visitors are often surprised that this city in the Mecsek Hills, about 100 miles southwest of Budapest, packs such a cultural punch. They shouldn't be. After all, Pécs has been around for 2,000 years and has the sights to prove it. Its religious monuments run the gamut, from an Early Christian mausoleum to a sublime Neo-Classical basilica, with a pair of 16th-century mosques and a grand 19th-century synagogue thrown in for good measure. Pécs has been a university center since 1367, and that adds to its cachet, enabling the city to support an arts community more vibrant than you'd otherwise expect in a city of only 160,000 inhabitants. Along with museums devoted to native sons—like Vilmos Zsolnay, whose Art Nouveau tiles adorn local roofs and whose porcelain factory still operates here—there's a fine selection of private galleries featuring up-and-coming artists. Moreover, the city's ballet company and symphony orchestra have international reputations. ✉ *Pécs* 🌐 *visithungary.com/category/pecs-region.*

Szentendre

TOWN | This is the highlight of the Danube Bend, a romantic, lively little town with a flourishing artists' colony. With its profusion of enchanting church steeples, colorful Baroque houses, and winding, narrow cobblestone streets, it's no wonder Szentendre attracts swarms of visitors, tripling its population in peak season. Szentendre was first settled by Serbs and Greeks fleeing the advancing Turks in the 16th and 17th centuries. They built houses and churches in their own style—rich in reds and blues seldom seen elsewhere in Hungary. ✉ *Szentendre* 🌐 *iranyszentendre.hu.*

Where to Eat and Drink

★ Aranysárkány

$$$ | EASTERN EUROPEAN | A favorite of early-20th-century Hungarian writer Frigyes Karinthy, the Golden Dragon restaurant has been welcoming locals and tourists for decades. Set within a small, sloped-roof house, it's known for its charming Hungarian decor and its meat- and fish-heavy menu; highlights include the *velős pirítós* (bone marrow on toast), *sárkányerøleves* (dragon's bouillon) with quail eggs, and *mézes-mázas libasteak* (honey-glazed goose steak). **Known for:** serves international cuisine (not, as the name suggests, Chinese food); extensive wine list with many Hungarian choices; reservations a must in summer. 💲 *Average main: HUF6,100* ✉ *Alkotmány utca 1/a, Szentendre* ☎ *26/301–479* 🌐 *www.aranysarkany.hu* 🕒 *Closed Mon.*

Borkonyha Winekitchen

$$$$ | HUNGARIAN | Not far from the Basilica, Borkonyha is a restaurant where Hungarian-influenced dishes take on new life, and there seems to be a wine pairing for everything on the menu. The six-course degustation menu is a roller coaster of flavors for all tastes, making the most of Hungary's wide range of ingredients by sourcing only the best. **Known for:** foie gras; all-Hungarian wine list; seasonally changing menus. 💲 *Average main: Ft10000* ✉ *Sas u 3* ☎ *12/660–835* 🌐 *borkonyha.hu* 🕒 *Closed Sun. No lunch weekdays.*

Gettó Gulyás

$$ | HUNGARIAN | If you are looking for the Hungarian national dish, this modest restaurant in the old Jewish quarter should be your first port of call. Gulyás (i.e., "goulash"), is a hearty soup that originated in Hungary as a filling meal prepared by herdsmen. **Known for:** főzelék vegetable stews (change seasonally); chicken and veal paptrikash; reservations essential. *Average main: Ft4040* ✉ *Wesselényi u. 18, Budapest* ☎ *20/376–4480* 🌐 *www.facebook.com/gettogulyas/.*

Hímesudvar Winery
WINE BARS | Sampling the famous wines of the Tokaj region is a must when in Hungary, so why not head into the heart of Tokaj itself and do just that? Smack-bang in the center of town, Hímesudvar is a charming winery with more than 30 years of expertise to its name, making it the perfect place to drop in and sample a glass or three. Checking out the cellar is free, but plumping out for an in-depth tour of the entire vineyard (19,900ft) is highly recommended. The building itself originates from the 16th century and has plenty of stories to tell. ✉ *Bem József u. 2, Tokaj* ☎ *47/352–416* 🌐 *www.himesudvar.hu.*

★ **Szimpla Kert** (*Szimpla Garden*)
The oldest and best-known of Budapest's uniquely Hungarian romkerts, Szimpla Kert has won various international awards for its wild, exuberant, grungy style, and set the bar for all the ruin bars to follow in its footsteps. Built inside a former stove factory, this maze of dark rooms, eclectic furnishings, local art, and crazy light installations attracts a raucous crowd of locals and tourists working their way through the night with wild abandon. Expect a noisy, lively night here with the occasional patron's dog darting here and there between the tables while its owner sips on a hookah (available to rent). Visit by day to get a better feel for the decor, although you should expect to be joined by a steady stream of camera-toting tour groups as this is one of the city's top attractions. Szimpla also hosts a weekly farmers' market featuring all-natural products on Sunday from 9 am to 2 pm, runs an antique shop next door, and rents bikes. ✉ *Kazinczy utca 14, Jewish Quarter* ☎ *20/261–8669* 🌐 *www.en.szimpla.hu* Ⓜ *M2: Astoria.*

Cool Places to Stay

★ **Aria Hotel Budapest**
$$$$ | **HOTEL** | Five-star luxury hotel Aria's music theme starts at the piano footpath at the entrance and extends past the space-age piano, to the subterranean Harmony Spa, throughout the hotel, and to the sky bar. **Pros:** unique music-themed rooms; complimentary wine-and-cheese afternoons; rooftop bar with great views of St. Stephen's Basilica. **Cons:** no views from rooms; small gym; some rooms are nicer than others. *Rooms from: Ft171,640* ✉ *Hercegprímás utca 5, Parliament* ☎ *1/445–4055* 🌐 *www.ariahotelbudapest.com* *49 rooms* *Free Breakfast.*

★ **Corinthia Hotel**
$$$$ | **HOTEL** | The Corinthia first opened as the luxurious Grand Royal Hotel in time for the Magyar Millennium in 1896, and, despite being destroyed during Hungary's 1956 revolution, it's just as luxurious today. **Pros:** opulent setting without a break-the-bank price; amazing spa and spa package deals; great restaurants. **Cons:** may be too big and too formal for some; non-spa packages don't offer the same value for money; service can be inconsistent. *Rooms from: Ft100,210* ✉ *Erzsébet körút 43–49, Jewish Quarter* ☎ *1/479–4000* 🌐 *www.corinthia.com* *440 rooms* *No Meals* Ⓜ *M1: Oktogon, Blaha Lujza tér; tram 4, 6 to Király utca.*

Matild Palace

$$$$ | **HOTEL** | Built by Princess Marie Clotilde of Saxe-Coburg and Gotha during La Belle Époque, this grand old building is now home to one of the city's most elegant luxury hotels, complete with a dizzying array of drinking and dining options. **Pros:** elegant rooms and sumptuous suites; unique bathrooms inspired by thermal baths; vast rooftop bar open year-round. **Cons:** different room styles means an odd mix of guests; situated on a busy main road; recently opened so still finding its feet. *Rooms from: HUF75,000* *Váci utca 36, Belváros* *1/550–5000* *www.marriott.com* *130 rooms* *No Meals* *M3: Ferenciek tere.*

Mystery Hotel

$$$ | **HOTEL** | Originally designed as a 19th-century Freemasons lodge, the gorgeously picturesque Mystery Hotel, which opened in 2019, is proof that Insta-worthy hotels don't need to be met with eye-rolls. **Pros:** attrractively designed rooms; beautifully vaulted central hall; popular rooftop terrace bar. **Cons:** very small sauna in spa; standard rooms are on the small side and noisy (if on the train station side); average breakfast is an expensive addition. *Rooms from: €140* *Podmaniczky u. 45, Budapest* *1/616–6000* *www.mysteryhotelbudapest.com* *82 rooms* *No Meals.*

Poland

Poland can claim several superlatives—including the world's biggest medieval town square, largest gothic brick castle, and probably the best vodka, to name just a few. From tourist hotspots like Krakow and Warsaw to less-visited areas like the Mazury Lakes, the country has myriad attractions. And if that's not enough to land your time, then the Central European country's year-round appeal surely will.

This is a place where four distinct seasons fill itineraries with soul-enriching experiences, like watching ancient Easter traditions celebrated while the world turns green in the spring; whiling away the hours in a medieval town square or at the beach in summer; taking to the mountains to watch the colors change in the fall; or enjoying a well-deserved mulled wine after a day's skiing in the winter.The setting for all these activities is impressive indeed, from the belt of silver sands fringed by fragrant pines on the Baltic shore, all the way up to the sharp granite peaks of the Tatra mountains. Countless lakes, vast forests, and picturesque rolling plains filled with unspoiled nature are the pride of the country — nearly 40% of the land is covered by protected areas, including some special protection zones designated by the European Union.And yet there is much more to Poland than great landscapes. What most attracts visitors is the wealth of culture and history, with important treasures of art and architecture, many of them with UNESCO World Heritage status. It's not just churches and castles either: historic sites range from prehistoric settlements to World War II fortifications. In addition to time-weathered monuments and works of art in every style of the last millennium, you'll find contemporary art alive and kicking in Poland's vibrant cities. Famous towns with character include dreamlike, medieval Kraków, the old Hanseatic port of Gdańsk, the ever-changing capital of Warsaw, and many more dynamic urban centers across the country.

Wawel Hill

Kraków's Royal Capstone

Wawel Hill dominates the old part of Kraków, and an entire day could be spent exploring its every corner. During the 8th century, it was topped with a tribal stronghold. In the 10th century, the first royal residence was constructed, and in the 14th century, a cathedral was built (consecrated in 1364). Little room for expansion has secured the structures' preservation, though a few Renaissance- and baroque-era chapels were constructed around the existing cathedral. Most noteworthy is the Kaplica Zygmuntowska (Sigismund Chapel), built in the 1520s by Florentine architect Bartolomeo Berrecci—widely considered the finest Renaissance chapel north of the Alps.

Don't Miss

The current Royal Castle, containing important works of Polish art, dates from the early 16th century. King Sigismund the Old brought artists and craftsmen from Italy to create it, and despite baroque reconstruction after a fire in the late 16th century, several sections of the original Renaissance castle endure, including the beautiful arcaded courtyard. It wasn't just the fire that threatened it—it narrowly escaped destruction in 1945, when Nazis almost demolished it as a parting shot.

Wawel Cathedral. ✉ *Wawel Hill* 🌐 *www.katedra-wawelska.pl* 🎫 *zł 22 Wawel*

Zamek Królewski (Royal Castle). ✉ *Wawel Hill* 🌐 *www.wawel.krakow.pl* 🎫 *From zł 5, but each exhibit or touring option is ticketed separately Wawel*

Nowa Huta

A Model Socialist Town

A story is often told that when Fidel Castro visited Kraków, he refused to see the famous royal castle and the largest medieval square in Europe: "Take me to the steelworks," he commanded instead. Although we don't propose to follow the Comandante's example to the letter, a visit to Nowa Huta is definitely worth your while. You'll feel the change not just in the sweeping scale of urban planning but also in the spirit of the place. The model socialist town was created in the 1950s to house workers at a giant steel factory. Its ideological heritage notwithstanding, Nowa Huta is an interesting example of urban planning and architecture. Paradoxically, the town played a key role in the downfall of Communism, when it became a stronghold of the Solidarity movement.

Don't Miss

The Arka Pana (meaning "The Lord's Ark") is an amazing modern church with a facade made of round river stones. These were brought by the people of Nowa Huta to the building site when authorities cut the town's supplies in an effort to stop the church's construction.

Getting Here

Nowa Huta is a 20- to 30-minute tram ride from Kraków's center—take Tram 4 or 15 from Kraków Główny. It's not easy to cover Nowa Huta's sights by walking—it's better to use a bike, tram, or car. Or better do it in a vintage Trabant on a guided tour from Crazy Guides.

Arka Pana. ✉ *Obrońców Krzyża 1, Kraków* ☎ *012/680–82–01* 🌐 *www.arkapana.pl*

Crazy Guides. 🌐 *www.crazyguides.com* 🎫 *Tours from €100*

Mountain Hiking in the High Tatras

A Walk on Poland's High Side

Just south of Kraków, Poland's great plains give way to the gently folding foothills of the Carpathians, building to the High Tatras on the Slovak border. Here, the Gorczański, Pieniński, and Tatrzański national parks all have awe-inspiring and unforgettable hiking territory. The routes are well-marked, and there are maps at entrance points that give the distances, times, and degrees of difficulty of the trails. The Tatras are serious mountains—magnificent, and not to be trifled with—so exercising appropriate mountain safety is a must.

Don't Miss

There are easy trails just outside of Zakopane, including to Siklawica Waterfall (for more casual hikers). Adventurous (and experienced) climbers will leap to the challenges of the Orla Perć ("Eagles' Perch"), and the last section of the ascent to the Tatra's highest peak, Rysy (the "Rifts")—which both have elements of*via ferrata*, routes where permanent chains are attached to the mountain wall for getting up the steeper slopes.

When to Go

Late spring to early autumn is the best time to visit the Małopolska region. November and March can be rainy and cold, and temperatures will drop to freezing or below during the winter. Most attractions remain open year-round, but you may have a close encounter with snow in May or even as late as June.

Getting Here

Zakopane, in the Małopolska region, is the most popular entry point. The best way to get there is by bus from Kraków, a two-hour trip. Even though the trails are well-marked, never walk in the Tatras without a detailed map, and let someone at your hotel know where you are going.

Warsaw's Stare Miasto

A City Reborn

The rebuilding of Warsaw's historic Stare Miasto (Old Town) is a real phoenix-from-the-ashes story. Postwar architects, who were determined to get it exactly as it was before, turned to old prints, photographs in family albums, and paintings—in particular the detailed 18th-century views of Bernardo Bellotto (the nephew of Canaletto). Curiously, they discovered that some of Bellotto's views were painted not from real life but from sketches of projects that were never realized. Whatever your feelings about reproduction architecture—and there's a lot of it in Warsaw—it seems to have worked. The Old Town is closed to traffic, and in its narrow streets you can leave the 21st century behind and relax for a while.

Don't Miss

The Rynek Starego Miasta (Old Town Square) is the heart of the Old Town, where settlers first arrived in the 10th and 11th centuries. Legend has it that a peasant named Wars was directed to the site by a mermaid named Sawa—hence the name of the city in Polish, *Warszawa*. For a taste of the square's history, visit the Muzeum Historyczne Warszawy. After being almost completely destroyed during World War II, the house was meticulously reconstructed using old prints, plans, and paintings.

Historyczne Warszawy. ✉ *Rynek Starego Miasta 28–42, Stare Miasto* ☎ *22/277–44–02* 🌐 *muzeum-warszawy.pl* 🎫 *zł5* 🕒 *Closed Mon.*

MuzeumWarsaw Tourist Information. ✉ *Plac Defilad 1, Śródmieście* ☎ *022/656–68–54* 🌐 *www.warsawtour.pl*

Mazury Lake District

Poland's Great Lakes

The Mazury Lake District is one of the most famous vacation regions of Poland, with excellent sailing and kayaking. The area contains some 2,700 large lakes and "lakelets," connected by rivers, streams, and canals, which spill through the region's flower-studded meadows and marshlands. In the center are the Mazurian Great Lakes (Kraina Wielkich Jezior Mazurskich); where nearly a third of the land is submerged. The area includes two of Poland's largest, Śniardwy and Mamry. The gateway, and a popular resort, is the town of Mikołajki.

Don't Miss

Hitler's onetime bunker, at Gierłoż, called Wilczy Szaniec (Wolf's Lair). Its massively fortified concrete bunkers were blown up, but you can still climb among the remains for a feel for his megalomania. Here, a small group of German patriots tried—and failed—to assassinate him on July 20, 1944.

Do This

The Krutynia River is considered one of the loveliest lowland kayaking trails in Poland, perhaps even in Europe. It meanders through stunning lakes and the ancient forest of Puszcza Piska. The infrastructure for tourists (equipment rental, simple dining, and lodging) is well-developed.

Getting Here

To explore fully it's best to have your own car. By public transport, aim for Mikołajki, which is reachable by bus from Warsaw. Journey time is three to four hours (with at least one change).

Mikołajki Tourist Information. *Plac Wolności 7* *874/216–850* *www.mikolajki.pl.* *Closed weekends*

Wilczy Szaniec. *Gierłoż* *089/52–44–29* *www.wolfsschanze.pl* *zł 20*

Gdańsk

Maritime Solidarity

Maybe it's the sea air, or maybe it's the mixture of the city's cultural importance and political tumult. Whatever the reason, Gdańsk is special to Poles—and to Scandinavians and Germans, who visit the region in great numbers. Gdańsk was almost entirely destroyed during World War II, but the streets of its Główne Miasto (Main Town) have since been restored to reflect their historic and cultural richness. The Stare Miasto (Old Town) contains modern hotels and shops, but several churches and the beautifully reconstructed Old Town Hall justify its name. At the north end of the Old Town are the shipyards. The site—whose clashes between workers and militarized police in the 1970s and '80s caught the world's attention—has now settled back into the daily grind. That story of how Poland broke its shackles is now told in the European Solidarity Center.

Don't Miss

Kościół Najświętszej Marii Panny (St. Mary's Church) is the largest brick church in the world—and the largest church of any kind in Poland, with space for 25,000 worshippers. The enormous 14th-century construction underwent major restoration after World War II. It contains a 500-year-old, 25-foot-high astronomical clock, which keeps track of solar and lunar progressions.

Getting Here

Gdańsk can be reached by train from Warsaw in three hours. Kościół Mariacki is a 15-minute walk from the main train station.

European Solidary Center. ✉ *Solidarity 1* 🌐 *ecs.gda.pl* 🎫 *zł 30 (permanent exhibit), zł 15 (shipyard exhibition)*

Kościół Najświętszej Marii Panny. ✉ *Podkramarska 5, at ul. Piwna, Stare Miasto* 🌐 *www.bazylikamariacka.gdansk.pl* 🎫 *Free; Tower zł 14*

Wieliczka Salt Mine

A Subterranean Wonderland

Visiting the 700-year-old mines of Wieliczka combines the aesthetic pleasure of the underground salt chambers, with a lesson in history and geology. Its "healthy, balsamic air," famous for its medicinal properties, attracted famous fans including Polish kings, Nicolaus Copernicus, Johann Wolfgang von Goethe, Tsar Alexander I, and Austro-Hungarian Emperor Franz Josef. If all these arguments were not enough, this first-rate tourist attraction is a UNESCO World Heritage Site, too. The underground itinerary takes you to several chapels that have been carved from the salt; huge, fantastically shaped multilevel chambers; and salty subterranean lakes that send off fantasmagorical reflections of light.

Don't Miss

Look for the 17th-century Chapel of St. Anthony, with the saints' expressions softened with the moisture coming through the shaft. The colossal Chapel of the Blessed Kinga is rather like a cathedral hewn out of salt.

Getting Here

From Kraków, take the suburban train for 20 minutes to Wieliczka Rynek Kopalnia, from where it's a few minutes' walk to the mine. Visitors usually descend into the mine on foot (378 stairs, 210 feet) and return by elevator, but it is possible to take the elevator down for an additional fee. It is a long walk, so make sure you wear comfortable walking shoes. The temperature in the mine is 15°C (60°F) year-round, so dress accordingly.

✉ *Daniłowicza 10, Wieliczka* 🌐 *www.wieliczka-saltmine.com* 🎫 *zł 109*

Memorial and Museum Auschwitz-Birkenau

Acknowledging a Painful Past

Between 1940 and 1945 more than 1½ million people, 90% of them Jews from Poland and throughout Europe, died at Auschwitz and Birkenau, the largest Nazi-operated death-camp complex. The camp in the small town of Oświęcim (better known by its German name, *Auschwitz*) has come to be seen as the epicenter of the moral collapse of the West, proof of the human capacity for tremendous evil. The first inmates were Polish political prisoners, and the first gas victims were Russian POWs; the dead eventually included Poles, Jews, Romanies (Gypsies), homosexuals, Jehovah's Witnesses, and so-called criminals. More prisoners lived and died at Birkenau than at Auschwitz, including hundreds of thousands who went directly to gas chambers from boxcars in which they had been locked up for days. The Birkenau camp has been preserved to look much the way it did after the Nazis abandoned it.

Don't Miss

Begin with the heart-rending movie filmed by Soviet troops on January 27, 1945, the day they liberated those left behind by the retreating Germans. The English version runs a few times a day.

Getting There

Visiting begins at the Auschwitz site (Auschwitz I), and an hourly shuttle bus connects it with Birkenau (Auschwitz II). Buses and trains from Kraków stop at the nearby town of Oswiecim (61 km [38 miles] west of Kraków), from where local buses operate to the site, about 1 mile away.

✉ *Więźniów Oświęcimia 20, Oświęcim* ☎ *33/844–80–00* 🌐 *www.auschwitz.org* 🎫 *Free; guided tour from zł 85*

When in Poland

★ **Katedra w Oliwie** (*Oliwa Cathedral*)
CHURCH | The district of Oliwa, northwest of Gdansk's Old Town, is worth visiting if only for its magnificent cathedral complex. Originally part of a Cistercian monastery, the church was erected during the 13th century. Like most other structures in Poland, it has been rebuilt many times, resulting in a hodgepodge of styles from Gothic to Renaissance to Rococo, including an impressive Rococo organ. Demonstrations of the organ and a brief narrated church history are given almost hourly on weekdays in summer (May through September), less frequently the rest of the year. ✉ *Ul. Cystersów 10, Oliwa* 🌐 *www.archikatedraoliwa.pl* ⏲ *Museum closed Sun. and mid-Sept.–June.*

Kazimierz Dolny
TOWN | This small town is so pleasing to the eyes that it has thrived for more than a century as an artists' colony and vacation spot on a steep, hilly bank of the placid Vistula River. Although the first settlement existed here in the 12th century, the town was formally founded by King Kazimierz the Great, after whom it was named. This Kazimierz received the nickname Dolny (the Lower) to distinguish it from another newly founded Kazimierz upriver, now part of Kraków. Kazimierz Dolny prospered as a river port during the 16th and 17th centuries, but the partitioning of Poland left it cut off from the grain markets of Gdańsk. Thereafter, the town fell into decline until it was rediscovered by painters and writers during the 19th century. ✉ *Kazimierz Dolny*

Malbork Castle
CASTLE/PALACE | In 1230, the Teutonic Knights arrived on the banks of the Vistula River and built this castle. It passed into Polish hands after the second Toruń Treaty in 1466 concluded the 13-year war between the Poles and the Teutonic Knights. For the next three centuries, Malbork served as the royal residence for Polish kings during their annual visits to Pomerania. Although heavily damaged during World War II, it was later restored. Two-hour guided tours offer the best way to see the castle, which is often a day-trip from Gdańsk, but there is a hotel on the castle grounds if you want to spend the night. ✉ *Rte. 50, Malbork* ☎ *055/647–09–78* 🌐 *www.zamek.malbork.pl* 🎫 *zł 70.*

★ **Park Łazienkowski** (*Łazienki Park*)
CITY PARK | **FAMILY** | This 180-acre park, commissioned during the late 18th century by King Słanisław August Poniatowski, runs adjacent to the Vistula River. Peacocks wander through the park, as well as sweet red squirrels affectionately named "Basia" in Poland. One of the most beloved sights in Łazienki Park is the Pomnik Fryderyka Chopina (Chopin Memorial), a sculpture under a streaming willow tree that shows the composer in a typical romantic pose. The magnificent Pałac Łazienkowski is the focal point of the park. The neoclassical summer residence was so faithfully reconstructed after World War II that there is still no electricity. The palace has splendid 18th-century furniture, as well as part of the art collection of King Słanisław August Poniatowski. ✉ *Agrykola 1, Lazienki* ☎ *022/621–62–41* 🎫 *zł 40 (free Fri.)* ⏲ *Closed Mon.*

★ **Rynek Główny** (*Main Market Square*)
PLAZA/SQUARE | Europe's largest medieval marketplace, which is surrounded by many historic buildings, is on a par in size and grandeur with St. Mark's Square in Venice. It even has the same plague of pigeons, although legend tells us the ones here are no ordinary birds: they are allegedly the spirits of the knights of Duke Henry IV Probus, who in the 13th century were cursed and turned into birds. Once a large open marketplace, its commercial activity is limited to a few flower sellers under colorful umbrellas and some portable souvenir stalls. Above all, Rynek is Kraków's largest outdoor

Poland
SWEDEN
Baltic Sea
LATVIA
LITHUANIA
RUSSIA
(Kaliningrad Oblast)
POLAND
CZECH REPUBLIC
SLOVAKIA
UKRAINE
AUSTRIA
HUNGARY
ROMANIA
0 50 mi
0 50 km
Jelgava
Liepaga
Šiauliai
Panevežys
Klaipeda
Kaunas
Kaliningrad
Gdynia
Katedra w Oliwie
Gdańsk
Nowa Huta
Koszalin
Elbląg
Malbork Castle
Mazury Lake District
Ełk
Hrodna
Olsztyn
Grudziądz
Szczecin
Białystok
Bydgoszcz
Inowrocław
Warsaw's Stare Miasto
Park Łazienkowski
Brest
Poznań
Żelazowa Wola
Warsaw
Zielona Gó
Łódź
Lublin
Kazimierz Dolny
Kielce
Wrocław
Opole
Wawel Hill
Rynek Główny
Katowice
Memorial and Museum Auschwitz-Birkenau
Kraków
Wieliczka Salt Mine
Rzeszów
Prague
Ostrava
Mountain Hiking in the High Tatras
Olomouc
Jihlava
Brno
Prešov
Uzhgorod
Zvolen
Miskolc
Vienna
Bratislava
Budapest
Oradea
E28
E65
E30
E36
E40
E67
E55
E75
E77
E261
E372
E371
E50
E272
E28
22
25
10
11
12
16
19

café, from spring through autumn, with more than 20 cafés scattered around the perimeter of the square. ✉ *Stare Miasto.*

Żelazowa Wola

HISTORIC HOME | A mecca for all Frédéric Chopin lovers, the composer's birthplace is a small 19th-century manor house, still with its original furnishings and now a museum dedicated to telling the story of the composer's life. When Chopin was born here on February 22 (or March 1), 1810, his father was a live-in tutor for the children of the wealthy Skarbek family. Although the family soon moved to Warsaw, Chopin often returned for holidays, and the house — not to mention the sounds and sights of the Mazovian countryside — is said to have influenced him in his early years. The manor is surrounded by a beautifully landscaped park, designed by Franciszek Krzywda Polkowski in the 1930s. The house is reachable by PKS bus and by private minibuses running from Warsaw's main bus station, but several companies also offer guided tours. ✉ *Żelazowa Wola 15, Zelazowa Wola* ☎ *046/863–33–00* 🌐 *www.muzeum.nifc.pl* 🎫 *zł 22 (free Wed.)* 🕒 *Closed Mon.*

Where to Eat and Drink

Bąkowo Zohylina

$$ | POLISH | Friendly waiters in folk costumes serve hearty regional dishes while the band plays fiery folk music in the background—rather loudly. This kind of food is designed—and guaranteed—to keep you warm, be it potato pancakes, a "mountaineer's cauldron" (a dense, goulash-like soup), or hot *oscypek* cheese with cranberries. **Known for:** rye soup; always busy; homey, rustic atmosphere. 💲 *Average main: zł70* ✉ *Ul. Piłsudskiego 6, Zakopane* ☎ *018/206–62–16* 🌐 *www.niznio.pl.*

Farina

$$$ | MEDITERRANEAN | True to its logo (a sack of flour and a fish), this restaurant offers consistently good fish, seafood, and homemade pasta. In addition to Mediterranean fare, there is also a selection of typically Polish dishes. **Known for:** good wine selection; great seafood; signature appetizer of truffle and mushroom pâté. 💲 *Average main: zł90* ✉ *Św. Marka 16, Stare Miasto* ☎ *519/399–474* 🌐 *www.farina.com.pl* 🕒 *Closed Mon.*

Motlava

$$ | POLISH | This sleek and contemporary restaurant, just a stone's throw from the Motława River, serves reimagined traditional Polish cuisine. Dishes include pork cheeks stewed in beer and served with confit shallots, or blood sausage served with stewed leeks, and pickled cucumber. **Known for:** vegetarian stuffed cabbage; hand-made dumplings; apple pie. 💲 *Average main: zł60* ✉ *Stara Stocznia 2/1, Gdansk* ☎ *058/719–51–00* 🌐 *www.motlava.pl.*

Restauracja Polska Różana

$$$ | POLISH | This elegant restaurant has a wide-open salon furnished with pretty antiques, and decorated with large bouquets of fresh flowers. Importantly, you can't go wrong here with the food, especially if you try the homemade *pierogi*, or pike perch fillet in white-leek sauce. **Known for:** great desserts; peaceful, if formal, atmosphere; delicious pierogi. 💲 *Average main: zł95* ✉ *Chocimska 7, Centrum* ☎ *022/848–12–25* 🌐 *www.restauracjarozana.com.pl.*

Restauracja Wentzl

$$$ | POLISH | The owners of this upscale establishment have reincarnated Jan Wentzl's restaurant (a celebrated 18th-century Polish restaurateur), which opened in the same building in 1792. On the menu, traditional Polish cuisine meets classic French decadence—you'll see dishes like duck roasted with nuts and apples, and served with gingerbread sauce, or Mazurian crayfish and cognac stew. **Known for:** formal service; great views of Market Square; beautifully decorated dining room. *Average main: zł95* *Rynek Główny 19, Stare Miasto* *012/429–57–12.*

Cool Places to Stay

Grand Hotel

$$$ | HOTEL | Without question, this hotel around the corner from Kraków's main square is the most elegant address for visitors to the city and the one most accessible to the major sights. **Pros:** great location; charming public areas. **Cons:** some rooms may be noisy, especially on weekend nights; a bit too old-fashioned for some. *Rooms from: zł819* *Ul. Sławkowska 5–7, Stare Miasto* *012/424–08–00* *www.grand.pl* *64 rooms* *Free Breakfast.*

Hotel Copernicus

$$$$ | HOTEL | Hotel Copernicus is a tastefully adapted medieval tenement house on the oldest and, arguably, the most charming street in Kraków. **Pros:** oozes history and charm—inside and out; lots of modern amenities. **Cons:** on the pricey side; some quirks (like tubs and no showers, or vice versa, in some bathrooms). *Rooms from: zł1150* *Ul. Kanonicza 16, Stare Miasto* *012/424–34–00* *www.hotelcopernicus.com* *29 rooms* *Free Breakfast.*

★ Hotel Gródek

$$$ | HOTEL | Hidden away from the noise in a cozy cul-de-sac next to the Planty Park and the Dominican convent, this boutique hotel is one of Kraków's finest. **Pros:** loads of character; great location; free and fast Wi-Fi. **Cons:** on the pricey side; sauna but otherwise limited amenities. *Rooms from: zł870* *Ul. Na Gródku 4, Stare Miasto* *012/431–90–30* *www.hotelgrodek.com* *23 rooms* *Free Breakfast.*

Hotel Podewils

$$$$ | HOTEL | This luxurious boutique hotel, housed in a sophisticated 18th-century building with Baroque features, is located on the edge of the Old Town, and conveniently opposite the Gdańsk Główny train station. **Pros:** completely renovated historic structure; rooms facing the river have great views; nice marble bathrooms. **Cons:** not all the rooms are equally nice; no restaurant in the hotel (just a breakfast room); rooms can be cold in winter. *Rooms from: zł320* *Ul. Szafarnia 2, Stare Miasto* *058/300–95–60* *www.podewils.pl* *10 rooms* *Free Breakfast.*

Le Regina

$$$ | HOTEL | This luxurious boutique hotel—a remodeled 18th-century palace—is an oasis within the busy capital with a superb location at the north end of the Old Town. **Pros:** deluxe service; hotel very central but peaceful and quiet. **Cons:** expensive rates; some overpriced extras including breakfast and valet parking. *Rooms from: zł820* *Kościelna 12, Stare Miasto* *022/531–60–00* *www.maisonleregina.com* *61 rooms* *Free Breakfast.*

★ Polonia Palace Hotel

$$ | HOTEL | When this hotel opened in 1913, it was the best address in Warsaw, and following decades of faded glory it underwent a large-scale restoration, reopening in 2005 in a condition that once again became worthy of its name. **Pros:** excellent location; excellent breakfast. **Cons:** busy reception; expensive extras (room service, in-room Wi-Fi). *Rooms from: zł690* *Al. Jerozolimskie 45, Centrum* *22/318–28–00* *www.poloniapalace.com* *206 rooms* *Free Breakfast.*

Slovakia

East of the Czech Republic and about one-third as large as its neighbor, Slovakia became an independent state on January 1, 1993. Although they speak a language closely related to Czech, the Slovaks had managed to maintain a strong sense of national identity throughout their common statehood as part of Czechoslovakia. In the end, it was the Slovaks' very different history that split them from the Czechs, and it's this history that makes this a unique travel destination.

Part of the Great Moravian Empire in the 9th century, the Slovaks were conquered a century later by the Magyars and remained under Hungarian and Habsburg rule. Following the Tartar invasions in the 13th century, many Saxons were invited to resettle the land and develop the economy, including cultivating the region's rich mineral resources. During the 15th and 16th centuries, Romanian shepherds migrated from Walachia through the Carpathian Mountains into Slovakia, and the merging of these varied groups with the resident Slavs bequeathed to the region a rich folk culture and some unique forms of architecture, especially in the east.

Today, most visitors to Slovakia come for one of two things: the cultural capital of Bratislava, with its charming Staré mesto (Old Town)—a beautiful city center set along the Danube that affords visitors a glimpse of the capital's former glories, though is surrounded by less appealing Communist-era high rises—and the soaring peaks of the Vysoké Tatry (High Tatras), which is set up perfectly to cater to tourists, especially hikers and skiers. Yet people often overlook Slovakia's many other charms, such as exquisite medieval towns like Spiš in the plains and valleys below the High Tatras, and the beautiful 18th-century wooden country churches farther east. Taking the time to explore a little farther afield in Slovakia is a very rewarding experience.

Old Town, Bratislava

Slovakia's Historic Heart

Since Slovakia joined the European Union in 2014, Bratislava has blossomed into a thriving, modern European capital. Yet it has still retained its charming Old Town. This historic center is perhaps best exemplified by two squares: Hlavné námestie, home to a landmark fountain and a ring of beautiful Gothic and Baroque buildings—look out for the Stará radnica (Old Town Hall), a mishmash of different houses built at various stages from the 14th century onward—and Hviezdoslavovo námestie, a lovely, tree-shaded promenade lined with grand buildings and odd sculptures. Other highlights include Michalská brána (Michael's Gate), the last gate standing from Bratislava's original 13th-century city walls; Primaciálny palác (Primate's Palace), a gorgeous Neoclassical building built for the Archbishop József Batthyány; and Katedrála svätého Martina (St Martin's Cathedral), the coronation church of many Hungarian and Austrian monarchs; look for the golden crown and cushion on its spire.

Don't Miss

Bratislava's most striking Secession-style building, the Kostol svätej Alžbety (Church of St. Elizabeth)—better known as the Blue Church—is noted for its powder blue exterior, which extends all the way up to its 120-foot round tower.

Best Quick Bite

High-quality gelato is popular here, and if you have time for only one scoop, opt for Koun (pronounced "cone"). ✉ *Paulínyho 1, Bratislava* 🌐 *www.koun.sk*

Getting Here

The Old Town is a 10-minute bus/tram ride (or a 20-minute walk) from the main train station.

Visit Bratislava. 🌐 *www.visitbratislava.com*

Bratislava Castle

A Picture-Book Fortress

With roots dating back more than a millennium—it was first mentioned in AD 907 for its role in a battle between Bavarians and Hungarians—the wonderfully imposing Bratislavský hrad (Bratislava Castle) was significantly rebuilt in the Renaissance style in the mid-16th century. It's this enormous, rectangular form with four stocky towers that you can see today, although it incorporates architectural features from throughout its history (and the dazzling white paint job is distinctly 20th-century handiwork). From the Old Town, walk up the (steep) castle hill and pass through one of the four entrance gates—probably Viedenská brána or Leopoldova brána— for incredible views of the town and the winding Danube below. The grounds are free to enter, so you can soak up the vistas as long as you like. You only need to pay if you want to head inside the castle, either for the SNM-Historical Museum, which is a little sparse but does include access to the Crown Tower via a narrow passageway, or any of the regularly-changing temporary exhibits.

Don't Miss

While you're at the castle, take time to explore the beautiful Baroková záhrada (Baroque Garden) and take a stroll through the woods around the castle walls.

Getting Here

It's a short but steep walk up from the Old Town to Bratislava Castle. Trams 44 and 47 spare you the climb, and drop you off right by the entrance gate; you can pick them up from just outside the Presidential Palace.

✉ *Zámocká 2, Bratislava* ☎ *02/204–831–10* 🌐 *www.bratislava-hrad.sk.* 🎫 *€12*

Banská Štiavnica

A Medieval Town Frozen in Time

Since the 11th century, this little town has earned its wealth from mining, and today it's essentially one large mining museum. German miners arrived here to exploit rich gold and silver deposits, and their success is apparent in some of the town's remaining monuments, such as the golden Trinity column on Trinity Square. At the Slovenské banské múzeum you can view some of the town's original mining machinery from the early 13th century and take a trip down into a pit mine. You can also explore two castles: the New Castle (Nový zámok), a six-story Renaissance fortification built in the 1500s, and the Old Castle (Starý zámo), built above town in the early 13th century. Just outside of town lies the charming late-baroque château Svätý Anton.

Don't Miss

Romantic Bojnice Hrad (Bojnice Castle), dating from before 1175, has all the necessary elements of a fairy-tale palace: multilevel turrets with decorative spires, ornate parapets, and a sparkling moat. The interior is beautifully restored and furnished in 12th-century style, and it's just over an hour's drive northwest of Banská Štiavnica.

Getting Here and Around

Banská Štiavnica is accessible by train from Bratislava, but it's twice as fast to drive.

Bojnice Hrad. ✉ *Zámok a okolie 1, Bojnice* 🌐 *bojnicecastle.sk* 🎫 *From €11* 🕓 *Closed Mon. in Apr., May, and Oct. Closed Mon. and Tues. Nov.–Mar.*

Slovenské banské múzeum. ✉ *J. K. Hella 12, Banská Štiavnica* 🌐 *www.muzeumbs.sk* 🎫 *€14, guided tour in English €20* ✍ *Reservations essential*

Hiking or Skiing in the High Tatras

Mythic Mountains

A visit to the Vysoké Tatry (High Tatras) alone makes a trip to Slovakia worthwhile. Although the range is relatively compact—just 32 km (20 miles) from end to end—its peaks seem wilder and more starkly beautiful than those of the Alps. The highest is Gerlachovský štít, at 8,710 feet, though some 20 others exceed 8,000 feet, and the best way to see them is on foot or on skis. From spring to autumn, a reasonably fit person of any age should have little trouble with any of the well-marked walking trails. Be sure to wear proper shoes with good ankle support. In winter, the entire region is crisscrossed with cross-country skiing paths, as well as several dedicated downhill ski slopes. The ski season usually lasts from the end of December through April, though the best months are January and February.

Stay Here

Grand Hotel Praha. There are a few main resort towns in the Tatras, but Tatranská Lomnica has a near-perfect combination of peace, convenience, and atmosphere. Moreover, the lift behind the Grandhotel Praha brings some of the best walks in the Tatras to your doorstep. ✉ *Tatranská Lomnica 8, Vysoké Tatry* ☎ *44 290 13 38* 🌐 *www.tmrhotels.com/grandhotel-praha*

Best Restaurant

Bilíkova chata. Take a break with a warm beverage at this rustic and cozy restaurant and hotel just before you reach Hrebienok. ✉ *Hrebienok, Starý Smokovec* ☎ *949 579 777* 🌐 *bilikova-chata.sk*

Getting Here

Poprad is the gateway to the mountains. There are regular trains from Bratislava and Košice, as well as twice-weekly Wizzair flights from London.

Spiš Castle

Sprawling Castle Complex

In the heart of Eastern Slovakia, looking down on the village of Žehra, lies one of the largest castle ruins anywhere in Europe. Spišský hrad (Spiš Castle) has been occupied by the overlords of the Spiš region since the 12th century, first the Kings of Hungary, then various Hungarian noble families, then the states of Czechoslovakia and Slovakia. The site's UNESCO-listed fortifications are mostly in ruins today, but in the section that has been preserved there's a museum of medieval history, featuring a collection of torture devices. The hilltop location affords a beautiful view of the surrounding hills and town; climb the 22-meter-high tower for an even better panorama.

Don't Miss

To the southwest of Spiš Castle, beyond the town of Levoča, lies Slovenský Raj (Slovak Paradise), a wonderfully wild and romantic area of cliffs, caves, and waterfalls. It's a dream for adventurous hikers, with some gorges only accessible by narrow but secure iron ladders.

Best Restaurant

Visit family-owned restaurant U Janusa for a taste of Slovak culture as well as cuisine. Try one of the local specialties, such as bryndzové halušky (small potato dumplings with soft sheep cheese, bacon and chives). ✉ *Kláštorská 22, Levoča* ☎ *534 514 592* 🌐 *ujanusa.sk*

Getting Here

A car is the easiest way to reach Spiš Castle. However, a bus does run from Poprad to the town of Spišské Podhradie, about an hour's walk from the castle. ✉ *Žehra* ☎ *053/454–13–36* 🌐 *www.spisskyhrad.sk* 🎫 *€8* 🕒 *Closed Nov.–Mar.*

When in Slovakia

Bardejov

TOWN | Bardejov is a great surprise, tucked away in this remote corner of Slovakia. Recognized as a UNESCO World Heritage Site, it is an exceptionally complete and well-preserved example of a fortified medieval town and possesses one of the nation's most enchanting squares. Indeed, Bardejov owes its splendors to its location astride the ancient trade routes to Poland and Russia. It's hard to put a finger on exactly what makes the square so captivating—it could be the lack of arcades in front of the houses, the high pointed roofs, or the colorful pastels and decorative scenes painted on the facades, which have a light, almost comic effect. Shopping along the pedestrian square is quite pleasant. The Šariš (Icon Museum) houses a collection of icons from as early as the 15th century and paintings taken from the area's numerous Greek Catholic and Orthodox churches. Many of the icons depict the story of St. George slaying the dragon (for the key to the princess's chastity belt!). The legend of St. George, which probably originated in pre-Christian mythology, was often used to attract the peasants of the area to the more abstemious stories of Christianity. Pick up the short commentary in English when you buy your ticket; for more detailed information, purchase the Slovak/English book Ikony from the reception area. ✉ *Bardejov* ✣ *80 km (50 miles) north of Košice* 🌐 *tik.bardejov.travel.*

Devínsky hrad (*Devín Castle*)

CASTLE/PALACE | Located on the confluence of the Morava and Danube rivers that form the border between Slovakia and Austria, just 10½ kilometers (6½ miles) west of Bratislava, lies this extraordinary ruined castle. Built on the top of a high crag, the enormous Devín Castle is one of the oldest in the region, first mentioned in written sources in 864. You can learn about the history of the castle and the village (all the way back to Neolithic times) in a fascinating exhibition within the castle walls. Enjoy the sweeping views from the top of the ruined Upper Castle, and take a snap of the famous **Maiden's Tower**, a tiny watchtower precariously balanced on a lone rock that has spawned countless legends of imprisoned women leaping to their deaths. In summer, there are kid-friendly medieval-themed events held in and around the castle. To reach Devín, take Bus 29 from Bratislava (30 minutes) or drive west out of the city on Devínska cesta. ✉ *Muránská 1050/10, Bratislava* ☎ *02/657–301–05* 🌐 *www.muzeum.bratislava.sk* 🎫 *€5* ⏲ *Closed Mon.*

Grasalkovičov palác (*Grassalkovich Palace*)

GOVERNMENT BUILDING | This grand Rococo-style summer residence was built in 1780 for Count Anton Grassalkovich, advisor to Empress Maria Theresa (who was crowned in Bratislava in 1761). Today, it's the official residence of the President of the Slovak Republic so it isn't possible to see inside, but come at 1 pm any day of the week to witness the ceremonial Changing of the Guard. You can also head around the back of the palace to explore the lovely Prezidentská záhrada (Presidental Garden), a public park that's an oasis of manicured lawns, sculpted hedges, and gorgeous flower displays. It also has a number of avant garde sculptures, including the playful *Fountain of Youth* by Slovak sculptor Tibor Bártfay. ✉ *Hodžovo námestie 2978/1, Bratislava* ☎ *02/578–881–55* 🌐 *www.prezident.sk.*

Košice

TOWN | In Košice you leave rural Slovakia behind. Though rich historically and with an interesting old town square, Košice is a sprawling, modern city, the second largest in Slovakia after Bratislava. Positioned along the main trade route between Hungary and Poland, the city

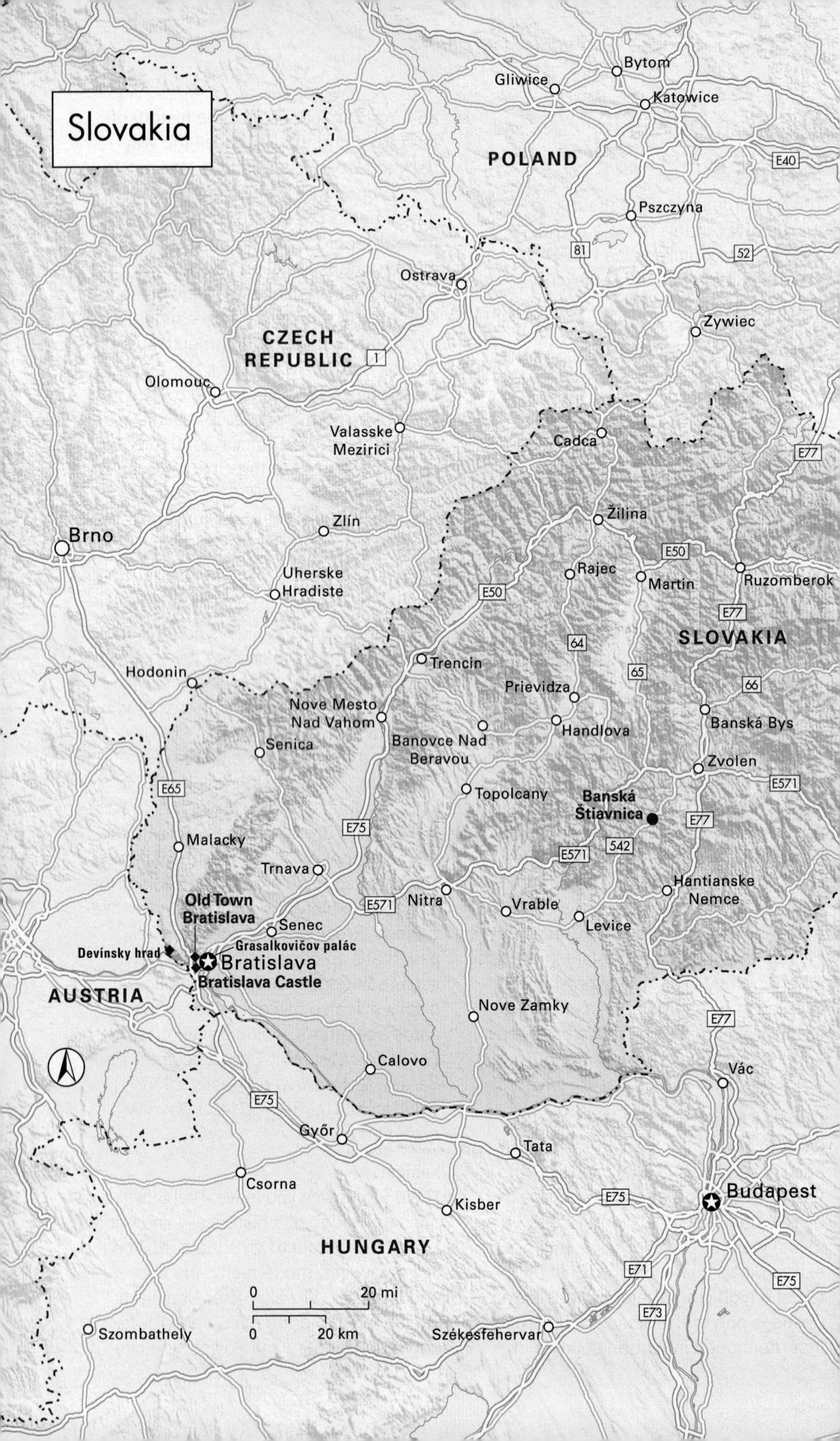
Slovakia
Bytom
Gliwice
Katowice
POLAND
E40
Pszczyna
81
52
Ostrava
Zywiec
CZECH
REPUBLIC
1
Olomouc
Valasske
Mezirici
Cadca
E77
Žilina
Zlín
Brno
E50
Rajec
Martin
Ruzomberok
Uherske
Hradiste
E50
E77
SLOVAKIA
64
Trencin
65
66
Hodonin
Prievidza
Nove Mesto
Nad Vahom
Handlova
Banská Bys
Senica
Banovce Nad
Beravou
Zvolen
E65
E571
Topolcany
Banská
Štiavnica
E75
E77
542
Malacky
E571
Trnava
Hantianske
Nemce
Nitra
E571
Vrable
Old Town
Bratislava
Levice
Senec
Grasalkovičov palác
Devínsky hrad
Bratislava
Bratislava Castle
AUSTRIA
Nove Zamky
E77
Calovo
Vác
E75
Győr
Tata
Csorna
E75
Budapest
Kisber
HUNGARY
E71
0
20 mi
E75
E73
0
20 km
Szombathely
Székesfehervar

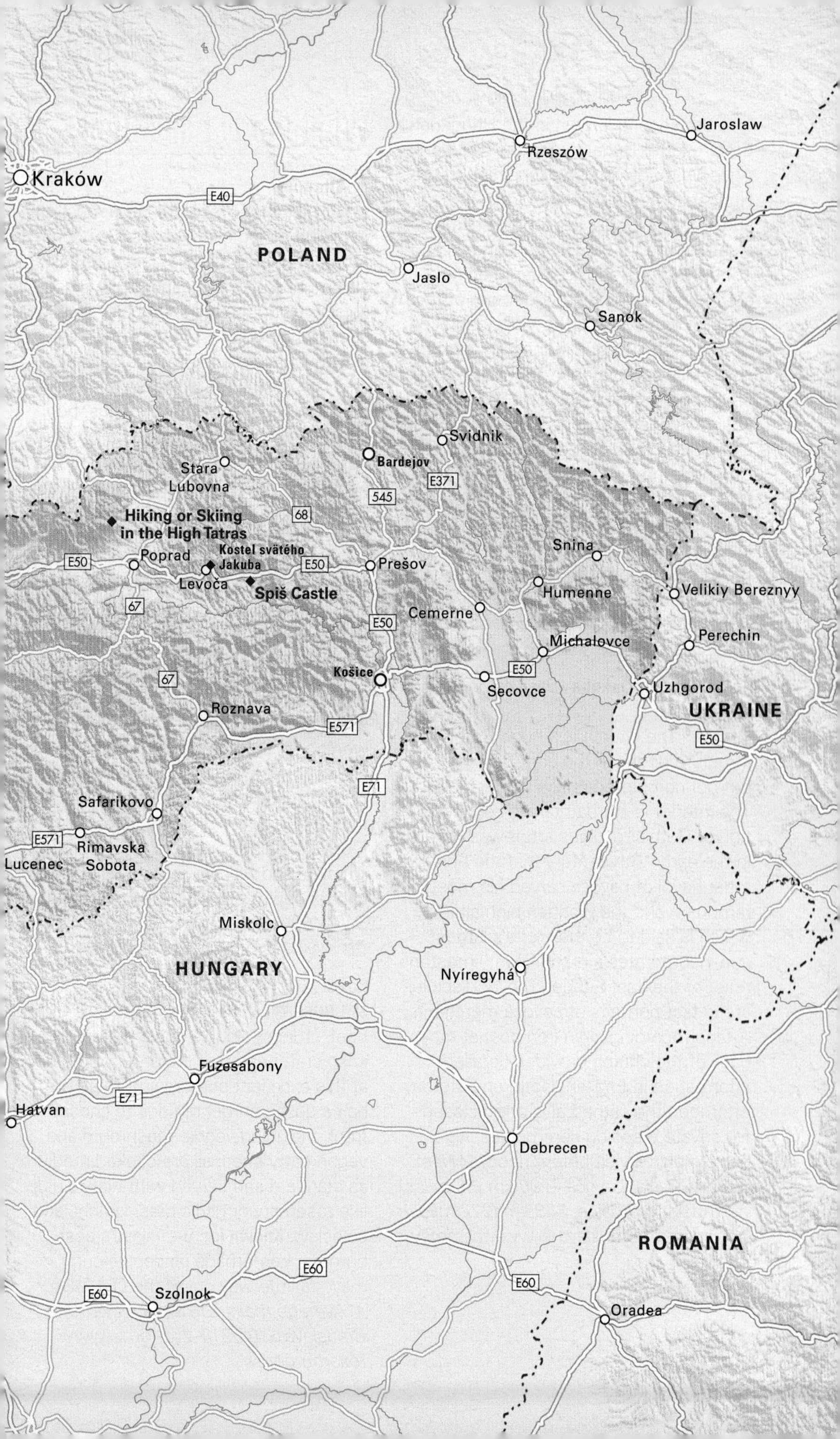

Kraków
E40
Rzeszów
Jaroslaw
POLAND
Jaslo
Sanok
Svidnik
Stara
Lubovna
Bardejov
E371
545
68
Hiking or Skiing
in the High Tatras
Kostel svätého
Jakuba
Snina
E50
Poprad
E50
Prešov
Levoča
Spiš Castle
Humenne
Velikiy Bereznyy
67
Cemerne
E50
Michalovce
Perechin
67
Košice
E50
Secovce
Uzhgorod
UKRAINE
Roznava
E571
E50
E71
Safarikovo
E571
Rimavska
Sobota
Lucenec
Miskolc
HUNGARY
Nyíregyhá
Fuzesabony
E71
Hatvan
Debrecen
ROMANIA
E60
E60
E60
Szolnok
Oradea

was the second largest in the Hungarian Empire (after Buda) during the Middle Ages. With the Turkish occupation of the Hungarian homeland during the 16th and 17th centuries, the town became a safe haven for the Hungarian nobility. The town square is dominated on its southern flank by the huge tower of the Gothic Dóm svätej Alžbety (Cathedral of St. Elizabeth). Begun in the 15th century and finally completed in 1508, the cathedral is the largest in Slovakia. Inside the church is one of Europe's largest Gothic altarpieces, a 35-foot-tall medieval wood carving attributed to the master Erhard of Ulm. Most of the great Hungarian leader Francis Rákoczi II's remains were placed in a crypt under the north transept of the cathedral (he left his heart in Paris). ✉ *Košice* ✣ *100 km 62 miles) southeast of Levoča, 402 km (250 miles) east of Bratislava* 🌐 *visitkosice.org.*

Kostol svätého Jakuba (*Basilica of St. James*)
CHURCH | The church is a huge Gothic structure begun in the early 14th century but not completed until a century later. The interior is a breathtaking concentration of Gothic religious art. It was here in the early 16th century that the Spiš artist Pavol of Levoča carved his most famous work: the wooden high altar, which is said to be the world's largest and incorporates a magnificent limestone relief of the Last Supper. The 12 disciples are in fact portraits of Levoča merchants. A tape recording in an iron post at the back of the church provides detailed information in English. Note: on Saturday afternoon the cathedral is often closed for private wedding ceremonies; it's best to plan a visit before noon. ✉ *Nám. majstra Pavla, Levoča* ✣ *90 km (56 miles) northwest of Košice, 358 km (222 miles) northeast of Bratislava* 🌐 *www.chramsv-jakuba.sk.*

Where to Eat and Drink

★ **Albrecht**
$$$$ | **FRENCH** | One of the city's most elegant fine dining experiences, Restaurant Albrecht near Bratislava Castle serves sumptuous, strictly seasonal French cuisine using the highest quality locally sourced ingredients; menus often list individual farms and producers. Head chef Jaroslav Žídek is known for his elaborate, multicourse tasting menus, but you can also order the dishes à la carte: opt for the tuna ceviche to start, the lamb back with sheep-cheese ravioli for main, and the plum dumplings to finish. **Known for:** multicourse tasting menus; great value lunch menu; five minutes by taxi from the Old Town. $ *Average main: €30* ✉ *Mudroňova 4237/82, Bratislava* ☎ *902–333–888* 🌐 *www.hotelalbrecht.sk/restauracia* 🕒 *Closed Sun.*

★ **Kláštorný pivovar**
For a great-tasting, great-value beer, you won't beat the home brew at this popular brewpub—it's just €3.70 for a whole liter of Monastic Beer served straight from the tap. Enjoy it with tasty Slovak pub food like grilled sausages, baked pork knuckle, and *halušky* (potato dumplings with sheep's cheese). ✉ *Námestie SNP 469/8, Bratislava* ☎ *907–976–284* 🌐 *www.klastornypivovar.sk.*

Roxor
$$ | **BURGER** | Melt-in-the-mouth eco-farm beef, crunchy double-cooked fries, and crisp craft beers are the order of the day at this excellent burger joint. There are half a dozen burger options to choose from, including veggie mushroom and vegan patty ones; all are cooked medium as standard and served with tasty sides like rosemary or garlic fries, kimchi, and coleslaw. **Known for:** Bratislava's best burgers; homemade pineapple-curry mayo; a little way out of the Old Town. $ *Average main: €15* ✉ *Šancová 19, Bratislava* ☎ *02/210–205–00* 🌐 *www.roxorburger.sk.*

Zylinder

$$$ | **AUSTRIAN** | With dishes based on traditional Austro-Hungarian recipes, this well-located café and restaurant makes a pleasant stop for lunch or dinner. Expect everything from traditional Austrian schnitzel and *tafelspitz* (boiled beef served with minced apples) to Hungarian beef goulash and *somlói galuska* (sponge trifle), as well as Slovakian specialties like *halušky* (small potato dumplings with sheep cheese, sautéed bacon, and sour cream). **Known for:** tasty beef broth with noodles; great location on Hviezdoslav Square; big portions and good value for area. *Average main: €16 ✉ Hviezdoslavovo námestie 19, Bratislava ☎ 903–123–134 🌐 www.zylinder.sk.*

Cool Places to Stay

Arcade Hotel

$$ | **HOTEL** | This 16th-century building on the main square is an ideal place to stay, with rooms and apartments varying in size, comfort, and cost, but each equipped with the basic creature comforts. **Pros:** atmospheric on-site restaurant; historic charm; free Wi-Fi. **Cons:** pet-friendly; no elevator. *Rooms from: €138 ✉ Nám. SNP 5, Banská Bystrica ☎ 48 43 02 111 🌐 www.arcade.sk 18 rooms Free Breakfast.*

Hotel Bankov

$ | **HOTEL** | Formerly a 19th-century spa resort, Bankov is now a peaceful respite surrounded by hiking trails in the cool hills a 10-minute drive outside Košice. **Pros:** nice summer terrace; beautiful building; luxurious touches unusual outside of Bratislava. **Cons:** not in town, so requires a car; can be busy with group events; cheapest rooms are not nearly as charming as the others. *Rooms from: €84 ✉ Dolný Bankov 2, Košice ☎ 556–324–522 🌐 www.hotelbankov.sk 29 rooms Free Breakfast.*

Loft Hotel

$$ | **HOTEL** | Standing out from the Old Town crowd with its industrial-style decor incorporating exposed brick walls, distressed wooden floors, shabby leather sofas, and retro advertising prints, Loft offers a different kind of hotel experience. **Pros:** sixth floor rooms have gorgeous garden views; free snacks and wine for guests; popular Fabrika brewpub downstairs. **Cons:** industrial decor isn't to all tastes; underground parking is €20 a day; wood floors can be noisy. *Rooms from: €85 ✉ Štefánikova 864/4, Bratislava ☎ 901–902–680 🌐 www.lofthotel.sk 111 rooms No Meals.*

★ Marrol's Boutique Hotel

$$$ | **HOTEL** | A romantic boutique gem in the heart of the Old Town, Marrol's is set within a 19th century burgher's house and oozes period charm, with its opulent chandeliers, deep leather armchairs, and charming wood paneling. **Pros:** free minibar full of drinks; lovely plant-covered Summer Terrace; underground parking available. **Cons:** breakfast is nothing special; service isn't always with a smile; noise in corridors carries. *Rooms from: €110 ✉ Tobrucká 6953/4, Bratislava ☎ 02/577–846–00 🌐 www.hotelmarrols.sk 54 rooms Free Breakfast.*

Chapter 8

ITALY AND MALTA

WELCOME TO ITALY AND MALTA

TOP REASONS TO GO

★ **The Vatican:** This tiny independent state in central Rome holds some of the city's most spectacular sights.

★ **Ancient Rome:** The Colosseum and the Roman Forum are remarkable ruins from Rome's past.

★ **Pompeii:** The excavated ruins of Pompeii offer a unique glimpse into everyday life—and sudden death—in Roman times.

★ **Venice's Grand Canal:** A trip down Venice's "Main Street," whether by water bus or gondola, is a signature Italian experience.

★ **Galleria degli Uffizi, Florence:** The museum contains dozens of Renaissance masterpieces.

★ **Ravello:** High above the Amalfi Coast, this place is a contender for the title of most beautiful village in the world.

★ **Valletta:** Malta's cultural crown jewel.

1 Rome. No other city has such powerful evocations of a long and spectacular past.

2 Florence. It's hard to think of a place that's more closely linked to the 15th-century Renaissance.

3 The Amalfi Coast and Naples. Italy's third-largest city is densely packed. The world's most beautiful coastal drive links Positano, Amalfi, and Ravello.

4 Venice. Canals and an atmosphere of faded splendor that practically defines the word decadent characterize Venice.

5 Sicily. Italy's largest island has bustling cities, Baroque towns, beautiful beaches, archaeological sites and vineyards.

6 The Rest of Italy and Sardinia. From fashion-forward Milan, the ski resorts of the Dolomites, and glamorous Lake Como to the rustic *trulli* homes of Puglia and the hill towns of Umbria.

7 Malta. Hulking megalithic temples, ornate Baroque churches, and hilltop citadels are Malta's human legacy. Dizzying limestone cliffs, sparkling Mediterranean seas, and charming rural landscapes make up its natural beauty.

AUSTRIA
Graz
Klagenfurt
HUNGARY
Maribor
Bolzano
Ljubljana
Trento
SLOVENIA
Zagreb
Milan
Trieste
4
Venice
CROATIA
Verona
Gulf of Venice
Belgrade
Parma
Ferrara
Pula
BOSNIA AND HERZEGOVINA
SERBIA
Bologna
Ravenna
Zadar
Sarajevo
2
San Marino
Pisa
Florence
Ancona
Livorno
Arezzo
Split
Siena
Adriatic Sea
Perugia
ELBA
Bastia
Dubrovnik
Podgorica
Pescara
L'Aquila
MONTENEGRO
Civitavecchia
1
Rome
ITALY
Tirana
Foggia
Bari
ALBANIA
Benevento
Olbia
3
Naples
Vesuvius
ISCHIA
Brindisi
CAPRI
Salerno
Taranto
Lecce
GREECE
Tyrrhenian Sea
Ionian Sea
Catanzaro
AEOLIAN ISLANDS
Messina
EGADI ISLANDS
Palermo
Sea
Marsala
Etna
5
Catania
Bizerte
Siracusa
Tunis
SICILY
PANTELLERIA
TUNISIA
8
MALTA
Sousse
MALTA
Valletta

WHAT TO EAT IN ITALY AND MALTA

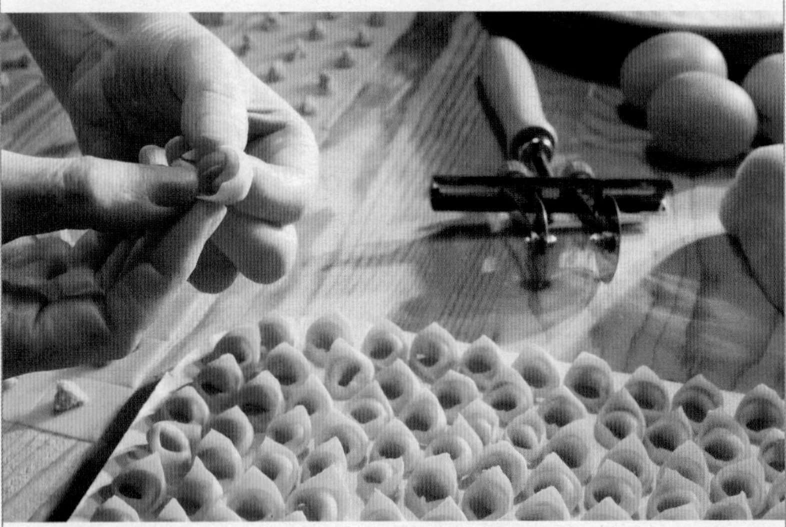

Pasta

PASTA

There are hundreds of pasta shapes and a seemingly infinite number of sauces for them. Be sure to try regional dishes like *carbonara* in Rome, *pici* in Florence and Tuscany, and *orecchiette* in Puglia.

PIZZA

Naples may be the birthplace of pizza, but you'll find it all over Italy in many different forms. The main ones to know are *pizza tonda* (round pizza) and *pizza al taglio* (baked in sheet pans and sold by the slice).

SOUPS AND STEWS

In the winter, there's nothing better than a hearty soup like Tuscan *ribollita* or a rustic *minestrone*. In Malta, the national dish is a rabbit stew called *fenek*.

RISOTTO

When Italians eat rice it's usually in the form of risotto, a dish made with starchy, short-grain rice cooked in broth until it becomes creamy; it's typically embellished with vegetables, cheese, mushrooms, seafood, or meat. Try a classic *risotto alla pescatora* or *risotto alla milanese*.

AFFETTATI

Cold cuts are a classic antipasto served throughout Italy, though the particular kind of ham and sausage varies. Look for *prosciutto crudo* (cured pork), *salame* (dry sausage), and *mortadella* (emulsified pork sausage served thinly sliced). Eat them unadorned, draped on bread or in sandwiches.

CHEESE

Cheeses, too, are regional, though you can often find cheeses like *parmigiano reggiano* all over. Try *mozzarella di bufala* from Campania, *burrata* from Puglia, Sicilian *ricotta, fontina* from the Aosta Valley and *taleggio* from Lombardy.

MEAT AND FISH
Meat and seafood usually appear on menus as *secondi*. In coastal regions, fish is often served whole roasted in the oven or grilled. Meat ranges from hearty steaks to lamb chops or *porchetta* (pork grilled on a spit and flavored with fennel and herbs). In Malta try *lampuki* (a savory fish pie).

STREET FOOD
Popular throughout Italy and Malta, street foods are often eaten as a snack. Try versions of fried rice balls, known as *supplì* in Rome and *arancini* in Sicily, fried fish like anchovies, or Maltese *pastizzi* (savory pastries filled with ricotta or curried peas).

WINE
There are more than 300 official Italian wine varieties. At wine bars and restaurants, you can usually order *un bicchiere* (a glass), a bottle, or sometimes a liter, *mezzo litro* (half liter) or *quarto* (quarter of a liter) of house wine. In Malta, local wine is usually a medium-dry white.

PASTRIES
The most common breakfast throughout Italy is a cappuccino and *cornetto* (croissant), but there are plenty of other delicious pastries worth trying, like *sfogliatella* in Naples and Campania, *pasticciotto* in Puglia, and *maritozzo* in Rome.

Gelato

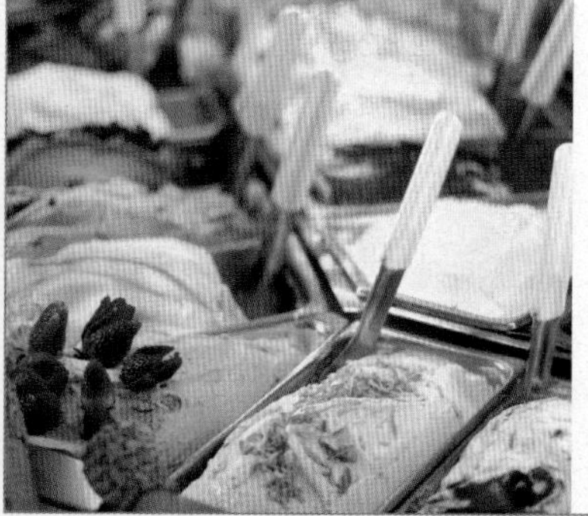

Pizza

GELATO
Softer and silkier than ice cream, gelato is the perfect treat on a hot day. Beware that not all gelato is created equal—look for gelaterias serving all-natural gelato made with fresh ingredients.

TRUFFLES
More truffles are found in Umbria than anywhere else in Italy. Spoleto and Norcia are prime territory for the tartufo nero, prized for its extravagant flavor and intense aroma. But the milder summer truffle is in season from May through December, and the autumn truffle is found from October to December.

SWEETS
Said to have originated in Venice, tiramisu lovers will have ample opportunity to sample this creamy delight made from ladyfingers soaked in espresso and rum or brandy and covered with mascarpone cream and cinnamon. Semifreddo (soft homemade ice cream) is often found on Venetian (and other) menus.

Italy and Malta Snapshot

Know Before You Go

BOOK IN ADVANCE.

Avoid waiting in line for hours by buying museum tickets online before your visit. Also, the earlier you buy high-speed train tickets in Italy, the less expensive they're likely to be (regional trains and seat reservation are not cheaper).

LACE UP YOUR WALKING SHOES.

The best way to see a city is on foot. While public transport in Italy works well, in recent years many city and town centers have been pedestrianized. Fall in with a weekend afternoon passeggiata in smaller towns, where Italians stroll the main street dressed in their Sunday best.

USE BUSES IN MALTA.

Malta does not have a well-developed train system, but modern buses go virtually everywhere. Transportation for locals is free, while tourists must buy an Explore or ExplorePlus card for seven days of bus transit.

Planning Your Time

Although breakfast is generally served from 7 to 10:30, other mealtimes vary by region. In the north, lunch is noon to 2, whereas restaurants in the south often serve it until 3. You may have difficulty finding dinner in the north after 9 pm, when most southerners are just sitting down to eat (restaurants there tend not to open until 7:30). And shoppers take note: many stores close from 1 to 4:30. Mealtimes in Malta are more similar to those in southern Italy.

Great Trips

3 days. You can't see all of Rome in three days, but you can see the major sights and perhaps squeeze in a side trip to the nearby hill towns known as the Castelli Romani.

4 days. Pair a day in Naples with three days exploring the Amalfi Coast or the nearby islands of Capri and Ischia.

5 days. Combine a couple of days in Florence with three days exploring Tuscany's countryside and hill towns such as Lucca, Siena, and San Gimignano.

3 days. Spend a day exploring Valletta, one exploring the Three Cities and Sliema, and take a day trip to the beaches of Gozo.

Big Events

Carnival. In both Venice and Malta, Carnival (the period in February leading up to Lent) is a big celebration.

Biennale di Venezia. Come springtime in even-numbered years, the contemporary art world descends on Venice. In odd years leading architects display their creations. 🌐 *www.labiennale.org*

Milan Design Week. For a week in April Italy's northern powerhouse city hosts the biggest gathering of the design world. 🌐 *www.salonemilano.it*

Fiera Internazionale del Tartufo Bianco. From early October to early December, Alba hosts an internationally famous truffle fair. The fourth Sunday of September sees the Palio degli Asini, a hilarious donkey race, a lampoon of Asti's eminently serious horse race. 🌐 *www.fieradeltartufo.org*

What To...

READ

The Neapolitan novels, Elena Ferrante. These novels and the HBO TV series bring multilayered postwar Naples to life.

Italian Folk Tales, Italo Calvino. The Cuban-born and Liguria-raised magical realist published this fabulous collection in 1956.

The Leopard, Giuseppe Tommasi di Lampedusa. The Italian literary classic chronicles the tumultuous, revolutionary years of the Risorgimento (1860s–early 20th century) in Sicily.

SPQR: A History of Ancient Rome, Mary Beard. The renowned classicist set out to understand how a small village became the center of a powerful empire.

WATCH

La Dolce Vita, Federico Fellini. One of the great masterpieces of Italian cinema.

The Great Beauty, Paolo Sorrentino. This Oscar-winning 2013 film about an aging journalist is set in Rome.

Call Me By Your Name, Luca Guadagnino. Set in 1980s northern Italy, this film is a bit of a coming of age story and a bit of a love story.

Stanley Tucci: Searching for Italy. The Italian-American actor goes on a culinary and cultural adventure around Italy.

Troy. The big screen adaptation of Homer's epic was shot across Malta.

LISTEN TO

Volare, Nel Blu Dipinto di Blu. 1958, Domenico Modugno and Franco Migliacci

Tu Vuò Fa' l'Americano. 1956 jazz song

Quando Quando Quando. 1962, Tony Renis

Palla Al Centro. 2022, Jovanotti and Elisa

BUY

Hand-painted pottery: from Grottaglie in Puglia, Deruta in Umbria, Vietri sul Mare on the Amalfi Coast, and Sciacca in Sicily. *Ganutell* (intricately woven wire flowers) in Malta.

Fashion: Make sure to browse the smaller boutiques and not just flagship stores.

Leather: top-quality bags, as well as wallets, belts, and jackets.

Food: From specialty shops like Tartufi Morra in Alba for truffle products to wine shops selling bottles impossible to find back home. Gozo produces exceptional cheese.

Contacts

AIR

Major Airports: Leonardo Da Vinci Fiumicino Airport (Rome, FCO); Malpensa International Airport (Milan, MXP); Marco Polo International Airport (Venice, VCE); Gallileo Gallei International Airport (Florence, PSA); Naples International Airport (NAP); Catania Fontanarossa Airport (Sicily, CTA); Olbia Costa Smeralda Airport (Sardinia, OLB); Malta International Airport (MLA).

BOAT

Alilauro. Hydrofoils between Naples, Capri, Ischia, Sorrento, and the Aeolian Islands. 🌐 *www.alilauro.it*

Gozo Channel Ferries. Car and passenger service. 🌐 *www.gozochannel.com*

SNAV. Ferries in Sicily, Sardinia, and the Pontine Islands. 🌐 *www.snav.it*

Tirrenia. Connects Civitavecchia and Naples to Sicily and Sardinia. 🌐 *www.tirrenia.it*

Valletta Ferry Services. Connects Valletta with Sliema and the Three Cities. 🌐 *www.vallettaferryservices.com*

Virtu Ferries. Car and passenger service between Malta and Sicily. 🌐 *www.virtuferries.com*

TRAIN

Italo. 🌐 *www.italotreno.it*

Trenital ia. 🌐 *www.trenitalia.com*

VISITOR INFORMATION

Italian Ministry of Tourism. 🌐 *www.italia.it*

Malta Tourism Authority. 🌐 *www.visitmalta.com*

Rome and the Vatican

The timeless city to which all roads lead, Mamma Roma enthralls visitors today as she has since time immemorial. Here the ancient Romans made us heirs-in-law to what we call Western Civilization; where centuries later Michelangelo painted the Sistine Chapel; and where Gian Lorenzo Bernini's Baroque nymphs and naiads still dance in their marble fountains.

Today the city remains a veritable Grand Canyon of culture. Ancient Rome rubs shoulders with the medieval, the modern runs into the Renaissance, and the result is like nothing so much as an open-air museum, this one filled with churches, piazzas, and winding streets through picturesque neighborhoods.

But always remember: "*Quando a Roma vai, fai come vedrai*" (When in Rome, do as the Romans do). Don't feel intimidated by the press of art and culture. Instead, contemplate the grandeur from a table at a sun-drenched café on Piazza della Rotonda; let Rome's colorful life flow around you without feeling guilty because you haven't seen everything. It can't be done, anyway. There's just so much here that you'll have to come back, so be sure to throw a coin in the Trevi Fountain.

It's important to remember that the Vatican is *in* Rome but it isn't *Rome.* Instead, it's a city-state unto itself, even if the only "citizens" are the pope and his priests. For good Catholics and sinners alike, the Vatican is an exercise in spirituality, requiring patience but delivering joy. Some come here for a transcendent glimpse of a heavenly Michelangelo fresco; others come in search of a direct connection with the divine. But what all visitors share, for a few hours, is an awe-inspiring landscape that offers a famous sight for every taste: rooms decorated by Raphael, antique sculptures like the Apollo Belvedere, famous paintings by Giotto and Bellini, and, perhaps most of all, the Sistine Chapel—for the lover of beauty, few places are as historically important as this epitome of faith and grandeur.

The Colosseum

Gladiators and Glory

The most spectacular extant edifice of ancient Rome, the Colosseum has a history that is half gore, half glory. Once able to house 50,000 spectators, it was built to impress Romans with its spectacles involving wild animals and fearsome gladiators from the farthest reaches of the empire. Senators had marble seats up front and the vestal virgins took the ringside position, while the plebs sat in wooden tiers at the back, then the masses above on the top tier. Looming over all was the amazing *velarium*, an ingenious system of sail-like awnings rigged on ropes and maneuvered by sailors from the imperial fleet, who would unfurl them to protect the arena's occupants from sun or rain.

Don't Miss

By booking a guided tour, you can visit the *hypogeum:* the subterranean passageways that were the architectural engine rooms that made the slaughter above proceed like clockwork. In a scene prefiguring something from Dante's Inferno, hundreds of beasts would wait to be eventually launched via a series of slave-powered hoists and lifts into the bloodthirsty sand of the arena above.

Stay Here

If you dream of waking up to head-on views of the Colosseum, look no further than Palazzo Manfredi. ✉ *Via Labicana, 125* 🌐 *www.manfredihotels.com*

✉ *Piazza del Colosseo* ☎ *06/39967700* 🌐 *www.coopculture.it* 🎫 *€16 for 24-hr ticket, €22 Full Experience ticket* ✍ *To avoid long lines, tickets should be purchased in advance* 🚆 *Colosseo stop on metro line B or Tram 3*

The Roman Forum

The Heart of Ancient Rome

Whether it's from the main entrance on Via dei Fori Imperali or by the entrance at the Arch of Titus, descend into the extraordinary archaeological complex that is the Foro Romano and the Palatine Hill, once the very heart of the Roman world. The Forum began life as a marshy valley between the Capitoline and Palatine Hills—a valley crossed by a mud track and used as a cemetery by Iron Age settlers. Over the years, a market center and some huts were established here, and after the land was drained in the 6th century BC, the site eventually became a political, religious, and commercial center: the Forum. Hundreds of years of plunder reduced the Forum to its current desolate state. But this enormous area was once Rome's pulsating hub, filled with stately and extravagant temples, palaces, and shops, and crowded with people from all corners of the empire.

Don't Miss

Standing at the northern approach to the Palatine Hill on the Via Sacra, the Arco di Tito was erected in AD 81 to celebrate the sack of Jerusalem 10 years earlier, after the First Jewish–Roman War. Under the arch are two great sculpted reliefs, both showing scenes from Titus's triumphal parade along this very Via Sacra.

✉ *Entrance at Via dei Fori Imperiali, Monti* ☎ *06/39967700* 🌐 *www.coopculture.it* 🎫 *An €18 combined ticket includes single entry to Palatine Hill–Forum site and single entry to Colosseum (if used within 24 hrs); S.U.P.E.R. ticket €22 (€24 with online reservation) includes access to Houses of Augustus and Livia, Palatine Museum, Aula Isiaca, Santa Maria Antiqua, and Temple of Romulus; audio guide €5 Advance tickets strongly encouraged, especially in high season* 🚇 *Colosseo*

St. Peter's Basilica

The World's Largest Church

The world's largest church, built over the tomb of St. Peter, is the most imposing and breathtaking architectural achievement of the Renaissance (although much of the lavish interior dates to the Baroque). No fewer than five of Italy's greatest artists—Bramante, Raphael, Peruzzi, Antonio da Sangallo the Younger, and Michelangelo—died while striving to erect this new St. Peter's. Highlights include the Loggia delle Benedizioni (Benediction Loggia), the balcony where newly elected popes are proclaimed; Michelangelo's *Pietà;* and Bernini's great bronze canopy, as well as many other Bernini masterpieces.

Don't Miss

For views of both the dome above and the piazza below, take the elevator or stairs to the roof; the apex of the dome can be reached via a spiral staircase.

Those who don't wish to go high can go low; the Grotte Vaticana, where you can see over 90 tombs of former popes, royalty, and dignitaries, including St. Peter himself.

Best Souvenir

If you are Catholic (or perhaps even if you aren't), you can purchase a vial shaped like the Virgin Mary in the gift shop and have it filled with holy water.

✉ Viale Vaticano, near intersection with Via Leone IV, Vatican 🌐 www.vatican.va 🎫 Free (but security lines to enter the basilica can be very long) ⏲ Closed during Papal Audience (Wed. until 1 pm) and during other ceremonies in piazza 🚊 Ottaviano

Vatican Museums

Treasures Beyond Measure

Other than the pope and his papal court, the occupants of the Vatican are some of the most famous artworks in the world. The Vatican Palace, residence of the popes since 1377, consists of an estimated 1,400 rooms, chapels, and galleries. The pope and his household occupy only a small part; most of the rest is given over to the Vatican Library and Museums. The collection is extraordinarily rich: highlights include the great antique sculptures (including the celebrated Apollo Belvedere in the Octagonal Courtyard and the Belvedere Torso in the Hall of the Muses); the Stanze di Raffaello (Raphael Rooms), with their famous gorgeous frescoes; and the Old Master paintings, such as Leonardo da Vinci's beautiful (though unfinished) *St. Jerome in the Wilderness*, some of Raphael's greatest creations, and Caravaggio's gigantic *Deposition in the Pinacoteca* ("Picture Gallery").

Don't Miss

The famous Capella Sistina (Sistine Chapel), where popes are elected, is part of the Vatican Museums. If you visit, a pair of binoculars helps greatly, as does a small mirror. Lines are shorter after 2:30 in the afternoon, but the chapel can become so uncomfortably crowded that this is the one place that is well worth splurging for an expensive after- or before-hours private tour. The Vatican Gardens are also included with admission to the museums.

✉ Viale Vaticano, near intersection with Via Leone IV, Vatican ☎ 06/698 83145 🌐 www.museivaticani.va 🎫 €17; tours start at €34 Closed Sun. and church holidays 🚇 Cipro–Musei Vaticani or Ottaviano–San Pietro; Bus 64 or 40 ✍ Advance reservations strongly encouraged

The Pantheon

Rome's Most Perfect Ancient Building

The best preserved ancient building in the city, this former Roman temple is a marvel of architectural harmony and proportion. It was entirely rebuilt by the emperor Hadrian around AD 120 on the site of an earlier Pantheon (from the Greek: *pan*, all, and *theon*, gods) erected in 27 BC by Augustus's right-hand man and son-in-law, Agrippa. The most striking thing about the Pantheon is not its size, immense though it is, nor even the phenomenal technical difficulties posed by so massive a construction; rather, it's the remarkable unity of the building. The diameter described by the dome is exactly equal to its height. It's the use of such simple mathematical balance that gives classical architecture its characteristic sense of proportion and its nobility. The opening at the apex of the dome, the oculus, is nearly 30 feet in diameter and was intended to symbolize the "all-seeing eye of the heavens." One of the reasons the Pantheon is so well preserved is the result of it being consecrated as a church in AD 608.

Don't Miss

The Pantheon is also one of the city's important burial places. Its most famous tomb is that of Raphael (between the second and third chapels on the left as you enter).

✉ *Piazza della Rotonda* ☎ *06/68300230* 🌐 *www.pantheonroma.com* 🎫 *Free; audio guide €9* 🚊 *The Spagna and Barberini metro stops are both about a 15-min walk away. Alternatively, take a bus to Largo Argentina or Corso Rinascimento*

Piazza Navona

Rome's Most Breathtaking Baroque Piazza

Always camera-ready, the beautiful Baroque plaza known as Piazza Navona has Bernini sculptures, three gorgeous fountains, a magnificently Baroque church (Sant'Agnese in Agone), and under it all the remains of a Roman athletics track. Pieces of the arena are still visible near the adjacent Piazza Sant'Apollinare, and the ancient spirit of entertainment lives on in the buskers and mimes who populate the piazza today. The piazza took on its current look during the 17th century, after Pope Innocent X of the Pamphilj family decided to make over his family palace (now the Brazilian embassy and an ultraluxe hotel) and the rest of the piazza.

Don't Miss

Center stage is the Fontana dei Quattro Fiumi, created for Innocent by Bernini in 1651. Bernini's powerful figures of the four rivers represent the longest rivers of the four known continents at the time: the Nile (his head covered because the source was unknown); the Ganges; the Danube; and the Plata (the length of the Amazon was then unknown). Popular legend has it that the figure of the Plata—the figure closest to Sant'Agnese in Agone—raises his hand before his eyes because he can't bear to look upon the church's "inferior" facade designed by Francesco Borromini, Bernini's rival.

Getting Here

The metro stops Spagna and Barberini are both about a 20-minute walk away, but several buses stop nearby on Corso Rinascimento or Corso Vittorio Emanuele II.

The Spanish Steps

The Staircase Known Around the World

The iconic Spanish Steps (often called simply *la scalinata*, or "the staircase," by Italians) and the Piazza di Spagna from which they ascend both get their names from the Spanish Embassy to the Vatican on the piazza—even though the staircase was built with French funds by an Italian in 1723. In honor of a diplomatic visit by the King of Spain, the hillside was transformed by architect Francesco de Sanctis with a spectacular piece of urban planning to link the church of Trinità dei Monti at the top with the Via Condotti below. In an allusion to the church, the staircase is divided by three landings (beautifully lined by potted azaleas mid-April–mid-May).

Don't Miss

Bookending the bottom of the steps are two beloved holdovers from the 18th century, when the area was known as the "English Ghetto": to the right, the Keats-Shelley House, and to the left, Babington's Tea Rooms—both beautifully redolent of the era of the Grand Tour. At the bottom of the steps, Bernini's splendid "Barcaccia" (sinking ship) fountain dates to the early 17th century and still spouts drinking water from the ancient Aqua Vergine aqueduct.

Best Spot for Coffee

Antico Caffè Greco. Pricey, this is a national landmark and Rome's oldest café. It has served the likes of Byron, Shelley, Keats, Goethe, and Casanova. It serves a perfect espresso. $ *Average main: €12* ✉ *Via dei Condotti 86, Piazza di Spagna* ☎ *06/6791700* 🌐 *www.caffegreco.shop* 🚇 *Spagna*

Getting Here

Piazza di Spagna is a short walk from Piazza del Popolo, the Pantheon, and the Trevi Fountain. One of Rome's handiest subway stations, Spagna, is tucked just left of the steps.

The Trevi Fountain

The World's Most Famous Fountain

Alive with rushing waters commanded by an imperious sculpture of Oceanus, the Fontana di Trevi has been all about theatrical effects from the start; it is an aquatic marvel in a city filled with them. The fountain's unique drama is largely due to its location: its vast basin is squeezed into the tight confluence of three little streets (the *tre vie*, which may give the fountain its name), with cascades emerging as if from the wall of Palazzo Poli. The dream of a fountain emerging full-force from a palace was first envisioned by Bernini and Pietro da Cortona from Pope Urban VIII's plan to rebuild an older fountain, which had earlier marked the end-point of the ancient Acqua Vergine aqueduct, created in 18 BC by Agrippa. Three popes later, under Pope Clement XIII, Nicola Salvi finally broke ground with his winning design.

Don't Miss

Everyone knows the famous legend that if you throw a coin into the Trevi Fountain you will ensure a return trip to the Eternal City, but not everyone knows how to do it the right way. You must toss a coin with your right hand over your left shoulder, with your back to the fountain. One coin means you'll return to Rome; two, you'll return and fall in love; three, you'll return, find love, and marry.

Getting Here

The Barberini metro stop on Line A is less than a 10-minute walk away.

Trastevere

Rome's Most Picturesque Neighborhood

Across the Tiber from the Jewish Ghetto is Trastevere (literally "across the Tiber"), long cherished as Rome's Greenwich Village and now subject to rampant gentrification. In spite of this, Trastevere remains about the most tightly knit community in the city, the Trasteverini proudly proclaiming their descent from the ancient Romans. Ancient bridges—the Ponte Fabricio and the Ponte Cestio—link Trastevere and the Ghetto to Isola Tiberina (Tiber Island), a diminutive sandbar and one of Rome's most picturesque sights.

Don't Miss

Money was no object to the extravagant Agostino Chigi, a banker from Siena who financed many papal projects. His munificence is evident in Villa Farnesina, built for him about 1511. He was especially proud of the decorative frescoes in the airy loggias, some painted by Raphael himself, notably a luminous Triumph of Galatea. In the magnificent Loggia of Psyche on the ground floor, Giulio Romano and others worked from Raphael's designs. Raphael's lovely Galatea is in the adjacent room.

Getting Here

From the Vatican or Spanish Steps, expect a 30- to 40-minute walk. From Termini station, take Bus No. 40 Express or No. 64 to Largo di Torre Argentina, where you can switch to Tram No. 8 to get to Trastevere.

Best Bar

Freni & Frizioni. This bar has a cute artist vibe, and is great for an afternoon coffee, tea, or aperitivo, or for late-night socializing. Though the vibe is laid-back, the bartenders take their cocktails seriously—and have the awards to prove it. ✉ *Via del Politeama 4, Trastevere* 🌐 *www.freniefrizioni.com*

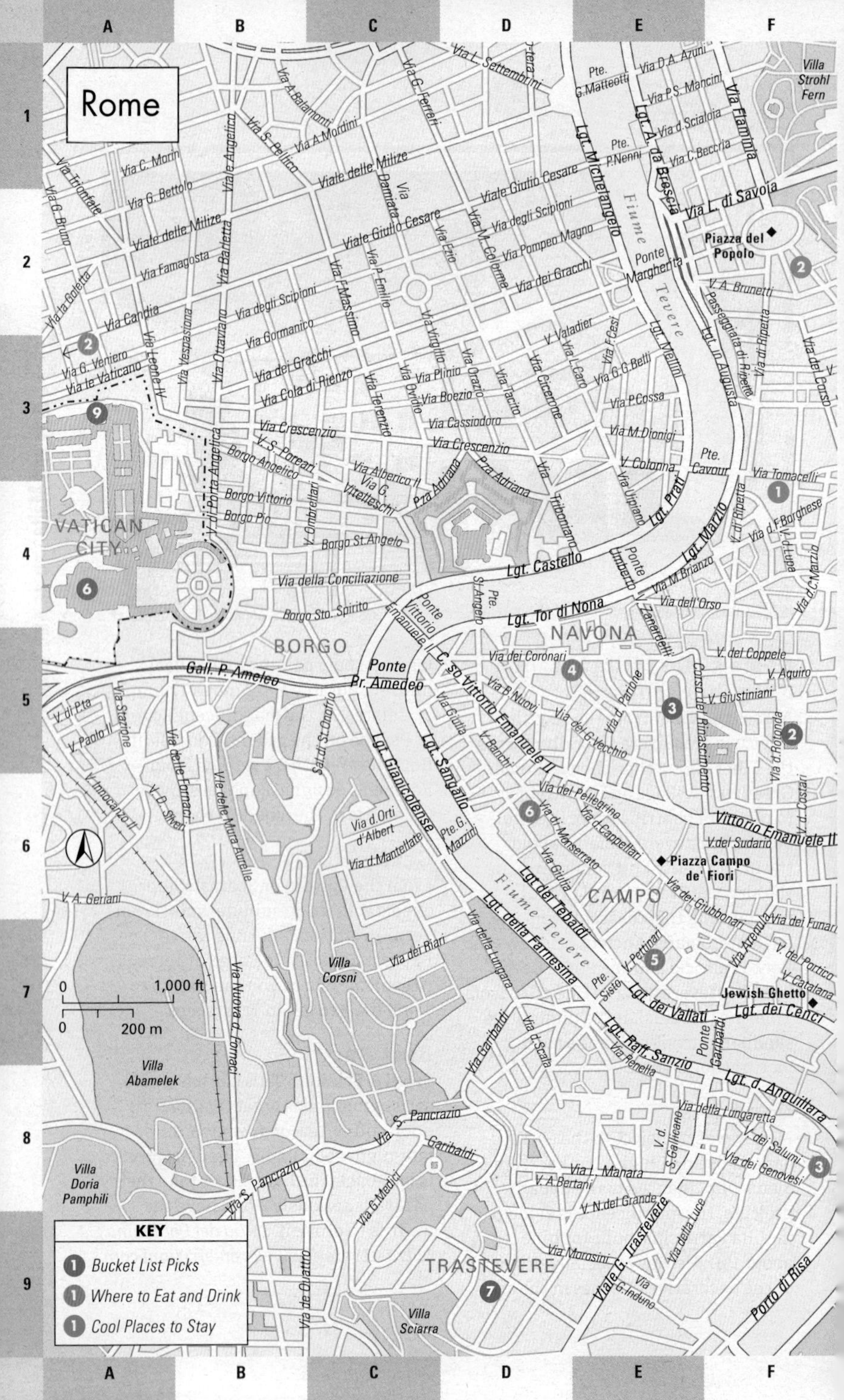

Rome
A
B
C
D
E
F
1
2
3
4
5
6
7
8
9
Villa Strohl Fern
Piazza del Popolo
Via L. Settembrini
Pte. G.Matteotti
Via D.A. Azuni
Via P.S. Mancini
Via d. Scialoia
Via C. Beccria
Via Flaminia
Lgt. A. da Brescia
Pte. P.Nenni
Via L. di Savoia
Lgt. Michelangelo
Fiume Tevere
Ponte Margherita
V. A. Brunetti
Passeggiata di Ripetta
Lgt. in Augusta
Via di Ripetta
Via del Corso
Via A.Balamonti
Via G. Ferrari
Via S. Pellico
Via A. Mordini
Viale Angelico
Via C. Morin
Via Trionfale
Via G. Bruno
Via G. Bettolo
Viale delle Milizie
Via Damiata
Viale Giulio Cesare
Via degli Scipioni
Via Pompeo Magno
Via dei Gracchi
Via M. Colonna
Via Ezio
Via P. Emilio
Via F. Massimo
Via Famagosta
Via Barletta
Via la Goletta
Via Candia
Via Vespasiano
Via Ottaviano
Via Leone IV
Via Gormanico
Via Cola di Rienzo
Via G. Veniero
Via le Vaticano
Via Terenzio
Via Ovidio
Via Plinio
Via Boezio
Via Virgilio
Via Orazio
Via Tacito
Via Cicerone
V. Valadier
Via L. Caro
Via F. Cesi
Via G.G. Belli
Lgt. Mellini
Via P. Cossa
Via M. Dionigi
Via Cassiodoro
Via Crescenzio
V. Colonna
Pte. Cavour
Via Tomacelli
Lgt. Prati
Via Ulpiano
Via Tribroniano
Via Alberico II
Via G. Vitelleschi
V.S. Porcari
Borgo Angelico
Borgo Vittorio
Borgo Pio
V. di Porta Angelica
V. Ombrellari
Borgo St. Angelo
Pza Adriana
VATICAN CITY
Via della Conciliazione
Borgo Sto. Spirito
Lgt. Castello
Ponte Umberto
Lgt. Marzio
Via M. Brianzo
Via dell'Orso
V. d. F. Borghese
V. d. Lupa
Via d. C. Marzio
V. di Ripetta
Ponte Vittorio Emanuele II
Pte. St. Angelo
Lgt. Tor di Nona
NAVONA
V. Zanardelli
BORGO
Via dei Coronari
Corso del Rinascimento
V. del Coppele
V. Aquiro
V. Giustiniani
Via d. Rotonda
Gall. P. Ameleo
Ponte Pr. Amedeo
C. so Vittorio Emanuele II
Via B. Nuovi
Via del G. Vecchio
Via d. Parione
V. di Pta
V. Paolo II
Via Stazione
V. Innocenzo II
V. D. Silvei
Via delle Fornaci
V. le delle Mura Aurelie
Sal. di St. Onofrio
Lgt. Gianicolense
Lgt. Sangallo
Via Giulia
V. Banchi
Via del Pellegrino
Via d. Cappellari
Vittorio Emanuele II
V. del Sudario
V. d. Costari
Via d. Orti d'Albert
Via d. Mantellate
Pte. G. Mazzini
Via di Monserrato
Piazza Campo de' Fiori
CAMPO
Via dei Giubbonari
Via dei Funari
V. A. Geriani
Lgt. dei Tebaldi
Lgt. della Farnesina
Via della Lungara
Via dei Riari
Villa Corsni
V. Pettinari
Via Arenula
V. del Portico
V. Catalana
Jewish Ghetto
Lgt. dei Cenci
Pte. Sisto
Lgt. dei Vallati
0
1,000 ft
200 m
Via Nuova d. Fornaci
Villa Abamelek
Via Garibaldi
Via d. Scala
Lgt. Raff. Sanzio
Via Renella
Ponte Garibaldi
Lgt. d. Anguillara
Via della Lungaretta
V. dei Salumi
Via dei Genovesi
Via S. Pancrazio
Garibaldi
Villa Doria Pamphili
Via S. Pancrazio
V. A. Bertani
Via L. Manara
V. d. S. Gallicano
V. N. del Grande
Via G. Medici
Via della Luce
Viale G. Trastevere
Via Morosini
TRASTEVERE
Via G. Induno
Porto di Risa
Via de Quattro
Villa Sciarra
KEY
Bucket List Picks
Where to Eat and Drink
Cool Places to Stay

Bucket List Picks

1 The Colosseum I8
2 The Pantheon F5
3 Piazza Navona E5
4 The Roman Forum H7
5 The Spanish Steps G3
6 St. Peter's Basilica A4
7 Trastevere D9
8 The Trevi Fountain H5
9 Vatican Museums A3

Where to Eat and Drink

1 Ai Tre Scalini I6
2 Bonci Pizzarium A3
3 Da Enzo F8
4 Gelateria del Teatro E5
5 Pianostrada E7
6 Pierluigi D6

Cool Places to Stay

1 Hotel Vilòn F4
2 Hotel de Russie F2
3 Palazzo Manfredi J8

When in Rome and the Vatican

★ Catacombe di San Sebastiano (*Catacombs of St. Sebastian*)

CEMETERY | The 4th-century church at this site was named after the saint who was buried in its catacomb, which burrows underground on four different levels. This was the only early Christian cemetery to remain accessible during the Middle Ages, and it was from here that the term "catacomb" is derived—it's in a spot where the road dips into a hollow, known to the Romans as a *catacumba* (Greek for "near the hollow"). ✉ *Via Appia Antica 136, Via Appia Antica* ☎ *06/7850350* 🌐 *www.catacombe.org* 🎫 *€10* ⏲ *Closed Dec.*

★ Galleria Borghese

ART MUSEUM | The luxury-loving Cardinal Scipione Borghese had this museum custom-built in 1612 as a showcase for his fabulous collection of both antiquities and more "modern" works. One of the collection's most famous works is Canova's Neoclassical sculpture, *Pauline Borghese as Venus Victorious*. Nearby are three key early Baroque sculptures by Bernini: *David, Apollo and Daphne,* and *The Rape of Persephone* . You'll also find masterpieces by Caravaggio, Raphael (including his moving *Deposition*), Pinturicchio, Perugino, Bellini, and Rubens. Probably the gallery's most famous painting is Titian's allegorical *Sacred and Profane Love*. **TIP→ Admission to the Galleria Borghese is by reservation only. Visitors are admitted in two-hour shifts 9–5. Prime-time slots sell out days in advance, so reserve and directly (and early) through the museum's website.** ✉ *Piazzale Scipione Borghese 5, off Via Pinciana, Villa Borghese* ☎ *06/32810 reservations, 06/8413979 info* 🌐 *galleria-borghese.beniculturali.it* 🎫 *€15, including €2 reservation fee; increased fee during temporary exhibitions* ⏲ *Closed Mon.* ✍ *Reservations essential.*

★ Jewish Ghetto

HISTORIC DISTRICT | The very first Jewish ghetto in Europe also contains the continent's highest density of Renaissance-era synagogues, and visiting them on a guided tour is interesting not only culturally but also aesthetically. In 1516, the Venetian Senate voted to confine Jews to an island in Cannaregio, whose gates were locked at night and whose canals were patrolled. In the 16th century, the community grew with refugees from the Inquisition. Although the gates were pulled down after Napoléon's 1797 arrival, the ghetto was reinstated during the Austrian occupation. Full freedom wasn't realized until 1866 with the founding of the Italian state. Many Jews fled Italy after Mussolini's 1938 racial laws, but of the remainder, all but eight were killed by the Nazis. You can visit some of the historic buildings of the ghetto on guided tours, which run in English every hour from 10 am to 5 pm (starting 9 am on Fridays) every day except Saturday. ✉ *Campo del Ghetto Nuovo, Cannaregio* ☎ *055/2989815* 🌐 *www.ghettovenezia.com* 🎫 *€12 for guided tour* ⏲ *No guided tours on Sat. or Jewish holidays.*

★ Musei Capitolini

ART MUSEUM | Surpassed in size and richness only by the Musei Vaticani, the world's first public museum—with the greatest hits of Roman art through the ages, from the ancients to the Baroque—is housed in the Palazzo dei Conservatori and the Palazzo Nuovo, which mirror one another across Michelangelo's famous piazza. The collection was begun by Pope Sixtus IV (the man who built the Sistine Chapel) in 1473, when he donated a room of ancient statuary to the people of the city. This core of the collection includes the She Wolf, which is the symbol of Rome, and the piercing gaze of the Capitoline Brutus. Buy your ticket and enter the Palazzo dei Conservatori where, in the first courtyard, you'll see the giant head, foot, elbow, and imperially raised finger of the fabled seated statue of

Constantine, which once dominated the Basilica of Maxentius in the Forum. As you walk between the two halves of the museum, be sure to take the staircase to the Tabularium gallery and its unparalleled view over the Forum. ✉ *Piazza del Campidoglio 1, Piazza Venezia* ☎ *06/0608* 🌐 *www.museicapitolini.org* 🎫 *€11.50 (€16 with exhibitions); €18 with access to Centrale Montemartini; €7 audio guide* Ⓜ *Colosseo.*

Piazza Campo de' Fiori

MARKET | FAMILY | A bustling marketplace in the morning (Monday through Saturday from 8 to 2) and a trendy meeting place the rest of the day and night, this piazza has plenty of down-to-earth charm. After lunch, it becomes a circus of bars particularly favored by study-abroad students, tourists, and young expats. Brooding over the piazza is a hooded statue of the philosopher Giordano Bruno, who was burned at the stake here in 1600 for heresy. ✉ *Intersection of Via dei Baullari, Via Giubbonari, Via del Pellegrino, and Piazza della Cancelleria, Campo de' Fiori.*

★ Piazza del Popolo

PLAZA/SQUARE | FAMILY | With its obelisk and twin churches, this immense square marks what was, for centuries, Rome's northern entrance, where all roads from the north converged and where visitors, many of them pilgrims, got their first impression of the Eternal City. The desire to make this entrance to Rome something special was a pet project of popes and their architects for more than three centuries. Although it was once crowded with fashionable carriages, the piazza today is a pedestrian zone. At election time, it's the scene of huge political rallies, and on New Year's Eve, Rome stages a mammoth alfresco party here. ✉ *Piazza del Popolo* Ⓜ *Flaminio.*

Where to Eat and Drink

★ Ai Tre Scalini

WINE BARS | An ivy-covered wine bar in the center of Monti, Rome's trendiest 'hood, Ai Tre Scalini has a warm and cozy menu of delicious antipasti and light entrées to go along with its enticing wine list. After about 8 pm, if you haven't booked, be prepared to wait—this is one extremely popular spot with locals. ✉ *Via Panisperna 251, Monti* ☎ *06/48907495* 🌐 *www.aitrescalini.org* Ⓜ *Cavour.*

★ Bonci Pizzarium

$ | PIZZA | FAMILY | This tiny storefront by famed pizzaiolo Gabriele Bonci is the city's most famous place for pizza al taglio (by the slice). It serves more than a dozen versions, from the standard margherita to slices piled high with prosciutto and other tasty ingredients. **Known for:** Rome's best pizza al taglio; over a dozen flavors; long lines. Ⓢ *Average main: €5* ✉ *Via della Meloria 43, Prati* ☎ *06/39745416* 🌐 *www.bonci.it* ⏲ *Closed Mon.* Ⓜ *Cipro.*

★ Da Enzo

$ | ROMAN | In the quieter part of Trastevere, the family-run Da Enzo is everything you would imagine a classic Roman trattoria to be. There are just a few tables, but diners from around the world line up to eat here—a testament to the quality of the food. **Known for:** cacio e pepe (pasta with pecorino-cheese sauce and black pepper), carbonara, and other Roman classics; boisterous, authentic atmosphere; small space with long waits. Ⓢ *Average main: €14* ✉ *Via dei Vascellari 29, Trastevere* ☎ *06/5812260* 🌐 *www.daenzoal29.com* ⏲ *Closed Sun. and 2 wks in Aug.*

★ Gelateria Del Teatro

$ | ICE CREAM | FAMILY | In a window next to the entrance of this renowned gelateria, you can see the fresh fruit being used to create the day's flavors, which highlight the best of Italy—from Amalfi lemons to Alban hazelnuts. In addition to traditional options, look for interesting combinations like raspberry and sage or white chocolate with basil. **Known for:** sublime gelato; seasonal, all natural ingredients; charming location on a cobblestone street. Ⓢ *Average main: €3* ✉ *Via dei Coronari 65/66, Piazza Navona* ☎ *06/45474880* 🌐 *www.gelateriadelteatro.it.*

★ Pianostrada

$$ | MODERN ITALIAN | This restaurant has an open kitchen, where you can watch the talented women owners cook up a storm of inventive delights—this is a "kitchen *lab*," after all, where top local ingredients are whipped into delicious plates. The spaghetti with tomato sauce, smoked ricotta, parmigiano, basil, and lemon peel is one of the signature dishes, and the amped-up traditional recipe is a delicious indication of how interesting the food can get. **Known for:** freshly baked focaccia with various toppings; creative burgers and salads; secret garden seating. Ⓢ *Average main: €20* ✉ *Via delle Zoccolette 22, Campo de' Fiori* ☎ *06/89572296* ⏲ *Closed Mon. No lunch Tues.–Fri.*

★ Pierluigi

$$$$ | SEAFOOD | This popular seafood restaurant is a fun spot on balmy summer evenings, where elegant diners sip crisp white wine at tables out on the pretty Piazza de' Ricci. As at most Italian restaurants, fresh fish is sold per hectogram (100 grams, or about 3.5 ounces), so you may want to double-check the cost after it's been weighed. **Known for:** top-quality fish and seafood; tables on the pretty pedestrianized piazza; elegant atmosphere with great service. Ⓢ *Average main: €38* ✉ *Piazza de' Ricci 144, Campo de' Fiori* ☎ *06/6868717* 🌐 *www.pierluigi.it.*

Cool Places to Stay

★ Hotel de Russie

$$$$ | HOTEL | Occupying a 19th-century hotel that once hosted royalty, Picasso, and Cocteau, the Hotel de Russie is now the first choice in Rome for government bigwigs and Hollywood high rollers seeking ultimate luxury in a secluded retreat. **Pros:** big potential for celebrity sightings; well-equipped gym and world-class spa; excellent Stravinskij cocktail bar has courtyard tables. **Cons:** faster Internet comes at a fee; breakfast not included; very expensive. Ⓢ *Rooms from: €1,100* ✉ *Via del Babuino 9, Piazza del Popolo* ☎ *06/328881* 🌐 *www.roccofortehotels.com/hotels-and-resorts/hotel-de-russie* *120 rooms* 🍽 *No Meals* Ⓜ *Flaminio.*

★ Hotel Vilòn

$$$$ | HOTEL | Set in a 16th-century mansion annexed to Palazzo Borghese and tucked behind a discreet entrance, this intimate hotel might be Rome's best-kept secret. **Pros:** gorgeous design; attentive staff; fantastic location. **Cons:** no spa or gym; some rooms are a bit small; not much communal space. Ⓢ *Rooms from: €460* ✉ *Via dell'Arancio 69, Piazza di Spagna* ☎ *06/878187* 🌐 *www.hotelvilon.com* *18 rooms* 🍽 *Free Breakfast* Ⓜ *Spagna.*

Palazzo Manfredi

$$$$ | HOTEL | If you dream of waking up to head-on views of the Colosseum, book into this boutique hotel, which is set in a 17th-century palazzo built over the ruins of the Ludus Magnus, the gymnasium used by Roman gladiators, and offers refined luxury. **Pros:** incredible views; unparalleled location; excellent restaurant and cocktail bar. **Cons:** not all rooms have Colosseum views; some guests complain about noise; no spa. Ⓢ *Rooms from: €550* ✉ *Via Labicana 125, Colosseo* ☎ *06/77591380* 🌐 *www.manfredihotels.com* *20 rooms* 🍽 *No Meals* Ⓜ *Colosseo.*

Florence

The magical combination of beauty and history has drawn people to Florence for centuries. *Firenze* offers myriad moments of personal illumination before its palazzi, churches, art museums, as well as in interaction with the people you meet. Florence has captivated visitors for centuries, probably ever since the powerful Medici family first staged jousts and later lavish pageants to celebrate their weddings.

Its mostly sober beauty continued to attract people from all over Europe intent on taking in the achievements of the past on their Grand Tour of Europe, as you'll read in E.M. Forster's *A Room with a View.* Sometimes this heady combination of art and beauty has proven overwhelming, as it did for French author and diplomat Stendhal in 1817, whose visit to the church of Santa Croce occasioned palpitations and a fainting spell. Today, however, visitors are more often overwhelmed by the press of their own numbers on tightly scheduled tours. Florence has always been visitor-friendly—the historical center of the city can be crossed on foot in less than half an hour, and the picturesque surrounding hills are a short bus ride away. But the flood of tourists has made the natives more reticent.

Few Florentines, these days, can afford to live in the center. Even the university has pulled out to a suburb. By day, the city is overrun with day-trippers; come evening by U.S. study-abroad students intent on immersion in the native *aperitivo* culture.

Where have all the Italians gone, you wonder? Fear not, they appear on Sundays to walk in family groups along the major shopping streets; local school groups still pack museums; and residents still hold parades in Renaissance costumes to mark various historical or religious occasions. Caffè and Enoteca (wine bar) culture thrive, drawing in both visitors and locals. All is revealed to those who dodge the crowds and look just around the corner onto a quieter piazza, or neighborhood.

Duomo

Firenze's Colorful Cathedral

In 1296, Arnolfo di Cambio was commissioned to build "the loftiest, most sumptuous edifice human invention could devise" in the Romanesque style. The immense Duomo (or Cattedrale di Santa Maria del Fiore) was not completed until 1436, the year it was consecrated. The imposing facade dates only from the 19th century; its neo-Gothic style somewhat complements Giotto's genuine Gothic 14th-century campanile. The interior is a fine example of Florentine Gothic, though much of the cathedral's best-known art has been moved to the nearby Museo dell'Opera del Duomo.

Don't Miss

The real glory of the Duomo is Filippo Brunelleschi's dome, presiding over the cathedral with a dignity and grace that few domes to this day can match. Brunelleschi's cupola was one of the great engineering breakthroughs of all time: most of Europe's later domes, including that of St. Peter's in Rome, were built employing Brunelleschi's methods, and today the Duomo has come to symbolize Florence in the same way that the Eiffel Tower symbolizes Paris.

Getting Here

It's quickest to take the 10-minute walk to the Duomo pedestrianized area from Stazione Santa Maria Novella, as Florentine buses and taxis can get caught in traffic.✍

✉ *Piazza del Duomo* ☎ *055/230–2885* 🌐 *duomo.firenze.it* 🎫 *Church free; admission to cupola is via the €30 Brunelleschi Pass, a 3-day combo ticket that also includes the Battistero, Campanile, Museo dell'Opera del Duomo, and Santa Reparata Basilica Cripta* ✍ *Timed-entry reservations required for the cupola*

Galleria degli Uffizi

Venus in a Renaissance Gallery

The Medici installed their art collections—including a cornucopia of Roman, Greek, and Renaissance statues and busts—at Europe's first modern museum. It was open to the public (at first only by request) in 1591. Among the highlights are Paolo Uccello's *Battle of San Romano* ; the portraits of the Renaissance duke Federico da Montefeltro and his wife Battista Sforza by Piero della Francesca; the *Madonna of the Goldfinch* by Raphael; Michelangelo's *Doni Tondo* ; the *Venus of Urbino* by Titian; and the splendid *Bacchus* by Caravaggio.

Don't Miss

Many visitors make a beeline to a pair of beautiful Sandro Botticelli canvases. One of the most recognizable artworks of the Renaissance is the oft-imitated *Nascita di Venere* (*Birth of Venus*) painted around the 1480s, depicting the alluring goddess standing on a scallop shell. Beside it is *Primavera* (*Spring*) a large panel painting in tempera (1480), depicting an assembly of mythological figures in a flower-filled orange grove. It was inspired by classical and Renaissance writers including ancient Roman poet Ovid. At center stage is a red-draped Venus who once again returns and challenges our gaze.

Getting Here

The Gallery is just under a mile from the main train station where you can catch the C1 bus to within 700 feet of its sumptuous salons.

✉ *Piazzale degli Uffizi 6, Piazza della Signoria* ☎ *055/294883* 🌐 *www.uffizi.it* 🎫 *From €20* 🕒 *Closed Mon.* 🎫 *For a €4 fee, advance tickets (strongly recommended) can be reserved by phone, online, or at the Uffizi reservation booth on the Piazza Pitti at least 1 day in advance of your visit*

Ponte Vecchio

Florence's Most Famous Bridge

The charmingly simple "Old Bridge" over the River Arno was built in 1345 to replace an earlier bridge swept away by floods. Its shops first housed butchers, then grocers, blacksmiths, and other merchants. But in 1593, the Medici grand duke Ferdinand I, whose private corridor linking the Medici palace (Palazzo Pitti) with the Medici offices (the Uffizi) crossed the bridge atop the shops, decided that all this plebeian commerce and its accompanying pungent whiff beneath his feet was unseemly. So he threw out the butchers and blacksmiths and installed 41 goldsmiths and 8 jewelers. The bridge has been devoted solely to these two trades ever since. Although it's a must-visit sight, to avoid crowded times and get a view and photo of its higgledy-piggledy allure head to the nearby bridge Ponte Santa Trinità.

Don't Miss

The Corridoio Vasariano, the private Medici elevated passageway, was built by Vasari in 1565. It was most likely designed so that the Medici family wouldn't have to walk amid the commoners. By reservation visitors can walk its recently refurbished length (minus the celebrated collection of self-portraits, which were moved to the Uffizi), starting on the ground floor of the Uffizi, passing over Ponte Vecchio as far as the Boboli Gardens and Pitti Palace.

Getting Here

From Santa Maria Novella train station it's around a 20-minute walk, or 15 minutes from nearby bus stop Stazione Via Pazani aboard the electric C2 bus.

Corridoio Vasariano. ✉ *Piazzale degli Uffizi 6, Piazza della Signoria* ☎ *055/294883* 🌐 *www.uffizi.it*

Santa Croce

The Pantheon of Florence

The Santa Croce quarter, on the southeast fringe of the historic center, arose in the Middle Ages outside the second set of medieval city walls. The centerpiece of the neighborhood was (and is) the basilica of Santa Croce; the vast piazza could accommodate any overflow of worshippers and also served as a fairground and a staging ground for no-holds-barred soccer games. A center of leatherworking since the Middle Ages, the neighborhood is still packed with leatherworkers and leather shops.

Don't Miss

The collection of art within this Gothic church is by far the most important of any church in Florence. The most famous works are the Giotto frescoes in the two chapels immediately to the right of the high altar. They illustrate scenes from the lives of St. John the Evangelist and St. John the Baptist (in the right-hand chapel), as well as those from the life of St. Francis (in the left-hand chapel). Among the church's other highlights are Donatello's *Annunciation;* 14th-century frescoes by Taddeo Gaddi (circa 1300–66) illustrating scenes from the life of the Virgin Mary; and Donatello's *Crucifix,* criticized by Brunelleschi for making Christ look like a peasant. Illustrious Italians buried here include Galileo, Ghiberti, Machiavelli, Michelangelo, and Puccini

Getting Here

From Santa Maria Novella railway station it's a scenic 20-minute walk, via Piazza del Duomo. The C2 bus from Stazione Via Panzani should be a few minutes quicker.

✉ *Piazza Santa Croce 16, Santa Croce* ☎ *055/246–6105* 🌐 *www.santacroceopera.it* 🎫 *Church and museum €8* ⏲ *Closed Tues.*

The Oltrarno

Charms South of the Arno

A walk through the Oltrarno (literally "the other side of the Arno") takes in very different aspects of Florence: the splendor of the Medici, manifest in the riches of the mammoth Palazzo Pitti and the gracious Giardino di Boboli with manicured lawns, fountains and sculptures including the humorous portly Nano Morgante (aka Fontana del Bacchino) depicting the famed dwarf court jester of the Medici. Then there's the charm of the Oltrarno itself, a slightly gentrified neighborhood with artisan workshops, galleries, antique shops, and trendy eateries. Head to leafy cobblestoned Piazza Santo Spirito for wonderful outdoor eating, market goods (food and antiques), and chilled neighborhood vibes.

Don't Miss

Piazzale Michelangelo offers a marvelous view of Florence and the hills around it, rivaling the vista from the Forte di Belvedere. A copy of Michelangelo's *David* overlooks outdoor cafés packed with tourists during the day and with Florentines in the evening. In May, the Giardino dell'Iris (Iris Garden) off the piazza is abloom with more than 2,500 varieties of the flower. The Giardino delle Rose (Rose Garden) on the terraces below the piazza is also in full bloom in May and June.

Getting Here

From Stazione Santa Maria Novella, walk to Via Il Prato to catch bus C3 for the quickest route to Palazzo Pitti. It's a 20-minute walk from the Boboli Gardens (near the Forte di San Giorgio) to climb up to Piazzale Michelangelo, passing Villa Bardini en route. A cab will cost around €16.

Galleria dell'Accademia

A Michelangelo Marvel

Although the collection of Florentine paintings is largely unremarkable, it's the sculptures by Michelangelo that put this museum on your bucket list. The unfinished Slaves, fighting their way out of their marble prisons, were meant for the tomb of Michelangelo's overly demanding patron Pope Julius II. But the focal point is the original *David* (perhaps his most famous single work), commissioned in 1501 by the Opera del Duomo, which gave the 26-year-old sculptor a leftover block of ruined marble.

Don't Miss

A sculptor, painter, architect, and poet, Florentine native son Michelangelo was a consummate genius, and some of his finest creations remain in the San Lorenzo *quartiere* not far from the Accademia. The Biblioteca Medicea Laurenziana is perhaps his most fanciful work of architecture. But a key to understanding Michelangelo's genius can be found in the magnificent Cappelle Medicee, where both his sculptural and architectural prowess can be clearly seen. Planned frescoes were never completed but would have shown in one space the artistic triple threat that he certainly was.

Getting Here

Galleria dell'Accademia. ✉ *Via Ricasoli 60, San Marco* ☎ *055/294883 reservations* 🌐 *www.polomuseale.firenze.it* 🎫 *€12* 🕒 *Closed Mon.* ✍ *Reservations strongly encouraged*

Biblioteca Medicea Laurenziana. ✉ *Piazza San Lorenzo 9, entrance to left of San Lorenzo, San Lorenzo* 🌐 *www.bmlonline.it* 🎫 *Special exhibitions €3 Open days can vary wildly; always check in advance of a visit*

Cappelle Medicee. ✉ *Piazza di Madonna degli Aldobrandini, San Lorenzo* ☎ *055/294883 reservations* 🌐 *www.cappellemedicee.it* 🎫 *€9* 🕒 *Closed Tues.*

Piazza Santa Maria Novella

A Gorgeous Open Space in Central Florence

Piazza Santa Maria Novella is a gorgeous, pedestrian-only square, with grass (laced with roses) and plenty of places to sit and rest your feet. The streets in and around the piazza have their share of architectural treasures including some of Florence's most tasteful palaces, the Dominican splendor of the Santa Maria Novella basilica facade, and the Museo Novecento, which is dedicated to Italian art of the 20th century. Between Santa Maria Novella and the Arno is Via Tornabuoni, Florence's swankiest shopping street.

Don't Miss

The Museo Salvatore Ferragamo is a shrine to footwear. The shoes in this dramatically displayed collection were designed by Salvatore Ferragamo (1898–1960) beginning in the early 20th century. Born in southern Italy, Ferragamo jump-started his career in Hollywood by creating shoes for the likes of Mary Pickford and Rudolph Valentino. He then returned to Florence and set up shop in the 13th-century Palazzo Spini Ferroni. The collection includes about 16,000 shoes, and those on display are frequently rotated. Special exhibitions are also mounted here and are well worth visiting—past shows have been devoted to Audrey Hepburn, Greta Garbo, and Marilyn Monroe. An audio guide and guided tours (with reservation) are free. ✉ *Via dei Tornabuoni 2, Santa Maria Novella* ☎ *055/356–2846* 🌐 *museo.ferragamo.com* 🎫 *€8*

Fiesole

Hilltop Delights and Roman Sights

A half-day excursion to Fiesole, in the hills 8 km (5 miles) above Florence, gives you a pleasant respite from museums and a wonderful view of the city. From here the view of the Duomo gives you a new appreciation for what the Renaissance accomplished. Fiesole began life as an ancient Etruscan—later Roman—village. Eventually it gave up its independence in exchange for Florence's protection. The medieval cathedral, ancient Roman amphitheater, and lovely old villas behind garden walls are clustered on a series of hilltops. A walk around Fiesole can take from one to two or three hours, depending on how far you stroll from the main piazza.

Don't Miss

The beautifully preserved, 2,000-seat Anfiteatro Romano, near the Duomo, dates from the 1st century BC and is still used for summer concerts. To the right of the amphitheater are the remains of the Terme Romani (Roman Baths), where you can see the gymnasium and baths.

Getting Here

Take Bus no. 7 from Piazza Adua (25-minute trip). By car, the drive takes 20 to 30 minutes. Drive to Piazza della Libertà and cross the Ponte Rosso heading in the direction of the SS65/SR65. Turn right on to Via Salviati and continue on to Via Roccettini, then a left turn onto Via Vecchia Fiesolana. For the adventurous, it's a two-hour walk from central Florence to Fiesole.

Anfiteatro Romano. ✉ *Via Portigiani 1, Fiesole* ☎ *055/596–1293* 🌐 *www.museidifiesole.it* 🎫 *€12, includes access to archaeological park and museums* ⏲ *Museo Bandini closed Mon.–Thurs.*

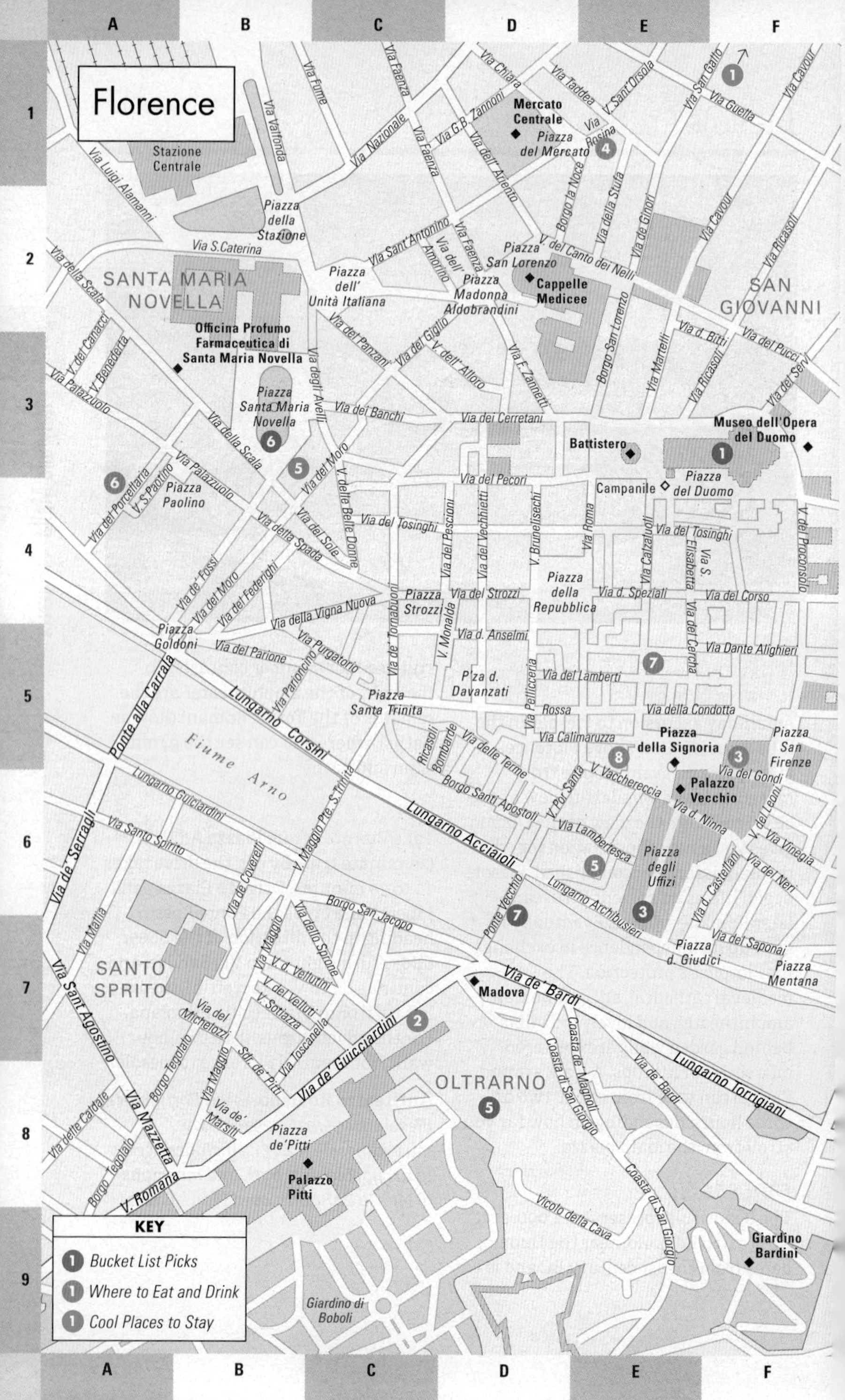

Florence
A
B
C
D
E
F
1
2
3
4
5
6
7
8
9
Stazione Centrale
Via Luigi Alamanni
Via Valfonda
Via Fiume
Via Faenza
Via Nazionale
Via Chiara
Via G.B. Zannoni
Mercato Centrale
Piazza del Mercato
Via dell' Ariento
Via Taddea
V. Sant'Orsola
Via Rosina
Via San Gallo
Via Guelfa
Via Cavour
Piazza della Stazione
Via S.Caterina
Via della Scala
SANTA MARIA NOVELLA
Piazza dell' Unità Italiana
Via Sant'Antonino
Via dell' Amorino
Via Faenza
Piazza San Lorenzo
Piazza Madonna Aldobrandini
Cappelle Medicee
V. del Canto dei Nelli
Borgo la Noce
Via della Stufa
Via de Ginori
Via Cavour
Via Ricasoli
SAN GIOVANNI
Officina Profumo Farmaceutica di Santa Maria Novella
V. del Canacci
V. Benedetta
Via Palazzuolo
Via del Panzani
Via del Giglio
V. dell' Alloro
Via F. Zannetti
Borgo San Lorenzo
Via Martelli
Via d. Bitti
Via Ricasoli
Via del Pucci
Via dei Servi
Piazza Santa Maria Novella
Via degli Avelli
Via dei Banchi
Via dei Cerretani
Museo dell'Opera del Duomo
Battistero
Via della Scala
Via del Moro
V. della Belle Donne
Via del Pecori
Campanile
Piazza del Duomo
Via del Porcellana
V. S. Paolino
Via Palazzuolo
Piazza Paolino
Via della Spada
Via del Sole
Via del Tosinghi
Via del Pescioni
Via del Vecchietti
V. Brunelleschi
Via Roma
Via Calzaiuoli
Via del Tosinghi
Via S. Elisabetta
V. del Proconsolo
Via de' Fossi
Via del Moro
Via del Federighi
Via della Vigna Nuova
Piazza Strozzi
Via del Strozzi
Piazza della Repubblica
Via d. Speziali
Via del Corso
Piazza Goldoni
Via del Parione
Via Purgatorio
Via de' Tornabuoni
V. Monalda
Via d. Anselmi
Via del Cercha
Via Dante Alighieri
Ponte alla Carraia
Lungarno Corsini
Via Parioncino
Piazza Santa Trinita
P'za d. Davanzati
Via Pellicceria
Via del Lamberti
Rossa
Via della Condotta
Fiume Arno
Ricasoli
Bombarde
Via delle Terme
Via Calimaruzza
Piazza della Signoria
Piazza San Firenze
Via del Gondi
Lungarno Guicciardini
V. Maggio Pte. S. Trinita
Borgo Santi Apostoli
V. Por Santa
V. Vacchereccia
Palazzo Vecchio
Via d. Ninna
Via del Leoni
Via Santo Spirito
Lungarno Acciaioli
Via Lambertesca
Piazza degli Uffizi
Via Vinegia
Via de' Serragli
Via de Coverelli
Lungarno Archibusieri
Via d. Castellani
Via del Neri
Via Maffia
Borgo San Jacopo
Via dello Sprone
Ponte Vecchio
Via del Saponai
Piazza d. Giudici
Piazza Mentana
SANTO SPRITO
Via Maggio
V. d. Velluti
V. del Velluti
V. Sdrucciolo
Madova
Via de' Bardi
Via Sant Agostino
Via del Michelozzi
Via Toscanella
Via de' Guicciardini
Coasta de' Magnoli
Coasta di San Giorgio
Via de' Bardi
Lungarno Torrigiani
Borgo Tegolaio
Via Maggio
Sdr. de' Pitti
OLTRARNO
Via Mazzetta
Via de' Marsili
Via delle Caldaie
Piazza de'Pitti
Palazzo Pitti
Borgo Tegolaio
V. Romana
Vicolo della Cava
Coasta di San Giorgio
Giardino Bardini
KEY
Bucket List Picks
Where to Eat and Drink
Cool Places to Stay
Giardino di Boboli

Bucket List Picks

1 Duomo F3
2 Fiesole J1
3 Galleria degli Uffizi E6
4 Galleria dell'Accademia G1
5 The Oltrarno D8
6 Piazza Santa Maria Novella B3
7 Ponte Vecchio D7
8 Santa Croce H6

Where to Eat and Drink

1 Cibrèo Ristorante J4
2 Fuori Porta H9
3 Gucci Osteria F5
4 Mario E1
5 'ino E6
6 La Sostanza A4
7 Perché No! E5
8 Rivoire E5

Cool Places to Stay

1 Antica Dimora Johlea F1
2 Hotel La Scaletta C7
3 Monna Lisa H3
4 Morandi alla Crocetta I1
5 The Place Firenze B3
6 Villa San Michele J1

When in Florence

Battistero (*Baptistery*)
RELIGIOUS BUILDING | The octagonal Baptistery is one of the supreme monuments of the Italian Romanesque style and one of Florence's oldest structures. The round Romanesque arches on the exterior date from the 11th century, and the interior dome mosaics from the beginning of the mid-13th century are justly renowned, but they could never outshine the building's famed bronze Renaissance doors decorated with panels crafted by Lorenzo Ghiberti. Michelangelo declared them so beautiful that they could serve as the Gates of Paradise. ✉ *Piazza del Duomo, Duomo* ☎ *055/2645789* 🌐 *duomo.firenze.it* 🎫 *Admission is via one of 3 combo tickets, each valid for 3 days: €30 Brunelleschi Pass (with Campanile, Cupola of the Duomo, Museo dell'Opera del Duomo, and Santa Reparata Basilica Cripta); €20 Giotto Pass (with Campanile, Museo dell'Opera, and Cripta); €15 Ghiberti Pass (with Museo dell'Opera and Cripta).*

Casa Buonarroti
ART MUSEUM | If you really enjoy walking in the footsteps of the great genius, you may want to complete the picture by visiting the Buonarroti family home. Michelangelo lived here from 1516 to 1525, and later gave it to his nephew, whose son, Michelangelo il Giovane (Michelangelo the Younger), turned it into a gallery dedicated to his great-uncle. The artist's descendants filled it with art treasures, some by Michelangelo himself. Two early marble works—the *Madonna of the Stairs* and *Battle of the Centaurs*—demonstrate his genius. ✉ *Via Ghibellina 70, Santa Croce* ☎ *055/241752* 🌐 *www.casabuonarroti.it* 🎫 *€8* 🕓 *Closed Tues.*

Giardino Bardini
GARDEN | Garden lovers, those who crave a view, and those who enjoy a nice hike should visit this lovely villa, whose history spans centuries. It had a walled garden as early as the 14th century; its "Grand Stairs"—a zigzag ascent well worth scaling—have been around since the 16th. The garden is filled with irises, roses, and heirloom flowers. It also has a Japanese garden and statuary. ✉ *Costa San Giorgio 2, San Niccolò* ☎ *055/2638599* 🌐 *www.villabardini.it* 🎫 *€6 garden only, €10 garden and exhibits* 🕓 *Closed Mon. (with occasional exceptions).*

★ **Madova**
HATS & GLOVES | Complete your winter wardrobe with a pair of high-quality leather gloves, available in a rainbow of colors and a choice of linings (silk, cashmere, and unlined), from Madova. It's been in business for more than100 years. ✉ *Via Guicciardini 1/r, Palazzo Pitti* ☎ *055/2396526* 🌐 *www.madova.com.*

★ **Mercato Centrale**
MARKET | **FAMILY** | Some of the food at this huge, two-story market hall is remarkably exotic. The ground floor contains meat and cheese stalls, as well as some very good bars that have panini. The upstairs food hall is eerily reminiscent of food halls everywhere, but the quality of the food served more than makes up for this. The downstairs market is closed on Sunday; the upstairs food hall is always open. ✉ *Piazza del Mercato Centrale, San Lorenzo* ☎ *055/2399798* 🌐 *www.mercatocentrale.it/firenze.*

★ **Museo dell'Opera del Duomo** (*Cathedral Museum*)
ART MUSEUM | A seven-year restoration, completed in 2015, gave Florence one of its most modern, up-to-date museums. The exhibition space was doubled, and the old facade of the cathedral, torn down in the 1580s, was re-created with a 1:1 relationship to the real thing. Both sets of Ghiberti's doors adorn the same room. Michelangelo's *Pietà* finally has the space it deserves, as does Donatello's *Mary Magdalene.* ✉ *Piazza del Duomo 9, Duomo* ☎ *055/2302885* 🌐 *duomo.*

firenze.it 🎫 *Admission is via one of 3 combo tickets, each valid for 3 days: €30 Brunelleschi Pass (with Battistero, Campanile, Cupola of the Duomo, and Santa Reparata Basilica Cripta); €20 Giotto Pass (with Battistero, Campanile, and Cripta); €15 Ghiberti Pass (with Battistero and Cripta)* ⏲ *Closed 1st Tues. of month.*

★ Officina Profumo Farmaceutica di Santa Maria Novella

PERFUME | The essence of a Florentine holiday is captured in the sachets of this Art Nouveau emporium of herbal cosmetics and soaps that are made following centuries-old recipes created by friars. ✉ *Via della Scala 16, Santa Maria Novella* ☎ *055/216276* 🌐 *www.smnovella.it.*

Palazzo Pitti

ART MUSEUM | This enormous palace is one of Florence's largest architectural set pieces.The original palazzo, built for the Pitti family around 1460, consisted of the main entrance and the sections extending as far as three windows on either side. In 1549, the property was sold to the Medici, and Bartolomeo Ammannati was called in to make substantial additions. Today, the palace houses several museums. The Museo degli Argenti displays a vast collection of Medici treasures and the Galleria d'Arte Moderna holds a collection of 19th- and 20th-century paintings, mostly Tuscan. ✉ *Piazza Pitti, Palazzo Pitti* ☎ *055/294883* 🌐 *www.uffizi.it/palazzo-pitti* 🎫 *From €10* ⏲ *Closed Mon.*

Palazzo Vecchio (*Old Palace*)

CASTLE/PALACE | **FAMILY** | Florence's forbidding, fortresslike city hall was begun in 1299, presumably designed by Arnolfo di Cambio, and its massive bulk and towering campanile dominate Piazza della Signoria. It was built as a meeting place for the guildsmen governing the city at the time; today, it is still City Hall. The main attraction is on the second floor, the opulently vast Sala dei Cinquecento (Room of the Five Hundred), named for the 500-member Great Council that met here. ✉ *Piazza della Signoria, Piazza della Signoria* ☎ *055/2768325* 🌐 *museicivicifiorentini.comune.fi.it* 🎫 *From €12.50.*

Piazza della Signoria

PLAZA/SQUARE | This is by far the most striking square in Florence. It was here, in 1497 and 1498, that the famous "bonfire of the vanities" took place, when the fanatical Dominican friar Savonarola induced his followers to hurl their worldly goods into the flames. The statues in the square and in the 14th-century Loggia dei Lanzi on the south side vary in quality. Cellini's famous bronze *Perseus* holding the severed head of Medusa is certainly the most important. ✉ *Piazza della Signoria, Florence.*

San Miniato al Monte

CHURCH | This abbey, like the Baptistery a fine example of Romanesque architecture, is one of the oldest churches in Florence, dating from the 11th century. A 12th-century mosaic topped by a gilt bronze eagle, emblem of San Miniato's sponsors, the Calimala (cloth merchants' guild), crowns the green-and-white marble facade. Inside are a 13th-century inlaid-marble floor and apse mosaic. Artist Spinello Aretino (1350–1410) covered the walls of the Sagrestia with frescoes of scenes from the life of St. Benedict. ✉ *Via delle Porte Sante 34, San Niccolò* ☎ *055/2342731* 🌐 *www.sanminiatoalmonte.it.*

Where to Eat and Drink

★ Cibrèo Ristorante

$$$$ | **TUSCAN** | This upscale trattoria serves sumptuous options like the creamy crostini di fegatini (with a savory chicken-liver spread) and melt-in-your-mouth desserts. Many Florentines hail this as the city's best restaurant, and justifiably so—chef-owner Fabio Picchi knows Tuscan food better than anyone, and it shows. **Known for:** authentic Tuscan food; seasonal menu; multilingual staff. 💲 *Average main: €40*

✉ Via A. del Verrocchio 8/r, Santa Croce ☎ 055/2341100 🌐 www.cibreo.com/en/cibreo-restaurant ⏲ Closed Sun. and Mon.

★ Fuori Porta

$ | **WINE BAR** | One of Florence's oldest wine bars serves cured meats and cheeses, pastas, salads, and daily specials. Crostini and *crostoni*—grilled breads topped with a mélange of cheeses and meats—are the house specialty, but the verdure sott'olio are divine, too. **Known for:** lengthy wine list; crostini and crostoni; changing daily specials. *$ Average main: €11 ✉ Via Monte alle Croci 10, San Niccolò ☎ 055/2342483 🌐 www.fuoriporta.it.*

★ Gucci Osteria

$$$ | **FUSION** | Chef, artist, and visionary Massimo Bottura has joined forces with the creative folk at Gucci to develop a marvelous menu that is both classic and innovative. Though he trained with Ducasse and Adrià, his major influence was his grandmother's cooking. **Known for:** tortellini in crema di Parmigiano Reggiano; an ever-changing menu; outdoor seating in one of Florence's most beautiful squares. *$ Average main: €35 ✉ Piazza della Signoria 10, Piazza della Signoria ☎ 055/75927038 🌐 www.gucciosteria.com.*

★ 'ino

$ | **ITALIAN** | This is the perfect place to grab a bite and/or a glass of wine after a visit to the nearby Uffizi. Only the very best ingredients go into owner Alessandro Frassica's delectable panini. **Known for:** top-notch ingredients; interesting panini combinations; delicious bread. *$ Average main: €8 ✉ Via dei Georgofili 3/r–7/r, Piazza della Signoria ☎ 055/214154 🌐 www.inofirenze.com ⏲ Closed Mon. and Tues.*

★ La Sostanza

$$ | **TUSCAN** | Since opening its doors in 1869, this trattoria has been serving top-notch, unpretentious food to Florentines who like their bistecca very large and, of course, very rare, as that's the only way to eat it. The *tartino di carciofi* (artichoke tart) and the *pollo al burro* (chicken with butter) are signature dishes. **Known for:** delicious desserts (especially the semifreddo); Tuscan classics; no-frills, 19th-century decor. *$ Average main: €17 ✉ Via del Porcellana 25/r, Lungarno North ☎ 055/212691 🌐 www.facebook.com/trattoriasostanzailtroia ▭ No credit cards ⏲ Closed Sun.*

★ Mario

$ | **TUSCAN** | Florentines flock to this narrow, family-run trattoria near San Lorenzo to feast on Tuscan favorites served at simple tables under a wooden ceiling dating from 1536. A distinct cafeteria feel and genuine Florentine hospitality prevail: you'll be seated wherever there's room, which often means with strangers. **Known for:** grilled meats; roasted potatoes; festive atmosphere. *$ Average main: €13 ✉ Via Rosina 2/r, corner of Piazza del Mercato Centrale, San Lorenzo ☎ 055/218550 🌐 www.trattoriamario.com ⏲ Closed Sun. and Aug. No dinner Mon.-Wed and Sat.*

★ Perché No!

$ | **ICE CREAM** | **FAMILY** | What many consider the best gelateria in the centro storico embodies the "practice makes perfect" adage. It's been making ice cream since 1939. **Known for:** gelati made daily; one of the oldest gelaterias in the city; unusual flavors and vegan options. *$ Average main: €3 ✉ Via dei Tavolini 19r, Duomo ☎ 055/2398969 🌐 www.facebook.com/GelateriaPercheNo.*

★ Rivoire

$$ | **ITALIAN** | One of the best spots in Florence for people-watching offers stellar service, light snacks, and terrific aperitivi. It's been around since the 1860s, and has been famous for its hot and cold chocolate (with or without cream) for more than a century. **Known for:** hot chocolate; friendly bartenders; the view on the piazza. *$ Average main: €15 ✉ Piazza*

della Signoria 5/R, Piazza della Signoria ☏ *055/214412* 🌐 *rivoire.it/en.*

Cool Places to Stay

★ Antica Dimora Johlea

$$$ | B&B/INN | In addition to guest rooms with four-poster beds and sweeping drapes, this 19th-century palazzo has a charming, flower-filled terrace where you can sip a glass of wine while taking in a view of Brunelleschi's cupola. **Pros:** great staff; cheerful rooms; honor bar. **Cons:** staff goes home at 7:30; staircase to roof terrace is narrow; steps to breakfast room. $ *Rooms from: €263* ✉ *Via San Gallo 80, San Marco* ☏ *055/4633292* 🌐 *www.antichedimorefiorentine.it* *6 rooms* *Free Breakfast.*

Hotel La Scaletta

$$ | HOTEL | In addition to a tremendous view of the Boboli Gardens, this cozy pensione near the Ponte Vecchio and Palazzo Pitti has simply furnished but large rooms and a sunny breakfast room. **Pros:** in-house restaurant with stunning views; wonderful, multilingual staff; in a lively neighborhood. **Cons:** small elevator, many steps; books up quickly; neighborhood can be noisy. $ *Rooms from: €169* ✉ *Via Guicciardini 13, Palazzo Pitti* ☏ *055/283028* 🌐 *www.hotellascaletta.it* *36 rooms* *Free Breakfast.*

★ Monna Lisa

$$ | HOTEL | Although some rooms are small, all are tastefully decorated and housed in a 15th-century palazzo that retains its original staircase and some of its wood-coffered ceilings. **Pros:** lavish buffet breakfast; cheerful, multilingual staff; pretty garden. **Cons:** rooms in annex are less charming than those in palazzo; street noise in some rooms; thin walls have been noted. $ *Rooms from: €186* ✉ *Borgo Pinti 27, Santa Croce* ☏ *055/2479751* 🌐 *www.monnalisa.it* *48 rooms* *Free Breakfast.*

★ Morandi alla Crocetta

$$ | B&B/INN | You're made to feel like friends of the family at this charming and distinguished residence, furnished comfortably in the classic style of a gracious Florentine home and former convent. **Pros:** interesting, offbeat location near the sights; affable staff; historic touches like fragments of a 17th-century fresco. **Cons:** books up quickly; far from the "true" historical center; some say breakfast could be better. $ *Rooms from: €207* ✉ *Via Laura 50, Santissima Annunziata* ☏ *055/2344747* 🌐 *www.hotelmorandi.it* *10 rooms* *Free Breakfast.*

★ The Place Firenze

$$$$ | HOTEL | Hard to spot from the street, this sumptuous place provides all the comforts of a luxe home away from home—expect soothing earth tones in the guest rooms, free minibars, crisp linens, and room service offering organic dishes. **Pros:** private, intimate feel; stellar staff; small dogs allowed. **Cons:** breakfast at a shared table; books up quickly; might be too trendy for some. $ *Rooms from: €660* ✉ *Piazza Santa Maria Novella 7, Santa Maria Novella* ☏ *055/2645181* 🌐 *www.theplacefirenze.com* *20 rooms* *Free Breakfast.*

Villa San Michele

$$$$ | HOTEL | The cypress-lined driveway provides an elegant preamble to this incredibly gorgeous (and very expensive) hotel nestled in the hills of Fiesole. **Pros:** exceptional convent conversion; stunning views; shuttle bus makes frequent forays to and from Florence. **Cons:** money must be no object; some rooms are small; you must either depend on the shuttle bus or have a car. $ *Rooms from: €1715* ✉ *Via Doccia 4, Fiesole* ☏ *055/5678200* 🌐 *www.belmond.com/hotels/europe/italy/florence/belmond-villa-san-michele* *Closed Nov.–May* *45 rooms* *Free Breakfast.*

Tuscany and Umbria

No place better epitomizes the beauty and splendor of Italy than the central regions of Tuscany and Umbria. They are both characterized by midsize cities and small hilltop towns, each with its own rich history and art treasures. In between, the gorgeous countryside produces some of Italy's finest wine and produce, which are showcased in the wonderful restaurants and enoteche (wine bars).

Any mention of Tuscany may conjure honey-hued scenes of architectural stage-sets backdropped by cypress tree-dotted rolling hills. There's Pisa and its Leaning Tower; Siena, home of the Palio and enchanting shell-shape Piazza del Campo; Assisi, the city of St. Francis, pilgrims and Giotto's magnificent frescoes; the medieval towers of hilltop San Gimignano; and the handsome walled city of Lucca.

The beauty of the landscape here proves the perfect foil for the region's abundance of outstanding art and architecture. Many of the cities and towns in this region have retained the same fundamental character over the past 500 years. Civic rivalries that led to bloody battles centuries ago have given way to serious soccer rivalries. Renaissance pomp lives on in the celebration of local feast days and centuries-old traditions such as the Palio in Siena.

As the birthplace of the Renaissance, Tuscany often gets the plaudits as the epitome of a certain Chianti-quaffing, escapist way of life; but Umbria is no slouch with its wonderful art, architecture, and wine, plus its rugged, mountainous landscapes, resourceful people, and hearty food gives it a more down-to-earth feel. Orvieto's cathedral and Assissi's basilica are two of the most important sights in Italy.

Leaning Tower of Pisa

Tuscany's Most Famous Failed Structure

There may be a heap of kitsch in the stalls around the Leaning Tower, but this remains a must-visit sight in a city that offers wonderful Arno river walks. Work on the Leaning Tower (Torre Pendente), built as a campanile (bell tower) for the Duomo, started in 1173. The lopsided settling began when construction reached the third story. The architects attempted to compensate through such methods as making the remaining floors slightly taller on the leaning side, but the extra weight only made the problem worse. The settling continued, and, by the late 20th century, it had accelerated to such a point that many feared the tower would simply topple over, despite all efforts to prop it up. The structure has since been firmly anchored to the earth. Work to restore the tower to its original tilt of 300 years ago was launched in early 2000 and finished two years later. Note, though, that children under eight aren't allowed to climb.

Don't Miss

Pisa's treasures aren't as abundant as those of Florence, to which it is inevitably compared, but the cathedral-baptistery-tower complex on the Piazza del Duomo (Campo dei Miracoli, or Field of Miracles) is among the most dramatic settings in Italy.

Getting Here

Pisa is an easy hour's train ride from Florence. By car it's a straight shot on the Firenze–Pisa–Livorno ("Fi-Pi-Li") autostrada.

✉ *Piazza del Duomo, Pisa*
☎ *050/835011* 🌐 *www.opapisa.it*
🎫 *€20* ✍ *Reservations, which are essential, can be made online or by calling the Museo dell'Opera del Duomo*

San Gimignano

A Hilltop Medieval Wonder

When you're on a hilltop surrounded by soaring medieval towers silhouetted against the sky, it's difficult not to fall under the spell of San Gimignano. Its tall walls and narrow streets are typical of Tuscan hill towns, but it's the medieval "skyscrapers" that set the town apart from its neighbors. Today 14 towers remain, but at the height of the Guelph–Ghibelline conflict there was a forest of more than 70, and it was possible to cross the town by rooftop rather than by road.

Don't Miss

Behind the simple facade of the Romanesque Collegiata lies a treasure trove of fine frescoes, covering nearly every wall. Bartolo di Fredi's 14th-century fresco cycle of Old Testament scenes extends along one wall. Their distinctly medieval feel, with misshapen bodies, buckets of spurting blood, and lack of perspective, contrasts with the much more reserved scenes from the Life of Christ (attributed to 14th-century artist Lippo Memmi) painted on the opposite wall just 14 years later.

Best Restaurant

Cum Quibus. This is one of the region's most creative restaurants—an intimate place with a menu that's mostly Tuscan but not traditional. $ *Average main: €26* ✉ *Via San Martino 17, San Gimignano* ☎ *0577/943199* 🌐 *www.mktn.it/cumquibus* ⏱ *Closed Tues. and Jan. and Feb.*

Getting Here

You can reach San Gimignano by car from the superstrada (exit at Poggibonsi Nord). Buses run between Siena or Florence and Poggibonsi.

Collegiata. ✉ *Piazza Pecori 1–2, San Gimignano* 🌐 *www.duomosangimignano.it* 🎫 *€5* ⏱ *Closed Jan. 1, 15–31, and Nov. 15–30*

Siena

A Campo for All Seasons

With its narrow streets and steep alleys, a Gothic Duomo, a bounty of early Renaissance art, and the glorious Palazzo Pubblico overlooking its magnificent fan-shape Campo (venue of the famous twice-annual Palio horse race, held on July 2 and August 16), Siena is often described as Italy's best-preserved medieval city. Make a point of catching the *passeggiata* (evening stroll), when locals throng the Via di Città, Banchi di Sopra, and Banchi di Sotto, the city's three main streets.

Don't Miss

Siena's Duomo is one of the finest Gothic churches in Italy. The multicolor marbles and painted decoration are typical of the Italian approach to Gothic architecture—lighter and much less austere than the French. The amazingly detailed facade has few rivals. It was completed in two brief phases at the end of the 13th and 14th centuries. The statues and decorative work were designed by Nicola Pisano and his son Giovanni, although much of what's seen today are copies, the originals having been removed to the adjacent Museo dell'Opera Metropolitana. The gold mosaics are 18th-century restorations. The Campanile (no entry) is among central Italy's finest.

Getting Here

Take the Florence–Siena superstrada for speed or the Via Cassia (SR2) for a scenic route. SITA provides an excellent direct bus service (quicker than the train) between Florence and Siena.

Siena Duomo. ✉ *Piazza del Duomo, Città* 🌐 *operaduomo.siena.it* 🎫 *€13 combined ticket includes Cripta, Battistero, and Museo dell'Opera*

Siena Tourism. 🌐 *www. terresiena.it*

Wine Tasting in Chianti

Vineyards, Vino, and Views

Both sides of the Strada Chiantigiana (SR222) are embraced by glorious panoramic views of vineyards, olive groves, and castle towers. Traveling south from Florence, you first reach the aptly named one-street town of Strada in Chianti. Farther south, the number of vineyards on either side of the road dramatically increases—as do the signs inviting you in for a free tasting. Beyond Strada lies Greve in Chianti, completely surrounded by wineries and filled with wineshops. There's art to be had as well: Passignano, west of Greve, has an abbey that shelters a 15th-century *Last Supper*by Domenico and Davide Ghirlandaio. Farther still, along the Strada Chiantigiana, are Panzano and Castellina in Chianti, both hill towns with food and wine-making pedigrees.

Don't Miss

A visit to Castello di Brolio combines the region's finest castle with a wonderful wine-tasting experience. It was built about AD 1000, but the Ricasoli family have been in possession since 1141. Bettino Ricasoli (1809–80) was one of the founders of modern Italy and is said to have invented the original formula for Chianti wine. Brolio, one of Chianti's best-known labels, is still justifiably famous.

Getting Here

Driving from Florence or Siena: Greve, Radda, Panzano, and Castellina are reached via the Strada Chiantigiana (SR222). SITA buses travel frequently between Florence and Greve.

Castello di Brolio. ✉ *Località Madonna a Brolio, Gaiole in Chianti* ☎ *0577/7301* 🌐 *www.ricasoli.com* 🎫 *€7 gardens and wine tasting, cellar and castle tours (with tastings) from €30* 🕒 *Closed Dec. No tours Dec.–Mar. Museum closed Mon.* ✍ *Reservations required for castle and cellar tours*

Galleria Nazionale dell'Umbria

Umbria's Best Art Experience

The Galleria Nazionale dell'Umbria is the region's most comprehensive art gallery. Housed in the handsome Palazzo dei Priori in Perugia, the collection features native artists—most notably Pintoricchio (1454–1513) and Perugino (circa 1450–1523). In addition to paintings, the gallery has frescoes, sculptures, and some superb examples of crucifixes from the 13th and 14th centuries.

Don't Miss

Perugia is a majestic, handsome, wealthy city, and with its trendy boutiques, refined cafés, and grandiose architecture, it doesn't try to hide its affluence. A student population of around 30,000 means that the city, with a permanent population of about 165,000, is abuzz with activity throughout the year. Umbria Jazz, one of the region's most important music festivals, attracts music lovers from around the world every July, and Eurochocolate, the international chocolate festival, is an irresistible draw each October for anyone with a sweet tooth. Join the evening Perugina *passeggiata*stroll and aperitivo crowd on Corso Vannucci.

Getting Here

Perugia is well connected by train. Buses from the train station connect to Piazza d'Italia, the heart of the old town. If you're in a hurry, take the minimetro, a one-line subway, to Stazione della Cupa.

Galleria Nazionale dell'Umbria. *Corso Vannucci 19, Piazza IV Novembre, Perugia* *gallerianazionaledellumbria.it* €8 *Closed Mon.*

Perugia Tourism. *turismo.comune.perugia.it*

Assisi

A Pilgrimage to Giotto's Frescoes

The small town of Assisi is one of the Christian world's most important pilgrimage sites and home of the Basilica di San Francesco—built to honor St. Francis (1182–1226) and erected swiftly after his death. Once you've seen the basilica, stroll through the town's narrow winding streets to see beautiful vistas of the nearby hills and valleys peeking through openings between the buildings.

Don't Miss

The Basilica di San Francesco is a two-tiered monolith begun in 1228, covered floor to ceiling with some of Europe's finest frescoes. In the Upper Church, the magnificent frescoes from 13th-century Italian painter Giotto, painted when he was only in his twenties, show that he was a pivotal artist in the development of Western painting. He broke away from the stiff, unnatural styles of earlier generations to move toward realism and three-dimensionality. The Lower Church features frescoes by celebrated Sienese painters Simone Martini and Pietro Lorenzetti, as well as by Giotto (or his assistants).

Getting Here

Assisi lies on the Terontola–Foligno rail line, with almost hourly connections to Perugia and direct trains to Rome and Florence several times a day. The Stazione Centrale is 4 km (2½ miles) from town, with a bus service about every half-hour. By car, Assisi is easily reached via the A1/E35 autostrada (Rome–Florence) and the SS75 highway. The walled town is closed to traffic, so cars must be left in the parking lots.

Basilica di San Francesco. ✉ *Piazza di San Francesco, Assisi* ☎ *075/8190084* 🌐 *www.sanfrancescoassisi.org* 🎫 *Free*

Hiking in the Umbrian Hills

Green Hills, Blue Mountains

Magnificent scenery makes Umbria excellent walking, hiking, and mountaineering country. Head to the area around Spoleto for several pleasant, easy, and well-signed trails that begin at the far end of the Ponte delle Torri bridge over Monteluco. From Cannara, an easy half-hour walk leads to the fields of Pian d'Arca, the site of St. Francis's sermon to the birds. For slightly more arduous walks, follow the saint's path uphill from Assisi to the Eremo delle Carceri, and then continue along the trails that crisscross Monte Subasio. At 4,250 feet, the treeless summit affords views of Assisi, Perugia, far-off Gubbio, and the distant mountain ranges of Abruzzo. For even more challenging hiking, the northern reaches of the Valnerina are exceptional; the mountains around Norcia should not be missed. Throughout Umbria and the Marches, most recognized trails are marked with the distinctive red-and-white blazes of the Club Alpino Italiano.

Don't Miss

A spectacular 4000-feet-above-sea-level mountain plain Piano Grande sits amid the Sibillini or "Blue Mountains." It's a hang glider's paradise and a wonderful place for a hike, picnic, or camping out under a spellbindingly starry sky free of light pollution.

Getting Here

From Spoleto, drive along the SS395-SS685 superhighway to Norcia and Castelluccio, the gateway to the Piano Grande. You can head into the Valnerina area from Terni on the S209, or on the SP395 bis north of Spoleto.

Parco Nazionale dei Monti Sibillini. 🌐 *www.sibillini.net*

Umbria Tourism. 🌐 *www.umbriatourism.it*

Orvieto

Rock-Carved Citadel

Carved from an enormous plateau of volcanic rock high above a green valley, Orvieto has natural defenses that made the high walls seen in many Umbrian towns unnecessary. The Etruscans were the first to settle here, digging a honeycombed network of more than 1,200 wells and storage caves out of the soft stone. The Romans attacked, sacked, and destroyed the city in 283 BC. Since then, it has grown up out of the rock into an enchanting maze of alleys and squares. Orvieto was solidly Guelph in the Middle Ages, and, for several hundred years, popes sought refuge in the city, at times needing protection from their enemies, at times seeking respite from the summer heat in Rome.

Don't Miss

Orvieto's stunning cathedral (Duomo) was built to commemorate the Miracle at Bolsena, when a young priest's just-blessed wafer began to drip blood (or microbes say some scientists). Beyond the vibrant mosaic-filled Gothic facade is a vast interior. The Cappella di San Brizio holds one of Italy's greatest fresco cycles, notable for its influence on Michelangelo's *Last Judgment*, as well the extraordinary beauty of the figuration.

Best Restaurant

Le Grotte di Funaro. Dine on hearty traditional Umbrian grilled meat, vegetables, and pizzas inside the atmospheric tufa caves. *Average main: €16* ✉ *Via Ripa Serancia 41, Orvieto* ☎ *0763/343276* 🌐 *www.grottedelfunaro.com* 🕓 *Closed Mon. and 10 days in July*

Getting Here

Orvieto is well connected by train to Rome, Florence, and Perugia.

Duomo di Orvieto. ✉ *Piazza del Duomo, Orvieto* 🌐 *www.opsm.it* 🎟 *€5*

When in Tuscany and Umbria

Arezzo

TOWN | Arezzo is best known for the magnificent Piero della Francesca frescoes in the church of San Francesco. It's also the birthplace of the poet Petrarch (1304–74), the Renaissance artist and art historian Giorgio Vasari, and Guido d'Arezzo (aka Guido Monaco), the inventor of contemporary musical notation. Arezzo thrived as an Etruscan capital from the 7th to the 4th century BC, and was one of the most important cities in the Etruscans' anti-Roman 12-city federation, resisting Rome's rule to the last. The city eventually fell and in turn flourished under the Romans. In 1289 Florentine Guelphs defeated Arezzo in a famous battle at Campaldino. Among the Florentine soldiers was Dante Alighieri (1265–1321), who often referred to Arezzo in his Divine Comedy. At the 14th century, Arezzo lost its independence to Florence. ✉ *Arezzo* ✣ *63 km (39 miles) northeast of Siena, 81 km (50 miles) southeast of Florence* 🌐 *www.arezzointuscany.it.*

Cascata delle Marmore

WATERFALL | **FAMILY** | The road east of Terni (SS3 Valnerina) leads 10 km (6 miles) to the Cascata delle Marmore (Waterfalls of Marmore), which, at 541 feet, are the highest in Europe. A canal was dug by the Romans in the 3rd century BC to prevent flooding in the nearby agricultural plains. Nowadays, the waters are often diverted to provide hydroelectric power for Terni, reducing the roaring falls to an unimpressive trickle, so check with the information office at the falls (there's a timetable on its website) or with Terni's tourist office before heading here. On summer evenings, when the falls are in full spate, the cascading water is floodlit to striking effect. The falls are usually at their most energetic at midday and at around 4 pm. This is a good place for hiking, except in December and January, when most trails may be closed. ✉ *SP79, Terni* ✣ *10 km (6 miles) east of Terni* ☎ *0744/67561* 🌐 *www.cascatadellemarmore.info* 🎫 *€12.*

Gubbio

TOWN | There's something otherworldly about this jewel of a medieval town, tucked away on the slopes of Monte Ingino. Even in the height of summer, the so-called Città del Silenzio (City of Silence) stays comparatively cool, and its dramatically steep streets remain relatively serene. At Christmas, kitsch is king. From December 7 to January 10, colored lights are strung down the mountainside in a shape resembling an evergreen, creating the world's largest Christmas tree. Parking in the central Piazza dei Quaranta Martiri—named for 40 hostages murdered by the Nazis in 1944—is easy and secure. It's wise to leave your car there and explore the narrow streets on foot. ✉ *Gubbio* ✣ *39 km (24 miles) northeast of Perugia, 92 km (57 miles) east of Arezzo* 🌐 *www.ilikegubbio.com.*

★ La Fortezza

CASTLE/PALACE | **FAMILY** | Providing refuge for the last remnants of the Sienese army during the Florentine conquest of 1555, the battlements of this 14th-century fortress are still in excellent condition. Climb the narrow, spiral steps for the 360-degree view of most of southern Tuscany. An on-site enoteca serves delicious snacks that pair beautifully with the local wines. ✉ *Piazzale Fortezza, Montalcino* ☎ *0577/849221 enoteca* 🌐 *www.enotecalafortezza.com* 🎫 *Fortress free, walls €4* ⏲ *Closed Mon. Nov.–Mar.*

Lucca

TOWN | Ramparts built in the 16th and 17th centuries enclose a charming fortress town filled with churches (99 of them), terra-cotta–roofed buildings, and narrow cobblestone streets, along which locals maneuver bikes to do their daily shopping. Here Caesar, Pompey,

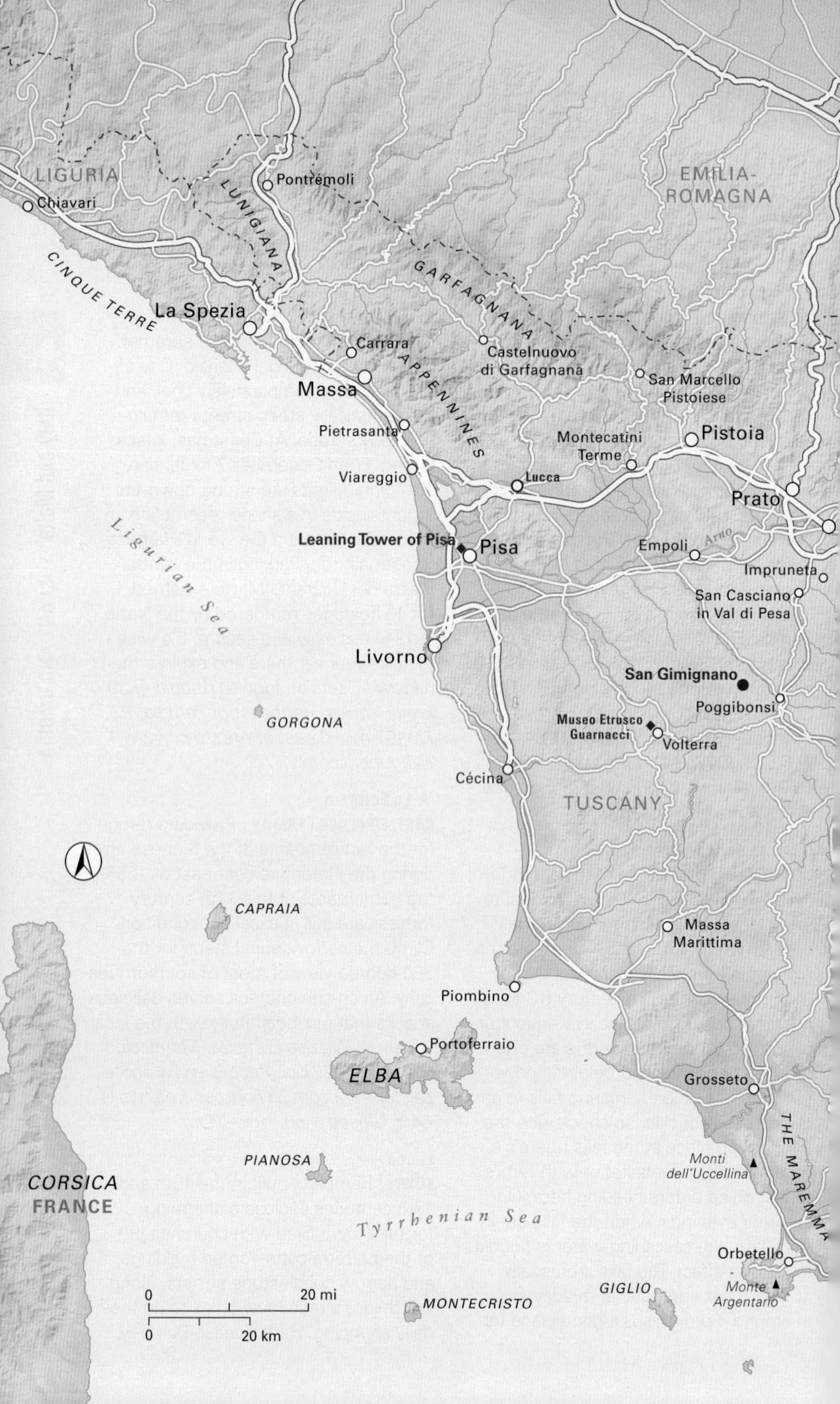

LIGURIA
Chiavari
Pontremoli
LUNIGIANA
EMILIA-ROMAGNA
CINQUE TERRE
GARFAGNANA
La Spezia
Carrara
Castelnuovo di Garfagnana
APPENNINES
Massa
San Marcello Pistoiese
Pietrasanta
Montecatini Terme
Pistoia
Viareggio
Lucca
Prato
Ligurian Sea
Leaning Tower of Pisa
Pisa
Empoli
Arno
Impruneta
San Casciano in Val di Pesa
Livorno
San Gimignano
Poggibonsi
GORGONA
Museo Etrusco Guarnacci
Volterra
Cécina
TUSCANY
CAPRAIA
Massa Marittima
Piombino
Portoferraio
ELBA
Grosseto
THE MAREMMA
PIANOSA
Monti dell'Uccellina
CORSICA
FRANCE
Tyrrhenian Sea
Orbetello
Monte Argentario
0
20 mi
0
20 km
MONTECRISTO
GIGLIO

Tuscany and Umbria
Bologna
Ravenna
Ímola
Faensa
Cervia
Forlì
Cesenatico
Cesena
Adriatic Sea
Rímini
SAN MARINO
Riccione
Cattolica
SAN MARINO
Pésaro
Fano
MUGELLO
Borgo San Lorenzo
Florence
Poppi
Bibbiena
PRATOMAGNO
Urbino
CHIANTI
THE MARCHES
Sansepolcro
Pérgola
Cagli
Arezzo
Città di Castello
Sasso-ferrato
Wine Tasting in Chianti
Monte San Savino
Siena
Gubbio
Fabriano
Cortona
Lake Trasimene
Gualdo Tadino
Galleria Nazionale dell'Umbria
Nocera Umbra
La Fortozza
Pienza
Montepulciano
Montalcino
Perugia
Assisi
Chianciano Terme
Chiusi
VAL D'ORCIA
Spello
Foligno
VALNERINA
Montefalco
UMBRIA
Todi
Hiking in the Umbrian Hills
Orvieto
Spoleto
Scansano
Cascota delle Marmore
Manciano
Lake Bolsena
Amelia
Terni
Montefiascone
Narni
Tuscania
Viterbo
Rieti
LAZIO

and Crassus agreed to rule Rome as a triumvirate in 56 BC; Lucca was later the first Tuscan town to accept Christianity. The town still has a mind of its own, and when most of Tuscany was voting Communist as a matter of course, Lucca's citizens rarely followed suit. The famous composer Giacomo Puccini (1858–1924) was born here; he is celebrated during the summer Opera Theater and Music Lucca. The ramparts circling the centro storico are the perfect place to stroll, bicycle, or just admire the view. ✉ *Lucca* ✣ *95 km (39 miles) west of Florence* 🌐 *www.luccaturismo.it.*

Montefalco

TOWN | Nicknamed the "balcony over Umbria" for its high vantage point over the valley that runs from Perugia to Spoleto, Montefalco began as an important Roman settlement along the Via Flaminia. The town owes its current name ("Falcon's Mount") to Emperor Frederick II (1194–1250). He destroyed the ancient town in 1249, and built in its place what would later become Montefalco. Almost no traces remain of the old Roman center. However, Montefalco has more than its fair share of interesting art and architecture and is well worth the drive up the hill. It's also a good place to stop for a meal, as is nearby Bevagna. You need go no farther than the main squares to find a restaurant or bar with a hot meal, and most establishments—both simple and sophisticated—offer a splendid combination of history and small-town hospitality ✉ *Montefalco* ✣ *34 km (21 miles) south of Assisi, 48 km (30 miles) southeast of Perugia* 🌐 *stradadelsagrantino.it.*

Montepulciano

TOWN | Perched on a hilltop, Montepulciano is made up of a pyramid of redbrick buildings set within a circle of cypress trees. At an altitude of almost 2,000 feet, it is cool in summer and chilled in winter by biting winds sweeping down its spiraling streets. The town has an unusually harmonious look, the result of the work of three architects: Antonio da Sangallo "il Vecchio" (circa 1455–1534), Vignola (1507–73), and Michelozzo (1396–1472). The group endowed it with fine palaces and churches in an attempt to impose Renaissance architectural ideals on an ancient Tuscan hill town. ✉ *Montepulciano* ✣ *65 km (40 miles) southeast of Siena, 114 km (70 miles) southeast of Florence* 🌐 *wwww.prolocomontepulciano.it.*

★ **Museo Etrusco Guarnacci**

HISTORY MUSEUM | An extraordinary collection of Etruscan relics is made all the more interesting by clear explanations in English. The bulk of the collection is comprised of roughly 700 carved funerary urns. The oldest, dating from the 7th century BC, were made from tufa (volcanic rock). A handful are made of terra-cotta, but most—dating from the 3rd to 1st century BC—are done in alabaster. The urns are grouped by subject, and, taken together, they form a fascinating testimony about Etruscan life and death. ✉ *Via Don Minzoni 15, Volterra* ☎ *0586/894563* 🌐 *www.comune.volterra.pi.it/musei/museo-etrusco-guarnacci* 🎫 *From €10.*

Spello

TOWN | With well-appointed hotels, this hilltop town at the edge of Monte Subasio, just a short drive or train ride from Perugia or Assisi, makes an excellent base for exploring the region. Spello's art scene includes first-rate frescoes by Pinturicchio and Perugino, and contemporary artists can be observed at work in studios around town. If antiquity is your passion, the town also has some intriguing Roman ruins. And the warm, rosy-beige tones of the local pietra rossa stone on the buildings brighten even cloudy days. ✉ *Spello* ✣ *30 km (19 miles) southeast of Perugia, 12 km (7 miles) southeast of Assisi* 🌐 *www.umbriatourism.it.*

Where to Eat and Drink

★ Il Giglio

$$$ | TUSCAN | Divine, cutting-edge food and Tuscan classics are served in this one-room space, where in winter, there's a roaring fireplace and, in warmer months, there's outdoor seating on a pretty little piazza. If mushrooms are in season, try the *tacchoni con funghi,* a homemade pasta with mushrooms and a native herb called *nepitella.* A local favorite during winter is the *coniglio con olive* (rabbit stew with olives). **Known for:** creative menu with seasonal ingredients; fine service; the wine list, especially its selection of local wines. *Average main: €35 Piazza del Giglio 2, Lucca 0583/494508 www.ristorantegiglio.com Closed Tue. and Wed. and 15 days in Nov.*

★ Osteria Piazzetta dell'Erba

$$ | UMBRIAN | Hip service and sophisticated presentations attract locals, who enjoy Italian cuisine with unusual twists (think porcini mushroom risotto with blue cheese and blueberries), a nice selection of salads—unusual for an Umbrian restaurant—plus sushi options and intriguing desserts. The enthusiastic young team keep things running smoothly and the energy high. **Known for:** friendly staff; inventive dishes; intimate ambience. *Average main: €20 Via San Gabriele dell'Addolorata 15/b, Assisi 075/815352 www.osteriapiazzetta-dellerba.it Closed Mon. and a few wks in Jan. or Feb.*

★ Redibis

$$ | MODERN ITALIAN | Housed in a Roman theater—built in the 1st century AD but brought up-to-date with mid-century modern furniture and sleek chandeliers—this restaurant has an atmosphere that's as unique as the food. The seasonally changing menu, featuring mainly zero kilometer products, aims to adapt ancient ingredients like Roveja wild peas of Colfiorito to sophisticated modern tastes, while offering a fine selection of Umbrian wines. **Known for:** fascinating cavelike atmosphere; focus on local producers; beautifully presented dishes. *Average main: €23 Via dell'Anfiteatro 3, Bevagna 8 km (5 miles) northwest of Montefalco 0742/362120 www.foodie.bio Closed Tues.*

★ Ristorante Apollinare

$$ | UMBRIAN | Low wooden ceilings and flickering candlelight make this monastery from the 10th and 11th centuries Spoleto's most romantic spot; in warm weather, you can dine under a canopy on the piazza. The kitchen serves sophisticated, innovative variations on local dishes, including long, slender strengozzi pasta with such toppings as cherry tomatoes, mint, and a touch of red pepper or (in season) porcini mushrooms or truffles. **Known for:** modern versions of traditional Umbrian dishes; intimate and elegant setting; impeccable service. *Average main: €22 Via Sant'Agata 14, Spoleto 0743/223256 www.ristoranteapollinare.it Closed Tues.*

★ Ristoro di Lamole

$$ | TUSCAN | Up a winding road lined with olive trees and vineyards, this place is worth the effort it takes to find. The view from the outdoor terrace is divine, as is the simple, exquisitely prepared Tuscan cuisine—start with the bruschetta drizzled with olive oil or the sublime *verdure sott'olio* (marinated vegetables) before moving on to any of the fine secondi. **Known for:** coniglio is a specialty; sweeping view from the terrace; your hosts Paolo and Filippo. *Average main: €20 Via di Lamole 6, Località Lamole, Greve in Chianti 055/8547050 www.ristorodilamole.it Closed Nov.–Apr.*

Cool Places to Stay

★ Castello di Petroia

$$ | HOTEL | This atmospheric, 12th-century castle 15 km (9 miles) from Gubbio has spacious, antiques-filled, individually decorated rooms—some with decorated or beamed ceilings and stained glass, many with whirlpool tubs—as well as excellent in-house breakfasts and dinners. **Pros:** charming atmosphere; lovely breakfast buffet with handmade cakes and jams; seasonal outdoor swimming pool. **Cons:** decor is on the simple side; beds could be comfier; temperature can be difficult to regulate in guest rooms. *Rooms from: €160 Località Petroia, Gubbio 075/920287 www.petroia.it Closed early Jan.–late Mar. 13 rooms Free Breakfast.*

★ Castiglion del Bosco

$$$$ | RESORT | This estate, one of the largest still in private hands in Tuscany, was purchased at the beginning of this century and meticulously converted into a second-to-none resort that incorporates a medieval *borgo* (village) and surrounding farmhouses and has luxurious suites, as well as opulent three- to five-bedroom villas, each with its own pool. **Pros:** exclusive and tranquil location; breathtaking scenery; acclaimed golf course. **Cons:** well off the beaten track, the nearest town is 12 km (7½ miles) away; private transportation required; truly exorbitant prices. *Rooms from: €1107 Località Castiglion del Bosco, Montalcino 0577/1913001 www.castigliondelbosco.com 53 units No Meals.*

★ Il Falconiere

$$$$ | B&B/INN | Accommodation options at this sumptuous property include rooms and suites in an 18th-century villa, or for more seclusion, private suites and villas at the far end of the property. **Pros:** attractive setting in the valley beneath Cortona; excellent service; elegant, but relaxed. **Cons:** a car is a must; some find rooms in main villa a little noisy; might be too isolated for some. *Rooms from: €576 Località San Martino 370, Cortona 3 km (2 miles) north of Cortona 0575/612679 www.ilfalconiere.it Closed Nov.–Jan. 33 rooms Free Breakfast.*

★ Nun Assisi Relais & Spa Museum

$$$$ | HOTEL | Within walking distance of Assisi's restaurants and shops, this monastery built in 1275 has been converted into a thoroughly contemporary, high-end place to stay with a fabulous spa carved out of 2,000-year-old Roman baths. **Pros:** fantastic blend of the historical and modern; excellent restaurant; wonderful place to relax. **Cons:** on the expensive side; on-site parking costs extra; split-level rooms with stairs difficult for those with mobility issues. *Rooms from: €590 Via Eremo delle Carceri 1A, Assisi 075/8155150 www.nunassisi.com 18 rooms Free Breakfast.*

★ Posta Donini 1579 – UNA Esperienze

$$ | HOTEL | FAMILY | Beguilingly comfortable guest rooms set on lovely grounds—where gardeners go quietly about their business—along with a small but charming spa and a well-regarded restaurant make this historical hotel south of Perugia worth a stay. **Pros:** plush atmosphere; a quiet and private getaway; great restaurant. **Cons:** outside Perugia; uninteresting village; parking area can get full. *Rooms from: €152 Via Deruta 43, San Martino in Campo 075/609132 www.postadonini.it 48 rooms Free Breakfast.*

★ Villa Bordoni

$$ | B&B/INN | Scottish expats David and Catherine Gardner transformed a ramshackle, 16th-century villa into a stunning retreat where no two rooms are alike—all have stenciled walls; some have four-poster beds, others small mezzanines. **Pros:** splendidly isolated in the hills above Greve; beautiful decor; wonderful hosts. **Cons:** on a long and bumpy dirt road; need a car to get around; books up quickly. *Rooms from: €175 Via San Cresci 31/32, Greve in Chianti 055/8546230 www.villabordoni.com Closed Dec.–Feb. 12 rooms Free Breakfast.*

The Amalfi Coast and Naples

A region of evocative names—Naples, Capri, Sorrento, Pompeii, Positano, Amalfi—Campania conjures up visions of cliff-shaded, sapphire-hue coves, sun-dappled waters, and mighty ruins. Naples, the third-largest city in Italy, is a draw in itself, but more travelers visit this corner than any other in southern Italy, and it's no wonder.

Home to Vesuvius and the Campi Flegrei supervolcano, the area's unique geology is responsible for Campania's photogenic landscape and fertile soil, which yields some of the tastiest produce on the planet. A spectacular coastline stretches out along a deep blue sea, punctuated by three notable islands: Capri, a limestone spur off the Sorrentino Peninsula, has a jet-set rep, chic shopping, and prices to match; while Ischia and Procida, two islands spewed from the multiple-crater Campi Flegrei volcanic caldera have an earthier, more down-to-earth vibe and more affordable resorts.

Through the ages, the area's temperate climate, warm sea, fertile soil, and natural beauty have attracted Greek colonists, then Roman emperors—who called the region "Campania Felix," or "the happy land"—and later Saracen raiders and Spanish invaders. The result has been a rich and varied history, reflected in everything from architecture to mythology. The highlights span millennia: the near-intact Roman towns of Pompeii and Herculaneum, the Greek temples in Paestum, the Norman and Baroque churches in Naples, the white-dome fisherman's houses of Positano, the dolce vita resorts of Capri. Campania piles them all onto one mammoth must-see sandwich.

The region's complex identity is most intensely felt in its major metropolis, Naples. Few who visit remain ambivalent. You needn't participate in the mad whirl of the city, however. The best pastime in Campania is simply finding a spot with a stunning view and indulging in *il dolce far niente* ("the sweetness of doing nothing").

Positano

Fishing Village Turned Chic Resort

The most photographed fishing village in the world, this fabled locale is home to some 4,000 Positanesi, who are joined daily by thousands arriving via the scenic SS163 Amalfi Drive road, as well as by ferry and yacht. The town clings to the Monti Lattari with arcaded, cubist buildings, set in tiers up the mountainside, in pastel shades of rose, peach, purple, and ivory.

Don't Miss

The walkway from Piazza Flavio Gioia leads down to Spiaggia Grande, Positano's main beach, bordered by an esplanade and some of the town's busiest restaurants. Surrounded by the spectacular amphitheater of houses and villas that leapfrog up the hillsides of Monte Comune and Monte Sant'Angelo, this remains one of the most picturesque beaches in the world.

When to Go

Avoid the stifling summer heat by booking for the cooler and less crowded months May or October, when you can still enjoy swimming in the sea and walking in the Monti Lattari. Many hotels and restaurants close between November and Easter.

Getting Here

Feeling bold? Hire a vehicle to negotiate the winding, cliff-hugging and busy Amalfi Drive. SITA buses leave from the Circumvesuviana train station in Sorrento. Buses also run from Naples and, in summer, directly from Rome. There is a ferry from Sorrento in the summer months.

Positano Tourism. ✉ *Ufficio di Turismo Via Regina Giovanna 13* ☎ *334/9118563*

Ravello

Gardens, Fairytale Architecture, and Serenity

Positano may focus on pleasure, and Amalfi on history, but cool, serene Ravello revels in refinement. Thrust over the S163 and the Bay of Salerno on a mountain buttress, below forests of chestnut and ash, and above terraced lemon groves and vineyards, it early on beckoned the affluent with its island-in-the-sky views and secluded defensive positioning. Gardens out of the Arabian Nights, pastel palazzi, tucked-away piazzas with medieval fountains, architecture ranging from Romano-Byzantine to Norman-Saracen, and those sweeping blue-water, blue-sky vistas have inspired a panoply of large personalities. Today, visitors flock here to discover its lofty charms, its celebrated two-month-long summer music festival (the Ravello Festival), and to stroll through the hillside streets to gape at the bluer-than-blue panoramas of sea and sky.

Don't Miss

To the south of Ravello's main square, a hilly 15-minute walk along Via San Francesco brings you to Ravello's showstopper, the Villa Cimbrone (now a hotel), whose dazzling gardens perch 1,500 feet above the sea. This medieval-style fantasy was created in 1905 by England's Lord Grimthorpe and made world famous in the 1930s when Greta Garbo found sanctuary from the press here.

Getting Here

Buses from Amalfi make the 20-minute trip along white-knuckle roads.

Villa Cimbrone. ✉ *Via Santa Chiara 26, Ravello* ☎ *089/857459* 🌐 *www.villacimbrone.it* 🎫 €7

Pompeii

Roman Life (and Death) Frozen in Time

Petrified memorial to Vesuvius's eruption in 79 AD, Pompeii is the largest, most accessible, and most famous excavation anywhere. Ancient Pompeii had a population of 10,000 to 20,000 and covered about 170 acres on the seaward end of the Sarno Plain. Today it attracts more than 2 million visitors every year, but if you come in the quieter late afternoon, you can truly fall under the site's spell.

Don't Miss

Highlights include the Foro (Forum), which served as Pompeii's cultural, political, commercial, and religious hub; homes that were captured in various states by the eruption of Vesuvius, including the Casa del Poeta Tragico (House of the Tragic Poet), a middle-class residence with a canine floor mosaic, and the Casa dei Vettii (House of the Vettii), a wealthy merchant's home; the Villa dei Misteri (Villa of the Mysteries), a palatial abode with frescoes; and the Anfiteatro (Amphitheater), built around 70 BC.

Getting Here

The archaeological site of Pompeii has its own stop (Pompei–Villa dei Misteri) on the Circumvesuviana line to Sorrento, close to the main entrance at the Porta Marina, which is the best place from which to start a tour. To get to Pompeii by car, take the A3 Napoli–Salerno highway to the Pompei exit and follow signs for the nearby "Scavi." It's a sprawling sight, exposed to the Mezzogiorno sun, so bring good walking shoes, a hat, water, and snacks. ✉ *Pompeii* ☎ *081/8575347* 🌐 *www.pompeiisites.org* 🎫 *From €16; Tickets available at www.ticketone.it/en/artist/scavi-pompei*

Naples's Centro Storico

The City's Beating Heart

To experience the true essence of Naples, you need to explore the Centro Storico, an unforgettable neighborhood that is the heart of old Naples. This is the Naples of peeling building facades and hanging laundry, with small alleyways fragrant with fresh flowers laid at the many shrines to the Blessed Virgin. Here the cheapest pizzerias in town feed the locals like kings, and the raucous street carnival of Neapolitan daily life is punctuated with oases of spiritual calm. All the contradictions of Naples—splendor and squalor, palace and slum, triumph and tragedy—meet here and sing a full-throated chorale. It would take many lifetimes to unravel all the layers of this fascinating district. A full day's dive can take in the Santa Chiara cloisters, Sansevero chapel, Via Gregorio Armeno, the Duomo, and Museo Nazionale.

Don't Miss

It's only fitting that the Museo Archeologico Nazionale—the single most important and remarkable museum of Greco-Roman antiquities in the world—sits in the district first settled by the ancient Greeks (Neapolis) and then the Romans.

Getting Here

The Centro Storico can be reached quickly via the Metropolitana (it spans 5 different stops). Much of the ancient Decumanus, a gridlike street plan, can be explored on foot, following Spaccanapoli (literally "Split Naples") and Via Tribunali, which brim with street-life, beautiful artworks, dazzling churches, superstitious rituals, and an eerie underground network of tunnels.

Museo Archeologico Nazionale. ✉ *Piazza Museo 19, Centro Storico* ☎ *081/4422111* 🌐 *mannapoli.it* 🎫 *€15* ⏲ *Closed Tues.* 🚇 *Museo*

Naples Tourism. 🌐 *www.visitnaples.eu*

Pizza Napoletana

Pizza Where It Was Invented

Pizza in its modern form was created by impoverished Neapolitans on the streets, and there is no place better to enjoy its flavorsome local ingredients and wood-fired texture than in the heart of Naples. To follow the purest Neapolitan pizza path start off with either a Marinara (olive oil, tomato salsa, and oregano) or Margherita (San Marzano tomatoes, mozzarella, or fior di latte, fresh basil, salt, and extra-virgin olive oil). The latter was invented in 1889 by Pizzeria Brandi's pizzaiolo (pizza maker), in honor of the Queen of Italy, Margherita of Savoy. Its colors of tomato (red), mozzarella (white) and basil (green) marked the tricolor of Italian Unification.

Don't Miss

Look out for the "True Neapolitan Pizza" (*Verace Pizza Napoletana*) logo, denoting that a pizzeria and its trained *pizzaioli*are part of the AVPN association that protects and promotes the local tradition and use the best ingredients. Famous true pizza associates include Trianon da Ciro, Umberto, Di Matteo, and Sorbillo. Some fine historic *pizzerie*—like Da Michele and Brandi—are not part of AVPN but still uphold traditions.

The President's Pizza

Di Matteo. Bill Clinton enjoyed a Margherita here when the G8 was held in Naples in 1994. Today the superlative *pizzaioli* turn out a wide array of perfect pizzas. 💲 *Average main: €6* ✉ *Via Tribunali 94, Centro Storico* ☎ *081/455262* 🌐 *www.pizzeriadimatteo.com*

Getting Here

The best pizzerie are on Via dei Tribunali in the Centro Storico. Choose either the Piazza Dante or Museo metro stop, and then walk.

Associazane Verace Pizza Napoletana. 🌐 *www.pizzanapoletana.org*

Certosa e Museo di San Martino

Palatial Clifftop Monastery

Atop a rocky promontory with a fabulous view of the entire city and bay; and grand salons now housing an eclectic art collection, the Certosa di San Martino is a monastery that seems more like a palace. This *certosa* (charter house), which started in 1325, was so sumptuous that by the 18th century Ferdinand IV was threatening to halt the religious order's government subsidy. Although the Angevin heritage can be seen in the pointed arches and cross-vaulted ceiling of the certosa church, over the years dour Gothic was traded in for varicolored Neapolitan Baroque. Highlights include the cappella del Tesoro, with Luca Giordano's ceiling fresco of Judith holding aloft Holofernes's head and Jusepe de Ribera's masterful *Pietà;* the *Quarto del priore* (Prior's Quarters), an extravaganza of salons filled with frescoes, majolica-tile floors, and paintings; and the Sezione Presepiale, the world's greatest collection of Christmas cribs.

Don't Miss

For sublime Bay views amid Florentine-style gardens, saintly statues and macabre skull statues by architect and sculptor Cosimo Fanzago, head out to the Chiostro Grande (Great Cloister).

Getting Here

You can take the Metropolitana line 1 to Vanvitelli followed by a half-mile walk. For a shorter walk and experience of the city's celebrated funicular railway, take either the Funicolare di Montesanto to Morgen or Funcicolare Centrale to Piazza Fuga.

✉ *Piazzale San Martino 8, Vomero* ☎ *081/2294503* 🌐 *www.beniculturali.it/luogo/certosa-e-museo-di-san-martino* 🎫 *€6* 🕒 *Closed Wed.*

Capri

A Green and Glam Island

Gorgeous grottoes, soaring conical peaks, caverns great and small, plus villas of the emperors and thousands of legends brush Capri with an air of whispered mystery. Emperor Augustus was the first to tout the island's pleasures by nicknaming it Apragopolis (City of Sweet Idleness), and Capri has drawn escapists of all kinds ever since. Ancient Greek and Roman goddesses made way for Jacqueline Onassis, Elizabeth Taylor, and Brigitte Bardot, who made the island into a paparazzi playground in the 1960s. Today, new generations of glitterati continue to answer the island's call. Life on Capri gravitates around the two centers of Capri Town and Anacapri, higher up (902 feet), the former full of chic shops and the latter with a more native, friendly charm.

Don't Miss

Once you're lofted up to Anacapri, the island's "second city," by bus, you can reach the island heights by taking the spectacular chairlift that ascends to the top of Monte Solaro (1,932 feet). From this serene vantage point, on clear days there are jaw-dropping views of Campania's shimmering bays and even as far as the smoking cone volcano island Stromboli.

Getting Here

Capri is well connected to the mainland (with more sailings from April to October from Naples and Sorrento). On arriving at the main harbor, the Marina Grande, take the funicular to Capri Town. Tiny orange buses ply the hairpin bends of the island. To avoid the crowds splurge on a taxi.

Capri Tourism. 🌐 *www.capritourism.com*

Monte Solaro. ✉ *Piazza Vittoria, Anacapri* ☎ *081/8371428* 🌐 *www.capriseggiovia.it* 🎫 *€9 one-way, €12 return* ⏱ *Closes in adverse weather*

Paestum

Visions of a Lost Civilization

One of Italy's most majestic sights lies on the edge of a flat coastal plain: the remarkably preserved Greek temples of Paestum. This is the site of the ancient city of Poseidonia, founded by Greek colonists probably in the 6th century BC. When the Romans took it over in 273 BC, they Latinized the name to Paestum and changed the layout of the settlement, adding an amphitheater and a forum. Much of the archaeological material found on the site is displayed in the Museo Nazionale here, with several rooms devoted to the unique tomb paintings—rare examples of Greek and pre-Roman pictorial art—discovered in the area.

Don't Miss

The Tempio di Nettuno (Temple of Poseidon), is a showstopping Doric edifice with 36 fluted columns that rivals those of the finest temples in Greece. Beyond is the so-called Basilica. It dates from the early 6th century BC. The name is an 18th-century misnomer, though, since it was, in fact, a temple to Hera, the wife of Zeus. Try to see the temples in the early morning or late afternoon when the stone takes on a golden hue.

Getting Here

By car, take the A3 autostrada south from Salerno, take the Battipaglia exit to SS18. Exit at Capaccio Scala. You can also take a CSTP or SCAT bus (departs hourly) or an FS train from Salerno. The archaeological site is a 10-minute walk from the station.

Via Magna Grecia, Paestum 0828/811023 www.museopaestum.beniculturali.it €12, Dec.–Feb. €6

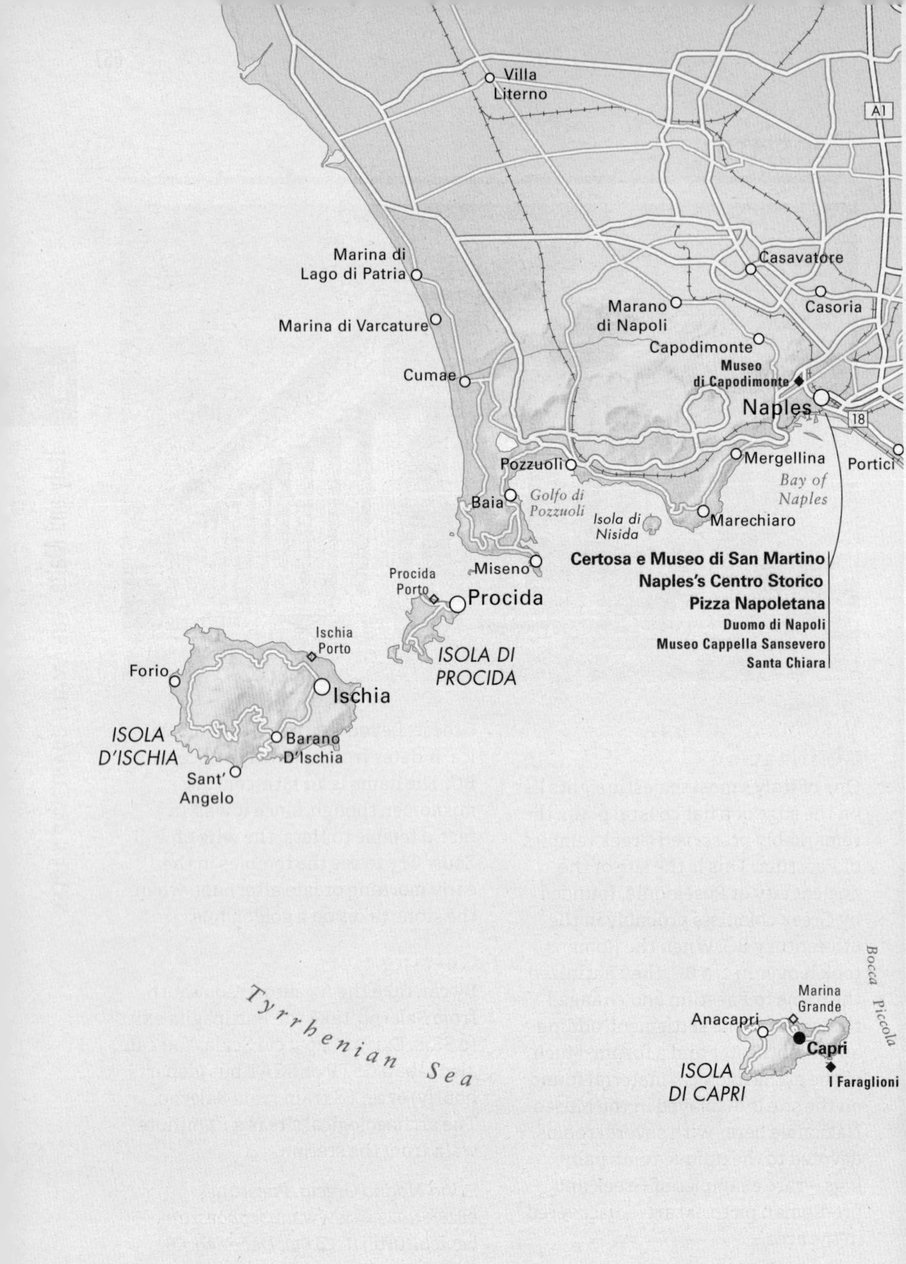

The Amalfi Coast and Naples

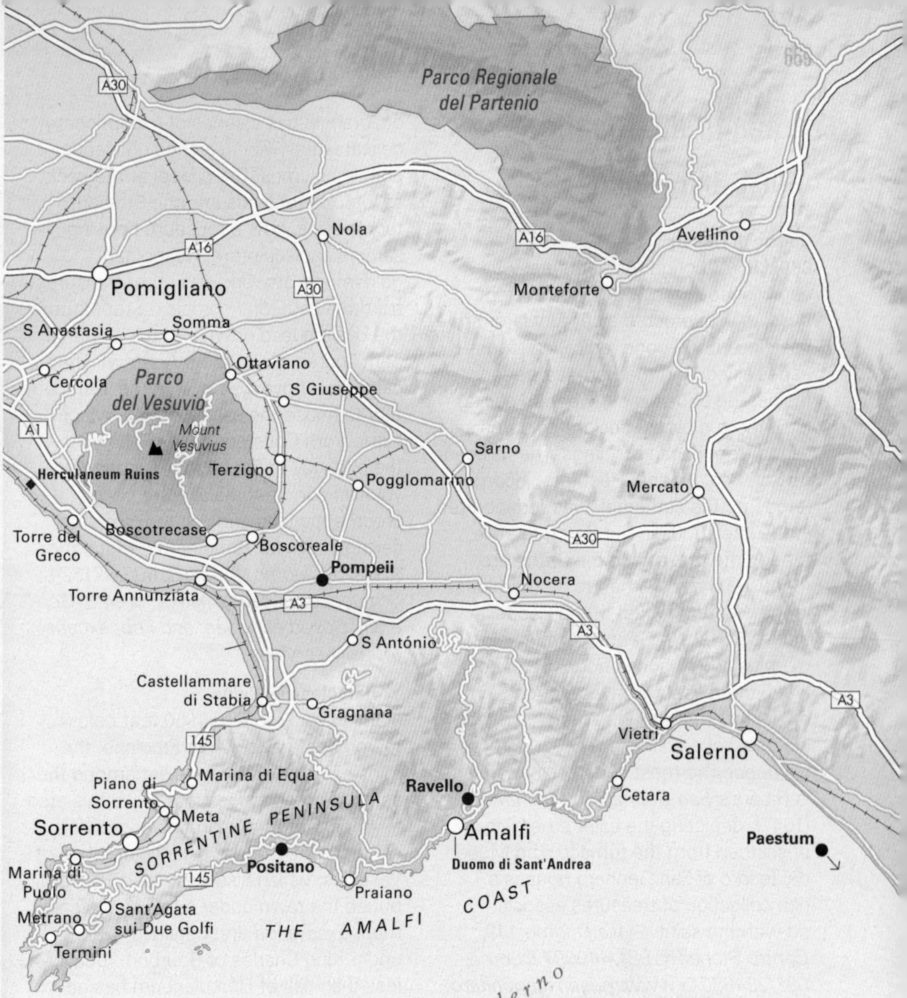

Parco Regionale del Partenio
A30
A16
Nola
A16
Avellino
Pomigliano
A30
Monteforte
S Anastasia
Somma
Ottaviano
Cercola
Parco del Vesuvio
S Giuseppe
A1
Mount Vesuvius
Sarno
Herculaneum Ruins
Terzigno
Pogglomarino
Mercato
Torre del Greco
Boscotrecase
Boscoreale
A30
Pompeii
Nocera
Torre Annunziata
A3
A3
S António
Castellammare di Stabia
Gragnana
A3
Vietri
145
Salerno
Marina di Equa
Piano di Sorrento
Ravello
Cetara
Meta
SORRENTINE PENINSULA
Sorrento
Amalfi
Paestum
Marina di Puolo
145
Positano
Duomo di Sant'Andrea
Praiano
Metrano
Sant'Agata sui Due Golfi
Termini
THE AMALFI COAST
Bay of Salerno

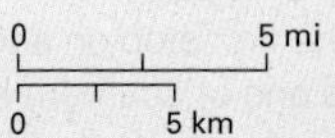

When in the Amalfi Coast and Naples

Duomo di Napoli

CHURCH | Although the cathedral was established in the 1200s, the current building was erected a century later and has since undergone radical changes—especially during the Baroque period. Inside, the 350-year-old wooden ceiling is supported by 110 ancient columns salvaged from pagan buildings. The 4th-century church of Santa Restituta, incorporated into the cathedral, was redecorated in the late 1600s in the Baroque style, though the mosaics in the Battistero (Baptistery) are claimed to be the oldest in the Western world. In the Cappella del Tesoro di San Gennaro, multicolor marbles and frescoes honor St. Januarius, the miracle-working patron saint of Naples. Three times a year his dried blood is believed to liquefy during rites in his honor. The most spectacular painting is Ribera's *San Gennaro in the Furnace* (1647), depicting the saint emerging unscathed from the furnace. The Museo del Tesoro di San Gennaro houses a rich collection of treasures associated with the saint. ✉ *Via Duomo 149, Centro Storico* ☎ *081/449097 Duomo, 081/294980* 🌐 *www.museosangennaro.it* 🎫 *Cappella del Tesoro di San Gennaro with audioguide from €5; museum and chapel with audioguide €12; guided visits from €20* Ⓜ *Duomo, Cavour.*

★ **Duomo di Sant'Andrea**

CHURCH | Complicated, grand, delicate, and dominating, the 9th-century Amalfi cathedral has been remodeled over the years with Romanesque, Byzantine, Gothic, and Baroque elements, but retains a predominantly Arab-Norman style. Built around 1266 as a burial ground for Amalfi's elite, the cloister, the first stop on a tour of the cathedral, is one of southern Italy's architectural treasures. Its flower-and-palm-filled quadrangle has a series of exceptionally delicate intertwining arches on slender double columns. The chapel at the back of the cloister leads into the 9th-century basilica, now a museum housing sarcophagi, sculpture, Neapolitan goldsmiths' artwork, and other treasures from the cathedral complex. Steps from the basilica lead down into the Cripta di Sant'Andrea (Crypt of St. Andrew). The cathedral above was built in the 13th century to house the saint's bones, which came from Constantinople. Following the one-way traffic up to the cathedral, you can admire the elaborate polychrome marbles and painted, coffered ceilings from its 18th-century restoration. ✉ *Piazza Duomo, Amalfi* ☎ *089/871324* 🌐 *museodiocesanoamalfi.it* 🎫 *€4* ⏲ *Generally closed early Jan. and Feb. except for daily services.*

★ **Herculaneum Ruins**

RUINS | Lying more than 50 feet below the present-day town of Ercolano, the ruins of Herculaneum are set among the acres of greenhouses that make this area an important European flower-growing center. In AD 79, the gigantic eruption of Vesuvius, which also destroyed Pompeii, buried the town under a tide of volcanic mud. Excavation first began in 1738 under King Charles of Bourbon. Today less than half of Herculaneum has been excavated. Nevertheless, what has been found is generally better preserved than Pompeii. In some cases you can even see the original wooden beams, doors, and staircases. At the entrance, pick up a free map showing the gridlike layout of the dig. Splurge on an audio guide app via 🌐 *www.ercolano.tours* (€10): the standard audio guide (€8 for one, €13 for two) may be available for those without a smartphone. You can also join a group with a local guide (around €15 per person). Most of the houses are open, and a representative cross-section of domestic, commercial, and civic buildings can be seen. ✉ *Corso Resina 6, Ercolano* ☎ *081/7777008* 🌐 *ercolano.beniculturali.it*

€13; €15 with Teatro Antico Closed Wed.

★ **I Faraglioni**

NATURE SIGHT | Few landscapes set more artists dreaming than that of the famous Faraglioni—three enigmatic, pale-ocher limestone colossi that loom out of the sea just off the Punta Tragara on the southern coast of Capri. Soaring almost 350 feet above the water, the Faraglioni have become for most Italians a beloved symbol of Capri and have been poetically compared to Gothic cathedrals or modern skyscrapers. The first rock is called Faraglione di Terra, since it's attached to the land; at its base is the famous restaurant and bathing lido Da Luigi, where a beach mattress may accompany the luncheon menu. The second is called Faraglione di Mezzo, or Stella, and little boats can often be seen going through its picturesque tunnel, which was caused by sea erosion. The rock farthest out to sea is Faraglione di Scopolo and is inhabited by a wall lizard species with a striking blue belly, considered a local variant by biologists although legend has it that they were originally brought as pets from Greece to delight ancient Roman courtiers. ✉ *End of Via Tragara, Capri.*

★ **Museo Cappella Sansevero** (*Sansevero Chapel Museum*)

NOTABLE BUILDING | The dazzling funerary chapel of the Sangro di Sansevero princes combines noble swagger, overwhelming color, and a touch of the macabre—which expresses Naples perfectly. The chapel was begun in 1590 by Prince Giovan Francesco di Sangro to fulfill a vow to the Virgin if he were cured of a dire illness. The seventh Sangro di Sansevero prince, Raimondo, had the building modified in the mid-18th century and is generally credited for its current Baroque styling, the noteworthy elements of which include the splendid marble-inlay floor and statuary, including Giuseppe Sanmartino's spine-chillingly lifelike *Cristo Velato* (Veiled Christ). ✉ *Via Francesco de Sanctis 19, off Vicolo Domenico Maggiore, Centro Storico* ☎ *081/5518470* 🌐 *www.museosansevero.it* *€10* *Closed Tues.* Ⓜ *Dante.*

★ **Museo di Capodimonte**

ART MUSEUM | The grandiose, 18th-century, neoclassical, Bourbon royal palace houses fine and decorative art in 124 rooms. The main galleries on the first floor are devoted to the Farnese collection, as well as work from the 13th to the 18th century, including many pieces by Dutch masters, as well as an El Greco and 12 Titian paintings. On the second floor look for stunning paintings by Simone Martini (circa 1284–1344) and Caravaggio (1573–1610). ✉ *Via Miano 2, Capodimonte* ☎ *081/7499111* 🌐 *capodimonte.cultura.gov.it, www.amicidicapodimonte.org* *€15* *Closed Wed.*

★ **Santa Chiara**

RELIGIOUS BUILDING | Offering a stark and telling contrast to the opulence of the nearby Gesù Nuovo, Santa Chiara is the leading Angevin Gothic monument in Naples. The fashionable house of worship for the 14th-century nobility and a favorite Angevin church from the start, the church of St. Clare was intended to be a great dynastic monument by Robert d'Anjou. His second wife, Sancia di Majorca, added the adjoining convent for the Poor Clares to a monastery of the Franciscan Minors; this was the first time the two sexes were combined in a single complex. Built in a Provençal Gothic style between 1310 and 1328 (probably by Gagliardo Primario) and dedicated in 1340, the church had its aspect radically altered in the Baroque period. A six-day fire started by Allied bombs on August 4, 1943, put an end to all that. Around the left side of the church is the **Chiostro delle Clarisse**, the most famous cloister in Naples. ✉ *Piazza Gesù Nuovo, Centro Storico* ☎ *081/5516673* 🌐 *www.monasterodisantachiara.it* *Museum and cloister €6* *Cloister closed Sun. afternoon* Ⓜ *Dante, Università.*

Where to Eat and Drink

★ Da Gelsomina

$$$ | SOUTHERN ITALIAN | Amid its own terraced vineyards with inspiring views to the island of Ischia and beyond, this is much more than just a well-reputed restaurant. The owner's mother was a friend of Axel Munthe, and he encouraged her to open a food kiosk, which evolved into Da Gelsomina; today the specialties include *pollo a mattone,* chicken grilled on bricks, and locally caught rabbit. **Known for:** opened in the 1960s with family links to Axel Munthe; chicken grilled on bricks; fresh produce and wine from their verdant gardens. *Average main: €35 Via Migliara 72, Anacapri 081/8371499 www.dagelsomina.com Closed Nov.–Mar.*

★ Don Alfonso 1890

$$$$ | SOUTHERN ITALIAN | A gastronomic giant and pioneer in upscale farm-to-table cuisine (it even grows its own produce on a small farm nearby), Don Alfonso is considered one of Italy's best restaurants. It's a family affair, with mamma (Livia) handling the dining room, papà (former chef Alfonso Iaccarino) tending to the organic plot, one son working as the current chef (preparing classic dishes alongside edgier creations), and the other serving as maître d'. **Known for:** stellar tasting menus; slow food pioneer; Punta Campanella local garden produce. *Average main: €160 Corso Sant'Agata 13, Sant'Agata sui Due Golfi SITA Bus to via Nastro Verde or taxi from Sorrento. 081/8780026 www.donalfonso.com Closed Mon. and Tues. and Nov.–Apr. No lunch weekdays.*

★ Enoteca Belledonne

WINE BARS | Between 8 and 9 in the evening, it seems as though the whole upscale Chiaia neighborhood has descended into this tiny space for an aperitivo. The small tables and low stools are notably uncomfortable, but the cozy atmosphere and the pleasure of being surrounded by glass-front cabinets full of wine bottles with beautiful labels more than makes up for it. Excellent local wines are available by the glass at great prices. *Vico Belledonne a Chiaia 18, Chiaia 081/403162 www.enoteca-belledonne.it San Pasquale.*

★ Tenuta Vannulo—Buffalo Farm and Shop

FARM/RANCH | FAMILY | Foodies, families, and the curious flock to this novel farm attraction that celebrates humane animal husbandry, organic mozzarella di bufala, and other wonderful products. A tour of the ranch run by the Palmieri family—headed by the serene octogenerian Antonio—brings you nose to glistening snout with probably the most pampered buffalo in the world. Some 600 of them wallow in pools, get a mechanical massage, and flap their ears to classical music. The shop/restaurant is the place to taste and take away cheese, ice cream, yogurt, chocolate, and leather products. *Contrada Vannulo, Via Galileo Galilei 101, Capaccio, Paestum 0828/727894 www.vannulo.it €5 guided tours; book in advance.*

★ Umberto

$$ | SOUTHERN ITALIAN | Run by the Di Porzio family since 1916, Umberto is one of the city's classic restaurants, combining the classiness of its neighborhood, Chiaia, and the friendliness one finds in other parts of Naples. Try the *paccheri 'do tre dita* ("three-finger" pasta with octopus, tomato, olives, and capers); it bears the nickname of the original Umberto, who happened to be short a few digits. **Known for:** authentic Pizza DOC (smaller, with chunky cornicione rim); charming hosts; classic Neapolitan meat sauce alla Genovese. *Average main: €17 Via Alabardieri 30–31, Chiaia 081/418555 www.umberto.it No lunch Mon. Chiaia.*

Cool Places to Stay

★ **Albergo Il Monastero**
$$ | HOTEL | The Castello Aragonese, on its own island, is the unrivaled location for this unique hotel with a peaceful ambience and simple but comfortable rooms overlooking the Mediterranean. **Pros:** stunning views and peaceful garden; situated inside the castle; great restaurant on terrace. **Cons:** a long way from the entrance to your room; perhaps too far from the town's action; some may not like the understated decor. *Rooms from: €170 ✉ Castello Aragonese 3, Ischia Ponte ☎ 081/992435 🌐 www.albergoilmonastero.it ⏲ Closed Nov.–late Apr. 21 rooms Free Breakfast.*

★ **Anantara Hotel Convento di Amalfi**
$$$$ | HOTEL | This fabled medieval monastery was lauded by such guests as Longfellow and Wagner, and after a 2022 overhaul it still retains its historic charm and features, including a celebrated Arab-Sicilian cloister and Baroque church; once stark monk cells are now comfy contemporary guest room cocoons, some with vibrant artworks and suites with terrace hot tubs—two restaurants provide fine dining and Gino Sorbillo's classic Neapolitan pizza menu. **Pros:** a slice of paradise; impeccable service; sublime terrace and garden walkways. **Cons:** traditionalists will miss some of its old-world charm; a 10-minute walk to town; noise from occasional wedding and event. *Rooms from: €2000 ✉ Via Annunziatella 46, Amalfi ☎ 089/8736711 🌐 www.ghconventodiamalfi.com ⏲ Closed Jan.–mid-Mar. 53 rooms Free Breakfast.*

★ **Hotel Palazzo Decumani**
$$ | HOTEL | This contemporary upscale hotel near the Centro Storico's major sights occupies an early-20th-century palazzo, but you won't find heavy, ornate furnishings—the emphasis is on light and space, both in short supply in old Naples. **Pros:** guests-only lounge-bar; large rooms and bathrooms; service on par with fancier hotels. **Cons:** can be hard to find—follow signs from Corso Umberto; some may find decor a tad sparse; soundproofing not the best. *Rooms from: €200 ✉ Piazzetta Giustino Fortunato 8, Centro Storico ☎ 081/4201379 🌐 www.palazzodecumani.com 28 rooms Free Breakfast Ⓜ Duomo.*

★ **Hotel Villa Cimbrone**
$$$$ | HOTEL | Suspended over the azure sea and set amid legendary rose-filled gardens, this Gothic-style castle was once home to Lord Grimthorpe and a hideaway for Greta Garbo; since the 1990s, it's been an exclusive if pricey visitors haven, with guest rooms ranging from palatial to cozy. **Pros:** gorgeous pool and views; surrounded by beautiful gardens; top-rated restaurant. **Cons:** a longish hike from town center (porters can help with luggage); daily arrival of respectful day-trippers; special place comes at a price. *Rooms from: €990 ✉ Via Santa Chiara 26, Ravello ☎ 089/857459 🌐 www.villacimbrone.com ⏲ Closed Nov.–mid-Apr. 19 rooms Free Breakfast.*

★ **J. K. Place**
$$$$ | HOTEL | Occupying an 1876 villa above Marina Grande harbor, southern Italy's most glamorous hotel makes other Capri accommodations seem dull. **Pros:** exquisite pool; pleasant walk to the magical Tiberio beach; free shuttle to town. **Cons:** expensive; only for high rollers; pool visible from main road. *Rooms from: €1273 ✉ Via Provinciale Marina Grande 225, Capri ☎ 081/8384001 🌐 www.jkcapri.com ⏲ Closed mid-Oct.–mid-Apr. 22 rooms Free Breakfast.*

Venice

Venice is often called La Serenissima, or "the most serene," a reference to the majesty, wisdom, and power of this city that was for centuries a leader in trade between Europe and Asia and a major center of European culture. Built on water by people who saw the sea as both a defender and an ally—and who constantly invested in its splendor with magnificent architectural projects—Venice is a city unlike any other.

No matter how often you've seen it in photos and films, the real thing is more dreamlike than you could ever imagine. Its most notable landmarks, the Basilica di San Marco and the Palazzo Ducale, are exotic mixes of Byzantine, Romanesque, Gothic, and Renaissance styles, reflecting Venice's ties with the rest of Italy and with Constantinople to the east.

Shimmering sunlight and silvery mist soften every perspective here; it's easy to understand how the city became renowned in the Renaissance for its artists' use of color. It's full of secrets, inexpressibly romantic, and frequently given over to pure, sensuous enjoyment. You'll see Venetians going about their daily affairs in *vaporetti* (canal boats), in the *campi* (squares), and along the *calli* (narrow streets). Despite their many challenges (including more frequent flooding and overcrowding), they are proud of their city and its history and are still quite helpful to those who show proper respect for Venice and its way of life.

The city is built across a small archipelago of 118 islands, all connected by some 400 bridges in a bay at the mouth of the Po and Piave rivers.

You can walk across Venice proper in a couple of hours, even counting a few minutes for getting lost—which can be a pleasure in itself, as you might wind up coming across a traditional wine bar or a quirky shop that turns out to be the highlight of your afternoon. That said, vaporetti will save wear and tear on tired feet, and are a hugely scenic way to get around.

Cruising the Grand Canal

Venice's "Main Street"

Venice's Grand Canal is one of the world's great thoroughfares. It winds its way from Piazzale Roma to Piazza San Marco, passing 200 palazzi built from the 13th to the 18th centuries by Venice's richest and most powerful families. There's a theatrical quality to a boat ride on the canal: it's as if each pink- or gold-tinted facade is trying to steal your attention from its rival across the way. In medieval and Renaissance cities, wars and sieges required defense to be an element of design; but in rich, impregnable Venice, you could safely show off what you had. But more than being simply an item of conspicuous consumption, a Venetian's palazzo was an embodiment of their person—not only their wealth, but also their erudition and taste.

Don't Miss

Ca' d'Oro (1421–38) is a splendid example of Venetian Gothic domestic design. Inspired by stories of Nero's Domus Aurea (Golden House) in Rome, the first owner had parts of the facade gilded with 20,000 sheets of gold leaf. The gold has long worn away, but the Ca' d'Oro is still Venice's most beautiful Gothic palazzo.

Getting Around

The easiest and cheapest way to see the Grand Canal is to take the Line 1 vaporetto from Piazalle Roma to San Marco. The ride takes about 35 minutes. Invest in a day ticket, and you can spend the better part of a day hopping on and off at the vaporetto's many stops, visiting the sights along the banks.

ACTV. ☎ *041/041041* 🌐 *www.actv.it*

Basilica di San Marco

The Cultural Mosaic of Venice

Standing at the heart of Venice, the spectacular Basilica di San Marco has been, for about a millennium, the city's religious center. Like other great churches—and even more so—it's also an expression of worldly accomplishments and aspirations. As you take in the shimmering mosaics and elaborate ornamentation, you begin to grasp the pivotal role Venice has played for centuries in European culture. The basilica was the doges' personal chapel, linking its religious function to the political life of the city, and was endowed with all the riches the Republic's admirals and merchants could carry off from the Orient (as the Byzantine Empire was then known), earning it the nickname "Chiesa d'Oro" (Golden Church).

Don't Miss

The glory of the basilica is its brilliant, floor-to-ceiling mosaics. The mosaics of the atrium, or porch, represent the Old Testament, while those of the interior show the stories of the Gospel and saints, ending with the image of Christ in Glory (a Renaissance copy) in the apse. Look especially for the beautiful 12th-century mosaics in the dome of the Pentecost, the first dome in the nave of the basilica as you enter the church, and for the 12th-century mosaics in the dome of the ascension. ✉ *Piazza San Marco, San Marco 328, San Marco* ☎ *041/2708311* 🌐 *www.basilicasanmarco.it* 🎫 *Basilica €3, sanctuary and Pala d'Oro €5, museum €7* 🚆 *Vaporetto: Zaccaria, Vallaresso*

Palazzo Ducale (Doge's Palace)

Jewel of Gothic Design

Rising majestically above Piazzetta San Marco, this Gothic fantasia of pink-and-white marble—the doges' residence from the 10th century and the central administrative center of the Venetian Republic—is a majestic expression of Venetian prosperity and power. Upon entering, you'll find yourself in an immense courtyard with some of the first evidence of Venice's Renaissance architecture, including Antonio Rizzo's 15th-century Scala dei Giganti (Stairway of the Giants). Though ordinary mortals must use the central interior staircase, its upper flight is the lavishly gilded Scala d'Oro (Golden Staircase), designed by Sansovino. The popular Secret Itineraries tour lets you visit the doge's private apartments and hidden passageways.

Don't Miss

The palace's sumptuous chambers have walls and ceilings covered with works by Venice's greatest artists. The ceiling of the Sala del Senato (Senate Chamber), featuring *The Triumph of Venice* by Tintoretto, is magnificent, but it's dwarfed by his masterpiece *Paradise* in the Sala del Maggiore Consiglio (Great Council Hall), the world's largest oil painting. The room's carved gilt ceiling is breathtaking, especially with Veronese's majestic *Apotheosis of Venice* filling one of the center panels. In the Anticollegio you'll find *The Rape of Europa* by Veronese and Tintoretto's *Bacchus and Ariadne Crowned by Venus.*

✉ Piazza San Marco 1, San Marco ☎ 041/42730892 🌐 palazzoducale.visitmuve.it 🎫 Museums of San Marco Pass €25; museum Pass €36; Secret Itineraries tour €28 🚊 Vaporetto: San Zaccaria,Vallaresso

Gallerie dell'Accademia

The Greatest Collection of Venetian Art

Gallerie dell'Accademia was founded by Napoléon in 1807 on the site of a religious complex he had suppressed. The galleries were carefully and subtly restructured between 1945 and 1959 by the renowned Venetian architect Carlo Scarpa. One highlight is *The Tempest* by Giorgione (1477–1510), a revolutionary work that has intrigued viewers and critics for centuries. It is unified not only by physical design elements, as was usual, but more importantly by a mysterious, somewhat threatening atmosphere. Also look out for *Feast in the House of Levi*, which got Veronese summoned to the Inquisition over its depiction of dogs, jesters, and other extraneous and unsacred figures. Plus, don't miss several of Tintoretto's finest works, plus the views of 15th- and 16th-century Venice by Carpaccio and Gentile Bellini—you'll easily recognize many places you've seen on your walks around the city.

Don't Miss

Jacopo Bellini is considered the father of the Venetian Renaissance, and you can compare his *Madonna and Child with Saints* with such later works as *Madonna of the Orange Tree* by Cima da Conegliano (circa 1459–1517) and *Ten Thousand Martyrs of Mt. Ararat* by Vittore Carpaccio (circa 1455–1525). Jacopo's more accomplished son Giovanni (circa 1430–1516) attracts your eye not only with his subject matter but also with his rich color.

✉ *Campo de la Carità, Dorsoduro 1050* ☎ *041/5222247, 041/5243354* 🌐 *www.gallerieaccademia.it* 🎫 *€12* ✍ *Reservations strongly advised* 🚊 *Vaporetto: Accademia, Zattere*

Ponte di Rialto

A Landmark with Amazing Views

The competition to design a stone bridge across the Grand Canal attracted the best architects of the late 16th century, including Michelangelo, Palladio, and Sansovino, but the job went to the less famous (if appropriately named) Antonio da Ponte (1512–95). His pragmatic design, completed in 1591, featured shop space and was high enough for galleys to pass beneath. Putting practicality and economy over aesthetic considerations—unlike the classical plans proposed by his more famous contemporaries—da Ponte's bridge essentially followed the design of its wooden predecessor. But it kept decoration and cost to a minimum at a time when the Republic's coffers were low, due to continual wars against the Turks and competition brought about by the Spanish and Portuguese opening of oceanic trade routes. Climb the Rialto Bridge using one of its three sets of stairs to enjoy one of the city's most famous views: the Grand Canal vibrant with boat traffic.

Don't Miss

During the day, check out the shops built into the Rialto Bridge's central stair section, though their goods tend to be pricier than other places in the city. In the evening, the bridge makes the perfect spot for a romantic stroll. If you head to the Rialto Bridge from San Marco, continue across to the Rialto Market, a lively produce and fish market that's still frequented by locals.

Getting Here

Take vaporetti lines 1 or 2 to the Rialto stop.

Riding in a Gondola

A Musical Trip

Taking a trip along one of the back canals aboard a sleek, black gondola with a singing driver clad in black pants and a striped shirt is the quintessential Venetian experience and is not to be missed despite the high price. Gondolas ply fixed routes at fixed prices, so it's important to enter at the correct place to get the best trip, and it's important to pick a gondolier who is both fun and engaging.

Don't Miss

If you want to take a gondola home with you, seek out the workshop of Gilberto Penzo in the San Polo district. He makes kits that will allow you to build your own gondola once you get home, and it's considerably cheaper than the real ride . ✉ *Calle Seconda dei Saoneri, San Polo 2681, San Polo* ☎ *041/5246139* 🌐 *www.veniceboats.com* 🚉 *Vaporetto: San Tomà*

When and Where to Go

It's best to pick a time when it's not too hot or busy. Especially in summer, go in the morning (there's no shade on a gondola for either you or the gondolier). Sunset is also a wonderful time to take a trip, but rates go up after 7 pm, and your gondolier may be getting tired. Avoid gondolas around San Marco, which tend to travel only on the Grand Canal, but the area around Ponte San Polo is an ideal place. You can also get a shared gondola (and pay only for your seats).

Rental Details

Gondolas can be hired near most major bridges and campos. Fares are €80 for 25 to 30 minutes; €100 after 7 pm or before 8 am (payable in cash only); rates are set, and gondoliers will not negotiate. Maximum of 5 people per gondola. Prebook a trip with Get Your Guide (🌐 *getyourguide.com*).

Murano

Island of Outstanding Glass Artistry

In the 13th century, the Republic, concerned about fire hazards and anxious to maintain control of its artisans' expertise, moved its glassworks to Murano. Today, this bustling island in the northern Venetian Lagoon is still renowned for its glass creations. As in Venice, bridges here link a number of small islands, which are dotted with houses that once were—and still largely are—workmen's cottages. Many of them line the Fondamenta dei Vetrai, the canalside walkway leading from the Colonna vaporetto landing. If you're looking to buy Murano glass, more elaborate pieces can cost thousands of dollars, but you can take home a modest but lovely piece, such as a drinking glass, for a more affordable price.

Don't Miss

The compact yet informative Museo Vetro (Glass Museum) displays glass items dating from the 3rd century AD to today. You'll learn all about techniques introduced through the ages (many of which are still in use), including 15th-century gold-leaf decoration, 16th-century filigree work that incorporated thin bands of white or colored glass into the crystal, and the 18th-century origins of Murano's iconic chandeliers.

Getting Here

To avoid being pressured to buy glass, take the regular vaporetto from Piazzale Roma or the Fondamente Nuove to Murano instead of succumbing to the hawkers offering you a "free" trip to Murano.

Museo del Vetro. ✉ *Fondamenta Marco Giustinian 8, Murano* ☎ *041/739586* 🌐 *museovetro.visitmuve.it* 🎫 *€11* 🕒 *Closed Mon.–Wed.* 🚆 *Vaporetto: Murano Museo*

Venice Carnevale

World's Best Costume Ball

For the 12 days leading up to *quaresima* (Lent), the city of Venice celebrates, with more than half a million people attending masquerade balls, historical processions, concerts, plays, street performances, fashion shows, and all other manner of revelry. The first record of the Venice Carnevale dates back to 1097, but it was in the 18th century that Venice earned its international reputation as the "city of Carnevale." During that era the partying began after Epiphany (January 6) and transformed the city for over a month into one ongoing masquerade. After the Republic's fall in 1797, Carnevale was periodically prohibited by the French and then the Austrian occupiers. Carnevale was not revived until 1979, when the municipality saw a way of converting the unruly antics of throwing water balloons in the days preceding Lent into a more pleasant celebration.

Don't Miss

Carnevale events and schedules change from year to year. Many of Carnevale's costume balls are open to the public—but they come with an extravagant price tag, and the most popular of them need to be booked well in advance. But you don't have to blow the bank on a masquerade ball in order to take part in Carnevale—many people go simply for the exuberant street life. Be aware, though, that the crowds are enormous, and ball or no ball, prices for everything absolutely skyrocket.

Carnevale di Venezia. 🌐 *www.carnevale.venezia.it*

When in Venice

★ Jewish Ghetto

HISTORIC DISTRICT | The very first Jewish ghetto in Europe also contains the continent's highest density of Renaissance-era synagogues, and visiting them on a guided tour is interesting not only culturally but also aesthetically. In 1516, the Venetian Senate voted to confine Jews to an island in Cannaregio, whose gates were locked at night and whose canals were patrolled. In the 16th century, the community grew with refugees from the Inquisition. Although the gates were pulled down after Napoléon's 1797 arrival, the ghetto was reinstated during the Austrian occupation. Full freedom wasn't realized until 1866 with the founding of the Italian state. Many Jews fled Italy after Mussolini's 1938 racial laws, but of the remainder, all but eight were killed by the Nazis. You can visit some of the historic buildings of the ghetto on guided tours, which run in English every hour from 10 am to 5 pm (starting 9 am on Fridays) every day except Saturday. ✉ *Campo del Ghetto Nuovo, Cannaregio* ☎ *055/2989815* 🌐 *www.ghettovenezia.com* 🎫 *€12 for guided tour* ⊗ *No guided tours on Sat. or Jewish holidays.*

★ San Giorgio Maggiore

CHURCH | There's been a church on this island since the 8th century. Today's refreshingly airy and simply decorated church of brick and white marble was begun in 1566 by Palladio and displays his architectural hallmarks of mathematical harmony and classical influence. *The Last Supper* and the *Gathering of Manna*, two of Tintoretto's later works, line the chancel. To the right of the entrance hangs *The Adoration of the Shepherds* by Jacopo Bassano. Ask to see Carpaccio's *St. George and the Dragon*, which hangs in a private room. The campanile (bell tower) dates from 1791. **■ TIP→ Climb to the top of the campanile for unparalleled 360-degree views of the lagoon, islands, and Venice itself.** ✉ *Isola di San Giorgio Maggiore, San Giorgio Maggiore* ☎ *041/5227827* 🌐 *www.abbaziasangiorgio.it* 🎫 *Church free, campanile €6* Ⓜ *Vaporetto: San Giorgio.*

★ Santa Maria Gloriosa dei Frari

CHURCH | Completed in 1442, this immense Gothic church of russet-color brick, known locally as "I Frari," is famous for its array of spectacular Venetian paintings and historic tombs. In the sacristy, see Giovanni Bellini's 1488 triptych *Madonna and Child with Saints*. The Corner Chapel is graced by Bartolomeo Vivarini's altarpiece *St. Mark Enthroned* and *Saints John the Baptist, Jerome, Peter, and Nicholas*. In the first south chapel of the chorus, there is a fine sculpture of St. John the Baptist by Donatello, dated 1438, with a psychological intensity rare for early Renaissance sculpture. ✉ *Campo dei Frari, San Polo* ☎ *041/2728611* 🌐 *www.basilicadeifrari.it* 🎫 *€3 (free with Chorus Pass)* Ⓜ *Vaporetto: San Tomà.*

★ Scuola di San Giorgio degli Schiavoni

HISTORIC SIGHT | Founded in 1451 by the Dalmatian community, this small scuola, or confraternity, was, and still is, a social and cultural center for migrants from what is now Croatia. It contains one of Italy's most beautiful rooms, harmoniously decorated between 1502 and 1507 by Vittore Carpaccio. Although Carpaccio generally painted legendary and religious figures against backgrounds of contemporary Venetian architecture, here is perhaps one of the first instances of "Orientalism" in Western painting. **■ TIP→ Opening hours are quite flexible. Since this is a must-see site, book in advance so you won't be disappointed.** ✉ *Calle dei Furlani, Castello 3259/A, Castello* ☎ *041/5228828* 🌐 *www.scuoladalmatavenezia.com* 🎫 *€5* Ⓜ *Vaporetto: Arsenale, San Zaccaria.*

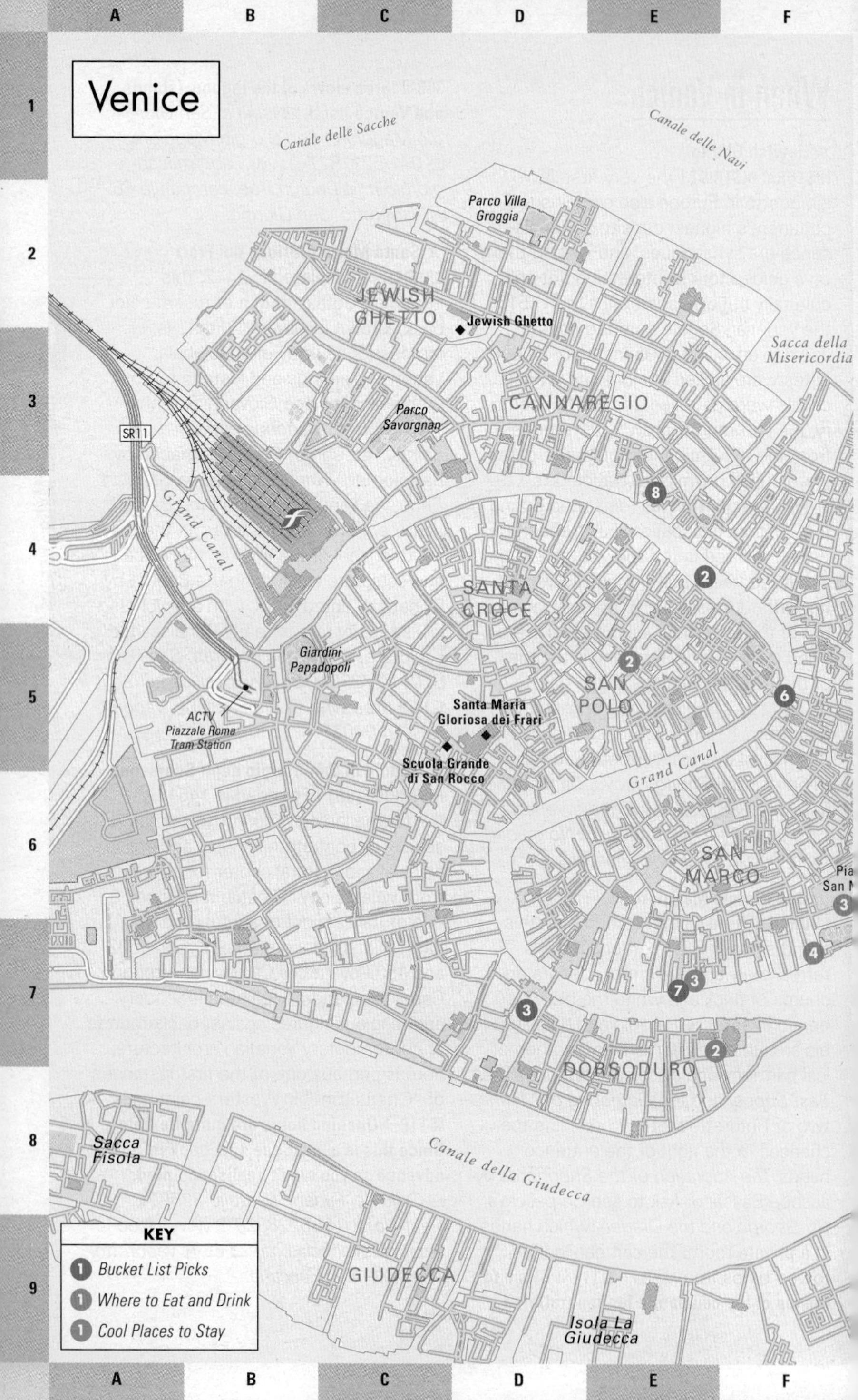
Venice
A
B
C
D
E
F
1
2
3
4
5
6
7
8
9
Canale delle Sacche
Canale delle Navi
Parco Villa Groggia
JEWISH GHETTO
Jewish Ghetto
Sacca della Misericordia
CANNAREGIO
Parco Savorgnan
SR11
Grand Canal
SANTA CROCE
Giardini Papadopoli
SAN POLO
ACTV Piazzale Roma Tram Station
Santa Maria Gloriosa dei Frari
Scuola Grande di San Rocco
Grand Canal
SAN MARCO
DORSODURO
Sacca Fisola
Canale della Giudecca
GIUDECCA
Isola La Giudecca
KEY
Bucket List Picks
Where to Eat and Drink
Cool Places to Stay

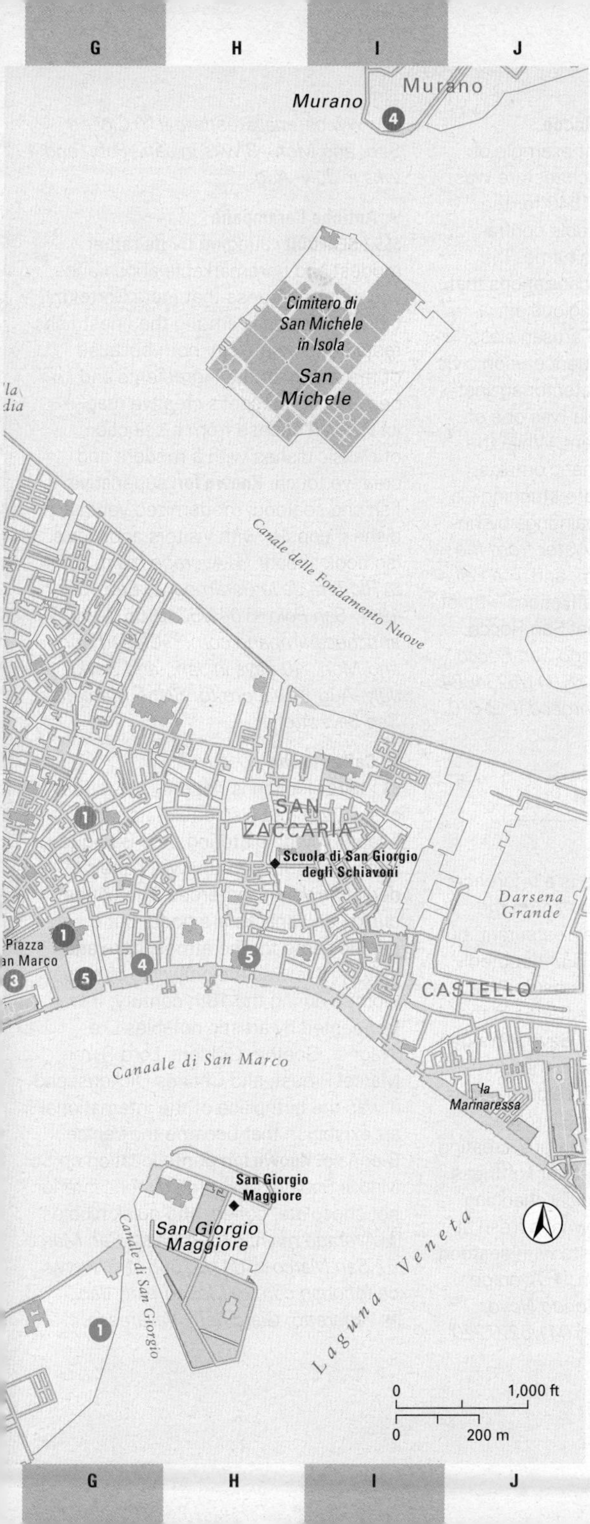

Bucket List Picks

1 Basilica di San Marco G6
2 Cruising the Grand Canal E4
3 Gallerie dell'Accademia D7
4 Murano I1
5 Palazzo Ducale (Doge's Palace) G6
6 Ponte di Rialto.......................... F5
7 Riding in a Gondola................ E7
8 Venice Carnevale................... E4

Where to Eat and Drink

1 Alle Testiere........................ G5
2 Antiche Carampane E5
3 Caffè Florian........................ F6
4 Harry's Bar F7

Cool Places to Stay

1 Belmond Hotel Cipriani G9
2 Ca Maria Adele E7
3 The Gritti Palace E7
4 Hotel Danieli......................... G6
5 Metropole H6

★ Scuola Grande di San Rocco

ART MUSEUM | This elegant example of Venetian Renaissance architecture was built between 1516 and 1549 for the essentially secular charitable confraternity bearing the saint's name. The Venetian *scuole* were organizations that sometimes had loose religious affiliations, through which the artisan class could exercise some influence upon civic life. San Rocco was a protector against the plague, and his scuola was one of the city's most magnificent. While the building is bold and dramatic outside, its contents are even more stunning—a series of more than 60 paintings by Tintoretto. *Moses Striking Water from the Rock, The Brazen Serpent,* and *The Fall of Manna* represent three afflictions—thirst, disease, and hunger—that San Rocco sought to relieve. ✉ *Campo San Rocco, San Polo 3052, San Polo* ☎ *041/5234864* 🌐 *www.scuolagrandesanrocco.it* 🎫 *€10* Ⓜ *Vaporetto: San Tomà.*

Where to Eat and Drink

★ Alle Testiere

$$$ | **VENETIAN** | The name is a reference to the old headboards that adorn the walls of this tiny, informal restaurant, but the food (not the decor) is undoubtedly the focus. Local foodies consider this one of the most refined eateries in the city thanks to chef Bruno Gavagnin's gently creative take on classic Venetian fish dishes; the chef's artistry seldom draws attention to itself, but simply reveals new dimensions of familiar fare, creating dishes that stand out for their lightness and balance. **Known for:** daily changing fish offerings, based on what's fresh at the market; excellent pasta with seafood; wonderful wine selection. $ *Average main: €28* ✉ *Calle del Mondo Novo, Castello 5801, Castello* ☎ *041/5227220* 🌐 *www.osterialletestiere.it* ⏲ *Closed Sun. and Mon., 3 wks in Jan.–Feb., and 4 wks in July–Aug.*

★ Antiche Carampane

$$$ | **SEAFOOD** | Judging by its rather modest and unremarkable appearance, you wouldn't guess that Piera Bortoluzzi Librai's trattoria is among the finest fish restaurants in the city both because of the quality of the ingredients and because of the chef's creative magic. You can choose from a selection of classic dishes with a modern and creative touch. **Known for:** superlative fish and seafood; modernized Venetian dishes; popular with visitors and locals (so book ahead). $ *Average main: €30* ✉ *Rio Terà delle Carampane, San Polo 1911, San Polo* ☎ *041/5240165* 🌐 *www.antichecarampane.com* ⏲ *Closed Sun. and Mon., 10 days in Jan., and 3 wks July–Aug.* Ⓜ *Vaporetto: Rialto Mercato, San Silvestro.*

★ Caffè Florian

$$ | **CAFÉ** | Florian is not only Italy's first café (1720), but also one of its most beautiful, with glittering, neo-Baroque decor and 19th-century wall panels depicting Venetian heroes. The coffee, drinks, and snacks are good, but most people come for the atmosphere and history: this was the only café to serve women during the 18th century; it was frequented by artistic notables like Wagner, Goethe, Goldoni, Lord Byron, Marcel Proust, and Charles Dickens; and it was the birthplace of the international art exhibition that became the Venice Biennale. **Known for:** prime location on St. Mark's Square; beautiful, historic interior; hot chocolate, coffee, and quick nibbles. $ *Average main: €16* ✉ *Piazza San Marco 57, San Marco* ☎ *041/5205641* 🌐 *www.caffeflorian.com* ⏲ *Closed early Jan.* Ⓜ *Vaporetto: Giardinetti, Vallaresso.*

★ Harry's Bar

$$$$ | VENETIAN | For those who can afford it, lunch or dinner at Harry's Bar is as much a part of a visit to Venice as a walk across Piazza San Marco or a vaporetto ride down the Grand Canal. Inside, the suave, subdued beige-on-white decor is unchanged from the 1930s, and the classic Venetian fare is carefully and excellently prepared. **Known for:** being the birthplace of the Bellini cocktail; see-and-be-seen atmosphere; signature crepes flambées and famous Cipriani chocolate cake. *Average main: €58* *Calle Vallaresso, San Marco 1323, San Marco* *041/5285777* *www.cipriani.com* *Vaporetto: Vallaresso.*

Cool Places to Stay

★ Belmond Hotel Cipriani

$$$$ | HOTEL | With amazing service, wonderful rooms, fab restaurants, and a large pool and spa—all just a five-minute boat ride from Piazza San Marco (the hotel water shuttle leaves every 15 minutes, 24 hours a day)—the Cipriani is Venetian luxe at its best. **Pros:** old-world charm meets modern luxury; Olympic-size heated saltwater pool; Michelin-starred restaurant. **Cons:** very expensive; may be too quiet for some; gym not open 24 hours. *Rooms from: €1400* *Giudecca 10, Giudecca* *041/240801* *www.belmond.com* *Closed mid-Nov.–late Mar.* *96 rooms* *Free Breakfast* *Vaporetto: Zitelle.*

★ Ca Maria Adele

$$$$ | HOTEL | One of the city's most intimate and elegant getaways blends terrazzo floors, dramatic Murano chandeliers, and antique-style furnishings with contemporary touches, particularly in the African-wood reception area and breakfast room. **Pros:** quiet and romantic; imaginative decor; tranquil yet convenient spot near Santa Maria della Salute. **Cons:** no elevator and lots of stairs; bathrooms on the small side; no restaurant (just breakfast room). *Rooms from: €419* *Campo Santa Maria della Salute, Dorsoduro 111, Dorsoduro* *041/5203078* *www.camariaadele.it* *Closed 3 wks in Jan.* *12 rooms* *Free Breakfast* *Vaporetto: Salute.*

★ The Gritti Palace

$$$$ | HOTEL | With handblown chandeliers, sumptuous textiles, and sweeping canal views, this grande dame (whose history dates from 1525, when it was built as the residence of the prominent Gritti family) represents aristocratic Venetian living at its best. **Pros:** truly historical property; Grand Canal location; classic Venetian experience. **Cons:** major splurge; food served at the hotel gets mixed reviews; few spa amenities. *Rooms from: €1450* *Campo Santa Maria del Giglio 2467, San Marco* *041/794611* *www.thegrittipalace.com* *82 rooms* *No Meals* *Vaporetto: Giglio.*

★ Hotel Danieli

$$$$ | HOTEL | One of the city's most famous lodgings—built in the 14th century and run as a hotel since 1822—lives up to its reputation: the chance to explore the wonderful, highly detailed lobby is itself a reason to book an overnight stay, plus the views along the lagoon are fantastic, the rooms gorgeous, and the food fabulous. **Pros:** historical and inviting lobby; amazing rooftop views; tasty cocktails at Bar Dandolo. **Cons:** lots of American tourists; some rooms feel dated; service can be indifferent. *Rooms from: €1200* *Riva degli Schiavoni, Castello 4196, Castello* *041/5226480* *hoteldanieli.com* *210 rooms* *No Meals* *Vaporetto: San Zaccaria.*

★ **Metropole**
$$$$ | HOTEL | Atmosphere prevails in this labyrinth of opulent, intimate spaces featuring classic Venetian decor combined with Eastern influences: common areas and sumptuously appointed guest rooms are filled with an assortment of antiques and curiosities. **Pros:** hotel harkens back to the gracious Venice of a bygone era; suites have private roof terraces with water views; great food and cocktails in the gorgeous Oriental Bar & Bistrot. **Cons:** one of the most densely touristed locations in the city; rooms with views are considerably more expensive; quirky, eccentric collections on display not for everyone. *Rooms from: €355* *Riva degli Schiavoni, Castello 4149, Castello* *041/5205044* *www.hotelmetropole.com* *67 rooms* *Free Breakfast* *Vaporetto: San Zaccaria.*

Sicily

The island of Sicily has an abundance of history. Some of the world's best-preserved Byzantine mosaics stand adjacent to magnificent Greek temples and Roman ampitheaters. Add the spectacular sight of Mt. Etna plus Sicily's unique cuisine—mingling Arab and Greek spices, Spanish, and French techniques—and you understand why visitors continue to be drawn here.

The island has beckoned seafaring wanderers since the trials of Odysseus were first sung in Homer's *Odyssey*—an epic that is sometimes called the world's first travel guide.

Strategically poised between Europe and Africa, Sicily has hosted two of the most enlightened capitals of the West: Siracusa and Palermo. And it has been a melting pot of every great civilization on the Mediterranean—Greek and Roman, then Arab and Norman, and finally French, Spanish, and Italian. Invaders through the ages weren't just attracted by the strategic location of this mystical, three-cornered land, however; they recognized a paradise in Sicily's deep blue skies and temperate climate, in its lush vegetation and rich marine life—all of which prevail to this day.

In modern times, the traditional graciousness and nobility of the Sicilian people have survived alongside the destructive influences of the Mafia under Sicily's semiautonomous government. The island has more recently emerged as something of an international travel hot spot, drawing an increasing number of visitors year-round to such archaeological hot spots as Agrigento, Siracusa, and Segesta.

In high season, tour groups seem to outnumber the locals in chi-chi Taormina and the elegant Baroque hill towns of the southeast. Some are coming for their own *White Lotus* experience, and they are being welcomed at the ultra-luxurious Four Seasons resort in Taormina.

And yet, in Sicily's agricultural heartlands, vineyards, olive groves, and lovingly kept dirt roads leading to family farmhouses still tie Sicilians to the land and to tradition, forming a happy connectedness that can't be defined by economic measures.

Parco Archeologico della Neapolis

Lush Gardens and Greek Drama

Siracusa, known to English speakers as Syracuse, was founded in 734 BC by Greek colonists and became one of the great ancient capitals of Western civilization. The dramatic set of Greek and Roman ruins in the modern city's Parco Archeologico (Archaeological Zone) are considered to be some of the best archaeological sites in all of Italy. Highlights include the Latomia del Paradiso (Quarry of Paradise), a lush tropical garden that once served as a prison for the city's enslaved Athenian enemies; the Anfiteatro Romano (Roman Amphitheater), used for combative sports and circuses; and the huge Teatro Greco, the most complete Greek theater surviving from antiquity, where the plays of Aeschylus were first staged. Classical dramas are still performed here every year. A visit to the park should be combined with a stop at Siracusa's archaeological museum, nearby.

Don't Miss

At one end of the quarries is the famous Orecchio di Dionisio (Ear of Dionysius), a cave with an ear-shape entrance and unusual acoustics.

When to Go

A visit in May and June will allow you to view a performance of one of the Greek tragedies annually performed in the Teatro Greco.

Getting Here

Siracusa is easily accessed by bus, train, or car. The sprawling Parco Archeologico is accessible from Viale Teracati, at the northern end of Corso Gelone in the modern city, and best reached by car or public transport.

✉ *Viale Teocrito, Siracusa* ☎ *0931/66206* 🎫 *€17, combined ticket with Museo Archeologico €22; free 1st Sun. of month*

La Martorana

A Perfect Marriage of Cultures

Virtually every great European empire ruled Sicily's strategically positioned capital at some point, evident in its richly diverse architecture, and perhaps most impressively in this triumphant synthesis of Byzantine, Arab, and Norman art. Erected in 1143, the church of La Martorana still retains its elegant Norman campanile, but its comparatively low-key exterior and bijou proportions give no hint of the splendors that lie within, in the form of some of the oldest and best-preserved mosaic artwork of the Norman period. The glittering parade of rich golds, vivid greens, and intense blues is in no way diminished by the considerable alterations the church underwent during the Baroque period. And it is the images of Christ, numerous saints, and lavishly winged angels high along the western wall that command most attention. Elsewhere, note the bejeweled Byzantine stole in which King Roger II is garbed, reflecting the Norman court's penchant for all things Byzantine, while archangels along the ceiling wear the same stole wrapped around their shoulders and arms.

Don't Miss

One of La Martorana's most fascinating mosaics shows King Roger II being crowned by Christ; it's located near the entrance.

Getting Here

Palermo is easily reached by plane (from Europe) or train and bus (from elsewhere in Sicily), but driving within the city should be avoided. Once you are there, most city sights are reachable on foot.

✉ *Piazza Bellini 3, Quattro Canti, Palermo* ☎ *345/8288231* 🎫 *€2* ⏲ *Closed Sun. and Mon.*

Duomo di Monreale

Sicily's Finest Norman Church

The main reason to visit the sleepy town of Monreale is to see the spectacular gold mosaics inside its splendid cathedral. Built between 1174 and 1185, Monreale's Duomo is a glorious fusion of Eastern and Western influences and is widely regarded as the finest example of Norman architecture in Sicily. The lavishly executed 68,220 square feet of mosaics decorating the cathedral interior illustrate events from the Old and New Testaments. Christ Pantocrator dominates the apse area; the nave contains narratives of the Creation; and scenes from the life of Christ adorn the walls of the aisles and the transept. Bonnano Pisano's bronze doors, completed in 1186, depict 42 biblical scenes and are considered among the most important medieval artifacts still in existence. Barisano da Trani's 42 panels on the north door, dating from 1179, present saints and evangelists.

Don't Miss

Adjacent to the Duomo, the cloister of the abbey was built at the same time as the church but enlarged in the 14th century. The lovely enclosure is surrounded by 216 intricately carved double columns.

When to Go

Try to arrive early in the morning or later in the afternoon to avoid the tour bus hordes.

Getting Here

Monreale is 10 km (6 miles) southwest of Palermo, a short drive from the capital. If you don't have a car, take one of the frequent buses from Palermo's Piazza Indipendenza or the central station.

✉ *Piazza del Duomo, Monreale* 🌐 *www.monrealeduomo.it* 🎫 *€4; €10 with Cloister*

Tempio Dorico, Segesta

An Unfinished Ancient Masterpiece

Segesta is the site of one of Sicily's most imposing temples, constructed on the side of a barren windswept hill overlooking a valley of giant fennel. Virtually intact today, the Tempio Dorico (Doric Temple) is considered by some to be finer in its proportions and setting than any other Doric temple left standing. The temple was actually started in the 5th century BC by the Elymians, who may have been refugees from Troy—or at least non-Greeks, since it seems they often sided with Carthage. The style of the temple is in many ways Greek, but it was never finished; the walls and roof never materialized, and the columns were never fluted. Wear comfortable shoes if you're up for the hike of a little more than 1 km (½ mile) to the remains of a fine theater with impressive views (there's also a shuttle bus if you aren't up for the hike).

When to Go

Try to be here at sunset for the best views; in summer concerts and plays are staged in the theater.

Getting Here

Segesta is 85 km (53 miles) southwest of Palermo. The site is easily reached via the A29 autostrada. Park your car in the lot at the bottom of the hill and walk about five minutes up to the temple. Trains from Palermo and Trapani stop at the Segesta–Tempio station, necessitating a 20-minute uphill walk to the site. There are also daily buses from Trapani (except on Sunday). ✉ *Calatafimi-Segesta* ☎ *0924/952356* 🌐 *www.parcodisegesta.com* 🎫 *€6*

Valley of the Temples, Agrigento

Breathtaking Greek Temples

Not even in Athens will you find Greek temples as finely preserved as this stunning set of ruins proudly perched above the sea in a grove of almond trees. Originally erected as a showpiece to flaunt the Greek victory over Carthage, they include the beautiful, semi-ruined Tempio di Giunone (Temple of Juno); the Tempio della Concordia (Temple of Concord), almost perfectly complete; the Tempio di Ercole (Temple of Hercules), the valley's oldest surviving temple; and the Tempio di Giove (Temple of Jupiter), intended to be the largest in the complex but never completed. At night, when the temples are floodlit, they make an unforgettable sight.

Don't Miss

The Temple of Juno is perhaps the most beautiful of all the temples, commanding an exquisite view of the valley (especially at sunset).

When to Go

The best time to go is early morning or a couple of hours before sunset. If you are in Agrigento in high summer, you might consider a night visit. In January and February, the valley is awash in the fragrant blossoms of thousands of almond trees

Getting Here

The bus and train stations are centrally located in Agrigento; the archaeological park is reachable by bus in about 15 or 20 minutes. Motorists should arrive via the coastal SS115 and, from Palermo, by the SS189. The best place to park is at the entrance to the site. The temples are a bit spread out, but the site is all walkable and usually toured on foot. There is a shuttle bus (€2) to the theater.

✉ *Zona Archeologica, Via dei Templi, Agrigento* ☎ *0922/1839996* 🌐 *www.parcovalledeitempli.it* 🎟 *€10, €14 with museum (free 1st Sun. of month)*

Villa Romana del Casale

Gorgeous Roman Mosaics

Some of Italy's most vivid and colorful Roman mosaics—and among the finest mosaics of the Roman world anywhere—can be visited in a peaceful rural spot outside the inland town of Piazza Armerina. Belonging to an exceptionally well-preserved Imperial Roman Villa that is thought to have been a hunting lodge of the emperor Maximian (3rd 4th century AD), the artful mosaics were probably made by North African artisans and cover more than 12,000 square feet, depicting hunting and fishing scenes, nymphs, a Neptune, and enslaved people massaging bathers. The entrance was through a triumphal arch that led into an atrium surrounded by a portico of columns, which line the way to the *thermae*, or bathhouse. The peristyle leads to the main villa, where in the Salone del Circo you look down on mosaics illustrating scenes from the Circus Maximus in Rome. A theme running through many of the mosaics—especially the long hall flanking one entire side of the peristyle courtyard—is the capturing and shipping of wild animals, which may have been a major source of the owner's wealth.

Don't Miss

One of the site's most famous mosaics shows girls wearing the ancient equivalent of bikinis, going through what looks like a fairly rigorous set of training exercises.

Getting Here

Villa Romana del Casale is 4 km (2½ miles) southwest of Piazza Armerina, and is best reached by car.

✉ *SP15, Contrada Casale* ☎ *0935/680036* 🌐 *www.piazzaarmerina.org* 🎫 *€10 (free 1st Sun. of month)*

Ascending Mount Etna

A Close Encounter with Mamma Etna

The most iconic symbol of Sicily and the largest and highest volcano in Europe, Mt. Etna is so important to locals that it's often affectionately called "Mamma Etna." You'll get wonderful vistas of Etna from various vantage points on Sicily's eastern coast, but it's also rewarding to see the mountain up close on a hike or climb. You can find routes suitable for every fitness level, or join an organized tour. Traveling to the proximity of the crater depends on Mt. Etna's temperament, but it's usually possible to wander up and down the enormous lava dunes and explore the moonlike surface of dead craters. You can also circle Mt. Etna on the Circumetnea, a private railroad that runs around the base of the volcano.

Don't Miss

Mt. Etna has become a popular destination for wine lovers thanks to the many boutique wineries on its slopes; most accept visitors with an appointment.

When to Go

Etna is very active, so you should always verify whether access is restricted due to volcanic events.

Getting Here

Reaching the lower slopes of Mt. Etna by car or bus from Catania is easy. Getting to the more interesting, higher levels requires taking one of the four-wheel-drive minibuses that leave from Piano Provenzana or Rifugio Sapienza. A cable car, the Funivia dell'Etna, departs from Rifugio Sapienza.

Circumetnea. ✉ *Via Caronda 352, Catania* 🌐 *www.circumetnea.it* 🎫 *€8 one-way* ⏲ *Closed Sun.*

Funivia dell'Etna. ✉ *Rifugio Sapienza* 🌐 *www.funiviaetna.com*

Parco dell'Etna. 🌐 *www.parcoetna.it*

Taormina's Teatro Greco

Unforgettable Vistas in Sicily's Best Resort

The Greeks put a premium on finding impressive locations to stage their dramas, and they truly excelled when choosing Taormina's jagged, cactus-covered cliffs to build this theater. Beyond the columns, the view of the town's rooftops spilling down the hillside, the arc of the coastline, and Mt. Etna in the distance is as close to perfection as a panorama can get. Who can resist the photo-opportunity offered by white puffs of smoke rising from the snowcapped volcano against a brilliant, blue sky? And after sunset, when the marvelous vistas of the sparkling Ionian Sea are shrouded in darkness, the glow of Italy's most famous volcano can sometimes be seen in the distance. The theater was built during the 3rd century BC and rebuilt by the Romans in the 2nd century AD. Its acoustics are exceptional: even today a stage whisper can be heard in the last rows.

Don't Miss

Even when overrun with tourists, Taormina's boutique-lined main streets are worth a leisurely meander, with plentiful opportunities for refreshment.

When to Go

In summer, the Teatro Greco hosts music and dance performances. Taormina becomes a ghost town in January and February, with almost every hotel and restaurant closed.

Getting Here

Buses from Messina and Catania arrive near the center of Taormina, a short walk from the theater. Trains pull in at the station at the bottom of the hill, connected to the hilltop town by local buses.

Via Teatro Greco, Taormina *0942/23220* *www.parconaxostaormina.com* *€10*

Sicily

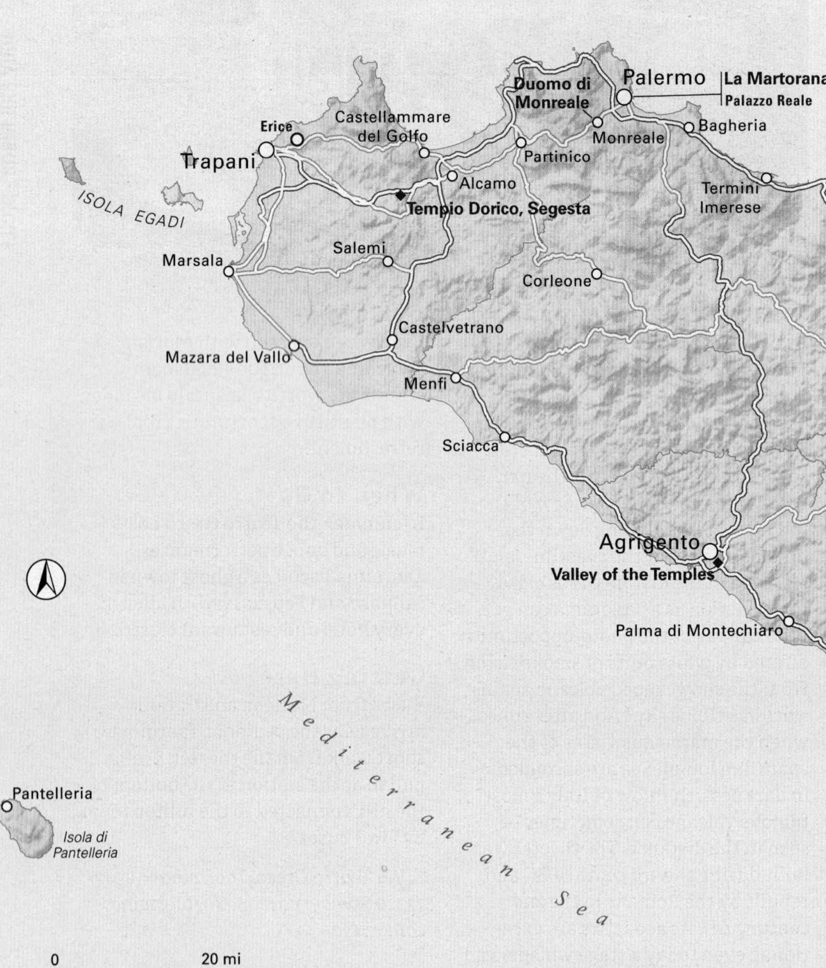

Isola di Ustica
Palermo
La Martorana
Palazzo Reale
Duomo di Monreale
Monreale
Bagheria
Castellammare del Golfo
Erice
Trapani
Partinico
Alcamo
Termini Imerese
ISOLA EGADI
Tempio Dorico, Segesta
Salemi
Marsala
Corleone
Castelvetrano
Mazara del Vallo
Menfi
Sciacca
Agrigento
Valley of the Temples
Palma di Montechiaro
Mediterranean Sea
Pantelleria
Isola di Pantelleria
0
20 mi
0
20 km

Tyrrhenian Sea
Isola Stromboli
ISOLE AEOLIAN
Isola Alicudi
Isola Filicudi
Island Hopping in the Aeolians
Isola Salina
Isola Lipari
Lipari
Isola Vulcano
Milazzo
Messina
Capo d'Orlando
Sant'Agata di Militello
Cefalù
Parco dei Nebrodi
Parco delle Madonie
Randazzo
Taormina's Teatro Greco
Taormina
Mt. Etna 3,340m
Bronte
Parco dell' Etna
Mascali
Riposto
Nicosia
Adrano
Leonforte
Ascending Mount Etna
Acireale
Enna
Aci Castello
Caltanissetta
SICILY
Catania
Barrafranca
Villa Romana del Casale
Palagonia
Riesi
Ravanusa
Lentini
Caltagirone
Francofonte
Augusta
Melilli
Priolo Gargallo
Parco Archeologico della Neapolis
Licata
Gela
Siracusa
Duomo di Siracusa
Ortigia
Ionian Sea
Vittoria
Ragusa
Noto
Avola
Modica
Rosolini
Ispica
Pachino

When in Sicily

Cefalù

TOWN | Cefalù is the jewel of the Tyrrhenian Coast, a classically appealing old Sicilian town built on a spur jutting out into the sea. Its medieval origins have left behind many interesting historical sites such as the Palazzo Maria in Piazza Duomo and the Osteria Magno in Corso Ruggero. Both were owned by the Ventimiglia family, who dominated this part of the island in the middle ages. Cefalù's medieval washhouse is also fascinating; carved out of rustic lava stone and fed by the waters of the Cefalino River, which flow out from 22 iron lion-shaped mouths, it was used until the early 20th century. There are the ornate facades of the church of the Monte della Pietà (1716) and the stunning Church of Purgatory (1668). The town's historical center is dotted with endless architectural details. ✉ *Cefalù* ✣ *39 km (22 miles) northeast of Caccamo* 🌐 *wwww. cefalu.it.*

★ **Duomo di Siracusa**

RELIGIOUS BUILDING | Siracusa's Duomo is an archive of more than 2,000 years of island history, and has creatively incorporated ruins through the many time periods it has survived, starting with the bottommost, where excavations have unearthed remnants of Sicily's distant past, when the Siculi inhabitants worshipped their deities here. During the 5th century BC (the same time Agrigento's Temple of Concord was built), the Greeks erected a temple to Athena over it, and in the 7th century, Siracusa's first Christian cathedral was built on top of the Greek structure. The massive columns of the original Greek temple were incorporated into the present structure and are clearly visible, embedded in the exterior wall along Via Minerva. The Greek columns were also used to dramatic advantage inside, where on one side they form chapels connected by elegant wrought-iron gates. The Baroque facade, added in the 18th century, displays a harmonious rhythm of concaves and convexes. In front, the sun-kissed stone piazza is encircled by pink and white oleanders and elegant buildings ornamented with filigree grillwork, and is typically filled with frolicking children and street musicians. Check with the tourist office for guided tours of its underground tunnels, which are located to the right when you stand facing the cathedral. ✉ *Piazza del Duomo, Ortigia* ☎ *0931/65328* 🌐 *arcidiocesi.siracusa.it/chiesa-cattedrale* 🎫 *€2.*

Erice

TOWN | Perched 2,450 feet above sea level, Erice is an enchanting medieval mountaintop aerie of palaces, fountains, and cobblestone streets. Shaped like an equilateral triangle, the town was the ancient landmark Eryx, dedicated to Aphrodite (Venus). When the Normans arrived, they built a castle on Monte San Giuliano, which offers striking views of Trapani, the Egadi Islands offshore, and, on a very clear day, Cape Bon and the Tunisian coast. Because of Erice's elevation, clouds conceal much of the view for most of winter. Sturdy shoes (for the cobblestones) and something warm to wear are recommended. ✉ *Erice* ✣ *38 km (24 miles) south of San Vito Lo Capo, 15 km (9 miles) northeast of Trapani.*

Island Hopping in the Aeolians

ISLAND | The seven inhabited islands that make up the Aeolian archipelago are reachable—and interconnected by—a good service of ferries and hydrofoils, making leisurely trips between them viable, or you can stay for a night or two. Each has its own distinctive character. **Lipari** is the largest and most developed of the group, its main town busy with bars and restaurants; visitors come to its close neighbor, **Vulcano,** to soak in its strong-smelling but health-giving sulfur springs; with its twin volcanic peaks, the archipelago's highest island, **Salina,** is also the most fertile, producing excellent Malvasia wine; **Panarea** has some of the most dramatic scenery, including wild caves carved out of rock and dazzling flora; Stromboli, the northernmost of the Aeolians, is still an active volcano, and, like Vulcano, has beaches of black sand; the two westernmost isles, **Alicudi** and **Filicudi,** are famous for their unusual volcanic rock formations, excellent hiking possibilities, and remote style of life. ✉ *Lipari* ✣ *1 hr by hydrofoil; 60–75 min from Reggio di Calabria and Messina by ferry.*

Noto

TOWN | If Siracusa's Baroque beauty whets your appetite for that over-the-top style, head to Noto. About 40 minutes away on the A18, the compact and easy-to-navigate city is doable as a day trip—though staying overnight lets you see the lovely buildings glow in the setting sun after the tourist hordes have departed. Despite being decimated by an earthquake in 1693, Noto has remarkable architectural integrity. It presents a pleasing ensemble of honey-color buildings, strikingly uniform in style but never dull. Simply walking Corso Vittorio Emanuele, the pedestrianized main street, qualifies as an aesthetic experience. ✉ *Noto* ✣ *38 km (23 miles) southwest of Siracusa* 🌐 *www.notoinforma.it.*

Ortigia

ISLAND | The island of Ortigia (spelled "Ortygia" by English speakers), the ancient city first inhabited by the Greeks that juts out into the Ionian Sea, is connected to mainland Siracusa by two small bridges. Ortigia has become increasingly popular with tourists, and although it's filled with lots of modern boutiques (and tourist shops), it still retains its charm despite the crowds, and it's compact enough to make walking the easiest way to enjoy those pleasures. Coming from the train station, it's a 15-minute trudge to Ortigia along Via Francesco Crispi and Corso Umberto. If you're not up for that, take one of the free electric buses leaving every 10 minutes from the station around the corner. ✉ *Siracusa* 🌐 *www.siracusaturismo.net.*

★ **Palazzo Reale** (*Royal Palace*)

CASTLE/PALACE | This historic palace, also called Palazzo dei Normanni (Norman Palace), was the seat of Sicily's semiautonomous rulers for centuries; the building is a fascinating mesh of 10th-century Norman and 17th-century Spanish structures. Because it now houses the Sicilian Parliament, parts of the palace are closed to the public from Tuesday to Thursday when the regional assembly is in session, but the must-see Cappella Palatina (Palatine Chapel) remains open. Built in 1132, it's a dazzling example of the harmony of artistic elements produced under the Normans. Upstairs are the royal apartments, including the Sala di Re Ruggero (King Roger's Hall), decorated with ornate medieval mosaics of hunting scenes. From Friday to Monday, the Sala is included with entry to the palace or chapel. ✉ *Piazza del Parlamento, Near Palazzo Reale* ☎ *091/7055611* 🌐 *www.federicosecondo.org* 🎫 *€14.50 Fri.–Mon.; €10 Tues.–Thurs.* ⏲ *Royal Apartments closed Tues.–Thurs.*

Where to Eat and Drink

★ **Cave Ox**

$ | **ITALIAN** | This casual osteria is frequented by local winemakers who come for pizza dinners and rustic daily lunch specials, but most visitors are smitten with the small but amazing cellar focused on Etna natural wines. Everything's fresh, simple, and delicious—and made to pair with one of the delightful wines suggested by owner and wine enthusiast Sandro. **Known for:** superlative selection of natural wines from Etna; filling lunches and pizza dinners; local winemaker crowd. 💲 *Average main: €12* ✉ *Via Nazionale Solicchiata 159* ☎ *0942/986171* 🌐 *www.caveox.it* ⏲ *Closed Tues.*

★ **Don Camillo**
$$$ | **SICILIAN** | A gracious series of delicately arched rooms at this beloved local eatery are lined with wine bottles and sepia-tone images of the old town. À la carte preparations bring together fresh seafood and inspired creativity: sample, for instance, the sublime spaghetti *delle Sirene* (with sea urchin and shrimp in butter) or cod with saffron from the Ibleian hills with a courgette puree. If you want, you can put yourself in the hands of the chef and opt for one of the exquisite tasting menus, which start at €75 excluding wine. **Known for:** fish, meat, and vegetarian tasting menus; helpful service; fantastic wine list. *Average main: €20 Via Maestranza 96, Ortigia 0931/67133 www.ristorantedoncamillosiracusa.it Closed Sun., 2 wks in Jan., and 2 wks in July.*

★ **Il Re di Girgenti**
$$ | **SICILIAN** | You might not expect to find an ultramodern—even hip—place to dine within a few minutes' drive of Agrigento's ancient temples, yet Il Re di Girgenti offers up pleasing versions of Sicilian classics in a trendy, country-chic atmosphere (think funky black-and-white tile floors mixed with shelves lined with old-fashioned crockery) popular with young locals. The thoughtful wine list offers good prices on both local wines and those from throughout Sicily. **Known for:** Sicilian dishes with a twist; contemporary setting with lovely views; delightful wine selections. *Average main: €20 Via Panoramica dei Templi 51, Agrigento 0922/401388 www.ilredigirgenti.it Closed Tues.*

★ **Trattoria Il Barcaiolo**
$$ | **SEAFOOD** | Just behind the public beach in Mazzarò Bay, this intimate little terrace restaurant is shrouded by an enormous old grapevine and looks out onto postcard-perfect views of paradise. Since 1981, the family-owned trattoria has been serving pristine seafood to discerning locals and in-the-know tourists. **Known for:** extensive wine list; swordfish carpaccio with citrus and capers; cassata and cannoli for dessert. *Average main: €18 Via Castelluccio 43, Taormina 379/2089564 mobile www.barcaiolo.altervista.org.*

Cool Places to Stay

★ **Domus Mariae**
$$ | **HOTEL** | On Ortigia's eastern shore, this hotel, in an unusual twist, is owned by Ursuline nuns, who help to make the mood placid and peaceful, but the elegant accommodations are far from monastic. **Pros:** nice breakfast; gorgeous sea views and rooftop terrace; enthusiastic staff. **Cons:** stairs to climb; not much street parking near the hotel; small rooms and not all rooms have sea views. *Rooms from: €164 Via Vittorio Veneto 76, Ortigia 0931/60087 www.domusmariaebenessere.com 12 rooms Free Breakfast.*

★ **Eurostars Centrale Palace**
$$ | **HOTEL** | A stone's throw from Palermo's main historic sites, this hotel in the heart of the old town was once a stately private palace; built in 1717, it weaves old-world charm with modern comfort. **Pros:** great rooftop restaurant; location in the center of it all; comfortable

rooms. **Cons:** showing its age a bit; very limited parking; some rooms have no views. *Rooms from: €170* *Corso Vittorio Emanuele 327, Quattro Canti* *091/336666* *www.eurostarscentralepalace.com* *104 rooms* *Free Breakfast.*

★ **Monaci delle Terre Nere**

$$$$ | **HOTEL** | This cozy boutique hotel in the foothills of Mount Etna features spacious rustic-chic rooms on a working organic farm with vineyards, along with an elegant Slow Food–inspired restaurant. **Pros:** eco-conscious atmosphere and policies; delicious food and wine; pool with countryside views. **Cons:** accommodations may be a little quirky for some; no televisions in bedrooms; bathrooms can be quite minimalist. *Rooms from: €900* *Via Monaci, Zafferana Etnea* *095/7083638* *www.monacidelleterrenere.it* *Closed Jan.–mid-Mar.* *27 rooms* *Free Breakfast.*

★ **San Domenico Palace, A Four Seasons Hotel**

$$$$ | **HOTEL** | The sweeping views of the castle, the sea, and Mount Etna from this converted 14th-century Dominican monastery will linger in your mind, along with the equally memorable levels of luxury and wonderful food in the hotel's highly lauded restaurant, Principe Cerami. **Pros:** strong sense of history and grandeur; gorgeous infinity pool with amazing views; quiet and restful. **Cons:** very expensive; parking €50 per day; beach access through partner affiliates. *Rooms from: €3000* *Piazza San Domenico 5, Taormina* *0942/613111* *www.fourseasons.com/taormina* *Closed early Jan.–mid-Mar.* *111 rooms* *Free Breakfast.*

★ **Villa Athena**

$$$$ | **HOTEL** | The 18th-century Villa Athena, updated into a sleek, luxurious place to stay, complete with gorgeous manicured gardens and swimming pool, holds a privileged position directly overlooking the Temple of Concordia, a 10-minute walk away—an amazing sight both during the day and when it's lit up at night. **Pros:** unbeatable location for the Valle dei Templi, with phenomenal temple views; good restaurant and spa; plenty of free parking. **Cons:** lobby on the small side; very expensive compared to other area options; lack of information on local attractions. *Rooms from: €667* *Via Passeggiata Archeologica 33, Agrigento* *0922/596288* *www.hotelvillaathena.it* *27 rooms* *Free Breakfast.*

Rest of Italy and Sardinia

Italy's blend of great art, delicious food and wine, monumental buildings, and enchanting countryside draw legions of visitors throughout the year, but the vast majority of these confine themselves to a small, well-trodden circuit, leaving most of the country free for more leisurely wanderings.

Outside the triangle of its three most-visited cities—Rome, Florence, and Venice—and popular areas such as the Amalfi Coast, Tuscany, and Umbria, this generously endowed peninsula offers layers of history, culture, and sheer hedonistic pleasure which repay adventurous excursions off the beaten path.

Milan, for example, the commercial and forward-looking pulse of the nation, might seem disappointingly modern and congested to some, but its historic buildings and art collections in many ways rival those of Florence and Rome, while its status as one of the world's great fashion centers and shopping experiences beat those other cities hands down.

A short distance north, the great lakes of northern Italy—Como, Maggiore, Garda, Iseo, and Orta—have few equals for sheer beauty, not least for the 18th- and 19th-century villas, exotic formal gardens, and dozens of Belle Époque-era resorts that line their shores.

South of Milan, you can pamper yourself in the glamorous harbor village of Portofino before roaming the trails that connect the postcard-pretty Cinque Terre settlements of the Italian Riviera, while crossing to the Adriatic coast allows you to admire the breathtaking collection of glittering mosaics left from Byzantine rule in the city of Ravenna.

The deep south of the peninsula presents a series of charms of a different order, ranging from the intriguing cave dwellings of Matera—now a chic hub of trendy hotels and restaurants—to the delicate, Baroque beauty of Lecce. And for awesome mountain landscapes and golden beaches, all it takes is a ferry ride across the Tyrrhenian Sea to uncover the hidden glories of the island of Sardinia.

A Night at La Scala

Watch an Opera in Its Italian Shrine

What the Louvre is to art, Milan's La Scala is to the world of opera. You need know nothing of opera to sense that La Scala is closer to a cathedral than a concert hall. Hearing any opera sung in this magical setting is an unparalleled experience: it is, after all, where Verdi established his reputation and where Maria Callas sang her way into opera lore. It stands as a symbol—both for the performer who dreams of singing here and for the opera buff—and its notoriously demanding audiences are apt to jeer performers who do not measure up. If you are lucky enough to be here during the season, do whatever is necessary to attend. Tickets go on sale two months before the first performance and are usually sold out the same day. Although you might not get seats for the more popular operas with big-name stars, it is worth trying; ballets are easier. There are also reduced-visibility balcony tickets available for each performance on a first-come, first-served basis.

Don't Miss

The Museo Teatrale alla Scala displays an extensive collection of librettos, paintings of the famous names of Italian opera, posters, costumes, antique instruments, and design sketches for the theater. It is also possible to take a look at the theater itself. Special exhibitions reflect current productions.

Teatro alla Scala. ✉ *Piazza della Scala, Largo Ghiringhelli 1, Duomo* ☎ *02/72003744 theater, 02/88797473 museum* 🌐 *www.teatroallascala.org* 🎫 *Museum €10* 🚇 *Duomo or Cordusio; Tram No. 1*

Da Vinci's *Last Supper*

One of the World's Most Famous Paintings

Leonardo da Vinci's *The Last Supper*, housed in the church of Santa Maria delle Grazie, a former Dominican monastery, has had an almost unbelievable history of bad luck and neglect. Its near destruction in an American bombing raid in August 1943 was only the latest chapter in a series of misadventures, including—if one 19th-century source is to be believed—being whitewashed over by monks. Well-meant but disastrous attempts at restoration have done little to rectify the problem of the work's placement: it was executed on a wall unusually vulnerable to climatic dampness. After years of restorers patiently shifting from one square centimeter to another, Leonardo's masterpiece is free of centuries of retouching, grime, and dust. Astonishing clarity and luminosity have been regained, helped by lighting, and a timed entry system where small groups are ushered into climate-controlled rooms with automatic glass doors, to prevent humidity. Before and after viewing the masterpiece you can read displays about the restoration process.

Don't Miss

The painting was executed in what was the order's refectory, which is now referred to as the Cenacolo Vinciano. Take a moment to visit Santa Maria delle Grazie itself. It's a handsome, completely restored church with a fine dome and a cloister, both of which Bramante added around the time Leonardo was commissioned to paint *The Last Supper*.

✉ Piazza Santa Maria delle Grazie 2, off Corso Magenta, Sant'Ambrogio ☎ 02/92800360 reservations, 02/4676111 church 🌐 www.cenacolovinciano.net 🎫 €15 🕐 Closed Mon. 🚆 Cadorna or Conciliazione; tram No. 18 ✍ Reservations are required

Shopping in Milan

High Sophistication and World-Class Shopping

As a capital of sophisticated, international fashion, Milan is also famed for its fashionable shops, which rival those of New York and Paris. The city offers experiences and goods for every taste, not just the fabulous outlets for such global fashion giants as Armani, Prada, Versace, Salvatore Ferragamo, and Ermenegildo Zegna, but stores where you can find the creations of less famous designers. Discriminating shoppers might start their explorations at Galleria Vittorio Emanuele II, a spectacular late-19th-century Belle Époque monument that is essentially a select shopping mall. The heart of Milan's shopping activity is the Quadrilatero della Moda district, north of the Duomo, where the world's leading designers compete for shoppers' attention in stores that are themselves works of high style. Corso Buenos Aires in northeastern Milan is one of the busiest in the city with more than 350 stores and outlets to choose from, while there's no limit on what you can spend on upscale Via Montenapoleone. The charming Brera neighborhood has smaller shops with some appealing offerings from lesser-known names, and Corso di Porta Ticinese has a more edgy street style.

Don't Miss

Wealthy Brera residents flock to the neighborhood's Monday- and Thursday-morning markets, whose food stands are interspersed with clothing and shoe stalls popular with Milan's sartorial connoisseurs.

Getting Here

Milan's city center is compact and walkable; trolleys, trams, and the efficient Metropolitana (subway) provide access to locations farther afield. Driving in Milan is difficult, and drivers in the center must pay a daily congestion charge on weekdays.

Lake Como

Europe's Deepest Lake

One of the most beautiful lakes in the world—and Europe's deepest—Lake Como boasts picture-book villages, stately villas, and Edenic gardens, all set against the majestic backdrop of the snowcapped Alps. Many travelers head directly to Bellagio, which sits at the center of the lake's three branches and is sometimes called the prettiest town in Europe. From here you can catch a ferry to Varenna, whose principal sight is the spellbinding garden of the Villa Monastero. Other lakeside settlements include dreamy Tremezzo, home to the magnificent Villa Carlotta and its 14 acres of azaleas and rhododendrons, and the former silk town of Como, where elegant cobblestone pedestrian streets thread through its medieval center.

Best Activities

Lake Como offers many ways to stay active and outdoors, from windsurfing at the lake's northern end, to boating, sailing, and Jet Skiing at Como and Cernobbio. Lake Como is also quite swimmable in summer, and for hikers there are lovely paths weaving around the lake.

Don't Miss

Villa del Balbianello is relentlessly picturesque and known from cameos in many films; it's reached by boat from Como and Bellagio.

When to Go

For the best of the blossoms in Lake Como's celebrated gardens, come in late April or early May.

Getting Here

Como, on the south shore of the lake, is just 49 km (30 miles), an easy drive or regional train ride from Milan. Seasonal car ferries and vaporetti crisscross the waters.

Como Tourism Office. ✉ *Via Albertolli 7, Como* 🌐 *www.visitcomo.eu/en*

Hiking in the Cinque Terre

Perched Villages Overlooking the Deep Blue Sea

"Charming" and "breathtaking" are adjectives that get a workout when you're traveling in Italy, but it's rare that both apply to a single location. The Cinque Terre, clinging to the cliffs along a gorgeous stretch of the Ligurian coast, is such a place. Despite the summer crowds, each of the five old fishing villages that make up the "Five Lands" (Monterosso al Mare, Vernazza, Corniglia, Manarola, and Riomaggiore) has maintained its own distinct charm. Footpaths winding through the steep terrain were for centuries the only way to travel between the villages, and today these provide one of the most rewarding ways to experience the Cinque Terre, offering beautiful views of the rocky coast tumbling into the sea as well as access to secluded beaches and grottoes.

Don't Miss

The 2½-hour hike between Monterosso and Levanto affords glorious views of the Cinque Terre to the south, Corsica to the west, and the Alps to the north. Monterosso itself is the region's only place offering both sand and decent swimming.

When to Go

The ideal times to visit the Cinque Terre are September and May, when the weather is mild and the summer tourist season isn't in full swing.

Getting Here

The towns have limited parking, so it's easier to arrive by frequent but often crowded trains from La Spezia or Levanto.

Cinque Terre Tourism. 🌐 *www.cinqueterre.com* 🌐 *www.lecinqueterre.org* 🌐 *www.parconazionale-5terre.it* 🎫 *A 1-day pass, which includes a trail map and an information leaflet, costs €8*

Portofino

The Jewel of the Italian Riviera

One of Europe's well-known playgrounds for the rich and famous, the chic resort town of Portofino is one of the most photographed places on the Ligurian coast, with a decidedly romantic and highly affluent aura. Most visitors are content to browse at the pricey boutiques or sip a coffee while people-watching, perhaps followed by a stroll around the harbor to gaze at the yachts framed by the sapphire Ligurian Sea and the cliffs of Santa Margherita. More active pursuits include visiting the local castle and weaving through the picture-perfect cliff-side gardens. There are also several tame, photo-friendly hikes, such as the 15-minute walk to Punta Portofino, from where pristine views can be had from the deteriorating *faro* (lighthouse). Further afield, well-marked trails lead to nearby villages in the hills; maps are available at tourist information offices.

Don't Miss

The medieval stronghold of Abbazia di San Fruttuoso protects a minuscule fishing village that can be reached only on foot or by water. The restored abbey contains the tombs of illustrious members of the Doria family and occasionally hosts temporary exhibitions.

Getting Here and Around

Trying to reach Portofino by bus or car on the single, narrow road can be a nightmare in summer and on holiday weekends. Train-travelers must stop at Santa Margherita Ligure, then take a bus or boat to Portofino.

Portofino Tourism Office. ✉ *Via Roma 35, Portofino* ☎ *0185/269024* 🌐 *www.turismoinliguria.it*

Ravenna

Glittering, Breathtaking Treasures

The small, quiet, and well-heeled city of Ravenna has brick palaces, cobblestone streets, magnificent monuments, and spectacular Byzantine mosaics. Following its conquest by the Byzantines in AD 540, Ravenna spent much of its past looking east and its greatest art treasures show that Byzantine influence. Churches and tombs with the most unassuming exteriors contain within them walls covered with sumptuous and beautifully preserved Byzantine mosaics, the best-known and most elaborate examples of which can be admired in the Basilica di San Vitale and the adjacent tomb, Mausoleo di Galla Placidia. Equally compelling are the mosaics displayed in the church of Sant'Apollinare Nuovo and the Battistero Neoniano. Just outside Ravenna, the town of Classe reveals even more mosaic gems, displayed in the church of Sant'Apollinare in Classe.

Don't Miss

A small neoclassical building contains the tomb of Italy's greatest scribe, the Tomba di Dante. Exiled from his native Florence, the author of *The Divine Comedy* died in Ravenna in 1321.

Getting Here

By train, there are one or two services hourly from Bologna, taking 70 minutes. Most of the city's sights can be easily reached on foot; for Classe, take Bus No. 4 or the local train from Ravenna's station, or use the cycle path from the city center.

Basilica San Vitale. ✉ *Via San Vitale, off Via Salara, Ravenna* ☎ *0544/541688 for info,800/303999 for info (toll-free)* 🌐 *www.ravennamosaici.it* 🎫 *€11 combination ticket, includes 4–5 diocesan monuments*

Ravenna Tourism Office. ✉ *Piazza San Francesco 7, Ravenna* ☎ *0544/35755* 🌐 *www.turismo.ra.it*

Sassi di Matera

Ancient European Cave Dwellings

Deep in Italy's Mezzogiorno, the town of Matera is one of southern Italy's most intriguing places, perched on the verge of a steep gully that is honeycombed with ancient cave dwellings and rock-hewn churches. The oldest of these, called Sassi, date from Paleolithic times, when they were truly just caves, and over time were transformed into enclosed houses, which came to resemble a Dante-esque vision of squalor and poverty. Most inhabitants were moved out of their troglodytic abodes in the 1960s, and since the area was designated as a UNESCO World Heritage site in 1993, many of the Sassi have been transformed into modern-day homes, chic bars and restaurants, and swanky hotels. You can enjoy stellar views from Matera's upper town, but don't be put off exploring the area on foot, either independently or on a walking tour. The Baroque churches and elegant palazzi of Matera's so-called New Town are also worth a prolonged wander, the broad piazzas filled to bursting during the evening *passeggiata*.

Don't Miss

Santa Maria de Idris is the most spectacular of the *chiese rupestri*, or rock-hewn churches.

Getting Here

Driving from Bari, take the SS96 to Altamura, then the SS99 to Matera. Drivers should be careful not to enter Matera's restricted traffic areas to avoid an unwelcome ticket when you get home. Roughly one train per hour (Ferrovie Appulo Lucane) leaves Bari Centrale for Matera.

Proloco Matera Città dei Sassi (Tourism Office). ✉ *Via Ridola 60, Matera* ☎ *328/9333548* 🌐 *www.proloco-matera2019.it*

Lecce

The Baroque Heel of the Boot

The crown jewel of the Mezzogiorno, Lecce has been called "the Florence of the south," but that term doesn't do justice to Lecce's uniqueness. Although its pretty boutiques, bustling streets, and laid-back student cafés draw comparisons to the cultural capitals of the north, Lecce's impossibly intricate Baroque architecture and its hyperanimated crowds are distinctively southern. The city's ornate appearance was the result of a citywide impulse in the 17th century to redo the town in an exuberant fashion, endowing it with a lighter, more fanciful air than the heavy and monumental style that often characterizes Baroque architecture. Nor has Lecce lost its Pugliese charm: two steps from the idyllic Otranto–Brindisi coastline and a hop from the olive groves of Puglia, the town exudes an optimism and youthful joie de vivre unparalleled in any other Baroque showcase.

Don't Miss

Lecce's magnificent Duomo, Santa Maria Assunta, often leaves viewers open-mouthed. The piazza surrounding the Duomo is especially beautiful when illuminated at night.

Getting Here

By car from Bari, take the main coast road via Brindisi and continue along the SS613 to Lecce. Frequent trains run along the coast from Bari and beyond. The closest airport is in Brindisi.

Duomo. ✉ *Piazza Duomo, off Corso Vittorio Emanuele II, Lecce* ☎ *0832/308557* *www.cattedral-edilecce.it* 🎫 *Duomo €6; LeccEcclesiae ticket €9*

Lecce Tourism Office. ✉ *Corso Vittorio Emanuele II 16, Lecce* ☎ *0832/682985* 🌐 *www.turismo.ilecce.it/infopoint*

Costa Smeralda

Sardinia's Emerald Coast

The rugged granite landscape of Sardinia's northeast is probably best known for the Costa Smeralda (Emerald Coast), a short strip of gorgeous coast studded with elite hotels and beaches. Previously a high-class hideaway for celebrities, these days the area is more accessible, with budget dining and lodging options among the luxury resorts. Day-trippers are drawn to the Costa Smeralda's "capital," **Porto Cervo**, a jet-setter enclave where the uber-rich have anchored their yachts since the 1960s. The Piazzetta here is the place to see and be seen while sipping over-priced cocktails. The nearby beaches, which rank among the most exclusive in Europe, also get crowded with summer sun worshippers. With fine golden sand sheltered by red cliffs and fronting azure waters, many of the beaches can only be reached by boat, and there are regular launches from Porto Cervo. Rentals of sun beds and towels are as expensive as you'd expect.

Don't Miss

The Spiaggia del Principe is among the less developed of the Costa Smeralda's five-star beaches, tucked well away from the crowds.

When to Go

Avoid August, if possible, for its inflated prices and crowded beaches. During the winter months, many restaurants, hotels, and shops are closed.

Getting Here

Sardinia is linked to the mainland by frequent ferries and flights. The nearest port and airport to the Costa Smeralda are in Olbia, from where buses and taxis run to Porto Cervo and around.

Sardinia Tourism. 🌐 *www.sardegnaturismo.it*

When in Italy and Sardinia

★ **Cappella degli Scrovegni** (*The Arena Chapel*)

CHURCH | The spatial depth, emotional intensity, and naturalism of the frescoes illustrating the lives of Mary and Jesus in this world-famous chapel broke new ground in Western art. Enrico Scrovegni commissioned these frescoes to atone for the sins of his deceased father, Reginaldo, the usurer condemned to the Seventh Circle of the Inferno in Dante's *Divine Comedy.* Giotto and his assistants worked on the frescoes from 1303 to 1305, arranging them in tiers to be read from left to right. Opposite the altar is a *Last Judgment,* most likely designed and painted by Giotto's assistants.

To preserve the artwork, doors are opened only every 15 minutes. A maximum of 25 visitors must spend 15 minutes in an acclimatization room before making a 15-minute chapel visit (20 minutes in certain months). Tickets should be picked up at least one hour before your reservation. It's sometimes possible to buy admission on the spot. A good place to get some background before visiting the chapel is the multimedia room. ✉ *Piazza Eremitani 8, Padua* ☎ *049/2010020 reservations* 🌐 *www.cappelladegliscrovegni.it* 🎫 *€14, includes Musei Civici and Palazzo Zuckermann.*

Ferrara

TOWN | When the legendary Ferrarese filmmaker Michelangelo Antonioni called his beloved hometown "a city that you can see only partly, while the rest disappears to be imagined," perhaps he was referring to the low-lying mist that rolls in off the Adriatic each winter and shrouds Ferrara's winding knot of medieval alleyways, turreted palaces, and ancient wine bars—once frequented by the likes of Copernicus—in a ghostly fog. But perhaps Antonioni was also suggesting that Ferrara's striking beauty often conceals a dark and tortured past. Today you're likely to be charmed by Ferrara's prosperous air and meticulous cleanliness, its excellent restaurants and chic bars (for coffee and any other liquid refreshment), and its lively wine-bar scene. Although Ferrara is a UNESCO World Heritage site, the city draws amazingly few tourists—which only adds to its appeal. ✉ *Ferrara* ✣ *47 km (29 miles) northeast of Bologna, less than an hour by train* 🌐 *www.ferrarainfo.com.*

Skiing in Piedmont and the Valle d'Aosta

SKIING & SNOWBOARDING | Skiing is the major sport in both Piedmont and the Valle d'Aosta. Excellent facilities abound at resort towns such as Courmayeur and Breuil-Cervinia. The so-called Via Lattea (Milky Way)—five skiing areas near Sestriere with 400 km (almost 250 miles) of linked runs and more than 100 ski lifts—provides practically unlimited skiing. Lift tickets, running around €40 for a day's pass, are a good deal compared to those at major U.S. resorts. The Matterhorn straddles the border between Switzerland and Italy at Breuil-Cervinia, which is connected to Zermatt by a cable car that opened in summer 2023. ✉ *Breuil-Cervinia* 🌐 *www.cervinia.it.*

Tropea

TOWN | Ringed by cliffs and wonderful sandy beaches, the Tropea promontory is still just beginning to be discovered by foreign tourists. The main town of Tropea, its old palazzi built in simple golden stone, easily wins the contest for prettiest town on Calabria's Tyrrhenian Coast. On a clear day the seaward views from the waterfront promenade take in Stromboli's cone and at least four of the other Aeolian Islands; you can visit them by motorboat, departing daily in summer. Accommodations are good, and beach addicts won't be disappointed by the choice of magnificent sandy bays within easy reach. The beach beside Santa Maria dell'Isola is said to be one of the Mediterranean's most beautiful, but there are other fine beaches south

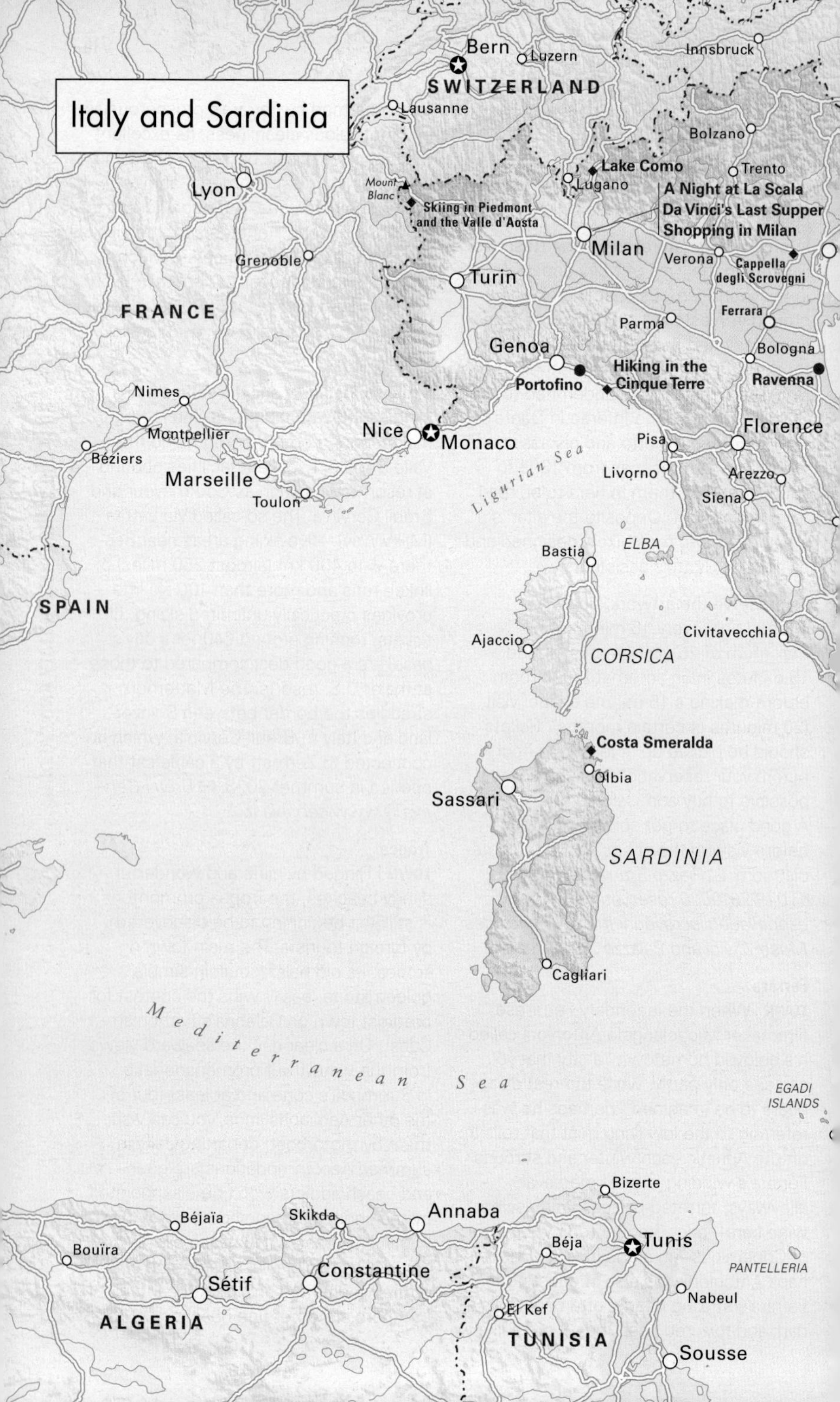

Italy and Sardinia
Bern
Luzern
Innsbruck
SWITZERLAND
Lausanne
Bolzano
Lake Como
Trento
Lugano
A Night at La Scala
Da Vinci's Last Supper
Shopping in Milan
Mount Blanc
Skiing in Piedmont and the Valle d'Aosta
Lyon
Milan
Verona
Cappella degli Scrovegni
Grenoble
Turin
FRANCE
Ferrara
Parma
Genoa
Bologna
Hiking in the Cinque Terre
Portofino
Ravenna
Nimes
Montpellier
Béziers
Nice
Monaco
Florence
Pisa
Marseille
Livorno
Arezzo
Toulon
Ligurian Sea
Siena
Bastia
ELBA
SPAIN
Civitavecchia
Ajaccio
CORSICA
Costa Smeralda
Olbia
Sassari
SARDINIA
Cagliari
Mediterranean Sea
EGADI ISLANDS
Bizerte
Béjaïa
Skikda
Annaba
Bouïra
Béja
Tunis
PANTELLERIA
Constantine
Sétif
Nabeul
ALGERIA
El Kef
TUNISIA
Sousse

AUSTRIA
Graz
HUNGARY
Klagenfurt
Maribor
Szeged
Pécs
ROMANIA
Ljubljana
Timişoara
SLOVENIA
Zagreb
Osijek
Trieste
CROATIA
Novi Sad
Venice
Gulf of Venice
Banja Luka
Belgrade
Pula
BOSNIA AND HERZEGOVINA
SERBIA
Zadar
Sarajevo
San Marino
Ancona
Split
Mostar
Adriatic Sea
Perugia
MONTENEGRO
Pristina
KOSOVO
Dubrovnik
Podgorica
Pescara
Shkodër
Skopje
L'Aquila
NORTH MACEDONIA
Rome
ITALY
Foggia
Tirana
Bitola
Bari
Benevento
ALBANIA
Sassi di Matera
Naples
Vesuvius
Brindisi
ISCHIA
Salerno
CAPRI
Lecce
Taranto
Ioannina
Corfu
GREECE
Tyrrhenian Sea
Ionian Sea
Catanzaro
AEOLIAN ISLANDS
Tropea
Messina
Palermo
Pirgos
Marsala
Etna
Catania
Siracusa
SICILY
0
100 mi
0
100 km
MALTA
MALTA
Valletta

at Capo Vaticano and north at Briatico. ✉ *Tropea* ✥ *120 km (75 miles) southwest of Cosenza* 🌐 *www.prolocotropea.eu.*

Where to Eat and Drink

★ Ceresio 7 Pools & Restaurant

$$$$ | **CONTEMPORARY** | Book well in advance for one of Milan's most fashionable eateries, where the tables are lacquered red and modern artwork crowds the walls—exactly what you'd expect from the twin brothers, Dean and Dan Caten, behind the fashion label Dsquared2. The food cred matches the scene—with fresh, creative, sophisticated pastas and other dishes. **Known for:** luxe ingredients like lobster, king crab, and truffles; place for seeing and being seen; swimming pools and terrace views. $ *Average main: €37* ✉ *Via Ceresio 7, Garibaldi* ☎ *02/31039221* 🌐 *www.ceresio7.com* Ⓜ *Garibaldi; Tram No. 2, 4, 12, or 14; Bus No. 37 or 190.*

Le Zie Trattoria Casereccia

$$ | **SOUTHERN ITALIAN** | **FAMILY** | Local families favor this tiny old-fashioned trattoria, where no-frills charm is matched by wholesome, unfussy food. *Cucina casereccia* (home-cooked) specialties include *polpo in teglia* (stewed octopus), *baccalà al forno* (baked salt cod), and the ubiquitous rustic *purè di fave e cicoria* (bean puree with wild chicory). **Known for:** warm hospitality; genuine local color and cuisine; best to book ahead. $ *Average main: €17* ✉ *Via Costadura 19, Lecce* ☎ *0832/245178* ⏲ *Closed Mon. No dinner Sun.*

★ Ristorante Belforte

$$ | **LIGURIAN** | High above the sea in one of Vernazza's remaining medieval stone towers is this unique spot serving delicious Cinque Terre cuisine such as branzino *sotto sale* (cooked under salt), *tagliolini al nero di seppia con gamberi* (fresh pasta with squid ink sauce and prawns), and *polpo di scoglio alla griglia* (grilled octopus). The setting is magnificent, so try for an outdoor table. **Known for:** incredible views; grilled octopus; lively atmosphere. $ *Average main: €20* ✉ *Via Guidoni 42, Vernazza* ☎ *0187/812222* 🌐 *www.ristorantebelforte.it* ⏲ *Closed Tues. and Nov.–late Mar.*

★ Ristorante La Punta

$$ | **ITALIAN** | When tourist-heavy Bellagio starts to wear you down, seek respite at this charming restaurant located on the town's very northernmost point, a scenic 10-minute walk from the center, with amazing lake views of Varenna to the north and Tremezzo to the west. As you might expect, the menu is heavy on lake fish; although the dishes aren't innovative, they're fresh and well prepared, and the view makes the experience even better. **Known for:** superfresh fish; superlative Lake Como views; friendly service. $ *Average main: €23* ✉ *Via Eugenio Vitali 19, Bellagio* ☎ *031/951888* 🌐 *www.ristorantelapunta.it* ⏲ *Closed Nov.–Mar.*

★ Vitantonio Lombardo

$$$$ | **MODERN ITALIAN** | An open kitchen and contemporary table lamps heighten the culinary theater of Matera's fanciest restaurant, set in a cool, minimalist Rione Sassi grotto. The chef's innovative tasting menus feature vibrant seasonal creations served on artsy ceramics and in wooden bowls. **Known for:** glass-screened wine cellar; imaginative, changing tasting menu; exquisite bread and olive oil. $ *Average main: €130 for 6-course tasting menu* ✉ *Via Madonna delle Virtù 13/14, Matera* ☎ *0835/335475* 🌐 *www.vlristorante.it* ⏲ *Closed Tues. No lunch Wed.–Fri.*

Cool Places to Stay

★ Armani Hotel Milano

$$$$ | **HOTEL** | This minimalist boutique hotel looks like it has been plucked from the pages of a sleek magazine, and it should: it was designed by fashion icon Giorgio Armani to evoke the same sculptural, streamlined aesthetic—and tailored comfort—as his signature clothing. **Pros:** complimentary (except for alcohol) minibar; lovely spa area and 24-hour gym; great location near major shopping streets. **Cons:** breakfast (only included in some rates) not up to par; some noise issues from neighboring rooms; a few signs of wear and tear. *Rooms from: €1050 Via Manzoni 31, Quadrilatero 02/88838888 www.armanihotelmilano.com 95 rooms No Meals Montenapoleone.*

★ Cala di Volpe

$$$$ | RESORT | Long a magnet for the beautiful people, this hyperglamorous Marriott Luxury Collection hotel was designed by Jacques Couëlle to resemble an ancient Sardinian fishing village, complete with its own covered bridge; the exterior is complemented by a rustic-elegant interior with beamed ceilings, terra-cotta floors, Sardinian arts and crafts, and porticoes overlooking the Cala di Volpe Bay. There's an Olympic-size saltwater pool, boat service to a private beach, and access to the Pevero Golf Club. **Pros:** stunning architecture and grounds; luxurious ambience; professional staff. **Cons:** some rooms disappoint; astronomical rates for room, additional amenities, drinks, and meals; car necessary. *Rooms from: €1431 Cala di Volpe, Porto Cervo 0789/976111, 800/4484066 toll-free www.caladivolpe.com Closed late Oct.–early Apr. 121 rooms Free Breakfast.*

Grand Hotel et de Milan

$$$$ | HOTEL | Only blocks from La Scala, you'll find everything you would expect from a traditionally elegant European hotel, where tapestries and persimmon velvet enliven a 19th-century look without sacrificing dignity and luxury. **Pros:** traditional and elegant; great location off Milan's main shopping streets; staff go above and beyond to meet guest needs. **Cons:** gilt decor may not suit those who like more modern design; no spa; some small rooms. *Rooms from: €682 Via Manzoni 29, Quadrilatero 02/723141 www.grandhoteletdemilan.it 72 rooms, 23 suites No Meals Montenapoleone.*

★ Locanda di San Martino

$$ | HOTEL | Situated at the bottom of the Sassi ravine on Via Fiorentini (limited car access), the Locanda is a more upscale cave-dwelling hotel, with all modern comforts, including an elevator to whisk you up the cliff to your room. **Pros:** convenient location if you come by car; comfortable rooms; on-site ancient Roman–style spa. **Cons:** rooms reached via outdoor walkway; limited parking nearby; spa may be a tad intimate for some. *Rooms from: €155 Via Fiorentini 71, Matera 0835/256600 www.locandadisanmartino.it 40 rooms Free Breakfast.*

Patria Palace

$$$ | HOTEL | Lecce's grandest hotel—impeccable from top to bottom, with vaulted ceilings, frescoes, and antique furnishings—also happens to have a stellar location in front of the monumental Santa Croce Basilica, the crown jewel of Lecce Baroque. **Pros:** many sumptuous, high-ceilinged rooms; fabulous roof terrace; valet parking for guests. **Cons:** a few rooms overlook noisy backstreets; some rooms outdated and less grand; style of the lobby doesn't match that of the handsome facade. *Rooms from: €297 Piazzetta Riccardi 13, Lecce 0832/245111 www.patriapalace.com 67 rooms Free Breakfast.*

Malta

Despite having few resources, Malta has suffered a long history of invasion, sandwiched as it is—strategically and culturally—between North Africa and Europe and between Islam and Christianity. In its 7,000 years of inhabitation, the island's shores have been overrun by just about every major power in the Mediterranean and beyond, from Phoenicians to French.

No invader did more to shape Malta than the Knights of the Order of St. John, a Catholic military order gifted the islands by King Charles V of Spain in 1530. They built gilded Baroque palaces and churches, and raised vast city walls to fend off attacks and reshape the land. Stroll the cobbled citadels of Mdina, Valletta, and the Three Cities (Vittoriosa, Senglea, and Conspicua), and you can soak in their legacy.

Later came the British, wrenching Malta from the grasp of Napoleon's French in 1800 and holding fast as the islands fell under the gunsights of the Axis powers during World War II. Some 6,700 bombs fell on the capital Valletta alone over 154 days, but Malta and its people resisted and survived. The legacy of that time can now be felt in countless museums, forts, and even Valletta's Lascaris War Rooms, in which the Allied forces plotted.

Since Malta gained independence in 1964, it has since joined both the European Union (in 2004) and adopted the euro as its official currency (in 2008). Tourists have been quick to claim its history and turquoise waters for their own. Resorts and malls have colonized the northeastern bays of the mainland, giving visitors all the more reason to stick to its historic sights, fishing villages, and rural west, or head to the tiny island of Gozo, a 25-minute ferry ride off the north coast, and a land of quiet villages, bracing clifftops, and crystal-clear waters for diving, kayaking, and snorkeling. With a population of just 30,000 people, it somehow has two opera houses and 47 places of worship.

Lascaris War Rooms

The Rooms That Changed the Course of World War II

In 1943, the Lascaris War Rooms arguably decided the course of World War II. It was then that President Eisenhower and the Allied commanders were plotting the invasion of Sicily (known as Operation Husky)—one of the first major assaults to retake Europe from the Axis powers. Although the nearby Grand Harbour of Valletta was being almost constantly bombed at the time, the location of this complex of underground tunnels—deep within the bedrock below the city—kept it safe from harm. The top-secret British HQ was later used by NATO to track Soviet subs right up until 1977, but after the end of the Cold War it was carefully restored to reflect its 1940s heyday. Guided tours (you are also free to explore on your own) will take you through the intricacies of planning such a game-changing operation long before computers were able to plot each movement—complicated military coordination was done with phones, string, and a chalkboard.

Don't Miss

The main Map Room, where the movements of both Allied and Axis shipping and aircraft across the central Mediterranean were plotted in real time, is the highlight of any tour.

Getting Here

The entrance to the war rooms is up at the Saluting Battery, beside the Upper Barrakka Gardens, with steps leading down from there. The gardens are just a few minutes on foot from both downtown Valletta and the main bus station.

✉ *Lascaris Ditch, Valetta* ☎ *21/234–717*
🌐 *www.lascariswarrooms.com* 🎫 *€14*

Ħal Saflieni Hypogeum

Six Thousand Years of History

Carved under the town of Paola, not far from the capital Valletta, Ħal Saflieni Hypogeum—a labyrinth of underground chambers—was used as a subterranean necropolis and funeral hall. It dates back to around 4000 BC, making it around 1,500 years older than the Pyramids of Giza, and it remains the only excavation of its kind in Europe. Many of its atmospheric chambers are decorated with red ocher or fine carvings, including the Oracle Room, which was cleverly shaped to amplify sound. Because of its delicate state (even the carbon dioxide exhaled by visitors can damage its walls), only 10 visitors per hour, for a maximum of eight hours a day, are allowed inside. As this limits capacity, book tickets at least a month in advance.

Don't Miss

A 5-minute walk from Ħal Saflieni, the four interconnecting Tarxien Temples have curious carvings, oracular chambers, and altars, all dating from about 2800 BC. Recovered stone figures of the broad-hipped fertility goddess, now lying in Valletta's National Archeology Museum, indicate it was dedicated to the Earth Mother. An audio guide accessed via a downloadable app narrates the history of the site and shows images of artifacts now covered for their protection. 🌐 *www.heritagemalta.org*

Getting Here

Bus Nos. 81, 83, 85 and 88 all make the journey from Valletta Bus Station to the Hypogeum in around 15 minutes.

✉ *Burial St., on road to Santa Lucija, Paola* ☎ *21/805–019* 🌐 *www.heritagemalta.org/hal-saflieni-hypogeum/* 🎫 *From €35*

St. John's Co-Cathedral

Malta's Incredibly Ornate Main Church

What appears to be a rather functional-looking building from the outside is deceiving. On the inside, the St. John's Co-Cathedral is one of the world's most lavishly decorated baroque cathedrals, the discrepancy between its outer and inner aspects reflecting the different eras through which it has stood. Completed in 1578 by the Knights of the Order of St. John as their own church, by the 17th century the order's mounting treasures from the Holy Land and desire to build a church to rival those of Rome saw it get a spectacular makeover. The floor is made up of a patchwork of colored-marble tombstones (housing 375 knights and officers of the order), and it shines beneath a breathtakingly intricate arched ceiling decorated by the Calabrian artist and knight Mattia Preti.

Don't Miss

In the Oratory is Caravaggio's only signed work, the dramatic and unsparing *Beheading of John the Baptist* (1607), which hangs above the very spot where the rogue artist was defrocked and de-knighted following a brawl (he had already fled to Malta to escape punishment for murder). Also hanging here is another of his works, the touchingly frail image of *Saint Jerome Writing* (1606), which found infamy after it was stolen in 1984 and held hostage.

Getting Here

The Co-Cathedral is a few minutes' walk from Valletta Bus Station. The public entrance (main ticket office) is on Republic Street.

✉ *Pjazza San Gwann, Valetta* ☎ *21/239–628* 🌐 *www.stjohnscocathedral.com* 🎫 *€10* 🕒 *Closed Sun.*

Mdina

A City Frozen in Time

Traffic is limited to residents' cars in Malta's ancient, walled capital—the longtime stronghold of the island's nobility—and the noise of the world outside barely penetrates its thick, golden walls. The streets are lined with sometimes block-long, still-occupied noble palaces, best visited toward the end of the day, when the coach tours thin. At the center, the baroque St. Paul's Cathedral (dating from 1703) is famed for Mattia Preti's intricate 17th-century apse mural *The Shipwreck of St. Paul.* Together with the 900-year-old Irish bogwood doors to its sacristy, this was one of few surviving relics of the 1693 earthquake that destroyed the original Norman-era church that stood on this site. Just as compelling are the labyrinth of catacombs that lie below neighboring suburb of Rabat, which was once part of an influential Roman city.

Don't Miss

The sweeping vista from the city walls at sunset takes in half the island, including Valetta and the coast.

Best Restaurant

Fontanella Tea Garden. A Mdina institution, this café offers some of the most scrumptious cakes in Malta, paired with delicious freshly brewed coffee. It's not just the food that attracts a regular stream of clients; the terrace tables have magnificent views across the Maltese countryside. $ *Average main: €7* ✉ *1 Bastion St., Mdina* ☎ *2145–4264* 🌐 *www.fontanellateagarden.com*

Getting Here

Bus Nos. 51, 52, and 53 link Mdina to Valletta in 30 minutes. Once here, everything is within a few minutes' walk.

St. Paul's Cathedral. ✉ *Archbishop Sq., Mdina* ☎ *21/454–679* 🌐 *www.metropolitanchapter.com* 🎫 *€10*

Gozo

Malta's Fiercely Independent Little Sister

Located just off the mainland, the island of Gozo is Malta in name only. Gozitans are a different breed to their flashier Maltese cousins—and even from each other. Villages, often just a few kilometers apart, typically have their own dialects. The island, a far cry from the traffic-snarled roads of mainland Malta, is quiet, rural, and beautiful. The northern coast is a wild series of lonely hiking trails and towering clifftops overlooking turquoise waters. Not much happens here, but that's the way the locals like it. The capital, Victoria (known locally as Rabat), is a charming old city with two main squares lined with cafés, and a hilltop Cittadella, built by the Knights of the Order of St. John and home to some fantastic views.

Don't Miss

The 5,800-year-old Ġgantija megalithic site is a complex of temples that are considered to be the world's oldest free-standing man-made structures, created 1,000 years before the Pyramids of Giza.

Best Restaurant

Ta' Rikardu. This is a truly authentic Gozitan experience, serving locally produced charcuterie and cheese in a vaulted stone medieval beside Gozo Cathedral. $ *Average main: €15* ✉ *4 Fosse St., The Citadel, Victoria* ☎ *21/555–953*

Getting Here

Ferries take 25 minutes to cross from Ċirkewwa on Malta to Mġarr on Gozo. A passenger-only fast ferry (45 minutes) also links Mgarr with the Grand Harbour in Valletta. Buses link Victoria with all major towns on Gozo.

Ġgantija Temples. ✉ *John Otto Bayer St., Xagħra, Gozo* ☎ *2155–3194* 🌐 *www.heritagemalta.org/ggantija-temples* 🎫 *€10*

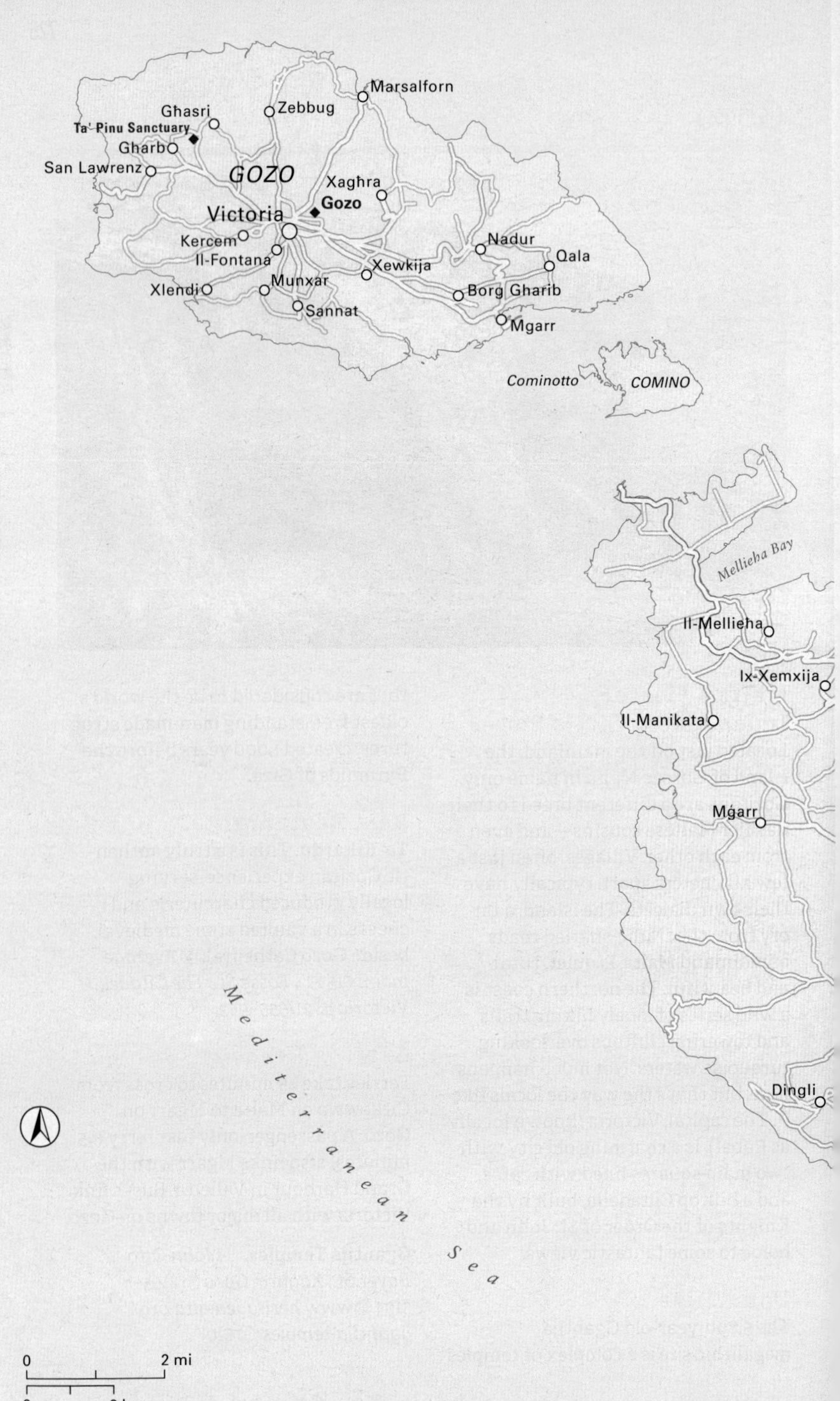

Marsalforn
Ghasri
Zebbug
Ta' Pinu Sanctuary
Gharb
San Lawrenz
GOZO
Xaghra
Victoria
Gozo
Kercem
Il-Fontana
Nadur
Qala
Xewkija
Munxar
Xlendi
Borg Gharib
Sannat
Mgarr
Cominotto
COMINO
Mellieħa Bay
Il-Mellieha
Ix-Xemxija
Il-Manikata
Mgarr
Mediterranean Sea
Dingli
0
2 mi
0
2 km

Malta

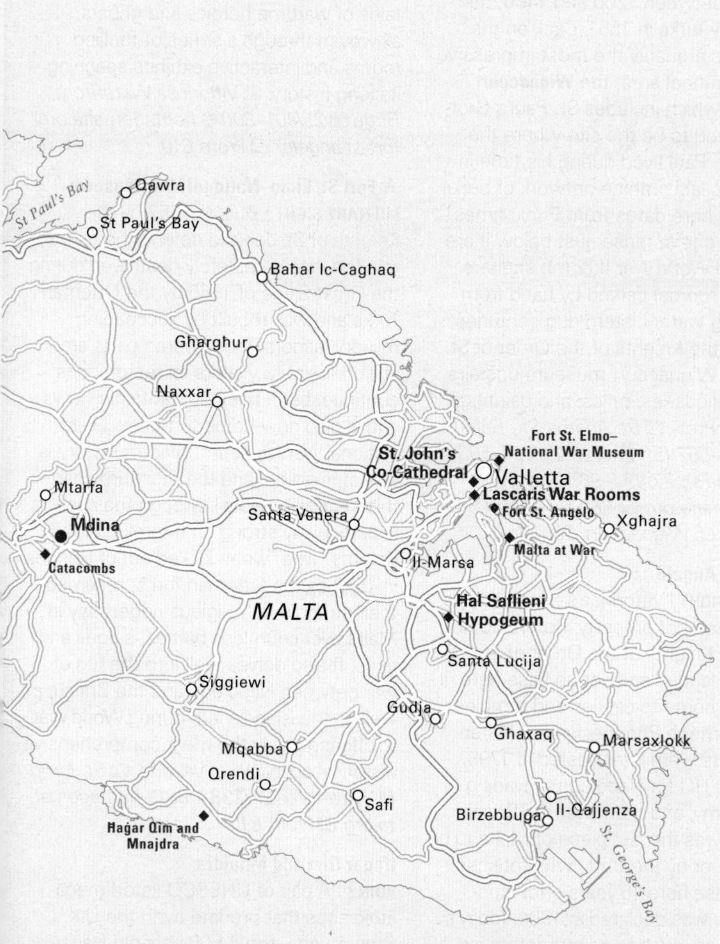
Mediterranean Sea
St Paul's Bay
Qawra
St Paul's Bay
Bahar Ic-Caghaq
Gharghur
Naxxar
Fort St. Elmo–
National War Museum
St. John's
Co-Cathedral
Valletta
Lascaris War Rooms
Fort St. Angelo
Xghajra
Mtarfa
Mdina
Catacombs
Santa Venera
Il-Marsa
Malta at War
MALTA
Hal Saflieni
Hypogeum
Santa Lucija
Siggiewi
Gudja
Ghaxaq
Marsaxlokk
Mqabba
Qrendi
Safi
Il-Qajjenza
Birzebbuga
Hagar Qim and
Mnajdra
St. George's Bay

When in Malta

★ Catacombs

CEMETERY | Catacombs run under much of Rabat. Up Saint Agatha Street from Parish Square, the **Catacombs of St. Paul** are clean of bones but full of carved-out burial troughs and feature the most comprehensive information on the rituals of the city's underground world, including why each tomb is a different shape. **St. Agatha's Crypt and Catacombs,** farther up the street, were beautifully frescoed between 1200 and 1480, then defaced by Turks in 1551. Back on the square lies arguably the most impressive surviving tunnel area, the **Wignacourt Complex ,** which includes St. Paul's Grotto—believed to be the site where the apostle St. Paul lived during his time in Malta. This labyrinthine network of burial chambers here dates from Punic times and holds one surprise: just below it are a series of World War II bomb shelters (some 50 rooms) carved by hand from an existing water cistern dug centuries earlier by the Knights of the Order of St. John. The Wignacourt museum upstairs houses reliquaries, relics, and paintings by Mattia Preti. ✉ *St. Agatha St., Rabat* ☎ *21/454–562 (St. Paul's), 21/454–503 (St. Agatha's), 27/494–905* 🌐 *www.heritagemalta.org* 🎫 *€6 St. Paul's; €6 St. Agatha's; €6 Wignacourt Complex.*

★ Fort St. Angelo

MILITARY SIGHT | Vittoriosa's headland has always been hot property. Before 1530, when the Knights of the Order of St. John first landed and set up base here, it had been home to castles and temples dating from the Phoenecian era. When the Knights were later ousted in 1798, it became HQ for Napoleon's invading French army, and then later the British Navy—it was the last piece of Malta to be handed over by the Brits, who retained a naval base here 15 years after independence was declared in 1964. Today's layout owes much to its strengthening in 1690 by the engineer Don Carlos de Grunenberg. So successful was his design that, some 250 years later, it was able to withstand 69 direct hits by World War II bombers. Nazi propaganda even famously claimed it had "sunk HMS St Angelo" (as the fort was then known by the British) despite it not being a ship. But its starring moment was during the Great Siege of 1565, when it repelled wave after wave of Ottoman Turks over three long, hot summer months. Following extensive renovations, completed in 2016, it reopened as a **museum**, narrating tales of wartime heroics and ghosts, all woven through a series of thrilling rooms and interactive exhibits spanning its long history. ✉ *Vittoriosa Waterfront, Birgu* ☎ *25/401–800* 🌐 *heritagemalta.org/fort-st-angelo/* 🎫 *From €10.*

★ Fort St. Elmo–National War Museum

MILITARY SIGHT | Built in 1552 by the Knights of St. John to defend the harbor, this fort was completely destroyed during the Great Siege of 1565 by the Ottoman Turks and was rebuilt by succeeding military leaders. Today, some parts are still off-limits to visitors as restorations continue, but it has both fantastic views and is also now home to the excellent National War Museum. Malta's history is one of invasion, and the museum charts this in gripping detail through the ages. It is particularly strong on the reign of the Knights, who, when kicked out of Rhodes in 1522 by the Ottoman Turks, resumed their struggle for religious hegemony in Malta over countless battles, sieges and raids. It also delves well into the tug of war between Napoleon and the British, as well as the island's fate during World War II, offering easily the most comprehensive historical overview of Valletta. ✉ *St. Elmo Pl., Valletta* ☎ *21/233–088* 🌐 *heritagemalta.org* 🎫 *From €10.*

Ħaġar Qim and Mnajdra

RUINS | A pair of UNESCO-listed megalithic sites that predate even the U.K.'s Stonehenge, the 4,800-year-old Ħaġar

Qim ("*ha*-jar eem") gives a clear picture of the massive scale of Malta's ancient limestone temples. Along the external wall you'll find the largest megaliths, some weighing close to 20 tons. The altars are well preserved, though some are reproductions. Just a short walk away lies Mnajdra, a series of three temples encircled by hard coralline limestone walls. Built between 3600 BC and 2500 BC, what survives is thought to be the remains of a much larger complex. Visitor centers for both sites offer as many answers as fascinating mysteries about their use. ✉ *Triq Haġar Qim, Qrendi* ☎ *21/424–231* 🌐 *www.heritagemalta.org* 🎫 *€10* Ⓜ *Bus: 201 (Rabat).*

Malta at War

MILITARY SIGHT | There's no shortage of museums unraveling Malta's military history, but few are as intimate. Housed inside an 18th-century army barracks and labyrinthine, rock-cut, underground air-raid shelter, it focuses on the period from 1940 to 1943, when World War II and the Blitz came to Malta—then a strategically vital outpost for the Allied Forces and stepping stone to Fascist Italy. Through artifacts, newsreels, and a stirring propaganda documentary, narrated by Laurence Olivier and released by King George VI in January 1943 to pluck up the spirits of his battered Maltese subjects, it shows daily life as the bombs fell and hope was all but lost and then found again. ✉ *Couvre Port, Birgu* ☎ *21/800–992* 🌐 *www.maltaatwarmuseum.com* 🎫 *€14.*

★ Ta' Pinu Sanctuary

What was once a tiny chapel servicing an equally miniscule village found fame in 1883 when a local woman was said to hear the voice of the Virgin here. Pilgrims flocked to it, overwhelming the chapel, so a wealthy local man paid to build what is now Ta' Pinu Sanctuary around it in the 1920s (the chapel still exists in part behind the altar, along with the tomb of the woman who heard the "miracle"). It's an impressive building, constructed in soft Maltese stone, which meant they could carve intricate Romanesque flourishes. Perhaps the most remarkable sight is the votive offerings in the rear, left by visitors who have experienced "miracles" of their own and who wish to thank the Virgin. From broken bicycle wheels to plaster casts, all manner of personal memorabilia is strewn across the walls, with written stories accompanying each and making for fascinating reading. ✉ *Triq ta' Pinu, Gharb* ☎ *21/556–187* 🌐 *www.tapinu.org/* Ⓜ *Bus: 308 (Victoria/Rabat).*

Where to Eat and Drink

★ Beati Paoli

$$ | MEDITERRANEAN | FAMILY | One of the buzziest restaurants in the capital is the family-run Beati Paoli, an impossibly cozy, friendly affair that still flies under the radar of most visitors. It has that neighborhood feel, boasting of its "local fresh rabbit" on the blackboard frontage, yet serves up subtly crafted, on-point Maltese and Mediterranean dishes with a changing specials menu that never fails to delight. **Known for:** friendly service; excellently crafted local dishes; good selection of Maltese wines. 💲 *Average main: €20* ✉ *Valletta* ☎ *99/309–319* ⏲ *Closed for dinner Sun.; closed for lunch Mon. and Sat.*

★ Noni

$$$ | MEDITERRANEAN | One of the current rising stars of Malta's dining scene is Jonathan Brincat, owner-chef of the much talked-about Noni, a chic, cozy escape set in a former jazz bar. The menu is a studied, elegant affair taking a number of Maltese and Mediterranean classics and fine-tuning them with a bit of French flair, from saddle of rabbit with confit croquette to a crackling smoked rib "gyoza" that accompanies the pork to smoky chorzio bean puree. **Known for:** imaginative cooking; hip atmosphere; good selection of local wines and craft beers. 💲 *Average main: €27* ✉ *211*

Republic St., Valletta ☎ *21/221–441* 🌐 *noni.com.mt* 🕒 *Closed Sun. No lunch Mon.–Wed.*

Ta' Frenċ

$$$ | MEDITERRANEAN | You'll find refined service and classic cuisine in this old limestone farmhouse. Using produce from its vegetable garden, a seasonal menu includes boat-fresh seafood dishes, fresh pasta, and a fine suckling pig. **Known for:** classic dishes; farmhouse-meets-fine dining setting; plenty of fresh seafood. $ *Average main: €28* ✉ *Ghajn Damma St., Xaghra* ✣ *Halfway between Victoria and Marsalforn* ☎ *21/553–888* 🌐 *www.tafrenc.mt* 🕒 *Closed Tues.*

★ Ta' Kris

$$ | ITALIAN | This is one of the last remaining traditional Maltese trattorias along the tourist strip, and local families, along with a few in-the-know visitors, flock to this relaxed eatery. The chef is famed for his homemade succulent *braġjoli* (thin beef steak stuffed with pork herbs and breadcrumbs, then rolled and cooked) and mouth-watering slow-cooked rabbit. **Known for:** great Maltese food; bustling atmosphere; atmospheric setting in an old Maltese bakery. $ *Average main: €14* ✉ *80 Fawwara La., Sliema* ☎ *2133–7367, 7933–7367* 🌐 *www.takrisrestaurant.com.*

Cool Places to Stay

Cornucopia

$ | HOTEL | A haven of peace and quiet in the heart of the Gozitan countryside, Cornucopia is the perfect place to bring the novels you always hoped to read but never found the time to—it has two pools after all. **Pros:** countryside setting; friendly staff; children/family pool. **Cons:** fixtures and fittings need updating; free Wi-Fi only in reception; no sea views. $ *Rooms from: €90* ✉ *10 Gnien Imrik St., Xaghra* ☎ *21/556–486* 🌐 *www.cornucopiahotel.com* ⇆ *61 rooms.*

★ Palazzo Consiglia

$$ | HOTEL | This property is part of the wave of boutique hotels that has swept over the old city in recent years, turning aging palazzo town houses into enviably chic stays with minimal rooms and high prices. **Pros:** the decadent underground spa; located on a quiet street, away from the crowds but still a two-minute walk to the center; rooftop pool has great views. **Cons:** few of the bedrooms have windows facing outward; no real parking area; breakfast area is a little squashed. $ *Rooms from: €169* ✉ *102 St. Ursula St., Valletta* ☎ *21/244–222* 🌐 *palazzoconsiglia.com/* ⇆ *13 rooms* 🍴 *Free Breakfast.*

The Snop House

$$ | HOTEL | What was once the social club of Malta's Labour Party has, somewhat ironically, been transformed into a rather bijou boutique by its owners, a pair of charming French expats who fell in love with Malta. **Pros:** the rooftop has wonderful views over the sleepy town; rooms are slickly decorated; an elevator means there's good access to every floor. **Cons:** the church bells respect the sleep of no one; the lift is one of the slowest around; the breakfast space is rather cramped. $ *Rooms from: €110* ✉ *Triq il-Vitorja, Senglea* ☎ *27/029–324* 🌐 *thesnophouse.com* ⇆ *6 rooms* 🍴 *Free Breakfast.*

★ The Xara Palace Relais and Chateaux

$$$ | HOTEL | When the last tourists leave Mdina at night and the "Silent City" finally lives up to its nickname, there are no more elegant stays than this. **Pros:** you get to stay in Malta's most beautiful walled city; great facilities for a boutique hotel; valet parking solves the usual "where to park" issue. **Cons:** the crowds during the day are a pain (and noisy in the morning); the pool is actually in a different location, though hotel transport is available; there are few dining options in town. $ *Rooms from: €209* ✉ *Misrah Il Kunsill, Mdina* ☎ *21/450–560* 🌐 *xarapalace.com.mt/* ⇆ *17 rooms* 🍴 *Free Breakfast.*

Chapter 9

THE BALKANS

WELCOME TO THE BALKANS

TOP REASONS TO GO

★ **Nature:** If you are after unspoiled nature that ticks every box, you'll find it here.

★ **Nightlife:** In the Balkans, the parties never seem to stop.

★ **History:** At turns inspiring and tumultuous, history is a living, breathing thing in these parts.

★ **Food:** Carnivores will be in dreamland, but vegetarians will be pleasantly surprised (and satisfied).

★ **Beaches:** The excellence of Croatia's coastline is well-documented, but Montenegro and Albania aren't far behind.

★ **People:** The best storytellers in Europe? Look no further than the Balkans.

The ten countries that make up the Balkan region are quite diverse.

1 Slovenia. You have Europe in miniature, a vibrant country of artists and steeples packed with stunning nature and picture-perfect towns.

2 Croatia. Next door to Slovenia is increasingly popular Croatia, with its brilliant coastline and echoes of empires long gone.

3 Bulgaria. East of Croatia is Bulgaria, the southernmost frontier of Eastern and Central Europe that straddles the line between gorgeous tradition and innovative futurism.

4 Romania. The sweeping plains and medieval cities of beautiful Romania speak for themselves.

5 Southern Balkans. Bosnia and Herzegovina, Serbia, Montenegro, North Macedonia, Kosovo, and Albania comprise the Southern Balkans, six thrilling destinations where tangible history nestles next to an exciting future, all fueled by some of the best coffee on the continent.

Kraków
Lvov
POLAND
UKRAINE
SLOVAKIA
Budapest
HUNGARY
Iaşi
Chişinău
MOLDOVA
Cluj-Napoca
BacÄƒu
ROMANIA
4
Sibiu
Focşani
Tulcea
Belgrade
Piteşti
Bucharest
Constanta
Sarajevo
SERBIA
Varna
MONTENEGRO
Pristina
Sofia
BULGARIA
3
Burgas
Black Sea
KOSOVO
Podgorica
5
Skopje
NORTH MACEDONIA
Istanbul
Tirana
ALBANIA
Thessaloniki
Bursa
TURKEY
Ionian Sea
GREECE
Aegean Sea
Izmir
Patra
Athens

WHAT TO EAT AND DRINK IN THE BALKANS

Kavarma

GRILLED MEAT

It might seem a little obvious, but meat is ubiquitous throughout the region. This is particularly true in the Southern Balkans, where (minced-meat rolls) and (a spiced meat patty) are everywhere. The most popular meats are pork and lamb, but chicken is increasingly popular.

CRNI RIŽOT

Supremely popular on the Croatian coast, (black risotto) sings with the taste of the sea. The strange color of the dish comes from the ink of the cuttlefish, and it is unlike anything else on the continent.

SARMA

A traditional dish found everywhere from Bosnia and Herzegovina to Bulgaria, Sarma are rolled cabbage leaves filled with rice, meat, and more. Variations differ from country to country.

ŠTRUKLJI

A rolled pastry with savory and sweet fillings, štruklji has been a popular traditional dish in Slovene houses since the 16th century. Štruklji is usually served as a side, but what a delicious side.

MĂMĂLIGĂ

Before polenta, there was mămăligă, a mainstay throughout Romania, another type of porridge made from yellow cornmeal. What was once a rural staple has become increasingly common in gourmet establishments as a new generation of chefs gets in touch with their roots.

COFFEE

You should obviously drink coffee wherever you are, but prepare to be blown away by the stuff in Kosovo. Europe's youngest nation has developed a reputation as a caffeine lover's dream, and it only takes one sip to see why.

SHOPSKA SALAD

If you think the colors of your salad resemble those of the Bulgarian flag, that is no coincidence. Bulgaria's national dish is a refreshing salad of diced tomatoes, cucumbers, onions, and peppers topped with white cheese.

BUREK

Another staple throughout the region, are your best bet at breakfast. Or lunch. Or dinner. Actually, whenever you are hungry, go for burek. There are many varieties of this filled pastry classic (potatoes, cheese, leafy greens, eggplant, and mushrooms, for example), but the meat-filled remain king.

KREMŠNITA

The origins of this delightful custard cream cake are debated to this day, but there is something about devouring one on the shores of Slovenia's Lake Bled that really takes the, erm, cake.

CIORBĂ DE BURTĂ

Tripe soup might not sound like the most appetizing thing, but there are plenty of reasons that Romanians have been eating this for centuries. It is utterly delicious, first of all. If you like your soups creamy, you are in for a treat. It's made a bit sour by the addition of vinegar or lemon juice, creamy because of the addition of sour cream.

Štruklji

Kremšnita

RAKIJA

No meal is complete without the obligatory glass of. Enjoyed everywhere from Ljubljana to Tirana via Sofia, Zagreb, and the rest, rakija also happens to be the cure for everything. Many variations are available, but plum () is the most common, but it can be made from grapes (and is in Bulgaria).

ISTRIAN TRUFFLES

If you want to live the gourmet life, head to Istria and order the truffles. There is never a bad time to eat truffles, after all, but there is something about Istrian truffles that hits differently.

KAVARMA

The longer it takes to cook something, the more succulent it will be. That is a culinary rule, right? (a gorgeous slow-cooked stew of meat and vegetables prepared in a clay pot) proves it. You'll find kavarma in any traditional Bulgarian restaurant worthy of the name.

The Balkans Snapshot

Know Before You Go

WHEN TO GO

If you like seasonal variety, you are going to love this part of the world. Summers are scorching, winters are freezing, meaning spring and fall are gorgeously temperate. The shoulder seasons are almost always the best, although summer and winter are packed with events and excitement. The coastline (from Slovenia all the way down to Albania) pretty much shuts up shop during the winter, and most of the action moves to higher ground and the many ski resorts. Truth be told, there is no bad time to visit any of these spots, and when is best will largely depend on what type of weather you like best for exploring.

REGIONAL DIFFERENCES

There are 10 different countries in the Balkan region, so "differences" feels like somewhat of an understatement. Ljubljana is a world away from Tirana, and the Black Sea coast of Romania and Bulgaria is a different beast entirely from the Adriatic. Even within individual countries, differences are stark across short distances. It should go without saying, but the best way to approach every city, town, village, and resort is by doing so on its own merits. Blanket assumptions are a major no-no in these parts, whether talking about history, politics, culture, sports, language, or anything else. The great empires of the past left their marks on all these countries, but every one of them is defiantly proud of itself.

Planning Your Time

Getting around Slovenia, Croatia, and Serbia isn't too much of a problem, with extensive bus networks and a handful of train options. Even so, those bus journeys can often take longer than they should, with many stops and interminably winding roads. Things get harder the farther south you go, meaning a private vehicle remains the best mode of transport (if it is an option). If public transport if your only option, be prepared to travel slowly.

Great Trips

5 days: A tour of five of the former Yugoslav capitals (leaving out Podgorica): **Ljubljana, Zagreb, Sarajevo, Belgrade,** and **Skopje.**

5 days: The best of the best on that marvelous coastline: **Piran, Zadar, Dubrovnik, Perast,** and **Durrës.**

5 days: A little bit of everything in the south: **Mostar, Kotor, Tirana, Ohrid,** and **Prizren.**

Big Events

Kurentovanje, Slovenia. Few countries do carnival with as much joy and creativity as Slovenia. Get yourself to Cerknica for the most intense version.

Sarajevo Film Festival, Bosnia and Herzegovina. For a week in August, the Bosnian capital becomes a mecca for movie lovers worldwide.

Guča Trumpet Festival, Serbia. If you aren't into trumpets, grilled meat, and chaos, Guča probably isn't for you. This three-day festival in August is Serbia's most raucous party.

What To...

READ

The Balkans, Misha Glenny. Glenny remains one of the most authoritative voices on Balkan history.

Death and the Dervish, Meša Selimović. This slow-burning classic from one of Yugoslavia's finest writers is a striking tale of a soul at a crossroads.

The File on H, Ismail Kadare. Any of Kadare's novels could be included here, but the absurd twists and turns make this one mandatory for any reading list.

Natural Novel, Georgi Gospodinov. A postmodernist masterpiece, Gospodinov's experimental debut is ostensibly about a young couple on the cusp of divorce, but it's much more.

WATCH

The Death of Mr Lazarescu. A dark comedy from Romania about an elderly gentleman on the brink of death, shuttled from hospital to hospital as doctors refuse to take charge.

Before the Rain. Milcho Manchevski's masterpiece is a brilliantly weighted example of intertwining love stories and the universality of emotion.

I Even Met Happy Gypsies. A must-watch classic of Yugoslav cinema, this charming and impactful tale depicts Romani life in Vojvodina.

The World is Big and Salvation Lurks Around the Corner. Directed by Stefan Komandarev, this beautifully titled Bulgarian film is a coming-of-age story told through amnesia, tumult, and backgammon.

LISTEN TO

Dubioza Kolektiv, *Apsurdistan.*

Toše Proeski, *The Best Of.*

Rambo Amadeus, *Hoćemo gusle.*

George Enescu. Simply pick out a playlist and let the music sweep you away

BUY

Whether you enjoy a drink or not, a bottle of traditional booze, be it rakija, wine, beer, or any other, is the classic Balkan souvenir.

The intricate designs of traditional carpets can be difficult to resist. Head to Pirot (Serbia) and Oltenia (Romania) for the best.

Bags of salt can be bought across Slovenia (Piran salt is world famous) and make for a great souvenir.

The entire region is packed with old-fashioned craft workers still plying their trades, from metalworkers in Sarajevo to ceramics in Tirana.

Contacts

AIR

MAJOR AIRPORTS

Slovenia. Ljubljana Jože Pučnik Airport (LJU)

Croatia. Zagreb Airport (ZAG), Split Airport (SPU), Dubrovnik Airport (DBV)

Bulgaria. Sofia Airport (SOF)

Romania. Bucharest Airport (OTP)

Bosnia and Herzegovina. Sarajevo International Airport (SJJ)

Serbia. Belgrade Nikola Tesla Airport (BEG)

Kosovo. Prishtina International Airport (PRN)

Montenegro. Podgorica Airport (TGD)

North Macedonia. Skopje International Airport (SKP)

Albania. Tirana International Airport (TIA), Kukës International Airport (AFZ)

BUS

Purchase tickets at bus stations or from the driver.

SLOVENIA

Bus Station Ljubljana. ✉ *Trg Osvobodilne fronte 4, Ljubljana*

CROATIA

Autobusni Kolodvor Zagreb. ✉ *Avenija Marina Držića 4, Zagreb*

Autobusni Kolodvor Split. ✉ *Obala kneza Domagoja 12, Split*

BULGARIA

Central Bus Station Sofia. ✉ *Knyaginya Maria Luiza 100, Sofia*

Bus Station Plovdiv. ✉ *Hristo Botev 47, Plovdiv*

ROMANIA

MementoBUS Terminal. ✉ *Șoseaua Orhideelor 49, Bucharest*

BOSNIA AND HERZEGOVINA

Sarajevo Central Bus Station. ✉ *Put života 2, Sarajevo*

Sarajevo Istočno Bus Station. ✉ *Srpskih vladara 2, Istočno Sarajevo*

Mostar Bus Station. ✉ *Maršala Tita, Mostar*

SERBIA

Belgrade Bus Station. ✉ *Železnička 4, Belgrade*

Novi Sad Bus Station. ✉ *Bulevar Jaše Tomić 6, Novi Sad*

MONTENEGRO

Podgorica Bus Station. ✉ *1 Trg Golootočkih Žrtava, Podgorica*

Kotor Bus Station. ✉ *Put prvoboraca bb, Kotor*

NORTH MACEDONIA

Skopje Bus Station. ✉ *Vladimir Komarov, Skopje*

Ohrid Bus Station. ✉ *Vele Markov 9, Ohrid*

TRAIN

Purchase train tickets from the station.

MAJOR TRAIN STATIONS

Slovenia. Ljubljana (✉ *Trg Osvobodilne fronte 7*)

Croatia. Zagreb (✉ *Trg Kralja Tomislava 12*)

Bulgaria. Sofia Central Station (✉ *Orlandovtsi*)

Romania. Bucharest Gara de Nord (✉ *Piața Gării de Nord*)

Bosnia and Herzegovina. Sarajevo (✉ *Put života 2*)

Serbia. Belgrade Centre-Prokop (✉ *Prokupačka ulica*)

Kosovo. Prishtina railway station

Montenegro. Railway Station Bar. Podgorica train station (✉ *7 Trg Golootočkih Žrtava*)

North Macedonia. Railway Station Skopje (✉ *Bul. Kuzman Josifovski Pitu*)

VISITOR INFORMATION

Slovenia. 🌐 *www.slovenia.info/en*

Croatia. 🌐 *croatia.hr/en-gb*

Bulgaria. 🌐 *bulgariatravel.org*

Romania. 🌐 *visit-romania.eu*

Bosnia and Herzegovina. 🌐 *www.visitsarajevo.ba*

Serbia. 🌐 *www.serbia.travel*

Kosovo. 🌐 *www.destinationkosovo.com*

Montenegro. 🌐 *www.montenegro.travel/en*

North Macedonia. 🌐 *www.exploringmacedonia.com*

Albania. 🌐 *albania.al*

Slovenia

Slovenia may be the best-kept secret in Europe. Just half the size of Switzerland, the country is often treated as fly-over—or drive-through—territory by travelers heading to better-known places in Croatia or Italy. But it deserves more attention (and time) than most travelers expect.

The general lack of international tourists is good news for anyone choosing Slovenia as a destination, either in its own right or as a highlight during a visit to the region. It means fewer crowds—even in the peak summer touring months—fewer hassles and, in many ways, a more relaxed travel experience with a chance to get to know the friendly and sophisticated Slovenian people. While you can still expect to encounter some crowds during busy summer weekends in Ljubljana, the number of visitors pales compared to a more popular destination like Amsterdam, Rome, or Copenhagen. While Slovenia's beautiful artistic monuments and charming towns may lack the grandeur and historical importance found in neighboring Italy or Austria, they still cast a captivating spell. Every corner of the country is packed with beautiful towns and even more beautiful experiences.

And when it comes to natural beauty, Slovenia easily competes with other European countries. The Julian Alps northwest of the capital are every bit as spectacular as their sister Alpine ranges in Austria, Italy, and Switzerland, and the magnificent countryside and the quietly elegant charm of Ljubljana await those with the imagination to choose a destination that is off the beaten path. Lake Bled is one of the most beautiful lakes in all of Europe and well worth a visit in its own right.

That isn't to say that crowds are absent—far from it—and Slovenia's most magical spots are growing in popularity with every passing year. You can't blame the crowds, that's for sure, and Slovenia's reputation as Europe in miniature is well deserved. This is a country of romance, creativity, excitement, and beauty, where adorable towns built around picturesque churches are the norm. Slovenia is a true "something for everyone" destination, the sort of place that captures hearts and refuses to let go, and those hearts are all the better for it.

Lake Bled

Slovenia's Most Famous and Most Romantic Spot

Bled's famed lake is nestled within a rim of mountains and surrounded by forests, with a castle on one side and a promenade beneath stately chestnut trees on the other. Horse-drawn carriages clip-clop along the promenade, while swans glide on the water, creating the ultimate romantic scene. On a tiny island in the middle of the lake, the lovely Cerkev svetega Martina (St. Martin's Pilgrimage Church) stands within a circle of trees. Take a ride over to the island on a*pletna*; a traditional covered boat.

Don't Miss

The stately Bled Castle perches above the lake on the summit of a steep cliff against a backdrop of the Julian Alps and Triglav Peak. You can climb up to the castle for fine views of the lake, the resort, and the surrounding countryside. An exhibition traces the development of the castle through the centuries, with exhibits from archaeological artifacts to period furniture on display, but the view steals the show.

Getting Here

If traveling by train, the nearest station is in Lešče-Bled, 5 km to the east. bus is a much better option, with several options daily from Ljubljana. Buses also run directly from Ljubljana Airport. Bled is easily accessed by car; from Ljubljana, take E57 west, followed by E61.

Bled Tourist Information Center. ✉ *Cesta Svobode 10, Bled* ☎ *(386 4) 574–11–22* 🌐 *www.bled.si*

Triglav National Park

Everything That Is Great About Slovenia

Covering some 4% of Slovenia's entire landmass, it can be argued that Triglav National Park is the ideological and spiritual heart of the country. The iconic three peaks of Triglav (the highest point in the country) are found on Slovenia's coat of arms and its flag, placing this dreamland of gorges, caves, waterfalls, rivers, and forests front and center for the nation. Mountain huts dot the landscape offering affordable accommodations for those looking to wander the meadows. Slovenia's only national park, Triglav contains everything that makes Slovenian nature magnificent, all within 840 square km (324 square miles) of magic.

Don't Miss

Lake Bohinj is the quieter, wilder, and prettier sister of Bled and lies entirely within the Triglav National Park. The entire length of the north shore is wild, and accessible only by foot. The lake, at an altitude of 1,715 feet, is surrounded on three sides by the steep walls of the Julian Alps. The altitude means the temperature of the water rarely rises above a brisk but still swimmable 74°F. The small village of Ribčev Laz, on the eastern end of the lake, functions as the de facto town center.

Getting Here

Triglav National Park is accessed via public buses from nearby towns or private vehicles. The best way is to arrive via public bus from Kranjska Gora, over the dramatic Vršič Pass.

✉ *Bohinjsko Jezero* ☎ *(386 4) 578–0200*
🌐 *www.tnp.si*

Piran

Small but Perfectly Formed Pearl on Slovenia's Coast

The jewel of the Slovenian coast, the medieval walled Venetian town of Piran stands compact on a small peninsula, capped by a neo-Gothic lighthouse and presided over by a hilltop Romanesque cathedral. Narrow, winding, cobbled streets lead to the main square, Trg Tartini, which opens out onto a charming harbor. Historically, Piran's wealth was based on salt making. Culturally, the town is known as the birthplace of the 17th-century violinist and composer Giuseppe Tartini. A statue of the great man stands in the square that takes his name.

Don't Miss

Eating by the sea is a real privilege here. Highly regarded by the locals, the tiny, family-run TK focuses on all manner of local fish, grilled or fried; don't miss the grilled shrimp or calamari. Consistently well-cooked, this place is worth a visit. In summer, you can dine at tables along the quiet street. Less touristy and more affordable than the restaurants along the seafront, Neptun only serves local catches rather than the imported farmed fish from Italy and Greece, like so many of their neighboring establishments.

Getting Here

Several buses run from Ljubljana to Piran daily, from early in the morning until the afternoon. This is usually the best option, as parking in Piran is expensive. The nearest train station is Koper, a 45-minute bus ride from Piran.

Piran Tourist Information Center. ✉ *Tartinijev trg 2, Piran* ☎ *(386 5) 673–4440* 🌐 *www.portoroz.si*

Škocjan Caves

An Incredible Underworld Recognized by UNESCO

The 11 interconnected chambers that compose the Škocjan Jama stretch for almost 6 km (about 4 miles) through a dramatic, subterranean landscape so unique that UNESCO has named them a World Heritage Site. The 90-minute walking tour of the two chilly main chambers—the Silent Cave and the Murmuring Cave—is otherworldly as winds swirl around the dripstone sculptures, massive sinkholes, and stalactites and stalagmites that resemble the horns of a mythic creature. The Reka River is the reason for everything here, and the miraculous water also allows flora and fauna to survive in this magical underworld. Škocjan has been a protected area since 1996, but people have been expressing their love for this place for thousands of years.

Don't Miss

The highlight is Europe's largest cave hall, a gorge 479 feet high, 404 feet wide, and 984 feet long, spanned by a narrow bridge illuminated with footlights. Far below, the brilliant jade waters of the Reka River rush by on their underground journey. The view is nothing short of mesmerizing.

Getting Here

Getting to Škocjan from Ljubljana is relatively easy, with several buses and trains running from the capital to Divača daily. From there, it is a 3-km (2-mile) hike to the cave network, although the busy season sees plenty of shuttle buses and taxis making the trip considerably easier.

✉ *Škocjan 2, Divača* ☎ *(386 5) 7082–110*
🌐 *www.park-skocjanske-jame.si*

Kobilarna Lipica

Majestic Horses and More Than 400 Years of Heritage

Founded in 1580 by the Austrian Archduke Karl II, the Kobilarna Lipica was where the white Lipizzaners—the majestic horses of the famed Spanish Riding School in Vienna—originated. The horses are more gray than white, but that is just the tip of the iceberg; they are actually born dark and turn gray due to a mutated gene. Visitors see a range of shades today, and each horse is as beautiful as the last. These are modest yet intelligent beasts, easy to teach, and made for the performances they give three times a week during the summer. Today, the farm no longer sends its horses to Vienna but breeds them for its own performances and riding instruction. The impressive stables and grounds are open to the public. Riding classes are available, but lessons are geared toward experienced riders and must be booked in advance.

Don't Miss

There is no shortage of activities at Kobilarna Lipica, but interacting with these majestic animals is undoubtedly the highlight. The ultimate experience is the full house; a visit to the stud farm followed by some rigorous training, a serene carriage ride, and one of Lipica's trademark performances. You can also play golf if you are into that sort of thing.

Getting Here

From Ljubljana, buses run to Divača and Sežana, where local buses continue to Lipica. Trieste is a 25-minute drive away, and the Italian city is also the location of the nearest airport.

✉ *Lipica 5, Sežana* ☎ *(386 5) 739–1708*
🌐 *www.lipica.org*

When in Slovenia

★ Franja Partisan Hospital
MILITARY SIGHT | FAMILY | This is the best-preserved and the most exciting of WWII Partisan hospitals, which served as a clandestine aid center for wounded resistance soldiers, tucked away in a gorge and secluded ravine where the Nazis would not have looked. Named after the doctor that helped run it, Franja was attacked but never actually discovered at its location deep in the Pasice gorge in the village of Dolenji Novaki. From its opening in December 1943 to liberation in May 1945, a total of 522 wounded soldiers of various nationalities were treated there. Be it a 20-minute nature walk or few hours' exploration, experiencing the Franja Partisan Hospital is an ideal and active way to add variety to traditional museum excursions. Well-written information boards will lead you up a stunning path to 14 wooden cabins that served as the hospital complex. ✉ *Dolenji Novaki pri Cerknem, Cerkno* ☎ *05/372–3180* 🌐 *www.muzej-idrija-cerkno.si* ⏲ *Closed Nov.–Mar.*

★ Ljubljanski Grad (*Ljubljana Castle*)
CASTLE/PALACE | Ljubljana's hilltop castle affords views over the river and the Old Town's terracotta rooftops, spires, and green cupolas. On a clear day, the distant Julian Alps are a dramatic backdrop. The castle walls date from the early 16th century, although the tower was added in the mid-19th century. The surrounding park was landscaped by Plečnik in the 1930s. The castle also houses a virtual museum showcasing Slovenian history through digital technology. Take a step back through time and do the tour, it's a great introduction to Ljubljana. The castle is also home to the Museum of Puppetry, one of the most underrated museums in the city. ✉ *Studentovska ul, uphill from Vodnikov trg, Grajska planota 1, Ljubljana* ☎ *01/306–4293* 🌐 *www.ljubljanskigrad.si* 🎫 *€16 (including funicular).*

Logarska Dolina
Slovenia is one of the most beautiful countries on the planet, and every city, town and village seems to be picture-perfect in its own special way. The most beautiful view in the country? That might just go to Logarska Dolina, specifically the stunning entrance to this glacial Alpine valley. Pictures don't do it justice, but that doesn't mean you shouldn't take a snap or 10. Logarska Dolina is 75 km (47 miles) north of Ljubljana, not far from the border with Austria, and it is packed with natural sights and darling mountain hut restaurants. ✉ *Logarska Dolina 9, Solčavkso* ☎ *03/838–9004.*

Postojnska Jama (*Postojna Cave*)
CAVE | FAMILY | This is one of the largest networks of caves in the world, with 23 km (14 miles) of underground passageways. A miniature train takes you through the first 7 km (4½ miles) to reveal a succession of well-lighted rock formations. This strange underground world is home to the snakelike "human fish" on view in an aquarium in the Great Hall. Eyeless and colorless because of countless millennia of life in total darkness, these amphibians can live for up to 60 years. Temperatures average 8°C (46°F) year-round, so bring a sweater, even in summer. Tours leave every hour on the hour May through October and three to four times a day November to April. ✉ *Jamska 30, Postojna* ☎ *05/700–0100* 🌐 *www.postojnska-jama.eu* 🎫 *€28.*

Ptujski Grad (*Ptuj Castle*)
CASTLE/PALACE | The centerpiece of Slovenia's oldest town, Ptujski Grad stands atop a steep hill in the center of Ptuj. Planned around a Baroque courtyard, the castle houses a museum that houses musical instruments, an armory, 15th-century church paintings, and period furniture. The views from the castle are sublime, and there is a café for those looking to refresh themselves in a gorgeous setting. Ptuj is a beautiful little town 30 km (19 miles) south of Maribor

Slovenia
Liezen
Wiener Neus
S6
E57
Bruck
Leoben
Hartberg
E59
AUSTRIA
Graz
Zwischenwas
Spittal
Wolfsberg
S37
E55
E57
Villach
Klagenfurt
E55
Davograd
201
E652
E653
Vršic Pass
Jesenice
Maribor
Soteska Vintgar
Logarska Dolina
Ptujski Grad
Triglav National Park
Lake Bled
Radovljica
Slovenska B
Radovljica Chocolate Festival
Kranj
E59
Žalec Beer Fountain
Celje
Varazdin
ITALY
Most na Soc
Franja Partisan Hospital
E61
E57
102
Ljubljana
Ljubljanski Grad
Odprta Kuhna
Vrhnika
Visnja Gora
Krsko
E71
E61
E70
SLOVENIA
Postojnska Jama
Postonja
Zagreb
E70
Novo Mesto
Kobilarna Lipica
106
Trieste
Škocjan Caves
Kocevje
E70
Piran
E71
Karlovac
E61
E65
Rijeka
Ogulin
CROATIA
Labin
Slunj
Cres
Baskc
Senj
Pula
Plitvička
Cres
Bihac
BOSNIA AND HERZEGOVINA
E65
Adriatic Sea
Unije
Mali Losinj
Covici
Lošinj
Pag
Olib
0
20 mi
0
20 km
Gracac
Nin

and well worth a visit. ✉ *Grajska Raven, Na gradu 1, Ptuj* ☎ *02/748–0360* 🌐 *www.pmpo.si* 🎫 *€2.*

Soteska Vintgar (*Vintgar Gorge*)
CANYON | FAMILY | This gorge was cut between precipitous cliffs by the clear Radovna River, which flows down numerous waterfalls and through pools and rapids. The marked trail through the gorge leads over bridges and along wooden walkways and galleries. It was discovered almost by accident in 1891 by a photographer and local mayor, but the authorities were quick to recognise its potential. By 1893 it was open to the public, and this stunning 1.6km gorge of natural beauty has been stealing hearts ever since. The vertical walls of the Hom and Boršt hills create a real sense of drama. If you are heading to Triglav National Park from Bled, this is the most exciting (and beautiful) way to do it. ✉ *Zgornje Gorje Rd., Podhom 80, 5 km (3 miles) northwest of Bled, Bled* 🌐 *www.vintgar.si.*

Vršič Pass
MOUNTAIN | From Kranjska Gora, head south over the breathtaking Vršič Pass, some 5,253 feet above sea level. You'll then descend into the beautiful Soča Valley, winding through the foothills to the west of Triglav Peak and passing truly magnificent scenery in the process. From Trenta, continue west for about 20 km (12 miles) to reach the mountain adventure resort of Bovec. The Vršič Pass isn't for the faint of heart, and every hairpin turn is fraught with danger, but roads in Slovenia don't come much more exhilarating than this. The truly brave should make the journey via bus from Kranjska Gora.

Žalec Beer Fountain
OTHER ATTRACTION | Beer lovers, welcome to heaven. Žalec is Slovenia's beer capital, a small town in the centre of the country that is famous for its hops and the magic they make, and this place knows how to honor its traditions. In the center of the town is a beer fountain with a selection of brews available for sampling. Simply rock up to the kiosk, buy a glass, and enjoy your six samples from the world's first beer fountain. Žalec is a button-cute town with history around every corner, but the real magic lies in the beers that flow through its soul. ✉ *Savinjska cesta 11, Žalec.*

Where to Eat and Drink

★ Čokl
$ | CAFÉ | Ljubljana's caffeine-mecca, Čokl is a postage stamp-sized café that serves up the best coffee in the city, at least according to those in the know. The terrace is a lovely spot to spend an afternoon, especially taking into account how small the interior is. **Known for:** impressive coffee expertise; teeny-tiny interior; Ljubljana's best espresso. $ *Average main: €2* ✉ *Krekov trg 8, Ljubljana* ☎ *041/837–556.*

Daktari
CAFÉS | With its hodge-podge of furniture and an undeniable artistic streak running through the walls, Daktari is a veritable Ljubljana institution. A wide range of patrons regularly enjoys the packed schedule of events here or simply an evening of drinks and discussion, from early in the morning until late at night. You won't find a more eclectic crowd anywhere else in the city, in a more eclectic environment. Daktari is Ljubljana at its very best, with cold beer and hot coffee in abundance. ✉ *Krekov trg 7, Ljubljana* ☎ *05/9055-538* ✉ *info@daktari.si.*

★ Druga Violina
$ | SLOVENIAN | FAMILY | The gorgeous Stari trg location and a hearty menu filled with Slovenian classics would be enough to justify a cheerful lunch at Druga Violina, but there is more to this spot than initially meets the eye. The restaurant doubles up as an initiative to help people with disabilities in the region, a talented group of people who help grow the ingredients

on a nearby farm and work as the wait staff in the restaurant itself. **Known for:** fresh, locally grown produce; traditional Slovenian food; socially aware outlook. *Average main: €10* *Stari trg 21, Ljubljana* *82/052–506* *Closed Mon.*

★ Hiša Franko

$$$$ | **SLOVENIAN** | Hiša Franko, or the House of Franko, is Slovenia's highest-rated eatery. The internationally awarded chef, Ana Roš, makes use of homegrown vegetables and fresh trout from the nearby alpine-water creek with rare inventiveness and skill. **Known for:** first-class wine cellar; cheese produced on premises; creative menu. *Average main: €225* *Staro selo 1, Kobarid* *05/389–4120* *www.hisafranko.com* *Closed Mon, Tues.*

The Human Fish Taproom

BREWPUBS | Slovenia's original craft beer is best enjoyed at its brewery, located in Vrhnika, an easy 25-minute journey from Ljubljana. The selection of beers is extensive (including a no-alcohol Respectable Fish), and the terrace is a great spot for a quiet afternoon drink with great conversation. Matt is just about as friendly as hosts get, with a veritable well of stories and information. There is also an actual dartboard, and such things should always be celebrated. The taproom is closed Monday and Tuesday. *Tržaška cesta 27, Ljubljana* *030/381–473* *www.facebook.com/taproomvrhnika.*

Cool Places to Stay

★ Bohinj Park ECO Hotel

$$ | **HOTEL** | **FAMILY** | As the first ecological hotel in Slovenia, Park ECO has won a litany of awards, all for good reason. **Pros:** furnishings made from all-natural materials; vegetarian options; entertainment for all ages and skill levels. **Cons:** large, full hotel; conferences can seemingly take over the hotel; a little on the pricey side of things. *Rooms from: €150* *Triglavska cesta 17, Bohinjsko Jezero* *08/200–4140* *www.bohinj-eco-hotel.si* *102 rooms* *Free Breakfast.*

Hotel Grad Otočec

$$$$ | **HOTEL** | The medieval Otočec castle, dating from the 13th century, is now a luxury hotel, complete with period furniture. **Pros:** historic setting; beautiful rooms; nearby golf and thermal baths. **Cons:** few on-site amenities. *Rooms from: €294* *Grajska 1, Otocec* *07/384–8901* *booking.grad-otocec@terme-krka.si* *www.terme-krka.si* *16 rooms* *Free Breakfast.*

Vila Bled

$$ | **HOTEL** | Late Yugoslav president Tito was the gracious host to numerous 20th-century statesmen at this former royal residence amid 13 acres of gardens overlooking the lake. **Pros:** unforgettable lake views; old-school elegance; free Wi-Fi in rooms. **Cons:** rooms can seem a bit dated if you're not a fan of retro style; café and restaurant on the expensive side; hard to get to without private transport. *Rooms from: €150* *C. Svobode 26, Bled* *04/575–3710* *www.brdo.si/vila-bled* *31 rooms* *Free Breakfast.*

Croatia

With 1,778 km (1,111 miles) of coastline and more than a thousand islands, Croatia is one of Europe's most beautiful seaside destinations. Backed by dramatic mountains, Dalmatia's sapphire-blue waters are scattered with pine-scented islands and presided over by finely preserved, walled medieval towns packed with Venetian monuments. But like its Balkan neighbors, Croatia has a history shadowed by conflict and strife.

The region's earliest inhabitants were the Illyrians, and the principal tribe, the Delmata, gave their name to Dalmatia. The coastal region was colonized by Greece and later Rome. Dalmatia (excluding Dubrovnik, which remained an independent republic) eventually came under the rule of Venice. Lying on the trade route to the Orient, port towns such as Split and Hvar flourished, and many of Croatia's finest buildings date from this period. After Venice fell in 1797, all of Croatia was under Austro-Hungarian rule by the 19th century.

After Germany declared war on Yugoslavia in 1941, Josip Broz Tito founded the Partizan movement, aimed at pushing Fascist forces out of the area. When the war ended, Tito created the Socialist Federal Republic of Yugoslavia, with Croatia as one of six constituent republics. The Tito years saw a period of peace and prosperity, and during the 1960s, Croatia became a popular international tourist destination.

Following Tito's death in 1980, an economic crisis set in, and relations between Croatia and the Serb-dominated Yugoslav government deteriorated. In 1989, Franjo Tudjman founded the Croatian Democratic Union (HDZ), calling for an independent Croatia, while in Serbia the nationalist leader Slobodan Miloševic rose to power. In 1991 Croatia declared independence. The events that followed led to a horrendous civil war in which some 20,000 people were killed and hundreds of thousands were displaced. After the war, a decade of political and economic isolation ensued, as the country gradually reentered Europe, joining the European Union on July 1, 2013.

Diocletian's Palace

A Palace Fit for an Emperor in a Gorgeous Old Port City

The home of Split's thriving Old Town, Diocletian's Palace is a marvelous maze of restaurants, cafés, shops, and boutiques. The palace dates back to the late 3rd century AD and originally served as both a luxurious villa and a Roman garrison. Its rectangular shape has two main streets: Dioklecijanova Ulica, which runs north to south, and Poljana Krajlice Jelene, which runs east to west, dividing the palace complex into four quarters. Each of its four walls has a main gate, the largest and most important being the northern Zlatna Vrata (Golden Gate), which once opened onto the road to the Roman settlement of Salona. The Mjedna Vrata (Bronze Gate) on the south wall directly faces the sea and likely served as an entryway for sailors who docked by it during Roman times.

Don't Miss

The main body of the Cathedral of St. Domnius is the 3rd-century octagonal mausoleum designed as a shrine to Emperor Diocletian. The elegant, 200-foot, Romanesque-Gothic bell tower was constructed and reconstructed in stages between the 13th and 20th centuries. Climb to the top of the bell tower (sometimes closed in winter during bad weather) for a spectacular view of the entire palace, Split, and the surrounding Adriatic Sea.

Getting Here

Diocletian's Palace is the centerpiece of Split, a short walk from the bus station. The city itself is well-connected by plane, bus, and ferry.

✉ *Split, Splitsko-Dalmatinska*
🌐 *visitsplit.com*

Dubrovnik Old Town

A Stunning Old Town That Lives Up to the Hype

Nothing can prepare you for your first sight of Dubrovnik. Completely encircled by thick fortified walls with a maze of gleaming white streets within, it is truly one of the world's most beautiful cities. And it never gets old; whether admiring it from the top of Mt. Srđ, from a kayak out at sea, or standing in the middle of the Stradun looking around you in awe, your imagination will run wild picturing what it looked like when the walls were built eight centuries ago, without any suburbs or highways around it, just this magnificent stone city rising out of the sea.

Don't Miss

Dubrovnik's city walls define the Old Town and are one of the world's most stunning architectural achievements. A walk along the top is the ultimate Dubrovnik must-do for the magnificent views of the sea and Lokrum Island outside the walls and the terra-cotta rooftops within. The walls encircle the Old Town as part of a fortification system that also includes four gates, and the entire circuit takes a couple of hours if you stop for photos and maybe a drink along the way.

Getting Here

An official bus shuttles visitors from the airport to Dubrovnik bus station (buses depart 30 minutes after every flight arrival), and the old town is 3 km (3 miles) from the station. Local buses (lines 1A, 1B, 3) run frequently, and there is never a shortage of taxis.

Dubrovnik Tourist Information Center. ✉ *Stradun 21, Dubrovnik* ☎ *(385 20) 323–350* 🌐 *visitdubrovnik.hr*

Hvar Stari Grad

Sea Life and Cocktails on Croatia's Most Magnificent Island

Some locals claim that Stari Grad is the oldest town in Europe. Founded in the fourth century BC, this is the site of the original Greek settlement on Hvar, called *Pharos*by the Greeks. While much of the attraction in Stari Grad focuses on its ancient history, the city is still very much alive throughout the year. It features a beautiful, walkable riviera and forest path, as well as a number of cultural attractions. The island of Hvar bills itself as the "sunniest island in the Adriatic." And it even has the figures to back up this claim—an annual average of 2,760 hours of sunshine with a maximum of two foggy days a year.

Don't Miss

The 16th-century hilltop Fortica fortress is a symbol of Hvar Town. Climbing to the top takes about 25 minutes, and you get to take in the amazing Mediterranean plant garden as you go. Once you're at the top, you can explore the fortress's stone walls and behold breathtaking views of the city below, along with the sea and islands stretching over the horizon as far as the eye can see.

Getting Here

Frequent ferries run from Split to Hvar, taking between 50 minutes and two hours.

Hvar Tourist Information Center.
✉ *Trg Svetog Stjepana 42, Hvar*
☎ *(385 21) 741-059* 🌐 *visithvar.hr*

Plitvice Lakes National Park

A Miraculous Series of Glistening and Impossibly Green Terraced Lakes

This 8,000-acre park is home to 16 beautiful emerald lakes connected by cascading waterfalls, stretching 8 km (5 miles) through a valley flanked by high, forested hills home to deer, bears, wolves, wild boar, and the Eurasian lynx. Thousands of years of sedimentation of calcium, magnesium carbonate, algae, and moss have yielded the natural barriers between the lakes, and since the process is ongoing, new barriers, curtains, stalactites, channels, and cascades are constantly forming, and the existing ones changing. The deposited sedimentation, or tufa, also coats the beds and edges of the lakes, creating their sparkling, azure look.

Don't Miss

With unadorned log walls, wood-beam ceilings, white-curtained windows, lively Croatian folk music playing, and an open kitchen with an open hearth, **Lička Kuća** is exactly what a restaurant in a great national park should be.

Getting Here

The park is right on the main highway (E71) from Zagreb to Split, and it is certainly worth the three-hour trip from the capital. There are three entrances just off the main road about an hour's walk apart, creatively named Entrance 1, Entrance 2, and auxiliary Entrance Flora. There is a bus station by entrances 1 and 2, with direct buses to Zagreb and Karlovac.

✉ *Licko-Senjska* ☎ *(385 53) 751–014*
🌐 *np-plitvicka-jezera.hr*

Pula Arena

Travel Back in Time to Gladiator Days

Designed to accommodate 23,000 spectators, Pula's arena is the sixth-largest building of its type in the world (after the Colosseum in Rome and similar arenas in Verona, Catania, Capua, and Arles). Construction was completed in the 1st century AD under the reign of Emperor Vespasian, and the Romans staged gladiator games here until such bloodthirsty sports were forbidden during the 5th century. It has remained more or less intact, except for the original tiers of stone seats and numerous columns that were hauled away for other buildings. Today it is used for summer concerts (by musicians including Sting, James Brown, and Jose Carreras), opera performances, and the annual film festival in mid-July. The underground halls house a museum with large wooden oil presses and amphorae.

Don't Miss

The Pula Film Festival lights up the arena every summer with a national and international schedule of films for movie lovers. The Croatian film industry awards are usually presented at the festival, thought to be the oldest one of its type in the country. The setting is utterly perfect.

Getting Here

Pula arena is an easy 10-minute walk from the city's bus station, which is well-connected to other cities in Croatia and neighboring countries. Pula Airport is 6 km from the city center and has connections with several European cities, including London, Frankfurt, Brussels, and more.

✉ *Flavijevska ulica bb, Pula, Istarska, Croatia* ☎ *052/219–028* 🌐 *www.pulainfo.hr* 🎫 *70 Kn*

Zadar

Magical Music and Incredible Light Shows in Dalmatia's Old Capital

Zadar is too often passed over by travelers on their way to Split or Dubrovnik. What they miss out on is a city that is remarkably lovely and lively despite—and, in some measure, because of—its tumultuous history. The Old Town, separated from the rest of the city on a peninsula some 4 km (2½ miles) long and just 1,640 feet wide, is bustling and beautiful: the marble pedestrian streets are replete with Roman ruins, medieval churches, palaces, museums, archives, and libraries.

Don't Miss

Comprising 35 pipes under the quay stretching along a 230-foot stretch of Zadar's atmospheric Riva promenade, the Sea Organ yields a never-ending concert that delights one and all. The organ's sound resembles a whale song, but it is in fact the sea itself. Directly next to the organ is the whimsically named Greeting to the Sun, a 22-meter circle of multilayered glass plates set into the stone-paved waterfront. Under the glass, light-sensitive solar modules soak up the sun's energy during daylight hours, turning it into electrical energy. Just after sunset, it puts on an impressive light show, illuminating the waterfront in shades of blue, green, red, and yellow.

Getting Here

Zadar is well-connected, with an international airport with flights from several major European cities and a central bus station for connections within Croatia. There are also ferries to Ancona (Italy).

Zadar Tourist Board. ✉ *Jurja Barakovića 5, Zadar* ☎ *(385 23) 316–166* 🌐 *zadar.travel*

Zagreb's Christmas Markets

Eastern Europe's Best Christmas Market

Advent in Zagreb is the most wonderful time of the year at its most magical, when the entire city comes alive in a mass of festive cheer. The Croatian capital is a beautiful city year round, but Zagreb shimmers and sparkles at Christmas in a way that begs to be seen. Advent season in Zagreb usually runs from the end of November to the beginning of January, meaning there are plenty of opportunities to get merry in these most magical surroundings. All the classic Advent activities are found here, from button-cute stalls selling festive souvenirs to a conveyor belt of hearty food and heartier booze. The events schedule is packed with traditional and contemporary events, and there is always something to keep the kids busy while the adults focus on getting merry. Sure, the weather gets a little chilly, but Zagreb is at its lightest during Advent. If you're looking for somewhere to get festive, look no further than the charming Croatian capital.

Don't Miss

The ice-skating rink on Trg Kralja Tomislava is one of the highlights, and it can be as much fun watching the action as donning the skates yourself. This is especially true with a piping hot cup of glühwein in hand.

Getting Here

Flights from the U.S. to Zagreb require a connection in Europe. Once you are there, Advent covers much of the city, but the main action takes place in and around Trg Ban Jelačić, the main square.

Zagreb Tourist Information Center. ✉ *Trg Ban Jelačić 11, Zagreb* ☎ *(385 1) 48–14–051* 🌐 *www.infozagreb.hr*

Zlatni Rat

Croatia's Most Picturesque Beach, One That Changes Shape Every Day

Croatia has more than 100 blue flag beaches up and down its coast, but there is a reason Zlatni Rat is the poster boy of them all. Pure aesthetics, for a start, as there are few more beautiful beaches on the planet. Obviously, you'd need wings to get the complete picture of the beach's beauty, but the view from the pebbles is more than stunning enough. There is more to Zlatni Rat than meets the eye, although that which meets the eye is plenty stunning. The beach actually changes shape depending on the tides and winds, meaning no second trip to Zlatni Rat is technically the same as the first. Those winds encourage plenty of windsurfing in these parts, with adventures for experts and lessons for novices available nearby. If you prefer your beach visits to be of the nude variety, head to the westernmost tip for the nudist sections.

Don't Miss

Without sounding too obvious, what better activity on Croatia's best beach than lazing the day away in the sun with a good book? Embrace the serenity.

Getting Here

Zlatni Rat is a simple stroll from Bol on the southern side of Brač island, a peaceful amble through pine trees and serenity that ends with a slither of smooth pebbles and a slice of Dalmatian paradise. Brač itself is a 50-minute ferry from Split.

Brač Tourism. 🌐 *www.visitbrac.com*

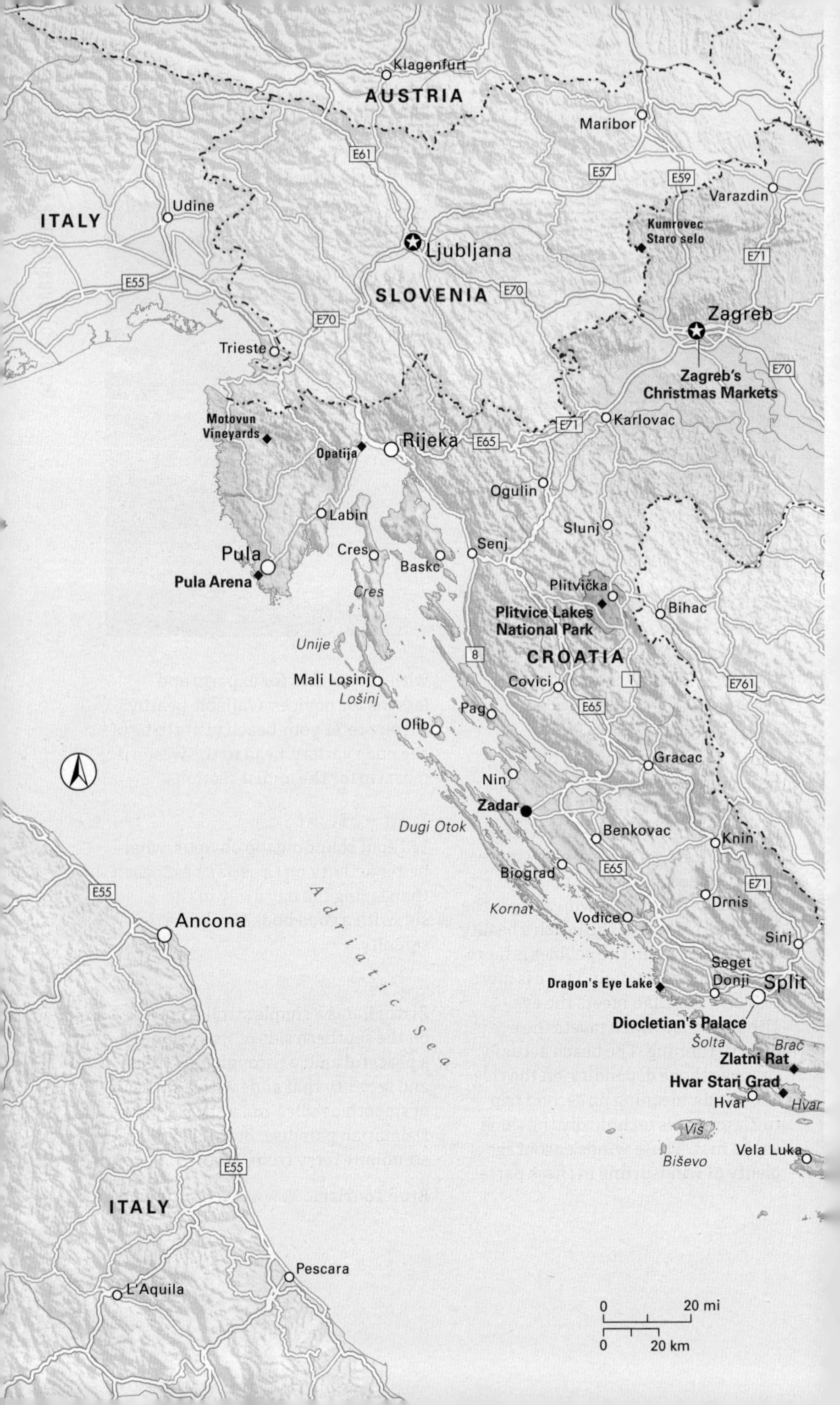

AUSTRIA
Klagenfurt
Maribor
E61
E57
E59
Varazdin
ITALY
Udine
Kumrovec Staro selo
Ljubljana
E71
SLOVENIA
E70
E55
Zagreb
Trieste
Zagreb's Christmas Markets
Motovun Vineyards
Opatija
Rijeka
E65
Karlovac
Ogulin
Labin
Slunj
Pula
Cres
Baskc
Senj
Pula Arena
Cres
Plitvička
Plitvice Lakes National Park
Bihac
Unije
CROATIA
Mali Losinj
Lošinj
Covici
E761
Pag
Olib
Gracac
Nin
Zadar
Dugi Otok
Benkovac
Knin
Biograd
Kornat
Drnis
Vodice
Ancona
Adriatic Sea
Sinj
Seget Donji
Split
Dragon's Eye Lake
Diocletian's Palace
Šolta
Brač
Zlatni Rat
Hvar Stari Grad
Hvar
Viš
Biševo
Vela Luka
ITALY
Pescara
L'Aquila
0 20 mi
0 20 km

Croatia
HUNGARY
E73
Kaposvár
Szeged
Pécs
2
Subotica
Virovitica
E73
45
Donji
Mihol
Podravska S
Kopački Rit
Nature Park
Daruvar
2
Osijek
E661
2
E73
Novska
Dakovo
Gradski
Muzej Vukovar
Zrenjanin
E70
Slavonski B
Novi Sad
Prijedor
E661
E70
Belgrade
Banja Luka
Šabac
E73
Tuzla
BOSNIA AND
HERZEGOVINA
SERBIA
Jajce
Zenica
E661
Valjevo
Gornji Vaku
Sarajevo
E761
Livno
Užice
Cačak
E761
Konjic
E762
Kraljevo
E73
E65
Mostar
Gdinj
Stolac
Novi Pazar
Bacina
MONTENEGRO
Korcula
Korcula
E762
E65
Mali Ston
Lastovo
Niksic
Mljet
Lastovo
Prozura
Brsecine
Pec
Dubrovnik
E80
Dubrovnik Old Town
KOSOVO
E65
Podgorica
Hercegnovi
Budva
ALBANIA

When in Croatia

Dragon's Eye Lake

BODY OF WATER | Nobody is entirely sure how it came to be, but visitors shouldn't trouble themselves with thoughts of origin. The Dragon's Eye Lake is a magnificent natural phenomenon, an oval lake surrounded by massive cliffs with water that gets warmer the deeper you go. A base of hydrogen sulfide explains the latter, although don't worry, it is completely safe to swim here. Dragon's Eye Lake is in Rogoznica, a small settlement 40km or so south of Šibenik, 55km from Split. ✉ *Rogoznica.*

★ Gradski Muzej Vukovar (*Vukovar Municipal Museum*)

The 18th-century palace Dvorac Eltz has housed the Gradski Muzej Vukovar since 1969. During the siege of Vukovar, the palace was severely damaged and the collection was moved to a Zagreb museum for safekeeping. After decades of reconstruction, the entire museum and all 2,000 of its pieces are once again open for viewing, a positive sign that Vukovar is back in business. Founded in 1946, the museum was originally housed in an old school and then a post office before the palace became its home. It has an excellent range of local archaeological artifacts, from the Vučedol culture that flourished around 3000 BC right up to the siege of Vukovar. ✉ *Županijska 2, Vukovar* ☎ *032/441–270* 🌐 *www.muzej-vukovar.hr* 🎫 *€5.30* ⏲ *Closed Mon.*

★ Kopački Rit Nature Park

SCENIC DRIVE | Kopački Rit Nature Park is one of the largest remaining wetlands along the Danube and a place of serene beauty. Embracing more than 74,100 acres immediately north of the Drava, 10 km (6 miles) northeast of Osijek, the park is covered with immense reed beds, willow, poplar, and oak forests, and crisscrossed by ridges, ponds, shallow lakes, and marshes. More than 300 bird species, hundreds of varieties of plants, and dozens of species of butterflies, mammals, and fish live here, and it is also a breeding area for numerous endangered species, including the white-tailed sea eagle, the black stork, and the European otter. Getting to Kopački Rit from Osijek is simple if you have a car—follow the signs once you're in Bilje. If you go by bus, get off in Bilje and follow the signs on foot for some 4 km (2½ miles) along rural roads to the entrance of the park or ride a bike from Osijek. ✉ *Information Center near Kopačevo, Kopacevo* ☎ *031/445–445* 🌐 *www.pp-kopacki-rit.hr* 🎫 *150 Kn for Beaver's Trail.*

★ Kumrovec Staro selo (*Kumrovec Old Village*)

MUSEUM VILLAGE | **FAMILY** | The old quarter of Kumrovec is an open-air museum with beautifully restored thatched cottages and wooden farm buildings, orchards, and a stream giving a lifelike reconstruction of 19th-century rural life. On weekends craftsmen, including a blacksmith, a candlemaker, and others, demonstrate their skills. This is the birthplace of Josip Broz Tito, the man who led Yugoslavia from the end of World War II until his death in 1980, so expect plenty of Yugostalgia. ✉ *Kumrovec BB, Kumrovec* ☎ *049/225–830* 🌐 *www.mss.mhz.hr* 🎫 *€5.30.*

Motovun Vineyards

WINERY | Croatia is a rising star on the European wine scene, and oenophiles owe it to themselves to pay a visit to the northern region of Istria. The village of Motovun, in particular, as this small spot is surrounded by stunning vineyards producing quality wines in a gorgeous setting. Several organized tours are available, jaunts that take thirsty visitors through many vineyards for tastings, education, food, and all the rest. Motovun is a medieval beauty in and of itself, a photogenic quality that only increases with every fresh glass of wine. That's how it works, right? ✉ *Motovun, Motovun.*

Opatija

TOWN | Croatia is a tourism hotspot these days, but it wasn't always like this. Rewind the clock back just 150 years, and things were very different. In fact, it wasn't until the building of Hotel Kvarner (1884) in Opatija that things began. Opatija has since become known as the home of Croatian Tourism, and the Istrian town is a byword for relaxation and bliss. Many of Croatia's oldest spas and wellness centers are here, making it the perfect spot for relaxation and rejuvenation. Add some fantastic seafood, the Croatian Walk of Fame, and one of the most romantic promenades in the country, and you've got a honeymoon destination like no other. ✉ *Opatija* 🌐 *www.visitopatija.com.*

Where to Eat and Drink

Marvlvs Library and Jazz Bar

Located in the house where Marko Marulić (the father of Croatian literature) was born, Marvlvs Library & Jazz Bar is one big love letter to creativity and all that influences it. The wine list is extensive and excellent, while the frequent live jazz concerts nestle alongside poetry readings and literary events on the calendar. The back room is arguably Split's most marvelous secret nook, and the staff are among the most engaging in the city. Marvlvs also serves a crisp pint of Guinness if you are after something a little heftier. ✉ *Papalićeva 4, Split* ☎ *98/963-7067.*

★ Noel

$$$$ | **MODERN EUROPEAN** | Zagreb's first Michelin-starred restaurant is completely deserving of that honor, serving up high-quality gastronomy with an extensive French, Italian, and Croatian wine list to match. And everything is offered in a charming location hidden among the narrow streets of the city center. **Known for:** great cocktail menu; vegetarian options; seasonal, predominately local produce and meat. $ *Average main: €176* ✉ *Ulica Popa Dukljanina 1, Zagreb* ☎ *1/4844–297* 🌐 *noel.hr* ⏲ *Closed Sun. No lunch.*

The Old Pharmacy Pub

PUBS | There is no shortage of British-style boozers across the continent these days, and many of them have rolled over into the world of caricature. Not so The Old Pharmacy Pub, a beer-focused establishment with a story to tell and the perfect environment for telling it. A fantastic place to enjoy any major sporting event or drink a bucketful (not literally) of beers with friends, The Old Pharmacy Pub is a guaranteed good time. ✉ *Ul. Andrije Hebranga 11a, Zagreb* ☎ *91/245-6183.*

★ Pelegrini

$$$$ | **MEDITERRANEAN** | In a carefully restored 14th-century palazzo opposite the historic St. James Cathedral in Šibenik sits the magnificent Pelegrini. The menu features traditional Dalmatian cuisine that is innovatively prepared, with exquisite flavor being the restaurant's guiding principle. **Known for:** excellent Dalmatian cuisine; extensive wine list; four-course minimum for dinner. $ *Average main: €110* ✉ *Jurja Dalmatinca 1, Šibenik* ☎ *022/213–701* 🌐 *www.pelegrini.hr/en.*

Restaurant 360

$$$$ | **MEDITERRANEAN** | This restaurant's terrace—atop Dubrovnik's historic city walls—is one of the most stunning dining settings in Croatia, a location that offers unbeatable views of the glimmering sea, with a menu that holds up its end of the bargain. The flavors and traditions of Dubrovnik and the Mediterranean dominate the menu, with subtle touches that keep diners coming back time and time again. **Known for:** extensive wine list with deep offerings from Croatia; local specialties like Ston Bay oysters and lamb from the country's mountainous interior; modern interpretations of traditional Croatian cuisine. $ *Average main: €128* ✉ *Sv. Dominka bb, Dubrovnik*

☎ *20/322–222* 🌐 *360dubrovnik.com* ⏲ *Closed Mon. No lunch.*

Cool Places to Stay

★ Grand Park Hotel Rovinj

$$$$ | HOTEL | FAMILY | Emerging from the fragrant pine forest, this hotel has an unbelievably perfect location on the waterfront opposite Sv. Katarina Island and the charming Old Town of Rovinj, an excellent restaurant, a top spa, and luxurious accommodations. **Pros:** spectacular location overlooking Old Town Rovinj; exceptional Cap Aureo Restaurant; indoor and outdoor pools. **Cons:** shared beach with Katarina Hotel on island across; outdoor infinity pool can get crowded; some suites on lower floors do not have views. $ *Rooms from: Kn3025* ✉ *Smareglijeva ulica 1A, Rovinj* ☎ *052/800–250* 🌐 *www.maistra.com/grand-park-hotel-rovinj* *209 rooms* *Free Breakfast.*

Ninon

$$$ | HOTEL | A quite gorgeous boutique hotel in a gorgeous village on the coast, Ninon leaves no stone unturned in the quest for that perfect stay. **Pros:** contemporary (yet somewhat austere) style; restaurant serving local food only to hotel guests; all rooms have breathtaking sea views. **Cons:** more of a retreat; 20 minutes drive from Dubrovnik; no children allowed. $ *Rooms from: €277* ✉ *Ulice Podubrave 1, Brsečine* ✣ *25 km northwest of Dubrovnik* ☎ *99/8888–525* 🌐 *www.myninon.com* *9 rooms* *Free Breakfast.*

★ San Canzian Village & Hotel

$$$$ | HOTEL | A luxurious boutique hotel has been created from several old houses found in the medieval village of Mužolini Donji, near Buje, Momjan, and Grožnjan. **Pros:** high-style interiors throughout; excellent restaurant with a knowledgeable sommelier; peaceful and restorative energy. **Cons:** more spa services needed; changing chefs; a drive to the beach. $ *Rooms from: €220* ✉ *Muzolini Donji 7, Grožnjan* ☎ *0992/302–0000* 🌐 *san-canzian.hr* ⏲ *Closed Jan.–Mar.* *24 rooms* *Free Breakfast.*

★ Villa Giardino (*Villa Giardino Heritage Boutique Hotel*)

$$ | B&B/INN | Set in a quiet garden full of Mediterranean greenery, this hotel is just a five-minute walk from the harbor. **Pros:** attentive staff; peaceful yet centrally located; breakfast served in lovely garden. **Cons:** often fully booked; limited facilities; on the expensive side. $ *Rooms from: Kn1285* ✉ *Novi put 2, Brac* ☎ *021/635–900* 🌐 *www.villagiardinobol.com* ⏲ *Closed Nov.–Apr.* *5 rooms* *Free Breakfast.*

Bulgaria

For many first-time visitors, Bulgaria still comes with a caveat. Maybe it's the lingering memories of communism and the Soviet Union—Bulgaria was always portrayed (accurately) as the most pro-Soviet of the Eastern bloc satellite states. The country's relatively remote location, tucked away in the far southeastern corner of Europe, helped to contribute to this image of intrigue and mystery. But that's already ancient history.

Foreign tourists are quickly discovering the country's charms. Bulgaria (along with neighboring Romania) is one of the fastest-growing tourist destinations in Europe. Visitors are drawn first and foremost to the Black Sea resorts. The coastal towns and resorts here are increasingly attracting visitors from Britain, Scandinavia, and Germany. And word of the mountain resorts, the secluded monasteries, and the charming, historically rich cities of Plovdiv and Veliko Târnovo is spreading quickly.

Bulgaria is one of Europe's oldest nations, founded in AD 681 by the Bulgars, but Bulgaria was a crossroads of civilization thousands of years before then. Archaeological finds in Varna, on the Black Sea coast, show evidence of inhabitance as early as 4600 BC.

Modern Bulgaria was formed at the end of the 19th century, with the country's liberation from the Ottoman Empire. Bulgaria weathered the two World Wars of the 20th century more or less intact but fell within the Soviet sphere of influence at the end of World War II. On January 1, 2007, nearly 20 years after throwing off their communist oppressors, Bulgarians achieved their long-sought-after objective of joining the European Union. Change is in the air. EU membership brought with it a flood of foreign investment in the form of new roads, office blocks, and apartments, and a plethora of new hotels and resorts, particularly on the Black Sea coast.

Rila Monastery

The Country's Most Significant Spiritual SIte

The perfect mixture of history, culture, nature, and spirituality? That'll be Rila Monastery. The story of the monastery's origins is one that touches on all of those aspects. Considered Bulgaria's first hermit, Saint John of Rila took to these mountains to live a life of intense piety, eschewing everything in the 10th century in favor of prayer and solitude. John's life became big news, and soon people were heading here in search of blessings and for a glimpse of a living saint. The number of followers grew, and eventually, this monastery was built. That was in AD 927, and Rila Monastery has been Bulgaria's most important monastery ever since. It was vital to keeping the Bulgarian flame alive during the long Ottoman centuries, giving life to language and culture, while it also acted as a hideout for many of Bulgaria's most significant revolutionaries.

Don't Miss

At 1,147 meters above sea level, the monastery is surrounded by astonishing greenery that only adds to the aura of tranquillity. The central church is a beauty, with religious scenes depicted in vivid color as Hreylo's Tower (the oldest building in the complex) stands proudly next door.

Getting Here

The best way to reach the secluded location in the Rila Mountains is with a private vehicle or on a guided tour. There is a direct return bus from Sofia (from Ovcha Kupel station) on weekdays at 10:20 am, and the journey takes two hours and 40 minutes.

✉ *Kyustendil* ☎ *(359) 7054–3383* 🌐 *rilski-manastir.org*

Buzludzha Monument

The Most Famous Abandoned Monument in Europe

Bulgaria's fascinating Buzludzha Monument has to be in the conversation when talking about abandoned monuments in Europe. Well, that is the Monument House of the Bulgarian Communist Party, to be exact, although maybe it is easier to stick with Buzludzha (the name of the mountain on which the building stands). As the lengthy moniker suggests, the building was constructed as a monument to a century of communism in Bulgaria, built on the spot where optimistic youths established the Bulgarian Social Democratic Party 100 years earlier. The end of Communism meant the end of maintaining the building, and it soon fell into ruin. Designating most of Europe's Communist monuments as "UFO-like" is lazy, but there is no getting around it here. The saucer shape of the building is from a different world, and it isn't difficult to see why this place has been the site of many music videos and movies.

Don't Miss

Most of the incredible mosaics that covered its walls have been lost to time, weather, or vandalism, and restoration efforts mean the monument is now guarded 24/7. The days of entering and exploring are over, but the exterior is more than awe-inspiring enough to make a trip up here a must.

Getting Here

It's not really close to a major destination, being 250 km (155 miles) from Sofia and 77 km (48 miles) from Veliko Tarnovo. There are two roads to the monument, one leading from Kazanlak in the south and another from Gabrovo in the north. There is no public transport.

🌐 *www.buzludzha-project.com*

Veliko Tarnovo

The City of Tsars Was Once the Capital of a Mighty State

One of Bulgaria's oldest settlements, Veliko Tarnovo is a popular weekend getaway for upper-middle-class urbanites and a beloved stop on the backpacker trail. It's an idyllic small town through which the Yantra River runs, and terra-cotta-roofed homes sit on the ridges above it. Despite its growing popularity and ever-growing abundance of expat-focused businesses, Veliko Tarnovo manages to maintain an air of old-world charm. It also happens to be spellbindingly beautiful, which is never a bad thing.

Don't Miss

A stupendous structure, Tsarvets was the Second Bulgarian Empire's most significant fortress from 1185 to 1393. The royal palaces were housed here, along with hundreds of quarters for the members of the court, guards, servants, churches, and workshops. Tsarevets, as you see today, is not the original (it has been sacked and destroyed many times), but a faithful restoration that was undertaken between 1930 and 1981. The views from the top of the fortress are magnificent. If you aren't feeling in the mood to climb all the way up, there is an elevator to the top of the bell tower.

Getting Here

Veliko Tarnovo is relatively easy to get to, no matter which direction you are traveling in. Direct buses run from Sofia, Varna, Plovdiv, Ruse, and Burgas, with trains coming from the latter three towns.

Veliko Tarnovo Tourist Information Center. ✉ *5 ul. Hristo Botev* ☎ *(359 62) 622–148* 🌐 *www.velikoturnovo.info*

Aleksandar Nevski Cathedral

Sofia's Most Magnificient Landmark

Named after the Russian Tsar who saved his country from invading Swedish troops in 1240 (and is also revered as a saint in Bulgaria), this imposing Neo-Byzantine building is one of the largest Orthodox churches in the world and dominates central Sofia. Built as a memorial to 200,000 Russian soldiers who died in the Russo-Turkish Liberation War (1877–78), the foundation stone was laid in 1882, but it was not completed until 1912. Covering an area of more than 30,000 square feet and said to be able to hold up to 10,000 people, it was worked on by some of Russia's and Bulgaria's best artists. Sofia wouldn't be Sofia without its beating heart of a cathedral.

Don't Miss

The external architecture is simply beautiful, and its multidomed roof reaches 175 feet at its highest point. The interior, which has five aisles, three altars, and plenty of imported Carrara marble, is gloomy and dimly lit, but this adds to the mystical atmosphere.

Getting Here

You can't really miss the cathedral, and you'll find it right in the center of the city. The cathedral can be visited between 7 am and 7 pm every day, with weekly worship services at 8 am and 5 pm.

✉ *Pl. Sveti Aleksandar Nevski, Sofia*
☎ *(359 2) 988–1704* 🌐 *www.cathedral.bg*

Shipka Memorial Church

A Gorgeous Church Dedicated to Bulgarian Fighters for Independence

The Shipka Memorial Church (also known as the Memorial Temple of the Birth of Christ) is one of the most striking churches in Bulgaria. It originally served as a Russian Orthodox Church but was passed over to the Bulgarian Orthodox counterpart following independence; still, the Russian influence is everywhere here. You can see it in the glistening onion domes peeking through the trees at the foot of the Stara Planina mountains. You can see it in the design of the exterior (17th-century Muscovite, for the record), and you can read it in the names that adorn the interior walls. Those names are of Bulgarian, Russian, and Ukrainian soldiers who died in the brutal Russo-Turkish War of 1877–78, a war that led to the reestablishment of the Bulgarian state after nearly 500 years of Ottoman rule. The church (and wider complex) is a living site, so be sure to dress respectfully and act as such, although such things should go without saying.

Don't Miss

Many soldiers are buried in stone sarcophagi found in the church's crypt. At the other end of the church, the 53-meter bell tower is gorgeous, and its bells were cast from cartridges used in the battles.

Getting Here

To visit the church, buses run directly from Plovdiv and Stara Zagora, although a scenic option is to meander along one of the many hiking trails that traverse the Shipka Pass.

✉ 6150 Shipka ☎ (359 88) 990–2368
🌐 bulgariatravel.org

When in Bulgaria

Baba Vida Fortress

CASTLE/PALACE | FAMILY | On the banks of the Danube is this well-preserved medieval fortress, which dates back to the 10th century and was a defensive stronghold through the Middle Ages. It was captured by the Ottomans and used as storage space for food and munitions and, after liberation in 1878, was used by the Bulgarian army. It opened as a museum in the mid-1950s and is today a popular spot for filming. From the tops of the towers and the walls, take in panoramic views of the Danube River and the surrounding cityscape. ✉ *Ul. Baba Vida, near Ul. Kazarmina, Vidin* ☎ *094/601–705* 🎫 *BGN 4.*

Balchik Old Town

TOWN | Balchik can trace its history back more than 2,000 years to the Ancient Thracians. That history is not as immediately obvious, but it is still a charming old town, some 15 miles north of Varna, with plenty to keep visitors interested. It enjoys an attractive location, pinned to the Black Sea Coast by being at the foot of sandy cliffs that dominate it from above. Much of its appeal lies in wandering the streets lined with whitewashed houses. The picturesque setting has attracted generations of artists who come to paint the scene—Balchik seascapes are regularly seen in galleries across the country. The lack of beach here has kept mass tourism at bay, giving the town a sleepy feel that only adds to its charms. Between the two World Wars, the town found itself part of the Kingdom of Romania, and during this time, the Balchik Palace was built as a summer residence for Queen Marie and her family. The elegant whitewashed villa (open daily) and the adjacent Botanical Gardens are the town's most popular landmarks to this day. ✉ *Balchik Sq. 21 September Sq., Balchik* 🌐 *www.balchik.bg.*

Belogradchik Rocks

MOUNTAIN | FAMILY | Running along the western slopes of the Balkans Mountains are these gorgeous rock formations, some of which stand more than 650 feet (200 meters) tall. The rocks, made of sandstone and conglomerate, are believed to have started forming a cool 230 million years ago. They're mostly reddish brown in color with some yellow tinges and look especially beautiful as the sun sets and illuminates their cliffs. The groups of rocks closest to central Belogradchik have interesting names based on local legends, like the Schoolgirl, the Madonna, and the Mushrooms. Whether you hike up to the plateau or walk leisurely around the lower levels, the views over the forest are phenomenal. You can see the rocks on a day-trip from Sofia. ✉ *Belogradchik* ☎ *93/630–01* 🌐 *belogradchishki-skali.weebly.com.*

Carnival of Humor and Satire

ARTS FESTIVALS | You can never have enough laughter in your life, and Bulgaria's House of Humor and Satire is well aware of this. The cultural center in Gabrovo was established in 1972 with the expressed aim of bringing laughter into as many lives as possible, through exhibitions, live events, a packed library, and more. The week-long Carnival of Humor and Satire is the crowning glory of the House, a festival of joy that takes place every May. Expect theater shows, exhibitions, and all sorts of fun at the carnival, a blast of color unlike anything else in Europe. ✉ *Bryanska 68, Gabrovo* ☎ *66/807–229* 🎫 *BGN 6* 🕒 *Closed Mon.*

Lake Atanasovsko

BODY OF WATER | Did you know Bulgaria has a pink lake that is home to a large population of flamingos? You do now. Just north of Burgas on the Black Sea, Lake Atanasovsko is a treasure trove of biodiversity, with over 230 species of plants and more than 300 different types of birds calling it home. Flora and fauna aside, Lake Atanasovsko is absolutely

Bulgaria
MOLDOVA
ROMANIA
E574
E85
E60
Focşani
Braşov
Galati
E81
Tulcea
Buzău
Rimnicu Vil
E574
Ploieşti
E85
Piteşti
E87
E81
Drobeta-Tur
A2
E70
Bucharest
Constanta
Călăraşi
Craiova
E70
Ruse
Vidin
Baba Vida Fortress
Dobrich
Magura Winery
E70
E87
Belogradchik Rocks
Balchik Old Town
E83
Pobiti Kamani
Montana
Pleven
Shumen
Varna
E85
E79
Prohodna Cave
Lovec
SERBIA
Vratsa
Veliko Tarnovo
E772
Aleksandar Nevski Cathedral
Carnival of Humor and Satire
Buzludzha Monument
E87
Black Sea
Lake Atanasovsko
Shipka Memorial Church
Sliven
Sofia
E871
Burgas
Pernik
E80
BULGARIA
E871
Stara Zagor
Plovdiv Ampitheater
Kyustendil
Skiing on Borovets
E85
E80
E79
Plovdiv
Rila Monastery
Khaskovo
E87
E80
Edirne
Lüleburgaz
E80
TURKEY
Xanthi
E79
Seres
E84
E90
Kavala
Alexandroup
E75
GREECE
Thessaloniki
E90
Aegean Sea
Çanakkale
Katerini
Balıkesir
E87
Larissa
0
50 mi
0
50 km
Volos

beautiful, an immensely photogenic landscape of salt, swamps, and sun, with healing mud-bathing to boot. The Lake Atanasovsko Nature Reserve is a 20-minute drive north of Burgas, with a taxi or private vehicle being your best bet. ✉ *Lake Atanasovsko, Burgas.*

★ Magura Winery

WINERY | Whether you're a keen oenophile or just enjoy a good glass of wine, touring Magura Winery's cellars is a really fun way to pass an afternoon. The winery, in the village of Rabisha, 20 km (12½ miles) from Belogradchik, opened in 1967. Growing conditions in the region are favorable and, as such, the grapes here produce some of the country's best sparkling wine. Bottles are stored in the 15-million-year-old Magura Cave. Three levels of guided tastings are available, starting from 25 leva per person on weekdays. All tastings include a selection of wine and a platter of cheese and cold appetizers. ✉ *Village of Rabisha, Vidin district, Rabisha* ☎ *093/29–6230* 🌐 *www.magurawinery.bg* 🎫 *BGN 25.*

Plovdiv Amphitheater

RUINS | Plovdiv is an absolute must-visit for many reasons, from its charming old town to its thriving culinary scene. It also has a strong claim to being the oldest continually inhabited city in Europe. The main event? That will be the remarkable 2nd-century amphitheater, or the Roman theater of Philippopolis, to be exact. One of the finest preserved Roman amphitheaters on the planet, it once held around 7,000 spectators and has been restored to its former glory, becoming one of the most incredible venues in Europe along the way. It is all the more incredible that the amphitheater was lost to the world until a landslide in 1972. ✉ *Plovdiv* ☎ *32/621–040* 🌐 *www.oldplovdiv.bg* 🎫 *BGN 5.*

Pobiti Kamani

NATURE SIGHT | Bulgaria's stone desert is different, to say the least. This is the only desert in Eastern Europe, after all, and one of only two in Europe (Spain's Tabernas Desert is the other) that formed naturally. Nobody is entirely sure how it all came about, but that doesn't deter visitors, who head to this miraculous spot near Varna in search of cacti, desert reptiles, and seven groups of stone pillars that are supremely photogenic. Despite being such a unique phenomenon, the Stone Desert is strangely quiet, so visitors can expect to have much of it to themselves. Pobiti Kamani is a half-hour drive east of Varna. Alternatively, get the scenic train to Beloslav and pick up a taxi from there. ✉ *Varna* ✥ *24 km (15 miles) west of Varna.*

Prohodna Cave

CAVE | Dare you gaze into the Eyes of God? Okay, not the literal eyes of a deity, but the two holes that poke out the ceiling of Prohodna Cave have earned that moniker. The holes were formed by years of erosion and are found in the cave's central chamber, letting light flood into an otherwise pitch-black world. There is more to the cave than deity peepers, and the big entrance has developed into a wildly popular spot for bungee jumping. That entrance also happens to be the biggest cave arch in Bulgaria, yet another reason to visit Prohodna. The Eyes of God take center stage (quite literally), with accommodation available in a nearby mountain hostel. ✉ *Karlukovo*

Skiing on Borovets

SKIING & SNOWBOARDING | Bulgaria offers some of the best-value skiing in Europe, and Borovets might be the best value within the country itself. Bansko might be bigger and more celebrated, but the variety of things on offer at Borovets makes it a favorite of all who visit. There are plenty of tree-lined slopes for all abilities, while the postskiing activities at the resort are borderline famous. Let's just say that many a second morning's ski has been delayed because of late breakfasts. Night skiing is also available, another bucket list experience found on beautiful Borovets. Sofia is 70 km (44 miles) north of Borovets, and the drive takes around 80 minutes. ✉ *Rila Hotel, Borovets* ☎ *889/607–000* 🌐 *www.rilaborovets.com.*

Where to Eat and Drink

Cosmos

$$ | **EASTERN EUROPEAN** | Sofia's most exciting restaurant is a culinary experience from another world and one of the best restaurants in Bulgaria, make no mistake about it. Not literally, of course, but Cosmos is committed to taking diners from the streets of the capital into the stars via a dizzying universe of flavors and techniques, not to mention a hefty dose of creativity. **Known for:** great service; good Balkan wine list; reasonable prices for such sophisticated cuisine. $ *Average main: leva25* ✉ *Lavele St. 19, Sofia* ☎ *888/200–700* 🌐 *cosmosbg.com.*

Ethno Restaurant Burgas

$$ | **MEDITERRANEAN** | This charming spot in Burgas will exceed your expectations every time. Blue and white checkerboard cloths adorn the tables as one traditional meal after another flies out of the kitchen. **Known for:** good seafood offerings; cash only; vegetarian-friendly. $ *Average main: leva16* ✉ *Aleksandrovska 49, Burgas* ☎ *88/787–7999* 💳 *No credit cards.*

Izbata Tavern

$$ | **EASTERN EUROPEAN** | Sofia has no shortage of international restaurants focused on the future of food, but Izbata takes diners in a different direction. The past is king here, where a traditional interior makes the perfect environment for hearty Bulgarian classics like *kavarma* (a pork and vegetable stew), *dolma* (pork wrapped in cabbage leaves), and *kapama* (sauerkraut with a difference). **Known for:** wide selection of Bulgarian wines; menu full of traditional favorites; meat-heavy menu with some vegetarian choices. $ *Average main: leva24* ✉ *Slavyanska 18, Sofia* ☎ *29/895–533* 🌐 *tavern.izbata.bg.*

Mehana Chiflika

$ | **EASTERN EUROPEAN** | Tradition is everything at Chiflika. Located in the small city of Ruse, this old-school tavern transports diners to the villages via homely recipes and a veritable cavalcade of folk music, bringing the comforts of the mountains into the heart of the city. **Known for:** nightly entertainment; popular for large groups; historic setting. $ *Average main: leva7* ✉ *Otetz Paisiy 2, Ruse* ☎ *88/744–8348* 🌐 *chiflika.eu.*

Philippopolis

$$ | **EUROPEAN** | Named after the grand amphitheater that attracts visitors to Plovdiv from all over the world, Philippopolis is a gorgeous garden restaurant in the old town. This is the sort of place that bridges the divide between high-class business dinners and ultraromantic date nights, with a menu of international classics expertly cooked. **Known for:** lovely garden for outdoor dining; wide selection of fine Balkan wines; feels like eating dinner in an art museum. $ *Average main: leva28* ✉ *Suborna 29, Plovdiv* ☎ *32/622–742* 🌐 *www.philippopolis.com* ⏲ *No lunch.*

Vodenitzata

$$ | **EASTERN EUROPEAN** | An old Bulgarian proverb states that it is not the size of the table that matters, but the size of the heart, something taken seriously at Vodenitzata. This is Bulgarian hospitality at its most pure, embellished with traditional food and a desire to make everyone feel at home. **Known for:** inviting garden for outdoor dining when the weather is nice; cold tarator soup and barbecued lamb; nightly folk music and dancing. $ *Average main: leva19* ✉ *Kv. Dragalevtsi, Park Vitosha, Sofia* ☎ *29/671–058* 🌐 *vodenitzata.com.*

Cool Places to Stay

Belchin Spring

$$$ | **RESORT** | The modern world is a hectic place, and taking time to relax and reset is more important than ever, making this full-service spa resort an inviting destination. **Pros:** full-service spa; family-friendly; excellent sports facilities. **Cons:** restaurant could be better; quite expensive rates for Bulgaria; staff are not always friendly and helpful. *Rooms from: leva280 c. Belchin 2025, Belchin www.belchin-spring.com 48 rooms, 14 villas Free Breakfast.*

Grand Hotel Sofia

$$$ | **HOTEL** | Fancy some five-star pampering in the heart of Sofia at three-star prices? Hotels in Bulgaria can offer fabulous value to visitors from the U.S. and Western Europe, and the Grand is living proof of this. **Pros:** very reasonable rates; close to everything; rooms are spacious and comfortable. **Cons:** fine furnishings may be overwhelming to guests looking for simplicity; breakfast gets a mixed review; some guests report slow check-in. *Rooms from: leva185 Ul. Gurko 1, Sofia 02/811–0811 www.grandhotel-sofia.bg 105 rooms Free Breakfast.*

Jägerhof

$$ | **HOTEL** | A slice of Bavarian brilliance in Plovdiv, Jägerhof is an exercise in high-class quality and impeccable service. **Pros:** modern design; great service; good on-site brewery. **Cons:** can be busy with large meetings; can't easily adjust room temperature; food in restaurant gets mixed reviews. *Rooms from: leva133 Saedinenie Str 2, Trakia, Plovdiv 32/347–060 jagerhof.bg 50 rooms No Meals.*

Sol Marina Palace

$$$ | **RESORT** | This really is a palace, make no mistake; it's a place defined by opulence, grace, and class. **Pros:** modern rooms; convenient location near the sights and beach; helpful staff. **Cons:** food in restaurant doesn't always match up to the quality of the hotel; small pool; attracts some large, loud groups. *Rooms from: leva230 Ivan Vazov 7, Nessebar 55/420–600 www.melia.com 123 rooms All-Inclusive.*

Romania

For most of the 21st century, tourism to Romania by international visitors has been growing at a steady clip by about 10 percent every year. Outdated notions of Romania from the 1980s and 1990s have begun to be replaced by a more forward-looking vision that acknowledges the country's charming villages, gorgeous scenery, and inviting locals.

Admittedly, the 40 years the country spent under Communism, especially the last decade of Nicolae Ceaușescu's reign in the 1980s were brutal, and Romania has had to cope with serious problems, including the long-known issues with overcrowded and inadequate orphanages that were long a source for international adoptions. But look beyond the stereotypes, and you'll see a totally different side to the story.

It's no stretch to say Romania may be Europe's last great, unspoiled frontier. In the remote areas of Maramureș and Transylvania, you'll find vast tracts of pristine wilderness and a traditional way of life that remains untouched by modern civilization. The Carpathian mountains cut north to south through the center of the country, affording marvelous hikes through fir-covered forests.

Several Transylvanian cities claim intact medieval districts, and fortified churches dominate the villages. To the northeast, the beautiful and intricately painted monasteries of Bucovina are UNESCO World Heritage monuments (the country now has nine UNESCO-designated sights). In the southeast, you'll find a watery wilderness where the Danube River ends its long journey across Europe and empties into the Black Sea. Even the capital city Bucharest seems to sparkle with new energy and vitality these days. On January 1, 2007, Romania achieved its long-term goal of joining the European Union, but the country is still working slowly to reform its economy so that it can adopt the euro. Nevertheless, EU entry has brought hundreds of millions of dollars of investment capital and, more importantly, a renewed sense of pride and confidence to Romania. More than 30 years after the 1989 revolution, Romania has not only arrived—it appears poised for prime time, a destination where tourism is growing faster than in almost any other country in Europe.

Transfâgăraşan Highway

One of the World's Great Road Trips

An appearance on *Top Gear* in 2009 brought international fame to the Transfâgăraşan Highway, but those in the know have been aware of its majesty for years. Romania's most famous road is one of the great driving adventures of Europe. The highway was built between 1970 and 1974, as an increasingly paranoid Nicolae Ceauşescu demanded a route to move troops north should Communist Romania be invaded by the Soviet Union. While that never happened, Ceauşescu's anxiety created a spectacularly scenic route. The road is filled with dramatic hairpins, sharp descents, and serpentine stretches, meaning it isn't for amateurs. The road closes between October and May, as winter weather makes it too dangerous.

Don't Miss

The road traverses more than 150 km (93 miles) and reaches heights of 2,042 meters. Along the way you can see a former residence of Vlad the Impaler and a statue of Prometheus. Arguably, Lake Bâlea, a glacial lake high up in the Făgăraș Mountains, is the highlight. Driving the entire road without stopping should take four hours, but neglecting the sights and sounds would be foolish. There are a handful of food options along the road, while accommodation is best enjoyed on either end. For the best experience (and to ease yourself in somewhat), start in the south near the small town of Bascov.

Getting Here

The Transfâgăraşan (officially known as DN7C) starts near the village of Bascov and weaves through the Carpathians, marrying the regions of Transylvania and Wallachia. You'll need your own vehicle.

Bran Castle

It Was Never Dracula's Home

There are plenty of reasons to love Bran Castle, but a history of vampiric habitation is not among them. More puzzling perhaps is that Romania's most popular tourist attraction looks nothing like the description of Dracula's home in Bram Stoker's classic tale, nor does it have any direct relation to Vlad the Impaler, Dracula's historical inspiration. The location, however, is stunning, as the medieval fortress is dramatically perched on a hill near beautiful Brașov, overlooking what was once a hugely important and influential trade route. And its quick construction (begun in 1377) is but one of the structure's marvels.

Don't Miss

Now a museum dedicated to Marie, the beloved last Queen of Romania, the castle displays her furniture and art collection. Queen Marie used the castle as her summer residence and loved the place, turning it into a comfortable home. The castle is a veritable warren of winding corridors, elegant staircases, and ostentatious rooms, every bit the opulent palace one might expect.

Getting Here

The popularity of the castle makes it a relatively easy visit, with buses running frequently from Brașov to Bran, where plenty of taxis await the mass of visitors.

✉ *Strada General Traian Moșoiu 24, Bran* ☎ *(40 268) 237–700* 🌐 *www.bran-castle.com* 🎫 *From 55 lei*

Palace of the Parliament

The Heaviest Building in the World and a Relic of a Different Time

This mammoth modern building—one of the largest in the world—stands witness to the megalomania of the former dictator Nikolae Ceauşescu. Today, it houses the Romanian parliament. Unlike the royal palaces, every detail is Romanian, from the 24-karat gold on the ceilings to the huge handwoven carpet on the floor. Forty-five-minute tours of the ground-floor rooms depart from an entrance on the northern end of the building (the right-hand side as you stand facing the building from the front). Engineering estimates say it weighs a whopping 4.10 million tons, making it the heaviest building in the world. There's no shifting this one.

Don't Miss

With a building this massive, a guided tour is a must. There are plenty available, and all cover the same subjects, telling visitors about the building's construction with plenty of fascinating tidbits thrown in for good measure. It also doubles up as a decent workout; you'll be getting your steps in, that's for sure.

Getting Here

You would be right in assuming the heaviest building in the world is fairly easy to find. To get in, enter via B-dul Naţiunile Unite on the northern side of the behemoth, and bring identification.

✉ Strada Izvor 2–4, Bucharest ☎ (40 733) 558–0240 🌐 cic.cdep.ro 🎫 60 lei Tours are offered daily, but they must be reserved by phone 24 hrs in advance

Alba Carolina Citadel

The Star-Shape Citadel in Alba Iulia Is Utterly Unique

Why aren't all fortresses star-shape? A trip to Alba Iulia's star attraction (pun intended) certainly makes a case in favor of the shape. The Alba Carolina Citadel fortress was originally constructed in the 13th century, but it took its modern form in the 18th century, joining two previous fortresses with a fancy new design. The construction of the star-shape citadel was completed by more than 20,000 serfs, with Italian architects, craftsmen, and designers lending a hand along the way. Its purpose was to fortify some new territory acquired by the Habsburg Empire. The allure today is more to tourists and birds. Three of the original seven gates have been restored as faithfully as possible, and the fortress is a conveyor belt of stories, myths, legends, and history. The Union Museum and Union Hall offer plenty of the latter, being the site for the unification of Romania and Transylvania.

Don't Miss

Be sure to make time for the changing of the guards, one of the most fascinating traditions in these parts, with visitors encouraged to take photos with the various ranks on duty.

Getting Here

To get to Albaq Iulia, there are direct trains from Bucharest, Timișoara, Sibiu, Cluj-Napoca, and more. It is hard to miss Romania's biggest fortress once you're here.

✉ *Calea Moților, Numărul 5A, Alba Iulia* 🌐 *turism.apulum.ro* 🎫 *20 lei*

Sibiu Lutheran Cathedral

The Largest Organ in Southeastern Europe

Sibiu's Lutheran Cathedral of St. Mary is a highlight of any visit to the city. It's a monolith, with its 73-meter-high tower visible from all points. The views from the top are every bit as marvelous as you'd expect, though the climb up the steeple takes time and isn't for the short of breath—but the vistas awaiting you are worth the struggle. The Gothic beauty was built in stages over 170 years, with work starting in 1350 and finally coming to a conclusion in 1520. Work never ends on major cathedrals, and this one is no exception. The tomb of Mihnea Vodă cel Rău is found here, and the cathedral's use as a burial ground isn't entirely unusual. Many of Sibiu's most significant medieval personalities were laid to rest here, although that stopped at the end of the 18th century. The death theme continues with the four turrets outside; these informed visitors that the town had the right to sentence folks to death. Be warned, evildoers, be warned.

Don't Miss

The organ isn't just for show, and concerts are frequently held here during the summer. The acoustics are every bit as fantastic as you might assume, and the grandiose aura of the cathedral makes it an incredible music venue.

Getting Here

Sibiu is a major city in the Transylvania region of Romania, about 4 hours (285 km [177 miles]) northwest of Bucharest. A train from Bucharest takes almost six hours, while the direct bus makes the trip in five hours. Sibiu also has direct air service from several European destinations. The cathedral is visible from most of the city, standing proud on Piaţa Albert Huet.

✉ *Piaţa Albert Huet, Sibiu* 🌐 *sibiucity.ro* 🎫 *10 lei*

Romania
Kiev
Lutsk
Rivne
Zhytomyr
E85
Bila Tserkv
Lvov
POLAND
E40
E50
Ternopil
Khmelnytsky
Vinnytsya
UKRAINE
E50
Uman
E50
Ivano-Frank
Kamyanets-P
SLOVAKIA
Košice
Chernivtsi
E85
Miskolc
Merry Cemetery
Botoşani
Satu Mare
Baia Mare
Suceava
Voroneț Monastery
E576
Debrecen
Chişinău
HUNGARY
Iaşi
E58
Bistrita
Oradea
MOLDOVA
E60
Cluj-Napoca
Untold Festival
E671
Bacău
Salina Turda
Tirgu Mures
E85
E81
Arad
Alba Carolina Citadel
ROMANIA
E68
E574
E68
Timişoara
Sibiu
Focşani
Letea Forest
Sibiu Lutheran Cathedral
Braşov
Bran Castle
Galati
Berca Mud Volcanoes
Peleş Castle
Tulcea
E7
Transfăgărașan Highway
Buzău
Fishing in the Danube Delta
Reşita
Rimnicu Vil
Ploieşti
E70
E85
Piteşti
E87
E81
Belgrade
Drobeta-Tur
Bucharest
A2
Palace of the Parliament
E574
Constanța
Călăraşi
Constanta Casino
Craiova
Comana Natural Park
E70
Ruse
SERBIA
Dobrich
Varna
Vratsa
E772
Turnovo
0
50 mi
E87
0
50 km
Pristina
BULGARIA
Sofia
KOSOVO
Burgas
Stara Zagor
Black Sea
Plovdiv
Skopje
Edirne
NORTH MACEDONIA
Istanbul
GREECE
TURKEY
Aegean Sea
Thessaloniki
Bursa

When in Romania

Berca Mud Volcanoes

HOT SPRING | Getting muddy has never been more perplexingly beautiful. Of course,.the Berca Mud Volcanoes don't shower onlookers in mud (it tends to solidify at the surface), but this natural phenomenon is truly fascinating nonetheless. The whole thing feels a bit like being on the moon, if the moon were in eastern Romania. This unique landscape is also home to strange flora that only add to the otherworldly feel of it all. Be sure to dress appropriately (it is all pretty muddy, after all), and don't expect public transport to make its way to these parts. A private vehicle is the way to go. ✉ *Pâclele*

Comana Natural Park

Southern Romania's largest protected area is in Comana, a commune of five small villages. The park covers more than 60 acres and its management has done a great job catering to families and outdoors enthusiasts. Bike trails run through the forest (bicycles are available for hire), and there are tennis and basketball courts, a pick-your-own garden with herbs and vegetables, a few restaurants serving local cuisine, and an adventure park where kids (and eager adults) can climb trees and a rock wall, ride horses, and practice archery. You can fish, kayak, and canoe within the park and watch birds in the protected bird area. Weekends are quite crowded; come early. ✉ *Strada Gellu Naum 608, Comana* ☎ *37/299–8863* 🌐 *www.comanaparc.ro.*

Constanta Casino

NOTABLE BUILDING | Visiting abandoned buildings has become wildly popular in the social media age, and abandoned buildings in Romania don't come more beguiling than the stunning Art Nouveau wonder that is (was?) Constanta Casino. The casino opened in the late 19th century but didn't take on its current form until 1910, although the violence of the two World Wars put a stop to the entertainment. Romania's communist government turned it into a House of Culture, but maintaining the place became almost impossible as time passed. It shut in 1990 and has been neglected ever since. Occasional attempts to renovate mean visiting isn't always possible. ✉ *Bd. Regina Elisabeta 4, Constanta* 🌐 *cazino-constanta.ro.*

Fishing in the Danube Delta

FISHING | The Danube is one of the most important rivers in Europe, a behemoth that flows through countries and gave birth to a wide range of hugely influential cities. The hustle and bustle of the city is a world away from the tranquillity of its delta, and there are few experiences more serene than a spot of fishing in these parts. What can you catch? Everything from pike to carp, with plenty of variety between, although fishing in the Danube Delta is less about the catch and more about the experience. A range of tours is available through Discover Danube Delta, from day trips to week-long extravaganzas, with plenty of education to be had along the way. Make the musical city of Tulcea your base. 🌐 *www.discoverdanubedelta.com* *Day trips from €80.*

Letea Forest

FOREST | The oldest natural reservation in Romania, Letea Forest is the elder statesman of the country's natural wonders. There was a reason for its early protection (established in 1938): the unbelievable biodiversity found within. A vast number of unique trees are found in Letea, including everything from English oaks to black poplars, silver limes, common alders, and many more. There are plenty of animals here, too, including falcons, eagles, and snakes, as well as more than 1,600 different types of insects. Don't let the creepy-crawlies put you off, though: Letea Forest is a glorious adventure playground. The jewel of the Danube Delta? That might just be Letea

Forest. It is best seen on a day-long excursion from Tulcea. ✉ *Letea Forest* 🌐 *www.info-delta.ro.*

Merry Cemetery

CEMETERY | Thought all cemeteries were solemn affairs? Get yourself to Săpânța and have your perspective changed. Found in a small village near Romania's border with Ukraine, the Merry Cemetery is packed with colorful tombs and witty epitaphs, making it arguably the most unique graveyard in Europe. Established in the 1930s, the Merry Cemetery takes an irreverent look at death, focusing instead on humor and warmth as opposed to sadness and grief. The cemetery was started by Ioan Stan Pătraș, and his life and times are celebrated in a small museum just 400 meters or so from the cemetery's entrance. ✉ *Săpânța* 🎫 *Free.*

Peleș Castle

CASTLE/PALACE | **FAMILY** | A fairy-tale castle come to life, Peleș is a stunning Neo-Renaissance/Gothic structure that sits tall upon the Carpathian Mountains. It dates to 1883 and is estimated to have cost a whopping 16,000,000 gold Romanian lei (roughly $120 million today). The former royal residence has more than 150 rooms, each more stunning than the last, a bubble of gold and carved wood. It's estimated that the castle's art and antiquities collection includes nearly 4,000 pieces of armor and armaments and 2,000 paintings. Audio guides are available, and if you're on a time crunch, these are a better option than the tour guides, who may not be available immediately. Part of the complex is the splendid Art Nouveau–style **Pelișor Castle**, built by King Carol I for his nephew, the future King Ferdinand, and finished in 1902. It's less castle and more stately home, but still well worth a visit, and it's much less crowded than Peleș. ✉ *Aleea Peleșului 2, Sinaia* ☎ *244/310–918* 🌐 *peles.ro* 🎫 *From 50 lei* ⏲ *Closed weekends.*

Salina Turda

MINE | No matter your interest level in salt, a trip to the incredible Turda Salt Mine is a must. It might just be the most impressive salt mine on the planet, after all. Located just outside Cluj-Napoca, the mine only opened to visitors in 1992, but they have since come in their droves, eager to view one of the most beautiful underground secrets in the world. The mine is a conveyor belt of amazing sights, from the stunning chambers to salt chapels and much, much more. Salina Turda is 35 km (22 miles) south of Cluj and 1.2 km (about 1 mile) from the village that gives the mine its name. ✉ *Aleea Durgăului 7, Turda* ☎ *364/260–940* 🌐 *www.salinaturda.eu* 🎫 *50 lei.*

Untold Festival

MUSIC FESTIVALS | The largest electronic music festival in Romania has grown and grown since its first edition in 2015. The August extravaganza turns charming Cluj-Napoca into a cauldron of trance, techno, house, and the rest, with many of the world's most popular artists taking to the stage and sending hundreds of thousands of revelers into a frenzy. More than 370,000 partygoers attended Untold in 2019, and the festival has won its fair share of awards along the way. What does the future hold for Untold Festival? Time will tell, but its place on the European festival calendar is assured. Romania's biggest party is also its best. ✉ *Aleea Stadionului 2, Cluj-Napoca* 🌐 *untold.com.*

Voroneț Monastery

RELIGIOUS BUILDING | There are plenty of painted monasteries in the historic Bukovina region, but none are as achingly beautiful as Voroneț Monastery. Established in 1488 and dedicated to Saint George, this Romanian Orthodox monastery is a triumph of Moldavian architecture and a celebration of color, with a particularly intense shade of blue at the heart of it all. Legend has it that the monastery was founded by Stephen the Great after he made a promise to a famous hermit called Daniil, and there is a palpable air of importance here. The monastery church is one of the most beloved in Romania, a must-see in its own right. ✉ *Strada Voroneț 166, Voroneț* ☎ *230/235–323* 🌐 *www.manastireavoronet.ro* 🎫 *5 lei.*

Where to Eat and Drink

Baracca

$$ | ITALIAN | Cluj-Napoca's finest Italian restaurant is also one of the city's most romantic settings, but the menu is all about innovation and experience, not to mention a vibrant love of life and the magic it brings. Everything begins with the ingredients, fresh produce from the region that is put into the more than capable hands of a band of extremely creative chefs. **Known for:** house-made pastas; elaborate tasting menus; substantial wine menu. 💲 *Average main: L100* ✉ *Strada Napoca 8A, Cluj-Napoca* ☎ *732/155–177* 🌐 *www.baracca.ro* 🕒 *Closed Sun. No lunch.*

Bistro de l'Arte

$ | EUROPEAN | Helmed by the irrepressible Oana Coantâ (a former Woman Chef of the Year winner), Bistro de l'Arte is as much about playfulness as it is delicious, delicious food. The homely interior puts comfort first, safe in the knowledge that the quality of the menu is assured. **Known for:** daily changing menu; celebrated chef at the helm; popular weekend brunch. 💲 *Average main: L44* ✉ *Piața George Enescu 11Bis, Brasov* ☎ *720/535–566* 🌐 *bistrodelarte.ro.*

Cavalerul Medieval

$$ | EASTERN EUROPEAN | Ever wanted to dine in a medieval castle? Cavalerul Medieval offers that and a whole lot more, in a space designed to evoke the 12th- and 13th-century defensive castles of medieval England but with a modernized menu that even includes some vegetarian choices. **Known for:** refined versions of medieval-style dishes; lots of grilled meat and fish (but also a few vegetarian offerings); theme entertainment. 💲 *Average main: L53* ✉ *Soseaua Iasi - Ciurea nr.58* ☎ *332/419–628* 🌐 *www.cavalerulmedieval.ro.*

Fix Me A Drink

COCKTAIL LOUNGES | Cocktails should be all about innovation, about bringing new ingredients together in search of perfection. Few bars take this as seriously as Bucharest's Fix Me a Drink, although do take the use of the word "seriously" with a big pinch of salt. This is a joyful spot in the capital that makes the most of region-specific ingredients and creates magic in the process. Add a minimalist interior and regular art exhibitions, and you have somewhere to be celebrated. ✉ *Strada Ion Brezoianu 23–25, Bldg. B, fl. 1, Bucharest* ☎ *771/707–869* 🌐 *fixmad.com.*

Privo

$$ | INTERNATIONAL | Hotel Privo's restaurant might be its most prized asset, and it will become clear from the first bite. The food here is fantastic and uses local ingredients to craft international cuisine of the highest distinction. **Known for:** grilled steaks and fish; extensive wine selections; excellent service. 💲 *Average main: L73* ✉ *Hotel Privo, Strada Urcușului 1, Târgu Mureș* ☎ *365/424–442* 🌐 *www.privo.ro.*

Vatra

$ | EASTERN EUROPEAN | Tradition, tradition, tradition: would you like a little tradition with your tradition? From the decor to the dishes, Vatra is a place that embraces all things Romanian, with a fabulous array of stews to a delicious selection of meals made using a traditional cast-iron pot. **Known for:** pork and potato stew; lots of grilled meat; large portions. 💲 *Average main: L53* ✉ *Strada Ion Brezoianu 19, Bucharest* ☎ *721/200–800* 🌐 *vatra.ro.*

Cool Places to Stay

Casa Comana

$$ | HOTEL | FAMILY | Home to the restaurant of the same name, this boutique hotel in Comana Natural Park (a 45-minute drive from Giurgiu) is well-suited for families with young children. **Pros:** free Wi-Fi; a boat ride is included in the price; nice spa. **Cons:** thin walls; service could use some improvement; the restaurant is very popular and thus crowded. *Rooms from: L250* ✉ *Strada Gelu Naum, Comana* ☎ *743/079–934* ⊕ *www.casacomana.ro* *21 rooms* *Free Breakfast.*

Casa Timiș Resort

$$$ | RESORT | There is an undeniable elegance to every aspect of a stay at Casa Timiș Resort, which offers a homey feel in the midst of a vineyard, albeit a home that comes with a total multi-sensory experience, delectable cuisine, and all the comfort one could want. **Pros:** very comfortable beds; beautiful pool area; large, comfortably appointed rooms. **Cons:** expensive restaurants; some guests report inconsistent service; isolated location. *Rooms from: L920* ✉ *Florica Romalo 4, Chitorani* ☎ *723/682–568* ⊕ *casatimis.ro* *26 suites* *Free Breakfast.*

Complex Egreta

$$$ | HOTEL | Romania's first lake resort is a unique experience in all of Europe, with cottages suspended on stilts above the Danube in a beautiful location. **Pros:** decks for lounging and watching the river; lots of attractions nearby; large, pine-paneled, two-level rooms. **Cons:** limit of three adults in each room; not many off-site dining options nearby, and dinner isn't offered; no pets allowed. *Rooms from: L400* ✉ *DN57, Berzasca* ☎ *721/841–556* ⊕ *complex-egreta.ro* *15 rooms* *Free Breakfast.*

Pensiunea Dealul Verde

$$$ | B&B/INN | A two-hour drive west of Brașov, Pensiunea Dealul Verde may remind you of a certain Hobbit town since its rooms have been carved out of the green hills (hence the name "Green Hill"). **Pros:** lots of activities in the nearby area; particularly pet-friendly; hearty breakfast and dinner included (served family-style). **Cons:** since rooms are underground, there are no windows except in the front (though whitewashed walls amplify the natural light); somewhat isolated location; few on-site facilities except for sauna and steamroom. *Rooms from: L1145* ✉ *Porumbacu de Jos* ☎ *745/021–418* ⊕ *pensiuneadealulverde.ro* *8 rooms* *All-Inclusive.*

Southern Balkans

Six beautiful countries—each magnificent in its own way—makes up the southern Balkan region, and all are ready and waiting for the tourism floodgates to open. The tumult of the 20th century has given way to the optimism of the 21st, and the occasional bump in the road hasn't been enough to stop regional tourism from growing.

Bosnia and Herzegovina might be Europe's most surprising country. Visitors never fail to be amazed by the jaw-dropping natural beauty, delicious food, and convivial people in a country of storytellers with plenty of stories to tell.

Neighboring **Serbia** marries excitement with serenity and is the sort of place where you are just as likely to welcome the sunrise on top of a mountain as you are after a night of partying. Belgrade has become one of the great capital cities of Europe, but it is just the tip of the iceberg. **Kosovo** is more than just Europe's youngest nation. It is also the continent's best-kept coffee secret, and its relative youth belies centuries of history and culture.

Albania's development from a Communist basketcase to Europe's undisputed king of hospitality has been thrilling, and its coastline won't stay so quiet forever.

Speaking of coastlines, **Montenegro** is fast becoming the darling of the European seaside scene, while the magic of its mountainous interior offers a captivating juxtaposition.

North Macedonia? It offers all of the above, along with Europe's deepest lake and scenery for days. Just check out the view from the top of Kruševo, for starters.For travelers who are willing to dip their toes into the waters of these six countries (sometimes literally), it's rather easy to find superlatives since so much of this region is relatively undiscovered—at least by Americans—who may be swept up in a sea of energy, excitement, and extremely good times.

Ajvatovica, Bosnia and Herzegovina

The Largest Islamic Cultural Event in Europe

Care to guess where Europe's largest Islamic cultural, traditional, and religious event takes place? If you guessed a tiny village of 1,000 or so people in the hills of Central Bosnia, you are correct. For 364 days of the year, Prusac is a sleepy settlement with fabulous views across the valley, a handful of pretty mosques, and one café. Its people go about their business, tilling their fields, and commuting in and out of Bugojno and Donji Vakuf, the largest towns in the vicinity. *Ajvatovica* is named after Ajvaz-dedo, a hardworking Muslim who strove to improve the fortunes of his people, but there is much more to his accomplishments than industriousness and commitment. Legend has it that Prusac was once threatened by a disastrously long drought. With the situation looking dire, Ajvaz-dedo found a spring nearby, but it was cut off by a massive rock. After 40 days of prayer, the rock miraculously split in half, and water finally returned to Prusac. Pilgrimages soon began, and Ajvatovica grew into the spectacle it has become.

When to Go

For one day at the end of every June, Prusac becomes the center of Islamic Europe as thousands descend on the village to celebrate a 16th-century miracle.

Getting Here

From Sarajevo, daily buses run to the central towns of Bugojno and Donji Vakuf. Local buses to Prusac leave from both, although a taxi is easier. The drive from Sarajevo to Prusac takes just over two hours. Expect accommodation in Bugojno and Donji Vakuf to be booked up in advance ahead of Ajvatovica. Both towns have a handful of good food options (Orhideja in Donji Vakuf is particularly excellent).

Belgrade Fortress, Serbia

Belgrade's Best Site Offers History and Views for Days

This ancient fortification overlooking the confluence of the Sava and Danube rivers is now one of Belgrade's prettiest city parks. The fortress was built, expanded, destroyed, and built again between the 1st and 18th centuries, but the current structure dates largely to the Ottoman period in the 18th century. It's split into the Upper Town (Despot's Gate, the Clock Tower, the Roman Well, and the Statue of the Victor) and Lower Town (Nebojša Tower, the Turkish bath, and the Gate of Charles VI). The lovely Kalemegdan Park surrounds it all. With spectacular views of the city and perfect sunsets over the rivers, this is one of the most romantic spots in the city. Kids will love the military museum's enormous collection of cannons and tanks, the Grand Stairway, the zoo, and the children's park. There are a few cafés and restaurants if you need a break. Some attractions charge a nominal fee.

Don't Miss

The most magical time here is sunset (or sunrise, for the early birds) over the confluence of the Sava and Danube rivers. The area gets pretty busy, but there is plenty of room for people looking for the most romantic view in town.

Getting Here

Belgrade is well-connected by plane, train, bus, and car, with direct connections to most major cities around the continent. Kalemegdan is right in the center of town, at the end of the bustling Knez Mihailova pedestrian street.

✉ *Terazije 3/V, Belgrade* ☎ *(381 112) 620–685* 🌐 *www.beogradskatvrdjava.co.rs*

Lake Ohrid, North Macedonia

Europe's Deepest Lake is Picture-Perfect

North Macedonia's most magnificent spot isn't just a pretty picture. Lake Ohrid, which straddles the border between North Macedonia and Albania, is one of the oldest and deepest lakes in Europe, with water that plummets to depths of 286 meters. Swimming in the lake is a must, as is taking a lazy boat out onto the waters to consider the lake's eponymous town from a different angle. The town of Ohrid is plenty interesting, home to a range of quality hotels, restaurants, and bars. Aside from the lake, the town is famous for its churches, supposedly having one for every day of the year. What this means during leap years isn't entirely clear, but ticking off all 365 of them is quite the task.

Don't Miss

The most famous image associated with Lake Ohrid is the birthday cake–perfect Church of Saint John the Theologian, perched on a small hill above the lake. No visit to Ohrid is complete without visiting the church and taking that photo. It is the image that continues to put Lake Ohrid on bucket lists.

Getting Here

Ohrid International Airport (served by Wizz Air flights from several different European airports) is 9 km (5½ miles) northwest of town, and the city is connected to Skopje via a three-hour bus journey.

Ohrid Tourist Association. ✉ *Jane Sandanski 147, 6000 Ohrid, North Macedonia* ☎ *(389 70) 684–428* 🌐 *ohridtouristassociation.com*

Ostrog Monastery, Montenegro

A Jaw-Dropping Monastery Built into the Side of a Vertical Cliff-Face

The creation of Ostrog would seem to be impossible. After all, how do you carve a monastery into a vertical cliff face? Established in the 17th century, this Serbian Orthodox monastery (the most important pilgrimage site in the country) took on its current whitewashed form in the early 20th century, after the original monastery was destroyed by a fire. Dedicated to Saint Basil of Ostrog, the monastery is divided into two parts (the upper and lower monastery), with several small chapels and rooms you can visit. There is serenity here, enough to soften even the most cynical of hearts, and it remains both an active monastery and a place of worship for those who come to be blessed by the relics of St. Basil. Be sure to dress respectfully, and get ready for that jaw to drop.

Don't Miss

Ostrog is a living, working monastery, and visiting during times of worship is a beautiful experience. The warren of chapels and quiet rooms within the main building are gorgeous, and the views out across the valley are stunning,

Getting Here

Getting to Ostrog isn't the easiest of endeavors. A train from Podgorica to Ostrog is quick (less than an hour) and cheap, and there are several trains a day; you can hike up to the lower monastery in about an hour from Ostrog station. But most tourists are coming from Kotor or Dubrovnik, from which it's a two-hour bus trip to Nikšić; from there, you can get a 30-minute taxi ride. In the summer, companies offer guided bus tours from both Dubrovnik and Kotor.

✉ *Dabojevići, Nikšić* ☎ *(382 68) 330–336*
🌐 *manastirostrog.com*

Perast, Montenegro

The Most Magnificent Spot on the Montenegrin Coast

Tiny Perast is a peaceful bayfront village of stone villas with gardens of fig trees and oleander. It was built by wealthy local sea captains during the 17th and 18th centuries, a time when it was prosperous enough to play host to a fleet of some 100 merchant ships navigating the oceans. In fact, Perast's naval skills were so respected that in the early 18th century, the Russian czar Peter the Great sent his young officers to study at the Perast Maritime Academy.

Don't Miss

Two islands are easily visible from the Perast waterfront. St. George's is a natural island, but its sibling, Our Lady of the Rocks, is man-made. Folklore has it that in 1452, local sailors found an icon depicting the Virgin and Child cast upon a rock jutting up from the water. Taking this as a sign from God, they began placing stones on and around the rock, slowly building an island over it. By 1630 they had erected a church on the new island, which still stands. The other island (which is closed to the public) is home to the Monastery of St. George, which dates to the 12th century; it became a favorite burial spot for local sea captains around the 18th century, and those crypts remain today. To visit Our Lady of the Rocks, hop on a taxi boat from Perast's waterfront (a five-minute trip that costs €5 round-trip); there is no shortage of options.

Getting Here

Perast is a 12-km (7-mile) drive north of Kotor, while Tivat International Airport is 20 km (12 miles) south. Our Lady of the Rocks is a popular day excursion from Kotor if you aren't staying over in Perast.

Visit Kotor. ✉ *Stari Grad 315, Kotor* ☎ *(382 32) 325 950* 🌐 *kotor.travel*

Prizren, Kosovo

The Cultural Capital of Kosovo

Kosovo's second-largest city is its most alluring. A dazzling location in the valley of the Sharr mountains helps, but there is more to this southern stunner than a picture-perfect location. Prizren has history and culture in spades, not to mention the best café scene in Kosovo, which is the continent's most underrated. Pizren is also the perfect base to explore the sweeping natural landscape of Kosovo's south, with adrenaline-heavy activities nestled next to serene scenes. As for sights, Prizren packs a punch. Its cobbled streets give way to languid mosques and a tangible sense of history, and the Old Stone Bridge is a real thing of beauty. Be sure to make the steep climb up to the Prizren Fortress, a place of power and security for ages.

Don't Miss

Prizren is Kosovo's festival capital, with a fantastic year-round schedule of traditional and contemporary events. **Dokufest** is a brilliant documentary festival that takes over town in August, while the wild **40 Bunar Fest** is just about as eccentric as adventure festivals get (it's a tubing race down the Lumbardhi River). This is just the tip of a particularly packed iceberg, with an array of events showcasing the vast cultural diversity found here.

Getting Here

The most convenient way to visit Prizren is via bus from Prishtina, with other direct options from Istanbul, Skopje, Tirana, and Belgrade.

Rozafa Castle, Albania

A Castle Packed with Myths and Legends

Shkodra is one of Albania's most exciting cities, a vibrant place of culture, entertainment, and history. It also happens to be the country's cycling capital, which can be a shock after visiting the traffic-heavy cities farther south. The most amazing attraction? That'll be the jaw-dropping Rozafa Castle. Locations don't come much more strategically vital than this, so civilizations have been building here since the beginning of time, and the castle features in many regional myths and legends. The most notable of these is the story of three brothers, their three wives, and the struggle to build a castle that would stand. According to legend, one of the wives was buried in the castle walls, a necessary sacrifice to ensure its stability. Told as a metaphor for the sacrificial strength of women, it is just one of many myths associated with this incredible place.

Don't Miss

Rozafa Castle houses a small museum that tells the story of the castle, as well as showcasing the only mosaics found in Northern Albania. The museum is fascinating and deserves attention when visiting the castle, but the awesome sense of history and scope outweighs everything up here. The views are predictably stunning.

Getting Here

Podgorica Airport (Montenegro) is 40 km (25 miles) away and has the best air connections in the vicinity. Why not do as the locals do and traverse the short journey from Shkodra on two wheels? Rozafa is 3½ km (2 miles) south of Shkodra, a major town close to Albania's border with Montenegro.

✉ *Rozafa* 🎫 *€2, additional €2 for museum*

Stari Most, Bosnia and Herzegovina

A Stunning Stone Bridge that Defies Gravity

There are many beautiful stone bridges in Bosnia and Herzegovina, but none is as iconic as Mostar's stunning Stari Most (Old Bridge). Construction on the original began in 1557 and finished nine years later, but the demands of Sultan Suleiman the Magnificent were ambitious. Mimar Hayruddin (an apprentice of famous Ottoman architect Mimar Sinan) was in charge of its construction, and legend has it that he was so pessimistic about the structure's stability that he vanished on the day of its completion, convinced it wouldn't stand. The original bridge stood for 427 years, until it was obliterated in 1993 during the Bosnian War by some 60 shells. UNESCO coordinated a rebuilding project, and the rebuilt bridge was unveiled in 2004, with a promise from locals that this one would eventually last for many more than 400 years. The bridge is in the heart of Mostar's old town, surrounded by shops, cafés, restaurants, and mosques. The bridge gets very busy in summer, but you can't fault the masses for their judgment.

Don't Miss

Experienced locals dive from the bridge frequently during summer, although not until enough money has been collected from excited onlookers. It is an impressive feat, best enjoyed from the "beach" area directly in front of the bridge.

Getting Here

Herzegovina's largest city, Mostar is 130 km (81 miles) south of Sarajevo. The best way to visit is via train from the capital, a gorgeous 2½-hour ride that snakes alongside the Neretva river. Alternatively, buses run between the two cities throughout the day.

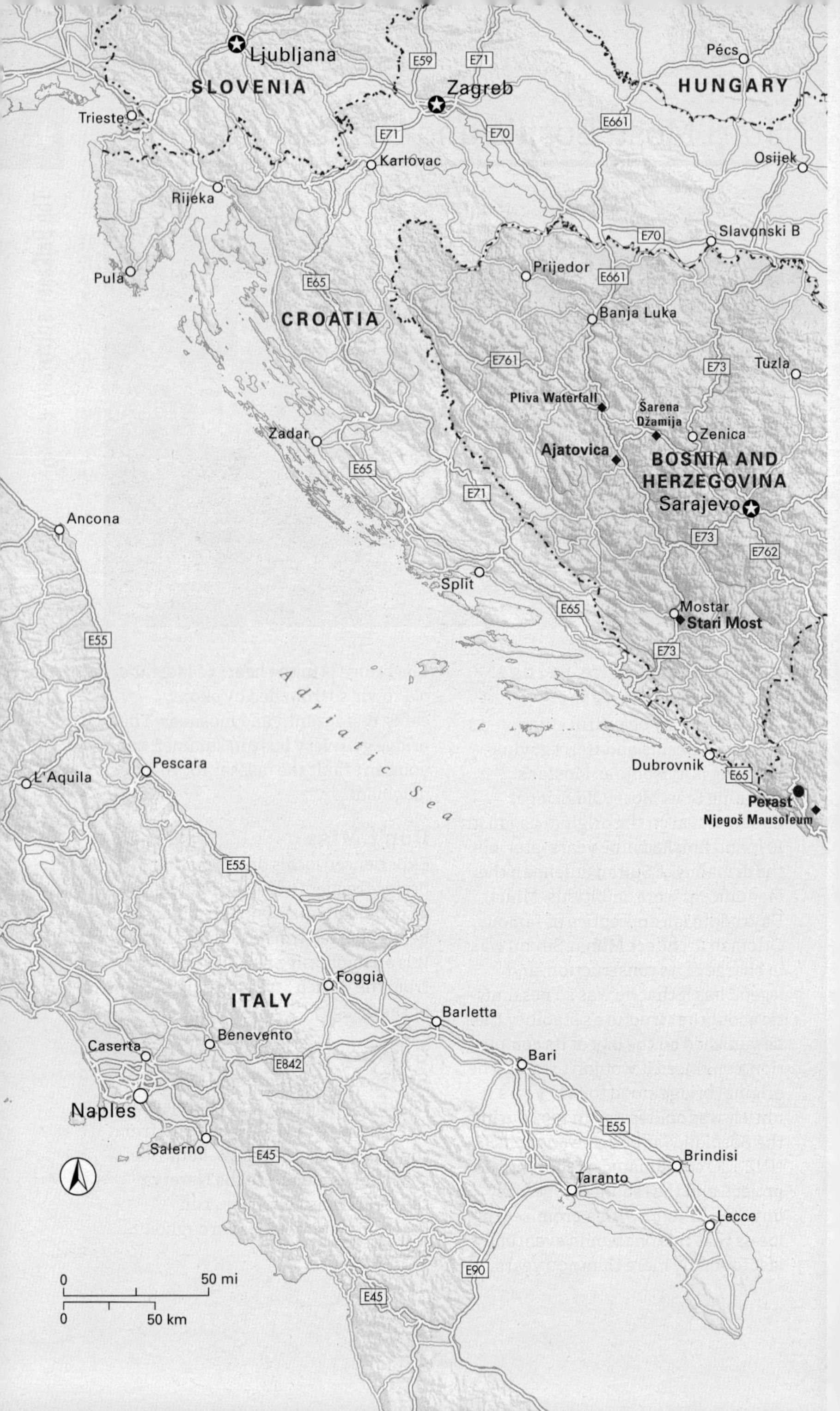

Ljubljana
SLOVENIA
Zagreb
HUNGARY
Pécs
Trieste
Karlovac
Rijeka
Osijek
Slavonski B
Pula
Prijedor
Banja Luka
CROATIA
Tuzla
Pliva Waterfall
Šarena Džamija
Zenica
Zadar
Ajatovica
BOSNIA AND HERZEGOVINA
Sarajevo
Ancona
Split
Mostar
Stari Most
Adriatic Sea
Dubrovnik
Perast
Njegoš Mausoleum
Pescara
L'Aquila
Foggia
ITALY
Barletta
Benevento
Caserta
Bari
Naples
Salerno
Brindisi
Taranto
Lecce
E59
E71
E70
E661
E65
E761
E73
E762
E55
E842
E45
E90
0
50 mi
0
50 km

The Southern Balkans
Arad
Subotica
E75
Timişoara
Zrenjanin
Novi Sad
E70
Reşita
ROMANIA
Rimnicu Vil
E70
Belgrade Fortress
E70
Šabac
Belgrade
Drobeta-Tur
E75
E70
E763
Craiova
Valjevo
E79
E70
House on the Drina
Kragujevac
Čačak
E761
SERBIA
E761
Užice
Kraljevo
E75
Kruševac
Uvac Canyon Kayaking
Niš
E79
Vratsa
Novi Pazar
E80
Leskovac
MONTENEGRO
E80
Kosovska Mi
E65
Niksic
Sofia
Ostrog Monastery
Pec
Pristina
E871
Pernik
Gračanica Monastery
E75
Podgorica
KOSOVO
BULGARIA
Gjakova
E65
E80
Kyustendil
Prizren
E871
E79
Shkodër
Skopje
Rozafa Castle
Tetovo
Gostivar
NORTH MACEDONIA
E75
Tirana
Kruševo
Bunk'Art 1
E65
Durrës
Seres
Elbasan
Lake Ohrid
Bitola
E79
ALBANIA
E9
Thessaloniki
GREECE
E75
Vlorë
Katerini
E65
Gjirokastra World Heritage Site
E90
Aegean Sea
Corfu
Ioanina
Larissa

When in the Southern Balkans

Bunk'Art 1

OTHER MUSEUM | Much has been written about the strange concrete bunkers that are found all across Albania. Ostensibly built as war shelters as the increasingly neurotic Communist dictator Enver Hoxha isolated the country further and further, they were, predictably, never used for their intended purpose. In the years after Communism, the bunkers have been repurposed for everything from cafés to animal shelters. Tirana's Bunk'Art Museum is a fabulous example. There are actually two Bunk'Art locations, telling the complicated and traumatic story of Albania's Communist years with grace and fortitude. ✉ *Rruga Fadil Deliu* ☎ *672/072–905* *Free* *Closed Mon. and Tues.*

Gjirokastra World Heritage Site

TOWN | North of Sarandë, at 940 feet above sea level, this ancient city offers dramatic views, along with the opportunity to visit the fascinating Islamic Monastic Sufi Sect of Bektashi. Gjirokastra, where traces of human habitation dating back to the 1st century BC have been discovered, is located on the slopes of the Mali i Gjerë overlooking the Drinos River. The city was probably founded sometime in the 12th century AD around a fortress on the hillside. Now a picturesque town with traditional houses, it has a medieval citadel that was converted into a prison under the Nazis and currently houses a weapons museum. Gjirokastra was also home of the dictator Hoxha, who ruled Albania with a Stalinist-type regime for decades. ✉ *Gjirokastra* ✣ *56 km (34 miles) north of Sarande (hourly buses)* 🌐 *www.gjirokastra.org.*

Gračanica Monastery

CHURCH | History is never far from any conversation in Kosovo, and visitors are best advised to simply listen (and listen only). That doesn't mean you should avoid history completely, however, and Kosovo is home to some seriously important Serbian Orthodox monasteries. One of the most important is Gračanica, just a short drive from Prishtina. Constructed in 1321 under the auspices of Serbian King Stefan Milutin, Gračanica has played a huge role in regional history and culture, and it transmits an aura that is undeniable. All of these monasteries have stories to tell, stories of birth, tumult, rebirth, and more tumult, while the aesthetics alone make them must-sees. Three others are on the UNESCO World Heritage list: Visoki Dečani (in Dečan), Peć (in Peja), and Our Lady of Ljeviš (Prizren). ✉ *Graçanicë 10500.*

House on the Drina

NOTABLE BUILDING | This tiny house is perched atop a rock in the middle of the Drina River, a seemingly miraculous sight. The house came into being in 1968, the brainchild of a group of swimming enthusiasts from the region who wanted somewhere more comfortable than a rock to rest after battling the current of the powerful Drina river. Unfortunately, the flowing river means constant repairs are required (and it also means that several iterations of the house have been destroyed and rebuilt). International attention finally arrived in the 21st century thanks to a darling photo in *National Geographic,* but no camera truly does justice to the amazing House on the Drina. ✉ *Bajina Bašta*

Kruševo

TOWN | North Macedonia's highest town might also be its most enchanting. Kruševo packs a heck of a lot into its tiny boundaries, from incredible monuments to beloved pop stars and some of the best views in the entire country. The Makedonium Monument is an eccentric structure that pays homage to those who have died defending the town over the centuries, while Kruševo is also the final resting place of much-missed pop icon Toše Proeski. The views deserve extra attention, spreading far and wide across Pelagonia with excellence that must be seen. Visit Kruševo in summer, winter, spring, or autumn; there are no bad options. ✉ *Kruševo*

Njegoš Mausoleum

TOMB | Montenegro's Lovćen National Park really does feel like a different world. The incredible views offered at its plateau are fit for a king, although in this case, they are fit for the poet prince who modernized Montenegro and left his indelible mark on the past, present, and future of this small nation. The Njegoš Mausoleum peacefully sits 1,655 meters into the sky on the summit of Jezerski Vrh, and it is no great shock to hear that it is the most visited point in this beautiful park. The hike covers 5 km (3 miles) of relatively sedate gradients before rising steeply in the final moments, although most choose to drive to the car park and clamber up the 461 steps instead. ✉ *Lovćen National Park, Lovćen.*

Pliva Waterfall

WATERFALL | Jajce is a town of real historical significance in Bosnia and Herzegovina, from its role in the rise and fall of the medieval Bosnian state to its vital importance in the development of socialist Yugoslavia. But the real pull for tourists is Pliva Waterfall, situated in the center of Jajce and the anchor around which this beautiful town grows. The confluence of the Pliva and Vrbas rivers is accentuated by these dramatic cascades as the water plunges 22 meters with stunning results. ✉ *Jajce* 🌐 *jajce.ba/turizam/* 🎫 *4 KM.*

Šarena Džamija

MOSQUE | Tetovo's Šarena Džamija (which means "Decorated Mosque") is undoubtedly one of Europe's most beautiful mosques. As North Macedonia's largest Albanian-majority town, Tetovo is a sufficiently fascinating place in of itself, but the vivid panels of its central mosque are its crowning glory. The mosque was unusual from the start, financed as it was by two sisters from the town, and they pulled out all the stops when it came to decoration. Keep an eye out for the depiction of Mecca, thought to be the only one of its type in Europe. Tetovo is a 50-minute drive west of Skopje, the North Macedonian capital. ✉ *Braka Milladinovi, Tetovo.*

Uvac Canyon Kayaking

KAYAKING | Meandering rivers don't come much more dreamy than this one. The dramatic bends of Serbia's Uvac Canyon must be seen to be believed, although don't be surprised to doubt the validity of your eyes after enjoying this masterpiece of nature. In the west of Serbia (not too far from the border with Bosnia and Herzegovina), the extravagant bends of the Uvac River are accentuated by vultures, eagles, lakes, caves, and more, making the Uvac Canyon a real celebration of Serbia's brilliant nature. Numerous kayak and boating tours are available along with myriad hiking trails that lead to some seriously stunning views. Tours can be organized through Wild Serbia, with departures from Belgrade. ✉ *Priboj* 🌐 *wildserbia.com.*

Where to Eat and Drink

Cetinjska

BARS | Belgrade's nightlife is internationally famous, but the *splavs* (party boats) and traditional *kafanas* (taverns) leave a little to be desired. For an altogether more authentic experience, head to Cetinjska, a former car park turned nightlife hotbed just a short walk from Belgrade's old Bohemian quarter. There is spontaneity in spades here, with new bars and cafes cropping up all the time, many disappearing as quickly as they arrived. Many have stood the test of time, however, with **Zaokret** and **Ljubimac** two of the best. Rock up early and expect to leave late. Cetinjska is the center of Belgrade's alternative nightlife scene, a magnet for locals looking to imbibe deep into the night. ✉ *Cetinjska, Belgrade.*

Dveri

$$ | **EASTERN EUROPEAN** | Although Sarajevo's Baščaršija is packed with restaurants, few stand out, but delightful Dveri remains the exception, and long may that be the case. This tiny restaurant has an interior that is entirely its own, the perfect accompaniment to a menu of local and international dishes, accentuated by brilliant staff and some of the best homemade bread (pogača) in the city. **Known for:** nice selection of Balkan wines; excellent bread; mućkalica (a meat and vegetable stew). $ *Average main: KM15* ✉ *Prote Bakovića 12, Sarajevo* ☎ *33/537–020* 🌐 *dveri.co.ba* ▭ *No credit cards.*

Etno Selo Timčevski

$$$ | **EASTERN EUROPEAN** | If you're looking to embrace Macedonian culture and tradition while devouring simple, divine food, then this is the place to go. In the far north of the country, the restaurant is attached to a private winery and pours its own vintages along with plenty of grilled meat and other delicacies. **Known for:** beautiful terrace overlooking the river; Tikveshka zolta (local grape brandy); grilled meat. $ *Average main: MD2700* ✉ *Vojnik* ✣ *25 km (16 miles) northeast of Kumanovo.*

★ Konoba Scala Santa

$$ | **SEAFOOD** | Believed to be the oldest restaurant in Kotor, this rustic eatery is one of the best places in town for lobster, mussels, and fresh fish, such as simple barbecued *zubatac* (dentex) drizzled with olive oil and served with a wedge of lemon. The candlelit dining room has exposed stone walls, a wood-beam ceiling hung with fishing equipment and a big open fireplace. **Known for:** oldest tavern in the Old Town; great Montenegrin seafood dishes; big open fireplace and outdoor dining in the summer. $ *Average main: €12* ✉ *Trg od Salate, Kotor* ☎ *067/393–458.*

Princessa Gresa

$ | **INTERNATIONAL** | Prishtina might just be one of the more underrated food destinations in the southern Balkan region, and hungry visitors are well advised to make Princessa Gresa their first port of call. Mediterranean flavors dominate the menu, with an eye on quality and both ears firmly focused on the environment. **Known for:** delicious grilled fish; great value prix-fixe options; good steaks and other grilled meats. $ *Average main: €4* ✉ *23 Fehmi Agani, Prishtina* ☎ *38/245–841* 🌐 *www.restaurantgresa-ks.com.*

Uka Farm

$$ | **EASTERN EUROPEAN** | Agro-tourism is on the rise in Albania, as more and more people open up their gorgeous farms and produce to an increasing number of curious (and hungry) visitors. Uka Farm is one such spot, a small holding on the outskirts of Tirana that feels like a world away from the hustle and bustle of the capital. **Known for:** literally farm-to-table cuisine; very good wines made on-site; menu heavy on grilled meat. $ *Average main: L1361* ✉ *Rruga Adem Jashari, Laknas* ☎ *67/203–9909* ▭ *No credit cards.*

Cool Places to Stay

Eko Selo Natura Art

$$$$ | B&B/INN | Eko Selo Natura Art sits on the edge of Una National Park, and serves as the perfect base from which to explore Bosnia's most magnificent river. **Pros:** access to farm animals for kids; large and comfortable (if basic) apartments; magnificent riverside setting. **Cons:** inconsistent service; need a car; isolated location means you are reliant on the hotel's restaurant (though it's good). *$ Rooms from: KM250 ✉ Turističko naselje Natura Art, Lohovo ☎ 60/313-8767 🌐 www.opalhoteli.com 💳 No credit cards 🛏 3 rooms 🍽 No Meals.*

Epidamn Hotel

$$$ | HOTEL | Despite being one of the more popular stops on Albania's northern coast, Durres isn't overflowing with excellent hotel options, but this one ticks every box. **Pros:** popular restaurant and bar in the hotel; friendly, welcoming service; inviting spa. **Cons:** limited parking options; old-fashioned, old-world decor might not be to every taste; doesn't have its own website for booking (but appears on several third-party sites). *$ Rooms from: L9500 ✉ Bd. Epidamn ☎ 67/661-1110 🛏 17 rooms 🍽 Free Breakfast.*

Hotel Conte

$$ | HOTEL | These four stone buildings dating from the 15th and 16th centuries have been tastefully converted into well-appointed apartments, some with kitchens and one with a Jacuzzi. **Pros:** lovely old building; tastefully furnished; good breakfast. **Cons:** Muzak in the restaurant not for everyone; steep steps up to some apartments; proximity to church means early morning bells. *$ Rooms from: €100 ✉ Obala Kapitana Martka Martinovica, Perast ☎ 067/257-387 🌐 www.hotel-conte.me 🛏 18 rooms 🍽 Free Breakfast.*

Viceroy Kopaonik

$$$ | HOTEL | Kopaonik offers some of the best skiing in Serbia, and the Viceroy Hotel is the only luxury option around, dishing up five-star elegance in the dizzying heights of the country's largest ski resort. **Pros:** excellent spa; large, comfortable rooms; easy access to the slopes. **Cons:** spa is small; restaurants don't match the quality of the rest of the hotel; somewhat large and impersonal hotel. *$ Rooms from: RSD15000 ✉ Trg Josifa Pancica 12, Kopaonik ☎ 36/5155-500 🌐 www.viceroyhotelsandresorts.com 🛏 119 rooms 🍽 Free Breakfast.*

Chapter 10

GREECE, CYPRUS, AND ISTANBUL

WELCOME TO GREECE, CYPRUS, AND ISTANBUL

TOP REASONS TO GO

★ **The Acropolis, Greece:** The great emblem of Classical Greece has loomed above Athens (whose harbor of Piraeus is the gateway to all the Greek Islands) for 2,500 years.

★ **Delphi, Greece:** Perched on the slopes of Mount Parnassus, this was the ancient site of the most venerated and consulted Greek oracle.

★ **Santorini, Greece:** One of the world's most picturesque islands cradles the sunken caldera of a volcano that last erupted in 1650 BC.

★ **Topkapı Palace, Turkey:** Once accessible only to the privileged, today anyone with the price of admission can visit Istanbul's Topkapı Palace to see its grandeur, including the sultan's private Harem.

★ **Troödos Region, Cyprus:** Visit the mountains of Troödos to see a collection of UNESCO-listed Byzantine churches whose interiors were exquisitely frescoed in the 11th and 15th centuries.

1 **Athens.** The capital has a rich cultural life, regenerated neighborhoods, a sleek subway, and great restaurants and bars.

2 **Mainland Greece.** Beyond Athens you'll discover magnificent ruins, scenic gorges, rock-topped monasteries, and Byzantine glories.

3 **The Cyclades.** The Cyclades aren't all blue-domed villages, but beaches, billionaires, and nightclubs abound.

4 **Other Greek Islands.** Greece spans more than 6,000 islands, from Rhodes to Crete.

5 **Cyprus.** Its Greek and Turkish Cypriot communities might still be divided by a border, but ancient history, windswept sands, and incredible food are found across both sides of the island.

6 **Istanbul.** Straddling Europe and Asia, Istanbul is the undisputed cultural, economic, and historical capital of Turkey.

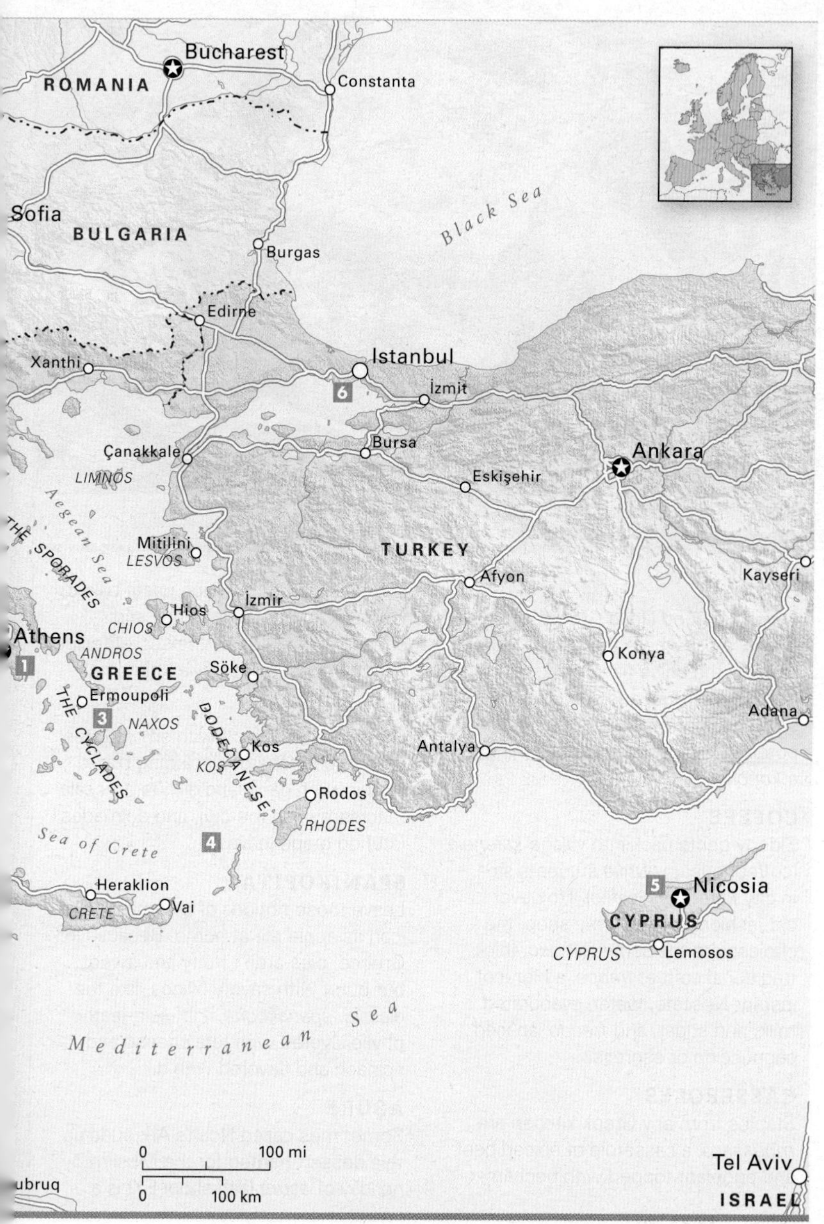
Bucharest
ROMANIA
Constanta
Black Sea
Sofia
BULGARIA
Burgas
Edirne
Xanthi
Istanbul
6
İzmit
Bursa
Çanakkale
LIMNOS
Aegean Sea
THE SPORADES
Mitilini
LESVOS
Ankara
Eskişehir
TURKEY
Afyon
Kayseri
İzmir
Hios
CHIOS
Athens
ANDROS
1
GREECE
Söke
Ermoupoli
THE CYCLADES
3
NAXOS
DODECANESE
Kos
KOS
Konya
Adana
Antalya
Rodos
RHODES
Sea of Crete
4
Heraklion
Vai
CRETE
5
Nicosia
CYPRUS
CYPRUS
Lemosos
Mediterranean Sea
0
100 mi
0
100 km
Tel Aviv
ISRAEL

WHAT TO EAT IN GREECE, CYPRUS, AND ISTANBUL

Horiatiki

OUZO

Savor the good life in Greece in an *ouzeri,* a bar where the star of the show is the anise-flavored liquor made from grape must and served with a small plate of mezedes. The clear, potent liquid is sipped from a tall glass, a *konokia.*

COFFEE

Elderly gents pack into village *kafeneia* (coffeehouses), while students sip in city *kafeterias* (cafés). However old-fashioned or chic the shop, the choices are the same: *elliniko,* thick traditional coffee; *frappe,* a blend of instant Nescafe, water, evaporated milk, and sugar; and *freddo,* an iced cappuccino or espresso.

CASSEROLES

Staples from any Greek kitchen are *moussaka,* a casserole of spiced beef and eggplant topped with bechamel, and *pastitsio,* tube-shape pasta baked with spiced beef, bechamel, and cheese. Cooks follow the secret recipe handed down from *yiayia* (grandma).

MEZEDES

Greek meals kick off with small plates meant to be shared, including tzaziki (yogurt with garlic and dill), taramosalata (creamy fish roe dip), and dolmades (stuffed grape leaves).

SPANIKOPITA

Leave those notions of being as American as apple pie at home. Because in Greece, pies aren't fruity and sweet but burst with savory fillings, like the classic, *spanakopita,* light-as-a-feather phyllo layered with feta cheese and spinach and flavored with dill.

AŞURE

Sometimes called Noah's Ark pudding, this dessert named for the Muslim holiday of *aşure* (aah-shoor-EY) is a porridge with a base of grains and nuts with dried fruits, pomegranate seeds, chickpeas, beans, and rose water.

MANTI

Every culture has a take on dumplings, and in the Turkish version small pockets of minced meat are doused in garlicky yogurt and topped with melted butter or oil, plus a dusting of mint and red pepper flakes.

RAKI

Turkey's national drink isn't just a beverage—it's an experience. Like Greek ouzo and French pastis, *rakı* is a clear anise liquor that turns milky white when diluted with water (it's sometimes referred to as "lion's milk").

MIDYE DOLMA

One of the most satisfying of Istanbul's street snacks are rice-stuffed mussels served with a spritz of lemon juice.

SIMIT

Sold on every Istanbul street corner, simit is a bready circle encrusted with sesame seeds: it's crunchy on the outside and soft on the inside.

TOMATOKEFTEDES

Among Santorini's great gifts to the world, one of the most traditional dishes on the island consists of fried tomato fritters that are best when topped with tzatziki or another dip and

Casseroles

Midye dolma

served with a crisp glass of wine or a glass of ouzo.

SAGANAKI

Slabs of *graviera* cheese dredged in flour, fried to golden perfection in a pan (called a *saganaki*), and drizzled with lemon. Cut it into bite-size pieces and serve it for all to enjoy.

GYROS AND SOUVLAKI

Gyro are shaved from meat, often pork or lamb, that's roasted on a vertical spit, while souvlaki is the same meat that's been skewered then grilled. They're the street food of choice everywhere in Greece and often stuffed inside pitas for a portable feast.

AMYGDALOTA

You've probably had baklava, but on your travels in Greece you're likely to discover another favorite sweet: almond cookies, often served alongside coffee. There's usually a plate in the kitchen at the ready to bring out to guests.

HORIATIKI

What the rest of the world knows as Greek salad is best in the homeland, bursting with flavorful tomatoes, onions, olives, and cucumbers, and topped with a generous slab of creamy feta cheese.

Greece, Cyprus, and Istanbul Snapshot

Know Before You Go

APPROPRIATE DRESS IS A CONSIDERATION.

In Turkey, standards of dress differ across the country. The urban garb you'd wear in any big city will fit in fine in Istanbul, but casual and conservative attire is best in small towns; the coasts tolerate somewhat skimpier clothes. In Greece, similar rules apply to visiting its religious sites, which impose a dress code for visitors: usually no shorts or bare shoulders.

BUSES GO JUST ABOUT EVERYWHERE.

In Greece, train coverage is spotty, especially in large, rural areas such as the Peloponnese, where rail has mostly yet to penetrate; on the islands it is nonexistent. Buses and minibuses take their place and can ferry you to most cities and towns. There is no centralized booking system, so plotting long routes can often mean logistical gymnastics.

THE "EVIL EYE" IS MEANT TO PROTECT YOU.

The ubiquitous blue, eye-shaped amulet (*nazar boncuğu* in Turkish; *mati* in Greek) is often referred to as an "evil eye," but rather than casting a nasty spell, it's actually meant to protect its wearer against them. Tiny versions are pinned to baby's clothes; larger ones are displayed inside houses and shops.

Planning Your Time

It would take months to explore every island, peninsula, and city of Greece, which has hundreds of inhabited islands, while Istanbul alone warrants at least a week of your time. So pick an area and do it justice: a visit to the ancient cities, citadels, and mountains of Greece's Peloponnese, for example, can easily eat up a fortnight. Cyprus is, in some ways, a handy middle ground, albeit one with a tragic history, with both cultures straddling this scenic and historic bite-size island.

Great Trips

5 days in the Peloponnese. Eleusis, Corinth, Mycenae, Tiryns, Epidaurus, Kalamata, Mystras, and Monemvasia.

4 days in the Dodecanese. Island-hop from Rhodes to Symi to Kos to Patmos.

3 days in Istanbul. Aya Sofya Blue Mosque, Topkapı Palace, and a cruise on the Bosphorus.

6 days in the Cyclades and Crete. Mykonos to Santorini to Crete.

Big Events

Athens and Epidaurus Festival, Greece: June to October. A full schedule of theater, opera, orchestra, and dance performances fills venues across Athens and the ancient Theatre of Epidauros. 🌐 *www.greekfestival.gr*

Anastenaria Fire Walking Festival, Greece: May 21–23. Outside of Thessaloniki, the ritual always begins on St. Constantine Day, lasting for three days.

Istanbul International Music Festival, Turkey: June. Three weeks of international and local artists, including classical performances and special venues.

What To...

READ

Memed, My Hawk, Yaşar Kemal. This classic 1950s novel vividly depicts a harsh rural life.

The Other Side of the Mountain, Erendiz Atasü. The feminist and activist author of this modern classic created a rich, multigenerational tale of Turkish women dating back to the Ottoman Empire.

Mani: Travels in the Southern Peloponnese, Patrick Leigh Fermor. A great British travel writer travels down Greece's Mani peninsula, where he lived for more than half a century.

The Greek Way, Edith Hamilton. The author and classicist puts into perspective the Golden Age of the 5th century BC.

WATCH

Once Upon a Time in Anatolia. A dark, soulful film by Nuri Bilge Ceylan from 2011 follows a group of men from a small town searching for a dead body.

Kedi. This 2017 documentary explores the lives of cats in Istanbul, a staple of local street life for thousands of years.

Before Midnight. The third installment of director Richard Linklater's Before trilogy sees Europe-trotting protagonists Celine and Jesse travel Greece's southern Peloponnese to resurrect their rocky marriage.

The Trip to Greece. British actors Steve Coogan and Rob Brydon follow in the footsteps of Odysseus.

LISTEN TO

Tarkan. Easily the best-known Turkish singer of the last few decades.

Timur Selçuk. The grandaddy of Turkish pop competed in the Eurovision Song Contest, twice.

Vassilis Tsitsanis. The composer and bouzouki master among the biggest rebetiko stars from its heyday in the 1950s.

Vangelis. A pioneer of early electronica, who scored such films as *Blade Runner* and *Chariots of Fire.*

BUY

Intricately painted earthenware is produced all over Turkey but the tiles and other ceramics made in Iznik are rightly celebrated.

Hydrated magnesium silicate (meerschaum) is a white, ivory-like substance found in Turkey and often used to make carved pipes and jewelry.

Rare mastic resin is produced only in Chios; it is used in everything from liqueurs to perfume.

Kompoloi (or worry beads) provide the sound of old Greece and Cyprus, but you'll find them everywhere.

Contacts

AIR

Major Airports: Athens International Airport (ATH); Thessaloniki Airport (SKG); Santorini/Thira Airport (JTR), Mykonos Airport (JMK); Crete-Heraklion (HER), Corfu (CFU), Rhodes (RHO); Istanbul Airport (IST); Larnaca International Airport (Cyprus, LCA); Paphos International Airport (Cyprus, PFO)

TRAIN

Hellenic Train. ☎ *14511, general line; 21301/21451, international line* 🌐 *www.hellenictrain.gr*

Türkiye Cumhuriyeti Devlet Demiryolları [Turkish State Railways]. ☎ *444–8233, no area code required in Turkey* 🌐 *www.tcdd.gov.tr* 🌐 *ebilet.tcddtasimacilik.gov.tr, for tickets*

VISITOR INFORMATION

Cyprus Tourism Organization. 🌐 *www.visitcyprus.com*

Greek National Tourism Organization. 🌐 *www.visitgreece.gr*

Turkish Culture and Tourism Office. 🌐 *www.goturkiye.com*

Athens

It's no wonder that all roads in Greece lead to the fascinating and paradoxical metropolis of Athens. Lift your eyes 200 feet above the city to the Parthenon, its honeycomb-colored marble columns rising from a massive limestone base, and you'll behold architectural perfection that has not been surpassed in 2,500 years. Today, this shrine of classical form dominates a 21st-century boom town.

One of the world's oldest cities, Athens is home to just over 3 million souls, many of whom spend the day philosophizing about the city's issues, including budget woes, red tape, overcrowding, transport strikes, immigration problems, and unemployment. These analysis sessions are usually accompanied by excellent coffee, a stream of meze dishes, or artfully mixed cocktails, since Athenians refuse to stay indoors in any weather or mood.

But while Athens can initially be a difficult city to love, it's also a difficult city to leave, and many temporary visitors end up settling here for years or consistently returning without ever having expected to.

The financial crisis that began in 2009 served to inspire Greeks to try out new jobs and start innovative and sophisticated entrepreneurial pursuits, while the blossoming urban arts scene earned the Greek capital the title of being a hothouse for major artistic initiatives by leading global film, theater, and music directors as well as painters.

To experience Athens— in Greek—fully is to understand the essence of Greece: ancient monuments surviving in a sea of cement, startling views of mountains and the sea from unremarkable urban locations, folkish tradition and vintage kitsch juxtaposed with ultramodern concepts. There is a growing sense of being completely "on par" with the most advanced capitals in the world, but retaining a sense of near-anarchic freedom that can rarely be sensed elsewhere.

To appreciate Athens is to appreciate life with all its refreshing surprises and paradoxical complexities.

The Acropolis

Towering over Athens

One of the most inspiring surviving ancient temples, it symbolizes Greece's Golden Age. The stunning centerpiece, the Parthenon, was commissioned in the 5th century BC by the great Athenian leader Pericles as part of an elaborate building program designed to epitomize the apex of an iconic culture. Most of the notable structures, the Propylaia, the Erechtheion, and the Temple of Athena Nike on this flat-top limestone outcrop, 512 feet high, were built from 461 to 406 BC by the architects Iktinos, Kallikrates, and Mnesikles, and the master sculptors Pheidias, Agorakritus, and Alkamenes. Thousands of years later, the Acropolis pulls the patriotic heartstrings of modern Greeks and seduces millions of annual visitors back to an ancient time.

Don't Miss

Monument of Filopappus at the summit of Lofos Mousson (Hill of the Muses), whose peak offers the city's best view of the Parthenon.

When to Go

In general, the earlier you start out the better. In summer, by noon the heat is blistering and the reflection of the light thrown back by the rock and the marble ruins is almost blinding, though by 5 pm, the light is best for taking photographs.

Getting Here

Take the metro to the Acropolis station, then follow the pedestrianized street Dionyssiou Areopagitou to the entrance at the Beulé Gate. Another way up is along the rock's northern face via the Peripatos, a paved path from the Plaka district.

Acropolis. ✉ *Dionyssiou Areopagitou, Acropolis* 🌐 *odysseus.culture.gr* 🎫 *€20 Acropolis and Theater of Dionysus; €30 joint ticket for all Unification of Archaeological Sites* 🚇 *Acropolis*

National Archaeological Museum

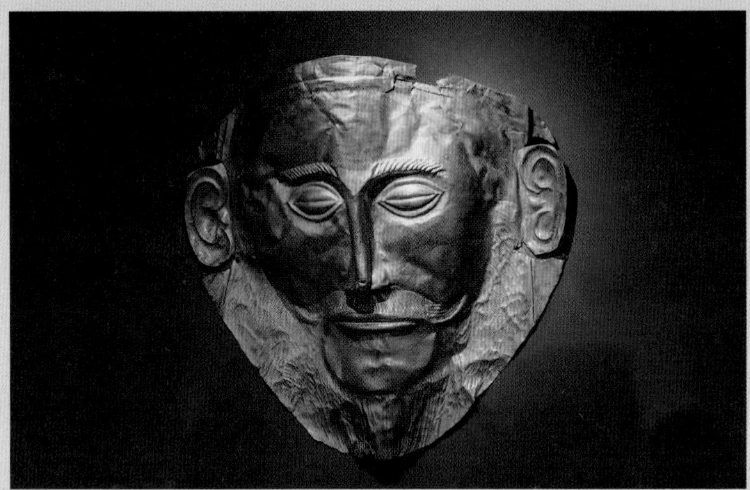

Greece's Greatest Treasures

Many of the greatest achievements in ancient Greek sculpture and painting are housed here in the most important museum in Greece. Artistic highlights from every period of its ancient civilization, from Neolithic to Roman times, make this a treasure trove beyond compare. The museum's most celebrated display is the Mycenaean Antiquities. The funeral mask of a bearded king (once thought to be the image of Agamemnon); a splendid silver bull's-head libation cup; and the 15th-century BC Vapheio Goblets (masterworks in embossed gold). Not to be missed are the beautifully restored frescoes from Santorini, delightful murals depicting daily life in Minoan Santorini. Other stars of the museum include the works of Geometric and Archaic art (10th to 6th century BC), the stelae of the warrior Aristion signed by Aristokles, and the unusual Running Hoplite.

Don't Miss

The collection of Classical art (5th to 3rd century BC) contains some of the most renowned surviving ancient statues, including the Jockey of Artemision and the Varvakios Athena.

Best Restaurant

Yiantes. Between the National Archaeological Museum and Lycabettus Hill, this restaurant's flower-filled courtyard is matched by a menu that reads like an honest culinary journey through the far reaches of Greece. *Average main: €20* *Valtetsiou 44, Exarcheia* *210/330–1369* *Closed Mon.* *Panepistimio*

Getting Here

Somewhat removed from the main tourist areas, the museum is best reached by taxi. Victoria Metro Station is a 10-minute walk. *28 Oktovriou (Patission) 44, Exarcheia* *www.namuseum.gr* *€12* *Omonia,Victoria*

Ancient Agora

The Commercial Hub of Ancient Athens

The Agora was once lined with statues and expensive shops, the favorite strolling ground of fashionable Athenians and a mecca for merchants and students. The long colonnades offered shade in summer and protection from rain in winter to the throng of people who transacted the day-to-day business of the city, and, under their arches, Socrates discussed matters with Plato, and Zeno expounded the philosophy of the Stoics (whose name comes from the six stoas, or colonnades of the Agora). Besides administrative buildings, the schools, theaters, workshops, houses, stores, and market stalls of a thriving town surrounded it. The Agora's showpiece was the Stoa of Attalos II, which has been re-created as a modern museum.

Don't Miss

On the low hill called Kolonos Agoraios in the Agora's northwest corner stands the best-preserved Doric temple in all Greece, the Hephaistion, sometimes called the Thission because of its friezes showing the exploits of Theseus. A little older than the Parthenon, it is surrounded by 34 columns and is 104 feet in length, and was once filled with sculptures. It never quite makes the impact of the Parthenon, in large part due to the fact that it lacks a noble site and can never be seen from below.

Ancient Agora. ✉ *3 entrances: from Monastiraki on Adrianou; from Thission on Apostolou Pavlou; and descending from Acropolis on Polygnotou St. (near the church of Ayion Apostolon), Monastiraki* 🌐 *odysseus.culture.gr* 🎫 *€10; €30 joint ticket for all Unification of Archaeological Sites* 🚆 *Monastiraki*

Syntagma Square

The Heart of Athens

At the top of the city's main square stands the Greek Parliament, formerly King Otto's royal palace, completed in 1838 for the new monarchy. It seems a bit austere and heavy for a southern landscape, but it was proof of progress, the symbol of the new ruling power. The building's saving grace is the stone's magical change of color from off-white to gold to rosy-mauve as the day progresses. On a wall behind the Tomb of the Unknown Soldier, the bas-relief of a dying soldier is modeled after a sculpture on the Temple of Aphaia in Aegina; the text is from the funeral oration said to have been given by Pericles. Pop into the gleaming Syntagma metro station to examine artfully displayed artifacts uncovered during subway excavations. A floor-to-ceiling cross-section of earth behind glass shows finds in chronological layers, ranging from a skeleton in its ancient grave to traces of the 4th-century BC road to Mesogeia to an Ottoman cistern.

Don't Miss

Watch the Changing of the Evzones Guards at the Tomb of the Unknown Soldier, in front of Parliament. On Sunday the honor guard of tall young men don their dress costumes, which includes a short white and very heavy *foustanella* (kilt) with 400 neat pleats, one for each year of the Ottoman occupation.

Drink Here

Oinoscent. If you'd like to learn about Greek wine using both your mind and your taste buds, this modern bar is the best spot. ✉ *Voulis 45–47, Syntagma* ☏ *210/322–9374* 🚊 *Syntagma*

National Garden

A Green Respite in Central Athens

When you can't take the city noise anymore, step into this oasis completed in 1860 as part of King Otto and Queen Amalia's royal holdings. With 38 acres of shady copses, manicured lawns littered with antiquities (some replicas commissioned by the queen), and water features, the garden provides refuge to old men who argue politics on the benches, children who career freely amid the tropical nature, runners who count early-morning jogging laps, and animal lovers who feed the stray cats. Some of the trees you'll spot are washingtonia palms, casuarinas, judas, and Chinese trees of heaven. At the east end is the neoclassical Zappeion Hall, built in 1888 as an Olympic building (with funds from Greek benefactor Evangelos Zappas). Next door, the open-air cinema attracts Athenians year-round. Children appreciate the duck, koi, and terrapin ponds, the small zoo, and the playground at the east end.

Don't Miss

Across the main avenue at the bottom of the Garden is the dazzling white pentelic marble Kallimarmaro (Panathenaic) Stadium, which was built on the very site of an ancient stadium for the revived Olympic Games in 1896.

Best Restaurant

Aegli Zappiou. Nestled among fountains and flowering trees next to the Zappio Exhibition Hall in the National Garden, it's an ideal spot to sample a fresh dessert, have a cup of Greek coffee, or eat some haute cuisine. [$] *Average main: €15* ✉ *Zappio Megaro, Syntagma 210/336–9300* 🌐 *www.aeglizappiou.gr* 🚇 *Syntagma*

✉ *Syntagma* 🌐 *www.zappeion.gr*
🕒 *Gates shut at sunset* 🚇 *Syntagma or Acropolis (then a walk past Hadrian's Arch)*

Thisseo

One of the Oldest Parts of Athens

A former red-light district has now become one of the most sought-after residential neighborhoods in Athens. Easily accessible by metro and offering a lovely view of the Acropolis, it has one of the liveliest café and restaurant scenes in Athens. Mainly on Adrianou Street along the rail track, you'll find excellent *rakadika* and *ouzeri*—publike eateries that offer plates of appetizers to accompany *raki*, a fiery grape spirit, or the ever-appealing *ouzo*. On a summer evening, walk to the main strip on the Nileos pedestrian zone to sit at an outdoor table scattered around the old tram lines, or perch yourself under the Acropolis on Apostolou Pavlou Street taking in the amazing views slowly sipping an iced coffee or a cold beer. Browse hand-made jewelry and crafts from vendors who line the street with their makeshift stalls. The rest of the neighborhood is quiet, an odd mix of mom-and-pop stores and dilapidated houses that are slowly being renovated.

Don't Miss

The Temple of Hephaestus is one of the best-preserved Temples in all of Greece. Built by Iktinos—best known as one of the creators of the Parthenon—in the mid-5th century BC, it was dedicated to the god of fire and smithery as well as to Athina Ergani, goddess of craftspeople.

Getting Here

Thisseo has a metro station, but it is only a short walk from Monastiraki. Much of the district is pedestrianized.

Best Restaurant

Kuzina. Sleek and dazzlingly decorated, the restaurant serves inventive seafood and pasta, among the best in Athens. $ *Average main: €30* ✉ *Adrianou 9, Thissio* ☎ *210/324–0133* 🌐 *www.kuzina.gr* 🚇 *Thissio*

Lycabettus Hill

The Best Sunset in Athens

Myth claims that Athens's highest hill came into existence when Athena removed a piece of Mt. Pendeli, intending to boost the height of her temple on the Acropolis. While she was en route, a crone brought her bad tidings, and the flustered goddess dropped the rock in the middle of the city. Dog-walkers and joggers have made it their daily stomping grounds, and kids love the ride up the steeply inclined *teleferique* (funicular) to the summit (one ride every 30 minutes), crowned by whitewashed Agios Georgios chapel with a bell tower donated by Queen Olga. On a clear day, not only can you see the Acropolis, Piraeus port, and Aegina island but also the mountains of the Peloponnese beyond. Cars park up at the top at sunset for swoon-inducing magic-hour views of the city lights going on, as the moon rises over "violet-crowned" Mt. Hymettus. Refreshments and snacks are available from the modest canteen popular with concertgoers, who flock to events at the hill's open-air theater during summer months.

Don't Miss

Hunt out the church of Agios Isidoros, which is built into a sparkling quartz cave on the western slopes of Lycabettus.

Getting Here

The base is a 15-minute walk northeast of Syntagma Sq. A funicular runs every 30 minutes (every 10 minutes during rush hour) from the corner of Ploutarchou and Aristippou (take Bus 060 from Kanari or Kolonaki Square); the terminal is on Aristippou Street (walk all the way up Ploutarchou Street, right to the top of the stairs).

Lucabettus Hill. ☎ *210/721–0701 funicular information* 🌐 *www.lycabettushill.com* 🎟 *Funicular €8 round-trip, €5 one-way* 🚆 *Evangelismos*

Anafiotika

A Village Under the Acropolis

In the shadow of the Acropolis, part whitewashed and part earth-hued, Anafiotika is still populated by some descendants of the Anafi stonemasons who arrived from that small Cycladic island. Wander around and try to get as lost as possible as the village remains an enchanting area of simple stone houses, many nestled right into the bedrock of the sacred rock of Acropolis, most little changed over the years, others reverently restored. Cascades of bougainvillea and pots of geraniums and marigolds enliven the balconies and rooftops, and the prevailing serenity is in blissful contrast to the cacophony of modern Athens. In classical times, this district was abandoned because the Delphic Oracle claimed it as sacred ground. The buildings here were constructed by masons, who came to find work in the rapidly expanding Athens of the 1840s and 1850s. They took over this area, whose rocky terrain was similar to Anafi's, hastily erecting homes overnight and taking advantage of an Ottoman law that decreed that if you could put up a structure between sunset and sunrise, the property was yours.

Don't Miss

Perched on the bedrock of the Acropolis is Ayios Georgios tou Vrachou (St. George of the Rock), which marks the southeast edge of the village. One of the most beautiful churches of Athens, it is still in use today.

Getting Here

From Acropolis or Syntagma metro stations head into Plaka. At the western edge of the Plaka under the Acropolis you'll come across the first narrow alleys of the Anafiotika.

Varvakeio Agora

Feeding Athens for over a Century

Athens's raucous Central Market is on Athinas Street, which runs down from Omonia Square to Monastiraki Square: on one side are open-air stalls selling fruit and vegetables, with a few stores selling mainly eastern European foods tucked at the back. Across the street, in the huge neoclassical covered market, built between 1870 and 1884 (and renovated in 1996), are the meat market surrounding the fish market, juxtaposing the surrealistic composition of suspended carcasses and shimmering fish on marble counters. The shops at the north end of the market, to the right on Sofokleous, sell the best cheese, olives, halvah, bread, spices, and cold cuts—including *pastourma* (spicy cured beef)—available in Athens. Nearby is Evripidou Street, lined with herb and spice shops all the way down. Small restaurants serving traditional fare and *patsa* (tripe soup) used to dot the market, staying open until dawn and were popular stops with weary clubbers trying to ease their hangovers. Today only one remains.

Don't Miss

Ipeiros. The last remaining Ksechinathiko-style taverna, Ipeiros is more than just a place to eat, it's a legendary Athenian experience. ✉ *Filopoimenos 4, Varvakeio Agora* ☎ *210/3240773*

When to Go

The market rumbles into life in the early hours of the morning around 6 am until 3 pm. If you're after seafood or fish, earlier means fresher.

✉ *Athinas St., Monastiraki* ⏲ *Closed Sun.* *Monastiraki*

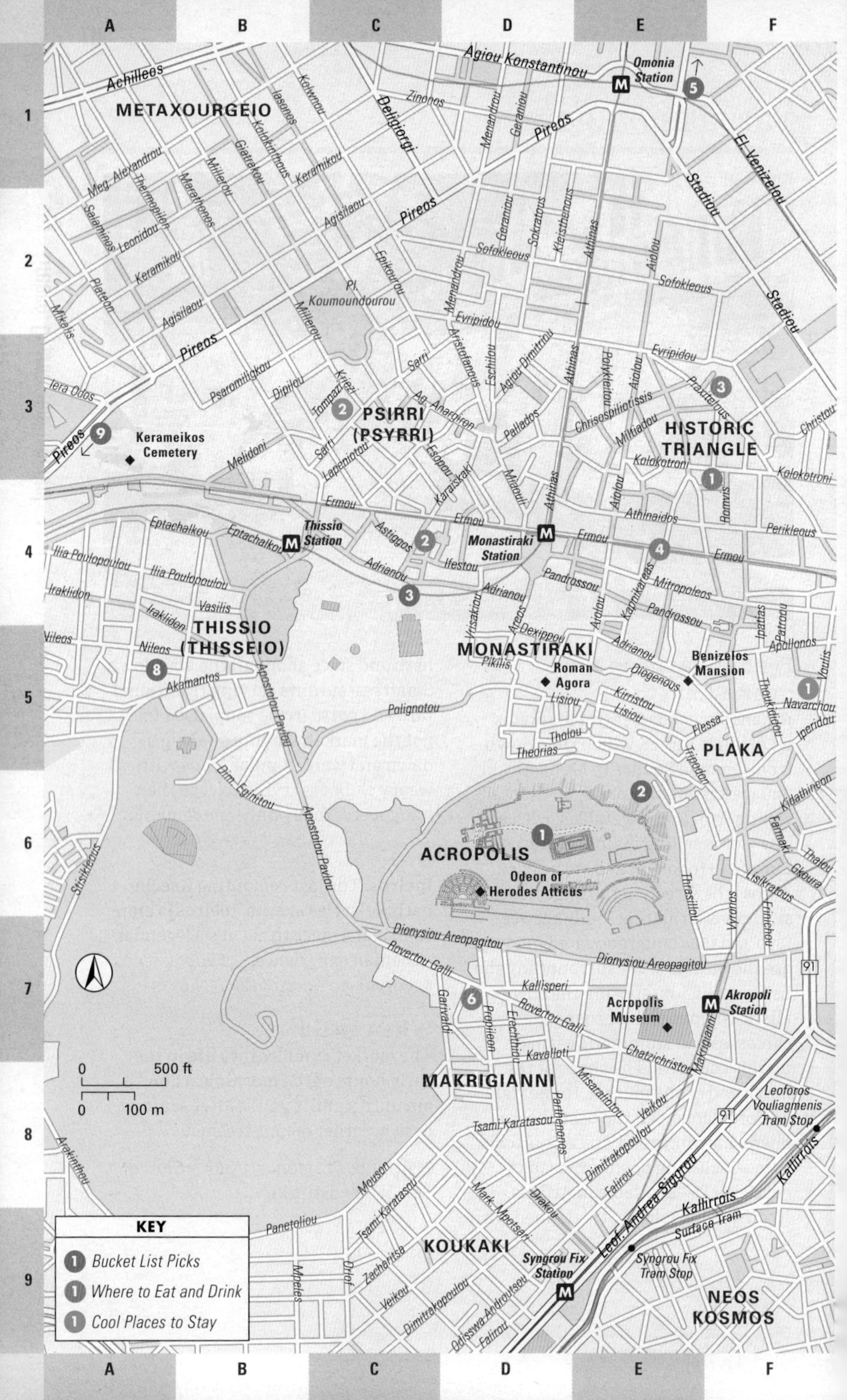

METAXOURGEIO
PSIRRI (PSYRRI)
HISTORIC TRIANGLE
THISSIO (THISSEIO)
MONASTIRAKI
PLAKA
ACROPOLIS
MAKRIGIANNI
KOUKAKI
NEOS KOSMOS
Omonia Station
Thissio Station
Monastiraki Station
Akropoli Station
Syngrou Fix Station
Kerameikos Cemetery
Roman Agora
Benizelos Mansion
Odeon of Herodes Atticus
Acropolis Museum
Leoforos Vouliagmenis Tram Stop
Syngrou Fix Tram Stop
Surface Tram
0 500 ft
0 100 m
KEY
Bucket List Picks
Where to Eat and Drink
Cool Places to Stay

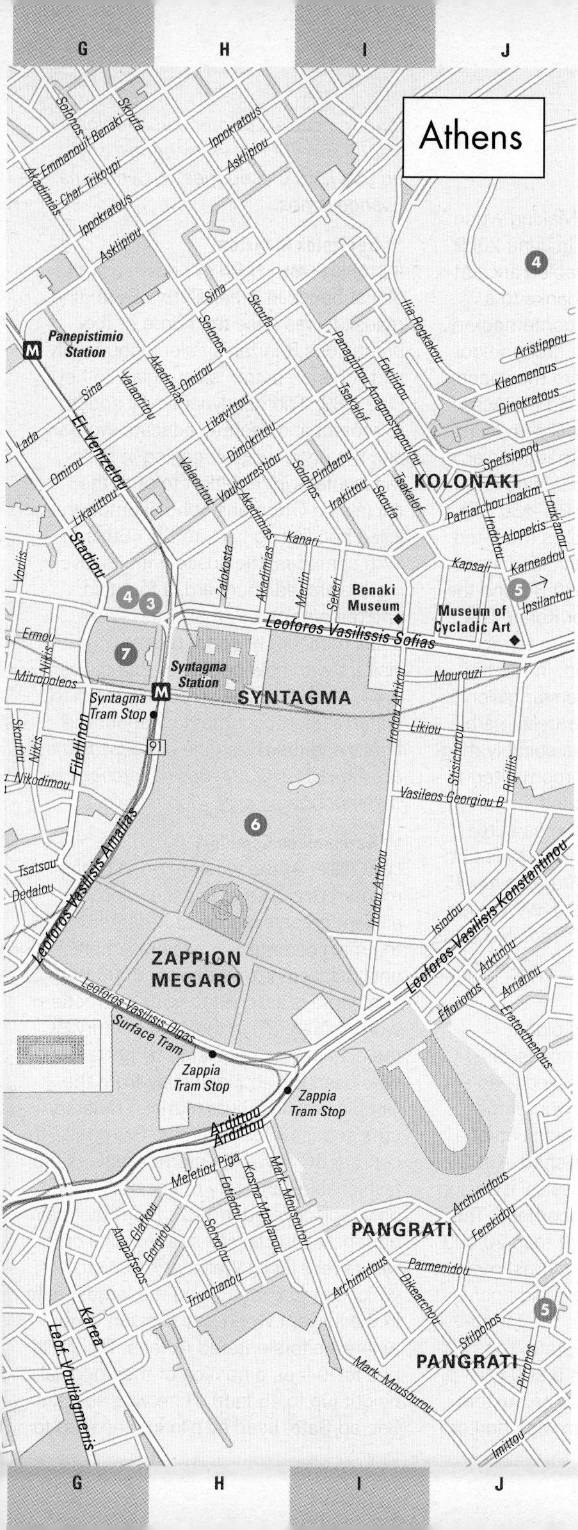

Athens

Bucket List Picks ▼

1 The Acropolis **D6**
2 Anafiotika **E6**
3 Ancient Agora **C4**
4 Lycabettus Hill **J2**
5 National Archaeological Museum **E1**
6 National Garden **H5**
7 Syntagma Square **G4**
8 Thisseo **A5**
9 Varvakeio Agora **A3**

Where to Eat and Drink ▼

1 Baba Au Rum **F4**
2 Café Avissinia **C4**
3 The Clumsies **F3**
4 Kapnikarea **E4**
5 Spondi **J8**
6 Strofi **D7**

Cool Places to Stay ▼

1 Electra Palace **F5**
2 The Foundry **C3**
3 Grande Bretagne **G4**
4 King George Athens **G4**
5 The Modernist **J4**

When in Athens

★ Acropolis Museum

HISTORY MUSEUM | FAMILY | Making world headlines when it opened in June 2009, the museum nods to the fabled ancient hill above it but speaks—thanks to a spectacular building—in a contemporary architectural language. The ground-floor exhibit features objects from the sanctuaries and settlements around the Acropolis, including theatrical masks and vases from the sanctuary of the matrimonial deity Nymphe. The first floor is devoted to the Archaic period (650 BC–480 BC), with rows of precious statues mounted for 360-degree viewing, including stone lions gorging a bull from 570 BC and the legendary five Caryatids (or Korai). The second floor is devoted to the terrace and restaurant–coffee shop. In the top-floor atrium, don't miss the star gallery devoted to the temple's Pentelic marble decorations, consisting of a suitably magnificent, rectangle-shaped room tilted to align with the Parthenon itself and empty spaces that can hold the pieces Lord Elgin whisked off to the British Museum in London. ✉ *Dionyssiou Areopagitou 15, Acropolis* ☎ *210/900–0900* 🌐 *www.theacropolismuseum.gr* 🎫 *€10, reduced to €5* ⏲ *Closed Mon. Nov.–Mar.* Ⓜ *Acropolis.*

★ Benaki Museum

HISTORY MUSEUM | Greece's oldest private museum, which emphasizes the country's later heritage, received a spectacular face-lift in the year of the Athens Olympics with the addition of a hypermodern wing. Established in 1926, it is in an imposing Neoclassical mansion in the posh Kolonaki neighborhood. The permanent collection (more than 20,000 items are on display in 36 rooms) moves chronologically from the ground floor upward, from prehistory to the formation of the modern Greek state. You might see anything from a 5,000-year-old hammered-gold bowl to an austere Byzantine icon of the Virgin Mary to Lord Byron's pistols. ✉ *Koumbari 1, Kolonaki* ☎ *210/367–1000* 🌐 *www.benaki.org/en* 🎫 *€12* ⏲ *Closed Tues.* Ⓜ *Syntagma, Evangelismos.*

★ Benizelos Mansion

HISTORIC HOME | FAMILY | Known as "the oldest house in Athens," this Byzantine mansion was once the home of the prestigious Benizelos Paleologou family, and Athens's patron saint Agia Filothei (1522–89). Filothei dynamically sought to protect and secretly educate women and the poor, while engaging in diplomatic affairs in her effort to oust the occupying Ottomans, who eventually killed her. Dating back to the 16th and 17th centuries, the space with its lovely marble-arched courtyard, a fountain, and remains of a Roman wall is now a folk museum of sorts, presenting visitors with how people of that caliber lived. There is also a screening room to watch a short documentary about the family and the Byzantine era. ✉ *Adrianou 96, Plaka* ☎ *210/324–8861* 🌐 *archontiko-mpenizelon.gr* Ⓜ *Monastiraki.*

★ Kerameikos Cemetery

CEMETERY | At the western edge of the modern Gazi district lies the wide, ancient green expanse of Kerameikos, the main cemetery in ancient Athens until Sulla destroyed the city in 86 BC. The name is associated with the modern word "ceramic": in the 12th century BC the district was populated by potters who used the abundant clay from the languid Iridanos River to make funerary urns and grave decorations. From the 7th century BC onward, Kerameikos was the fashionable cemetery of ancient Athens, only rediscovered in 1861. From the main entrance, you can still see remains of the Makra Teixi (Long Walls) of Themistocles, which ran to Piraeus, and the largest gate in the ancient world, the Dipylon Gate, where visitors entered Athens. The walls rise to 10 feet, a fraction of their original height (up to 45 feet). Here was also the Sacred Gate, used by pilgrims headed to

Eleusis. Between the two gates are the foundations of the Pompeion, the starting point of the Panathenaic procession. On the Street of Tombs, a number of the distinctive stelae (funerary monuments) remain, including a replica of the marble relief of Dexilios, a knight who died in the war against Corinth (394 BC). To the left of the site's entrance is the Oberlaender Museum, also known as the Kerameikos Museum, whose displays include sculpture, terra-cotta figures, and some striking red-and-black-figured pottery. ✉ *Ermou 148, Gazi-Kerameikos* ☎ *210/346–3552* 🌐 *odysseus.culture.gr* 🎫 *Full: €8 site and museum; €30 joint ticket for all Unification of Archaeological Sites* Ⓜ *Kerameikos.*

★ **Museum of Cycladic Art**

ART MUSEUM | FAMILY | Also known as the Nicholas P. and Dolly Goulandris Foundation, and funded by one of Greece's richest families, this museum has an outstanding collection of 350 Cycladic artifacts dating from the Bronze Age, including many of the enigmatic marble figurines whose slender shapes fascinated such artists as Picasso, Modigliani, and Brancusi. Along with Cycladic masterpieces, a wide array from other eras is also on view, ranging from the Bronze Age through the 6th century AD. The third floor is devoted to Cypriot art, while the fourth floor showcases a fascinating exhibition on "scenes from daily life in antiquity." A glass corridor connects the main building to the gorgeous, 19th-century, Neoclassical Stathatos Mansion, where temporary exhibits are mounted. ✉ *Neofitou Douka 4, Kolonaki* ☎ *210/7228–3215* 🌐 *www.cycladic.gr* 🎫 *€7* ⏲ *Closed Tues.* Ⓜ *Evangelismos.*

★ **Odeon of Herodes Atticus**

NOTABLE BUILDING | Hauntingly beautiful, this ancient theater was built in AD 160 by the affluent Herodes Atticus in memory of his wife, Regilla. Known as the Irodion and visited throughout the summer by culture vultures, it is nestled Greek-style into the hillside, but with typically Roman arches in its three-story stage building and barrel-vaulted entrances. The theater, which holds 5,000, was restored and reopened in 1955 for the Athens Epidaurus Festival. ✉ *Dionyssiou Areopagitou, Acropolis* ✥ *Near Propylaion* ☎ *210/928–2900 box office, 210/322–1897 persons with disabilities* 🌐 *aefestival.gr* Ⓜ *Acropolis.*

★ **Roman Agora**

HISTORIC SIGHT | FAMILY | The city's commercial center from the 1st century BC to the 4th century AD, the Roman Market was a large rectangular courtyard with a peristyle that provided shade for the arcades of shops. Its most notable feature is the west entrance's Bazaar Gate, or Gate of Athena Archegetis, completed around AD 2. On the north side stands one of the few remains of the Turkish occupation, the Fethiye (Victory) Mosque; eerily beautiful, it dates from the late 15th century. Surrounded by a cluster of old houses on the western slope of the Acropolis, the world-famous Tower of the Winds (Aerides), now open to the public for visits, is the most appealing and well-preserved of the Roman monuments of Athens. ✉ *Pelopidas and Aiolou, Plaka* ☎ *210/324–5220* 🌐 *odysseus.culture.gr* 🎫 *€8; €30 5-day joint ticket for all Unification of Archaeological Sites* Ⓜ *Monastiraki.*

Where to Eat and Drink

★ **Baba Au Rum**

COCKTAIL LOUNGES | Rum is the star at this trendy, popular bar in the heart of Monastiraki. All the liqueurs, syrups, and essences to flavor highly original and delicious cocktails are made in-house. The vibe is buzzy both indoors—where the decor has stylish yet quirky vintage touches like stained-glass lamps and antique drinking glasses—and out, where crowds gather especially on weekends. From tiki-inspired beverages to dark rum, chocolate, and lemon creations, you can spend hours experimenting here. Voted as one of the top 50 bars worldwide. ✉ *Klitiou 6, Monastiraki* ☎ *211/710–9140* 🌐 *babaaurum.com* Ⓜ *Monastiraki.*

★ Café Avissinia

$$ | GREEK | Facing hoary and merchant-packed Abyssinia Square, this timeworn but exceptional eatery is popular with locals who want home-cooked traditional food with heavy Asia Minor influences and endless servings of the excellent barrel wine and ouzo. Diners love to settle within the elegant glass-and-wood interior to sample mussels and rice pilaf, wine-marinated octopus with pasta, fresh garden salad, or any of the dips. **Known for:** delicious spinach-enriched moussaka and Soutzoukakia; an air of nostalgia but with style; live music on weekend afternoons. $ *Average main: €15* ✉ *Abyssinia Sq., Kynetou 7, Psirri* ☎ *210/321–7047* 🌐 *www.cafeavissinia.net* ⏲ *Closed Mon.* Ⓜ *Thissio, Monastiraki.*

The Clumsies

COCKTAIL LOUNGES | Located between Syntagma and Psirri, this innovative and wildly popular bar-restaurant is among the most popular in Athens. The impressively decorated, multilevel venue even has a private room, where clients can order bespoke drinks. Despite its appeal to people of all ages and styles, The Clumsies is generally unpretentious, and the unique cocktails that fall under the categories happiness, excitement, tenderness (there's a degustation menu that offers the chance of tasting four to five smaller versions) are top quality. ✉ *Praxitelous 30, Monastiraki* ☎ *210/323–2682* 🌐 *www.theclumsies.gr* Ⓜ *Monastiraki, Syntagma.*

★ Kapnikarea

LIVE MUSIC | Down-to-earth, local, unpretentious, Kapnikarea is named after the sunken Byzantine church that it flanks. Come here to relax after some sightseeing or shopping on busy Ermou Street where live rembetika music swirls mesmerically around a little alleyway every day until midnight. Locals love it and sit for hours on end, morphing into impromptu choirs, intoning their favorite songs. This little spot has been around for ages and is not to be missed. ✉ *Hristopoulou 2, at Ermou 57, Monastiraki* ✣ *Behind Kapnikarea church* ☎ *210/322–7394* Ⓜ *Monastiraki.*

Strofi

$$ | GREEK | It's the place where the likes of Rudolph Nureyev, Maria Callas, and Elizabeth Taylor dined after performances at the Odeon of Herodes Atticus nearby, and its walls are lined with images attesting to its glamorous past. Once a humble taverna with a fantastic Acropolis view, its current modernist renovated version and simple traditional Greek menu are still pleasing to tourists and politicians alike. **Known for:** a lovely view of the Parthenon; a reliable Greek menu; grilled meats. $ *Average main: €25* ✉ *Rovertou Galli 25, Makriyianni* ☎ *210/921–4130* 🌐 *www.strofi.gr* ⏲ *Closed Mon.* Ⓜ *Acropolis.*

Cool Places to Stay

Electra Palace

$$$$ | HOTEL | If you want luxurious elegance, good service, and a great location, this is the hotel for you: rooms from the fifth floor up have a view of the Acropolis, and, in summer, you can bask in the sunshine at the outdoor swimming pool (taking in the view of Athens's greatest monument) or catch the sunset from the rooftop garden—if you're not enjoying some serious pampering in the spa. **Pros:** gorgeous rooms; great location; shady garden and rooftop pool. **Cons:** air-conditioning can be problematic; pool is small and gets busy; traffic jams on road in front. $ *Rooms from: €300* ✉ *Nikodimou 18–20, Plaka* ☎ *210/337–0000* 🌐 *www.electrahotels.gr* *154 rooms* 🍽 *Free Breakfast* Ⓜ *Syntagma.*

★ **The Foundry**

$$$ | HOTEL | FAMILY | Tucked away in the far corner of Psiri, The Foundry, housed in an early industrial building that fuses vintage mid-century design with restrained luxury, is perfect for couples and families visiting the capital. **Pros:** outstanding design; great service; easy access to Athens's best sights. **Cons:** no parking; few rooms; hot items in the breakfast basket aren't always hot. *Rooms from: €236 Sarri 40, Psirri 211/182–4604 www.thefoundrysuitesathens.com 12 rooms Free Breakfast Monastiraki.*

★ **Grande Bretagne**

$$$$ | HOTEL | FAMILY | With a guest list that includes more than a century's worth of royals, rock stars, and heads of state, the landmark Grande Bretagne remains the most exclusive and architecturally majestic hotel in Athens. **Pros:** all-out luxury; exquisite rooms; excellent café, spa, and pool lounge. **Cons:** expensive; decor may not suit all tastes; demonstrations usually take place at Syntagma Square. *Rooms from: €450 Vasileos Georgiou A'1 at Syntagma Sq., Syntagma 210/333–0000, 210/331–5555 www.grandebretagne.gr 320 rooms Free Breakfast Syntagma.*

★ **King George Athens**

$$$$ | HOTEL | One of the most historic and luxurious hotels in Athens, the King George is where numerous celebrities stay (often in the Royal Penthouse suite), and first impressions tell you why: a spacious lobby done in marble, mahogany, velvet, leather, and gold trim lures you into a world where antique crystal lamps and frosted glass shower stalls with mother-of-pearl tiles raise standards of luxury to dizzying heights. **Pros:** sophisticated dining; luxurious rooms; attentive service. **Cons:** slow elevators; thin walls in some rooms; no pool. *Rooms from: €401 3 Vasileos Georgiou A, Syntagma 210/322–2210 www.kinggeorgeathens.com 102 rooms Free Breakfast Syntagma.*

★ **The Modernist**

$$ | HOTEL | Opened in the summer of 2021, this boutique hotel is setting the benchmark for the industry in the capital for refined and elegant design, Acropolis views, and trendy touches like a record player or a Polaroid camera in the rooms, not to mention a magic formula to make guests feel well looked after. **Pros:** standout service; cool designer boutique hotel; gym. **Cons:** no kid-friendly meals; no parking; some hot-cold tap issues. *Rooms from: €204 I.Gennadiou 4, Kolonaki 216/000–2130 www.themodernisthotels.com/athens 38 rooms Free Breakfast Evangelismos.*

Mainland Greece

The sight greets you time and again in Greece—a line of solid, sun-bleached masonry silhouetted against a clear blue sky. If you're lucky, a cypress waves gently to one side. What makes the scene all the more fulfilling is the realization that a kindred spirit looked up and saw the same temple or theater some 2,000 or more years ago.

Temples, theaters, statues, a stray Doric column or two, the fragment of a Corinthian capital: these traces of the ancients are thick on the ground in Greece.

Greece still remains an agelessly impressive land. Western poetry, music, architecture, politics, medicine, and law all had their birth centuries ago here. The Greek countryside itself remains a stunning presence, dotted with cypress groves, vineyards, and olive trees; carved into gentle bays or dramatic coves bordered with startling white sand; or articulated into rolling hills and rugged mountain ranges that plunge into the sea. Indeed, you cannot travel far across the land without encountering the sea, or far across the sea without encountering one of its roughly 2,000 islands. Approximately equal in size to New York State, Greece has 15,019 km (9,312 miles) of coastline, more than any other country of its size.

From Attica in the southeast to the wilder reaches of Epirus and Thessaly in the northwest to Macedonia in the northeast, Greece offers a wide variety of changing landscapes, from windswept plains to towering mountains. One of the highlights is the vast, rugged Peloponnese Peninsula, which nourished kingdoms and empires.

Wherever you head, you should explore this fascinating country with open eyes. Chances are you'll enjoy it in all its forms: its slumbering cafés and buzzing tavernas, its elaborate religious rituals, and its stark, bright beauty. As the lucky traveler soon learns, although their countryside may be bleached and stony, the Greeks themselves provide the vibrant color that has long since vanished from classical monuments once saturated with blue, gold, and vermilion pigment under the eye-searing Aegean sun.

Sounion

Where Attica Meets the Aegean

Poised at the edge of a rugged 195-foot cliff, the Temple of Poseidon hovers between sea and sky here. The archaeological site at Sounion is one of the most photographed in Greece. In antiquity, the view from the cliff was matched emotion for emotion by the sight of the cape (called the "sacred headland" by Homer) and its mighty temple when viewed from the sea—a sight that brought joy to sailors, knowing upon spotting the massive temple that they were close to home. Aegeus, the legendary king of Athens, threw himself off the cliff when he saw the approaching ship of his son, Theseus, with black sails leading him to believe his son was dead. To honor Aegeus, the Greeks named their sea, the Aegean, after him.

Don't Miss

The National Park of Sounion has some great trails to hike, through pine forests past antiquities and Byzantine chapels. Remember to bring your swimming gear and plenty of water.

When to Go

Arrange your visit so that you enjoy the panorama of sea and islands from this airy platform either early in the morning, before the summer haze clouds visibility and the tour groups arrive, or at dusk, when the promontory has one of the most spectacular sunset vantage points in Attica.

Getting Here

From Athens there's a regular bus service from Ktel Attica; however, the best way to go is by taxi, on an organized tour, or by renting a car.

Temple of Poseidon. ✉ *Cape Sounion* ☎ *22920/39363* 🌐 *odysseus.culture.gr* 🎫 *€10*

Meteora

Nearer to Heaven

Here in a remote area of central Greece, landscape and legend conspire to twist reality into fantasy. Soaring skyward out of dense orchards looms a different kind of forest: gigantic rock pinnacles, the loftiest of which rises 984 feet. But even more extraordinary than these stone pillars are the monasteries that perch atop the stalagmitic skyscrapers. Funded by Byzantine emperors, run by ascetic monks, and once scaled by James Bond, these saintly castles-in-air are almost literally "out of this world." The name Meteora comes from the Greek word ("to hang in midair"). These world-famous monasteries seem to do just that. Legend would have it that they are remnants of an epic battle between the Titans and the Olympian Gods. If you visit just two, choose Megalo Meteora and Varlaam.

Don't Miss

The Museum of Geological Formations of Meteora takes visitors back 30 million years to when the geological morphology at Meteora is believed to have taken shape. An audio-visual installation details the events leading to the present-day phenomenon and explores the geology of Greece.

Getting Here

Just outside Kalambaka, the monasteries are easily accessible by both train and bus (there are regular services from both Athens and Thessaloniki); you can also visit on a long full-day tour from Athens (🌐 *visitmeteora.travel*).

Meteora. ✉ *Megalo Meteora* 🕓 *Closed Tues. and Tues.–Thurs (Nov.–Mar.); Ayia Triada closed Thurs.; Varlaam closed Fri. and Thurs.–Fri. (Nov.–Mar.); Ayia Barbara closed Wed. (Nov.–Mar.); Ayios Stephanos closed Mon.* 🎫 *€3 for each monastery*

Delphi

An Ancient Oracle

High in the mountains, Delphi, the home of the most famous oracle of antiquity, is an extraordinary ancient site perched dramatically on the edge of a grove leading to the sea. When the archaeological site is first seen from the road, it would appear that there is hardly anything left to attest to the existence of what was once an expansive city. True, only the Treasury of the Athenians and a few other columns are left standing, but once you are within the precincts, ascending the slopes, the plan becomes clearer and the layout is revealed in such detail that it is possible to conjure up a vision of what the scene must have once been, when Delphi was the holiest place in all Greece. Most impressive are The Temple of Apollo from the 4th century BC and, above it, the well-preserved stadium, which seated 5,000.

Don't Miss

The museum of Delphi is home to a wonderful collection of art and architectural sculpture, its centerpiece being one of the greatest surviving ancient bronzes on display anywhere, which commands a prime position in a spacious hall: *The Bronze Charioteer.*

Getting Here

KTEL Fokidas buses from Athens that go to Arachova continue on to Delphi (three hours). The first KTEL bus leaves Athens Terminal B (Liossion) typically at 7:30 am or 10:30 am, depending on the day.

Ancient Delphi. ✉ *Delphi Rd. to Arachova, immediately east of modern Delphi* ☎ *22650/82313* 🌐 *odysseus.culture.gr* 🎫 *€12, includes the Sanctuary of Athena and Delphi Museum*

Mount Olympus

The Home of the Gods

Mount Olympus, mythological home of the Ancient Greek gods, has some of the most beautiful nature trails in Europe. Hundreds of species of wildflowers and herbs bloom in spring, more than 85 of which are found only on this mountain. There are basically three routes to Zeus's mountaintop, all beginning in Litochoro. The most-traveled road is Via Prionia; the others are by Diastavrosi (literally, *crossroads*) and along the Enipeos. You can climb all the way on foot, drive up, or negotiate a taxi ride to the end of the road at Prionia (where there's a taverna) and then trek the rest of the way on foot (six hours or so) up to snow-clad Mytikas summit—Greece's highest peak at 9,570 feet. The climb to Prionia takes about four hours; the ride, on a bumpy gravel road—with no guardrails between you and breathtakingly precipitous drops—takes little less than an hour, depending on your nerves. If you can manage to take your eyes off the road, the scenery is magnificent.

Don't Miss

Dion Archaeological Park, at the base of sacred Olympus, was once a sacred city for the Macedonians, devoted primarily to the worship of Zeus and his daughters, the nine Muses.

Getting Here

Trains from Athens and Thessaloniki stop at Litochoro, but by bus you'll need to make one change at Katerini.

Dion Archaeological Site. ✉ *Dion is 7 km (4½ miles) north of Litochoro, off E75/1A, Thessaloniki–Athens road 23510/53484* 🌐 *ancientdion.org* 🎫 *€8, including museum*

Mount Olympus. Plan a solo or organized hike carefully. 🌐 *www.mountolympus.gr*

Vergina

The Royal Macedonian Tombs

At the Aigai Archaeological Site, some of antiquity's greatest treasures await you at the Royal Tombs of Vergina. Today the complex, including a museum, is a fitting shrine to the original capital of the kingdom of Macedonia, then known as Aigai. The entrance is appropriately stunning: you walk down a white-sandstone ramp into the partially underground structure, roofed over by a large earth-covered dome approximately the size of the original (mounded grave). Here on display are some of the legendary artifacts from the age of Philip II of Macedonia. This was the first intact Macedonian tomb ever found—imposing and exquisite, with a huge frieze of a hunting scene, a masterpiece similar to those of the Italian Renaissance but 1,800 years older, along with a massive yet delicate fresco depicting the abduction of Persephone (a copy of which is displayed along one wall of the museum).

Don't Miss

The ancient village ruins of Pellas and its museum—both best known for their intricate, artful, and beautifully preserved floor mosaics, mainly of mythological scenes—are on either side of the main road toward Edessa (where the waterfalls are also well worth a visit).

Getting Here

Public transportation to Vergina is convoluted, so the easiest way to get to Vergina is by car or through an organized tour from Thessaloniki.

Aigai Archaeological Site. ✉ *Vergina, Off E90, near Veria* ☎ *23310/92347* 🌐 *www.aigai.gr* 🎫 *€12; €6 Nov.–Mar.*

Ladadika

The Place to Drink and Dine in Thessaloniki

The food and nightlife epicenter of Greece's second city, with pedestrianized Katouni Street as its key thoroughfare, is near the port. The area was named after the oil (*ladi*) vendors who moved to the area after the great fire of 1917, as this is where oil, spices, and foods were stored. Protected as a historic district from the building frenzy of the mid-1980s, the Ladadika was instead colonized by entrepreneurs who opened cheap tavernas (filling tables with inviting mezedes and carafes of ouzo) and bars in the restored late 19th-century buildings. Locals thronged to the lively area, and more and more establishments opened up and spilled over into the surrounding streets and alleys. Even so, Ladadika still has buckets of charm and hosts many of the city's best and trendiest restaurants and drinking establishments.

Don't Miss

Thessaloniki's most famous landmark—and a symbol of Macedonia—the White Tower is the only medieval defensive tower left standing along the seafront (the other remaining tower, the Trigoniou, is in the Upper City). Now a part of the Museum of Byzantine Culture, its six floors offer an excellent multimedia introduction to the city's history.

Best Restaurant

To Full Tou Meze. Ordering your meal from the eccentric waiters at this busy spot the heart of the bustling Ladadika part of the fun. It is one of the best places in town for mezedes. $ *Average main: €10* ✉ *Katouni 3, Ladadika, Thessaloniki* ☎ *2310/524700* 🌐 *www.fullmeze.gr*

Getting Here

Thessaloniki has an airport with flights from across Europe, so it's possible to fly directly, but it's about a 6-hour train trip from Athens.

Metsovo

A Proud Traditional Village

The quaintly traditional village of Metsovo cascades down a mountain at about 3,300 feet above sea level, below the 6,069-foot Katara pass, which is the highest in Greece and marks the border between Epirus and Thessaly. Even in summer, the temperatures may be in the low 20s C (70s F), and February's average highs are just above freezing. Early evening is a wonderful time to arrive. As you descend through the mist, dazzling lights twinkle in the ravine. Stone houses with gray-slate roofs and sharply projecting wooden balconies line steep, serpentine alleys. In the square, especially after the Sunday service, old men—dressed mostly in black—sit on benches, like crows on a tree branch. Should you arrive on a religious feast day, many villagers will be decked out in traditional costume. Older women often wear dark blue or black dresses with embroidered trim every day, augmenting these with brightly colored aprons, jackets, and scarves with floral embroidery on holidays.

Don't Miss

The fascinating Averoff Museum of regional paintings and sculptures showcases the outstanding art collection amassed by politician and intellectual Evangelos Averoff (1910–90). The 19th- and 20th-century paintings depict historical scenes, local landscapes, and daily activities.

Getting Here

There is no regular train or bus service to Metsovo, so the only feasible options are private car or taxi. From Ioannina, the trip takes about 45 minutes.

Anilio Adventure Park. ✉ *Metsovo* ✣ *6 km (4 miles) south of Metsovo* 🌐 *www.aniliopark.gr*

Averoff Museum. ✉ *Main Sq., Metsovo* 🌐 *www.averoffmuseum.gr* 🎫 *€3* 🕑 *Closed Tues.*

Nissi Island

Just 10 Minutes and a World Away

This small island in Pamvotis Lake, which hosts the third-largest monastic community in Greece, is a quiet refuge from busy Ioannina. As you look back at the outline of Ioannina's citadel and its mosques, the 10-minute boat ride to Nissi seems to take you back in time. No outside vehicles are allowed, and without the din of motorcycles and cars, the picturesque village seems to be in a different world. Ali Pasha once kept deer here for hunting. With its neat houses and flower-trimmed courtyards, pine-edged paths, runaway chickens, and reed-filled backwater, it's the perfect place to relax, have lunch, visit some of the island's fabled monasteries (dress appropriately and carry a small flashlight to make it easier to see the magnificent frescoes), then have a pleasant dinner before returning to the 21st century.

Don't Miss

The main attraction on Nissi is the 16th-century Ayios Pandeleimonos Monastery, now the Ali Pasha Museum. Ali Pasha, the despotic Ottoman ruler of Ioannina in the late 18th and early 19th century, was killed here in the monks' cells on January 17, 1822.

Stay Here

Kastro Hotel. The stylish vibe of old aristocracy coupled with minimalist good taste infuses this neoclassical mansion. $ *Rooms from: €60* ✉ *Andronikou Paleologou 57, Ioannina* ☎ *26510/22866* 🌐 *whotelkastro.gr*

Getting Here

Many European cities have direct flights to Ioannina Airport. There are also daily flights from Athens with Olympic Air. Boats to Nisi leave from the Molos close to Mavili Square.

Vikos Gorge

The World's Deepest Gorge

To get to the famed gorge—the deepest in the world—you follow a precipitous route from the upper limestone tablelands of Monodendri, down almost 3,300 feet to the clear, rushing waters of the Voidomatis trout stream (no swimming allowed) as it flows north into Albania. It's a strenuous but exhilarating eight-hour hike on which you are likely to see dramatic vistas, birds of prey, waterfalls, flowers and herbs, and hooded shepherds tending their flocks. Make sure you have proper footwear, hiking gear, food and water, and emergency supplies and provisions, and never hike in heavy rains or go far in groups of fewer than four. Your safest bet is to go on a guided walk; a number of outfitters schedule gorge hikes and other invigorating activities.

Don't Miss

Papingo, 59 km (37 miles) north of Ioannina, has traditional stone houses topped with the silvery blue slate, varied scenery, and friendly locals. It's divided into two villages, Megalo (Large) and Mikro (small) Papingo. The village is near the Voidomatis River, which has excellent rafting and canoeing.

When to Go

In late summer and autumn the temperature is pleasant and the landscape welcoming.

Getting Here

There's a paltry bus service from Ioannina a couple of times a week. Your best bet for getting here and around is by rental car, taxi, or with a tour company.

Trekking Hellas. This well-established and reliable outfitter offers activities and excursions throughout Greece and uses the best local experts as guides. ✉ *Spiro Lamprou 7, Zagorohoria* ☎ *26510/71703* 🌐 *www.trekking.gr* 🎫 *From €70*

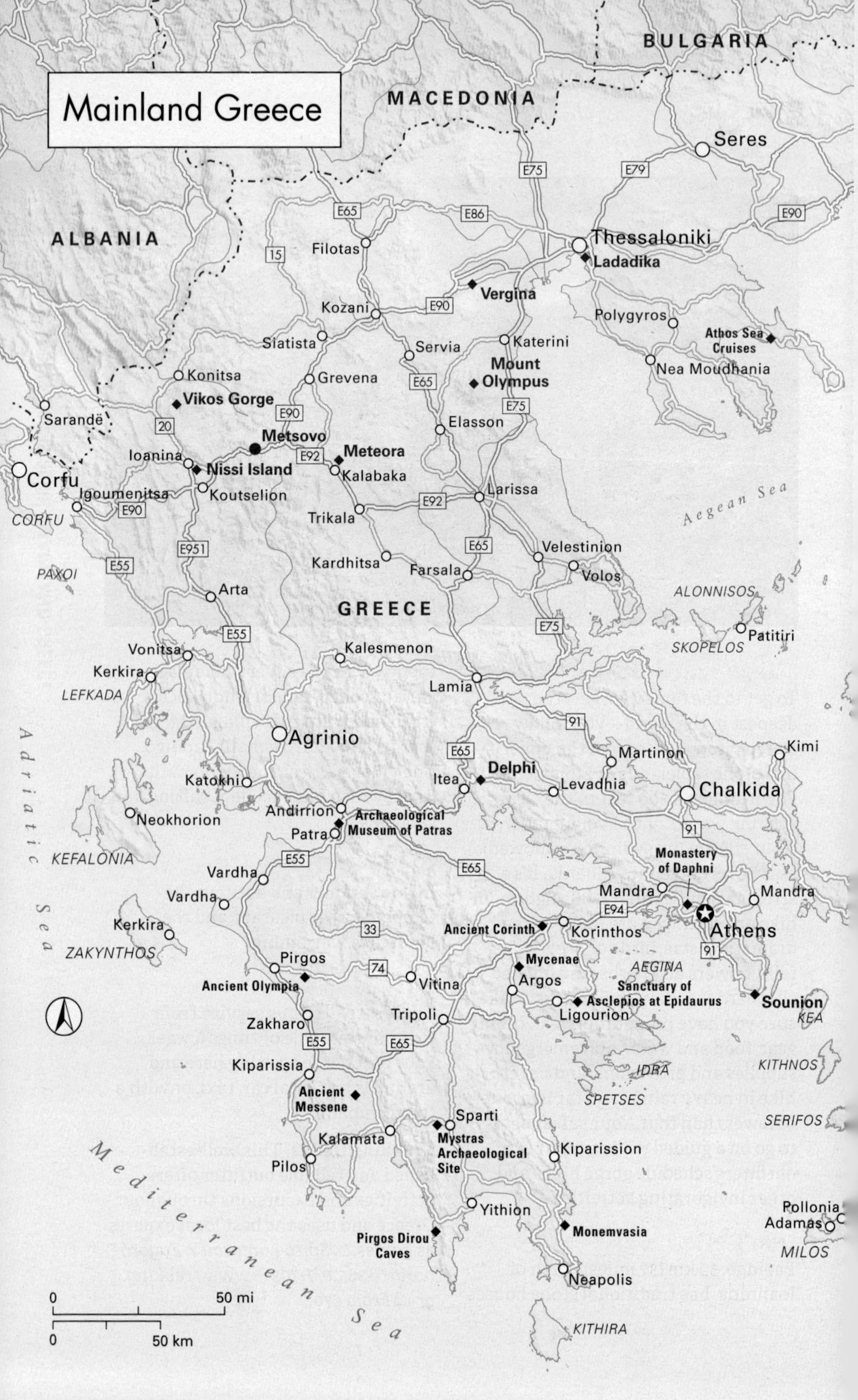

Mainland Greece
BULGARIA
MACEDONIA
ALBANIA
GREECE
Seres
Thessaloniki
Ladadika
Filotas
Vergina
Kozani
Polygyros
Athos Sea Cruises
Siatista
Katerini
Servia
Mount Olympus
Nea Moudhania
Konitsa
Grevena
Vikos Gorge
Sarandë
Elasson
Metsovo
Ioanina
Meteora
Nissi Island
Kalabaka
Corfu
Igoumenitsa
Koutselion
Larissa
CORFU
Trikala
Aegean Sea
PAXOI
Kardhitsa
Velestinion
Farsala
Volos
Arta
ALONNISOS
Patitiri
SKOPELOS
Vonitsa
Kalesmenon
Kerkira
LEFKADA
Lamia
Adriatic Sea
Agrinio
Martinon
Kimi
Delphi
Katokhi
Itea
Levadhia
Chalkida
Neokhorion
Andirrion
Archaeological Museum of Patras
Patra
KEFALONIA
Monastery of Daphni
Vardha
Vardha
Mandra
Mandra
Kerkira
Ancient Corinth
Korinthos
Athens
ZAKYNTHOS
Pirgos
Mycenae
AEGINA
Ancient Olympia
Argos
Vitina
Sanctuary of Asclepios at Epidaurus
Sounion
Ligourion
KEA
Tripoli
Zakharo
KITHNOS
Kiparissia
IDRA
Ancient Messene
SPETSES
Sparti
SERIFOS
Kalamata
Mystras Archaeological Site
Kiparission
Pilos
Mediterranean Sea
Yithion
Pollonia
Adamas
Monemvasia
Pirgos Dirou Caves
MILOS
Neapolis
0
50 mi
0
50 km
KITHIRA
E75
E79
E65
E86
E90
15
E90
E65
E75
20
E90
E92
E92
E90
E951
E55
E65
E75
E55
91
E65
91
E55
E65
E94
33
74
91
E55
E65

When in Greece

★ Ancient Corinth

RUINS | FAMILY | Excavations of one of the great cities of classical and Roman Greece have gone on since 1896, exposing ruins on the slopes of Acrocorinth and northward toward the coast. In ancient times, goods and often entire ships were hauled across the isthmus on a paved road between Corinth's two ports—Lechaion on the Gulf of Corinth and Kenchreai on the Saronic Gulf—ensuring a lively trade with colonies and empires throughout Europe and the Middle East. Most of the buildings that have been excavated are from the Roman era. The highlight is the Temple of Apollo and seven of its original 38 columns. ✉ *Corinth* ✥ *Off E94, 7 km (4½ miles) west of Corinth* ☎ *27410/31207* 🌐 *www.culture.gr* 🎫 *€8 combined ticket (Ancient Corinth and Archeological Museum).*

★ Ancient Messene

RUINS | In terms of footprints, this is one of the most awe-inspiring sites of ancient Greece, thanks to its impressive walls, famed entry gates, vast theater arenas, and temples. One temple alone, the Asklepion, was thought to be an entire town by archaeologists until recently (see 🌐 *www.ancientmessene.gr* for an excellent scholarly take on the site). The most striking aspect of the ruins is the city's circuit wall, a feat of defensive architecture that rises and dips across the hillsides for an astonishing 9 km (5½ miles). Four gates remain; the best preserved is the north or Arcadian Gate, a double set of gates separated by a round courtyard. ✉ *Mavromati* ✥ *From modern town of Messene, turn north at intersection of signposted road to Mavromati* ☎ *27240/51201* 🌐 *www.culture.gr* 🎫 *€10.*

★ Ancient Olympia

RUINS | FAMILY | One of the most celebrated archaeological sites in Greece is located at the foot of the pine-covered Kronion hill and set in a valley where the Kladeos and Alpheios rivers join. Just as athletes from city-states throughout ancient Greece made the journey to compete in the ancient Olympics—the first sports competition—visitors from all over the world today make their way to the small modern Arcadian town. The Olympic Games, first staged around the 8th century BC, were played here in the stadium, hippodrome, and other venues for some 1,100 years. Today, the venerable ruins of these structures attest to the majesty and importance of the first Olympiads. Modern Olympia, an attractive mountain town surrounded by pleasant hilly countryside, has hotels and tavernas, convenient for visitors to the ancient site. ✉ *Off Ethnikos Odos 74, Olympia* ✥ *Ancient site is a 10-minute walk from the Archeological Museum* ☎ *26240/22517* 🌐 *odysseus.culture.gr* 🎫 *€12, combined ticket with Museums, €6 Nov.–Mar.*

★ Athos Sea Cruises

BOAT TOURS | FAMILY | Some travelers prefer to cruise past the area's monasteries since they are off-limits to women. Athos Sea Cruises has six separate cruises that sail here from April to October embarking at either 9:30 or 10:30 am, with an additional afternoon departure at 2 pm from May to October; tours last three hours. There is commentary in English, French, Russian, and German. Tickets can be bought from the Ouranoupolis central square. ✉ *Ouranoupolis* ✥ *Near tower on main road* ☎ *23770/71370 Mr. Rodokalakis, 23770/71606 Ms. Rodokalaki, 23770/71071 Mr. Riga* 🌐 *www.athos-cruises.gr* 🎫 *From €18.*

★ Monastery of Daphni

HISTORIC SIGHT | Sacked by Crusaders, inhabited by Cistercian monks, and desecrated by Turks, this UNESCO World Heritage site remains one of the most splendid Byzantine monuments in Greece. Dating mostly from the 11th century (the golden age of Byzantine art), the church contains a series of miraculously preserved mosaics without parallel: powerful portraits of figures from the Old and New Testaments, images of Christ and the Virgin Mary in the *Presentation of the Virgin*, and, in the golden dome, a stern *Pantokrator* ("ruler of all") surrounded by the 16 Old Testament prophets who predicted his coming. An ongoing restoration project makes it hard to see some of the mosaics, but this doesn't take away much of the awe inspired by the Byzantine masters. ✉ *Peristeri* ✣ *At the end of Iera Odos, at Athinon* ☎ *21058/11558* 🌐 *www.culture.gr* 🎫 *Free* ⏲ *Closed Mon. and Tues.*

Monemvasia

TOWN | The eastern "finger" dangling off the southern edge of the Peloponnese is the dramatic setting for this Byzantine town that clings to the side of the 1,148-foot rock that was once a headland until it was separated from the mainland by an earthquake in AD 375. The Laconians, who settled here in the 6th century, found it to be such an effective defense that a millennia later this became the last outpost of the Byzantine empire to hold out against the Turks. Now just 10 families live here, but the citadel is wonderfully preserved, with the Upper Town, where most of the great ruins lie. It is a delight to wander the back lanes and along the old walls and spend the night. ✉ *Monemvasia* ✣ *140 km (85 miles) east of Gythion* 🌐 *monemvasia.gr.*

★ **Mycenae**

RUINS | FAMILY | The gloomy, gray ruins are hardly distinguishable from the rock beneath; it's hard to believe that this kingdom was once so powerful that it ruled a large portion of the Mediterranean world, from 1500 BC to 1100 BC. The major archaeological artifacts from the dig are now in the National Archaeological Museum in Athens (particularly the so-called "Death Mask of Agamemnon," so seeing those first will add to your appreciation of the ruined city, though both the museums of nearby Nafplion and at the site offer plenty of context for what you'll see. ✉ *Mycenae* ✣ *21 km (13 miles) north of Nafplion* ☎ *27510/76585* 🌐 *www.culture.gr* 🎫 *Combined ticket with Treasury of Atreus and Mycenae Archaeological Museum €12.*

★ **Mystras Archaeological Site**

RUINS | FAMILY | In this Byzantine city, abandoned gold-and-stone palaces, churches, and monasteries line serpentine paths; the scent of herbs and wildflowers permeates the air; goat bells tinkle; and walnut, fig, and lime trees scatter the ground with their fruit. An intellectual and cultural center where philosophers like Chrysoloras, "the sage of Byzantium," held forth on the good and the beautiful, Mystras seems an appropriate place for the last hurrah of the Byzantine emperors. Today the splendid ruins are a UNESCO World Heritage site and one of the most impressive sights in the Peloponnese. ✉ *Ano Chora, Mystras* ☎ *27310/23315* 🌐 *odysseus.culture.gr* 🎫 *€12.*

★ **Pirgos Dirou Caves**

CAVE | FAMILY | Carved out of the limestone by the slow-moving underground river Vlychada on its way to the sea, the vast Pirgos Dirou caves—actually two main caves, Glyfada and Alepotrypa—are one of Greece's more popular natural attractions. The eerie caverns, places of worship in Paleolithic and Neolithic times, were believed to be entrances to the underworld by the ancient Greeks, and served as hiding places millennia later for Resistance fighters during World War II. Today you climb aboard a boat for a 25-minute tour of Glyfada's scenic grottoes. ✉ *Pirgos Dirou* ✣ *10 km (6 miles) southwest of Areopolis, 5 km (3 miles) west of Areopolis–Vathia road* ☎ *27330/52222* 🎫 *€15 (€10 if booked online).*

★ **Sanctuary of Asklepios at Epidaurus**

RUINS | FAMILY | What was once the most famous healing center in the ancient world is today best known for its remarkably well preserved theater, which was buried at some time in antiquity and remained untouched until it was uncovered in the late 19th century. Built in the 4th century BC by the architect Polykleitos the Younger, the 14,000-seat theater was never remodeled in antiquity, and because it was rather remote, the stones were never quarried for secondary building use. In addition, the acoustics are so perfect that even from the last of the 55 tiers every word can be heard. It's the setting for a highly acclaimed summer drama festival. ✉ *Epidaurus* ✥ *Off Hwy. 70, near Ligourio* ☎ *27530/22009* 🌐 *www.culture.gr* 🎫 *€12.*

Where to Eat and Drink

★ Baobab

LIVE MUSIC | Minimalist bar where the people take center stage over the decor. As the night intensifies so does the music, which morphs from easy-on-the-ear jazz, afro beat, and soul to dance-inducing electric sounds. If you're into good sounds look no further as the late-night live DJs are the bees knees. The cocktails aren't too bad either. ✉ *23 Ernestou Emprar, Kentro* ☎ *23155/38460* 🌐 *www.facebook.com/baobab.skg.*

★ Duck Private Cheffing

$$$ | **GREEK FUSION** | **FAMILY** | A gourmet dining experience based on fresh, seasonal ingredients with an ever-changing menu, Duck offers the opportunity to sample an array of local seafood prepared in contemporary ways. You might be served fish carpaccio or shrimp *kritharoto* (barley pasta cooked risotto-style), scallops with celeriac cream or ravioli with beef ragout, Gorgonzola sauce, and almonds. **Known for:** fresh, seasonal ingredients; elevated cuisine; reservations-only dining. $ *Average main: €30* ✉ *Chalkis 3, Patriarchika Pileas, Aerodromio* ✥ *Near the airport* ☎ *23155/19333* 🌐 *www.facebook.com/duckprivatecheffing* ⊗ *Closed Mon.*

★ Gastrodromio En Olympo

$$ | **GREEK** | Self-taught and ever-evolving chef Andreas Gavris creates seasonal delights fit for the gods in his justifiably popular restaurant. Standouts include the melon soup with prawns and mint; *bourani,* a rich rice dish with nettles, wild mushrooms, and a Gruyère-like cheese from Crete; and black pig of Olympus stew and mountain lamb, cooked with mushroom and wheat puree. **Known for:** tastefully elevated Greek cuisine; professional and friendly service; an extensive wine list. $ *Average main: €19* ✉ *Agios Nikolaou 36, Litochoro* ✥ *Opposite the town hall* ☎ *23520/21300* 🌐 *www.gastrodromio.gr.*

★ Mourga

$ | **SEAFOOD** | A successful cooperative venture that has been delighting locals with their delicious seafood and veggie innovations for a few years now. Apart from the regular table seating there is a stainless steel bar in front of the open kitchen where you can watch the chefs strut their stuff up close as you chow down. **Known for:** excellent seafood; good value; great atmosphere. $ *Average main: €13* ✉ *Christopoulou 12, Kentro* ☎ *23102/68826.*

★ O Kritikos

$$$ | **SEAFOOD** | Want sublime seafood pasta or risotto? Head to a place like this one, where the owner is a local fisherman and everything served is the catch of the day. **Known for:** fresh fish and seafood; excellent service; it's busy (reservations strongly recommended). $ *Average main: €26* ✉ *Main road, away from the tower, Ouranoupolis* ☎ *23770/71222* 🌐 *www.okritikos.com.*

★ 7 Thalasses

$$ | **SEAFOOD** | One of the better and most creative seafood restaurants in Thessaloniki offers a menu that maintains the delicate flavors of its ingredients but also manages to add a modern twist. For instance, the marinated sea bass tartare, seasoned with fleur de sel, lemon, and olive oil, is then covered with a sprinkling of roe, bringing to mind a wave gently breaking against your tongue. **Known for:** elevated dining in a modern setting; supremely fresh seafood; good desserts. *Average main: €25 ✉ Kalapothaki 8–10, Kentro ☎ 23102/33173 ⊕ 7thalasses.eu.*

Cool Places to Stay

★ Daios Luxury Living Hotel

$$$ | HOTEL | A minute's walk from the White Tower, this upscale contemporary hotel in shimmering glass stands out for all the right reasons: a prime seafront location, cool and chic interiors, and exemplary, discreet service. **Pros:** right in the heart of the city with outstanding views of the Thermaikos Gulf; free minibar in all rooms; the best luxury suites in town at good prices out of season. **Cons:** no pool; expensive nightly parking fee; some road noise in the lower-floor rooms. *Rooms from: €250 ✉ Nikis 59, Faliro ☎ 23102/50200 ⊕ www.daioshotels.com 49 rooms Free Breakfast.*

★ Doupiani House

$ | B&B/INN | A stay here means residing in a traditional stone-and-wood hotel set amid vineyards in the upper reaches of the idyllic village of Kastraki, where each room—with a luxurious carved double bed, oak floors, and closets—has a balcony with panoramic views of both Meteora and Kastraki. **Pros:** excellent and helpful staff have extensive local knowledge; ideal combo of comfort and tradition; wonderful hearty breakfast. **Cons:** not all rooms have the stunning view of the monasteries; small bathrooms; a little out of the way, but close to the monasteries. *Rooms from: €99 ✉ Kastrakiou, Kastraki ✣ Left off main road to Meteora, near Cave Camping ☎ 24320/75326, 24320/77555 ⊕ www.doupianihouse.gr 17 rooms Free Breakfast.*

★ Hotel Bitouni

$ | HOTEL | FAMILY | Local craftsmen fashioned the elegantly carved wooden ceilings in this traditional-style Metsovo mansion—at its heart a large fireplace in the main reception room nicely warms the cozy hotel. **Pros:** great breakfast with many homemade treats; excellent and helpful service; great value lodging also has free parking. **Cons:** luxury lovers, look elsewhere; only a few basic in-room amenities; not all rooms have the mountain views. *Rooms from: €55 ✉ Tositsa St., Metsovo ✣ On the main street leading up from main square ☎ 26560/41217 30 rooms Free Breakfast.*

★ The Modernist

$$ | HOTEL | The Modernist is a minimalist concept boutique hotel, where guests' needs are met to the highest of standards with the minimum of fuss. **Pros:** high-quality staff, who also offer top city tips; understated luxury; great central location. **Cons:** no parking; no restaurant facilities (lunch/dinner); small balconies. *Rooms from: €175 ✉ 32 Ermou St., Kentro ☎ 23160/09990 ⊕ www.themodernisthotels.com 40 rooms Free Breakfast.*

★ Skités

$$ | B&B/INN | Find peace and privacy on a bluff off a gravel road south of town at this charming complex of garden bungalows, comprised of small and rustic, pertinently monastic, but by no means ascetic rooms, and staffed by folks who want to make you feel comfortable. **Pros:** private and peaceful; very personal service; delicious vegetables from the owner's own plot. **Cons:** no nightlife; the rustic style is not to everyone's taste; Wi-Fi patchy in areas. *Rooms from: €135 ✉ 1 km (½ mile) south of town, Ouranoupolis ✣ If you need directions, ask for the hotel of Mrs. Pola Bohn ☎ 23770/71140, 23770/71141 ⊕ www.skites.gr Closed Nov.–late Apr. 25 rooms Free Breakfast.*

Cyclades

If the Greek islands suggest blazing sun and sea, bare rock and mountains, olive trees and vineyards, white rustic architecture and ancient ruins, fresh fish, and fruity oils, the Cyclades are your isles of quintessential plenty, the ultimate Mediterranean archipelago.

Named after the circle they form around the sacred isle of Delos, the 220 or so Cyclades are the most Greek of all the islands. If Zeus shook and threw the isles like dice across the Aegean, the islands of the Cyclades were particularly blessed.

All the top spots—poster pin-up Santorini, battle-scarred Milos, cliff-clinging Folegandros, the twins of ample comfort Paros and Naxos, elegant and stately Syros, marvelous cosmopolitan Mykonos, divine Delos, and pilgrim pulling Tinos—are beloved for their postcard-perfect whitewashed cubist houses, blue-roofed churches, twisting Bougainvillea-clad alleyways, pristine natural landscapes, and sparkling bays of enamel blue.

No matter which of these islands you head for, the Cyclades offer both culture and hedonism: countless classical sites, Byzantine castles, monasteries, churches, wineries, and villages wait to be explored, as do some of the most varied beaches in Greece. The best reason to visit the islands may simply be the enjoyment of the evening walk, the beauty of the surroundings, and the hospitality shown to strangers but a vibrant and varied nightlife is also to be found with beach parties, bustling tavernas and star-lit bars.

"My God, how much blue you spend, so we cannot see you," wrote Nobel Prize-winning poet Odysseas Elytis with reference to his homeland. The Cyclades are where everything gets bluer, where the horizon gets bigger, life is reduced to bare elements—rock, sky, sea—and the landscape gets more binary. If you have never understood the beauty of the setting sun, just come here, and it will all become clear.

"The islands with their drinkable blue volcanoes," as our poet imagines are the brightest stars in the constellation of the Aegean. These are the island archetypes we know and dream of—lone trees bent over by the wind, gorges and gaping ravines only scaled by goats, plunging cliffs, and all around the fusion of sunlight and aqua sparkle. Find your favorite and abandon yourself to the rhythm of their days.

Tinos Mountain Villages

Traditional Cycladic Village Life

Tinos's magnificently rustic villages are what make it unique: the dark arcades of Arnados, the vine-shaded sea views of Isternia, the gleaming marble squares of Pirgos. Tiny Volax is the most spectacular, with a landscape that seems to be straight out of *Lord of the Rings*. Windswept and remote, Volax is surrounded by hundreds of giant, granite boulders. Smooth and weatherworn, geologists are still undecided as to their origin—are they the result of volcanic eruption, or meteorites that landed in prehistoric times?

Don't Miss

Tinos is renowned for its 1,300 dovecotes (peristerines), which, unlike those on Mykonos or Andros, are mostly well-maintained; in fact, new ones are being built. Two stories high, with intricate stonework, carved-dove finials, and thin schist slabs arranged in intricate patterns resembling traditional stitchery, the dovecotes were introduced by the Venetians for breeding pigeons for their meat and high quality manure.

Best Restaurant

To Thalassaki. Sitting on a platform on the edge of Ormos Isternion Bay, right up against the Aegean Sea with views of Syros, chef and owner Antonia Zarpa produces innovative, well-thought-out dishes that capture the local flavors of her beloved island. *Average main: €30 ✉ Ornos, Tinos ☎ 22830/31366 ⏲ Closed Nov.–Mar.*

Getting Here

Many ferries stop at Tinos, as it is on the Mykonos line, and crossings take four to five hours from Piraeus. Buses run daily from Chora to the many villages in Tinos, and in summer buses are added for beaches.

Mykonos Nightlife

Decadent Days, Endless Nights

The nightlife on Mykonos beats to an obsessive rhythm until undetermined hours—little wonder the world's gilded youth come here just for the night scene. The party begins in the late afternoon at the beach clubs, while the bars along Little Venice don't start to fill up until after 11 pm. Much happens after midnight; you can either choose to club-hop around town or head south to the glamorous, outdoor clubs along Paradise and Super Paradise beaches. In the summer, flyers advertise which of the hottest DJs are booked and the promise of a packed, friendly, flirtatious young crowd keeps the party going well into the night.

Don't Miss

Many of the early ships' captains built distinguished houses directly on the seafront, with elaborate buttressed wooden balconies hanging over the water, earning the neighborhood the name Little Venice. Architecturally unique, it is one of the most attractive areas in all the islands, and many of these fine old houses now host elegant bars. A sunset drink here to the sound of the waves is a Mykonos must-do.

Best Bar

Galleraki. For more than 30 years, Galleraki has attracted happy, stylish, summer crowds. A compelling reason is its prime location, so close to the water in picturesque Little Venice that you may get sprayed when a boat passes. ✉ *Mykonos Town* ☎ *22890/27188* 🌐 *www.galleraki.gr*

Getting Here

There are daily 45-minute flights from Athens and also direct flights from Europe. The ferry from Piraeus or Rafina takes from two to five hours depending on your route and boat. Once on the island, water taxis and buses run between the old and new ports and to the beaches.

Delos

Birthplace of Apollo

Delos, dry and shadeless but encircled by other islands (and, indeed, that circling gave the Cyclades their name), was once the religious and political center of the Aegean. The Ionians had made the mythological birthplace of Apollo their religious center by 1000 BC. In 543 BC, the oracle at Delphi decreed that the Athenians should purify the island, and thereafter no one was allowed to be born or die there, but it thrived as a financial capital and free port for almost 400 years, well into the years of Roman rule. Delos flourished until the king of Pontus sacked the island and killed all its inhabitants in 88 BC. By 69 BC, the island was abandoned, and no serious excavation happened until 1872.

Don't Miss

One of the most evocative and recognizable sights of Delos is the 164-foot-long Avenue of the Lions. The five marble beasts, which were carved in Naxos, crouch on their haunches, vigilant guardians of the Sacred Lake. They are the survivors of a line of at least nine lions that were erected in the second half of the 7th century BC. One statue, removed in the 17th century, now guards the Arsenal of Venice, the remaining originals are in the Archaeological Museum on the island.

Best View

A dirt path leads up the base of Mt. Kynthos, which is the highest point on the island. There is an amazing panorama of Mykonos, Naxos, Paros, Rineia, and Syros from the top of the mountain.

Getting Here

Most visitors arrive from Mykonos on boats organized by tour companies whose offices are located at the old harbor (tour boats also leave from Tinos, Paros, Syros, and Naxos).

Folegandros

Peace in the Cyclades

If Santorini is the Hollywood leading lady of the Greek islands, Folegandros is the demure, younger sister, star of offbeat independent cinema. Built between the walls of a Venetian fort, its main town of Chora is pinch-yourself pretty, clinging to the edge of precipitous cliffs above brooding seas, a cozy huddle of whitewashed houses, flower-filled alleys, and brightly painted woodwork that has been lovingly preserved by the islanders. Five squares, closed to vehicles, host restaurants and cafés shaded by bougainvillea and hibiscus. Some of the buildings are set into the walls of the Venetian fort, or Kastro, built by the Duke of Naxos in the 13th century. A street circles the Kastro and is strikingly lined with cube houses that form a wall atop the towering cliff.

Don't Miss

The spectacularly photogenic Church of Komisis tis Theotkou (or Dormition of the Mother of God) dominates the town and stands on the foundations of the ancient settlement near the top of the cliff. The path that zigzags its way to the church is quite a climb but the rewards are the enchanting views over the town and the island.

Best Restaurant

Irini. Part grocery store, part taverna, this step back in time is the real deal for home-cooked dishes, where you dine amid tins, vegetables, and bottles of oil. $ *Average main: €10* ✉ *Ano Meria, Folegandros* ☎ *22860/41436*

Getting Here

Folegandros has no airport; ferries from Piraeus and Lavrio take four to nine hours depending on the route and the type of boat, but fast ferries from Milos and Santorini take an hour or less. Once on the island, buses meet the boats and run from the port to Chora hourly. In summer, small caïques (taxi boats) run between beaches.

Sarakiniko Beach, Milos

Multicolor Volcanic Beauty

Having been mined for millennia for its rich mineral deposits, Milos is known more these days for its eerie beauty, not the least of which can be seen in the sculpted inlet and beach of Sarakiniko, the main draw for tourists. The eerily sculpted inlet, whose bone-white rocks lie in the sea like vast Henry Moore abstract forms, was on the seabed 2 million years ago, and fish and shell fossils can often be seen in the rocks. Try to get there before 7 am, as the sunrise is spectacular and you will be largely alone; later, crowds will arrive for sunbathing, swimming, and cliff diving—or to view the shipwreck half-submerged or explore the abandoned mine tunnels. Beware though, there is no shade and the light reflecting from the white rocks is mesmerizing and intense.

Don't Miss

Almost as famous as its neighbor, Mandraki is home to the distinctive and colorful dwellings known as *syrmata*, the two-story houses built into the soft volcanic rock right at the water's edge with the ground floor acting as a boat house. The fishing hamlet of Klima on the opposite coast has similar kaleidoscopic buildings.

Best Restaurant

Medusa. On a cliffside setting by the brilliantly painted huts of Mandrakia is the island's best fish taverna. The very essence of summer is to be had on the large terrace on the waterfront. $ *Average main: €18* ✉ *Plaka, Milos, Mandraki* ☎ *22870/23670* 🌐 *www.medusamilos.gr*

Getting Here

The tiny airport on Milos is 5 km (3.1 miles) south of Adamas, the port, and the flight from Athens lasts 40 minutes. Ferries leave Piraeus and Lavrio daily in high season, with journeys taking between three and six hours. Once you land on the island, there is an extensive bus network.

Sunset in Santorini

Sensational Sunets

Every summer evening, travelers from all over the world congregate at the Santorini's caldera rim—sitting on whitewashed fences, staircases, beneath the town's windmill, on the old Kastro—each looking out to sea in anticipation of the performance: the Ia sunset. If you ever wondered why you might pay through the nose for a room with a view, this is the reason. The three-hour walk along the caldera's rim from Ia to Fira at this hour is unforgettable. In the middle of the brooding caldera, the volcano smolders away eerily, adding an air of suspense to an already awe-inspiring scene. The sunset in Ia may not really be much more spectacular than in Fira, and certainly not better than in Imerovigli, but nevertheless, there is something tribally satisfying at the sight of so many people gathering in one spot to celebrate pure beauty.

Don't Miss

The locals say that in Santorini there is more wine than water, and it may be true; Santorini produces more wine than any other Cyclades island. Conditions are especially ideal for the production of Assyrtiko, a distinctive white wine. A highlight of any Santorini trip is a visit to one or more of its many wineries. Santorini Wine Tours offers informative and fun trips guided by professional sommeliers and local experts to a variety of wineries and their associated vineyards. 🌐 *www.santoriniwinetour.com*

Getting Here

The island's airport has frequent flights from Athens, but the approach to Santorini through its caldera to the new port beneath its soaring cliffs is truly breathtaking.

Naxos Beaches

Sweetness and Tranquillity

"Great sweetness and tranquility" is how Nikos Kazantzakis, premier novelist of Greece, described Naxos. The greenest, largest, and most fertile of the southern Cyclades, Naxos has been inhabited for 6,000 years. While it's full of history and monuments—classical temples, medieval monasteries, Byzantine churches, Venetian towers—the many summer tourists can attest that Naxos has the best beaches in the Cyclades. The southwest coast of Naxos, facing Paros and the sunset, offers the Cyclades's longest stretches of sandy beaches, and the further from Naxos Town you go, the more untouched and undeveloped they become. The water around Naxos is some of the clearest in Greece. Agios Prokopios Beach may be among the best, with fine white sand and protection from island winds.

Don't Miss

The island's most famous landmark is ancient: the Portara, a massive doorway that leads to nowhere. Standing on the islet of Palatia, in the 3rd millennium BC it was to be the entrance to an unfinished Temple of Apollo that faces Delos, the god's birthplace. Although the rest of the temple was repurposed by later Venetian and Turkish rulers, the gate, built with four blocks of marble each weighing 20 tons, was so large it couldn't be demolished, and so it remains today.

Getting Here

Flights from Athens to Naxos take 35 minutes. Naxos is also a major ferry hub and is very well connected. Ferries from Piraeus and Lavrio take from four to six hours depending on the route and boat. Since it's the largest island in the Cyclades, a rental car can be very helpful.

Naousa, Paros

The Pearl of Paros

No longer a quaint fishing village, Naousa long ago discovered the benefits of tourism, but thankfully, the pretty little harbor is still in use as a fishing port, and white and blue boats rub gently together as fishermen repair their nets. The taverna-filled waterfront is the big draw, charmingly backed by Venetian townhouses, and the half-submerged ruins of the Venetian fortifications still remain and still make a handsome sight when lit up at night. Compared to Paros Town, the scene in Naousa is chicer, with a more intimate array of shops, bars, and restaurants. Although the nightlife is on a par with Paros Town, many visitors base themselves here for the local beaches.

Don't Miss

Kolymbithres beach, which is noted for its unusual rock formations, is also considered to be one of Paros's best, attracting its share of crowds to the small, sandy cove. The granite formations create shallow pools of water popular with the kids.

Best Restaurant

Siparos. For many repeat visitors a trip to Paros is unthinkable without a visit here. This storied eatery is along the coast of Naousa Bay in the beach town of Santa Maria and well deserves its reputation as one of the island's finest. [$] *Average main: €25* ✉ *Xifara, Santa Maria* 22840/52785 🌐 *www.siparos.gr*

Getting Here

Flights from Athens take 40 minutes, but Paros is well served by ferries—there are at least 15 of them daily. Once on the island, there is a bus service to the major destinations, but you may wish to consider renting a moped or car to explore the island interior.

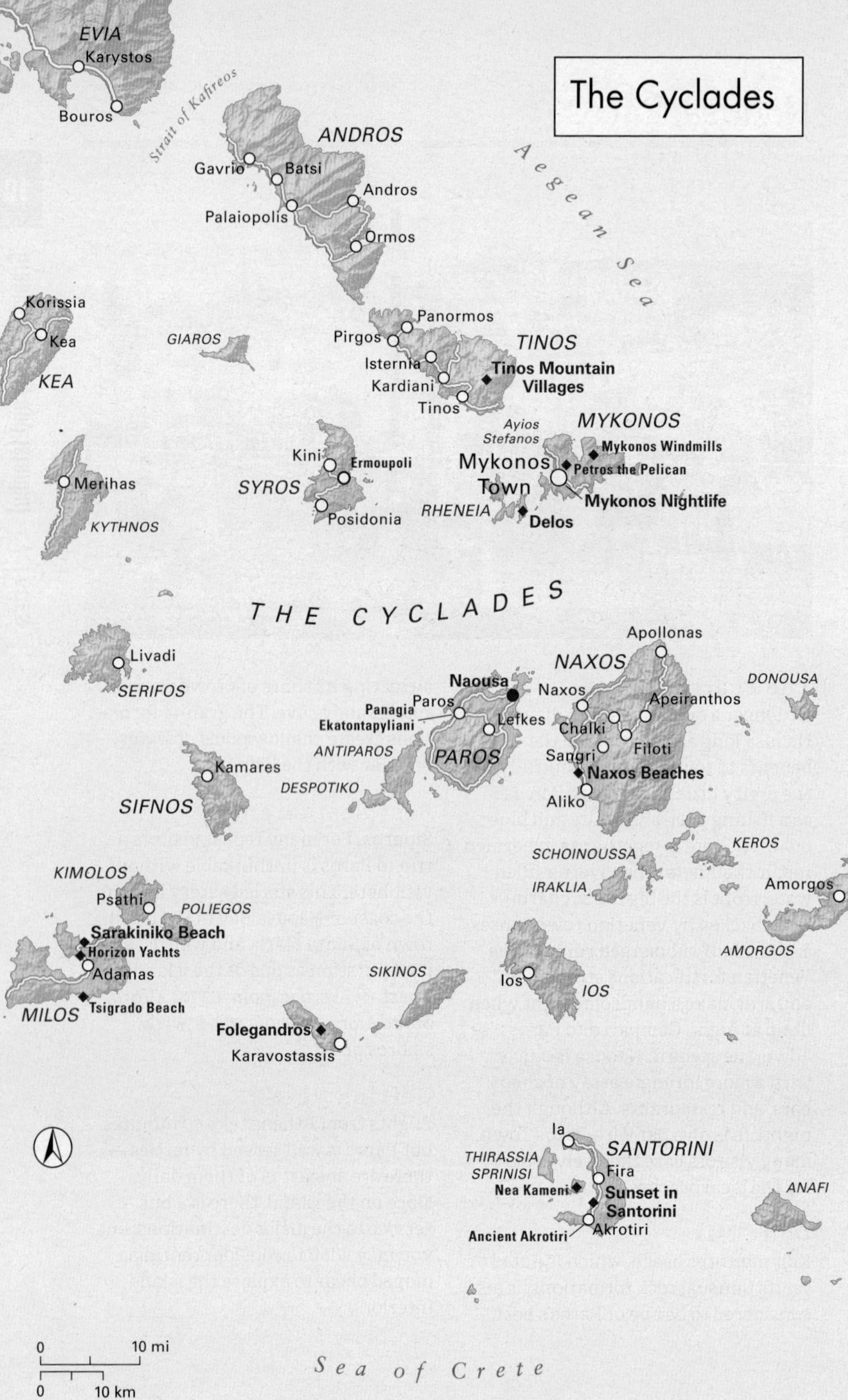

The Cyclades
EVIA
Karystos
Bouros
Strait of Kafireos
ANDROS
Gavrio
Batsi
Andros
Palaiopolis
Ormos
Aegean Sea
Korissia
Kea
KEA
GIAROS
Panormos
Pirgos
TINOS
Isternia
Tinos Mountain Villages
Kardiani
Tinos
Ayios Stefanos
MYKONOS
Mykonos Windmills
Kini
Ermoupoli
Mykonos Town
Petros the Pelican
Merihas
SYROS
Mykonos Nightlife
RHENEIA
Delos
Posidonia
KYTHNOS
THE CYCLADES
Apollonas
Livadi
NAXOS
SERIFOS
Naousa
DONOUSA
Naxos
Paros
Apeiranthos
Panagia Ekatontapyliani
Lefkes
Chalki
Filoti
ANTIPAROS
PAROS
Sangri
Kamares
Naxos Beaches
DESPOTIKO
Aliko
SIFNOS
KEROS
SCHOINOUSSA
KIMOLOS
IRAKLIA
Amorgos
Psathi
POLIEGOS
Sarakiniko Beach
Horizon Yachts
AMORGOS
Adamas
SIKINOS
Ios
IOS
MILOS
Tsigrado Beach
Folegandros
Karavostassis
Ia
THIRASSIA
SANTORINI
SPRINISI
Fira
Nea Kameni
Sunset in Santorini
ANAFI
Ancient Akrotiri
Akrotiri
0
10 mi
0
10 km
Sea of Crete

When in the Cyclades

★ Ancient Akrotiri

RUINS | If Santorini is known as the "Greek Pompeii," it is because of the archaeological site of ancient Akrotiri, near its southern tip. The entire enclosed site, once buried under volcanic ashes, is now covered by a protective canopy. The city was discovered in the 1860s, having been frozen in time by ash from an eruption 3,600 years ago, long before Pompeii's disaster. In 1967 excavations began, but only about one-thirtieth of the huge site has been excavated. Akrotiri was settled as early as 3000 BC and reached its peak after 2000 BC, when it developed trade and agriculture and settled the present town. ✉ *Akrotiri* ✥ *South of modern Akrotiri* ☎ *22860/81939* 🌐 *odysseus.culture.gr* 🎫 *€12; €15 for combined ticket for archaeological sites and museum in Fira* ⏲ *Closed Tues. Nov.–Mar.*

Emeroupoli

TOWN | The mercantile bustle of modern Ermoupoli—Syros's elegant port, capital, and the archipelago's business hub since the 18th century—often makes people do a double take. Seen from a distance out at sea, the city looks like a Cycladic village—one, albeit, raised to the *nth* dimension, with thousands of houses climbing their way up twin conical hills. The closer you get, the more impressive things look and as you pull into the harbor, lined with mansions and towering churches, you see that the city is a 19th-century neoclassical jewel. ✉ *Ermoupoli* ✥ *35 km (22 miles) west of Mykonos* 🌐 *www.visitsyros.com.*

★ Horizon Yachts

SAILING | Sail past sea stacks as big as houses and enter Kleftiko, a pirates lair with dazzling turquoise water that looks photoshopped. Swim up to the Cave of Sykia and lie on the small beach staring at the sky through the hole in the collapsed roof. Numbers are kept small on the company yachts and if the weather is right, sail on to Polyaigos, the largest uninhabited island in Greece and one of the best natural environments in the Aegean. Unless you have your own superyacht, you won't see Milos better. ✉ *Adamantas Tourist Yacht Shelter, Milos, Adamas* ✥ *On harbor* ☎ *22870/24083* 🌐 *www.horizonyachts.gr.*

Mykonos Windmills

WINDMILL | Across the water from Little Venice, set on a high hill, are the famous Mykonos windmills, echoes of a time when wind power was used to grind the island's grain. The area from Little Venice to the windmills is called Alefkandra, which means "whitening": women once hung their laundry here. A little farther toward the windmills, the bars that teeter on shoreside decks are barely above sea level, and as the north wind gets up, surf splashes the tables. Farther on, the shore spreads into an unprepossessing beach, and tables are placed on sand or pebbles. ✉ *Alefkandra.*

Nea Kameni

VOLCANO | To peer into a live, sometimes smoldering volcano, join one of the popular excursions to Nea Kameni, the larger of the two Burnt Isles. After disembarking, you hike 430 feet to the top and walk around the edge of the crater, wondering if the volcano is ready for its fifth eruption during the last 100 years—after all, the last was in 1956. Some tours continue on to the island of Therassia, where there is a village. Many operators on the island offer volcano tours.

★ Panagia Ekatontapyliani (*Hundred Doors Church*)

CHURCH | When St. Helen (mother to Emperor Constantine the Great) set daily for the Holy Land in AD 326, she stopped on Paros, had a vision, and vowed to build a church there. Constantine built that church in 328, and Justinian the Great added the splendid dome some two centuries later. It is one of the oldest unaltered churches in the world and is renowned pilgrimage, second only to Megalochari on TInos. ✉ *Paros Town* ✣ *750 feet east of dock* ☎ *22840/21243* 🌐 *www.ekatontapyliani.gr.*

Petros the Pelican

OTHER ATTRACTION | Can an animal be a noted landmark? If that is at all possible, then Mykonos has one. By the time the morning open-air fish market picks up steam in Mykonos Town, Petros the Pelican—the town mascot—is preening and cadging breakfast. In the 1950s, a group of migrating pelicans passed over Mykonos, leaving behind a single exhausted bird. A local fisherman nursed it back to health, and locals say that the pelican who roams the harbor is the original Petros. He is, in fact not, because the original bird died in 1985. But there is now a small group of birds, all known as "Petros" and all roaming the waterfront. If you spend any time around Little Venice or the windmills, you are bound to see one of them. Find him on Instagram: *@petrospelican_official-mykonos.* ✉ *Mykonos Town.*

Where to Eat and Drink

★ Bill and Coo Gastronomy Project

$$$$ | GREEK FUSION | Alongside the infinity pool at the Bill and Coo Hotel, complete with shining stars that twinkle from the bottom, is served some of the finest food in Mykonos. A futuristic glass box or the outdoor terrace on balmier nights is the setting, for a master class in modern Mediterranean cooking. **Known for:** stunning setting; staff are pitch-perfect—unstuffy and fun; wine pairings are spot on. $ *Average main: €50* ✉ *Megali Ammos, Mykonos Town* ☎ *22890/26292* 🌐 *www.bill-coo-hotel.com.*

★ Gioras Bakery

$ | BAKERY | Descend into the rustic interior of this bakery and you will feel like you have stepped back in time; Gioras dates back to the 18th century and is the oldest working wood-fired bakery in the Cyclades. Take a couple of pies for the beach, or sit with a coffee and a slice of baklava and breathe in the history. **Known for:** time capsule interior; run by the Varmvakourides family for two centuries; astonishing range of sweets and breads. $ *Average main: €3* ✉ *Aghiou Efthimiou, Mykonos Town* ☎ *22890/27784.*

★ Kalokeri

$$ | MODERN GREEK | A bright and fresh room, wistfully painted with sea creatures and cacti, is the backdrop to this bijou establishment on the main street. Refined Aegean cuisine with jewel-like presentation is the order of the day—this is food that you devour with your eyes first. **Known for:** the gourmet spot on the island; delightful staff; reservations a must. $ *Average main: €20* ✉ *Main St., Antiparos Town* ☎ *22840/63037.*

★ Selene

$$$$ | MODERN GREEK | Back in Fira, the restaurant that set Santorini on its own gastronomic trail continues to entice and impress in its new incarnation in the imposing setting of an 18th-century Catholic monastery. The ingredients of the Cyclades are redefined under the watch of Michelin-starred chef Ettore Botrini for a one of a kind experience—some of the finest dining in Greece. **Known for:** culinary landmark on the island; elaborate multicourse menus; astonishing wine cellar. $ *Average main: €50* ✉ *Catholic monastery of Dominican sisters, Fira* ✣ *Katikies garden* ☎ *22860/22249* 🌐 *selene.gr.*

★ Stou Fred

$$$$ | FRENCH FUSION | Globe-trotting chef Fred Chesneau finally set down roots in Paros, bringing French-influenced dining to the island. A romantic flower-filled garden with white ironwork furniture is a pretty match for the bi-weekly changing fixed menu that features the best locally sourced seasonal produce. Just 30 lucky diners each night get to experience a food journey that may take them from Paros to Paris via Bangkok and Tokyo. **Known for:** genial host Fred guides you through his creations; intriguing wine list of small French producers; five-course cosmopolitan fixed-price menu. *Average main: €65 Alexandrou Mayrou 16, Paros Town 69704/48763 www.stoufredparos.com Closed Sun. and Oct.–May.*

Cool Places to Stay

★ Anemomilos Boutique Hotel
$$$ | HOTEL | Perched on the towering cliff overlooking the sea and set amid a series of small garden terraces, this complex with truly breathtaking vistas of sea and sky is the best place to stay in Folegandros. **Pros:** sublime views; alluring pool; warm staff. **Cons:** always books up early; village-facing studios can be noisy; high-season rates can be prohibitive. *Rooms from: €270 Chora Edge of town 22860/41309 www.anemomiloshotel.com Closed Oct.–May 17 rooms Free Breakfast.*

★ Bill and Coo Suites and Lounge
$$$$ | HOTEL | From afar, Bill and Coo may look like any whitewashed Cycladic hotel, but inside a world of polished contemporary design and high-level service awaits—the infinity pool is one of the most photogenic on the island, overlooking the Megali Ammos beach area and sea, just outside Mykonos Town. **Pros:** excellent service; beautiful infinity pool; one of the top restaurants on Mykonos is here. **Cons:** pricey summer suite rates; not in easy reach of the beach or party scene; not in easy walking distance to Mykonos Town. *Rooms from: €600 Mykonos Town Megali Ammos 22890/26292 www.bill-coo-hotel.com Closed Nov.–Apr. 50 rooms Free Breakfast.*

★ Perivolas
$$$$ | HOTEL | A travel magazine favorite, Perivolas lives up to the hype and then some—that infinity pool still makes you gasp and the rest of the hotel is no slouch. **Pros:** the best infinity pool on Santorini; attentive but relaxed service; beautiful and tranquil surroundings. **Cons:** lots of steps; a walk to town; high-roller price tag. *Rooms from: €800 Nomikou, Ia Ia cliff face, east of center 22860/71308 www.perivolas.gr Closed Nov.–Mar. 22 rooms Free Breakfast.*

★ Vaos Windmill
$$ | HOTEL | One of the most unique accommodations in the Southern Aegean, Vaos is a converted windmill in the village of Trypiti. **Pros:** five-star views; unique, historic, and atmospheric; fully equipped kitchen to prepare your own food. **Cons:** in a pedestrian area with parking 200 meters away; steep stairs over three floors; the clue is in the name—it can get windy. *Rooms from: €220 Plaka 26103/21742 2 rooms No Meals.*

Other Greek Islands

Greece lays claim to some 6,000 isles and islets, but only 227 are inhabited. Some of these have become tourism powerhouses, but many are occupied by only a handful of hardy farmers and fisher-folk. They range in size from arid dots on the map like Symi and Hydra to mighty Crete, at 170 miles long the fifth-largest island in the Mediterranean.

Terrain and microclimate are equally varied: Rhodes, Greece's sunniest isle, claims 300 days of sunshine a year, while snow lies on the slopes of Cretan mountains until early summer. And, of course, Greece's archipelagos are steeped in history, from Europe's first civilizations through a trio of empires to the birth of independent Greece.

Since tourism dawned in the 1960s, the photogenic islands of the Cyclades with their white villages and tiny blue-domed churches have hogged the limelight. But if you look beyond that storied group, you'll discover a plethora of other isles and unforgettable experiences.

When Athenians want a break, they make a quick crossing to the idyllic islands of the Saronic Gulf. If you have to choose just one, make it boho-chic, car-free Hydra.The Dodecanese chain offers a baker's dozen of stylish isles and sandy beaches that are closer geographically to Turkey than mainland Greece. The top trio of Rhodes, Kos, and Symi are all popular destinations known for their medieval castles, Byzantine churches, and beaches. But Patmos stands out for its Biblical connections to the Book of Revelation of St. John.

In the Ionian Islands, Corfu Town resembles a stage set for a Verdi opera with colorful landmarks from its Venetian, French, and British past, while Kefalonia combines verdant vineyards, natural wonders, and enchanting harbor villages.

Lapped by the blue Aegean and the Libyan Sea, Crete—Greece's largest island—is almost a country within a country, with its own customs, rugged mountain gorges between soaring peak wildflower meadows, historic towns, and abundant reminders of an incredibly deep past. So many islands: so little time.

Rhodes Old Town

City of the Knights

Romans, Crusaders, Turks, and 20th-century Italians have all left their mark on Rhodes. The Old Town is the jewel of the island, filled with Orthodox and Catholic churches and a scattering of Ottoman mosques. When The Knights of St. John arrived in 1309, they built over the original fortifications, creating one of the great medieval monuments in the Mediterranean—a 2 ½ mile (4km) circuit of walls enclosing a labyrinth of cobbled streets. On Odos Ippoton, the Street of the Knights, they built the seven Inns of the Tongues, each home to one of the subdivisions of the Order. The most elaborate is the Inn of France, whose ornately carved facade bears heraldic patterns, fleur de lis, and an inscription that dates the building to 1492. No other walled city in Europe is quite as charming.

Don't Miss

The grand Palace of the Grand Master of the Knights of Rhodes was partly destroyed in 1856 by a gunpowder explosion but rebuilt in the 1930s; the exterior is true to the original, but the grandiose interior owes much to the febrile imagination of Italian dictator Benito Mussolini.

When to Go

Go in April, May, September, or October for the best sightseeing weather and fewer crowds. Many sights are closed November to March.

Getting Here

Rhodes is best reached by air, but there are overnight ferries from Athens. No taxis or buses operate within the Old Town, but there's free electric buggy service on request.

Palace of the Grand Master. ✉ *Ippoton, Old Town* 🌐 *www.odysseus.culture.gr* 🎫 *€8* ⏲ *Closed Tues. and Nov.–Mar.*

Rhodes Tourism. 🌐 *www.rhodes.gr*

Symi

An Island Idyll

Tiny Symi is an enchanting, peaceful island haven that has escaped big-time tourism. Life centers on sparkling Yialos Harbor—lined with candy-color neoclassical buildings—and the hillside town of Chorio, high above. Its merchants grew rich from the sponge trade, building the stylish mansions that line the narrow streets of Chorio and the Yialos quayside. In its heyday, Symi had some 20,000 inhabitants, but after it was seized by Italy in 1912 it fell into decline. Though many old houses still stand dilapidated, others have been restored as boutique hotels or vacation homes. Most beaches, like Aghia Marina, Aghios Nikolaos, Aghios Giorghios, Aghios Marathountas, and Nanou, are reachable only by boat, and so remain pristine. A more accessible option is Pedi Bay, a quieter version of the main harbor, with a calm beach and several tavernas.

Don't Miss

The unexpectedly huge Monastery of Taxiarchis Michael Panormitis, beneath pine-covered slopes above the little Gulf of Panormitis, is dedicated to Symi's patron saint, the protector of sailors. A multitier bell-tower surmounts the entrance to the black-and-white pebble mosaic courtyard, and the frescoed interior contains an ornate wooden iconostasis, flanked by a larger-than-life representation of Michael, all but his face covered with silver.

Getting Here

Ferry services link Yialos with neighboring Rhodes (60 to 90 minutes), as well as Kos and and Piraeus. On the island, buses link Yialos with Chorio and Pedi, as well as Panormitis. Taxi-boats leave Yialos several times daily for the beaches around the island.

Visit Symi. 🌐 *visitsymi.gr*

Asklepion of Kos

Island of Healing

Kos has lush fields and tree-clad mountains, but also miles of beaches that make it a tourism hot spot and lure to young partiers from around Europe. But there's more to Kos than sun, sea, and sand. In Kos Town, the tumbled marble blocks of Roman and Hellenistic ruins lie scattered inland from a harbor dominated by an imposing medieval fortress. You can still see an ancient plane tree under which Hippocrates (460–370 BC), father of medicine, supposedly taught. Archaeologists have unearthed extensive ruins that date from the 4th-century BC through Roman times, including parts of the old city walls, a Hellenistic stoa, and foundations of temples to Aphrodite and Hercules.

Don't Miss

The multitier Asklepion complex dedicated to the god of medicine flourished until the decline of the Roman Empire as the greatest center of healing in the Roman-Hellenic world. On its vast terraces stand Ionic and Doric temples.

When to Go

Go in spring (when the ruin sites are covered with brightly colored flowers) or autumn to avoid the summer crowds. But summer is the time if you are looking for fun and sun.

Getting Here

Ferries connect Kos with Piraeus, Rhodes, Patmos, and the Cyclades. There are also flights from Athens and (in summer) other European cities. Buses serve most of the island.

☒ Off Agiou Demetriou, Platani ✣ Take local bus from Kos Town to hamlet of Platani and walk to ruins from there ☎ 22420/28326 ⊕ odysseus.culture.gr €8 ⊙ Closed Tues. and Nov.–Mar.

Monastery of St. John, Patmos

A Divine Sanctuary

Tiny Patmos is a revered place of pilgrimage for the Greek Orthodox faithful but most famous as the place where the exiled St. John dictated the Book of Revelation in the Sacred Grotto in the first century AD; it is now part of the 17th-century Monastery of the Apocalypse. The quiet whitewashed houses of the hilltop Chora conceal Byzantine mansions and townhouses, now the enviable retreats of wealthy expats. But it also has a sybaritic side: even Orthodox priggishness has failed to deter nude sunbathing on the more remote beaches (though it has no long, sandy ones, which has probably saved it from the excesses of mass tourism). The most popular beach on Patmos stretches for 1.6 km (1 mile) or so along pebbly Kambos Bay. The most beautiful beach, though, is remote Psili Ammos, a scallop of rare golden sand.

Don't Miss

Above Chora, the 11th-century Monastery of St. John the Theologian is one of the world's best-preserved fortified medieval monastic complexes and has been endowed it with fabulous works of religious art.

Getting Here

There is no airport. Ferries from Rhodes to Patmos also call at Symi and Kos. Ferries from Piraeus (Athens) take seven to nine hours and also call at Mykonos. On the island, water taxis take you from Skala to most beaches, and buses connect Skala with Chora and Kambos.

Monastery of the Apocalypse. ⊕ 2 *km south of Chora* ☎ *22470/31276* 🎫 €2

Monastery of St. John the Theologian. ✉ *Chora* ☎ *22470/20800* 🌐 *www.patmosmonastery.gr* 🎫 €4

Patmos Municipal Tourism Office. 🌐 *www.patmosweb.gr*

Corfu Old Town

An Elegant Gem

This sophisticated little gem of a city glows with reminders of its checkered past: Venetian town houses, French arcades, and a handful of grand Georgian public buildings. The medieval Campiello quarter is an atmospheric labyrinth of narrow, winding streets, steep stairways, and little squares watched over by old churches and Venetian palazzi. The Spianada (esplanade) is a huge, open parade ground, bordered by the arcaded Liston, built by the French under Napoléon and meant to resemble the Rue du Rivoli in Paris. Standing in the center are reminders of British rule: an ornate Victorian bandstand and an Ionic rotunda built to honor the first British lord high commissioner. The most impressive of Corfu Town's many churches is the Church of St. Spyridon, landmarked by a distinctive red-domed tower. Built in 1596, its most prized treasure is the silver reliquary holding Spyridon's remains.

Don't Miss

Built by the Venetians in 1546, the formidable Old Fortress was once home to Corfu Town's entire population. Its ramparts withstood a Turkish assault in 1716, but most of the fortifications inside the fortress were destroyed by the British. From the highest point there are splendid views over the town and the mountainous mainland.

Getting Here

Several airlines fly to Corfu, and there are also frequent ferries from Igoumenitsa on the mainland. Corfu Town is easily walkable, while buses go to more distant parts of the island.

Old Fortress. ✉ *On eastern point of Corfu Town peninsula* ☎ *26610/48120* 🌐 *odysseus.culture.gr* 🎫 *€6*

Visit Corfu. 🌐 *www.visitcorfu.gr*

Kefalonia

Captain Corelli's Island

Although the island and its capital are probably best known as the setting for the 1990s novel, Kefalonia's charms lie mainly in its rugged, unspoiled hinterland and radiant seas: an earthquake in 1953 destroyed most of the Venetian-era buildings, though a couple of charming villages have survived. Mount Ainos dominates dominates the island's center, its slopes blanketed by wildflower meadows and fir forests and its lower slopes cloaked by vineyards. The one section of the island that survived the 1953 quake almost intact was the wild northern tip. Today, yachts outnumber fishing boats in the harbor of boho-chic Fiskardo, while its colorful waterfront Venetian buildings now house eateries and café-bars.

Don't Miss

Open to the sky, Melissani Cave and its cobalt-blue lake, fed by the sea almost 32 km (20 miles) away, was a place of worship during antiquity. Rowboats await to ferry visitors through a tunnel into its magical interior.

Getting Here

You can fly from Athens (1 hour). Ferries connect Sami, Kefalonia's busiest port, with Astakos (2 1/2 hours) and Patras (3 hours) on the mainland. Ferries also sail between Poros, south of Sami, and mainland Kyllini (1¼ hours). On the island, buses connect Argostoli with Sami, Poros, and Fiskardo, but to explore Kefalonia thoroughly you need a car.

Kefalonia Tourism. 🌐 *www.visitgreece.gr*

Melissani Cave. ✉ *Karavomylos, Sami* ☎ *26740/22997* 🎫 *€6* 🕓 *Closed Nov.–Apr.*

Mount Ainos National Park. ✉ *Mount Ainos* ☎ *26710/29258* 🌐 *aenosnationalpark.gr*

Palace of Knossos

Minoan Magnificence

When British archaeologist Sir Arthur Evans began excavating Knossos in 1899, this amazing archaeological site was finally uncovered after more than a millennium. The first palace was constructed here around 1900 BC; a second incarnation was built 1700 BC, after an earthquake destroyed the original. Knossos survived another disaster around 1450 BC, when other Minoan palaces were razed, but around 1380 BC it was destroyed by fire, and around 1100 BC the site was abandoned. Over the years it was buried. Evans uncovered the cool, dark throne-room complex (the wavy-back gypsum throne is the oldest in Europe) and the even more spectacular grand staircase, as well as many frescoes.

Don't Miss

Star exhibits at the Heraklion Archaeological Museum include engraved seal stones, the enigmatic Phaistos Disk, and a magnificent *rhyton* (libation vessel) carved from dark serpentine in the shape of a bull's head. Even more arresting are the frescoes of agile young men and women somersaulting over the back of a charging bull.

Getting Here

Crete is connected by air with many major airports in Europe and by ferry with Athens. Municipal bus No. 2 travels to Knossos every 20 minutes or so from Heraklion.

Heraklion Archaeological Museum. 🌐 *www.heraklionmuseum.gr* 🎫 *€12; €20 combined ticket with Palace of Knossos*

Knossos. 🌐 *www.odysseus.culture.gr* 🎫 *€15; €20, combined ticket with Archaeological Museum in Heraklion*

Gortyna

Birthplace of Christian Crete

Impressive Roman and Byzantine remains scattered around this site evoke its place at the heart of Cretan civilization for more than a thousand years. First settled by the Minoans (and celebrated by Homer), Gortyna outlived that culture's mysterious eclipse to thrive in the Dorian era, rising by the 2nd century BC to become Crete's paramount city-state and eventually its Roman-era provincial capital. At its peak, as many as 100,000 people lived here. It was the earliest Christian Cretan city and became the seat of Apostle Titus, first bishop of Crete. The soaring apse and side chapels of the Byzantine Basilica of Agios Titus (St. Titus), have been restored; next to it is the Odeion, a Roman theater leveled by an earthquake and rebuilt by Emperor Trajan. On the other side of the road that bisects the site are the Praetorium, the 2nd century AD palace of the Roman governor of Crete, and the Nymphaeum, a public bath originally supplied by an aqueduct. Climb to the hilltop Acropolis for a view of the site and the fertile fields and citrus groves of the southern plan that surrounds it.

Don't Miss

Within the walls of the Odeion, seek out the wall-mounted stone tablets, on which are engraved the 600 lines of the Gortyna Law Code, an inscription from the 5th century BC, and the earliest known written Greek law.

Getting Here

Buses from Heraklion to Moires, 8 km (5 miles) from Gortyna, take around 90 minutes. From Moires, you can take a local taxi to the archaeological site. A better option is to rent a car. ✉ *Agioi Deka, Phaistos* ☎ *28920/31144* 🌐 *www.odysseus.culture.gr* 🎫 *€6*

Samaria Gorge

Crete's Grand Canyon

Hiking the Samaria Gorge, Europe's longest, you'll encounter vivid wildflower meadows and fast-flowing streams, and may even glimpse the elusive Cretan wild goat (*kri kri*) and see lammergeier vultures wheeling high above. Starting south of Chania, the deep, verdant crevice extends 16 km (10 miles) from near the village of Xyloskalo all the way to the Libyan Sea. The canyon carves its way through the aptly named White Mountains, a trackless, treeless massif of almost lunar-looking limestone summits that are snow-capped as late as June, and melting snow feeds the torrent that flows through it. This magnificent landscape is the most traveled of the dozens of gorges that cut through Crete's mountains, but it is thrilling nonetheless, sometimes just a few feet wide. It takes five to six hours to walk down.

Don't Miss

Dwarfed by mountains on either side, two evocative ghost villages, abandoned in the 1960s, are gradually becoming little more than tumbled stone walls; fig trees still grow in their abandoned gardens.

When to Go

The gorge is closed October 15–May 1. Go in May or early October for best walking weather and to avoid crowds.

Getting Here

Samaria is 35 km (22 miles) south of Chania. Take the bus to the trailhead and a boat back from Agia Roumeli, at the mouth of the gorge, back in the afternoon to Chora Sfakion, from where buses return to Chania.

Samaria National Park. *www.samaria.gr* *€5 (not including bus/boat fare)*

Hydra

A Quick Athens Escape

For in-the-know Athenians, little Hydra is a favorite getaway from the noise and summer heat of Greece's sprawling capital. It's easy to see why. As your ferry approaches, the island appears mountainous and barren. But as the curved harbor suddenly comes into view, delight takes over. Two- and three-story gray-and-white houses with red tile roofs, many built between 1770 and 1821, at the height of the island's fortunes, rise in tiers above a quayside lined with bars and boutiques, and Hydra Town seems as fresh as when it was "discovered" in the 1960s by creatives like singer-songwriter Leonard Cohen and authors Lawrence Durrell and Henry Miller. Port and houses are protected monuments, so Hydra looks much as it did in its heyday. Even better, all motorized vehicles are banned, so the only traffic sounds are the clop of mules' hooves lightly echoing along narrow alleys. The almost uninhabited hinterland is crisscrossed with walking trails, some leading to tiny, pebbly beaches that can otherwise only be reached by boat.

Don't Miss

This Hydra Historical Archives and Museum commemorates Hydra's seafarers with displays of ships' figureheads from their vessels, weapons, charts, and portraits of island heroes, and quaint local costumes.

When to Go

The island is in full cultural swing in summer, and accommodations are at a premium from June through August.

Getting Here

Frequent ferries connect Hydra with Piraeus (90 minutes). On the island, water taxis carry visitors to beaches.

Hydra Tourist Information. 🌐 *www.hydra.gr*

When in the Greek Islands

★ Acropolis of Lindos

RUINS | FAMILY | A 15-minute climb (please don't take the donkey), from the village center up to the Acropolis of Lindos leads past a gauntlet of Lindian women who spread out their lace and embroidery like fresh laundry over the rocks. The final approach ascends a steep flight of stairs, past a marvelous 2nd-century BC relief of the prow of a Lindian ship, carved into the rock. The entrance takes you through the medieval castle built by the Knights of St. John, then to the Byzantine Chapel of St. John on the next level. The Romans, too, left their mark on the acropolis, with a temple dedicated to Diocletian. The Temple of Athena Lindia at the very top is surprisingly modest, given the drama of the approach. As was common in the 4th century BC, both the front and the rear are flanked by four Doric columns. ✉ *Lindos* ✣ *Above village* ☎ *22413/65200* 🌐 *odysseus.culture.gr* 🎫 *€12* ⏲ *Closed Tues. and Nov.–Mar.*

★ Archaeological Museum of Chania

HISTORY MUSEUM | In a magnificent new home, the rich collection from all over western Crete has been relocated to the new building and enriched with many new exhibits. The artifacts bear witness to the presence of Minoans, ancient Greeks, Romans, Venetians, and Ottomans with over 3,500 objects on show. The painted Minoan clay coffins and elegant late-Minoan pottery indicate that the region was as wealthy as the center of the island under the Minoans, though no palace has yet been located. ✉ *Skra 15, Chania* ☎ *28210/23315* 🌐 *www.amch.gr* 🎫 *€6.*

Boutari Winery

WINERY | Established by one of the oldest wine-making families in Greece, this state-of-the-art winery marries tradition with innovation, producing more than 100,000 bottles a year. There is a modern tasting room with great views over the vines to the hills beyond, for sampling some of the estate's award-winning offerings. You can buy the wines you have tasted, along with other local delicacies. ✉ *Skalani, Heraklion* ☎ *28107/31617* 🌐 *www.boutari.gr* 🎫 *Tastings from €10.*

Drogarati Cave

CAVE | A 4-km (2½ mile) drive from Sami, this 150-million-year-old cave was only discovered after a land collapse revealed its entrance. Earthquakes and trophy-seeking tourists have since damaged its more impressive stalactites but it remains a compelling sight, especially its 900-square-meter Chamber of Exaltation, which has also been known to double as a concert venue on occasion. ✉ *Chaliotata-Sami Rd., Sami* ☎ *26740/23302* 🎫 *€3* ⏲ *Closed Nov.–Mar.*

Mon Repos

HISTORIC HOME | The compact Neoclassical palace (really a villa) was built in 1831 by Sir Frederic Adam for his wife, and it was later the summer residence of the British lord high commissioners. After Greece won independence from Britain in 1864, Mon Repos was used as a summer palace for the royal family of Greece. Queen Elizabeth II's husband, Prince Philip, was born here in 1921. The Greek government opened the fully restored palace as a museum dedicated to the area's archaeological history. Displays of items found in the area—as well as interpretive displays, rooms showcasing Regency design, contemporary antiques, and botanical paintings—make for a truly eclectic museum collection. The room where Prince Philip was born (on the kitchen table, it is said) houses a 3D interactive map of Corfu Town and its environs. ✉ *Dairpfela 16, Kanoni* ✣ *2 km (1 mile) south of Old Fortress, following oceanfront walk* ☎ *26610/41369* 🌐 *odysseus.culture.gr* 🎫 *Grounds free; museum €4* ⏲ *Museum closed Tues.*

★ Palace of Phaistos

RUINS | The Palace of Phaistos was built around 1900 BC and rebuilt after a

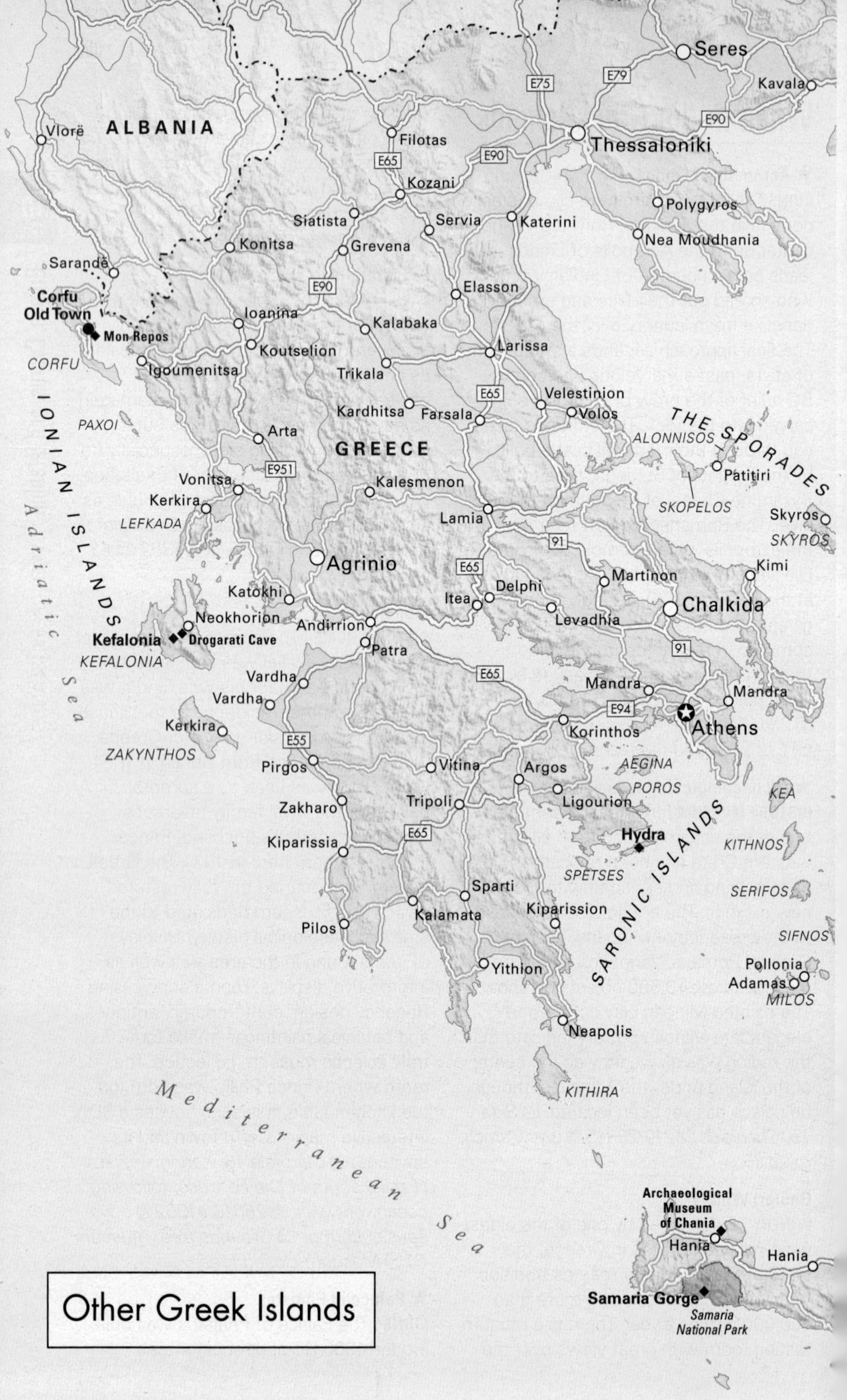

Other Greek Islands

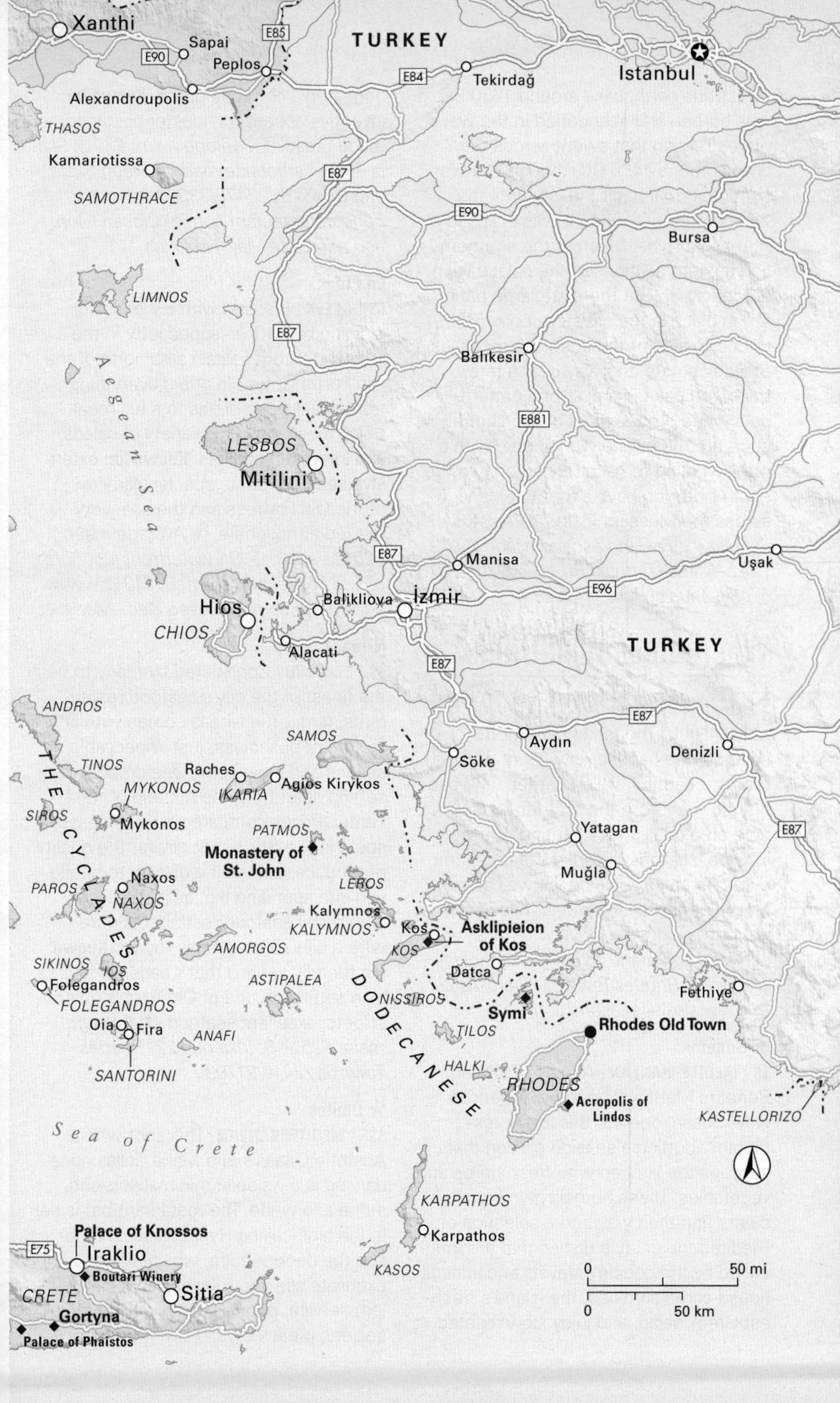

Xanthi
Sapai
Peplos
Alexandroupolis
THASOS
Kamariotissa
SAMOTHRACE
LIMNOS
TURKEY
Tekirdağ
Istanbul
Bursa
Balıkesir
Aegean Sea
LESBOS
Mitilini
Manisa
Uşak
İzmir
Balikliova
Hios
CHIOS
Alacati
TURKEY
ANDROS
SAMOS
Aydın
Denizli
Söke
TINOS
Raches
Agios Kirykos
MYKONOS
IKARIA
SIROS
Mykonos
PATMOS
Yatagan
Monastery of St. John
Muğla
THE CYCLADES
PAROS
Naxos
NAXOS
LEROS
Kalymnos
KALYMNOS
Kos
Asklipieion of Kos
KOS
AMORGOS
Datca
SIKINOS
IOS
ASTIPALEA
Folegandros
FOLEGANDROS
NISSIROS
Symi
Fethiye
Oia
Fira
ANAFI
TILOS
Rhodes Old Town
SANTORINI
HALKI
RHODES
DODECANESE
Acropolis of Lindos
KASTELLORIZO
Sea of Crete
KARPATHOS
Karpathos
Palace of Knossos
Iraklio
Boutari Winery
KASOS
CRETE
Sitia
Gortyna
Palace of Phaistos
0
50 mi
0
50 km
E85
E90
E84
E87
E90
E87
E881
E87
E96
E87
E87
E87
E75

disastrous earthquake around 1650 BC. It was burned and abandoned in the wave of destruction that swept across the island around 1450 BC, though Greeks continued to inhabit the city until the 2nd century BC, when it was eclipsed by Roman Gortyna. Much of the southern and eastern sections of the palace have eroded away. But there are large pithoi still in place in the old storerooms. On the north side of the court the recesses of an elaborate doorway bear a rare trace: red paint in a diamond pattern on a white ground. East of the central court are the palace workshops, with a metalworking furnace fenced off. On the south side, you have a memorable view across the Messara Plain. ✉ *Phaistos* ✣ *Follow signs and ascend hill off Ayii Deka–Mires–Timbaki Rd.* ☎ *28920/42315* 🌐 *odysseus.culture.gr* 🎫 *€8.*

Where to Eat and Drink

★ Alexis 4 Seasons

$$ | **SEAFOOD** | Though known for its seafood, the handsomely decorated old rooms, beautiful walled garden, and panoramic view from the roof terrace found here are equalling enchanting. Mussels in wine, scallops in vodka sauce, shrimp risotto in an ouzo sauce, as well as simply grilled fish fill the menu. **Known for:** gourmet seafood; city-view terrace; good service. [$] *Average main: €25* ✉ *Aristotelous 33, Rhodes Town* ☎ *22410/70522* 🌐 *www.alexis4seasons.com.*

★ Benetos

$$ | **MEDITERRANEAN** | A native Patmian, Benetos Matthaiou, and his American wife, Susan, operate this lovely restaurant abutting a seaside garden that supplies the kitchen with fresh herbs and vegetables. These homegrown ingredients find their way into a selection of Mediterranean-style dishes that are influenced by the couple's travels and include house-cured sardines, the island's freshest Greek salad, and juicy slow-roasted pork atop a chickpea puree. **Known for:** inventive appetizers; lobster pasta; homemade bread. [$] *Average main: €20* ✉ *Skala* ✣ *On harborside road between Skala and Grikos* ☎ *22470/33089* 🌐 *www.benetosrestaurant.com* ⏲ *Closed Mon. and mid-Oct.–May. No lunch.*

En Plo

$$ | **GREEK** | Blessed with a wonderful location by a wave-lapped jetty in the little waterfront Faliraki area north of the Old Fortress, En Plo offers everything from snacks and pizzas to a full meal. Enjoy mezedes, a big variety of salads, and interesting pastas. **Known for:** extensive seafood menu; spectacular view of the Old Fortress and the sea; very relaxed atmosphere. [$] *Average main: €20* ✉ *Faliraki* ✣ *On waterfront just north of Old Fortress* ☎ *26610/81813* 🌐 *www.enplocorfu.com* ⏲ *Closed Dec.–Mar.*

Nireas

$$ | **SEAFOOD** | Considered by many to be the finest of the city's seafood restaurants, family-run Nireas comes with little fanfare or pushiness, just impeccable service and a peaceful, vine-draped setting apart from the hubbub of the center. Prices compare well with lesser spots in the city, especially for the quality of produce, and staff won't try to hustle you into spending big, as is the case with many seafood restaurants here where bills can suddenly rocket. **Known for:** friendly service that's eager to help; a nice setting on one of Old Town's quieter streets; excellent seafood. [$] *Average main: €25* ✉ *Sofokleous 22, Rhodes Town* ☎ *22410/21703.*

★ Omilos

$$$ | **MEDITERRANEAN** | This spot where Aristotle Onassis and Maria Callas once danced is a vision in minimalist island stone and white. The restaurant-bar is set in the high-ceiling Hydra Nautical Club and the deck outside, which affords an exquisite sea view. **Known for:** excellent service; popular with visiting high society; great views. [$] *Average main:*

€35 ✉ Hydra port, Hydra Town ✣ On way to Hydronetta ☎ 22980/53800 ⏲ Closed Mon.–Thurs. Oct.–Apr.

Taverna Sigelakis
$ | **GREEK** | Residents from villages for miles around come to the town of Sivas to enjoy a meal of *stifado* (meat in a rich tomato sauce), artichokes with avgolemono (egg and lemon sauce), and other specialties, including delicious roasted lamb and chicken, all served on the vine-dappled front terrace in warm seasons or in the hearth-warmed dining room when the weather is cold. A meal comes with friendly service and a free glass of raki and a sweet. **Known for:** true traditional Cretan cooking; authentic stone-walled surroundings; hospitable owner. [$] *Average main: €14 ✉ Sivas ✣ 6 km (4 miles) northeast of Matala ☎ 28920/42748 🌐 www.sigelakis-studios.gr.*

★ **Venetian Well**
$$ | **MEDITERRANEAN** | The scene is as delicious as the food in this wonderfully romantic restaurant arranged around a 17th-century well on the most beautiful little square in the Old Town. Expect creative Greek and Mediterranean cuisine, with a menu that changes regularly according to the availability of the always fresh ingredients. **Known for:** sous vide lamb cooked for 24 hours; veal sweetbreads with smoked cream, salsify and truffle sauce; fine presentation and attentive service. [$] *Average main: €20 ✉ Kremasti Sq., Campiello ✣ Across from Church of the Panagia ☎ 26615/50955 🌐 www.venetianwell.gr ⏲ No lunch. Closed Sun.*

Cool Places to Stay

★ **Albergo Gelsomino Hotel**
$$ | **HOTEL** | Built in 1928, back when Kos was under the thumb of Fascist Italy, this beautiful building was originally created as a hotel for prominent military officials. **Pros:** an iconic building with a fascinating history; beachside breakfasts and good cocktails at the bar; free vintage bikes for guests to use. **Cons:** there's no pool or gym; you certainly pay for what you get; the glass "smoking booth" is a clever idea but very weird to look at. [$] *Rooms from: €200 ✉ Vasileos Georgiou V, Kos Town ☎ 22420/20200 🌐 www.gelsomino-hotel.com ⇆ 8 rooms 🍽 Free Breakfast.*

Bratsera Hotel
$$$ | **HOTEL** | An 1860 sponge factory was transformed into this charming character hotel (doors made out of old packing crates still bearing the "Piraeus sponge" stamp, etc.), which has a bevy of alluring delights, including guest-room decor accented with framed portraits, old engravings, four-poster ironwork beds, and cozy natural wood lofts, and the hotel restaurant—considered one of the island's best—which is set in the oleander-and-bougainvillea-graced courtyard. **Pros:** excellent restaurant; the relaxing-by-the-pool experience; free Wi-Fi. **Cons:** fitness room is small; some small, dark bathrooms; limited pool hours. [$] *Rooms from: €270 ✉ Hydra Town ✣ On left of port up Tompazi, then follow alley straight ahead as Tompazi veers to right ☎ 22980/53971, 22980/52794 restaurant 🌐 bratserahotel.com ⏲ Closed mid-Oct.–Mar. ⇆ 25 rooms 🍽 Free Breakfast.*

Cavalieri Hotel
$$ | **HOTEL** | This hotel occupies a landmark 18th-century building with a wonderful location equidistant between the Liston and the sea; it's one of the few hotels here to remain open year-round. Guest rooms have nice bathrooms and simple but comfortable furnishings. **Pros:** attractive historic building; great views over the Esplanade and the sea; short walk to the sights of the historic center. **Cons:** small public rooms; the area can be noisy; no dedicated parking. [$] *Rooms from: €150 ✉ Kapodistriou 4, Corfu Town ☎ 26610/39041 🌐 www.cavalieri-hotel.com ⇆ 50 rooms 🍽 Free Breakfast.*

Kalimera Archanes Village

$$ | **B&B/INN** | An especially appealing base for exploring Knossos and Heraklion is the well-kept wine village of Archanes, where four 19th-century stone houses tucked into a garden are fitted out with traditional furnishings and all the modern comforts. **Pros:** highly atmospheric and very comfortable; near many sights but provides a nice dose of Greek village life; beautiful interiors and outdoor spaces. **Cons:** beaches and Heraklion are a 20-minute drive away; a pool would be the icing on the cake; own transport needed. *Rooms from: €200* *Theotokopoulou, Tsikritsi, Archanes* *Off Leof. Kapetanaki, left after Likastos Taverna* *28107/52999* *www.archanes-village.com* *4 houses* *Free Breakfast.*

★ Marco Polo Mansion

$$ | **HOTEL** | Entering this renovated 15th-century Ottoman mansion in the maze of the Old Town's colorful Turkish section is like stepping into another world. **Pros:** a quiet, historic retreat in the back alleys; breakfast served in the garden is a thing of joy; the courtyard restaurant is wonderful. **Cons:** rooms are reached via several sets of stairs; hotel can only be reached on foot and is tricky to find; come here to live like a pasha, not to indulge in modern amenities. *Rooms from: €160* *Aghiou Fanouriou 40–42, Rhodes Town* *22410/25562* *www.marcopolomansion.gr* *Closed Nov.–Apr.* *10 rooms* *Free Breakfast.*

★ The Old Markets

$$$ | **HOTEL** | Symi's historic trading halls have been restored as a delightfully atmospheric inn where centuries-old surroundings are accented by stone floors and antiques. **Pros:** extremely comfortable accommodations, including a lavish suite; the only hotel with a pool on Symi; fantastic views for dinner and breakfast. **Cons:** the market rooms can be a little dark; steps to reach the hotel; the pool is indoors. *Rooms from: €240* *Kali Strata, Yialos* *22460/71440* *www.theoldmarkets.com* *Closed Nov.–Apr.* *7 rooms, 3 suites* *Free Breakfast.*

★ Petra Hotel & Suites

$$ | **HOTEL** | One of Greece's truly special retreats sits high above Grikos Bay, south of Skala, and provides a luxurious yet informal getaway, with large and sumptuous guest quarters, delightful outdoor lounges, a welcoming pool, and soothing sea views. **Pros:** wonderful outdoor spaces; superb service and hospitality; beach is just steps away. **Cons:** the hotel climbs a series of terraces reached only by steps; minimum three-night stay; not within walking distance to main sights of Patmos. *Rooms from: €170* *Skala* *22470/34020* *www.petrahotel-patmos.com* *Closed mid-Oct.–May* *11 rooms* *Free Breakfast.*

Cyprus

Cyprus's strategic position in the Eastern Mediterranean has made it subject to regular invasions by powerful empires. Greeks, Phoenicians, Assyrians, Egyptians, Persians, Romans, and Byzantines all have either ruled or breezed through here. It remains a divided island, with the north controlled by Turkey and the south an independent member of the EU.

In 1191, Richard the Lionheart, leader of the Third Crusade, took possession of Cyprus. A year later he sold Cyprus to the Knights Templar, who within a year resold it to Guy de Lusignan, the deposed king of Jerusalem. Guy's descendants ruled the island until the late 15th century, when it was annexed by the Venetians. The Turks wrested the island from Venice and ruled it from the 16th through 19th centuries. Cyprus became a British colony in 1914 and finally gained its independence in 1960.

Vestiges of the diverse cultures that have ruled here dot the island, from remnants of Neolithic settlements and ancient Greek and Roman temple sites, such as the spectacular cliffside site of Kourion, to Early Christian basilicas and painted Byzantine churches. Paphos has been designated a World Heritage site by UNESCO, and many fortifications built by the Crusaders and the Venetians still stand throughout the island. A piece of the true cross is said to be kept in the monastery of Stavrovouni, and Paphos has the remains of a pillar to which St. Paul was allegedly tied when he was beaten for preaching Christianity.

Since a 1974 Turkish invasion that resulted in forced population shifts, Cyprus has been divided by a thin buffer zone called the "Green Line" between the now mainly Turkish Cypriot north and predominantly Greek Cypriot south. The zone cuts right through the capital city of Nicosia. Cyprus joined the European Union in 2004—but without a resolution of the island's division, only the Greek Cypriot south flies the EU flag.

Today's tourists come to appreciate the golden sandy beaches and the clear blue seas. Glorious mountains tumble to the stunning coastline while peaceful villages with winding streets nestle amid vineyards and olive groves. A beguiling mix of the ancient and the modern, Cyprus is a distinctive destination that shows the influence of competing empires in its timeless beauty.

Nicosia

A Divided Capital

The capital of Cyprus is twice-divided. Its picturesque Old City is contained within 16th-century Venetian fortifications that separate it from the wide, tree-lined streets, large hotels, and high-rises of the modern section. The second division is political and more noticeable. The so-called Green Line set up by the United Nations divides the island between the Republic of Cyprus and Turkish-occupied Northern Cyprus, making it the last divided city in Europe. Laiki Geitonia, at the southern edge of the Old City in the Greek section, is an area of winding alleys and traditional architecture that has been restored to its historic charm. Tavernas, cafés, and craft workshops line the shaded, cobbled streets. You can travel across to the north via one of two pedestrian checkpoints, but be sure to bring your passport.

Don't Miss

Lefkosia on the Turkish side of the divided city makes a good half-day trip to see the sights and perhaps do some shopping for colorful fabrics and Turkish delight. Stop in the lively open bazaar around Arasta Sokagi, or visit the Bandabulya, the Municipal Market and pick up a kebab or Turkish pizza if you want a quick bite.

Getting Here and Around

Nicosia is easily navigable on foot with most of the restaurants, bars, and major historical sights falling within a fairly small radius within the Old Town. If you travel to the north, be sure to bring your passport.

Kourion

The Descendants of Argos

Kourion was one of the most important city-kingdoms of ancient Cyprus, whose inhabitants believed they were descents from Argos, the ancient Peloponnesian Kingdom. The archaeological site, west of Limassol, has both Greek and Roman ruins. Classical and Shakespearean plays are sometimes staged in the impressive amphitheater. Next to the theater is the Villa of Eustolios, a summer house built by a wealthy Christian with interesting mosaic floors from the 5th century AD; nearby is the partially rebuilt Roman stadium.

Don't Miss

East of Kourion is Limassol, a major commercial port, cruise-ship port of call, and wine-making center on the south coast. It's a bustling, cosmopolitan town with some of the liveliest nightlife on the island. Luxury hotels and apartments stretch along 12 km (7 miles) of seafront. Above the Old Port looms Limassol Castle, much damaged over the years from various invaders and from destructive earthquakes. A luxurious new marina can hold 650 yachts, as well as houses, apartments, shops, and restaurants.

Learn About Wine

The history of wine-making in Cyprus dates from at least 2000 BC; the best-known Cypriot wine is the sweet red Commandaria, which reminded Marc Antony of Cleopatra's kisses. There are dozens of other world-class wines from Cyprus. Learn about them in the Cyprus Wine Museum, about ten minutes west of Limassol in the village of Erimi, where you can also get wine samples. ✉ *Paphou 42, Erími* ☎ *25/873808* 🌐 *www.cypruswinemuseum.com* 🎫 *€6, €10 with tasting*

Kourion. ✣ *On main Paphos road, 19 km (12 miles) west of Limassol 25/934250* 🌐 *www.mcw.gov.cy* 🎫 *€5*

Kato Paphos Archaeological Park

Cyprus's Resort Hub

On the west end of Cyprus, Paphos combines a marvelous seaside location with stellar archaeological sites and buzzing nightlife. Since the late 1990s it has hosted some of the most lavish resorts on the island. The surrounding area is one of the most scenic in Cyprus, especially the untrammeled Akamas Peninsula. Nearby are the elaborate 2nd- to 5th-century AD Roman mosaics in the Roman Villa of Theseus, and the Houses of Dionysos, Aion, and Orpheus—all part of a UNESCO World Heritage site, the Kato Paphos Archaeological Park. The impressive mosaics are an easy walk from the harbor and were unearthed in 1962 by a farmer plowing his fields.

Don't Miss

Also at the archaeological park, the Tombs of the Kings, an early necropolis, date from 300 BC. Contrary to the name, no actual kings were buried here; rather, the tombs held aristocrats and high officials. The coffin niches are empty, but a powerful sense of mystery remains, but the underground tombs are impressive with columnated atriums.

Bathe Like a Goddess

The Baths of Aphrodite, 48 km (30 miles) north of Paphos, are a series of natural pools where the goddess is said to have seduced Adonis when he stopped for a drink while hunting. From the baths, a trail to the west follows the coastline, passing magnificent views out to sea and other secluded swimming spots. ✉ *Neo Chorio, Pólis* 🎫 *Free*

Getting Here

Paphos is the most pedestrian-friendly town in Cyprus, with a long beachside path running alongside most of the hotels all the way down to the pleasant leisure harbor, anchored by the medieval fortress. ☎ *26/306295* 🌐 *www.mcw.gov.cy* 🎫 *€3*

Petra tou Romiou

Birthplace of Aphrodite

The mythological birthplace of the Goddess of Love is a large offshore rock just off the southwest coast of Paphos. Swimming around Aphrodite's Rock three times is purported to bring you eternal love. Whether or not you believe the legend, it's a dramatic place to stop for a snack or picnic lunch and a look at the unquestionably romantic views where you may be tempted to swim or stay for sunset. It's doubly famous, as it is also associated with the Byzantine hero Digenes Akritas, who is said to have thrown the rocks into the sea to keep the plundering Saracens away from his love interest.

Don't Miss

Akamas National Park is a 230-sq km (89-sq mile) peninsula on the western tip of Cyprus. Diverse in its landscape, it is one of the most beautiful areas of the island with deep gorges, wide sandy bays, and hidden coves. Protected from development, the nature reserve has unique flora and fauna endemic to the region. Here is also the Blue Lagoon, one of the best destinations on the island for snorkeling and exploring the transparent sea. Its natural beauty is stunning, all the more so for not being completely undeveloped.

Getting Here and Around

Petra tou Romiou is between Phaphos and Limassol. Using Polis as a gateway, regular boat trips leave from the harbor at Latchi. You can also rent 4x4 vehicles and quads and drive out, but perhaps the most rewarding way to travel is to hike or cycle the numerous paths that crisscross the reserve.

Hiking in the Troodos Mountains

The Green Heart of Cyprus

North of Limassol, these mountains, which rise to 6,500 feet, have shady cedar and pine forests and cool springs with myriad trails that are ideal for hiking and mountain biking excursions. Small, painted Byzantine churches in the foothills are rich examples of a rare indigenous art form. In winter, visitors can ski in the Troodos mountains in the morning and sunbathe on the beach in the afternoon.

Don't Miss

In the foothills of Mount Olympos, the 11th-century Agios Nikolaos tis Stegis—the Church of St. Nicholas of the Roof—is so named for its steep, pitched roof, built for protection against the weather; it's a UNESCO World Heritage site that contains stunning frescoes.

Stop for a Drink

One of the prettiest villages in Cyprus, Omodos is an ancient wine-making town centered on a historic Byzantine monastery, Timios Stavros. As you wander the narrow cobblestone streets, be sure to stop into one of the many wine-tasting stalls for a sample or two of wines made from Cypriot grapes like Xynisteri (white) and Mavro (red); some still display old-fashioned grape presses and other wine-making paraphernalia.

Getting Here

You'll need a car to reach the Troodos Mountains and cover larger distances, but the area is ideal for biking and hiking and crisscrossed with many trails.

Agios Nikolaos tis Stegis. *5 km (3 miles) southwest of Kakopetria* *Free* *Closed Mon.*

Omodos. *www.omodosvillage.com*

Troodos Mountains Tourism. *mytroodos.com*

When in Cyprus

★ Agios Lazaros

CHURCH | In the town center stands one of the island's more important churches, resplendent with gold icons and unique wood carvings. Constructed in AD 890 by Byzantine Emperor Leo VI and restored to its glory in the 17th century, it is a beautiful example of Byzantine architecture. The church includes a fascinating crypt containing the sarcophagus of the Biblical Lazarus mentioned in Luke; Jesus is said to have resurrected Lazarus four days after his death, after which time Lazarus traveled to Kition, Larnaca's ancient city, where he became a bishop for 30 years. ✉ *Platia Agiou Lazarou* ☎ *24/652498* 🌐 *www.agioslazaros.org.cy* 🎫 *Free.*

Bellapais Monastery

RUINS | The majestic ruins of the former Bellapais Monastery (otherwise known as the Abbey of Peace), 6 km southeast of Girne, are just as impressive as those of St. Hilarion Kalesi. Founded by Augustinian monks in 1198, the abbey's original structure was considerably expanded by the Lusignans in the 13th century, and its spectacular Gothic architecture deserves to be explored. The rooftop offers gorgeous views of the coastal plains and the Mediterranean. The tranquil accompanying village with tiny streets was immortalized by Lawrence Durrell in his book *Bitter Lemons of Cyprus,* which chronicled his travails in buying a home in Bellapais. Every May the Bellapais Music Festival takes place inside the monastery. ✉ *Bellapais, Girne (Kyrenia).*

Famagusta (*Gazimağusa*)

TOWN | The chief port of Northern Cyprus has massive and well-preserved Venetian walls and the late 13th-century Gothic Cathedral of St. Nicholas, now Lala Mustafa Pasha Mosque. On August 1, 1571, the Venetians surrendered the town to the Turks, ending a brutal ten-month siege and signifying the end of their rule in Cyprus. A winged lion, symbol of the Republic of Venice, still graces the old Sea Gate, and in a nod to Cristoforo Moro, the Venetian administrator immortalized by Shakespeare, one of the battlements is named Othello's Tower. The Old Town, within the walls, is the most intriguing district to explore. ✉ *Famagusta* 🌐 *visitfamagusta.com.cy.*

Kyrenia (*Girne*)

TOWN | Of the coastal resorts, Kyrenia (called *Girne* by the Turks, who have occupied the city since 1974), with its yacht-filled harbor, has always been the most appealing to anyone with ambitions of empire—the Myceneans, Romans, Byzantines, Lusignans, Venetians, Ottomans, and the British all left their mark here. Probably the prettiest town in all of Cyprus, its horseshoe-shaped bay is flanked by a 12th-century castle, and there are excellent beaches to the east and west of the town. The harborfront buildings (once warehouses) are now home to lively bars and eateries. Craggy mountains that form the backdrop to the town help to keep the town cool and the surroundings areas noticeably green. ✉ *Girne (Kyrenia)* 🌐 *www.visitnorthcyprus.com.*

Larnaca Salt Lake

NATURE SIGHT | FAMILY | About 7 km (4 miles) southwest of Larnaca, near the airport, is the 2.2-sq. km Larnaca salt lake. It is a complex system of four main lakes: the main salt lake Alyki, Orphani, Soros, and the small Spiro lake. In winter it is a refuge for migrating birds, especially flamingoes, and in summer it dries up with salt deposits. Though you can't walk on the lake itself, there are plenty of nature trails and picnic spots around it. ✥ *Just off the airport road 7 km (4 miles) southwest of Larnaca.*

Lefkara

TOWN | This picturesque village—one of the prettiest in Cyprus—is best known for its lace: *lefkaritika* has been woven by hand here for centuries. Most

Cyprus

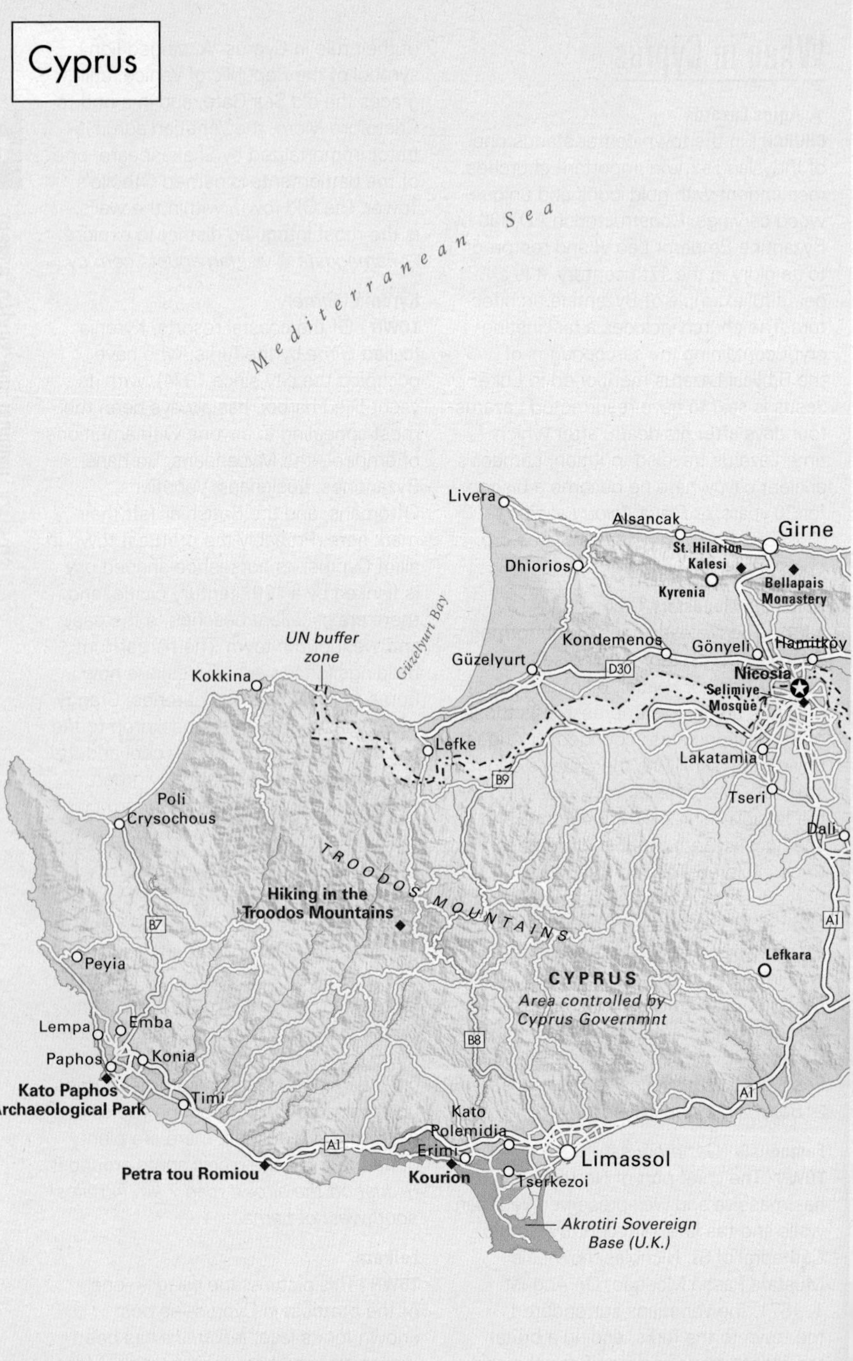

Mediterranean Sea
Livera
Alsancak
Girne
St. Hilarion Kalesi
Kyrenia
Bellapais Monastery
Dhiorios
Güzelyurt Bay
UN buffer zone
Kondemenos
Gönyeli
Hamitköy
Güzelyurt
D30
Nicosia
Selimiye Mosque
Kokkina
Lefke
Lakatamia
B9
Tseri
Poli Crysochous
Dali
TROODOS MOUNTAINS
Hiking in the Troodos Mountains
B7
A1
Lefkara
Peyia
CYPRUS
Area controlled by Cyprus Governmnt
Lempa
Emba
B8
Paphos
Konia
Kato Paphos Archaeological Park
Timi
A1
Kato Polemidia
A1
Erimi
Limassol
Petra tou Romiou
Kourion
Tserkezoi
Akrotiri Sovereign Base (U.K.)

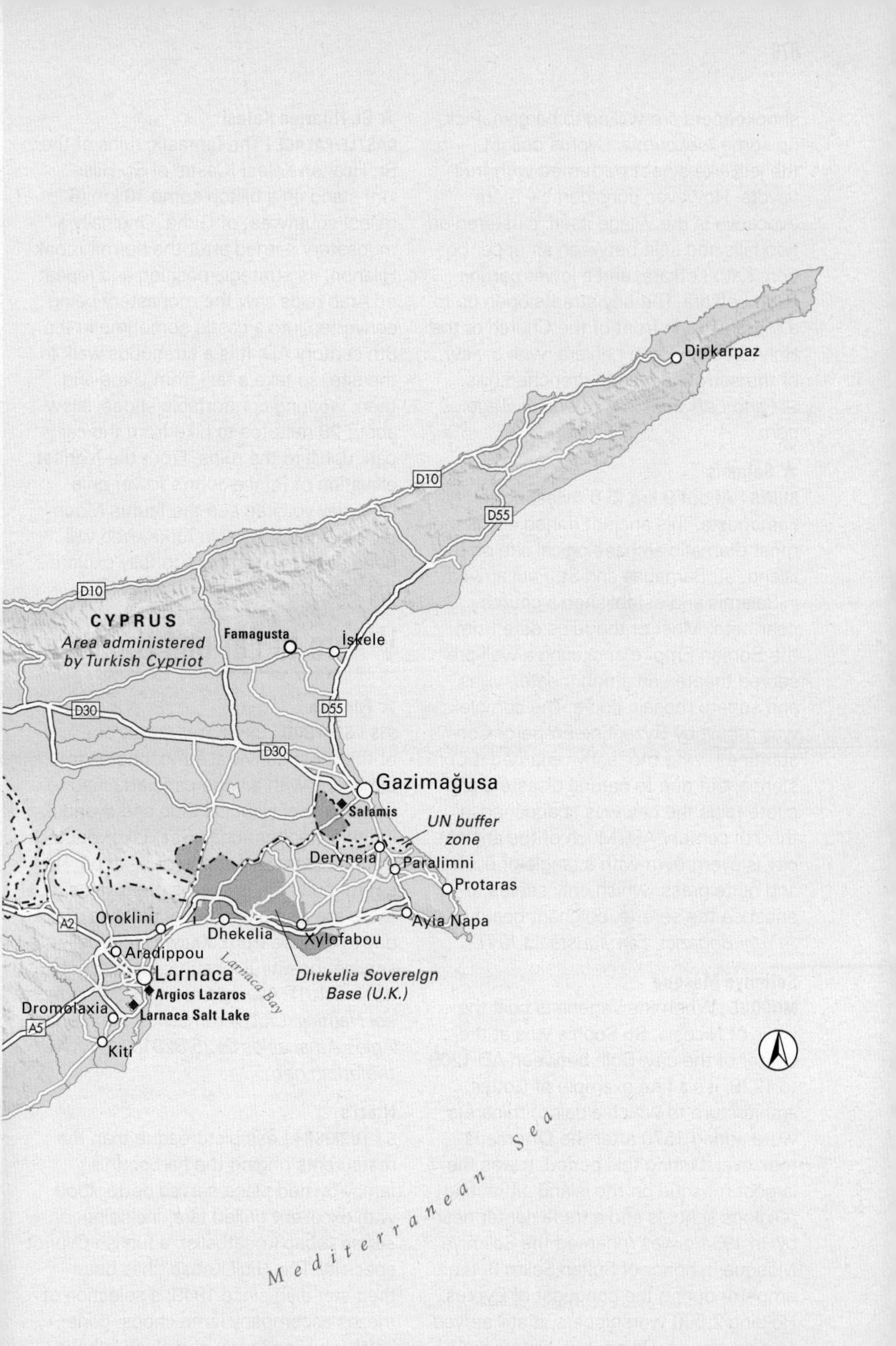

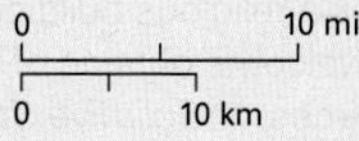
Dipkarpaz
D10
D55
D10
CYPRUS
Area administered
by Turkish Cypriot
Famagusta
İskele
D30
D55
D30
Gazimağusa
Salamis
UN buffer
zone
Deryneia
Paralimni
Protaras
Ayia Napa
Oroklini
A2
Dhekelia
Xylofabou
Aradippou
Larnaca
Larnaca Bay
Argios Lazaros
Dhekelia Sovereign
Base (U.K.)
Dromolaxia
Larnaca Salt Lake
A5
Kiti
Mediterranean Sea
0
10 mi
0
10 km

shopkeepers are willing to bargain. Pick up some *loukoumia*, Cyprus delight, the jelly-like sweet perfumed with fruit flavors. However, considerably more evocative is the village itself, clustered on two hills and split between an upper portion, Kato Lefkara, and a lower portion, Pano Lefkara. The tiny streets open up to a small plaza in front of the Church of the Holy Cross in Pano Lefkara, with a view of the surrounding sun-drenched hills. ✉ *Pano Lefkara* 🌐 *www.lefkaravillage.com.*

★ Salamis

RUINS | About 9 km (5.6 miles) north of Famagusta, this ancient ruined city is the most dramatic archaeological site on the island. St. Barnabas and St. Paul arrived in Salamis and established a church near here. Most of the ruins date from the Roman Empire, including a well-preserved theater, an amphitheater, villas, and superb mosaic floors. The complex was rebuilt by Byzantine Emperor Constantine I, who modestly renamed it Constantia, but due to natural disasters and pirate raids the city was abandoned in the 7th century AD. Much of the ancient city is overgrown with a tangle of bushes and dune grass, which only serves to enhance the serene, poignant beauty. ✉ *Yeni Bogazici, Famagusta* 🎫 *10 TL.*

Selimiye Mosque

MOSQUE | When the Venetians built the walls of Nicosia, St. Sophia was at the center of the city. Built between AD 1209 to 1228, it's a fine example of Gothic architecture to which a pair of minarets were added 1570 after the Ottomans took over. During this period, it was the largest mosque on the island, attracting religious schools and a trade center nearby. In 1954 it was renamed the Selimiye Mosque in honor of Sultan Selim II, the emperor during the conquest of Cyprus. Holding 2,500 worshippers, it still serves as a religious building, but visitors are welcome outside of the five daily prayer times. ✉ *Selimiye St., Nicosia* 🎫 *Free.*

★ St. Hilarion Kalesi

CASTLE/PALACE | The fantastic ruins of the St. Hilarion Kalesi (Castle of St. Hilarion) stand on a hilltop some 10 km (6 miles) southwest of Girne. Originally a monastery named after the hermit monk Hilarion, its strategic position and repeated Arab raids saw the monastery being converted into a castle sometime in the 8th century AD. It is a strenuous walk to the site, so take a taxi from Girne and then, wearing comfortable shoes, allow about 20 minutes to hike from the car park uphill to the ruins. From the highest elevation of Prince John's Tower on a clear day you can see the Taurus Mountains 60 miles away in Turkey. You will need at least two hours to fully explore the castle. ✉ *Girne (Kyrenia)* 🎫 *9 TL.*

Where to Eat and Drink

★ Fat Fish

$$$ | **SEAFOOD** | In what is surely one of the most convivial atmospheres in Limassol, with a wide patio attached to the Limassol Nautical Club and overlooking the Mediterranean Sea, take your pick from an extensive menu of seafood. The set-menu lunch is always great value, but there are also a handful of catches of the day to choose from. **Known for:** excellent service; beautiful location; wide variety of fresh fish. $ *Average main: €23* ✉ *Limassol Nautical Club, Promachon Eleftherias, Agios Athanasios* ☎ *25/828181* 🌐 *www.thefatfish.net.*

Niazi's

$ | **TURKISH** | Less picturesque than the restaurants ringing the harbor, this family-owned place serves better food with excellent grilled fare, including *şeftali kebab* (meatballs), a Turkish Cypriot specialty. The "Full Kebab" has been their star dish since 1949; a selection of mezes accompany lamb chops, doner, kofte, chicken kofte, and shish kebabs. **Known for:** their incredibly tasty full kebab menu; friendly service; great quality steaks. $ *Average main: TL40* ✉ *Kordonboyu Caddesi 22, Girne (Kyrenia)* ☎ *392/815-2160.*

★ Seven St. Georges Tavern

$$ | GREEK | This restaurant has not only the most delicious food in Paphos, but it is also the most charming place to dine. Everyone from locals to tourists in the know come to experience owner George's inventive Cypriot cooking, which includes a preponderance of fresh, seasonal, and often organic ingredients, and lots of options for vegetarians and vegans. **Known for:** attentive service; the delicious house red wine; the eclectic array of small dishes made with the freshest local ingredients. $ *Average main: €17* ✉ *Anthipolochagou Georgiou Savva 37* ☎ *99/655824* 🌐 *www.7stgeorges.com* ⏲ *Closed Mon.*

Cool Places to Stay

★ Almyra

$$$ | HOTEL | FAMILY | This hip, family-friendly resort has been renovated to good effect, with pure and crisp lines within earshot of the waves. **Pros:** lovely outdoor areas; kids' pool, club, babysitting, and kids' menus; excellent location above the beach pathway to the harbor area. **Cons:** some noise from the road; gets very busy with children in high season; parking could be an issue if you have a rental car. $ *Rooms from: €240* ✉ *Poseidonos 12* ☎ *26/888700* 🌐 *www.almyra.com* *187 rooms* *Free Breakfast.*

Amara

$$$$ | HOTEL | Newly built in 2019 and named after the ancient Greek word for everlasting, almost everything here is sparkling, new, and built to last. **Pros:** impeccable dining facilities; beautiful garden areas; discrete, respectful service. **Cons:** no private beach; sun beds get taken early in the day; luxury comes at a price. $ *Rooms from: €300* ✉ *Amathus Ave. 95, Agios Tychonas* ☎ *25/442222* 🌐 *www.amarahotel.com* *207 rooms* *Free Breakfast.*

★ Anassa

$$$$ | HOTEL | *Anassa* is the Greek word for "queen," and this upscale hotel is indeed one of the most luxurious on Cyprus—it is popular with visiting celebrities as well as with those looking to get away from it all. **Pros:** large, luxurious rooms; family-friendly with top-notch kids' club; genuine five star experience. **Cons:** somewhat remote location; lack of dining options nearby; prices fairly high in comparison to other hotels of same caliber. $ *Rooms from: €530* ✉ *Alekou Michalid 40, Neo Chorio, Pólis* ☎ *26/888000* 🌐 *www.anassa.com* ⏲ *Closed Nov.–Mar.* *166 rooms* *Free Breakfast.*

★ Sensatori Resort Aphrodite Hills

$$$ | RESORT | FAMILY | If you are a golfer or tennis player rather than a beach goer, the family-friendly Aphrodite Hills will be your dream come true—it offers an 18-hole championship course and a tennis academy with nine professional courts. **Pros:** plenty of activities on-site; nine dining destinations available; beautiful views of the Mediterranean sea and Aphrodite's Rock. **Cons:** no beach on property; not easy to get to Paphos without a car; main pool can get overcrowded. $ *Rooms from: €270* ✉ *Aphrodite 1* ☎ *26/829000* 🌐 *www.aphroditehills.com* *290 rooms* *Free Breakfast.*

Istanbul

The only city in the world that can lay claim to straddling two continents, Istanbul—once known as Constantinople, capital of the Byzantine and then the Ottoman Empire—has for centuries been a bustling metropolis with one foot in Europe and the other in Asia. It is also the largest city in Europe or the Middle East.

Visitors to this city built over the former capital of two great empires are likely to be just as impressed by the juxtaposition of old and new. Istanbul embraces this enviable position with both a certain chaos and inventiveness, ever-evolving as one of the world's most cosmopolitan crossroads. Office towers creep up behind historic palaces; peddlers' pushcarts vie with shiny BMWs for dominance on the noisy, narrow streets; and the Grand Bazaar gives the chic modern shopping malls a run for their money. As muezzins' call to prayer resounds from ancient mosques, hearty revelers still make their way home from nightclubs.

Most visitors to this sprawling city of over 15 million people will be drawn to the Old City, where the legacy of the Byzantine and Ottoman empires can be seen in monumental works of architecture, like the world-famous Aya Sofya, the magnificent Topkapı Palace, and the magnificent mosques built by classical-era architect Mimar Sinan. The winding streets are lined with restaurants, shops, and hotels, all vying for your attention.

Though it'd be easy to spend weeks exploring the historic center, situated on the city's Çatalca peninsula, visitors should venture beyond to experience the vibrancy of contemporary Istanbul. With a lively nightlife propelled by its young population and an exciting arts scene that's increasingly on the international radar, Istanbul is truly a city that never sleeps. Istanbul may be on the Bosphorus, but at heart it's a Mediterranean city, whose friendly inhabitants are effusively social and eager to share what they love most about their city.

Aya Sofya

Icon of an Ancient World

This soaring edifice is perhaps the greatest work of Byzantine architecture, commissioned in 537 by Emperor Justinian. For almost a thousand years it was the world's largest and most important religious monument—the cathedral of Constantinople and the scene of imperial coronations. The highlight is its immense dome, almost 18 stories high and more than 100 feet across. Look up into it and you'll witness a spectacle—thousands of gold tiles glittering in the light of 40 windows.

When Mehmet II conquered the city in 1453, he famously sprinkled dirt on his head before entering as a sign of humility. His first order was for it to be turned into a mosque, and, in keeping with the Islamic proscription against figural images, mosaics were plastered over. In 1935, president Atatürk began a restoration, uncovering the ancient mosaics. In 2020, Hagia Sophia reverted into an active mosque.

Don't Miss

The marble-and-brass Sacred Column is laden with legends. It's thought that the column weeps water that can work miracles. Over the centuries, believers have worn a hole in it as they attempt to access the water.

Getting Here

Situated in Sultanahmet, the heart of Istanbul's Old City, it's easily accessible by public transport. Take the T1 tram line and get off at Sultanahmet, from where it's about a five-minute walk. Guided tours can be booked on the website.

✉ *Sofya Sq., Sultanahmet* ☎ *212/522–1750* 🌐 *www.muze.gen.tr/muze-detay/ayasofya* 🕑 *Closed to non-Muslims during prayers* 🎫 *Free*

Blue Mosque

An Ottoman Marvel

Only after you enter do you understand why this is called the "blue" mosque. The inside is covered with 20,000 shimmering blue-green İznik tiles interspersed with 260 stained-glass windows, with Islamic calligraphy and intricate floral patterns painted lavishly on the ceiling. Architect Mehmet Ağa (a former student of Sinan) created this masterpiece of Ottoman craftsmanship at the behest of Sultan Ahmet I, starting in 1609 and completing it in eight years.

Ağa actually went a little too far. Having erected six minarets, he accidentally competed with the Holy City of Mecca's revered Masjid al-Haram. Subsequently, Ağa was sent to Mecca to build a seventh minaret for al-Haram, to re-establish its eminence. Sultan Ahmet I is interred in the *türbe* (mausoleum). From outside, you can admire a succession of domes that cover the huge interior space.

Don't Miss

The marble-crafted mihrab, a niche whose position (the *qibla*) faces the direction of prayer, which for Muslims is always in the direction of Mecca's Kabaa. To the right is the *minber* (pulpit), where the imam delivers sermons.

✉ *Sultanahmet Sq., Sultanahmet*
🌐 *www.sultanahmetcamii.org*
🎫 *Free* 🕒 *Closed Fri. after 1:30 PM; the mosque typically closes 1 hr before dusk; visitors must enter only in between the 5 daily prayers, when the mosque remains closed to nonworshippers for 90 mins at a time*

Topkapı Palace

The Medieval Seat of the Ottoman Empire

This vast palace was the residence of sultans and their harems and was the seat of Ottoman rule from the 1460s until the mid-19th century. Sultan Mehmet II built the original palace between 1459 and 1465, after his conquest of Constantinople. Over the centuries, it grew to include four courtyards and quarters for some 5,000 full-time residents, and is home to one of the world's largest collections of Ottoman wares.

Start at the impressive Imperial Gate and work your way to the beautiful Aya Irini, believed to stand on the site of the first church of Byzantium (separate admission). Experience the grandeur of the palace as you pass through Bab-üs Selam, taking you to the Treasury which contains famous jewels, including the 86-carat Spoonmaker's Diamond, the emerald-studded Topkapı Dagger, and two uncut emeralds (each weighing about 8 pounds).

Don't Miss

The opulent Imperial Harem (separate admission) was built as a home for sultans' female relatives, wives, concubines, and children. It's unusually situated in the right wing of the palace rather than at the back, which represented a shifting power dynamic between men and women of the palace.

✉ *Gülhane Parkı, Babıhümayun Cad., Sultanahmet (near Sultanahmet Sq.)* ☎ *212/512–0480* 🌐 *www.muze.gen.tr/muze-detay/topkapi* 🎫 *Palace TL200, Harem TL100, Aya Irini TL80* 🕓 *Closed Tues.*

Grand Bazaar

The World's Biggest Shopping Mall

Take a deep breath and plunge into this maze of 65 winding, covered streets crammed with 4,000 tiny shops, cafés, restaurants, mosques, and courtyards. It's said that this early version of a shopping mall, originally built by Mehmet II in 1461, contains the largest concentration of stores under one roof anywhere in the world, and that's easy to believe.

Streets in the bazaar are named after the tradespeople who traditionally had businesses there, with colorful names like "slipper-makers street," "fez-makers street," and "mirror-makers street." Today, although little of this correspondence remains, the bazaar is still organized roughly by type of merchandise: gold and silver jewelry shops line the prestigious main street, most of the leather stores are in their own wing, and carpet shops are clustered primarily in the center.

Don't Miss

The domed *iç bedesten* (inner bazaar) was once a secure fortress in the heart of the market, and is the oldest part of the bazaar where only the most valuable goods were kept. Today it's where you'll find quirky and unique items: you can find anything from antique pocket watches and vintage cigarette tins, to fine jewelry and Armenian and Greek religious items. Look for the double-headed Byzantine eagle over the door and you'll know you've found it.

Getting Here

Take the T1 tram line to Beyazit-Kapalicarsi, situated across the road from the entrance of the Grand Bazaar.

✉ *Yeniçeriler Cad. and Çadırcılar Cad.* ☎ *212/519–1248* 🌐 *www.kapali-carsi.com.tr* ⊗ *Closed Sun.*

A Food Tour of Istanbul

Eat in One of the Great Food Cities

Istanbul is a city made for food-lovers, where restaurants, from humble kebab joints to fancy fish venues, abound. A classic Istanbul meal, usually eaten at a rollicking *meyhane* (literally "drinking place"), starts with cold and hot meze, then a main course of grilled fish—accompanied by the anise-flavored spirit *rakı*, Turkey's national drink.

But you don't want to limit yourself to sit-down restaurants in a city where excellent street food is also on the menu. Try *borëk,*long coils of rolled-up phyllo dough stuffed with meat, potato, spinach, or cheese and baked until golden brown. *Kumpir* is something of a deluxe baked potato, crammed with a medley of ingredients like pickles, cheese, olives, and hot dog bits. Mussels are street food here, too—try *midye,* where shells are stuffed with mussels, rice, herbs, and spices.

For a delicious, cheap snack, try *balık ekmek*—literally "fish in bread"—it may become one of your most memorable seafood meals in Turkey. The recipe: a freshly grilled fillet of fish, served in a half loaf of crusty white bread and topped with onion and/or tomato slices.

Don't Miss

Turkey's legendary coffee: thick and almost chocolaty, it has an espresso-like foam on top and is usually served with a glass of water and a piece of *lokum* (Turkish delight). Turks drink their coffee four ways: *sade* (plain), *az* (a little sweet), *orta* (medium sweet), and *şekerli* (extra sweet).

Eat with an Expert

Culinary Backstreets runs a wide range of themed, friendly, small-group gastronomic walking tours of Istanbul's best neighborhoods for food. Most tours are $125 per person. (and are worth every penny). 🌐 *www.culinarybackstreets.com*

Basilica Cistern

Haunting Underground Halls

The major problem with the site of Byzantium was the lack of fresh water. So, for the city to grow, a great system of aqueducts and cisterns was built, the most famous of which is the Basilica Cistern (Yerebatan Sarnıcı), whose present form dates from the reign of Justinian in the 6th century. A journey through this ancient underground waterway takes you along dimly-lit walkways that weave around 336 marble columns rising 26 feet to support Byzantine arches and domes, from which water drips unceasingly. The cistern was always kept full as a precaution against long sieges, and fish, presumably descendants of those that arrived in Byzantine times, still flit through the dark waters. A hauntingly beautiful oasis of cool, shadowed, cathedral-like stillness (with instrumental music playing quietly in the background), the cistern is a relaxing place to get away from the hubbub of the Old City.

Don't Miss

The two most famous columns feature heads of Medusa, one on its side and one upside down. Dating from the late-Roman period, it's thought they were brought into the cistern either as a physical support, or to afford protection from her Gorgon devilry (being that they aren't the right way up).

✉ *Yerebatan Cad. at Divan Yolu, Sultanahmet* ☎ *212/512–1570* 🌐 *www.yerebatan.com* 🎫 *TL190* ✍ *Arrive early to avoid long queues*

Visit to a Turkish Hammam

A Traditional Turkish Scrub Down

A favorite pastime in Istanbul is to spend time in a hammam (Turkish bath), some of which are in exquisite buildings more than 500 years old. Hammams were how people kept clean before home plumbing—but they also became an important part of Ottoman social life, particularly for women. Men had the coffeehouse and women the hammam as a place to gossip and relax.

Most have separate facilities for men and women. Each has a *camekan*, a domed room for undressing, where you're clothed in a peştemal and slippers or wooden sandals. Then you'll continue through increasingly hotter rooms. First, the *soğukluk*, which also has showers and toilets for cooling down. The centerpiece is the *hararet*, a steamy, softly-lit room with marble washbasins for dousing yourself. In the middle is the *göbektaşı*, a marble, heated platform where people recline—and where you can opt for a traditional massage.

Don't Miss

Housed in a magnificent building dating from 1741, the Cağaloğlu Hamamı has long been considered one of the city's best. Florence Nightingale and Kaiser Wilhelm II once steamed here, and the clientele has remained generally upscale.

Getting Here

For Cağaloğlu Hamamı, take the T1 tram line and get off at Gülhane Istasyonu, from where it's a five-minute walk.

Cağaloğlu Hamamı. ✉ *Prof. Kazım İsmail Gürkan Cad. 24, Cağaloğlu, Sultanahmet* ☎ *212/522–2424* 🌐 *www.cagalogluhamami.com.tr* 🎫 *€50 (750TL) for a self-service visit; with a scrub and a massage it's about €70 (1050TL)*

Bosphorus Cruise

A Relaxing Waterbound Journey

A cruise on the Bosphorus Strait, whose shores are home to some of the prettiest parts of the city, is one of the most pleasant Istanbul experiences—and an easy way to escape the urban chaos. If you have a full day and want to go all the way to the mouth of the Black Sea, opt for a "full Bosphorus cruise." These leave from Eminönü and have multiple stops, arriving in the afternoon for a three-hour break at either Rumeli Kavağı (European side) or Anadolu Kavağı (Asian side), two fishing villages with fortresses at the opening to the Black Sea. They then zigzag back to Eminönü.

Don't Miss

Both sides of the strait are dotted with palaces, fortresses, and waterfront neighborhoods filled with old wooden summer homes, called *yalıs* (waterside mansions), built for the city's wealthier Ottoman-era residents. As you cruise up the Bosphorus, do disembark at some of these enclaves for an atmospheric stroll.

Getting Here

Eminönü is a transportation hub, and as such is well-served by public transport. Take the T1 tram line and get off at Eminönü, from where you can walk to the harbor and Galata Bridge (Galata Köprüsü), where boat trips depart.

Cruise Details

Bosphorus tours with Şehir Hatları depart daily from the first quay on the Bosphorus side of the Galata Bridge (look for the "Boğaz İskelesi" sign). There are two departures from early-June to mid-September, at 10:35 and 1:35, and at only 10:35 in other months. 🌐 *www.sehirhatlari.istanbul* 🎫 *TL5 one-way, TL25 round-trip*

When in Istanbul

★ İstanbul Arkeoloji Müzeleri (*Istanbul Archaeology Museums*)

HISTORY MUSEUM | FAMILY | Step into this vast repository of spectacular finds in a forecourt of Topkapı Palace to get a head-spinning look at the civilizations that have thrived for thousands of years in and around Turkey. The main museum was established in 1891. The most stunning pieces are sarcophagi, including the so-called Alexander Sarcophagus, found in Lebanon, carved with scenes from Alexander the Great's battles. The Çinili Köşk (Tiled Pavilion) is one of the most visually pleasing sights in all of Istanbul. The Eski Şark Eserleri Müzesi (Museum of the Ancient Orient) holds a 13th-century BC tablet on which is recorded the Treaty of Kadesh—perhaps the world's earliest known peace treaty—between the Hittite king Hattusili III and the Egyptian pharaoh Ramses II. ✉ *Alemdar Cad., Osman Hamdi Bey Yokuşu, Sultanahmet* ✥ *Inside Gülhane Park, next to Topkapı Palace* ☎ *212/520–7740* 🌐 *muze.gen.tr/muze-detay/arkeoloji* 🎫 *TL65.*

Princes' Islands

ISLAND | This cluster of nine islands in the Sea of Marmara are everything that Istanbul isn't: quiet, green, and car-less. Restrictions on development and a ban on automobiles—transportation is only on foot or by bicycle—help maintain the charmingly old-fashioned, quiet atmosphere. Indeed, the main draws are the laid-back ambience and natural beauty of the islands. During the Ottoman Empire, the islands were home to exiled notables, including princes—hence the name. By the mid-19th century, well-heeled Istanbul businessmen had staked their claim. The islands became known for their cosmopolitan lifestyle and were popular summer getaways for Istanbul's non-Muslim communities (Jews, Armenians, and Greeks). Atmospheric old ferryboats and more modern catamarans known as sea buses depart regularly from Katabaş and Eminönü. Ferries cost TL11.50 with an İstanbulkart and take around 90 minutes. ✉ *Istanbul* ✥ *12 miles off the coast of Istanbul from Sultanahmet.*

Spice Bazaar (*Mısır Çarşısı*)

MARKET | The enticing Spice Bazaar, also known as the Egyptian Bazaar, is much smaller than the Grand Bazaar but more colorful. When it was built in the 17th century, the bazaar was a vast pharmacy filled with burlap bags overflowing with herbs and spices fresh off the ships from Egypt and the Spice Islands. Today, although an increasing number of souvenir shops have opened up in the bazaar, you can buy spices (including highly sought-after Iranian saffron); dried fruit and nuts; and delicacies including *lokum* (Turkish delight), caviar, and Turkish coffee and tea. ✉ *Yeni Cami Meydanı, The Bazaar Quarter and Environs* ☎ *212/513–6597.*

★ Türk ve İslam Eserleri Müzesi (*Museum of Turkish and Islamic Arts*)

ART MUSEUM | Süleyman the Magnificent commissioned Sinan to build this grandiose stone palace overlooking the Hippodrome in about 1520 for his brother-in-law, the grand vizier Ibrahim Pasha, and it is one of the most important surviving examples of secular Ottoman architecture from its time. It now houses the Museum of Turkish and Islamic Arts, which has an exceptional collection of Islamic art and artifacts dating from the 7th through 20th century, including lavishly illustrated Korans; intricate metalwork; wood and stone carvings; an astrolabe from the 1200s; colorful ceramics; religious relics and artifacts; and one of the world's most highly regarded troves of antique carpets. ✉ *Atmeydanı 46, Sultanahmet* ☎ *212/518–1805* 🌐 *muze.gen.tr/muze-detay/tiem* 🎫 *TL60.*

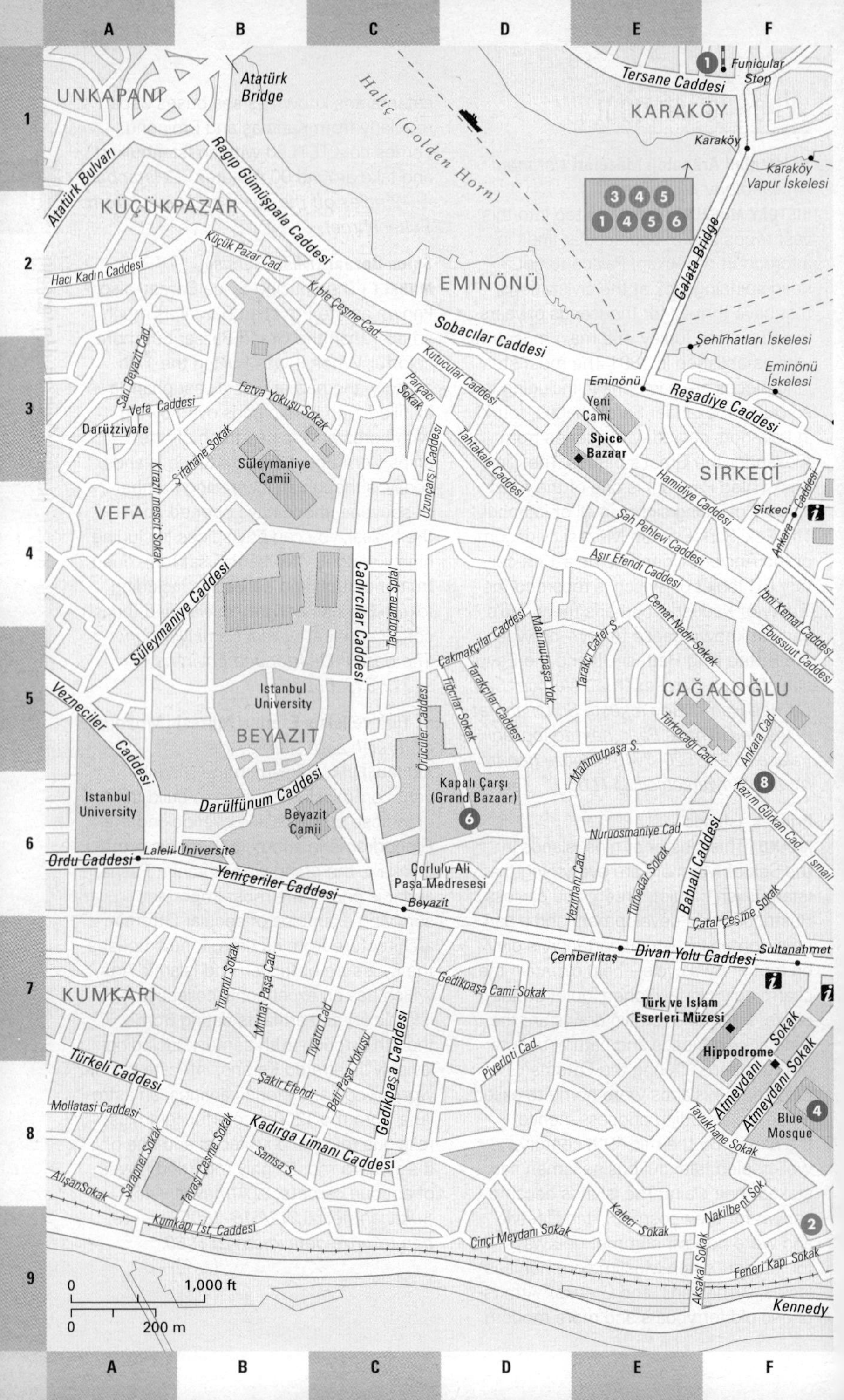

A
B
C
D
E
F
1
2
3
4
5
6
7
8
9
UNKAPANI
Atatürk Bridge
Haliç (Golden Horn)
Tersane Caddesi
Funicular Stop
KARAKÖY
Karaköy
Karaköy Vapur İskelesi
Atatürk Bulvarı
Ragıp Gümüşpala Caddesi
KÜÇÜKPAZAR
Küçük Pazar Cad.
Hacı Kadın Caddesi
Kıble Çeşme Cad.
EMINÖNÜ
Galata Bridge
Sobacılar Caddesi
Şehirhatları İskelesi
Eminönü İskelesi
Eminönü
Reşadiye Caddesi
Kutucular Caddesi
Parçacı Sokak
Sarı Beyazıt Cad.
Vefa Caddesi
Fetva Yokuşu Sokak
Darüzziyafe
Yeni Cami
Spice Bazaar
Şifahane Sokak
Süleymaniye Camii
Uzunçarşı Caddesi
Tahtakale Caddesi
SIRKECI
Hamidiye Caddesi
Sirkeci
Ankara Caddesi
Kirazlı mescit Sokak
VEFA
Şah Pehlevi Caddesi
Aşır Efendi Caddesi
Süleymaniye Caddesi
Cadırcılar Caddesi
Tacirjame Spital
Cemal Nadir Sokak
İbni Kemal Caddesi
Ebussuut Caddesi
Çakmakçılar Caddesi
Marımutpaşa Yok.
Tarakçı Cafer S.
Tarakçılar Caddesi
Tığcılar Sokak
Vezneciler Caddesi
Istanbul University
BEYAZIT
CAĞALOĞLU
Türkocağı Cad.
Örücüler Caddesi
Mahmutpaşa S.
Ankara Cad.
Kapalı Çarşı (Grand Bazaar)
Darülfünum Caddesi
Beyazit Camii
Istanbul University
Kazım Gürkan Cad.
Nuruosmaniye Cad.
Babıali Caddesi
Ordu Caddesi
Laleli-Üniversite
Yeniçeriler Caddesi
Çorlulu Ali Paşa Medresesi
Beyazit
Vezirhanı Cad.
Türbedar Sokak
Çatal Çeşme Sokak
Çemberlitaş
Divan Yolu Caddesi
Sultanahmet
Turanlı Sokak
Mithat Paşa Cad.
Gedikpaşa Cami Sokak
KUMKAPI
Tiyatro Cad
Türk ve Islam Eserleri Müzesi
Piyerloti Cad.
Hippodrome
Atmeydanı Sokak
Atmeydanı Sokak
Balı Paşa Yokuşu
Gedikpaşa Caddesi
Türkeli Caddesi
Şakir Efendi
Mollatasi Caddesi
Kadırga Limanı Caddesi
Tavukhane Sokak
Blue Mosque
Samsa S.
Şarapnel Sokak
Tavaşi Çeşme Sokak
AlişanSokak
Kaleci Sokak
Nakilbent Sok.
Kumkapı İst. Caddesi
Cinçi Meydanı Sokak
Aksakal Sokak
Feneri Kapı Sokak
Kennedy
0
1,000 ft
0
200 m
1
3
4
5
1
4
5
6
6
8
4
2

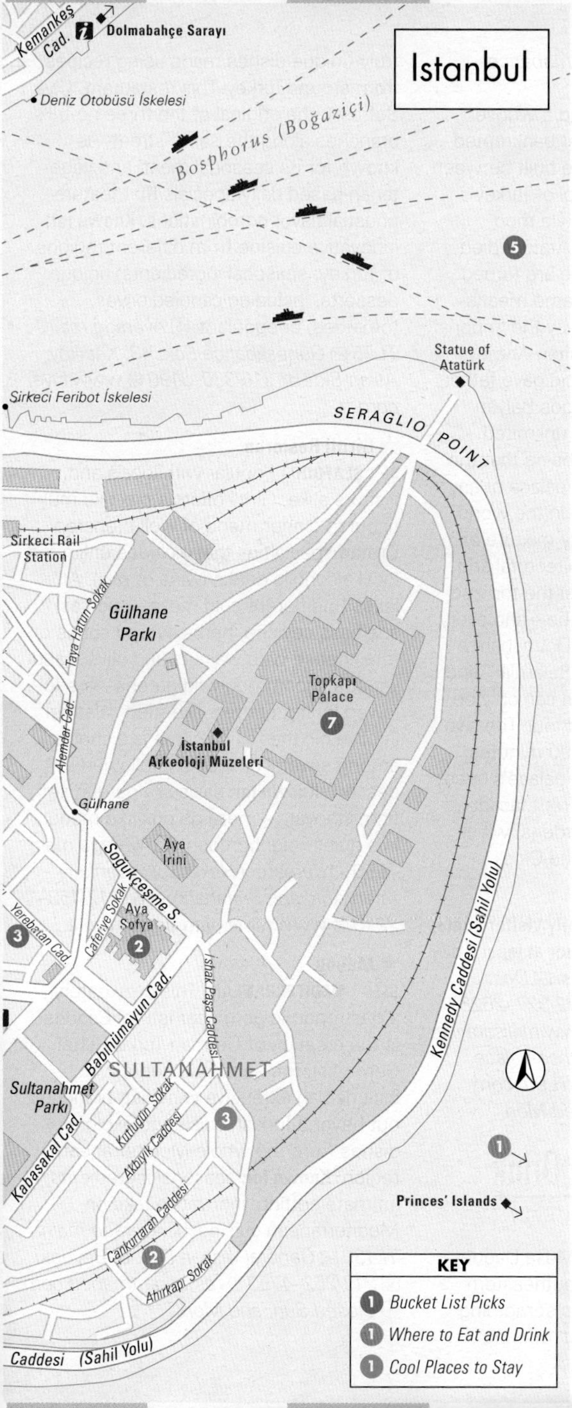

Istanbul

Bucket List Picks

1 A Food Tour of Istanbul F1
2 Aya Sofya.............................. G7
3 Basilica Cistern G7
4 Blue Mosque........................... F8
5 Bosphorus Cruise..................... J2
6 Grand Bazaar D6
7 Topkapı Palace........................ I5
8 Visit to a Turkish Hammam F6

Where to Eat and Drink

1 Çiya...................................... J8
2 Giritli Restoran H9
3 Mabou E2
4 Mikla E2
5 Yeni Lokanta........................... E2

Cool Places to Stay

1 Çırağan Palace Kempinski Istanbul E2
2 Dersaadet Hotel Istanbul F9
3 Esans Hotel............................ H8
4 Pera Palace Hotel E2
5 Sumahan on the Water E2
6 Tomtom Suites E2

Kemankeş Cad.
Dolmabahçe Sarayı
Deniz Otobüsü İskelesi
Bosphorus (Boğaziçi)
Statue of Atatürk
Sirkeci Feribot İskelesi
SERAGLIO POINT
Sirkeci Rail Station
Taya Hatun Sokak
Gülhane Parkı
Topkapı Palace
İstanbul Arkeoloji Müzeleri
Alemdar Cad.
Gülhane
Aya Irini
Soğukçeşme S.
Kennedy Caddesi (Sahil Yolu)
Yerebatan Cad.
Caferiye Sokak
Aya Sofya
İshak Paşa Caddesi
Babıhümayun Cad.
SULTANAHMET
Sultanahmet Parkı
Kutlugün Sokak
Akbıyık Caddesi
Kabasakal Cad.
Princes' Islands
Cankurtaran Caddesi
Ahırkapı Sokak
Caddesi (Sahil Yolu)

KEY

Bucket List Picks
Where to Eat and Drink
Cool Places to Stay

★ Dolmabahçe Sarayı (*Dolmabahçe Palace*)

CASTLE/PALACE | Abdülmecid I, whose free-spending lifestyle later bankrupted the empire, had this palace built between 1843 and 1856 as a symbol of Turkey's march toward European-style modernization. It's also where Atatürk died (and all clocks in the palace are turned to his time of death). Its name means "filled-in garden," inspired by the imperial garden planted here by Sultan Ahmet I (ruled 1603–17). Abdülmecid gave father and son Garabet and Nikoğos Balyan complete freedom and an unlimited budget, the only demand being that the palace "surpass any other palace of any other potentate anywhere in the world." The result, an extraordinary mixture of Turkish and European architectural and decorative styles, is as over-the-top and showy as a palace should be—and every bit as garish as Versailles. Dolmabahçe is divided into the public "Selamlık" and the private "Harem," which can only be seen on a separate guided tour. The two tours together take about 90 minutes. Afterward, stroll along the palace's nearly ½-km (¼-mile)-long waterfront facade and through the formal gardens, which have the Crystal Pavilion and Clock Museum.

TIP→ The palace has a daily visitor quota, so call the reservation number at least a day in advance to reserve tickets. ✉ *Dolmabahçe Cad., Besiktas* ☎ *212/327–2626 for reservations only* 🌐 *www.millisaraylar.gov.tr/en/palaces/dolmabahce-palace* 🎫 *Selamlık TL120, Harem TL90, combined ticket TL150* ⏲ *Closed Mon.*

Where to Eat and Drink

★ Çiya

$$ | TURKISH | Chef-owner Musa Dağdeviren, who hails from the southeastern Turkish city of Gaziantep, is something of a culinary anthropologist, offering truly unique dishes made using recipes from around Turkey. This restaurant, Çiya Sofrası—the original of the three no-frills branches along the same street—is known for its seasonal meat- and vegetarian-based daily specials that feature unusual flavor combinations. **Known for:** innovative cuisine from different regions of Turkey; seasonal ingredients; unique desserts, including candied olives, tomatoes, or eggplant. $ *Average main: TL75* ✉ *Güneşlibahçe Sok. 43, Kadıköy, Asian Side* ☎ *216/330–3190* 🌐 *www.ciya.com.tr.*

★ Giritli Restoran

$$ | SEAFOOD | Popular with locals and visitors alike, Giritli offers a prix-fixe multicourse dinner menu of well-prepared Cretan specialties that includes unlimited local alcoholic drinks (wine or rakı). At least 15 different cold meze—such as sea bass ceviche, herb-covered cubes of feta cheese with walnuts and olives, and various uncommon wild greens—are followed by hot starters like fried calamari in olive oil; the main course is a choice among several grilled fish, followed by dessert. **Known for:** oasis-like garden setting; innovative meze on prix-fixe menu; in a quiet neighborhood. $ *Average main: TL50* ✉ *Keresteci Hakkı Sok., Cankurtaran/Ahırkapı, Sultanahmet* ☎ *212/458–2270* 🌐 *www.giritlirestoran.com.*

★ Mabou

$$$$ | MEDITERRANEAN | This cozy eatery, a gastronomic gem near İstiklal Caddesi, is the creation of German-Turkish chef Cem Eksi. The seasonal menu, which includes an extensive wine list, branches out beyond Turkish cuisine to explore dishes from the whole Mediterranean region. **Known for:** seasonal ingredients; intimate setting; innovative take on Mediterranean cuisine. $ *Average main: TL130* ✉ *General Yazgan Sok. 8, Beyoglu* ☎ *212/252–4753* 🌐 *restaurantmabou.com* ⏲ *Closed Sun. and Mon.*

★ Mikla

$$$$ | **CONTEMPORARY** | With sleek, contemporary decor and a stunning 360-degree view of Istanbul from the top floor of the 18-story Marmara Pera Hotel, Mikla is the dramatic setting for prestigious American-trained Turkish-Finnish chef Mehmet Gürs's modern Anatolian cuisine. Sophisticated dishes of domestically sourced ingredients offer unique flavor combinations rarely seen in traditional Turkish cuisine, such as grilled dentex (a Mediterranean fish) served with olives, charred red peppers, and pistachio puree or a dessert of sour-cherry compote with bulgur wheat and *lor* cheese (similar to ricotta). **Known for:** prix-fixe menu and tasting menus only; extensive list of Turkish and international wines; sweeping views. *Average main: TL580 Marmara Pera Hotel, Meşrutiyet Cad. 15, Beyoglu 212/293–5656 www.miklarestaurant.com Closed Sun.*

★ Yeni Lokanta

$$$$ | **TURKISH** | Rising chef Civan Er puts a unique and contemporary twist on traditional Turkish dishes, using ingredients sourced from local producers in different regions of the country. The menu consists mainly of small plates that offer innovative flavor combinations, as in sweet-and-sour *kısır* (tabbouleh) made with a sour-cherry infusion or spicy, rustic *sucuk* sausage with walnuts served atop borlotti bean puree. **Known for:** contemporary vibe; dishes prepared in a wood-fired oven; tasting menu. *Average main: TL180 Kumbaracı Yokuşu 66, Beyoglu 212/292–2550 www.yenilokanta.com Closed Sun.*

Cool Places to Stay

★ Çırağan Palace Kempinski Istanbul

$$$$ | **HOTEL** | Once a residence for the Ottoman sultans, the late-19th-century Çırağan Palace (pronounced chi-rahn) is Istanbul's most luxurious hotel, with ornate public spaces that feel absolutely decadent and a breathtaking setting right on the Bosphorus—the outdoor infinity pool seems to hover on the water's edge and most rooms, full of Ottoman-inspired wood furnishings and textiles in warm colors, have balconies overlooking the Bosphorus as well. **Pros:** grand setting in incredible Bosphorus-front location; over-the-top feeling of luxury; infinity pool. **Cons:** exorbitant price of food and drinks; high rates, especially for rooms that have no Bosphorus view; service can be slow. *Rooms from: €565 Çırağan Cad. 32, Bosphorus 212/326–4646 www.kempinski.com/istanbul 313 rooms No Meals.*

★ Dersaadet Hotel Istanbul

$$ | **B&B/INN** | Dersaadet means "place of happiness" in Ottoman Turkish, and this small, cozy hotel lives up to its name—rooms have an elegant, even plush, feel, with colorful rugs, antique furniture, and ceilings hand-painted with traditional motifs. **Pros:** extraordinary level of service; lovely terrace; good value. **Cons:** some rooms are on the small side; no view from rooms on lower floors; walls are thin. *Rooms from: €60 Küçükayasofya Cad. Kapıağası Sok. 5, Sultanahmet 212/458–0760 hoteldersaadet.com 17 rooms Free Breakfast.*

★ Esans Hotel

$ | **B&B/INN** | The emphasis at this delightful, family-run, bed-and-breakfast is on guest satisfaction, and the 10 rooms in the restored wooden house are decorated with thoughtful attention to detail, like lovely Ottoman-Victorian-style wallpaper, upholstery, and linens; wooden floors and ceilings; and old-fashioned furniture. **Pros:** good value; on a quiet street; staff go out of their way to assist. **Cons:** no elevator; lack of soundproofing can be an issue; some rooms are small. *Rooms from: €45 Yeni Saraçhane Sok. 4, Sultanahmet 212/516–1902 www.esanshotel.com 10 rooms Free Breakfast.*

★ Pera Palace Hotel

$$$$ | HOTEL | Extensive restoration has brought this Istanbul landmark—founded in 1892 to provide upscale accommodations for travelers arriving on the Orient Express—back to its former glory, with beautifully outfitted rooms and plenty of period decorations and antique furniture. **Pros:** historic venue; luxurious facilities; attentive staff. **Cons:** some rooms have small bathrooms; rooms on back side look onto street with lots of traffic; expensive food and drinks. *Rooms from: €200 Meşrutiyet Cad. 52, Tepebaşı, Beyoglu 212/377–4000 www.perapalace.com 115 rooms No Meals.*

★ Sumahan on the Water

$$$$ | HOTEL | What was once a derelict distillery on the Asian waterfront of the Bosphorus is now one of Istanbul's chicest and most original places to stay, with comfortable rooms and suites—all with incredible water views and all decorated in a contemporary style with a few Turkish touches. **Pros:** stunning waterfront location; stylish and inviting public areas; secluded, romantic atmosphere. **Cons:** far from sights and commercial center; somewhat inconvenient to get to without the free (for guests) private launch; not all rooms are wheelchair-accessible. *Rooms from: €300 Kuleli Cad. 43, Çengelköy, Asian Side 216/422–8000 www.sumahan.com 13 rooms Free Breakfast.*

★ Tomtom Suites

$$$ | HOTEL | A restored 1901 residence that once housed Franciscan nuns offers superb accommodations and authentic character, with guest rooms furnished with warm woods, textiles in natural colors, high ceilings, and original artwork. **Pros:** historic building with romantic ambience; on a quiet street; helpful, welcoming staff. **Cons:** only upper room categories have sea views; reached via steep streets; rather high rates, especially considering lack of fitness facilities. *Rooms from: €130 Boğazkesen Cad., Tomtom Kaptan Sok. 18, Beyoglu 212/292–4949 www.tomtomsuites.com 20 suites Free Breakfast.*

Index

A

B

N

O

Photo Credits

Front Cover: Robert Harding / Alamy Stock Photo [Description: Stonehenge, UNESCO World Heritage Site, Salisbury Plain, Wiltshire, England, United Kingdom, Europe]. **Back cover, from left to right:** Anton_Ivanov/Shutterstock. Alessandro Colle/Shutterstock. Canadastock/ Shutterstock. **Spine:** Josefskacel/Dreamstime. **Interior, from left to right:** JackCoghlan/ Shutterstock (1). Pajor Pawel/Shutterstock (2-3). **Chapter 1: Experience Bucket List Europe:** F11photo/Dreamstime (6-7). Jim Prod/Otmsmn (10). Danbreckwoldt/Dreamstime (10). Mistervlad/Shutterstock (10). Kapitaen/iStockphoto (10). f11photo/Shutterstock (10). Dagmar Veselková/czechtourism (11). Lazar Mihai-Bogdan/ Shutterstock (11). Garrett1984/Dreamstime (11). Phant/Shutterstock (11). Jaro68/Shutterstock (11). Colin Keldie/ VisitScotland (12). Dan Courtice/Semitour Périgord (12). Lebasi0601/ Shutterstock (12). Getty Images/iStockphoto (12). Milosk50/Dreamstime (13). Savcoco/iStockphoto (14). SerrNovik/iStockphoto (15). SCStock/Shutterstock (16). Oksana Saman/Dreamstime (16). Botond Horvath/Shutterstock (16). RomanSlavik.com/Shutterstock (17). S.Borisov / Shutterstock (17). Pathara Buranadilok/Shutterstock (18). Stjepann/ Shutterstock (18). Josefskacel/Dreamstime (18). Rodrigolab/ Dreamstime (18). Sara Winter/Shutterstock (19). George KUZ/Shutterstock (19). Nataliya Hora / Shutterstock (19). Blue Planet Studio/Shutterstock (19). Muharremz/ Shutterstock (20). Jjkroese/Dreamstime (20). TomasSereda (20). J. Lekavicius/Shutterstock (21). Danbreckwoldt/Dreamstime (21). Guinness Storehouse (22). Barmalini/Dreamstime (23). Canadastock/Shutterstock (24). Graham King/Shutterstock (24). Dudlajzov/Dreamstime (24). Hike The World/Shutterstock (24). Givaga/Shutterstock (25). Cktravels.com/Shutterstock (26). The Lift Creative Services/ Shutterstock (26). Nina Alizada/Shutterstock (26). Anton_Ivanov/ Shutterstock (27). Dovapi/Dreamstime (27). Sergii Beck/Shutterstock (28). Trabantos/ Shutterstock (28). Daanholthausen/Dreamstime (28). Alessandro Colle/Shutterstock (29). Vladyslav Morozov/ Shutterstock (29). FooTToo/Shutterstock (30). Zoltangabor/ Dreamstime (30). Migel/Shutterstock (30). Marktucan/ Dreamstime (30). Tomas Marek/Shutterstock (31). Rcaucino/Dreamstime (32). Andrea Quartarone/Shutterstock (32). liner-pics/Shutterstock (32). Anton_Ivanov/Shutterstock (33). Magnus Kallstrom/Shutterstock (33). Belezonlar/Dreamstime (34). Dani Vincek/Shutterstock (35). **Chapter 2: England, Scotland, and Wales:** George KUZ/Shutterstock (39). Artfully Photographer/Shutterstock (42). Artyooran/Dreamstime (43). Brent Hofacker/Shutterstock (43). Adinabulina/ Dreamstime (47). Pajor Pawel/Shutterstock (48). Billybrown1410/Dreamstime (49). Alexey Fedorenko/Shutterstock (50). Claudio Divizia/Shutterstock (51). TTstudio/Shutterstock (52). David Steele/Shutterstock (53). Wadstock/Shutterstock (54). Danielbridge/Dreamstime (55). Mistervlad/Shutterstock (64). Deniskelly/Dreamstime (65). Blunker/Dreamstime (66). Phillt/Dreamstime (67). Alexey Fedorenko/Shutterstock (68). Xxlphoto/Dreamstime (69). The-Walker/Shutterstock (70). Gowithstock/Shutterstock (71). Chris_920/Shutterstock (72). Photofires/Dreamstime (73). Kmiragaya/Dreamstime (74). Vichie81/Dreamstime (81). Jaroslav Moravcik/Shutterstock (82). Jenifoto406/Dreamstime (83). Serge Bertasius Photography/Shutterstock (84). Fintastique/ Dreamstime (85). Jeffbanke/Dreamstime (93). Bobbrooky/Dreamstime (94). TTstudio/ Shutterstock (95). Jarcosa/Dreamstime (96). Scotland's scenery/Shutterstock (97). Tbures/Dreamstime (98). Jim6634/ Dreamstime (99). Valeria73/Dreamstime (100). PGregoryB/Dreamstime (101). AlizadaStudios/Dreamstime (102). Juleberlin/Dreamstime (103). Photoweges/Dreamstime (111). Tonybaggett/Dreamstime (112). Cktravels.com/ Shutterstock (113). Kanphiphat/Shutterstock (114). Crown Copyright (115). **Chapter 3: Ireland and Northern Ireland:** Sharkshock/Shutterstock (123). Natalia Ruedisueli/shutterstock (126). Courtesy of Celtic Whiskey Shop (127). Ireland Tourism (127). Nikolay100/Shutterstock (131). Salvador Maniquiz/Shutterstock (132). Donal Murphy (133). Ceri Breeze/ Shutterstock (134). Mikemike10/Shutterstock (135). Patryk Kosmider/Shutterstock (143). Patryk Kosmider/ Shutterstock (144). Gabriel12/Shutterstock (145). MNStudio/Shutterstock (146). Priscilla Goh/Shutterstock (147). Michael Cash Photography/Shutterstock (148). D. Ribeiro/Shutterstock (149). Yykkaa/iStock (150). Mark gusev/Shutterstock (151). Chrisdorney/Shutterstock (152). iLongLoveKing/Shutterstock (159). John Sones/Shutterstock (160). VanderWolfImages/ Dreamstime (161). Romrodinka/Dreamstime (162). Scukrov/Dreamstime (163). **Chapter 4: France and The Low Countries:** Milosk50/Shutterstock (171). Norikko/Shutterstock (174). Jonny Allen/Shutterstock (175). Wmaster890/ istockphoto (175). NaughtyNut/Shutterstock (180). Beboy/Shutterstock (181). Catarina Belova/Shutterstock (182). Givaga/ Shutterstock (183). Petr Kovalenkov/Shutterstock (184). Siaath/Shutterstock (185). Jaspe/Dreamstime (186). PhotoFires/ Shutterstock (187). Telly/Shutterstock (195). Richair/Dreamstime (196). Boris Stroujko/Shutterstock (197). Es70photo/ Dreamstime (198). Saintho/Dreamstime (199). ScStock/Shutterstock (200). Olrat/Shutterstock (201). Jorisvo/Shutterstock (202). Stephane Bidouze/Shutterstock (203). Pajor Pawel/Shutterstock (204). Vichie81/Shutterstock (213). BearFotos/ Shutterstock (214). Trabantos/Shutterstock (215). HBPhotographyFrance/ Shutterstock (216). Proslgn/Shutterstock (217). Alexey Fedorenko/ Shutterstock (218). Serhii Koval/Shutterstock (219). Dene' Miles/Shutterstock (220). Thipjang/ Shutterstock (229). Saiko3p/Shutterstock (230). Alexey Fedorenko/Shutterstock (231). Kollawat Somsri/ Shutterstock (232). Arnieby/Shutterstock (233). Vampy1/Dreamstime (234). Roberto Caucino/Shutterstock (235). Takashi Images/ Shutterstock (242). SigridSpinnnox.com (243). Milosk50/Shutterstock (244). Catalin Lazar/Shutterstock (245). Lolo ap

Photo Credits

wynn/ Shutterstock (246). Kobby Dagan/Shutterstock (247). Boris Stroujko/Shutterstock (255). Jesus Barroso/ hutterstock (256). Bossiema/Dreamstime (257). Ciwoa/Shutterstock (258). Amalasi/Shutterstock (259). Sandra Mori/ hutterstock (266). Siraanamwong/Dreamstime (267). Suratwadee Rattanajarupak/ Shutterstock (268). Neirfy/ hutterstock (269). Nataliya Nazarova/Shutterstock (270). Fortgens Photography/Shutterstock (271). Andre Bonn/ hutterstock (272). Olena Znak/Shutterstock (273). Nick N A/Shutterstock (274). Dennis van de Water/Shutterstock (275). **hapter 5: Spain and Portugal:** Taiga/Shutterstock (281). Patty Orly/Shutterstock (284). Miguel Tamayo Fotografia/ hutterstock (285). 54613/Shutterstock (285). Catarina Belova/Shutterstock (289). Noppasin Wongchum/iStockphoto 290). Christian Bertrand/Shutterstock (291). Jjfarquitectos/iStockphoto (292). Catarina Belova/Shutterstock (293). Dmitro2009/Shutterstock (294). Maks Ershov/Shutterstock (295). Helena Garcia Huertas/iStockphoto (296). Mistervlad/ Shutterstock (297). Valerie2000/Shutterstock (305). Xavier Dealbert/iStockphoto (306). Malajscy/Dreamstime (307). Trabantos/Shutterstock (308). Luciano Mortula-LGM/ Shutterstock (309). Vladislav Zolotov/iStockphoto (310). Sergii Figurnyi/Shutterstock (311). The Escape of Malee/Shutterstock (312). Nikolais/Dreamstime (320). Sopotnicki/ Shutterstock (321). Sorincolac/iStockphoto (322). Lucamarimedia/Shutterstock (323). KikoStock/Shutterstock (324). Pkazmierczak/iStockphoto (325). Agsaz/Shutterstock (326). Joserpizarro/Shutterstock (327). Agsaz/Shutterstock (328). Sean Pavone Photo/ iStockphoto (336). Fernando Avendano/Shutterstock (337). Karen Goncalves/iStockphoto (338). Jackf/Dreamstime (339). Leonori/Shutterstock (340). Digoarpi/Shutterstock (341). Rosmi Duaso/Alamy (342). Joserpizarro/Shutterstock (343). SCStock/Shutterstock (344). Mmeee/iStockphoto (345). Hans Harms/iStockphoto (354). Sara Winter/Shutterstock (355). Travelview/Shutterstock (356). Serenity-H/Shutterstock (357). Alberto Loyo/Shutterstock (358). ESB Professional/Shutterstock (365). Amnat30/Shutterstock (366). FCG/Shutterstock (367). Ico_k-pax/iStockphoto (368). Bruno Aleixo Photo/Shutterstock (369). Sergey Peterman/ Shutterstock (370). Joyfull/Shutterstock (371). Agsaz/ Shutterstock (372). Alicina/Shutterstock (378). DaLiu/Liubomir Paut/iStockphoto (379). Karol Kozlowski/Shutterstock (380). Iva Vagnerova/iStockphoto (381). Elakazal/Shutterstock (382). **Chapter 6: Scandinavia and the Baltic Region:** Gim42/iStockphoto (389). From my point of view/Shutterstock (392). Natalya Grisik/Dreamstime (393). Langoustine harbor/lobster harbor (393). Nick N A/Shutterstock (397). Aleh VaranishchaiStockphoto (398). Studio GM/ Shutterstock (399). LeManna/Shutterstock (400). Lukas Bischoff Photograph/Shutterstock (401). F-Focus by Mati Kose/ Shutterstock (402). Trabantos/Shutterstock (410). Stig Alenäs 2021 (411). Frank Bach/Shutterstock (412). Sukhoverkhova Viktoriia/Shutterstock (413). Stig Alenas/Shutterstock (414). Britta Paasch/Shutterstock (415). Uwe Aranas/Shutterstock (416). Smelov/Shutterstock (417). Pilguj/Shutterstock (418). Elena Lysenkova/Shutterstock (428). Tam and Trace Photography/Shutterstock (429). Tommi Selander/Shutterstock (430). Aleksei Verhovski/ Shutterstock (431). ArtBBNV/ Shutterstock (432). I love takeing photos and i think that is a really great opportunity for me to share them/iStockphoto (440). Miroslav_1/iStockphoto (441). Dudlajzov/Dreamstime (442). DanielFreyr/Shutterstock (443). Bzzup/Shutterstock (444). Alex Cimbal/Shutterstock (445). Menno Schaefer/Shutterstock (446). GrayKat (447). JackCoghlan/Shutterstock (448). Jan Jerman/Shutterstock (449). Anyaberkut/iStockphoto (458). Marco Allasio/Shutterstock (459). Ilinaolga/ Shutterstock (460). Yelo Jura/Shutterstock (461). MuYeeTing/iStockphoto (462). Scanrall/iStockphoto (463). Tomagn/ Dreamstime (464). Himanshu Saraf/Shutterstock (465). Kalin Eftimov/Shutterstock (474). Alizada Studios/ Shutterstock (475). Marco Calandra/Shutterstock (476). By-Studio/iStockphoto (477). Trabantos/Shutterstock (478). Rolf_52/ iStockphoto (479). Magnus Binnerstam/Shutterstock (480). V. Belov/Shutterstock (481). **Chapter 7: Central Europe:** SCStock/iStockphoto (487). Fusionstudio/Shutterstock (490). Festland/Dennis Savini/zeitlich und räumlich unbeschränkt (491). Dar1930/Shutterstock (491). Ecstk22/Shutterstock (495). Bhofack2/iStockphoto (496). Cyndi58/Shutterstock (497). James Davis Photography/Alamy Stock Photo (498). PytyCzech/iStockphoto (499). Elenaphotos/Dreamstime (500). Sina Ettmer Photography/ Shutterstock (501). Mistervlad/Shutterstock (502). Egeris/iStockphoto (503). BBA Photography/ Shutterstock (504). Noppasin Wongchum/iStockphoto (511). TTstudio/Shutterstock (512). Maciek Grabowicz/Shutterstock (513). Es70photo/Dreamstime (514). Tupungato/ Shutterstock (515). Pavel L Photo and Video/Shutterstock (523). Trabantos/Shutterstock (524). Sergey Borisov/iStockphoto (525). FotografieLink/iStockphoto (526). Barmalini/Shutterstock (527). SCStock/iStockphoto (528). Saiko3p/Shutterstock (529). Stefano Zaccaria/Shutterstock (530). FooTToo/Shutterstock (531). RudyBalasko/iStockphoto (532). Bluejayphoto/iStockphoto (533). Sergii Figurnyi/Shutterstock (534). Janoka82/ iStockphoto (541). Boris Stroujko/Shutterstock (542). Xantana/iStockphoto (543). Margouillatphotos/iStockphoto (544). Richard Cavalleri/Shutterstock (545). Xantana/Boris Stroujko/iStockphoto (546). Yangjlin/Shutterstock (547). Guitar photographer/Shutterstock (548). Matthew Dixon/iStockphoto (556). EyesTravelling/Shutterstock (557). RossHelen/ Shutterstock (558). DaLiu/Shutterstock (559). Radoslaw Maciejewski/Shutterstock (560). Ronstik/iStockphoto (561). JackF/iStockphoto (562). John_Silver/Shutterstock (563). Kaiser-v/Shutterstock (570). Posztos/Shutterstock (571). ZGPhotography/Shutterstock (572). Zedspider/Shutterstock (573). Ekaterina_Polischuk/ iStockphoto (574). Fotohalo/

Photo Credits

iStockphoto (575). TTstudio/Shutterstock (583). Sopotnicki/ Shutterstock (584). MNStudio/Shutterstock (585). Alefbet/ Shutterstock (586). Curioso.Photography/ Shutterstock (587). Patryk Kosmider/Shutterstock (588). Agsaz/ Shutterstock (589). Bondart Photography/Shutterstock (590). Milan Gonda/Shutterstock (596). Rasto SK/Shutterstock (597). Hike The World/Shutterstock (598). Jan Nedbal/ Shutterstock (599). Slawjanek_fotografia/Shutterstock (600). **Chapter 8: Italy and Malta:** Yasonya/ Shutterstock (607). Barbajones/Shutterstock (610). Bon Appetit / Alamy (611). Lisay/iStockphoto (611). Viacheslav Lopatin/Shutterstock (615). Vlas Telino studio/Shutterstock (616). Staraldo/Dreamstime (617). Byggarn.se/Shutterstock (618). Heracles Kritikos/Shutterstock (619). Nito100/Dreamstime (620). F11photo/Dreamstime (621). Anibal Trejo/Shutterstock (622). Vivida Photo PC/Shutterstock (623). Sevar82/Dreamstime (630). Libux77/Dreamstime (631). Boris Stroujko/Shutterstock (632). Blunker/Dreamstime (633). Vitalyedush/Dreamstime (634). Alexirina27000/ Dreamstime (635). Antanovich1985/Dreamstime (636). Cicloco/Dreamstime (637). James.Pintar/Shutterstock (645). Freesurf69/Dreamstime (646). Bogdan/Dreamstime (647). Katuka218/Dreamstime (648). Marcorubino/Dreamstime (649). Minnystock/Dreamstime (650). Paolo Paradiso/Shutterstock (651). Canadastock/ Shutterstock (652). IgorZh/Shutterstock (660). Jenifoto406/Dreamstime (661). Tigertim01/Dreamstime (662). Vividaphoto/Dreamstime (663). Fabioalfano/ Dreamstime (664). Sergii Figurnyi/Shutterstock (665). Boris Stroujko/ Shutterstock (666). Flaviu Boerescu/Dreamstime (667) CrackerClips Stock Media/Shutterstock (675). Swisshippo/Dreamstime (676). Dreamer4787/Shutterstock (677). Stimmungsbilder1/ Dreamstime (678). Emicristea/Dreamstime (679). Sergii Figurnyi/Shutterstock (680). Yasonya/ Dreamstime (681). Corrado Baratta/Shutterstock (682). Ali caliskan/Shutterstock (690). Kasto80/Dreamstime (691). Elesi/ Shutterstock (692). Slowmotiongli/Dreamstime (693). Leonid Andronov/Shutterstock (694). Lachris77/Dreamstime (695). Ppohudka/Dreamstime (696). IgorZh/Shutterstock (697). Siriocarnevalino/Dreamstime (705). Msalena/Dreamstime (706). Evgeniy Fesenko/Dreamstime (707). Photobyravis/Dreamstime (708). SimonDannhauer/ Dreamstime (709). Anton_Ivanov/Shutterstock (710). Canadastock/Shutterstock (711). Ermess/Dreamstime (712). Mitzo/Shutterstock (713). Alkan2011/ Dreamstime (714). PhotopankPL/Shutterstock (721). Viewingmalta.com (722). Efesenko/Dreamstime (723). Efesenko/ Dreamstime (724). Cecilialim/Dreamstime (725). **Chapter 9: The Balkans:** ZGPhotography/Shutterstock (731). Balevskiphoto/Dreamstime (734). Mankica/Shutterstock (735). Fomaa/Dreamstime (735). Roxana Bashyrova/Shutterstock (740). Gaspar Janos/Shutterstock (741). Evgeny Subbotsky/Shutterstock (742). Geza Kurka_Hungary/ Shutterstock (743). Vladiczech/Dreamstime (744). Pajor Pawel/Shutterstock (750). SchnepfDesign/Shutterstock (751). Alexey Fedorenko/ Shutterstock (752). Ivan Nemet/ Shutterstock (753). OPIS Zagreb/Shutterstock (754). Iurii Dzivinskyi/Shutterstock (755). Purple Images/iStockphoto (756). Mislaw/Shutterstock (757). Dennis van de Water/Shutterstock (764). Dudlajzov/ Dreamstime (765). Sergii Figurnyi/Shutterstock (766). Eivanov/Shutterstock (767). Trabantos/Shutterstock (768). Vaivodavlad/Dreamstime (775). Ecstk22/Shutterstock (776). Cristian M Balate/Shutterstock (777). Calin Stan/ Shutterstock (778). FrimuFilms/ Shutterstock (779). Tupungato/Shutterstock (786). Mykhailo Brodskyi/Shutterstock (787). Leonid Andronov/ Shutterstock (788). Nikolais/Dreamstime (789). Dmitrii Sakharov/Shutterstock (790). Milosk50/ Dreamstime (791). Milosk50/Dreamstime (792). MehmetO/Shutterstock (793). **Chapter 10: Greece, Cyprus, and Istanbul:** SCStock/Shutterstock (801). Pedjamilosavljevic/ Dreamstime (804). Esin Deniz/Shutterstock (805). Nina Firsova/Shutterstock (805). Rich Lynch/Shutterstock (809). Danflcreativo/Dreamstime (810). Scaliger/Dreamstime (811). Saiko3p/Shutterstock (812). Sangapark118/Dreamstime (813). Karnizz/Dreamstime (814). Milangonda/Dreamstime (815). Gtsichlis/Dreamstime (816). Alvaro German Vilela/Shutterstock (817). Aerial-motion/ Shutterstock (825). Npershaj/ Dreamstime (826). Mapics/Dreamstime (827). Kordoz/Dreamstime (828). KonstantinosLagos/Dreamstime (829). Pit Stock/ Shutterstock (830). Achilles/Dreamstime (831). Kostasgr/Shutterstock (832). Pit Stock/Shutterstock (833). Aerial-motion/ Shutterstock (840). Nick N A/Shutterstock (841). PanosKarapanagiotis/ iStockphoto (842). Giovanni Rinaldi/Shutterstock (843). Aerial-motion/Shutterstock (844). Fokke Baarssen/Shutterstock (845). Lukaszimilena/ Shutterstock (846). Pit Stock/ Shutterstock (847). Lals Stock/Shutterstock (853). Leoks/Shutterstock (854). Esin Deniz/Shutterstock (855). Tloventures/ Dreamstime (856). Andrew Mayovskyy/Shutterstock (857). SCStock/Shutterstock (858). Vladimir_Timofeev/ iStockphoto (859). Dmitry Naumov/Shutterstock (860). Dziewul/Shutterstock (861). Freeartist/iStockphoto (862). Dynamoland/ Dreamstime (870). Georgios Tsichlis/Shutterstock (871). Heracles Kritikos/Shutterstock (872). Kirillm/Dreamstime (873). Kirillm/Dreamstime (874). Artur Bogacki/Shutterstock (881). F11photo/Shutterstock (882). RuslanKphoto/Shutterstock (883). Epic_images/Shutterstock (884). Prometheus72/Shutterstock (885). RuslanKphoto/Shutterstock (886). FSYLN/ iStockphoto (887). Badahos/Shutterstock (888).

*Every effort has been made to trace the copyright holders, and we apologize in advance for any accidental errors. We would be happy to apply the corrections in the following edition of this publication.

Notes

Notes

Notes

Notes